SHOWCASE PRESENTS

ADAM STRANGE

VOLUME ONE

Dan DiDio Senior VP-Executive Editor

Julius Schwartz Editor-original series

Peter Hamboussi Editor-collected edition

Robbin Brosterman Senior Art Director

Paul Levitz President & Publisher

Georg Brewer VP-Design & DC Direct Creative

Richard Bruning Senior VP-Creative Director

Patrick Caldon Executive VP-Finance & Operations

Chris Caramalis VP-Finance

John Cunningham VP-Marketing

Terri Cunningham VP-Managing Editor

Alison Gill VP-Manufacturing

Hank Kanalz VP-General Manager, WildStorm

Jim Lee Editorial Director-WildStorm

Paula Lowitt Senior VP-Business & Legal Affairs

MaryEllen McLaughlin VP-Advertising & Custom Publishing

John Nee VP-Business Development

Gregory Noveck Senior VP-Creative Affairs

Sue Pohja VP-Book Trade Sales

Cheryl Rubin Senior VP-Brand Management

Jeff Trojan VP-Business Development, DC Direct

Bob Wayne VP-Sales

Cover illustration by Carmine Infantino and Bernard Sachs.
Front cover color by Richard and Tanya Horie.

SHOWCASE PRESENTS: ADAM STRANGE VOLUME ONE
Published by DC Comics. Cover and compilation
copyright © 2007 DC Comics. All Rights Reserved.

Originally published in single magazine form in SHOWCASE 17-19,
MYSTERY IN SPACE 53-84 Copyright © 1958-1963 DC Comics.
All Rights Reserved. All characters, their distinctive likenesses and related
elements featured in this publication are trademarks of DC Comics.
The stories, characters and incidents featured in this publication
are entirely fictional. DC Comics does not read or accept
unsolicited submissions of ideas, stories or artwork.

DC Comics, 1700 Broadway, New York, NY 10019
A Warner Bros. Entertainment Company
Printed in Canada. First Printing.
ISBN: 1-4012-1313-8
ISBN 13: 978-1-4012-1313-8

UNTIL THE 1970S IT WAS NOT COMMON PRACTICE IN THE COMIC BOOK INDUSTRY TO CREDIT ALL STORIES. IN THE PREPARATION OF THIS COLLECTION WE HAVE USED OUR BEST EFFORTS TO REVIEW ANY SURVIVING RECORDS AND CONSULT ANY AVAILABLE DATABASES AND KNOWLEDGEABLE PARTIES. WE REGRET THE INNATE LIMITATIONS OF THIS PROCESS AND ANY MISSING OR MISASSIGNED ATTRIBUTIONS THAT MAY OCCUR. ANY ADDITIONAL INFORMATION ON CREDITS SHOULD BE DIRECTED TO: EDITOR, COLLECTED EDITIONS, C/O DC COMICS.

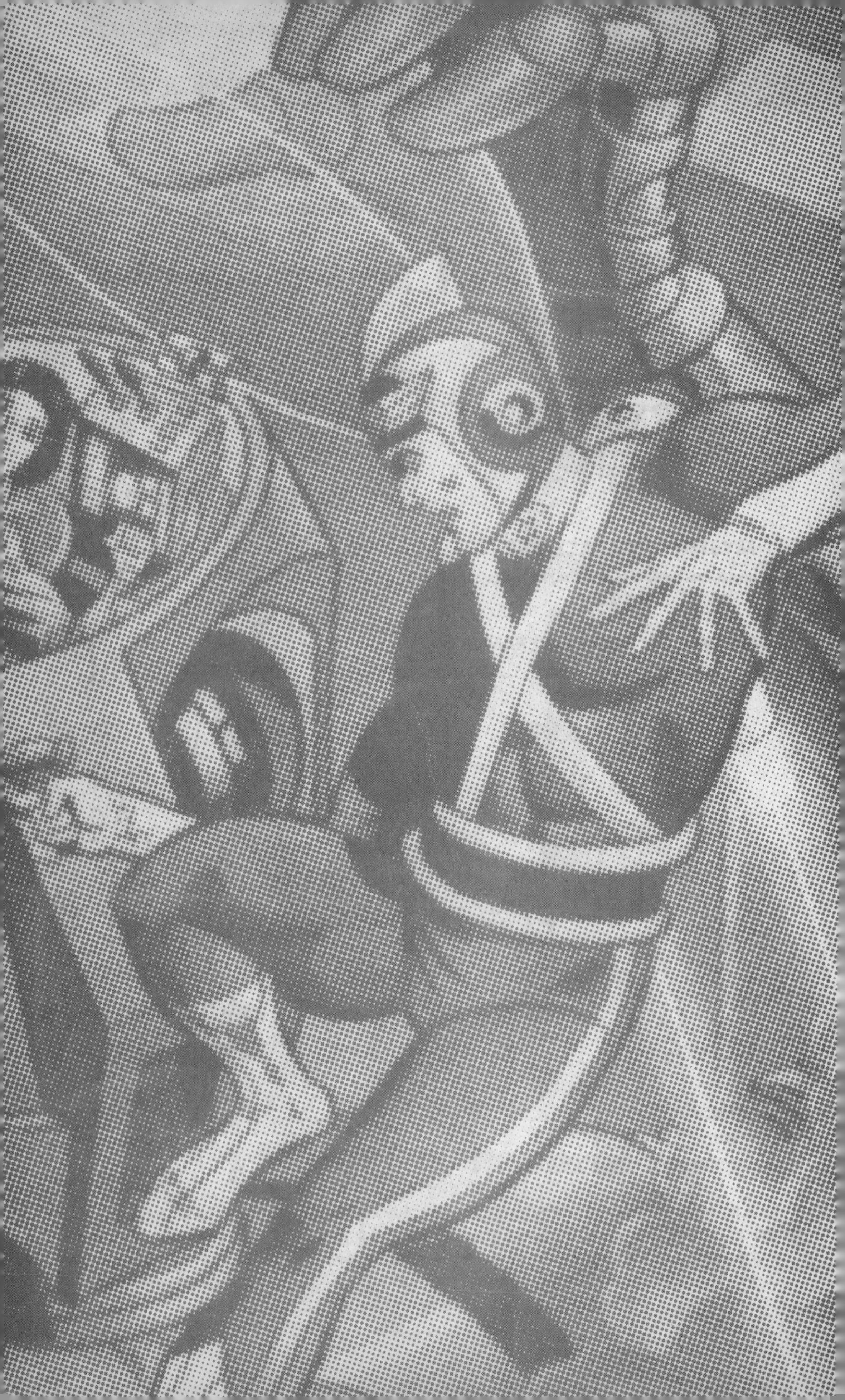

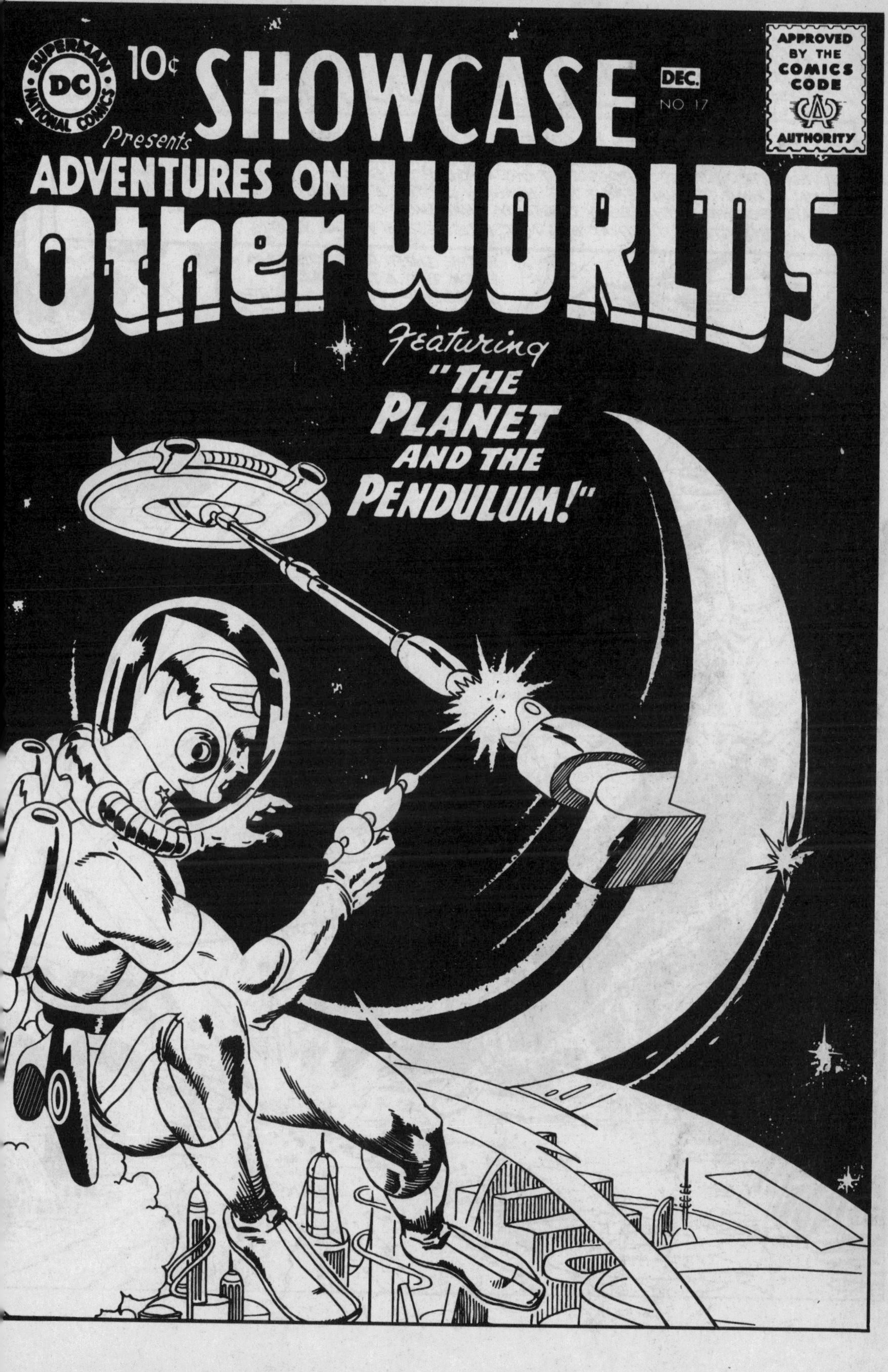
SUPERMAN DC NATIONAL COMICS
10¢
SHOWCASE
DEC. NO. 17
APPROVED BY THE COMICS CODE AUTHORITY
Presents
ADVENTURES ON
Other WORLDS
Featuring
"THE PLANET AND THE PENDULUM!"

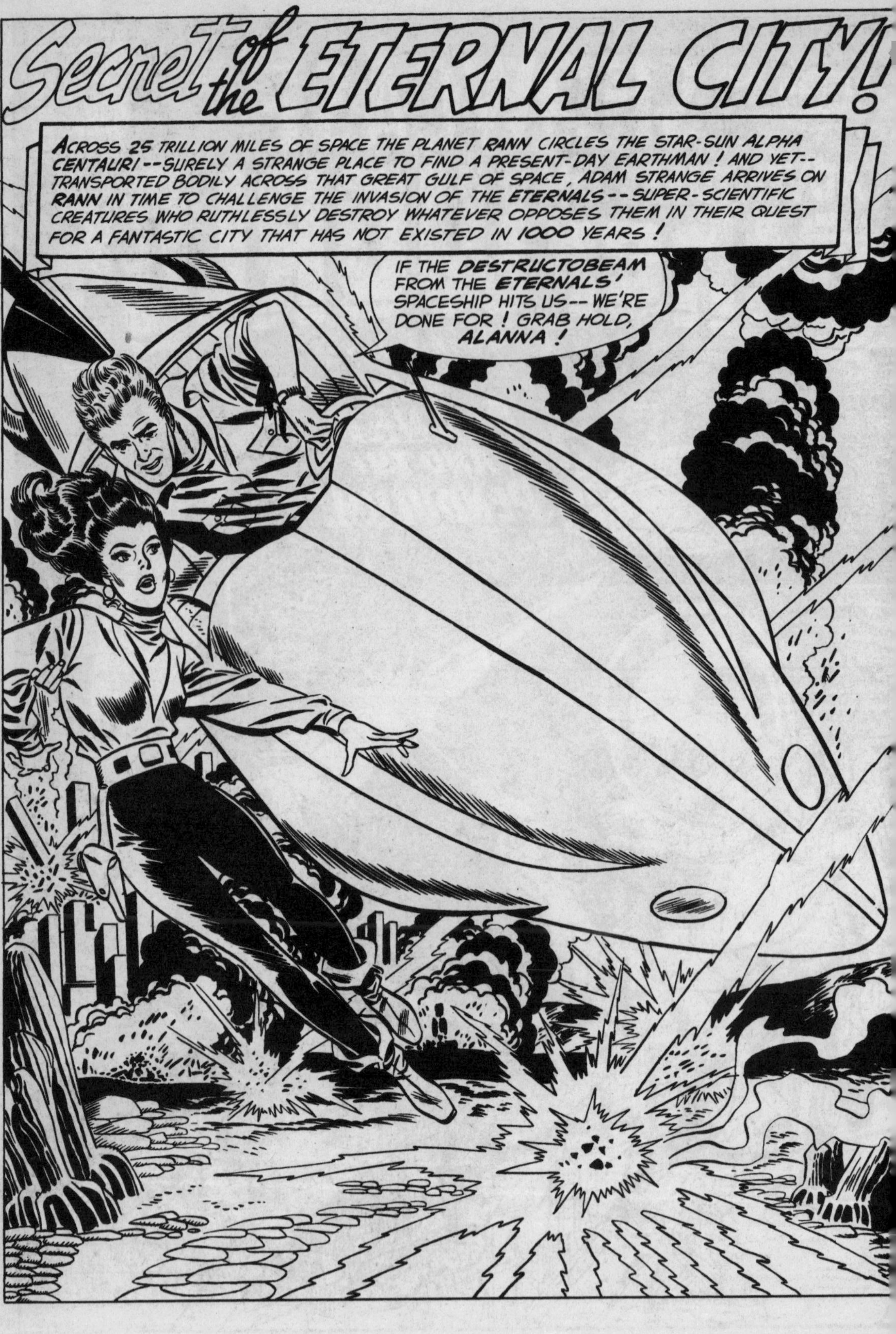
Secret of the ETERNAL CITY!
ACROSS 25 TRILLION MILES OF SPACE THE PLANET RANN CIRCLES THE STAR-SUN ALPHA CENTAURI--SURELY A STRANGE PLACE TO FIND A PRESENT-DAY EARTHMAN! AND YET--TRANSPORTED BODILY ACROSS THAT GREAT GULF OF SPACE, ADAM STRANGE ARRIVES ON RANN IN TIME TO CHALLENGE THE INVASION OF THE ETERNALS--SUPER-SCIENTIFIC CREATURES WHO RUTHLESSLY DESTROY WHATEVER OPPOSES THEM IN THEIR QUEST FOR A FANTASTIC CITY THAT HAS NOT EXISTED IN 1000 YEARS!
IF THE DESTRUCTOBEAM FROM THE ETERNALS' SPACESHIP HITS US--WE'RE DONE FOR! GRAB HOLD, ALANNA!

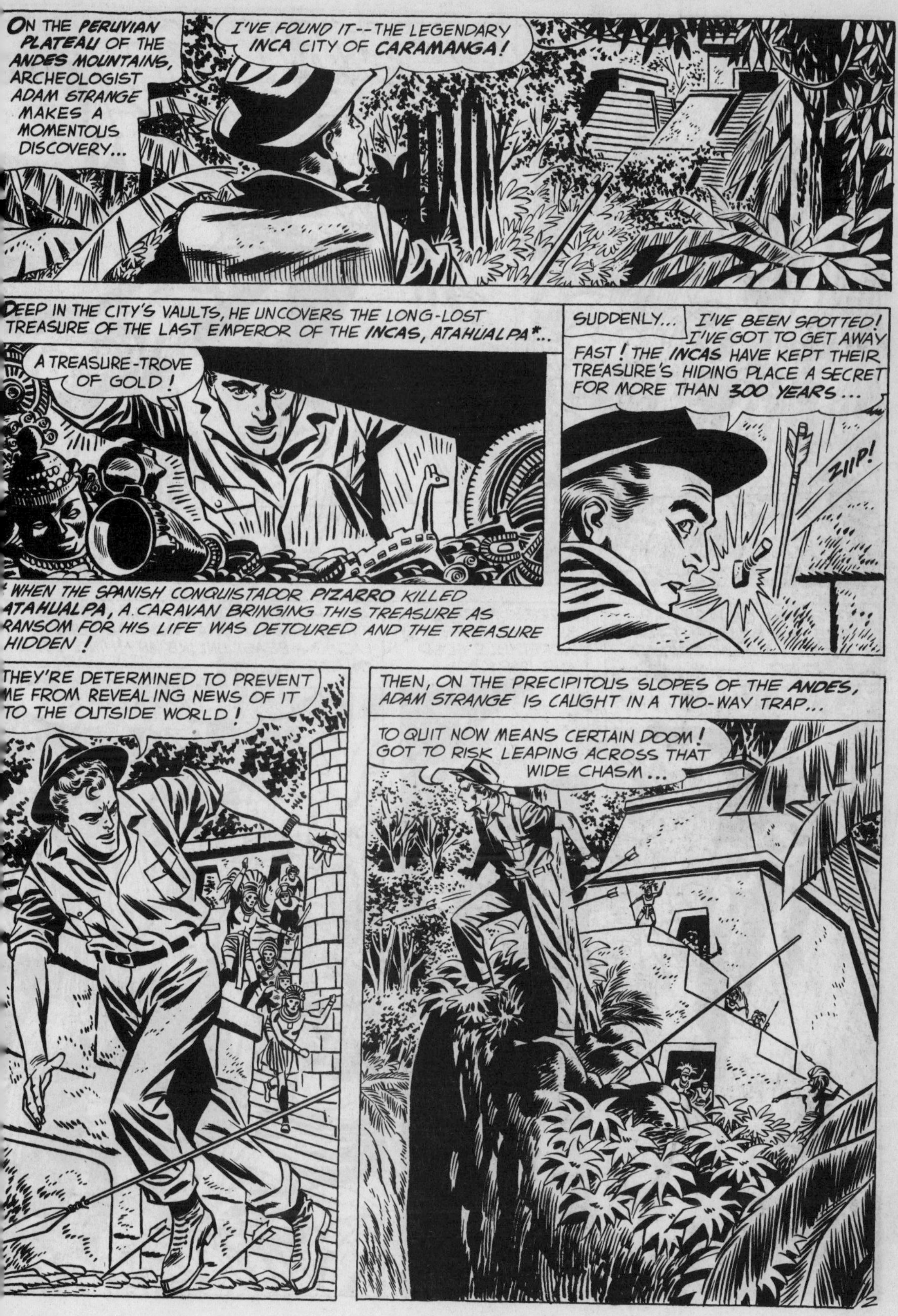
ON THE PERUVIAN PLATEAU OF THE ANDES MOUNTAINS, ARCHEOLOGIST ADAM STRANGE MAKES A MOMENTOUS DISCOVERY...
I'VE FOUND IT--THE LEGENDARY INCA CITY OF CARAMANGA!
DEEP IN THE CITY'S VAULTS, HE UNCOVERS THE LONG-LOST TREASURE OF THE LAST EMPEROR OF THE INCAS, ATAHUALPA*...
A TREASURE-TROVE OF GOLD!
*WHEN THE SPANISH CONQUISTADOR PIZARRO KILLED ATAHUALPA, A CARAVAN BRINGING THIS TREASURE AS RANSOM FOR HIS LIFE WAS DETOURED AND THE TREASURE HIDDEN!
SUDDENLY...
I'VE BEEN SPOTTED! I'VE GOT TO GET AWAY FAST! THE INCAS HAVE KEPT THEIR TREASURE'S HIDING PLACE A SECRET FOR MORE THAN 300 YEARS...
ZIIP!
THEY'RE DETERMINED TO PREVENT ME FROM REVEALING NEWS OF IT TO THE OUTSIDE WORLD!
THEN, ON THE PRECIPITOUS SLOPES OF THE ANDES, ADAM STRANGE IS CAUGHT IN A TWO-WAY TRAP...
TO QUIT NOW MEANS CERTAIN DOOM! GOT TO RISK LEAPING ACROSS THAT WIDE CHASM...

AFTER BACKING UP A LITTLE, THE ARCHEOLOGIST RACES ACROSS THE MOUNTAIN ROCKS...

IT'S AT LEAST A TWENTY-FIVE-FOOT LEAP!

WITH A POWERFUL KICK HE HURLS HIMSELF ACROSS SPACE...

AT THE APEX OF HIS LEAP THERE IS A BRILLIANT FLARE OF LIGHT, A THUNDERCLAP OF SOUND...

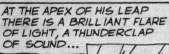

VROOOOM!

THERE IS A STABBING, BLINDING MOMENT OF INCREDIBLE COLD AND DARKNESS...

AND THE NEXT MOMENT ADAM STRANGE FINDS HIMSELF IN A TROPICAL JUNGLE FACING A BEAST UNLIKE ANYTHING SEEN ON EARTH!...

WH--WHERE IN THE WORLD DID I LEAP TO?

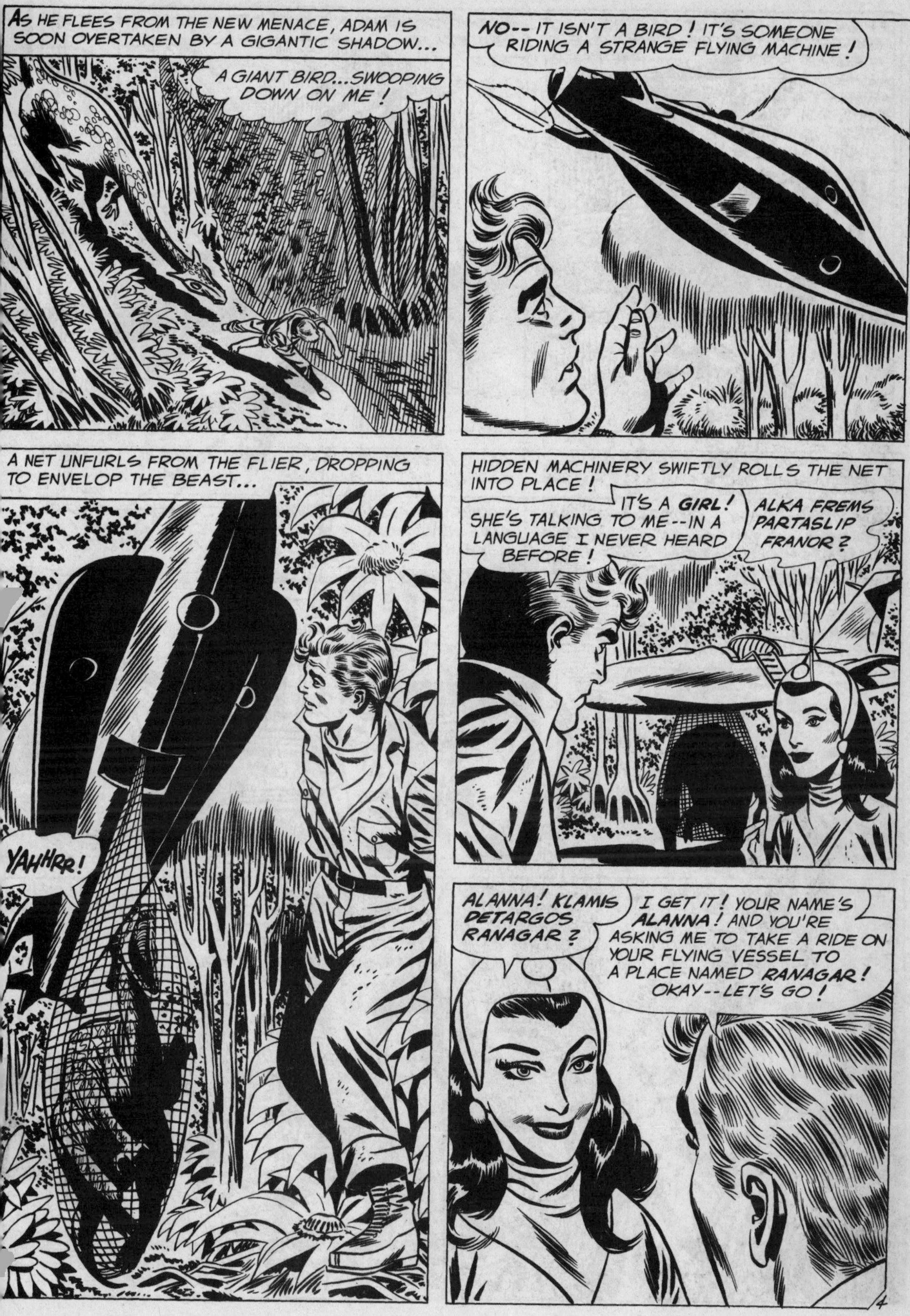
AS HE FLEES FROM THE NEW MENACE, ADAM IS SOON OVERTAKEN BY A GIGANTIC SHADOW...
A GIANT BIRD...SWOOPING DOWN ON ME!
NO-- IT ISN'T A BIRD! IT'S SOMEONE RIDING A STRANGE FLYING MACHINE!
A NET UNFURLS FROM THE FLIER, DROPPING TO ENVELOP THE BEAST...
YAHHRR!
HIDDEN MACHINERY SWIFTLY ROLLS THE NET INTO PLACE!
IT'S A GIRL! SHE'S TALKING TO ME--IN A LANGUAGE I NEVER HEARD BEFORE!
ALKA FREMS PARTASLIP FRANOR?
ALANNA! KLAMIS DETARGOS RANAGAR?
I GET IT! YOUR NAME'S ALANNA! AND YOU'RE ASKING ME TO TAKE A RIDE ON YOUR FLYING VESSEL TO A PLACE NAMED RANAGAR! OKAY--LET'S GO!
4

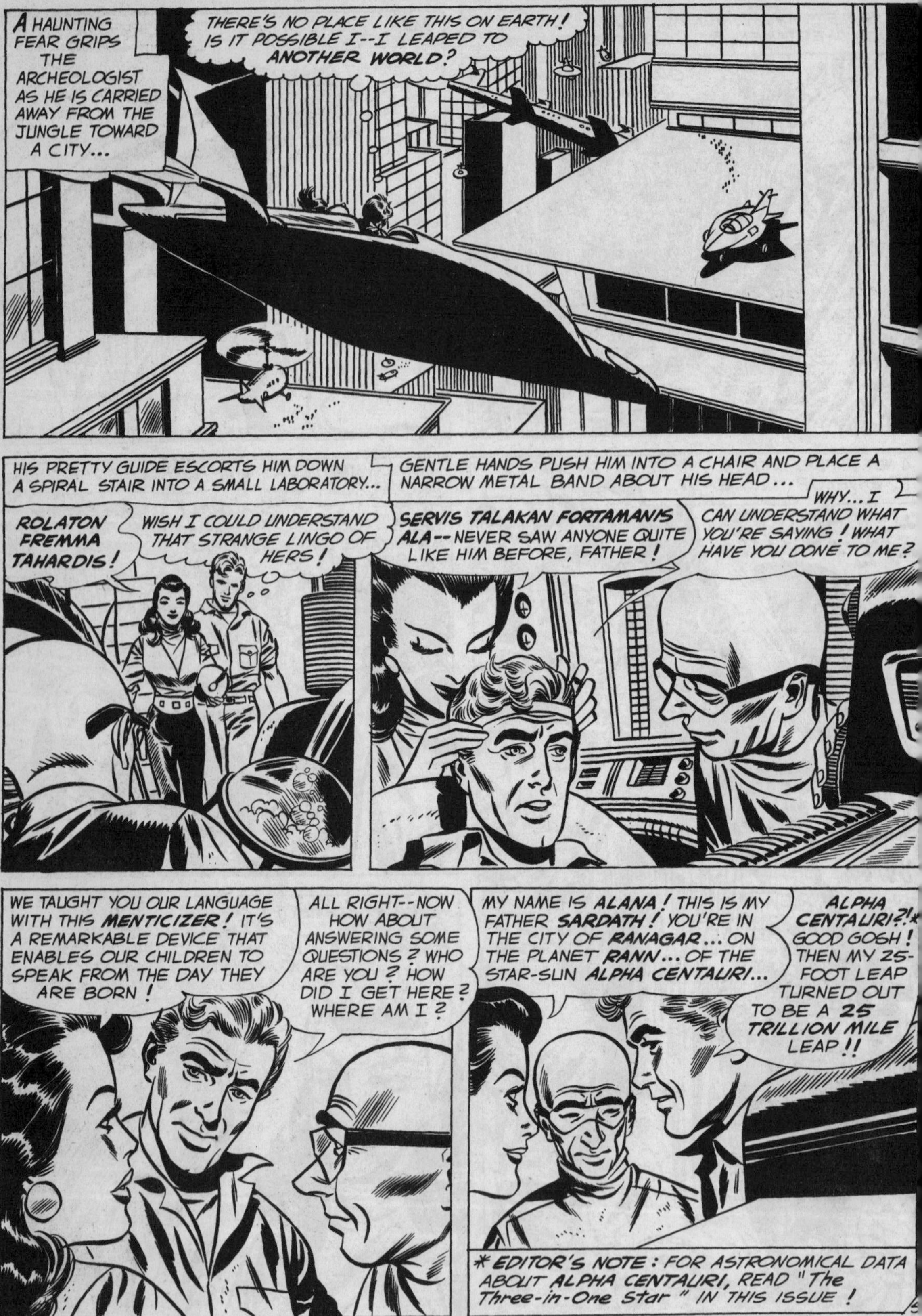
A HAUNTING FEAR GRIPS THE ARCHEOLOGIST AS HE IS CARRIED AWAY FROM THE JUNGLE TOWARD A CITY...
THERE'S NO PLACE LIKE THIS ON EARTH! IS IT POSSIBLE I--I LEAPED TO ANOTHER WORLD?
HIS PRETTY GUIDE ESCORTS HIM DOWN A SPIRAL STAIR INTO A SMALL LABORATORY...
ROLATON FREMMA TAHARDIS!
WISH I COULD UNDERSTAND THAT STRANGE LINGO OF HERS!
GENTLE HANDS PUSH HIM INTO A CHAIR AND PLACE A NARROW METAL BAND ABOUT HIS HEAD...
SERVIS TALAKAN FORTAMANIS ALA-- NEVER SAW ANYONE QUITE LIKE HIM BEFORE, FATHER!
WHY... I CAN UNDERSTAND WHAT YOU'RE SAYING! WHAT HAVE YOU DONE TO ME?
WE TAUGHT YOU OUR LANGUAGE WITH THIS MENTICIZER! IT'S A REMARKABLE DEVICE THAT ENABLES OUR CHILDREN TO SPEAK FROM THE DAY THEY ARE BORN!
ALL RIGHT--NOW HOW ABOUT ANSWERING SOME QUESTIONS? WHO ARE YOU? HOW DID I GET HERE? WHERE AM I?
MY NAME IS ALANA! THIS IS MY FATHER SARDATH! YOU'RE IN THE CITY OF RANAGAR... ON THE PLANET RANN... OF THE STAR-SUN ALPHA CENTAURI...
ALPHA CENTAURI?!* GOOD GOSH! THEN MY 25-FOOT LEAP TURNED OUT TO BE A 25 TRILLION MILE LEAP!!
*EDITOR'S NOTE: FOR ASTRONOMICAL DATA ABOUT ALPHA CENTAURI, READ "The Three-in-One Star" IN THIS ISSUE!

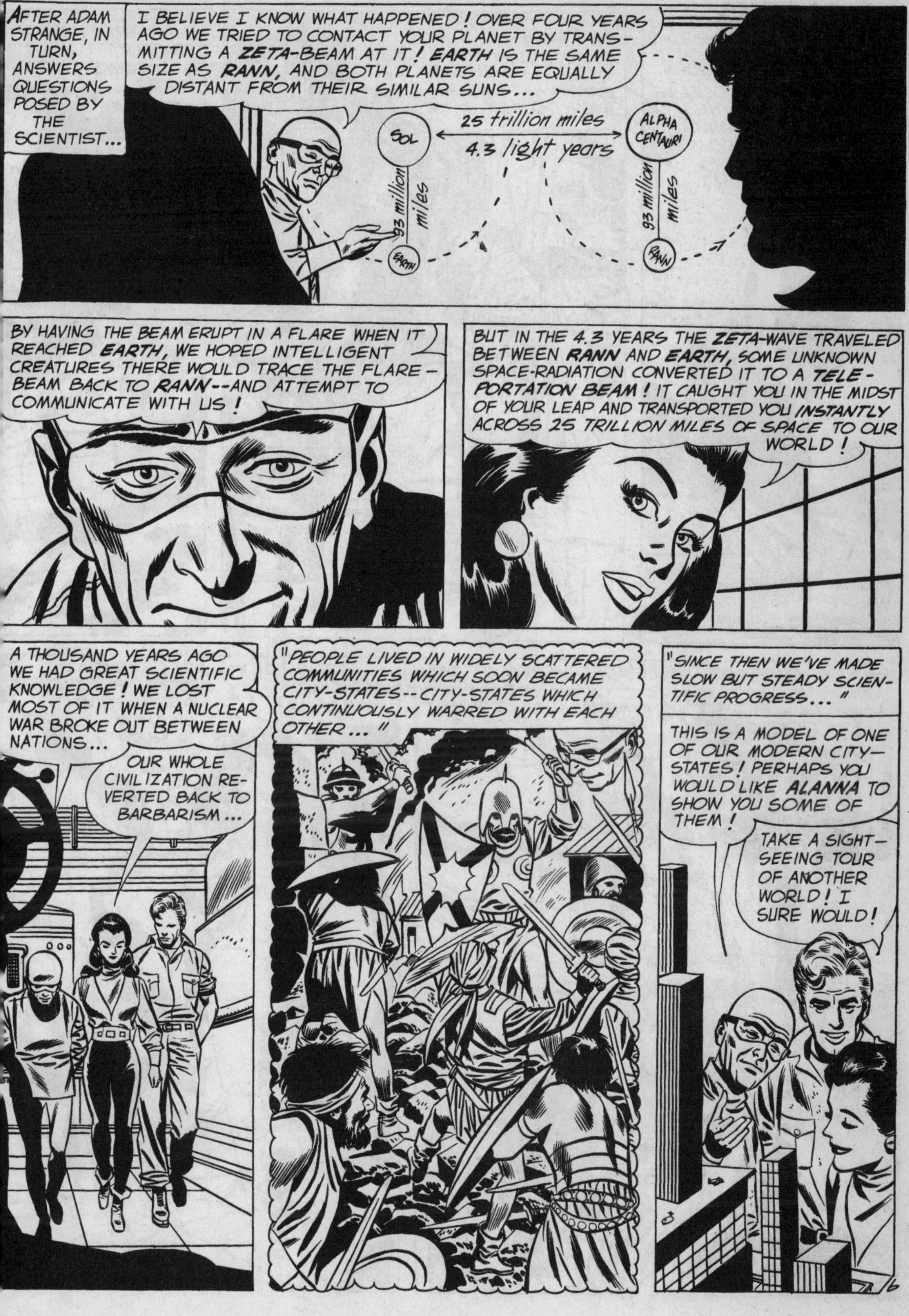
AFTER ADAM STRANGE, IN TURN, ANSWERS QUESTIONS POSED BY THE SCIENTIST...
I BELIEVE I KNOW WHAT HAPPENED! OVER FOUR YEARS AGO WE TRIED TO CONTACT YOUR PLANET BY TRANSMITTING A ZETA-BEAM AT IT! EARTH IS THE SAME SIZE AS RANN, AND BOTH PLANETS ARE EQUALLY DISTANT FROM THEIR SIMILAR SUNS...
SOL
EARTH
93 million miles
25 trillion miles
4.3 light years
ALPHA CENTAURI
RANN
93 million miles
BY HAVING THE BEAM ERUPT IN A FLARE WHEN IT REACHED EARTH, WE HOPED INTELLIGENT CREATURES THERE WOULD TRACE THE FLARE-BEAM BACK TO RANN--AND ATTEMPT TO COMMUNICATE WITH US!
BUT IN THE 4.3 YEARS THE ZETA-WAVE TRAVELED BETWEEN RANN AND EARTH, SOME UNKNOWN SPACE-RADIATION CONVERTED IT TO A TELEPORTATION BEAM! IT CAUGHT YOU IN THE MIDST OF YOUR LEAP AND TRANSPORTED YOU INSTANTLY ACROSS 25 TRILLION MILES OF SPACE TO OUR WORLD!
A THOUSAND YEARS AGO WE HAD GREAT SCIENTIFIC KNOWLEDGE! WE LOST MOST OF IT WHEN A NUCLEAR WAR BROKE OUT BETWEEN NATIONS...
OUR WHOLE CIVILIZATION REVERTED BACK TO BARBARISM...
"PEOPLE LIVED IN WIDELY SCATTERED COMMUNITIES WHICH SOON BECAME CITY-STATES--CITY-STATES WHICH CONTINUOUSLY WARRED WITH EACH OTHER..."
"SINCE THEN WE'VE MADE SLOW BUT STEADY SCIENTIFIC PROGRESS..."
THIS IS A MODEL OF ONE OF OUR MODERN CITY-STATES! PERHAPS YOU WOULD LIKE ALANNA TO SHOW YOU SOME OF THEM!
TAKE A SIGHT-SEEING TOUR OF ANOTHER WORLD! I SURE WOULD!
7A/6

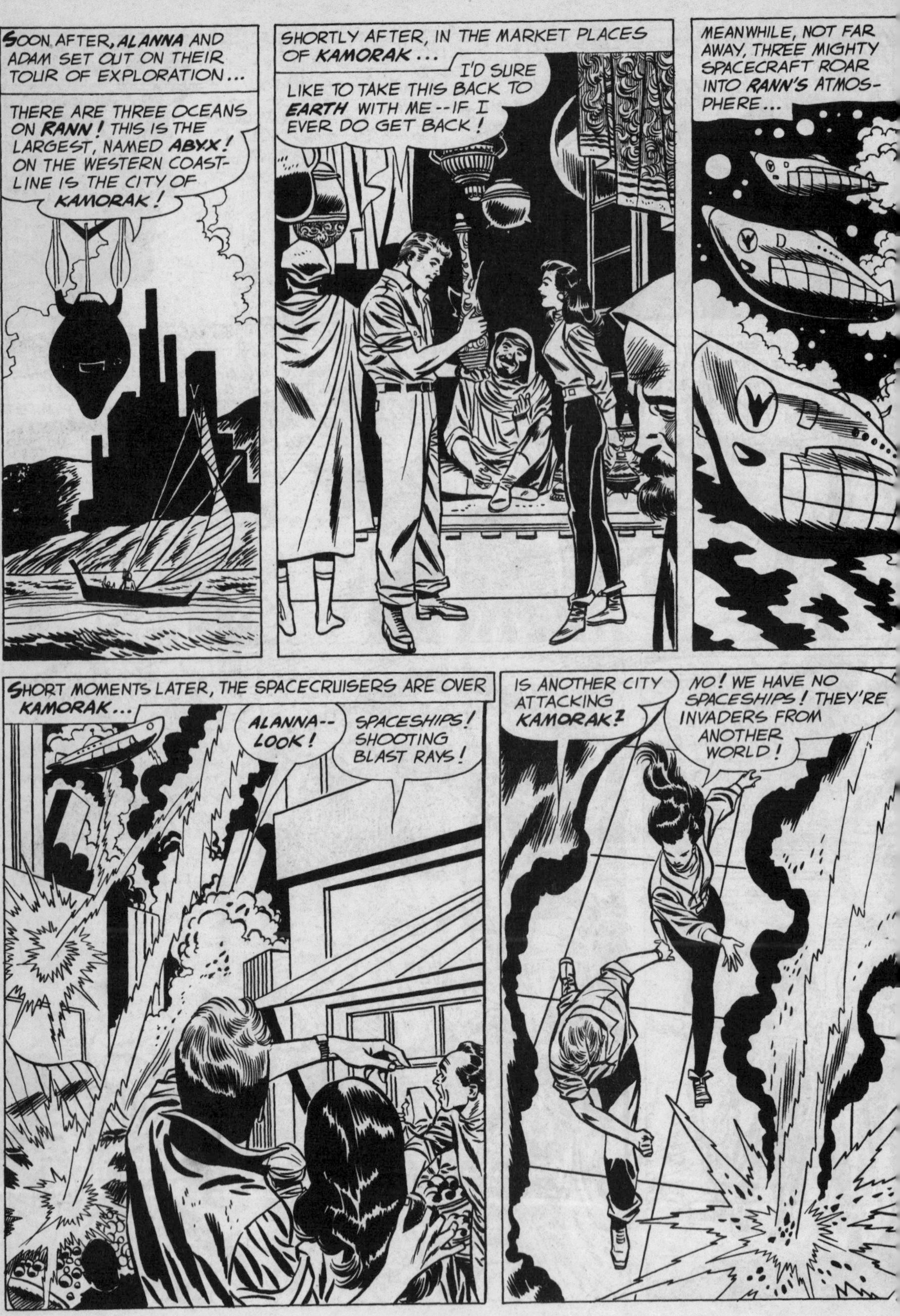
SOON AFTER, ALANNA AND ADAM SET OUT ON THEIR TOUR OF EXPLORATION...
THERE ARE THREE OCEANS ON RANN! THIS IS THE LARGEST, NAMED ABYX! ON THE WESTERN COAST-LINE IS THE CITY OF KAMORAK!
SHORTLY AFTER, IN THE MARKET PLACES OF KAMORAK...
I'D SURE LIKE TO TAKE THIS BACK TO EARTH WITH ME--IF I EVER DO GET BACK!
MEANWHILE, NOT FAR AWAY, THREE MIGHTY SPACECRAFT ROAR INTO RANN'S ATMOS-PHERE...
SHORT MOMENTS LATER, THE SPACECRUISERS ARE OVER KAMORAK...
ALANNA-- LOOK!
SPACESHIPS! SHOOTING BLAST RAYS!
IS ANOTHER CITY ATTACKING KAMORAK?
NO! WE HAVE NO SPACESHIPS! THEY'RE INVADERS FROM ANOTHER WORLD!

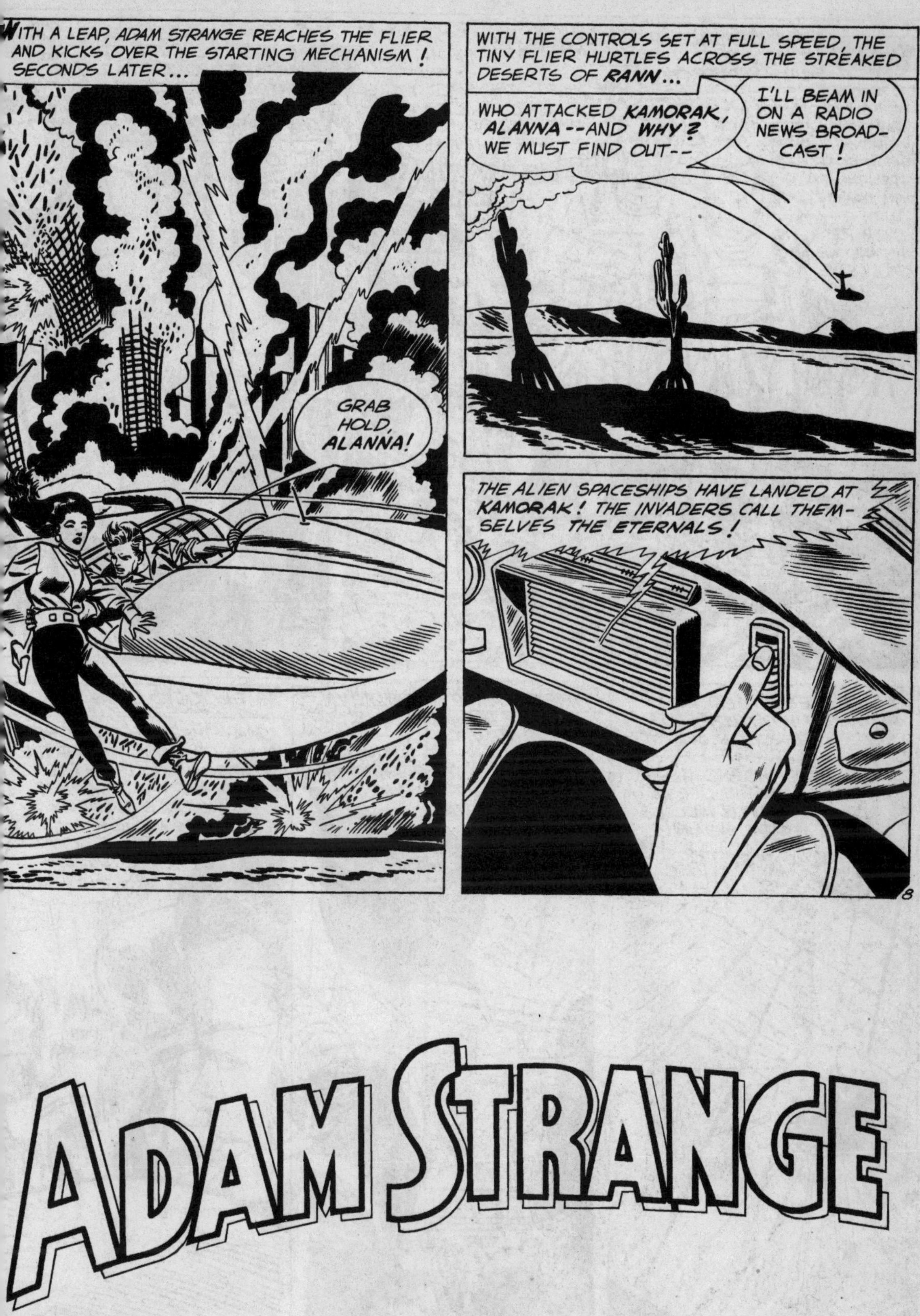
WITH A LEAP, ADAM STRANGE REACHES THE FLIER AND KICKS OVER THE STARTING MECHANISM! SECONDS LATER...
GRAB HOLD, ALANNA!
WITH THE CONTROLS SET AT FULL SPEED, THE TINY FLIER HURTLES ACROSS THE STREAKED DESERTS OF RANN...
WHO ATTACKED KAMORAK, ALANNA--AND WHY? WE MUST FIND OUT--
I'LL BEAM IN ON A RADIO NEWS BROADCAST!
THE ALIEN SPACESHIPS HAVE LANDED AT KAMORAK! THE INVADERS CALL THEMSELVES THE ETERNALS!
8

ADAM STRANGE

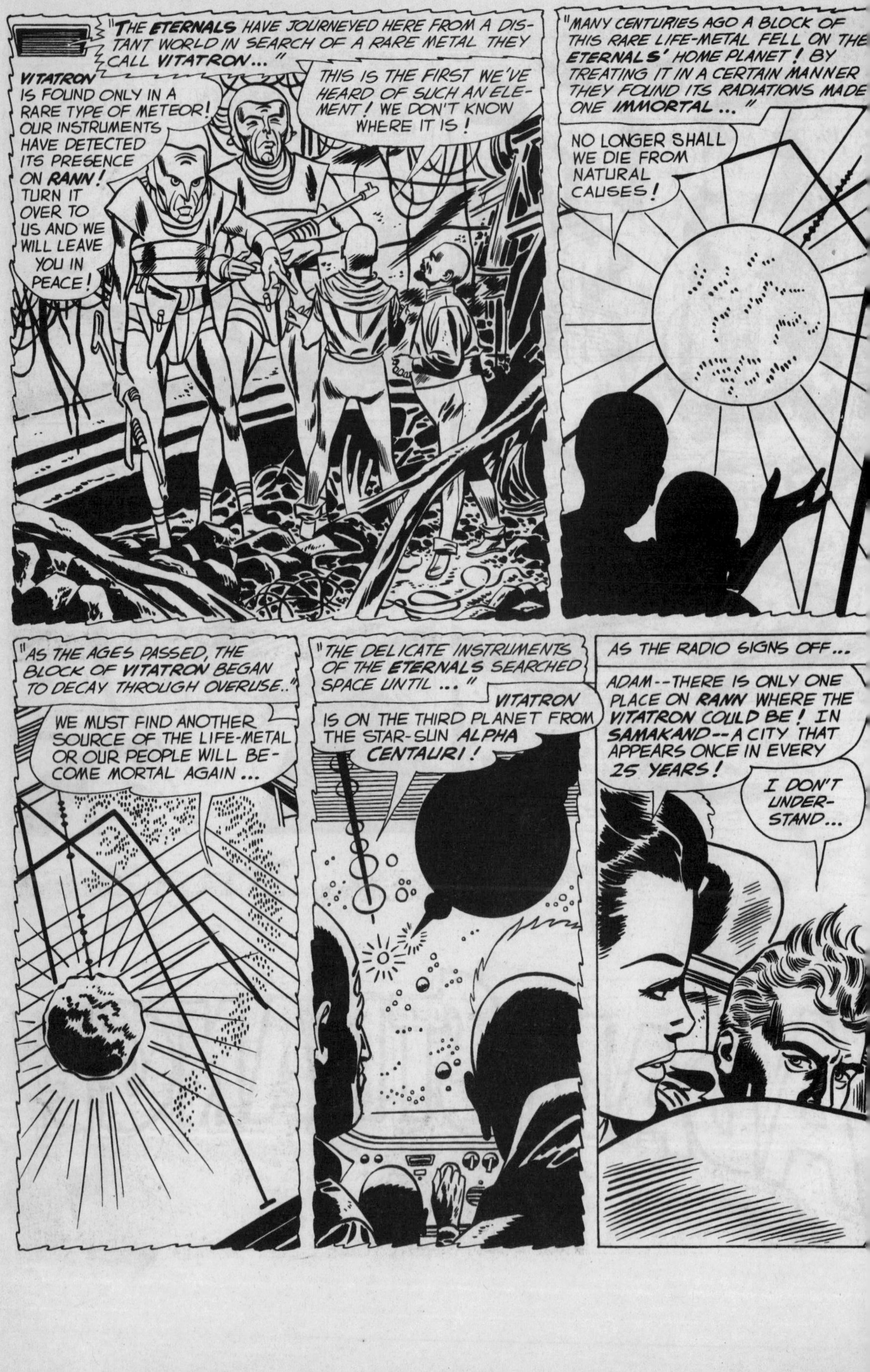
"THE ETERNALS HAVE JOURNEYED HERE FROM A DISTANT WORLD IN SEARCH OF A RARE METAL THEY CALL VITATRON..."
VITATRON IS FOUND ONLY IN A RARE TYPE OF METEOR! OUR INSTRUMENTS HAVE DETECTED ITS PRESENCE ON RANN! TURN IT OVER TO US AND WE WILL LEAVE YOU IN PEACE!
THIS IS THE FIRST WE'VE HEARD OF SUCH AN ELEMENT! WE DON'T KNOW WHERE IT IS!
"MANY CENTURIES AGO A BLOCK OF THIS RARE LIFE-METAL FELL ON THE ETERNALS' HOME PLANET! BY TREATING IT IN A CERTAIN MANNER THEY FOUND ITS RADIATIONS MADE ONE IMMORTAL..."
NO LONGER SHALL WE DIE FROM NATURAL CAUSES!
"AS THE AGES PASSED, THE BLOCK OF VITATRON BEGAN TO DECAY THROUGH OVERUSE.."
WE MUST FIND ANOTHER SOURCE OF THE LIFE-METAL OR OUR PEOPLE WILL BECOME MORTAL AGAIN...
"THE DELICATE INSTRUMENTS OF THE ETERNALS SEARCHED SPACE UNTIL..."
VITATRON IS ON THE THIRD PLANET FROM THE STAR-SUN ALPHA CENTAURI!
AS THE RADIO SIGNS OFF...
ADAM--THERE IS ONLY ONE PLACE ON RANN WHERE THE VITATRON COULD BE! IN SAMAKAND--A CITY THAT APPEARS ONCE IN EVERY 25 YEARS!
I DON'T UNDERSTAND...

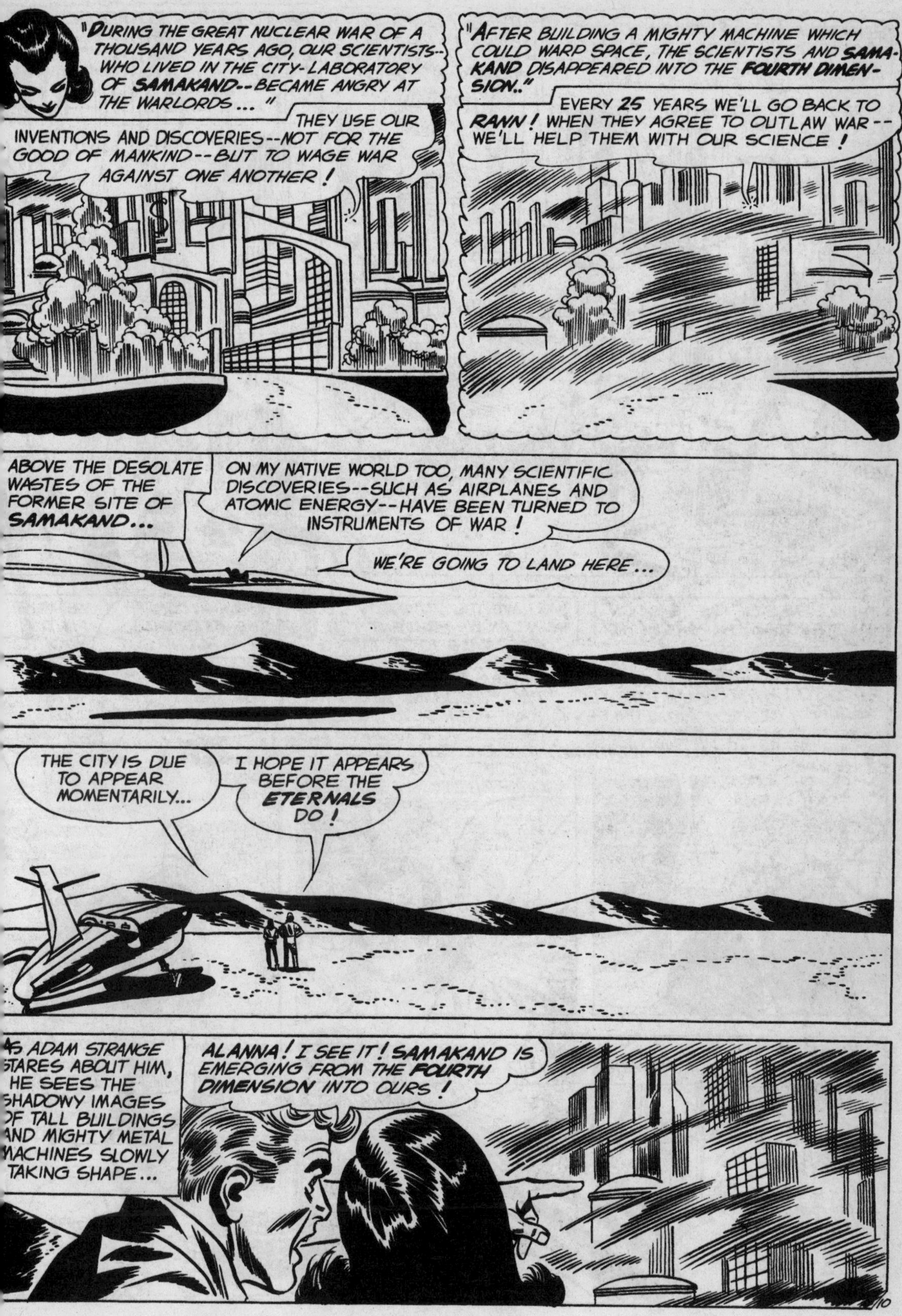
"DURING THE GREAT NUCLEAR WAR OF A THOUSAND YEARS AGO, OUR SCIENTISTS-- WHO LIVED IN THE CITY-LABORATORY OF SAMAKAND--BECAME ANGRY AT THE WARLORDS ..."
THEY USE OUR INVENTIONS AND DISCOVERIES--NOT FOR THE GOOD OF MANKIND--BUT TO WAGE WAR AGAINST ONE ANOTHER!
"AFTER BUILDING A MIGHTY MACHINE WHICH COULD WARP SPACE, THE SCIENTISTS AND SAMAKAND DISAPPEARED INTO THE FOURTH DIMENSION.."
EVERY 25 YEARS WE'LL GO BACK TO RANN! WHEN THEY AGREE TO OUTLAW WAR--WE'LL HELP THEM WITH OUR SCIENCE!
ABOVE THE DESOLATE WASTES OF THE FORMER SITE OF SAMAKAND...
ON MY NATIVE WORLD TOO, MANY SCIENTIFIC DISCOVERIES--SUCH AS AIRPLANES AND ATOMIC ENERGY--HAVE BEEN TURNED TO INSTRUMENTS OF WAR!
WE'RE GOING TO LAND HERE...
THE CITY IS DUE TO APPEAR MOMENTARILY...
I HOPE IT APPEARS BEFORE THE ETERNALS DO!
AS ADAM STRANGE STARES ABOUT HIM, HE SEES THE SHADOWY IMAGES OF TALL BUILDINGS AND MIGHTY METAL MACHINES SLOWLY TAKING SHAPE...
ALANNA! I SEE IT! SAMAKAND IS EMERGING FROM THE FOURTH DIMENSION INTO OURS!
10

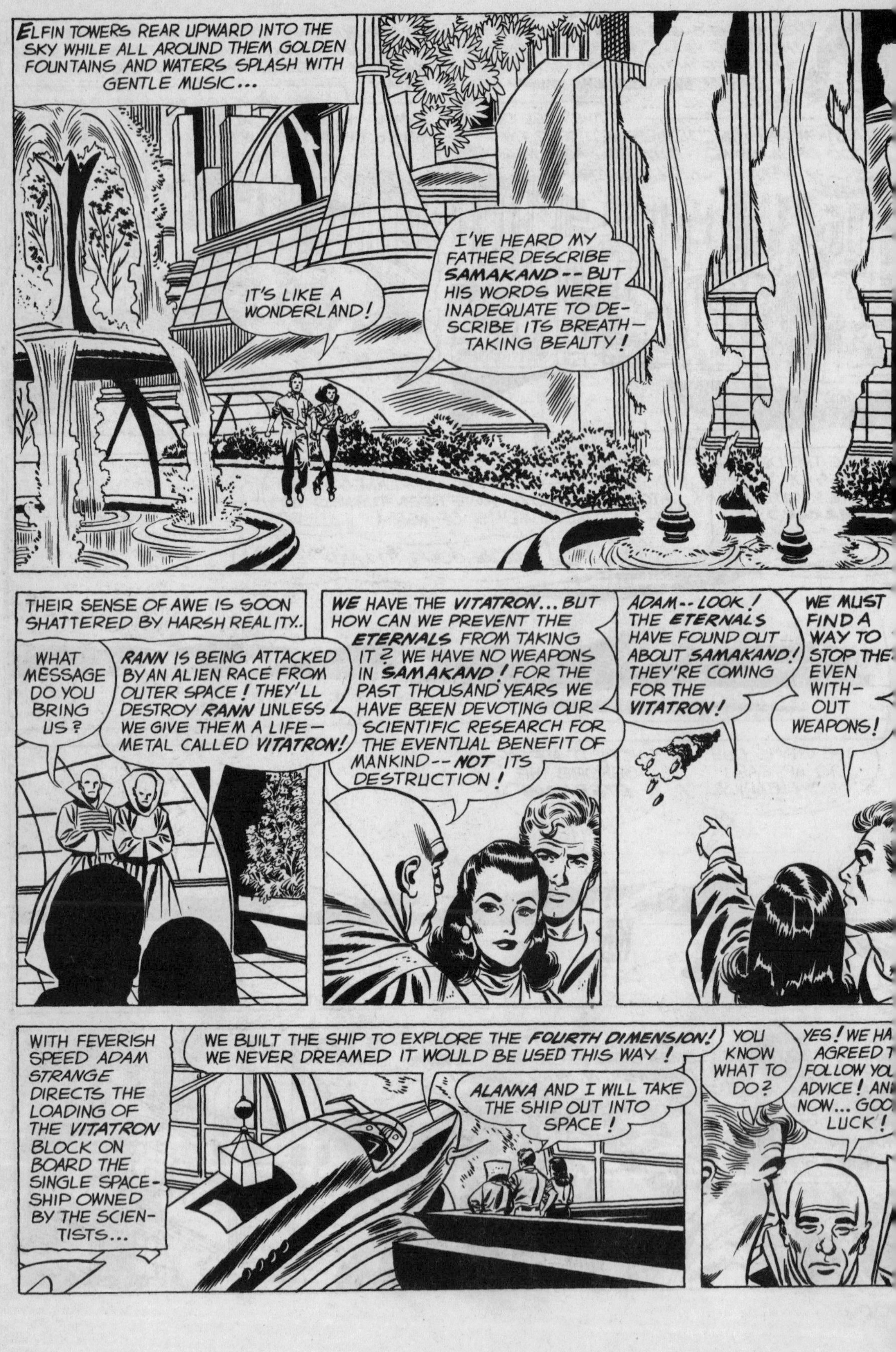
ELFIN TOWERS REAR UPWARD INTO THE SKY WHILE ALL AROUND THEM GOLDEN FOUNTAINS AND WATERS SPLASH WITH GENTLE MUSIC...
IT'S LIKE A WONDERLAND!
I'VE HEARD MY FATHER DESCRIBE SAMAKAND -- BUT HIS WORDS WERE INADEQUATE TO DESCRIBE ITS BREATH-TAKING BEAUTY!
THEIR SENSE OF AWE IS SOON SHATTERED BY HARSH REALITY..
WHAT MESSAGE DO YOU BRING US?
RANN IS BEING ATTACKED BY AN ALIEN RACE FROM OUTER SPACE! THEY'LL DESTROY RANN UNLESS WE GIVE THEM A LIFE-METAL CALLED VITATRON!
WE HAVE THE VITATRON... BUT HOW CAN WE PREVENT THE ETERNALS FROM TAKING IT? WE HAVE NO WEAPONS IN SAMAKAND! FOR THE PAST THOUSAND YEARS WE HAVE BEEN DEVOTING OUR SCIENTIFIC RESEARCH FOR THE EVENTUAL BENEFIT OF MANKIND -- NOT ITS DESTRUCTION!
ADAM -- LOOK! THE ETERNALS HAVE FOUND OUT ABOUT SAMAKAND! THEY'RE COMING FOR THE VITATRON!
WE MUST FIND A WAY TO STOP THE EVEN WITH-OUT WEAPONS!
WITH FEVERISH SPEED ADAM STRANGE DIRECTS THE LOADING OF THE VITATRON BLOCK ON BOARD THE SINGLE SPACE-SHIP OWNED BY THE SCIEN-TISTS...
WE BUILT THE SHIP TO EXPLORE THE FOURTH DIMENSION! WE NEVER DREAMED IT WOULD BE USED THIS WAY!
ALANNA AND I WILL TAKE THE SHIP OUT INTO SPACE!
YOU KNOW WHAT TO DO?
YES! WE HA AGREED T FOLLOW YO ADVICE! AN NOW... GOO LUCK!

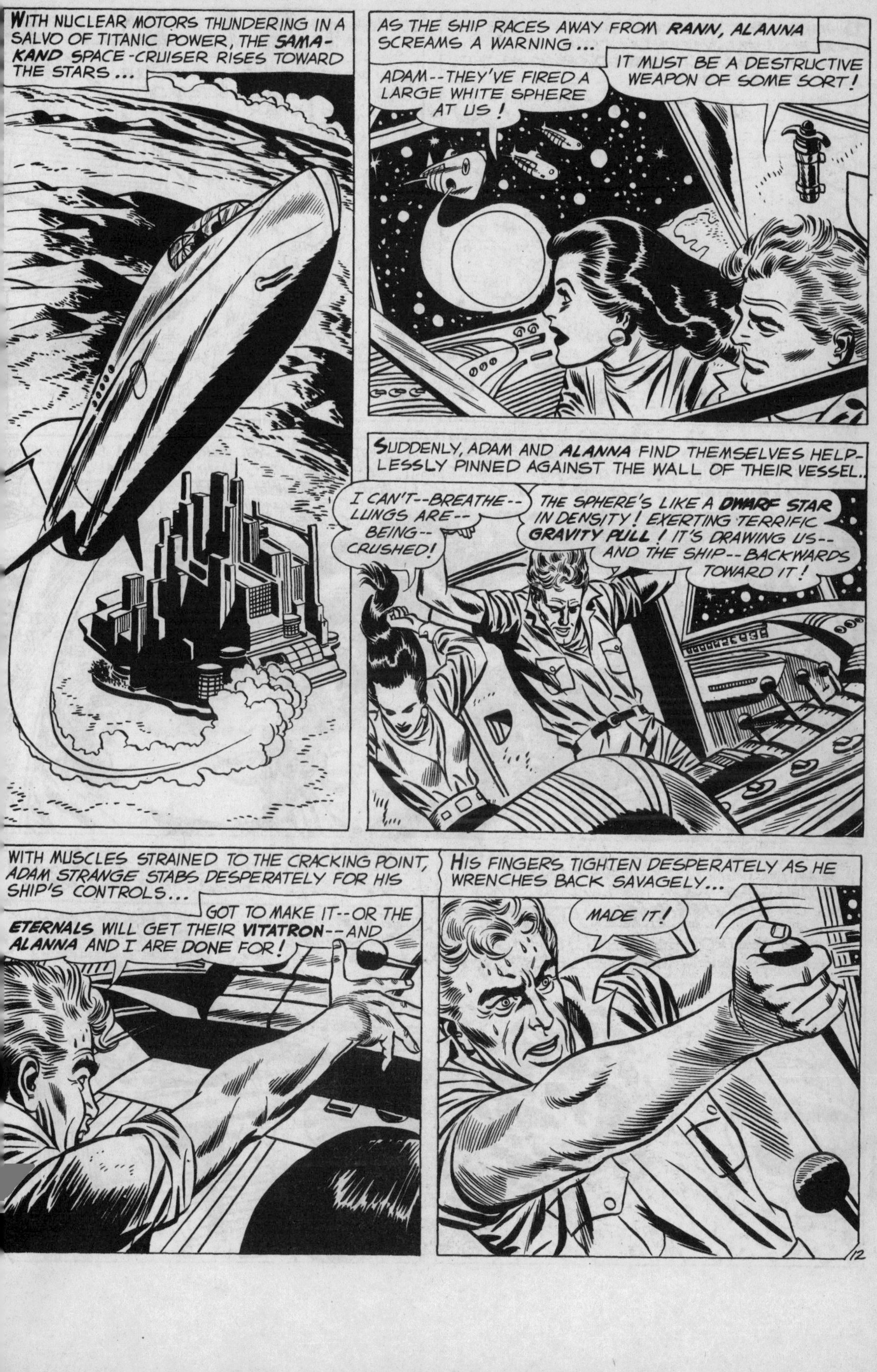
WITH NUCLEAR MOTORS THUNDERING IN A SALVO OF TITANIC POWER, THE SAMAKAND SPACE-CRUISER RISES TOWARD THE STARS ...
AS THE SHIP RACES AWAY FROM RANN, ALANNA SCREAMS A WARNING ...
ADAM--THEY'VE FIRED A LARGE WHITE SPHERE AT US!
IT MUST BE A DESTRUCTIVE WEAPON OF SOME SORT!
SUDDENLY, ADAM AND ALANNA FIND THEMSELVES HELPLESSLY PINNED AGAINST THE WALL OF THEIR VESSEL..
I CAN'T--BREATHE--LUNGS ARE--BEING--CRUSHED!
THE SPHERE'S LIKE A DWARF STAR IN DENSITY! EXERTING TERRIFIC GRAVITY PULL! IT'S DRAWING US--AND THE SHIP--BACKWARDS TOWARD IT!
WITH MUSCLES STRAINED TO THE CRACKING POINT, ADAM STRANGE STABS DESPERATELY FOR HIS SHIP'S CONTROLS...
GOT TO MAKE IT--OR THE ETERNALS WILL GET THEIR VITATRON--AND ALANNA AND I ARE DONE FOR!
HIS FINGERS TIGHTEN DESPERATELY AS HE WRENCHES BACK SAVAGELY...
MADE IT!
12

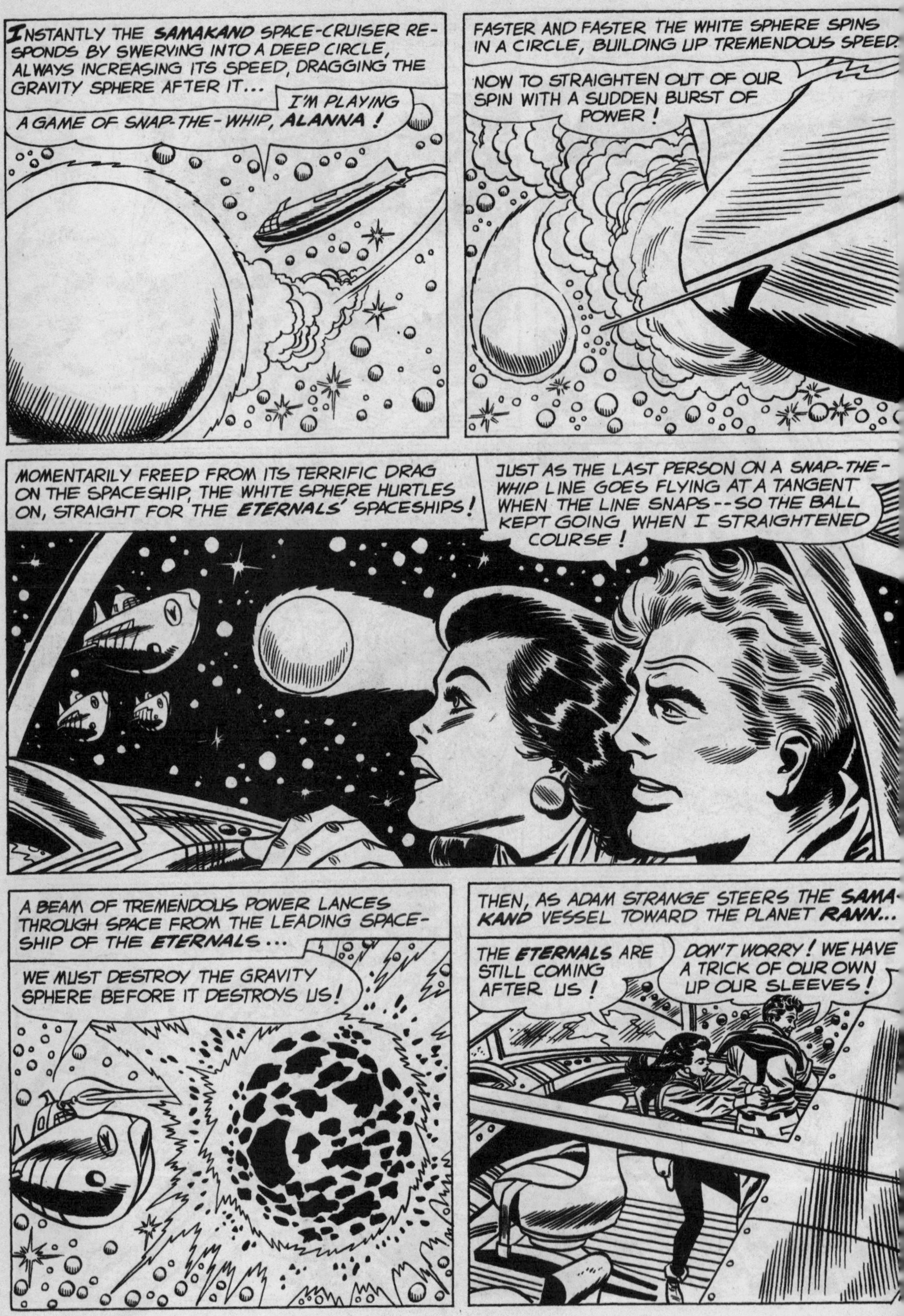
INSTANTLY THE SAMAKAND SPACE-CRUISER RESPONDS BY SWERVING INTO A DEEP CIRCLE, ALWAYS INCREASING ITS SPEED, DRAGGING THE GRAVITY SPHERE AFTER IT...
I'M PLAYING A GAME OF SNAP-THE-WHIP, ALANNA!
FASTER AND FASTER THE WHITE SPHERE SPINS IN A CIRCLE, BUILDING UP TREMENDOUS SPEED.
NOW TO STRAIGHTEN OUT OF OUR SPIN WITH A SUDDEN BURST OF POWER!
MOMENTARILY FREED FROM ITS TERRIFIC DRAG ON THE SPACESHIP, THE WHITE SPHERE HURTLES ON, STRAIGHT FOR THE ETERNALS' SPACESHIPS!
JUST AS THE LAST PERSON ON A SNAP-THE-WHIP LINE GOES FLYING AT A TANGENT WHEN THE LINE SNAPS--SO THE BALL KEPT GOING WHEN I STRAIGHTENED COURSE!
A BEAM OF TREMENDOUS POWER LANCES THROUGH SPACE FROM THE LEADING SPACESHIP OF THE ETERNALS...
WE MUST DESTROY THE GRAVITY SPHERE BEFORE IT DESTROYS US!
THEN, AS ADAM STRANGE STEERS THE SAMAKAND VESSEL TOWARD THE PLANET RANN...
THE ETERNALS ARE STILL COMING AFTER US!
DON'T WORRY! WE HAVE A TRICK OF OUR OWN UP OUR SLEEVES!

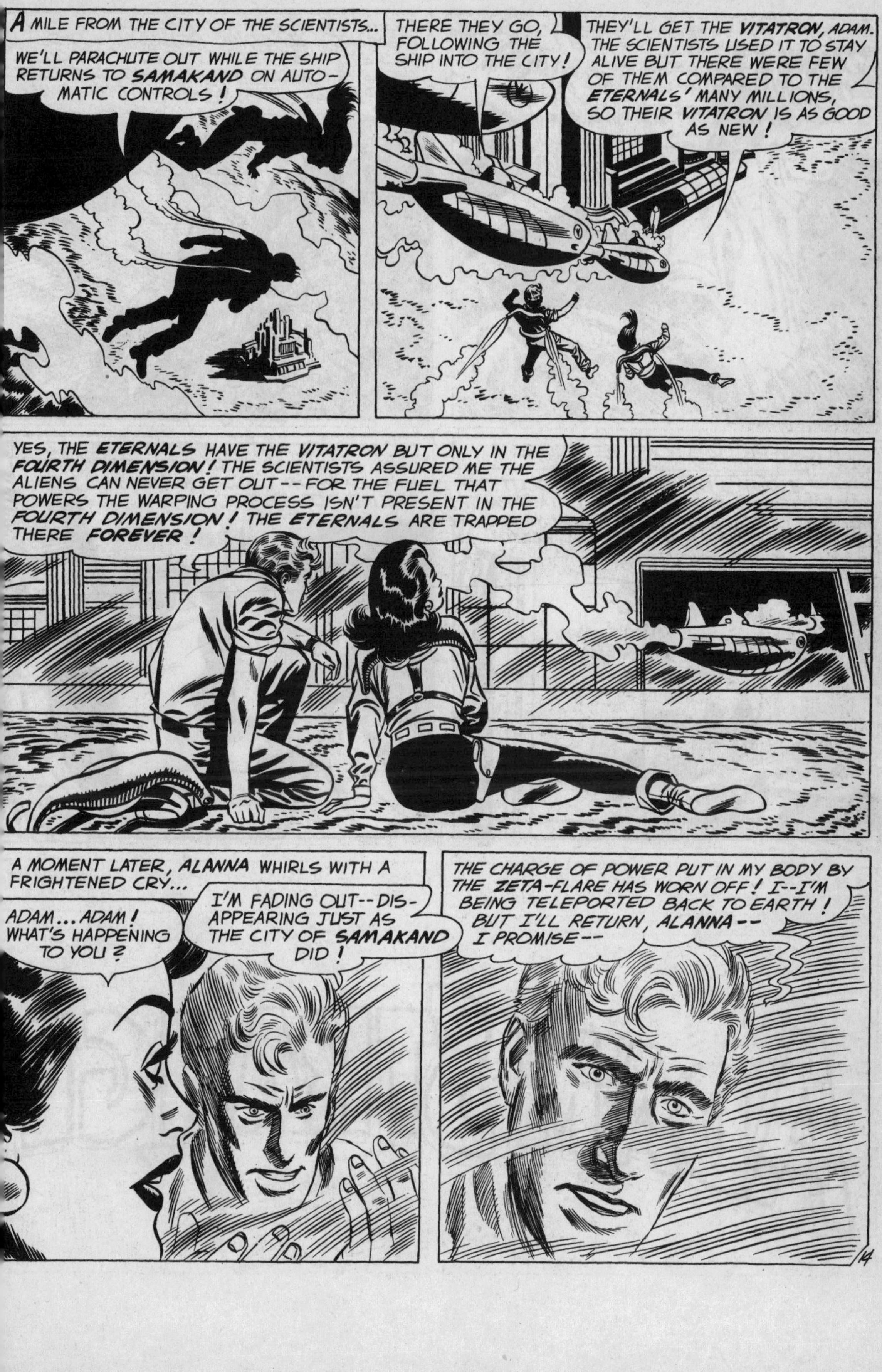
A MILE FROM THE CITY OF THE SCIENTISTS...
WE'LL PARACHUTE OUT WHILE THE SHIP RETURNS TO SAMAKAND ON AUTO-MATIC CONTROLS!
THERE THEY GO, FOLLOWING THE SHIP INTO THE CITY!
THEY'LL GET THE VITATRON, ADAM. THE SCIENTISTS USED IT TO STAY ALIVE BUT THERE WERE FEW OF THEM COMPARED TO THE ETERNALS' MANY MILLIONS, SO THEIR VITATRON IS AS GOOD AS NEW!
YES, THE ETERNALS HAVE THE VITATRON BUT ONLY IN THE FOURTH DIMENSION! THE SCIENTISTS ASSURED ME THE ALIENS CAN NEVER GET OUT--FOR THE FUEL THAT POWERS THE WARPING PROCESS ISN'T PRESENT IN THE FOURTH DIMENSION! THE ETERNALS ARE TRAPPED THERE FOREVER!
A MOMENT LATER, ALANNA WHIRLS WITH A FRIGHTENED CRY...
ADAM... ADAM! WHAT'S HAPPENING TO YOU?
I'M FADING OUT--DIS-APPEARING JUST AS THE CITY OF SAMAKAND DID!
THE CHARGE OF POWER PUT IN MY BODY BY THE ZETA-FLARE HAS WORN OFF! I--I'M BEING TELEPORTED BACK TO EARTH! BUT I'LL RETURN, ALANNA-- I PROMISE--
14

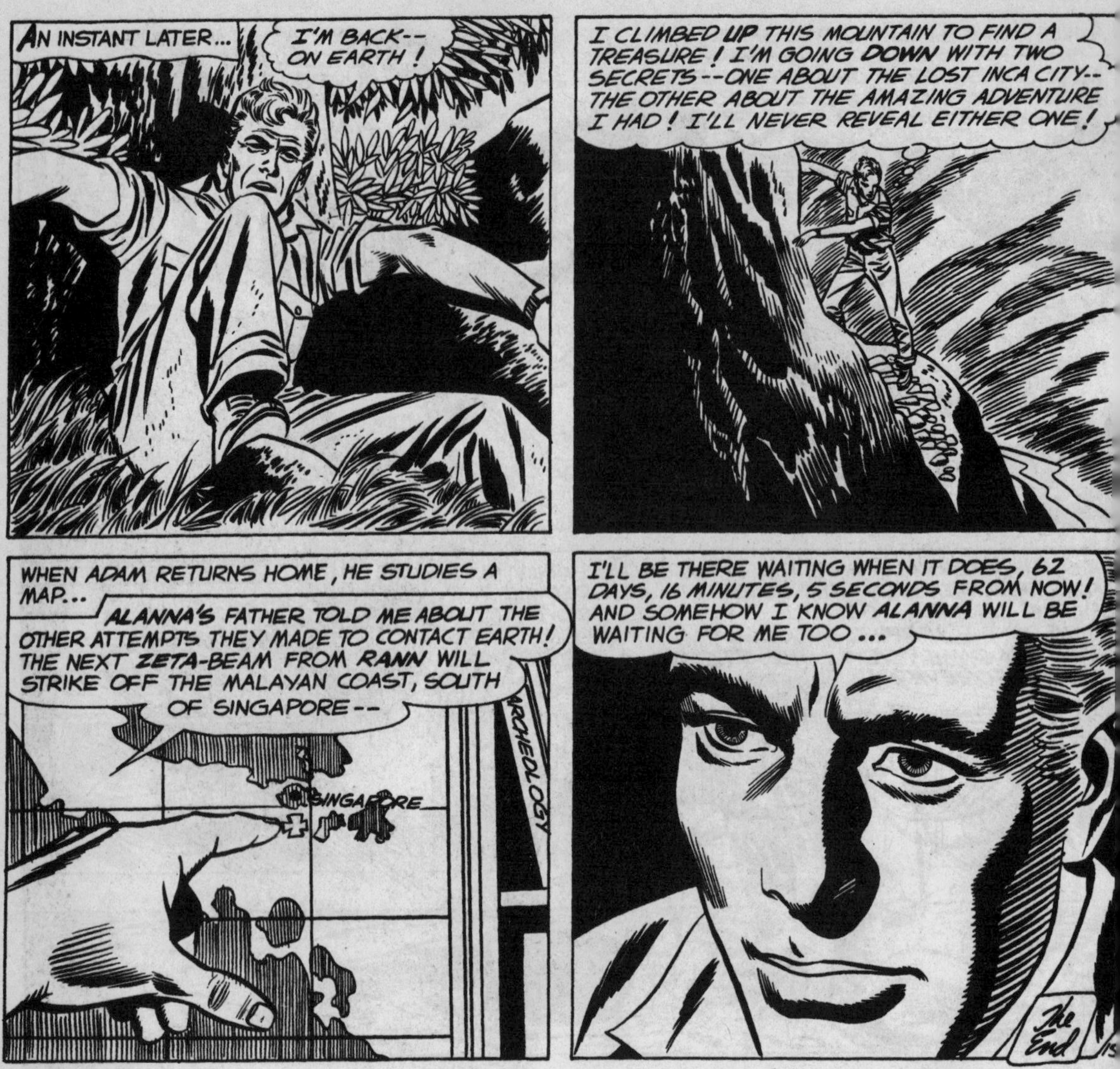
AN INSTANT LATER...
I'M BACK-- ON EARTH!
I CLIMBED UP THIS MOUNTAIN TO FIND A TREASURE! I'M GOING DOWN WITH TWO SECRETS--ONE ABOUT THE LOST INCA CITY-- THE OTHER ABOUT THE AMAZING ADVENTURE I HAD! I'LL NEVER REVEAL EITHER ONE!
WHEN ADAM RETURNS HOME, HE STUDIES A MAP...
ALANNA'S FATHER TOLD ME ABOUT THE OTHER ATTEMPTS THEY MADE TO CONTACT EARTH! THE NEXT ZETA-BEAM FROM RANN WILL STRIKE OFF THE MALAYAN COAST, SOUTH OF SINGAPORE--
SINGAPORE
ARCHEOLOGY
I'LL BE THERE WAITING WHEN IT DOES, 62 DAYS, 16 MINUTES, 5 SECONDS FROM NOW! AND SOMEHOW I KNOW ALANNA WILL BE WAITING FOR ME TOO...
The End
15

ADAM STRANGE

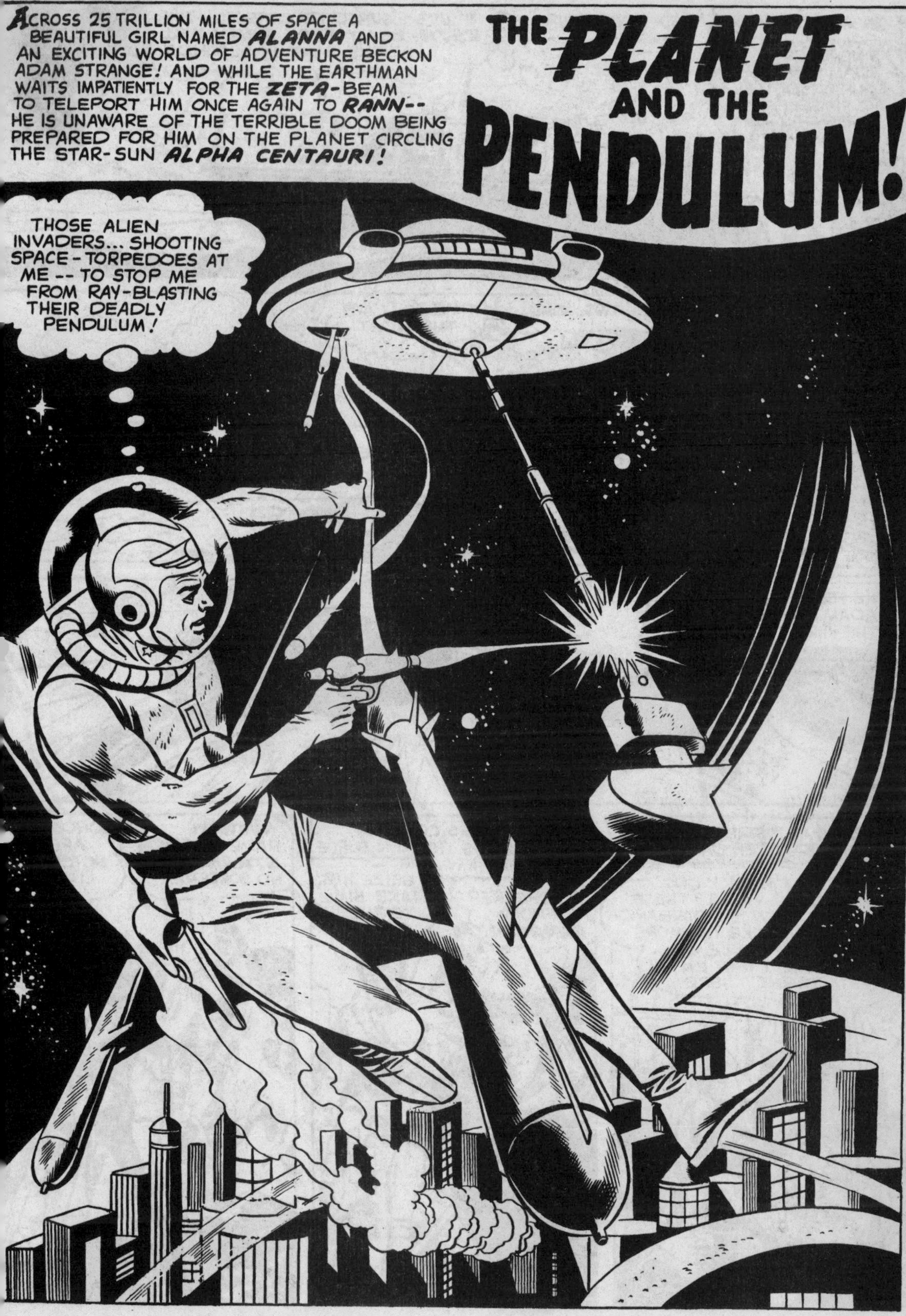
ACROSS 25 TRILLION MILES OF SPACE A BEAUTIFUL GIRL NAMED ALANNA AND AN EXCITING WORLD OF ADVENTURE BECKON ADAM STRANGE! AND WHILE THE EARTHMAN WAITS IMPATIENTLY FOR THE ZETA-BEAM TO TELEPORT HIM ONCE AGAIN TO RANN-- HE IS UNAWARE OF THE TERRIBLE DOOM BEING PREPARED FOR HIM ON THE PLANET CIRCLING THE STAR-SUN ALPHA CENTAURI!
THE PLANET AND THE PENDULUM!
THOSE ALIEN INVADERS... SHOOTING SPACE-TORPEDOES AT ME -- TO STOP ME FROM RAY-BLASTING THEIR DEADLY PENDULUM!

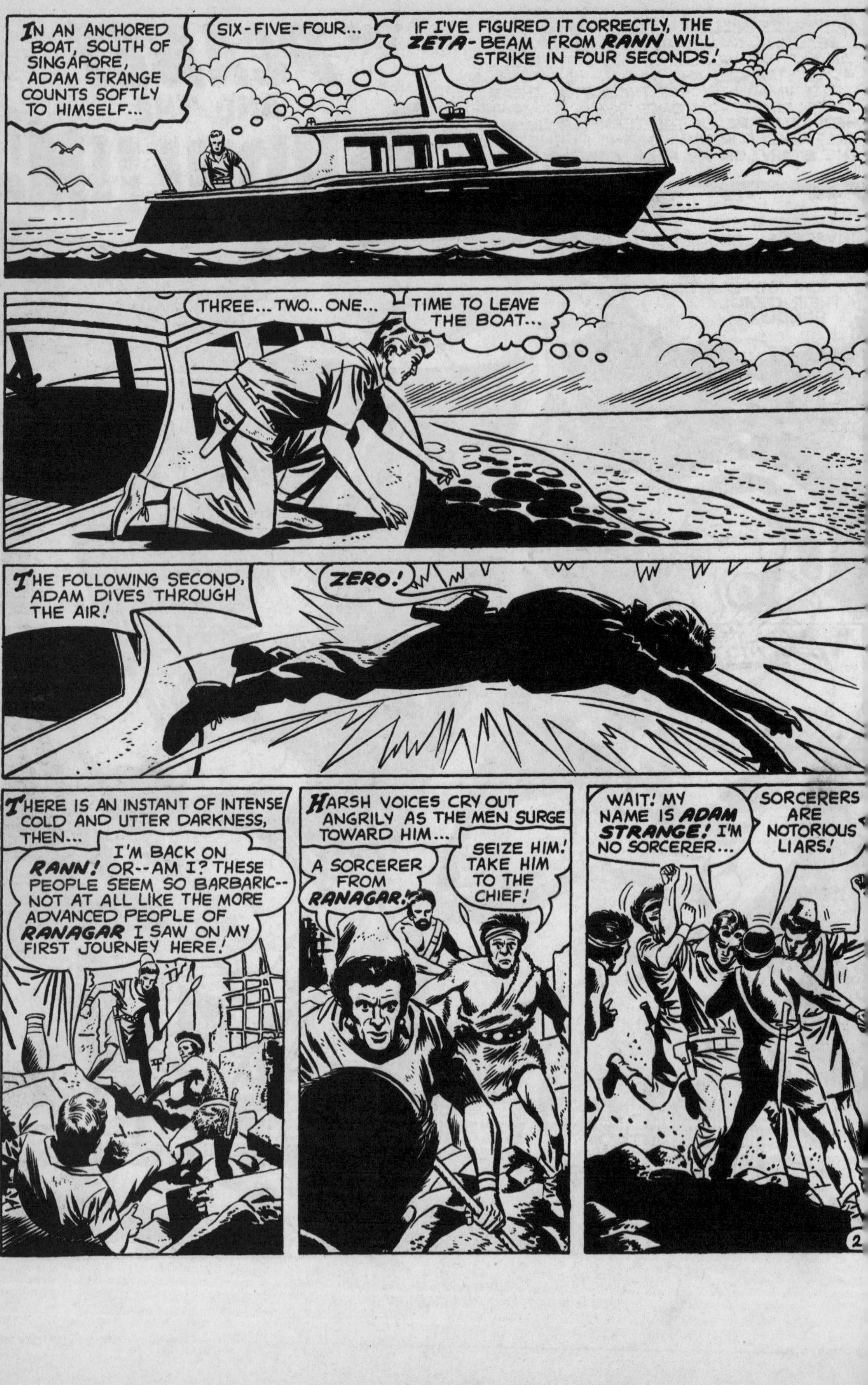
IN AN ANCHORED BOAT, SOUTH OF SINGAPORE, ADAM STRANGE COUNTS SOFTLY TO HIMSELF...
SIX-FIVE-FOUR...
IF I'VE FIGURED IT CORRECTLY, THE ZETA-BEAM FROM RANN WILL STRIKE IN FOUR SECONDS!
THREE...TWO...ONE...
TIME TO LEAVE THE BOAT...
THE FOLLOWING SECOND, ADAM DIVES THROUGH THE AIR!
ZERO!
THERE IS AN INSTANT OF INTENSE COLD AND UTTER DARKNESS, THEN...
I'M BACK ON RANN! OR--AM I? THESE PEOPLE SEEM SO BARBARIC--NOT AT ALL LIKE THE MORE ADVANCED PEOPLE OF RANAGAR I SAW ON MY FIRST JOURNEY HERE!
HARSH VOICES CRY OUT ANGRILY AS THE MEN SURGE TOWARD HIM...
A SORCERER FROM RANAGAR!
SEIZE HIM! TAKE HIM TO THE CHIEF!
WAIT! MY NAME IS ADAM STRANGE! I'M NO SORCERER...
SORCERERS ARE NOTORIOUS LIARS!
2

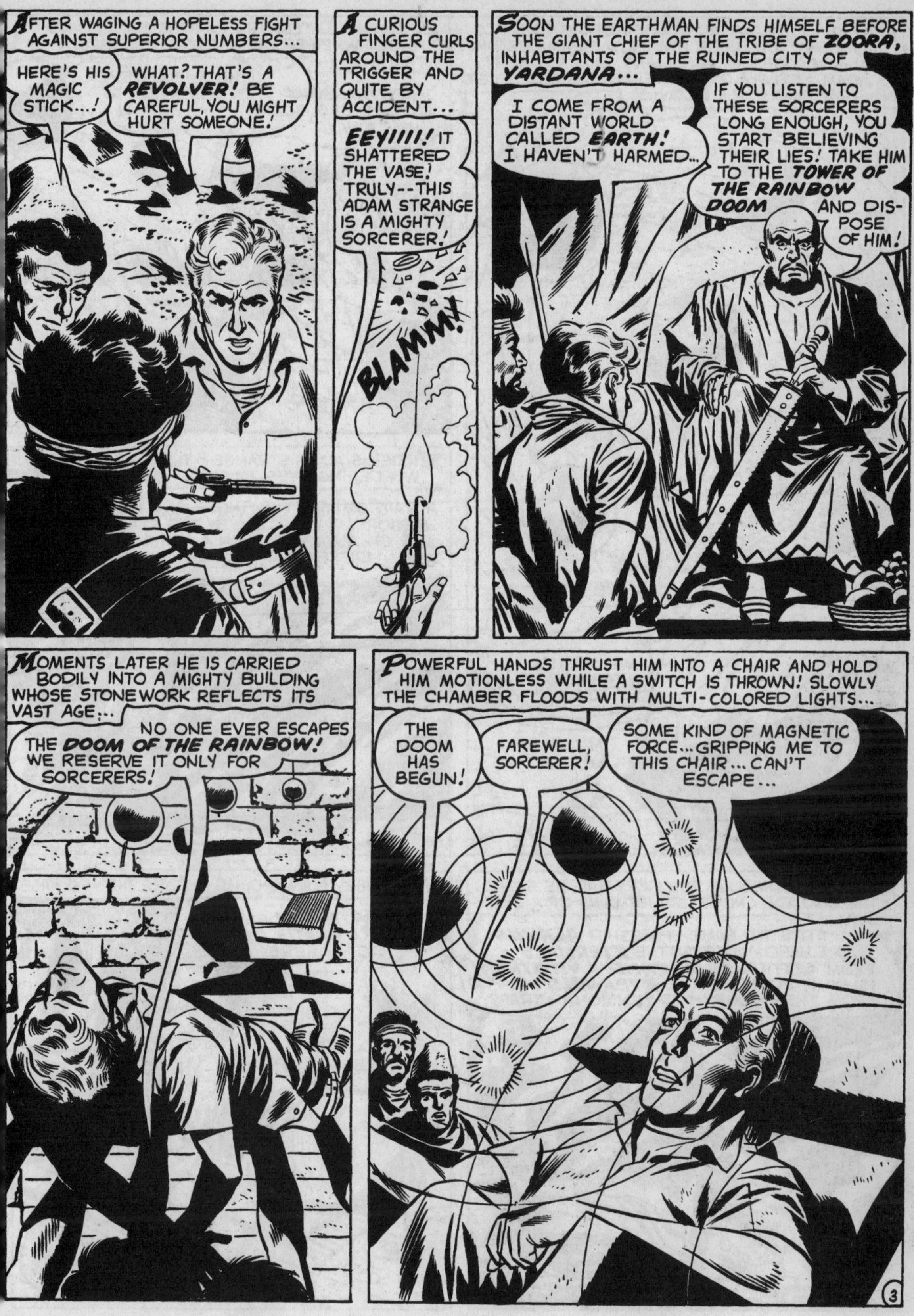
AFTER WAGING A HOPELESS FIGHT AGAINST SUPERIOR NUMBERS...
HERE'S HIS MAGIC STICK...!
WHAT? THAT'S A REVOLVER! BE CAREFUL, YOU MIGHT HURT SOMEONE!
A CURIOUS FINGER CURLS AROUND THE TRIGGER AND QUITE BY ACCIDENT...
EEYIIII! IT SHATTERED THE VASE! TRULY--THIS ADAM STRANGE IS A MIGHTY SORCERER!
BLAMM!
SOON THE EARTHMAN FINDS HIMSELF BEFORE THE GIANT CHIEF OF THE TRIBE OF ZOORA, INHABITANTS OF THE RUINED CITY OF YARDANA...
I COME FROM A DISTANT WORLD CALLED EARTH! I HAVEN'T HARMED...
IF YOU LISTEN TO THESE SORCERERS LONG ENOUGH, YOU START BELIEVING THEIR LIES! TAKE HIM TO THE TOWER OF THE RAINBOW DOOM AND DISPOSE OF HIM!
MOMENTS LATER HE IS CARRIED BODILY INTO A MIGHTY BUILDING WHOSE STONEWORK REFLECTS ITS VAST AGE...
NO ONE EVER ESCAPES THE DOOM OF THE RAINBOW! WE RESERVE IT ONLY FOR SORCERERS!
POWERFUL HANDS THRUST HIM INTO A CHAIR AND HOLD HIM MOTIONLESS WHILE A SWITCH IS THROWN! SLOWLY THE CHAMBER FLOODS WITH MULTI-COLORED LIGHTS...
THE DOOM HAS BEGUN!
FAREWELL, SORCERER!
SOME KIND OF MAGNETIC FORCE...GRIPPING ME TO THIS CHAIR... CAN'T ESCAPE...
3

OVERHEAD THE METAL GLOBES BEGIN TO CIRCLE MORE SWIFTLY! THEIR RAINBOW BEAMS BECOME A KALEIDOSCOPE OF BRILLIANT ENCHANTMENT AS ADAM FEELS A QUEER WEIGHTLESSNESS SPREADING THROUGHOUT HIS BODY...

WH-WHAT'S HAPPENING TO ME?

AN INSTANT LATER THE CHAIR IS EMPTY AND AWED WHISPERS RISE FROM BARBARIAN THROATS...

THE RAINBOW DOOM HAS BORNE HIM AWAY!

HE SHALL NEVER THREATEN US AGAIN!

WHERE IS ADAM STRANGE? THE EARTHMAN OPENS WONDERING EYES TO SEE...

A RAIN OF FIRE! NO...THOSE ARE BLAZING METEORS! I CAN TELL BY THE STARS I'M NOT ON RANN BUT ON A COMPLETELY DIFFERENT PLANET...

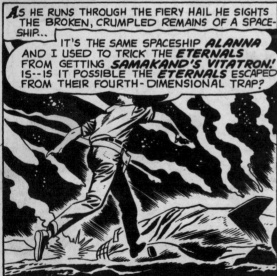

AS HE RUNS THROUGH THE FIERY HAIL HE SIGHTS THE BROKEN, CRUMPLED REMAINS OF A SPACE-SHIP...

IT'S THE SAME SPACESHIP ALANNA AND I USED TO TRICK THE ETERNALS FROM GETTING SAMAKAND'S VITATRON! IS--IS IT POSSIBLE THE ETERNALS ESCAPED FROM THEIR FOURTH-DIMENSIONAL TRAP?

HASTENING FORWARD, HE ENTERS THE WRECKAGE...

SARDATH...ALANNA'S FATHER! WHAT'S HE DOING HERE?

4

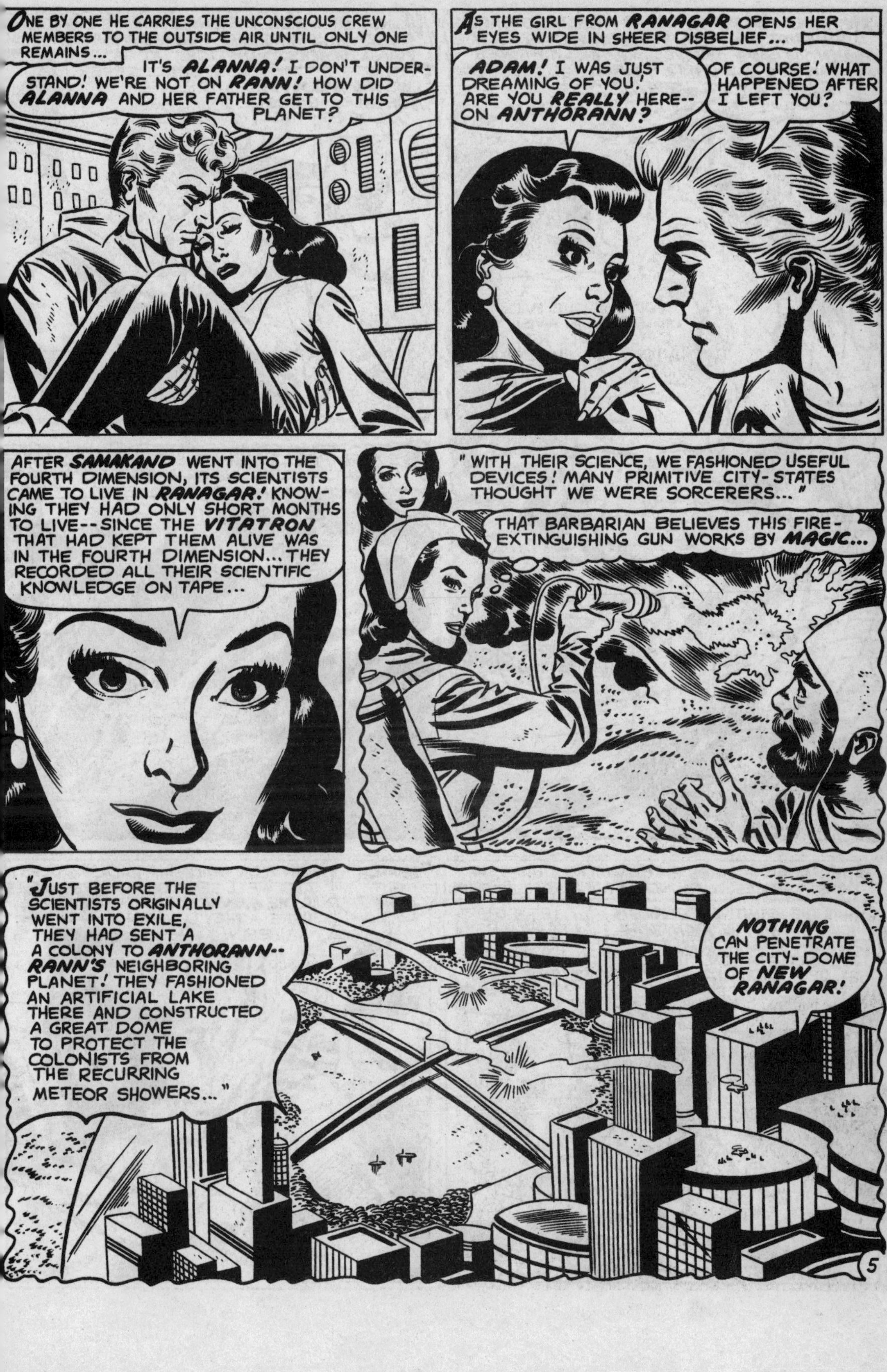
ONE BY ONE HE CARRIES THE UNCONSCIOUS CREW MEMBERS TO THE OUTSIDE AIR UNTIL ONLY ONE REMAINS...
IT'S ALANNA! I DON'T UNDERSTAND! WE'RE NOT ON RANN! HOW DID ALANNA AND HER FATHER GET TO THIS PLANET?
AS THE GIRL FROM RANAGAR OPENS HER EYES WIDE IN SHEER DISBELIEF...
ADAM! I WAS JUST DREAMING OF YOU! ARE YOU REALLY HERE-- ON ANTHORANN?
OF COURSE! WHAT HAPPENED AFTER I LEFT YOU?
AFTER SAMAKAND WENT INTO THE FOURTH DIMENSION, ITS SCIENTISTS CAME TO LIVE IN RANAGAR! KNOWING THEY HAD ONLY SHORT MONTHS TO LIVE--SINCE THE VITATRON THAT HAD KEPT THEM ALIVE WAS IN THE FOURTH DIMENSION...THEY RECORDED ALL THEIR SCIENTIFIC KNOWLEDGE ON TAPE...
"WITH THEIR SCIENCE, WE FASHIONED USEFUL DEVICES! MANY PRIMITIVE CITY-STATES THOUGHT WE WERE SORCERERS..."
THAT BARBARIAN BELIEVES THIS FIRE-EXTINGUISHING GUN WORKS BY MAGIC...
"JUST BEFORE THE SCIENTISTS ORIGINALLY WENT INTO EXILE, THEY HAD SENT A COLONY TO ANTHORANN--RANN'S NEIGHBORING PLANET! THEY FASHIONED AN ARTIFICIAL LAKE THERE AND CONSTRUCTED A GREAT DOME TO PROTECT THE COLONISTS FROM THE RECURRING METEOR SHOWERS..."
NOTHING CAN PENETRATE THE CITY-DOME OF NEW RANAGAR!
5

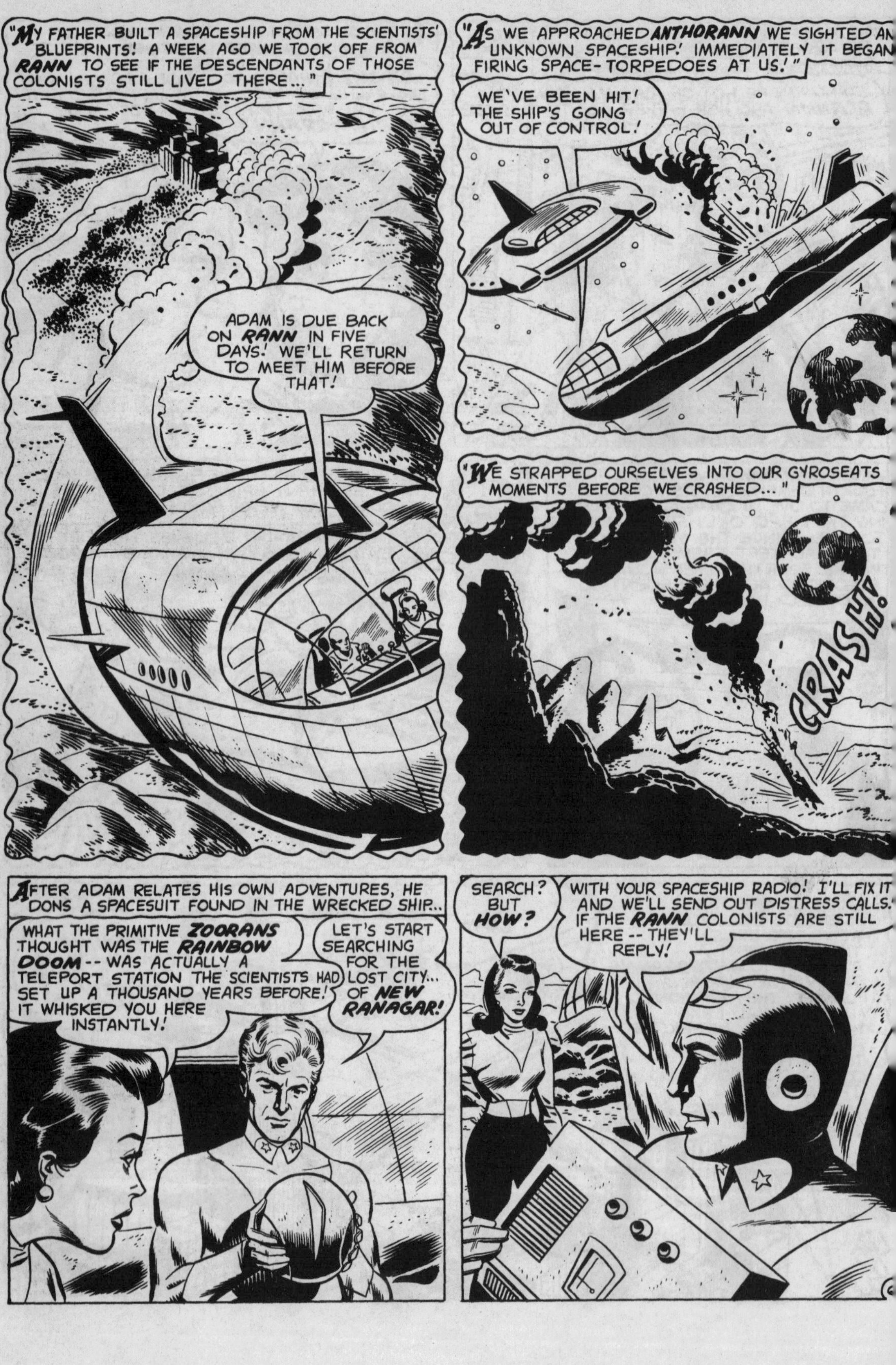
"MY FATHER BUILT A SPACESHIP FROM THE SCIENTISTS' BLUEPRINTS! A WEEK AGO WE TOOK OFF FROM RANN TO SEE IF THE DESCENDANTS OF THOSE COLONISTS STILL LIVED THERE..."
ADAM IS DUE BACK ON RANN IN FIVE DAYS! WE'LL RETURN TO MEET HIM BEFORE THAT!
"AS WE APPROACHED ANTHORANN WE SIGHTED AN UNKNOWN SPACESHIP! IMMEDIATELY IT BEGAN FIRING SPACE-TORPEDOES AT US!"
WE'VE BEEN HIT! THE SHIP'S GOING OUT OF CONTROL!
"WE STRAPPED OURSELVES INTO OUR GYROSEATS MOMENTS BEFORE WE CRASHED..."
CRASH!
AFTER ADAM RELATES HIS OWN ADVENTURES, HE DONS A SPACESUIT FOUND IN THE WRECKED SHIP...
WHAT THE PRIMITIVE ZOORANS THOUGHT WAS THE RAINBOW DOOM -- WAS ACTUALLY A TELEPORT STATION THE SCIENTISTS HAD SET UP A THOUSAND YEARS BEFORE! IT WHISKED YOU HERE INSTANTLY!
LET'S START SEARCHING FOR THE LOST CITY... OF NEW RANAGAR!
SEARCH? BUT HOW?
WITH YOUR SPACESHIP RADIO! I'LL FIX IT AND WE'LL SEND OUT DISTRESS CALLS. IF THE RANN COLONISTS ARE STILL HERE -- THEY'LL REPLY!

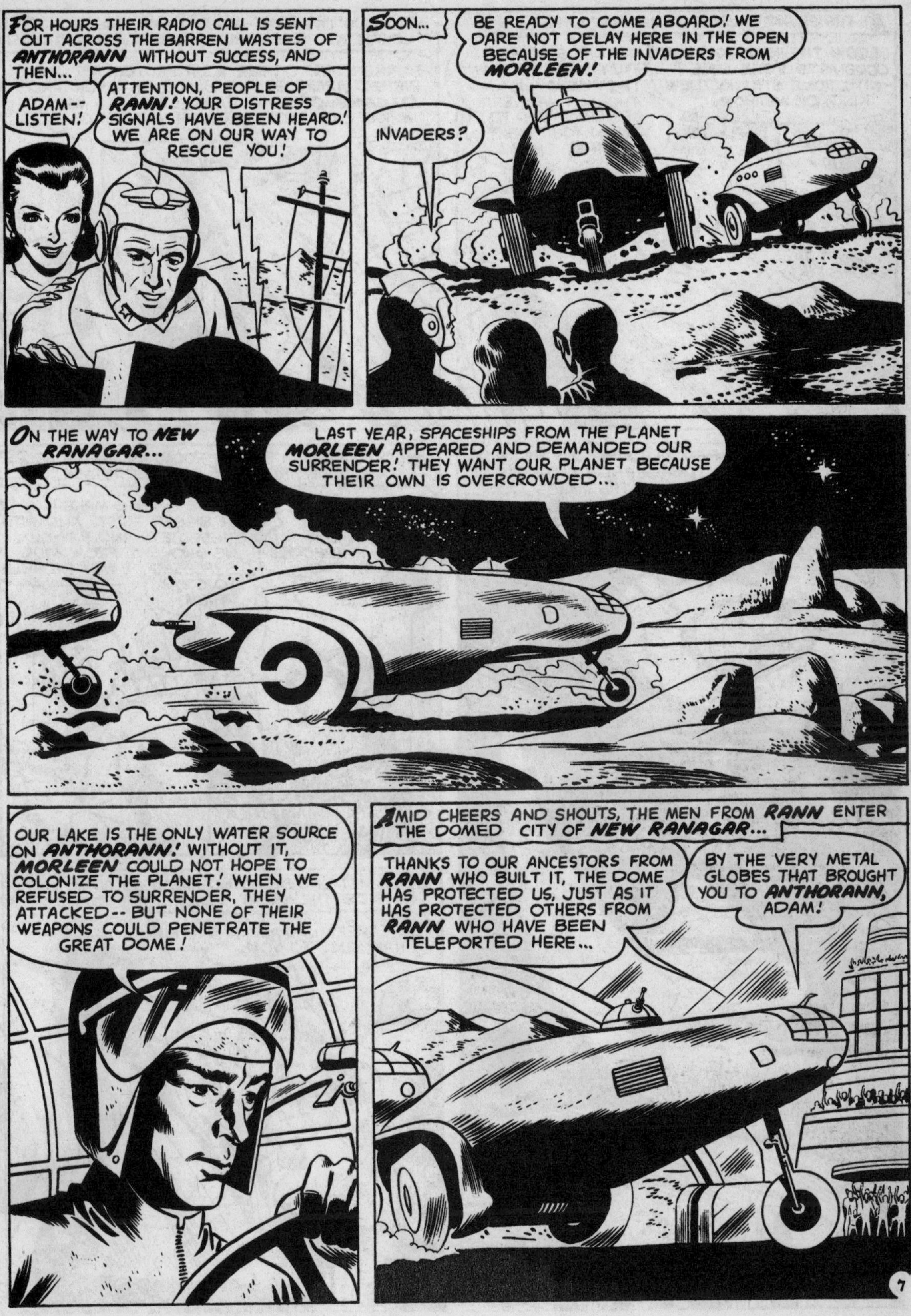
FOR HOURS THEIR RADIO CALL IS SENT OUT ACROSS THE BARREN WASTES OF ANTHORANN WITHOUT SUCCESS, AND THEN...
ADAM-- LISTEN!
ATTENTION, PEOPLE OF RANN! YOUR DISTRESS SIGNALS HAVE BEEN HEARD! WE ARE ON OUR WAY TO RESCUE YOU!
SOON...
BE READY TO COME ABOARD! WE DARE NOT DELAY HERE IN THE OPEN BECAUSE OF THE INVADERS FROM MORLEEN!
INVADERS?
ON THE WAY TO NEW RANAGAR...
LAST YEAR, SPACESHIPS FROM THE PLANET MORLEEN APPEARED AND DEMANDED OUR SURRENDER! THEY WANT OUR PLANET BECAUSE THEIR OWN IS OVERCROWDED...
OUR LAKE IS THE ONLY WATER SOURCE ON ANTHORANN! WITHOUT IT, MORLEEN COULD NOT HOPE TO COLONIZE THE PLANET! WHEN WE REFUSED TO SURRENDER, THEY ATTACKED-- BUT NONE OF THEIR WEAPONS COULD PENETRATE THE GREAT DOME!
AMID CHEERS AND SHOUTS, THE MEN FROM RANN ENTER THE DOMED CITY OF NEW RANAGAR...
THANKS TO OUR ANCESTORS FROM RANN WHO BUILT IT, THE DOME HAS PROTECTED US, JUST AS IT HAS PROTECTED OTHERS FROM RANN WHO HAVE BEEN TELEPORTED HERE...
BY THE VERY METAL GLOBES THAT BROUGHT YOU TO ANTHORANN, ADAM!
7

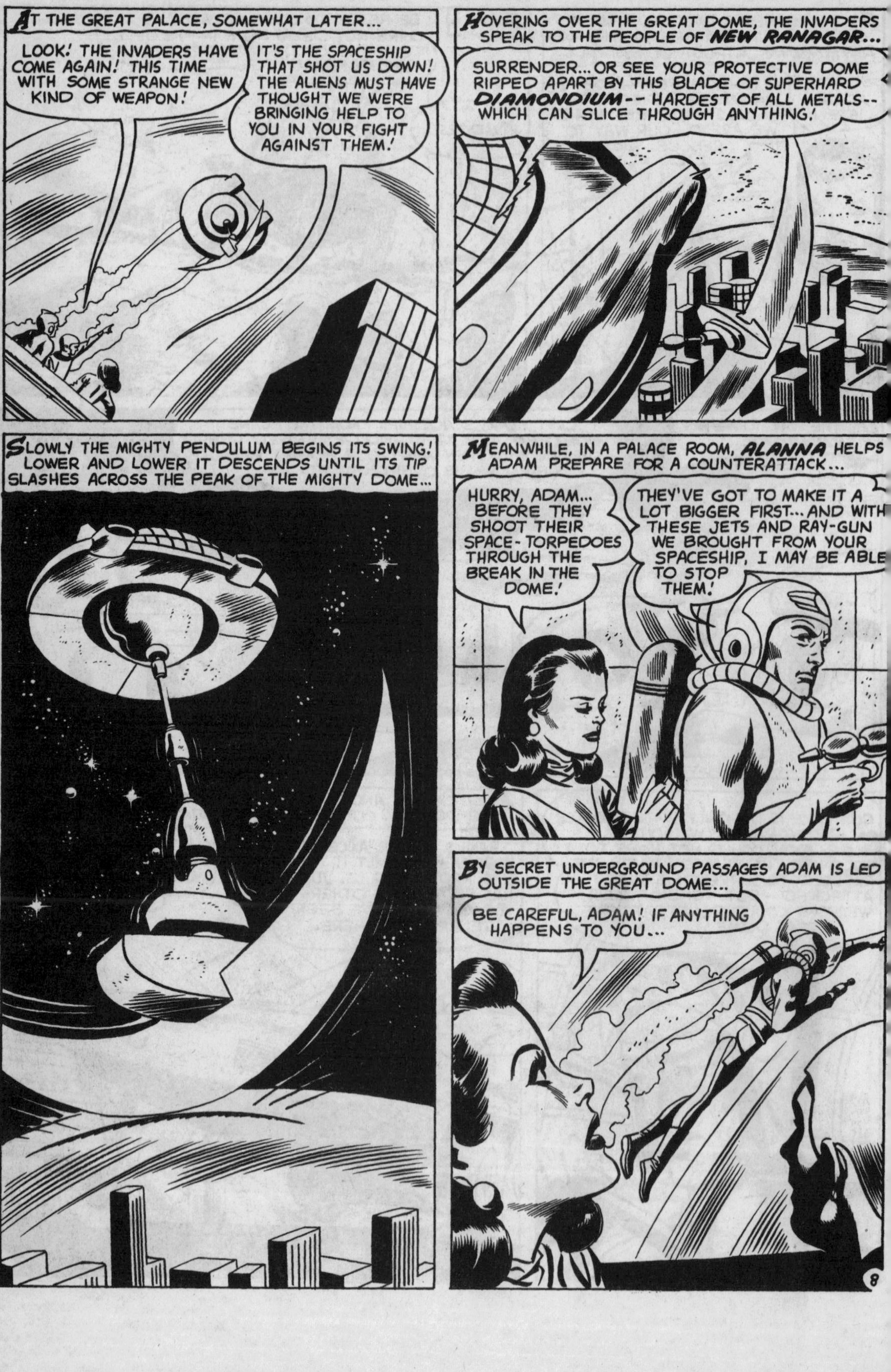
AT THE GREAT PALACE, SOMEWHAT LATER...
LOOK! THE INVADERS HAVE COME AGAIN! THIS TIME WITH SOME STRANGE NEW KIND OF WEAPON!
IT'S THE SPACESHIP THAT SHOT US DOWN! THE ALIENS MUST HAVE THOUGHT WE WERE BRINGING HELP TO YOU IN YOUR FIGHT AGAINST THEM!
HOVERING OVER THE GREAT DOME, THE INVADERS SPEAK TO THE PEOPLE OF NEW RANAGAR...
SURRENDER...OR SEE YOUR PROTECTIVE DOME RIPPED APART BY THIS BLADE OF SUPERHARD DIAMONDIUM-- HARDEST OF ALL METALS-- WHICH CAN SLICE THROUGH ANYTHING!
SLOWLY THE MIGHTY PENDULUM BEGINS ITS SWING! LOWER AND LOWER IT DESCENDS UNTIL ITS TIP SLASHES ACROSS THE PEAK OF THE MIGHTY DOME...
MEANWHILE, IN A PALACE ROOM, ALANNA HELPS ADAM PREPARE FOR A COUNTERATTACK...
HURRY, ADAM... BEFORE THEY SHOOT THEIR SPACE-TORPEDOES THROUGH THE BREAK IN THE DOME!
THEY'VE GOT TO MAKE IT A LOT BIGGER FIRST... AND WITH THESE JETS AND RAY-GUN WE BROUGHT FROM YOUR SPACESHIP, I MAY BE ABLE TO STOP THEM!
BY SECRET UNDERGROUND PASSAGES ADAM IS LED OUTSIDE THE GREAT DOME...
BE CAREFUL, ADAM! IF ANYTHING HAPPENS TO YOU...
8

SOARING HIGH INTO THE SKY OF *ANTHORANN*, ADAM STRANGE TRIGGERS HIS GUN AND SENDS A RAY-BLAST AT THE PENDULUM SHAFT!

GOT TO DESTROY THAT PENDULUM -- BEFORE IT DESTROYS THE DOME...

IN ANSWER TO HIS CHALLENGE, A DEADLY SPACE-TORPEDO IS FIRED AT HIM...

I'VE GOT TO DODGE... AND SHOOT... AT THE SAME TIME!

AS ADAM AVERTS FOLLOW-UP TORPEDOES, THEY EXPLODE HARMLESSLY ON THE GREAT DOME -- THEIR SHOCK WAVES TOSSING THE EARTHMAN ABOUT LIKE A LEAF IN A GALE!

DESPERATELY FIRING HIS BLASTER AND TWISTING TO AVOID THE TORPEDOES, ADAM STRANGE FIGHTS HIS GREATEST BATTLE...ONE MAN AGAINST THE ARMED MIGHT OF A SPACE-SHIP -- STRUGGLING TO SAVE THE LIFE OF THE WOMAN HE LOVES AND THE LIVES OF HER PEOPLE...

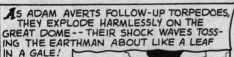

9

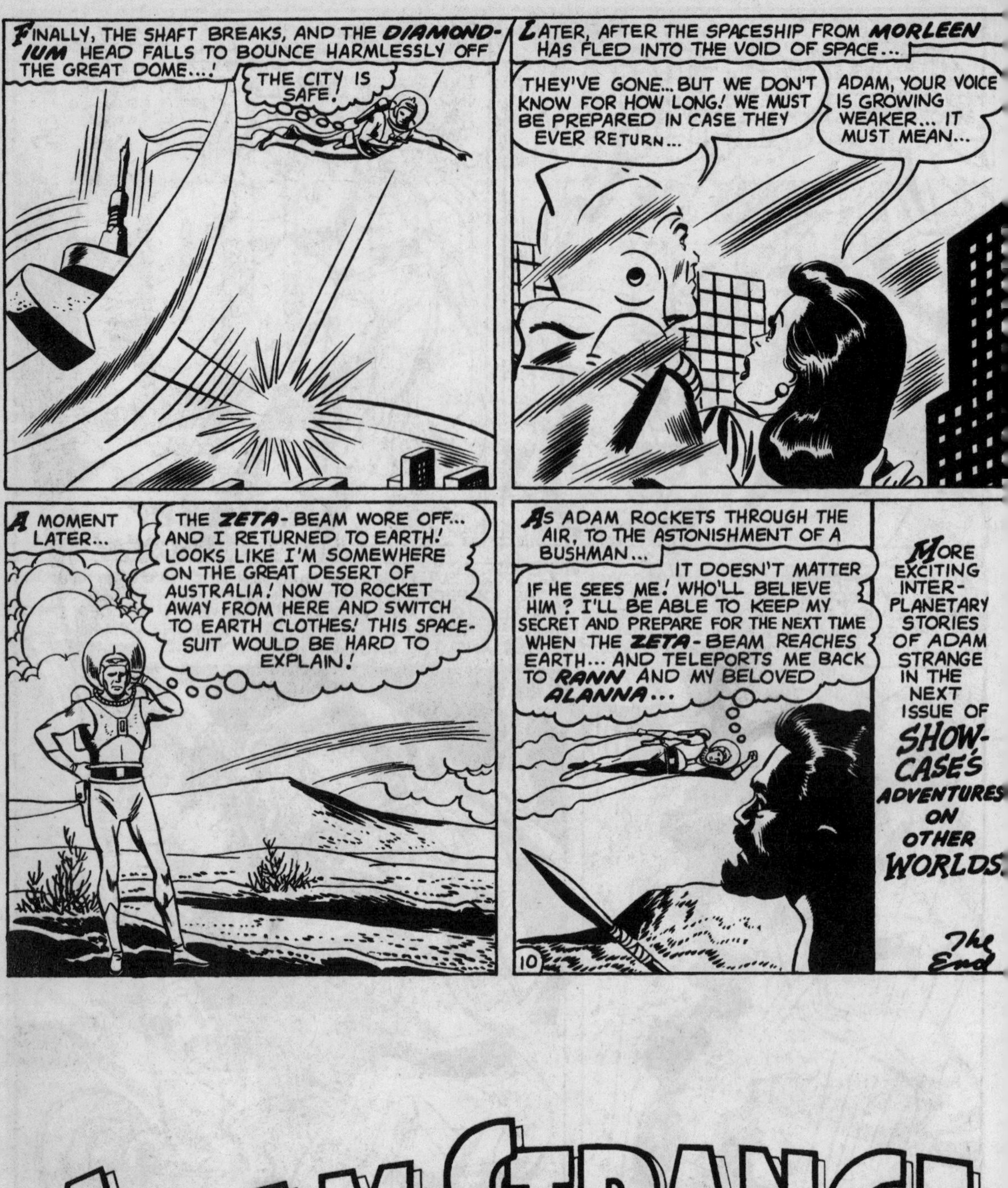
FINALLY, THE SHAFT BREAKS, AND THE DIAMONDIUM HEAD FALLS TO BOUNCE HARMLESSLY OFF THE GREAT DOME...!
THE CITY IS SAFE!
LATER, AFTER THE SPACESHIP FROM MORLEEN HAS FLED INTO THE VOID OF SPACE...
THEY'VE GONE... BUT WE DON'T KNOW FOR HOW LONG! WE MUST BE PREPARED IN CASE THEY EVER RETURN...
ADAM, YOUR VOICE IS GROWING WEAKER... IT MUST MEAN...
A MOMENT LATER...
THE ZETA-BEAM WORE OFF... AND I RETURNED TO EARTH! LOOKS LIKE I'M SOMEWHERE ON THE GREAT DESERT OF AUSTRALIA! NOW TO ROCKET AWAY FROM HERE AND SWITCH TO EARTH CLOTHES! THIS SPACE-SUIT WOULD BE HARD TO EXPLAIN!
AS ADAM ROCKETS THROUGH THE AIR, TO THE ASTONISHMENT OF A BUSHMAN...
IT DOESN'T MATTER IF HE SEES ME! WHO'LL BELIEVE HIM? I'LL BE ABLE TO KEEP MY SECRET AND PREPARE FOR THE NEXT TIME WHEN THE ZETA-BEAM REACHES EARTH... AND TELEPORTS ME BACK TO RANN AND MY BELOVED ALANNA...
10
MORE EXCITING INTER-PLANETARY STORIES OF ADAM STRANGE IN THE NEXT ISSUE OF SHOWCASE'S ADVENTURES ON OTHER WORLDS.
The End

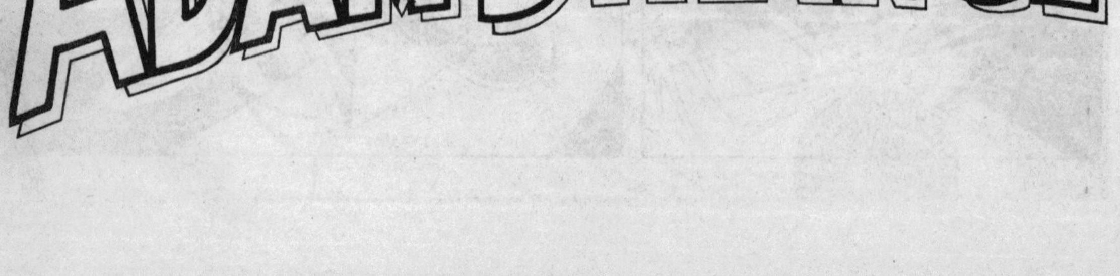
ADAM STRANGE

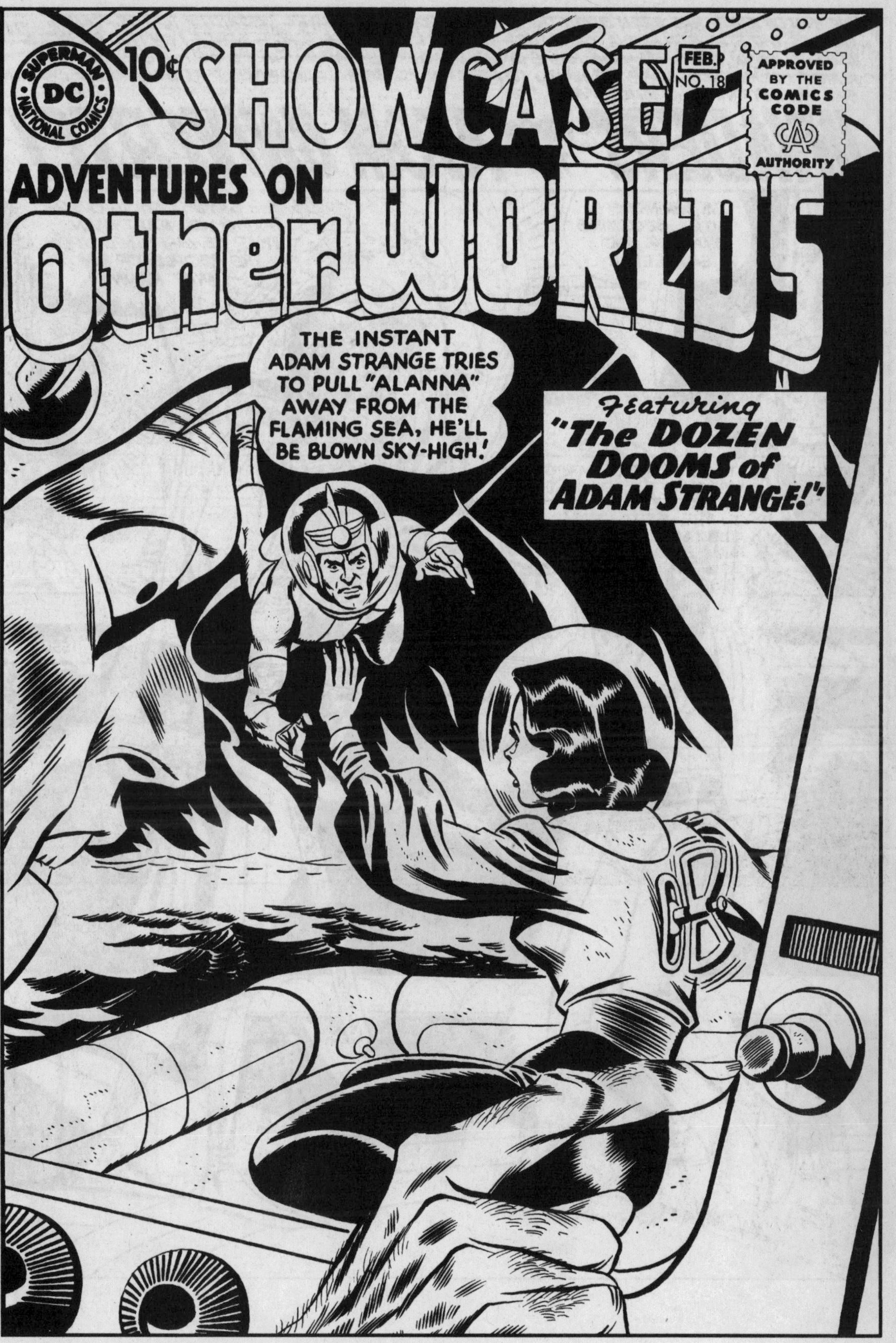
SUPERMAN DC NATIONAL COMICS
10¢ SHOWCASE
FEB. NO. 18
APPROVED BY THE COMICS CODE AUTHORITY
ADVENTURES ON Other WORLDS
THE INSTANT ADAM STRANGE TRIES TO PULL "ALANNA" AWAY FROM THE FLAMING SEA, HE'LL BE BLOWN SKY-HIGH!
Featuring "The DOZEN DOOMS of ADAM STRANGE!"

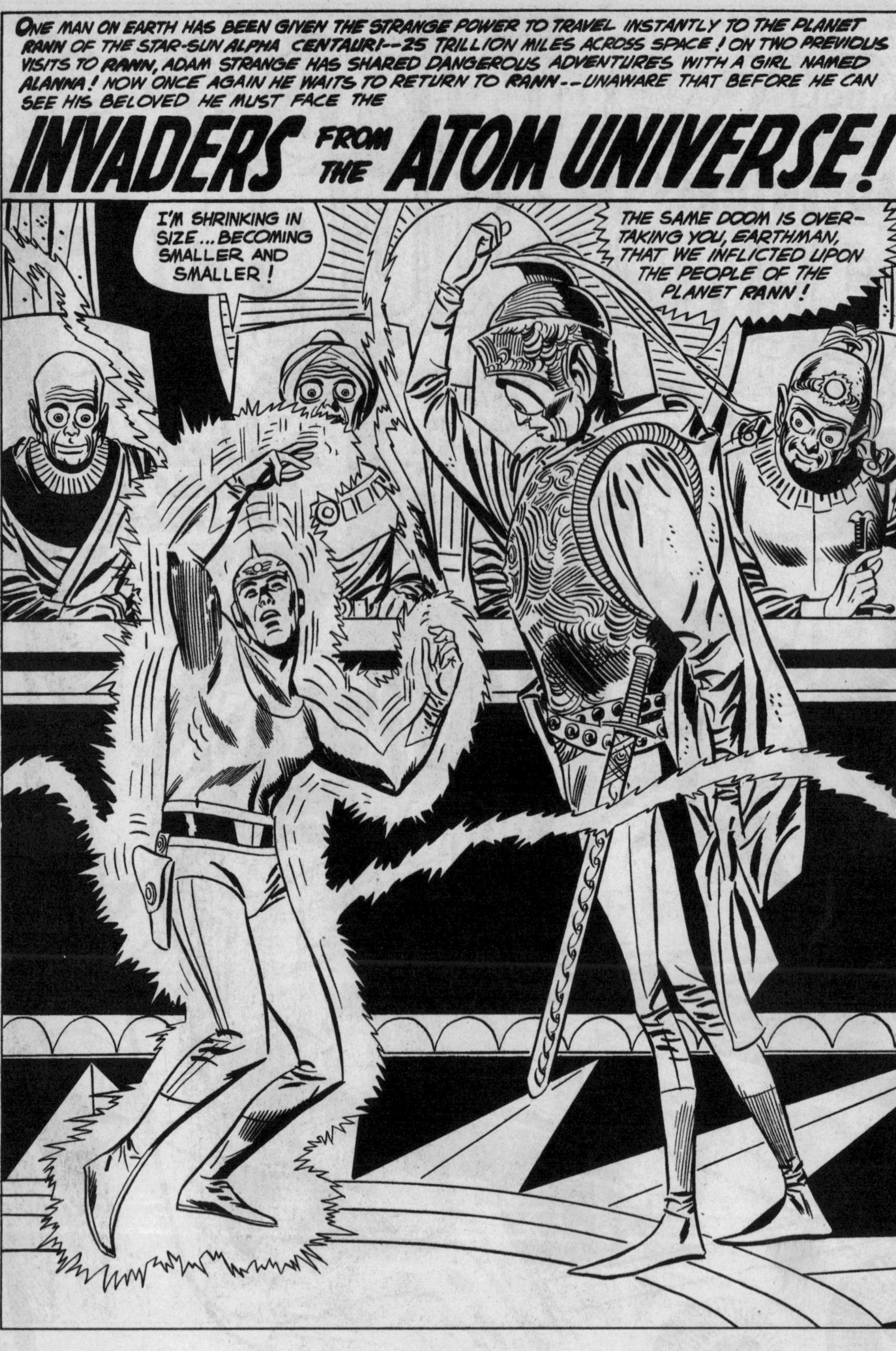
ONE MAN ON EARTH HAS BEEN GIVEN THE STRANGE POWER TO TRAVEL INSTANTLY TO THE PLANET RANN OF THE STAR-SUN ALPHA CENTAURI--25 TRILLION MILES ACROSS SPACE ! ON TWO PREVIOUS VISITS TO RANN, ADAM STRANGE HAS SHARED DANGEROUS ADVENTURES WITH A GIRL NAMED ALANNA ! NOW ONCE AGAIN HE WAITS TO RETURN TO RANN--UNAWARE THAT BEFORE HE CAN SEE HIS BELOVED HE MUST FACE THE
INVADERS FROM THE ATOM UNIVERSE!
I'M SHRINKING IN SIZE ... BECOMING SMALLER AND SMALLER !
THE SAME DOOM IS OVERTAKING YOU, EARTHMAN, THAT WE INFLICTED UPON THE PEOPLE OF THE PLANET RANN !

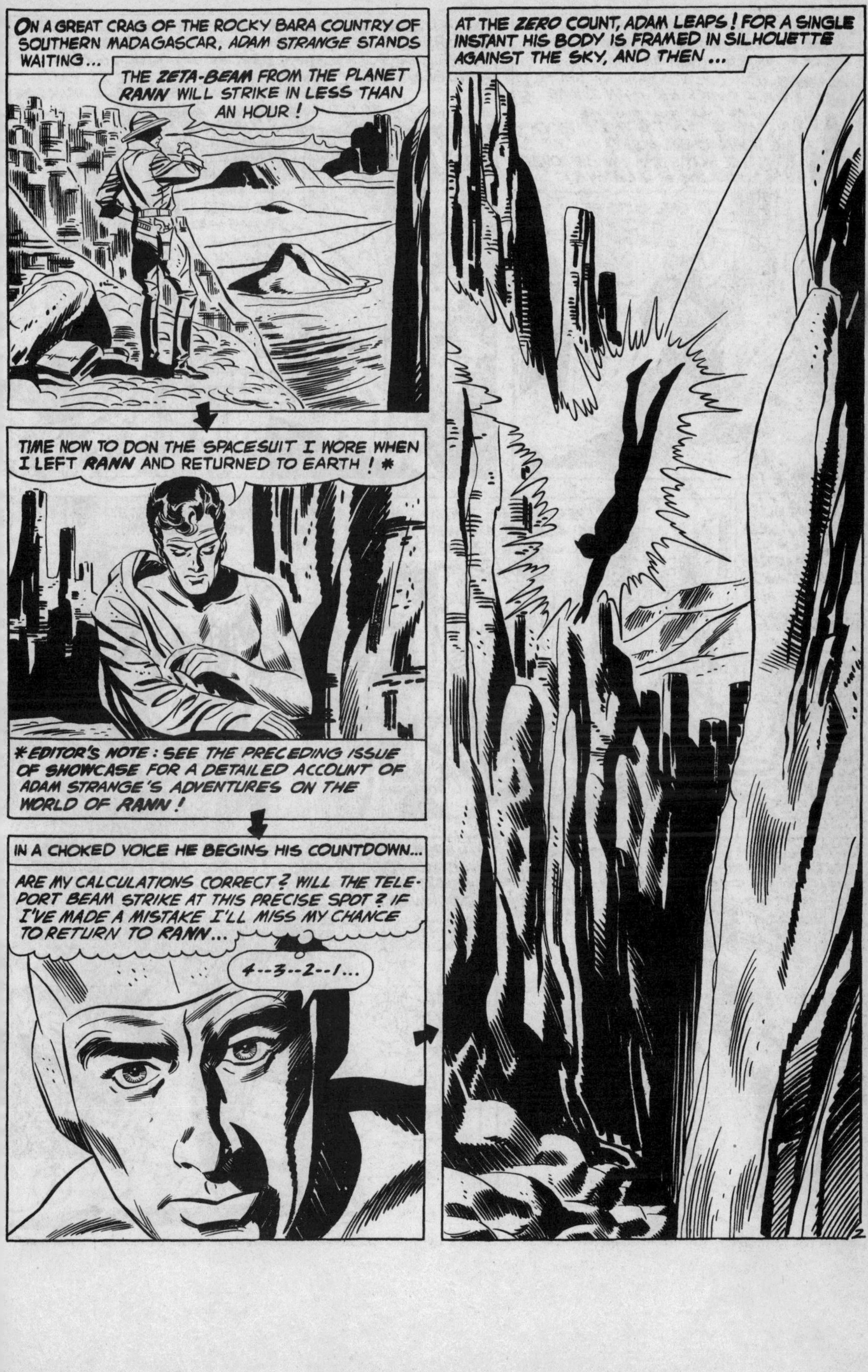
ON A GREAT CRAG OF THE ROCKY BARA COUNTRY OF SOUTHERN MADAGASCAR, ADAM STRANGE STANDS WAITING...
THE ZETA-BEAM FROM THE PLANET RANN WILL STRIKE IN LESS THAN AN HOUR!
TIME NOW TO DON THE SPACESUIT I WORE WHEN I LEFT RANN AND RETURNED TO EARTH! *
*EDITOR'S NOTE: SEE THE PRECEDING ISSUE OF SHOWCASE FOR A DETAILED ACCOUNT OF ADAM STRANGE'S ADVENTURES ON THE WORLD OF RANN!
IN A CHOKED VOICE HE BEGINS HIS COUNTDOWN...
ARE MY CALCULATIONS CORRECT? WILL THE TELE-PORT BEAM STRIKE AT THIS PRECISE SPOT? IF I'VE MADE A MISTAKE I'LL MISS MY CHANCE TO RETURN TO RANN...
4--3--2--1...
AT THE ZERO COUNT, ADAM LEAPS! FOR A SINGLE INSTANT HIS BODY IS FRAMED IN SILHOUETTE AGAINST THE SKY, AND THEN...
2

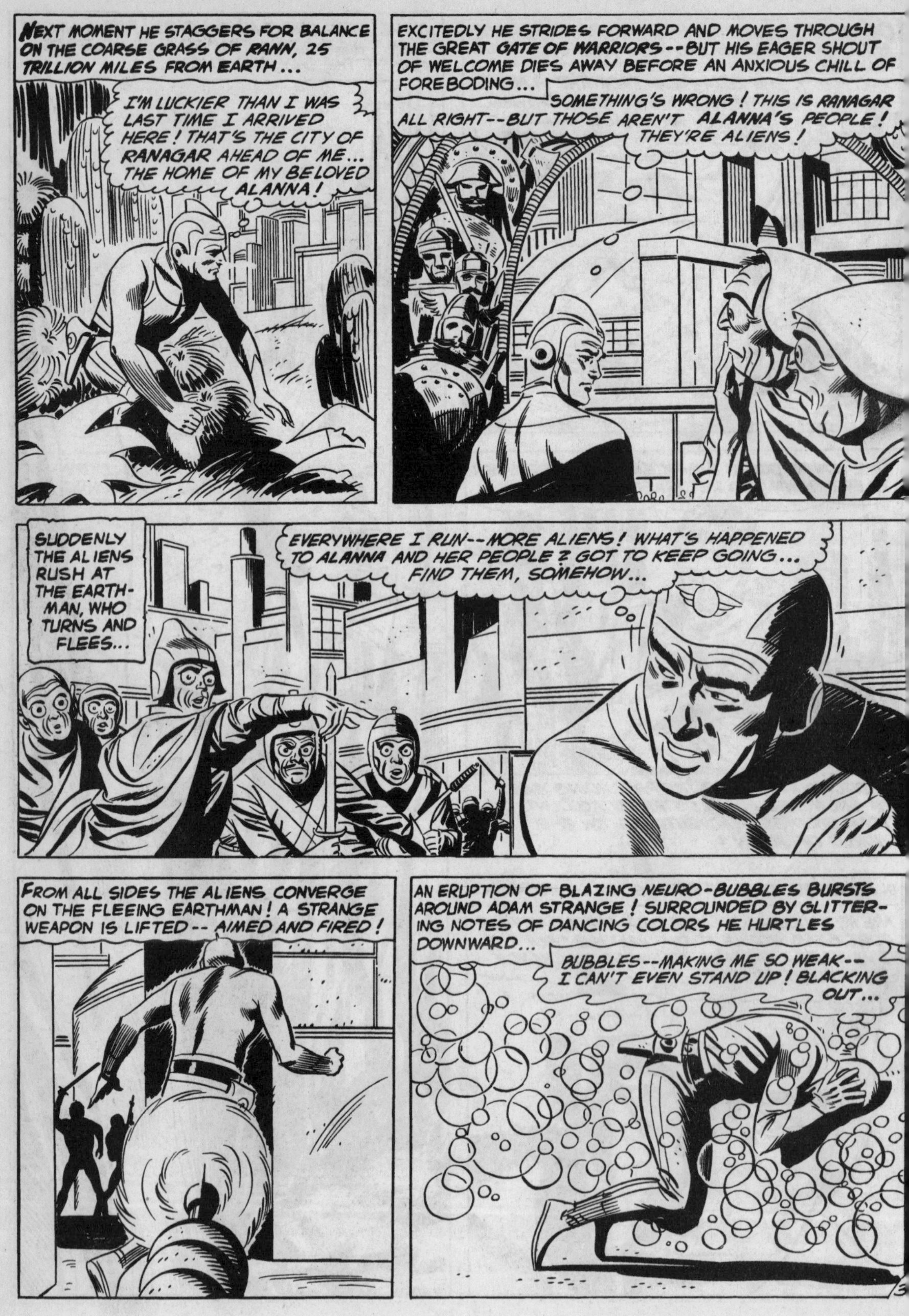
NEXT MOMENT HE STAGGERS FOR BALANCE ON THE COARSE GRASS OF RANN, 25 TRILLION MILES FROM EARTH...
I'M LUCKIER THAN I WAS LAST TIME I ARRIVED HERE! THAT'S THE CITY OF RANAGAR AHEAD OF ME... THE HOME OF MY BELOVED ALANNA!
EXCITEDLY HE STRIDES FORWARD AND MOVES THROUGH THE GREAT GATE OF WARRIORS--BUT HIS EAGER SHOUT OF WELCOME DIES AWAY BEFORE AN ANXIOUS CHILL OF FOREBODING...
SOMETHING'S WRONG! THIS IS RANAGAR ALL RIGHT--BUT THOSE AREN'T ALANNA'S PEOPLE! THEY'RE ALIENS!
SUDDENLY THE ALIENS RUSH AT THE EARTHMAN, WHO TURNS AND FLEES...
EVERYWHERE I RUN--MORE ALIENS! WHAT'S HAPPENED TO ALANNA AND HER PEOPLE? GOT TO KEEP GOING... FIND THEM, SOMEHOW...
FROM ALL SIDES THE ALIENS CONVERGE ON THE FLEEING EARTHMAN! A STRANGE WEAPON IS LIFTED-- AIMED AND FIRED!
AN ERUPTION OF BLAZING NEURO-BUBBLES BURSTS AROUND ADAM STRANGE! SURROUNDED BY GLITTERING NOTES OF DANCING COLORS HE HURTLES DOWNWARD...
BUBBLES--MAKING ME SO WEAK--I CAN'T EVEN STAND UP! BLACKING OUT...
3

WHEN HE RECOVERS CONSCIOUSNESS, HE FINDS HIM-SELF IN THE MASSIVE *HALL OF JUSTICE*...

WHO ARE YOU? WHERE DID YOU COME FROM?

YOU'RE COMMUNICATING BY MENTAL TELEPATHY...SO YOU'LL UNDER-STAND WHEN I SAY I'M ADAM STRANGE OF EARTH--A DISTANT PLANET! I'VE COME TO *RANN* BY TELEPORT BEAM!

BUT WHERE IS EVERYBODY? *ALANNA?* HER FATHER? ALL HER PEOPLE? WHAT HAPPENED TO THEM?

AS THE ALIEN CHIEF SNAPS AN ORDER, A SHOWER OF BRILLIANT LIGHTNINGS BURSTS INTO A FLAMEBALL AROUND THE EARTHMAN...

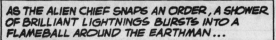

ALL YOUR QUESTIONS WILL BE ANSWERED SHORTLY, ADAM STRANGE! SENDAL-- TURN ON THE *ORKINOMIKRON!*

LIGHT SO BRIGHT-- CAN'T SEE!

THEN, TO HIS ASTONISHMENT, ADAM DISCOVERS HE IS SHRINKING SO SWIFTLY THAT IN SECONDS HE HAS BECOME A TINY MAN...

I'M GROWING SMALLER... SMALLER...

IN THE TIME NEEDED TO TAKE A SINGLE BREATH...

I'M AS SMALL AS AN ANT NOW! WHEN WILL THE SHRINKING PROCESS END?

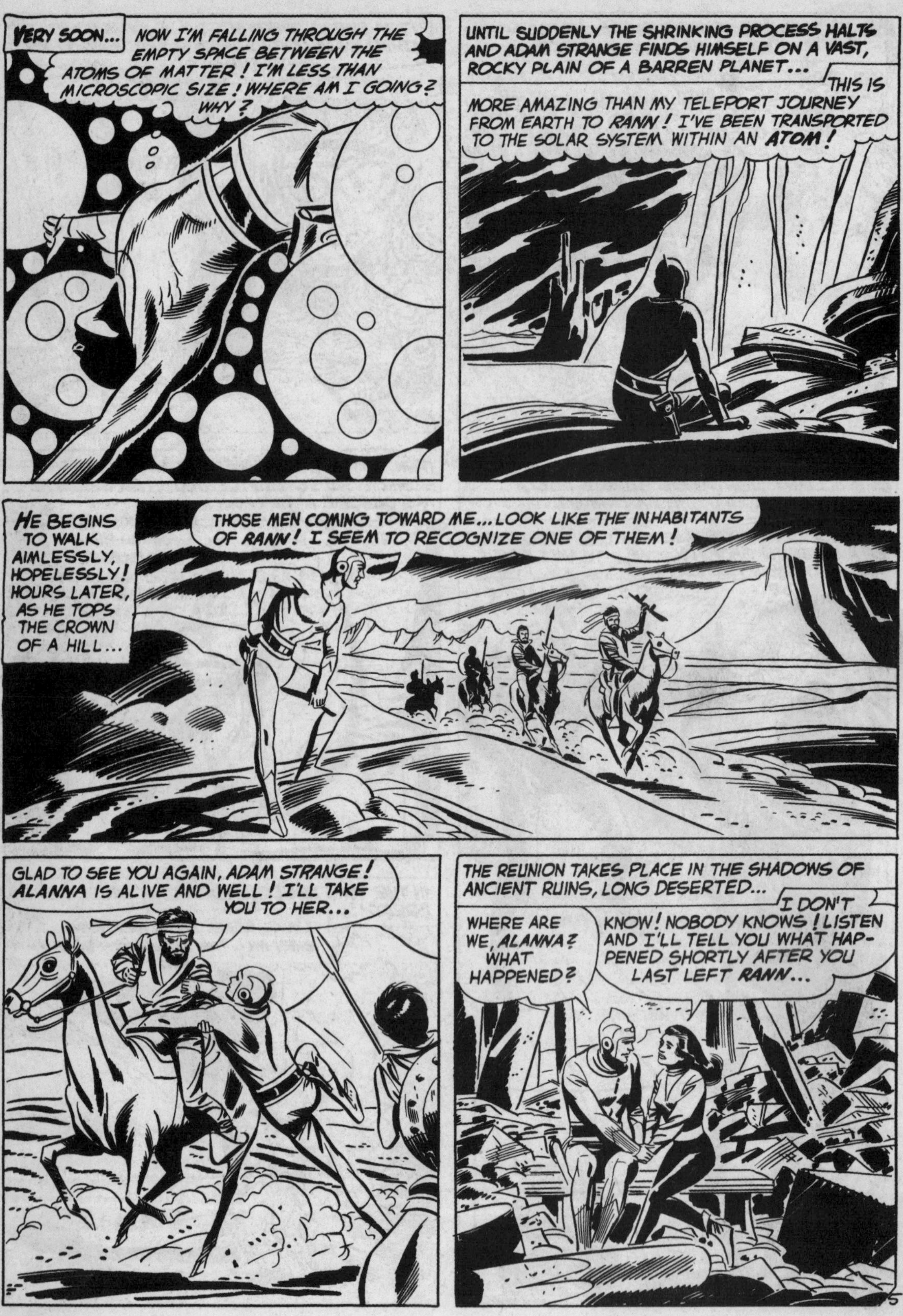
VERY SOON...
NOW I'M FALLING THROUGH THE EMPTY SPACE BETWEEN THE ATOMS OF MATTER! I'M LESS THAN MICROSCOPIC SIZE! WHERE AM I GOING? WHY?
UNTIL SUDDENLY THE SHRINKING PROCESS HALTS AND ADAM STRANGE FINDS HIMSELF ON A VAST, ROCKY PLAIN OF A BARREN PLANET...
THIS IS MORE AMAZING THAN MY TELEPORT JOURNEY FROM EARTH TO RANN! I'VE BEEN TRANSPORTED TO THE SOLAR SYSTEM WITHIN AN ATOM!
HE BEGINS TO WALK AIMLESSLY, HOPELESSLY! HOURS LATER, AS HE TOPS THE CROWN OF A HILL...
THOSE MEN COMING TOWARD ME... LOOK LIKE THE INHABITANTS OF RANN! I SEEM TO RECOGNIZE ONE OF THEM!
GLAD TO SEE YOU AGAIN, ADAM STRANGE! ALANNA IS ALIVE AND WELL! I'LL TAKE YOU TO HER...
THE REUNION TAKES PLACE IN THE SHADOWS OF ANCIENT RUINS, LONG DESERTED...
WHERE ARE WE, ALANNA? WHAT HAPPENED?
I DON'T KNOW! NOBODY KNOWS! LISTEN AND I'LL TELL YOU WHAT HAPPENED SHORTLY AFTER YOU LAST LEFT RANN...
5

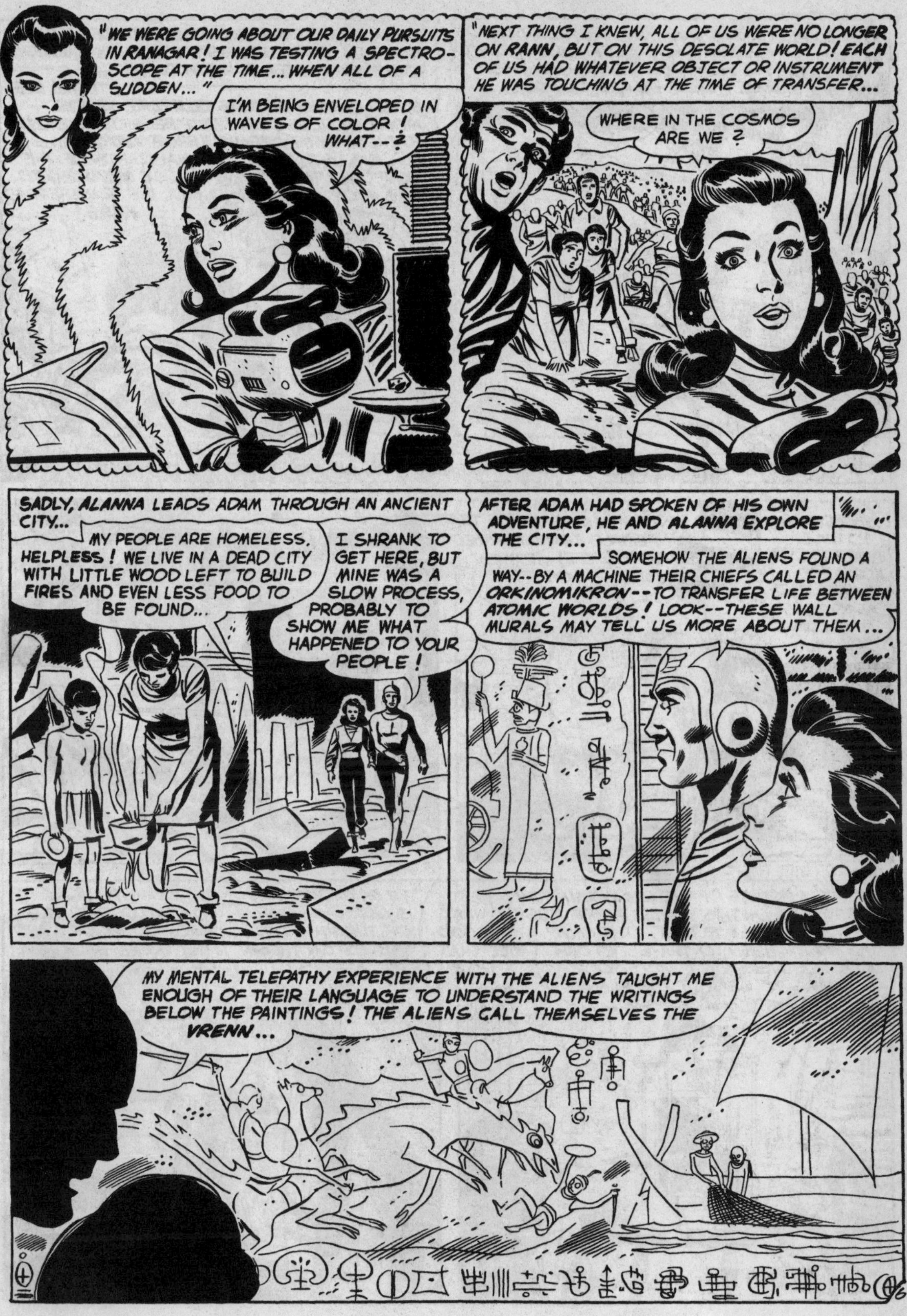
"WE WERE GOING ABOUT OUR DAILY PURSUITS IN RANAGAR! I WAS TESTING A SPECTROSCOPE AT THE TIME... WHEN ALL OF A SUDDEN..."
I'M BEING ENVELOPED IN WAVES OF COLOR! WHAT--?
"NEXT THING I KNEW, ALL OF US WERE NO LONGER ON RANN, BUT ON THIS DESOLATE WORLD! EACH OF US HAD WHATEVER OBJECT OR INSTRUMENT HE WAS TOUCHING AT THE TIME OF TRANSFER...
WHERE IN THE COSMOS ARE WE?
SADLY, ALANNA LEADS ADAM THROUGH AN ANCIENT CITY...
MY PEOPLE ARE HOMELESS, HELPLESS! WE LIVE IN A DEAD CITY WITH LITTLE WOOD LEFT TO BUILD FIRES AND EVEN LESS FOOD TO BE FOUND...
I SHRANK TO GET HERE, BUT MINE WAS A SLOW PROCESS, PROBABLY TO SHOW ME WHAT HAPPENED TO YOUR PEOPLE!
AFTER ADAM HAD SPOKEN OF HIS OWN ADVENTURE, HE AND ALANNA EXPLORE THE CITY...
SOMEHOW THE ALIENS FOUND A WAY--BY A MACHINE THEIR CHIEFS CALLED AN ORKINOMIKRON--TO TRANSFER LIFE BETWEEN ATOMIC WORLDS! LOOK--THESE WALL MURALS MAY TELL US MORE ABOUT THEM...
MY MENTAL TELEPATHY EXPERIENCE WITH THE ALIENS TAUGHT ME ENOUGH OF THEIR LANGUAGE TO UNDERSTAND THE WRITINGS BELOW THE PAINTINGS! THE ALIENS CALL THEMSELVES THE VRENN...

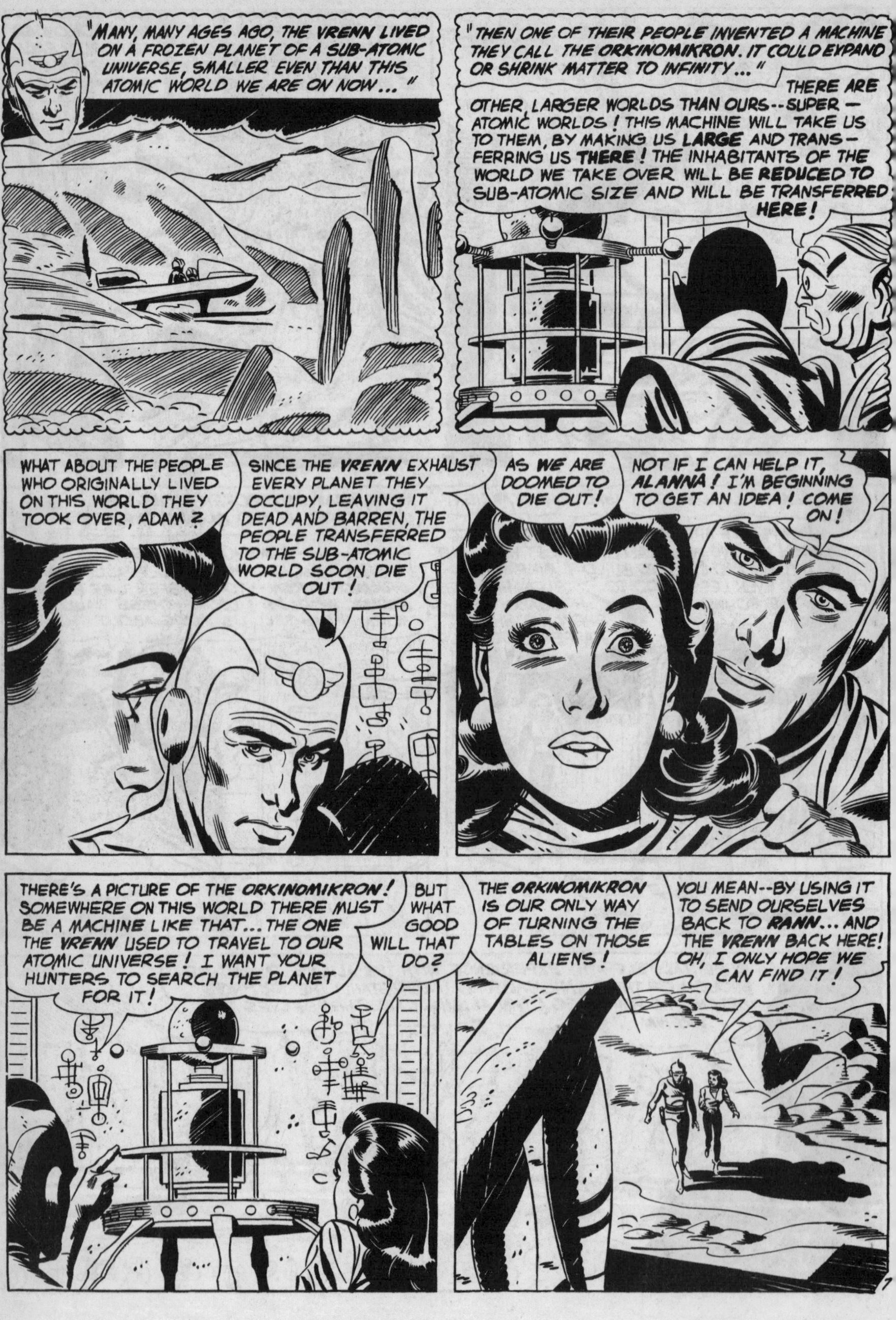
"MANY, MANY AGES AGO, THE VRENN LIVED ON A FROZEN PLANET OF A SUB-ATOMIC UNIVERSE, SMALLER EVEN THAN THIS ATOMIC WORLD WE ARE ON NOW..."
"THEN ONE OF THEIR PEOPLE INVENTED A MACHINE THEY CALL THE ORKINOMIKRON. IT COULD EXPAND OR SHRINK MATTER TO INFINITY..."
THERE ARE OTHER, LARGER WORLDS THAN OURS--SUPER-ATOMIC WORLDS! THIS MACHINE WILL TAKE US TO THEM, BY MAKING US LARGE AND TRANSFERRING US THERE! THE INHABITANTS OF THE WORLD WE TAKE OVER WILL BE REDUCED TO SUB-ATOMIC SIZE AND WILL BE TRANSFERRED HERE!
WHAT ABOUT THE PEOPLE WHO ORIGINALLY LIVED ON THIS WORLD THEY TOOK OVER, ADAM?
SINCE THE VRENN EXHAUST EVERY PLANET THEY OCCUPY, LEAVING IT DEAD AND BARREN, THE PEOPLE TRANSFERRED TO THE SUB-ATOMIC WORLD SOON DIE OUT!
AS WE ARE DOOMED TO DIE OUT!
NOT IF I CAN HELP IT, ALANNA! I'M BEGINNING TO GET AN IDEA! COME ON!
THERE'S A PICTURE OF THE ORKINOMIKRON! SOMEWHERE ON THIS WORLD THERE MUST BE A MACHINE LIKE THAT... THE ONE THE VRENN USED TO TRAVEL TO OUR ATOMIC UNIVERSE! I WANT YOUR HUNTERS TO SEARCH THE PLANET FOR IT!
BUT WHAT GOOD WILL THAT DO?
THE ORKINOMIKRON IS OUR ONLY WAY OF TURNING THE TABLES ON THOSE ALIENS!
YOU MEAN--BY USING IT TO SEND OURSELVES BACK TO RANN... AND THE VRENN BACK HERE! OH, I ONLY HOPE WE CAN FIND IT!
7

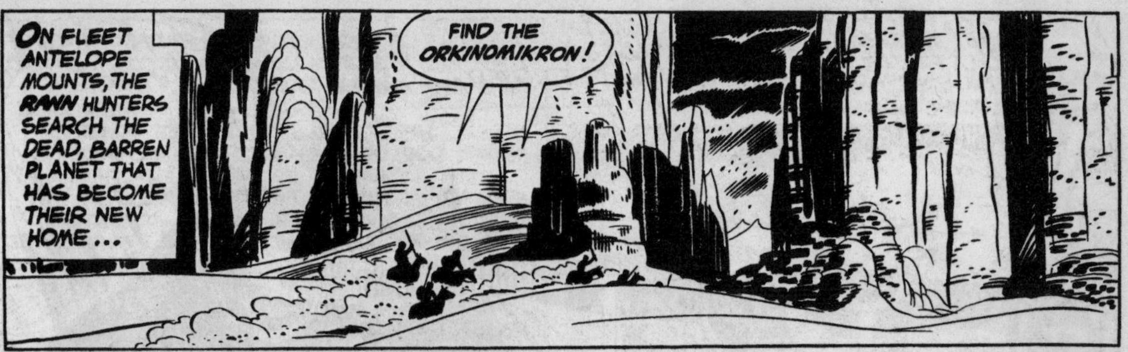
ON FLEET ANTELOPE MOUNTS, THE RANN HUNTERS SEARCH THE DEAD, BARREN PLANET THAT HAS BECOME THEIR NEW HOME...
FIND THE ORKINOMIKRON!

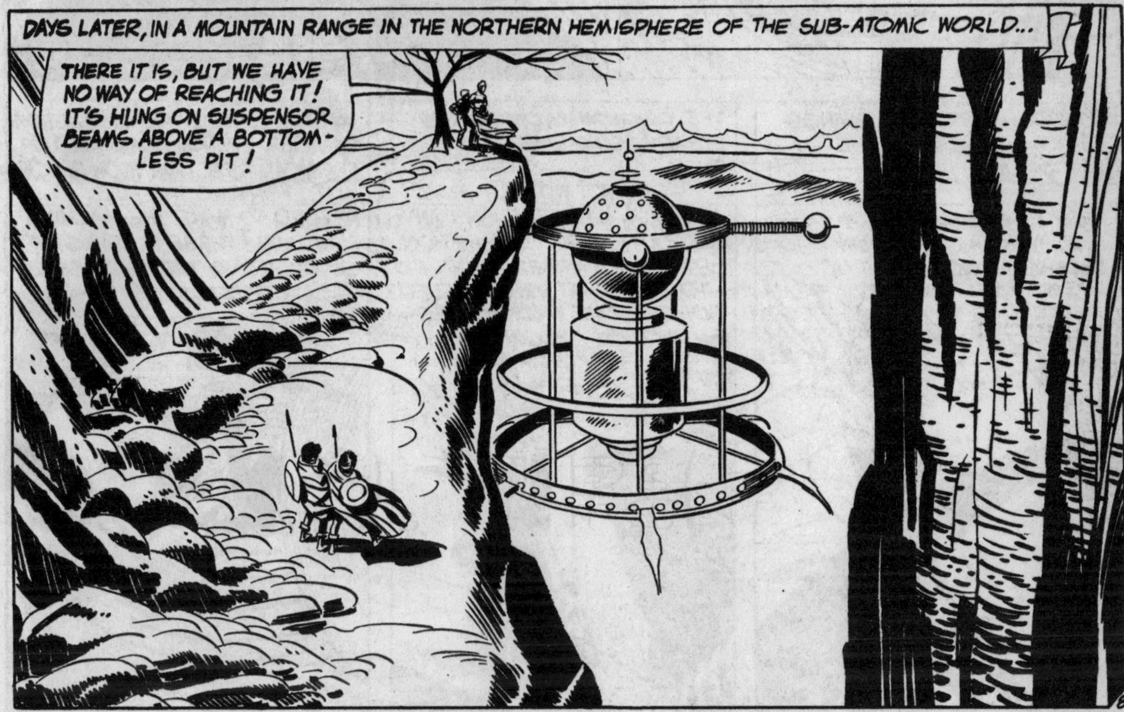
DAYS LATER, IN A MOUNTAIN RANGE IN THE NORTHERN HEMISPHERE OF THE SUB-ATOMIC WORLD...
THERE IT IS, BUT WE HAVE NO WAY OF REACHING IT! IT'S HUNG ON SUSPENSOR BEAMS ABOVE A BOTTOMLESS PIT!
8

ADAM STRANGE

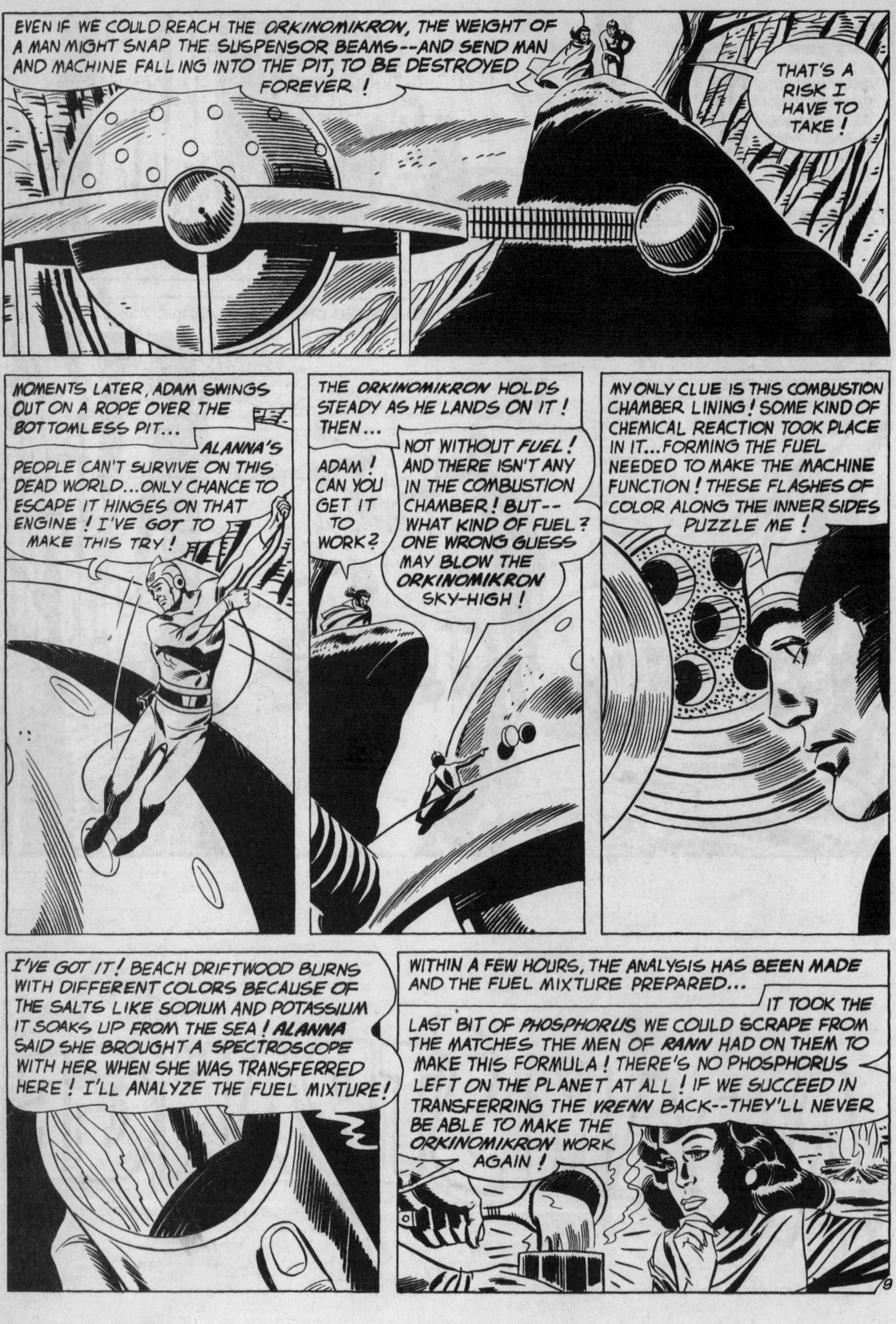
EVEN IF WE COULD REACH THE ORKINOMIKRON, THE WEIGHT OF A MAN MIGHT SNAP THE SUSPENSOR BEAMS--AND SEND MAN AND MACHINE FALLING INTO THE PIT, TO BE DESTROYED FOREVER!
THAT'S A RISK I HAVE TO TAKE!
MOMENTS LATER, ADAM SWINGS OUT ON A ROPE OVER THE BOTTOMLESS PIT...
ALANNA'S PEOPLE CAN'T SURVIVE ON THIS DEAD WORLD...ONLY CHANCE TO ESCAPE IT HINGES ON THAT ENGINE! I'VE GOT TO MAKE THIS TRY!
THE ORKINOMIKRON HOLDS STEADY AS HE LANDS ON IT! THEN...
ADAM! CAN YOU GET IT TO WORK?
NOT WITHOUT FUEL! AND THERE ISN'T ANY IN THE COMBUSTION CHAMBER! BUT--WHAT KIND OF FUEL? ONE WRONG GUESS MAY BLOW THE ORKINOMIKRON SKY-HIGH!
MY ONLY CLUE IS THIS COMBUSTION CHAMBER LINING! SOME KIND OF CHEMICAL REACTION TOOK PLACE IN IT...FORMING THE FUEL NEEDED TO MAKE THE MACHINE FUNCTION! THESE FLASHES OF COLOR ALONG THE INNER SIDES PUZZLE ME!
I'VE GOT IT! BEACH DRIFTWOOD BURNS WITH DIFFERENT COLORS BECAUSE OF THE SALTS LIKE SODIUM AND POTASSIUM IT SOAKS UP FROM THE SEA! ALANNA SAID SHE BROUGHT A SPECTROSCOPE WITH HER WHEN SHE WAS TRANSFERRED HERE! I'LL ANALYZE THE FUEL MIXTURE!
WITHIN A FEW HOURS, THE ANALYSIS HAS BEEN MADE AND THE FUEL MIXTURE PREPARED...
IT TOOK THE LAST BIT OF PHOSPHORUS WE COULD SCRAPE FROM THE MATCHES THE MEN OF RANN HAD ON THEM TO MAKE THIS FORMULA! THERE'S NO PHOSPHORUS LEFT ON THE PLANET AT ALL! IF WE SUCCEED IN TRANSFERRING THE VRENN BACK--THEY'LL NEVER BE ABLE TO MAKE THE ORKINOMIKRON WORK AGAIN!
9

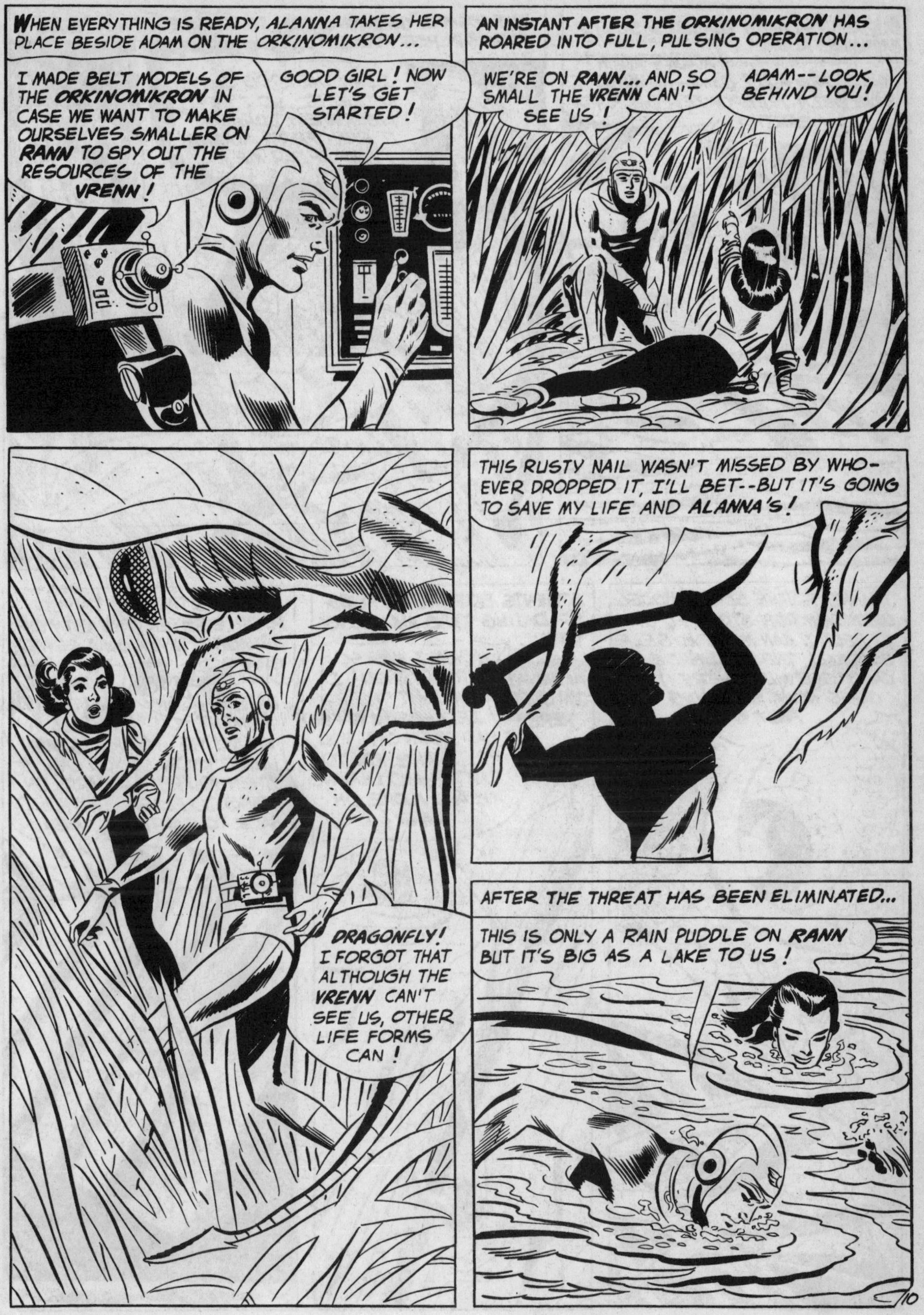
WHEN EVERYTHING IS READY, ALANNA TAKES HER PLACE BESIDE ADAM ON THE ORKINOMIKRON...
I MADE BELT MODELS OF THE ORKINOMIKRON IN CASE WE WANT TO MAKE OURSELVES SMALLER ON RANN TO SPY OUT THE RESOURCES OF THE VRENN!
GOOD GIRL! NOW LET'S GET STARTED!
AN INSTANT AFTER THE ORKINOMIKRON HAS ROARED INTO FULL, PULSING OPERATION...
WE'RE ON RANN... AND SO SMALL THE VRENN CAN'T SEE US!
ADAM--LOOK BEHIND YOU!
DRAGONFLY! I FORGOT THAT ALTHOUGH THE VRENN CAN'T SEE US, OTHER LIFE FORMS CAN!
THIS RUSTY NAIL WASN'T MISSED BY WHO-EVER DROPPED IT, I'LL BET--BUT IT'S GOING TO SAVE MY LIFE AND ALANNA'S!
AFTER THE THREAT HAS BEEN ELIMINATED...
THIS IS ONLY A RAIN PUDDLE ON RANN BUT IT'S BIG AS A LAKE TO US!
10

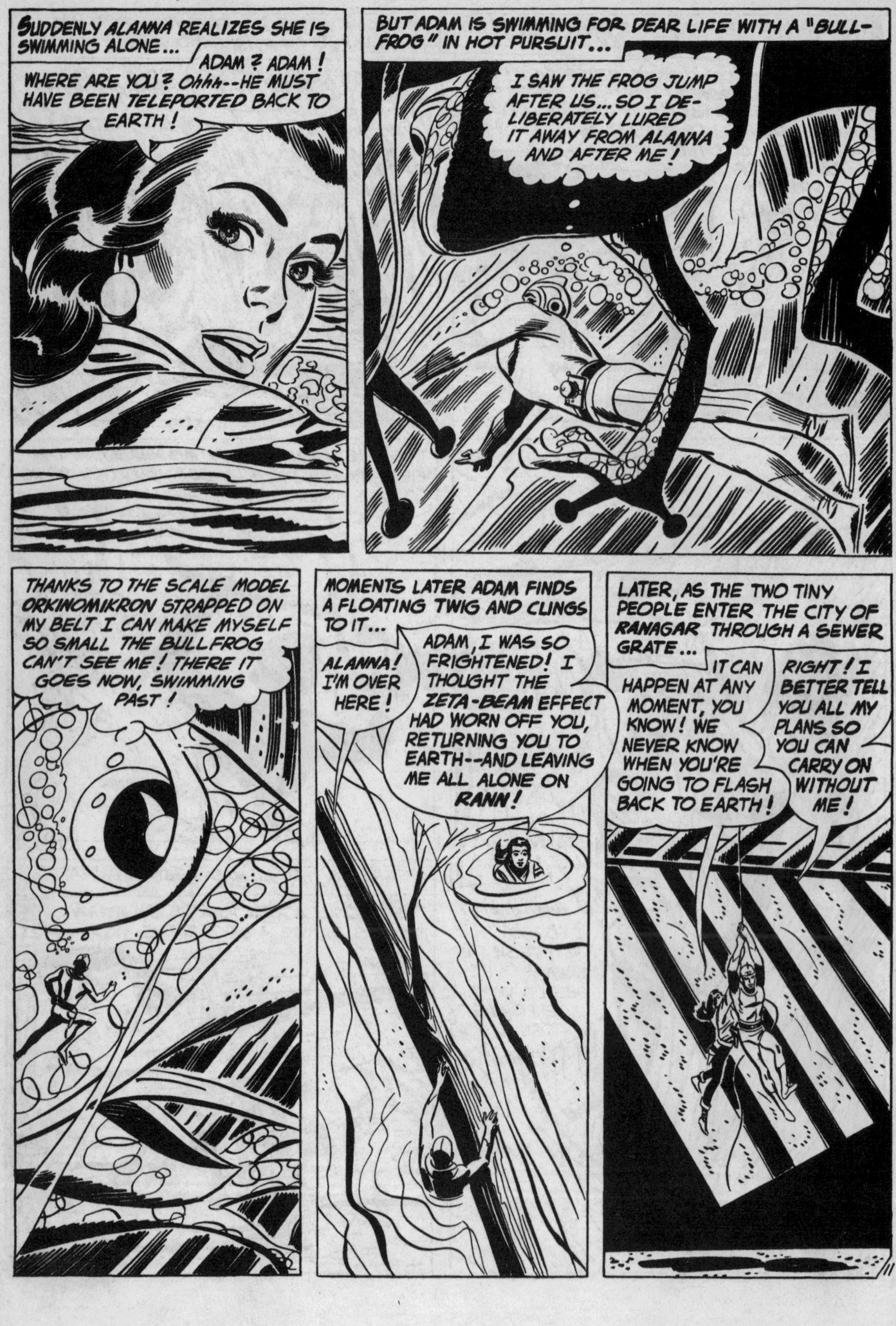
SUDDENLY ALANNA REALIZES SHE IS SWIMMING ALONE...
ADAM ? ADAM ! WHERE ARE YOU ? OHHH--HE MUST HAVE BEEN TELEPORTED BACK TO EARTH !
BUT ADAM IS SWIMMING FOR DEAR LIFE WITH A "BULL-FROG" IN HOT PURSUIT...
I SAW THE FROG JUMP AFTER US...SO I DE-LIBERATELY LURED IT AWAY FROM ALANNA AND AFTER ME !
THANKS TO THE SCALE MODEL ORKINOMIKRON STRAPPED ON MY BELT I CAN MAKE MYSELF SO SMALL THE BULLFROG CAN'T SEE ME ! THERE IT GOES NOW, SWIMMING PAST !
MOMENTS LATER ADAM FINDS A FLOATING TWIG AND CLINGS TO IT...
ALANNA! I'M OVER HERE !
ADAM, I WAS SO FRIGHTENED! I THOUGHT THE ZETA-BEAM EFFECT HAD WORN OFF YOU, RETURNING YOU TO EARTH--AND LEAVING ME ALL ALONE ON RANN!
LATER, AS THE TWO TINY PEOPLE ENTER THE CITY OF RANAGAR THROUGH A SEWER GRATE...
IT CAN HAPPEN AT ANY MOMENT, YOU KNOW! WE NEVER KNOW WHEN YOU'RE GOING TO FLASH BACK TO EARTH !
RIGHT ! I BETTER TELL YOU ALL MY PLANS SO YOU CAN CARRY ON WITHOUT ME !
11

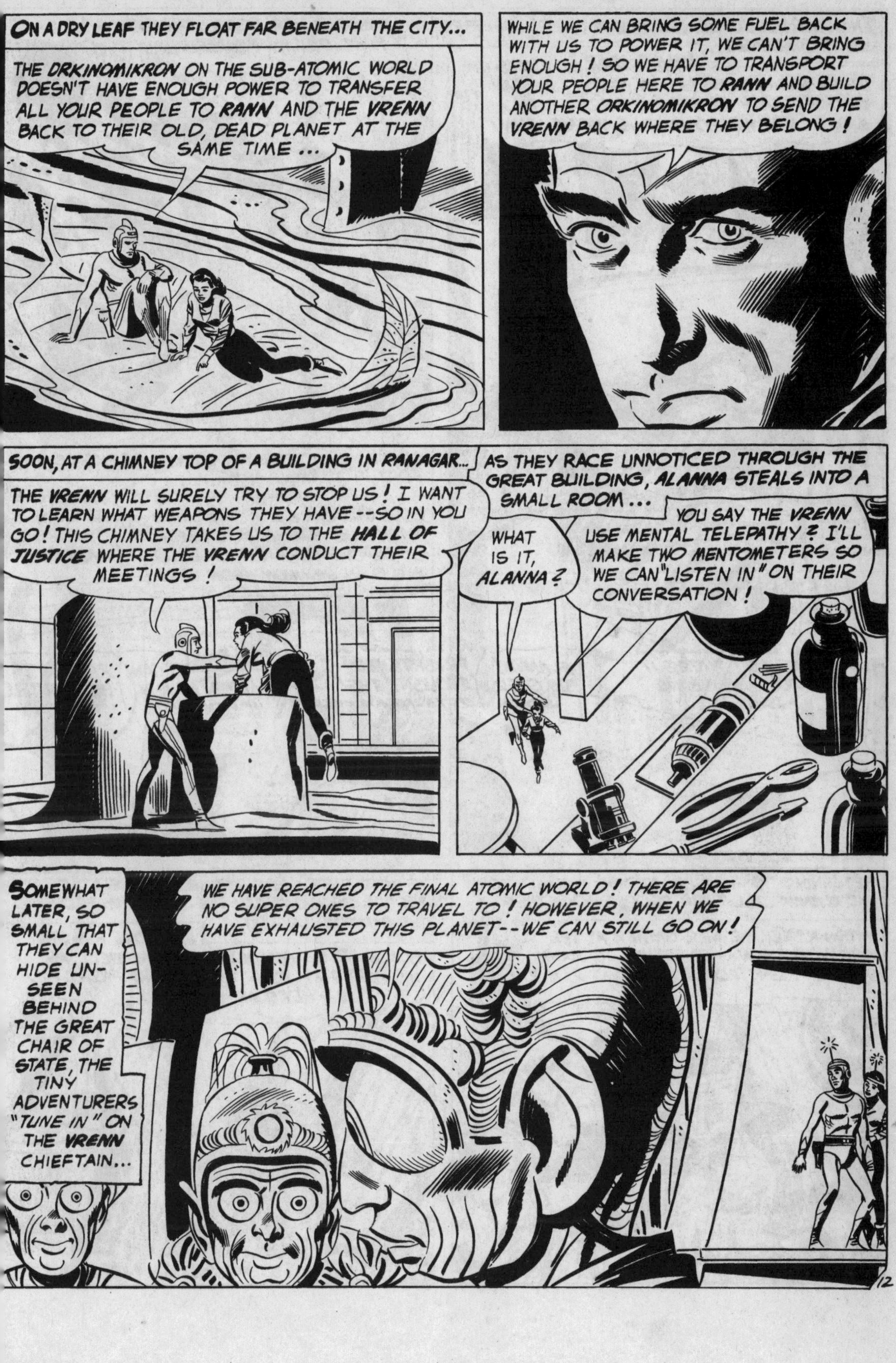
ON A DRY LEAF THEY FLOAT FAR BENEATH THE CITY...
THE ORKINOMIKRON ON THE SUB-ATOMIC WORLD DOESN'T HAVE ENOUGH POWER TO TRANSFER ALL YOUR PEOPLE TO RANN AND THE VRENN BACK TO THEIR OLD, DEAD PLANET AT THE SAME TIME ...
WHILE WE CAN BRING SOME FUEL BACK WITH US TO POWER IT, WE CAN'T BRING ENOUGH! SO WE HAVE TO TRANSPORT YOUR PEOPLE HERE TO RANN AND BUILD ANOTHER ORKINOMIKRON TO SEND THE VRENN BACK WHERE THEY BELONG!
SOON, AT A CHIMNEY TOP OF A BUILDING IN RANAGAR...
THE VRENN WILL SURELY TRY TO STOP US! I WANT TO LEARN WHAT WEAPONS THEY HAVE--SO IN YOU GO! THIS CHIMNEY TAKES US TO THE HALL OF JUSTICE WHERE THE VRENN CONDUCT THEIR MEETINGS!
AS THEY RACE UNNOTICED THROUGH THE GREAT BUILDING, ALANNA STEALS INTO A SMALL ROOM ...
WHAT IS IT, ALANNA?
YOU SAY THE VRENN USE MENTAL TELEPATHY? I'LL MAKE TWO MENTOMETERS SO WE CAN "LISTEN IN" ON THEIR CONVERSATION!
SOMEWHAT LATER, SO SMALL THAT THEY CAN HIDE UNSEEN BEHIND THE GREAT CHAIR OF STATE, THE TINY ADVENTURERS "TUNE IN" ON THE VRENN CHIEFTAIN...
WE HAVE REACHED THE FINAL ATOMIC WORLD! THERE ARE NO SUPER ONES TO TRAVEL TO! HOWEVER, WHEN WE HAVE EXHAUSTED THIS PLANET--WE CAN STILL GO ON!
12

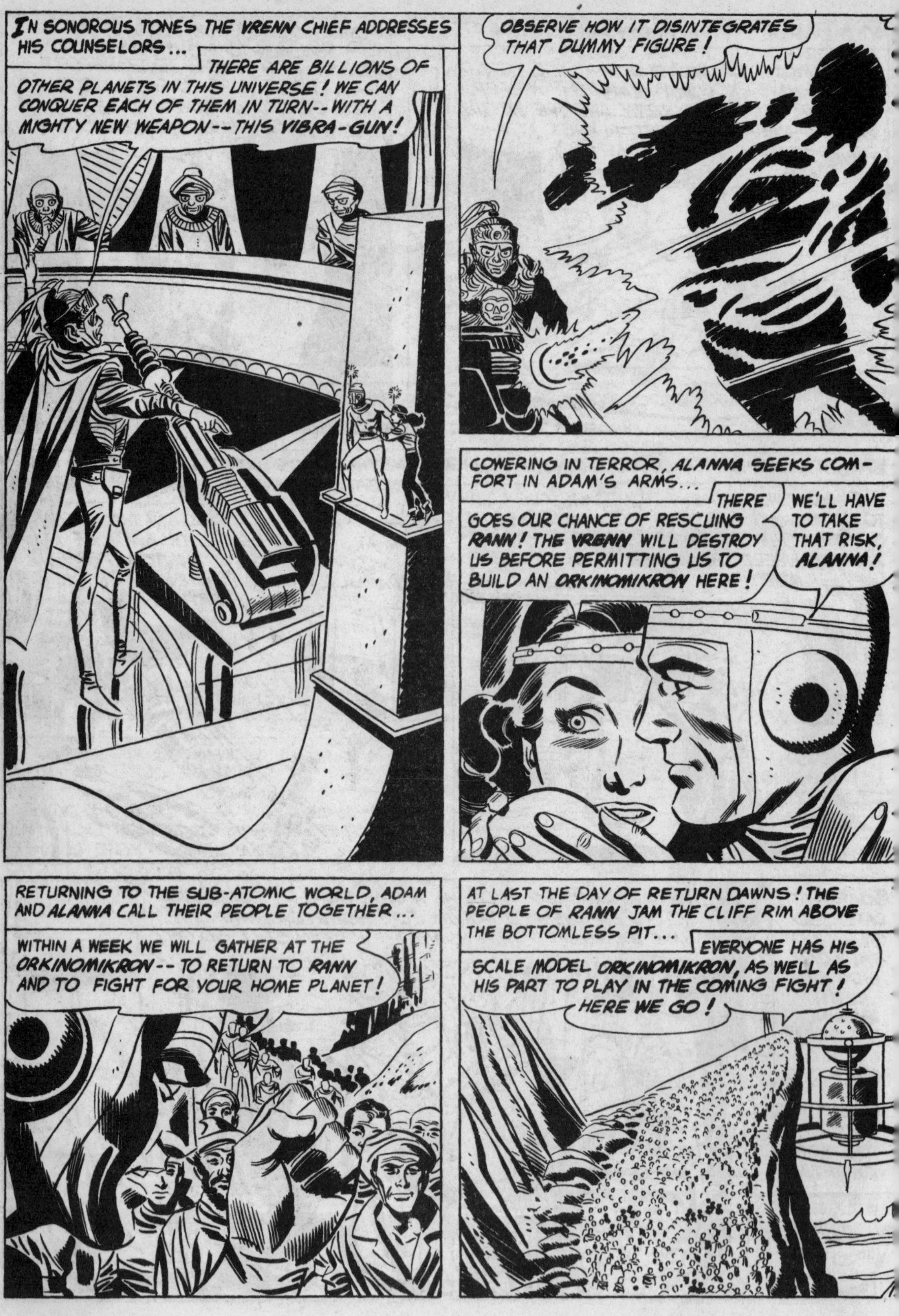
IN SONOROUS TONES THE VRENN CHIEF ADDRESSES HIS COUNSELORS...
THERE ARE BILLIONS OF OTHER PLANETS IN THIS UNIVERSE! WE CAN CONQUER EACH OF THEM IN TURN--WITH A MIGHTY NEW WEAPON--THIS VIBRA-GUN!
OBSERVE HOW IT DISINTEGRATES THAT DUMMY FIGURE!
COWERING IN TERROR, ALANNA SEEKS COMFORT IN ADAM'S ARMS...
THERE GOES OUR CHANCE OF RESCUING RANN! THE VRENN WILL DESTROY US BEFORE PERMITTING US TO BUILD AN ORKINOMIKRON HERE!
WE'LL HAVE TO TAKE THAT RISK, ALANNA!
RETURNING TO THE SUB-ATOMIC WORLD, ADAM AND ALANNA CALL THEIR PEOPLE TOGETHER...
WITHIN A WEEK WE WILL GATHER AT THE ORKINOMIKRON--TO RETURN TO RANN AND TO FIGHT FOR YOUR HOME PLANET!
AT LAST THE DAY OF RETURN DAWNS! THE PEOPLE OF RANN JAM THE CLIFF RIM ABOVE THE BOTTOMLESS PIT...
EVERYONE HAS HIS SCALE MODEL ORKINOMIKRON, AS WELL AS HIS PART TO PLAY IN THE COMING FIGHT!
HERE WE GO!

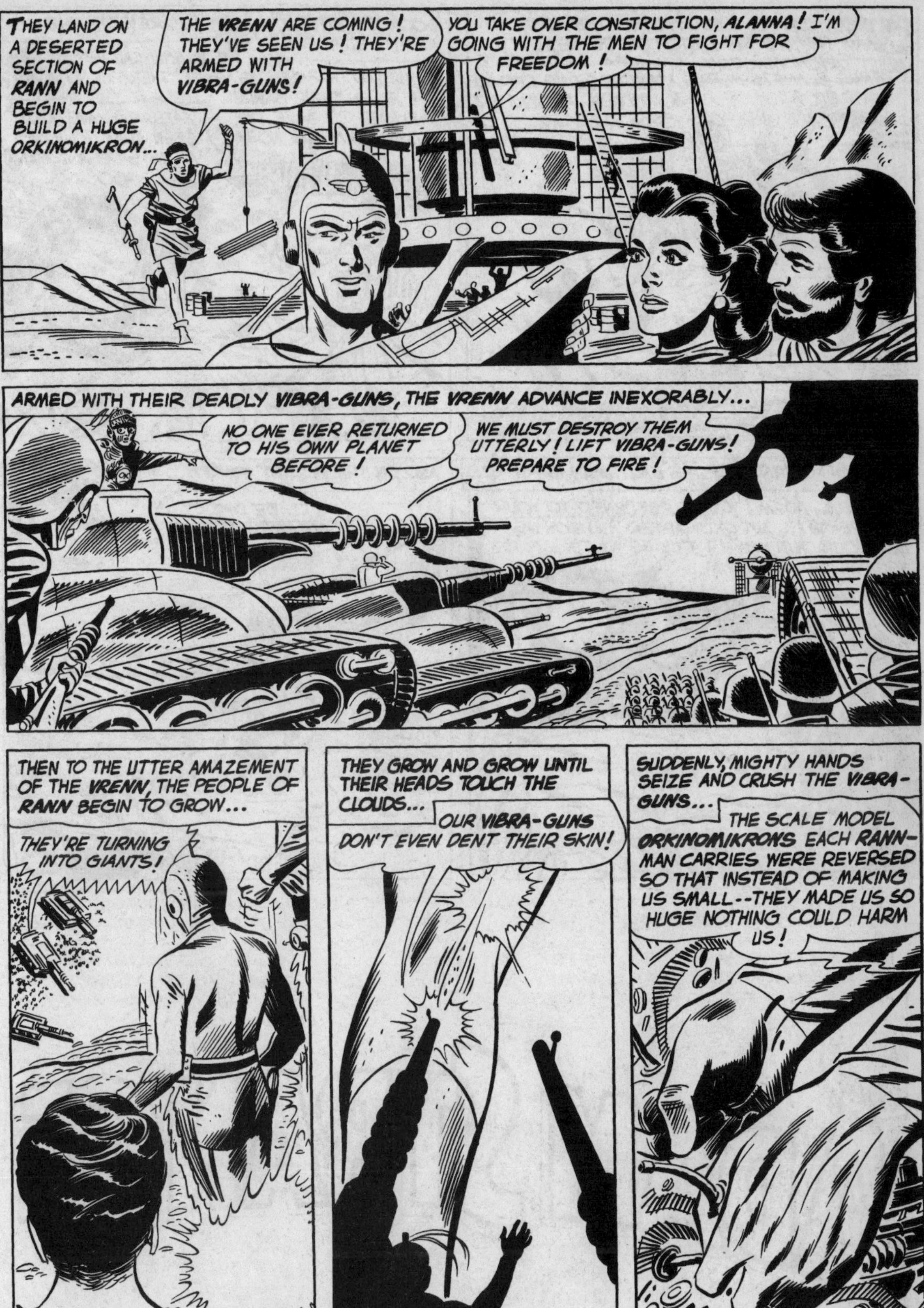
THEY LAND ON A DESERTED SECTION OF RANN AND BEGIN TO BUILD A HUGE ORKINOMIKRON...
THE VRENN ARE COMING! THEY'VE SEEN US! THEY'RE ARMED WITH VIBRA-GUNS!
YOU TAKE OVER CONSTRUCTION, ALANNA! I'M GOING WITH THE MEN TO FIGHT FOR FREEDOM!
ARMED WITH THEIR DEADLY VIBRA-GUNS, THE VRENN ADVANCE INEXORABLY...
NO ONE EVER RETURNED TO HIS OWN PLANET BEFORE!
WE MUST DESTROY THEM UTTERLY! LIFT VIBRA-GUNS! PREPARE TO FIRE!
THEN TO THE UTTER AMAZEMENT OF THE VRENN, THE PEOPLE OF RANN BEGIN TO GROW...
THEY'RE TURNING INTO GIANTS!
THEY GROW AND GROW UNTIL THEIR HEADS TOUCH THE CLOUDS...
OUR VIBRA-GUNS DON'T EVEN DENT THEIR SKIN!
SUDDENLY, MIGHTY HANDS SEIZE AND CRUSH THE VIBRA-GUNS...
THE SCALE MODEL ORKINOMIKRONS EACH RANN-MAN CARRIES WERE REVERSED SO THAT INSTEAD OF MAKING US SMALL--THEY MADE US SO HUGE NOTHING COULD HARM US!
14

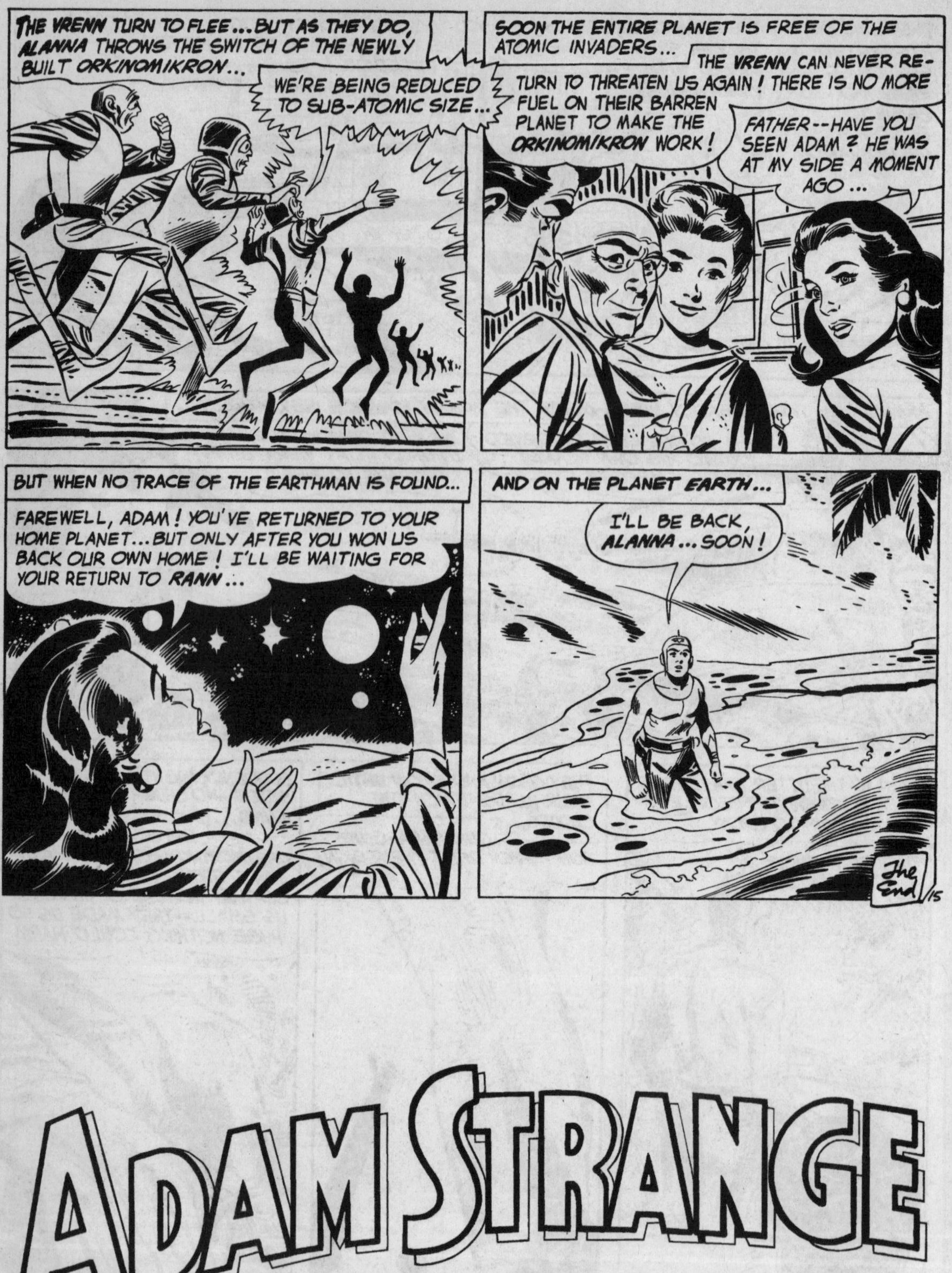
THE VRENN TURN TO FLEE...BUT AS THEY DO, ALANNA THROWS THE SWITCH OF THE NEWLY BUILT ORKINOMIKRON...
WE'RE BEING REDUCED TO SUB-ATOMIC SIZE...
SOON THE ENTIRE PLANET IS FREE OF THE ATOMIC INVADERS...
THE VRENN CAN NEVER RETURN TO THREATEN US AGAIN! THERE IS NO MORE FUEL ON THEIR BARREN PLANET TO MAKE THE ORKINOMIKRON WORK!
FATHER--HAVE YOU SEEN ADAM? HE WAS AT MY SIDE A MOMENT AGO...
BUT WHEN NO TRACE OF THE EARTHMAN IS FOUND...
FAREWELL, ADAM! YOU'VE RETURNED TO YOUR HOME PLANET...BUT ONLY AFTER YOU WON US BACK OUR OWN HOME! I'LL BE WAITING FOR YOUR RETURN TO RANN...
AND ON THE PLANET EARTH...
I'LL BE BACK, ALANNA...SOON!
The End
15

ADAM STRANGE

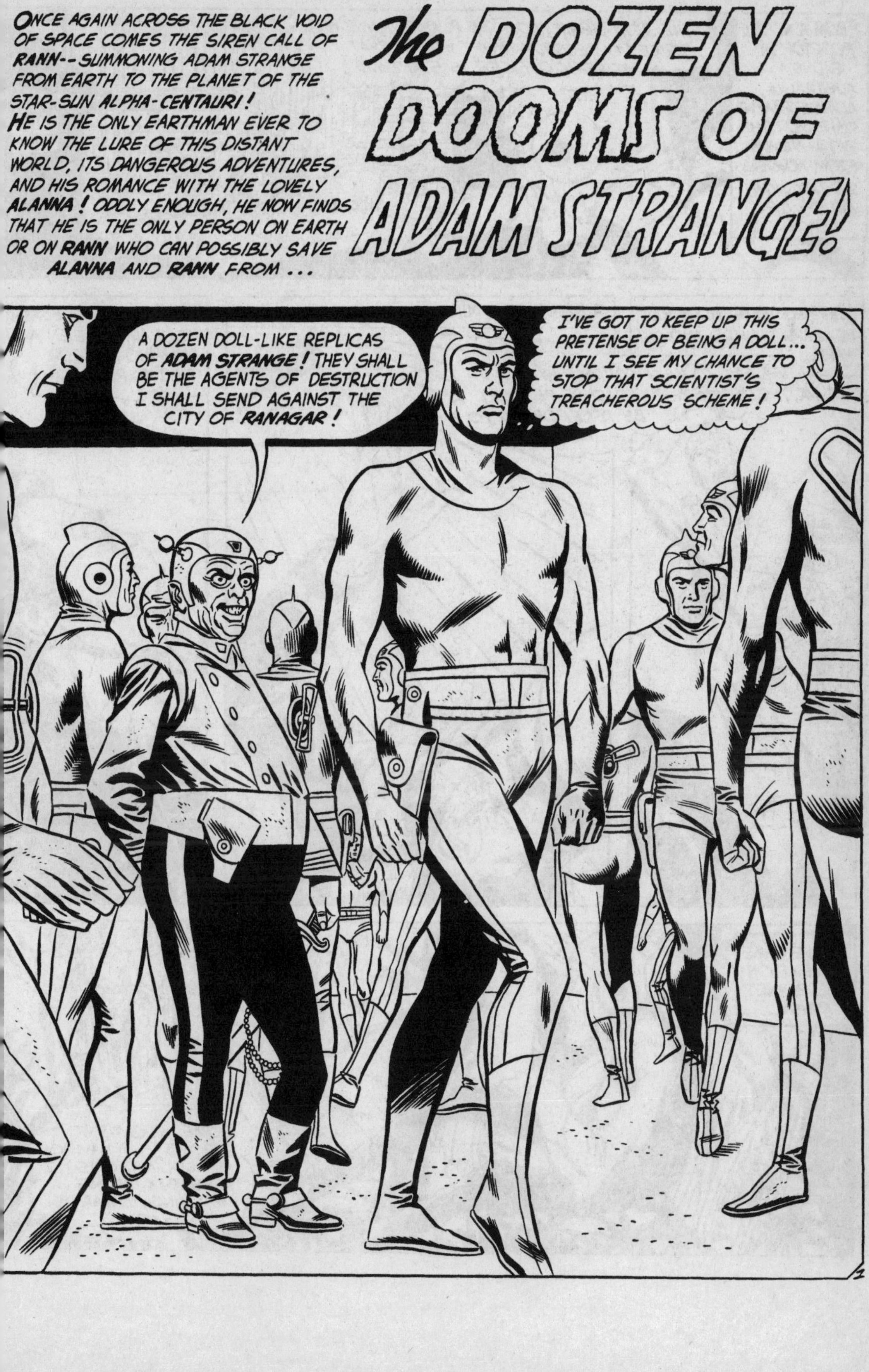
ONCE AGAIN ACROSS THE BLACK VOID OF SPACE COMES THE SIREN CALL OF RANN--SUMMONING ADAM STRANGE FROM EARTH TO THE PLANET OF THE STAR-SUN ALPHA-CENTAURI! HE IS THE ONLY EARTHMAN EVER TO KNOW THE LURE OF THIS DISTANT WORLD, ITS DANGEROUS ADVENTURES, AND HIS ROMANCE WITH THE LOVELY ALANNA! ODDLY ENOUGH, HE NOW FINDS THAT HE IS THE ONLY PERSON ON EARTH OR ON RANN WHO CAN POSSIBLY SAVE ALANNA AND RANN FROM ...
The DOZEN DOOMS OF ADAM STRANGE!
A DOZEN DOLL-LIKE REPLICAS OF ADAM STRANGE! THEY SHALL BE THE AGENTS OF DESTRUCTION I SHALL SEND AGAINST THE CITY OF RANAGAR!
I'VE GOT TO KEEP UP THIS PRETENSE OF BEING A DOLL... UNTIL I SEE MY CHANCE TO STOP THAT SCIENTIST'S TREACHEROUS SCHEME!

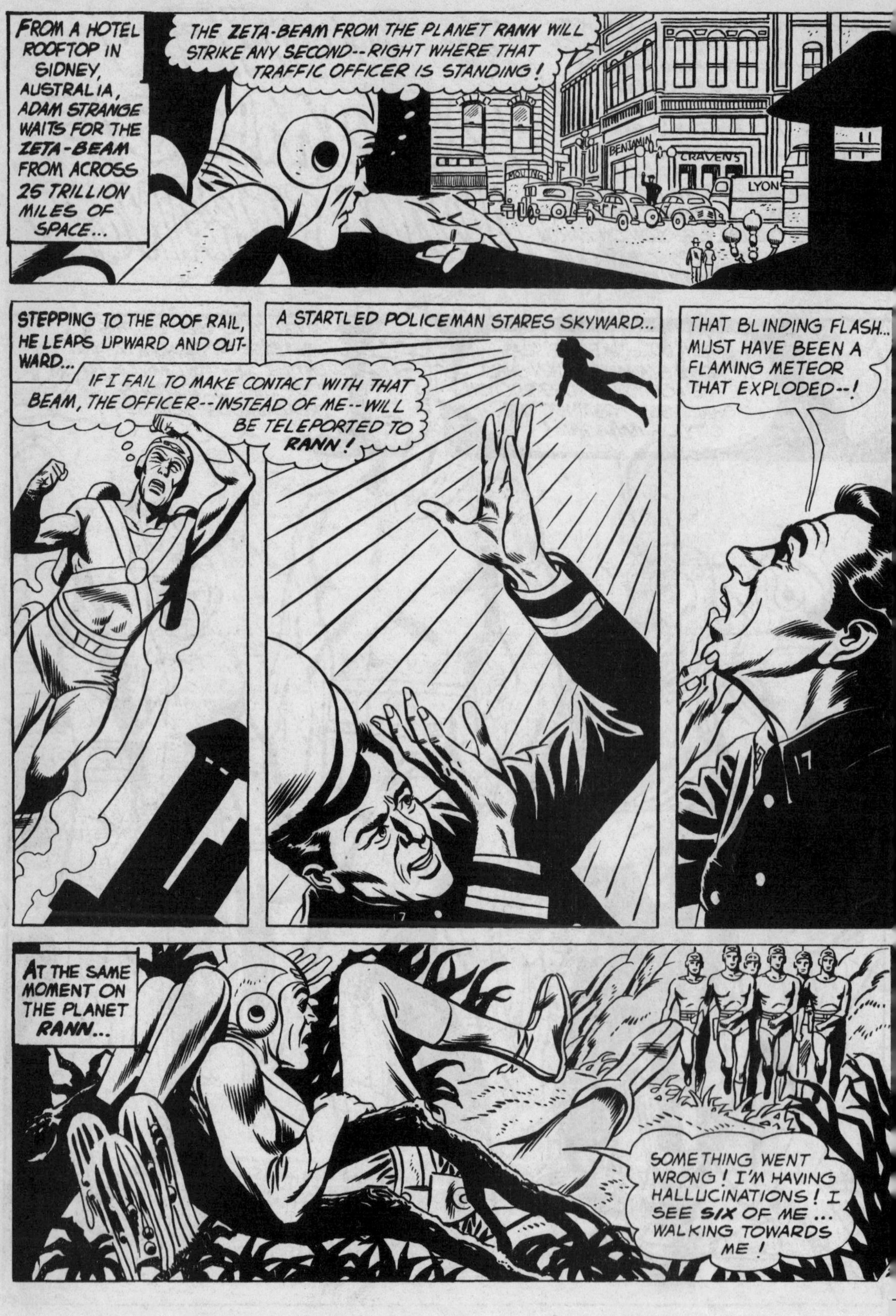
FROM A HOTEL ROOFTOP IN SIDNEY, AUSTRALIA, ADAM STRANGE WAITS FOR THE ZETA-BEAM FROM ACROSS 25 TRILLION MILES OF SPACE...
THE ZETA-BEAM FROM THE PLANET RANN WILL STRIKE ANY SECOND--RIGHT WHERE THAT TRAFFIC OFFICER IS STANDING!
BENJAMIN
CRAVENS
MOVING
LYON
STEPPING TO THE ROOF RAIL, HE LEAPS UPWARD AND OUTWARD...
IF I FAIL TO MAKE CONTACT WITH THAT BEAM, THE OFFICER--INSTEAD OF ME--WILL BE TELEPORTED TO RANN!
A STARTLED POLICEMAN STARES SKYWARD...
THAT BLINDING FLASH... MUST HAVE BEEN A FLAMING METEOR THAT EXPLODED--!
17
AT THE SAME MOMENT ON THE PLANET RANN...
SOMETHING WENT WRONG! I'M HAVING HALLUCINATIONS! I SEE SIX OF ME... WALKING TOWARDS ME!

SUDDENLY, A FAMILIAR VOICE CALLS OUT...

SURPRISE! SURPRISE!

ALANNA! SOMETHING TELLS ME YOU HAD SOMETHING TO DO WITH THOSE DUPLICATES OF ME!

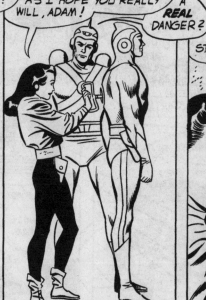

THESE ADAM STRANGE DOLLS ARE ALL THE RAGE IN RANAGAR! CHILDREN PLAY WITH THEM, MAKING BELIEVE "YOU'RE" SAVING THEM FROM ONE DANGER OR ANOTHER! AS I HOPE YOU REALLY WILL, ADAM!

A REAL DANGER?

LATER, IN THE CITY OF RANAGAR, ALANNA EXPLAINS...

HERE, BEYOND THE SEA OF MORMEEN AND CLOSE BY THE FLAMING SEA, IS THE CITY-STATE OF DYS! WE SUSPECT DYS IS PLANNING A SURPRISE ATTACK AGAINST RANAGAR--BUT HOW AND WHEN THE BLOW WILL STRIKE, WE DON'T KNOW!

FLAMING SEA

SEA OF MORMEEN

DYS HAS COMPLETELY CUT ITSELF OFF FROM THE REST OF RANN! NO ONE IS ALLOWED TO ENTER--ALL AIRCRAFT IS FORBIDDEN OVER ITS BOUNDARIES! WE FEAR THE LEADING SCIENTIST OF DYS--TAK VALL--IS PLOTTING THE INVASION!

I'VE VOLUNTEERED TO FLY A DOZEN ADAM STRANGE DOLLS TO DYS! I'M HOPING YOU WILL BE ONE OF THOSE "DOLLS," ADAM...!

IN THAT WAY I'LL BE SMUGGLED INTO DYS TO SPY ON TAK VALL! ASSIGNMENT ACCEPTED!

3

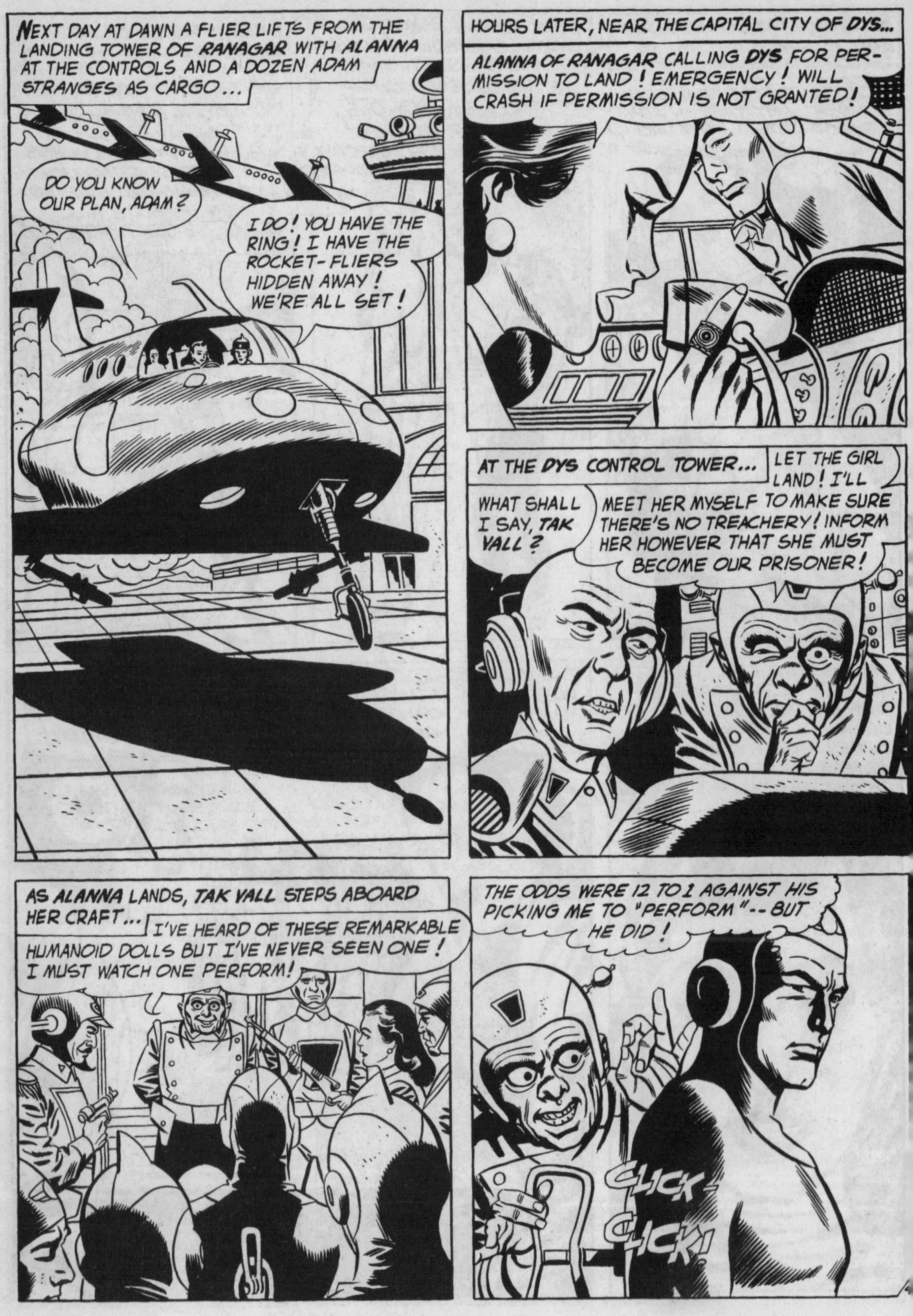
NEXT DAY AT DAWN A FLIER LIFTS FROM THE LANDING TOWER OF RANAGAR WITH ALANNA AT THE CONTROLS AND A DOZEN ADAM STRANGES AS CARGO...
DO YOU KNOW OUR PLAN, ADAM?
I DO! YOU HAVE THE RING! I HAVE THE ROCKET-FLIERS HIDDEN AWAY! WE'RE ALL SET!
HOURS LATER, NEAR THE CAPITAL CITY OF DYS...
ALANNA OF RANAGAR CALLING DYS FOR PERMISSION TO LAND! EMERGENCY! WILL CRASH IF PERMISSION IS NOT GRANTED!
AT THE DYS CONTROL TOWER...
WHAT SHALL I SAY, TAK VALL?
LET THE GIRL LAND! I'LL MEET HER MYSELF TO MAKE SURE THERE'S NO TREACHERY! INFORM HER HOWEVER THAT SHE MUST BECOME OUR PRISONER!
AS ALANNA LANDS, TAK VALL STEPS ABOARD HER CRAFT...
I'VE HEARD OF THESE REMARKABLE HUMANOID DOLLS BUT I'VE NEVER SEEN ONE! I MUST WATCH ONE PERFORM!
THE ODDS WERE 12 TO 1 AGAINST HIS PICKING ME TO "PERFORM"-- BUT HE DID!
CLICK-CLICK!

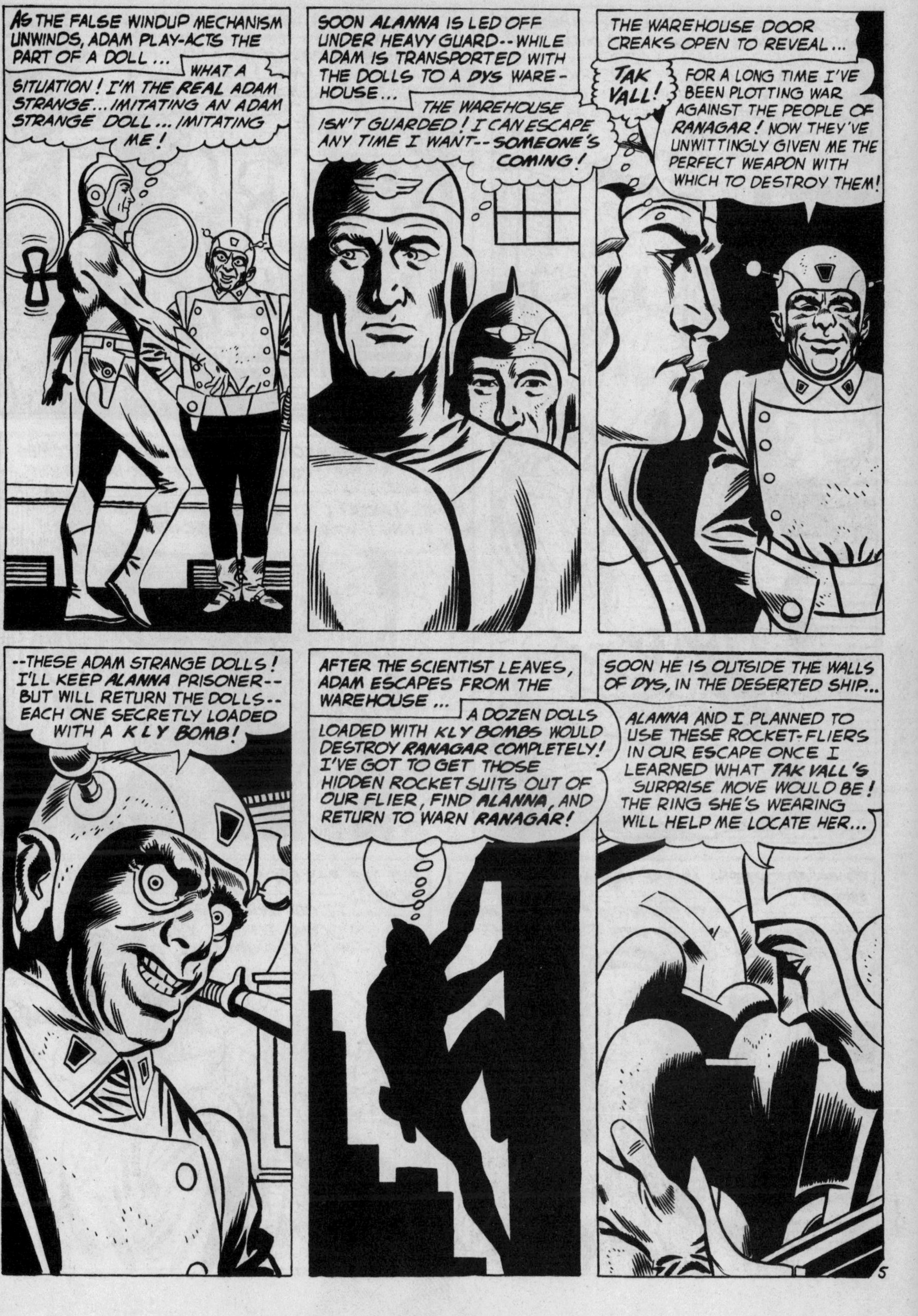
AS THE FALSE WINDUP MECHANISM UNWINDS, ADAM PLAY-ACTS THE PART OF A DOLL ...
WHAT A SITUATION! I'M THE REAL ADAM STRANGE... IMITATING AN ADAM STRANGE DOLL ... IMITATING ME!
SOON ALANNA IS LED OFF UNDER HEAVY GUARD--WHILE ADAM IS TRANSPORTED WITH THE DOLLS TO A DYS WARE-HOUSE...
THE WAREHOUSE ISN'T GUARDED! I CAN ESCAPE ANY TIME I WANT--SOMEONE'S COMING!
THE WAREHOUSE DOOR CREAKS OPEN TO REVEAL...
TAK VALL!
FOR A LONG TIME I'VE BEEN PLOTTING WAR AGAINST THE PEOPLE OF RANAGAR! NOW THEY'VE UNWITTINGLY GIVEN ME THE PERFECT WEAPON WITH WHICH TO DESTROY THEM!
--THESE ADAM STRANGE DOLLS! I'LL KEEP ALANNA PRISONER--BUT WILL RETURN THE DOLLS--EACH ONE SECRETLY LOADED WITH A KLY BOMB!
AFTER THE SCIENTIST LEAVES, ADAM ESCAPES FROM THE WAREHOUSE ...
A DOZEN DOLLS LOADED WITH KLY BOMBS WOULD DESTROY RANAGAR COMPLETELY! I'VE GOT TO GET THOSE HIDDEN ROCKET SUITS OUT OF OUR FLIER, FIND ALANNA, AND RETURN TO WARN RANAGAR!
SOON HE IS OUTSIDE THE WALLS OF DYS, IN THE DESERTED SHIP...
ALANNA AND I PLANNED TO USE THESE ROCKET-FLIERS IN OUR ESCAPE ONCE I LEARNED WHAT TAK VALL'S SURPRISE MOVE WOULD BE! THE RING SHE'S WEARING WILL HELP ME LOCATE HER...
5

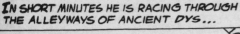

IN SHORT MINUTES HE IS RACING THROUGH THE ALLEYWAYS OF ANCIENT DYS...

HER RING GIVES OFF TINY ELECTRICAL VIBRATIONS WHICH ARE PICKED UP BY A FILAMENT WIRED TO MY TEETH! AS THOSE VIBRATIONS GROW STRONGER I KNOW I'M GETTING CLOSER TO HER!

THE VIBRATIONS ARE GROWING FAINT! I MADE A WRONG TURN SOMEWHERE! GOT TO RETRACE MY STEPS!

BY BACK ROADS AND MARKET SQUARES, ADAM COMES AT LAST TO THE GREAT PALACE OF TAK VALL WHERE...

PSSST, ALANNA! I'VE LEARNED TAK VALL'S PLANS! NOW WE MUST ESCAPE!

TO HIS AMAZEMENT AS THE WOMAN WHIRLS AROUND...

YOU AREN'T ALANNA!

ADAM STRANGE! HOW DID HE GET INTO DYS? SOUND THE ALARM, MOORA!

BUT THE MAN FROM EARTH MAKES THE NEXT MOVE...

I GOT INTO DYS AND I'M GOING TO GET OUT--WITH ALANNA!

16

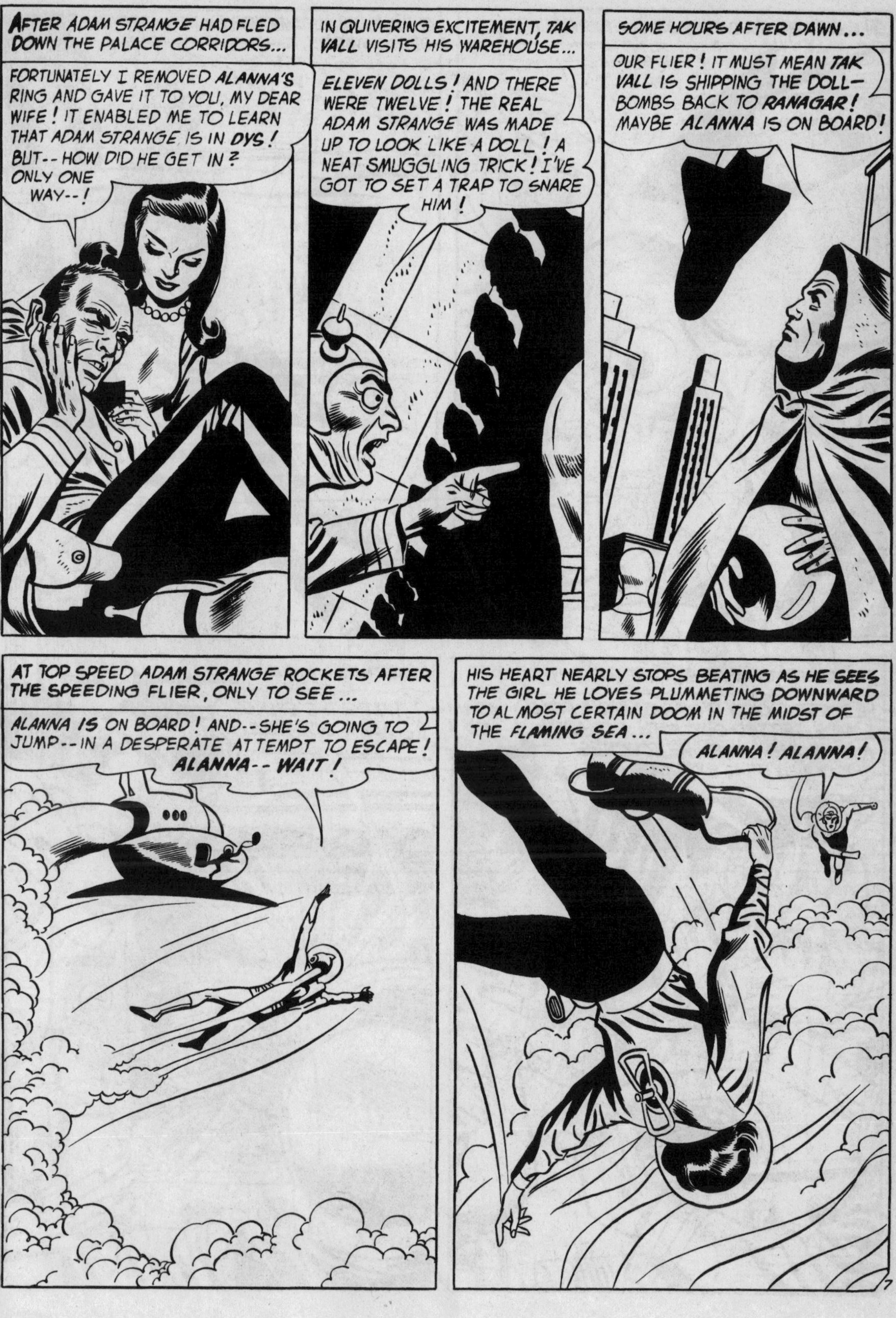
AFTER ADAM STRANGE HAD FLED DOWN THE PALACE CORRIDORS...
FORTUNATELY I REMOVED ALANNA'S RING AND GAVE IT TO YOU, MY DEAR WIFE! IT ENABLED ME TO LEARN THAT ADAM STRANGE IS IN DYS! BUT-- HOW DID HE GET IN? ONLY ONE WAY--!
IN QUIVERING EXCITEMENT, TAK VALL VISITS HIS WAREHOUSE...
ELEVEN DOLLS! AND THERE WERE TWELVE! THE REAL ADAM STRANGE WAS MADE UP TO LOOK LIKE A DOLL! A NEAT SMUGGLING TRICK! I'VE GOT TO SET A TRAP TO SNARE HIM!
SOME HOURS AFTER DAWN...
OUR FLIER! IT MUST MEAN TAK VALL IS SHIPPING THE DOLL-BOMBS BACK TO RANAGAR! MAYBE ALANNA IS ON BOARD!
AT TOP SPEED ADAM STRANGE ROCKETS AFTER THE SPEEDING FLIER, ONLY TO SEE...
ALANNA IS ON BOARD! AND--SHE'S GOING TO JUMP--IN A DESPERATE ATTEMPT TO ESCAPE! ALANNA-- WAIT!
HIS HEART NEARLY STOPS BEATING AS HE SEES THE GIRL HE LOVES PLUMMETING DOWNWARD TO ALMOST CERTAIN DOOM IN THE MIDST OF THE FLAMING SEA...
ALANNA! ALANNA!
7

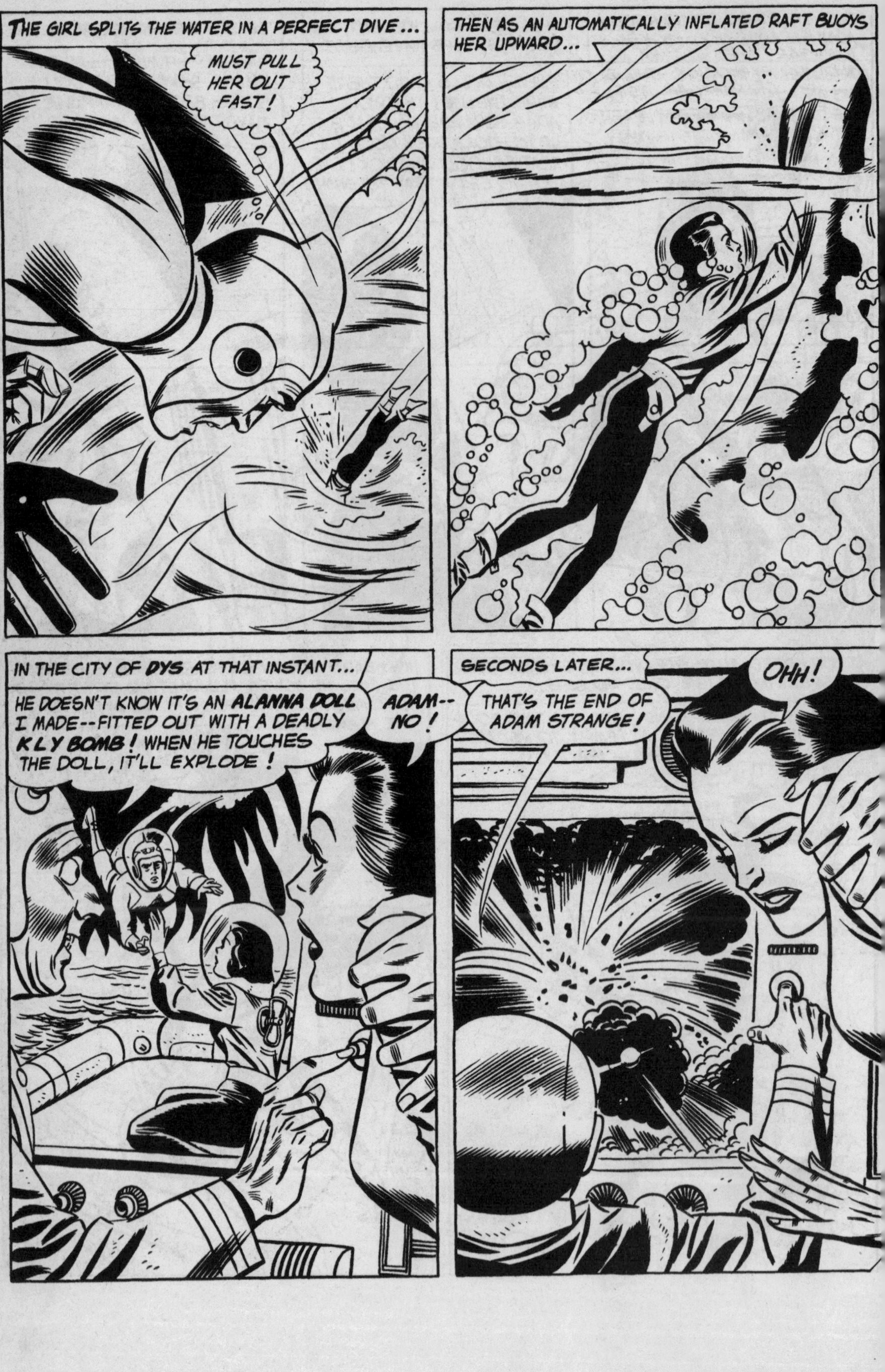
THE GIRL SPLITS THE WATER IN A PERFECT DIVE...
MUST PULL HER OUT FAST!
THEN AS AN AUTOMATICALLY INFLATED RAFT BUOYS HER UPWARD...
IN THE CITY OF DYS AT THAT INSTANT...
HE DOESN'T KNOW IT'S AN ALANNA DOLL I MADE--FITTED OUT WITH A DEADLY KLY BOMB! WHEN HE TOUCHES THE DOLL, IT'LL EXPLODE!
ADAM--NO!
SECONDS LATER...
THAT'S THE END OF ADAM STRANGE!
OHH!

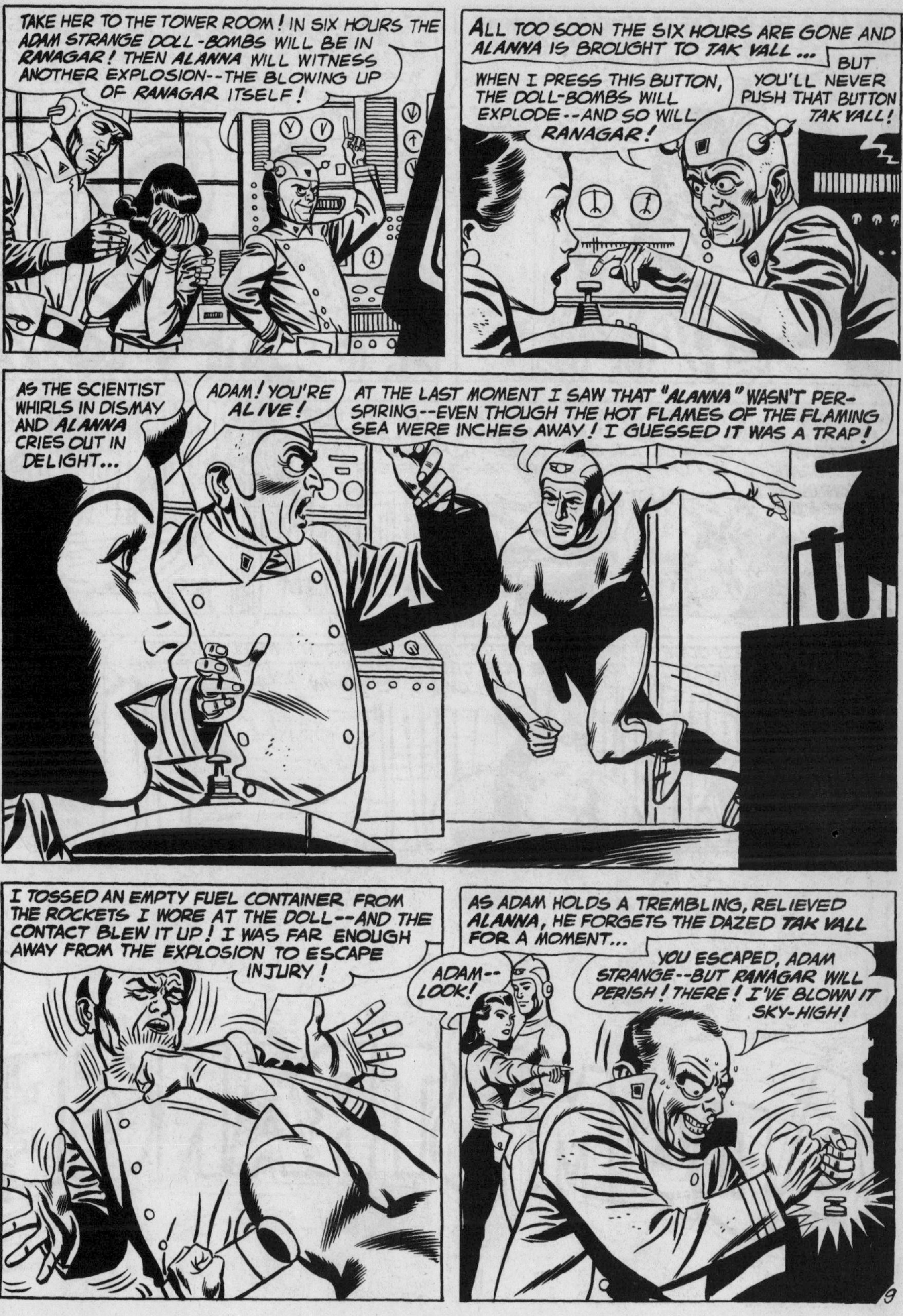
TAKE HER TO THE TOWER ROOM! IN SIX HOURS THE ADAM STRANGE DOLL-BOMBS WILL BE IN RANAGAR! THEN ALANNA WILL WITNESS ANOTHER EXPLOSION--THE BLOWING UP OF RANAGAR ITSELF!
ALL TOO SOON THE SIX HOURS ARE GONE AND ALANNA IS BROUGHT TO TAK VALL...
WHEN I PRESS THIS BUTTON, THE DOLL-BOMBS WILL EXPLODE--AND SO WILL RANAGAR!
BUT YOU'LL NEVER PUSH THAT BUTTON TAK VALL!
AS THE SCIENTIST WHIRLS IN DISMAY AND ALANNA CRIES OUT IN DELIGHT...
ADAM! YOU'RE ALIVE!
AT THE LAST MOMENT I SAW THAT "ALANNA" WASN'T PER-SPIRING--EVEN THOUGH THE HOT FLAMES OF THE FLAMING SEA WERE INCHES AWAY! I GUESSED IT WAS A TRAP!
I TOSSED AN EMPTY FUEL CONTAINER FROM THE ROCKETS I WORE AT THE DOLL--AND THE CONTACT BLEW IT UP! I WAS FAR ENOUGH AWAY FROM THE EXPLOSION TO ESCAPE INJURY!
AS ADAM HOLDS A TREMBLING, RELIEVED ALANNA, HE FORGETS THE DAZED TAK VALL FOR A MOMENT...
ADAM--LOOK!
YOU ESCAPED, ADAM STRANGE--BUT RANAGAR WILL PERISH! THERE! I'VE BLOWN IT SKY-HIGH!
9

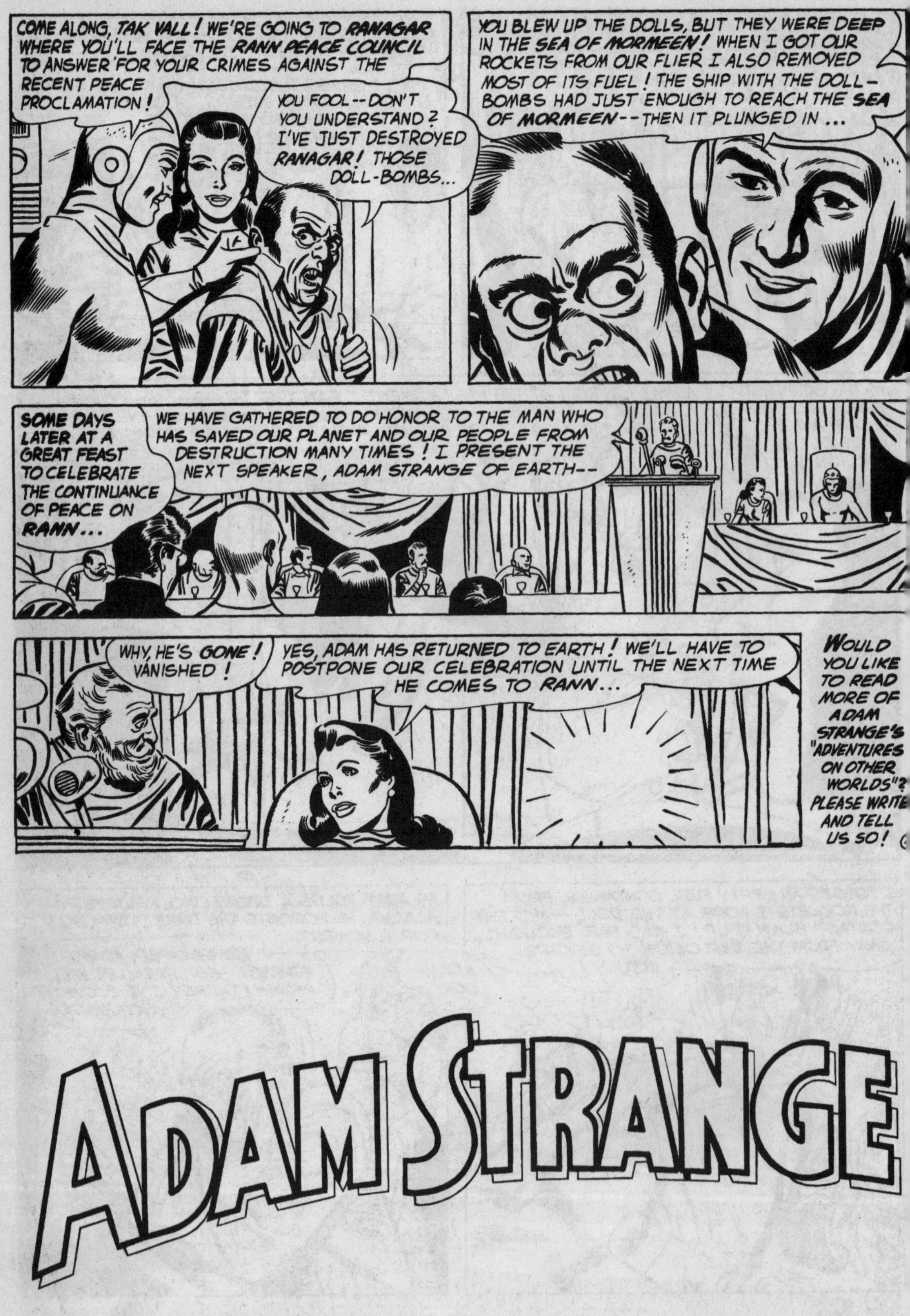
COME ALONG, TAK VALL! WE'RE GOING TO RANAGAR WHERE YOU'LL FACE THE RANN PEACE COUNCIL TO ANSWER FOR YOUR CRIMES AGAINST THE RECENT PEACE PROCLAMATION!
YOU FOOL--DON'T YOU UNDERSTAND? I'VE JUST DESTROYED RANAGAR! THOSE DOLL-BOMBS...
YOU BLEW UP THE DOLLS, BUT THEY WERE DEEP IN THE SEA OF MORMEEN! WHEN I GOT OUR ROCKETS FROM OUR FLIER I ALSO REMOVED MOST OF ITS FUEL! THE SHIP WITH THE DOLL-BOMBS HAD JUST ENOUGH TO REACH THE SEA OF MORMEEN--THEN IT PLUNGED IN...
SOME DAYS LATER AT A GREAT FEAST TO CELEBRATE THE CONTINUANCE OF PEACE ON RANN...
WE HAVE GATHERED TO DO HONOR TO THE MAN WHO HAS SAVED OUR PLANET AND OUR PEOPLE FROM DESTRUCTION MANY TIMES! I PRESENT THE NEXT SPEAKER, ADAM STRANGE OF EARTH--
WHY, HE'S GONE! VANISHED!
YES, ADAM HAS RETURNED TO EARTH! WE'LL HAVE TO POSTPONE OUR CELEBRATION UNTIL THE NEXT TIME HE COMES TO RANN...
WOULD YOU LIKE TO READ MORE OF ADAM STRANGE'S "ADVENTURES ON OTHER WORLDS"? PLEASE WRITE AND TELL US SO!

ADAM STRANGE

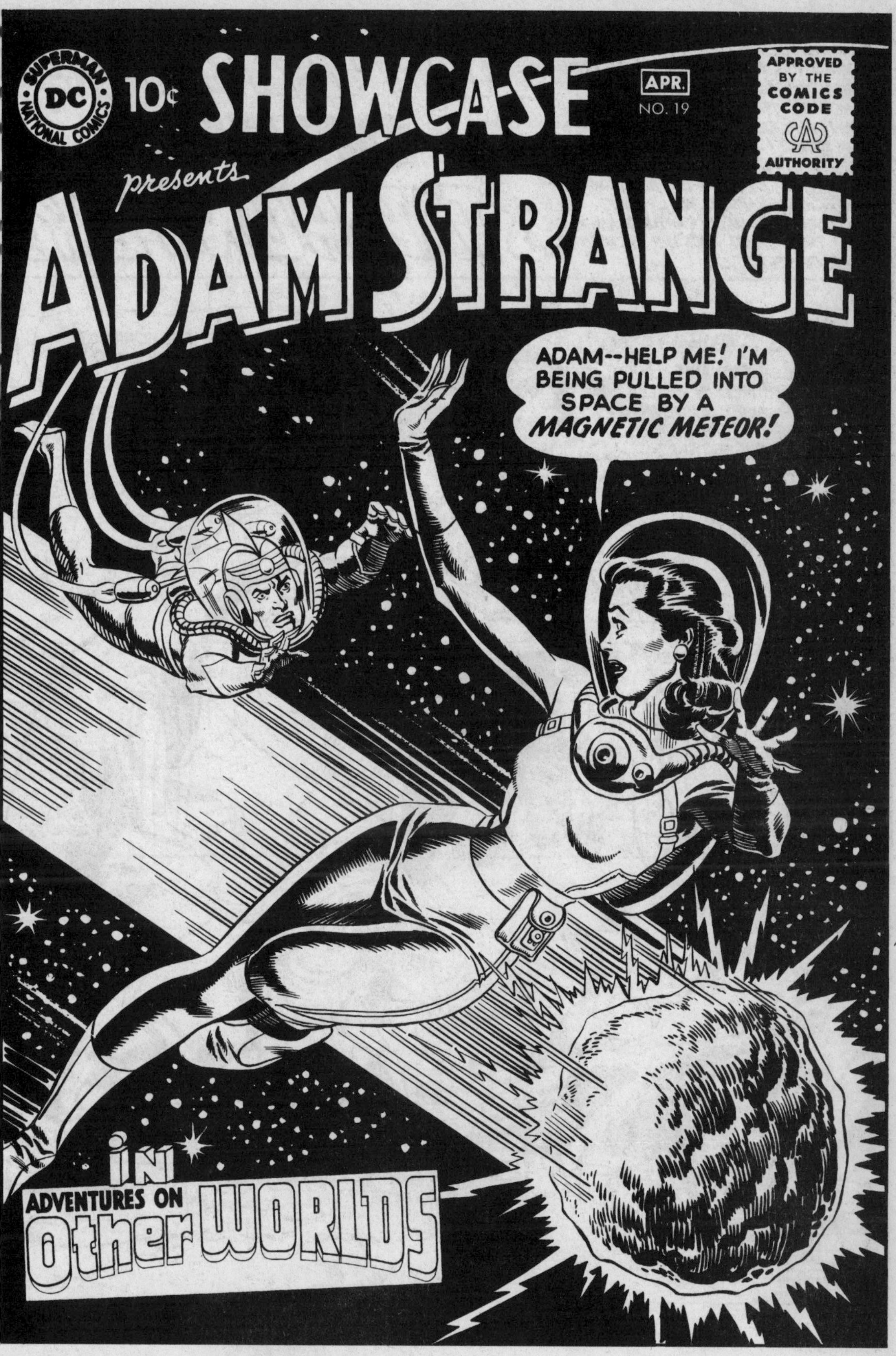
SUPERMAN DC NATIONAL COMICS
10¢
SHOWCASE
APR.
NO. 19
APPROVED BY THE COMICS CODE AUTHORITY
presents
ADAM STRANGE
ADAM--HELP ME! I'M BEING PULLED INTO SPACE BY A MAGNETIC METEOR!
IN
ADVENTURES ON
Other WORLDS

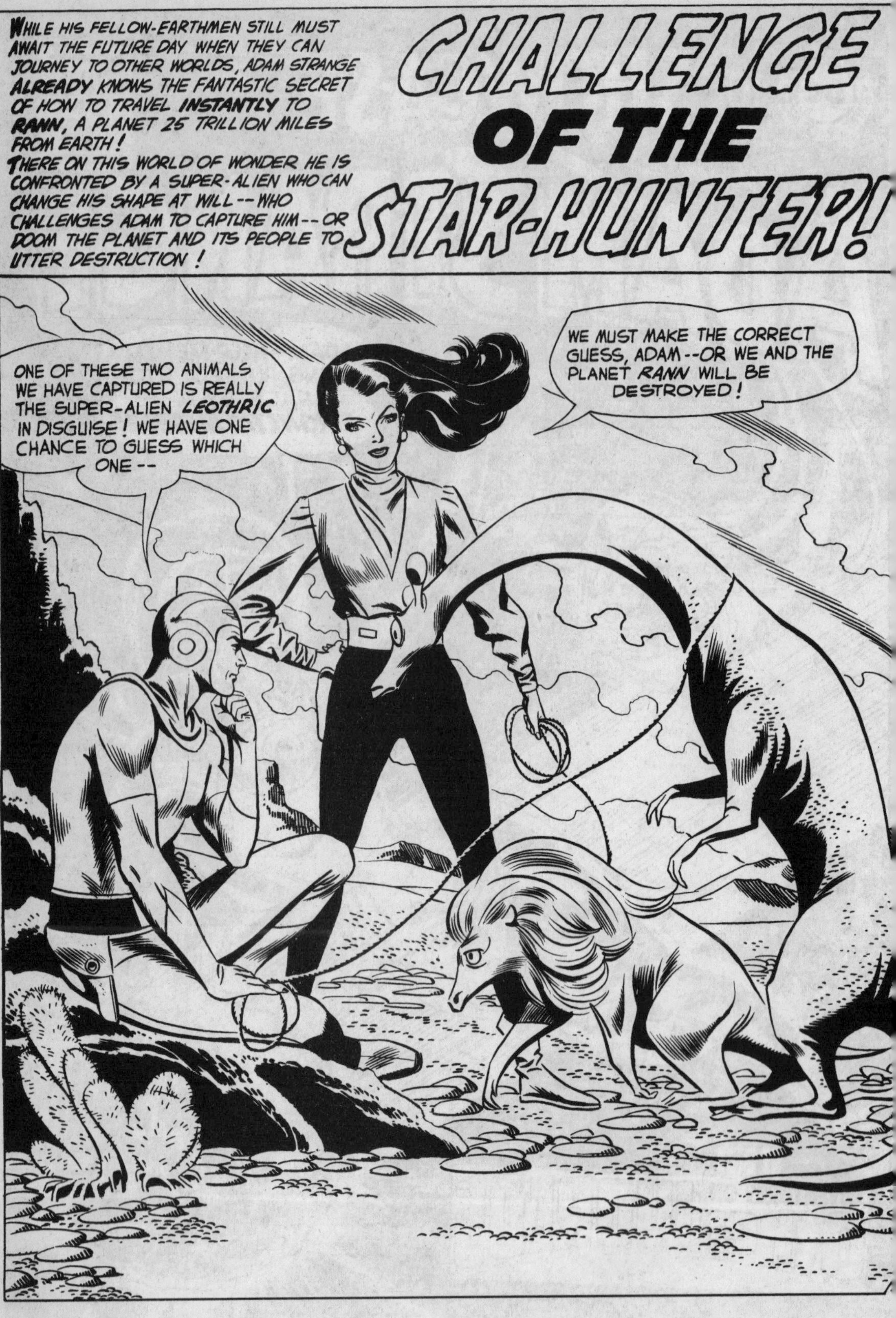
WHILE HIS FELLOW-EARTHMEN STILL MUST AWAIT THE FUTURE DAY WHEN THEY CAN JOURNEY TO OTHER WORLDS, ADAM STRANGE ALREADY KNOWS THE FANTASTIC SECRET OF HOW TO TRAVEL INSTANTLY TO RANN, A PLANET 25 TRILLION MILES FROM EARTH!
THERE ON THIS WORLD OF WONDER HE IS CONFRONTED BY A SUPER-ALIEN WHO CAN CHANGE HIS SHAPE AT WILL -- WHO CHALLENGES ADAM TO CAPTURE HIM -- OR DOOM THE PLANET AND ITS PEOPLE TO UTTER DESTRUCTION!
CHALLENGE OF THE STAR-HUNTER!
ONE OF THESE TWO ANIMALS WE HAVE CAPTURED IS REALLY THE SUPER-ALIEN LEOTHRIC IN DISGUISE! WE HAVE ONE CHANCE TO GUESS WHICH ONE --
WE MUST MAKE THE CORRECT GUESS, ADAM -- OR WE AND THE PLANET RANN WILL BE DESTROYED!

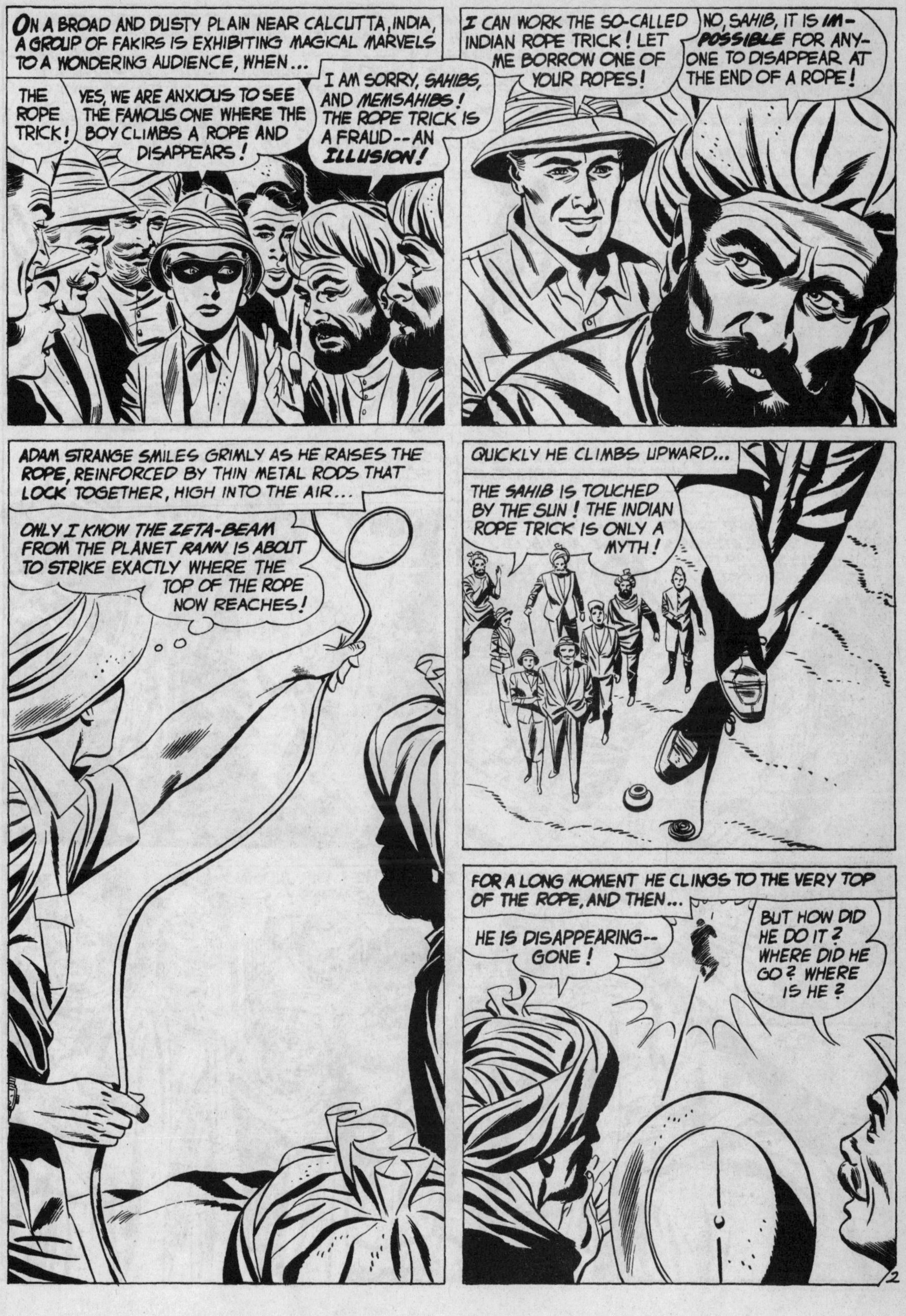
ON A BROAD AND DUSTY PLAIN NEAR CALCUTTA, INDIA, A GROUP OF FAKIRS IS EXHIBITING MAGICAL MARVELS TO A WONDERING AUDIENCE, WHEN...
THE ROPE TRICK!
YES, WE ARE ANXIOUS TO SEE THE FAMOUS ONE WHERE THE BOY CLIMBS A ROPE AND DISAPPEARS!
I AM SORRY, SAHIBS, AND MEMSAHIBS! THE ROPE TRICK IS A FRAUD--AN ILLUSION!
I CAN WORK THE SO-CALLED INDIAN ROPE TRICK! LET ME BORROW ONE OF YOUR ROPES!
NO, SAHIB, IT IS IMPOSSIBLE FOR ANYONE TO DISAPPEAR AT THE END OF A ROPE!
ADAM STRANGE SMILES GRIMLY AS HE RAISES THE ROPE, REINFORCED BY THIN METAL RODS THAT LOCK TOGETHER, HIGH INTO THE AIR...
ONLY I KNOW THE ZETA-BEAM FROM THE PLANET RANN IS ABOUT TO STRIKE EXACTLY WHERE THE TOP OF THE ROPE NOW REACHES!
QUICKLY HE CLIMBS UPWARD...
THE SAHIB IS TOUCHED BY THE SUN! THE INDIAN ROPE TRICK IS ONLY A MYTH!
FOR A LONG MOMENT HE CLINGS TO THE VERY TOP OF THE ROPE, AND THEN...
HE IS DISAPPEARING--GONE!
BUT HOW DID HE DO IT? WHERE DID HE GO? WHERE IS HE?
2

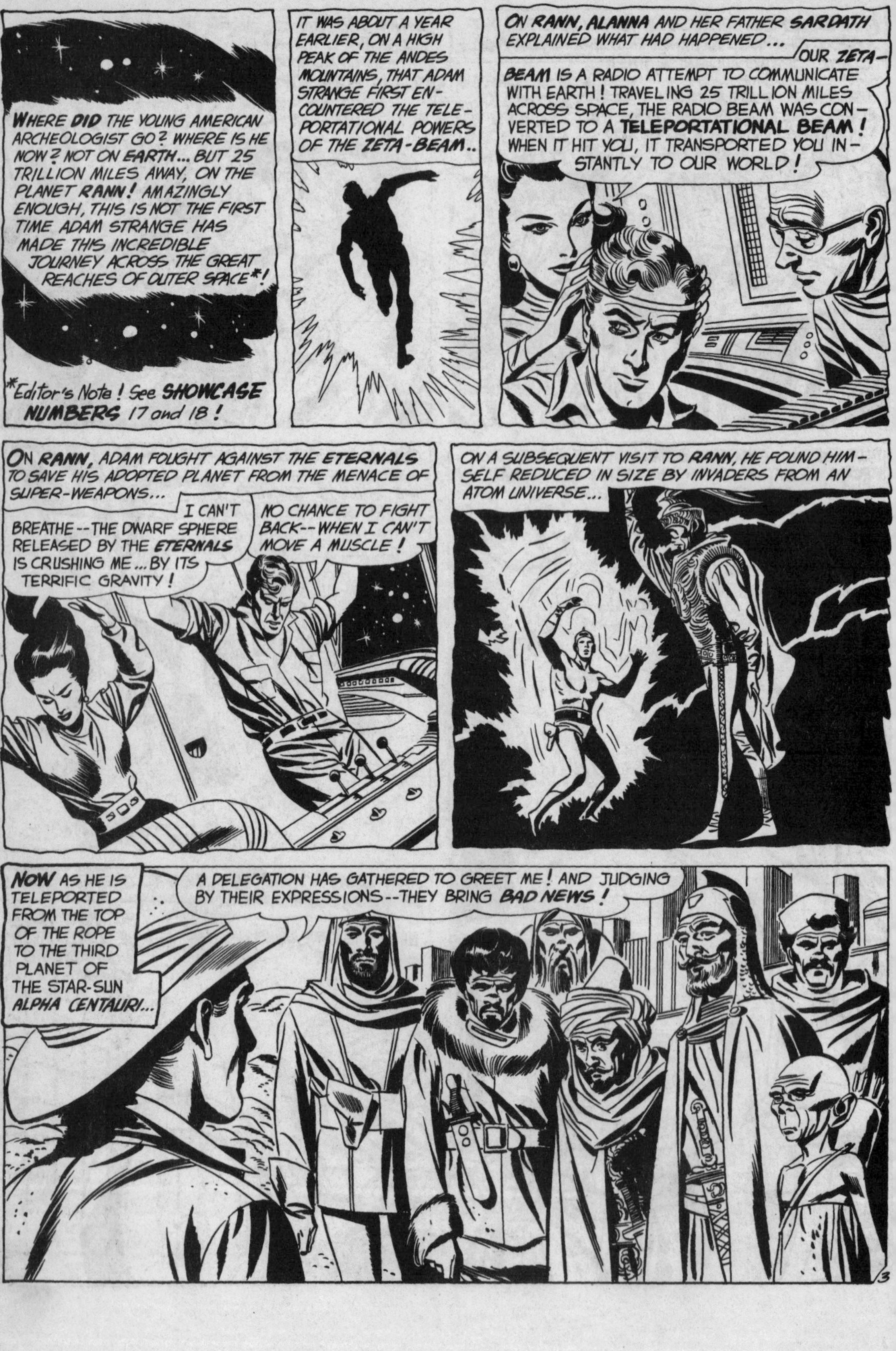
WHERE DID THE YOUNG AMERICAN ARCHEOLOGIST GO? WHERE IS HE NOW? NOT ON EARTH... BUT 25 TRILLION MILES AWAY, ON THE PLANET RANN! AMAZINGLY ENOUGH, THIS IS NOT THE FIRST TIME ADAM STRANGE HAS MADE THIS INCREDIBLE JOURNEY ACROSS THE GREAT REACHES OF OUTER SPACE*!
*Editor's Note! See SHOWCASE NUMBERS 17 and 18!
IT WAS ABOUT A YEAR EARLIER, ON A HIGH PEAK OF THE ANDES MOUNTAINS, THAT ADAM STRANGE FIRST ENCOUNTERED THE TELEPORTATIONAL POWERS OF THE ZETA-BEAM..
ON RANN, ALANNA AND HER FATHER SARDATH EXPLAINED WHAT HAD HAPPENED...
OUR ZETA-BEAM IS A RADIO ATTEMPT TO COMMUNICATE WITH EARTH! TRAVELING 25 TRILLION MILES ACROSS SPACE, THE RADIO BEAM WAS CONVERTED TO A TELEPORTATIONAL BEAM! WHEN IT HIT YOU, IT TRANSPORTED YOU INSTANTLY TO OUR WORLD!
ON RANN, ADAM FOUGHT AGAINST THE ETERNALS TO SAVE HIS ADOPTED PLANET FROM THE MENACE OF SUPER-WEAPONS...
I CAN'T BREATHE--THE DWARF SPHERE RELEASED BY THE ETERNALS IS CRUSHING ME...BY ITS TERRIFIC GRAVITY!
NO CHANCE TO FIGHT BACK--WHEN I CAN'T MOVE A MUSCLE!
ON A SUBSEQUENT VISIT TO RANN, HE FOUND HIMSELF REDUCED IN SIZE BY INVADERS FROM AN ATOM UNIVERSE...
NOW AS HE IS TELEPORTED FROM THE TOP OF THE ROPE TO THE THIRD PLANET OF THE STAR-SUN ALPHA CENTAURI...
A DELEGATION HAS GATHERED TO GREET ME! AND JUDGING BY THEIR EXPRESSIONS--THEY BRING BAD NEWS!
3

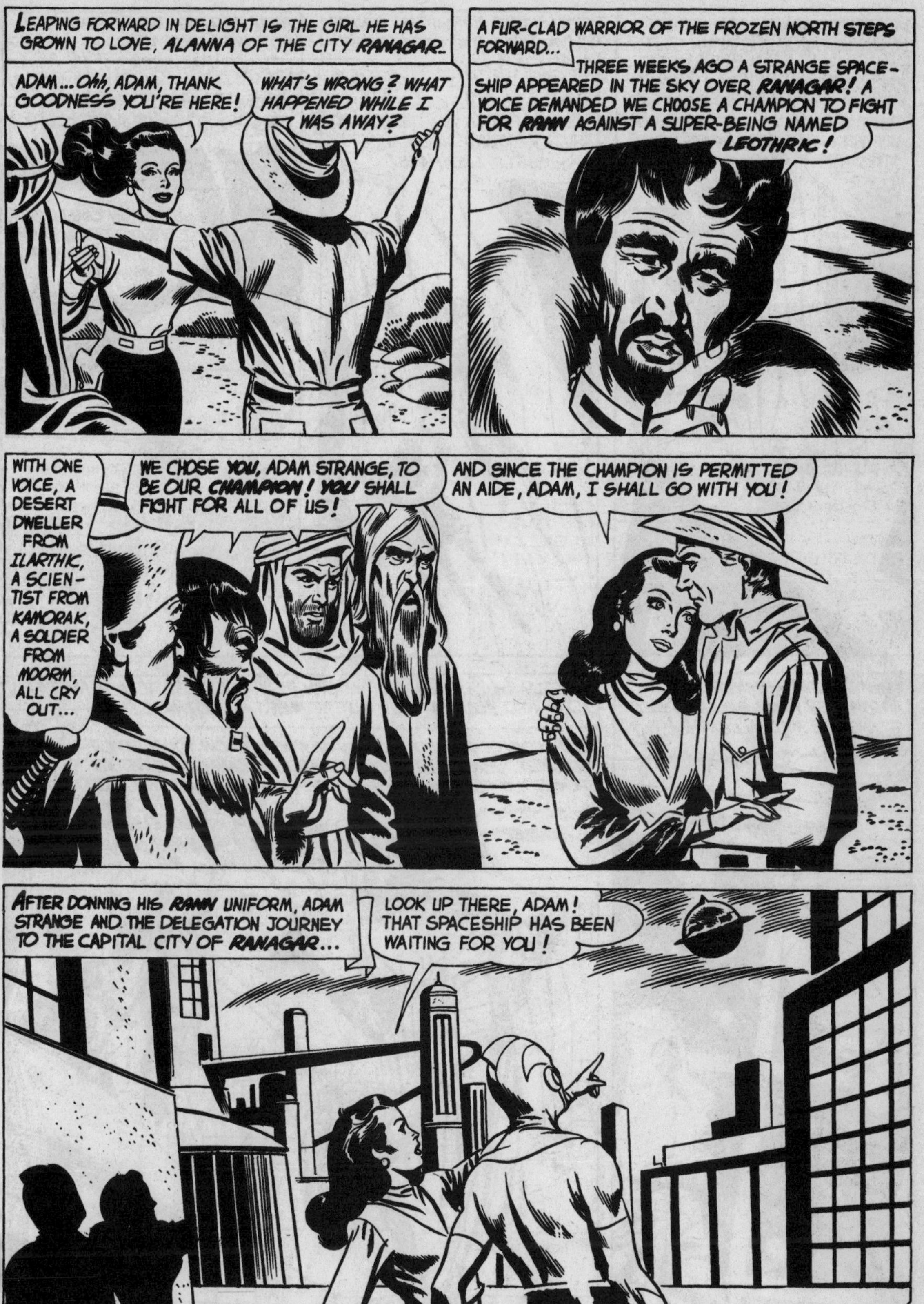
LEAPING FORWARD IN DELIGHT IS THE GIRL HE HAS GROWN TO LOVE, ALANNA OF THE CITY RANAGAR...
ADAM... OHH, ADAM, THANK GOODNESS YOU'RE HERE!
WHAT'S WRONG? WHAT HAPPENED WHILE I WAS AWAY?
A FUR-CLAD WARRIOR OF THE FROZEN NORTH STEPS FORWARD...
THREE WEEKS AGO A STRANGE SPACE-SHIP APPEARED IN THE SKY OVER RANAGAR! A VOICE DEMANDED WE CHOOSE A CHAMPION TO FIGHT FOR RANN AGAINST A SUPER-BEING NAMED LEOTHRIC!
WITH ONE VOICE, A DESERT DWELLER FROM ILARTHIC, A SCIEN-TIST FROM KAMORAK, A SOLDIER FROM MOORM, ALL CRY OUT...
WE CHOSE YOU, ADAM STRANGE, TO BE OUR CHAMPION! YOU SHALL FIGHT FOR ALL OF US!
AND SINCE THE CHAMPION IS PERMITTED AN AIDE, ADAM, I SHALL GO WITH YOU!
AFTER DONNING HIS RANN UNIFORM, ADAM STRANGE AND THE DELEGATION JOURNEY TO THE CAPITAL CITY OF RANAGAR...
LOOK UP THERE, ADAM! THAT SPACESHIP HAS BEEN WAITING FOR YOU!
4

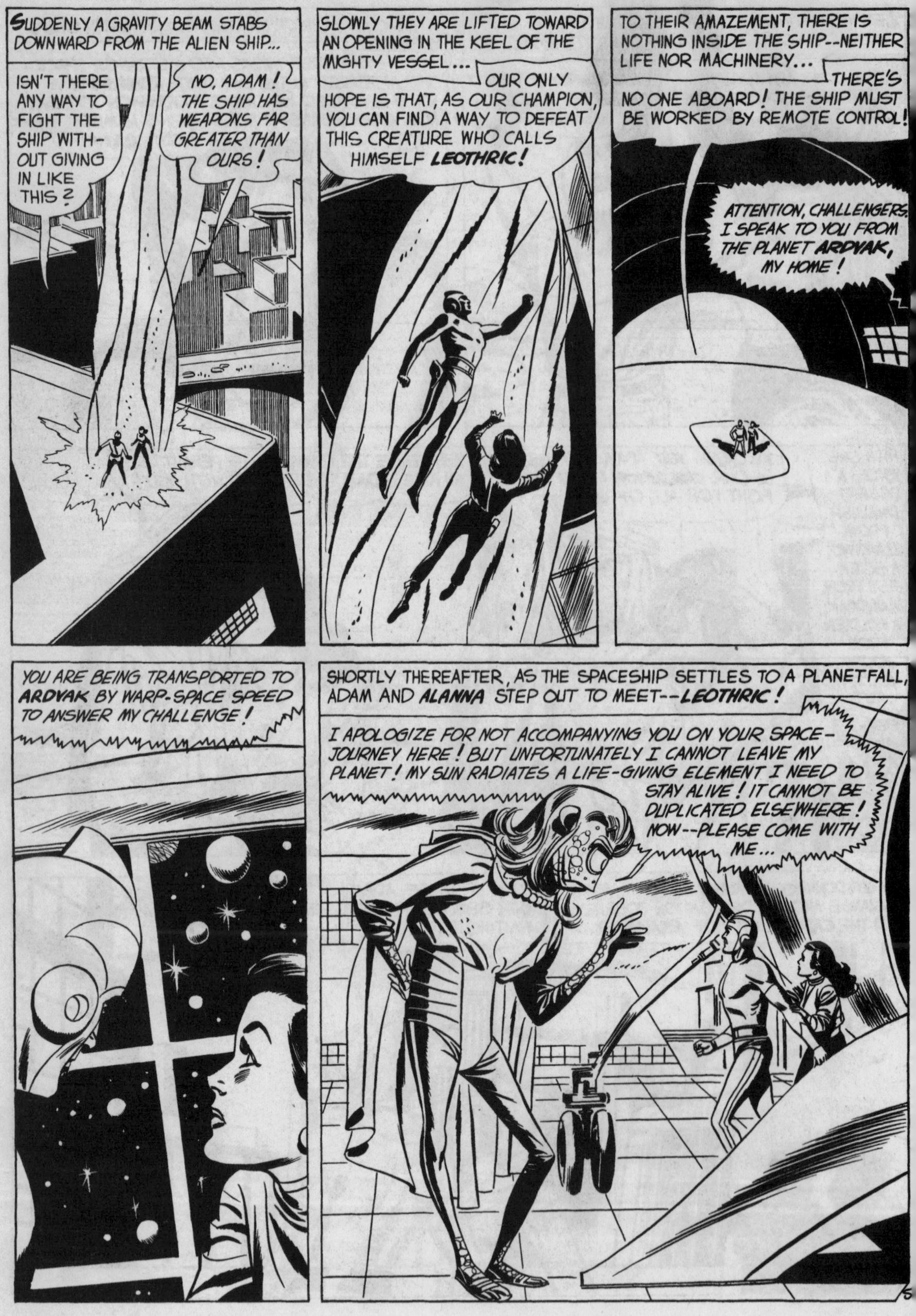
SUDDENLY A GRAVITY BEAM STABS DOWNWARD FROM THE ALIEN SHIP...
ISN'T THERE ANY WAY TO FIGHT THE SHIP WITH-OUT GIVING IN LIKE THIS?
NO, ADAM! THE SHIP HAS WEAPONS FAR GREATER THAN OURS!
SLOWLY THEY ARE LIFTED TOWARD AN OPENING IN THE KEEL OF THE MIGHTY VESSEL...
OUR ONLY HOPE IS THAT, AS OUR CHAMPION, YOU CAN FIND A WAY TO DEFEAT THIS CREATURE WHO CALLS HIMSELF LEOTHRIC!
TO THEIR AMAZEMENT, THERE IS NOTHING INSIDE THE SHIP--NEITHER LIFE NOR MACHINERY...
THERE'S NO ONE ABOARD! THE SHIP MUST BE WORKED BY REMOTE CONTROL!
ATTENTION, CHALLENGERS. I SPEAK TO YOU FROM THE PLANET ARDVAK, MY HOME!
YOU ARE BEING TRANSPORTED TO ARDVAK BY WARP-SPACE SPEED TO ANSWER MY CHALLENGE!
SHORTLY THEREAFTER, AS THE SPACESHIP SETTLES TO A PLANETFALL, ADAM AND ALANNA STEP OUT TO MEET--LEOTHRIC!
I APOLOGIZE FOR NOT ACCOMPANYING YOU ON YOUR SPACE-JOURNEY HERE! BUT UNFORTUNATELY I CANNOT LEAVE MY PLANET! MY SUN RADIATES A LIFE-GIVING ELEMENT I NEED TO STAY ALIVE! IT CANNOT BE DUPLICATED ELSEWHERE! NOW--PLEASE COME WITH ME...
5

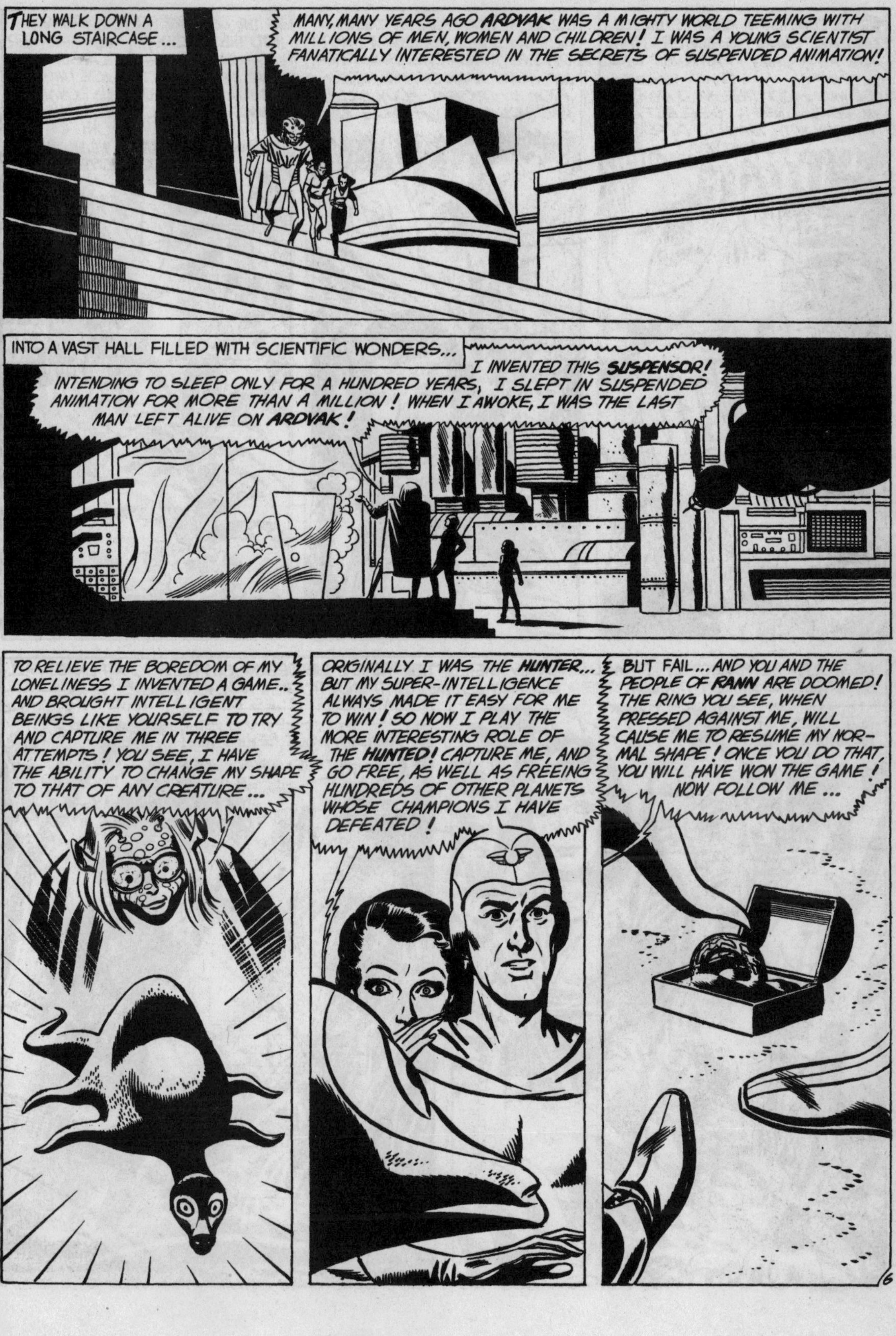
THEY WALK DOWN A LONG STAIRCASE...
MANY, MANY YEARS AGO ARDVAK WAS A MIGHTY WORLD TEEMING WITH MILLIONS OF MEN, WOMEN AND CHILDREN! I WAS A YOUNG SCIENTIST FANATICALLY INTERESTED IN THE SECRETS OF SUSPENDED ANIMATION!
INTO A VAST HALL FILLED WITH SCIENTIFIC WONDERS...
I INVENTED THIS SUSPENSOR! INTENDING TO SLEEP ONLY FOR A HUNDRED YEARS, I SLEPT IN SUSPENDED ANIMATION FOR MORE THAN A MILLION! WHEN I AWOKE, I WAS THE LAST MAN LEFT ALIVE ON ARDVAK!
TO RELIEVE THE BOREDOM OF MY LONELINESS I INVENTED A GAME.. AND BROUGHT INTELLIGENT BEINGS LIKE YOURSELF TO TRY AND CAPTURE ME IN THREE ATTEMPTS! YOU SEE, I HAVE THE ABILITY TO CHANGE MY SHAPE TO THAT OF ANY CREATURE...
ORIGINALLY I WAS THE HUNTER... BUT MY SUPER-INTELLIGENCE ALWAYS MADE IT EASY FOR ME TO WIN! SO NOW I PLAY THE MORE INTERESTING ROLE OF THE HUNTED! CAPTURE ME, AND GO FREE, AS WELL AS FREEING HUNDREDS OF OTHER PLANETS WHOSE CHAMPIONS I HAVE DEFEATED!
BUT FAIL... AND YOU AND THE PEOPLE OF RANN ARE DOOMED! THE RING YOU SEE, WHEN PRESSED AGAINST ME, WILL CAUSE ME TO RESUME MY NORMAL SHAPE! ONCE YOU DO THAT, YOU WILL HAVE WON THE GAME! NOW FOLLOW ME...
6

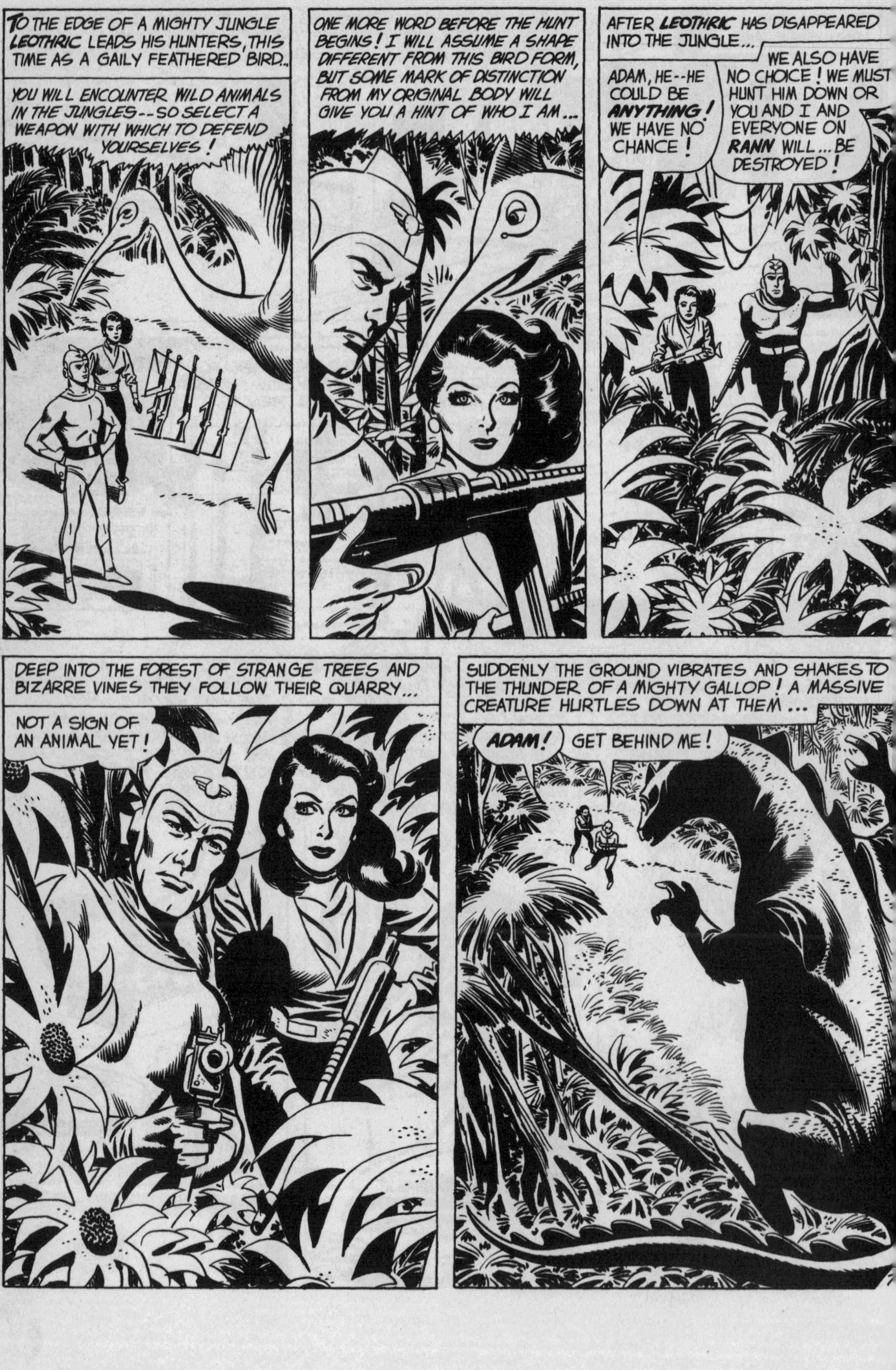
TO THE EDGE OF A MIGHTY JUNGLE LEOTHRIC LEADS HIS HUNTERS, THIS TIME AS A GAILY FEATHERED BIRD...
YOU WILL ENCOUNTER WILD ANIMALS IN THE JUNGLES--SO SELECT A WEAPON WITH WHICH TO DEFEND YOURSELVES!
ONE MORE WORD BEFORE THE HUNT BEGINS! I WILL ASSUME A SHAPE DIFFERENT FROM THIS BIRD FORM, BUT SOME MARK OF DISTINCTION FROM MY ORIGINAL BODY WILL GIVE YOU A HINT OF WHO I AM...
AFTER LEOTHRIC HAS DISAPPEARED INTO THE JUNGLE...
ADAM, HE--HE COULD BE ANYTHING! WE HAVE NO CHANCE!
WE ALSO HAVE NO CHOICE! WE MUST HUNT HIM DOWN OR YOU AND I AND EVERYONE ON RANN WILL... BE DESTROYED!
DEEP INTO THE FOREST OF STRANGE TREES AND BIZARRE VINES THEY FOLLOW THEIR QUARRY...
NOT A SIGN OF AN ANIMAL YET!
SUDDENLY THE GROUND VIBRATES AND SHAKES TO THE THUNDER OF A MIGHTY GALLOP! A MASSIVE CREATURE HURTLES DOWN AT THEM...
ADAM!
GET BEHIND ME!

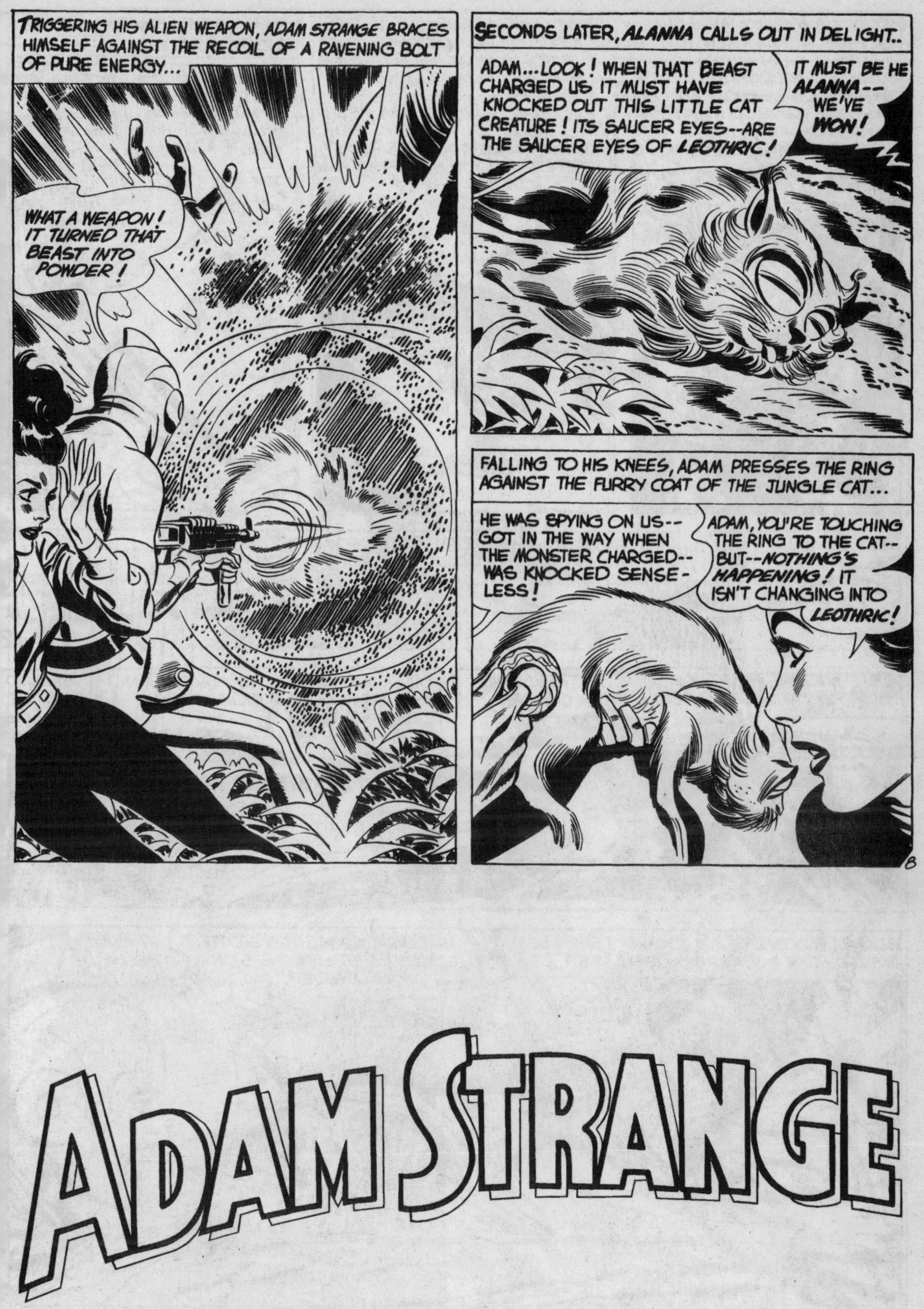
TRIGGERING HIS ALIEN WEAPON, ADAM STRANGE BRACES HIMSELF AGAINST THE RECOIL OF A RAVENING BOLT OF PURE ENERGY...
WHAT A WEAPON! IT TURNED THAT BEAST INTO POWDER!
SECONDS LATER, ALANNA CALLS OUT IN DELIGHT..
ADAM...LOOK! WHEN THAT BEAST CHARGED US IT MUST HAVE KNOCKED OUT THIS LITTLE CAT CREATURE! ITS SAUCER EYES--ARE THE SAUCER EYES OF LEOTHRIC!
IT MUST BE HE ALANNA-- WE'VE WON!
FALLING TO HIS KNEES, ADAM PRESSES THE RING AGAINST THE FURRY COAT OF THE JUNGLE CAT...
HE WAS SPYING ON US-- GOT IN THE WAY WHEN THE MONSTER CHARGED-- WAS KNOCKED SENSE-LESS!
ADAM, YOU'RE TOUCHING THE RING TO THE CAT-- BUT--NOTHING'S HAPPENING! IT ISN'T CHANGING INTO LEOTHRIC!
8

ADAM STRANGE

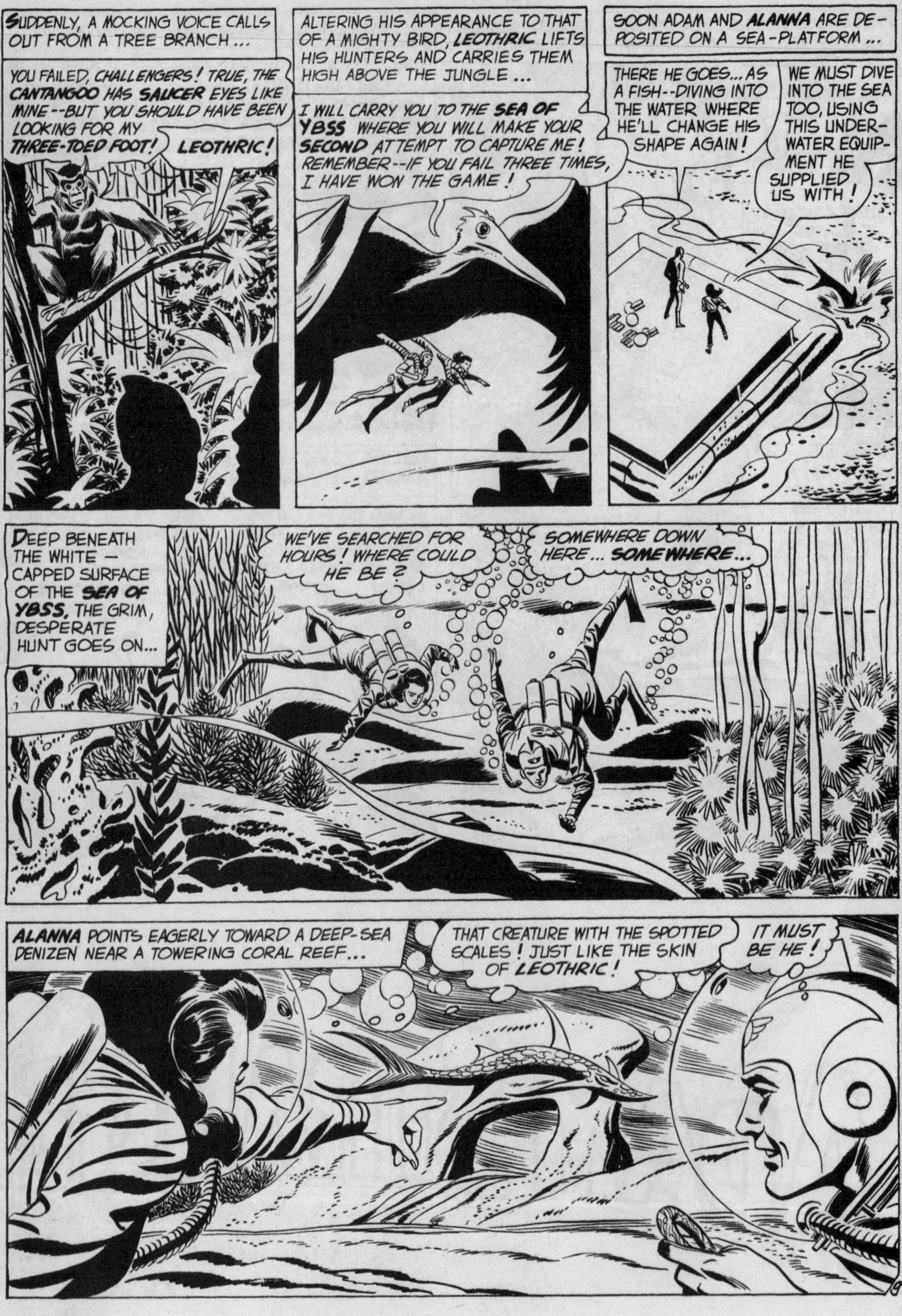
SUDDENLY, A MOCKING VOICE CALLS OUT FROM A TREE BRANCH...
YOU FAILED, CHALLENGERS! TRUE, THE CANTANGOO HAS SAUCER EYES LIKE MINE--BUT YOU SHOULD HAVE BEEN LOOKING FOR MY THREE-TOED FOOT!
LEOTHRIC!
ALTERING HIS APPEARANCE TO THAT OF A MIGHTY BIRD, LEOTHRIC LIFTS HIS HUNTERS AND CARRIES THEM HIGH ABOVE THE JUNGLE...
I WILL CARRY YOU TO THE SEA OF YBSS WHERE YOU WILL MAKE YOUR SECOND ATTEMPT TO CAPTURE ME! REMEMBER--IF YOU FAIL THREE TIMES, I HAVE WON THE GAME!
SOON ADAM AND ALANNA ARE DEPOSITED ON A SEA-PLATFORM...
THERE HE GOES... AS A FISH--DIVING INTO THE WATER WHERE HE'LL CHANGE HIS SHAPE AGAIN!
WE MUST DIVE INTO THE SEA TOO, USING THIS UNDER-WATER EQUIPMENT HE SUPPLIED US WITH!
DEEP BENEATH THE WHITE-CAPPED SURFACE OF THE SEA OF YBSS, THE GRIM, DESPERATE HUNT GOES ON...
WE'VE SEARCHED FOR HOURS! WHERE COULD HE BE?
SOMEWHERE DOWN HERE... SOMEWHERE...
ALANNA POINTS EAGERLY TOWARD A DEEP-SEA DENIZEN NEAR A TOWERING CORAL REEF...
THAT CREATURE WITH THE SPOTTED SCALES! JUST LIKE THE SKIN OF LEOTHRIC!
IT MUST BE HE!
9

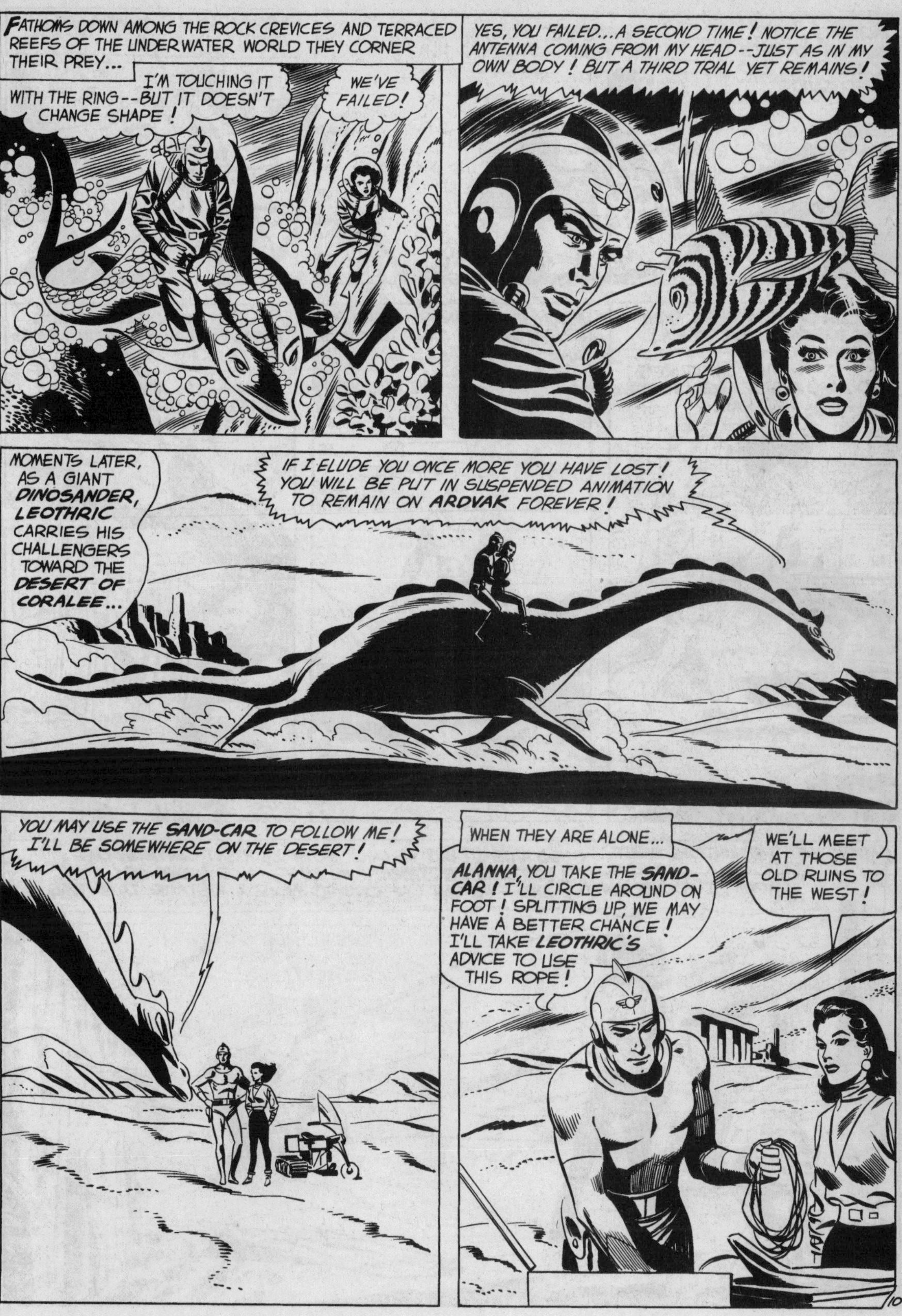
FATHOMS DOWN AMONG THE ROCK CREVICES AND TERRACED REEFS OF THE UNDERWATER WORLD THEY CORNER THEIR PREY...
I'M TOUCHING IT WITH THE RING--BUT IT DOESN'T CHANGE SHAPE!
WE'VE FAILED!
YES, YOU FAILED...A SECOND TIME! NOTICE THE ANTENNA COMING FROM MY HEAD--JUST AS IN MY OWN BODY! BUT A THIRD TRIAL YET REMAINS!
MOMENTS LATER, AS A GIANT DINOSANDER, LEOTHRIC CARRIES HIS CHALLENGERS TOWARD THE DESERT OF CORALEE...
IF I ELUDE YOU ONCE MORE YOU HAVE LOST! YOU WILL BE PUT IN SUSPENDED ANIMATION TO REMAIN ON ARDVAK FOREVER!
YOU MAY USE THE SAND-CAR TO FOLLOW ME! I'LL BE SOMEWHERE ON THE DESERT!
WHEN THEY ARE ALONE...
ALANNA, YOU TAKE THE SAND-CAR! I'LL CIRCLE AROUND ON FOOT! SPLITTING UP, WE MAY HAVE A BETTER CHANCE! I'LL TAKE LEOTHRIC'S ADVICE TO USE THIS ROPE!
WE'LL MEET AT THOSE OLD RUINS TO THE WEST!
10

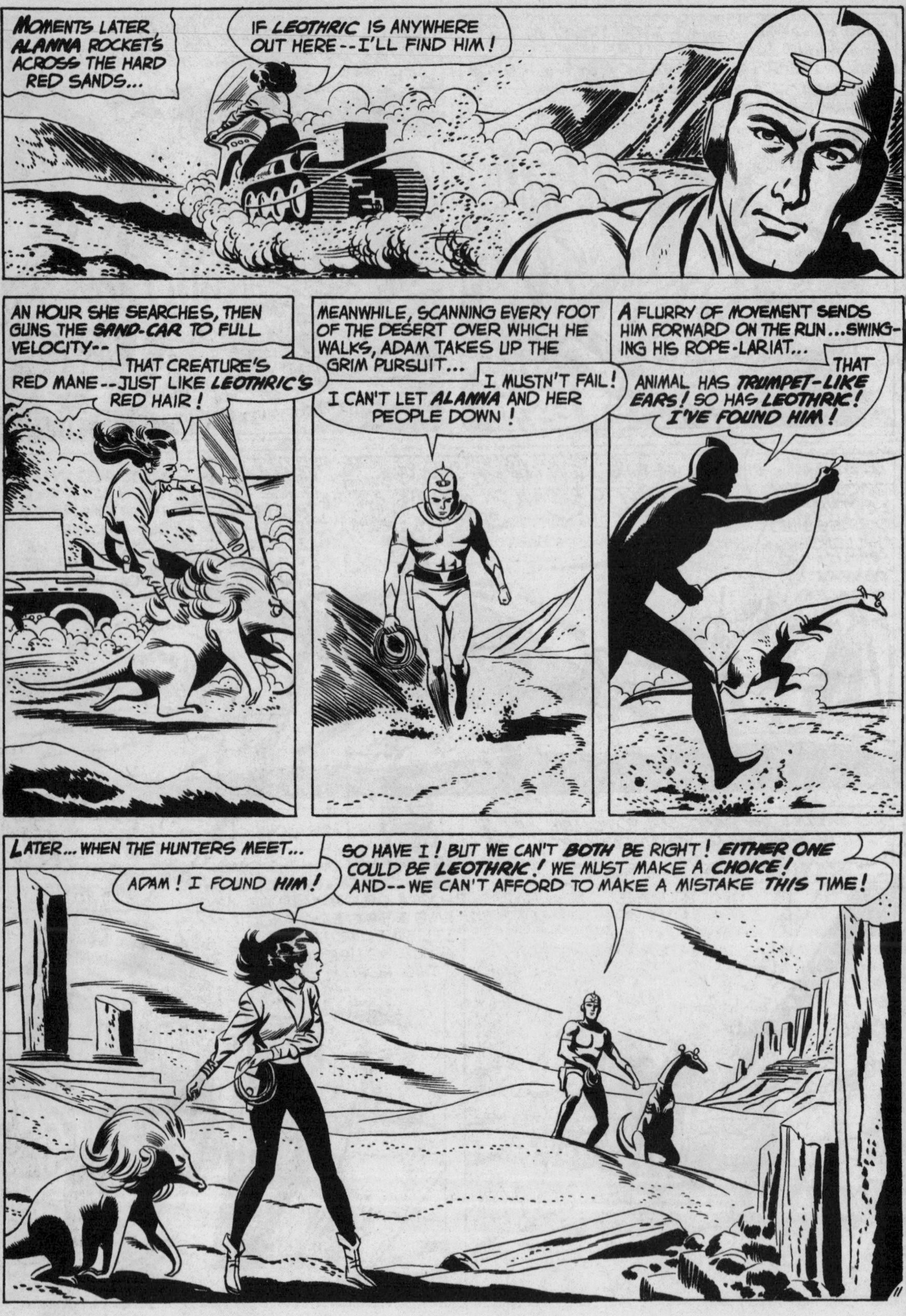
MOMENTS LATER, ALANNA ROCKETS ACROSS THE HARD RED SANDS...
IF LEOTHRIC IS ANYWHERE OUT HERE--I'LL FIND HIM!
AN HOUR SHE SEARCHES, THEN GUNS THE SAND-CAR TO FULL VELOCITY--
THAT CREATURE'S RED MANE--JUST LIKE LEOTHRIC'S RED HAIR!
MEANWHILE, SCANNING EVERY FOOT OF THE DESERT OVER WHICH HE WALKS, ADAM TAKES UP THE GRIM PURSUIT...
I MUSTN'T FAIL! I CAN'T LET ALANNA AND HER PEOPLE DOWN!
A FLURRY OF MOVEMENT SENDS HIM FORWARD ON THE RUN...SWINGING HIS ROPE-LARIAT...
THAT ANIMAL HAS TRUMPET-LIKE EARS! SO HAS LEOTHRIC! I'VE FOUND HIM!
LATER... WHEN THE HUNTERS MEET...
ADAM! I FOUND HIM!
SO HAVE I! BUT WE CAN'T BOTH BE RIGHT! EITHER ONE COULD BE LEOTHRIC! WE MUST MAKE A CHOICE! AND--WE CAN'T AFFORD TO MAKE A MISTAKE THIS TIME!
11

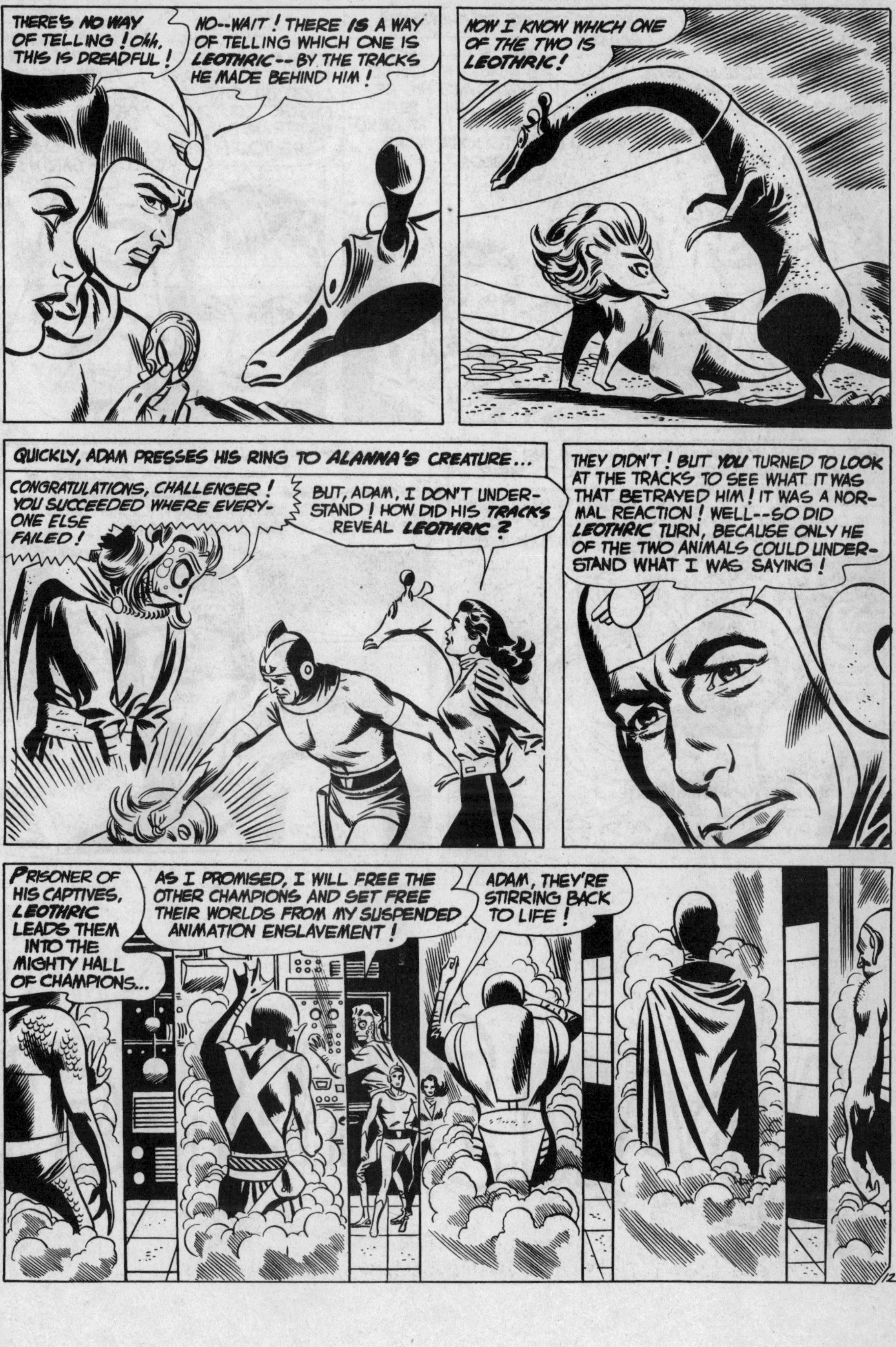
THERE'S NO WAY OF TELLING ! Ohh, THIS IS DREADFUL !
NO--WAIT ! THERE IS A WAY OF TELLING WHICH ONE IS LEOTHRIC-- BY THE TRACKS HE MADE BEHIND HIM !
NOW I KNOW WHICH ONE OF THE TWO IS LEOTHRIC !
QUICKLY, ADAM PRESSES HIS RING TO ALANNA'S CREATURE...
CONGRATULATIONS, CHALLENGER ! YOU SUCCEEDED WHERE EVERYONE ELSE FAILED !
BUT, ADAM, I DON'T UNDERSTAND ! HOW DID HIS TRACKS REVEAL LEOTHRIC ?
THEY DIDN'T ! BUT YOU TURNED TO LOOK AT THE TRACKS TO SEE WHAT IT WAS THAT BETRAYED HIM ! IT WAS A NORMAL REACTION ! WELL--SO DID LEOTHRIC TURN, BECAUSE ONLY HE OF THE TWO ANIMALS COULD UNDERSTAND WHAT I WAS SAYING !
PRISONER OF HIS CAPTIVES, LEOTHRIC LEADS THEM INTO THE MIGHTY HALL OF CHAMPIONS...
AS I PROMISED, I WILL FREE THE OTHER CHAMPIONS AND SET FREE THEIR WORLDS FROM MY SUSPENDED ANIMATION ENSLAVEMENT !
ADAM, THEY'RE STIRRING BACK TO LIFE !
12

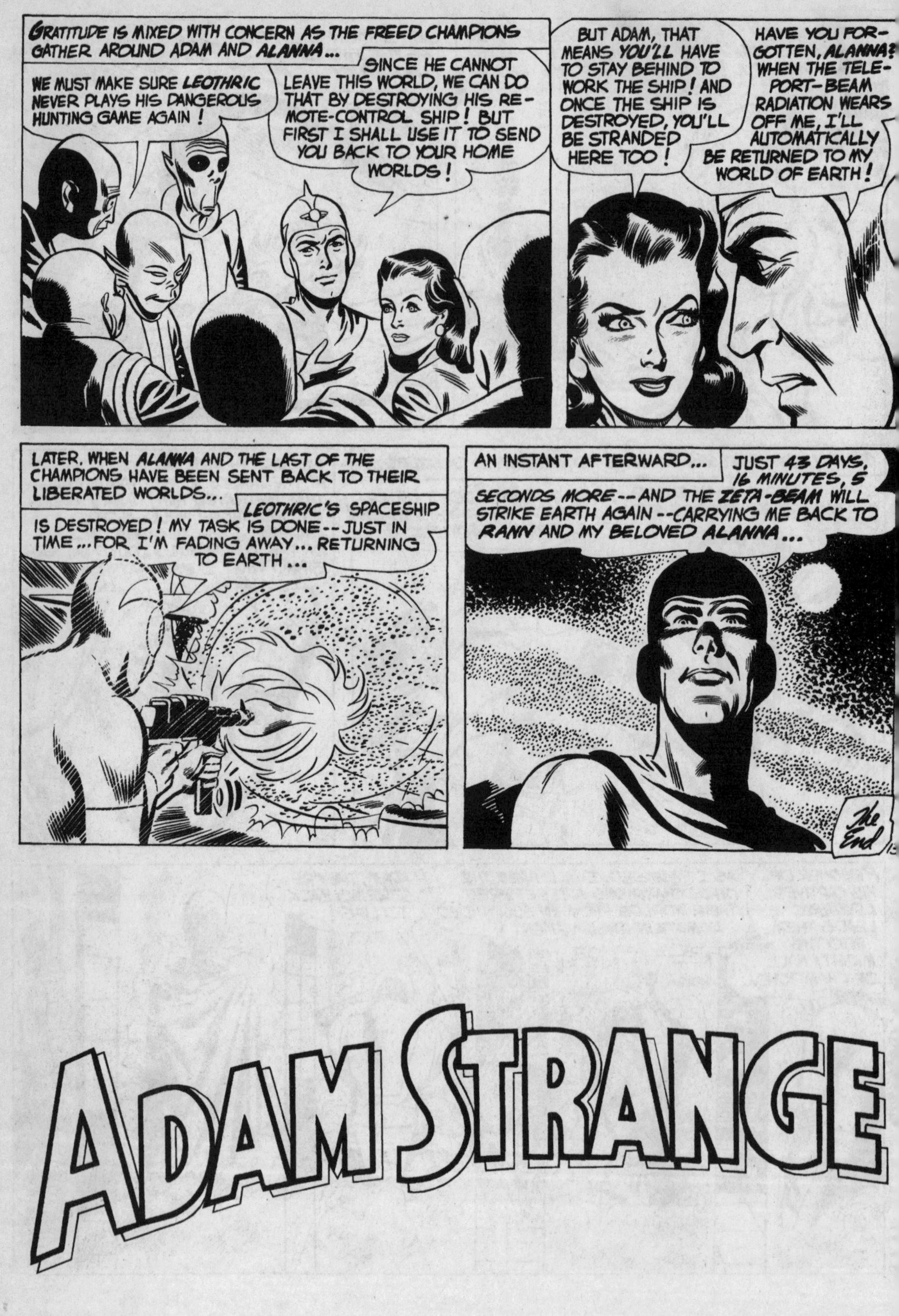
GRATITUDE IS MIXED WITH CONCERN AS THE FREED CHAMPIONS GATHER AROUND ADAM AND ALANNA...
WE MUST MAKE SURE LEOTHRIC NEVER PLAYS HIS DANGEROUS HUNTING GAME AGAIN!
SINCE HE CANNOT LEAVE THIS WORLD, WE CAN DO THAT BY DESTROYING HIS REMOTE-CONTROL SHIP! BUT FIRST I SHALL USE IT TO SEND YOU BACK TO YOUR HOME WORLDS!
BUT ADAM, THAT MEANS YOU'LL HAVE TO STAY BEHIND TO WORK THE SHIP! AND ONCE THE SHIP IS DESTROYED, YOU'LL BE STRANDED HERE TOO!
HAVE YOU FORGOTTEN, ALANNA? WHEN THE TELEPORT-BEAM RADIATION WEARS OFF ME, I'LL AUTOMATICALLY BE RETURNED TO MY WORLD OF EARTH!
LATER, WHEN ALANNA AND THE LAST OF THE CHAMPIONS HAVE BEEN SENT BACK TO THEIR LIBERATED WORLDS...
LEOTHRIC'S SPACESHIP IS DESTROYED! MY TASK IS DONE--JUST IN TIME...FOR I'M FADING AWAY... RETURNING TO EARTH...
AN INSTANT AFTERWARD...
JUST 43 DAYS, 16 MINUTES, 5 SECONDS MORE--AND THE ZETA-BEAM WILL STRIKE EARTH AGAIN--CARRYING ME BACK TO RANN AND MY BELOVED ALANNA...
The End
13

ADAM STRANGE

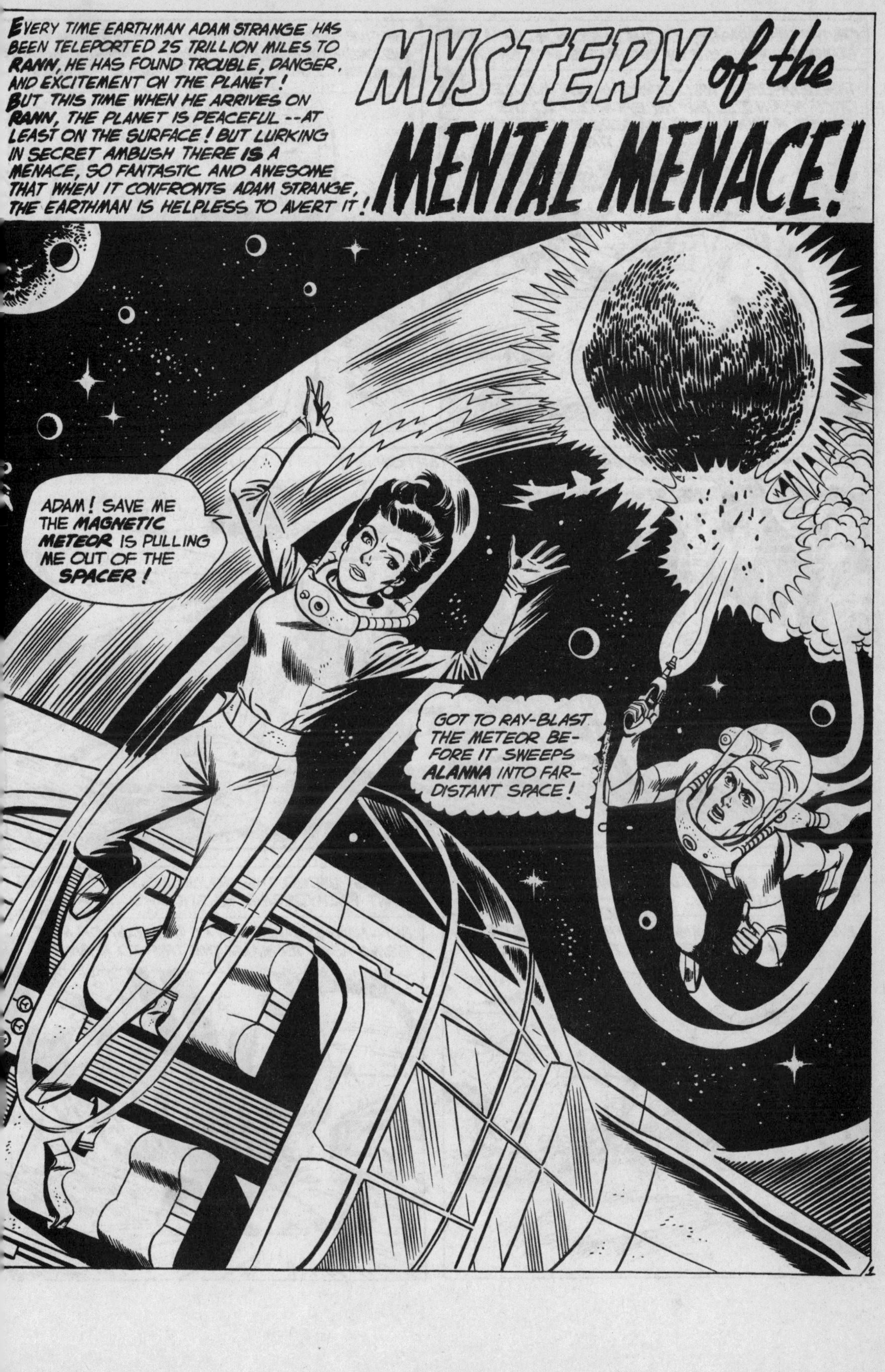
EVERY TIME EARTHMAN ADAM STRANGE HAS BEEN TELEPORTED 25 TRILLION MILES TO RANN, HE HAS FOUND TROUBLE, DANGER, AND EXCITEMENT ON THE PLANET! BUT THIS TIME WHEN HE ARRIVES ON RANN, THE PLANET IS PEACEFUL --AT LEAST ON THE SURFACE! BUT LURKING IN SECRET AMBUSH THERE IS A MENACE, SO FANTASTIC AND AWESOME THAT WHEN IT CONFRONTS ADAM STRANGE, THE EARTHMAN IS HELPLESS TO AVERT IT!
MYSTERY of the MENTAL MENACE!
ADAM! SAVE ME THE MAGNETIC METEOR IS PULLING ME OUT OF THE SPACER!
GOT TO RAY-BLAST THE METEOR BEFORE IT SWEEPS ALANNA INTO FAR-DISTANT SPACE!

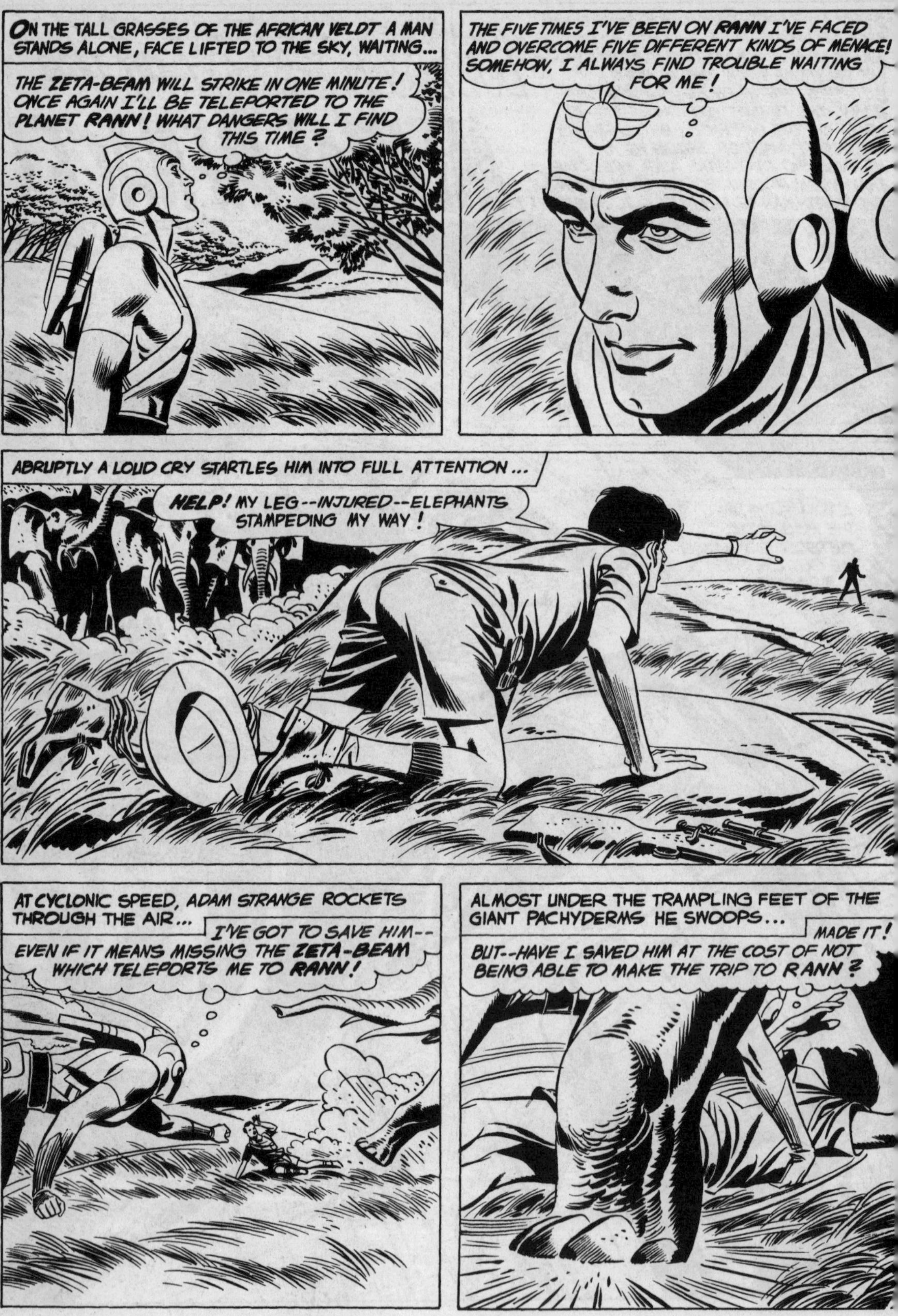
ON THE TALL GRASSES OF THE AFRICAN VELDT A MAN STANDS ALONE, FACE LIFTED TO THE SKY, WAITING...
THE ZETA-BEAM WILL STRIKE IN ONE MINUTE! ONCE AGAIN I'LL BE TELEPORTED TO THE PLANET RANN! WHAT DANGERS WILL I FIND THIS TIME?
THE FIVE TIMES I'VE BEEN ON RANN I'VE FACED AND OVERCOME FIVE DIFFERENT KINDS OF MENACE! SOMEHOW, I ALWAYS FIND TROUBLE WAITING FOR ME!
ABRUPTLY A LOUD CRY STARTLES HIM INTO FULL ATTENTION...
HELP! MY LEG--INJURED--ELEPHANTS STAMPEDING MY WAY!
AT CYCLONIC SPEED, ADAM STRANGE ROCKETS THROUGH THE AIR...
I'VE GOT TO SAVE HIM-- EVEN IF IT MEANS MISSING THE ZETA-BEAM WHICH TELEPORTS ME TO RANN!
ALMOST UNDER THE TRAMPLING FEET OF THE GIANT PACHYDERMS HE SWOOPS...
MADE IT! BUT--HAVE I SAVED HIM AT THE COST OF NOT BEING ABLE TO MAKE THE TRIP TO RANN?

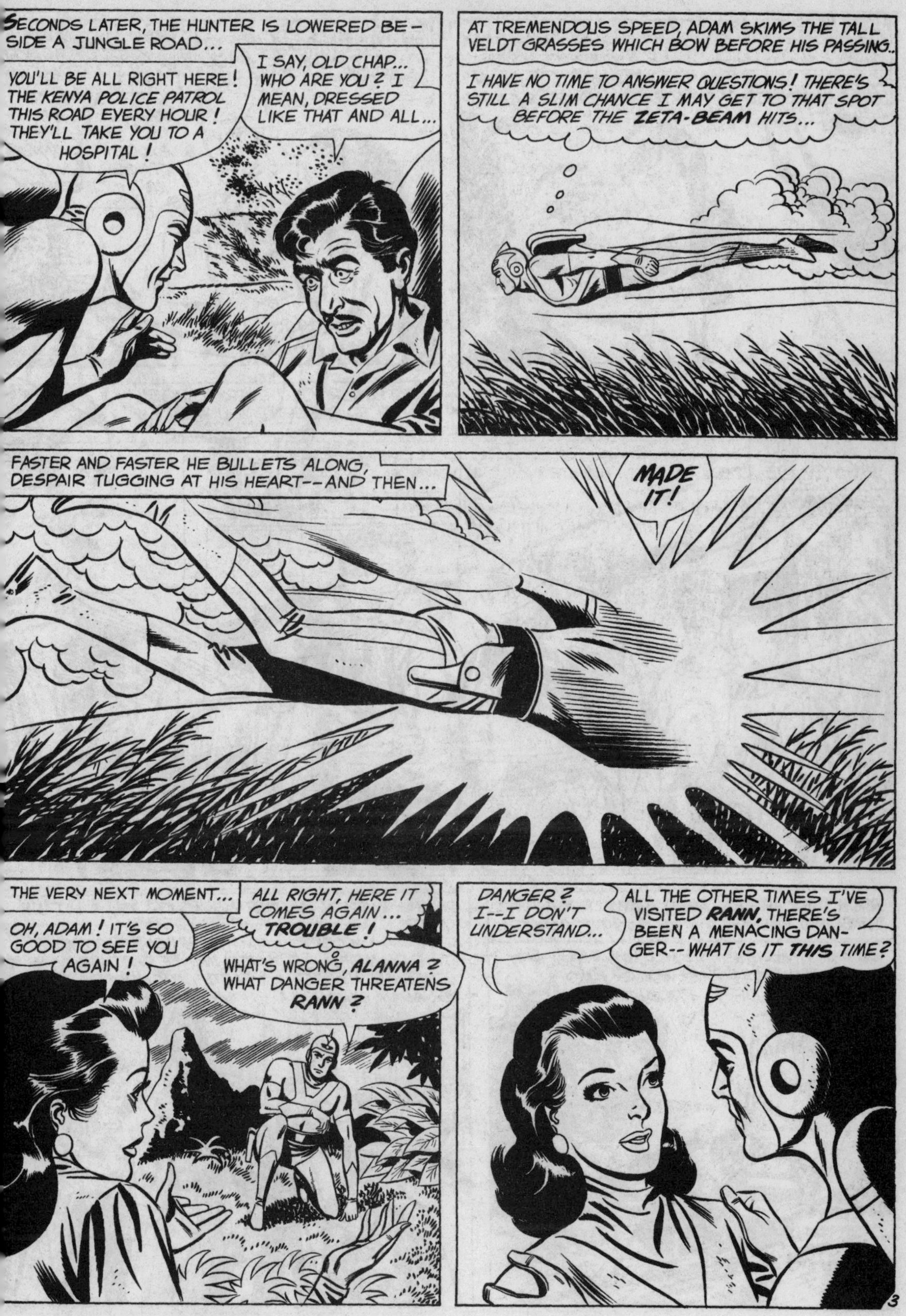
SECONDS LATER, THE HUNTER IS LOWERED BESIDE A JUNGLE ROAD...
YOU'LL BE ALL RIGHT HERE! THE KENYA POLICE PATROL THIS ROAD EVERY HOUR! THEY'LL TAKE YOU TO A HOSPITAL!
I SAY, OLD CHAP... WHO ARE YOU? I MEAN, DRESSED LIKE THAT AND ALL...
AT TREMENDOUS SPEED, ADAM SKIMS THE TALL VELDT GRASSES WHICH BOW BEFORE HIS PASSING..
I HAVE NO TIME TO ANSWER QUESTIONS! THERE'S STILL A SLIM CHANCE I MAY GET TO THAT SPOT BEFORE THE ZETA-BEAM HITS...
FASTER AND FASTER HE BULLETS ALONG, DESPAIR TUGGING AT HIS HEART--AND THEN...
MADE IT!
THE VERY NEXT MOMENT...
OH, ADAM! IT'S SO GOOD TO SEE YOU AGAIN!
ALL RIGHT, HERE IT COMES AGAIN... TROUBLE!
WHAT'S WRONG, ALANNA? WHAT DANGER THREATENS RANN?
DANGER? I--I DON'T UNDERSTAND...
ALL THE OTHER TIMES I'VE VISITED RANN, THERE'S BEEN A MENACING DANGER--WHAT IS IT THIS TIME?
3

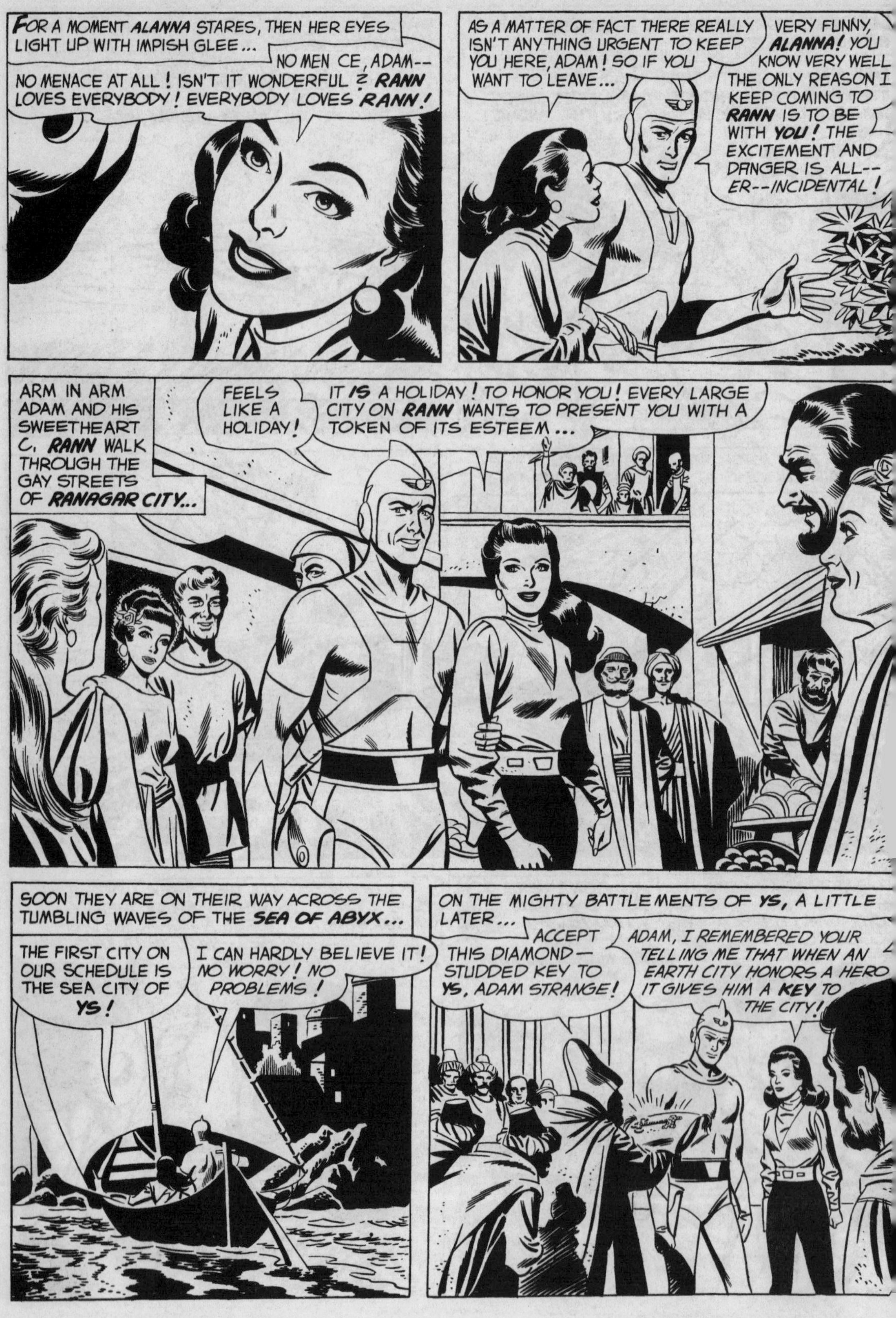
FOR A MOMENT ALANNA STARES, THEN HER EYES LIGHT UP WITH IMPISH GLEE...
NO MEN CE, ADAM-- NO MENACE AT ALL! ISN'T IT WONDERFUL? RANN LOVES EVERYBODY! EVERYBODY LOVES RANN!
AS A MATTER OF FACT THERE REALLY ISN'T ANYTHING URGENT TO KEEP YOU HERE, ADAM! SO IF YOU WANT TO LEAVE...
VERY FUNNY, ALANNA! YOU KNOW VERY WELL THE ONLY REASON I KEEP COMING TO RANN IS TO BE WITH YOU! THE EXCITEMENT AND DANGER IS ALL-- ER--INCIDENTAL!
ARM IN ARM ADAM AND HIS SWEETHEART C. RANN WALK THROUGH THE GAY STREETS OF RANAGAR CITY...
FEELS LIKE A HOLIDAY!
IT IS A HOLIDAY! TO HONOR YOU! EVERY LARGE CITY ON RANN WANTS TO PRESENT YOU WITH A TOKEN OF ITS ESTEEM...
SOON THEY ARE ON THEIR WAY ACROSS THE TUMBLING WAVES OF THE SEA OF ABYX...
THE FIRST CITY ON OUR SCHEDULE IS THE SEA CITY OF YS!
I CAN HARDLY BELIEVE IT! NO WORRY! NO PROBLEMS!
ON THE MIGHTY BATTLEMENTS OF YS, A LITTLE LATER...
ACCEPT THIS DIAMOND-STUDDED KEY TO YS, ADAM STRANGE!
ADAM, I REMEMBERED YOUR TELLING ME THAT WHEN AN EARTH CITY HONORS A HERO IT GIVES HIM A KEY TO THE CITY!

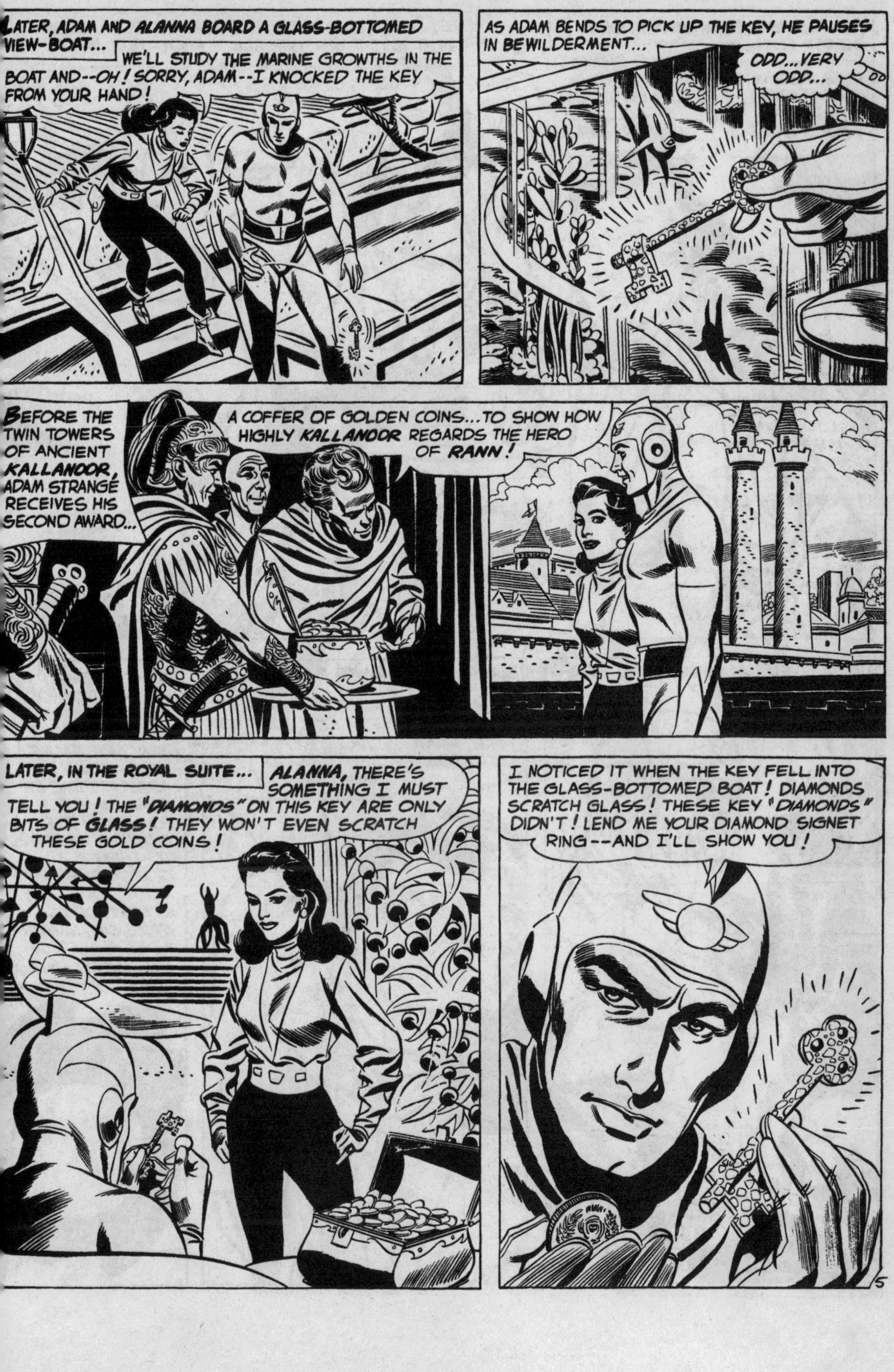
LATER, ADAM AND ALANNA BOARD A GLASS-BOTTOMED VIEW-BOAT...
WE'LL STUDY THE MARINE GROWTHS IN THE BOAT AND--OH! SORRY, ADAM--I KNOCKED THE KEY FROM YOUR HAND!
AS ADAM BENDS TO PICK UP THE KEY, HE PAUSES IN BEWILDERMENT...
ODD...VERY ODD...
BEFORE THE TWIN TOWERS OF ANCIENT KALLANOOR, ADAM STRANGE RECEIVES HIS SECOND AWARD...
A COFFER OF GOLDEN COINS...TO SHOW HOW HIGHLY KALLANOOR REGARDS THE HERO OF RANN!
LATER, IN THE ROYAL SUITE...
ALANNA, THERE'S SOMETHING I MUST TELL YOU! THE "DIAMONDS" ON THIS KEY ARE ONLY BITS OF GLASS! THEY WON'T EVEN SCRATCH THESE GOLD COINS!
I NOTICED IT WHEN THE KEY FELL INTO THE GLASS-BOTTOMED BOAT! DIAMONDS SCRATCH GLASS! THESE KEY "DIAMONDS" DIDN'T! LEND ME YOUR DIAMOND SIGNET RING--AND I'LL SHOW YOU!
5

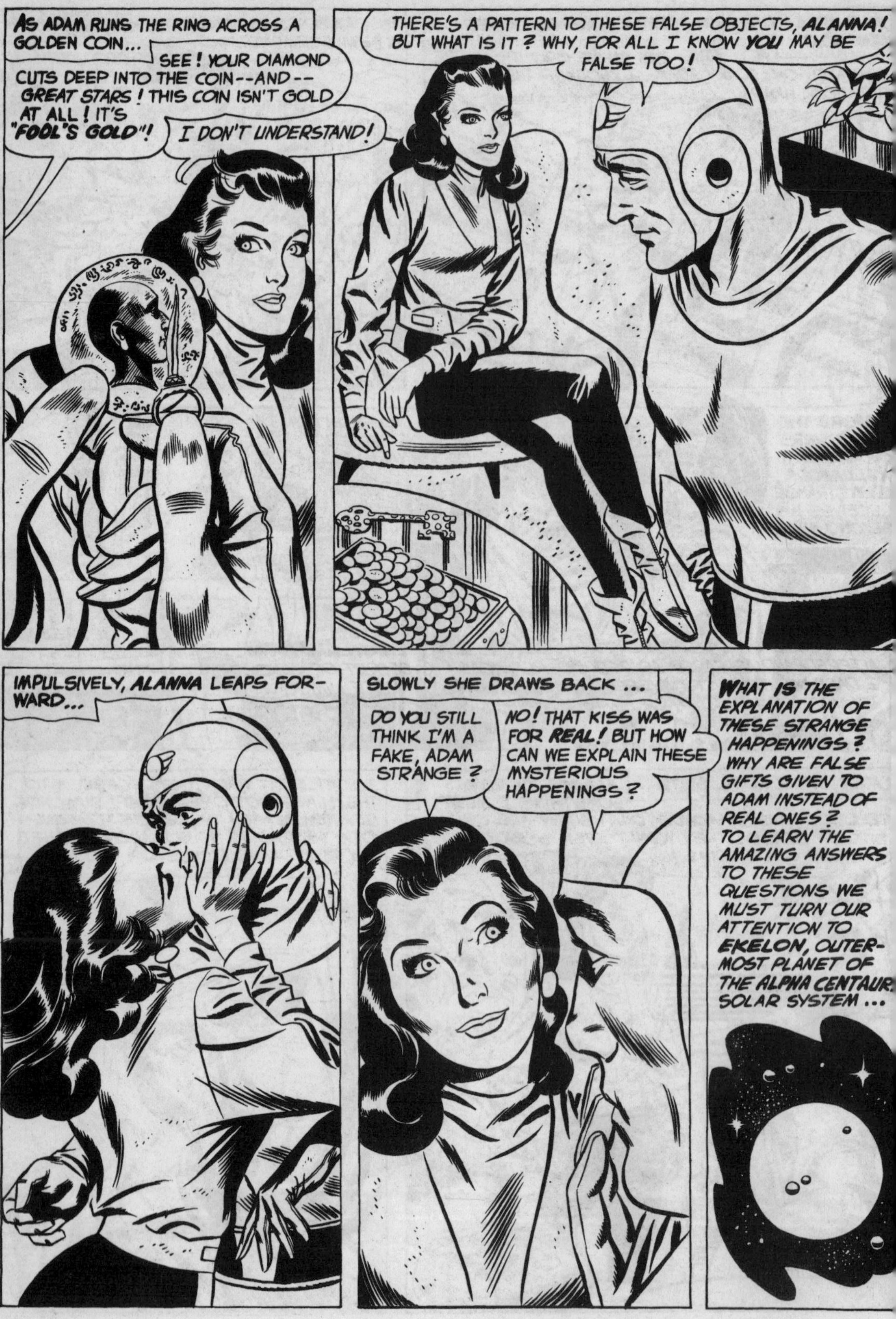
AS ADAM RUNS THE RING ACROSS A GOLDEN COIN...
SEE! YOUR DIAMOND CUTS DEEP INTO THE COIN--AND--GREAT STARS! THIS COIN ISN'T GOLD AT ALL! IT'S "FOOL'S GOLD"!
I DON'T UNDERSTAND!
THERE'S A PATTERN TO THESE FALSE OBJECTS, ALANNA! BUT WHAT IS IT? WHY, FOR ALL I KNOW YOU MAY BE FALSE TOO!
IMPULSIVELY, ALANNA LEAPS FOR-WARD...
SLOWLY SHE DRAWS BACK ...
DO YOU STILL THINK I'M A FAKE, ADAM STRANGE?
NO! THAT KISS WAS FOR REAL! BUT HOW CAN WE EXPLAIN THESE MYSTERIOUS HAPPENINGS?
WHAT IS THE EXPLANATION OF THESE STRANGE HAPPENINGS? WHY ARE FALSE GIFTS GIVEN TO ADAM INSTEAD OF REAL ONES? TO LEARN THE AMAZING ANSWERS TO THESE QUESTIONS WE MUST TURN OUR ATTENTION TO EKELON, OUTER-MOST PLANET OF THE ALPHA CENTAURI SOLAR SYSTEM ...

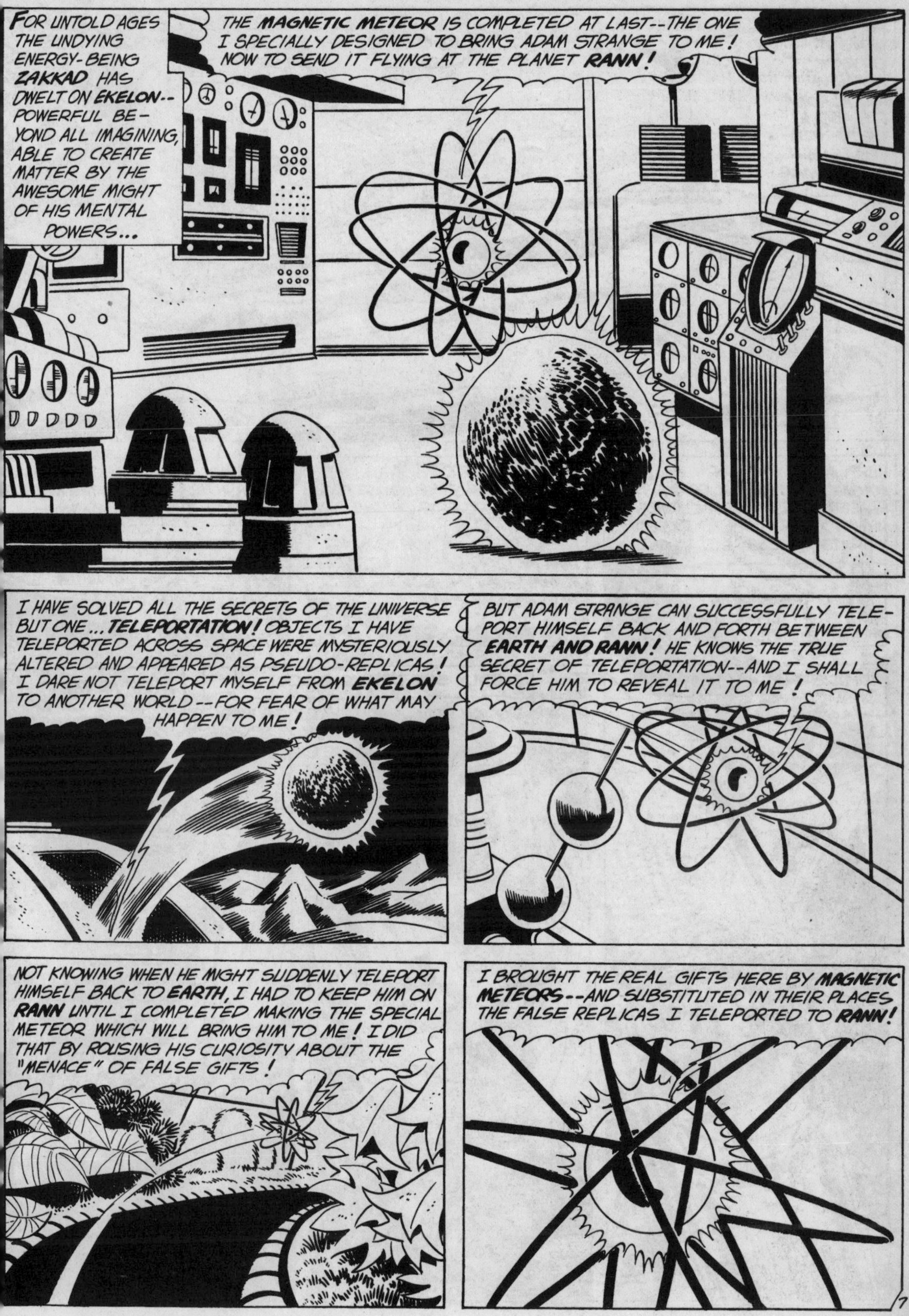
FOR UNTOLD AGES THE UNDYING ENERGY-BEING ZAKKAD HAS DWELT ON EKELON--POWERFUL BE-YOND ALL IMAGINING, ABLE TO CREATE MATTER BY THE AWESOME MIGHT OF HIS MENTAL POWERS...
THE MAGNETIC METEOR IS COMPLETED AT LAST--THE ONE I SPECIALLY DESIGNED TO BRING ADAM STRANGE TO ME! NOW TO SEND IT FLYING AT THE PLANET RANN!
I HAVE SOLVED ALL THE SECRETS OF THE UNIVERSE BUT ONE...TELEPORTATION! OBJECTS I HAVE TELEPORTED ACROSS SPACE WERE MYSTERIOUSLY ALTERED AND APPEARED AS PSEUDO-REPLICAS! I DARE NOT TELEPORT MYSELF FROM EKELON TO ANOTHER WORLD--FOR FEAR OF WHAT MAY HAPPEN TO ME!
BUT ADAM STRANGE CAN SUCCESSFULLY TELE-PORT HIMSELF BACK AND FORTH BETWEEN EARTH AND RANN! HE KNOWS THE TRUE SECRET OF TELEPORTATION--AND I SHALL FORCE HIM TO REVEAL IT TO ME!
NOT KNOWING WHEN HE MIGHT SUDDENLY TELEPORT HIMSELF BACK TO EARTH, I HAD TO KEEP HIM ON RANN UNTIL I COMPLETED MAKING THE SPECIAL METEOR WHICH WILL BRING HIM TO ME! I DID THAT BY ROUSING HIS CURIOSITY ABOUT THE "MENACE" OF FALSE GIFTS!
I BROUGHT THE REAL GIFTS HERE BY MAGNETIC METEORS--AND SUBSTITUTED IN THEIR PLACES THE FALSE REPLICAS I TELEPORTED TO RANN!
7

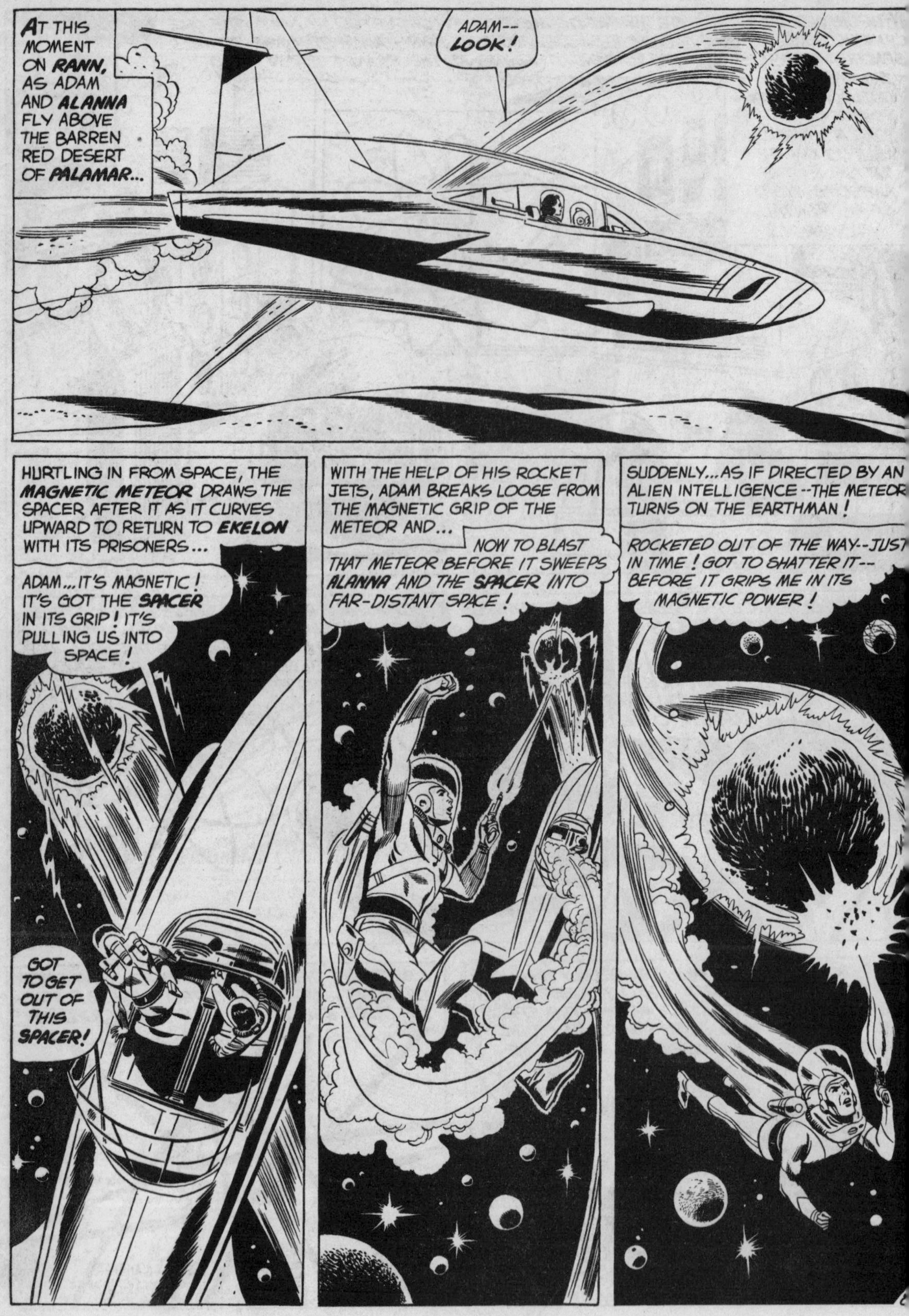
AT THIS MOMENT ON RANN, AS ADAM AND ALANNA FLY ABOVE THE BARREN RED DESERT OF PALAMAR...
ADAM-- LOOK!
HURTLING IN FROM SPACE, THE MAGNETIC METEOR DRAWS THE SPACER AFTER IT AS IT CURVES UPWARD TO RETURN TO EKELON WITH ITS PRISONERS...
ADAM... IT'S MAGNETIC! IT'S GOT THE SPACER IN ITS GRIP! IT'S PULLING US INTO SPACE!
GOT TO GET OUT OF THIS SPACER!
WITH THE HELP OF HIS ROCKET JETS, ADAM BREAKS LOOSE FROM THE MAGNETIC GRIP OF THE METEOR AND...
NOW TO BLAST THAT METEOR BEFORE IT SWEEPS ALANNA AND THE SPACER INTO FAR-DISTANT SPACE!
SUDDENLY... AS IF DIRECTED BY AN ALIEN INTELLIGENCE --THE METEOR TURNS ON THE EARTHMAN!
ROCKETED OUT OF THE WAY--JUST IN TIME! GOT TO SHATTER IT-- BEFORE IT GRIPS ME IN ITS MAGNETIC POWER!

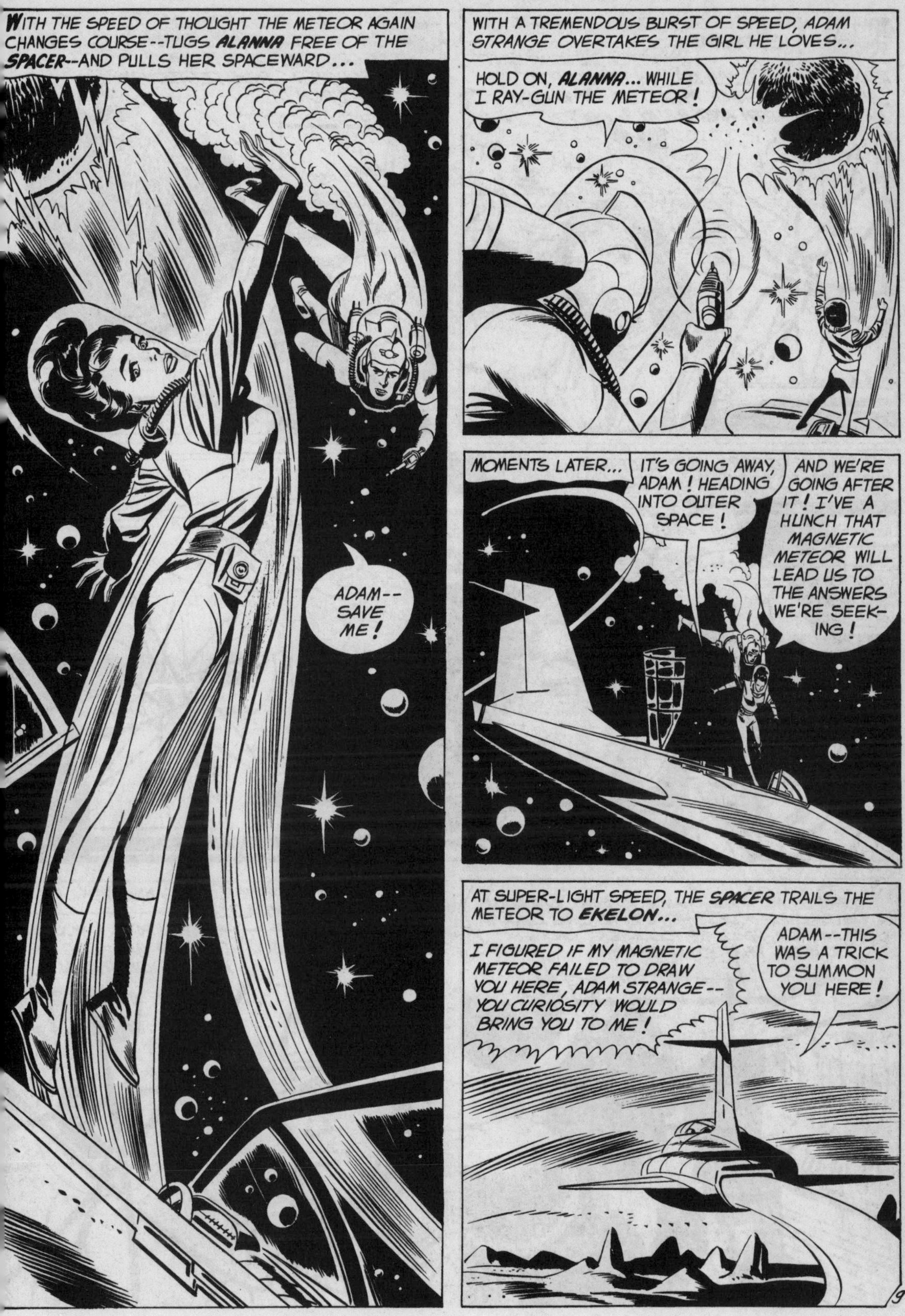
WITH THE SPEED OF THOUGHT THE METEOR AGAIN CHANGES COURSE--TUGS ALANNA FREE OF THE SPACER--AND PULLS HER SPACEWARD...
ADAM-- SAVE ME!
WITH A TREMENDOUS BURST OF SPEED, ADAM STRANGE OVERTAKES THE GIRL HE LOVES...
HOLD ON, ALANNA... WHILE I RAY-GUN THE METEOR!
MOMENTS LATER...
IT'S GOING AWAY, ADAM! HEADING INTO OUTER SPACE!
AND WE'RE GOING AFTER IT! I'VE A HUNCH THAT MAGNETIC METEOR WILL LEAD US TO THE ANSWERS WE'RE SEEKING!
AT SUPER-LIGHT SPEED, THE SPACER TRAILS THE METEOR TO EKELON...
I FIGURED IF MY MAGNETIC METEOR FAILED TO DRAW YOU HERE, ADAM STRANGE--YOU CURIOSITY WOULD BRING YOU TO ME!
ADAM--THIS WAS A TRICK TO SUMMON YOU HERE!
9

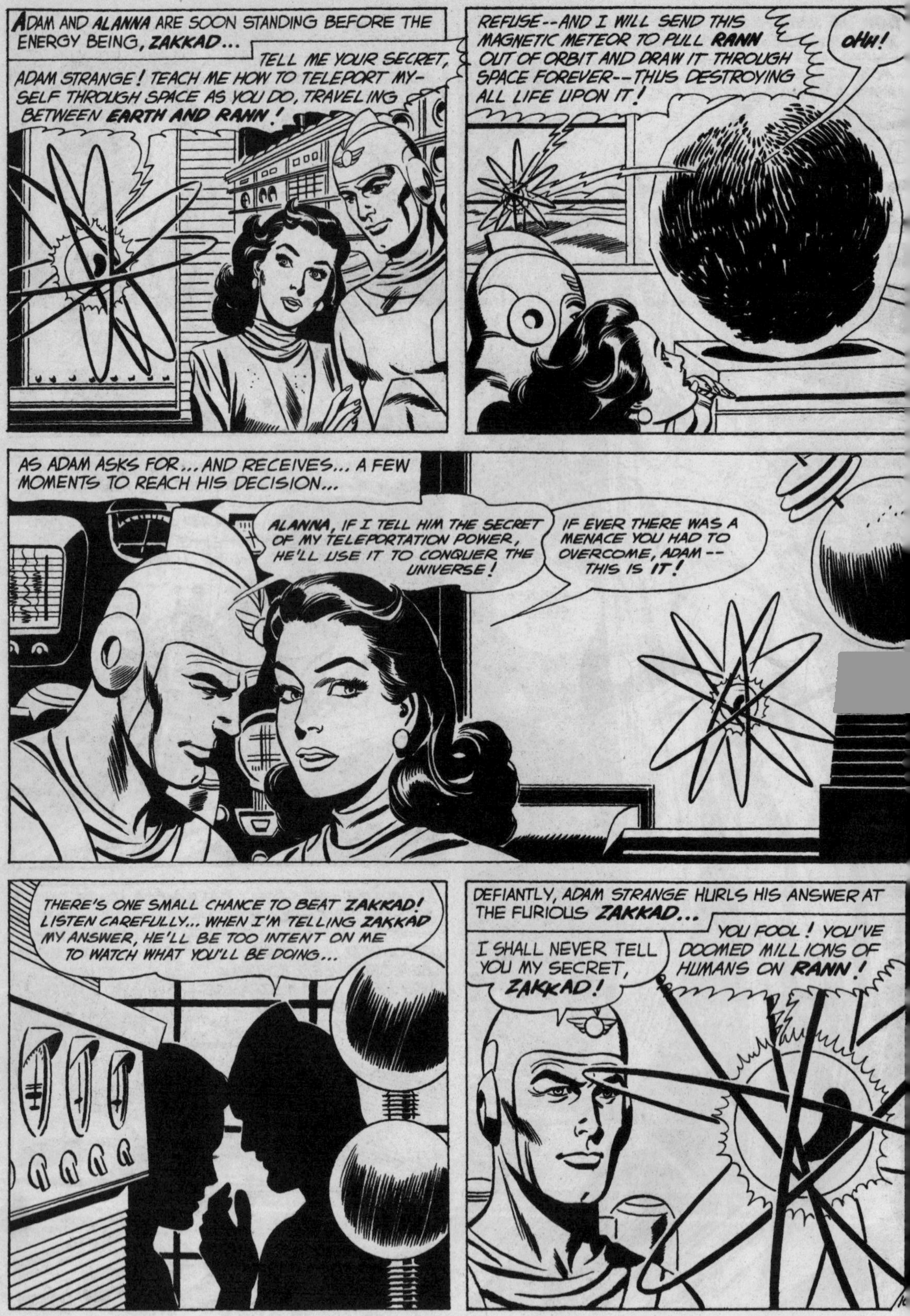
ADAM AND ALANNA ARE SOON STANDING BEFORE THE ENERGY BEING, ZAKKAD...
TELL ME YOUR SECRET, ADAM STRANGE! TEACH ME HOW TO TELEPORT MYSELF THROUGH SPACE AS YOU DO, TRAVELING BETWEEN EARTH AND RANN!
REFUSE--AND I WILL SEND THIS MAGNETIC METEOR TO PULL RANN OUT OF ORBIT AND DRAW IT THROUGH SPACE FOREVER--THUS DESTROYING ALL LIFE UPON IT!
OHH!
AS ADAM ASKS FOR... AND RECEIVES... A FEW MOMENTS TO REACH HIS DECISION...
ALANNA, IF I TELL HIM THE SECRET OF MY TELEPORTATION POWER, HE'LL USE IT TO CONQUER THE UNIVERSE!
IF EVER THERE WAS A MENACE YOU HAD TO OVERCOME, ADAM -- THIS IS IT!
THERE'S ONE SMALL CHANCE TO BEAT ZAKKAD! LISTEN CAREFULLY... WHEN I'M TELLING ZAKKAD MY ANSWER, HE'LL BE TOO INTENT ON ME TO WATCH WHAT YOU'LL BE DOING...
DEFIANTLY, ADAM STRANGE HURLS HIS ANSWER AT THE FURIOUS ZAKKAD...
I SHALL NEVER TELL YOU MY SECRET, ZAKKAD!
YOU FOOL! YOU'VE DOOMED MILLIONS OF HUMANS ON RANN!

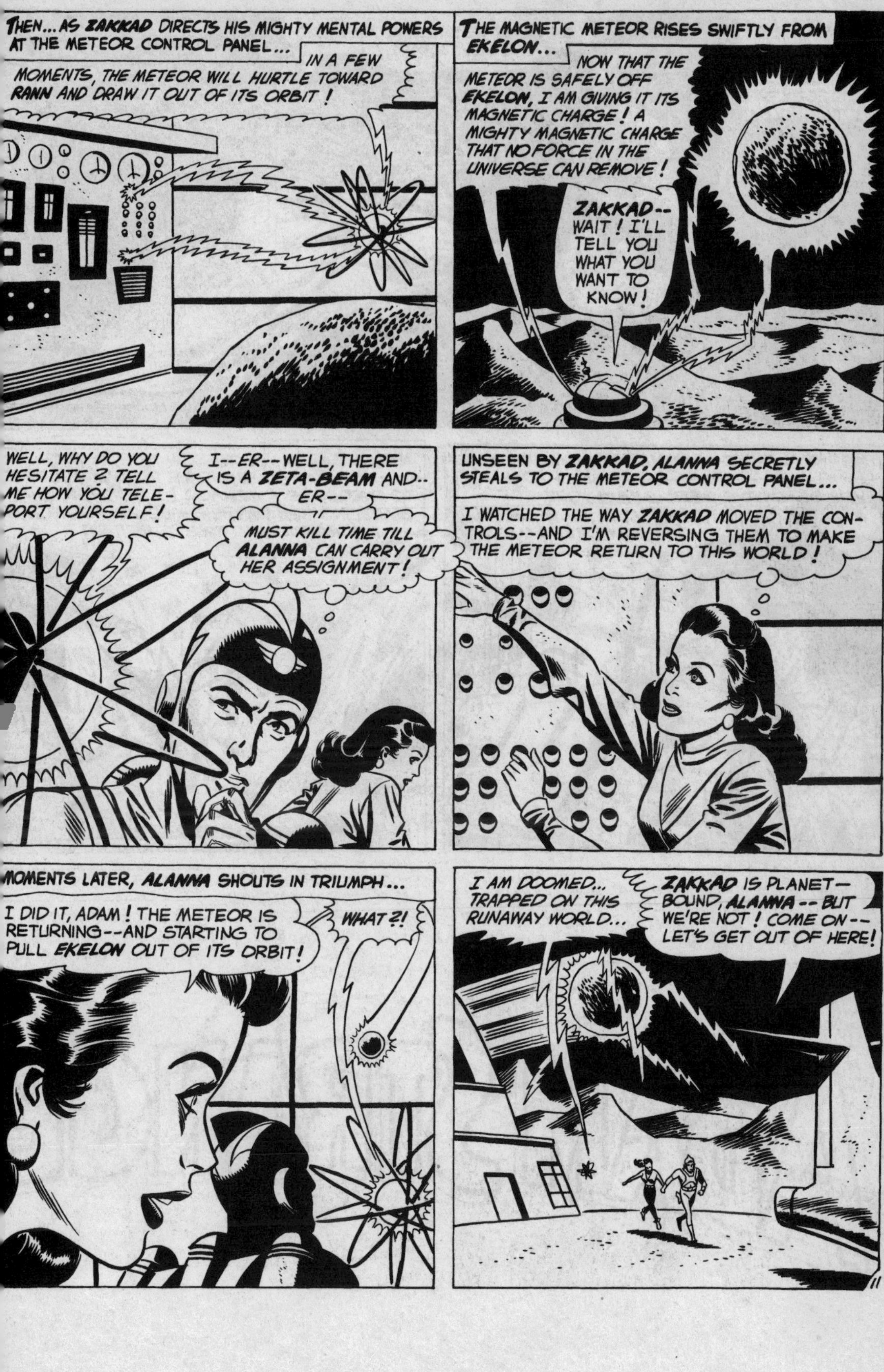
THEN... AS ZAKKAD DIRECTS HIS MIGHTY MENTAL POWERS AT THE METEOR CONTROL PANEL...
IN A FEW MOMENTS, THE METEOR WILL HURTLE TOWARD RANN AND DRAW IT OUT OF ITS ORBIT!
THE MAGNETIC METEOR RISES SWIFTLY FROM EKELON...
NOW THAT THE METEOR IS SAFELY OFF EKELON, I AM GIVING IT ITS MAGNETIC CHARGE! A MIGHTY MAGNETIC CHARGE THAT NO FORCE IN THE UNIVERSE CAN REMOVE!
ZAKKAD-- WAIT! I'LL TELL YOU WHAT YOU WANT TO KNOW!
WELL, WHY DO YOU HESITATE ? TELL ME HOW YOU TELE-PORT YOURSELF!
I--ER--WELL, THERE IS A ZETA-BEAM AND.. ER--
MUST KILL TIME TILL ALANNA CAN CARRY OUT HER ASSIGNMENT!
UNSEEN BY ZAKKAD, ALANNA SECRETLY STEALS TO THE METEOR CONTROL PANEL...
I WATCHED THE WAY ZAKKAD MOVED THE CON-TROLS--AND I'M REVERSING THEM TO MAKE THE METEOR RETURN TO THIS WORLD!
MOMENTS LATER, ALANNA SHOUTS IN TRIUMPH...
I DID IT, ADAM! THE METEOR IS RETURNING--AND STARTING TO PULL EKELON OUT OF ITS ORBIT!
WHAT ?!
I AM DOOMED... TRAPPED ON THIS RUNAWAY WORLD...
ZAKKAD IS PLANET-BOUND, ALANNA -- BUT WE'RE NOT! COME ON -- LET'S GET OUT OF HERE!
11

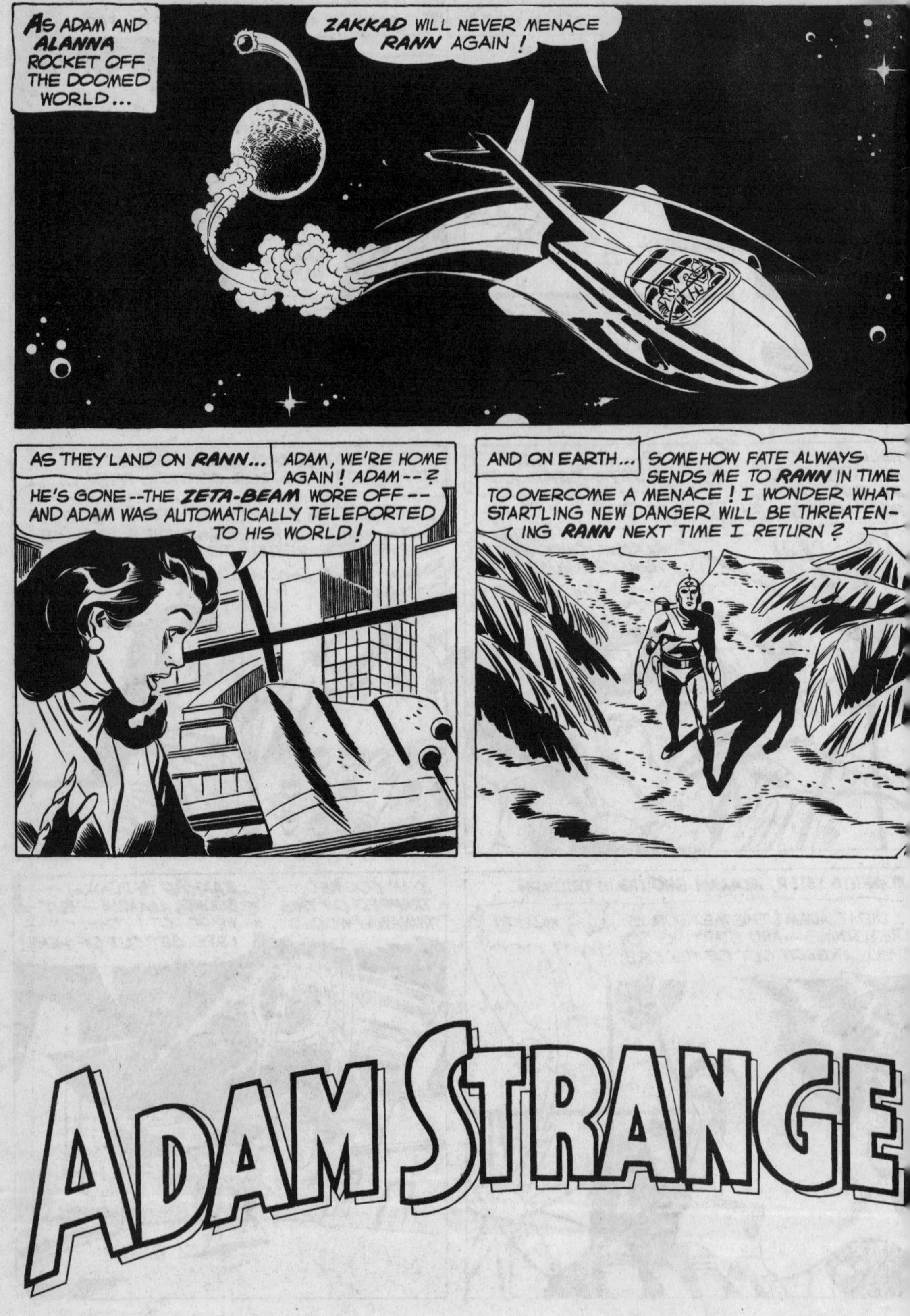
AS ADAM AND ALANNA ROCKET OFF THE DOOMED WORLD...
ZAKKAD WILL NEVER MENACE RANN AGAIN!
AS THEY LAND ON RANN...
ADAM, WE'RE HOME AGAIN! ADAM--?
HE'S GONE--THE ZETA-BEAM WORE OFF--AND ADAM WAS AUTOMATICALLY TELEPORTED TO HIS WORLD!
AND ON EARTH...
SOMEHOW FATE ALWAYS SENDS ME TO RANN IN TIME TO OVERCOME A MENACE! I WONDER WHAT STARTLING NEW DANGER WILL BE THREATENING RANN NEXT TIME I RETURN?

ADAM STRANGE

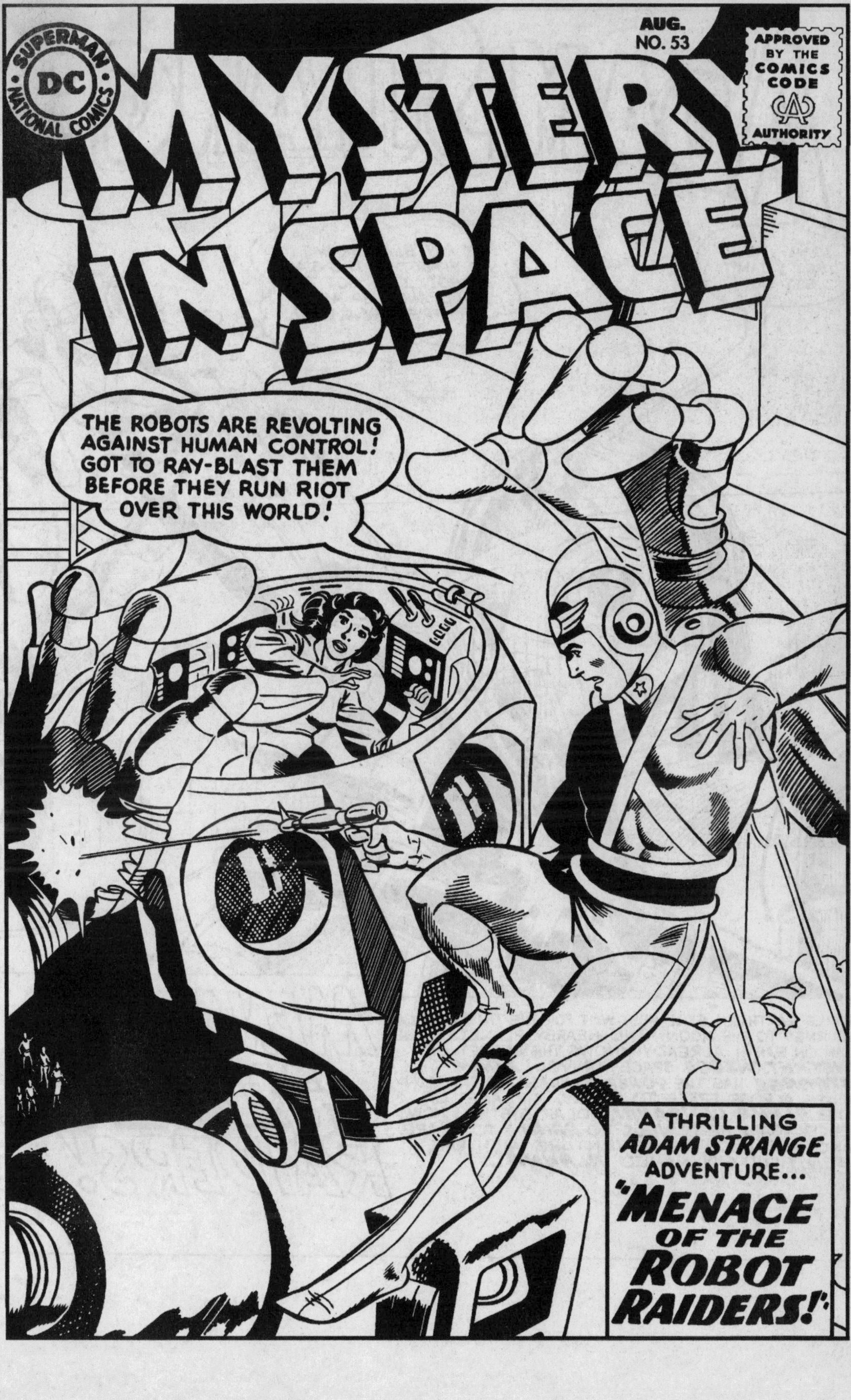
SUPERMAN DC NATIONAL COMICS
AUG. NO. 53
APPROVED BY THE COMICS CODE AUTHORITY
MYSTERY IN SPACE
THE ROBOTS ARE REVOLTING AGAINST HUMAN CONTROL! GOT TO RAY-BLAST THEM BEFORE THEY RUN RIOT OVER THIS WORLD!
A THRILLING ADAM STRANGE ADVENTURE...
"MENACE OF THE ROBOT RAIDERS!"

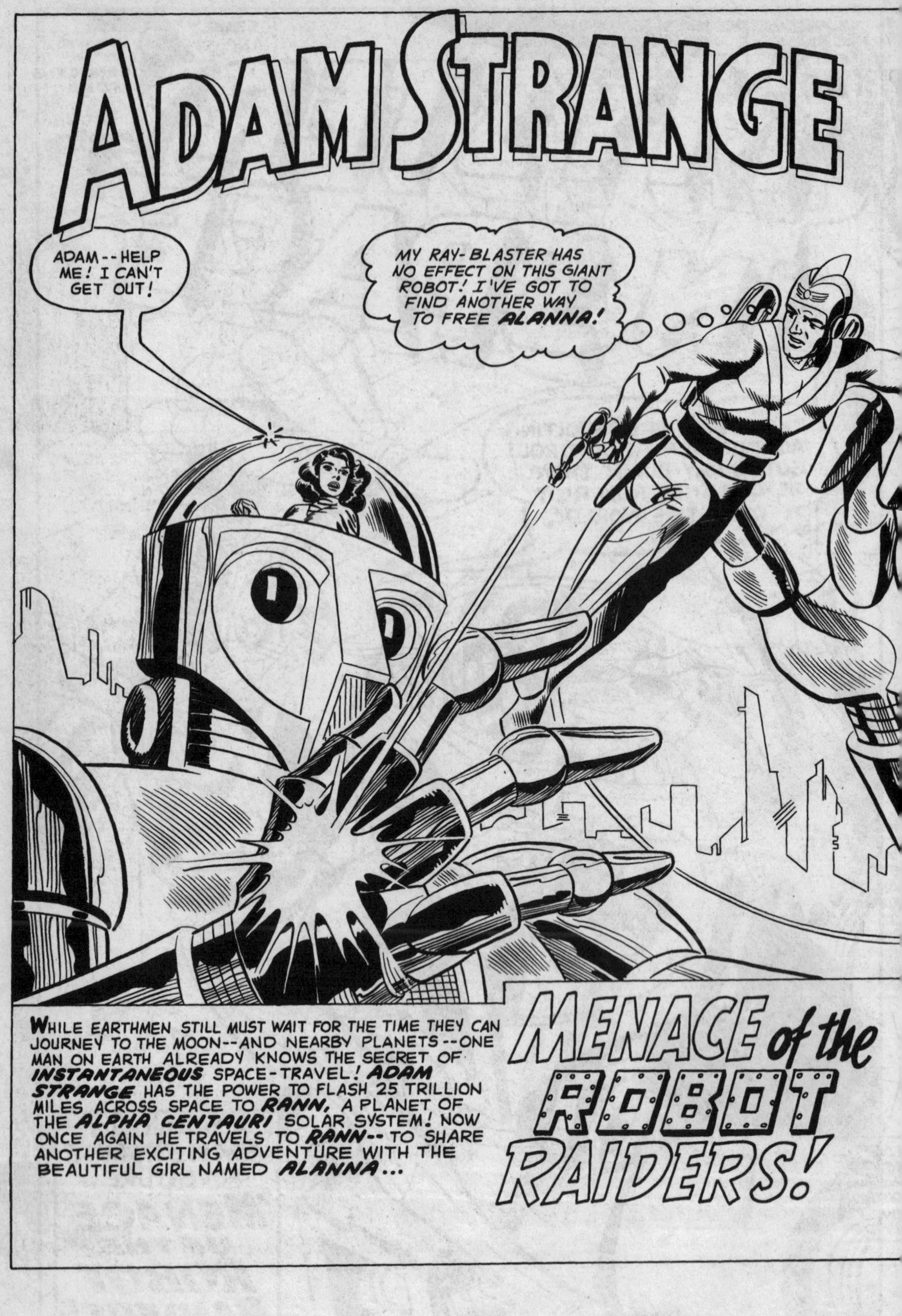
ADAM STRANGE
ADAM--HELP ME! I CAN'T GET OUT!
MY RAY-BLASTER HAS NO EFFECT ON THIS GIANT ROBOT! I'VE GOT TO FIND ANOTHER WAY TO FREE ALANNA!
WHILE EARTHMEN STILL MUST WAIT FOR THE TIME THEY CAN JOURNEY TO THE MOON--AND NEARBY PLANETS--ONE MAN ON EARTH ALREADY KNOWS THE SECRET OF INSTANTANEOUS SPACE-TRAVEL! ADAM STRANGE HAS THE POWER TO FLASH 25 TRILLION MILES ACROSS SPACE TO RANN, A PLANET OF THE ALPHA CENTAURI SOLAR SYSTEM! NOW ONCE AGAIN HE TRAVELS TO RANN-- TO SHARE ANOTHER EXCITING ADVENTURE WITH THE BEAUTIFUL GIRL NAMED ALANNA...
MENACE of the ROBOT RAIDERS!

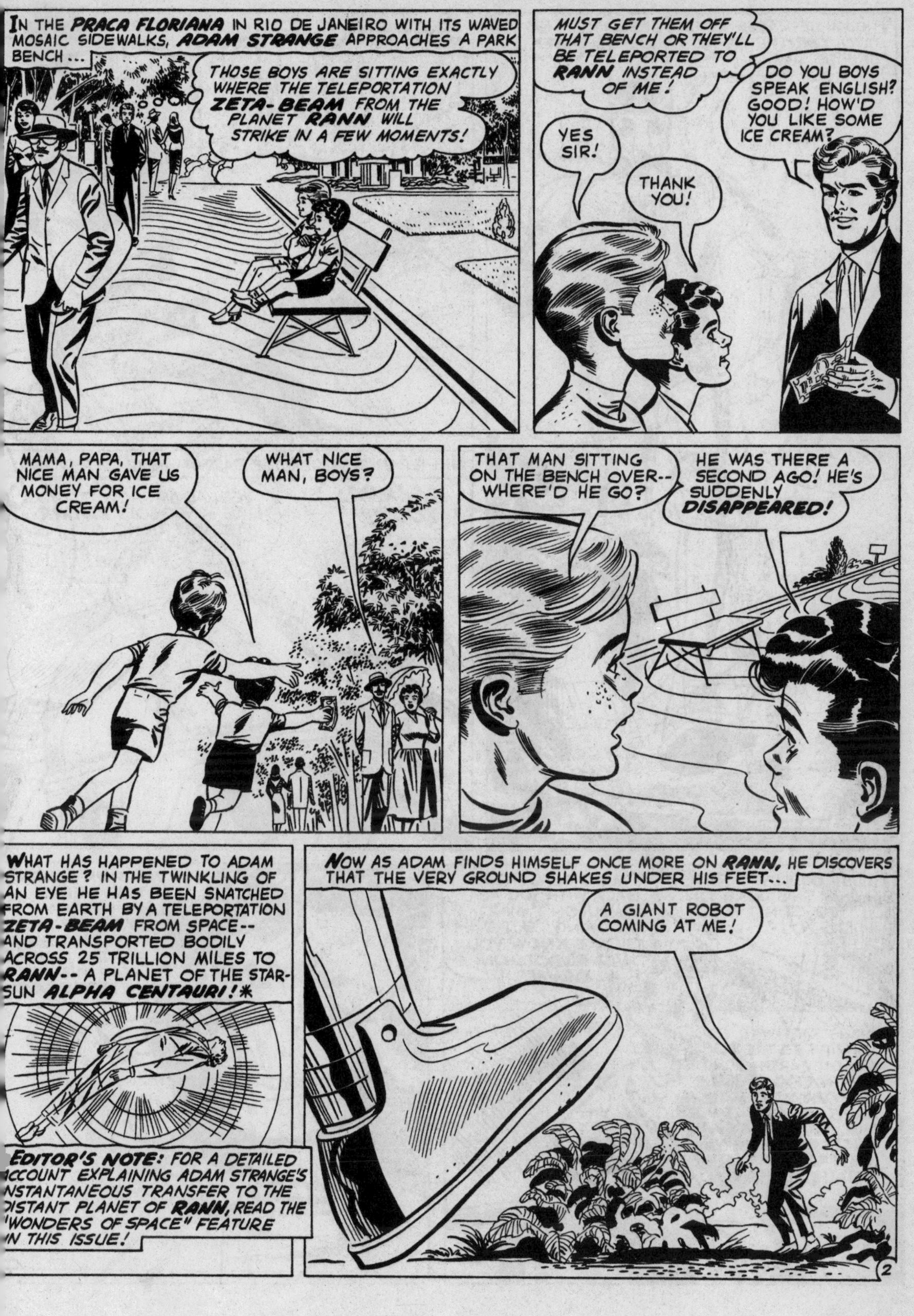
IN THE PRACA FLORIANA IN RIO DE JANEIRO WITH ITS WAVED MOSAIC SIDEWALKS, ADAM STRANGE APPROACHES A PARK BENCH...
THOSE BOYS ARE SITTING EXACTLY WHERE THE TELEPORTATION ZETA-BEAM FROM THE PLANET RANN WILL STRIKE IN A FEW MOMENTS!
MUST GET THEM OFF THAT BENCH OR THEY'LL BE TELEPORTED TO RANN INSTEAD OF ME!
DO YOU BOYS SPEAK ENGLISH? GOOD! HOW'D YOU LIKE SOME ICE CREAM?
YES SIR!
THANK YOU!
MAMA, PAPA, THAT NICE MAN GAVE US MONEY FOR ICE CREAM!
WHAT NICE MAN, BOYS?
THAT MAN SITTING ON THE BENCH OVER-- WHERE'D HE GO?
HE WAS THERE A SECOND AGO! HE'S SUDDENLY DISAPPEARED!
WHAT HAS HAPPENED TO ADAM STRANGE? IN THE TWINKLING OF AN EYE HE HAS BEEN SNATCHED FROM EARTH BY A TELEPORTATION ZETA-BEAM FROM SPACE-- AND TRANSPORTED BODILY ACROSS 25 TRILLION MILES TO RANN-- A PLANET OF THE STAR-SUN ALPHA CENTAURI!*
EDITOR'S NOTE: FOR A DETAILED ACCOUNT EXPLAINING ADAM STRANGE'S INSTANTANEOUS TRANSFER TO THE DISTANT PLANET OF RANN, READ THE "WONDERS OF SPACE" FEATURE IN THIS ISSUE!
NOW AS ADAM FINDS HIMSELF ONCE MORE ON RANN, HE DISCOVERS THAT THE VERY GROUND SHAKES UNDER HIS FEET...
A GIANT ROBOT COMING AT ME!
2

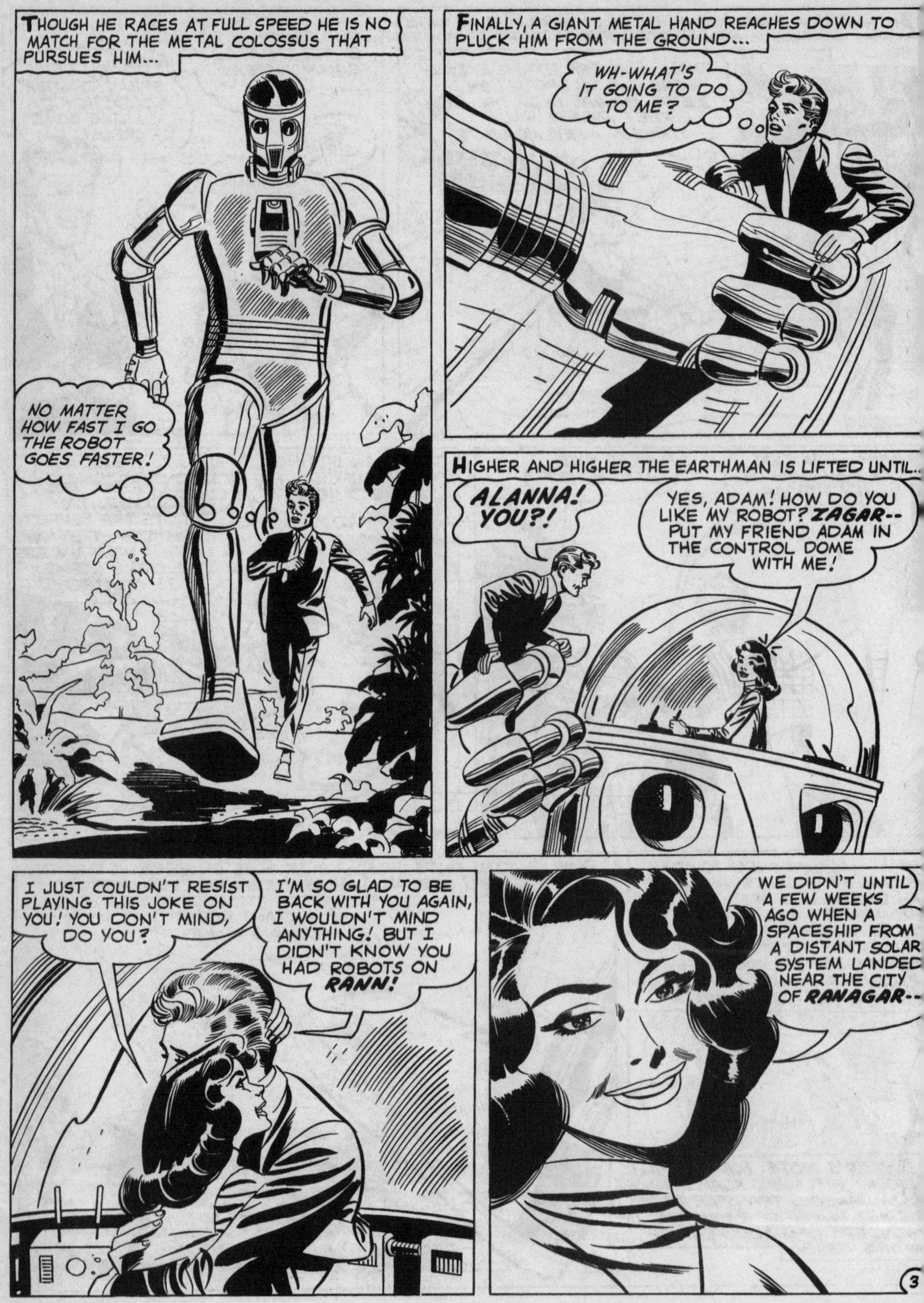
THOUGH HE RACES AT FULL SPEED HE IS NO MATCH FOR THE METAL COLOSSUS THAT PURSUES HIM...
NO MATTER HOW FAST I GO THE ROBOT GOES FASTER!
FINALLY, A GIANT METAL HAND REACHES DOWN TO PLUCK HIM FROM THE GROUND...
WH-WHAT'S IT GOING TO DO TO ME?
HIGHER AND HIGHER THE EARTHMAN IS LIFTED UNTIL...
ALANNA! YOU?!
YES, ADAM! HOW DO YOU LIKE MY ROBOT? ZAGAR-- PUT MY FRIEND ADAM IN THE CONTROL DOME WITH ME!
I JUST COULDN'T RESIST PLAYING THIS JOKE ON YOU! YOU DON'T MIND, DO YOU?
I'M SO GLAD TO BE BACK WITH YOU AGAIN, I WOULDN'T MIND ANYTHING! BUT I DIDN'T KNOW YOU HAD ROBOTS ON RANN!
WE DIDN'T UNTIL A FEW WEEKS AGO WHEN A SPACESHIP FROM A DISTANT SOLAR SYSTEM LANDED NEAR THE CITY OF RANAGAR--
3

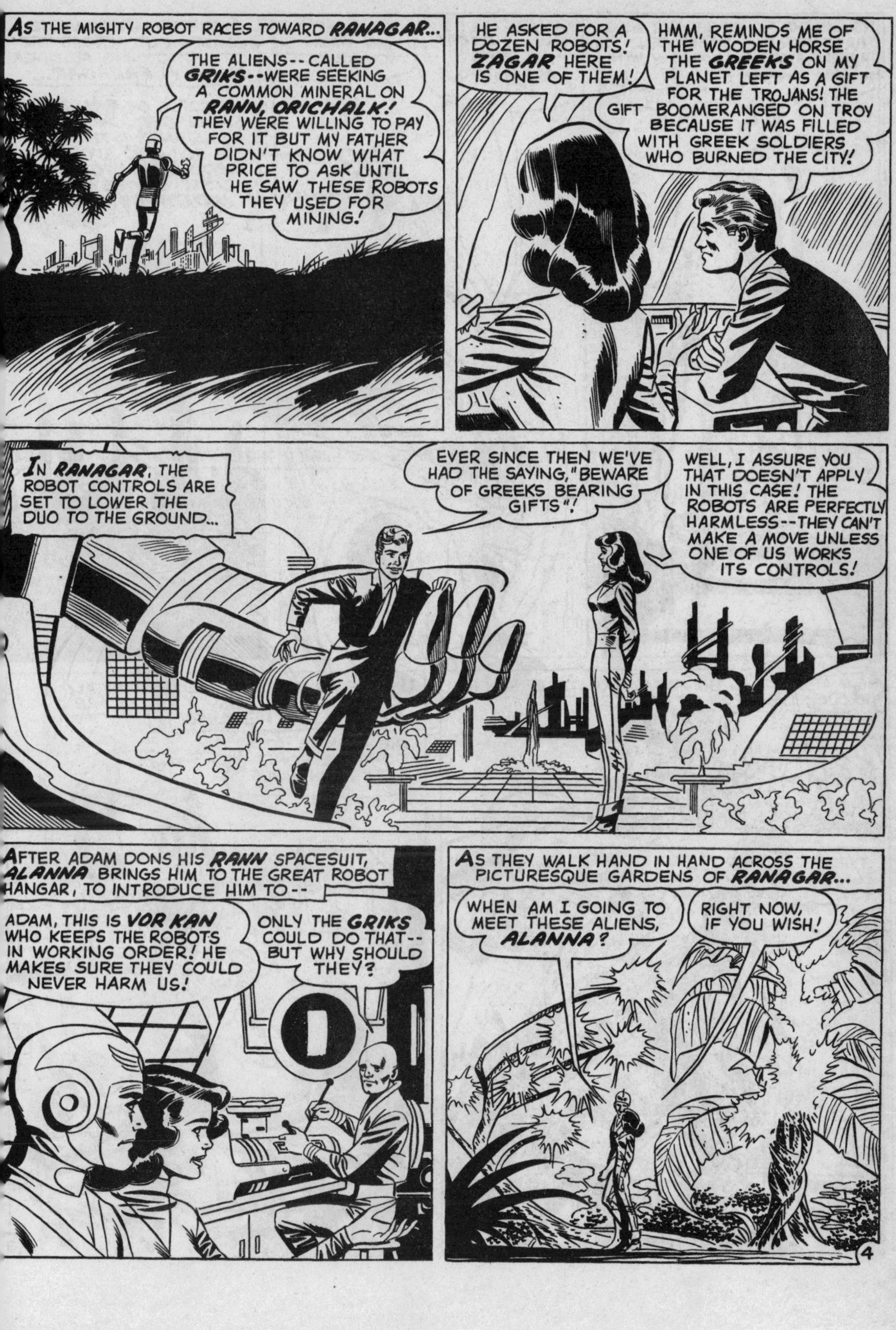
AS THE MIGHTY ROBOT RACES TOWARD RANAGAR...
THE ALIENS--CALLED GRIKS--WERE SEEKING A COMMON MINERAL ON RANN, ORICHALK! THEY WERE WILLING TO PAY FOR IT BUT MY FATHER DIDN'T KNOW WHAT PRICE TO ASK UNTIL HE SAW THESE ROBOTS THEY USED FOR MINING!
HE ASKED FOR A DOZEN ROBOTS! ZAGAR HERE IS ONE OF THEM!
HMM, REMINDS ME OF THE WOODEN HORSE THE GREEKS ON MY PLANET LEFT AS A GIFT FOR THE TROJANS! THE GIFT BOOMERANGED ON TROY BECAUSE IT WAS FILLED WITH GREEK SOLDIERS WHO BURNED THE CITY!
IN RANAGAR, THE ROBOT CONTROLS ARE SET TO LOWER THE DUO TO THE GROUND...
EVER SINCE THEN WE'VE HAD THE SAYING, "BEWARE OF GREEKS BEARING GIFTS"!
WELL, I ASSURE YOU THAT DOESN'T APPLY IN THIS CASE! THE ROBOTS ARE PERFECTLY HARMLESS--THEY CAN'T MAKE A MOVE UNLESS ONE OF US WORKS ITS CONTROLS!
AFTER ADAM DONS HIS RANN SPACESUIT, ALANNA BRINGS HIM TO THE GREAT ROBOT HANGAR, TO INTRODUCE HIM TO--
ADAM, THIS IS VOR KAN WHO KEEPS THE ROBOTS IN WORKING ORDER! HE MAKES SURE THEY COULD NEVER HARM US!
ONLY THE GRIKS COULD DO THAT--BUT WHY SHOULD THEY?
AS THEY WALK HAND IN HAND ACROSS THE PICTURESQUE GARDENS OF RANAGAR...
WHEN AM I GOING TO MEET THESE ALIENS, ALANNA?
RIGHT NOW, IF YOU WISH!
4

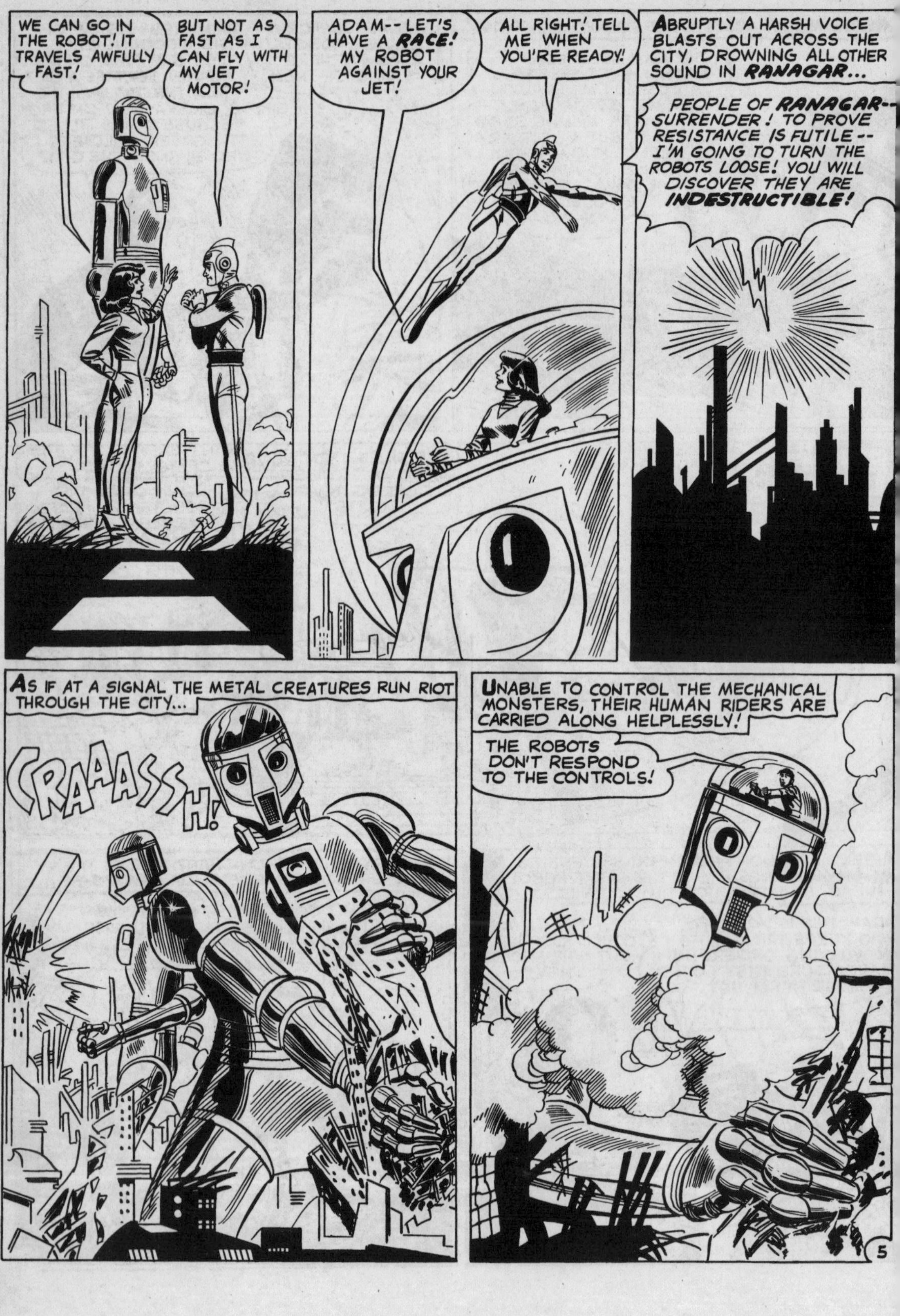
WE CAN GO IN THE ROBOT! IT TRAVELS AWFULLY FAST!
BUT NOT AS FAST AS I CAN FLY WITH MY JET MOTOR!
ADAM--LET'S HAVE A RACE! MY ROBOT AGAINST YOUR JET!
ALL RIGHT! TELL ME WHEN YOU'RE READY!
ABRUPTLY A HARSH VOICE BLASTS OUT ACROSS THE CITY, DROWNING ALL OTHER SOUND IN RANAGAR...
PEOPLE OF RANAGAR--SURRENDER! TO PROVE RESISTANCE IS FUTILE--I'M GOING TO TURN THE ROBOTS LOOSE! YOU WILL DISCOVER THEY ARE INDESTRUCTIBLE!
AS IF AT A SIGNAL THE METAL CREATURES RUN RIOT THROUGH THE CITY...
CRAAASSH!
UNABLE TO CONTROL THE MECHANICAL MONSTERS, THEIR HUMAN RIDERS ARE CARRIED ALONG HELPLESSLY!
THE ROBOTS DON'T RESPOND TO THE CONTROLS!
5

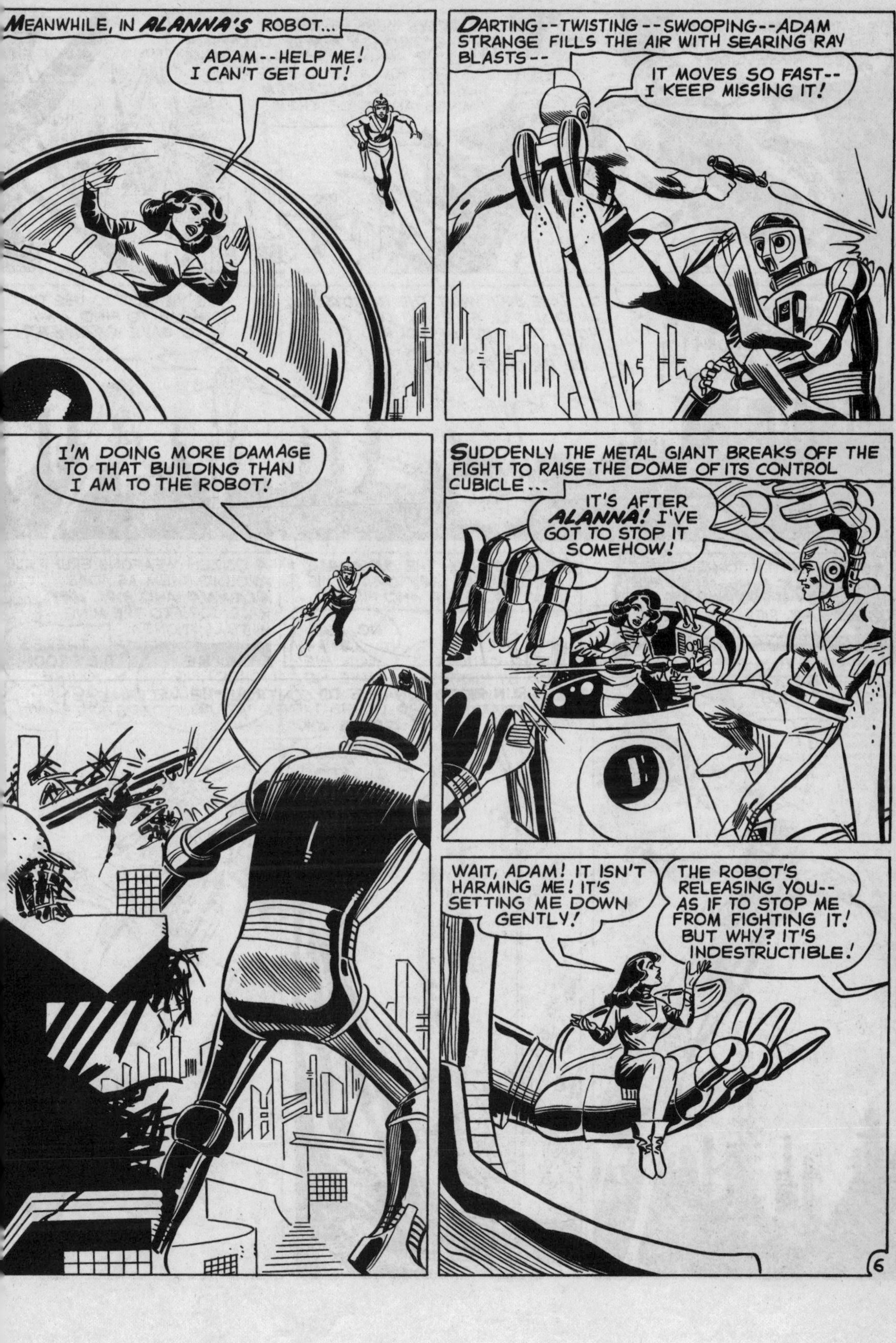
MEANWHILE, IN ALANNA'S ROBOT...
ADAM--HELP ME! I CAN'T GET OUT!
DARTING--TWISTING--SWOOPING--ADAM STRANGE FILLS THE AIR WITH SEARING RAY BLASTS--
IT MOVES SO FAST-- I KEEP MISSING IT!
I'M DOING MORE DAMAGE TO THAT BUILDING THAN I AM TO THE ROBOT!
SUDDENLY THE METAL GIANT BREAKS OFF THE FIGHT TO RAISE THE DOME OF ITS CONTROL CUBICLE...
IT'S AFTER ALANNA! I'VE GOT TO STOP IT SOMEHOW!
WAIT, ADAM! IT ISN'T HARMING ME! IT'S SETTING ME DOWN GENTLY!
THE ROBOT'S RELEASING YOU-- AS IF TO STOP ME FROM FIGHTING IT! BUT WHY? IT'S INDESTRUCTIBLE!
6

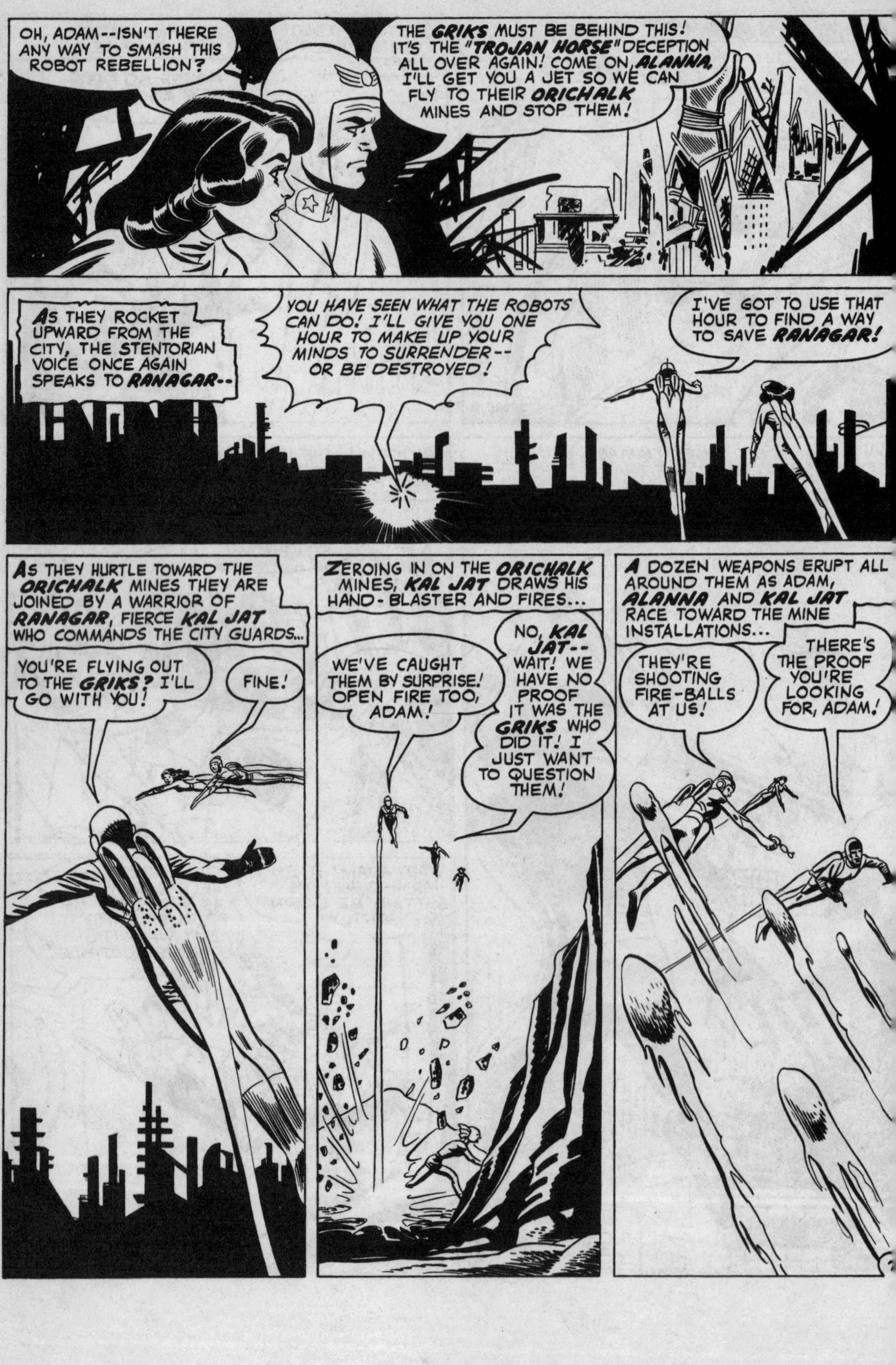
OH, ADAM--ISN'T THERE ANY WAY TO SMASH THIS ROBOT REBELLION?
THE GRIKS MUST BE BEHIND THIS! IT'S THE "TROJAN HORSE" DECEPTION ALL OVER AGAIN! COME ON, ALANNA, I'LL GET YOU A JET SO WE CAN FLY TO THEIR ORICHALK MINES AND STOP THEM!
AS THEY ROCKET UPWARD FROM THE CITY, THE STENTORIAN VOICE ONCE AGAIN SPEAKS TO RANAGAR--
YOU HAVE SEEN WHAT THE ROBOTS CAN DO! I'LL GIVE YOU ONE HOUR TO MAKE UP YOUR MINDS TO SURRENDER-- OR BE DESTROYED!
I'VE GOT TO USE THAT HOUR TO FIND A WAY TO SAVE RANAGAR!
AS THEY HURTLE TOWARD THE ORICHALK MINES THEY ARE JOINED BY A WARRIOR OF RANAGAR, FIERCE KAL JAT WHO COMMANDS THE CITY GUARDS...
YOU'RE FLYING OUT TO THE GRIKS? I'LL GO WITH YOU!
FINE!
ZEROING IN ON THE ORICHALK MINES, KAL JAT DRAWS HIS HAND-BLASTER AND FIRES...
WE'VE CAUGHT THEM BY SURPRISE! OPEN FIRE TOO, ADAM!
NO, KAL JAT-- WAIT! WE HAVE NO PROOF IT WAS THE GRIKS WHO DID IT! I JUST WANT TO QUESTION THEM!
A DOZEN WEAPONS ERUPT ALL AROUND THEM AS ADAM, ALANNA AND KAL JAT RACE TOWARD THE MINE INSTALLATIONS...
THEY'RE SHOOTING FIRE-BALLS AT US!
THERE'S THE PROOF YOU'RE LOOKING FOR, ADAM!

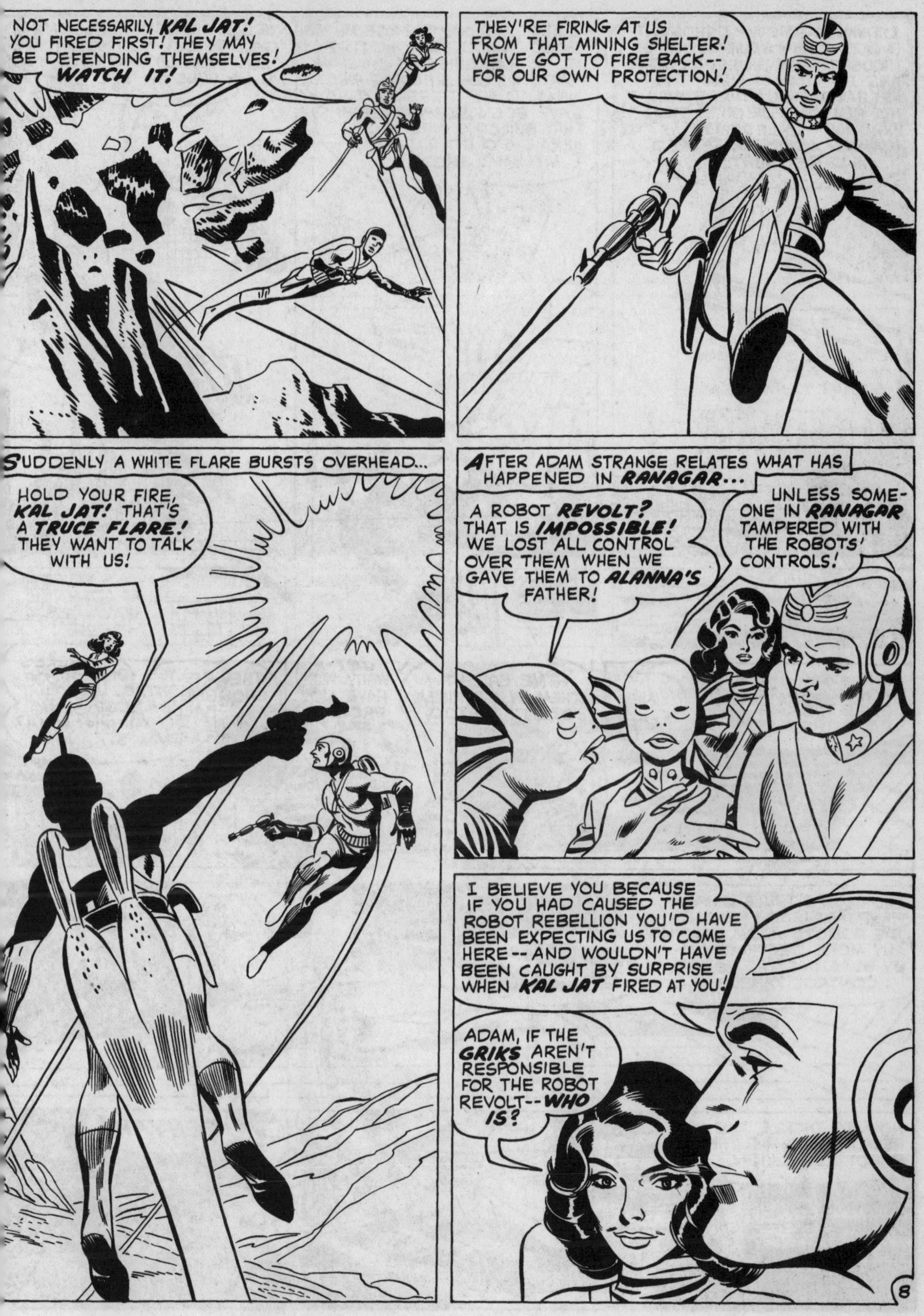
NOT NECESSARILY, KAL JAT! YOU FIRED FIRST! THEY MAY BE DEFENDING THEMSELVES! WATCH IT!
THEY'RE FIRING AT US FROM THAT MINING SHELTER! WE'VE GOT TO FIRE BACK-- FOR OUR OWN PROTECTION!
SUDDENLY A WHITE FLARE BURSTS OVERHEAD...
HOLD YOUR FIRE, KAL JAT! THAT'S A TRUCE FLARE! THEY WANT TO TALK WITH US!
AFTER ADAM STRANGE RELATES WHAT HAS HAPPENED IN RANAGAR...
A ROBOT REVOLT? THAT IS IMPOSSIBLE! WE LOST ALL CONTROL OVER THEM WHEN WE GAVE THEM TO ALANNA'S FATHER!
UNLESS SOME-ONE IN RANAGAR TAMPERED WITH THE ROBOTS' CONTROLS!
I BELIEVE YOU BECAUSE IF YOU HAD CAUSED THE ROBOT REBELLION YOU'D HAVE BEEN EXPECTING US TO COME HERE-- AND WOULDN'T HAVE BEEN CAUGHT BY SURPRISE WHEN KAL JAT FIRED AT YOU!
ADAM, IF THE GRIKS AREN'T RESPONSIBLE FOR THE ROBOT REVOLT--WHO IS?
8

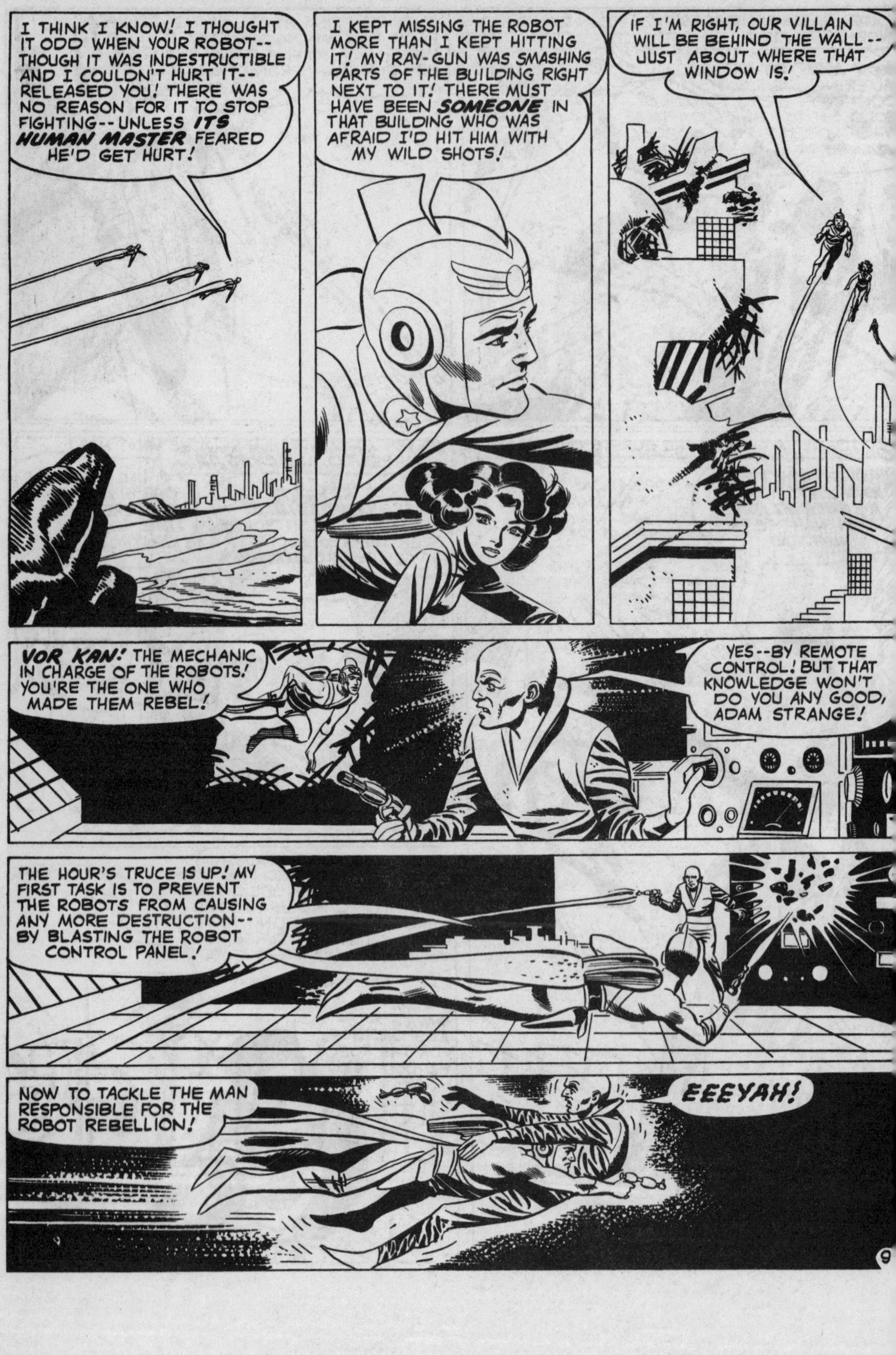
I THINK I KNOW! I THOUGHT IT ODD WHEN YOUR ROBOT-- THOUGH IT WAS INDESTRUCTIBLE AND I COULDN'T HURT IT-- RELEASED YOU! THERE WAS NO REASON FOR IT TO STOP FIGHTING--UNLESS ITS HUMAN MASTER FEARED HE'D GET HURT!
I KEPT MISSING THE ROBOT MORE THAN I KEPT HITTING IT! MY RAY-GUN WAS SMASHING PARTS OF THE BUILDING RIGHT NEXT TO IT! THERE MUST HAVE BEEN SOMEONE IN THAT BUILDING WHO WAS AFRAID I'D HIT HIM WITH MY WILD SHOTS!
IF I'M RIGHT, OUR VILLAIN WILL BE BEHIND THE WALL-- JUST ABOUT WHERE THAT WINDOW IS!
VOR KAN! THE MECHANIC IN CHARGE OF THE ROBOTS! YOU'RE THE ONE WHO MADE THEM REBEL!
YES--BY REMOTE CONTROL! BUT THAT KNOWLEDGE WON'T DO YOU ANY GOOD, ADAM STRANGE!
THE HOUR'S TRUCE IS UP! MY FIRST TASK IS TO PREVENT THE ROBOTS FROM CAUSING ANY MORE DESTRUCTION-- BY BLASTING THE ROBOT CONTROL PANEL!
NOW TO TACKLE THE MAN RESPONSIBLE FOR THE ROBOT REBELLION!
EEEYAH!
9

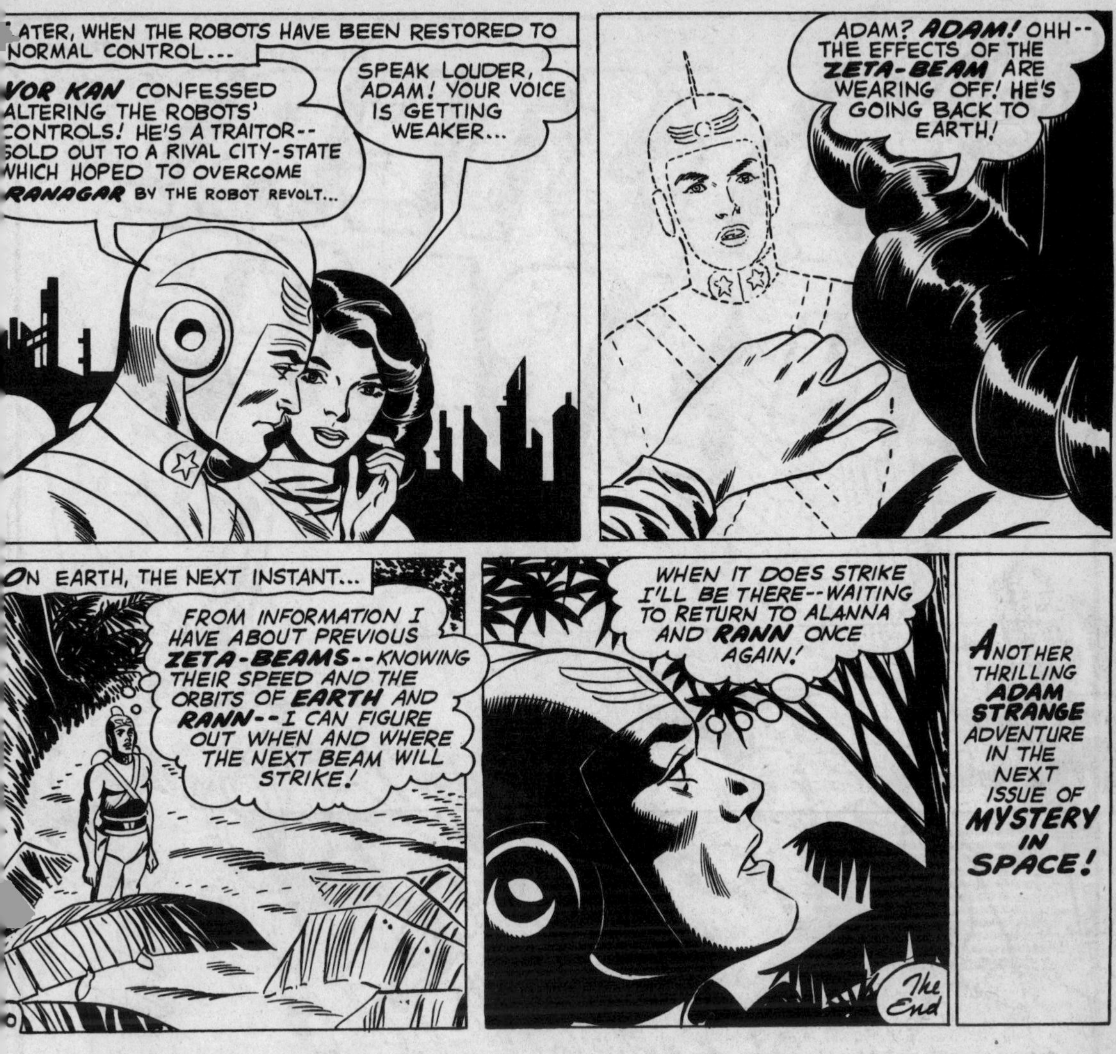
LATER, WHEN THE ROBOTS HAVE BEEN RESTORED TO NORMAL CONTROL...
VOR KAN CONFESSED ALTERING THE ROBOTS' CONTROLS! HE'S A TRAITOR--SOLD OUT TO A RIVAL CITY-STATE WHICH HOPED TO OVERCOME RANAGAR BY THE ROBOT REVOLT...
SPEAK LOUDER, ADAM! YOUR VOICE IS GETTING WEAKER...
ADAM? ADAM! OHH--THE EFFECTS OF THE ZETA-BEAM ARE WEARING OFF! HE'S GOING BACK TO EARTH!
ON EARTH, THE NEXT INSTANT...
FROM INFORMATION I HAVE ABOUT PREVIOUS ZETA-BEAMS--KNOWING THEIR SPEED AND THE ORBITS OF EARTH AND RANN--I CAN FIGURE OUT WHEN AND WHERE THE NEXT BEAM WILL STRIKE!
WHEN IT DOES STRIKE I'LL BE THERE--WAITING TO RETURN TO ALANNA AND RANN ONCE AGAIN!
The End
ANOTHER THRILLING ADAM STRANGE ADVENTURE IN THE NEXT ISSUE OF MYSTERY IN SPACE!

ADAM STRANGE

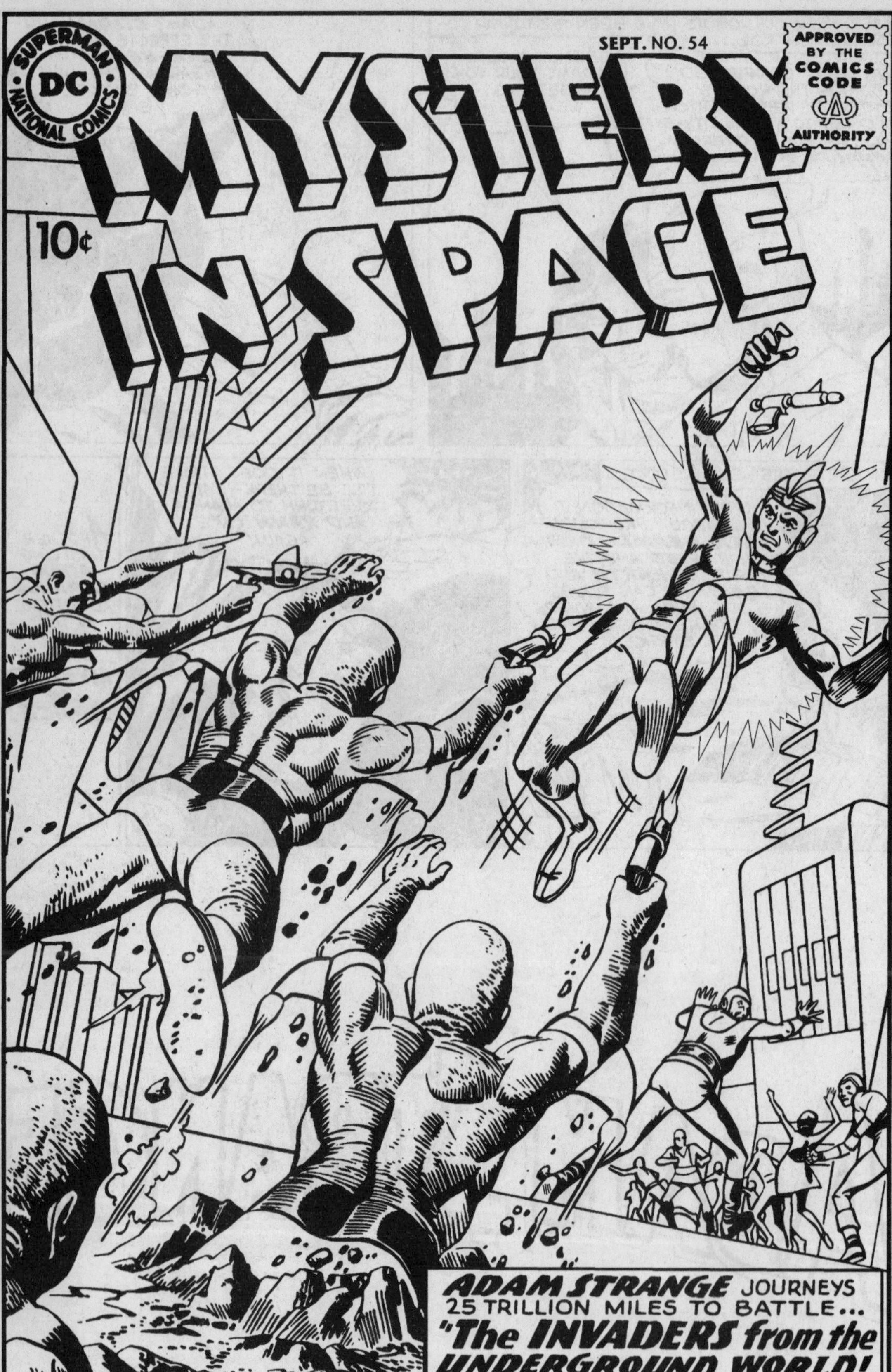
SUPERMAN DC NATIONAL COMICS
SEPT. NO. 54
APPROVED BY THE COMICS CODE AUTHORITY
MYSTERY IN SPACE
10¢
ADAM STRANGE JOURNEYS 25 TRILLION MILES TO BATTLE...
"The INVADERS from the UNDERGROUND WORLD!

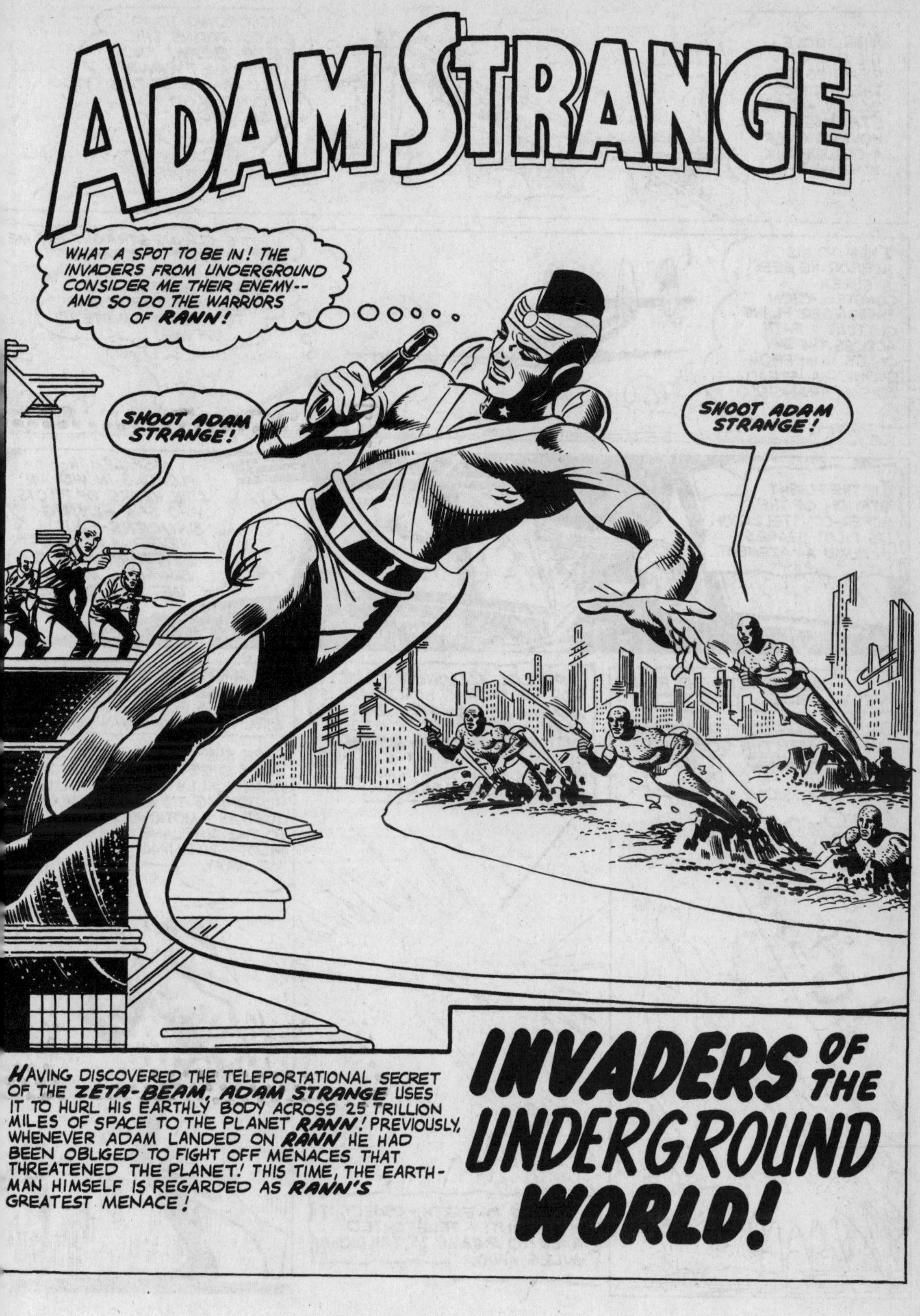
ADAM STRANGE
WHAT A SPOT TO BE IN! THE INVADERS FROM UNDERGROUND CONSIDER ME THEIR ENEMY-- AND SO DO THE WARRIORS OF RANN!
SHOOT ADAM STRANGE!
SHOOT ADAM STRANGE!
HAVING DISCOVERED THE TELEPORTATIONAL SECRET OF THE ZETA-BEAM, ADAM STRANGE USES IT TO HURL HIS EARTHLY BODY ACROSS 25 TRILLION MILES OF SPACE TO THE PLANET RANN! PREVIOUSLY, WHENEVER ADAM LANDED ON RANN HE HAD BEEN OBLIGED TO FIGHT OFF MENACES THAT THREATENED THE PLANET! THIS TIME, THE EARTH-MAN HIMSELF IS REGARDED AS RANN'S GREATEST MENACE!
INVADERS OF THE UNDERGROUND WORLD!

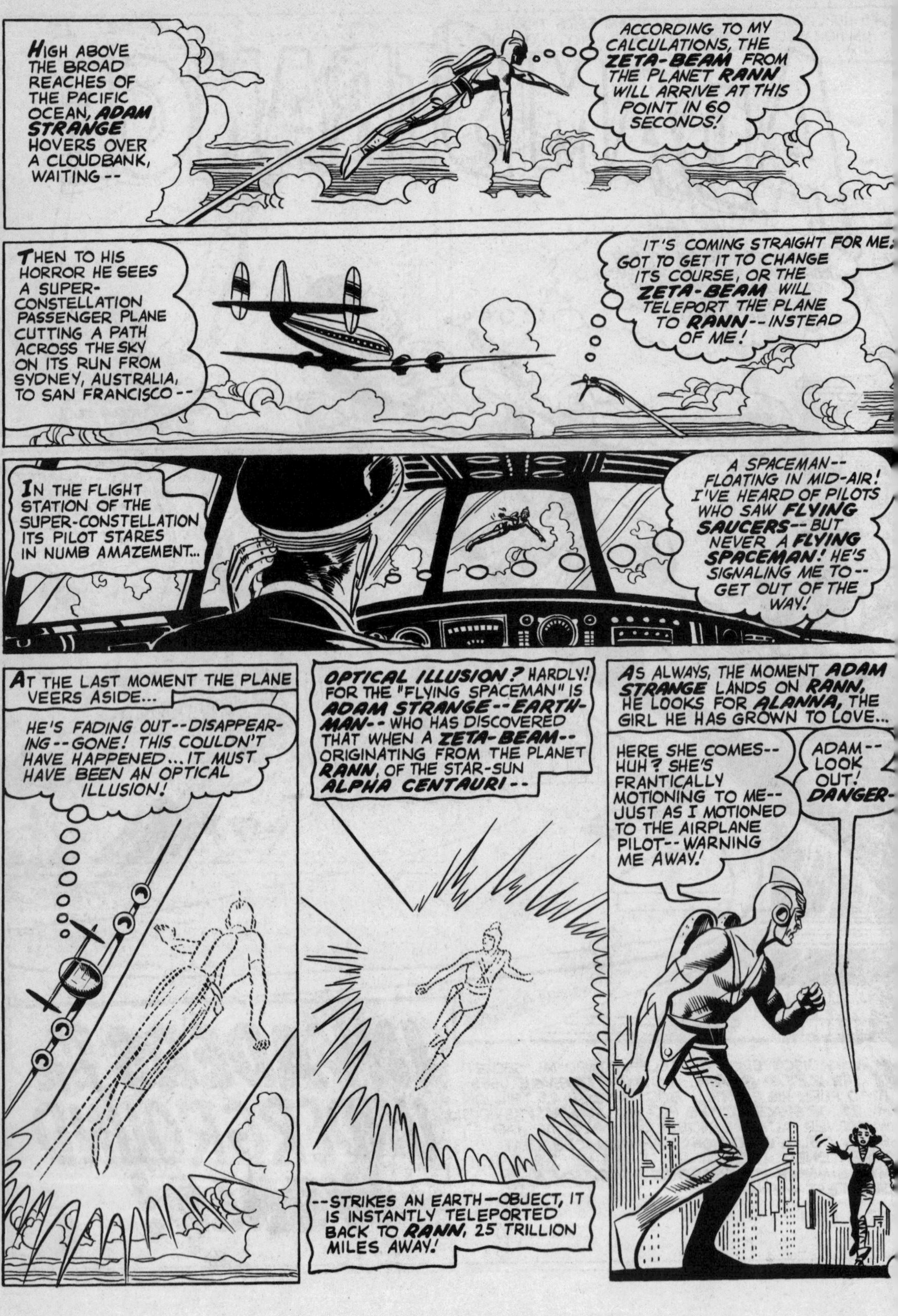
HIGH ABOVE THE BROAD REACHES OF THE PACIFIC OCEAN, ADAM STRANGE HOVERS OVER A CLOUDBANK, WAITING --
ACCORDING TO MY CALCULATIONS, THE ZETA-BEAM FROM THE PLANET RANN WILL ARRIVE AT THIS POINT IN 60 SECONDS!
THEN TO HIS HORROR HE SEES A SUPER-CONSTELLATION PASSENGER PLANE CUTTING A PATH ACROSS THE SKY ON ITS RUN FROM SYDNEY, AUSTRALIA, TO SAN FRANCISCO --
IT'S COMING STRAIGHT FOR ME! GOT TO GET IT TO CHANGE ITS COURSE, OR THE ZETA-BEAM WILL TELEPORT THE PLANE TO RANN -- INSTEAD OF ME!
IN THE FLIGHT STATION OF THE SUPER-CONSTELLATION ITS PILOT STARES IN NUMB AMAZEMENT...
A SPACEMAN -- FLOATING IN MID-AIR! I'VE HEARD OF PILOTS WHO SAW FLYING SAUCERS -- BUT NEVER A FLYING SPACEMAN! HE'S SIGNALING ME TO -- GET OUT OF THE WAY!
AT THE LAST MOMENT THE PLANE VEERS ASIDE...
HE'S FADING OUT -- DISAPPEARING -- GONE! THIS COULDN'T HAVE HAPPENED... IT MUST HAVE BEEN AN OPTICAL ILLUSION!
OPTICAL ILLUSION? HARDLY! FOR THE "FLYING SPACEMAN" IS ADAM STRANGE -- EARTH-MAN -- WHO HAS DISCOVERED THAT WHEN A ZETA-BEAM -- ORIGINATING FROM THE PLANET RANN, OF THE STAR-SUN ALPHA CENTAURI --
-- STRIKES AN EARTH-OBJECT, IT IS INSTANTLY TELEPORTED BACK TO RANN, 25 TRILLION MILES AWAY!
AS ALWAYS, THE MOMENT ADAM STRANGE LANDS ON RANN, HE LOOKS FOR ALANNA, THE GIRL HE HAS GROWN TO LOVE...
HERE SHE COMES -- HUH? SHE'S FRANTICALLY MOTIONING TO ME -- JUST AS I MOTIONED TO THE AIRPLANE PILOT -- WARNING ME AWAY!
ADAM -- LOOK OUT! DANGER-

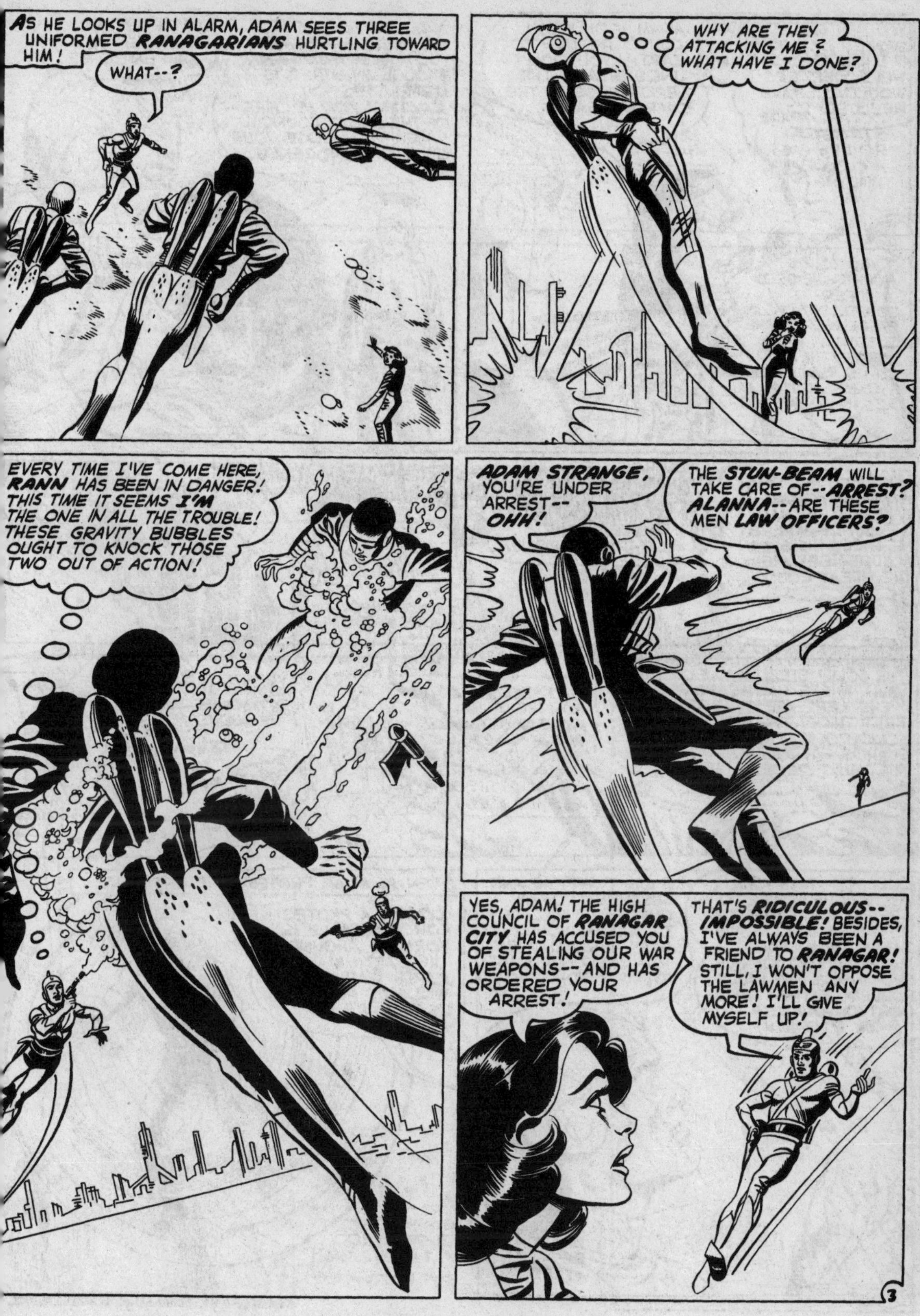
AS HE LOOKS UP IN ALARM, ADAM SEES THREE UNIFORMED RANAGARIANS HURTLING TOWARD HIM!
WHAT--?
WHY ARE THEY ATTACKING ME? WHAT HAVE I DONE?
EVERY TIME I'VE COME HERE, RANN HAS BEEN IN DANGER! THIS TIME IT SEEMS I'M THE ONE IN ALL THE TROUBLE! THESE GRAVITY BUBBLES OUGHT TO KNOCK THOSE TWO OUT OF ACTION!
ADAM STRANGE, YOU'RE UNDER ARREST-- OHH!
THE STUN-BEAM WILL TAKE CARE OF--ARREST? ALANNA--ARE THESE MEN LAW OFFICERS?
YES, ADAM! THE HIGH COUNCIL OF RANAGAR CITY HAS ACCUSED YOU OF STEALING OUR WAR WEAPONS--AND HAS ORDERED YOUR ARREST!
THAT'S RIDICULOUS--IMPOSSIBLE! BESIDES, I'VE ALWAYS BEEN A FRIEND TO RANAGAR! STILL, I WON'T OPPOSE THE LAWMEN ANY MORE! I'LL GIVE MYSELF UP!
3

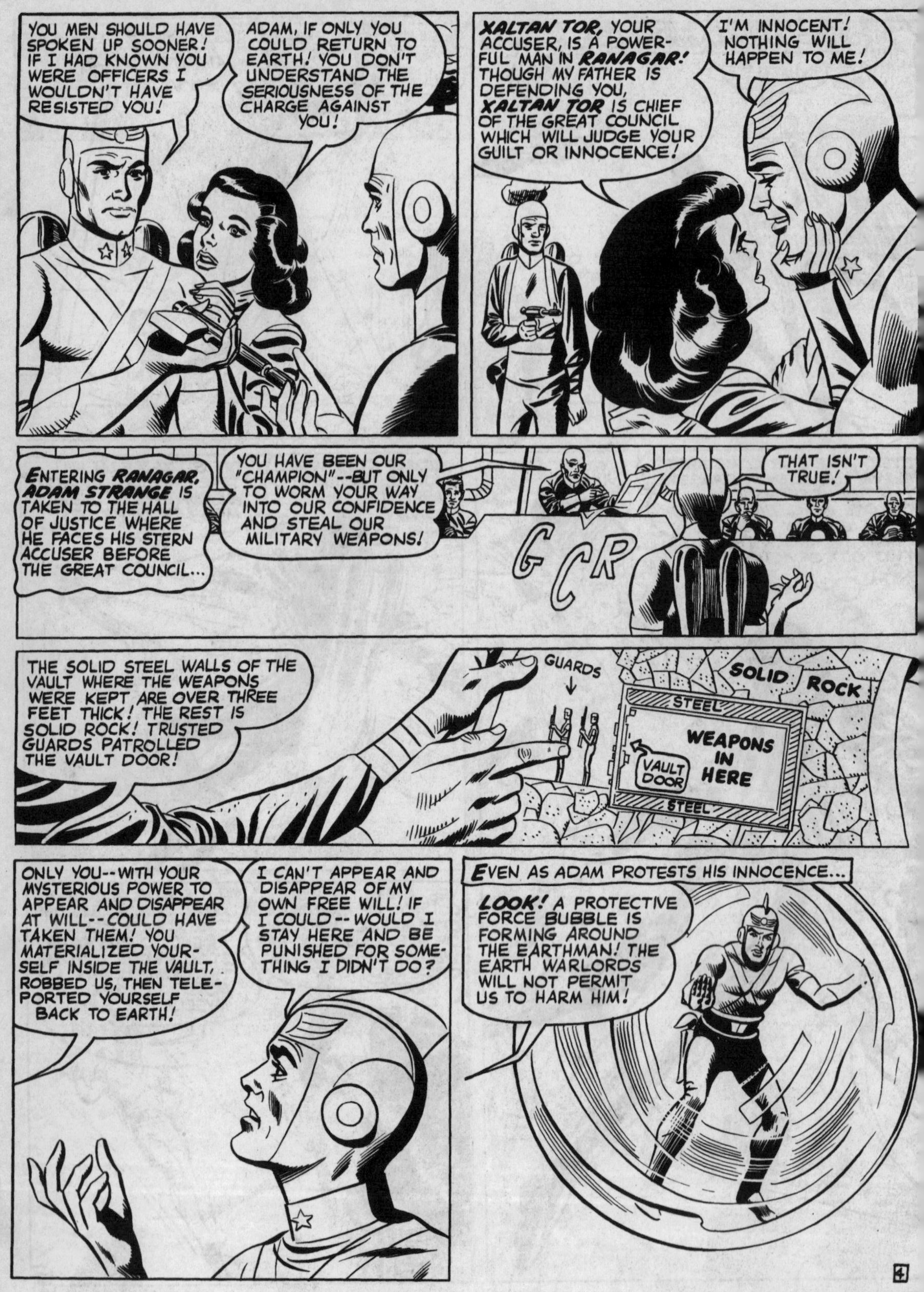
YOU MEN SHOULD HAVE SPOKEN UP SOONER! IF I HAD KNOWN YOU WERE OFFICERS I WOULDN'T HAVE RESISTED YOU!
ADAM, IF ONLY YOU COULD RETURN TO EARTH! YOU DON'T UNDERSTAND THE SERIOUSNESS OF THE CHARGE AGAINST YOU!
XALTAN TOR, YOUR ACCUSER, IS A POWERFUL MAN IN RANAGAR! THOUGH MY FATHER IS DEFENDING YOU, XALTAN TOR IS CHIEF OF THE GREAT COUNCIL WHICH WILL JUDGE YOUR GUILT OR INNOCENCE!
I'M INNOCENT! NOTHING WILL HAPPEN TO ME!
ENTERING RANAGAR, ADAM STRANGE IS TAKEN TO THE HALL OF JUSTICE WHERE HE FACES HIS STERN ACCUSER BEFORE THE GREAT COUNCIL...
YOU HAVE BEEN OUR "CHAMPION"--BUT ONLY TO WORM YOUR WAY INTO OUR CONFIDENCE AND STEAL OUR MILITARY WEAPONS!
THAT ISN'T TRUE!
GCR
THE SOLID STEEL WALLS OF THE VAULT WHERE THE WEAPONS WERE KEPT ARE OVER THREE FEET THICK! THE REST IS SOLID ROCK! TRUSTED GUARDS PATROLLED THE VAULT DOOR!
GUARDS
SOLID ROCK
STEEL
WEAPONS IN HERE
VAULT DOOR
STEEL
ONLY YOU--WITH YOUR MYSTERIOUS POWER TO APPEAR AND DISAPPEAR AT WILL--COULD HAVE TAKEN THEM! YOU MATERIALIZED YOURSELF INSIDE THE VAULT, ROBBED US, THEN TELEPORTED YOURSELF BACK TO EARTH!
I CAN'T APPEAR AND DISAPPEAR OF MY OWN FREE WILL! IF I COULD--WOULD I STAY HERE AND BE PUNISHED FOR SOMETHING I DIDN'T DO?
EVEN AS ADAM PROTESTS HIS INNOCENCE...
LOOK! A PROTECTIVE FORCE BUBBLE IS FORMING AROUND THE EARTHMAN! THE EARTH WARLORDS WILL NOT PERMIT US TO HARM HIM!
4

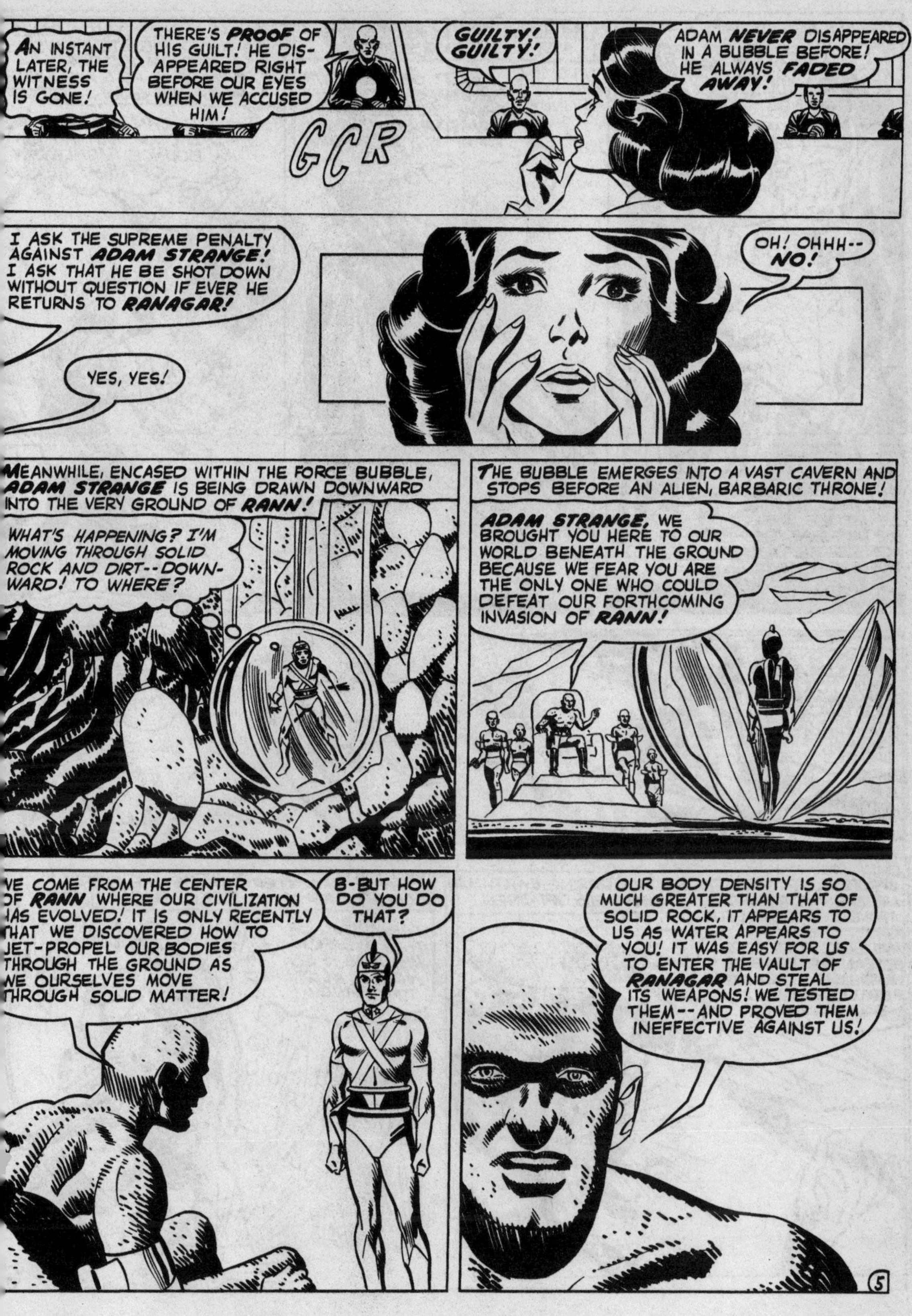
AN INSTANT LATER, THE WITNESS IS GONE!
THERE'S PROOF OF HIS GUILT! HE DIS-APPEARED RIGHT BEFORE OUR EYES WHEN WE ACCUSED HIM!
GUILTY! GUILTY!
ADAM NEVER DISAPPEARED IN A BUBBLE BEFORE! HE ALWAYS FADED AWAY!
GCR
I ASK THE SUPREME PENALTY AGAINST ADAM STRANGE! I ASK THAT HE BE SHOT DOWN WITHOUT QUESTION IF EVER HE RETURNS TO RANAGAR!
YES, YES!
OH! OHHH-- NO!
MEANWHILE, ENCASED WITHIN THE FORCE BUBBLE, ADAM STRANGE IS BEING DRAWN DOWNWARD INTO THE VERY GROUND OF RANN!
WHAT'S HAPPENING? I'M MOVING THROUGH SOLID ROCK AND DIRT--DOWN-WARD! TO WHERE?
THE BUBBLE EMERGES INTO A VAST CAVERN AND STOPS BEFORE AN ALIEN, BARBARIC THRONE!
ADAM STRANGE, WE BROUGHT YOU HERE TO OUR WORLD BENEATH THE GROUND BECAUSE WE FEAR YOU ARE THE ONLY ONE WHO COULD DEFEAT OUR FORTHCOMING INVASION OF RANN!
WE COME FROM THE CENTER OF RANN WHERE OUR CIVILIZATION HAS EVOLVED! IT IS ONLY RECENTLY THAT WE DISCOVERED HOW TO JET-PROPEL OUR BODIES THROUGH THE GROUND AS WE OURSELVES MOVE THROUGH SOLID MATTER!
B-BUT HOW DO YOU DO THAT?
OUR BODY DENSITY IS SO MUCH GREATER THAN THAT OF SOLID ROCK, IT APPEARS TO US AS WATER APPEARS TO YOU! IT WAS EASY FOR US TO ENTER THE VAULT OF RANAGAR AND STEAL ITS WEAPONS! WE TESTED THEM--AND PROVED THEM INEFFECTIVE AGAINST US!
5

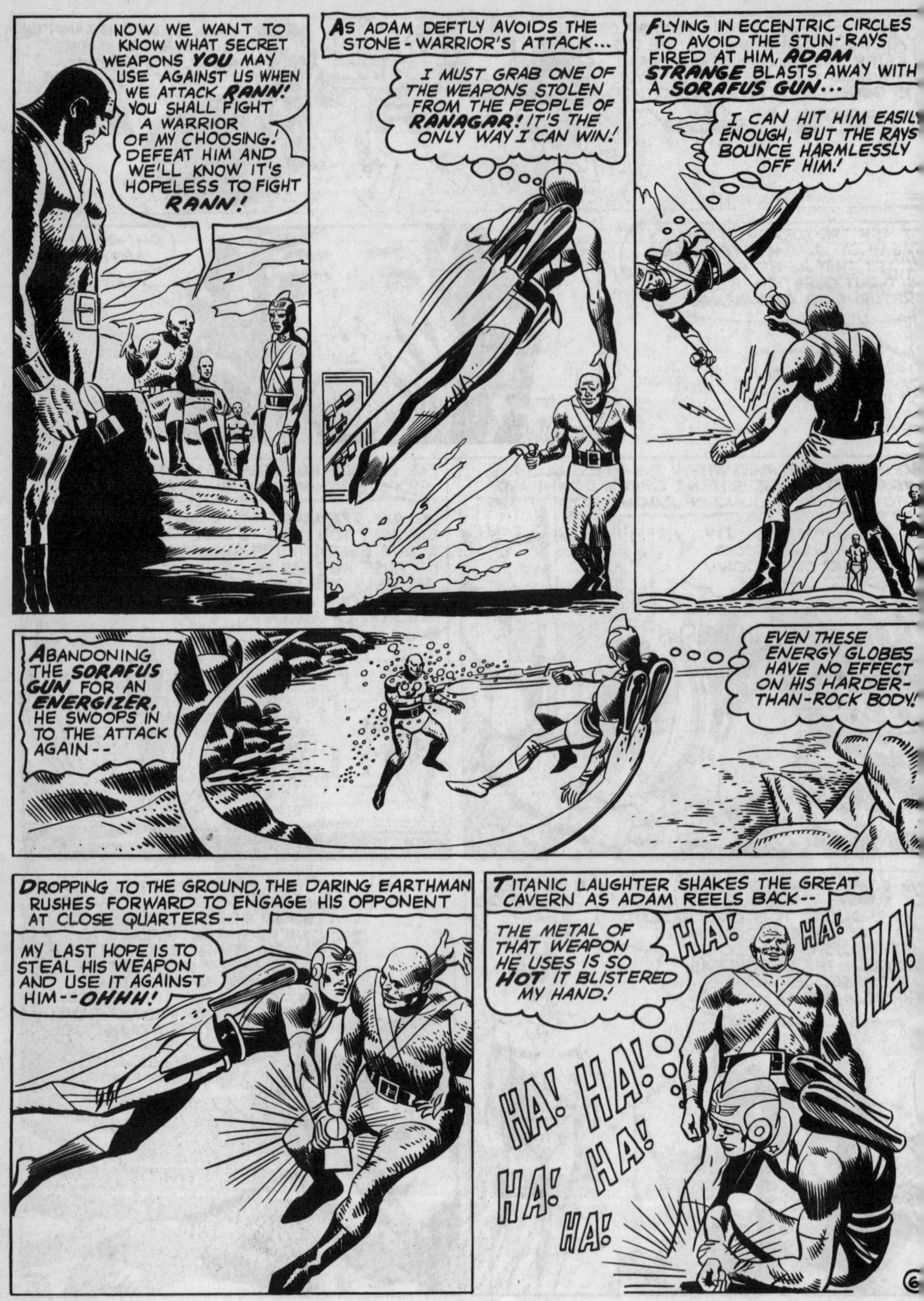

NOW WE WANT TO KNOW WHAT SECRET WEAPONS YOU MAY USE AGAINST US WHEN WE ATTACK RANN! YOU SHALL FIGHT A WARRIOR OF MY CHOOSING! DEFEAT HIM AND WE'LL KNOW IT'S HOPELESS TO FIGHT RANN!
AS ADAM DEFTLY AVOIDS THE STONE-WARRIOR'S ATTACK...
I MUST GRAB ONE OF THE WEAPONS STOLEN FROM THE PEOPLE OF RANAGAR! IT'S THE ONLY WAY I CAN WIN!
FLYING IN ECCENTRIC CIRCLES TO AVOID THE STUN-RAYS FIRED AT HIM, ADAM STRANGE BLASTS AWAY WITH A SORAFUS GUN...
I CAN HIT HIM EASILY ENOUGH, BUT THE RAYS BOUNCE HARMLESSLY OFF HIM!
ABANDONING THE SORAFUS GUN FOR AN ENERGIZER, HE SWOOPS IN TO THE ATTACK AGAIN--
EVEN THESE ENERGY GLOBES HAVE NO EFFECT ON HIS HARDER-THAN-ROCK BODY!
DROPPING TO THE GROUND, THE DARING EARTHMAN RUSHES FORWARD TO ENGAGE HIS OPPONENT AT CLOSE QUARTERS--
MY LAST HOPE IS TO STEAL HIS WEAPON AND USE IT AGAINST HIM--OHHH!
TITANIC LAUGHTER SHAKES THE GREAT CAVERN AS ADAM REELS BACK--
THE METAL OF THAT WEAPON HE USES IS SO HOT IT BLISTERED MY HAND!
HA! HA! HA!
HA! HA! HA! HA! HA!
6

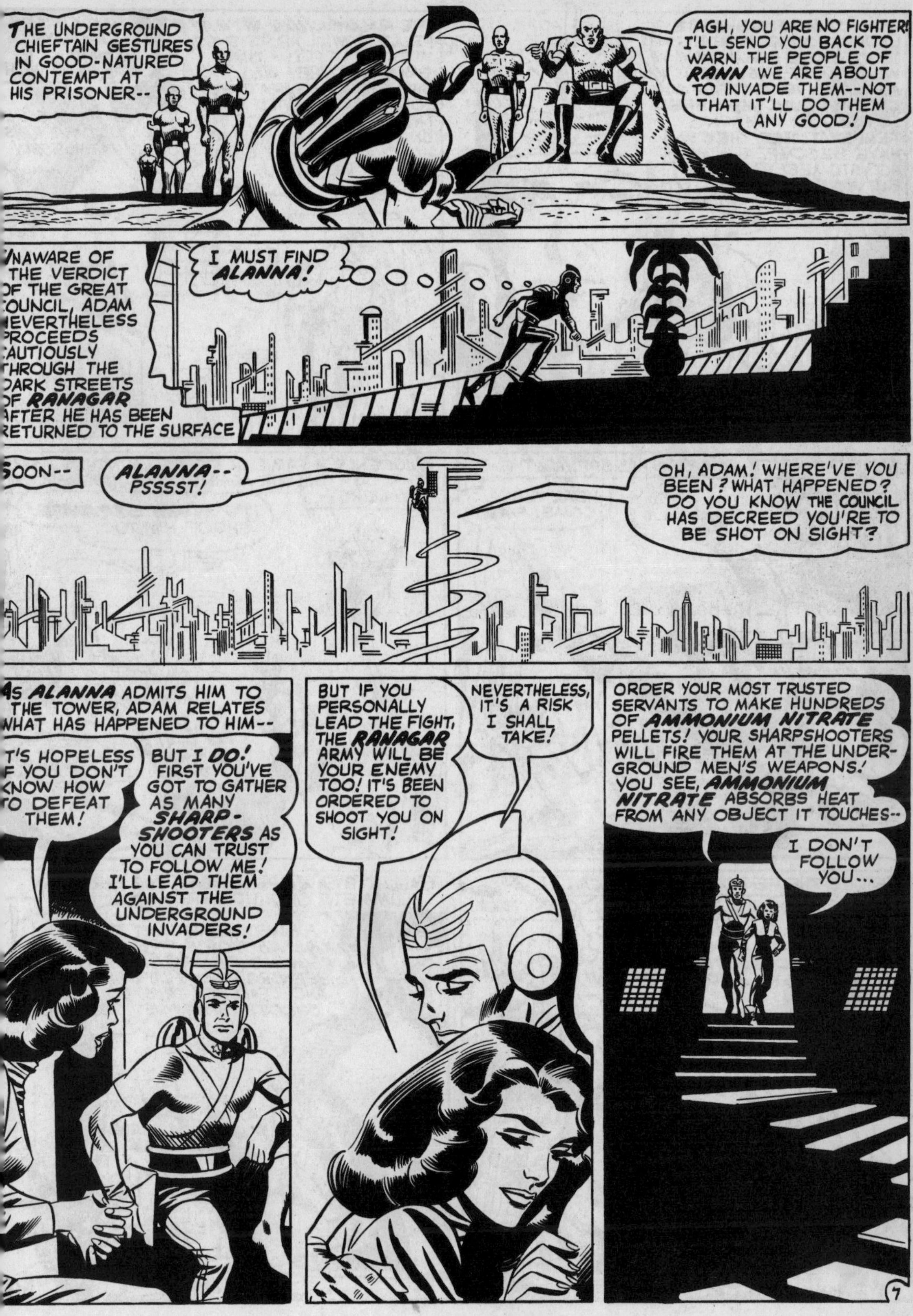
THE UNDERGROUND CHIEFTAIN GESTURES IN GOOD-NATURED CONTEMPT AT HIS PRISONER--
AGH, YOU ARE NO FIGHTER! I'LL SEND YOU BACK TO WARN THE PEOPLE OF RANN WE ARE ABOUT TO INVADE THEM--NOT THAT IT'LL DO THEM ANY GOOD!
UNAWARE OF THE VERDICT OF THE GREAT COUNCIL, ADAM NEVERTHELESS PROCEEDS CAUTIOUSLY THROUGH THE DARK STREETS OF RANAGAR AFTER HE HAS BEEN RETURNED TO THE SURFACE
I MUST FIND ALANNA!
SOON--
ALANNA-- PSSSST!
OH, ADAM! WHERE'VE YOU BEEN? WHAT HAPPENED? DO YOU KNOW THE COUNCIL HAS DECREED YOU'RE TO BE SHOT ON SIGHT?
AS ALANNA ADMITS HIM TO THE TOWER, ADAM RELATES WHAT HAS HAPPENED TO HIM--
IT'S HOPELESS IF YOU DON'T KNOW HOW TO DEFEAT THEM!
BUT I DO! FIRST YOU'VE GOT TO GATHER AS MANY SHARP-SHOOTERS AS YOU CAN TRUST TO FOLLOW ME! I'LL LEAD THEM AGAINST THE UNDERGROUND INVADERS!
BUT IF YOU PERSONALLY LEAD THE FIGHT, THE RANAGAR ARMY WILL BE YOUR ENEMY TOO! IT'S BEEN ORDERED TO SHOOT YOU ON SIGHT!
NEVERTHELESS, IT'S A RISK I SHALL TAKE!
ORDER YOUR MOST TRUSTED SERVANTS TO MAKE HUNDREDS OF AMMONIUM NITRATE PELLETS! YOUR SHARPSHOOTERS WILL FIRE THEM AT THE UNDERGROUND MEN'S WEAPONS! YOU SEE, AMMONIUM NITRATE ABSORBS HEAT FROM ANY OBJECT IT TOUCHES--
I DON'T FOLLOW YOU...
7

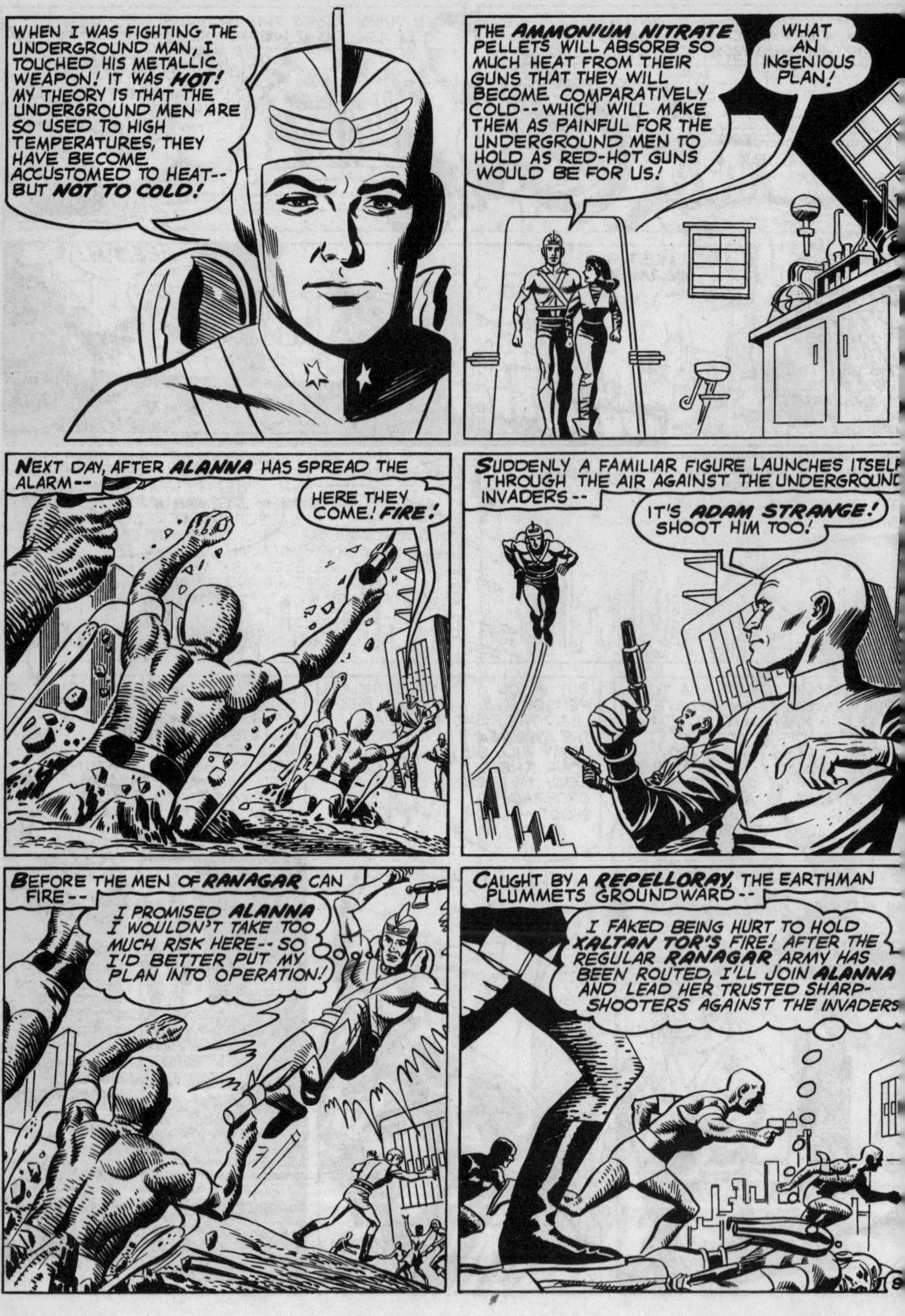
WHEN I WAS FIGHTING THE UNDERGROUND MAN, I TOUCHED HIS METALLIC WEAPON! IT WAS HOT! MY THEORY IS THAT THE UNDERGROUND MEN ARE SO USED TO HIGH TEMPERATURES, THEY HAVE BECOME ACCUSTOMED TO HEAT-- BUT NOT TO COLD!
THE AMMONIUM NITRATE PELLETS WILL ABSORB SO MUCH HEAT FROM THEIR GUNS THAT THEY WILL BECOME COMPARATIVELY COLD-- WHICH WILL MAKE THEM AS PAINFUL FOR THE UNDERGROUND MEN TO HOLD AS RED-HOT GUNS WOULD BE FOR US!
WHAT AN INGENIOUS PLAN!
NEXT DAY, AFTER ALANNA HAS SPREAD THE ALARM--
HERE THEY COME! FIRE!
SUDDENLY A FAMILIAR FIGURE LAUNCHES ITSELF THROUGH THE AIR AGAINST THE UNDERGROUND INVADERS--
IT'S ADAM STRANGE! SHOOT HIM TOO!
BEFORE THE MEN OF RANAGAR CAN FIRE--
I PROMISED ALANNA I WOULDN'T TAKE TOO MUCH RISK HERE-- SO I'D BETTER PUT MY PLAN INTO OPERATION!
CAUGHT BY A REPELLORAY, THE EARTHMAN PLUMMETS GROUNDWARD--
I FAKED BEING HURT TO HOLD XALTAN TOR'S FIRE! AFTER THE REGULAR RANAGAR ARMY HAS BEEN ROUTED, I'LL JOIN ALANNA AND LEAD HER TRUSTED SHARP-SHOOTERS AGAINST THE INVADERS!

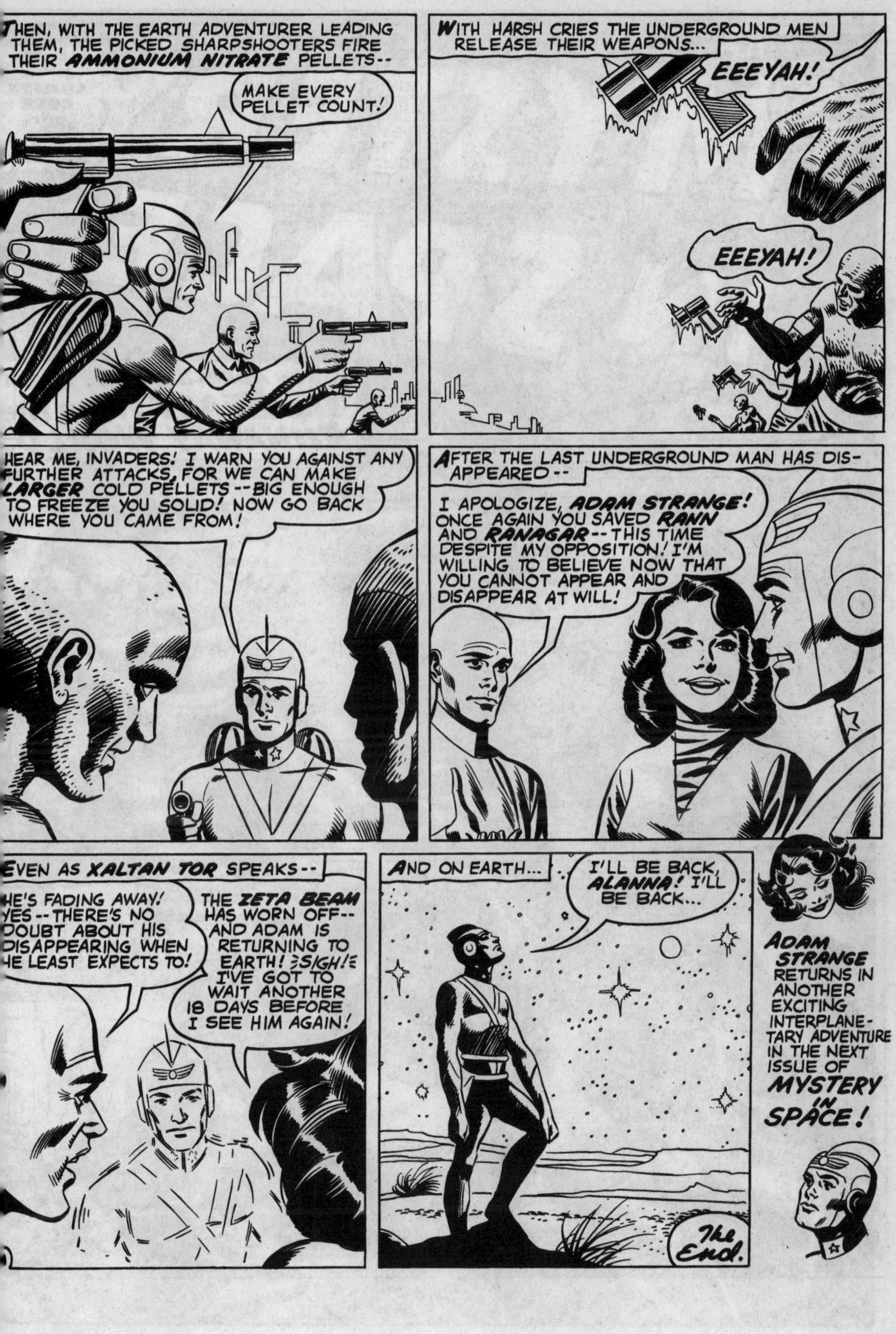
THEN, WITH THE EARTH ADVENTURER LEADING THEM, THE PICKED SHARPSHOOTERS FIRE THEIR AMMONIUM NITRATE PELLETS--
MAKE EVERY PELLET COUNT!
WITH HARSH CRIES THE UNDERGROUND MEN RELEASE THEIR WEAPONS...
EEEYAH!
EEEYAH!
HEAR ME, INVADERS! I WARN YOU AGAINST ANY FURTHER ATTACKS, FOR WE CAN MAKE LARGER COLD PELLETS--BIG ENOUGH TO FREEZE YOU SOLID! NOW GO BACK WHERE YOU CAME FROM!
AFTER THE LAST UNDERGROUND MAN HAS DISAPPEARED--
I APOLOGIZE, ADAM STRANGE! ONCE AGAIN YOU SAVED RANN AND RANAGAR--THIS TIME DESPITE MY OPPOSITION! I'M WILLING TO BELIEVE NOW THAT YOU CANNOT APPEAR AND DISAPPEAR AT WILL!
EVEN AS XALTAN TOR SPEAKS--
HE'S FADING AWAY! YES--THERE'S NO DOUBT ABOUT HIS DISAPPEARING WHEN HE LEAST EXPECTS TO!
THE ZETA BEAM HAS WORN OFF--AND ADAM IS RETURNING TO EARTH! SIGH! I'VE GOT TO WAIT ANOTHER 18 DAYS BEFORE I SEE HIM AGAIN!
AND ON EARTH...
I'LL BE BACK, ALANNA! I'LL BE BACK...
The End.
ADAM STRANGE RETURNS IN ANOTHER EXCITING INTERPLANETARY ADVENTURE IN THE NEXT ISSUE OF MYSTERY IN SPACE!

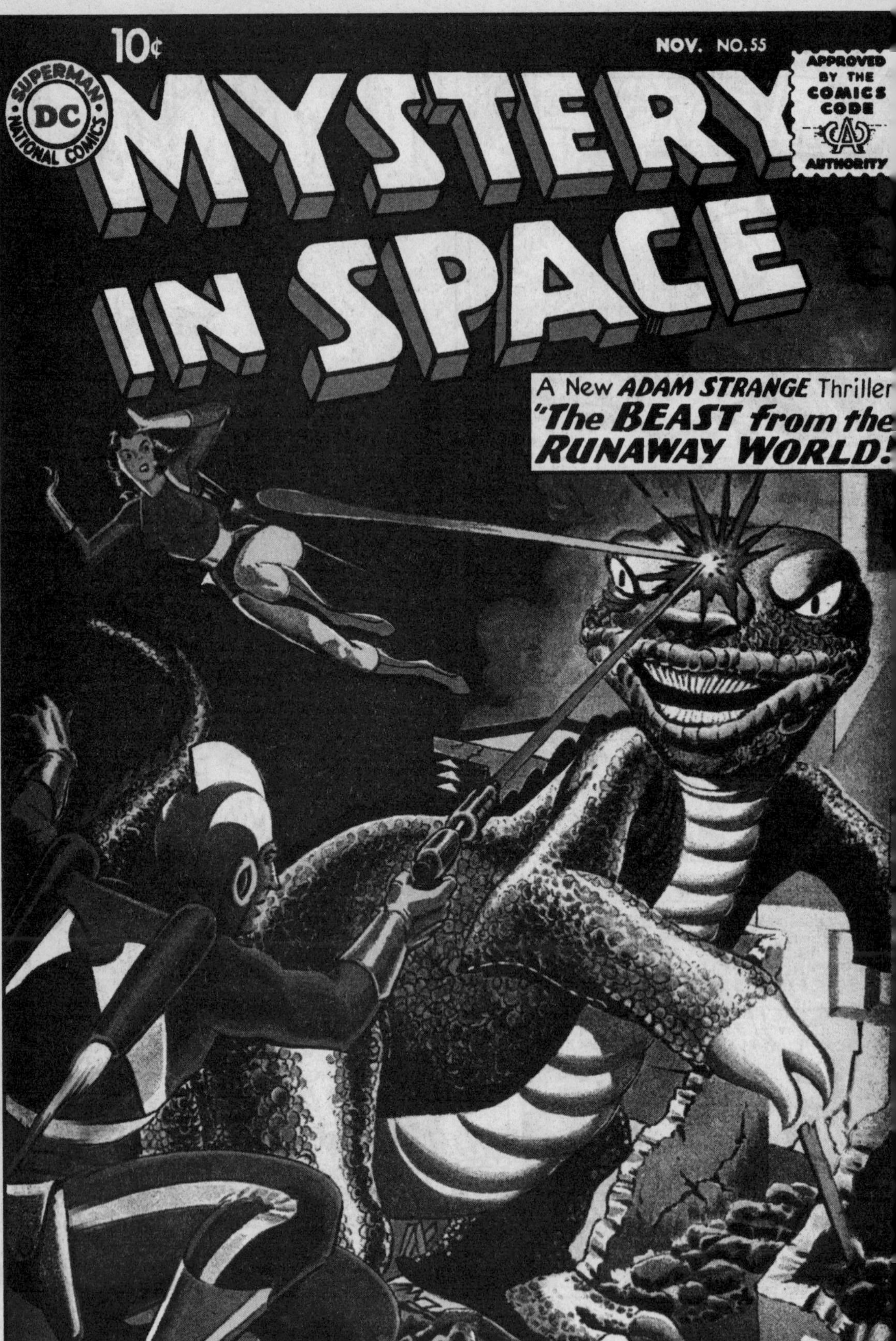
10¢
NOV. NO.55
SUPERMAN DC NATIONAL COMICS
APPROVED BY THE COMICS CODE AUTHORITY
MYSTERY IN SPACE
A New ADAM STRANGE Thriller
"The BEAST from the RUNAWAY WORLD!"

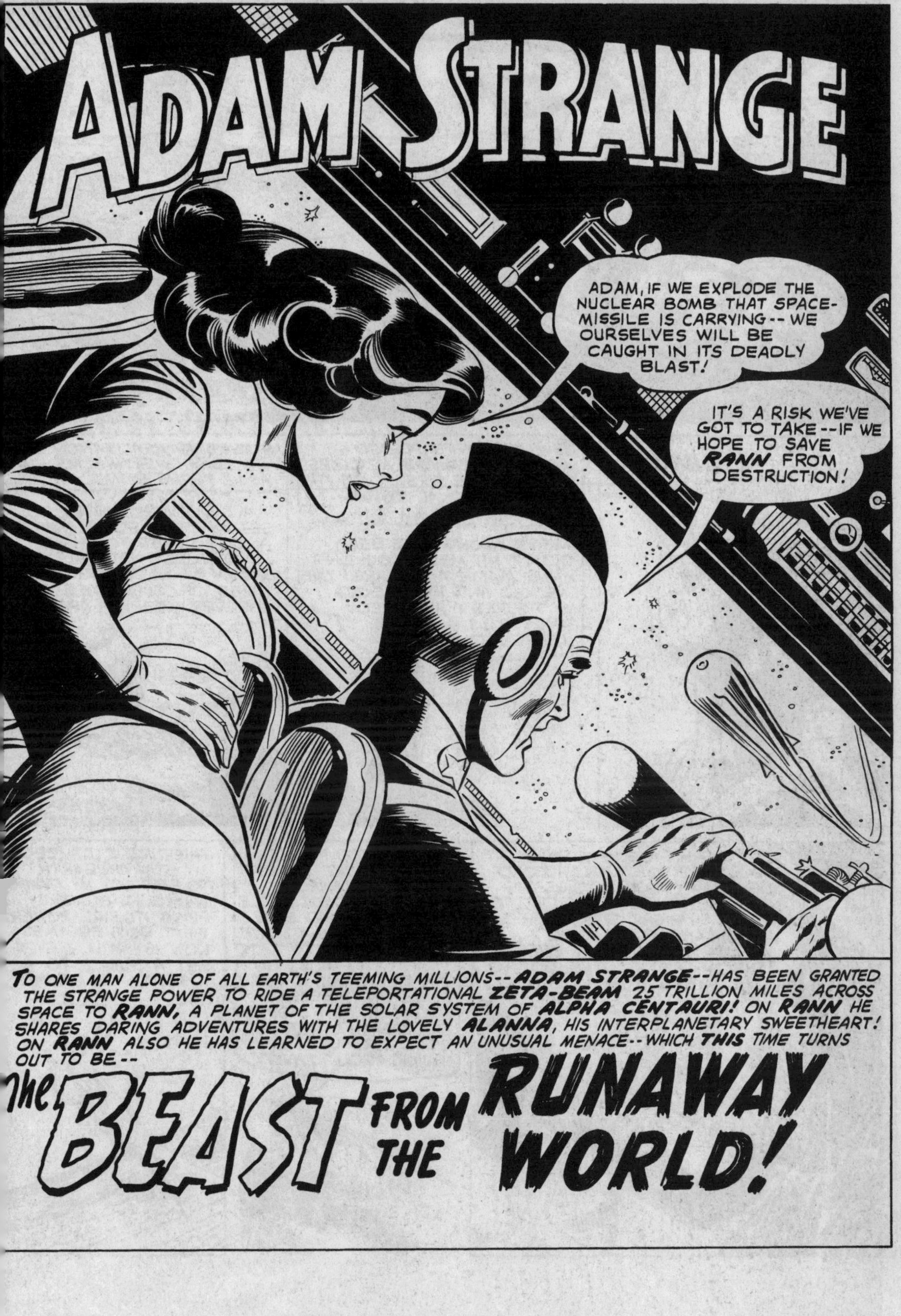
ADAM STRANGE
ADAM, IF WE EXPLODE THE NUCLEAR BOMB THAT SPACE-MISSILE IS CARRYING -- WE OURSELVES WILL BE CAUGHT IN ITS DEADLY BLAST!
IT'S A RISK WE'VE GOT TO TAKE -- IF WE HOPE TO SAVE RANN FROM DESTRUCTION!
TO ONE MAN ALONE OF ALL EARTH'S TEEMING MILLIONS -- ADAM STRANGE -- HAS BEEN GRANTED THE STRANGE POWER TO RIDE A TELEPORTATIONAL ZETA-BEAM 25 TRILLION MILES ACROSS SPACE TO RANN, A PLANET OF THE SOLAR SYSTEM OF ALPHA CENTAURI! ON RANN HE SHARES DARING ADVENTURES WITH THE LOVELY ALANNA, HIS INTERPLANETARY SWEETHEART! ON RANN ALSO HE HAS LEARNED TO EXPECT AN UNUSUAL MENACE -- WHICH THIS TIME TURNS OUT TO BE --
The BEAST FROM THE RUNAWAY WORLD!

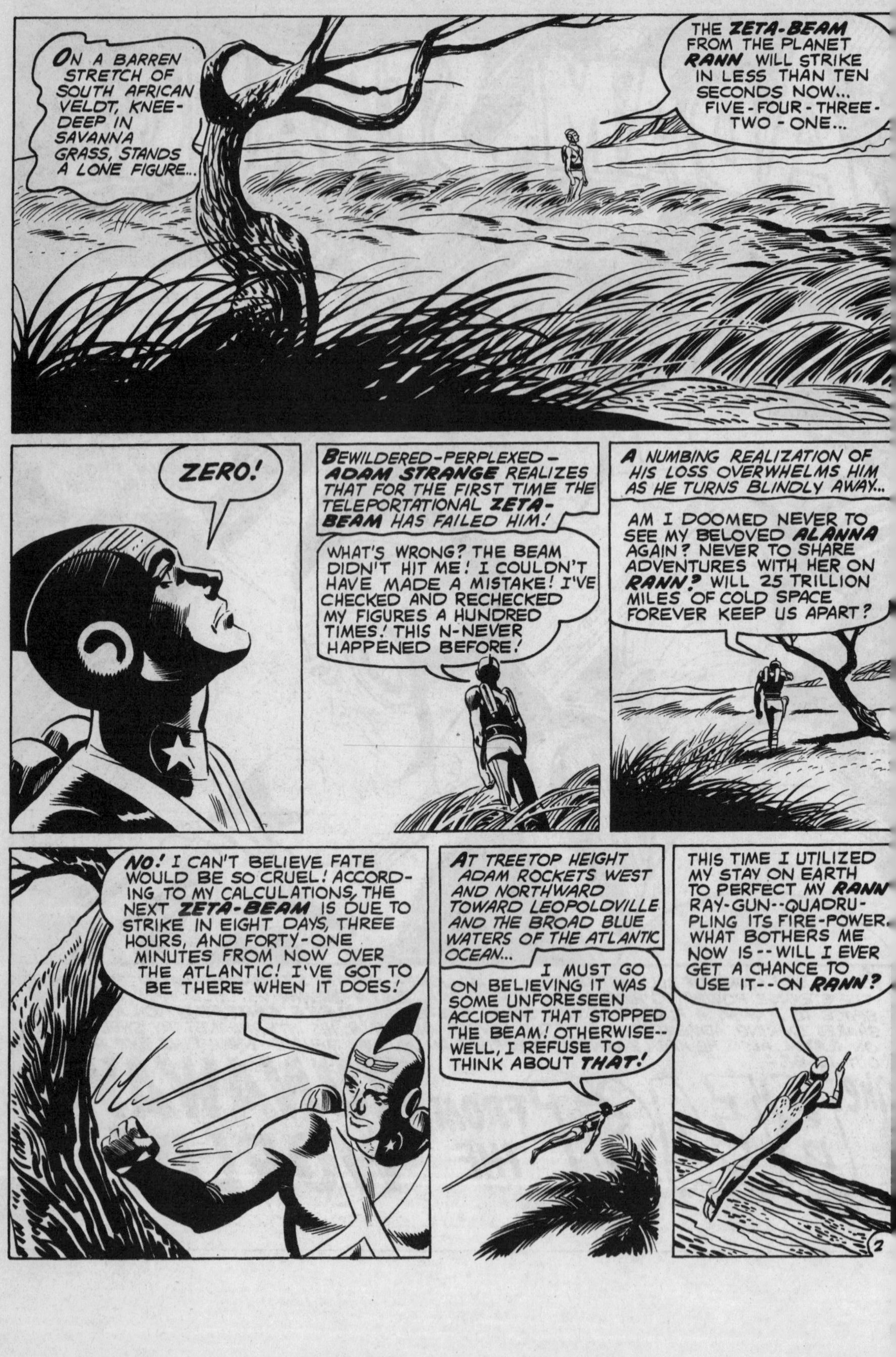
ON A BARREN STRETCH OF SOUTH AFRICAN VELDT, KNEE-DEEP IN SAVANNA GRASS, STANDS A LONE FIGURE...
THE ZETA-BEAM FROM THE PLANET RANN WILL STRIKE IN LESS THAN TEN SECONDS NOW... FIVE-FOUR-THREE-TWO-ONE...
ZERO!
BEWILDERED-PERPLEXED-ADAM STRANGE REALIZES THAT FOR THE FIRST TIME THE TELEPORTATIONAL ZETA-BEAM HAS FAILED HIM!
WHAT'S WRONG? THE BEAM DIDN'T HIT ME! I COULDN'T HAVE MADE A MISTAKE! I'VE CHECKED AND RECHECKED MY FIGURES A HUNDRED TIMES! THIS N-NEVER HAPPENED BEFORE!
A NUMBING REALIZATION OF HIS LOSS OVERWHELMS HIM AS HE TURNS BLINDLY AWAY...
AM I DOOMED NEVER TO SEE MY BELOVED ALANNA AGAIN? NEVER TO SHARE ADVENTURES WITH HER ON RANN? WILL 25 TRILLION MILES OF COLD SPACE FOREVER KEEP US APART?
NO! I CAN'T BELIEVE FATE WOULD BE SO CRUEL! ACCORDING TO MY CALCULATIONS, THE NEXT ZETA-BEAM IS DUE TO STRIKE IN EIGHT DAYS, THREE HOURS, AND FORTY-ONE MINUTES FROM NOW OVER THE ATLANTIC! I'VE GOT TO BE THERE WHEN IT DOES!
AT TREETOP HEIGHT ADAM ROCKETS WEST AND NORTHWARD TOWARD LEOPOLDVILLE AND THE BROAD BLUE WATERS OF THE ATLANTIC OCEAN...
I MUST GO ON BELIEVING IT WAS SOME UNFORESEEN ACCIDENT THAT STOPPED THE BEAM! OTHERWISE--WELL, I REFUSE TO THINK ABOUT THAT!
THIS TIME I UTILIZED MY STAY ON EARTH TO PERFECT MY RANN RAY-GUN--QUADRUPLING ITS FIRE-POWER. WHAT BOTHERS ME NOW IS--WILL I EVER GET A CHANCE TO USE IT--ON RANN?
2

EIGHT DAYS LATER, HOVERING ABOVE THE HEAVING WAVES OF THE SOUTH ATLANTIC, *ADAM STRANGE* WAITS WITH POUNDING HEART, MOUTH DRY, HOPE-FILLED EYES STRAINING SKYWARD...

WILL IT STRIKE? IT MUST-- IT *MUST*--

AND THEN SO SUDDENLY THAT HE IS CAUGHT COMPLETELY BY SURPRISE--FOR IN HIS ANXIETY HE HAS FORGOTTEN HIS COUNTDOWN-- THE *ZETA-BEAM* EXPLODES AROUND HIM!

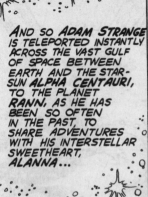

AND SO ADAM STRANGE IS TELEPORTED INSTANTLY ACROSS THE VAST GULF OF SPACE BETWEEN EARTH AND THE STAR-SUN *ALPHA CENTAURI,* TO THE PLANET *RANN,* AS HE HAS BEEN SO OFTEN IN THE PAST, TO SHARE ADVENTURES WITH HIS INTERSTELLAR SWEETHEART, *ALANNA*...

NOW AS HIS FEET TOUCH SOLID GROUND HE SEES ALANNA RACING TOWARD HIM...

OHH, ADAM! I-I WAS AFRAID I WAS NEVER GOING TO SEE YOU AGAIN!

WHY, *ALANNA*-- YOU'RE *CRYING*!

WHEN YOU DIDN'T APPEAR EIGHT DAYS AGO I WAS SURE SOMETHING TERRIBLE HAD HAPPENED TO YOU!

HERE, NOW! WHAT WAS THIS TERRIBLE THING YOU THOUGHT HAPPENED TO ME?

I TH-THOUGHT *ZARADAK* HA-HAD KILLED YOU!

ZARADAK?! WHO OR WHAT IN THE WORLD IS *ZARADAK?*

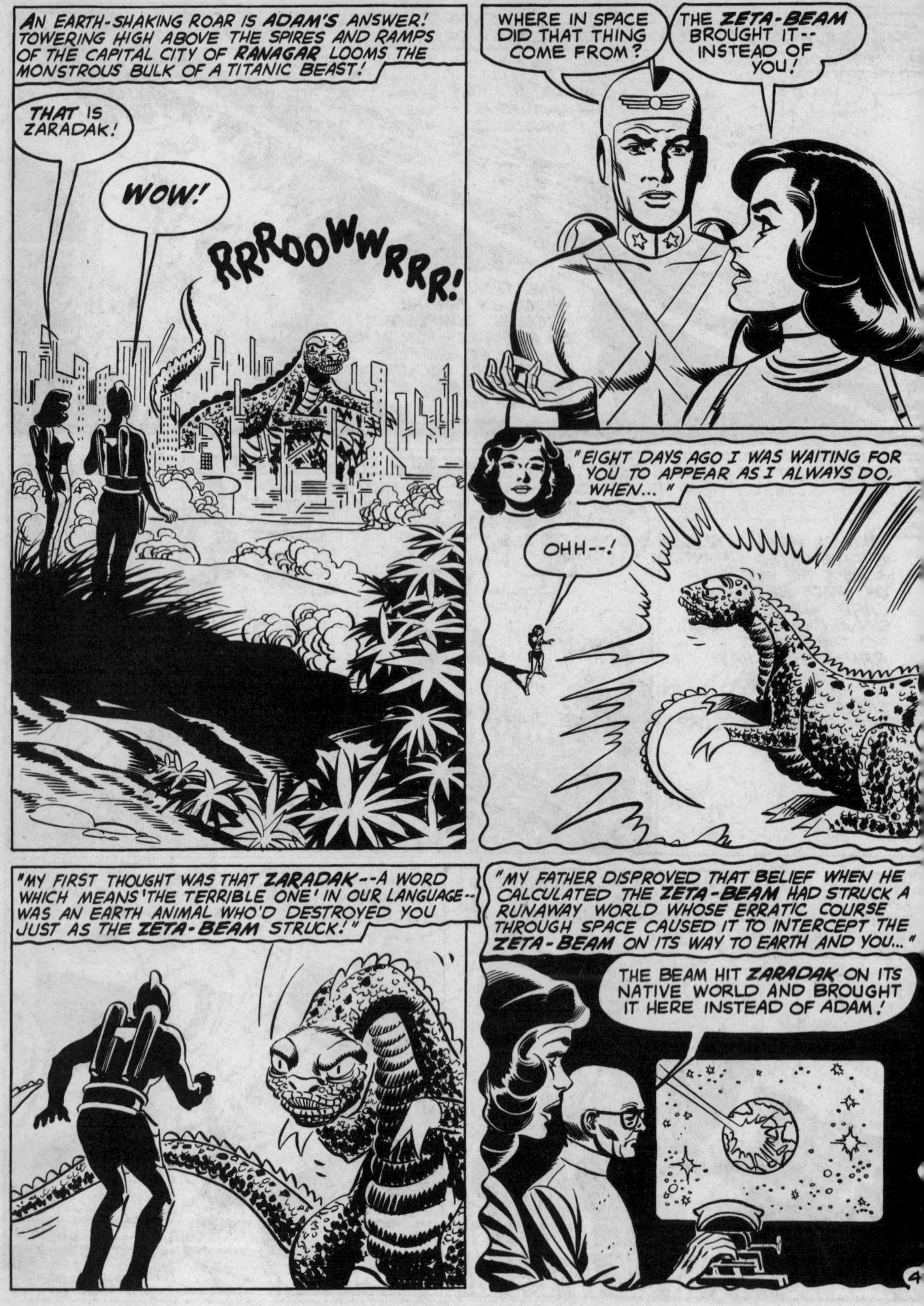
AN EARTH-SHAKING ROAR IS ADAM'S ANSWER! TOWERING HIGH ABOVE THE SPIRES AND RAMPS OF THE CAPITAL CITY OF RANAGAR LOOMS THE MONSTROUS BULK OF A TITANIC BEAST!
THAT IS ZARADAK!
WOW!
RRROOWWRRR!
WHERE IN SPACE DID THAT THING COME FROM?
THE ZETA-BEAM BROUGHT IT-- INSTEAD OF YOU!
"EIGHT DAYS AGO I WAS WAITING FOR YOU TO APPEAR AS I ALWAYS DO, WHEN..."
OHH--!
"MY FIRST THOUGHT WAS THAT ZARADAK--A WORD WHICH MEANS 'THE TERRIBLE ONE' IN OUR LANGUAGE--WAS AN EARTH ANIMAL WHO'D DESTROYED YOU JUST AS THE ZETA-BEAM STRUCK!"
"MY FATHER DISPROVED THAT BELIEF WHEN HE CALCULATED THE ZETA-BEAM HAD STRUCK A RUNAWAY WORLD WHOSE ERRATIC COURSE THROUGH SPACE CAUSED IT TO INTERCEPT THE ZETA-BEAM ON ITS WAY TO EARTH AND YOU..."
THE BEAM HIT ZARADAK ON ITS NATIVE WORLD AND BROUGHT IT HERE INSTEAD OF ADAM!
4

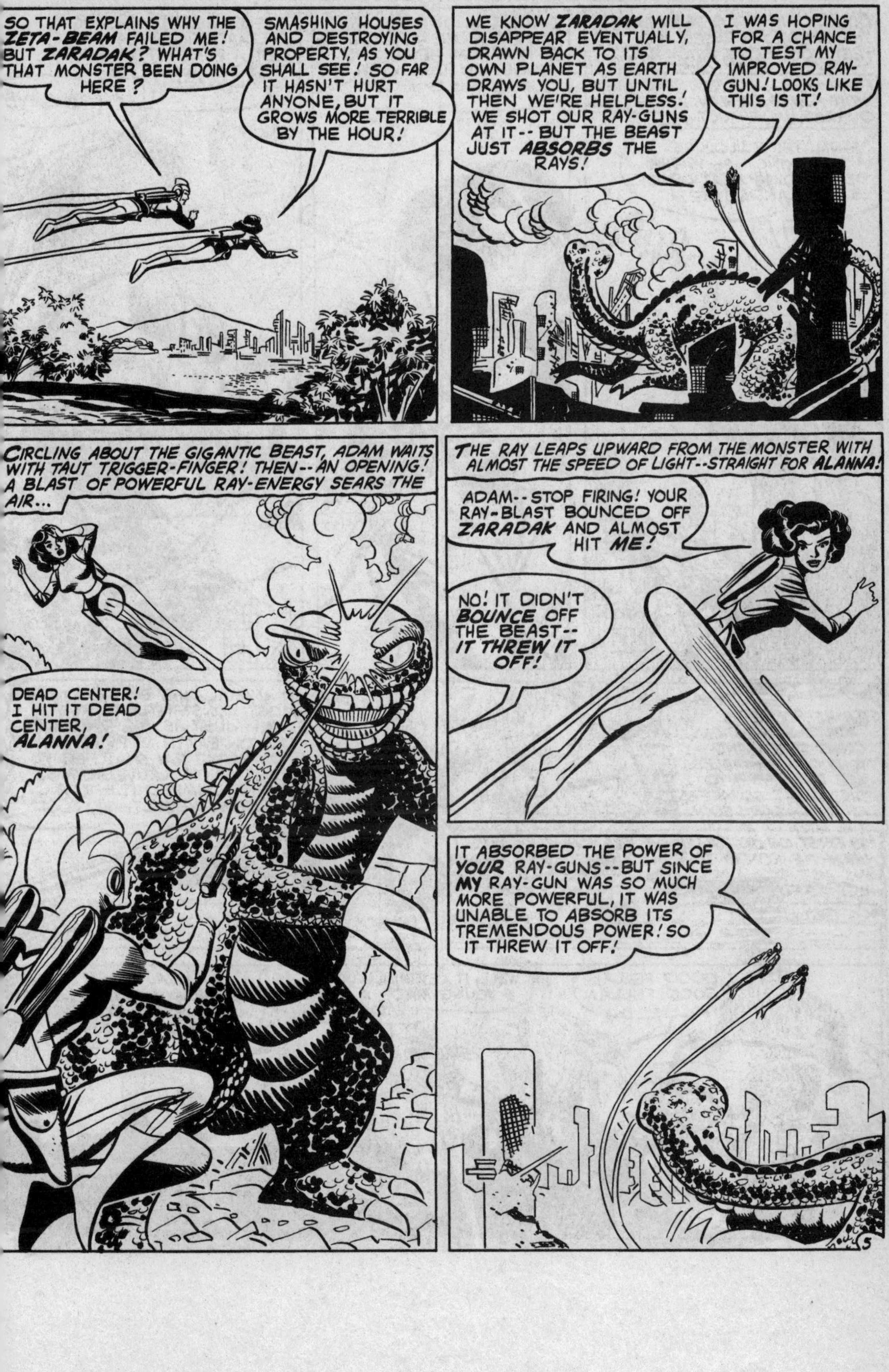
SO THAT EXPLAINS WHY THE ZETA-BEAM FAILED ME! BUT ZARADAK? WHAT'S THAT MONSTER BEEN DOING HERE?
SMASHING HOUSES AND DESTROYING PROPERTY, AS YOU SHALL SEE! SO FAR IT HASN'T HURT ANYONE, BUT IT GROWS MORE TERRIBLE BY THE HOUR!
WE KNOW ZARADAK WILL DISAPPEAR EVENTUALLY, DRAWN BACK TO ITS OWN PLANET AS EARTH DRAWS YOU, BUT UNTIL THEN WE'RE HELPLESS! WE SHOT OUR RAY-GUNS AT IT-- BUT THE BEAST JUST ABSORBS THE RAYS!
I WAS HOPING FOR A CHANCE TO TEST MY IMPROVED RAY-GUN! LOOKS LIKE THIS IS IT!
CIRCLING ABOUT THE GIGANTIC BEAST, ADAM WAITS WITH TAUT TRIGGER-FINGER! THEN--AN OPENING! A BLAST OF POWERFUL RAY-ENERGY SEARS THE AIR...
DEAD CENTER! I HIT IT DEAD CENTER, ALANNA!
THE RAY LEAPS UPWARD FROM THE MONSTER WITH ALMOST THE SPEED OF LIGHT--STRAIGHT FOR ALANNA!
ADAM--STOP FIRING! YOUR RAY-BLAST BOUNCED OFF ZARADAK AND ALMOST HIT ME!
NO! IT DIDN'T BOUNCE OFF THE BEAST-- IT THREW IT OFF!
IT ABSORBED THE POWER OF YOUR RAY-GUNS--BUT SINCE MY RAY-GUN WAS SO MUCH MORE POWERFUL, IT WAS UNABLE TO ABSORB ITS TREMENDOUS POWER! SO IT THREW IT OFF!
5

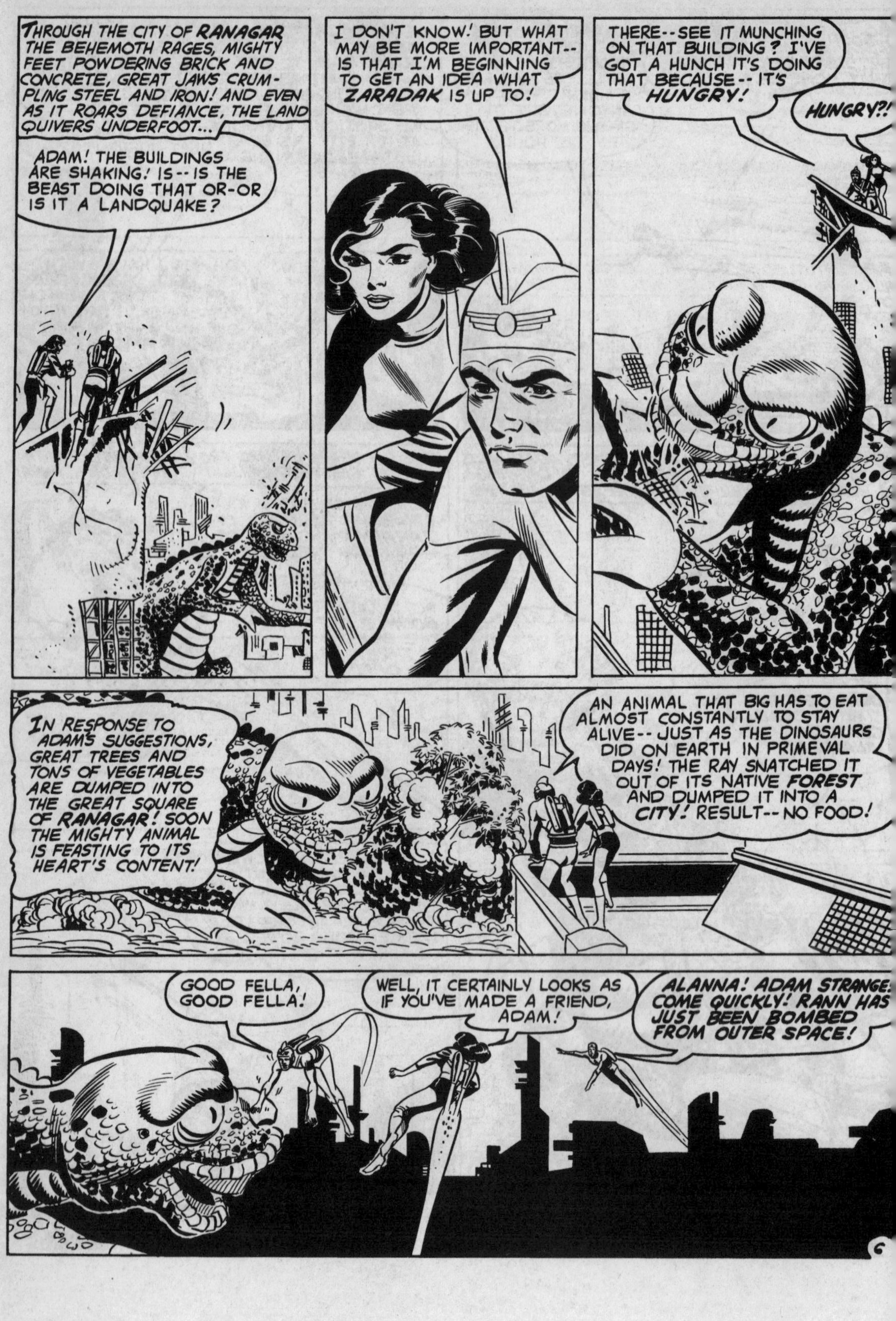
THROUGH THE CITY OF RANAGAR THE BEHEMOTH RAGES, MIGHTY FEET POWDERING BRICK AND CONCRETE, GREAT JAWS CRUMPLING STEEL AND IRON! AND EVEN AS IT ROARS DEFIANCE, THE LAND QUIVERS UNDERFOOT...
ADAM! THE BUILDINGS ARE SHAKING! IS--IS THE BEAST DOING THAT OR-OR IS IT A LANDQUAKE?
I DON'T KNOW! BUT WHAT MAY BE MORE IMPORTANT--IS THAT I'M BEGINNING TO GET AN IDEA WHAT ZARADAK IS UP TO!
THERE--SEE IT MUNCHING ON THAT BUILDING? I'VE GOT A HUNCH IT'S DOING THAT BECAUSE--IT'S HUNGRY!
HUNGRY?!
IN RESPONSE TO ADAM'S SUGGESTIONS, GREAT TREES AND TONS OF VEGETABLES ARE DUMPED INTO THE GREAT SQUARE OF RANAGAR! SOON THE MIGHTY ANIMAL IS FEASTING TO ITS HEART'S CONTENT!
AN ANIMAL THAT BIG HAS TO EAT ALMOST CONSTANTLY TO STAY ALIVE--JUST AS THE DINOSAURS DID ON EARTH IN PRIMEVAL DAYS! THE RAY SNATCHED IT OUT OF ITS NATIVE FOREST AND DUMPED IT INTO A CITY! RESULT--NO FOOD!
GOOD FELLA, GOOD FELLA!
WELL, IT CERTAINLY LOOKS AS IF YOU'VE MADE A FRIEND, ADAM!
ALANNA! ADAM STRANGE! COME QUICKLY! RANN HAS JUST BEEN BOMBED FROM OUTER SPACE!
6

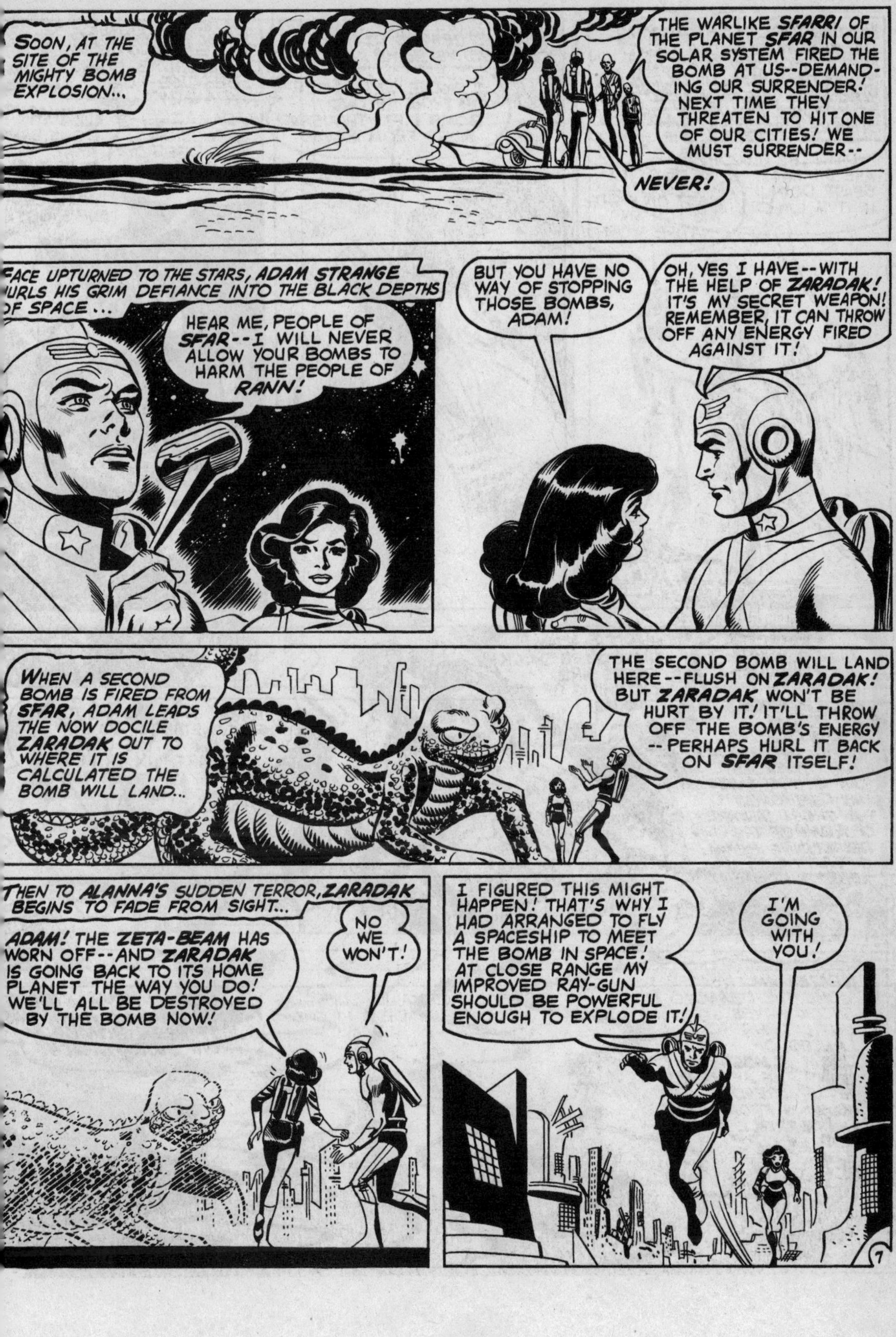
SOON, AT THE SITE OF THE MIGHTY BOMB EXPLOSION...
THE WARLIKE SFARRI OF THE PLANET SFAR IN OUR SOLAR SYSTEM FIRED THE BOMB AT US--DEMANDING OUR SURRENDER! NEXT TIME THEY THREATEN TO HIT ONE OF OUR CITIES! WE MUST SURRENDER--
NEVER!
FACE UPTURNED TO THE STARS, ADAM STRANGE HURLS HIS GRIM DEFIANCE INTO THE BLACK DEPTHS OF SPACE...
HEAR ME, PEOPLE OF SFAR--I WILL NEVER ALLOW YOUR BOMBS TO HARM THE PEOPLE OF RANN!
BUT YOU HAVE NO WAY OF STOPPING THOSE BOMBS, ADAM!
OH, YES I HAVE--WITH THE HELP OF ZARADAK! IT'S MY SECRET WEAPON! REMEMBER, IT CAN THROW OFF ANY ENERGY FIRED AGAINST IT!
WHEN A SECOND BOMB IS FIRED FROM SFAR, ADAM LEADS THE NOW DOCILE ZARADAK OUT TO WHERE IT IS CALCULATED THE BOMB WILL LAND...
THE SECOND BOMB WILL LAND HERE--FLUSH ON ZARADAK! BUT ZARADAK WON'T BE HURT BY IT! IT'LL THROW OFF THE BOMB'S ENERGY --PERHAPS HURL IT BACK ON SFAR ITSELF!
THEN TO ALANNA'S SUDDEN TERROR, ZARADAK BEGINS TO FADE FROM SIGHT...
ADAM! THE ZETA-BEAM HAS WORN OFF--AND ZARADAK IS GOING BACK TO ITS HOME PLANET THE WAY YOU DO! WE'LL ALL BE DESTROYED BY THE BOMB NOW!
NO WE WON'T!
I FIGURED THIS MIGHT HAPPEN! THAT'S WHY I HAD ARRANGED TO FLY A SPACESHIP TO MEET THE BOMB IN SPACE! AT CLOSE RANGE MY IMPROVED RAY-GUN SHOULD BE POWERFUL ENOUGH TO EXPLODE IT!
I'M GOING WITH YOU!
7

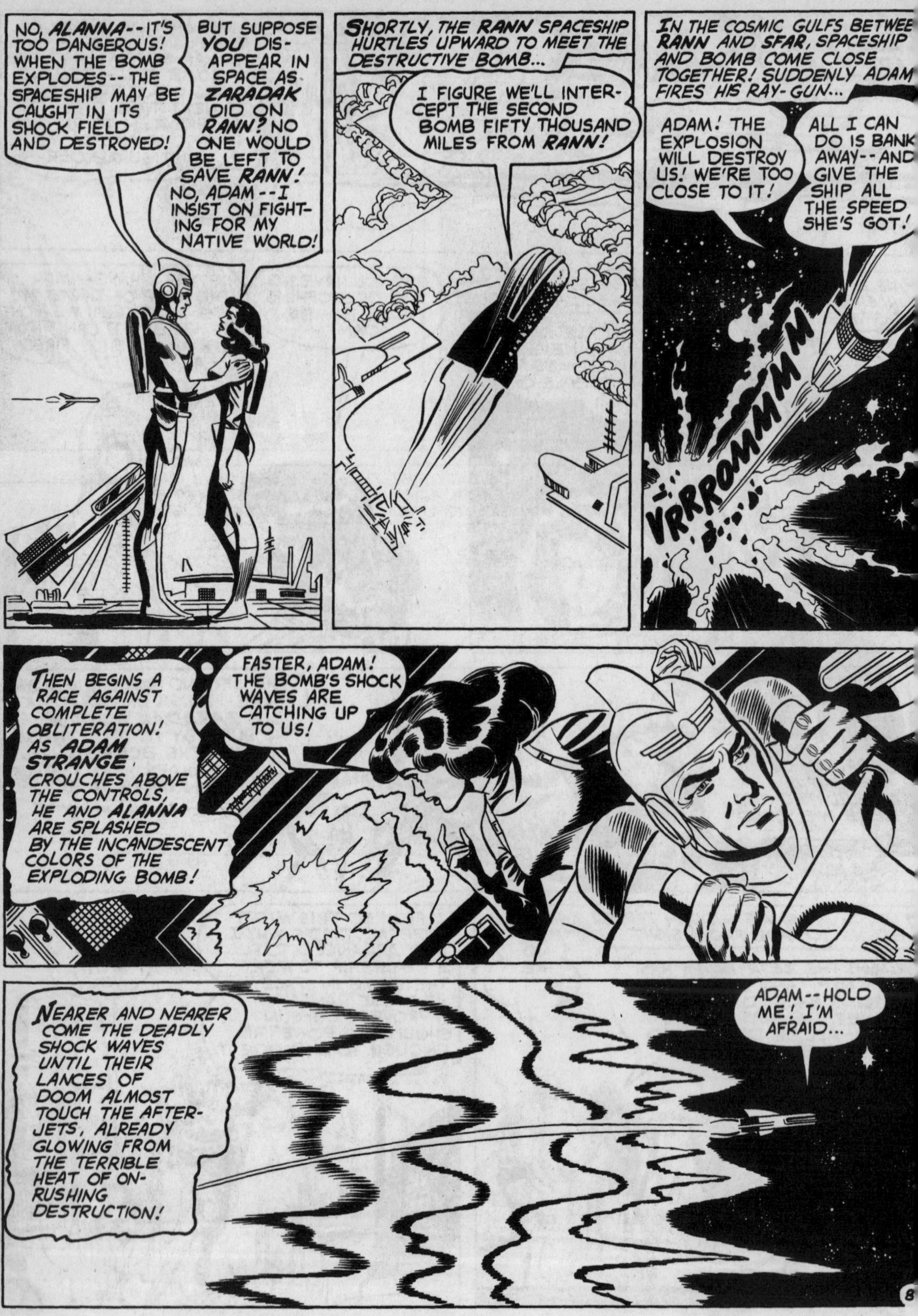
NO, ALANNA--IT'S TOO DANGEROUS! WHEN THE BOMB EXPLODES--THE SPACESHIP MAY BE CAUGHT IN ITS SHOCK FIELD AND DESTROYED!
BUT SUPPOSE YOU DISAPPEAR IN SPACE AS ZARADAK DID ON RANN? NO ONE WOULD BE LEFT TO SAVE RANN! NO, ADAM--I INSIST ON FIGHTING FOR MY NATIVE WORLD!
SHORTLY, THE RANN SPACESHIP HURTLES UPWARD TO MEET THE DESTRUCTIVE BOMB...
I FIGURE WE'LL INTERCEPT THE SECOND BOMB FIFTY THOUSAND MILES FROM RANN!
IN THE COSMIC GULFS BETWEE RANN AND SFAR, SPACESHIP AND BOMB COME CLOSE TOGETHER! SUDDENLY ADAM FIRES HIS RAY-GUN...
ADAM! THE EXPLOSION WILL DESTROY US! WE'RE TOO CLOSE TO IT!
ALL I CAN DO IS BANK AWAY--AND GIVE THE SHIP ALL THE SPEED SHE'S GOT!
VRRROMMMMM
THEN BEGINS A RACE AGAINST COMPLETE OBLITERATION! AS ADAM STRANGE CROUCHES ABOVE THE CONTROLS, HE AND ALANNA ARE SPLASHED BY THE INCANDESCENT COLORS OF THE EXPLODING BOMB!
FASTER, ADAM! THE BOMB'S SHOCK WAVES ARE CATCHING UP TO US!
NEARER AND NEARER COME THE DEADLY SHOCK WAVES UNTIL THEIR LANCES OF DOOM ALMOST TOUCH THE AFTER-JETS, ALREADY GLOWING FROM THE TERRIBLE HEAT OF ON-RUSHING DESTRUCTION!
ADAM--HOLD ME! I'M AFRAID...
8

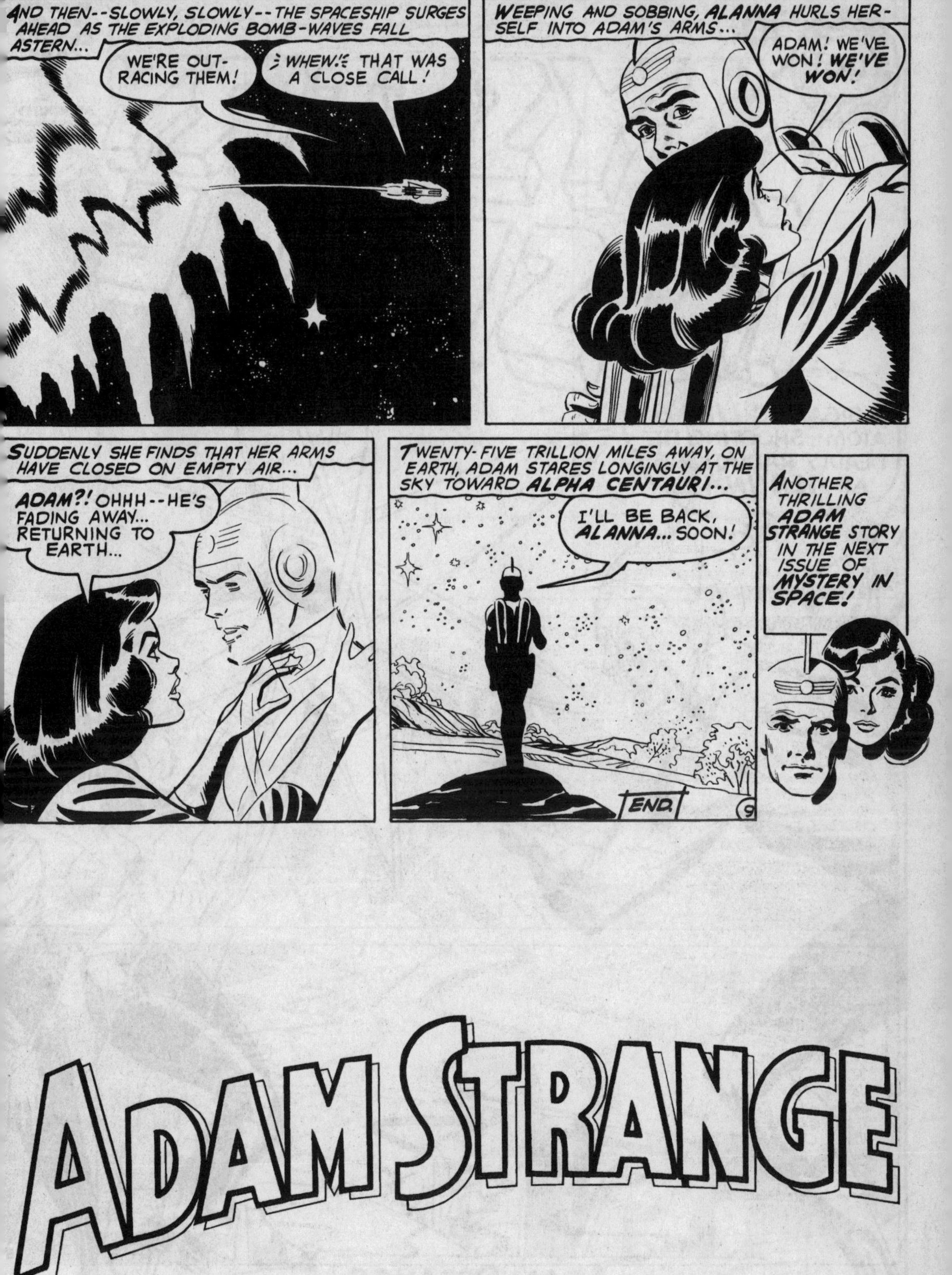
AND THEN--SLOWLY, SLOWLY--THE SPACESHIP SURGES AHEAD AS THE EXPLODING BOMB-WAVES FALL ASTERN...
WE'RE OUT-RACING THEM!
WHEW!! THAT WAS A CLOSE CALL!
WEEPING AND SOBBING, ALANNA HURLS HER-SELF INTO ADAM'S ARMS...
ADAM! WE'VE WON! WE'VE WON!
SUDDENLY SHE FINDS THAT HER ARMS HAVE CLOSED ON EMPTY AIR...
ADAM?! OHHH--HE'S FADING AWAY... RETURNING TO EARTH...
TWENTY-FIVE TRILLION MILES AWAY, ON EARTH, ADAM STARES LONGINGLY AT THE SKY TOWARD ALPHA CENTAURI...
I'LL BE BACK, ALANNA... SOON!
END
9
ANOTHER THRILLING ADAM STRANGE STORY IN THE NEXT ISSUE OF MYSTERY IN SPACE!

ADAM STRANGE

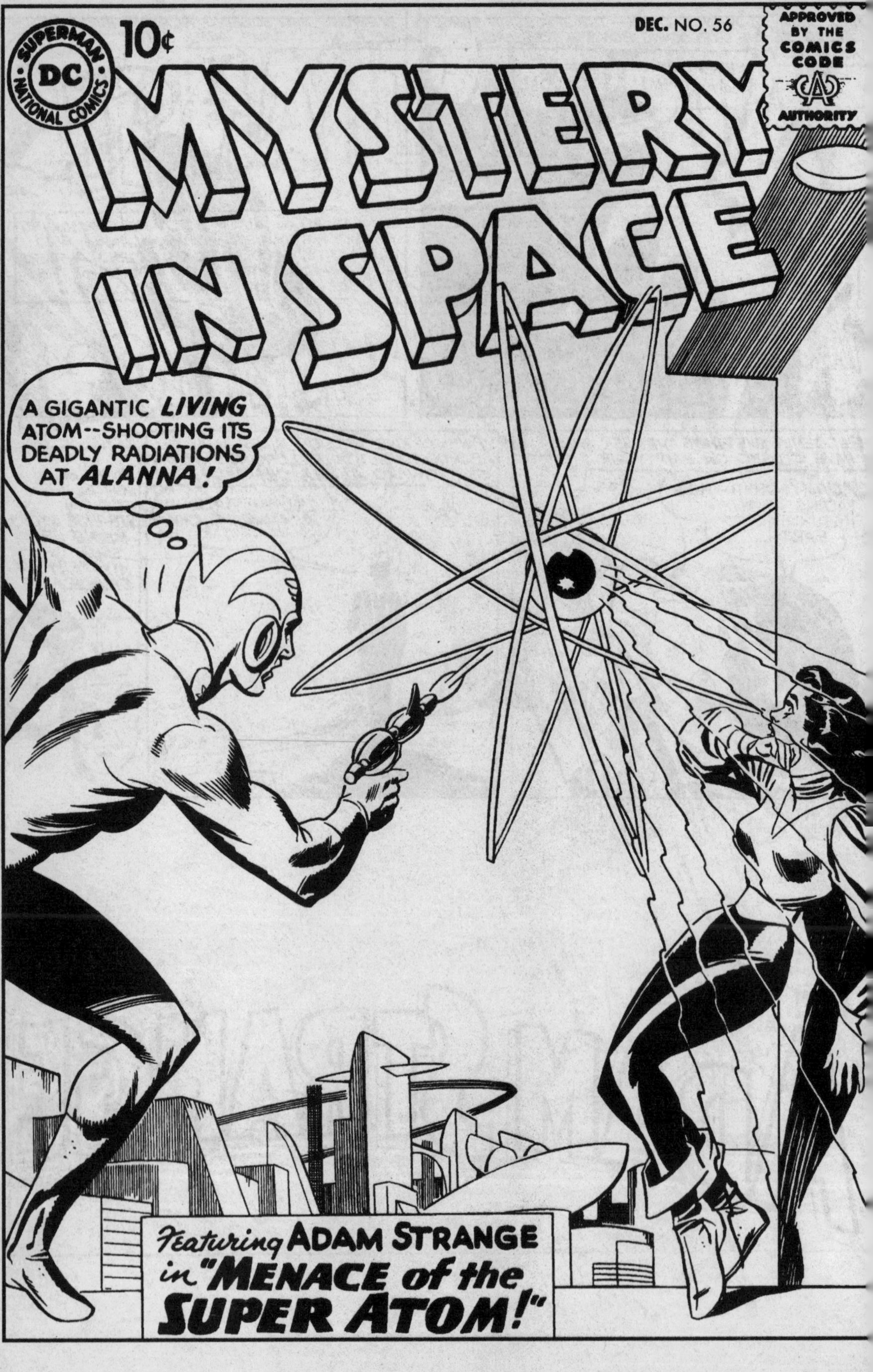
SUPERMAN DC NATIONAL COMICS
10¢
DEC. NO. 56
APPROVED BY THE COMICS CODE AUTHORITY
MYSTERY IN SPACE
A GIGANTIC LIVING ATOM--SHOOTING ITS DEADLY RADIATIONS AT ALANNA!
Featuring ADAM STRANGE in "MENACE of the SUPER ATOM!"

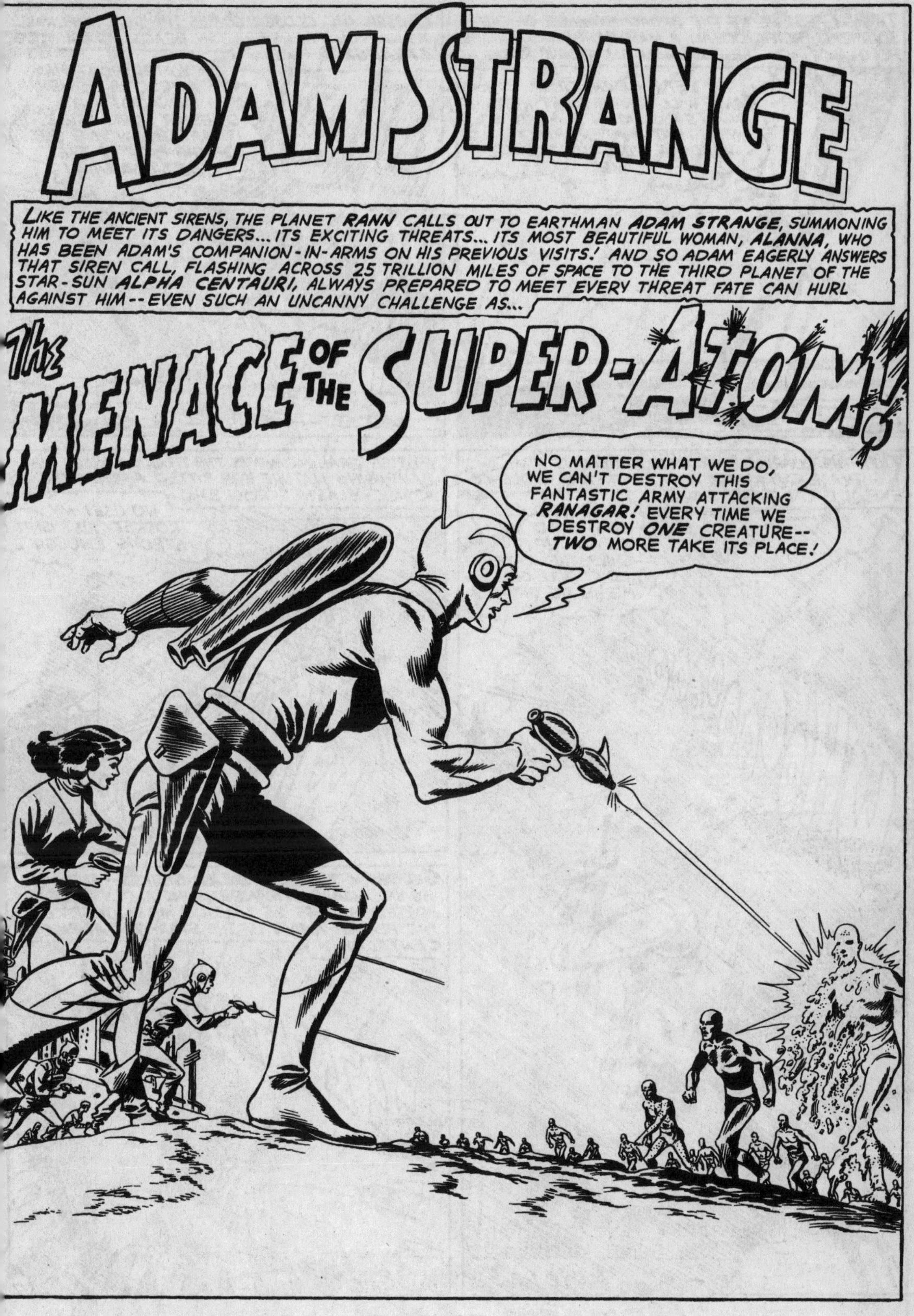
ADAM STRANGE
LIKE THE ANCIENT SIRENS, THE PLANET RANN CALLS OUT TO EARTHMAN ADAM STRANGE, SUMMONING HIM TO MEET ITS DANGERS... ITS EXCITING THREATS... ITS MOST BEAUTIFUL WOMAN, ALANNA, WHO HAS BEEN ADAM'S COMPANION-IN-ARMS ON HIS PREVIOUS VISITS! AND SO ADAM EAGERLY ANSWERS THAT SIREN CALL, FLASHING ACROSS 25 TRILLION MILES OF SPACE TO THE THIRD PLANET OF THE STAR-SUN ALPHA CENTAURI, ALWAYS PREPARED TO MEET EVERY THREAT FATE CAN HURL AGAINST HIM--EVEN SUCH AN UNCANNY CHALLENGE AS...
The MENACE OF THE SUPER-ATOM!
NO MATTER WHAT WE DO, WE CAN'T DESTROY THIS FANTASTIC ARMY ATTACKING RANAGAR! EVERY TIME WE DESTROY ONE CREATURE-- TWO MORE TAKE ITS PLACE!

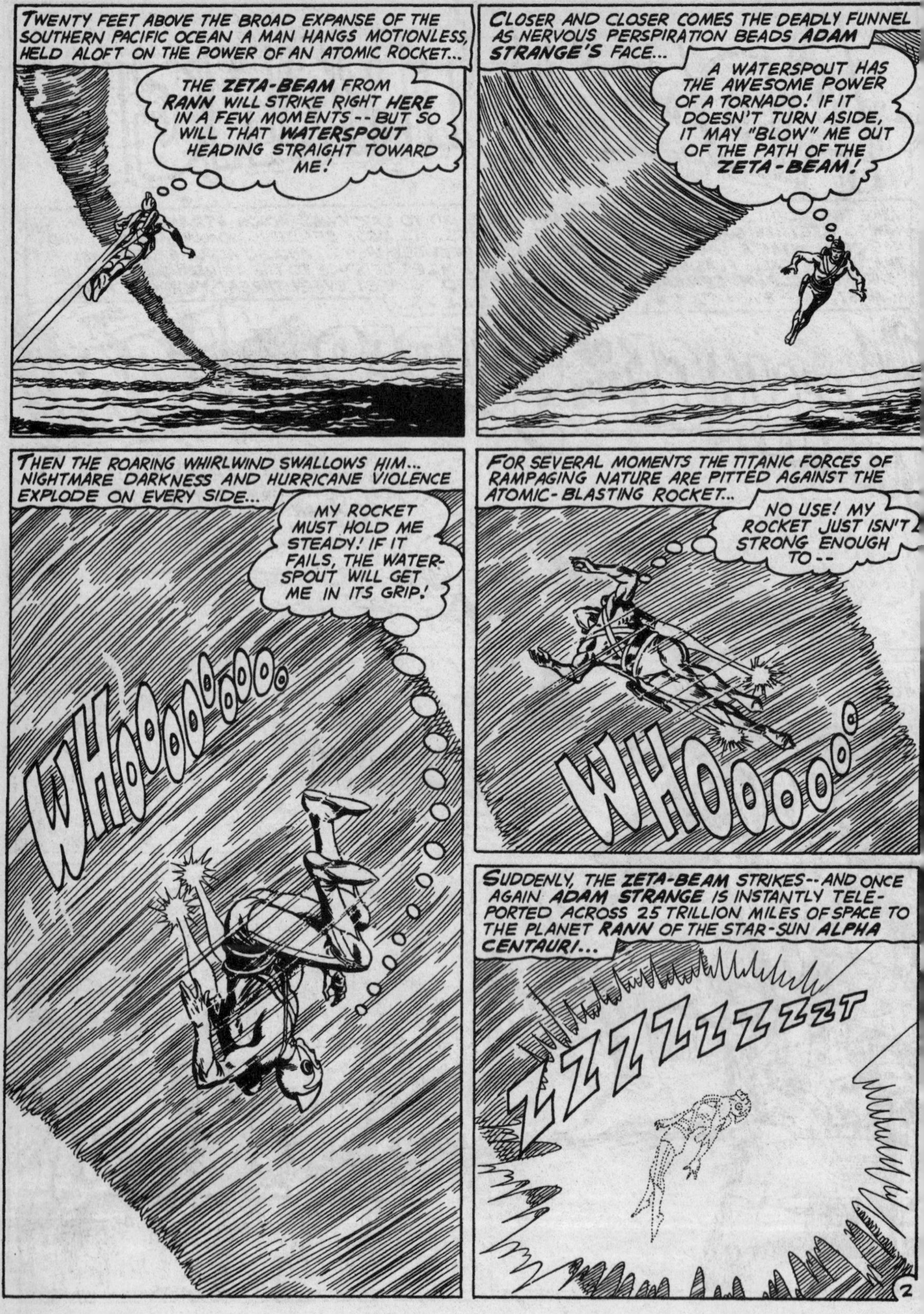
TWENTY FEET ABOVE THE BROAD EXPANSE OF THE SOUTHERN PACIFIC OCEAN A MAN HANGS MOTIONLESS, HELD ALOFT ON THE POWER OF AN ATOMIC ROCKET...
THE ZETA-BEAM FROM RANN WILL STRIKE RIGHT HERE IN A FEW MOMENTS -- BUT SO WILL THAT WATERSPOUT HEADING STRAIGHT TOWARD ME!
CLOSER AND CLOSER COMES THE DEADLY FUNNEL AS NERVOUS PERSPIRATION BEADS ADAM STRANGE'S FACE...
A WATERSPOUT HAS THE AWESOME POWER OF A TORNADO! IF IT DOESN'T TURN ASIDE, IT MAY "BLOW" ME OUT OF THE PATH OF THE ZETA-BEAM!
THEN THE ROARING WHIRLWIND SWALLOWS HIM... NIGHTMARE DARKNESS AND HURRICANE VIOLENCE EXPLODE ON EVERY SIDE...
MY ROCKET MUST HOLD ME STEADY! IF IT FAILS, THE WATER-SPOUT WILL GET ME IN ITS GRIP!
WHOOOOOOOOOO
FOR SEVERAL MOMENTS THE TITANIC FORCES OF RAMPAGING NATURE ARE PITTED AGAINST THE ATOMIC-BLASTING ROCKET...
NO USE! MY ROCKET JUST ISN'T STRONG ENOUGH TO --
WHOOOOOO
SUDDENLY, THE ZETA-BEAM STRIKES--AND ONCE AGAIN ADAM STRANGE IS INSTANTLY TELE-PORTED ACROSS 25 TRILLION MILES OF SPACE TO THE PLANET RANN OF THE STAR-SUN ALPHA CENTAURI...
ZZZZZZZZZT
2

AS HE LOOKS ABOUT THE ROLLING GRASSLANDS OF RANN...

THE OTHER TIMES I'VE LANDED ON *RANN*, ALANNA'S BEEN WAITING TO MEET ME! WHERE IS SHE NOW?

HERE COMES HER FLIER-- BUT *ALANNA* ISN'T IN IT! FOR SOME REASON SHE COULDN'T MEET ME--AND SENT THE FLIER TO BRING ME TO HER! I'LL GET IN AND LET THE ROBOT-FLIER TAKE ME TO HER!

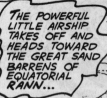

THE POWERFUL LITTLE AIRSHIP TAKES OFF AND HEADS TOWARD THE GREAT SAND BARRENS OF EQUATORIAL RANN...

I'VE NEVER VISITED THIS PLACE OF RANN BEFORE! I SEEM TO SEE RUINS UP AHEAD!

THE FLIER IS HEADING TOWARD THE RUINS-- GOING LOWER AND LOWER--ABOUT TO LAND NEAR THOSE STRANGE STATUES!

TO ADAM'S STUNNED AMAZEMENT THE "STATUES" COME TO LIFE, STRIDING FORWARD AS ADAM STEPS FROM HIS FLIER...

THE STATUES OF STONE... METAL... SAND... CHARGING AT ME!

AS SANDY HANDS REACH FOR HIM, ADAM FIGHTS BACK SAVAGELY...

I CAN'T LET THESE THINGS DETAIN ME! I'VE GOT TO FIND OUT WHERE ALANNA IS, AND FIND OUT WHAT HAS HAPPENED TO HER!

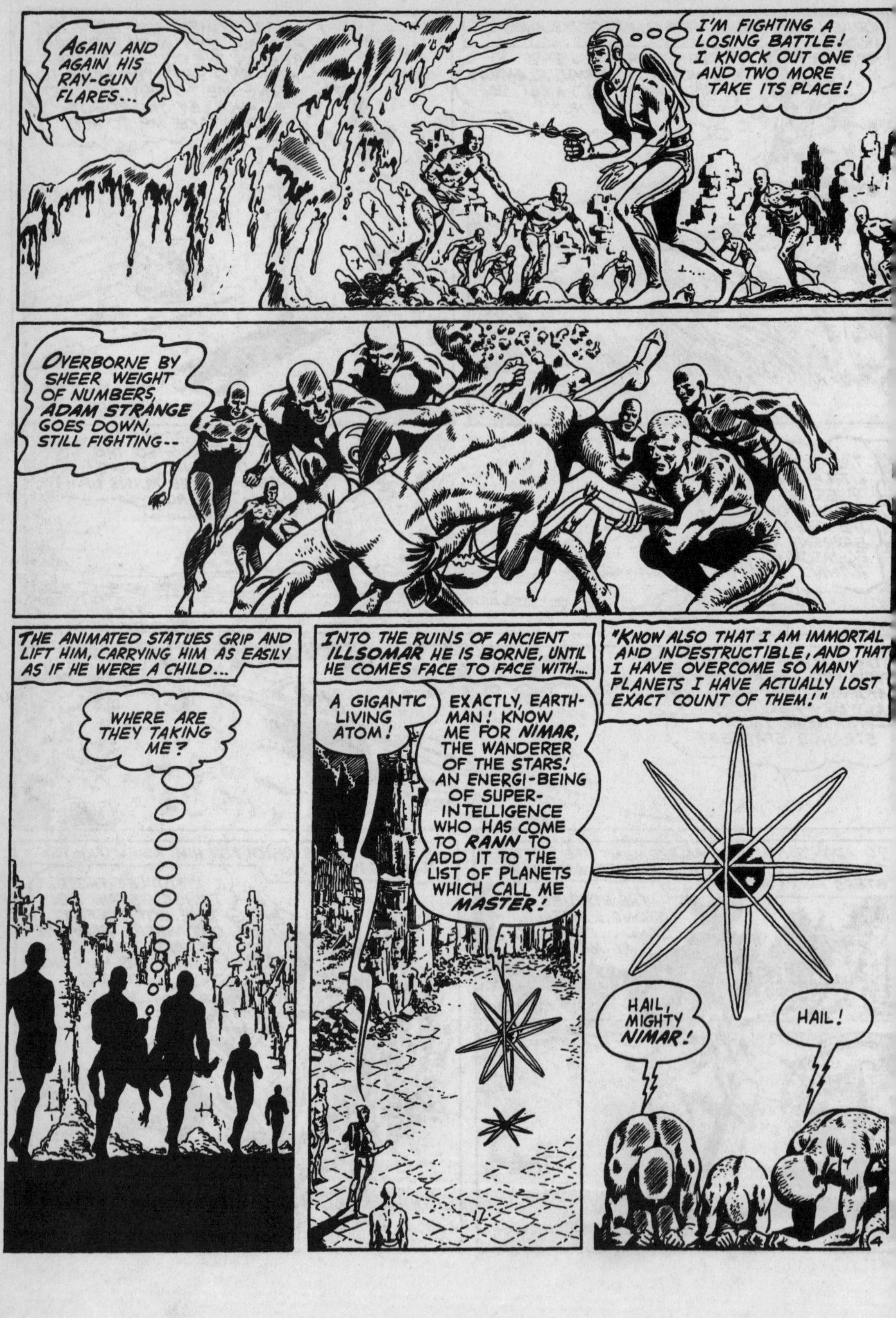

AGAIN AND AGAIN HIS RAY-GUN FLARES...
I'M FIGHTING A LOSING BATTLE! I KNOCK OUT ONE AND TWO MORE TAKE ITS PLACE!
OVERBORNE BY SHEER WEIGHT OF NUMBERS, ADAM STRANGE GOES DOWN, STILL FIGHTING--
THE ANIMATED STATUES GRIP AND LIFT HIM, CARRYING HIM AS EASILY AS IF HE WERE A CHILD...
WHERE ARE THEY TAKING ME?
INTO THE RUINS OF ANCIENT ILLSOMAR HE IS BORNE, UNTIL HE COMES FACE TO FACE WITH...
A GIGANTIC LIVING ATOM!
EXACTLY, EARTH-MAN! KNOW ME FOR NIMAR, THE WANDERER OF THE STARS! AN ENERGI-BEING OF SUPER-INTELLIGENCE WHO HAS COME TO RANN TO ADD IT TO THE LIST OF PLANETS WHICH CALL ME MASTER!
"KNOW ALSO THAT I AM IMMORTAL AND INDESTRUCTIBLE, AND THAT I HAVE OVERCOME SO MANY PLANETS I HAVE ACTUALLY LOST EXACT COUNT OF THEM!"
HAIL, MIGHTY NIMAR!
HAIL!
4

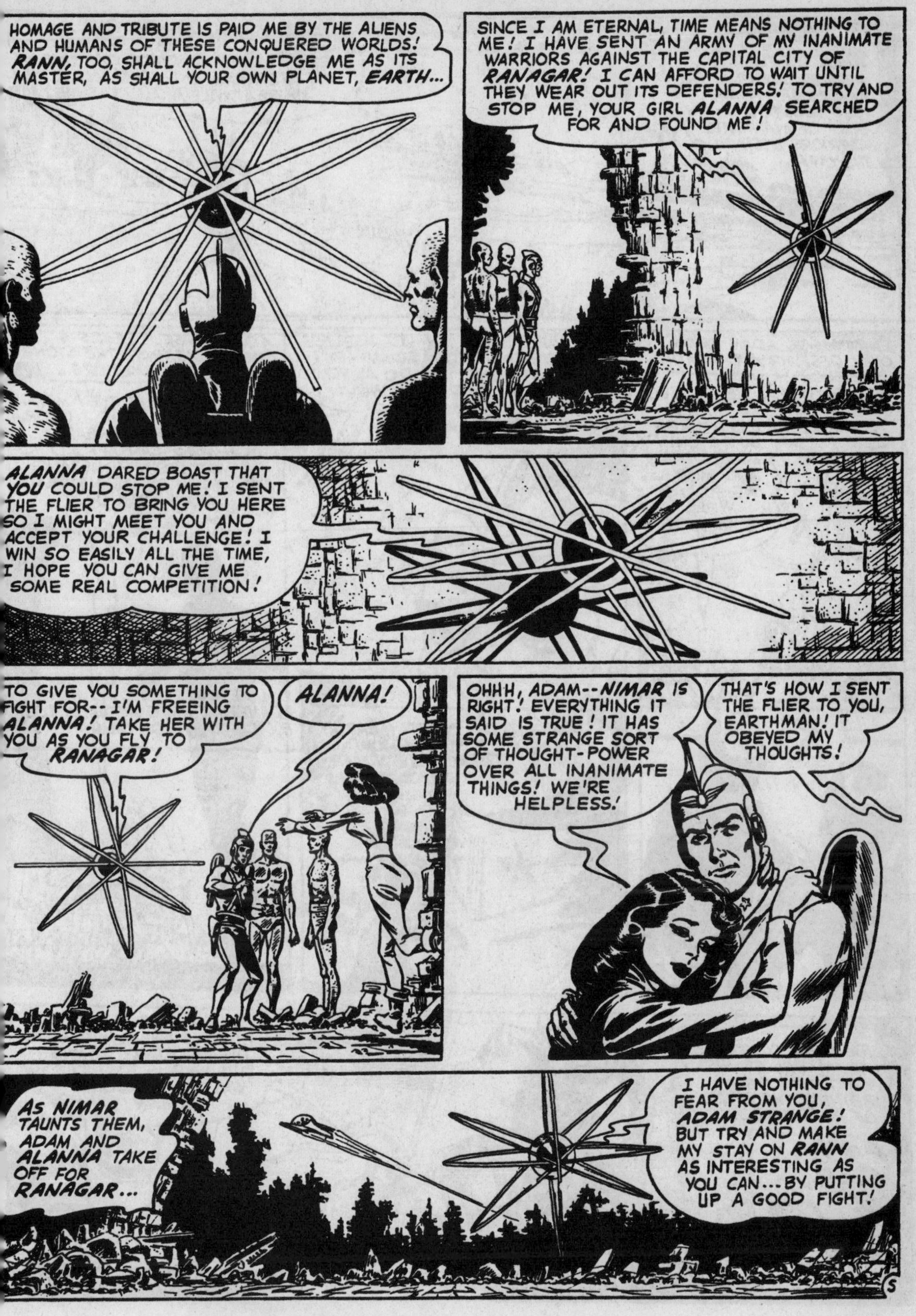
HOMAGE AND TRIBUTE IS PAID ME BY THE ALIENS AND HUMANS OF THESE CONQUERED WORLDS! RANN, TOO, SHALL ACKNOWLEDGE ME AS ITS MASTER, AS SHALL YOUR OWN PLANET, EARTH...
SINCE I AM ETERNAL, TIME MEANS NOTHING TO ME! I HAVE SENT AN ARMY OF MY INANIMATE WARRIORS AGAINST THE CAPITAL CITY OF RANAGAR! I CAN AFFORD TO WAIT UNTIL THEY WEAR OUT ITS DEFENDERS! TO TRY AND STOP ME, YOUR GIRL ALANNA SEARCHED FOR AND FOUND ME!
ALANNA DARED BOAST THAT YOU COULD STOP ME! I SENT THE FLIER TO BRING YOU HERE SO I MIGHT MEET YOU AND ACCEPT YOUR CHALLENGE! I WIN SO EASILY ALL THE TIME, I HOPE YOU CAN GIVE ME SOME REAL COMPETITION!
TO GIVE YOU SOMETHING TO FIGHT FOR-- I'M FREEING ALANNA! TAKE HER WITH YOU AS YOU FLY TO RANAGAR!
ALANNA!
OHHH, ADAM--NIMAR IS RIGHT! EVERYTHING IT SAID IS TRUE! IT HAS SOME STRANGE SORT OF THOUGHT-POWER OVER ALL INANIMATE THINGS! WE'RE HELPLESS!
THAT'S HOW I SENT THE FLIER TO YOU, EARTHMAN! IT OBEYED MY THOUGHTS!
AS NIMAR TAUNTS THEM, ADAM AND ALANNA TAKE OFF FOR RANAGAR...
I HAVE NOTHING TO FEAR FROM YOU, ADAM STRANGE! BUT TRY AND MAKE MY STAY ON RANN AS INTERESTING AS YOU CAN... BY PUTTING UP A GOOD FIGHT!
5

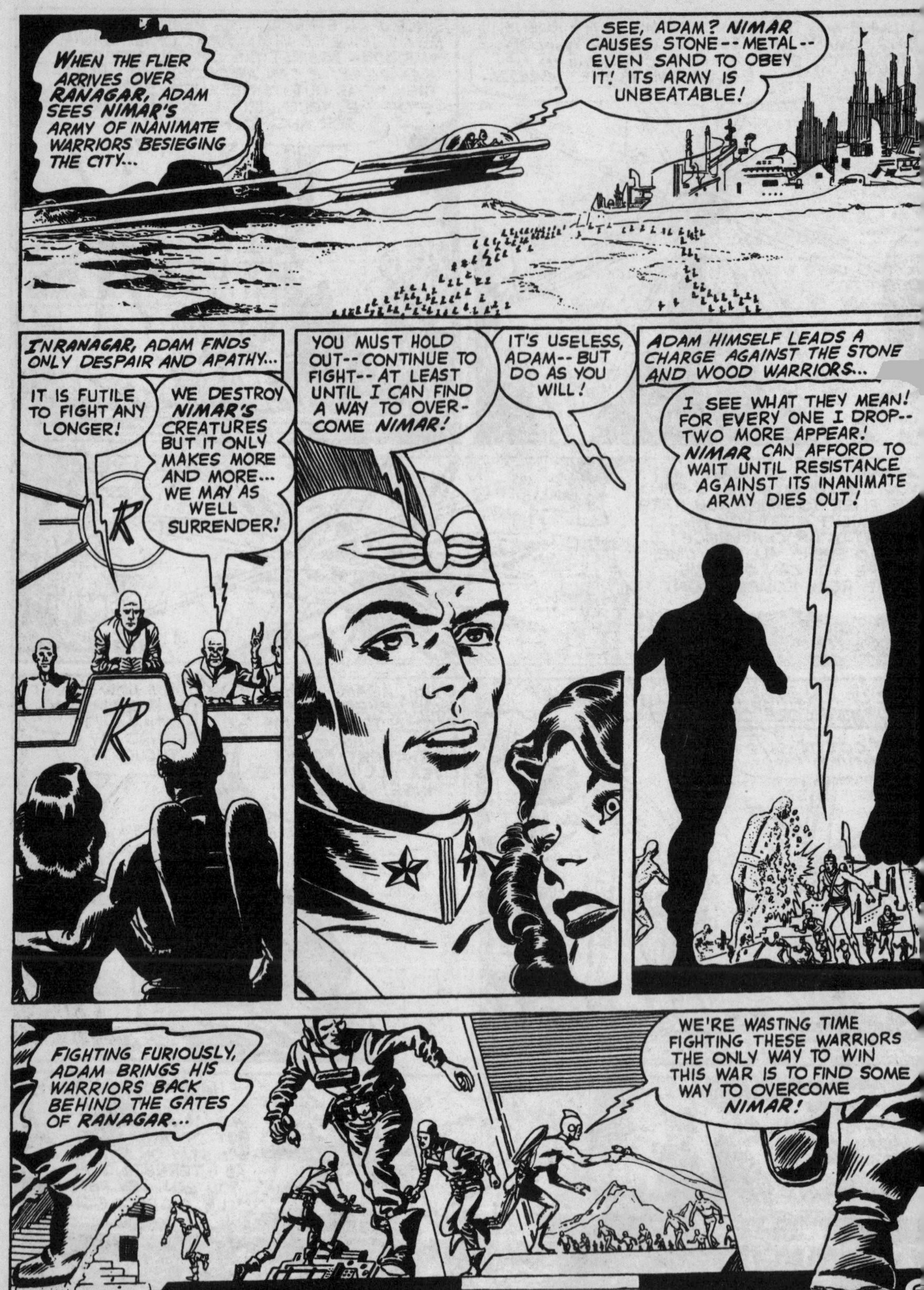
WHEN THE FLIER ARRIVES OVER RANAGAR, ADAM SEES NIMAR'S ARMY OF INANIMATE WARRIORS BESIEGING THE CITY...
SEE, ADAM? NIMAR CAUSES STONE--METAL--EVEN SAND TO OBEY IT! ITS ARMY IS UNBEATABLE!
IN RANAGAR, ADAM FINDS ONLY DESPAIR AND APATHY...
IT IS FUTILE TO FIGHT ANY LONGER!
WE DESTROY NIMAR'S CREATURES BUT IT ONLY MAKES MORE AND MORE... WE MAY AS WELL SURRENDER!
YOU MUST HOLD OUT--CONTINUE TO FIGHT--AT LEAST UNTIL I CAN FIND A WAY TO OVER-COME NIMAR!
IT'S USELESS, ADAM--BUT DO AS YOU WILL!
ADAM HIMSELF LEADS A CHARGE AGAINST THE STONE AND WOOD WARRIORS...
I SEE WHAT THEY MEAN! FOR EVERY ONE I DROP--TWO MORE APPEAR! NIMAR CAN AFFORD TO WAIT UNTIL RESISTANCE AGAINST ITS INANIMATE ARMY DIES OUT!
FIGHTING FURIOUSLY, ADAM BRINGS HIS WARRIORS BACK BEHIND THE GATES OF RANAGAR...
WE'RE WASTING TIME FIGHTING THESE WARRIORS THE ONLY WAY TO WIN THIS WAR IS TO FIND SOME WAY TO OVERCOME NIMAR!
6

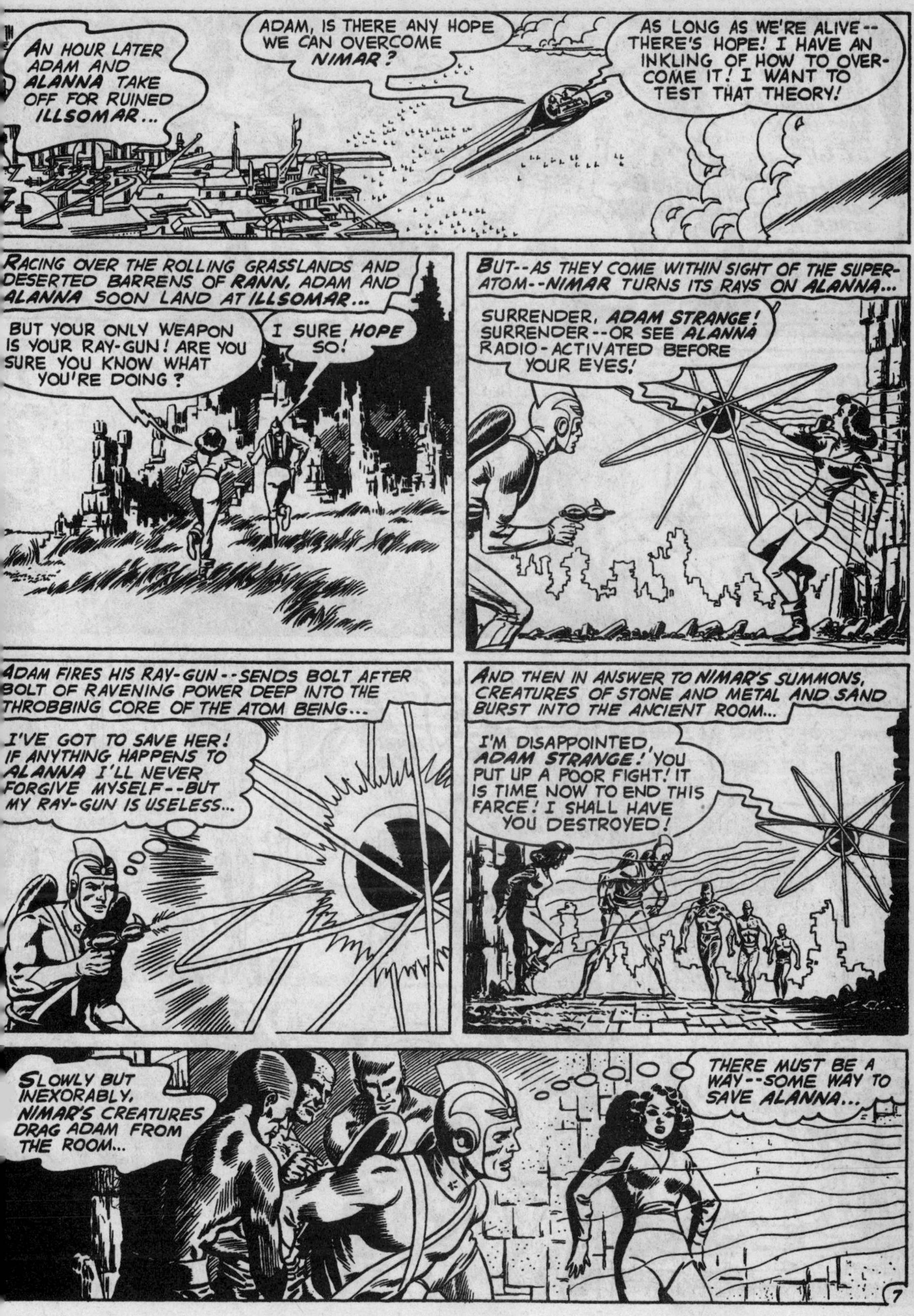
AN HOUR LATER ADAM AND ALANNA TAKE OFF FOR RUINED ILLSOMAR...
ADAM, IS THERE ANY HOPE WE CAN OVERCOME NIMAR?
AS LONG AS WE'RE ALIVE-- THERE'S HOPE! I HAVE AN INKLING OF HOW TO OVERCOME IT! I WANT TO TEST THAT THEORY!
RACING OVER THE ROLLING GRASSLANDS AND DESERTED BARRENS OF RANN, ADAM AND ALANNA SOON LAND AT ILLSOMAR...
BUT YOUR ONLY WEAPON IS YOUR RAY-GUN! ARE YOU SURE YOU KNOW WHAT YOU'RE DOING?
I SURE HOPE SO!
BUT--AS THEY COME WITHIN SIGHT OF THE SUPER-ATOM--NIMAR TURNS ITS RAYS ON ALANNA...
SURRENDER, ADAM STRANGE! SURRENDER--OR SEE ALANNA RADIO-ACTIVATED BEFORE YOUR EYES!
ADAM FIRES HIS RAY-GUN--SENDS BOLT AFTER BOLT OF RAVENING POWER DEEP INTO THE THROBBING CORE OF THE ATOM BEING...
I'VE GOT TO SAVE HER! IF ANYTHING HAPPENS TO ALANNA I'LL NEVER FORGIVE MYSELF--BUT MY RAY-GUN IS USELESS...
AND THEN IN ANSWER TO NIMAR'S SUMMONS, CREATURES OF STONE AND METAL AND SAND BURST INTO THE ANCIENT ROOM...
I'M DISAPPOINTED, ADAM STRANGE! YOU PUT UP A POOR FIGHT! IT IS TIME NOW TO END THIS FARCE! I SHALL HAVE YOU DESTROYED!
SLOWLY BUT INEXORABLY, NIMAR'S CREATURES DRAG ADAM FROM THE ROOM...
THERE MUST BE A WAY--SOME WAY TO SAVE ALANNA...
7

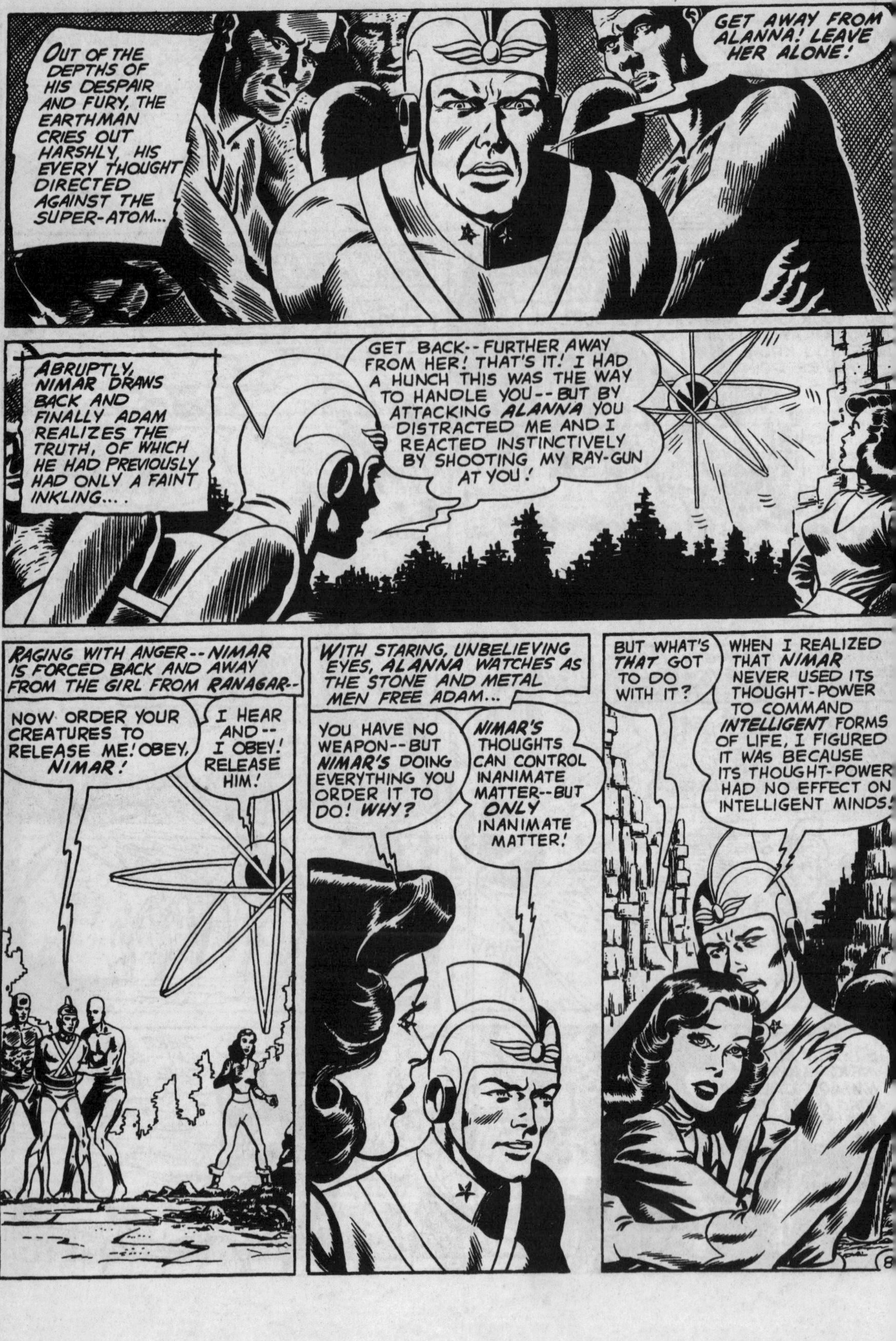
OUT OF THE DEPTHS OF HIS DESPAIR AND FURY, THE EARTHMAN CRIES OUT HARSHLY, HIS EVERY THOUGHT DIRECTED AGAINST THE SUPER-ATOM...
GET AWAY FROM ALANNA! LEAVE HER ALONE!
ABRUPTLY, NIMAR DRAWS BACK AND FINALLY ADAM REALIZES THE TRUTH, OF WHICH HE HAD PREVIOUSLY HAD ONLY A FAINT INKLING....
GET BACK--FURTHER AWAY FROM HER! THAT'S IT! I HAD A HUNCH THIS WAS THE WAY TO HANDLE YOU--BUT BY ATTACKING ALANNA YOU DISTRACTED ME AND I REACTED INSTINCTIVELY BY SHOOTING MY RAY-GUN AT YOU!
RAGING WITH ANGER--NIMAR IS FORCED BACK AND AWAY FROM THE GIRL FROM RANAGAR--
NOW ORDER YOUR CREATURES TO RELEASE ME! OBEY, NIMAR!
I HEAR AND--I OBEY! RELEASE HIM!
WITH STARING, UNBELIEVING EYES, ALANNA WATCHES AS THE STONE AND METAL MEN FREE ADAM...
YOU HAVE NO WEAPON--BUT NIMAR'S DOING EVERYTHING YOU ORDER IT TO DO! WHY?
NIMAR'S THOUGHTS CAN CONTROL INANIMATE MATTER--BUT ONLY INANIMATE MATTER!
BUT WHAT'S THAT GOT TO DO WITH IT?
WHEN I REALIZED THAT NIMAR NEVER USED ITS THOUGHT-POWER TO COMMAND INTELLIGENT FORMS OF LIFE, I FIGURED IT WAS BECAUSE ITS THOUGHT-POWER HAD NO EFFECT ON INTELLIGENT MINDS!
8

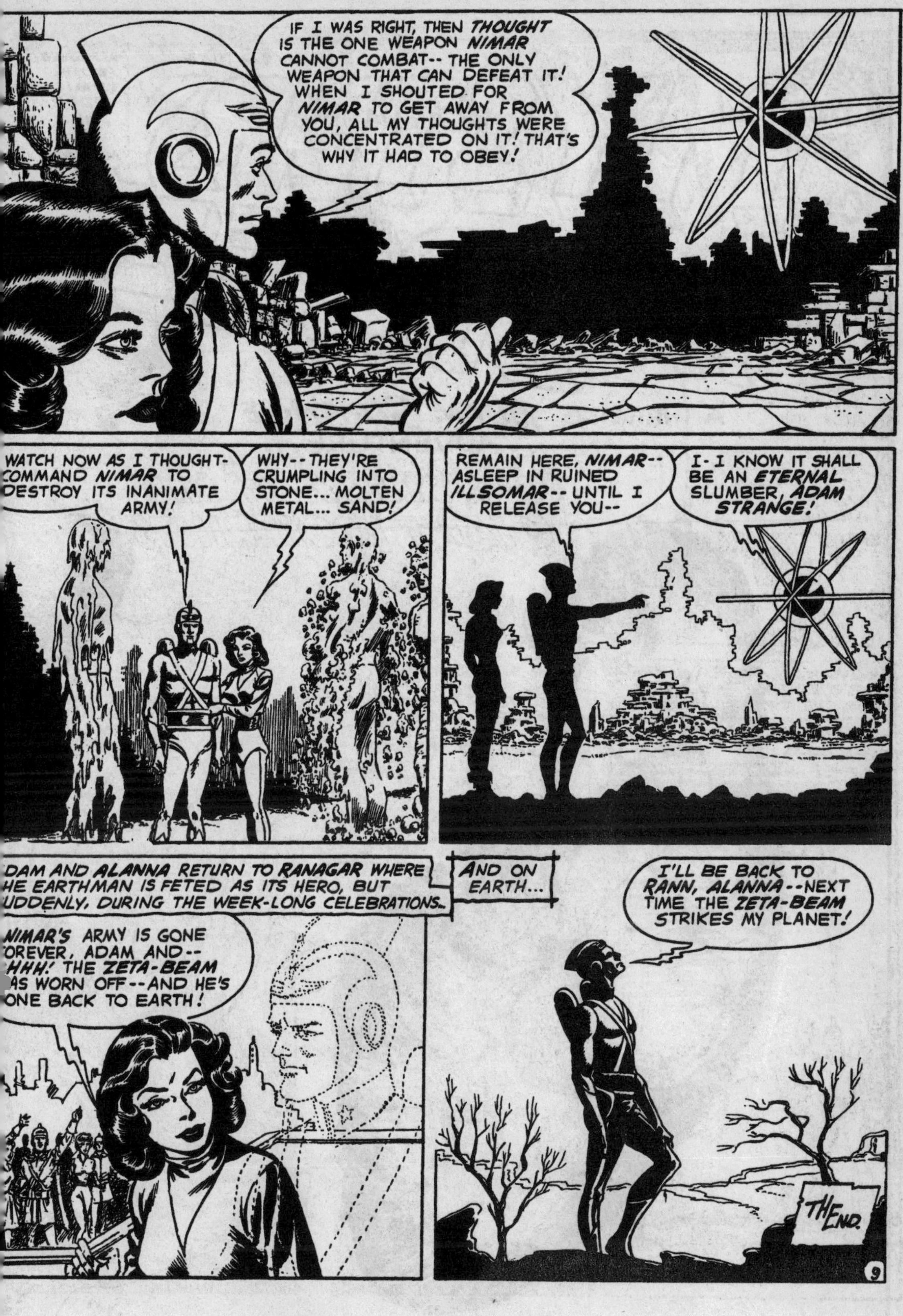
IF I WAS RIGHT, THEN THOUGHT IS THE ONE WEAPON NIMAR CANNOT COMBAT-- THE ONLY WEAPON THAT CAN DEFEAT IT! WHEN I SHOUTED FOR NIMAR TO GET AWAY FROM YOU, ALL MY THOUGHTS WERE CONCENTRATED ON IT! THAT'S WHY IT HAD TO OBEY!
WATCH NOW AS I THOUGHT-COMMAND NIMAR TO DESTROY ITS INANIMATE ARMY!
WHY--THEY'RE CRUMPLING INTO STONE... MOLTEN METAL... SAND!
REMAIN HERE, NIMAR-- ASLEEP IN RUINED ILLSOMAR-- UNTIL I RELEASE YOU--
I-I KNOW IT SHALL BE AN ETERNAL SLUMBER, ADAM STRANGE!
DAM AND ALANNA RETURN TO RANAGAR WHERE HE EARTHMAN IS FETED AS ITS HERO, BUT UDDENLY, DURING THE WEEK-LONG CELEBRATIONS..
NIMAR'S ARMY IS GONE OREVER, ADAM AND-- HHH! THE ZETA-BEAM AS WORN OFF--AND HE'S ONE BACK TO EARTH!
AND ON EARTH...
I'LL BE BACK TO RANN, ALANNA--NEXT TIME THE ZETA-BEAM STRIKES MY PLANET!
THE END.
9

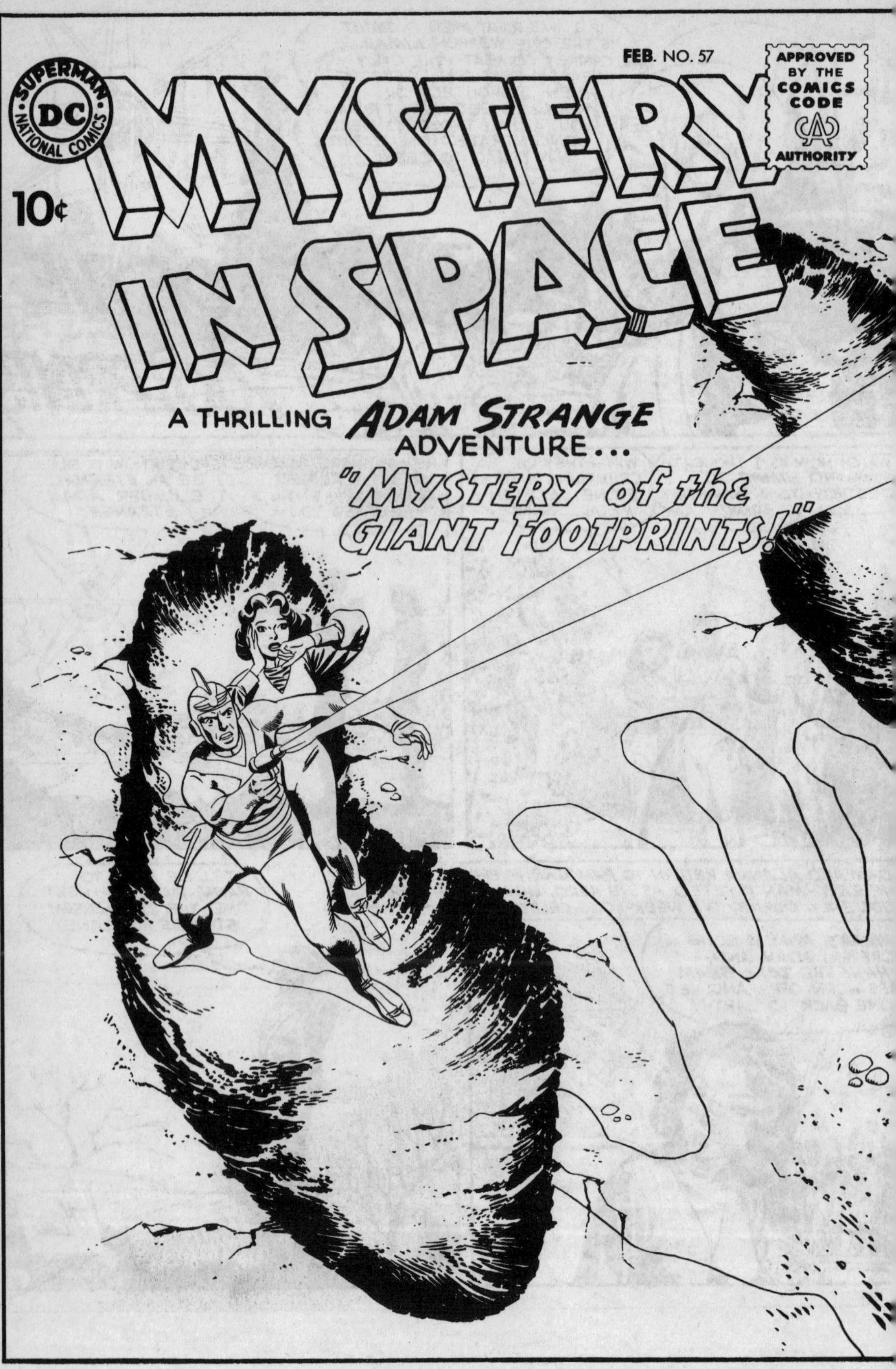
SUPERMAN DC NATIONAL COMICS
10¢
FEB. NO. 57
APPROVED BY THE COMICS CODE AUTHORITY
MYSTERY IN SPACE
A THRILLING ADAM STRANGE ADVENTURE...
"MYSTERY of the GIANT FOOTPRINTS!"

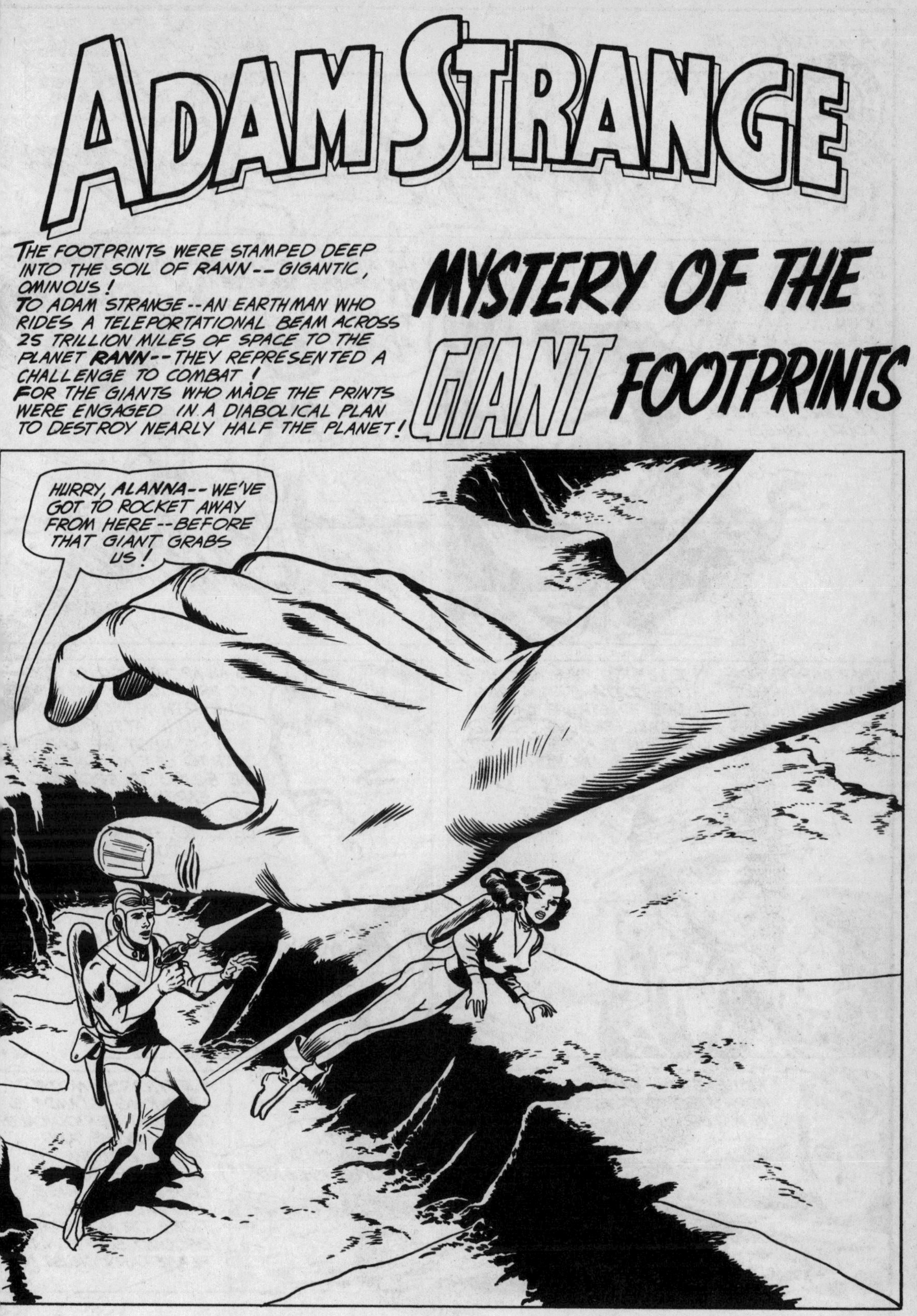
ADAM STRANGE
THE FOOTPRINTS WERE STAMPED DEEP INTO THE SOIL OF RANN-- GIGANTIC, OMINOUS!
TO ADAM STRANGE--AN EARTHMAN WHO RIDES A TELEPORTATIONAL BEAM ACROSS 25 TRILLION MILES OF SPACE TO THE PLANET RANN--THEY REPRESENTED A CHALLENGE TO COMBAT!
FOR THE GIANTS WHO MADE THE PRINTS WERE ENGAGED IN A DIABOLICAL PLAN TO DESTROY NEARLY HALF THE PLANET!
MYSTERY OF THE GIANT FOOTPRINTS
HURRY, ALANNA-- WE'VE GOT TO ROCKET AWAY FROM HERE--BEFORE THAT GIANT GRABS US!

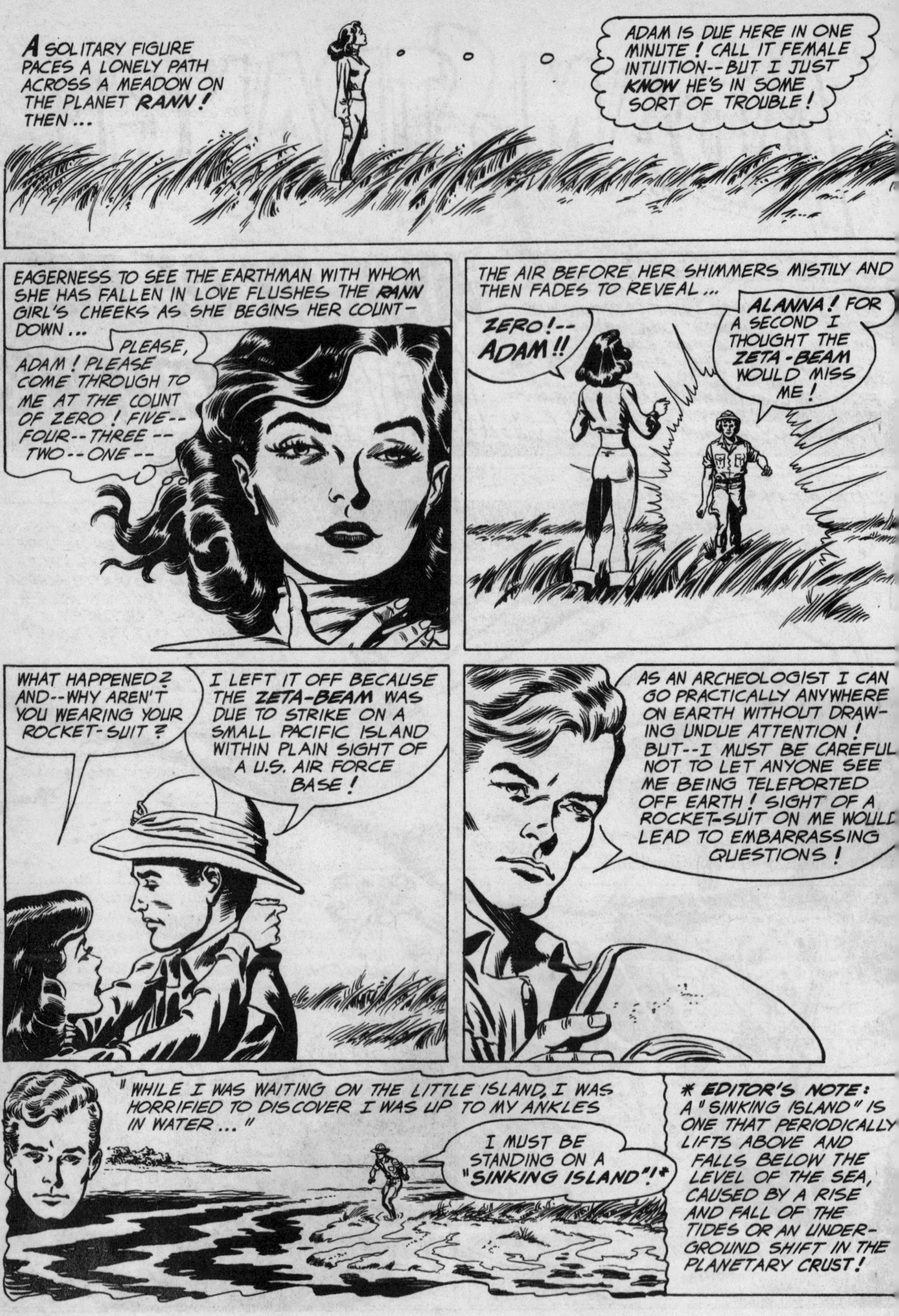
A SOLITARY FIGURE PACES A LONELY PATH ACROSS A MEADOW ON THE PLANET RANN! THEN ...
ADAM IS DUE HERE IN ONE MINUTE! CALL IT FEMALE INTUITION--BUT I JUST KNOW HE'S IN SOME SORT OF TROUBLE!
EAGERNESS TO SEE THE EARTHMAN WITH WHOM SHE HAS FALLEN IN LOVE FLUSHES THE RANN GIRL'S CHEEKS AS SHE BEGINS HER COUNT-DOWN...
PLEASE, ADAM! PLEASE COME THROUGH TO ME AT THE COUNT OF ZERO! FIVE--FOUR--THREE--TWO--ONE--
THE AIR BEFORE HER SHIMMERS MISTILY AND THEN FADES TO REVEAL...
ZERO!--ADAM!!
ALANNA! FOR A SECOND I THOUGHT THE ZETA-BEAM WOULD MISS ME!
WHAT HAPPENED? AND--WHY AREN'T YOU WEARING YOUR ROCKET-SUIT?
I LEFT IT OFF BECAUSE THE ZETA-BEAM WAS DUE TO STRIKE ON A SMALL PACIFIC ISLAND WITHIN PLAIN SIGHT OF A U.S. AIR FORCE BASE!
AS AN ARCHEOLOGIST I CAN GO PRACTICALLY ANYWHERE ON EARTH WITHOUT DRAWING UNDUE ATTENTION! BUT--I MUST BE CAREFUL NOT TO LET ANYONE SEE ME BEING TELEPORTED OFF EARTH! SIGHT OF A ROCKET-SUIT ON ME WOULD LEAD TO EMBARRASSING QUESTIONS!
"WHILE I WAS WAITING ON THE LITTLE ISLAND, I WAS HORRIFIED TO DISCOVER I WAS UP TO MY ANKLES IN WATER..."
I MUST BE STANDING ON A "SINKING ISLAND"!*
* EDITOR'S NOTE: A "SINKING ISLAND" IS ONE THAT PERIODICALLY LIFTS ABOVE AND FALLS BELOW THE LEVEL OF THE SEA, CAUSED BY A RISE AND FALL OF THE TIDES OR AN UNDERGROUND SHIFT IN THE PLANETARY CRUST!

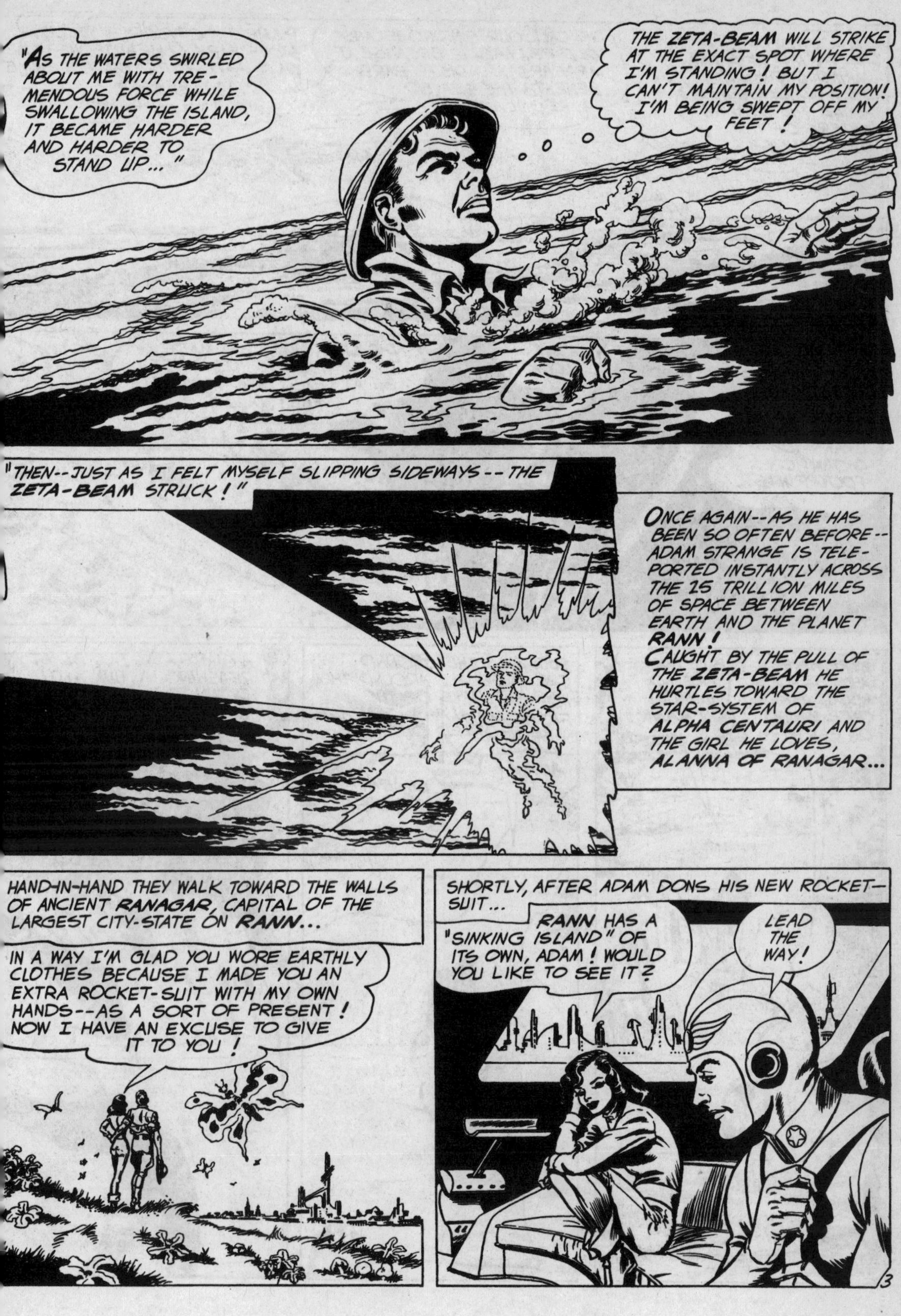
"AS THE WATERS SWIRLED ABOUT ME WITH TRE-MENDOUS FORCE WHILE SWALLOWING THE ISLAND, IT BECAME HARDER AND HARDER TO STAND UP..."
THE ZETA-BEAM WILL STRIKE AT THE EXACT SPOT WHERE I'M STANDING! BUT I CAN'T MAINTAIN MY POSITION! I'M BEING SWEPT OFF MY FEET!
"THEN--JUST AS I FELT MYSELF SLIPPING SIDEWAYS--THE ZETA-BEAM STRUCK!"
ONCE AGAIN--AS HE HAS BEEN SO OFTEN BEFORE--ADAM STRANGE IS TELE-PORTED INSTANTLY ACROSS THE 25 TRILLION MILES OF SPACE BETWEEN EARTH AND THE PLANET RANN! CAUGHT BY THE PULL OF THE ZETA-BEAM HE HURTLES TOWARD THE STAR-SYSTEM OF ALPHA CENTAURI AND THE GIRL HE LOVES, ALANNA OF RANAGAR...
HAND-IN-HAND THEY WALK TOWARD THE WALLS OF ANCIENT RANAGAR, CAPITAL OF THE LARGEST CITY-STATE ON RANN...
IN A WAY I'M GLAD YOU WORE EARTHLY CLOTHES BECAUSE I MADE YOU AN EXTRA ROCKET-SUIT WITH MY OWN HANDS--AS A SORT OF PRESENT! NOW I HAVE AN EXCUSE TO GIVE IT TO YOU!
SHORTLY, AFTER ADAM DONS HIS NEW ROCKET-SUIT...
RANN HAS A "SINKING ISLAND" OF ITS OWN, ADAM! WOULD YOU LIKE TO SEE IT?
LEAD THE WAY!
3

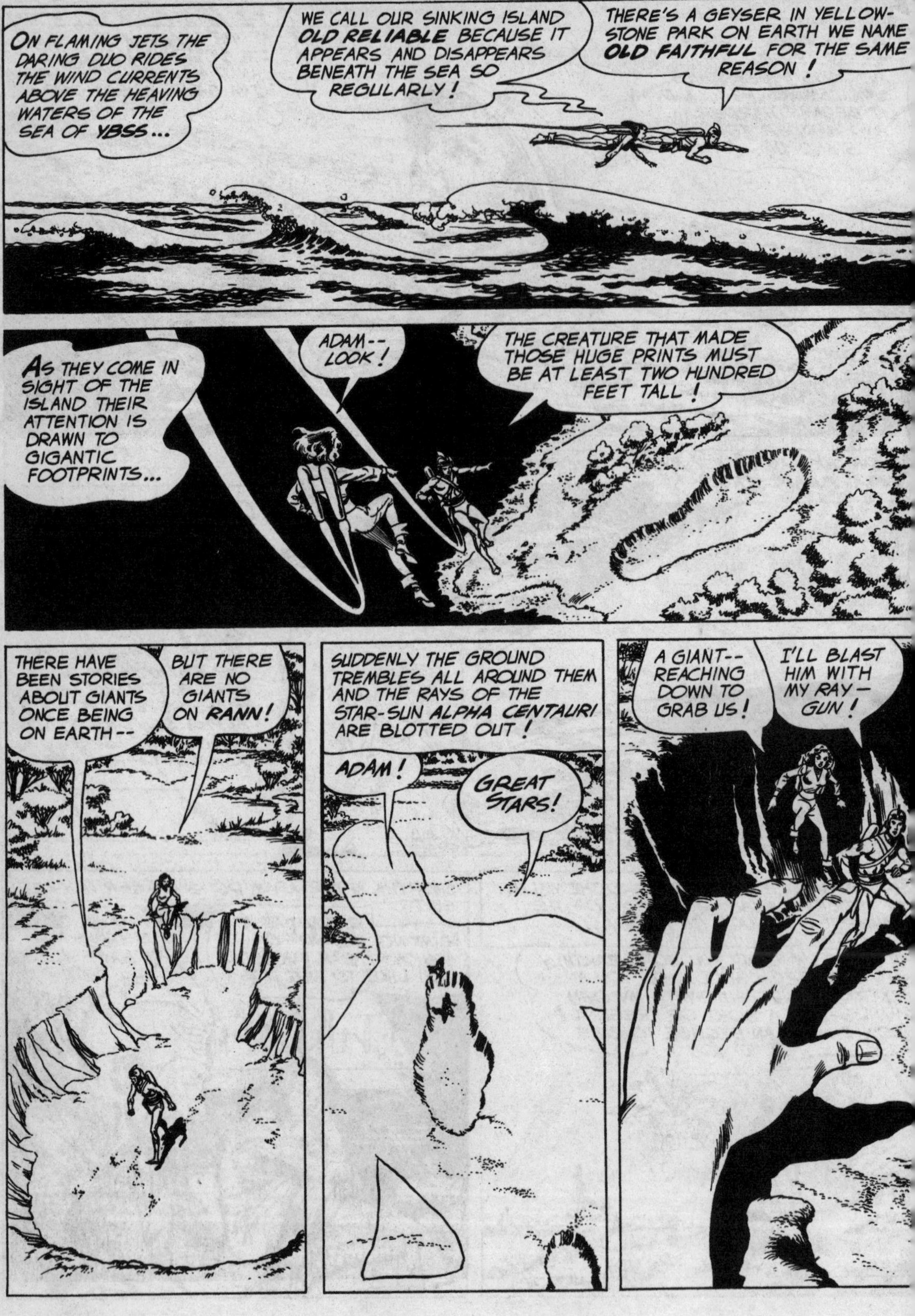
ON FLAMING JETS THE DARING DUO RIDES THE WIND CURRENTS ABOVE THE HEAVING WATERS OF THE SEA OF YBSS...
WE CALL OUR SINKING ISLAND OLD RELIABLE BECAUSE IT APPEARS AND DISAPPEARS BENEATH THE SEA SO REGULARLY!
THERE'S A GEYSER IN YELLOWSTONE PARK ON EARTH WE NAME OLD FAITHFUL FOR THE SAME REASON!
AS THEY COME IN SIGHT OF THE ISLAND THEIR ATTENTION IS DRAWN TO GIGANTIC FOOTPRINTS...
ADAM-- LOOK!
THE CREATURE THAT MADE THOSE HUGE PRINTS MUST BE AT LEAST TWO HUNDRED FEET TALL!
THERE HAVE BEEN STORIES ABOUT GIANTS ONCE BEING ON EARTH--
BUT THERE ARE NO GIANTS ON RANN!
SUDDENLY THE GROUND TREMBLES ALL AROUND THEM AND THE RAYS OF THE STAR-SUN ALPHA CENTAURI ARE BLOTTED OUT!
ADAM!
GREAT STARS!
A GIANT-- REACHING DOWN TO GRAB US!
I'LL BLAST HIM WITH MY RAY-GUN!

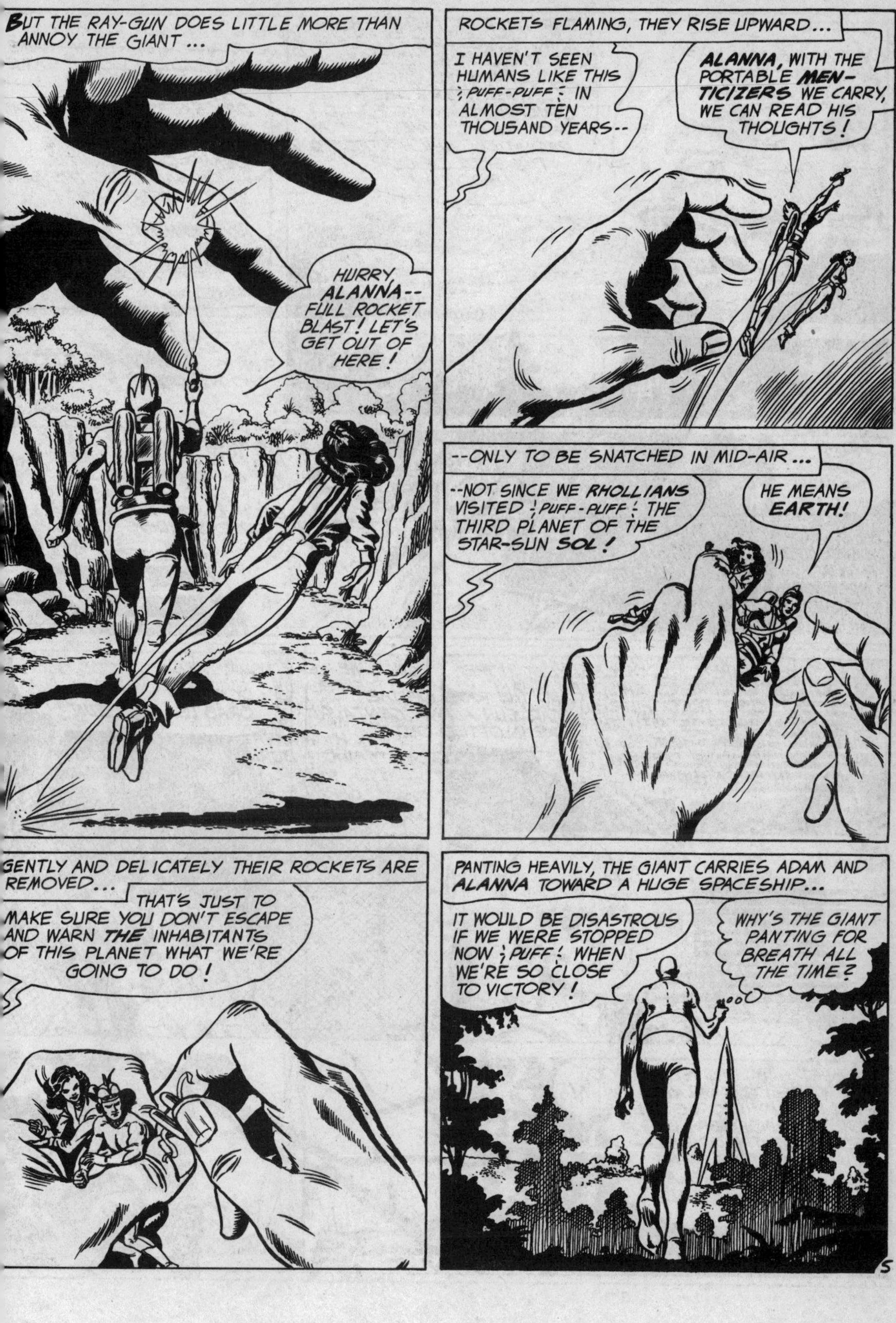
BUT THE RAY-GUN DOES LITTLE MORE THAN ANNOY THE GIANT ...
HURRY, ALANNA-- FULL ROCKET BLAST! LET'S GET OUT OF HERE!
ROCKETS FLAMING, THEY RISE UPWARD ...
I HAVEN'T SEEN HUMANS LIKE THIS ;PUFF-PUFF; IN ALMOST TEN THOUSAND YEARS--
ALANNA, WITH THE PORTABLE MENTICIZERS WE CARRY, WE CAN READ HIS THOUGHTS!
--ONLY TO BE SNATCHED IN MID-AIR ...
--NOT SINCE WE RHOLLIANS VISITED ;PUFF-PUFF; THE THIRD PLANET OF THE STAR-SUN SOL!
HE MEANS EARTH!
GENTLY AND DELICATELY THEIR ROCKETS ARE REMOVED ...
THAT'S JUST TO MAKE SURE YOU DON'T ESCAPE AND WARN THE INHABITANTS OF THIS PLANET WHAT WE'RE GOING TO DO!
PANTING HEAVILY, THE GIANT CARRIES ADAM AND ALANNA TOWARD A HUGE SPACESHIP ...
IT WOULD BE DISASTROUS IF WE WERE STOPPED NOW ;PUFF; WHEN WE'RE SO CLOSE TO VICTORY!
WHY'S THE GIANT PANTING FOR BREATH ALL THE TIME?
5

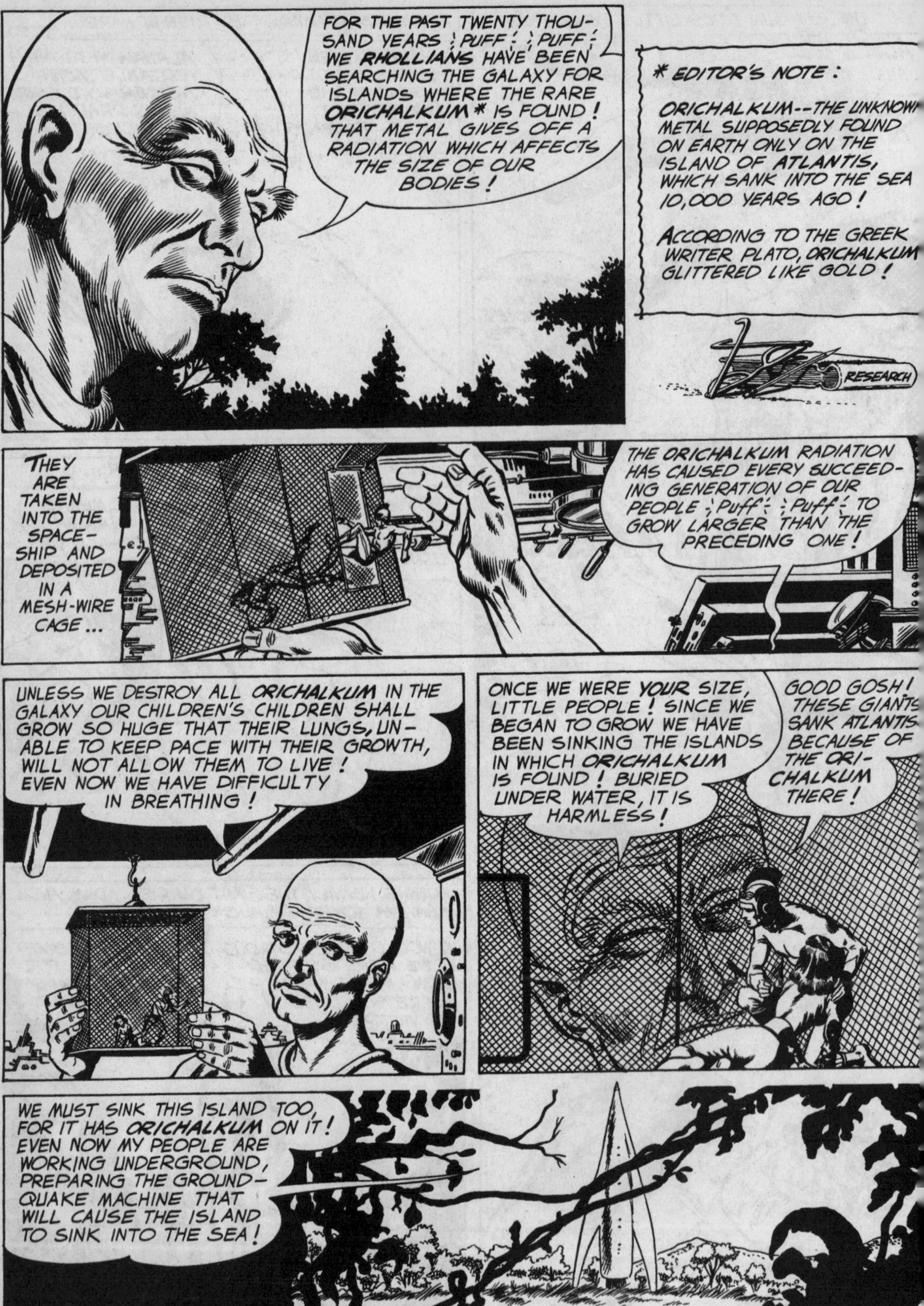
FOR THE PAST TWENTY THOUSAND YEARS -PUFF!- -PUFF!- WE RHOLLIANS HAVE BEEN SEARCHING THE GALAXY FOR ISLANDS WHERE THE RARE ORICHALKUM* IS FOUND! THAT METAL GIVES OFF A RADIATION WHICH AFFECTS THE SIZE OF OUR BODIES!
* EDITOR'S NOTE: ORICHALKUM--THE UNKNOWN METAL SUPPOSEDLY FOUND ON EARTH ONLY ON THE ISLAND OF ATLANTIS, WHICH SANK INTO THE SEA 10,000 YEARS AGO! ACCORDING TO THE GREEK WRITER PLATO, ORICHALKUM GLITTERED LIKE GOLD!
RESEARCH
THEY ARE TAKEN INTO THE SPACE-SHIP AND DEPOSITED IN A MESH-WIRE CAGE...
THE ORICHALKUM RADIATION HAS CAUSED EVERY SUCCEEDING GENERATION OF OUR PEOPLE -PUFF!- -PUFF!- TO GROW LARGER THAN THE PRECEDING ONE!
UNLESS WE DESTROY ALL ORICHALKUM IN THE GALAXY OUR CHILDREN'S CHILDREN SHALL GROW SO HUGE THAT THEIR LUNGS, UNABLE TO KEEP PACE WITH THEIR GROWTH, WILL NOT ALLOW THEM TO LIVE! EVEN NOW WE HAVE DIFFICULTY IN BREATHING!
ONCE WE WERE YOUR SIZE, LITTLE PEOPLE! SINCE WE BEGAN TO GROW WE HAVE BEEN SINKING THE ISLANDS IN WHICH ORICHALKUM IS FOUND! BURIED UNDER WATER, IT IS HARMLESS!
GOOD GOSH! THESE GIANTS SANK ATLANTIS BECAUSE OF THE ORICHALKUM THERE!
WE MUST SINK THIS ISLAND TOO, FOR IT HAS ORICHALKUM ON IT! EVEN NOW MY PEOPLE ARE WORKING UNDERGROUND, PREPARING THE GROUND-QUAKE MACHINE THAT WILL CAUSE THE ISLAND TO SINK INTO THE SEA!

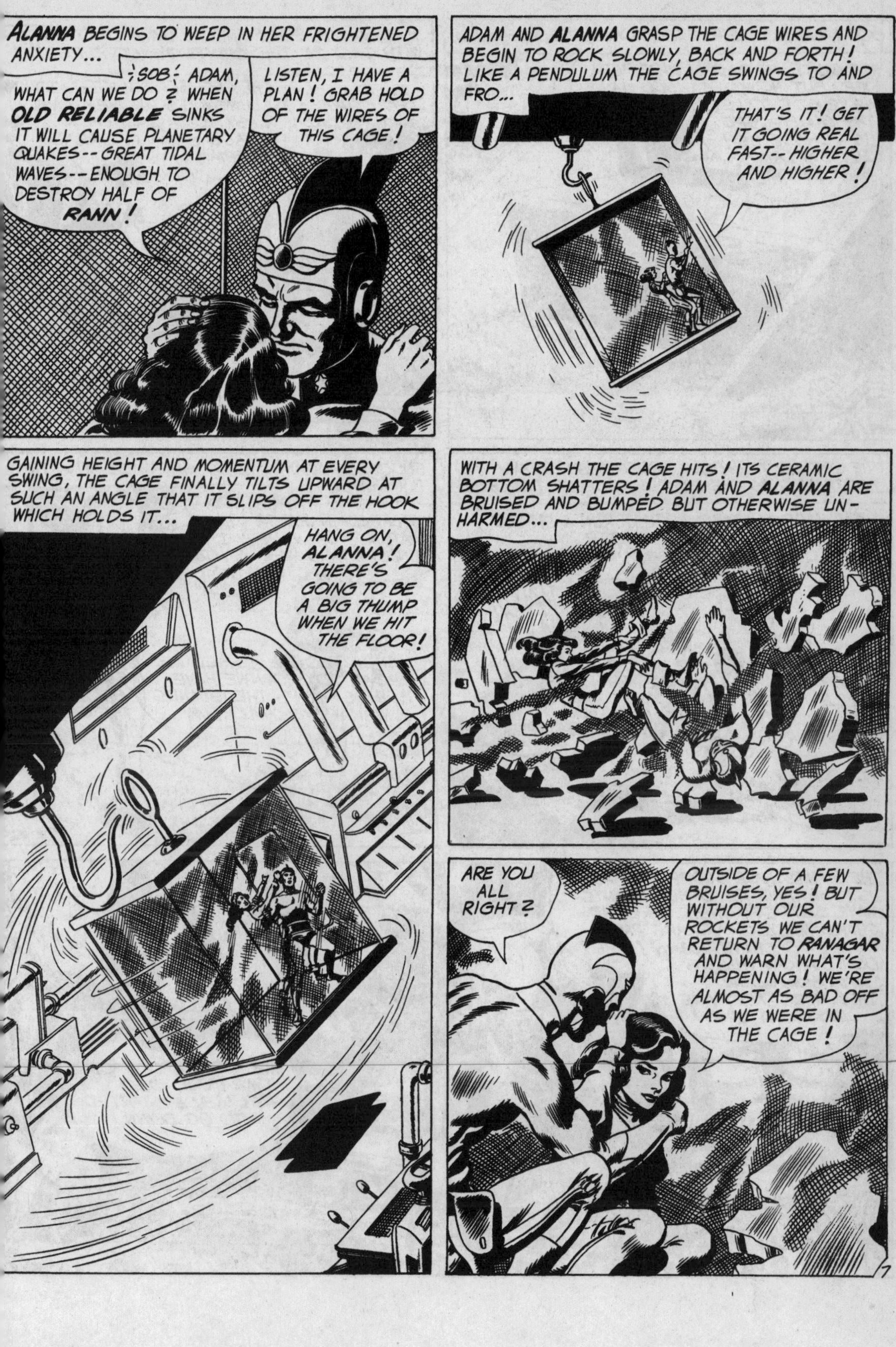
ALANNA BEGINS TO WEEP IN HER FRIGHTENED ANXIETY...
;SOB; ADAM, WHAT CAN WE DO ? WHEN OLD RELIABLE SINKS IT WILL CAUSE PLANETARY QUAKES--GREAT TIDAL WAVES--ENOUGH TO DESTROY HALF OF RANN!
LISTEN, I HAVE A PLAN! GRAB HOLD OF THE WIRES OF THIS CAGE!
ADAM AND ALANNA GRASP THE CAGE WIRES AND BEGIN TO ROCK SLOWLY, BACK AND FORTH! LIKE A PENDULUM THE CAGE SWINGS TO AND FRO...
THAT'S IT! GET IT GOING REAL FAST--HIGHER AND HIGHER!
GAINING HEIGHT AND MOMENTUM AT EVERY SWING, THE CAGE FINALLY TILTS UPWARD AT SUCH AN ANGLE THAT IT SLIPS OFF THE HOOK WHICH HOLDS IT...
HANG ON, ALANNA! THERE'S GOING TO BE A BIG THUMP WHEN WE HIT THE FLOOR!
WITH A CRASH THE CAGE HITS! ITS CERAMIC BOTTOM SHATTERS! ADAM AND ALANNA ARE BRUISED AND BUMPED BUT OTHERWISE UN-HARMED...
ARE YOU ALL RIGHT ?
OUTSIDE OF A FEW BRUISES, YES! BUT WITHOUT OUR ROCKETS WE CAN'T RETURN TO RANAGAR AND WARN WHAT'S HAPPENING! WE'RE ALMOST AS BAD OFF AS WE WERE IN THE CAGE!
7

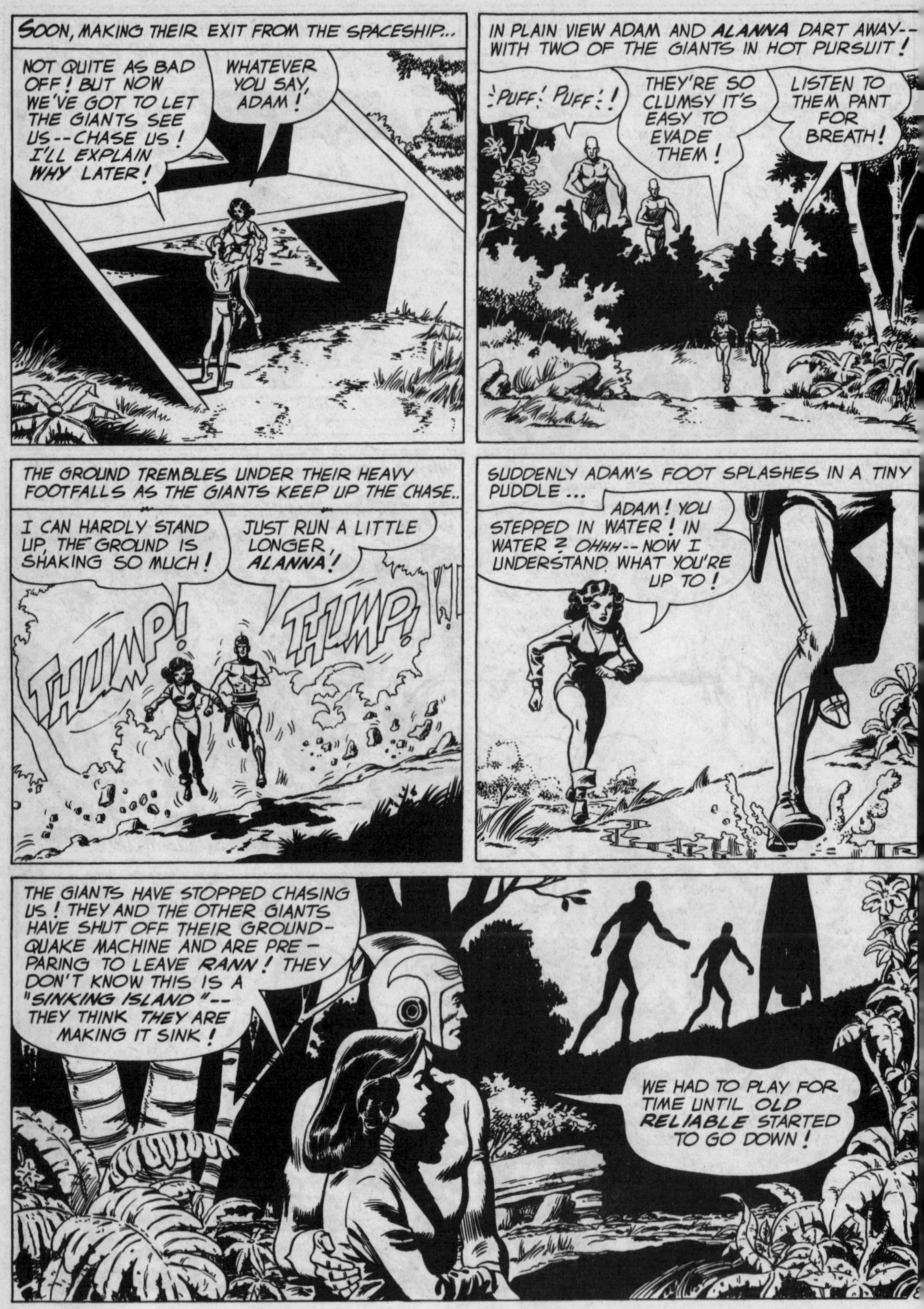
SOON, MAKING THEIR EXIT FROM THE SPACESHIP...
NOT QUITE AS BAD OFF! BUT NOW WE'VE GOT TO LET THE GIANTS SEE US--CHASE US! I'LL EXPLAIN WHY LATER!
WHATEVER YOU SAY, ADAM!
IN PLAIN VIEW ADAM AND ALANNA DART AWAY--WITH TWO OF THE GIANTS IN HOT PURSUIT!
PUFF! PUFF!
THEY'RE SO CLUMSY IT'S EASY TO EVADE THEM!
LISTEN TO THEM PANT FOR BREATH!
THE GROUND TREMBLES UNDER THEIR HEAVY FOOTFALLS AS THE GIANTS KEEP UP THE CHASE..
I CAN HARDLY STAND UP, THE GROUND IS SHAKING SO MUCH!
JUST RUN A LITTLE LONGER, ALANNA!
THUMP!
THUMP!
SUDDENLY ADAM'S FOOT SPLASHES IN A TINY PUDDLE...
ADAM! YOU STEPPED IN WATER! IN WATER? OHHH--NOW I UNDERSTAND WHAT YOU'RE UP TO!
THE GIANTS HAVE STOPPED CHASING US! THEY AND THE OTHER GIANTS HAVE SHUT OFF THEIR GROUND-QUAKE MACHINE AND ARE PRE-PARING TO LEAVE RANN! THEY DON'T KNOW THIS IS A "SINKING ISLAND"--THEY THINK THEY ARE MAKING IT SINK!
WE HAD TO PLAY FOR TIME UNTIL OLD RELIABLE STARTED TO GO DOWN!

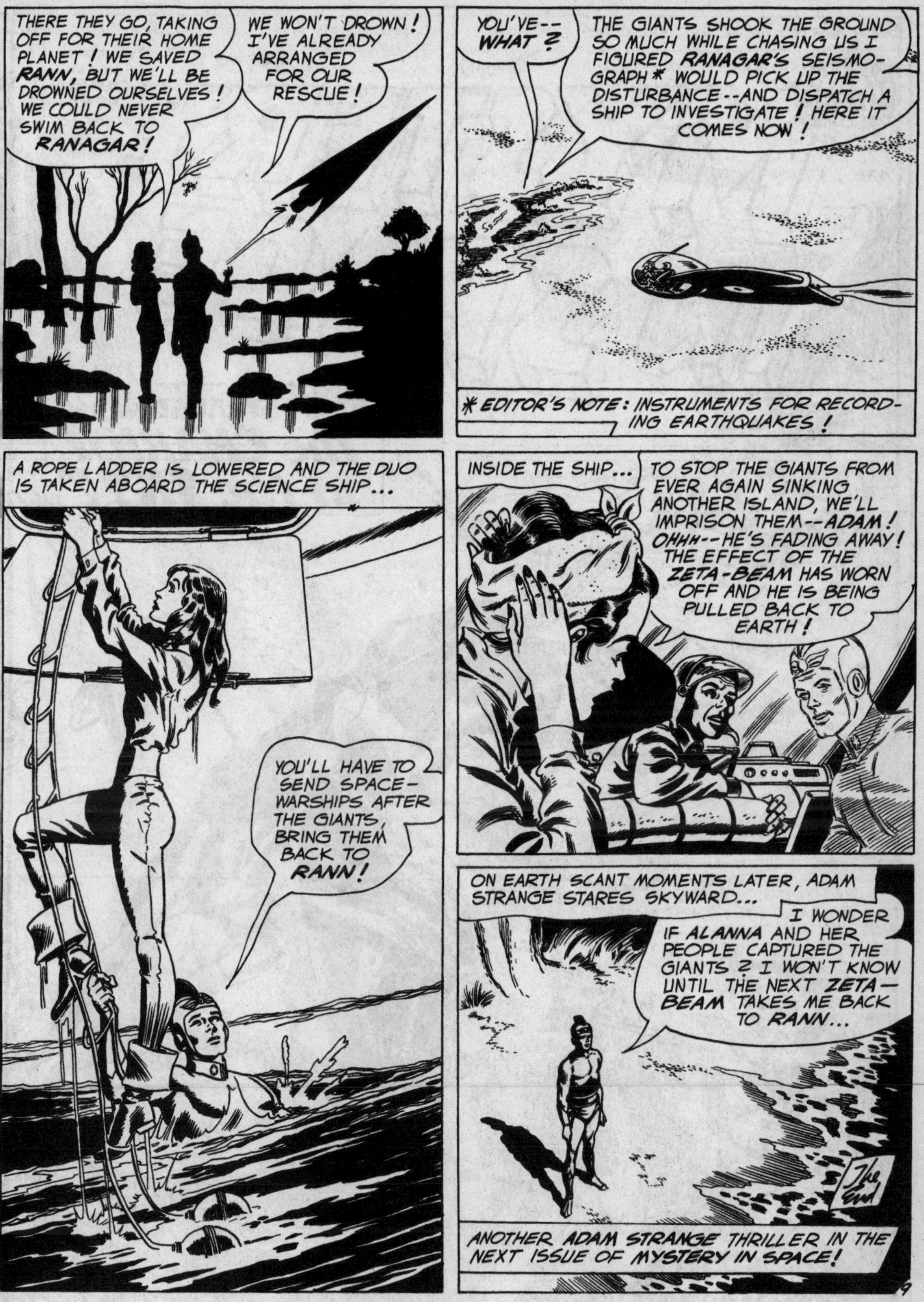
THERE THEY GO, TAKING OFF FOR THEIR HOME PLANET! WE SAVED RANN, BUT WE'LL BE DROWNED OURSELVES! WE COULD NEVER SWIM BACK TO RANAGAR!
WE WON'T DROWN! I'VE ALREADY ARRANGED FOR OUR RESCUE!
YOU'VE-- WHAT?
THE GIANTS SHOOK THE GROUND SO MUCH WHILE CHASING US I FIGURED RANAGAR'S SEISMOGRAPH* WOULD PICK UP THE DISTURBANCE--AND DISPATCH A SHIP TO INVESTIGATE! HERE IT COMES NOW!
*EDITOR'S NOTE: INSTRUMENTS FOR RECORDING EARTHQUAKES!
A ROPE LADDER IS LOWERED AND THE DUO IS TAKEN ABOARD THE SCIENCE SHIP...
YOU'LL HAVE TO SEND SPACE-WARSHIPS AFTER THE GIANTS, BRING THEM BACK TO RANN!
INSIDE THE SHIP...
TO STOP THE GIANTS FROM EVER AGAIN SINKING ANOTHER ISLAND, WE'LL IMPRISON THEM--ADAM! OHHH--HE'S FADING AWAY! THE EFFECT OF THE ZETA-BEAM HAS WORN OFF AND HE IS BEING PULLED BACK TO EARTH!
ON EARTH SCANT MOMENTS LATER, ADAM STRANGE STARES SKYWARD...
I WONDER IF ALANNA AND HER PEOPLE CAPTURED THE GIANTS? I WON'T KNOW UNTIL THE NEXT ZETA-BEAM TAKES ME BACK TO RANN...
The End
ANOTHER ADAM STRANGE THRILLER IN THE NEXT ISSUE OF MYSTERY IN SPACE!
9

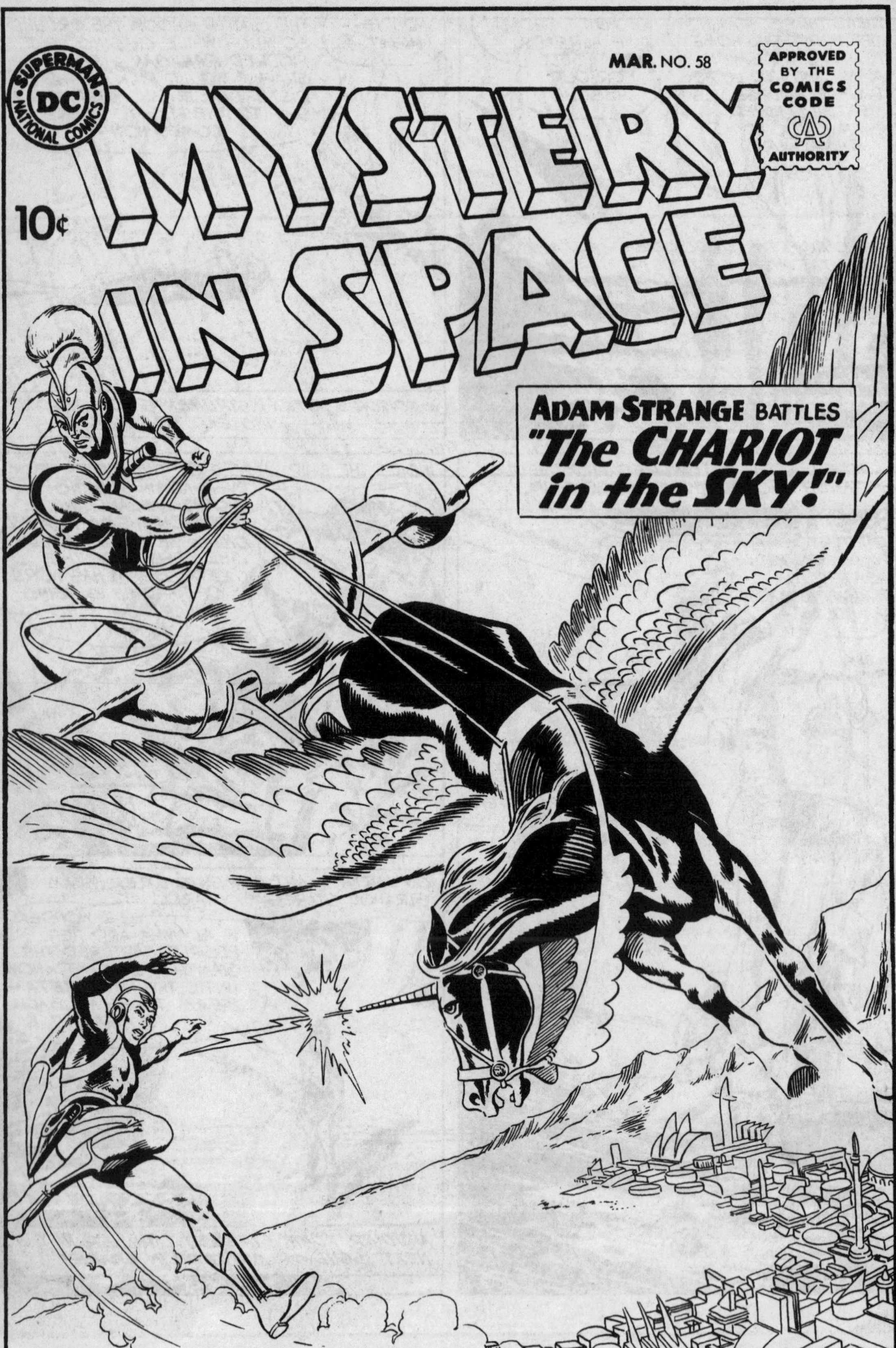
SUPERMAN
DC
NATIONAL COMICS
MAR. NO. 58
APPROVED BY THE COMICS CODE AUTHORITY
10¢
MYSTERY IN SPACE
ADAM STRANGE BATTLES "The CHARIOT in the SKY!"

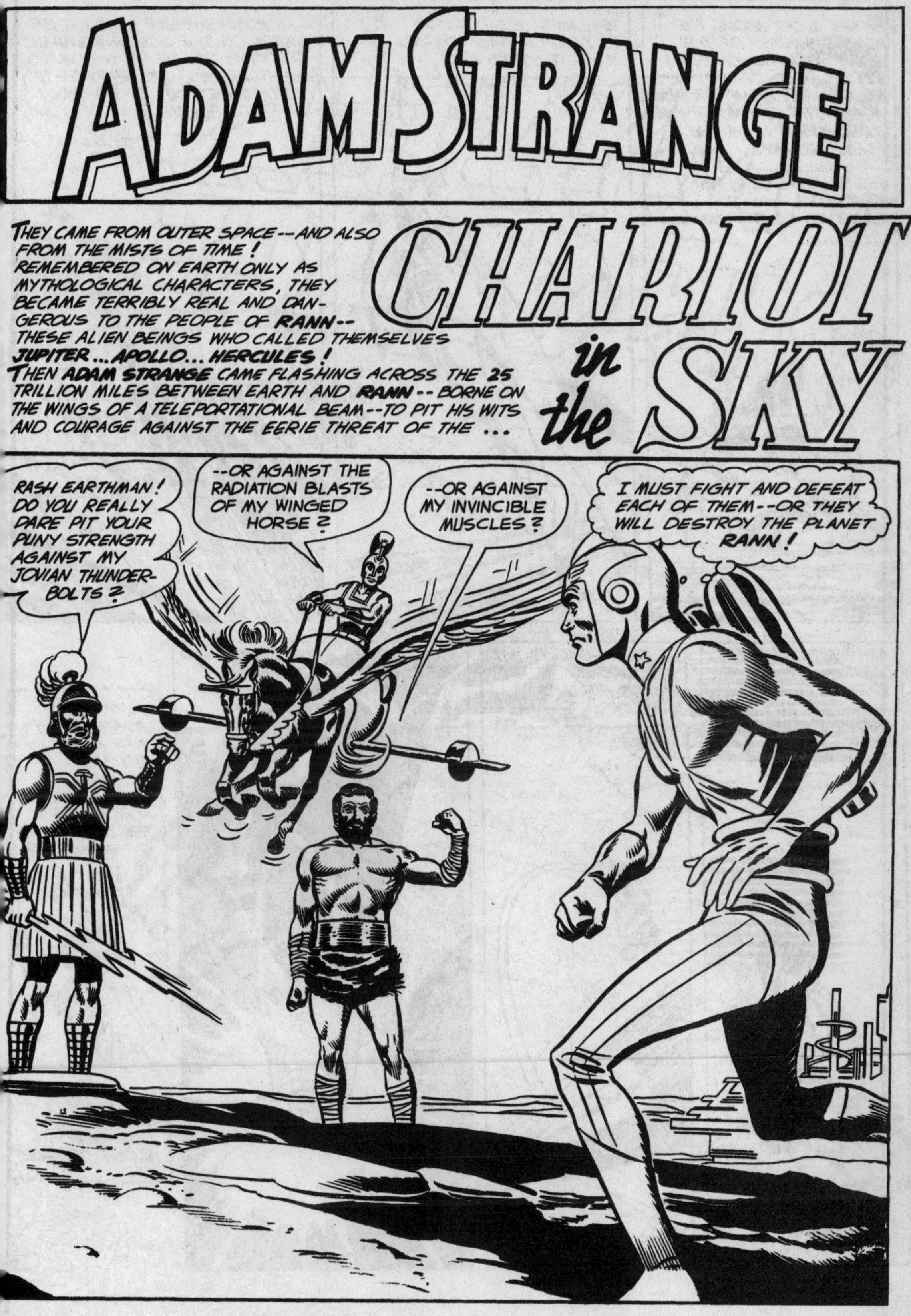
ADAM STRANGE
THEY CAME FROM OUTER SPACE--AND ALSO FROM THE MISTS OF TIME! REMEMBERED ON EARTH ONLY AS MYTHOLOGICAL CHARACTERS, THEY BECAME TERRIBLY REAL AND DANGEROUS TO THE PEOPLE OF RANN--THESE ALIEN BEINGS WHO CALLED THEMSELVES JUPITER... APOLLO... HERCULES! THEN ADAM STRANGE CAME FLASHING ACROSS THE 25 TRILLION MILES BETWEEN EARTH AND RANN--BORNE ON THE WINGS OF A TELEPORTATIONAL BEAM--TO PIT HIS WITS AND COURAGE AGAINST THE EERIE THREAT OF THE ...
CHARIOT in the SKY
RASH EARTHMAN! DO YOU REALLY DARE PIT YOUR PUNY STRENGTH AGAINST MY JOVIAN THUNDERBOLTS?
--OR AGAINST THE RADIATION BLASTS OF MY WINGED HORSE?
--OR AGAINST MY INVINCIBLE MUSCLES?
I MUST FIGHT AND DEFEAT EACH OF THEM--OR THEY WILL DESTROY THE PLANET RANN!

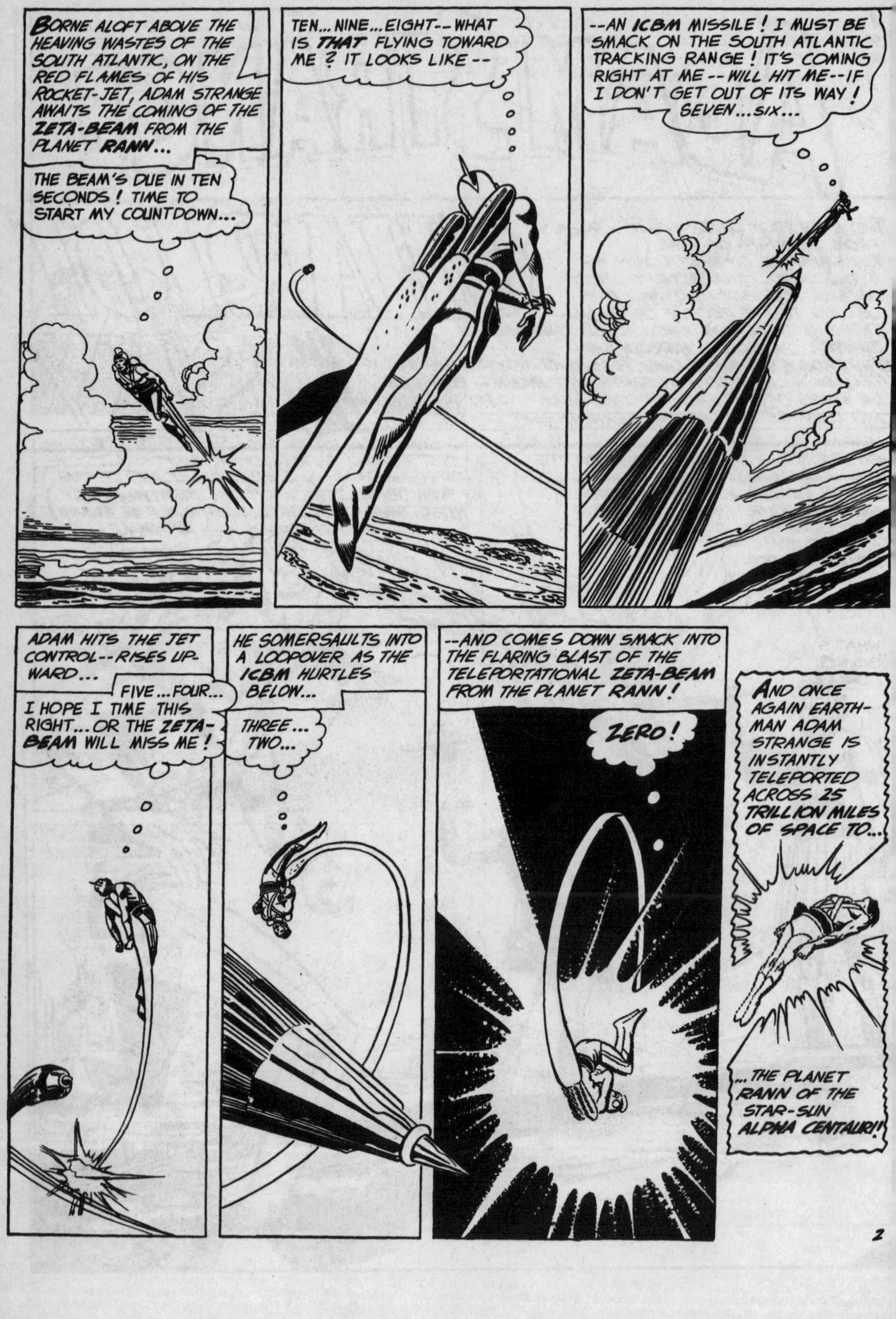
BORNE ALOFT ABOVE THE HEAVING WASTES OF THE SOUTH ATLANTIC, ON THE RED FLAMES OF HIS ROCKET-JET, ADAM STRANGE AWAITS THE COMING OF THE ZETA-BEAM FROM THE PLANET RANN...
THE BEAM'S DUE IN TEN SECONDS! TIME TO START MY COUNTDOWN...
TEN...NINE...EIGHT--WHAT IS THAT FLYING TOWARD ME? IT LOOKS LIKE--
--AN ICBM MISSILE! I MUST BE SMACK ON THE SOUTH ATLANTIC TRACKING RANGE! IT'S COMING RIGHT AT ME--WILL HIT ME--IF I DON'T GET OUT OF ITS WAY! SEVEN...SIX...
ADAM HITS THE JET CONTROL--RISES UPWARD...
FIVE...FOUR... I HOPE I TIME THIS RIGHT...OR THE ZETA-BEAM WILL MISS ME!
HE SOMERSAULTS INTO A LOOPOVER AS THE ICBM HURTLES BELOW...
THREE... TWO...
--AND COMES DOWN SMACK INTO THE FLARING BLAST OF THE TELEPORTATIONAL ZETA-BEAM FROM THE PLANET RANN!
ZERO!
AND ONCE AGAIN EARTHMAN ADAM STRANGE IS INSTANTLY TELEPORTED ACROSS 25 TRILLION MILES OF SPACE TO...
...THE PLANET RANN OF THE STAR-SUN ALPHA CENTAURI!
2

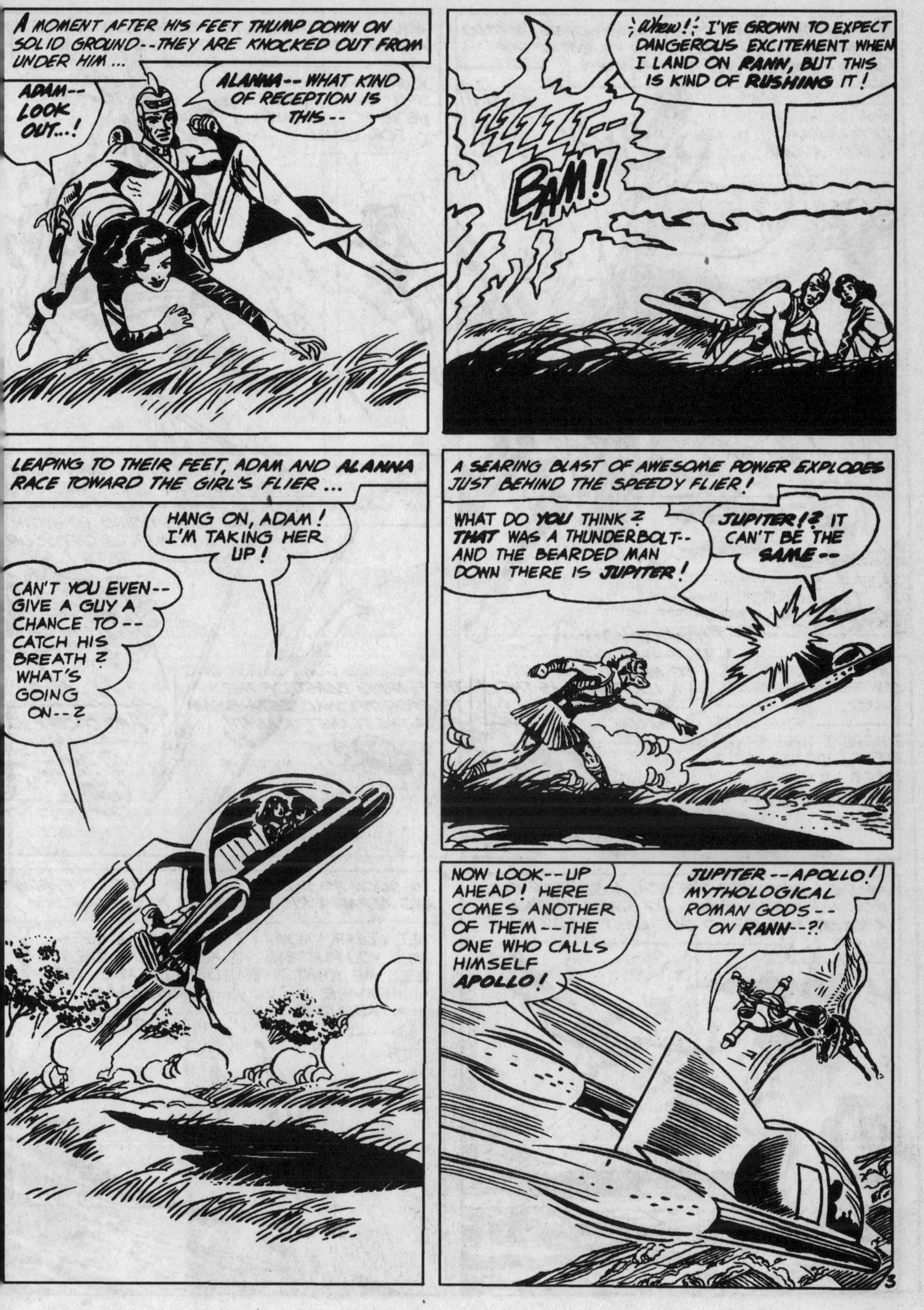
A MOMENT AFTER HIS FEET THUMP DOWN ON SOLID GROUND--THEY ARE KNOCKED OUT FROM UNDER HIM ...
ADAM-- LOOK OUT...!
ALANNA--WHAT KIND OF RECEPTION IS THIS--
WHEW! I'VE GROWN TO EXPECT DANGEROUS EXCITEMENT WHEN I LAND ON RANN, BUT THIS IS KIND OF RUSHING IT!
ZZZZT--
BAM!
LEAPING TO THEIR FEET, ADAM AND ALANNA RACE TOWARD THE GIRL'S FLIER ...
HANG ON, ADAM! I'M TAKING HER UP!
CAN'T YOU EVEN--GIVE A GUY A CHANCE TO--CATCH HIS BREATH? WHAT'S GOING ON--?
A SEARING BLAST OF AWESOME POWER EXPLODES JUST BEHIND THE SPEEDY FLIER!
WHAT DO YOU THINK? THAT WAS A THUNDERBOLT--AND THE BEARDED MAN DOWN THERE IS JUPITER!
JUPITER!? IT CAN'T BE THE SAME--
NOW LOOK--UP AHEAD! HERE COMES ANOTHER OF THEM--THE ONE WHO CALLS HIMSELF APOLLO!
JUPITER--APOLLO! MYTHOLOGICAL ROMAN GODS--ON RANN--?!
3

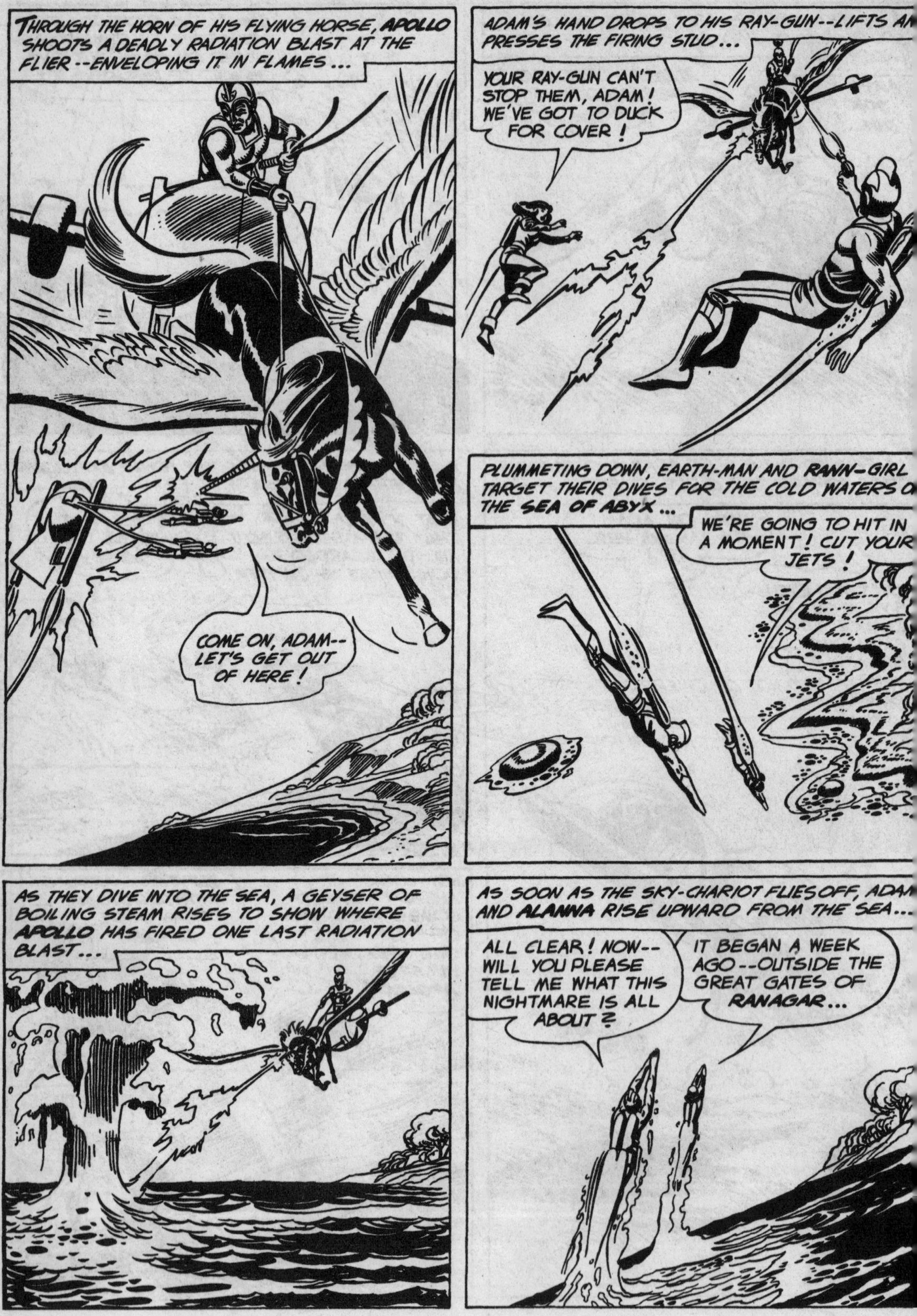
THROUGH THE HORN OF HIS FLYING HORSE, APOLLO SHOOTS A DEADLY RADIATION BLAST AT THE FLIER--ENVELOPING IT IN FLAMES...
COME ON, ADAM--LET'S GET OUT OF HERE!
ADAM'S HAND DROPS TO HIS RAY-GUN--LIFTS AN
PRESSES THE FIRING STUD...
YOUR RAY-GUN CAN'T STOP THEM, ADAM! WE'VE GOT TO DUCK FOR COVER!
PLUMMETING DOWN, EARTH-MAN AND RANN-GIRL TARGET THEIR DIVES FOR THE COLD WATERS O
THE SEA OF ABYX...
WE'RE GOING TO HIT IN A MOMENT! CUT YOUR JETS!
AS THEY DIVE INTO THE SEA, A GEYSER OF BOILING STEAM RISES TO SHOW WHERE APOLLO HAS FIRED ONE LAST RADIATION BLAST...
AS SOON AS THE SKY-CHARIOT FLIES OFF, ADAM AND ALANNA RISE UPWARD FROM THE SEA...
ALL CLEAR! NOW--WILL YOU PLEASE TELL ME WHAT THIS NIGHTMARE IS ALL ABOUT?
IT BEGAN A WEEK AGO--OUTSIDE THE GREAT GATES OF RANAGAR...

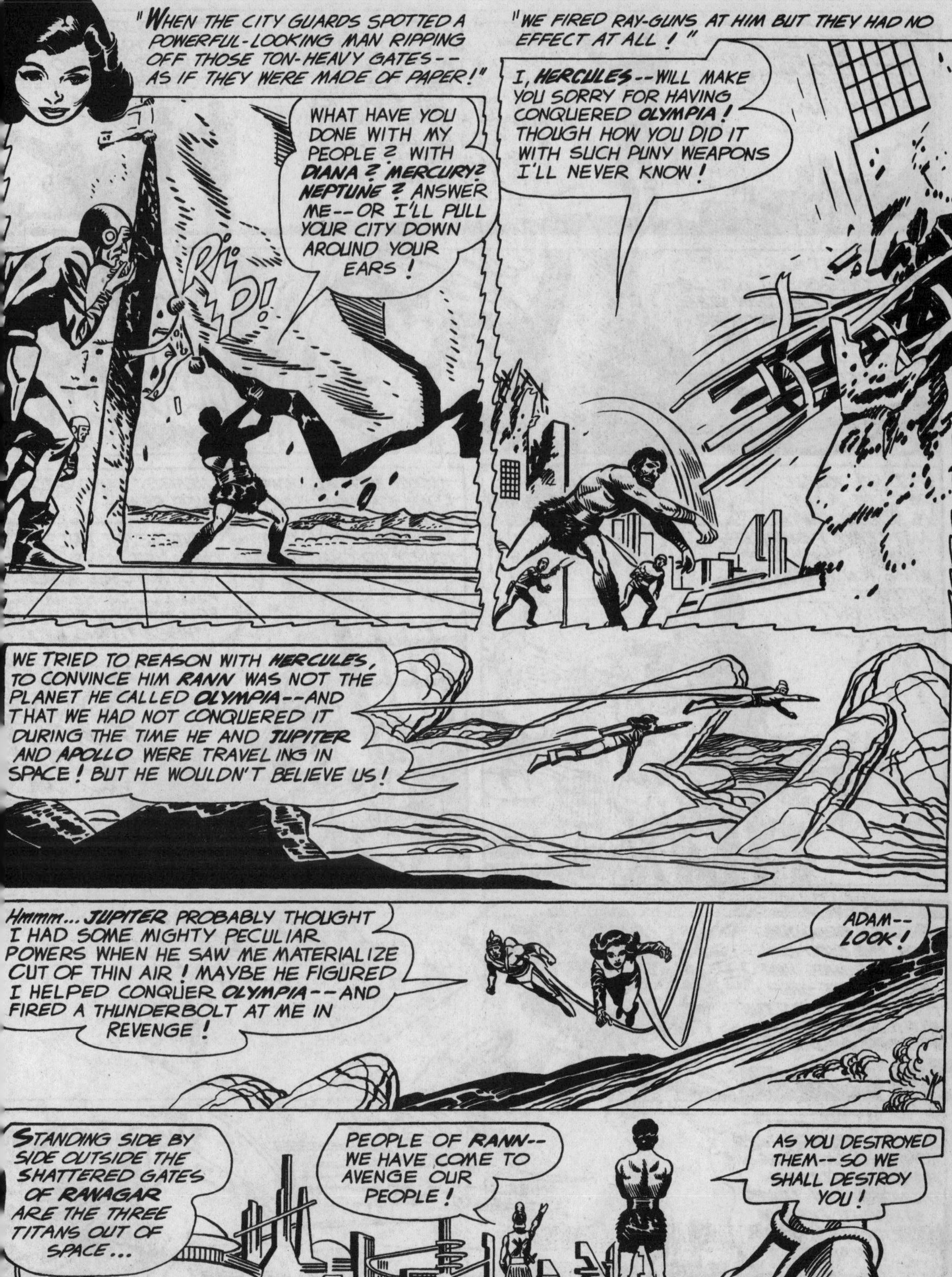
"WHEN THE CITY GUARDS SPOTTED A POWERFUL-LOOKING MAN RIPPING OFF THOSE TON-HEAVY GATES--AS IF THEY WERE MADE OF PAPER!"
WHAT HAVE YOU DONE WITH MY PEOPLE? WITH DIANA? MERCURY? NEPTUNE? ANSWER ME--OR I'LL PULL YOUR CITY DOWN AROUND YOUR EARS!
RIP!
"WE FIRED RAY-GUNS AT HIM BUT THEY HAD NO EFFECT AT ALL!"
I, HERCULES--WILL MAKE YOU SORRY FOR HAVING CONQUERED OLYMPIA! THOUGH HOW YOU DID IT WITH SUCH PUNY WEAPONS I'LL NEVER KNOW!
WE TRIED TO REASON WITH HERCULES, TO CONVINCE HIM RANN WAS NOT THE PLANET HE CALLED OLYMPIA--AND THAT WE HAD NOT CONQUERED IT DURING THE TIME HE AND JUPITER AND APOLLO WERE TRAVEL ING IN SPACE! BUT HE WOULDN'T BELIEVE US!
Hmmm... JUPITER PROBABLY THOUGHT I HAD SOME MIGHTY PECULIAR POWERS WHEN HE SAW ME MATERIALIZE OUT OF THIN AIR! MAYBE HE FIGURED I HELPED CONQUER OLYMPIA--AND FIRED A THUNDERBOLT AT ME IN REVENGE!
ADAM--LOOK!
STANDING SIDE BY SIDE OUTSIDE THE SHATTERED GATES OF RANAGAR ARE THE THREE TITANS OUT OF SPACE...
PEOPLE OF RANN--WE HAVE COME TO AVENGE OUR PEOPLE!
AS YOU DESTROYED THEM--SO WE SHALL DESTROY YOU!
5

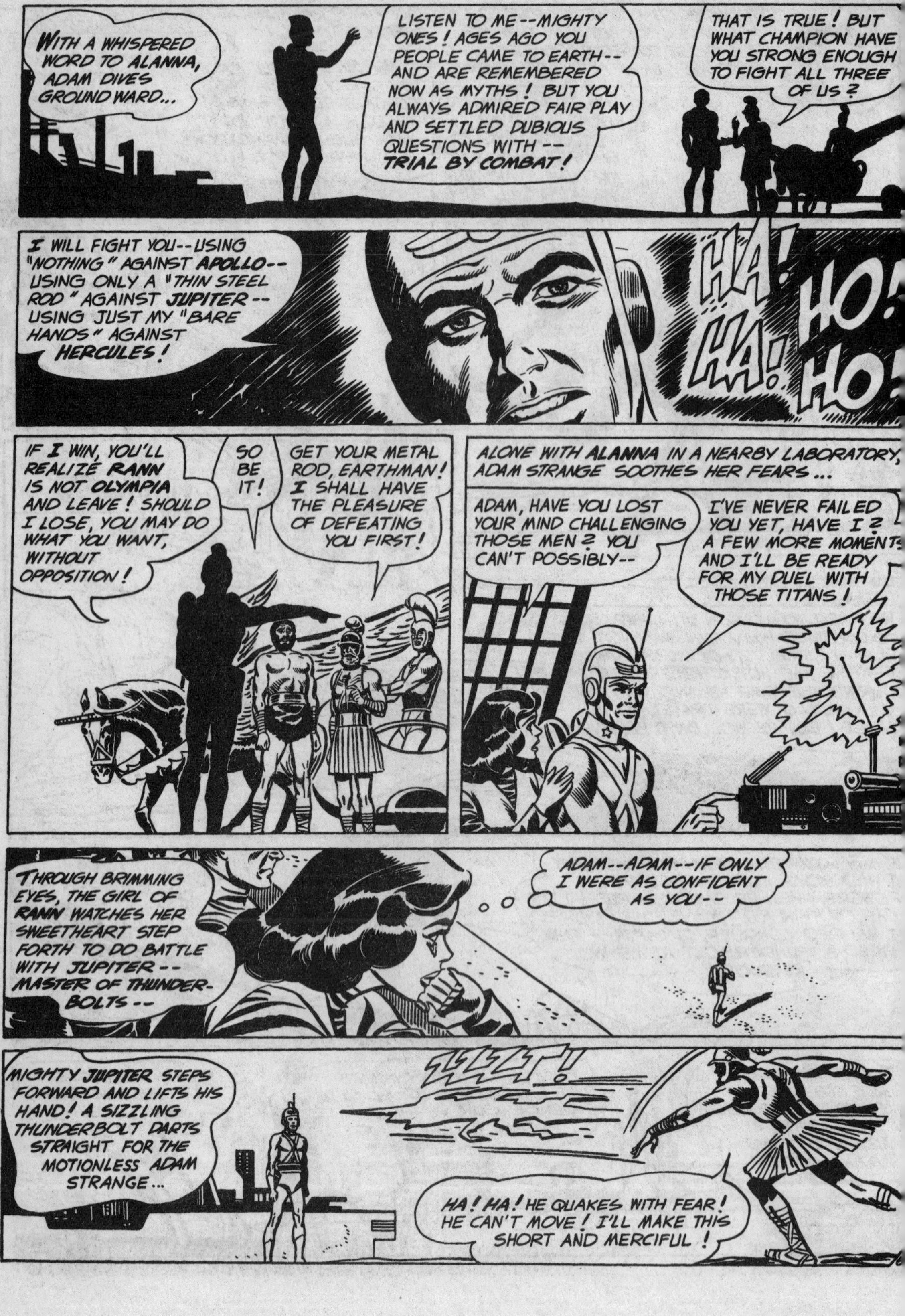
WITH A WHISPERED WORD TO ALANNA, ADAM DIVES GROUNDWARD...
LISTEN TO ME--MIGHTY ONES! AGES AGO YOU PEOPLE CAME TO EARTH--AND ARE REMEMBERED NOW AS MYTHS! BUT YOU ALWAYS ADMIRED FAIR PLAY AND SETTLED DUBIOUS QUESTIONS WITH--TRIAL BY COMBAT!
THAT IS TRUE! BUT WHAT CHAMPION HAVE YOU STRONG ENOUGH TO FIGHT ALL THREE OF US?
I WILL FIGHT YOU--USING "NOTHING" AGAINST APOLLO--USING ONLY A "THIN STEEL ROD" AGAINST JUPITER--USING JUST MY "BARE HANDS" AGAINST HERCULES!
HA! HA! HO! HO!
IF I WIN, YOU'LL REALIZE RANN IS NOT OLYMPIA AND LEAVE! SHOULD I LOSE, YOU MAY DO WHAT YOU WANT, WITHOUT OPPOSITION!
SO BE IT!
GET YOUR METAL ROD, EARTHMAN! I SHALL HAVE THE PLEASURE OF DEFEATING YOU FIRST!
ALONE WITH ALANNA IN A NEARBY LABORATORY, ADAM STRANGE SOOTHES HER FEARS...
ADAM, HAVE YOU LOST YOUR MIND CHALLENGING THOSE MEN? YOU CAN'T POSSIBLY--
I'VE NEVER FAILED YOU YET, HAVE I? A FEW MORE MOMENTS AND I'LL BE READY FOR MY DUEL WITH THOSE TITANS!
THROUGH BRIMMING EYES, THE GIRL OF RANN WATCHES HER SWEETHEART STEP FORTH TO DO BATTLE WITH JUPITER--MASTER OF THUNDER-BOLTS--
ADAM--ADAM--IF ONLY I WERE AS CONFIDENT AS YOU--
MIGHTY JUPITER STEPS FORWARD AND LIFTS HIS HAND! A SIZZLING THUNDERBOLT DARTS STRAIGHT FOR THE MOTIONLESS ADAM STRANGE...
ZZZT!
HA! HA! HE QUAKES WITH FEAR! HE CAN'T MOVE! I'LL MAKE THIS SHORT AND MERCIFUL!

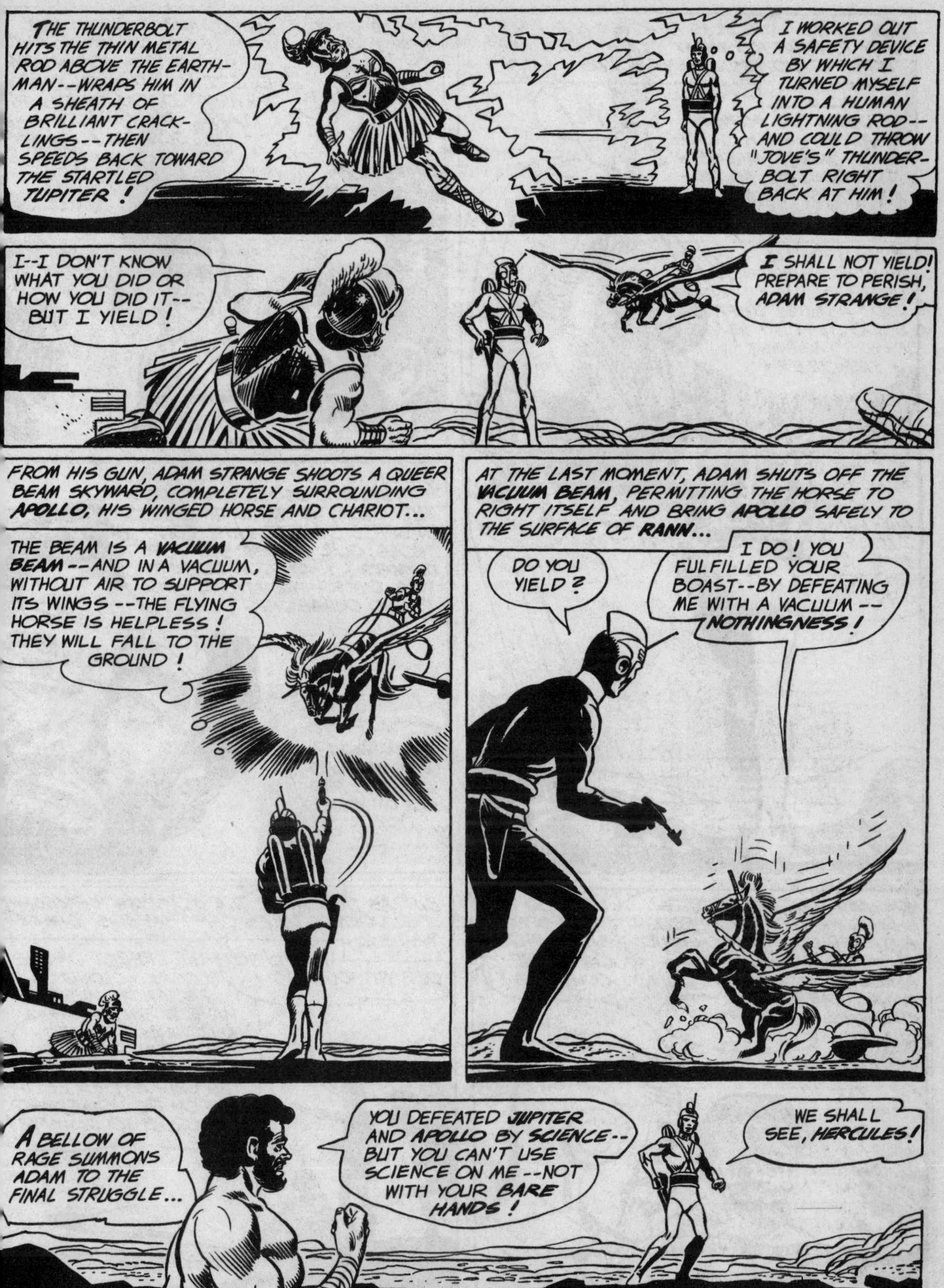
THE THUNDERBOLT HITS THE THIN METAL ROD ABOVE THE EARTH-MAN--WRAPS HIM IN A SHEATH OF BRILLIANT CRACK-LINGS--THEN SPEEDS BACK TOWARD THE STARTLED JUPITER!
I WORKED OUT A SAFETY DEVICE BY WHICH I TURNED MYSELF INTO A HUMAN LIGHTNING ROD--AND COULD THROW "JOVE'S" THUNDER-BOLT RIGHT BACK AT HIM!
I--I DON'T KNOW WHAT YOU DID OR HOW YOU DID IT--BUT I YIELD!
I SHALL NOT YIELD! PREPARE TO PERISH, ADAM STRANGE!
FROM HIS GUN, ADAM STRANGE SHOOTS A QUEER BEAM SKYWARD, COMPLETELY SURROUNDING APOLLO, HIS WINGED HORSE AND CHARIOT...
THE BEAM IS A VACUUM BEAM--AND IN A VACUUM, WITHOUT AIR TO SUPPORT ITS WINGS--THE FLYING HORSE IS HELPLESS! THEY WILL FALL TO THE GROUND!
AT THE LAST MOMENT, ADAM SHUTS OFF THE VACUUM BEAM, PERMITTING THE HORSE TO RIGHT ITSELF AND BRING APOLLO SAFELY TO THE SURFACE OF RANN...
DO YOU YIELD?
I DO! YOU FULFILLED YOUR BOAST--BY DEFEATING ME WITH A VACUUM--NOTHINGNESS!
A BELLOW OF RAGE SUMMONS ADAM TO THE FINAL STRUGGLE...
YOU DEFEATED JUPITER AND APOLLO BY SCIENCE--BUT YOU CAN'T USE SCIENCE ON ME--NOT WITH YOUR BARE HANDS!
WE SHALL SEE, HERCULES!
7

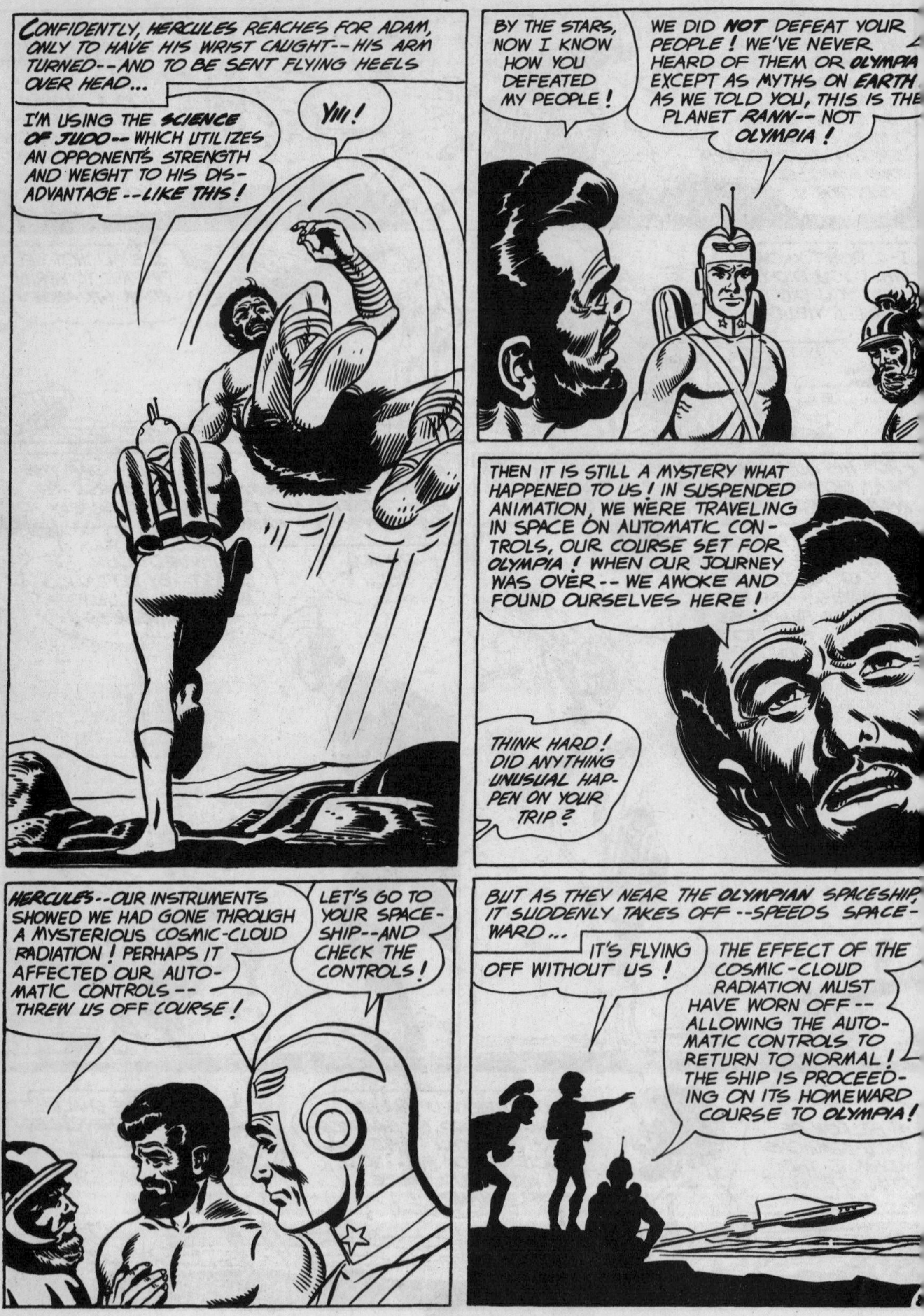
CONFIDENTLY, HERCULES REACHES FOR ADAM, ONLY TO HAVE HIS WRIST CAUGHT--HIS ARM TURNED--AND TO BE SENT FLYING HEELS OVER HEAD...
I'M USING THE SCIENCE OF JUDO--WHICH UTILIZES AN OPPONENT'S STRENGTH AND WEIGHT TO HIS DIS-ADVANTAGE--LIKE THIS!
YIII!
BY THE STARS, NOW I KNOW HOW YOU DEFEATED MY PEOPLE!
WE DID NOT DEFEAT YOUR PEOPLE! WE'VE NEVER HEARD OF THEM OR OLYMPIA EXCEPT AS MYTHS ON EARTH AS WE TOLD YOU, THIS IS THE PLANET RANN--NOT OLYMPIA!
THEN IT IS STILL A MYSTERY WHAT HAPPENED TO US! IN SUSPENDED ANIMATION, WE WERE TRAVELING IN SPACE ON AUTOMATIC CON-TROLS, OUR COURSE SET FOR OLYMPIA! WHEN OUR JOURNEY WAS OVER--WE AWOKE AND FOUND OURSELVES HERE!
THINK HARD! DID ANYTHING UNUSUAL HAP-PEN ON YOUR TRIP?
HERCULES--OUR INSTRUMENTS SHOWED WE HAD GONE THROUGH A MYSTERIOUS COSMIC-CLOUD RADIATION! PERHAPS IT AFFECTED OUR AUTO-MATIC CONTROLS--THREW US OFF COURSE!
LET'S GO TO YOUR SPACE-SHIP--AND CHECK THE CONTROLS!
BUT AS THEY NEAR THE OLYMPIAN SPACESHIP, IT SUDDENLY TAKES OFF--SPEEDS SPACE-WARD...
IT'S FLYING OFF WITHOUT US!
THE EFFECT OF THE COSMIC-CLOUD RADIATION MUST HAVE WORN OFF--ALLOWING THE AUTO-MATIC CONTROLS TO RETURN TO NORMAL! THE SHIP IS PROCEED-ING ON ITS HOMEWARD COURSE TO OLYMPIA!

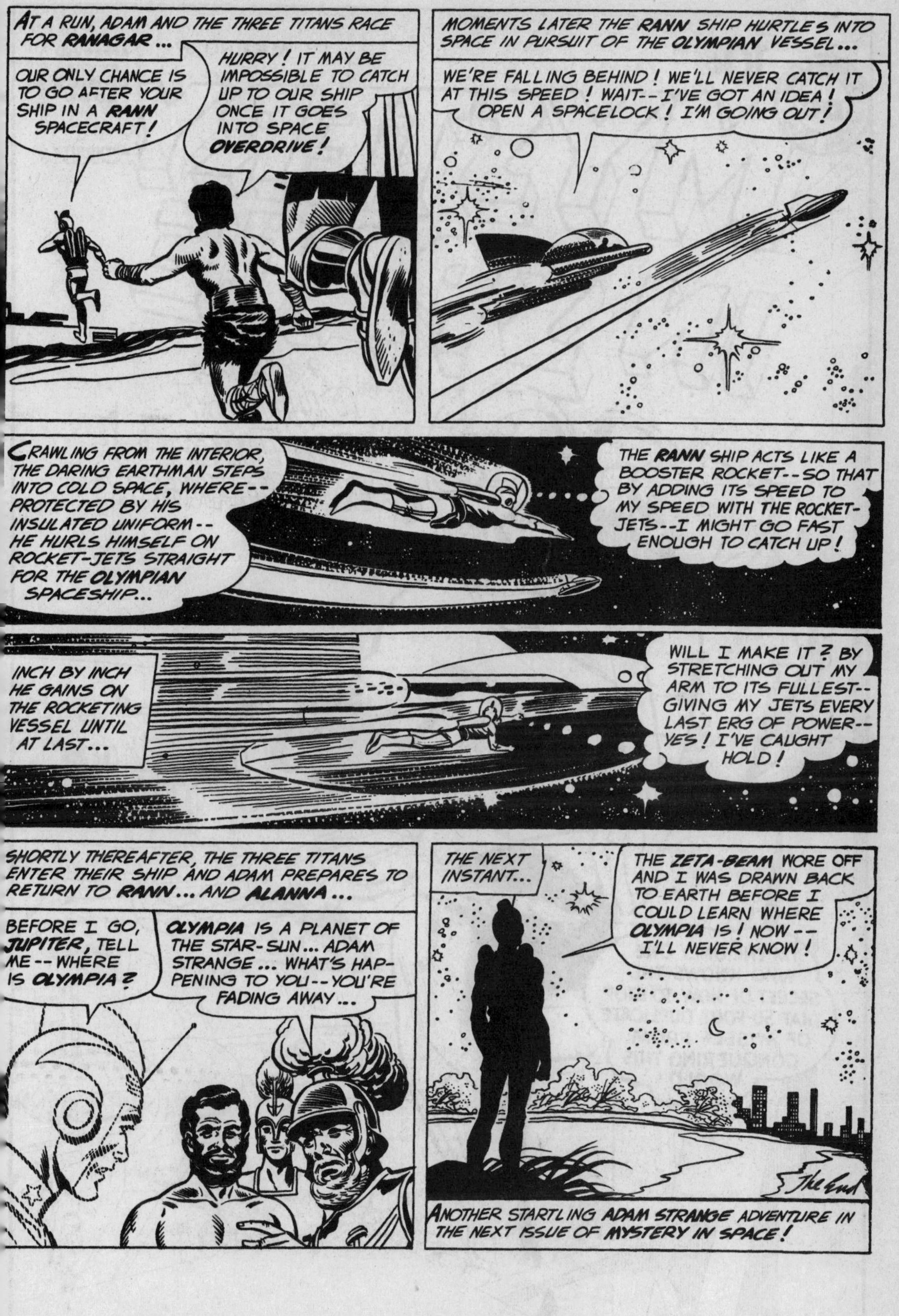
AT A RUN, ADAM AND THE THREE TITANS RACE FOR RANAGAR...
OUR ONLY CHANCE IS TO GO AFTER YOUR SHIP IN A RANN SPACECRAFT!
HURRY! IT MAY BE IMPOSSIBLE TO CATCH UP TO OUR SHIP ONCE IT GOES INTO SPACE OVERDRIVE!
MOMENTS LATER THE RANN SHIP HURTLES INTO SPACE IN PURSUIT OF THE OLYMPIAN VESSEL...
WE'RE FALLING BEHIND! WE'LL NEVER CATCH IT AT THIS SPEED! WAIT-- I'VE GOT AN IDEA! OPEN A SPACELOCK! I'M GOING OUT!
CRAWLING FROM THE INTERIOR, THE DARING EARTHMAN STEPS INTO COLD SPACE, WHERE-- PROTECTED BY HIS INSULATED UNIFORM-- HE HURLS HIMSELF ON ROCKET-JETS STRAIGHT FOR THE OLYMPIAN SPACESHIP...
THE RANN SHIP ACTS LIKE A BOOSTER ROCKET--SO THAT BY ADDING ITS SPEED TO MY SPEED WITH THE ROCKET-JETS--I MIGHT GO FAST ENOUGH TO CATCH UP!
INCH BY INCH HE GAINS ON THE ROCKETING VESSEL UNTIL AT LAST...
WILL I MAKE IT? BY STRETCHING OUT MY ARM TO ITS FULLEST-- GIVING MY JETS EVERY LAST ERG OF POWER-- YES! I'VE CAUGHT HOLD!
SHORTLY THEREAFTER, THE THREE TITANS ENTER THEIR SHIP AND ADAM PREPARES TO RETURN TO RANN... AND ALANNA...
BEFORE I GO, JUPITER, TELL ME-- WHERE IS OLYMPIA?
OLYMPIA IS A PLANET OF THE STAR-SUN... ADAM STRANGE... WHAT'S HAPPENING TO YOU--YOU'RE FADING AWAY...
THE NEXT INSTANT...
THE ZETA-BEAM WORE OFF AND I WAS DRAWN BACK TO EARTH BEFORE I COULD LEARN WHERE OLYMPIA IS! NOW-- I'LL NEVER KNOW!
The End
ANOTHER STARTLING ADAM STRANGE ADVENTURE IN THE NEXT ISSUE OF MYSTERY IN SPACE!

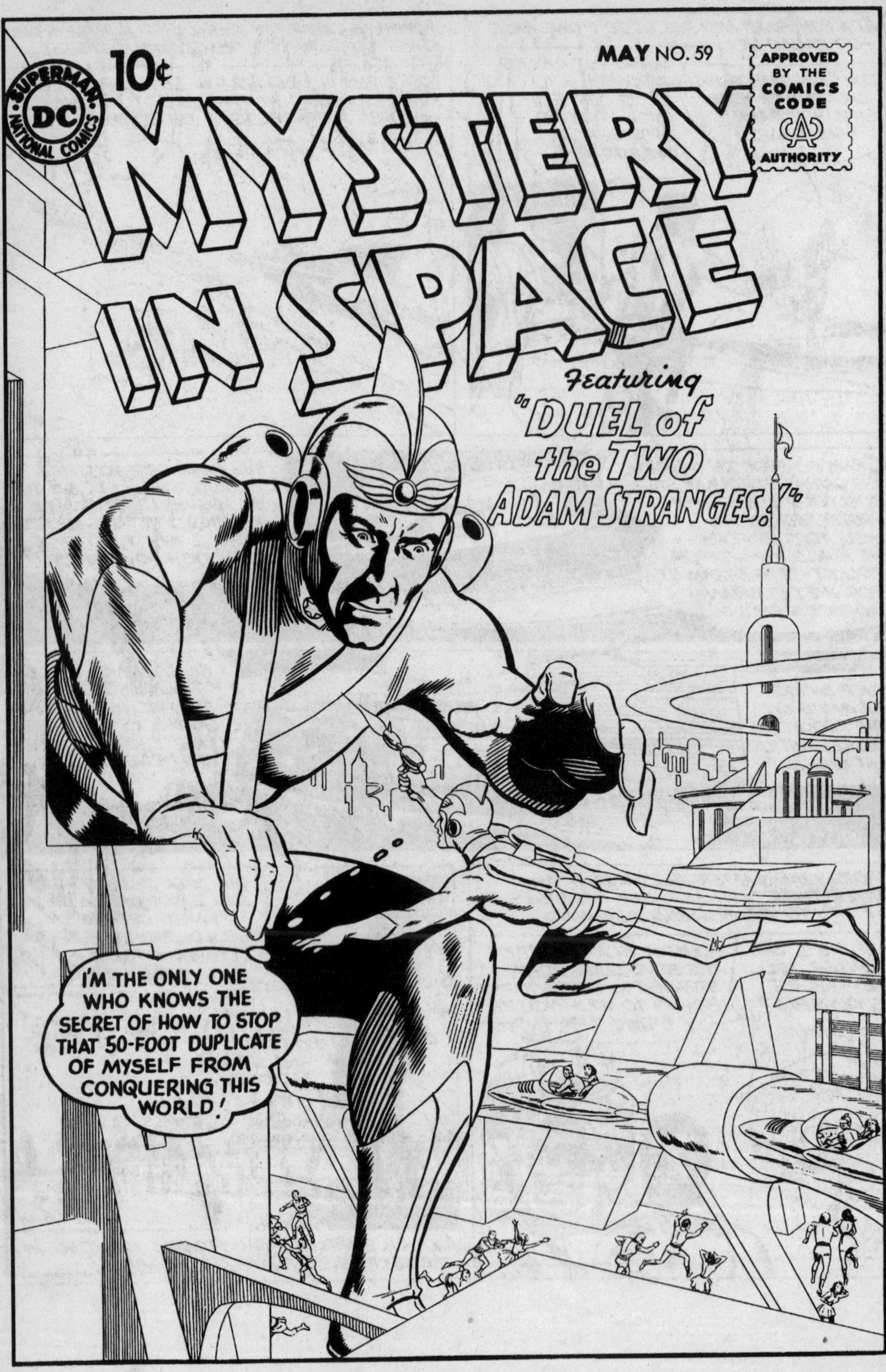
SUPERMAN DC NATIONAL COMICS
10¢
MAY NO. 59
APPROVED BY THE COMICS CODE AUTHORITY
MYSTERY IN SPACE
Featuring "DUEL of the TWO ADAM STRANGES!"
I'M THE ONLY ONE WHO KNOWS THE SECRET OF HOW TO STOP THAT 50-FOOT DUPLICATE OF MYSELF FROM CONQUERING THIS WORLD!

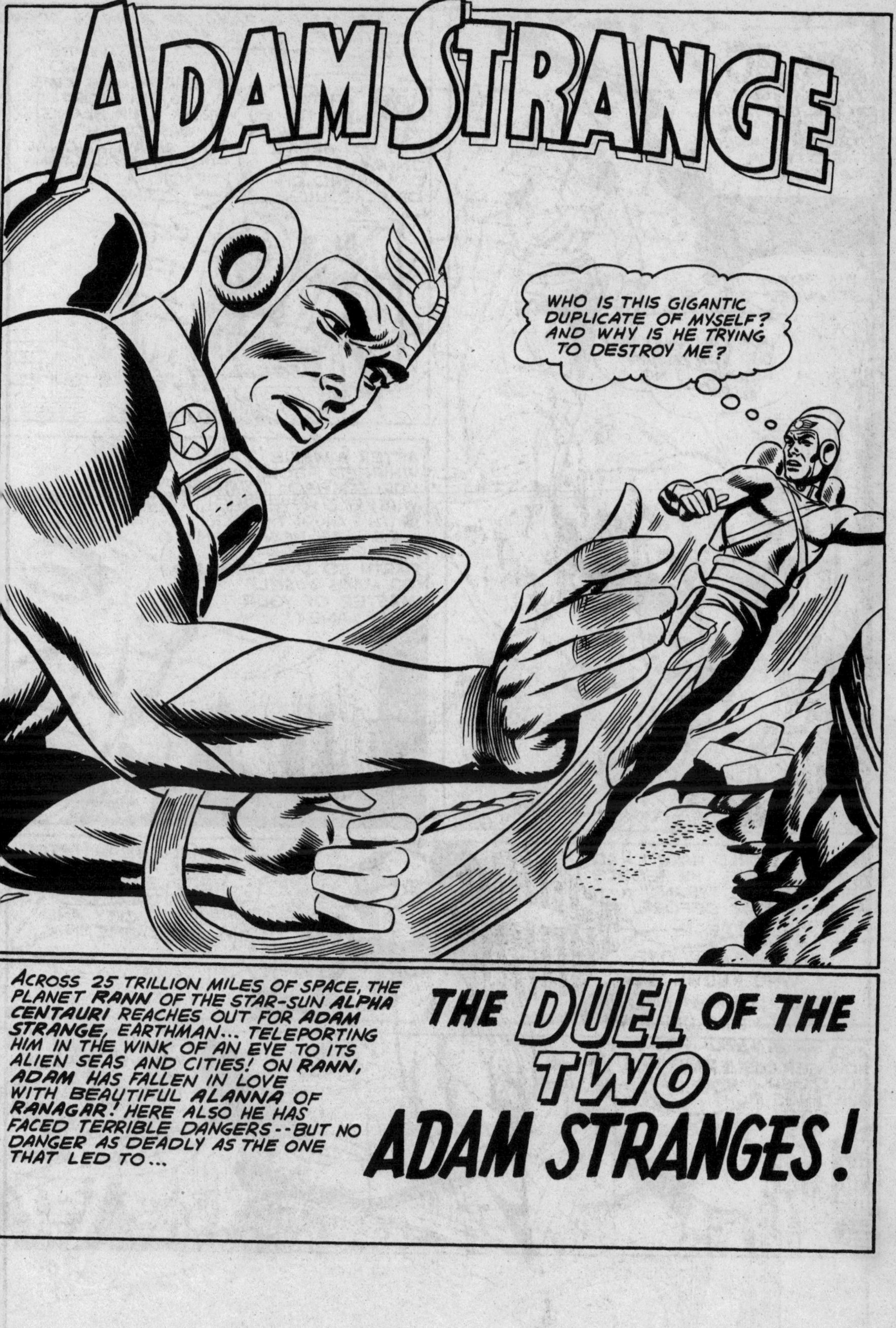
ADAM STRANGE
WHO IS THIS GIGANTIC DUPLICATE OF MYSELF? AND WHY IS HE TRYING TO DESTROY ME?
ACROSS 25 TRILLION MILES OF SPACE, THE PLANET RANN OF THE STAR-SUN ALPHA CENTAURI REACHES OUT FOR ADAM STRANGE, EARTHMAN... TELEPORTING HIM IN THE WINK OF AN EYE TO ITS ALIEN SEAS AND CITIES! ON RANN, ADAM HAS FALLEN IN LOVE WITH BEAUTIFUL ALANNA OF RANAGAR! HERE ALSO HE HAS FACED TERRIBLE DANGERS--BUT NO DANGER AS DEADLY AS THE ONE THAT LED TO...
THE DUEL OF THE TWO ADAM STRANGES!

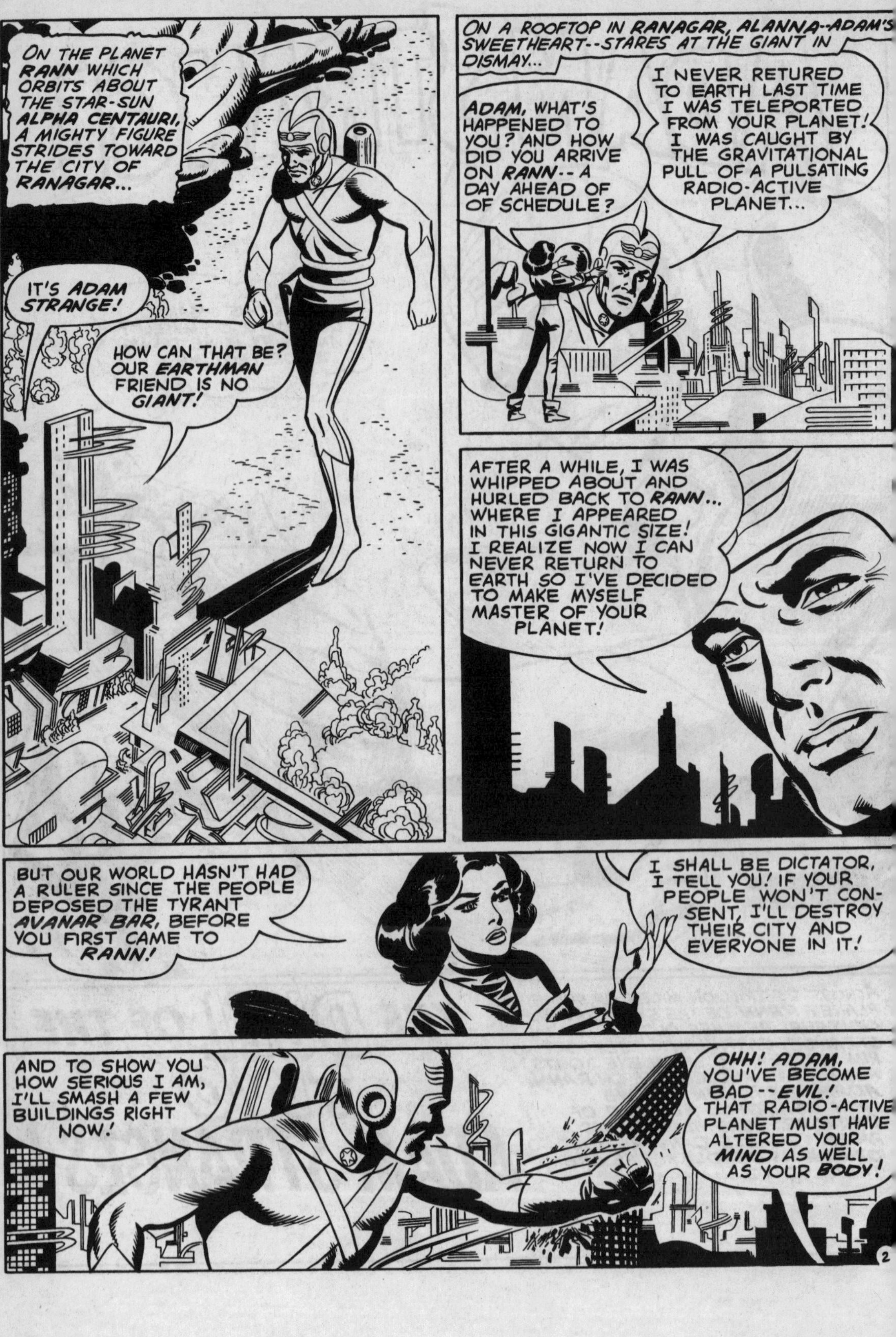
ON THE PLANET RANN WHICH ORBITS ABOUT THE STAR-SUN ALPHA CENTAURI, A MIGHTY FIGURE STRIDES TOWARD THE CITY OF RANAGAR...
IT'S ADAM STRANGE!
HOW CAN THAT BE? OUR EARTHMAN FRIEND IS NO GIANT!
ON A ROOFTOP IN RANAGAR, ALANNA--ADAM'S SWEETHEART--STARES AT THE GIANT IN DISMAY...
ADAM, WHAT'S HAPPENED TO YOU? AND HOW DID YOU ARRIVE ON RANN--A DAY AHEAD OF OF SCHEDULE?
I NEVER RETURED TO EARTH LAST TIME I WAS TELEPORTED FROM YOUR PLANET! I WAS CAUGHT BY THE GRAVITATIONAL PULL OF A PULSATING RADIO-ACTIVE PLANET...
AFTER A WHILE, I WAS WHIPPED ABOUT AND HURLED BACK TO RANN... WHERE I APPEARED IN THIS GIGANTIC SIZE! I REALIZE NOW I CAN NEVER RETURN TO EARTH SO I'VE DECIDED TO MAKE MYSELF MASTER OF YOUR PLANET!
BUT OUR WORLD HASN'T HAD A RULER SINCE THE PEOPLE DEPOSED THE TYRANT AVANAR BAR, BEFORE YOU FIRST CAME TO RANN!
I SHALL BE DICTATOR, I TELL YOU! IF YOUR PEOPLE WON'T CONSENT, I'LL DESTROY THEIR CITY AND EVERYONE IN IT!
AND TO SHOW YOU HOW SERIOUS I AM, I'LL SMASH A FEW BUILDINGS RIGHT NOW!
OHH! ADAM, YOU'VE BECOME BAD--EVIL! THAT RADIO-ACTIVE PLANET MUST HAVE ALTERED YOUR MIND AS WELL AS YOUR BODY!
2

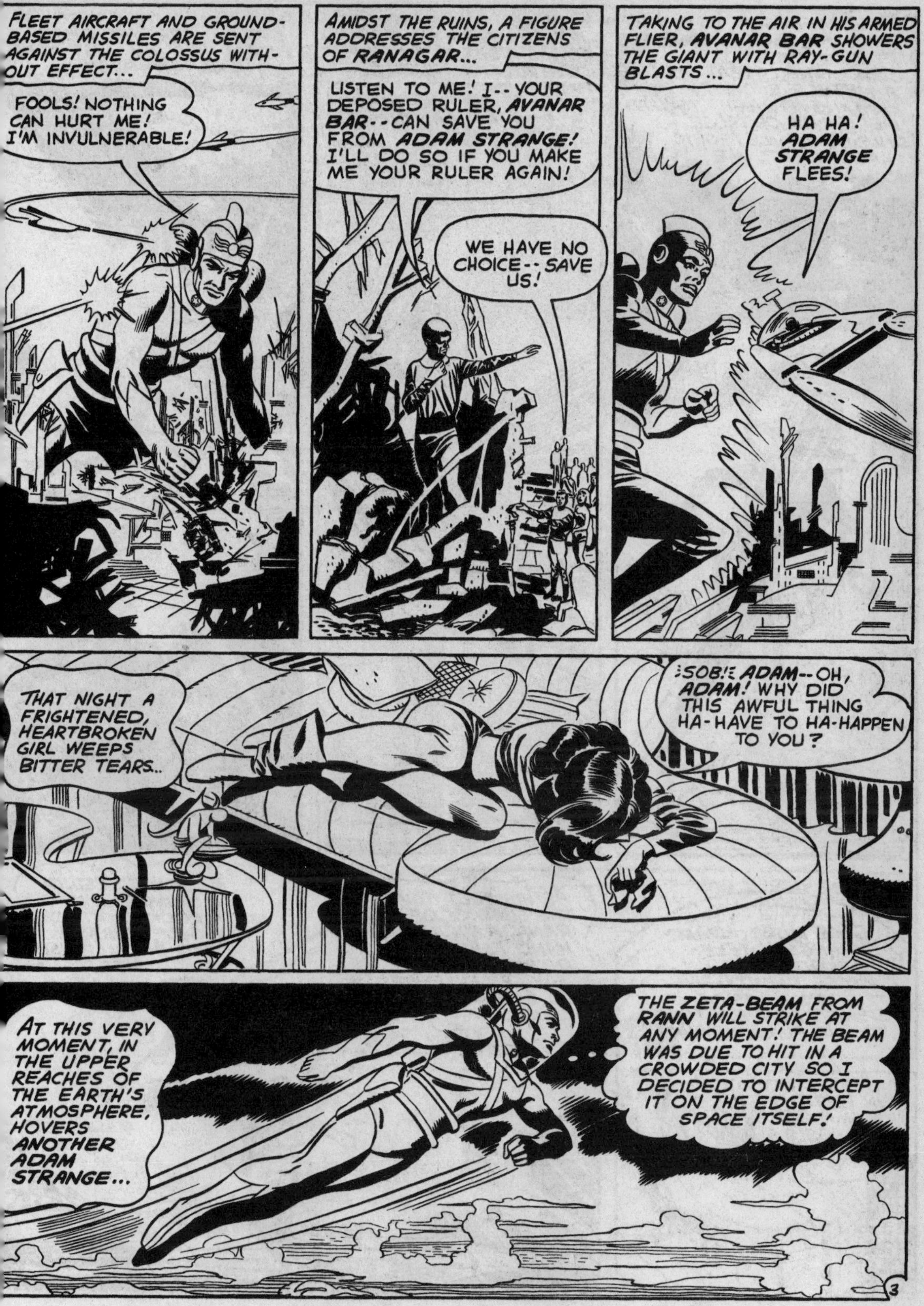
FLEET AIRCRAFT AND GROUND-BASED MISSILES ARE SENT AGAINST THE COLOSSUS WITHOUT EFFECT...
FOOLS! NOTHING CAN HURT ME! I'M INVULNERABLE!
AMIDST THE RUINS, A FIGURE ADDRESSES THE CITIZENS OF RANAGAR...
LISTEN TO ME! I-- YOUR DEPOSED RULER, AVANAR BAR-- CAN SAVE YOU FROM ADAM STRANGE! I'LL DO SO IF YOU MAKE ME YOUR RULER AGAIN!
WE HAVE NO CHOICE-- SAVE US!
TAKING TO THE AIR IN HIS ARMED FLIER, AVANAR BAR SHOWERS THE GIANT WITH RAY-GUN BLASTS...
HA HA! ADAM STRANGE FLEES!
THAT NIGHT A FRIGHTENED, HEARTBROKEN GIRL WEEPS BITTER TEARS..
SOB! ADAM--OH, ADAM! WHY DID THIS AWFUL THING HA-HAVE TO HA-HAPPEN TO YOU?
AT THIS VERY MOMENT, IN THE UPPER REACHES OF THE EARTH'S ATMOSPHERE, HOVERS ANOTHER ADAM STRANGE...
THE ZETA-BEAM FROM RANN WILL STRIKE AT ANY MOMENT! THE BEAM WAS DUE TO HIT IN A CROWDED CITY SO I DECIDED TO INTERCEPT IT ON THE EDGE OF SPACE ITSELF!
3

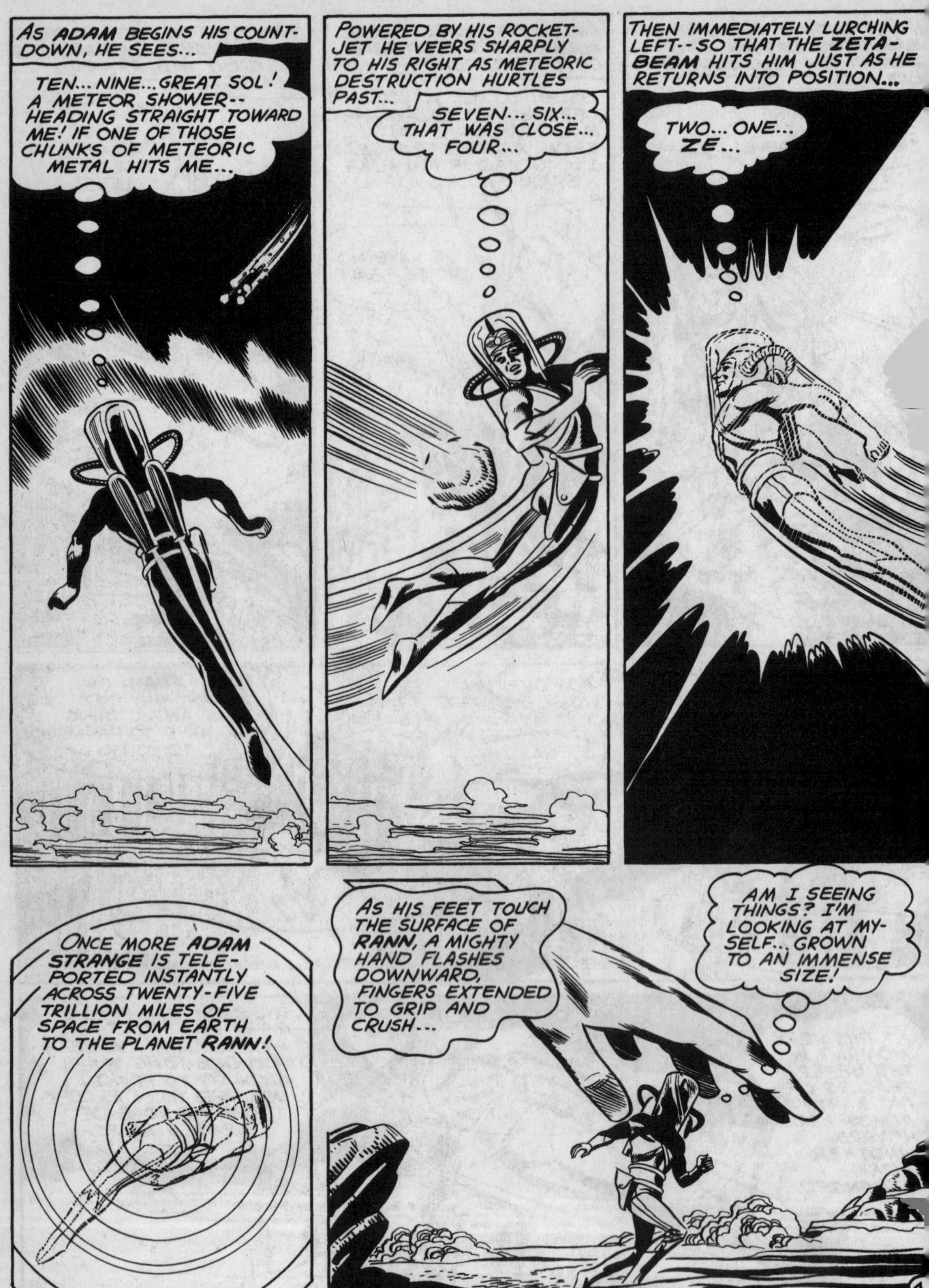
AS ADAM BEGINS HIS COUNT-DOWN, HE SEES...
TEN... NINE... GREAT SOL! A METEOR SHOWER-- HEADING STRAIGHT TOWARD ME! IF ONE OF THOSE CHUNKS OF METEORIC METAL HITS ME...
POWERED BY HIS ROCKET-JET HE VEERS SHARPLY TO HIS RIGHT AS METEORIC DESTRUCTION HURTLES PAST...
SEVEN... SIX... THAT WAS CLOSE... FOUR...
THEN IMMEDIATELY LURCHING LEFT--SO THAT THE ZETA-BEAM HITS HIM JUST AS HE RETURNS INTO POSITION...
TWO... ONE... ZE...
ONCE MORE ADAM STRANGE IS TELE-PORTED INSTANTLY ACROSS TWENTY-FIVE TRILLION MILES OF SPACE FROM EARTH TO THE PLANET RANN!
AS HIS FEET TOUCH THE SURFACE OF RANN, A MIGHTY HAND FLASHES DOWNWARD, FINGERS EXTENDED TO GRIP AND CRUSH...
AM I SEEING THINGS? I'M LOOKING AT MY-SELF... GROWN TO AN IMMENSE SIZE!
4

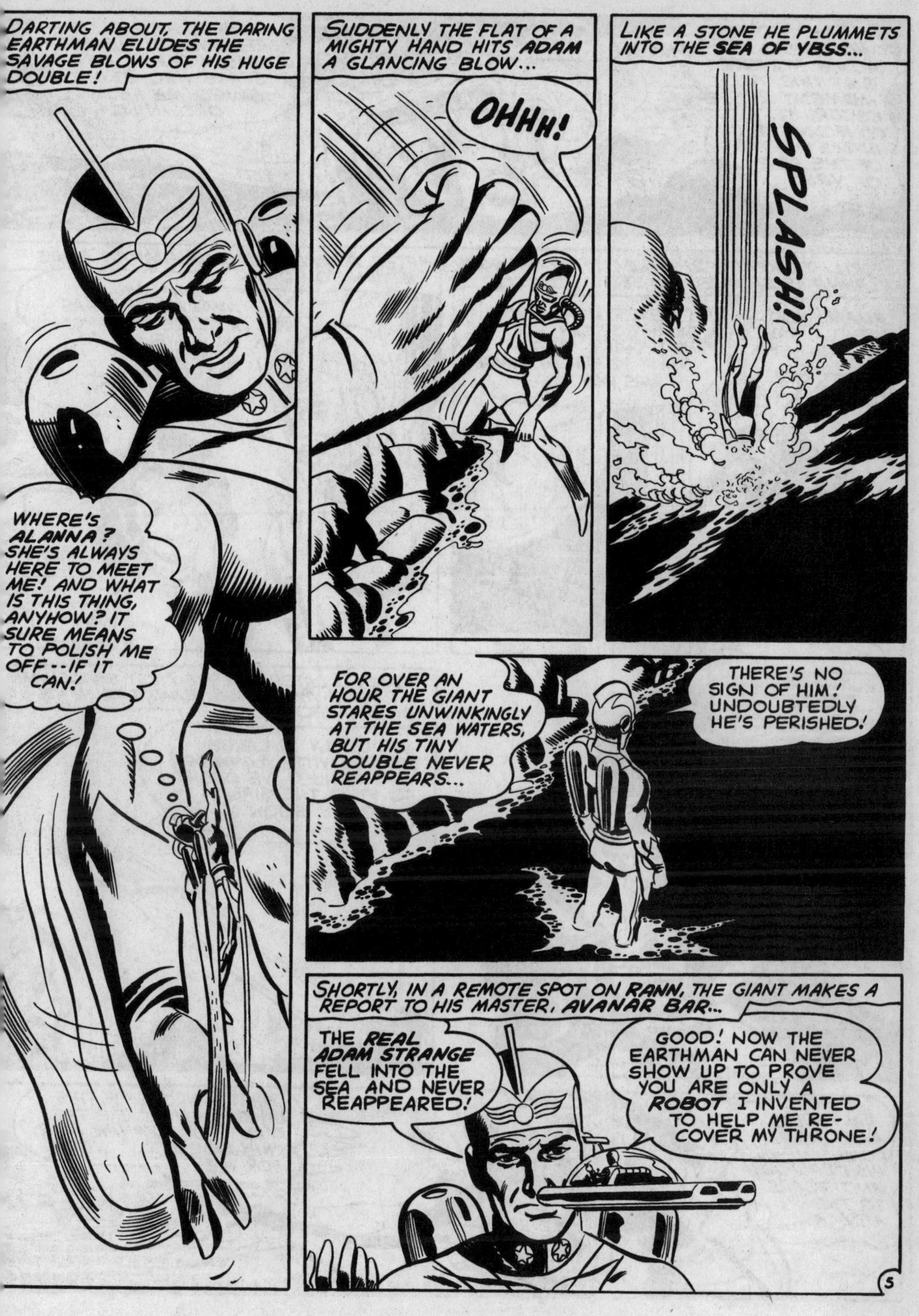
DARTING ABOUT, THE DARING EARTHMAN ELUDES THE SAVAGE BLOWS OF HIS HUGE DOUBLE!
WHERE'S ALANNA? SHE'S ALWAYS HERE TO MEET ME! AND WHAT IS THIS THING, ANYHOW? IT SURE MEANS TO POLISH ME OFF--IF IT CAN!
SUDDENLY THE FLAT OF A MIGHTY HAND HITS ADAM A GLANCING BLOW...
OHHH!
LIKE A STONE HE PLUMMETS INTO THE SEA OF YBSS...
SPLASH!!
FOR OVER AN HOUR THE GIANT STARES UNWINKINGLY AT THE SEA WATERS, BUT HIS TINY DOUBLE NEVER REAPPEARS...
THERE'S NO SIGN OF HIM! UNDOUBTEDLY HE'S PERISHED!
SHORTLY, IN A REMOTE SPOT ON RANN, THE GIANT MAKES A REPORT TO HIS MASTER, AVANAR BAR...
THE REAL ADAM STRANGE FELL INTO THE SEA AND NEVER REAPPEARED!
GOOD! NOW THE EARTHMAN CAN NEVER SHOW UP TO PROVE YOU ARE ONLY A ROBOT I INVENTED TO HELP ME RE-COVER MY THRONE!
5

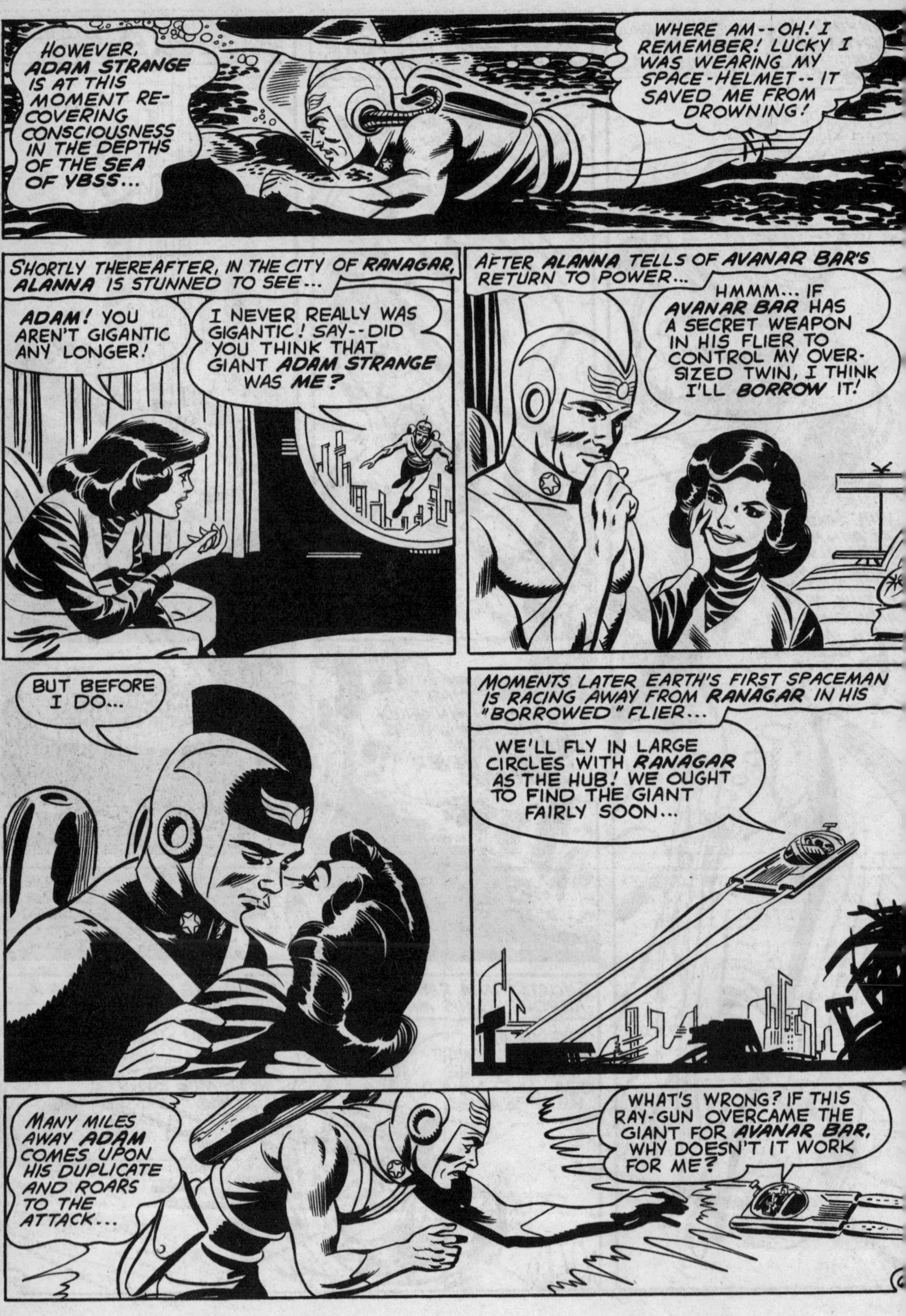
HOWEVER, ADAM STRANGE IS AT THIS MOMENT RECOVERING CONSCIOUSNESS IN THE DEPTHS OF THE SEA OF YBSS...
WHERE AM--OH! I REMEMBER! LUCKY I WAS WEARING MY SPACE-HELMET-- IT SAVED ME FROM DROWNING!
SHORTLY THEREAFTER, IN THE CITY OF RANAGAR, ALANNA IS STUNNED TO SEE...
ADAM! YOU AREN'T GIGANTIC ANY LONGER!
I NEVER REALLY WAS GIGANTIC! SAY--DID YOU THINK THAT GIANT ADAM STRANGE WAS ME?
AFTER ALANNA TELLS OF AVANAR BAR'S RETURN TO POWER...
HMMM... IF AVANAR BAR HAS A SECRET WEAPON IN HIS FLIER TO CONTROL MY OVER-SIZED TWIN, I THINK I'LL BORROW IT!
BUT BEFORE I DO...
MOMENTS LATER EARTH'S FIRST SPACEMAN IS RACING AWAY FROM RANAGAR IN HIS "BORROWED" FLIER...
WE'LL FLY IN LARGE CIRCLES WITH RANAGAR AS THE HUB! WE OUGHT TO FIND THE GIANT FAIRLY SOON...
MANY MILES AWAY ADAM COMES UPON HIS DUPLICATE AND ROARS TO THE ATTACK...
WHAT'S WRONG? IF THIS RAY-GUN OVERCAME THE GIANT FOR AVANAR BAR, WHY DOESN'T IT WORK FOR ME?

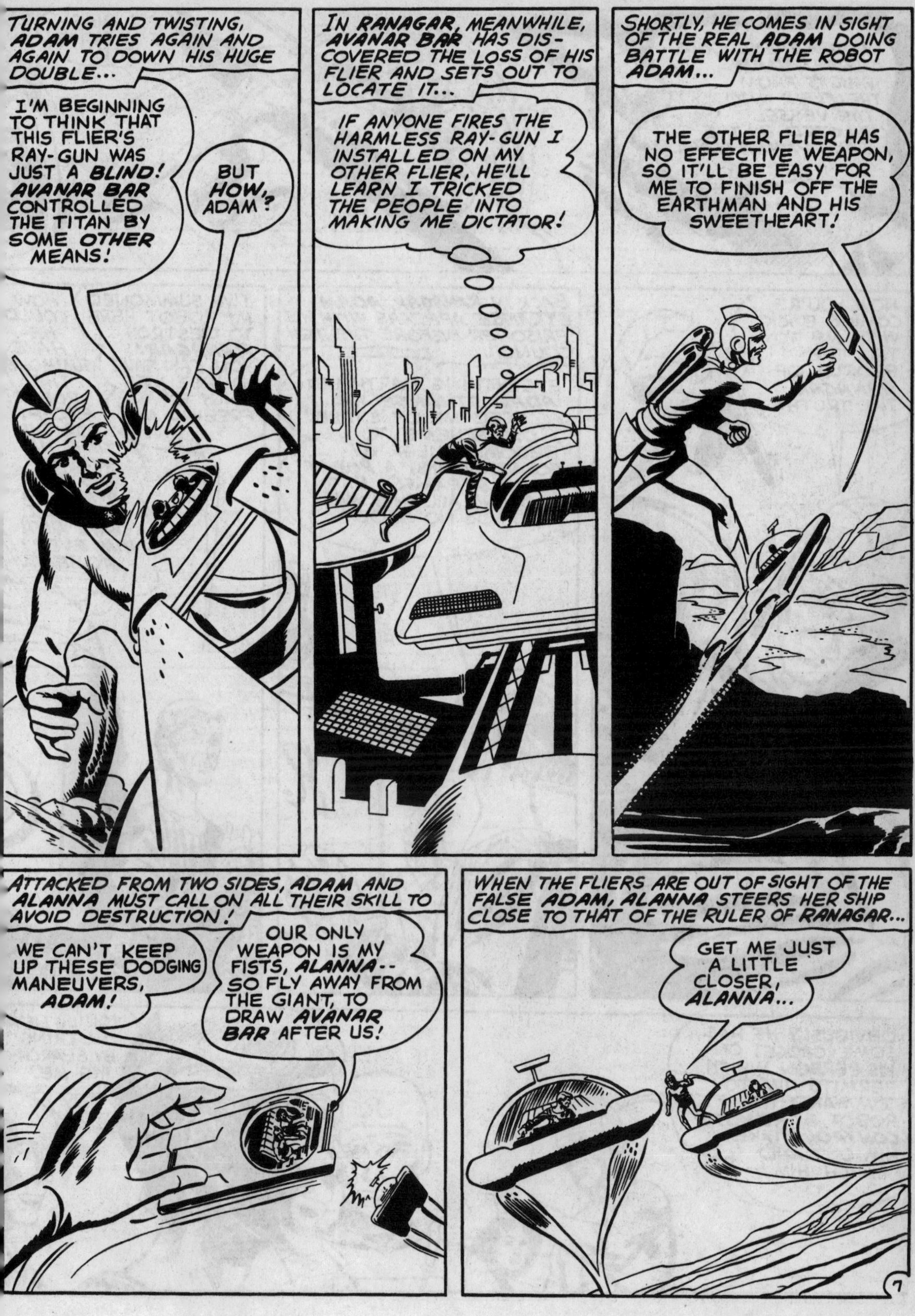
TURNING AND TWISTING, ADAM TRIES AGAIN AND AGAIN TO DOWN HIS HUGE DOUBLE...
I'M BEGINNING TO THINK THAT THIS FLIER'S RAY-GUN WAS JUST A BLIND! AVANAR BAR CONTROLLED THE TITAN BY SOME OTHER MEANS!
BUT HOW, ADAM?
IN RANAGAR, MEANWHILE, AVANAR BAR HAS DISCOVERED THE LOSS OF HIS FLIER AND SETS OUT TO LOCATE IT...
IF ANYONE FIRES THE HARMLESS RAY-GUN I INSTALLED ON MY OTHER FLIER, HE'LL LEARN I TRICKED THE PEOPLE INTO MAKING ME DICTATOR!
SHORTLY, HE COMES IN SIGHT OF THE REAL ADAM DOING BATTLE WITH THE ROBOT ADAM...
THE OTHER FLIER HAS NO EFFECTIVE WEAPON, SO IT'LL BE EASY FOR ME TO FINISH OFF THE EARTHMAN AND HIS SWEETHEART!
ATTACKED FROM TWO SIDES, ADAM AND ALANNA MUST CALL ON ALL THEIR SKILL TO AVOID DESTRUCTION!
WE CAN'T KEEP UP THESE DODGING MANEUVERS, ADAM!
OUR ONLY WEAPON IS MY FISTS, ALANNA-- SO FLY AWAY FROM THE GIANT, TO DRAW AVANAR BAR AFTER US!
WHEN THE FLIERS ARE OUT OF SIGHT OF THE FALSE ADAM, ALANNA STEERS HER SHIP CLOSE TO THAT OF THE RULER OF RANAGAR...
GET ME JUST A LITTLE CLOSER, ALANNA...
7

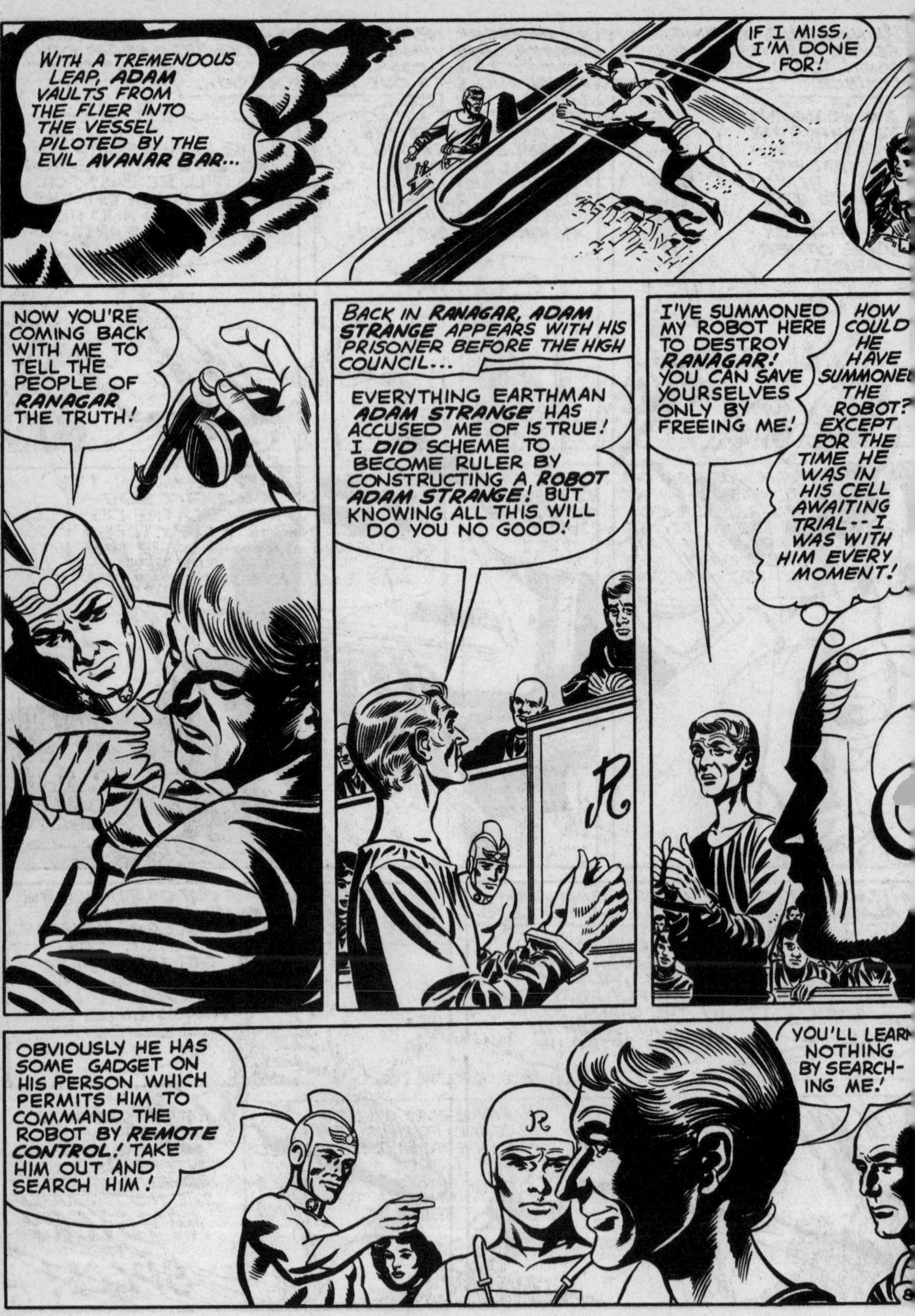
WITH A TREMENDOUS LEAP, ADAM VAULTS FROM THE FLIER INTO THE VESSEL PILOTED BY THE EVIL AVANAR BAR...
IF I MISS, I'M DONE FOR!
NOW YOU'RE COMING BACK WITH ME TO TELL THE PEOPLE OF RANAGAR THE TRUTH!
BACK IN RANAGAR, ADAM STRANGE APPEARS WITH HIS PRISONER BEFORE THE HIGH COUNCIL...
EVERYTHING EARTHMAN ADAM STRANGE HAS ACCUSED ME OF IS TRUE! I DID SCHEME TO BECOME RULER BY CONSTRUCTING A ROBOT ADAM STRANGE! BUT KNOWING ALL THIS WILL DO YOU NO GOOD!
I'VE SUMMONED MY ROBOT HERE TO DESTROY RANAGAR! YOU CAN SAVE YOURSELVES ONLY BY FREEING ME!
HOW COULD HE HAVE SUMMONE THE ROBOT? EXCEPT FOR THE TIME HE WAS IN HIS CELL AWAITING TRIAL--I WAS WITH HIM EVERY MOMENT!
OBVIOUSLY HE HAS SOME GADGET ON HIS PERSON WHICH PERMITS HIM TO COMMAND THE ROBOT BY REMOTE CONTROL! TAKE HIM OUT AND SEARCH HIM!
YOU'LL LEAR NOTHING BY SEARCH-ING ME!

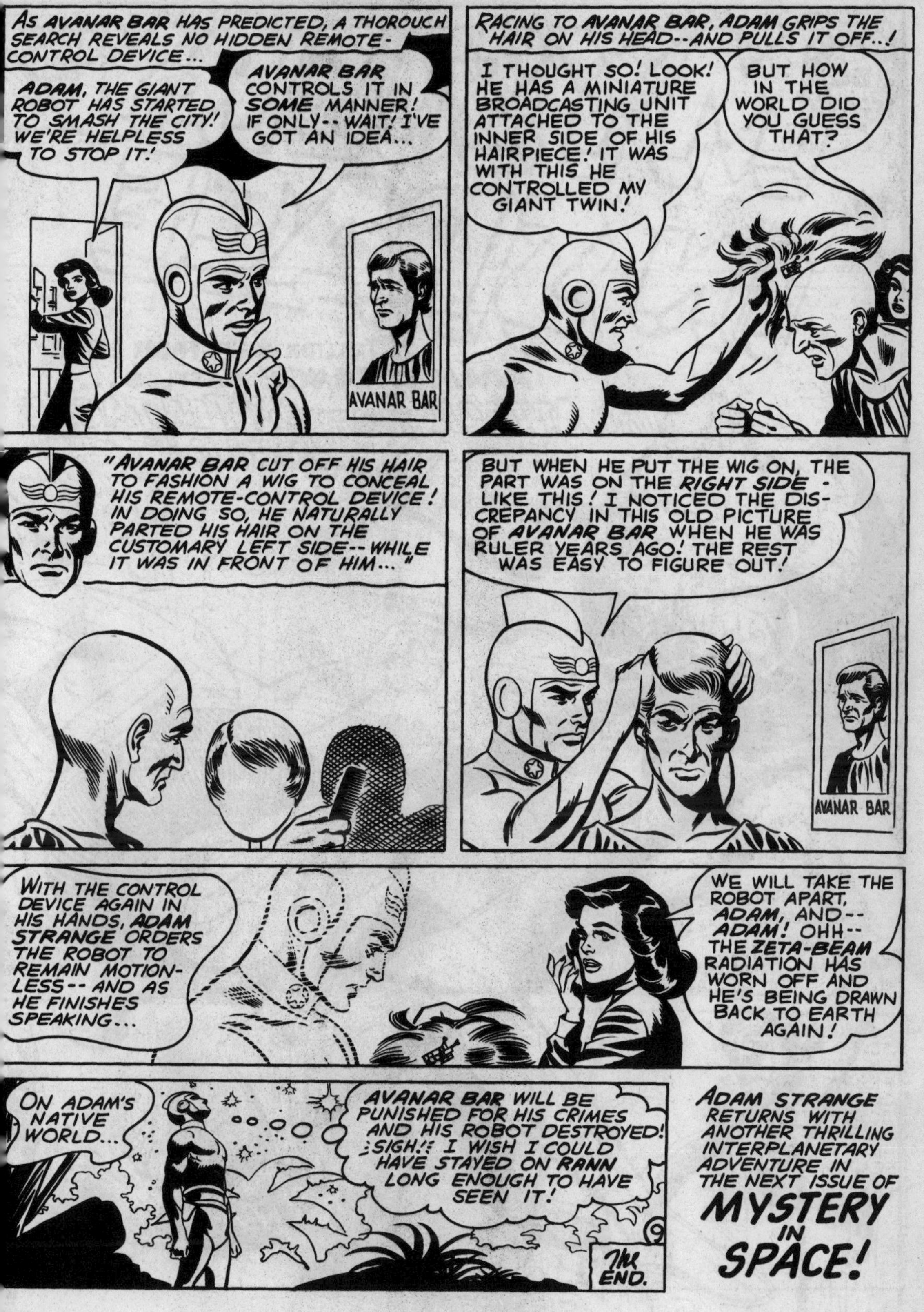
AS AVANAR BAR HAS PREDICTED, A THOROUCH SEARCH REVEALS NO HIDDEN REMOTE-CONTROL DEVICE...
ADAM, THE GIANT ROBOT HAS STARTED TO SMASH THE CITY! WE'RE HELPLESS TO STOP IT!
AVANAR BAR CONTROLS IT IN SOME MANNER! IF ONLY-- WAIT! I'VE GOT AN IDEA...
AVANAR BAR
RACING TO AVANAR BAR, ADAM GRIPS THE HAIR ON HIS HEAD--AND PULLS IT OFF..!
I THOUGHT SO! LOOK! HE HAS A MINIATURE BROADCASTING UNIT ATTACHED TO THE INNER SIDE OF HIS HAIRPIECE! IT WAS WITH THIS HE CONTROLLED MY GIANT TWIN!
BUT HOW IN THE WORLD DID YOU GUESS THAT?
"AVANAR BAR CUT OFF HIS HAIR TO FASHION A WIG TO CONCEAL HIS REMOTE-CONTROL DEVICE! IN DOING SO, HE NATURALLY PARTED HIS HAIR ON THE CUSTOMARY LEFT SIDE--WHILE IT WAS IN FRONT OF HIM..."
BUT WHEN HE PUT THE WIG ON, THE PART WAS ON THE RIGHT SIDE - LIKE THIS! I NOTICED THE DISCREPANCY IN THIS OLD PICTURE OF AVANAR BAR WHEN HE WAS RULER YEARS AGO! THE REST WAS EASY TO FIGURE OUT!
AVANAR BAR
WITH THE CONTROL DEVICE AGAIN IN HIS HANDS, ADAM STRANGE ORDERS THE ROBOT TO REMAIN MOTIONLESS-- AND AS HE FINISHES SPEAKING...
WE WILL TAKE THE ROBOT APART, ADAM, AND-- ADAM! OHH-- THE ZETA-BEAM RADIATION HAS WORN OFF AND HE'S BEING DRAWN BACK TO EARTH AGAIN!
ON ADAM'S NATIVE WORLD...
AVANAR BAR WILL BE PUNISHED FOR HIS CRIMES AND HIS ROBOT DESTROYED! SIGH! I WISH I COULD HAVE STAYED ON RANN LONG ENOUGH TO HAVE SEEN IT!
9
THE END.
ADAM STRANGE RETURNS WITH ANOTHER THRILLING INTERPLANETARY ADVENTURE IN THE NEXT ISSUE OF
MYSTERY IN SPACE!

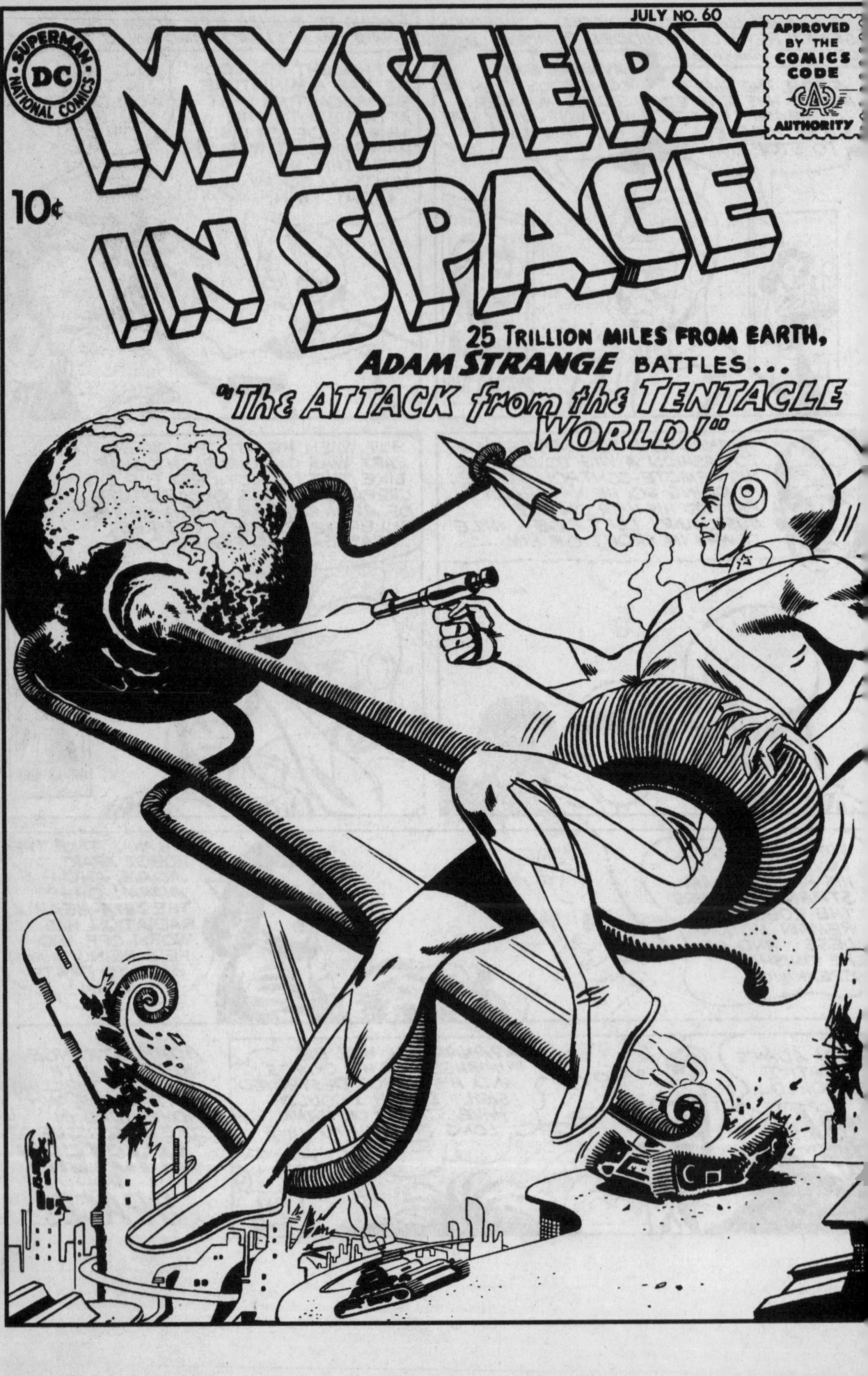
JULY NO. 60
SUPERMAN DC NATIONAL COMICS
APPROVED BY THE COMICS CODE AUTHORITY
MYSTERY IN SPACE
10¢
25 TRILLION MILES FROM EARTH,
ADAM STRANGE BATTLES...
"The ATTACK from the TENTACLE WORLD!"

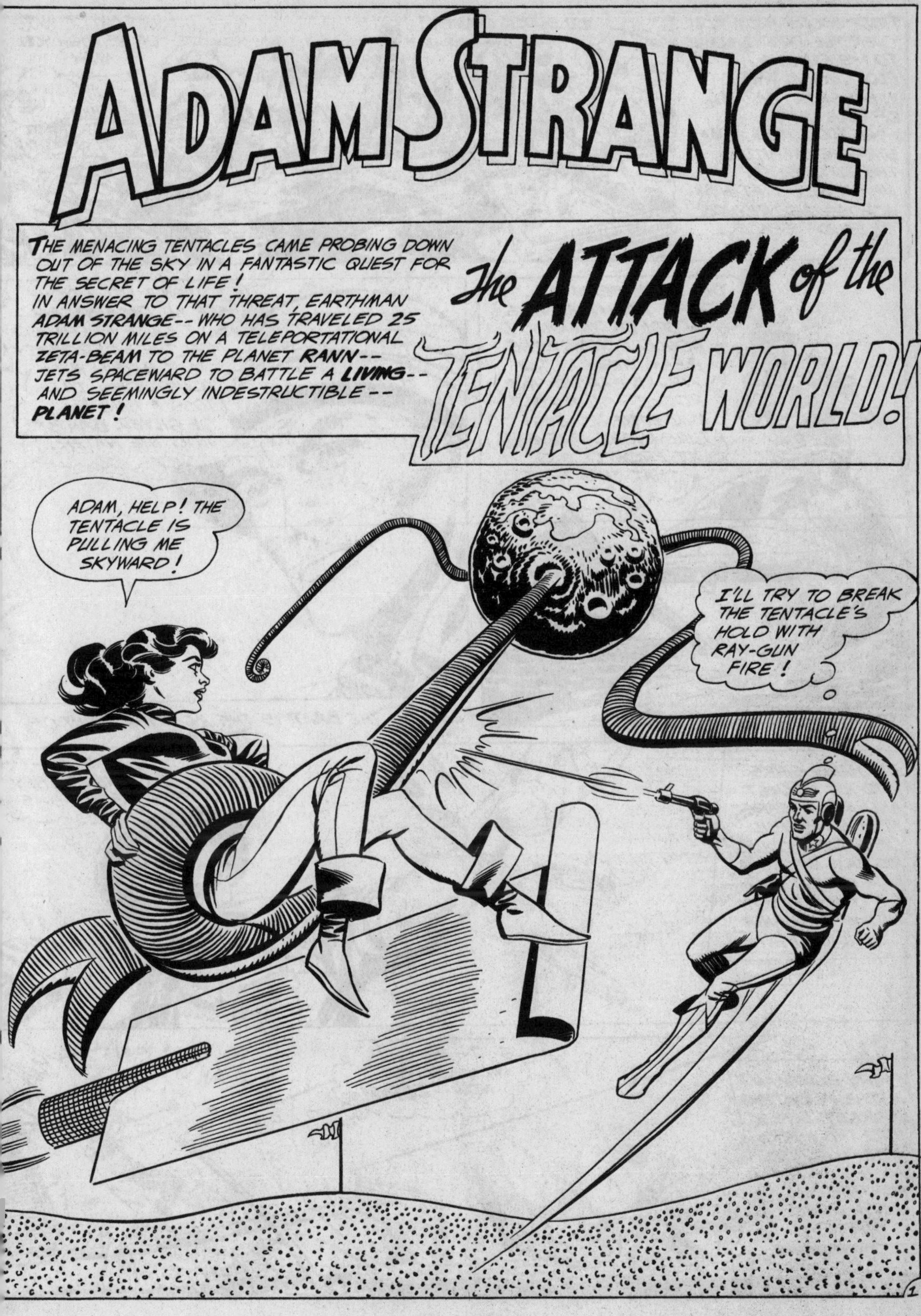
ADAM STRANGE
THE MENACING TENTACLES CAME PROBING DOWN OUT OF THE SKY IN A FANTASTIC QUEST FOR THE SECRET OF LIFE! IN ANSWER TO THAT THREAT, EARTHMAN ADAM STRANGE-- WHO HAS TRAVELED 25 TRILLION MILES ON A TELEPORTATIONAL ZETA-BEAM TO THE PLANET RANN-- JETS SPACEWARD TO BATTLE A LIVING-- AND SEEMINGLY INDESTRUCTIBLE -- PLANET!
The ATTACK of the TENTACLE WORLD!
ADAM, HELP! THE TENTACLE IS PULLING ME SKYWARD!
I'LL TRY TO BREAK THE TENTACLE'S HOLD WITH RAY-GUN FIRE!
1

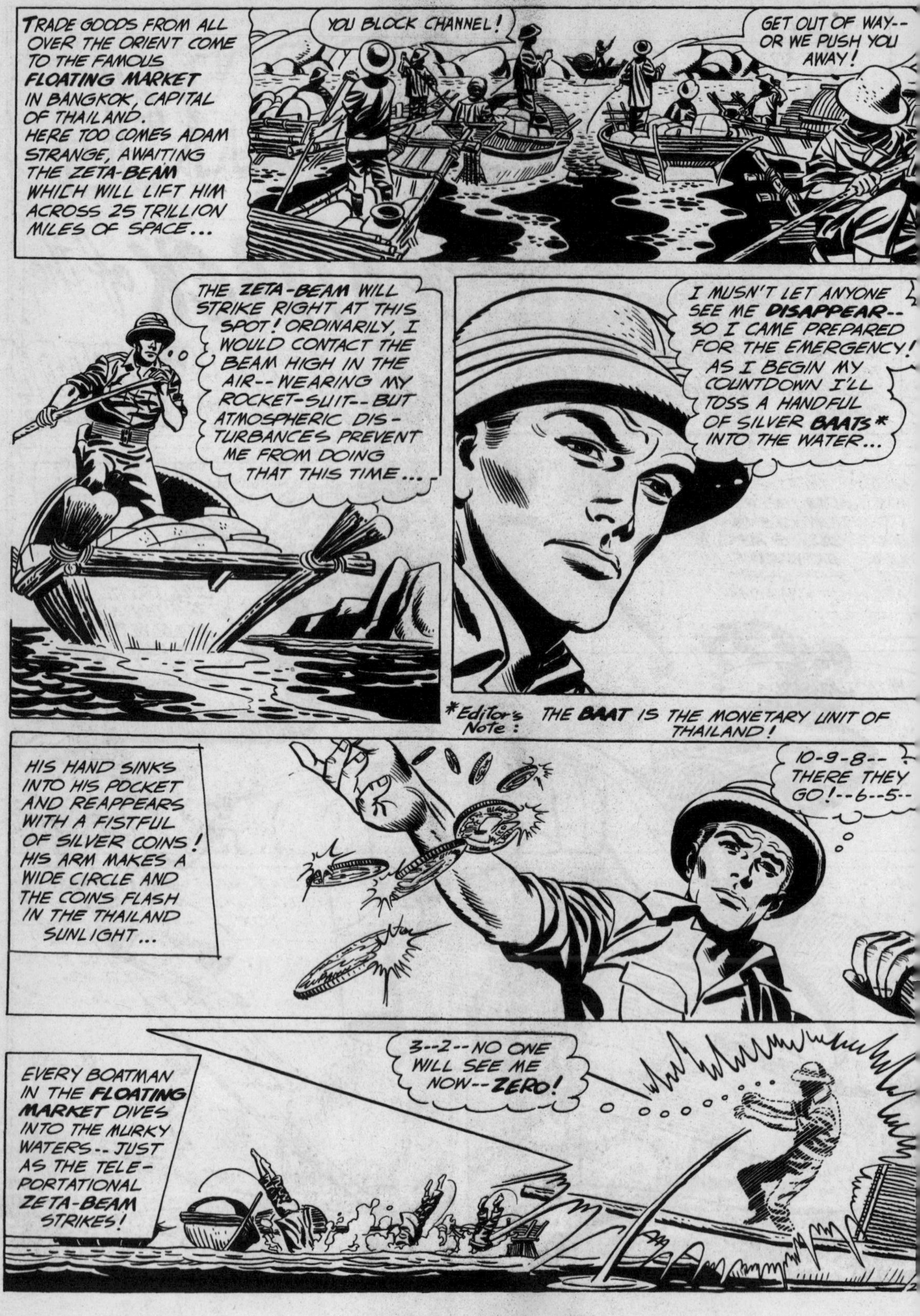
TRADE GOODS FROM ALL OVER THE ORIENT COME TO THE FAMOUS FLOATING MARKET IN BANGKOK, CAPITAL OF THAILAND. HERE TOO COMES ADAM STRANGE, AWAITING THE ZETA-BEAM WHICH WILL LIFT HIM ACROSS 25 TRILLION MILES OF SPACE...
YOU BLOCK CHANNEL!
GET OUT OF WAY-- OR WE PUSH YOU AWAY!
THE ZETA-BEAM WILL STRIKE RIGHT AT THIS SPOT! ORDINARILY, I WOULD CONTACT THE BEAM HIGH IN THE AIR--WEARING MY ROCKET-SUIT--BUT ATMOSPHERIC DIS-TURBANCES PREVENT ME FROM DOING THAT THIS TIME...
I MUSN'T LET ANYONE SEE ME DISAPPEAR-- SO I CAME PREPARED FOR THE EMERGENCY! AS I BEGIN MY COUNTDOWN I'LL TOSS A HANDFUL OF SILVER BAATS* INTO THE WATER...
*Editor's Note: THE BAAT IS THE MONETARY UNIT OF THAILAND!
HIS HAND SINKS INTO HIS POCKET AND REAPPEARS WITH A FISTFUL OF SILVER COINS! HIS ARM MAKES A WIDE CIRCLE AND THE COINS FLASH IN THE THAILAND SUNLIGHT...
10-9-8-- THERE THEY GO!--6--5--
EVERY BOATMAN IN THE FLOATING MARKET DIVES INTO THE MURKY WATERS--JUST AS THE TELE-PORTATIONAL ZETA-BEAM STRIKES!
3--2--NO ONE WILL SEE ME NOW--ZERO!

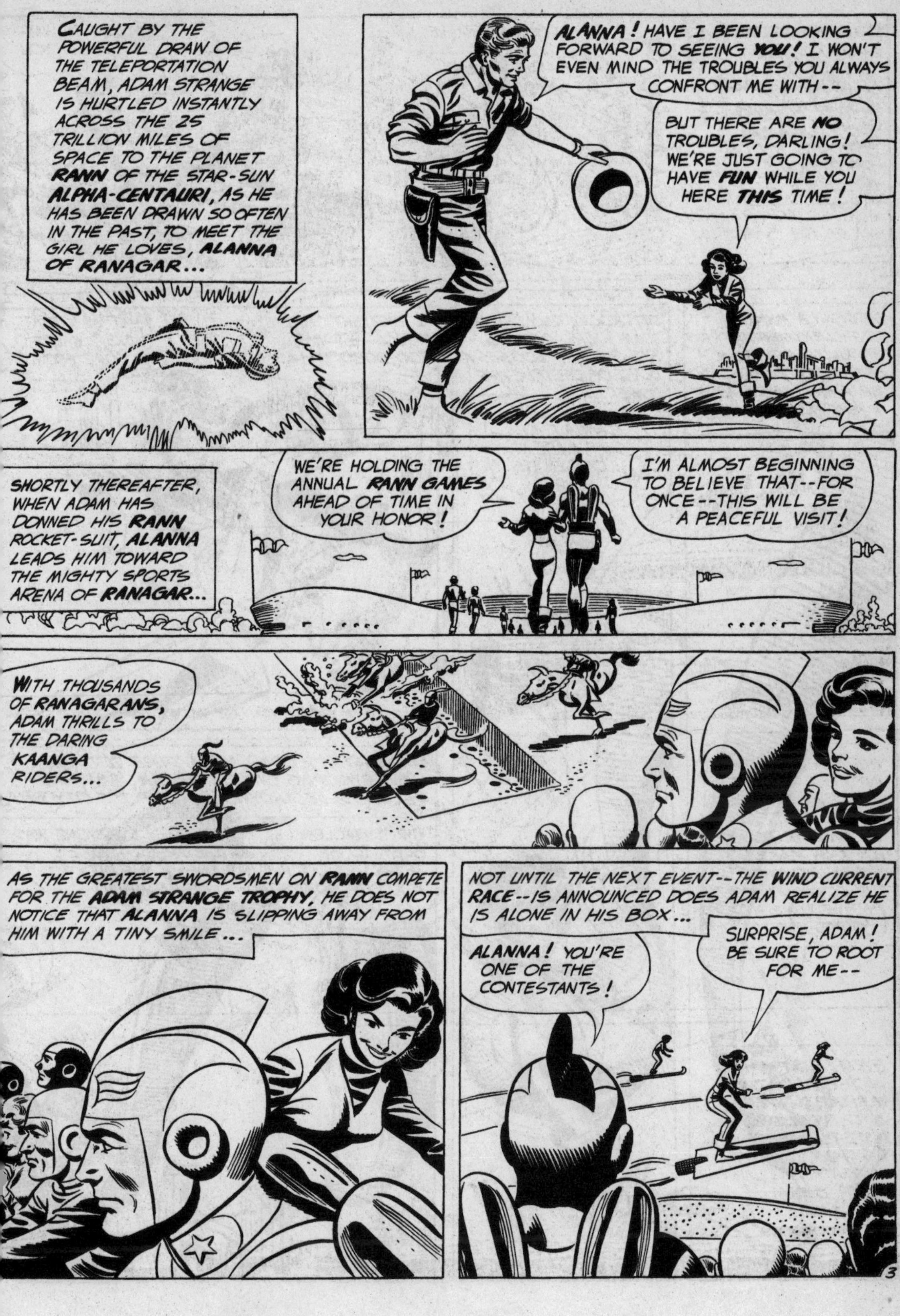
CAUGHT BY THE POWERFUL DRAW OF THE TELEPORTATION BEAM, ADAM STRANGE IS HURTLED INSTANTLY ACROSS THE 25 TRILLION MILES OF SPACE TO THE PLANET RANN OF THE STAR-SUN ALPHA-CENTAURI, AS HE HAS BEEN DRAWN SO OFTEN IN THE PAST, TO MEET THE GIRL HE LOVES, ALANNA OF RANAGAR...
ALANNA! HAVE I BEEN LOOKING FORWARD TO SEEING YOU! I WON'T EVEN MIND THE TROUBLES YOU ALWAYS CONFRONT ME WITH--
BUT THERE ARE NO TROUBLES, DARLING! WE'RE JUST GOING TO HAVE FUN WHILE YOU HERE THIS TIME!
SHORTLY THEREAFTER, WHEN ADAM HAS DONNED HIS RANN ROCKET-SUIT, ALANNA LEADS HIM TOWARD THE MIGHTY SPORTS ARENA OF RANAGAR...
WE'RE HOLDING THE ANNUAL RANN GAMES AHEAD OF TIME IN YOUR HONOR!
I'M ALMOST BEGINNING TO BELIEVE THAT--FOR ONCE--THIS WILL BE A PEACEFUL VISIT!
WITH THOUSANDS OF RANAGARANS, ADAM THRILLS TO THE DARING KAANGA RIDERS...
AS THE GREATEST SWORDSMEN ON RANN COMPETE FOR THE ADAM STRANGE TROPHY, HE DOES NOT NOTICE THAT ALANNA IS SLIPPING AWAY FROM HIM WITH A TINY SMILE...
NOT UNTIL THE NEXT EVENT--THE WIND CURRENT RACE--IS ANNOUNCED DOES ADAM REALIZE HE IS ALONE IN HIS BOX...
ALANNA! YOU'RE ONE OF THE CONTESTANTS!
SURPRISE, ADAM! BE SURE TO ROOT FOR ME--
3

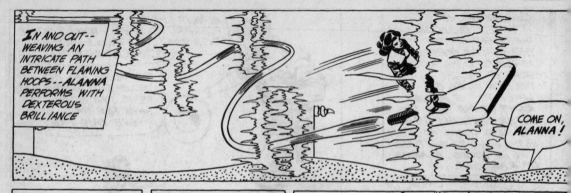

IN AND OUT-- WEAVING AN INTRICATE PATH BETWEEN FLAMING HOOPS--ALANNA PERFORMS WITH DEXTEROUS BRILLIANCE

COME ON, ALANNA!

SUDDENLY A MIGHTY TENTACLE COMES WHIPPING GROUNDWARD FROM A SEEMINGLY EMPTY SKY-- WRAPPING ITSELF ABOUT A TERRIFIED ALANNA...

OHHH--

JET-ROCKETING UPWARD, ADAM WHIPS OUT HIS RAY-GUN AND LOOSES A BLAST OF DESTRUCTIVE POWER...

JUMP, ALANNA! MY SHOT MADE IT LOOSEN ITS GRIP!

I THOUGHT THAT "PEACE" BIT WAS TOO GOOD TO LAST!

WHAT WAS THAT THING? WHERE'D IT COME FROM?

SUDDENLY A SECOND AND A THIRD TENTACLE COME SWOOPING ONTO RANAGAR, SMASHING BUILDINGS, DESTROYING PART OF THE CITY WALL...

THE TENTACLES SEEM TO BE TRYING TO CATCH HOLD OF SOME-THING...

FORTUNATELY EVERYONE WAS AT THE ARENA--THERE'S NO ONE IN THE CITY TO BE HARMED!

THE ARMED MIGHT OF ALL **RANN** SURGES TO THE ATTACK...

WE'RE SCORING HITS! THE TENTACLES ARE WITH— DRAWING!

WE AREN'T DESTROYING THOSE THINGS, HOW— EVER! WE JUST SEEM TO BE **STINGING THEM!**

ONLY FOR A MOMENT DO THE TANKS AND FLIERS HOLD THEIR ADVANTAGE, FOR SHORT MOMENTS LATER-- A TENTACLED WORLD COMES INTO VIEW...

HOW CAN THE TENTACLES WITHSTAND OUR WEAPON POWER? THEY RETREAT WHEN HIT, THEN SURGE BACK UN— HARMED!

AS ADAM AND **ALANNA** STARE SKY— WARD, A TELEPATHIC VOICE MAKES ITSELF HEARD...

PEOPLE OF **RANN**-- IT WILL DO YOU NO GOOD TO RESIST! NOTHING CAN DESTROY ME! I AM THE LIVING WORLD **YGGARDIS**, BORN IN THE COSMIC EXPLOSION WHICH ORIGINALLY SPAWNED THE PLANETS!

"TO ME ALONE OF ALL PLANETS IN THE UNIVERSE WAS LIFE GIVEN! I POSSESS A MIND JUST AS DO ALL OTHER LIFE- FORMS! AND POSSESSING LIFE AND A BRAIN, I GROW LONELY..."

HOW I YEARN TO HAVE LIVING CREATURES ROAM ABOUT MY SURFACE..AS DO OTHER WORLDS...

"FOR UNCOUNTED CENTURIES, I HAVE ROAMED THE UNIVERSE, RAIDING OTHER WORLDS FOR THEIR LIFE-FORMS, LIFTING THEM IN MY TENTACLES..."

I SHALL STEAL THE LIFE WHICH NATURE DENIED ME-- "PLANT" IT ON MY BODY-- GIVE IT SUSTAINING FOOD AND ATMOSPHERE...

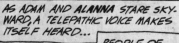

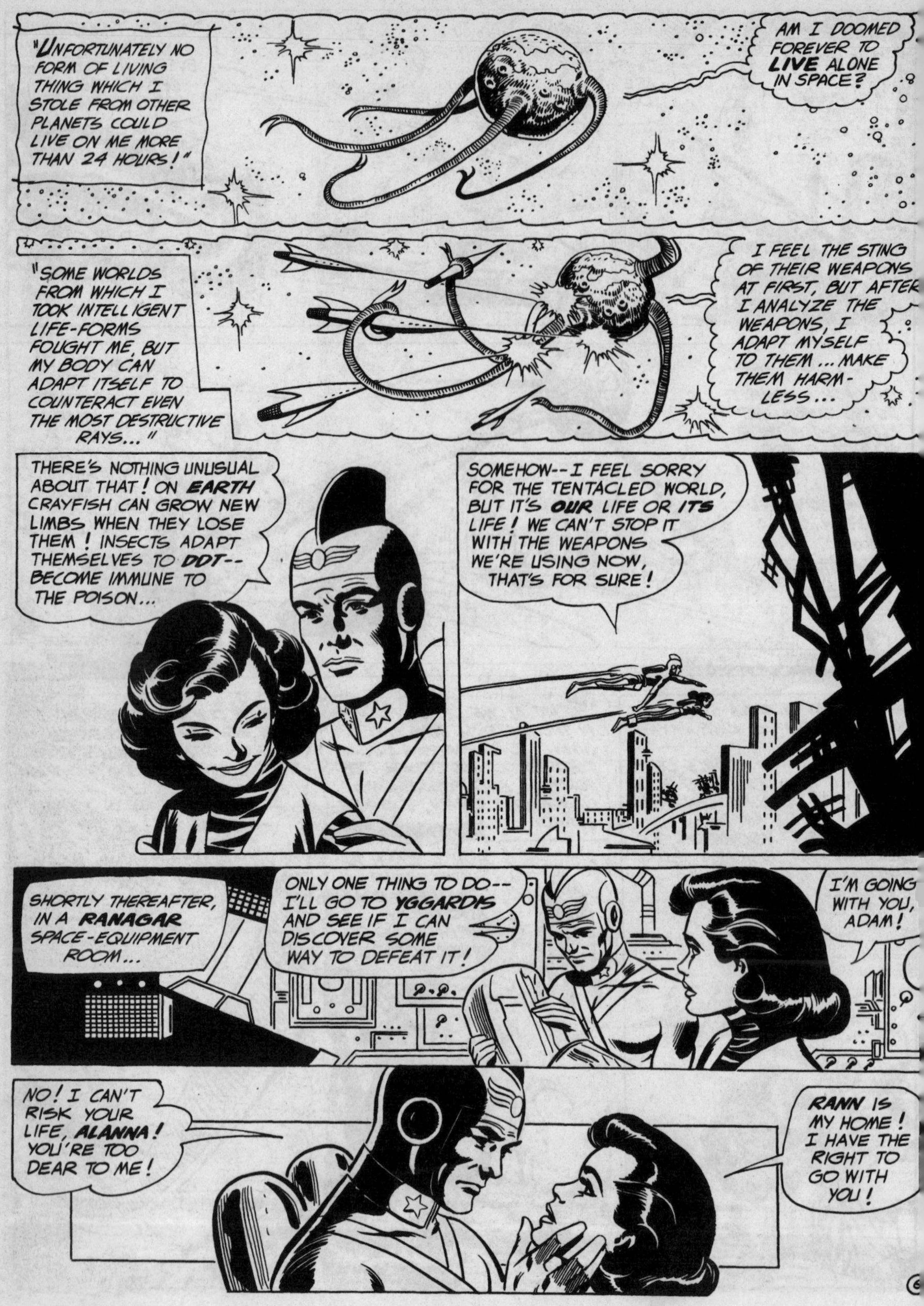
"UNFORTUNATELY NO FORM OF LIVING THING WHICH I STOLE FROM OTHER PLANETS COULD LIVE ON ME MORE THAN 24 HOURS!"
AM I DOOMED FOREVER TO LIVE ALONE IN SPACE?
"SOME WORLDS FROM WHICH I TOOK INTELLIGENT LIFE-FORMS FOUGHT ME, BUT MY BODY CAN ADAPT ITSELF TO COUNTERACT EVEN THE MOST DESTRUCTIVE RAYS..."
I FEEL THE STING OF THEIR WEAPONS AT FIRST, BUT AFTER I ANALYZE THE WEAPONS, I ADAPT MYSELF TO THEM ... MAKE THEM HARMLESS...
THERE'S NOTHING UNUSUAL ABOUT THAT! ON EARTH CRAYFISH CAN GROW NEW LIMBS WHEN THEY LOSE THEM! INSECTS ADAPT THEMSELVES TO DDT-- BECOME IMMUNE TO THE POISON...
SOMEHOW--I FEEL SORRY FOR THE TENTACLED WORLD, BUT IT'S OUR LIFE OR ITS LIFE! WE CAN'T STOP IT WITH THE WEAPONS WE'RE USING NOW, THAT'S FOR SURE!
SHORTLY THEREAFTER, IN A RANAGAR SPACE-EQUIPMENT ROOM...
ONLY ONE THING TO DO-- I'LL GO TO YGGARDIS AND SEE IF I CAN DISCOVER SOME WAY TO DEFEAT IT!
I'M GOING WITH YOU, ADAM!
NO! I CAN'T RISK YOUR LIFE, ALANNA! YOU'RE TOO DEAR TO ME!
RANN IS MY HOME! I HAVE THE RIGHT TO GO WITH YOU!

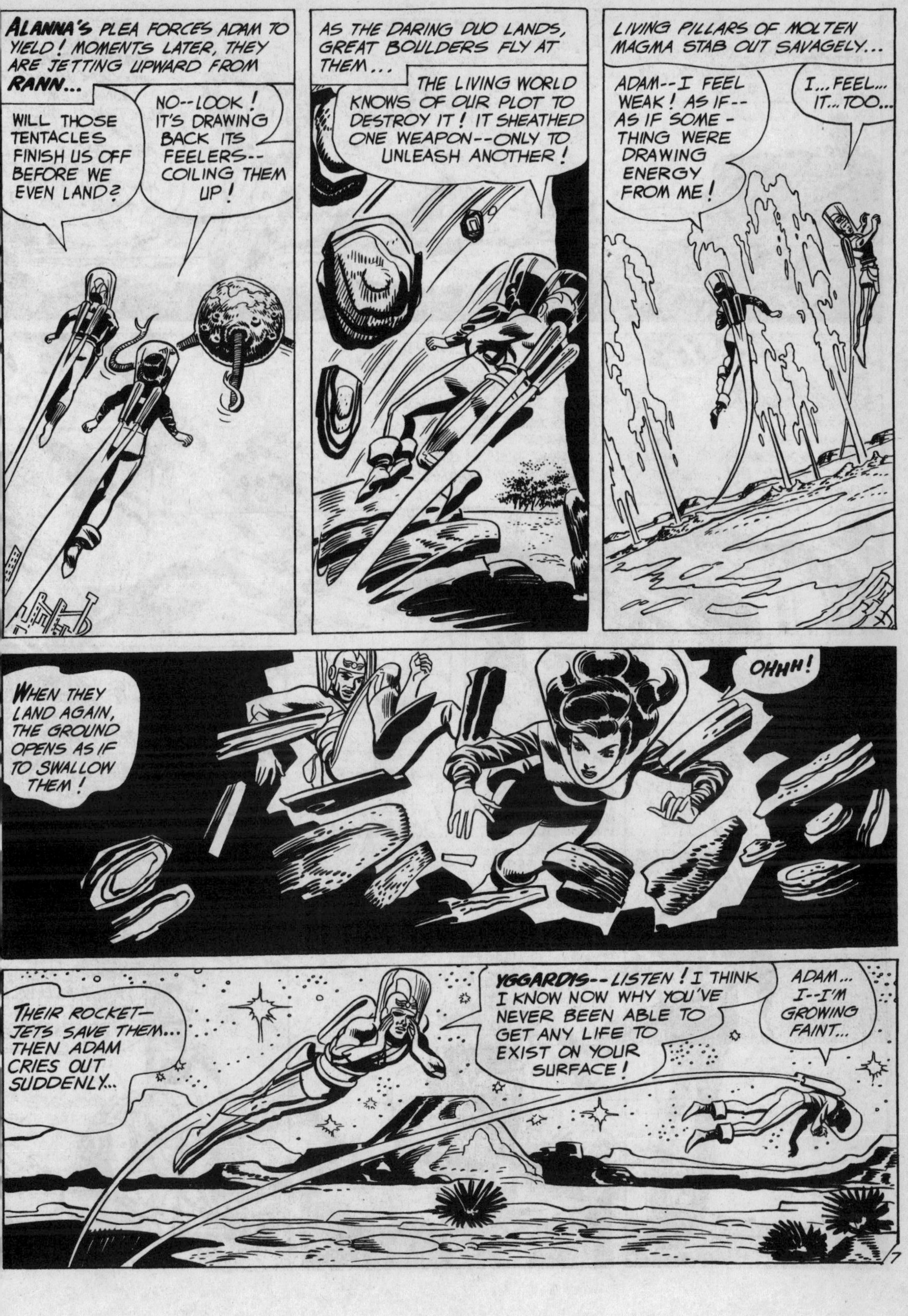
ALANNA'S PLEA FORCES ADAM TO YIELD! MOMENTS LATER, THEY ARE JETTING UPWARD FROM RANN...
WILL THOSE TENTACLES FINISH US OFF BEFORE WE EVEN LAND?
NO--LOOK! IT'S DRAWING BACK ITS FEELERS--COILING THEM UP!
AS THE DARING DUO LANDS, GREAT BOULDERS FLY AT THEM...
THE LIVING WORLD KNOWS OF OUR PLOT TO DESTROY IT! IT SHEATHED ONE WEAPON--ONLY TO UNLEASH ANOTHER!
LIVING PILLARS OF MOLTEN MAGMA STAB OUT SAVAGELY...
ADAM--I FEEL WEAK! AS IF--AS IF SOME-THING WERE DRAWING ENERGY FROM ME!
I...FEEL... IT...TOO...
WHEN THEY LAND AGAIN, THE GROUND OPENS AS IF TO SWALLOW THEM!
OHHH!
THEIR ROCKET-JETS SAVE THEM... THEN ADAM CRIES OUT SUDDENLY...
YGGARDIS--LISTEN! I THINK I KNOW NOW WHY YOU'VE NEVER BEEN ABLE TO GET ANY LIFE TO EXIST ON YOUR SURFACE!
ADAM... I--I'M GROWING FAINT...
7

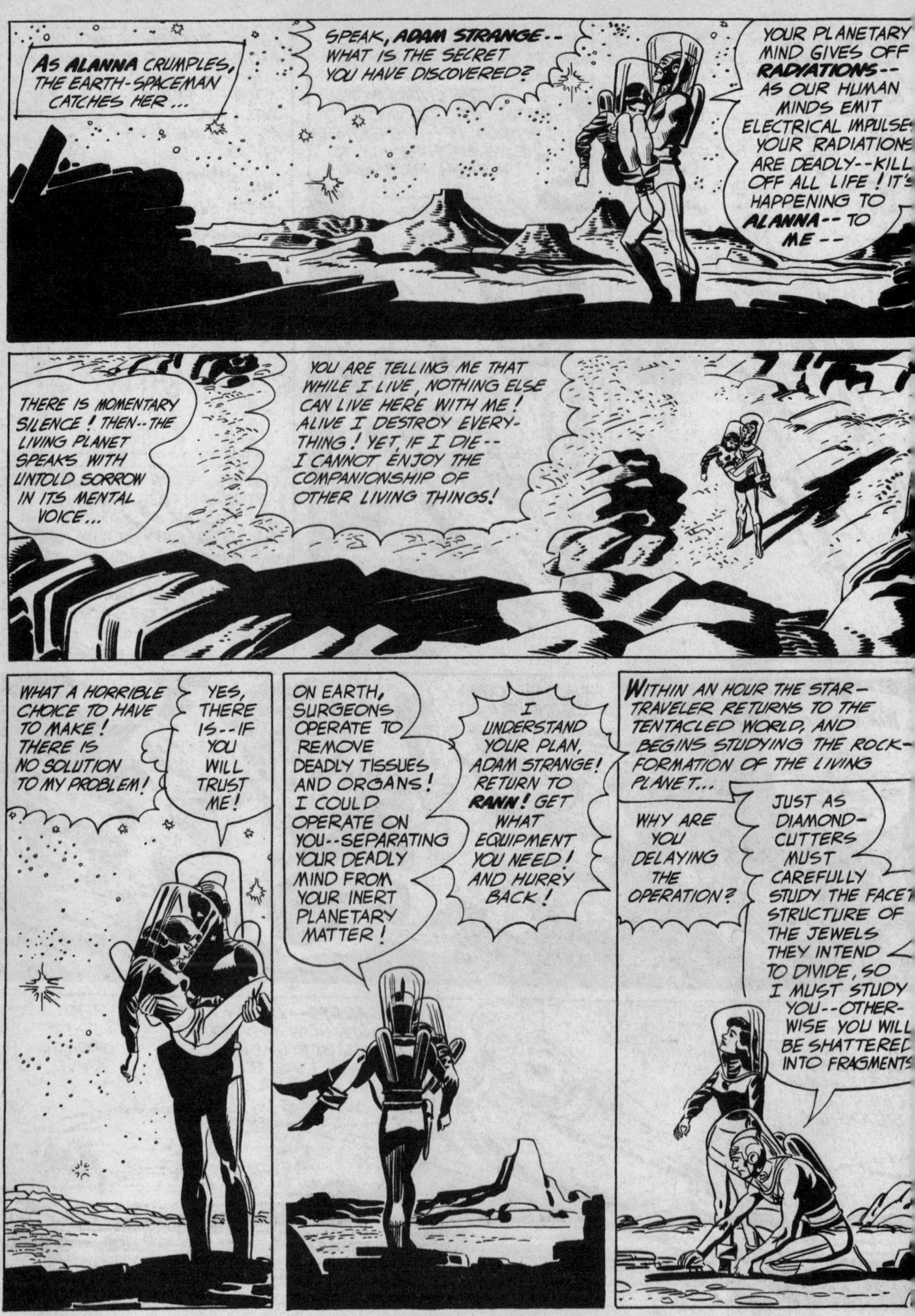
AS ALANNA CRUMPLES, THE EARTH-SPACEMAN CATCHES HER...
SPEAK, ADAM STRANGE-- WHAT IS THE SECRET YOU HAVE DISCOVERED?
YOUR PLANETARY MIND GIVES OFF RADIATIONS-- AS OUR HUMAN MINDS EMIT ELECTRICAL IMPULSES YOUR RADIATIONS ARE DEADLY--KILL OFF ALL LIFE! IT'S HAPPENING TO ALANNA-- TO ME--
THERE IS MOMENTARY SILENCE! THEN--THE LIVING PLANET SPEAKS WITH UNTOLD SORROW IN ITS MENTAL VOICE...
YOU ARE TELLING ME THAT WHILE I LIVE, NOTHING ELSE CAN LIVE HERE WITH ME! ALIVE I DESTROY EVERYTHING! YET, IF I DIE-- I CANNOT ENJOY THE COMPANIONSHIP OF OTHER LIVING THINGS!
WHAT A HORRIBLE CHOICE TO HAVE TO MAKE! THERE IS NO SOLUTION TO MY PROBLEM!
YES, THERE IS--IF YOU WILL TRUST ME!
ON EARTH, SURGEONS OPERATE TO REMOVE DEADLY TISSUES AND ORGANS! I COULD OPERATE ON YOU--SEPARATING YOUR DEADLY MIND FROM YOUR INERT PLANETARY MATTER!
I UNDERSTAND YOUR PLAN, ADAM STRANGE! RETURN TO RANN! GET WHAT EQUIPMENT YOU NEED! AND HURRY BACK!
WITHIN AN HOUR THE STAR-TRAVELER RETURNS TO THE TENTACLED WORLD, AND BEGINS STUDYING THE ROCK-FORMATION OF THE LIVING PLANET...
WHY ARE YOU DELAYING THE OPERATION?
JUST AS DIAMOND-CUTTERS MUST CAREFULLY STUDY THE FACET STRUCTURE OF THE JEWELS THEY INTEND TO DIVIDE, SO I MUST STUDY YOU--OTHERWISE YOU WILL BE SHATTERED INTO FRAGMENTS

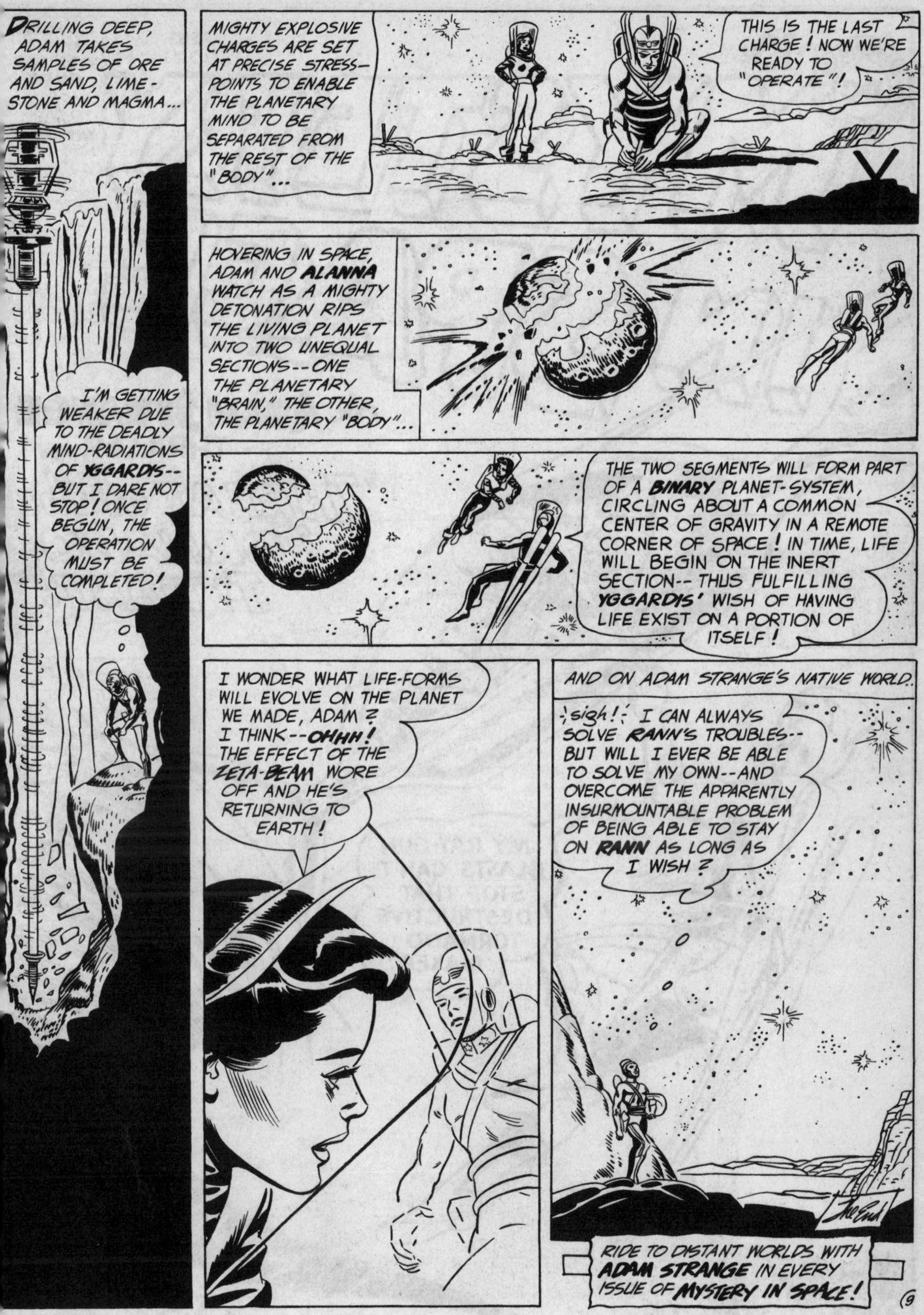
DRILLING DEEP, ADAM TAKES SAMPLES OF ORE AND SAND, LIME-STONE AND MAGMA...
I'M GETTING WEAKER DUE TO THE DEADLY MIND-RADIATIONS OF YGGARDIS-- BUT I DARE NOT STOP! ONCE BEGUN, THE OPERATION MUST BE COMPLETED!
MIGHTY EXPLOSIVE CHARGES ARE SET AT PRECISE STRESS-POINTS TO ENABLE THE PLANETARY MIND TO BE SEPARATED FROM THE REST OF THE "BODY"...
THIS IS THE LAST CHARGE! NOW WE'RE READY TO "OPERATE"!
HOVERING IN SPACE, ADAM AND ALANNA WATCH AS A MIGHTY DETONATION RIPS THE LIVING PLANET INTO TWO UNEQUAL SECTIONS--ONE THE PLANETARY "BRAIN," THE OTHER, THE PLANETARY "BODY"...
THE TWO SEGMENTS WILL FORM PART OF A BINARY PLANET-SYSTEM, CIRCLING ABOUT A COMMON CENTER OF GRAVITY IN A REMOTE CORNER OF SPACE! IN TIME, LIFE WILL BEGIN ON THE INERT SECTION-- THUS FULFILLING YGGARDIS' WISH OF HAVING LIFE EXIST ON A PORTION OF ITSELF!
I WONDER WHAT LIFE-FORMS WILL EVOLVE ON THE PLANET WE MADE, ADAM? I THINK--OHHH! THE EFFECT OF THE ZETA-BEAM WORE OFF AND HE'S RETURNING TO EARTH!
AND ON ADAM STRANGE'S NATIVE WORLD.
-sigh!- I CAN ALWAYS SOLVE RANN'S TROUBLES-- BUT WILL I EVER BE ABLE TO SOLVE MY OWN--AND OVERCOME THE APPARENTLY INSURMOUNTABLE PROBLEM OF BEING ABLE TO STAY ON RANN AS LONG AS I WISH?
The End
RIDE TO DISTANT WORLDS WITH ADAM STRANGE IN EVERY ISSUE OF MYSTERY IN SPACE!
9

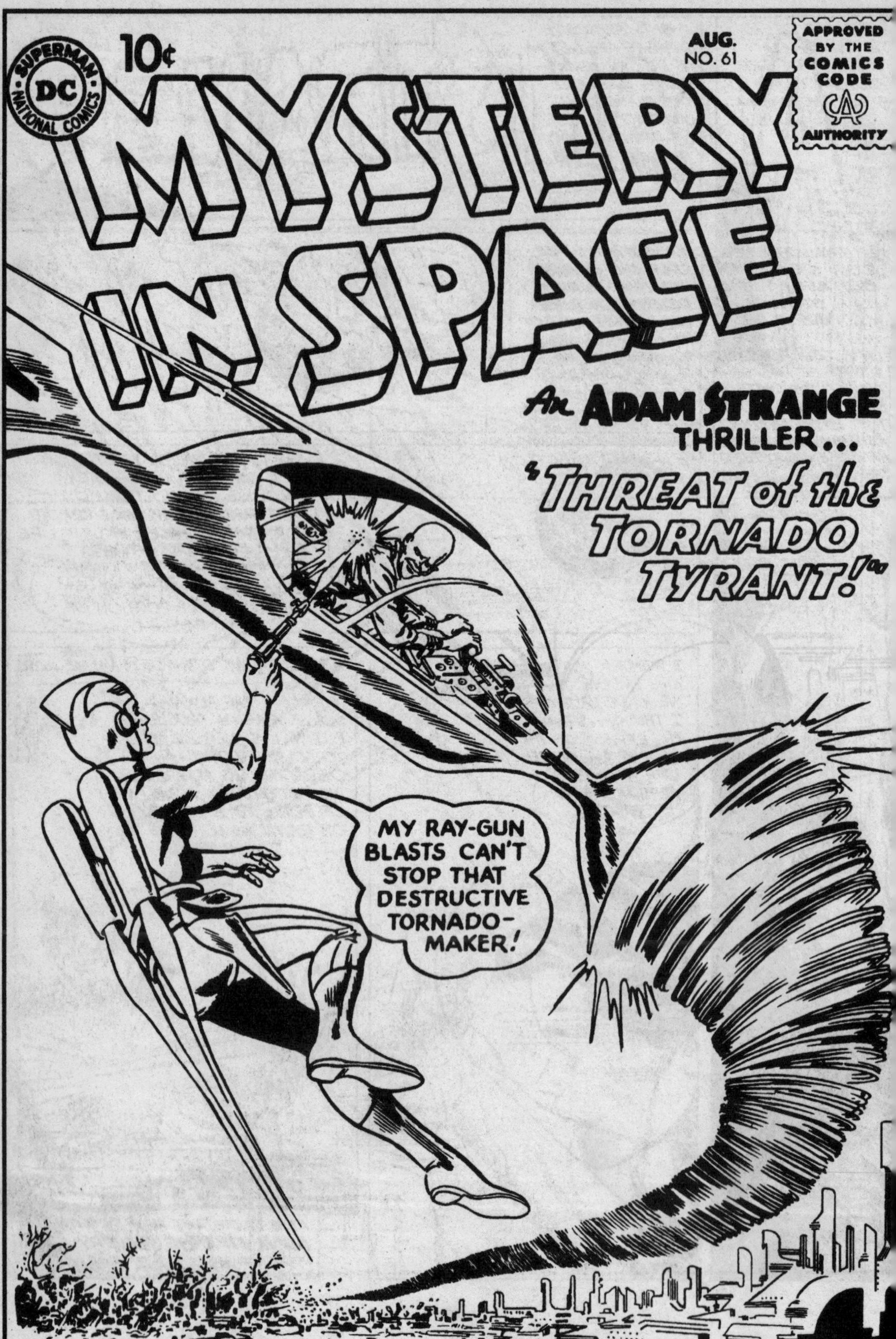
10¢
SUPERMAN DC NATIONAL COMICS
AUG.
NO. 61
APPROVED BY THE COMICS CODE AUTHORITY
MYSTERY IN SPACE
An ADAM STRANGE THRILLER...
"THREAT of the TORNADO TYRANT!"
MY RAY-GUN BLASTS CAN'T STOP THAT DESTRUCTIVE TORNADO-MAKER!

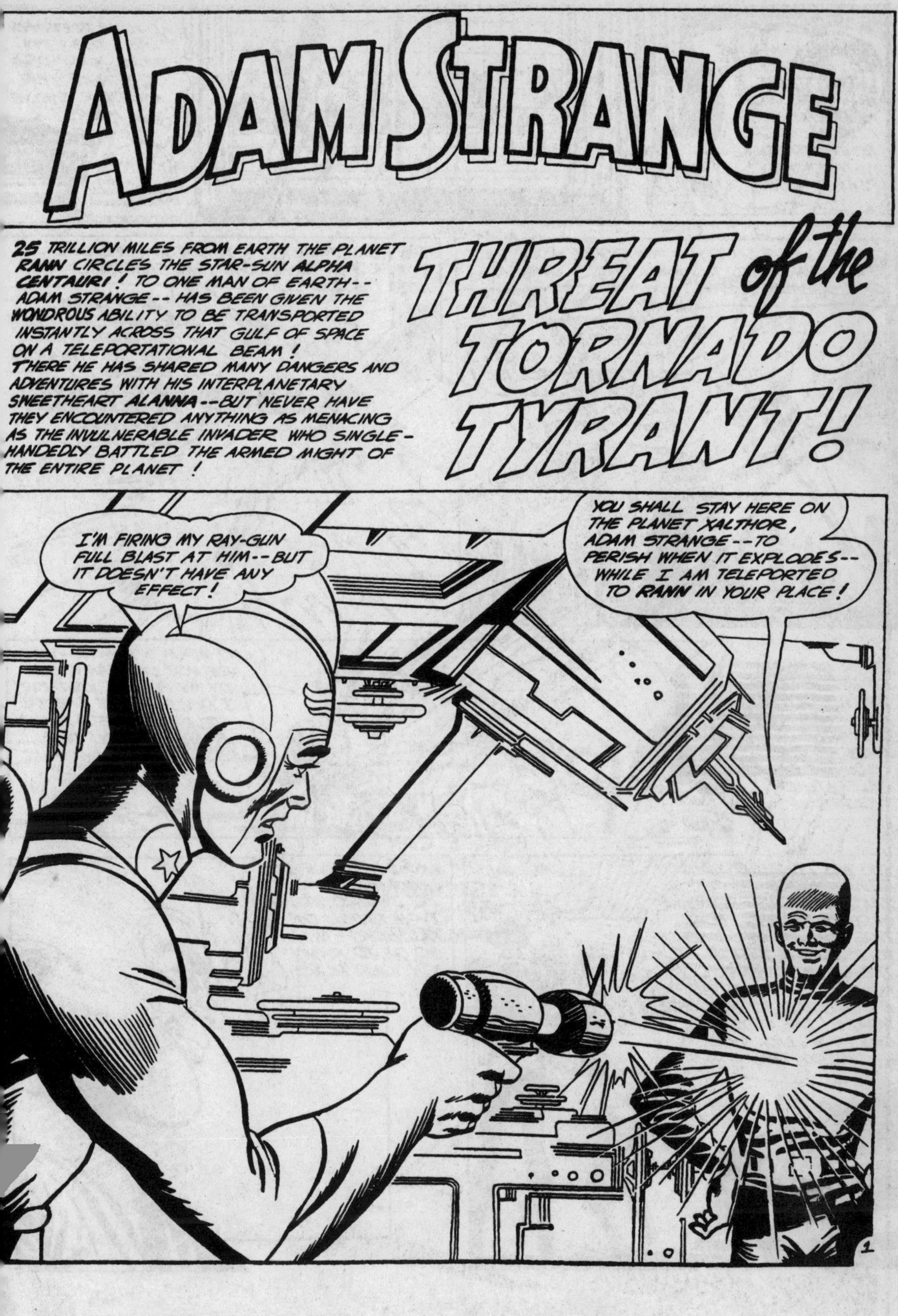
ADAM STRANGE
25 TRILLION MILES FROM EARTH THE PLANET RANN CIRCLES THE STAR-SUN ALPHA CENTAURI! TO ONE MAN OF EARTH--ADAM STRANGE--HAS BEEN GIVEN THE WONDROUS ABILITY TO BE TRANSPORTED INSTANTLY ACROSS THAT GULF OF SPACE ON A TELEPORTATIONAL BEAM! THERE HE HAS SHARED MANY DANGERS AND ADVENTURES WITH HIS INTERPLANETARY SWEETHEART ALANNA--BUT NEVER HAVE THEY ENCOUNTERED ANYTHING AS MENACING AS THE INVULNERABLE INVADER WHO SINGLE-HANDEDLY BATTLED THE ARMED MIGHT OF THE ENTIRE PLANET!
THREAT of the TORNADO TYRANT!
I'M FIRING MY RAY-GUN FULL BLAST AT HIM--BUT IT DOESN'T HAVE ANY EFFECT!
YOU SHALL STAY HERE ON THE PLANET XALTHOR, ADAM STRANGE--TO PERISH WHEN IT EXPLODES--WHILE I AM TELEPORTED TO RANN IN YOUR PLACE!
1

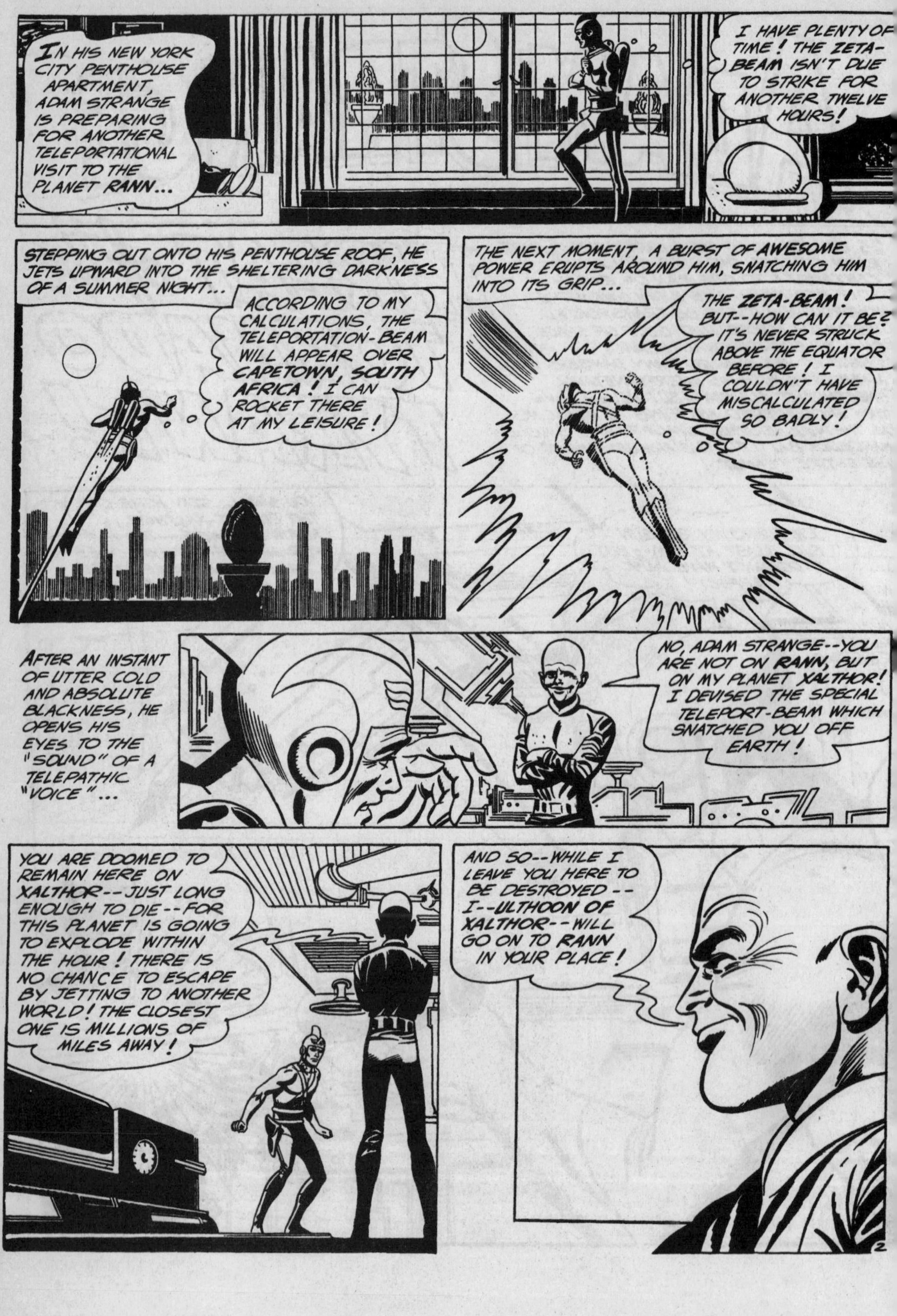
IN HIS NEW YORK CITY PENTHOUSE APARTMENT, ADAM STRANGE IS PREPARING FOR ANOTHER TELEPORTATIONAL VISIT TO THE PLANET RANN...
I HAVE PLENTY OF TIME! THE ZETA-BEAM ISN'T DUE TO STRIKE FOR ANOTHER TWELVE HOURS!
STEPPING OUT ONTO HIS PENTHOUSE ROOF, HE JETS UPWARD INTO THE SHELTERING DARKNESS OF A SUMMER NIGHT...
ACCORDING TO MY CALCULATIONS, THE TELEPORTATION-BEAM WILL APPEAR OVER CAPETOWN, SOUTH AFRICA! I CAN ROCKET THERE AT MY LEISURE!
THE NEXT MOMENT, A BURST OF AWESOME POWER ERUPTS AROUND HIM, SNATCHING HIM INTO ITS GRIP...
THE ZETA-BEAM! BUT--HOW CAN IT BE? IT'S NEVER STRUCK ABOVE THE EQUATOR BEFORE! I COULDN'T HAVE MISCALCULATED SO BADLY!
AFTER AN INSTANT OF UTTER COLD AND ABSOLUTE BLACKNESS, HE OPENS HIS EYES TO THE "SOUND" OF A TELEPATHIC "VOICE"...
NO, ADAM STRANGE--YOU ARE NOT ON RANN, BUT ON MY PLANET XALTHOR! I DEVISED THE SPECIAL TELEPORT-BEAM WHICH SNATCHED YOU OFF EARTH!
YOU ARE DOOMED TO REMAIN HERE ON XALTHOR--JUST LONG ENOUGH TO DIE--FOR THIS PLANET IS GOING TO EXPLODE WITHIN THE HOUR! THERE IS NO CHANCE TO ESCAPE BY JETTING TO ANOTHER WORLD! THE CLOSEST ONE IS MILLIONS OF MILES AWAY!
AND SO--WHILE I LEAVE YOU HERE TO BE DESTROYED--I--ULTHOON OF XALTHOR--WILL GO ON TO RANN IN YOUR PLACE!
2

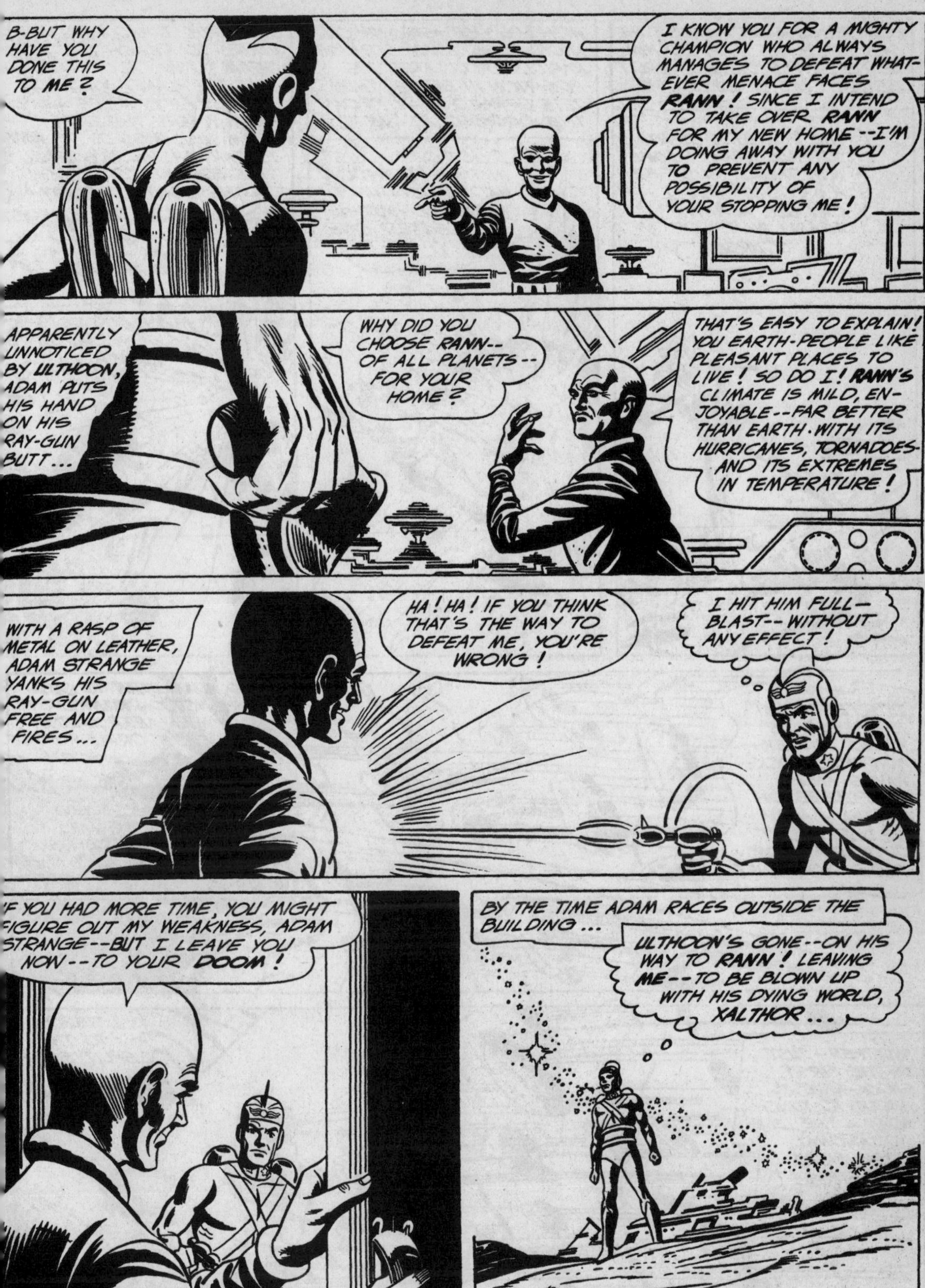
B-BUT WHY HAVE YOU DONE THIS TO ME?
I KNOW YOU FOR A MIGHTY CHAMPION WHO ALWAYS MANAGES TO DEFEAT WHATEVER MENACE FACES RANN! SINCE I INTEND TO TAKE OVER RANN FOR MY NEW HOME--I'M DOING AWAY WITH YOU TO PREVENT ANY POSSIBILITY OF YOUR STOPPING ME!
APPARENTLY UNNOTICED BY ULTHOON, ADAM PUTS HIS HAND ON HIS RAY-GUN BUTT...
WHY DID YOU CHOOSE RANN--OF ALL PLANETS--FOR YOUR HOME?
THAT'S EASY TO EXPLAIN! YOU EARTH-PEOPLE LIKE PLEASANT PLACES TO LIVE! SO DO I! RANN'S CLIMATE IS MILD, ENJOYABLE--FAR BETTER THAN EARTH WITH ITS HURRICANES, TORNADOES--AND ITS EXTREMES IN TEMPERATURE!
WITH A RASP OF METAL ON LEATHER, ADAM STRANGE YANKS HIS RAY-GUN FREE AND FIRES...
HA! HA! IF YOU THINK THAT'S THE WAY TO DEFEAT ME, YOU'RE WRONG!
I HIT HIM FULL-BLAST--WITHOUT ANY EFFECT!
IF YOU HAD MORE TIME, YOU MIGHT FIGURE OUT MY WEAKNESS, ADAM STRANGE--BUT I LEAVE YOU NOW--TO YOUR DOOM!
BY THE TIME ADAM RACES OUTSIDE THE BUILDING...
ULTHOON'S GONE--ON HIS WAY TO RANN! LEAVING ME--TO BE BLOWN UP WITH HIS DYING WORLD, XALTHOR...
3

EVEN AS HE RAILS AGAINST THE FATE WHICH HAS TRAPPED HIM, HE FEELS THE GROUND SPLIT BENEATH HIS SPACEBOOTS...

THE PLANET'S STARTING TO FALL APART! SOMEHOW THERE MUST BE A WAY OUT--SO I CAN SEE ALANNA AGAIN! WAIT--OF COURSE!

WITH HIS VAST ASTRONOMICAL KNOWLEDGE, ADAM STRANGE RAPIDLY CALCULATES HIS POSITION IN SPACE, THEN JETS UPWARD AWAY FROM THE DOOMED PLANET...

I GOT OFF--JUST IN TIME! ULTHOON HAD EVERYTHING PLANNED--BUT HE NEGLECTED ONE THING!

ON EARTH, I HAD TWELVE HOURS TO REACH THE ZETA BEAM! I'VE CALCULATED THAT THE PLANET XALTHOR IS ONLY FIFTY MILES AWAY FROM WHERE THE ZETA-BEAM WILL PASS ON ITS WAY TO EARTH! THERE'S STILL TIME FOR ME TO REACH THE CONTACT POINT!

JETS FLARING AT TOP SPEED, HE RACES THE EXPANDING SHOCK-WAVES AND STREAMERS OF MOLTEN MAGMA AS THEY ERUPT OUTWARD FROM THE DYING PLANET...

GOT TO OUT-DISTANCE THE EXPLOSION OR--I'M DONE FOR!

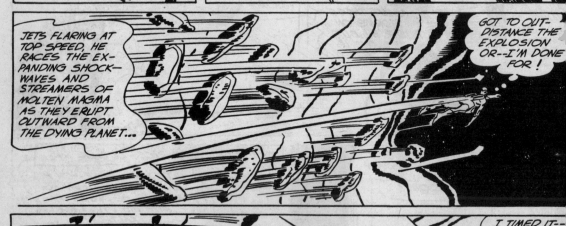

AND THEN--JUST AS THE FIRST SHOCK-WAVE IS ABOUT TO TOUCH ADAM--THE TELEPORTATIONAL BEAM FROM RANN STRIKES!

I TIMED IT-- TO THE SPLIT-SECOND

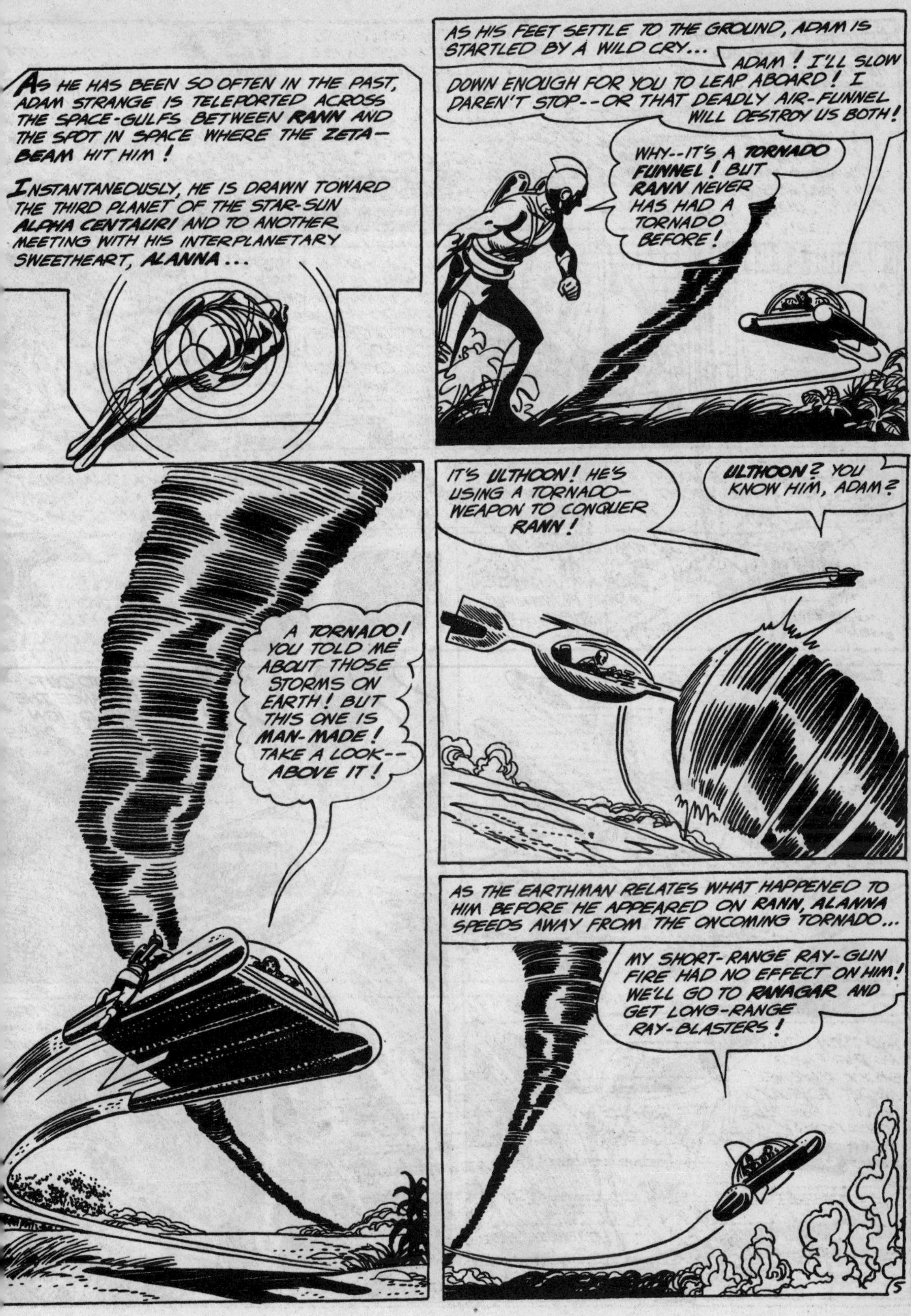
AS HE HAS BEEN SO OFTEN IN THE PAST, ADAM STRANGE IS TELEPORTED ACROSS THE SPACE-GULFS BETWEEN RANN AND THE SPOT IN SPACE WHERE THE ZETA-BEAM HIT HIM!
INSTANTANEOUSLY, HE IS DRAWN TOWARD THE THIRD PLANET OF THE STAR-SUN ALPHA CENTAURI AND TO ANOTHER MEETING WITH HIS INTERPLANETARY SWEETHEART, ALANNA...
AS HIS FEET SETTLE TO THE GROUND, ADAM IS STARTLED BY A WILD CRY...
ADAM! I'LL SLOW DOWN ENOUGH FOR YOU TO LEAP ABOARD! I DAREN'T STOP--OR THAT DEADLY AIR-FUNNEL WILL DESTROY US BOTH!
WHY--IT'S A TORNADO FUNNEL! BUT RANN NEVER HAS HAD A TORNADO BEFORE!
A TORNADO! YOU TOLD ME ABOUT THOSE STORMS ON EARTH! BUT THIS ONE IS MAN-MADE! TAKE A LOOK--ABOVE IT!
IT'S ULTHOON! HE'S USING A TORNADO-WEAPON TO CONQUER RANN!
ULTHOON? YOU KNOW HIM, ADAM?
AS THE EARTHMAN RELATES WHAT HAPPENED TO HIM BEFORE HE APPEARED ON RANN, ALANNA SPEEDS AWAY FROM THE ONCOMING TORNADO...
MY SHORT-RANGE RAY-GUN FIRE HAD NO EFFECT ON HIM! WE'LL GO TO RANAGAR AND GET LONG-RANGE RAY-BLASTERS!
5

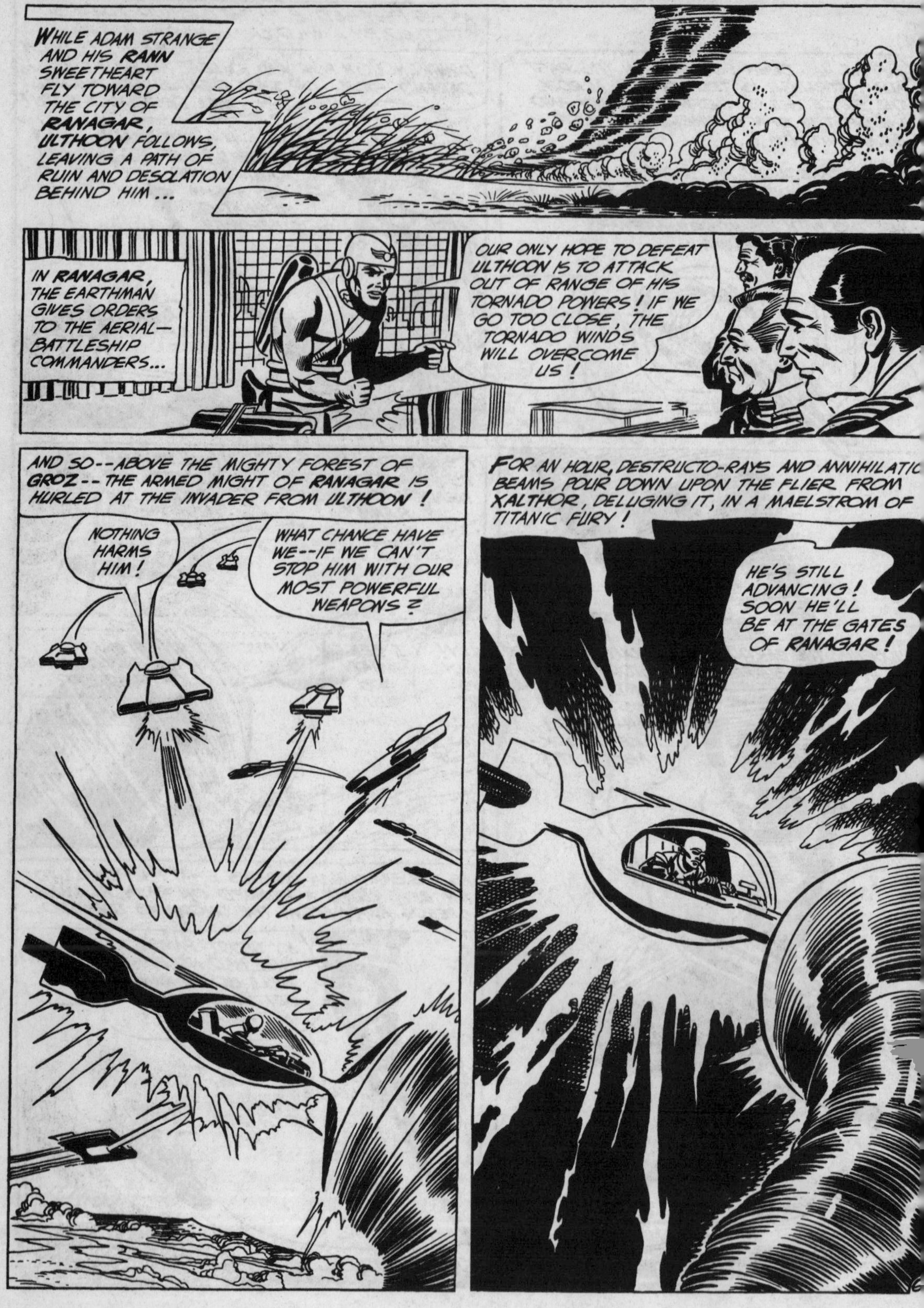
WHILE ADAM STRANGE AND HIS RANN SWEETHEART FLY TOWARD THE CITY OF RANAGAR, ULTHOON FOLLOWS, LEAVING A PATH OF RUIN AND DESOLATION BEHIND HIM...
IN RANAGAR, THE EARTHMAN GIVES ORDERS TO THE AERIAL-BATTLESHIP COMMANDERS...
OUR ONLY HOPE TO DEFEAT ULTHOON IS TO ATTACK OUT OF RANGE OF HIS TORNADO POWERS! IF WE GO TOO CLOSE, THE TORNADO WINDS WILL OVERCOME US!
AND SO--ABOVE THE MIGHTY FOREST OF GROZ--THE ARMED MIGHT OF RANAGAR IS HURLED AT THE INVADER FROM ULTHOON!
NOTHING HARMS HIM!
WHAT CHANCE HAVE WE--IF WE CAN'T STOP HIM WITH OUR MOST POWERFUL WEAPONS?
FOR AN HOUR, DESTRUCTO-RAYS AND ANNIHILATIC BEAMS POUR DOWN UPON THE FLIER FROM XALTHOR, DELUGING IT, IN A MAELSTROM OF TITANIC FURY!
HE'S STILL ADVANCING! SOON HE'LL BE AT THE GATES OF RANAGAR!

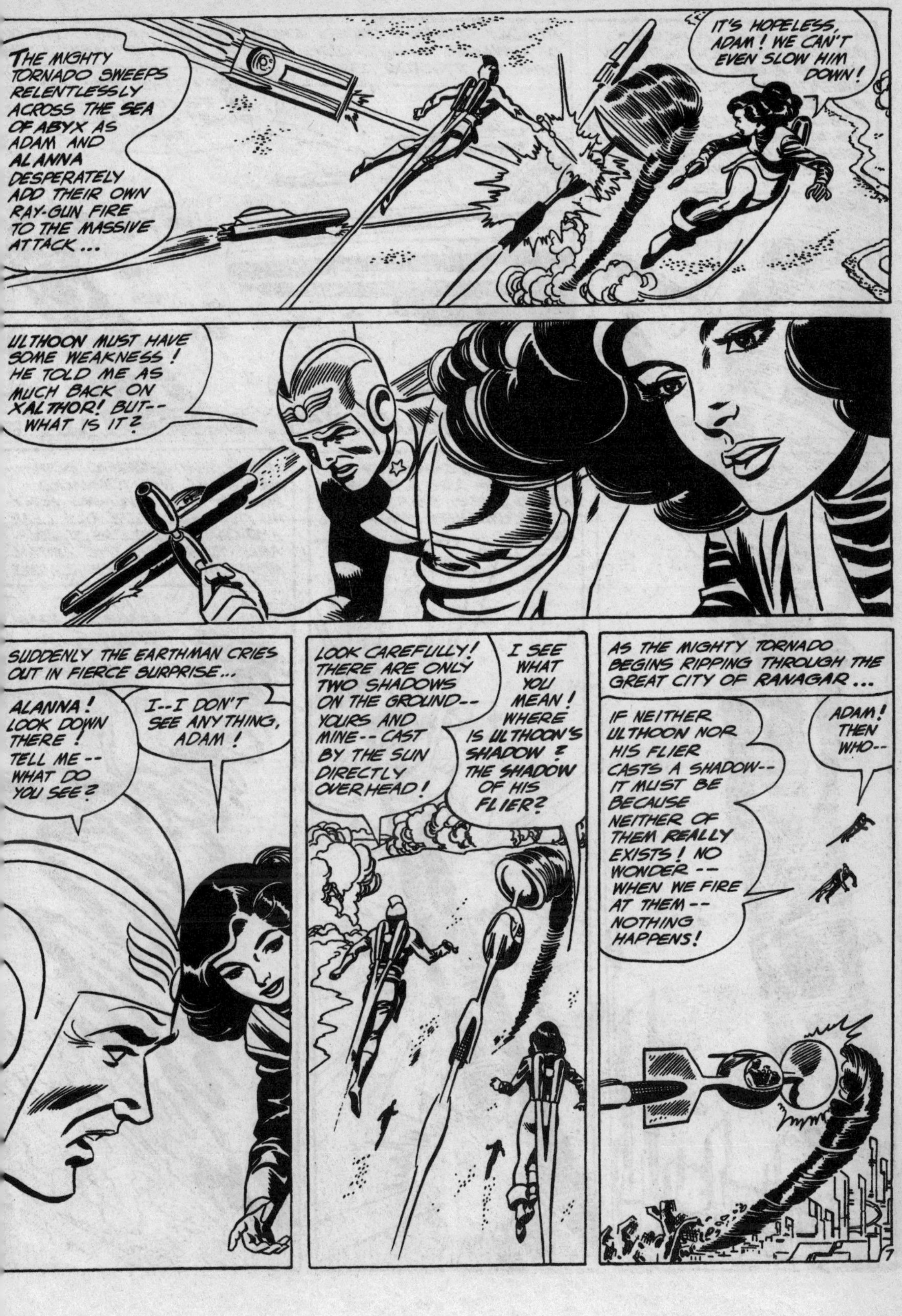
THE MIGHTY TORNADO SWEEPS RELENTLESSLY ACROSS THE SEA OF ABYX AS ADAM AND ALANNA DESPERATELY ADD THEIR OWN RAY-GUN FIRE TO THE MASSIVE ATTACK...
IT'S HOPELESS, ADAM! WE CAN'T EVEN SLOW HIM DOWN!
ULTHOON MUST HAVE SOME WEAKNESS! HE TOLD ME AS MUCH BACK ON XALTHOR! BUT-- WHAT IS IT?
SUDDENLY THE EARTHMAN CRIES OUT IN FIERCE SURPRISE...
ALANNA! LOOK DOWN THERE! TELL ME-- WHAT DO YOU SEE?
I--I DON'T SEE ANYTHING, ADAM!
LOOK CAREFULLY! THERE ARE ONLY TWO SHADOWS ON THE GROUND-- YOURS AND MINE-- CAST BY THE SUN DIRECTLY OVERHEAD!
I SEE WHAT YOU MEAN! WHERE IS ULTHOON'S SHADOW? THE SHADOW OF HIS FLIER?
AS THE MIGHTY TORNADO BEGINS RIPPING THROUGH THE GREAT CITY OF RANAGAR...
IF NEITHER ULTHOON NOR HIS FLIER CASTS A SHADOW-- IT MUST BE BECAUSE NEITHER OF THEM REALLY EXISTS! NO WONDER-- WHEN WE FIRE AT THEM-- NOTHING HAPPENS!
ADAM! THEN WHO--
7

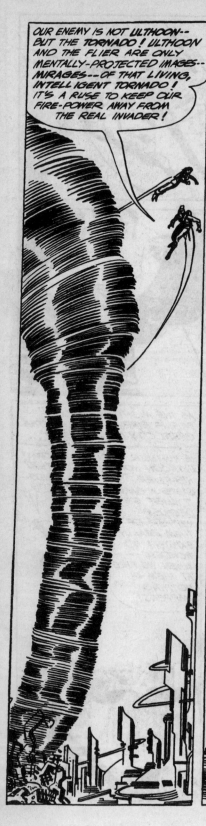

OUR ENEMY IS NOT *ULTHOON*-- BUT THE TORNADO! ULTHOON AND THE FLIER ARE ONLY MENTALLY-PROJECTED IMAGES-- MIRAGES--OF THAT LIVING, INTELLIGENT TORNADO! IT'S A RUSE TO KEEP OUR FIRE-POWER AWAY FROM THE REAL INVADER!

AT ADAM STRANGE'S ORDERS, EVERY AIRCRAFT IN THE GREAT FLE OF RANAGAR AIMS ITS GUNS--NOT AT THE FLIER--BUT AT THE SWIRLING TORNADO ITSELF...

FIRE AT THE TORNADO ON THE COUNT OF THREE! ONE! TWO! TH--

A TITANIC DISCHARGE OF RAY-BEAMS SEARS THE VERY AIR AS EVERY SHIP SHAKES TO MONUMENTAL BROAD- SIDES...

UNDER THAT TERRIFIC BOM- BARDMENT, THE TORNADO PULSES WITH RAVENING FURY AS ITS WISPY TENDRILS LEAP AND DART HELPLESSLY, UN- ABLE TO REACH THE AERIAL MIGHT WHICH IS DESTROYING IT!

IT IS AS I FEARED! ADAM STRANGE DIS- COVERED THE WAY TO DEFEAT ME!

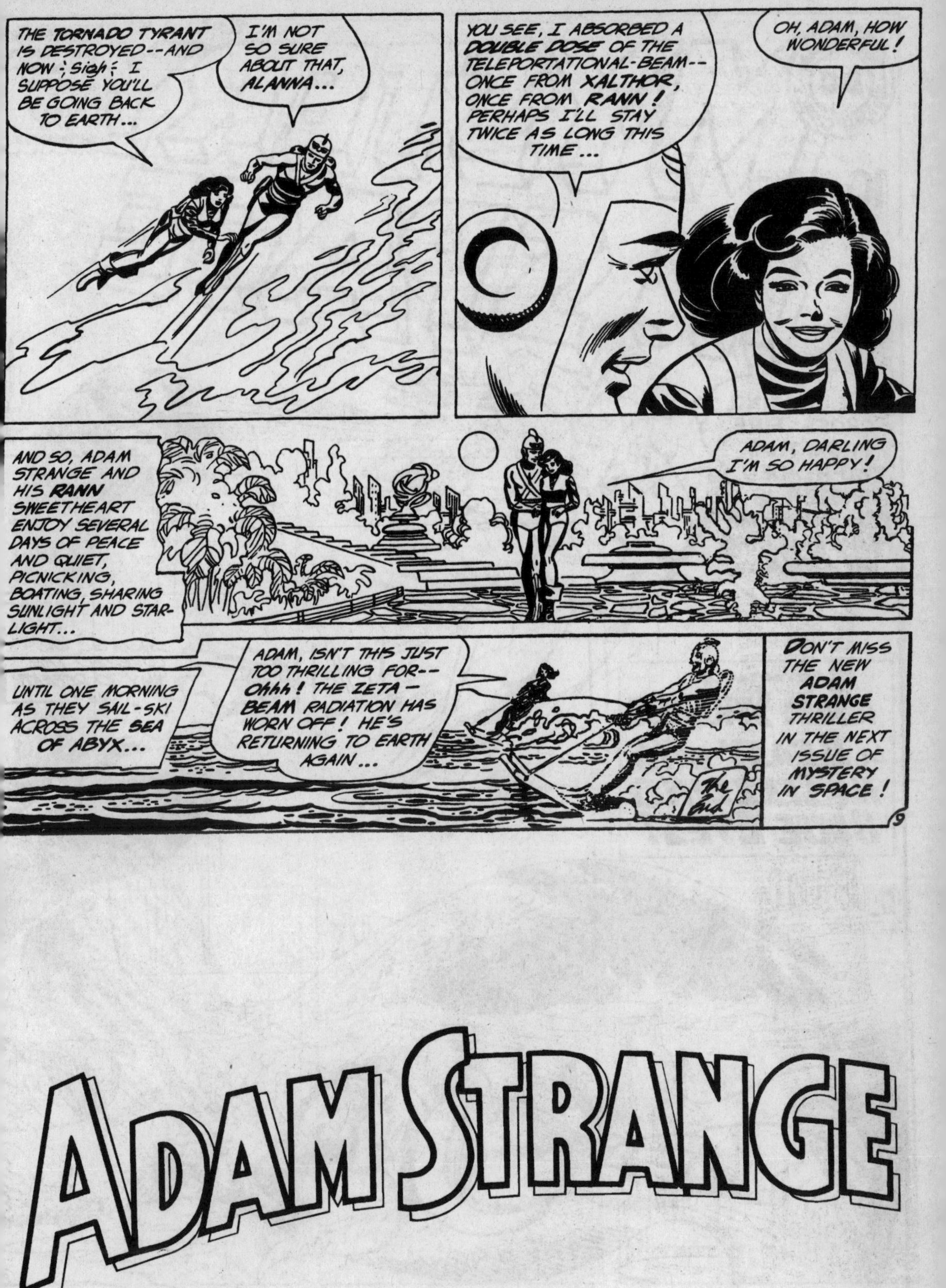
THE TORNADO TYRANT IS DESTROYED--AND NOW ; Sigh ; I SUPPOSE YOU'LL BE GOING BACK TO EARTH...
I'M NOT SO SURE ABOUT THAT, ALANNA...
YOU SEE, I ABSORBED A DOUBLE DOSE OF THE TELEPORTATIONAL-BEAM--ONCE FROM XALTHOR, ONCE FROM RANN! PERHAPS I'LL STAY TWICE AS LONG THIS TIME...
OH, ADAM, HOW WONDERFUL!
AND SO, ADAM STRANGE AND HIS RANN SWEETHEART ENJOY SEVERAL DAYS OF PEACE AND QUIET, PICNICKING, BOATING, SHARING SUNLIGHT AND STAR-LIGHT...
ADAM, DARLING I'M SO HAPPY!
UNTIL ONE MORNING AS THEY SAIL-SKI ACROSS THE SEA OF ABYX...
ADAM, ISN'T THIS JUST TOO THRILLING FOR--Ohhh! THE ZETA-BEAM RADIATION HAS WORN OFF! HE'S RETURNING TO EARTH AGAIN...
The End
DON'T MISS THE NEW ADAM STRANGE THRILLER IN THE NEXT ISSUE OF MYSTERY IN SPACE!
9

ADAM STRANGE

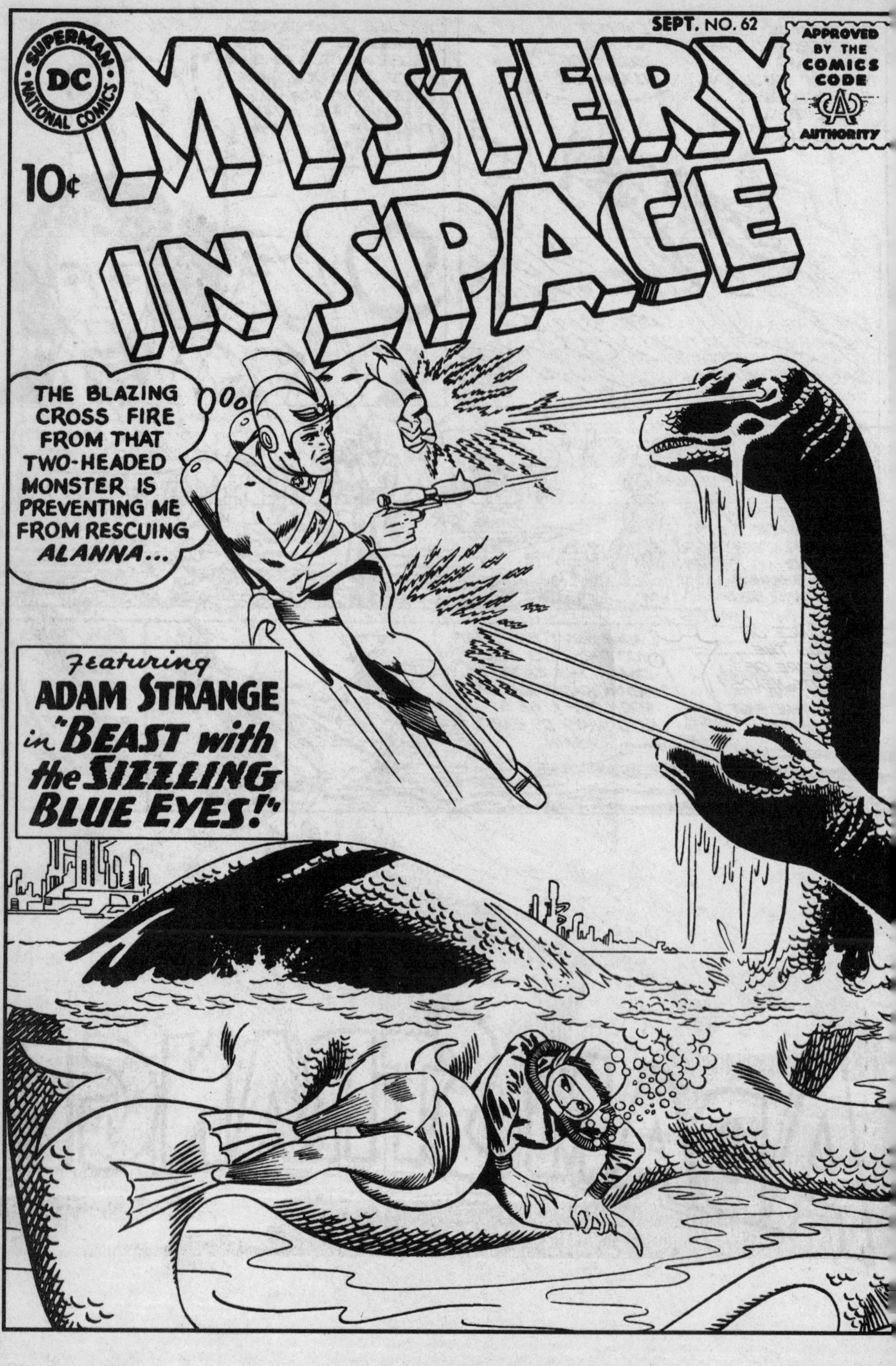
SUPERMAN DC NATIONAL COMICS
SEPT. NO. 62
APPROVED BY THE COMICS CODE AUTHORITY
MYSTERY IN SPACE
10¢
THE BLAZING CROSS FIRE FROM THAT TWO-HEADED MONSTER IS PREVENTING ME FROM RESCUING ALANNA...
Featuring ADAM STRANGE in "BEAST with the SIZZLING BLUE EYES!"

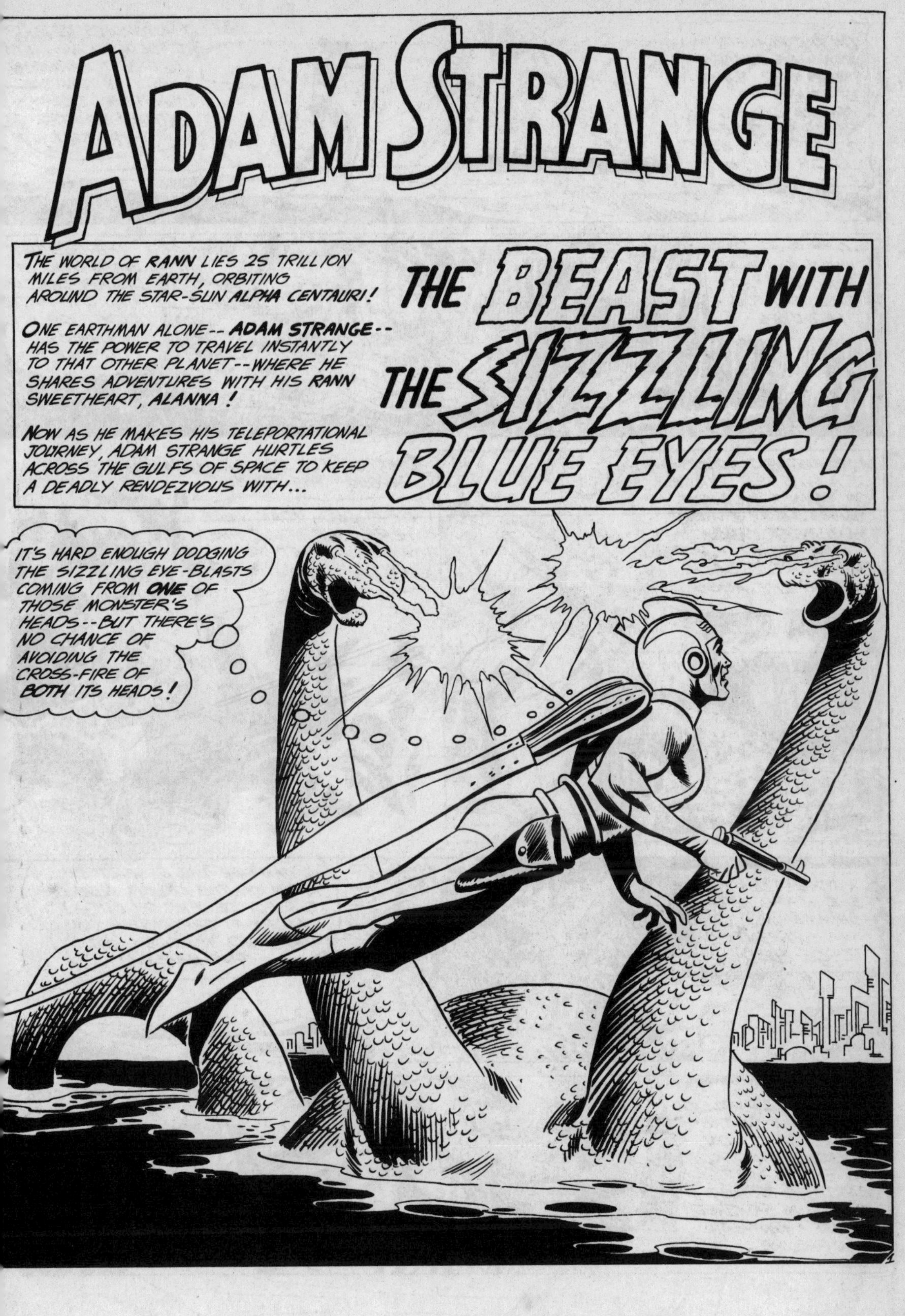
ADAM STRANGE
THE WORLD OF RANN LIES 25 TRILLION MILES FROM EARTH, ORBITING AROUND THE STAR-SUN ALPHA CENTAURI!
ONE EARTHMAN ALONE-- ADAM STRANGE-- HAS THE POWER TO TRAVEL INSTANTLY TO THAT OTHER PLANET--WHERE HE SHARES ADVENTURES WITH HIS RANN SWEETHEART, ALANNA!
NOW AS HE MAKES HIS TELEPORTATIONAL JOURNEY, ADAM STRANGE HURTLES ACROSS THE GULFS OF SPACE TO KEEP A DEADLY RENDEZVOUS WITH...
THE BEAST WITH THE SIZZLING BLUE EYES!
IT'S HARD ENOUGH DODGING THE SIZZLING EYE-BLASTS COMING FROM ONE OF THOSE MONSTER'S HEADS--BUT THERE'S NO CHANCE OF AVOIDING THE CROSS-FIRE OF BOTH ITS HEADS!
1

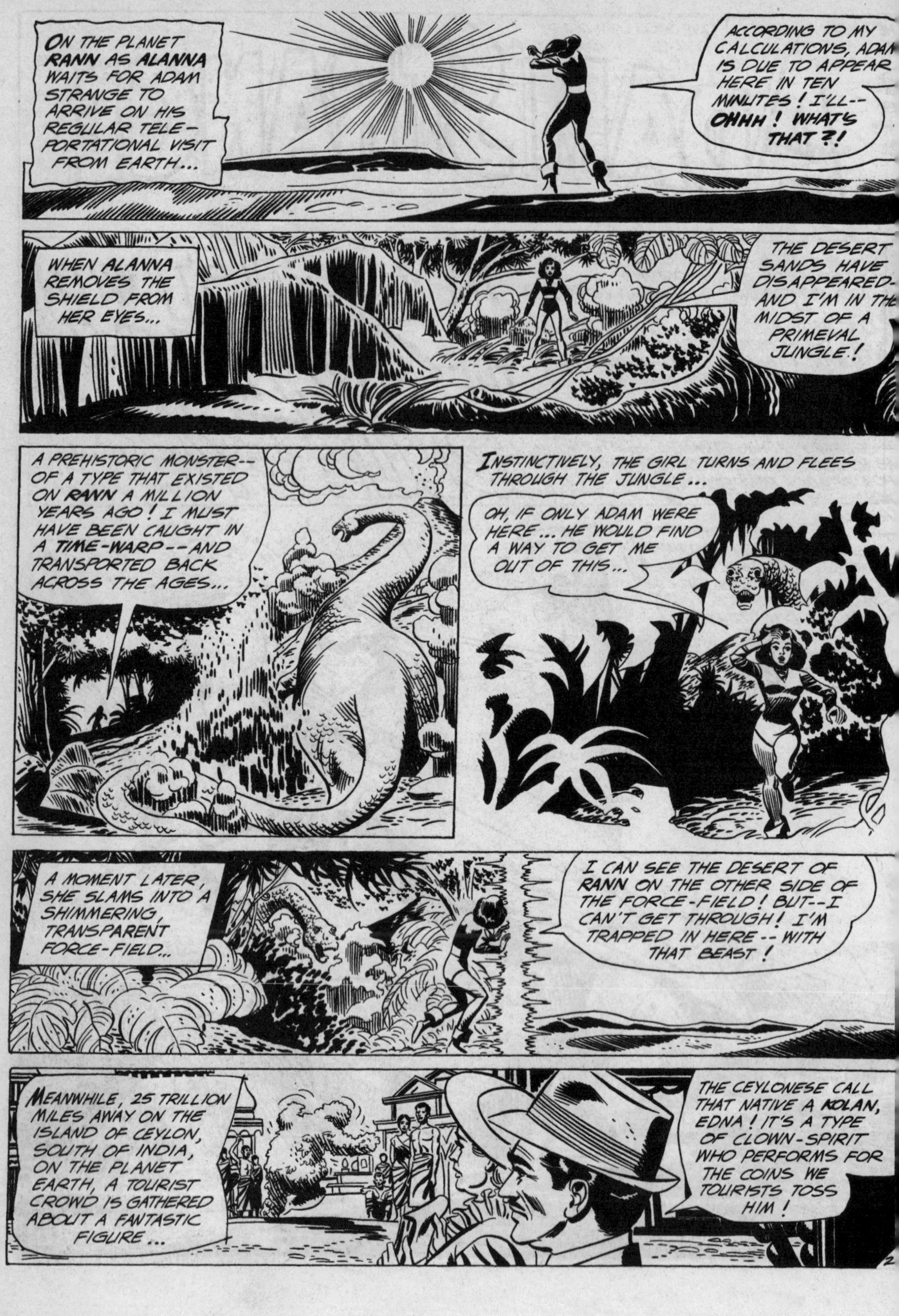
ON THE PLANET RANN AS ALANNA WAITS FOR ADAM STRANGE TO ARRIVE ON HIS REGULAR TELE-PORTATIONAL VISIT FROM EARTH...
ACCORDING TO MY CALCULATIONS, ADAM IS DUE TO APPEAR HERE IN TEN MINUTES! I'LL-- OHHH! WHAT'S THAT?!
WHEN ALANNA REMOVES THE SHIELD FROM HER EYES...
THE DESERT SANDS HAVE DISAPPEARED-- AND I'M IN THE MIDST OF A PRIMEVAL JUNGLE!
A PREHISTORIC MONSTER-- OF A TYPE THAT EXISTED ON RANN A MILLION YEARS AGO! I MUST HAVE BEEN CAUGHT IN A TIME-WARP--AND TRANSPORTED BACK ACROSS THE AGES...
INSTINCTIVELY, THE GIRL TURNS AND FLEES THROUGH THE JUNGLE...
OH, IF ONLY ADAM WERE HERE... HE WOULD FIND A WAY TO GET ME OUT OF THIS...
A MOMENT LATER, SHE SLAMS INTO A SHIMMERING, TRANSPARENT FORCE-FIELD...
I CAN SEE THE DESERT OF RANN ON THE OTHER SIDE OF THE FORCE-FIELD! BUT--I CAN'T GET THROUGH! I'M TRAPPED IN HERE -- WITH THAT BEAST!
MEANWHILE, 25 TRILLION MILES AWAY ON THE ISLAND OF CEYLON, SOUTH OF INDIA, ON THE PLANET EARTH, A TOURIST CROWD IS GATHERED ABOUT A FANTASTIC FIGURE...
THE CEYLONESE CALL THAT NATIVE A KOLAN, EDNA! IT'S A TYPE OF CLOWN-SPIRIT WHO PERFORMS FOR THE COINS WE TOURISTS TOSS HIM!
2

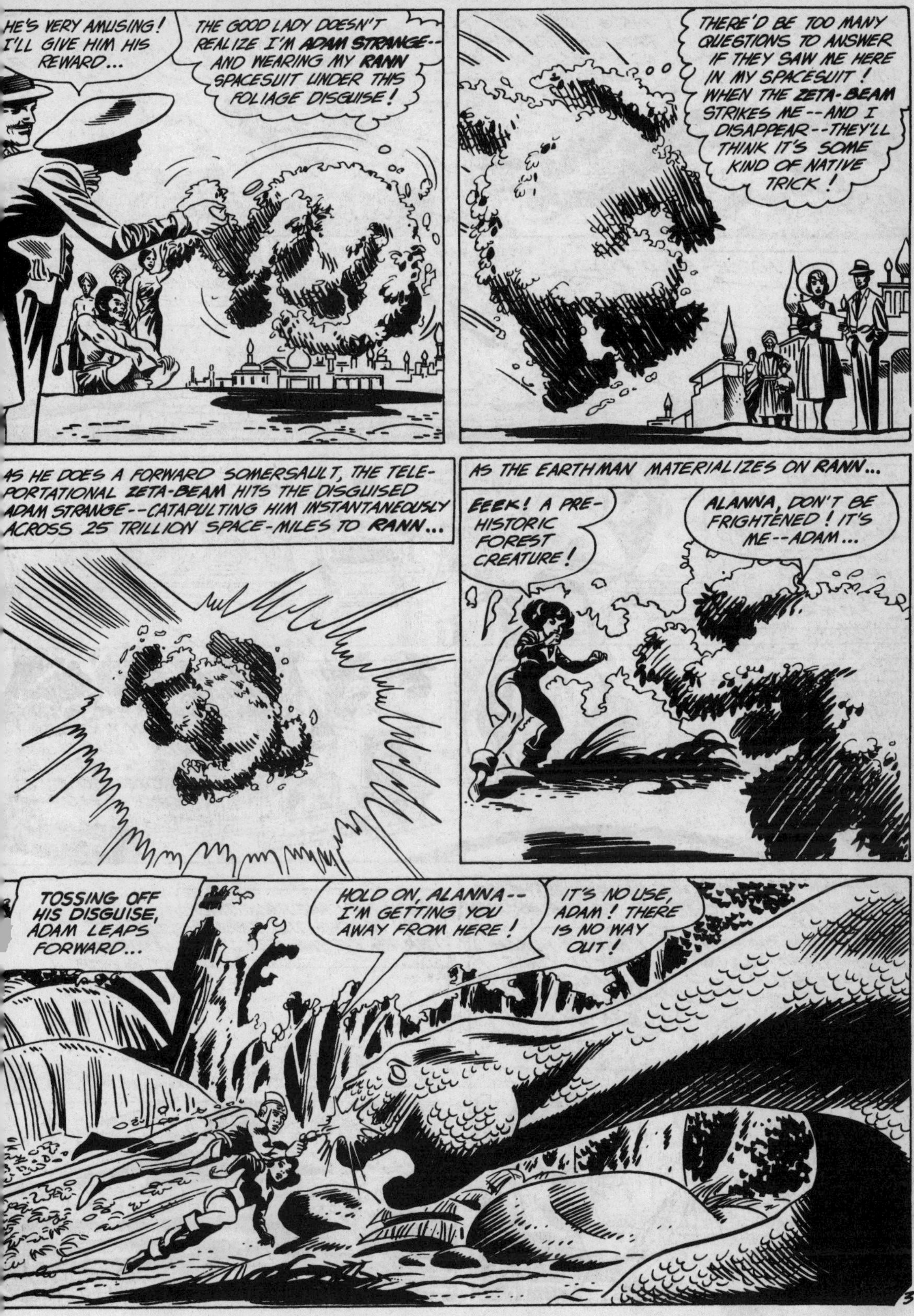
HE'S VERY AMUSING! I'LL GIVE HIM HIS REWARD...
THE GOOD LADY DOESN'T REALIZE I'M ADAM STRANGE--AND WEARING MY RANN SPACESUIT UNDER THIS FOLIAGE DISGUISE!
THERE'D BE TOO MANY QUESTIONS TO ANSWER IF THEY SAW ME HERE IN MY SPACESUIT! WHEN THE ZETA-BEAM STRIKES ME--AND I DISAPPEAR--THEY'LL THINK IT'S SOME KIND OF NATIVE TRICK!
AS HE DOES A FORWARD SOMERSAULT, THE TELE-PORTATIONAL ZETA-BEAM HITS THE DISGUISED ADAM STRANGE--CATAPULTING HIM INSTANTANEOUSLY ACROSS 25 TRILLION SPACE-MILES TO RANN...
AS THE EARTHMAN MATERIALIZES ON RANN...
EEEK! A PRE-HISTORIC FOREST CREATURE!
ALANNA, DON'T BE FRIGHTENED! IT'S ME--ADAM...
TOSSING OFF HIS DISGUISE, ADAM LEAPS FORWARD...
HOLD ON, ALANNA--I'M GETTING YOU AWAY FROM HERE!
IT'S NO USE, ADAM! THERE IS NO WAY OUT!
3

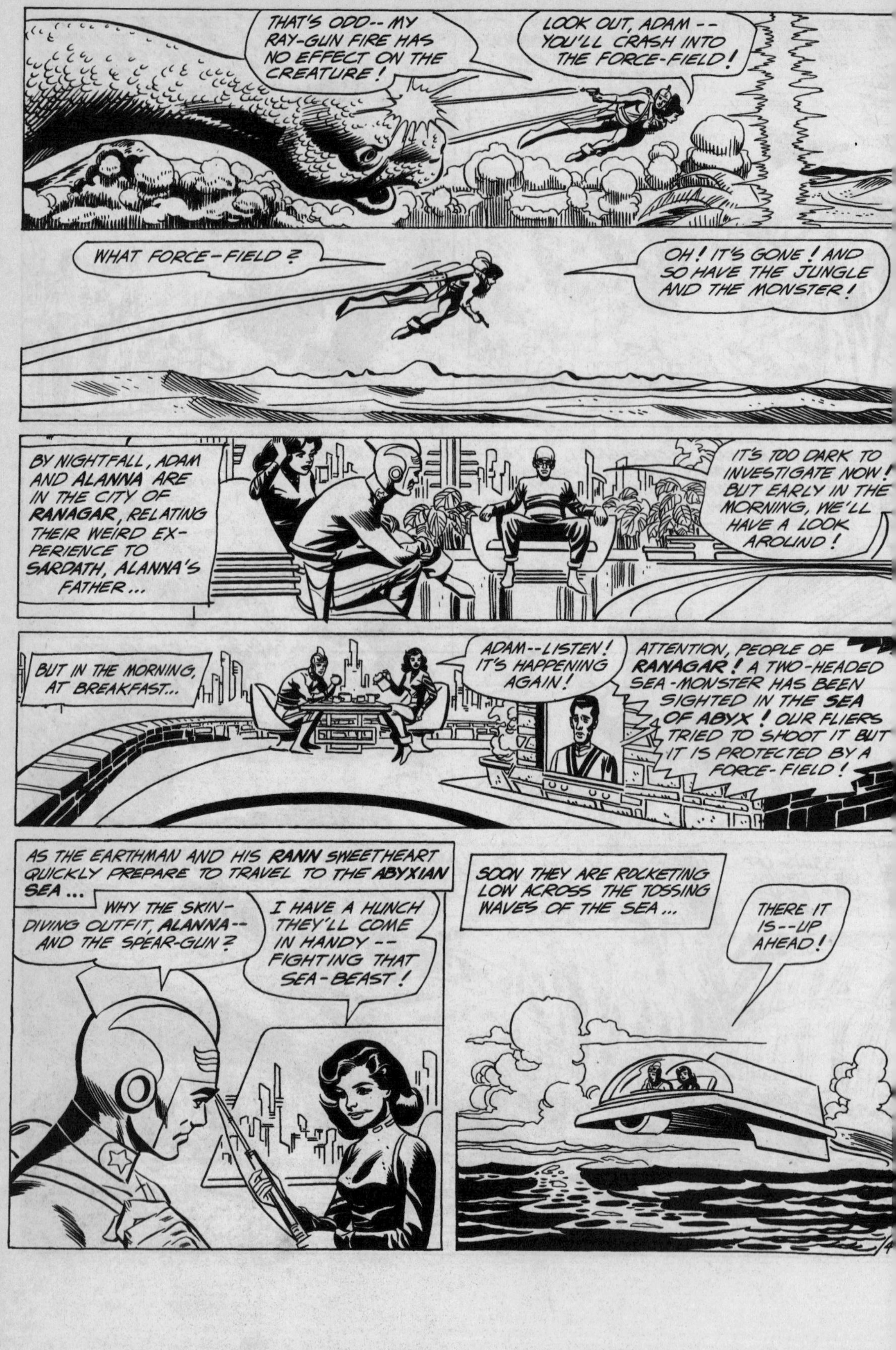
THAT'S ODD-- MY RAY-GUN FIRE HAS NO EFFECT ON THE CREATURE!
LOOK OUT, ADAM -- YOU'LL CRASH INTO THE FORCE-FIELD!
WHAT FORCE-FIELD?
OH! IT'S GONE! AND SO HAVE THE JUNGLE AND THE MONSTER!
BY NIGHTFALL, ADAM AND ALANNA ARE IN THE CITY OF RANAGAR, RELATING THEIR WEIRD EXPERIENCE TO SARDATH, ALANNA'S FATHER...
IT'S TOO DARK TO INVESTIGATE NOW! BUT EARLY IN THE MORNING, WE'LL HAVE A LOOK AROUND!
BUT IN THE MORNING, AT BREAKFAST...
ADAM--LISTEN! IT'S HAPPENING AGAIN!
ATTENTION, PEOPLE OF RANAGAR! A TWO-HEADED SEA-MONSTER HAS BEEN SIGHTED IN THE SEA OF ABYX! OUR FLIERS TRIED TO SHOOT IT BUT IT IS PROTECTED BY A FORCE-FIELD!
AS THE EARTHMAN AND HIS RANN SWEETHEART QUICKLY PREPARE TO TRAVEL TO THE ABYXIAN SEA...
WHY THE SKIN-DIVING OUTFIT, ALANNA-- AND THE SPEAR-GUN?
I HAVE A HUNCH THEY'LL COME IN HANDY -- FIGHTING THAT SEA-BEAST!
SOON THEY ARE ROCKETING LOW ACROSS THE TOSSING WAVES OF THE SEA...
THERE IT IS--UP AHEAD!

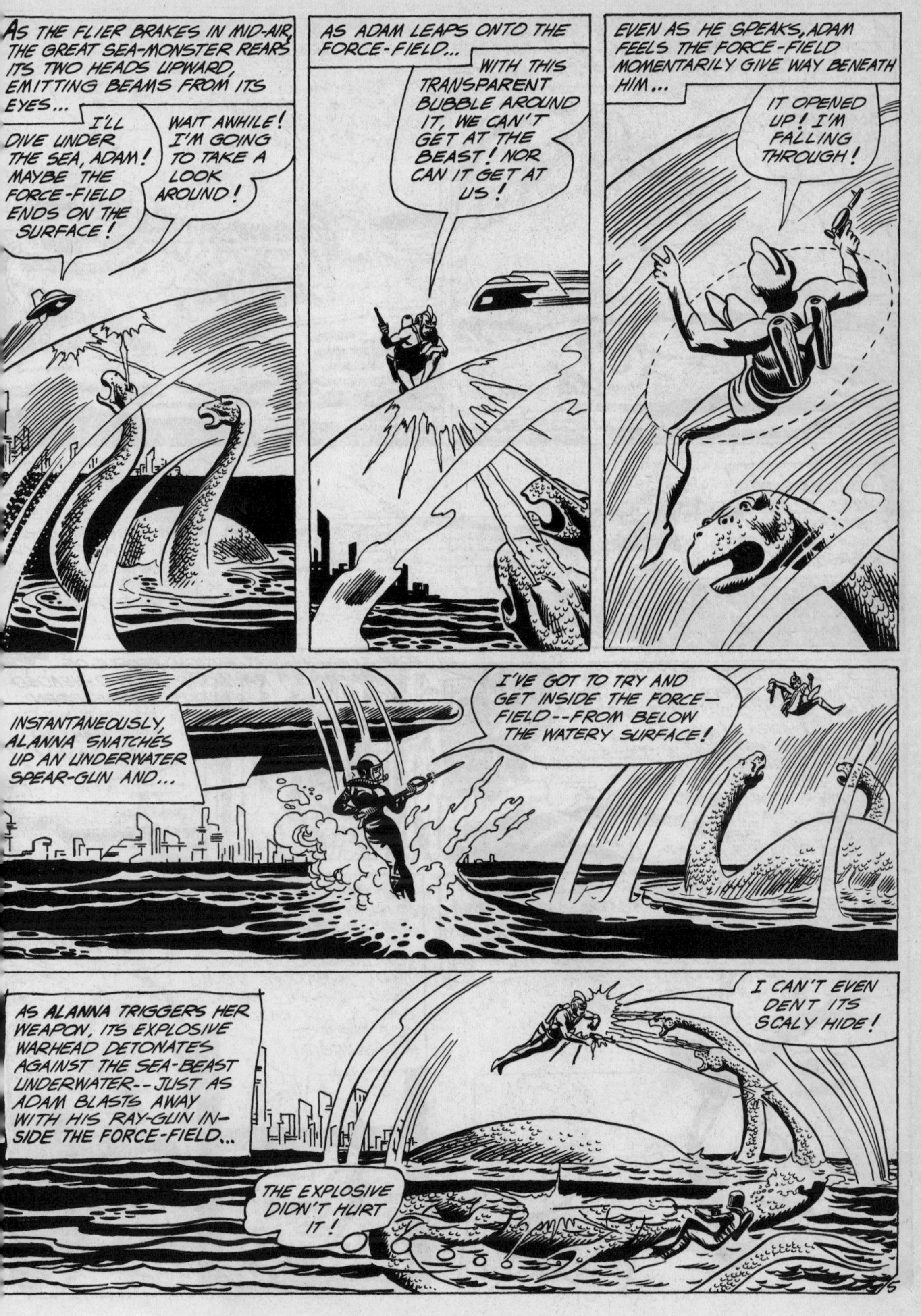
AS THE FLIER BRAKES IN MID-AIR, THE GREAT SEA-MONSTER REARS ITS TWO HEADS UPWARD, EMITTING BEAMS FROM ITS EYES...
I'LL DIVE UNDER THE SEA, ADAM! MAYBE THE FORCE-FIELD ENDS ON THE SURFACE!
WAIT AWHILE! I'M GOING TO TAKE A LOOK AROUND!
AS ADAM LEAPS ONTO THE FORCE-FIELD...
WITH THIS TRANSPARENT BUBBLE AROUND IT, WE CAN'T GET AT THE BEAST! NOR CAN IT GET AT US!
EVEN AS HE SPEAKS, ADAM FEELS THE FORCE-FIELD MOMENTARILY GIVE WAY BENEATH HIM...
IT OPENED UP! I'M FALLING THROUGH!
INSTANTANEOUSLY, ALANNA SNATCHES UP AN UNDERWATER SPEAR-GUN AND...
I'VE GOT TO TRY AND GET INSIDE THE FORCE-FIELD--FROM BELOW THE WATERY SURFACE!
AS ALANNA TRIGGERS HER WEAPON, ITS EXPLOSIVE WARHEAD DETONATES AGAINST THE SEA-BEAST UNDERWATER--JUST AS ADAM BLASTS AWAY WITH HIS RAY-GUN INSIDE THE FORCE-FIELD...
I CAN'T EVEN DENT ITS SCALY HIDE!
THE EXPLOSIVE DIDN'T HURT IT!
5

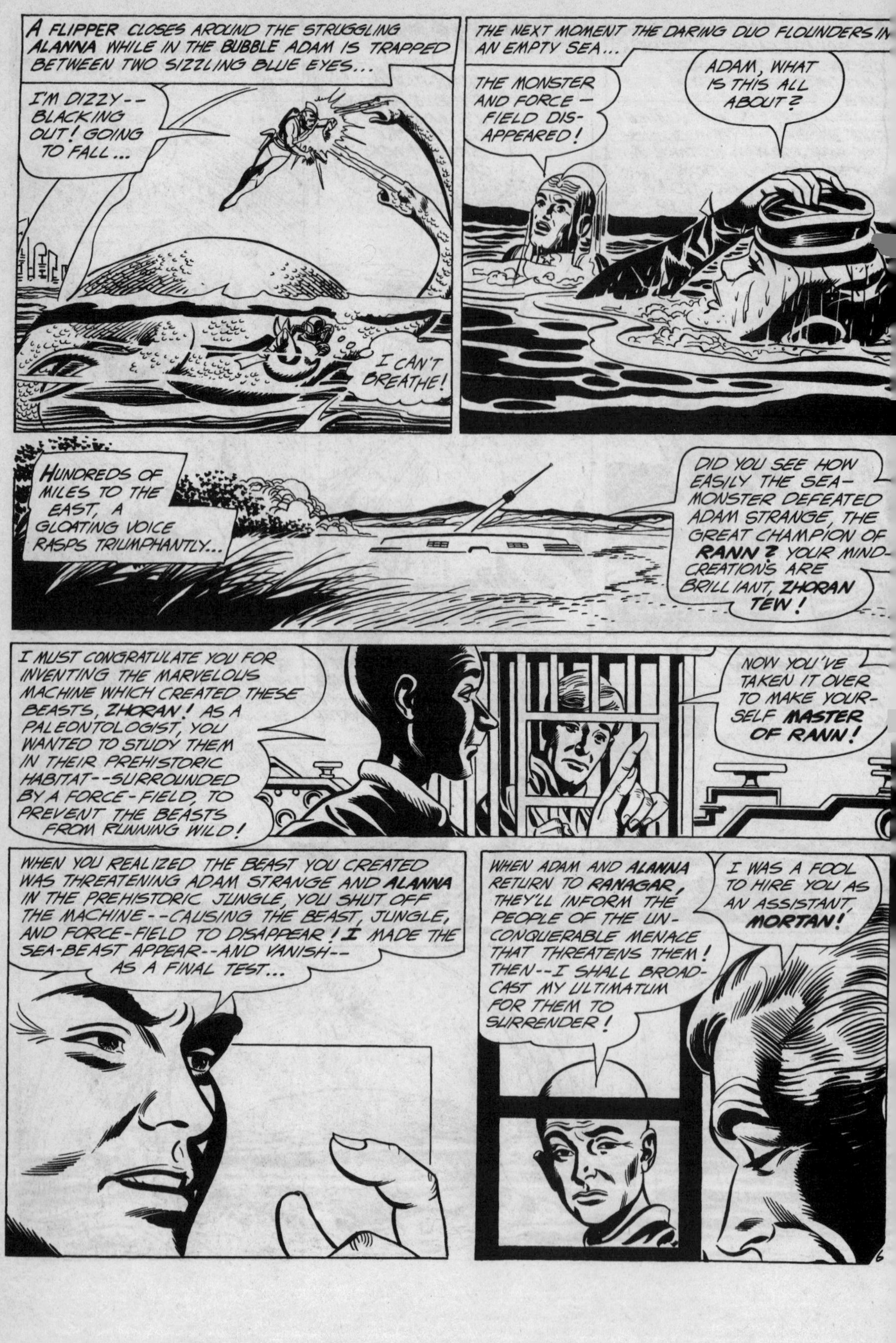
A FLIPPER CLOSES AROUND THE STRUGGLING ALANNA WHILE IN THE BUBBLE ADAM IS TRAPPED BETWEEN TWO SIZZLING BLUE EYES...
I'M DIZZY--BLACKING OUT! GOING TO FALL...
I CAN'T BREATHE!
THE NEXT MOMENT THE DARING DUO FLOUNDERS IN AN EMPTY SEA...
THE MONSTER AND FORCE-FIELD DISAPPEARED!
ADAM, WHAT IS THIS ALL ABOUT?
HUNDREDS OF MILES TO THE EAST, A GLOATING VOICE RASPS TRIUMPHANTLY...
DID YOU SEE HOW EASILY THE SEA-MONSTER DEFEATED ADAM STRANGE, THE GREAT CHAMPION OF RANN? YOUR MIND-CREATIONS ARE BRILLIANT, ZHORAN TEW!
I MUST CONGRATULATE YOU FOR INVENTING THE MARVELOUS MACHINE WHICH CREATED THESE BEASTS, ZHORAN! AS A PALEONTOLOGIST, YOU WANTED TO STUDY THEM IN THEIR PREHISTORIC HABITAT--SURROUNDED BY A FORCE-FIELD, TO PREVENT THE BEASTS FROM RUNNING WILD!
NOW YOU'VE TAKEN IT OVER TO MAKE YOURSELF MASTER OF RANN!
WHEN YOU REALIZED THE BEAST YOU CREATED WAS THREATENING ADAM STRANGE AND ALANNA IN THE PREHISTORIC JUNGLE, YOU SHUT OFF THE MACHINE--CAUSING THE BEAST, JUNGLE, AND FORCE-FIELD TO DISAPPEAR! I MADE THE SEA-BEAST APPEAR--AND VANISH--AS A FINAL TEST...
WHEN ADAM AND ALANNA RETURN TO RANAGAR, THEY'LL INFORM THE PEOPLE OF THE UNCONQUERABLE MENACE THAT THREATENS THEM! THEN--I SHALL BROADCAST MY ULTIMATUM FOR THEM TO SURRENDER!
I WAS A FOOL TO HIRE YOU AS AN ASSISTANT, MORTAN!
6

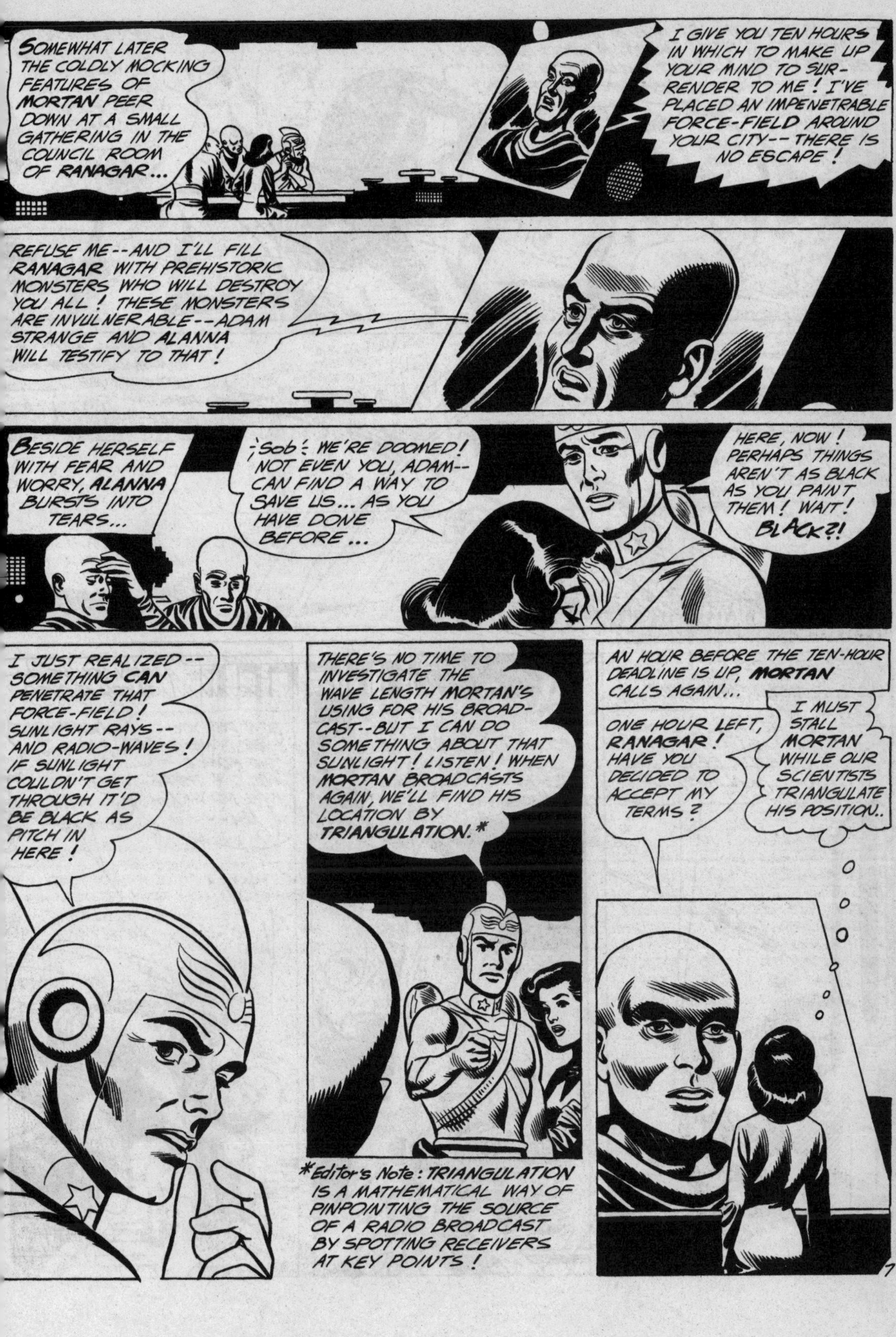
SOMEWHAT LATER THE COLDLY MOCKING FEATURES OF MORTAN PEER DOWN AT A SMALL GATHERING IN THE COUNCIL ROOM OF RANAGAR...
I GIVE YOU TEN HOURS IN WHICH TO MAKE UP YOUR MIND TO SURRENDER TO ME! I'VE PLACED AN IMPENETRABLE FORCE-FIELD AROUND YOUR CITY--THERE IS NO ESCAPE!
REFUSE ME--AND I'LL FILL RANAGAR WITH PREHISTORIC MONSTERS WHO WILL DESTROY YOU ALL! THESE MONSTERS ARE INVULNERABLE--ADAM STRANGE AND ALANNA WILL TESTIFY TO THAT!
BESIDE HERSELF WITH FEAR AND WORRY, ALANNA BURSTS INTO TEARS...
¡SOB! WE'RE DOOMED! NOT EVEN YOU, ADAM--CAN FIND A WAY TO SAVE US... AS YOU HAVE DONE BEFORE...
HERE, NOW! PERHAPS THINGS AREN'T AS BLACK AS YOU PAINT THEM! WAIT! BLACK?!
I JUST REALIZED--SOMETHING CAN PENETRATE THAT FORCE-FIELD! SUNLIGHT RAYS--AND RADIO-WAVES! IF SUNLIGHT COULDN'T GET THROUGH IT'D BE BLACK AS PITCH IN HERE!
THERE'S NO TIME TO INVESTIGATE THE WAVE LENGTH MORTAN'S USING FOR HIS BROADCAST--BUT I CAN DO SOMETHING ABOUT THAT SUNLIGHT! LISTEN! WHEN MORTAN BROADCASTS AGAIN, WE'LL FIND HIS LOCATION BY TRIANGULATION.*
*Editor's Note: TRIANGULATION IS A MATHEMATICAL WAY OF PINPOINTING THE SOURCE OF A RADIO BROADCAST BY SPOTTING RECEIVERS AT KEY POINTS!
AN HOUR BEFORE THE TEN-HOUR DEADLINE IS UP, MORTAN CALLS AGAIN...
ONE HOUR LEFT, RANAGAR! HAVE YOU DECIDED TO ACCEPT MY TERMS?
I MUST STALL MORTAN WHILE OUR SCIENTISTS TRIANGULATE HIS POSITION..
7

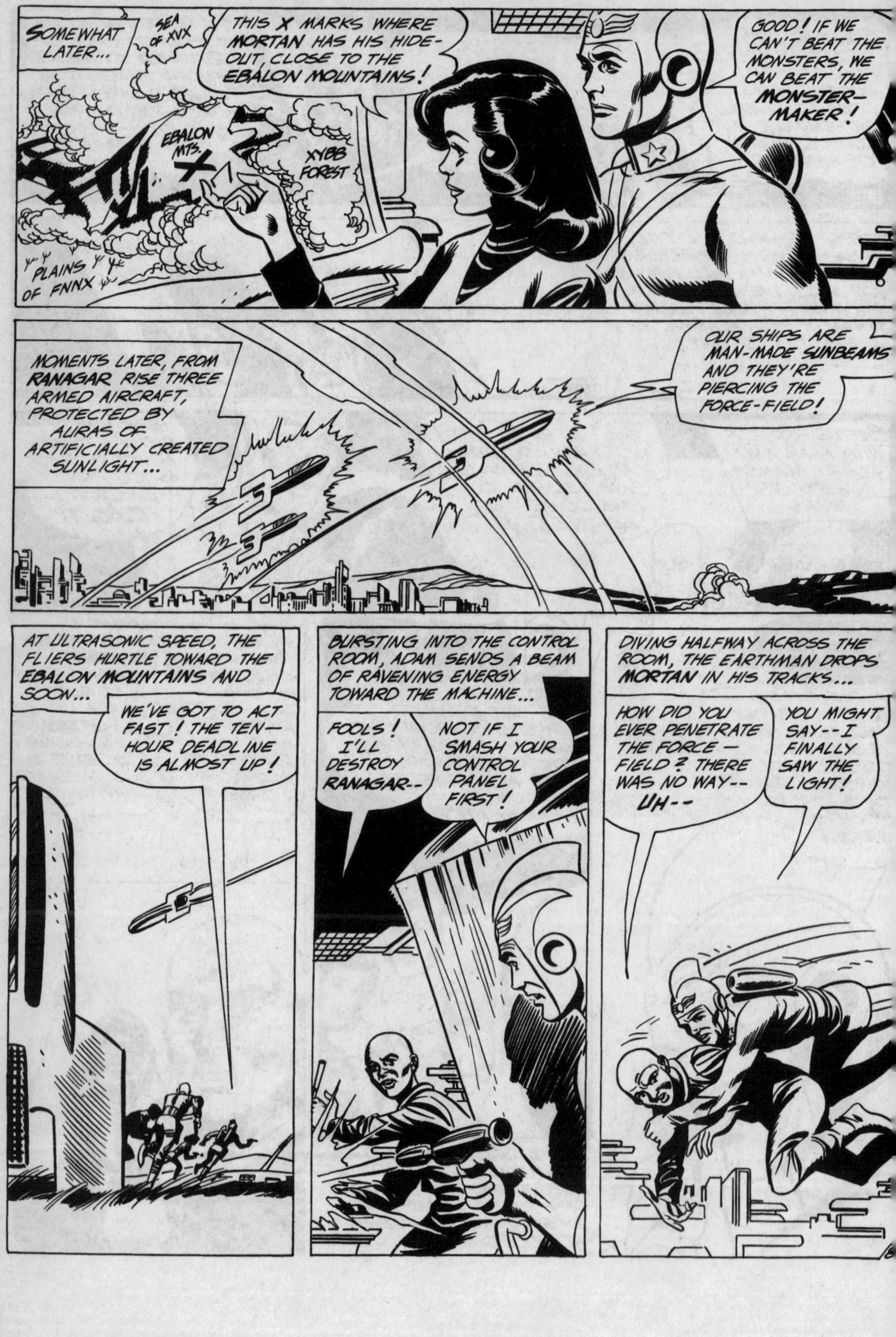
SOMEWHAT LATER...
SEA OF XVX
EBALON MTS.
XYBB FOREST
PLAINS OF FNNX
THIS X MARKS WHERE MORTAN HAS HIS HIDE-OUT, CLOSE TO THE EBALON MOUNTAINS!
GOOD! IF WE CAN'T BEAT THE MONSTERS, WE CAN BEAT THE MONSTER-MAKER!
MOMENTS LATER, FROM RANAGAR RISE THREE ARMED AIRCRAFT, PROTECTED BY AURAS OF ARTIFICIALLY CREATED SUNLIGHT...
OUR SHIPS ARE MAN-MADE SUNBEAMS AND THEY'RE PIERCING THE FORCE-FIELD!
AT ULTRASONIC SPEED, THE FLIERS HURTLE TOWARD THE EBALON MOUNTAINS AND SOON...
WE'VE GOT TO ACT FAST! THE TEN-HOUR DEADLINE IS ALMOST UP!
BURSTING INTO THE CONTROL ROOM, ADAM SENDS A BEAM OF RAVENING ENERGY TOWARD THE MACHINE...
FOOLS! I'LL DESTROY RANAGAR--
NOT IF I SMASH YOUR CONTROL PANEL FIRST!
DIVING HALFWAY ACROSS THE ROOM, THE EARTHMAN DROPS MORTAN IN HIS TRACKS...
HOW DID YOU EVER PENETRATE THE FORCE-FIELD? THERE WAS NO WAY-- UH--
YOU MIGHT SAY--I FINALLY SAW THE LIGHT!

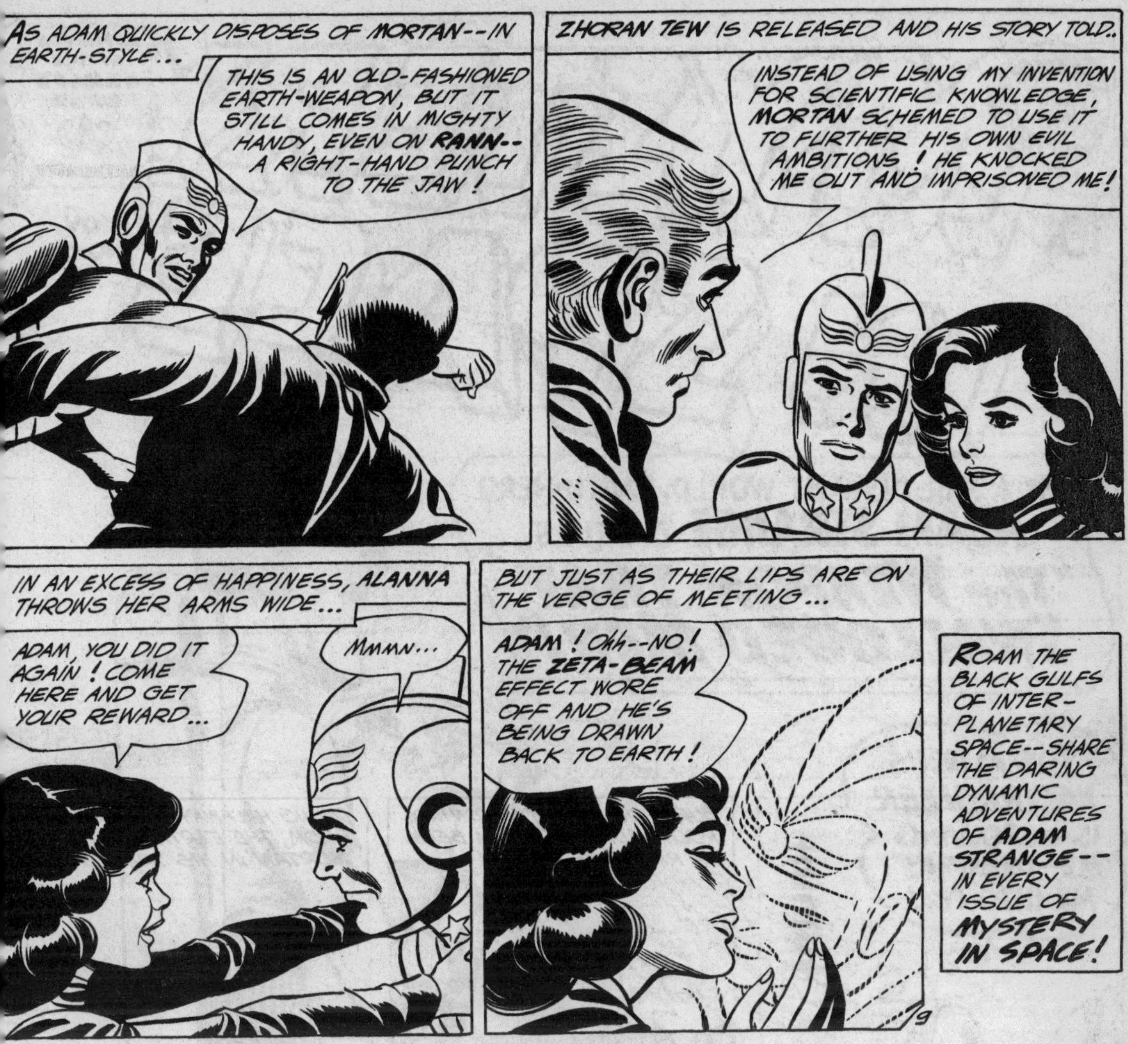
AS ADAM QUICKLY DISPOSES OF MORTAN--IN EARTH-STYLE...
THIS IS AN OLD-FASHIONED EARTH-WEAPON, BUT IT STILL COMES IN MIGHTY HANDY, EVEN ON RANN-- A RIGHT-HAND PUNCH TO THE JAW!
ZHORAN TEW IS RELEASED AND HIS STORY TOLD..
INSTEAD OF USING MY INVENTION FOR SCIENTIFIC KNOWLEDGE, MORTAN SCHEMED TO USE IT TO FURTHER HIS OWN EVIL AMBITIONS! HE KNOCKED ME OUT AND IMPRISONED ME!
IN AN EXCESS OF HAPPINESS, ALANNA THROWS HER ARMS WIDE...
ADAM, YOU DID IT AGAIN! COME HERE AND GET YOUR REWARD...
MMMN...
BUT JUST AS THEIR LIPS ARE ON THE VERGE OF MEETING...
ADAM! OHH--NO! THE ZETA-BEAM EFFECT WORE OFF AND HE'S BEING DRAWN BACK TO EARTH!
9
ROAM THE BLACK GULFS OF INTER-PLANETARY SPACE--SHARE THE DARING DYNAMIC ADVENTURES OF ADAM STRANGE--IN EVERY ISSUE OF MYSTERY IN SPACE!

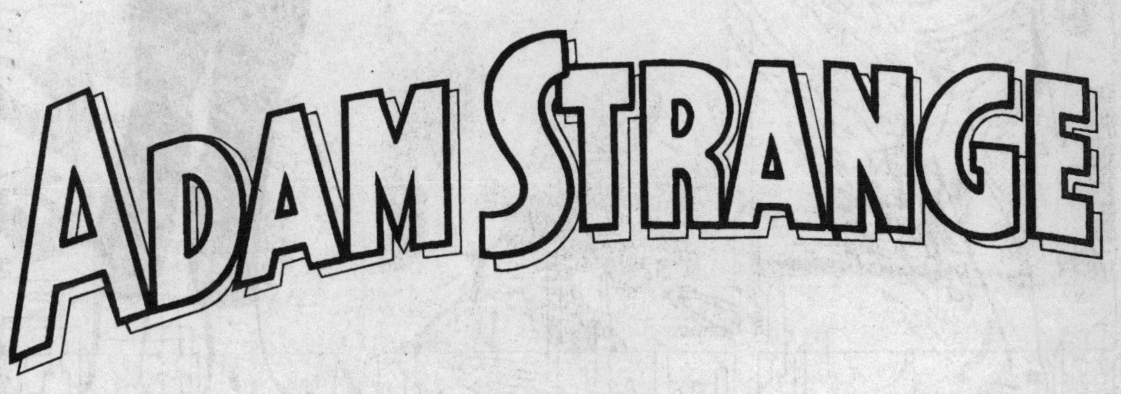
ADAM STRANGE

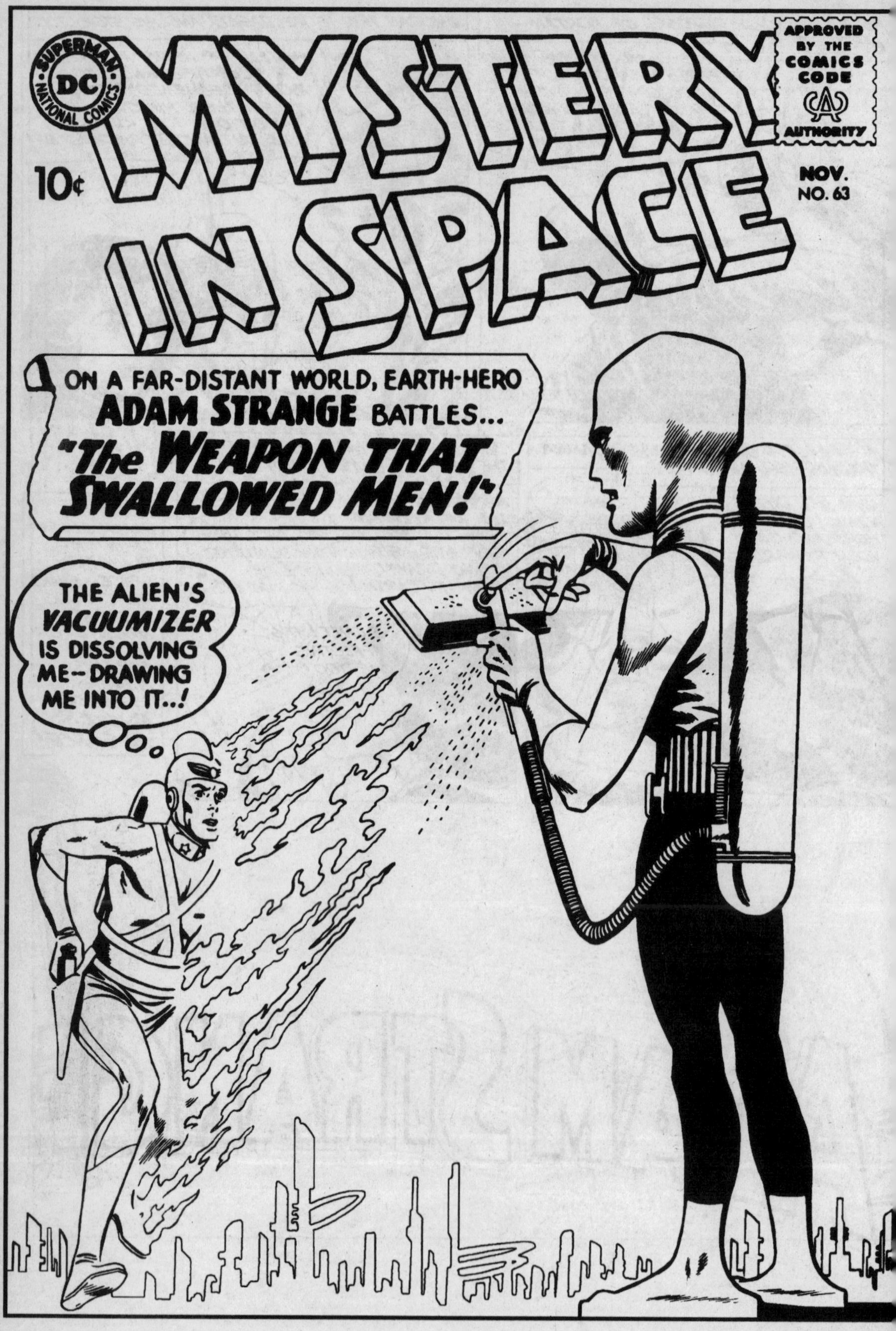
SUPERMAN DC NATIONAL COMICS
MYSTERY IN SPACE
APPROVED BY THE COMICS CODE AUTHORITY
10¢
NOV. NO. 63
ON A FAR-DISTANT WORLD, EARTH-HERO ADAM STRANGE BATTLES... "The WEAPON THAT SWALLOWED MEN!"
THE ALIEN'S VACUUMIZER IS DISSOLVING ME--DRAWING ME INTO IT..!

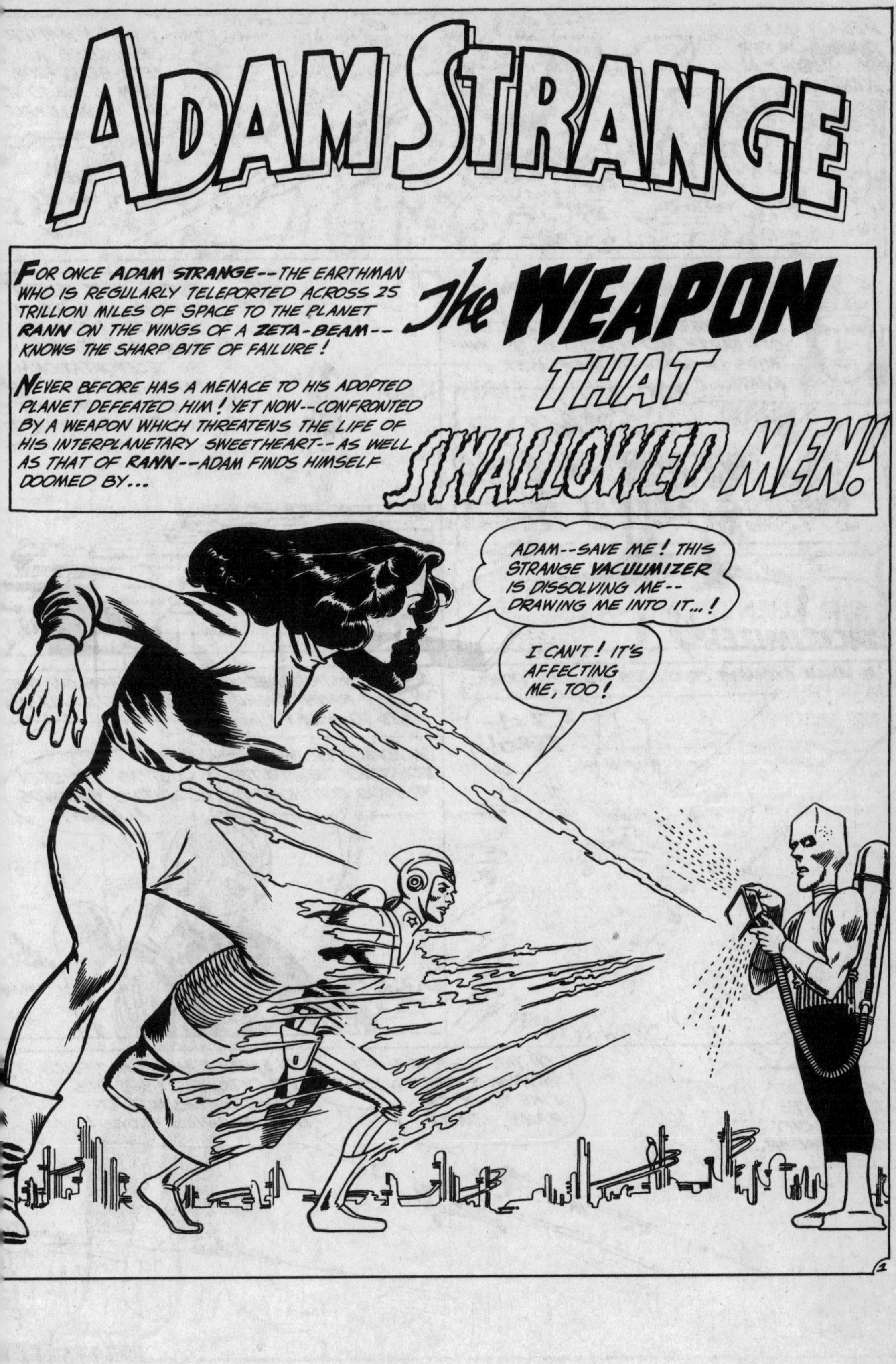
ADAM STRANGE
FOR ONCE ADAM STRANGE--THE EARTHMAN WHO IS REGULARLY TELEPORTED ACROSS 25 TRILLION MILES OF SPACE TO THE PLANET RANN ON THE WINGS OF A ZETA-BEAM--KNOWS THE SHARP BITE OF FAILURE!
NEVER BEFORE HAS A MENACE TO HIS ADOPTED PLANET DEFEATED HIM! YET NOW--CONFRONTED BY A WEAPON WHICH THREATENS THE LIFE OF HIS INTERPLANETARY SWEETHEART--AS WELL AS THAT OF RANN--ADAM FINDS HIMSELF DOOMED BY...
The WEAPON THAT SWALLOWED MEN!
ADAM--SAVE ME! THIS STRANGE VACUUMIZER IS DISSOLVING ME--DRAWING ME INTO IT...!
I CAN'T! IT'S AFFECTING ME, TOO!

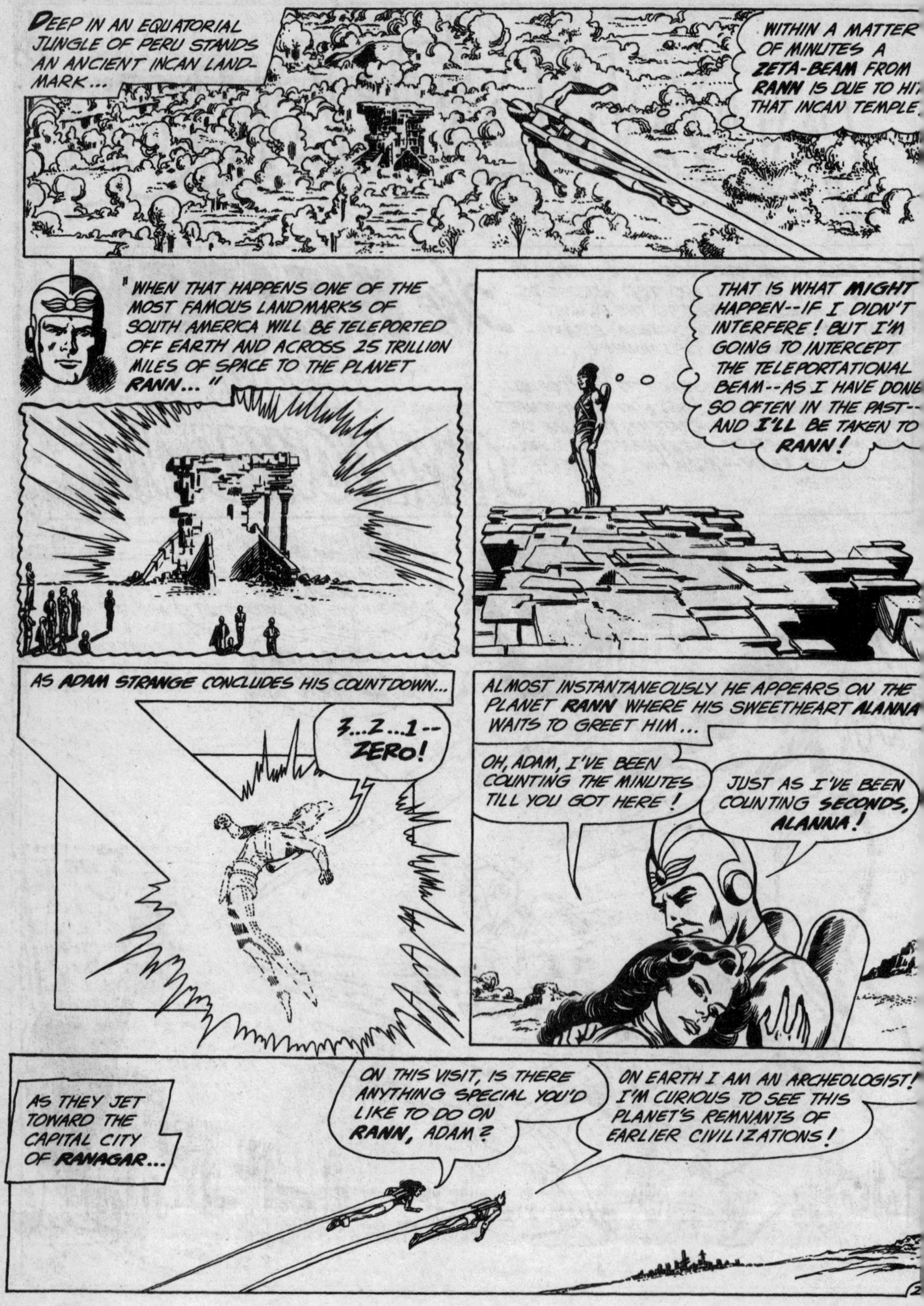
DEEP IN AN EQUATORIAL JUNGLE OF PERU STANDS AN ANCIENT INCAN LANDMARK...
WITHIN A MATTER OF MINUTES A ZETA-BEAM FROM RANN IS DUE TO HI THAT INCAN TEMPLE
"WHEN THAT HAPPENS ONE OF THE MOST FAMOUS LANDMARKS OF SOUTH AMERICA WILL BE TELEPORTED OFF EARTH AND ACROSS 25 TRILLION MILES OF SPACE TO THE PLANET RANN..."
THAT IS WHAT MIGHT HAPPEN--IF I DIDN'T INTERFERE! BUT I'M GOING TO INTERCEPT THE TELEPORTATIONAL BEAM--AS I HAVE DONE SO OFTEN IN THE PAST--AND I'LL BE TAKEN TO RANN!
AS ADAM STRANGE CONCLUDES HIS COUNTDOWN...
3...2...1--ZERO!
ALMOST INSTANTANEOUSLY HE APPEARS ON THE PLANET RANN WHERE HIS SWEETHEART ALANNA WAITS TO GREET HIM...
OH, ADAM, I'VE BEEN COUNTING THE MINUTES TILL YOU GOT HERE!
JUST AS I'VE BEEN COUNTING SECONDS, ALANNA!
AS THEY JET TOWARD THE CAPITAL CITY OF RANAGAR...
ON THIS VISIT, IS THERE ANYTHING SPECIAL YOU'D LIKE TO DO ON RANN, ADAM?
ON EARTH I AM AN ARCHEOLOGIST! I'M CURIOUS TO SEE THIS PLANET'S REMNANTS OF EARLIER CIVILIZATIONS!
2

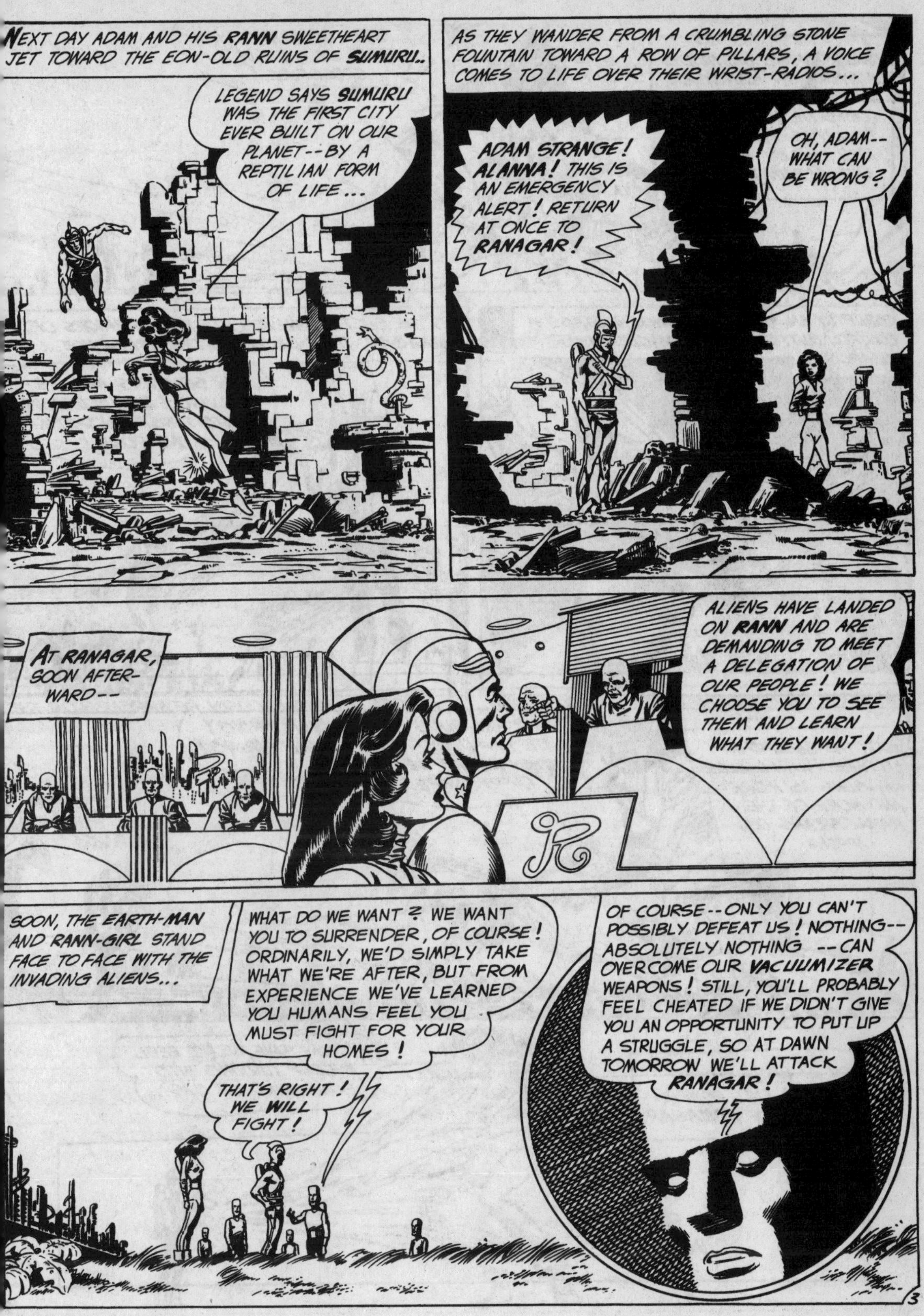
NEXT DAY ADAM AND HIS RANN SWEETHEART JET TOWARD THE EON-OLD RUINS OF SUMURU..
LEGEND SAYS SUMURU WAS THE FIRST CITY EVER BUILT ON OUR PLANET--BY A REPTILIAN FORM OF LIFE...
AS THEY WANDER FROM A CRUMBLING STONE FOUNTAIN TOWARD A ROW OF PILLARS, A VOICE COMES TO LIFE OVER THEIR WRIST-RADIOS...
ADAM STRANGE! ALANNA! THIS IS AN EMERGENCY ALERT! RETURN AT ONCE TO RANAGAR!
OH, ADAM--WHAT CAN BE WRONG?
AT RANAGAR, SOON AFTER-WARD--
ALIENS HAVE LANDED ON RANN AND ARE DEMANDING TO MEET A DELEGATION OF OUR PEOPLE! WE CHOOSE YOU TO SEE THEM AND LEARN WHAT THEY WANT!
SOON, THE EARTH-MAN AND RANN-GIRL STAND FACE TO FACE WITH THE INVADING ALIENS...
WHAT DO WE WANT? WE WANT YOU TO SURRENDER, OF COURSE! ORDINARILY, WE'D SIMPLY TAKE WHAT WE'RE AFTER, BUT FROM EXPERIENCE WE'VE LEARNED YOU HUMANS FEEL YOU MUST FIGHT FOR YOUR HOMES!
THAT'S RIGHT! WE WILL FIGHT!
OF COURSE--ONLY YOU CAN'T POSSIBLY DEFEAT US! NOTHING--ABSOLUTELY NOTHING --CAN OVERCOME OUR VACUUMIZER WEAPONS! STILL, YOU'LL PROBABLY FEEL CHEATED IF WE DIDN'T GIVE YOU AN OPPORTUNITY TO PUT UP A STRUGGLE, SO AT DAWN TOMORROW WE'LL ATTACK RANAGAR!
3

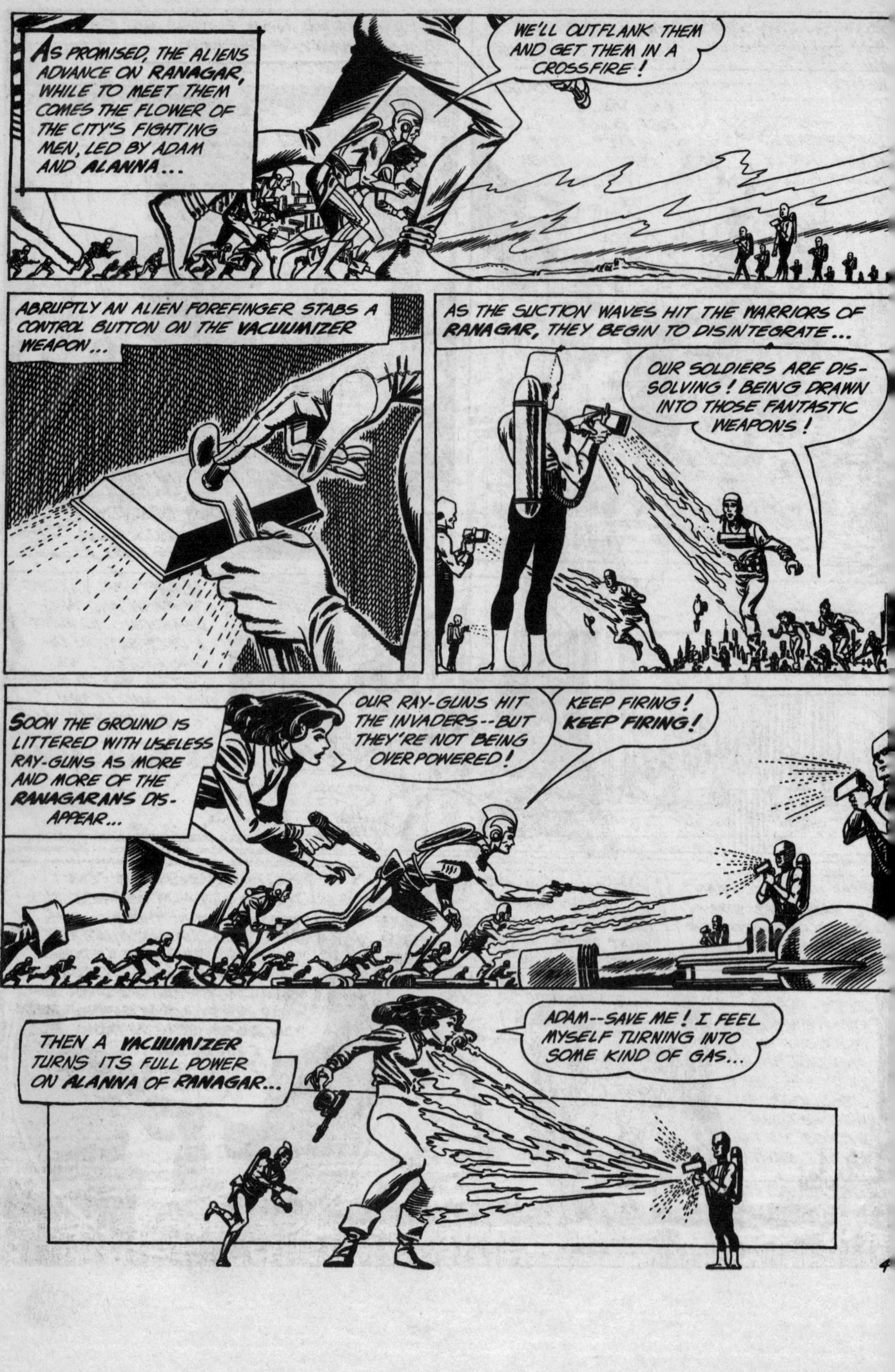
AS PROMISED, THE ALIENS ADVANCE ON RANAGAR, WHILE TO MEET THEM COMES THE FLOWER OF THE CITY'S FIGHTING MEN, LED BY ADAM AND ALANNA...
WE'LL OUTFLANK THEM AND GET THEM IN A CROSSFIRE!
ABRUPTLY AN ALIEN FOREFINGER STABS A CONTROL BUTTON ON THE VACUUMIZER WEAPON...
AS THE SUCTION WAVES HIT THE WARRIORS OF RANAGAR, THEY BEGIN TO DISINTEGRATE...
OUR SOLDIERS ARE DIS-SOLVING! BEING DRAWN INTO THOSE FANTASTIC WEAPONS!
SOON THE GROUND IS LITTERED WITH USELESS RAY-GUNS AS MORE AND MORE OF THE RANAGARANS DIS-APPEAR...
OUR RAY-GUNS HIT THE INVADERS--BUT THEY'RE NOT BEING OVERPOWERED!
KEEP FIRING! KEEP FIRING!
THEN A VACUUMIZER TURNS ITS FULL POWER ON ALANNA OF RANAGAR...
ADAM--SAVE ME! I FEEL MYSELF TURNING INTO SOME KIND OF GAS...
4

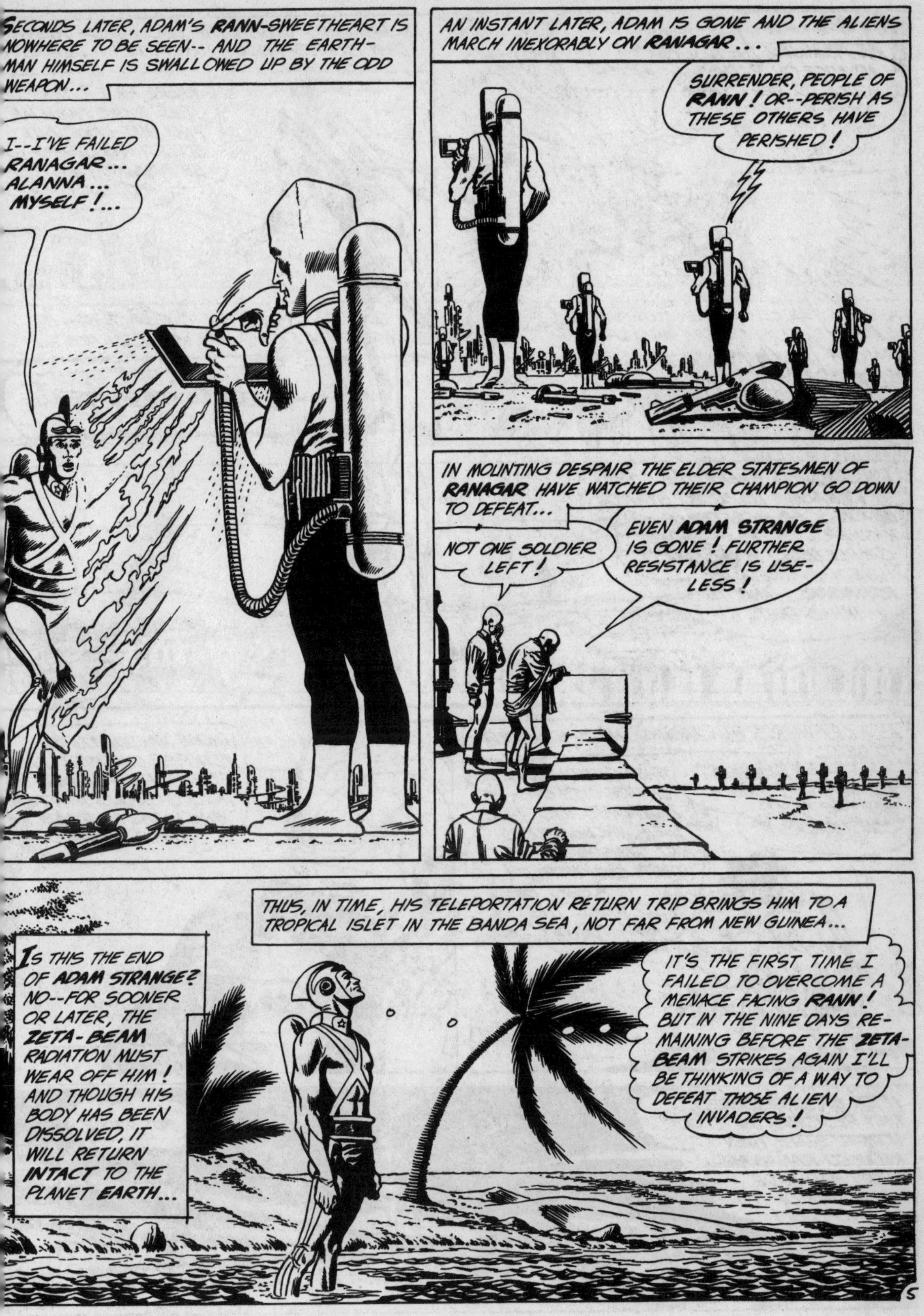
SECONDS LATER, ADAM'S RANN-SWEETHEART IS NOWHERE TO BE SEEN-- AND THE EARTH-MAN HIMSELF IS SWALLOWED UP BY THE ODD WEAPON...
I--I'VE FAILED RANAGAR... ALANNA... MYSELF!...
AN INSTANT LATER, ADAM IS GONE AND THE ALIENS MARCH INEXORABLY ON RANAGAR...
SURRENDER, PEOPLE OF RANN! OR--PERISH AS THESE OTHERS HAVE PERISHED!
IN MOUNTING DESPAIR THE ELDER STATESMEN OF RANAGAR HAVE WATCHED THEIR CHAMPION GO DOWN TO DEFEAT...
NOT ONE SOLDIER LEFT!
EVEN ADAM STRANGE IS GONE! FURTHER RESISTANCE IS USE-LESS!
IS THIS THE END OF ADAM STRANGE? NO--FOR SOONER OR LATER, THE ZETA-BEAM RADIATION MUST WEAR OFF HIM! AND THOUGH HIS BODY HAS BEEN DISSOLVED, IT WILL RETURN INTACT TO THE PLANET EARTH...
THUS, IN TIME, HIS TELEPORTATION RETURN TRIP BRINGS HIM TO A TROPICAL ISLET IN THE BANDA SEA, NOT FAR FROM NEW GUINEA...
IT'S THE FIRST TIME I FAILED TO OVERCOME A MENACE FACING RANN! BUT IN THE NINE DAYS RE-MAINING BEFORE THE ZETA-BEAM STRIKES AGAIN I'LL BE THINKING OF A WAY TO DEFEAT THOSE ALIEN INVADERS!
5

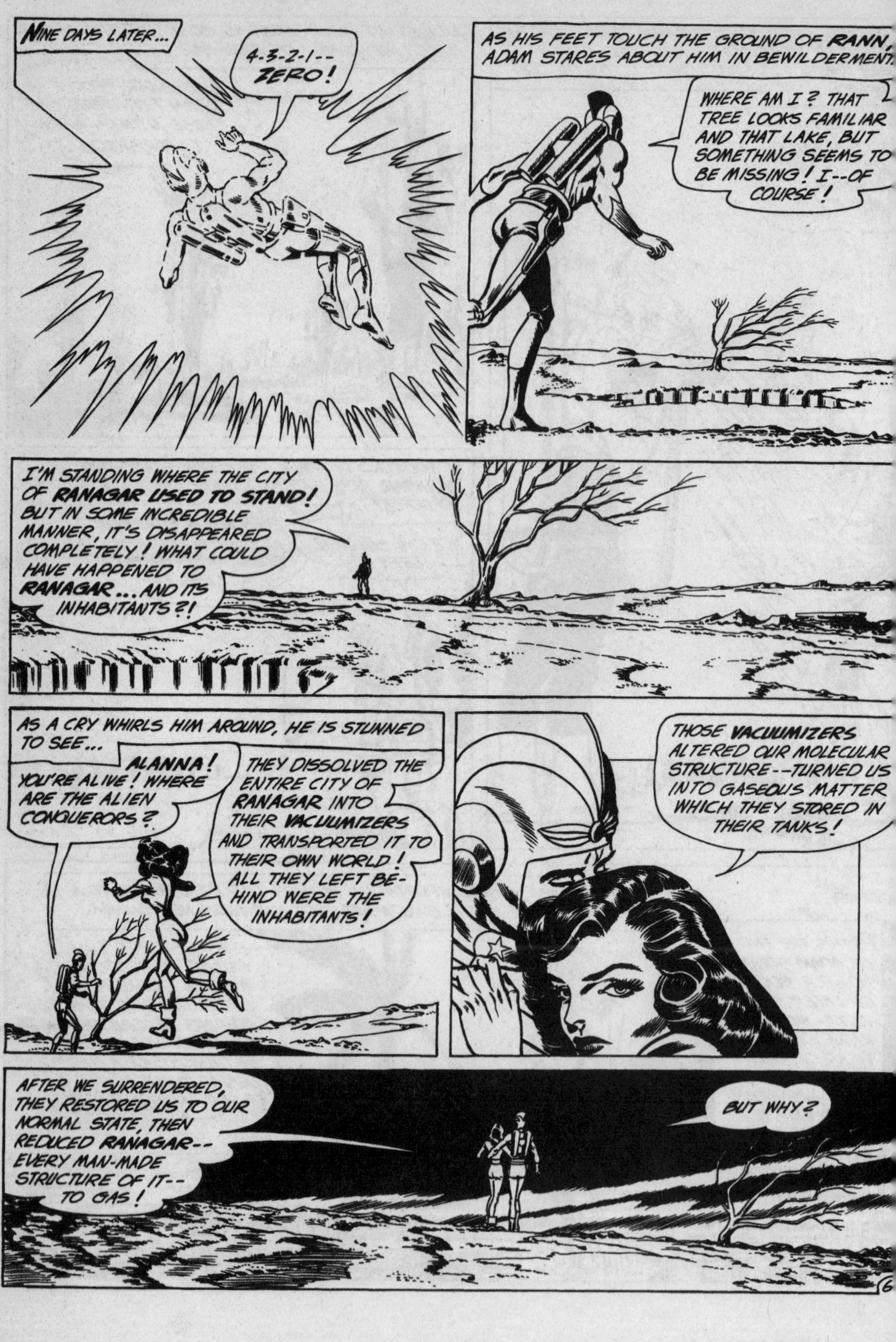
NINE DAYS LATER...
4-3-2-1-- ZERO!
AS HIS FEET TOUCH THE GROUND OF RANN, ADAM STARES ABOUT HIM IN BEWILDERMENT.
WHERE AM I? THAT TREE LOOKS FAMILIAR AND THAT LAKE, BUT SOMETHING SEEMS TO BE MISSING! I--OF COURSE!
I'M STANDING WHERE THE CITY OF RANAGAR USED TO STAND! BUT IN SOME INCREDIBLE MANNER, IT'S DISAPPEARED COMPLETELY! WHAT COULD HAVE HAPPENED TO RANAGAR... AND ITS INHABITANTS?!
AS A CRY WHIRLS HIM AROUND, HE IS STUNNED TO SEE...
ALANNA! YOU'RE ALIVE! WHERE ARE THE ALIEN CONQUERORS?
THEY DISSOLVED THE ENTIRE CITY OF RANAGAR INTO THEIR VACUUMIZERS AND TRANSPORTED IT TO THEIR OWN WORLD! ALL THEY LEFT BEHIND WERE THE INHABITANTS!
THOSE VACUUMIZERS ALTERED OUR MOLECULAR STRUCTURE--TURNED US INTO GASEOUS MATTER WHICH THEY STORED IN THEIR TANKS!
AFTER WE SURRENDERED, THEY RESTORED US TO OUR NORMAL STATE, THEN REDUCED RANAGAR--EVERY MAN-MADE STRUCTURE OF IT--TO GAS!
BUT WHY?
6

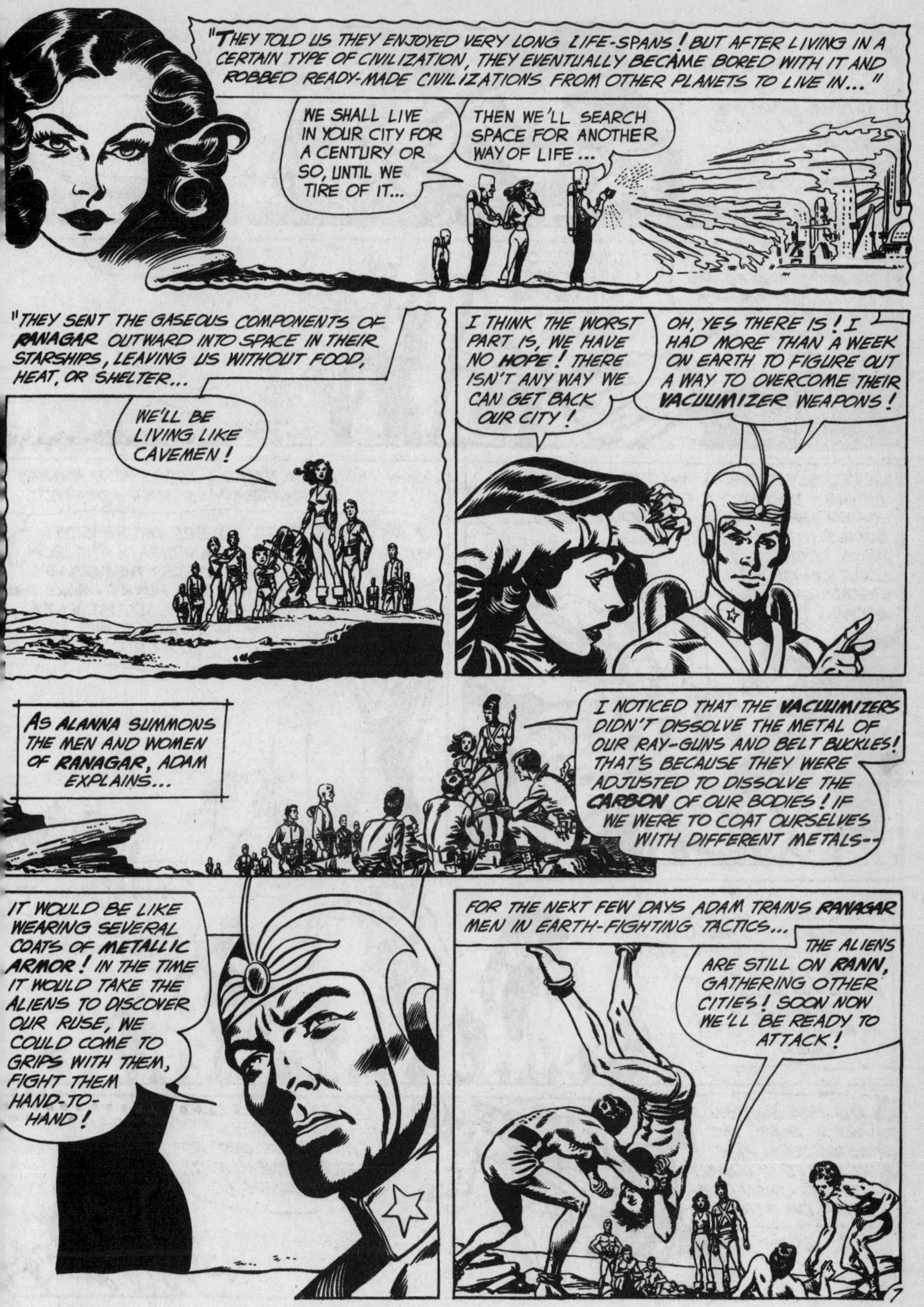
"THEY TOLD US THEY ENJOYED VERY LONG LIFE-SPANS! BUT AFTER LIVING IN A CERTAIN TYPE OF CIVILIZATION, THEY EVENTUALLY BECAME BORED WITH IT AND ROBBED READY-MADE CIVILIZATIONS FROM OTHER PLANETS TO LIVE IN..."
WE SHALL LIVE IN YOUR CITY FOR A CENTURY OR SO, UNTIL WE TIRE OF IT...
THEN WE'LL SEARCH SPACE FOR ANOTHER WAY OF LIFE...
"THEY SENT THE GASEOUS COMPONENTS OF RANAGAR OUTWARD INTO SPACE IN THEIR STARSHIPS, LEAVING US WITHOUT FOOD, HEAT, OR SHELTER...
WE'LL BE LIVING LIKE CAVEMEN!
I THINK THE WORST PART IS, WE HAVE NO HOPE! THERE ISN'T ANY WAY WE CAN GET BACK OUR CITY!
OH, YES THERE IS! I HAD MORE THAN A WEEK ON EARTH TO FIGURE OUT A WAY TO OVERCOME THEIR VACUUMIZER WEAPONS!
AS ALANNA SUMMONS THE MEN AND WOMEN OF RANAGAR, ADAM EXPLAINS...
I NOTICED THAT THE VACUUMIZERS DIDN'T DISSOLVE THE METAL OF OUR RAY-GUNS AND BELT BUCKLES! THAT'S BECAUSE THEY WERE ADJUSTED TO DISSOLVE THE CARBON OF OUR BODIES! IF WE WERE TO COAT OURSELVES WITH DIFFERENT METALS--
IT WOULD BE LIKE WEARING SEVERAL COATS OF METALLIC ARMOR! IN THE TIME IT WOULD TAKE THE ALIENS TO DISCOVER OUR RUSE, WE COULD COME TO GRIPS WITH THEM, FIGHT THEM HAND-TO-HAND!
FOR THE NEXT FEW DAYS ADAM TRAINS RANAGAR MEN IN EARTH-FIGHTING TACTICS...
THE ALIENS ARE STILL ON RANN, GATHERING OTHER CITIES! SOON NOW WE'LL BE READY TO ATTACK!
7

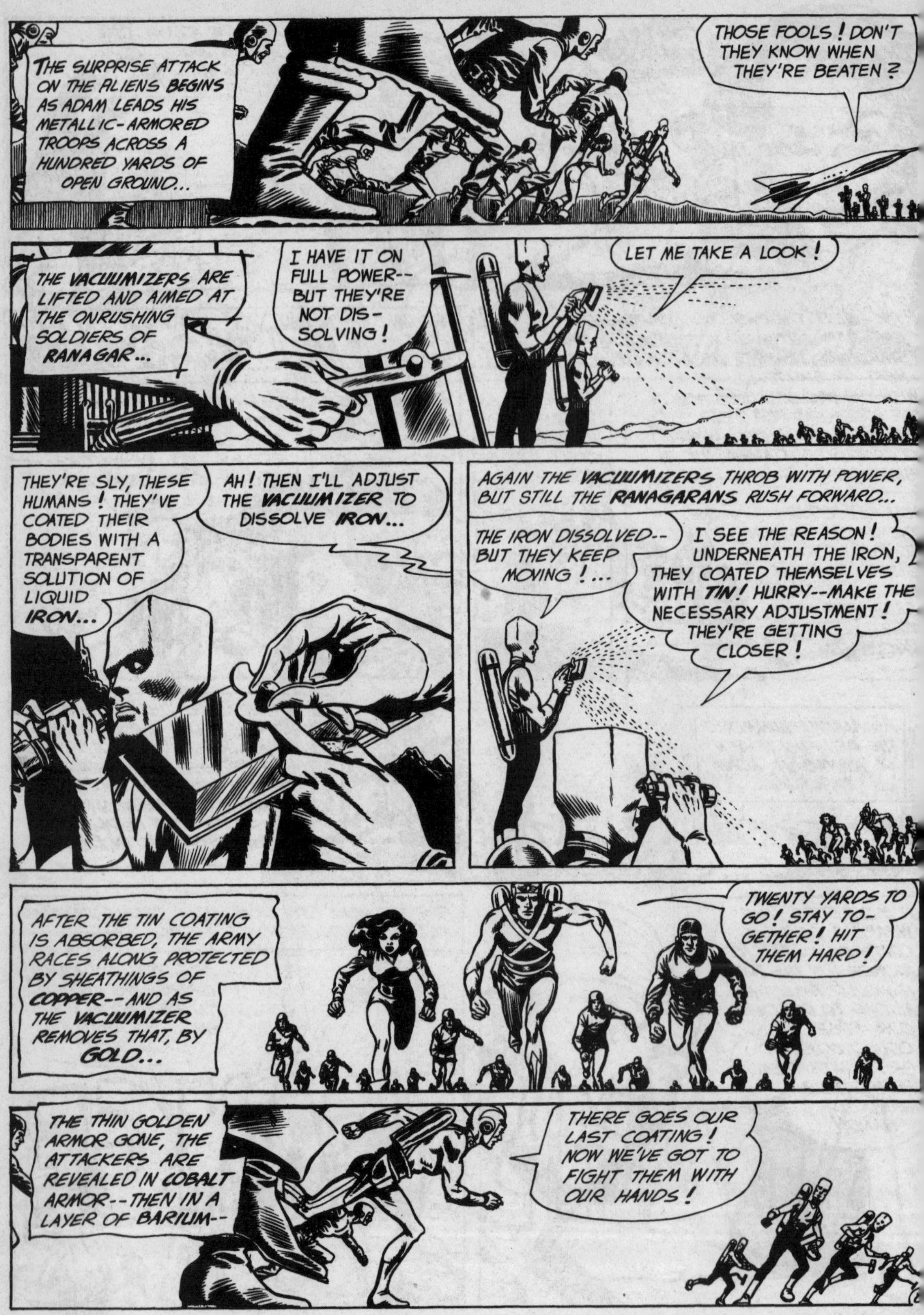
THE SURPRISE ATTACK ON THE ALIENS BEGINS AS ADAM LEADS HIS METALLIC-ARMORED TROOPS ACROSS A HUNDRED YARDS OF OPEN GROUND...
THOSE FOOLS! DON'T THEY KNOW WHEN THEY'RE BEATEN?
THE VACUUMIZERS ARE LIFTED AND AIMED AT THE ONRUSHING SOLDIERS OF RANAGAR...
I HAVE IT ON FULL POWER-- BUT THEY'RE NOT DIS-SOLVING!
LET ME TAKE A LOOK!
THEY'RE SLY, THESE HUMANS! THEY'VE COATED THEIR BODIES WITH A TRANSPARENT SOLUTION OF LIQUID IRON...
AH! THEN I'LL ADJUST THE VACUUMIZER TO DISSOLVE IRON...
AGAIN THE VACUUMIZERS THROB WITH POWER, BUT STILL THE RANAGARANS RUSH FORWARD...
THE IRON DISSOLVED-- BUT THEY KEEP MOVING!...
I SEE THE REASON! UNDERNEATH THE IRON, THEY COATED THEMSELVES WITH TIN! HURRY--MAKE THE NECESSARY ADJUSTMENT! THEY'RE GETTING CLOSER!
AFTER THE TIN COATING IS ABSORBED, THE ARMY RACES ALONG PROTECTED BY SHEATHINGS OF COPPER--AND AS THE VACUUMIZER REMOVES THAT, BY GOLD...
TWENTY YARDS TO GO! STAY TO-GETHER! HIT THEM HARD!
THE THIN GOLDEN ARMOR GONE, THE ATTACKERS ARE REVEALED IN COBALT ARMOR--THEN IN A LAYER OF BARIUM--
THERE GOES OUR LAST COATING! NOW WE'VE GOT TO FIGHT THEM WITH OUR HANDS!

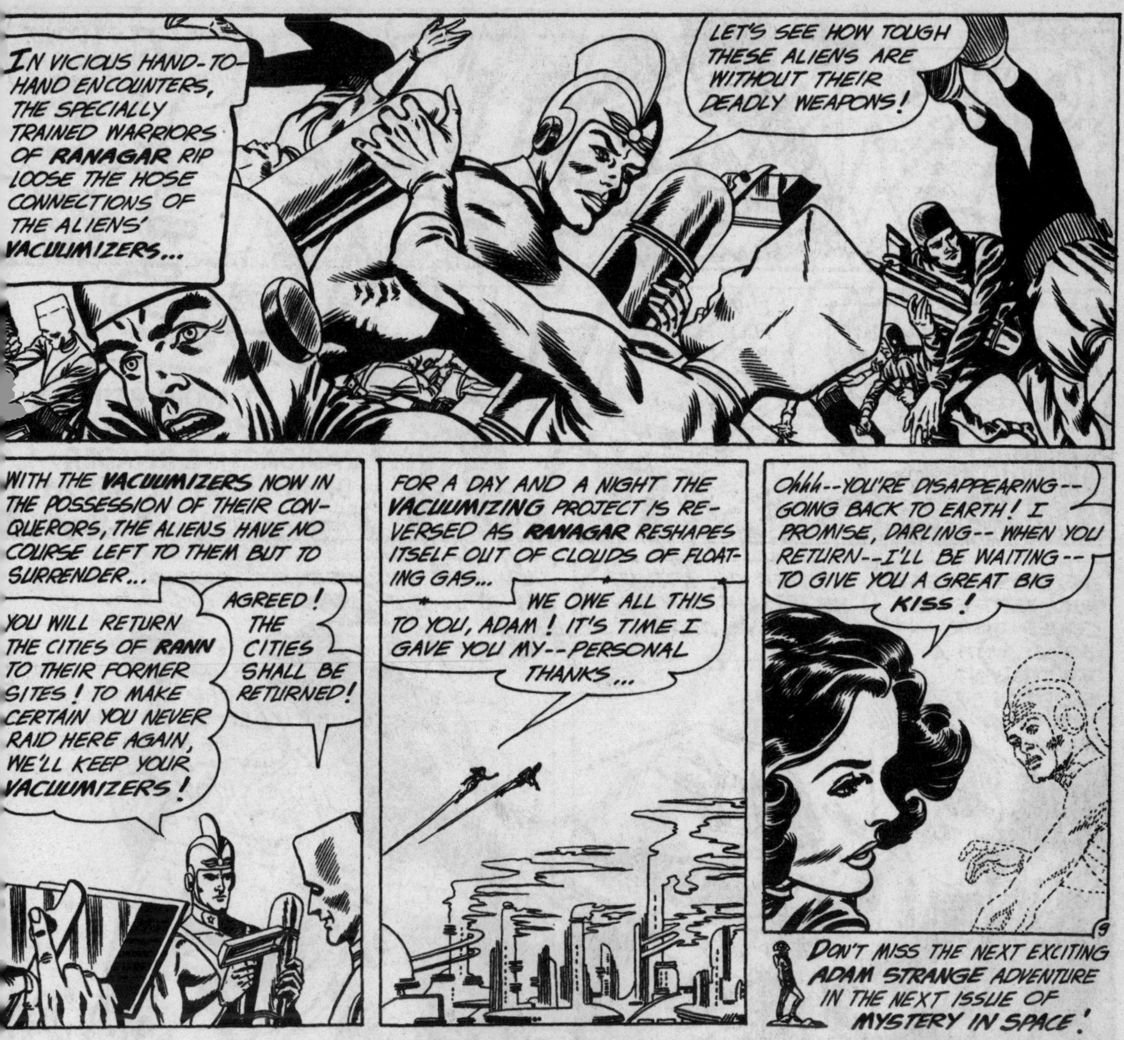
IN VICIOUS HAND-TO-HAND ENCOUNTERS, THE SPECIALLY TRAINED WARRIORS OF RANAGAR RIP LOOSE THE HOSE CONNECTIONS OF THE ALIENS' VACUUMIZERS...
LET'S SEE HOW TOUGH THESE ALIENS ARE WITHOUT THEIR DEADLY WEAPONS!
WITH THE VACUUMIZERS NOW IN THE POSSESSION OF THEIR CONQUERORS, THE ALIENS HAVE NO COURSE LEFT TO THEM BUT TO SURRENDER...
YOU WILL RETURN THE CITIES OF RANN TO THEIR FORMER SITES! TO MAKE CERTAIN YOU NEVER RAID HERE AGAIN, WE'LL KEEP YOUR VACUUMIZERS!
AGREED! THE CITIES SHALL BE RETURNED!
FOR A DAY AND A NIGHT THE VACUUMIZING PROJECT IS REVERSED AS RANAGAR RESHAPES ITSELF OUT OF CLOUDS OF FLOATING GAS...
WE OWE ALL THIS TO YOU, ADAM! IT'S TIME I GAVE YOU MY--PERSONAL THANKS...
Ohhh--YOU'RE DISAPPEARING--GOING BACK TO EARTH! I PROMISE, DARLING--WHEN YOU RETURN--I'LL BE WAITING--TO GIVE YOU A GREAT BIG KISS!
9
DON'T MISS THE NEXT EXCITING ADAM STRANGE ADVENTURE IN THE NEXT ISSUE OF MYSTERY IN SPACE!

ADAM STRANGE

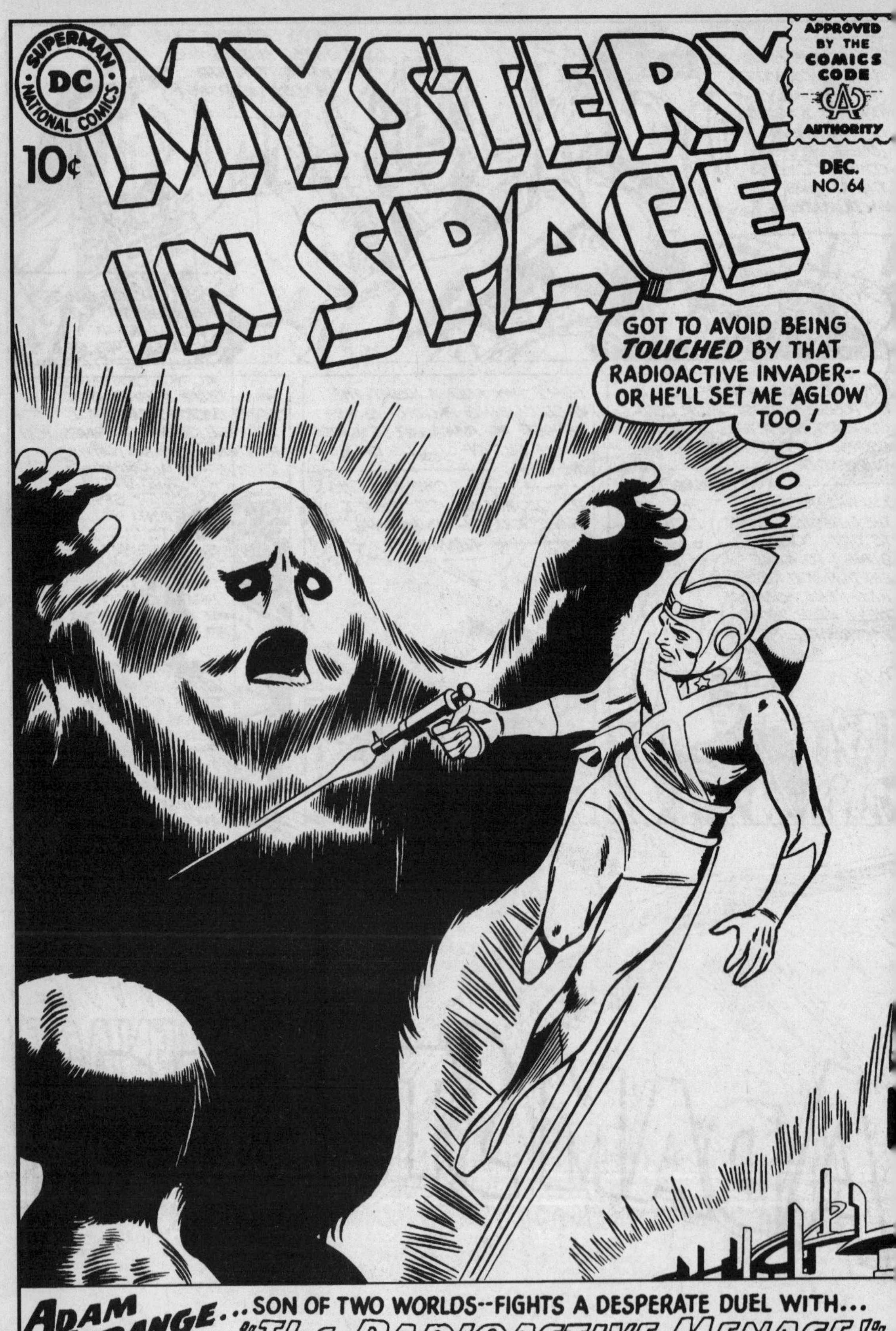
SUPERMAN DC NATIONAL COMICS
10¢
MYSTERY IN SPACE
APPROVED BY THE COMICS CODE AUTHORITY
DEC. NO. 64
GOT TO AVOID BEING TOUCHED BY THAT RADIOACTIVE INVADER-- OR HE'LL SET ME AGLOW TOO!
ADAM STRANGE... SON OF TWO WORLDS--FIGHTS A DESPERATE DUEL WITH...
"The RADIOACTIVE MENACE!"

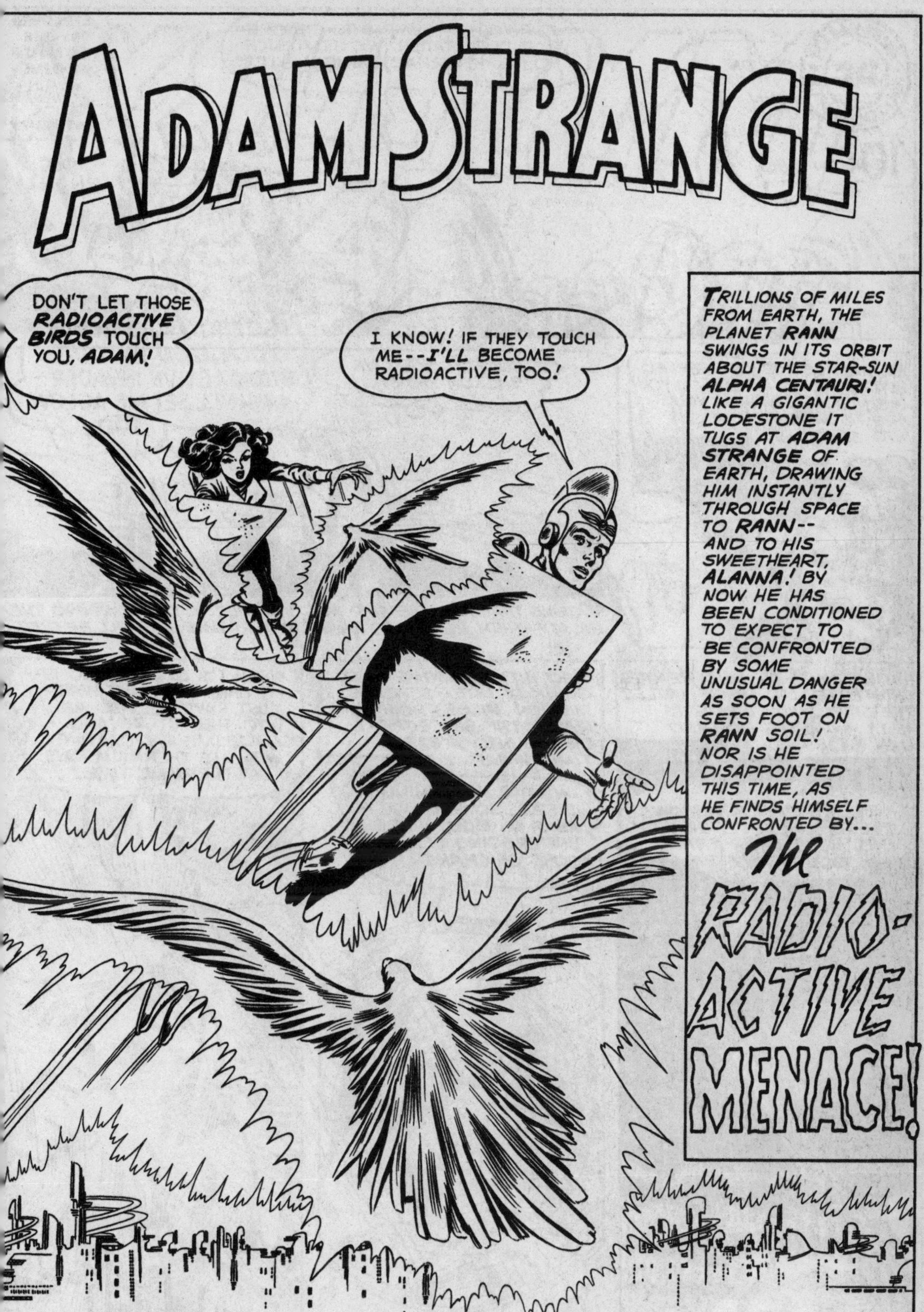
ADAM STRANGE
DON'T LET THOSE RADIOACTIVE BIRDS TOUCH YOU, ADAM!
I KNOW! IF THEY TOUCH ME--I'LL BECOME RADIOACTIVE, TOO!
TRILLIONS OF MILES FROM EARTH, THE PLANET RANN SWINGS IN ITS ORBIT ABOUT THE STAR-SUN ALPHA CENTAURI! LIKE A GIGANTIC LODESTONE IT TUGS AT ADAM STRANGE OF EARTH, DRAWING HIM INSTANTLY THROUGH SPACE TO RANN--AND TO HIS SWEETHEART, ALANNA! BY NOW HE HAS BEEN CONDITIONED TO EXPECT TO BE CONFRONTED BY SOME UNUSUAL DANGER AS SOON AS HE SETS FOOT ON RANN SOIL! NOR IS HE DISAPPOINTED THIS TIME, AS HE FINDS HIMSELF CONFRONTED BY...
The RADIO-ACTIVE MENACE!

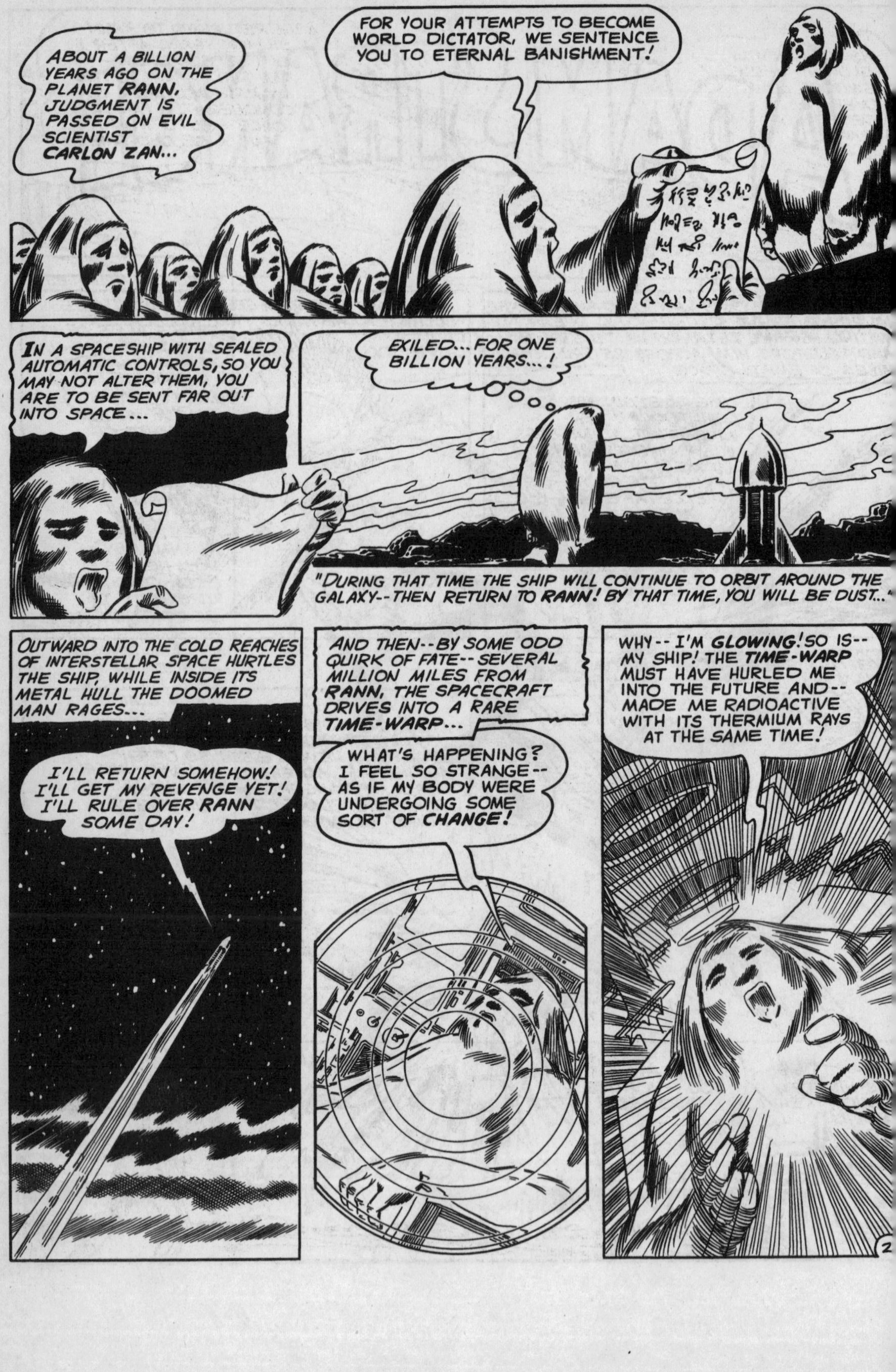
ABOUT A BILLION YEARS AGO ON THE PLANET RANN, JUDGMENT IS PASSED ON EVIL SCIENTIST CARLON ZAN...
FOR YOUR ATTEMPTS TO BECOME WORLD DICTATOR, WE SENTENCE YOU TO ETERNAL BANISHMENT!
IN A SPACESHIP WITH SEALED AUTOMATIC CONTROLS, SO YOU MAY NOT ALTER THEM, YOU ARE TO BE SENT FAR OUT INTO SPACE...
EXILED...FOR ONE BILLION YEARS...!
"DURING THAT TIME THE SHIP WILL CONTINUE TO ORBIT AROUND THE GALAXY--THEN RETURN TO RANN! BY THAT TIME, YOU WILL BE DUST..."
OUTWARD INTO THE COLD REACHES OF INTERSTELLAR SPACE HURTLES THE SHIP, WHILE INSIDE ITS METAL HULL THE DOOMED MAN RAGES...
I'LL RETURN SOMEHOW! I'LL GET MY REVENGE YET! I'LL RULE OVER RANN SOME DAY!
AND THEN--BY SOME ODD QUIRK OF FATE--SEVERAL MILLION MILES FROM RANN, THE SPACECRAFT DRIVES INTO A RARE TIME-WARP...
WHAT'S HAPPENING? I FEEL SO STRANGE--AS IF MY BODY WERE UNDERGOING SOME SORT OF CHANGE!
WHY--I'M GLOWING! SO IS--MY SHIP! THE TIME-WARP MUST HAVE HURLED ME INTO THE FUTURE AND--MADE ME RADIOACTIVE WITH ITS THERMIUM RAYS AT THE SAME TIME!
2

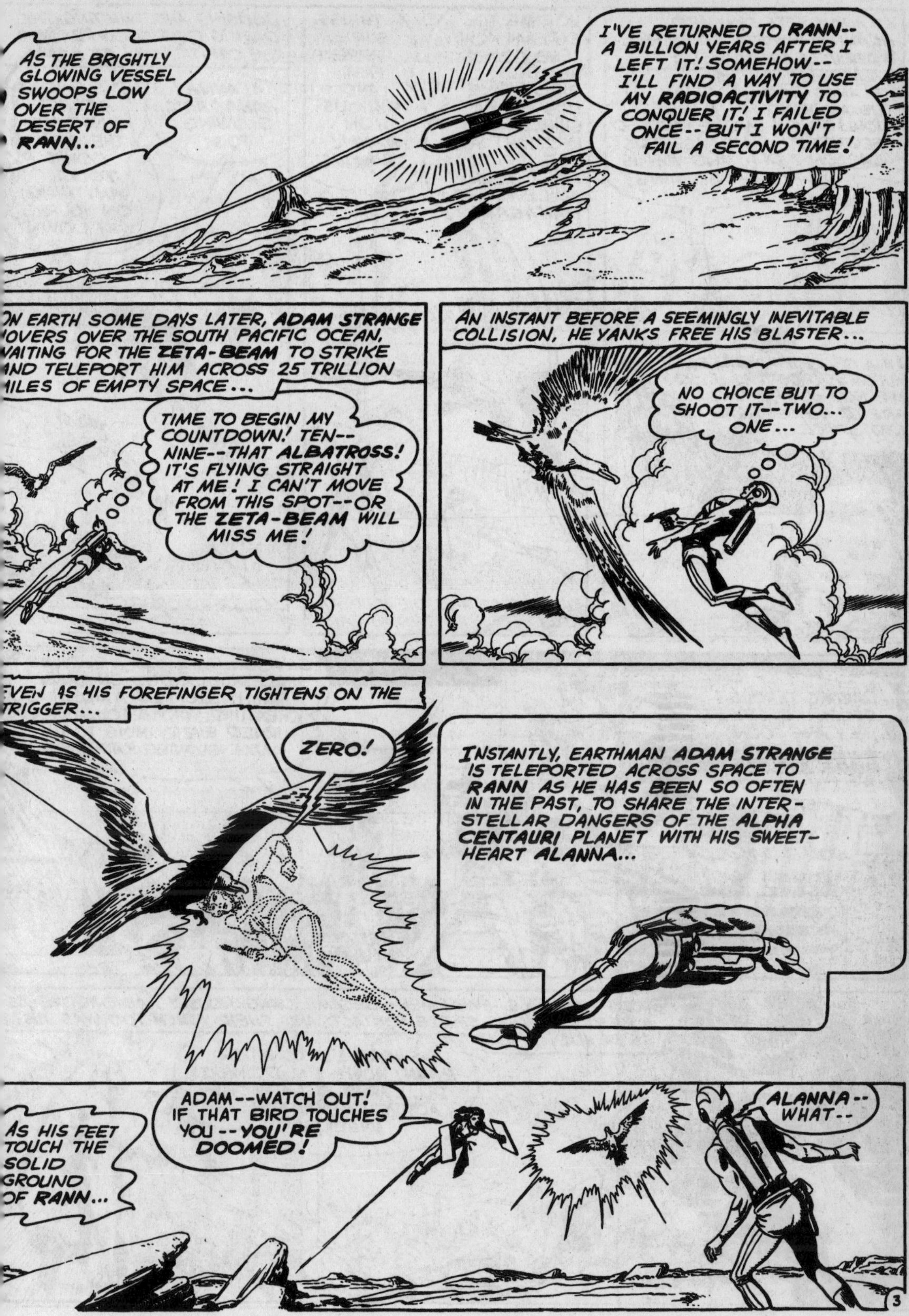
AS THE BRIGHTLY GLOWING VESSEL SWOOPS LOW OVER THE DESERT OF RANN...
I'VE RETURNED TO RANN-- A BILLION YEARS AFTER I LEFT IT! SOMEHOW-- I'LL FIND A WAY TO USE MY RADIOACTIVITY TO CONQUER IT! I FAILED ONCE--BUT I WON'T FAIL A SECOND TIME!
ON EARTH SOME DAYS LATER, ADAM STRANGE HOVERS OVER THE SOUTH PACIFIC OCEAN, WAITING FOR THE ZETA-BEAM TO STRIKE AND TELEPORT HIM ACROSS 25 TRILLION MILES OF EMPTY SPACE...
TIME TO BEGIN MY COUNTDOWN! TEN-- NINE--THAT ALBATROSS! IT'S FLYING STRAIGHT AT ME! I CAN'T MOVE FROM THIS SPOT--OR THE ZETA-BEAM WILL MISS ME!
AN INSTANT BEFORE A SEEMINGLY INEVITABLE COLLISION, HE YANKS FREE HIS BLASTER...
NO CHOICE BUT TO SHOOT IT--TWO... ONE...
EVEN AS HIS FOREFINGER TIGHTENS ON THE TRIGGER...
ZERO!
INSTANTLY, EARTHMAN ADAM STRANGE IS TELEPORTED ACROSS SPACE TO RANN AS HE HAS BEEN SO OFTEN IN THE PAST, TO SHARE THE INTER-STELLAR DANGERS OF THE ALPHA CENTAURI PLANET WITH HIS SWEET-HEART ALANNA...
AS HIS FEET TOUCH THE SOLID GROUND OF RANN...
ADAM--WATCH OUT! IF THAT BIRD TOUCHES YOU--YOU'RE DOOMED!
ALANNA-- WHAT--
3

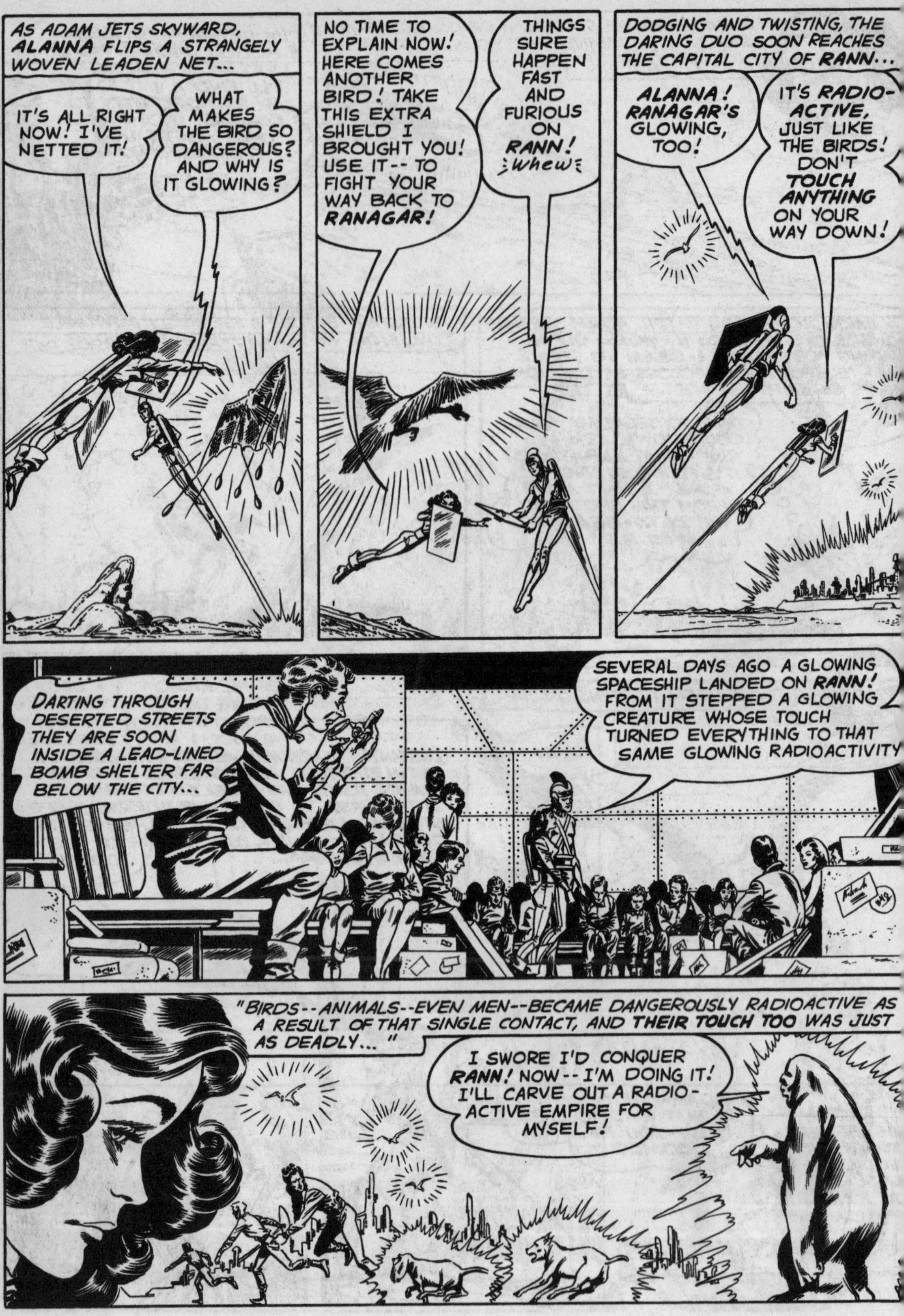
AS ADAM JETS SKYWARD, ALANNA FLIPS A STRANGELY WOVEN LEADEN NET...
IT'S ALL RIGHT NOW! I'VE NETTED IT!
WHAT MAKES THE BIRD SO DANGEROUS? AND WHY IS IT GLOWING?
NO TIME TO EXPLAIN NOW! HERE COMES ANOTHER BIRD! TAKE THIS EXTRA SHIELD I BROUGHT YOU! USE IT-- TO FIGHT YOUR WAY BACK TO RANAGAR!
THINGS SURE HAPPEN FAST AND FURIOUS ON RANN! WHEW
DODGING AND TWISTING, THE DARING DUO SOON REACHES THE CAPITAL CITY OF RANN...
ALANNA! RANAGAR'S GLOWING, TOO!
IT'S RADIO-ACTIVE, JUST LIKE THE BIRDS! DON'T TOUCH ANYTHING ON YOUR WAY DOWN!
DARTING THROUGH DESERTED STREETS THEY ARE SOON INSIDE A LEAD-LINED BOMB SHELTER FAR BELOW THE CITY...
SEVERAL DAYS AGO A GLOWING SPACESHIP LANDED ON RANN! FROM IT STEPPED A GLOWING CREATURE WHOSE TOUCH TURNED EVERYTHING TO THAT SAME GLOWING RADIOACTIVITY
"BIRDS--ANIMALS--EVEN MEN--BECAME DANGEROUSLY RADIOACTIVE AS A RESULT OF THAT SINGLE CONTACT, AND THEIR TOUCH TOO WAS JUST AS DEADLY..."
I SWORE I'D CONQUER RANN! NOW--I'M DOING IT! I'LL CARVE OUT A RADIO-ACTIVE EMPIRE FOR MYSELF!

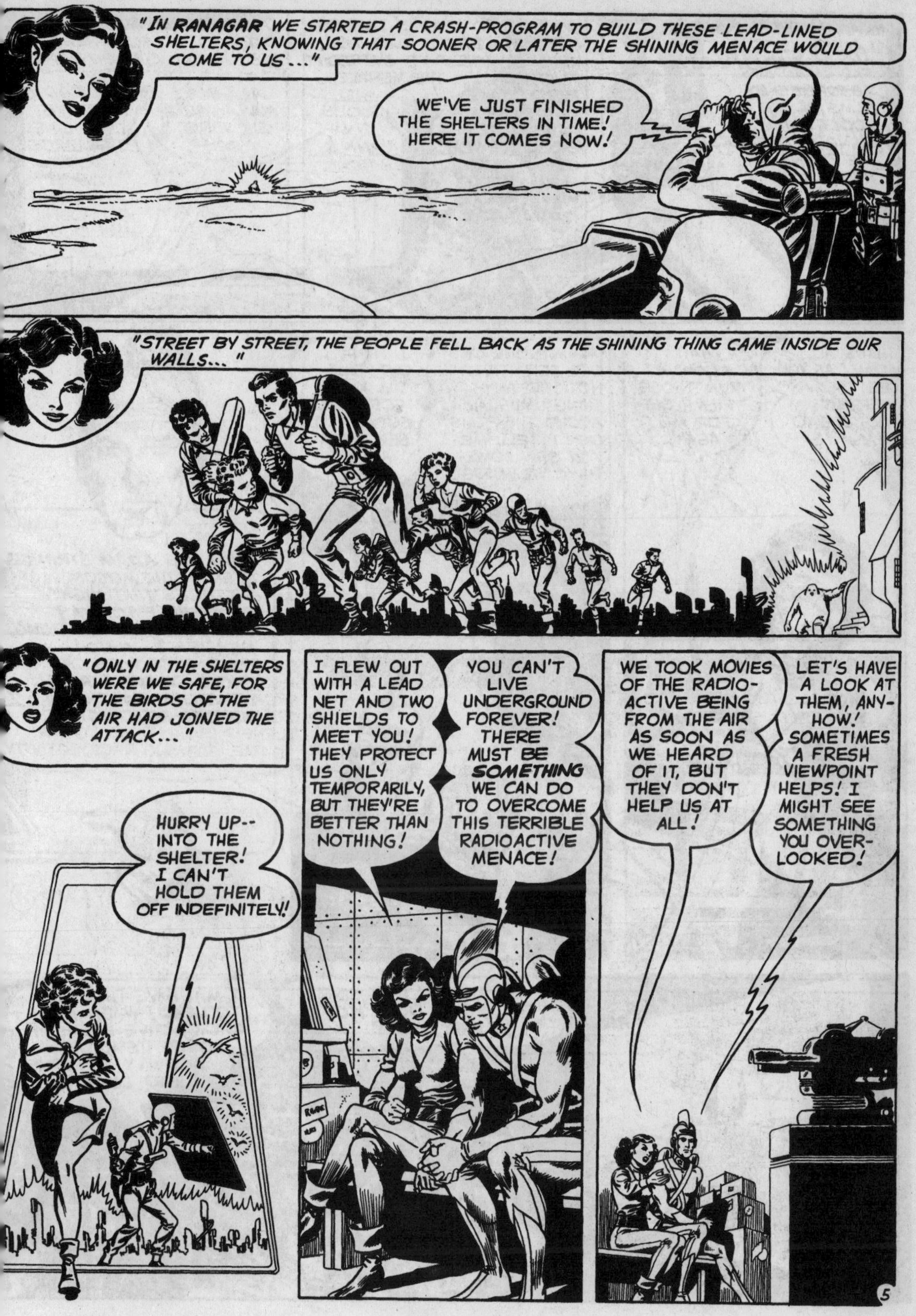
"IN RANAGAR WE STARTED A CRASH-PROGRAM TO BUILD THESE LEAD-LINED SHELTERS, KNOWING THAT SOONER OR LATER THE SHINING MENACE WOULD COME TO US..."
WE'VE JUST FINISHED THE SHELTERS IN TIME! HERE IT COMES NOW!
"STREET BY STREET, THE PEOPLE FELL BACK AS THE SHINING THING CAME INSIDE OUR WALLS..."
"ONLY IN THE SHELTERS WERE WE SAFE, FOR THE BIRDS OF THE AIR HAD JOINED THE ATTACK..."
HURRY UP-- INTO THE SHELTER! I CAN'T HOLD THEM OFF INDEFINITELY!
I FLEW OUT WITH A LEAD NET AND TWO SHIELDS TO MEET YOU! THEY PROTECT US ONLY TEMPORARILY, BUT THEY'RE BETTER THAN NOTHING!
YOU CAN'T LIVE UNDERGROUND FOREVER! THERE MUST BE SOMETHING WE CAN DO TO OVERCOME THIS TERRIBLE RADIOACTIVE MENACE!
WE TOOK MOVIES OF THE RADIO-ACTIVE BEING FROM THE AIR AS SOON AS WE HEARD OF IT, BUT THEY DON'T HELP US AT ALL!
LET'S HAVE A LOOK AT THEM, ANY-HOW! SOMETIMES A FRESH VIEWPOINT HELPS! I MIGHT SEE SOMETHING YOU OVER-LOOKED!
5

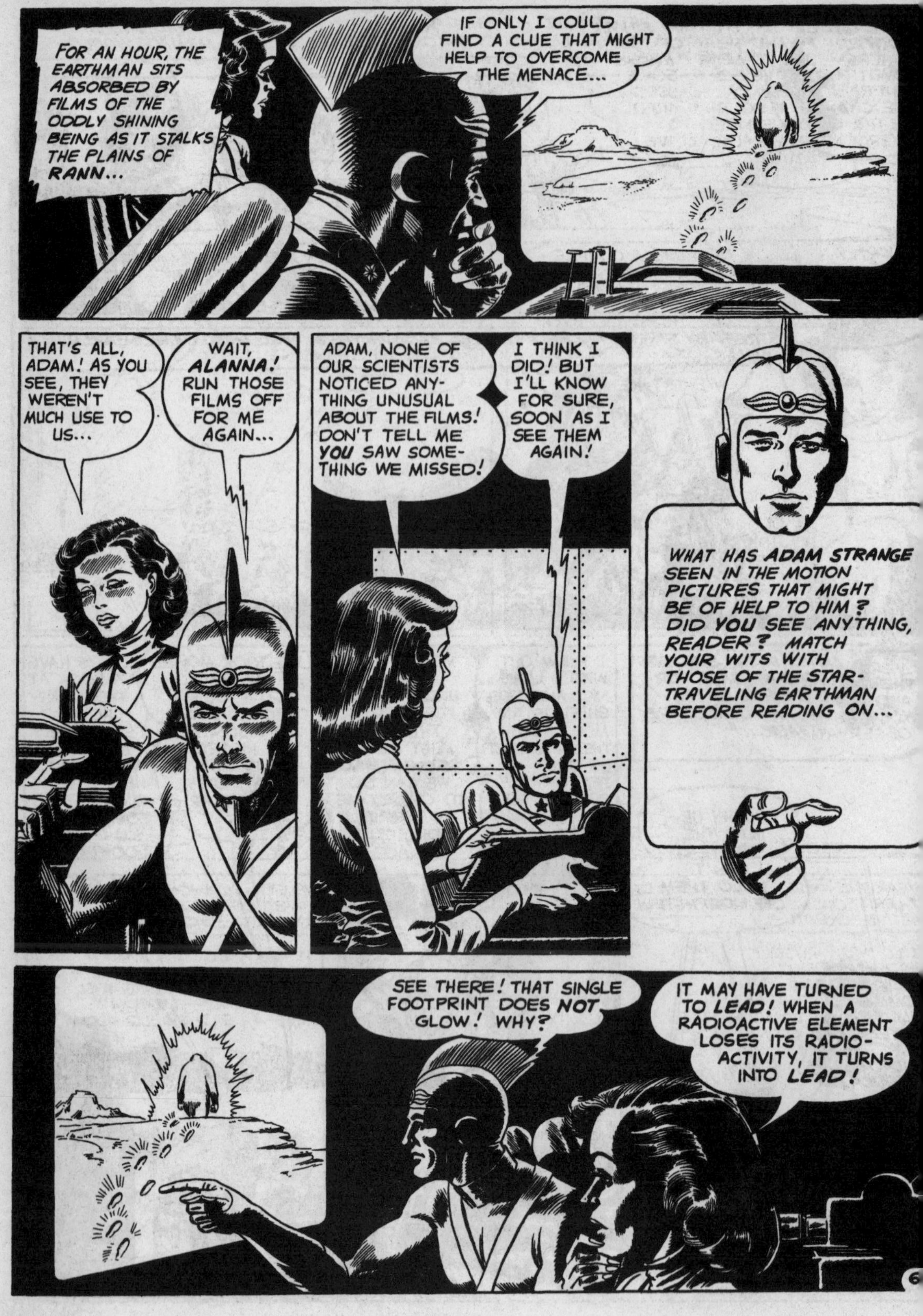
FOR AN HOUR, THE EARTHMAN SITS ABSORBED BY FILMS OF THE ODDLY SHINING BEING AS IT STALKS THE PLAINS OF RANN...
IF ONLY I COULD FIND A CLUE THAT MIGHT HELP TO OVERCOME THE MENACE...
THAT'S ALL, ADAM! AS YOU SEE, THEY WEREN'T MUCH USE TO US...
WAIT, ALANNA! RUN THOSE FILMS OFF FOR ME AGAIN...
ADAM, NONE OF OUR SCIENTISTS NOTICED ANYTHING UNUSUAL ABOUT THE FILMS! DON'T TELL ME YOU SAW SOMETHING WE MISSED!
I THINK I DID! BUT I'LL KNOW FOR SURE, SOON AS I SEE THEM AGAIN!
WHAT HAS ADAM STRANGE SEEN IN THE MOTION PICTURES THAT MIGHT BE OF HELP TO HIM? DID YOU SEE ANYTHING, READER? MATCH YOUR WITS WITH THOSE OF THE STAR-TRAVELING EARTHMAN BEFORE READING ON...
SEE THERE! THAT SINGLE FOOTPRINT DOES NOT GLOW! WHY?
IT MAY HAVE TURNED TO LEAD! WHEN A RADIOACTIVE ELEMENT LOSES ITS RADIO-ACTIVITY, IT TURNS INTO LEAD!
6

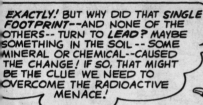

EXACTLY! BUT WHY DID THAT *SINGLE FOOTPRINT*--AND NONE OF THE OTHERS-- TURN TO *LEAD*? MAYBE SOMETHING IN THE SOIL -- SOME MINERAL OR CHEMICAL--CAUSED THE CHANGE! IF SO, THAT MIGHT BE THE CLUE WE NEED TO OVERCOME THE RADIOACTIVE MENACE!

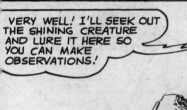

SHORTLY...

THE ONLY WAY WE'LL KNOW IS TO GO THERE!

WE HAVE A COUPLE OF FLIERS HIDDEN BEYOND *RANAGAR!* THE SCIENTISTS WILL JET THERE TO FETCH ONE WHILE YOU AND I GO ON TO THE SPOT WHERE THOSE FILMS WERE TAKEN!

AN HOUR LATER, ON THE GREAT PLAIN OF *KRANIMAR*...

TO DETERMINE WHAT MADE THIS FOOTPRINT CHANGE TO LEAD, WE MUST OBSERVE THE FOOTPRINT IN THE PROCESS OF CHANGING INTO LEAD!

YES, IT WOULD REQUIRE "ON THE SPOT" RESEARCH!

VERY WELL! I'LL SEEK OUT THE SHINING CREATURE AND LURE IT HERE SO YOU CAN MAKE OBSERVATIONS!

ADAM--BE CAREFUL!

NEAR THE ANCIENT RUINS OF DESERTED *TARRAZON* HE OVERTAKES THE RADIO-ACTIVE CREATURE...

I'LL SHOW MYSELF AND--THERE! IT'S SEEN ME! IT'S COMING FOR ME! ALL I HAVE TO DO IS KEEP OUT OF ITS WAY... AND ITS RADIOACTIVE TOUCH!

SUDDENLY FROM THE SKY--SUMMONED BY SOME QUEER MENTAL POWER OF THE RADIOACTIVE *CARLON ZAN*--TWO SWIFT BIRDS APPEAR...

I'M *TRAPPED!* IF I TURN BACK TO AVOID THE BIRDS-- THE RADIOACTIVE BEING WILL GET ME! AND--I DIDN'T BRING A LEAD SHIELD ALONG!

7

TIMING HIS FLIGHT TO THE EXACT INSTANT, ADAM DARTS BETWEEN TWO EON-OLD PILLARS...

CRASH!

I'LL USE THESE RUINS AS A SHIELD--AH! IT WORKED WITH THEM OUT OF THE WAY AND WITH NO OTHER BIRDS AROUND, I OUGHT TO BE SAFE ENOUGH!

SOON HE PASSES ABOVE THE SPOT WHERE THE NON-GLOWING FOOTPRINT WAS MADE...

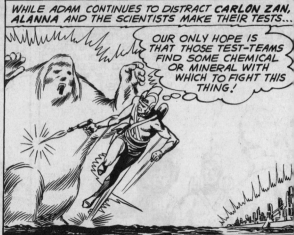

WHILE ADAM CONTINUES TO DISTRACT CARLON ZAN, ALANNA AND THE SCIENTISTS MAKE THEIR TESTS...

OUR ONLY HOPE IS THAT THOSE TEST-TEAMS FIND SOME CHEMICAL OR MINERAL WITH WHICH TO FIGHT THIS THING!

LOSING HIS PURSUER, ADAM JETS BACK TO ALANNA...

ADAM, WE FOUND IT! A RARE ELEMENT OF OUR SOIL WE CALL MALYBIUM! THE OTHER SCIENTISTS HAVE PUT SOME IN THIS "SPRAY" GUN!

MALYBIUM HASTENS THE DECOMPOSITION PROCESS OF THE RADIOACTIVE ELEMENT! ONCE THAT HAPPENS, THE ELEMENT TURNS TO LEAD!

LET'S TEST IT ON THAT BIRD!

IT HAS TO WORK, ADAM! IF IT DOESN'T--WE'RE DONE FOR!

HIGH IN THE AIR, THE EARTHMAN MEETS THE RADIO-ACTIVE BIRD WITH A CHARGE FROM THE MALYBIUM-GUN...

WILL IT WORK? WILL IT?

8

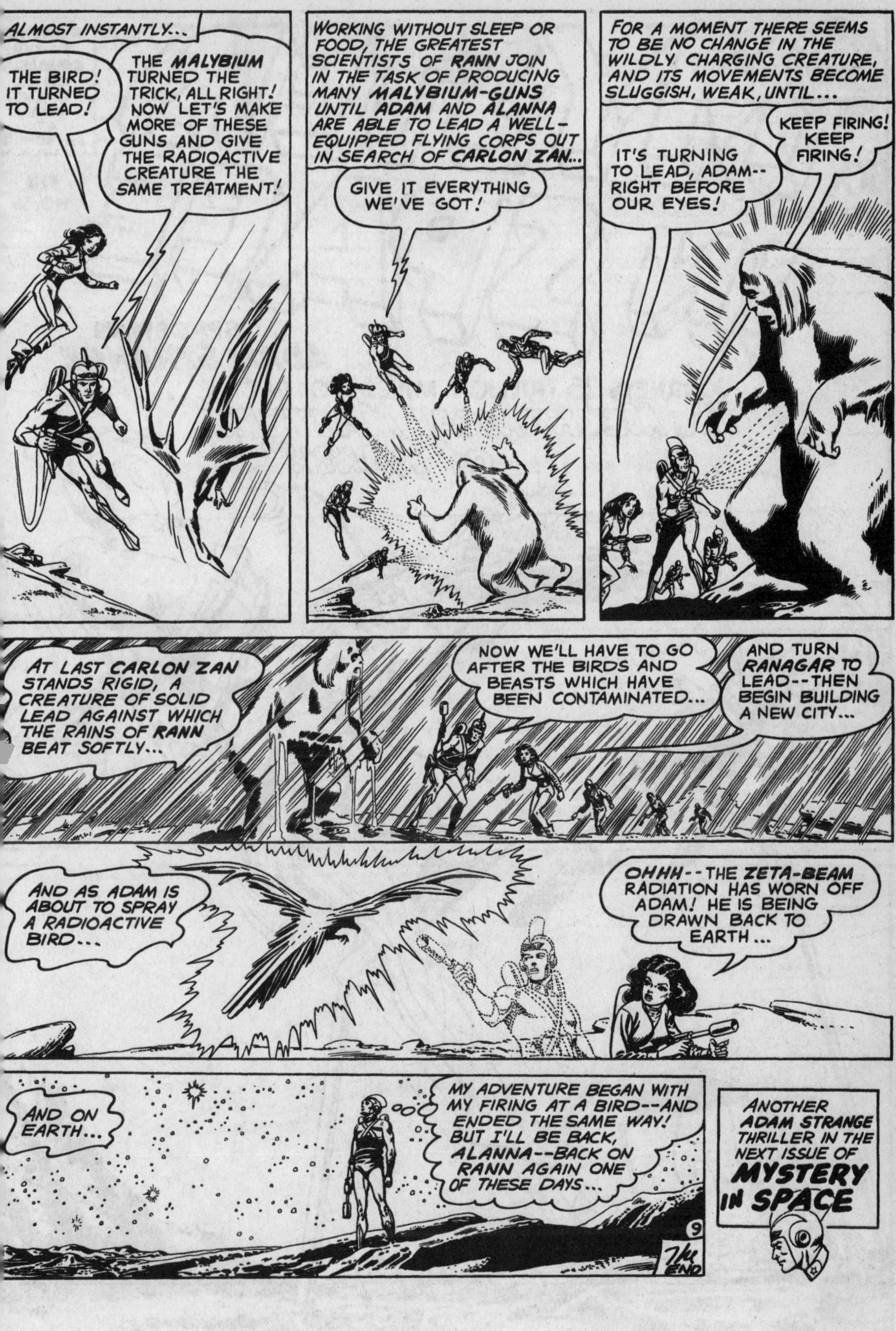
ALMOST INSTANTLY...
THE BIRD! IT TURNED TO LEAD!
THE MALYBIUM TURNED THE TRICK, ALL RIGHT! NOW LET'S MAKE MORE OF THESE GUNS AND GIVE THE RADIOACTIVE CREATURE THE SAME TREATMENT!
WORKING WITHOUT SLEEP OR FOOD, THE GREATEST SCIENTISTS OF RANN JOIN IN THE TASK OF PRODUCING MANY MALYBIUM-GUNS UNTIL ADAM AND ALANNA ARE ABLE TO LEAD A WELL-EQUIPPED FLYING CORPS OUT IN SEARCH OF CARLON ZAN...
GIVE IT EVERYTHING WE'VE GOT!
FOR A MOMENT THERE SEEMS TO BE NO CHANGE IN THE WILDLY CHARGING CREATURE, AND ITS MOVEMENTS BECOME SLUGGISH, WEAK, UNTIL...
IT'S TURNING TO LEAD, ADAM--RIGHT BEFORE OUR EYES!
KEEP FIRING! KEEP FIRING!
AT LAST CARLON ZAN STANDS RIGID, A CREATURE OF SOLID LEAD AGAINST WHICH THE RAINS OF RANN BEAT SOFTLY...
NOW WE'LL HAVE TO GO AFTER THE BIRDS AND BEASTS WHICH HAVE BEEN CONTAMINATED...
AND TURN RANAGAR TO LEAD--THEN BEGIN BUILDING A NEW CITY...
AND AS ADAM IS ABOUT TO SPRAY A RADIOACTIVE BIRD...
OHHH--THE ZETA-BEAM RADIATION HAS WORN OFF ADAM! HE IS BEING DRAWN BACK TO EARTH...
AND ON EARTH...
MY ADVENTURE BEGAN WITH MY FIRING AT A BIRD--AND ENDED THE SAME WAY! BUT I'LL BE BACK, ALANNA--BACK ON RANN AGAIN ONE OF THESE DAYS...
9
END
ANOTHER ADAM STRANGE THRILLER IN THE NEXT ISSUE OF MYSTERY IN SPACE

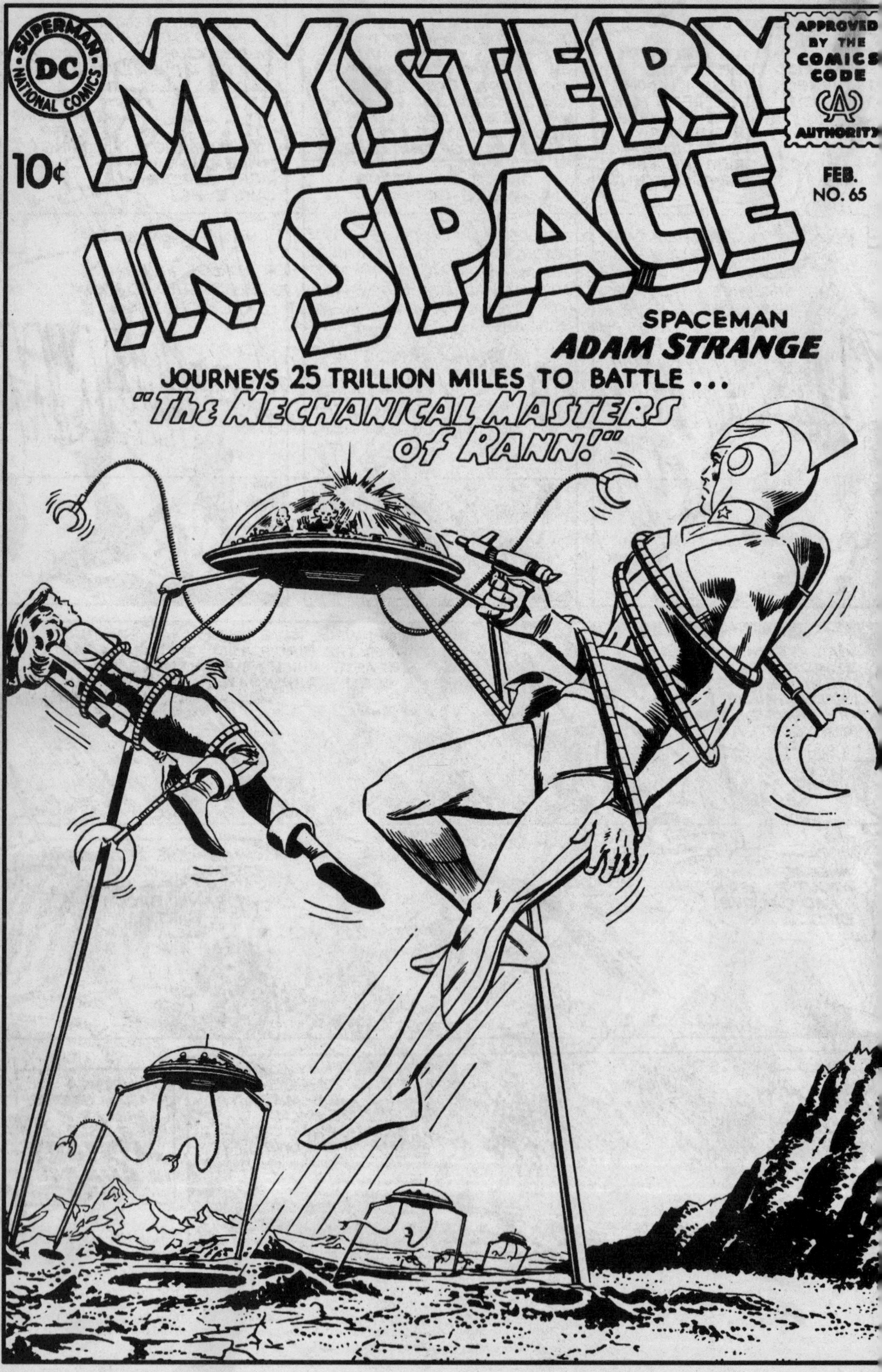
SUPERMAN DC NATIONAL COMICS
MYSTERY IN SPACE
APPROVED BY THE COMICS CODE AUTHORITY
10¢
FEB. NO. 65
SPACEMAN ADAM STRANGE
JOURNEYS 25 TRILLION MILES TO BATTLE...
"The MECHANICAL MASTERS of RANN!"

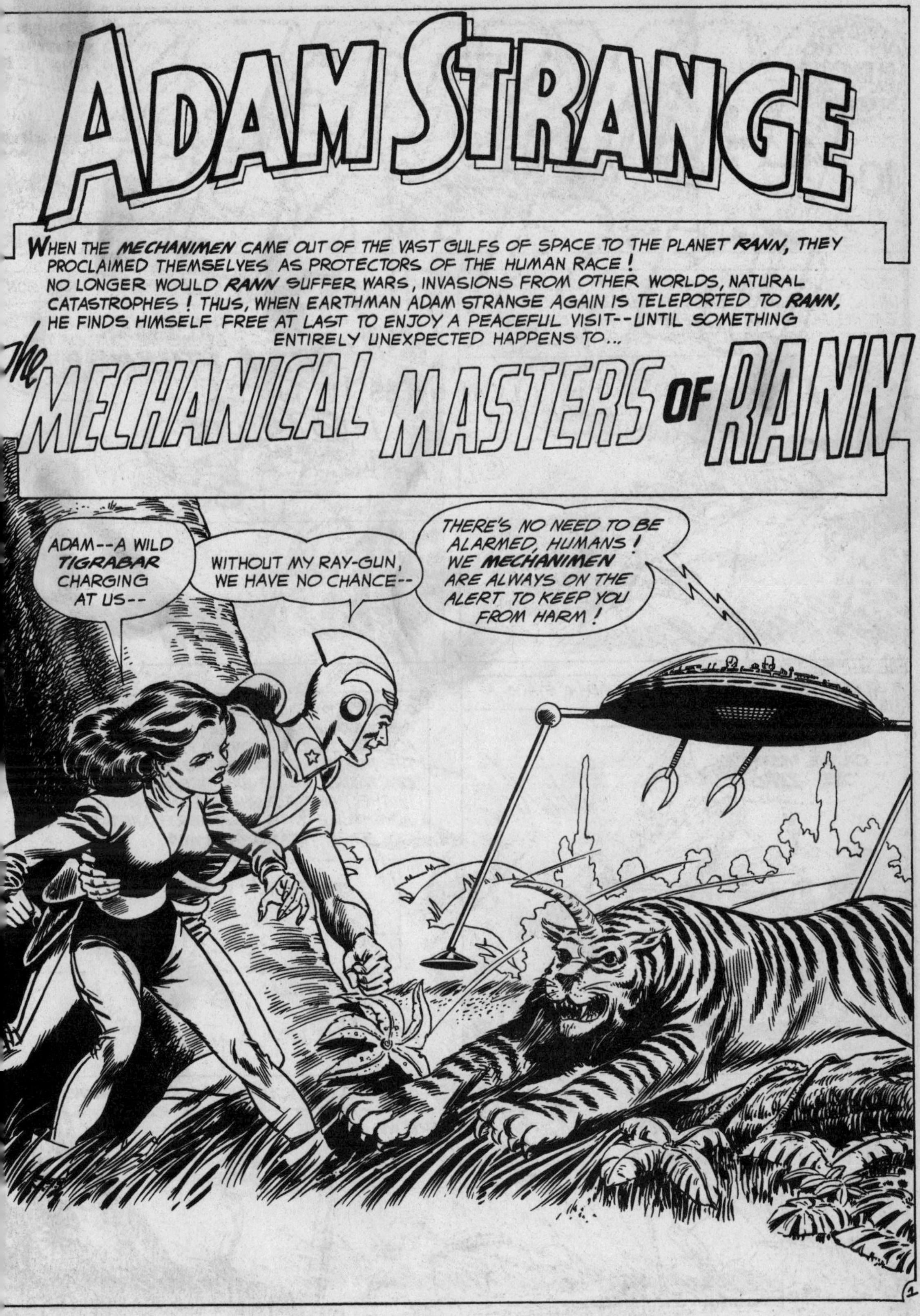
ADAM STRANGE
WHEN THE MECHANIMEN CAME OUT OF THE VAST GULFS OF SPACE TO THE PLANET RANN, THEY PROCLAIMED THEMSELVES AS PROTECTORS OF THE HUMAN RACE! NO LONGER WOULD RANN SUFFER WARS, INVASIONS FROM OTHER WORLDS, NATURAL CATASTROPHES! THUS, WHEN EARTHMAN ADAM STRANGE AGAIN IS TELEPORTED TO RANN, HE FINDS HIMSELF FREE AT LAST TO ENJOY A PEACEFUL VISIT--UNTIL SOMETHING ENTIRELY UNEXPECTED HAPPENS TO...
THE MECHANICAL MASTERS OF RANN
ADAM--A WILD TIGRABAR CHARGING AT US--
WITHOUT MY RAY-GUN, WE HAVE NO CHANCE--
THERE'S NO NEED TO BE ALARMED, HUMANS! WE MECHANIMEN ARE ALWAYS ON THE ALERT TO KEEP YOU FROM HARM!
1

In a little clearing of a tropical MADAGASCAR jungle, archeologist ADAM STRANGE awaits the coming of the ZETA-BEAM FROM RANN...

TIME TO BEGIN MY COUNTDOWN-- TEN, NINE ...

He is completely unaware of any danger until the tendril of the queer man-- eating plant which infests this corner of the jungle suddenly grip him ...

SEVEN, SIX-- WHAT IN THUNDER?

Frantically, his hand claws for his ray-gun!

THIS MONSTROUS PLANT'S SWUNG ME OUT OF THE ZETA-BEAM'S PATH-- FOUR... THREE...

Freed from the clutching plant, ADAM stabs at the controls of his jet-flyer...

NOW TO GET BACK ON THE "BEAM"-- ONE--ZERO!

CAUGHT by the teleportational pull of the ZETA-BEAM, the earthman is whirled across 25 trillion miles of space to the planet RANN of the star-sun ALPHA CENTAURI, as he has been so many times in the past, to share danger and adventure with his interplanetary sweetheart, ALANNA ...

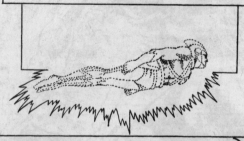

As his feet come to rest on the surface of the distant planet...

OH, ADAM--IT'S GOOD TO SEE YOU, AND DO I HAVE NEWS FOR YOU...!

OH--OH! HERE WE GO AGAIN! WHAT TROUBLE IS RANN IN NOW?

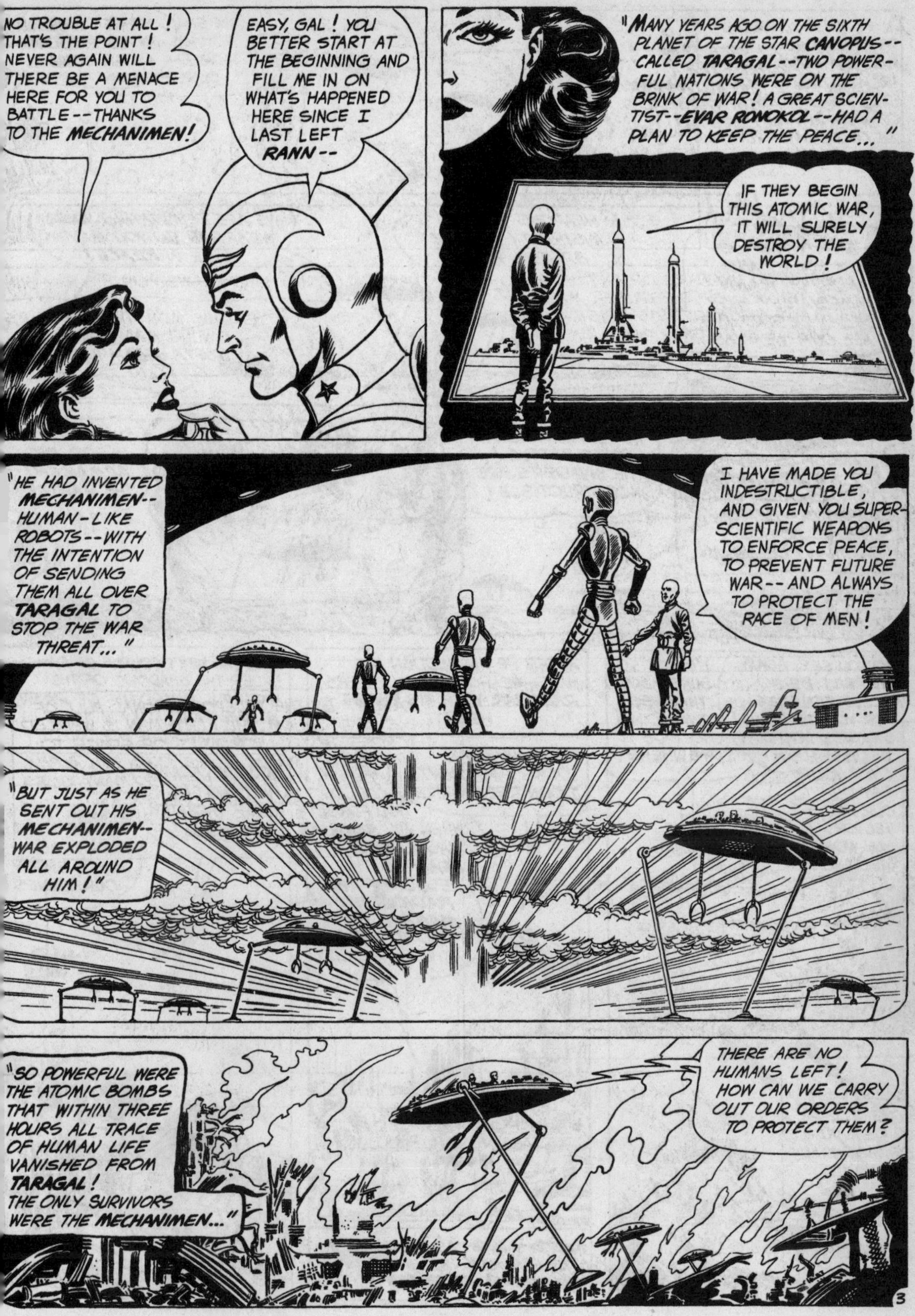
NO TROUBLE AT ALL! THAT'S THE POINT! NEVER AGAIN WILL THERE BE A MENACE HERE FOR YOU TO BATTLE--THANKS TO THE MECHANIMEN!
EASY, GAL! YOU BETTER START AT THE BEGINNING AND FILL ME IN ON WHAT'S HAPPENED HERE SINCE I LAST LEFT RANN--
"MANY YEARS AGO ON THE SIXTH PLANET OF THE STAR CANOPUS--CALLED TARAGAL--TWO POWERFUL NATIONS WERE ON THE BRINK OF WAR! A GREAT SCIENTIST--EVAR RONOKOL--HAD A PLAN TO KEEP THE PEACE..."
IF THEY BEGIN THIS ATOMIC WAR, IT WILL SURELY DESTROY THE WORLD!
"HE HAD INVENTED MECHANIMEN--HUMAN-LIKE ROBOTS--WITH THE INTENTION OF SENDING THEM ALL OVER TARAGAL TO STOP THE WAR THREAT..."
I HAVE MADE YOU INDESTRUCTIBLE, AND GIVEN YOU SUPER-SCIENTIFIC WEAPONS TO ENFORCE PEACE, TO PREVENT FUTURE WAR--AND ALWAYS TO PROTECT THE RACE OF MEN!
"BUT JUST AS HE SENT OUT HIS MECHANIMEN--WAR EXPLODED ALL AROUND HIM!"
"SO POWERFUL WERE THE ATOMIC BOMBS THAT WITHIN THREE HOURS ALL TRACE OF HUMAN LIFE VANISHED FROM TARAGAL! THE ONLY SURVIVORS WERE THE MECHANIMEN..."
THERE ARE NO HUMANS LEFT! HOW CAN WE CARRY OUT OUR ORDERS TO PROTECT THEM?
3

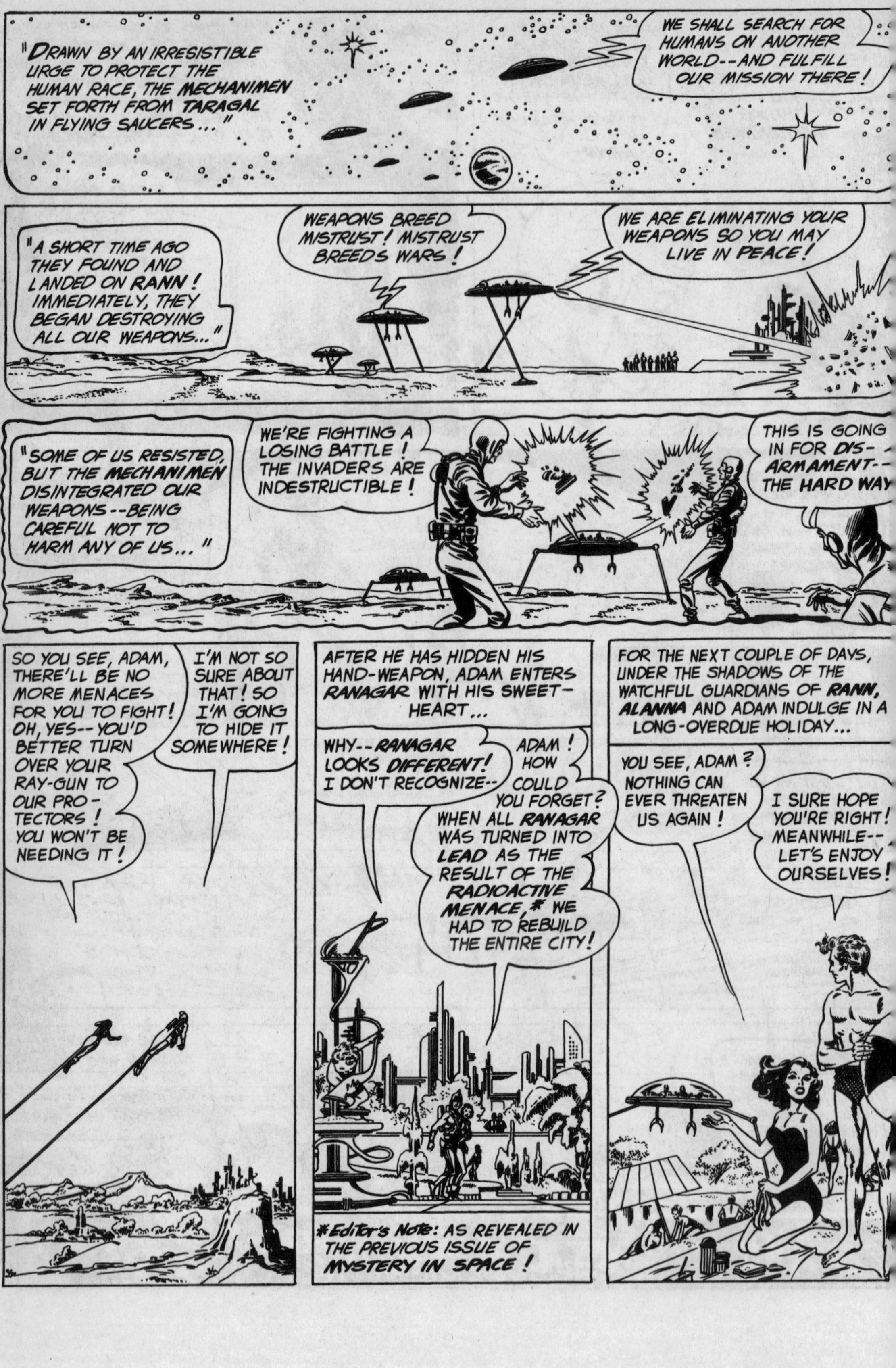
"DRAWN BY AN IRRESISTIBLE URGE TO PROTECT THE HUMAN RACE, THE MECHANIMEN SET FORTH FROM TARAGAL IN FLYING SAUCERS..."
WE SHALL SEARCH FOR HUMANS ON ANOTHER WORLD--AND FULFILL OUR MISSION THERE!
"A SHORT TIME AGO THEY FOUND AND LANDED ON RANN! IMMEDIATELY, THEY BEGAN DESTROYING ALL OUR WEAPONS..."
WEAPONS BREED MISTRUST! MISTRUST BREEDS WARS!
WE ARE ELIMINATING YOUR WEAPONS SO YOU MAY LIVE IN PEACE!
"SOME OF US RESISTED, BUT THE MECHANIMEN DISINTEGRATED OUR WEAPONS--BEING CAREFUL NOT TO HARM ANY OF US..."
WE'RE FIGHTING A LOSING BATTLE! THE INVADERS ARE INDESTRUCTIBLE!
THIS IS GOING IN FOR DIS-ARMAMENT--THE HARD WAY
SO YOU SEE, ADAM, THERE'LL BE NO MORE MENACES FOR YOU TO FIGHT! OH, YES--YOU'D BETTER TURN OVER YOUR RAY-GUN TO OUR PRO-TECTORS! YOU WON'T BE NEEDING IT!
I'M NOT SO SURE ABOUT THAT! SO I'M GOING TO HIDE IT SOMEWHERE!
AFTER HE HAS HIDDEN HIS HAND-WEAPON, ADAM ENTERS RANAGAR WITH HIS SWEET-HEART...
WHY--RANAGAR LOOKS DIFFERENT! I DON'T RECOGNIZE--
ADAM! HOW COULD YOU FORGET? WHEN ALL RANAGAR WAS TURNED INTO LEAD AS THE RESULT OF THE RADIOACTIVE MENACE,* WE HAD TO REBUILD THE ENTIRE CITY!
*Editor's Note: AS REVEALED IN THE PREVIOUS ISSUE OF MYSTERY IN SPACE!
FOR THE NEXT COUPLE OF DAYS, UNDER THE SHADOWS OF THE WATCHFUL GUARDIANS OF RANN, ALANNA AND ADAM INDULGE IN A LONG-OVERDUE HOLIDAY...
YOU SEE, ADAM? NOTHING CAN EVER THREATEN US AGAIN!
I SURE HOPE YOU'RE RIGHT! MEANWHILE--LET'S ENJOY OURSELVES!

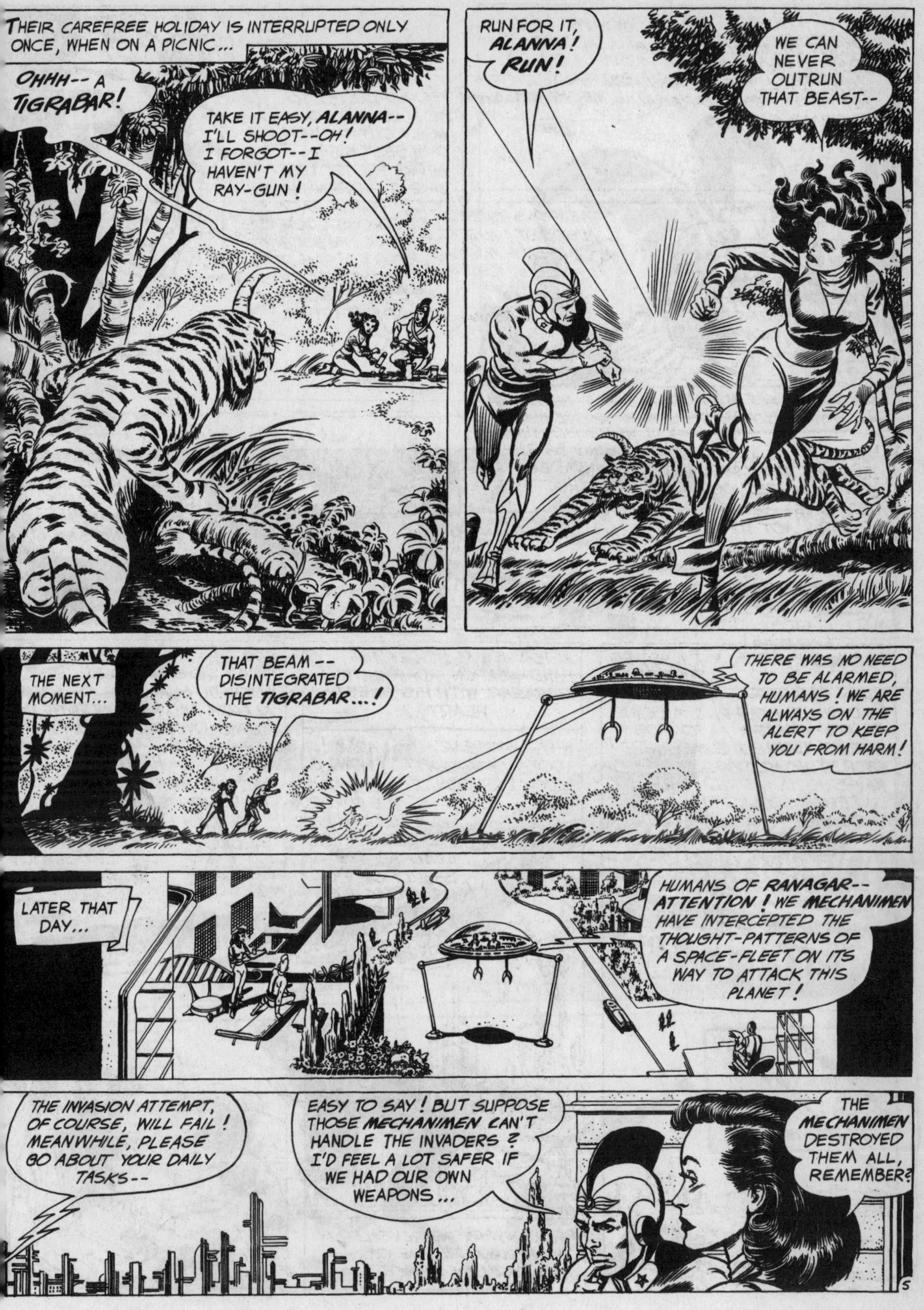
THEIR CAREFREE HOLIDAY IS INTERRUPTED ONLY ONCE, WHEN ON A PICNIC...
OHHH-- A TIGRABAR!
TAKE IT EASY, ALANNA-- I'LL SHOOT--OH! I FORGOT--I HAVEN'T MY RAY-GUN!
RUN FOR IT, ALANNA! RUN!
WE CAN NEVER OUTRUN THAT BEAST--
THE NEXT MOMENT...
THAT BEAM -- DISINTEGRATED THE TIGRABAR...!
THERE WAS NO NEED TO BE ALARMED, HUMANS! WE ARE ALWAYS ON THE ALERT TO KEEP YOU FROM HARM!
LATER THAT DAY...
HUMANS OF RANAGAR-- ATTENTION! WE MECHANIMEN HAVE INTERCEPTED THE THOUGHT-PATTERNS OF A SPACE-FLEET ON ITS WAY TO ATTACK THIS PLANET!
THE INVASION ATTEMPT, OF COURSE, WILL FAIL! MEANWHILE, PLEASE GO ABOUT YOUR DAILY TASKS--
EASY TO SAY! BUT SUPPOSE THOSE MECHANIMEN CAN'T HANDLE THE INVADERS? I'D FEEL A LOT SAFER IF WE HAD OUR OWN WEAPONS...
THE MECHANIMEN DESTROYED THEM ALL, REMEMBER?
5

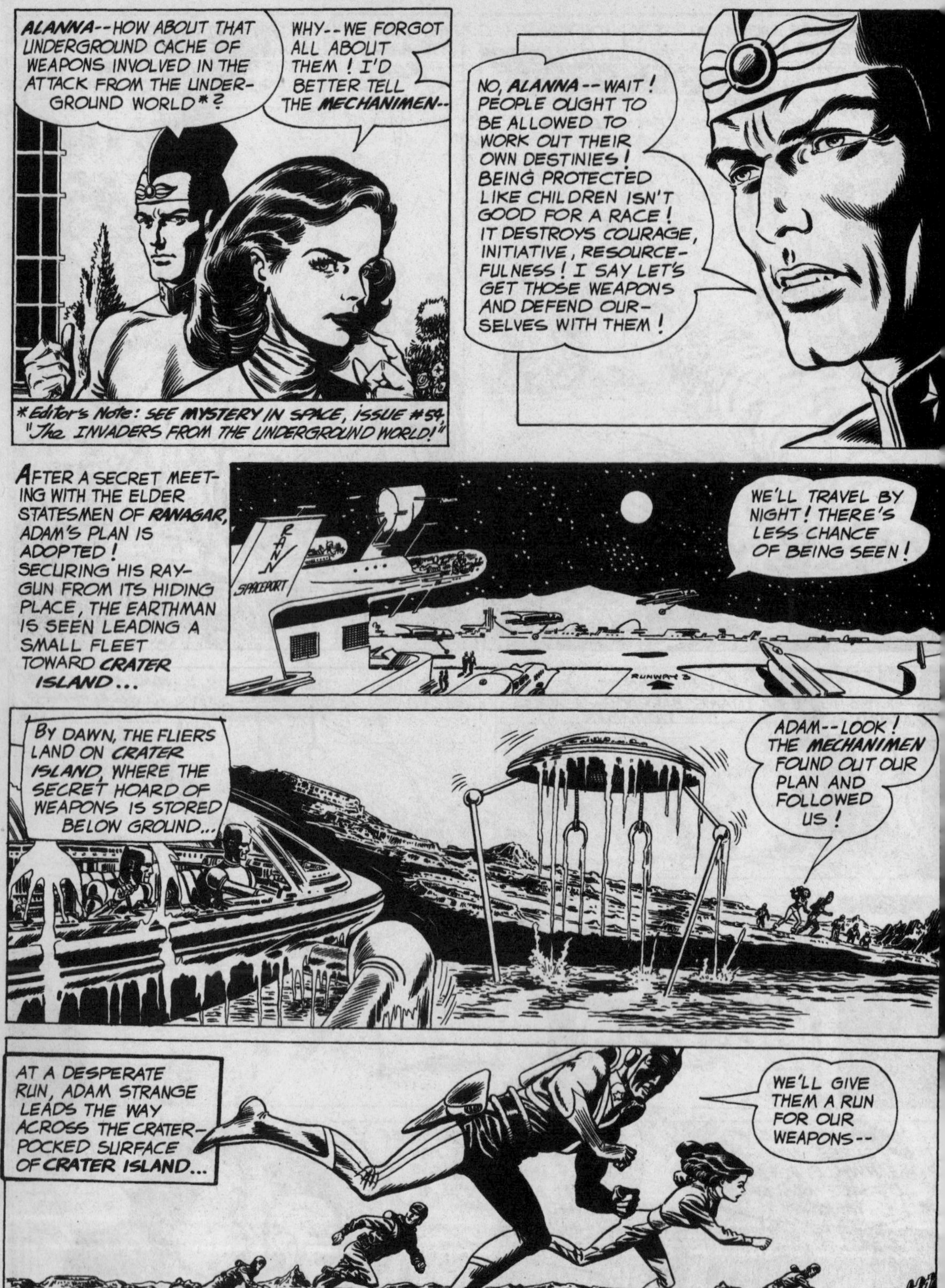
ALANNA--HOW ABOUT THAT UNDERGROUND CACHE OF WEAPONS INVOLVED IN THE ATTACK FROM THE UNDER-GROUND WORLD*?
WHY--WE FORGOT ALL ABOUT THEM! I'D BETTER TELL THE MECHANIMEN--
*Editor's Note: SEE MYSTERY IN SPACE, ISSUE #54, "The INVADERS FROM THE UNDERGROUND WORLD!"
NO, ALANNA--WAIT! PEOPLE OUGHT TO BE ALLOWED TO WORK OUT THEIR OWN DESTINIES! BEING PROTECTED LIKE CHILDREN ISN'T GOOD FOR A RACE! IT DESTROYS COURAGE, INITIATIVE, RESOURCE-FULNESS! I SAY LET'S GET THOSE WEAPONS AND DEFEND OUR-SELVES WITH THEM!
AFTER A SECRET MEET-ING WITH THE ELDER STATESMEN OF RANAGAR, ADAM'S PLAN IS ADOPTED! SECURING HIS RAY-GUN FROM ITS HIDING PLACE, THE EARTHMAN IS SEEN LEADING A SMALL FLEET TOWARD CRATER ISLAND...
RANN
SPACEPORT
RUNWAY 3
WE'LL TRAVEL BY NIGHT! THERE'S LESS CHANCE OF BEING SEEN!
BY DAWN, THE FLIERS LAND ON CRATER ISLAND, WHERE THE SECRET HOARD OF WEAPONS IS STORED BELOW GROUND...
ADAM--LOOK! THE MECHANIMEN FOUND OUT OUR PLAN AND FOLLOWED US!
AT A DESPERATE RUN, ADAM STRANGE LEADS THE WAY ACROSS THE CRATER-POCKED SURFACE OF CRATER ISLAND...
WE'LL GIVE THEM A RUN FOR OUR WEAPONS--
6

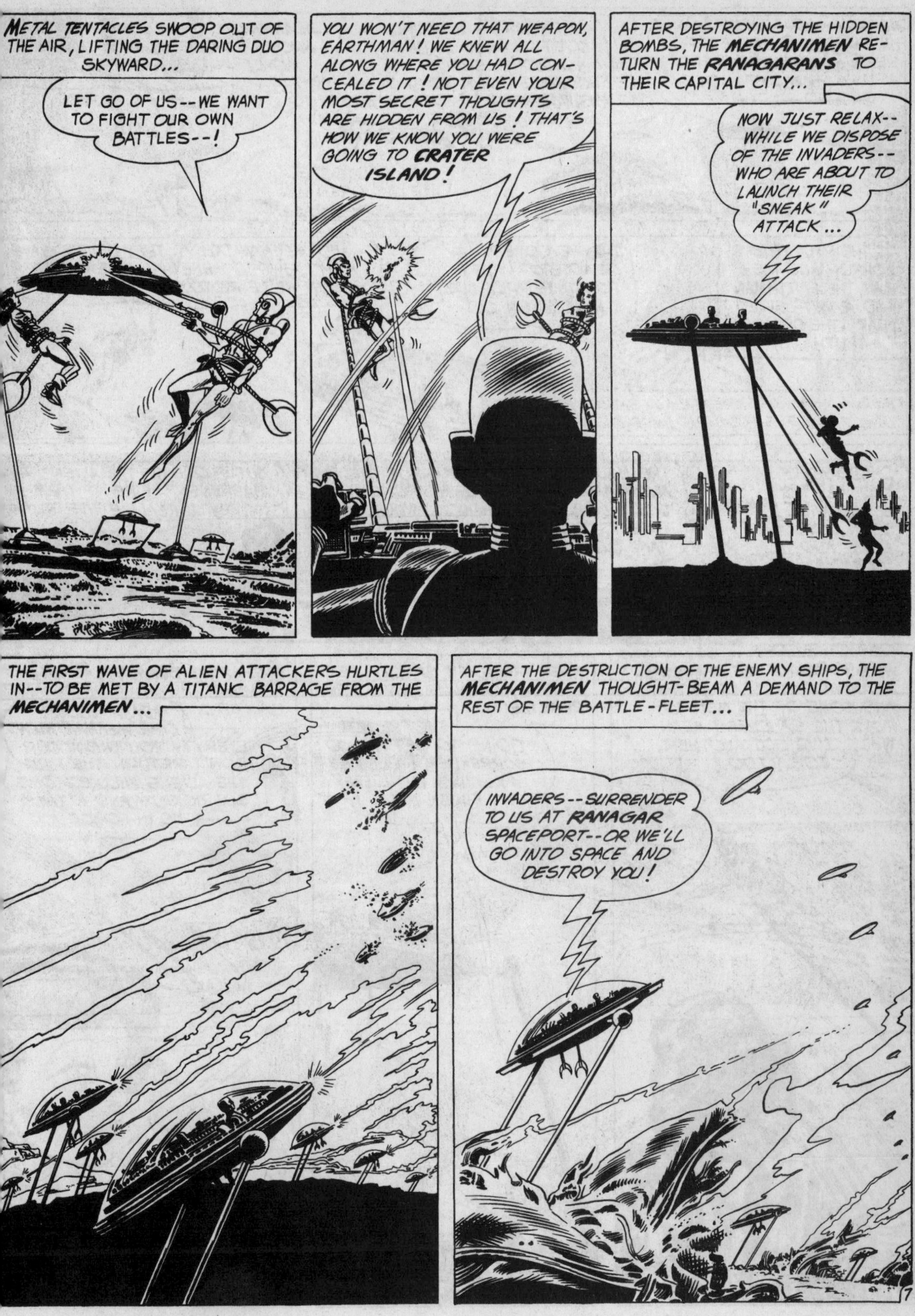
METAL TENTACLES SWOOP OUT OF THE AIR, LIFTING THE DARING DUO SKYWARD...
LET GO OF US--WE WANT TO FIGHT OUR OWN BATTLES--!
YOU WON'T NEED THAT WEAPON, EARTHMAN! WE KNEW ALL ALONG WHERE YOU HAD CONCEALED IT! NOT EVEN YOUR MOST SECRET THOUGHTS ARE HIDDEN FROM US! THAT'S HOW WE KNOW YOU WERE GOING TO CRATER ISLAND!
AFTER DESTROYING THE HIDDEN BOMBS, THE MECHANIMEN RETURN THE RANAGARANS TO THEIR CAPITAL CITY...
NOW JUST RELAX--WHILE WE DISPOSE OF THE INVADERS--WHO ARE ABOUT TO LAUNCH THEIR "SNEAK" ATTACK...
THE FIRST WAVE OF ALIEN ATTACKERS HURTLES IN--TO BE MET BY A TITANIC BARRAGE FROM THE MECHANIMEN...
AFTER THE DESTRUCTION OF THE ENEMY SHIPS, THE MECHANIMEN THOUGHT-BEAM A DEMAND TO THE REST OF THE BATTLE-FLEET...
INVADERS--SURRENDER TO US AT RANAGAR SPACEPORT--OR WE'LL GO INTO SPACE AND DESTROY YOU!
7

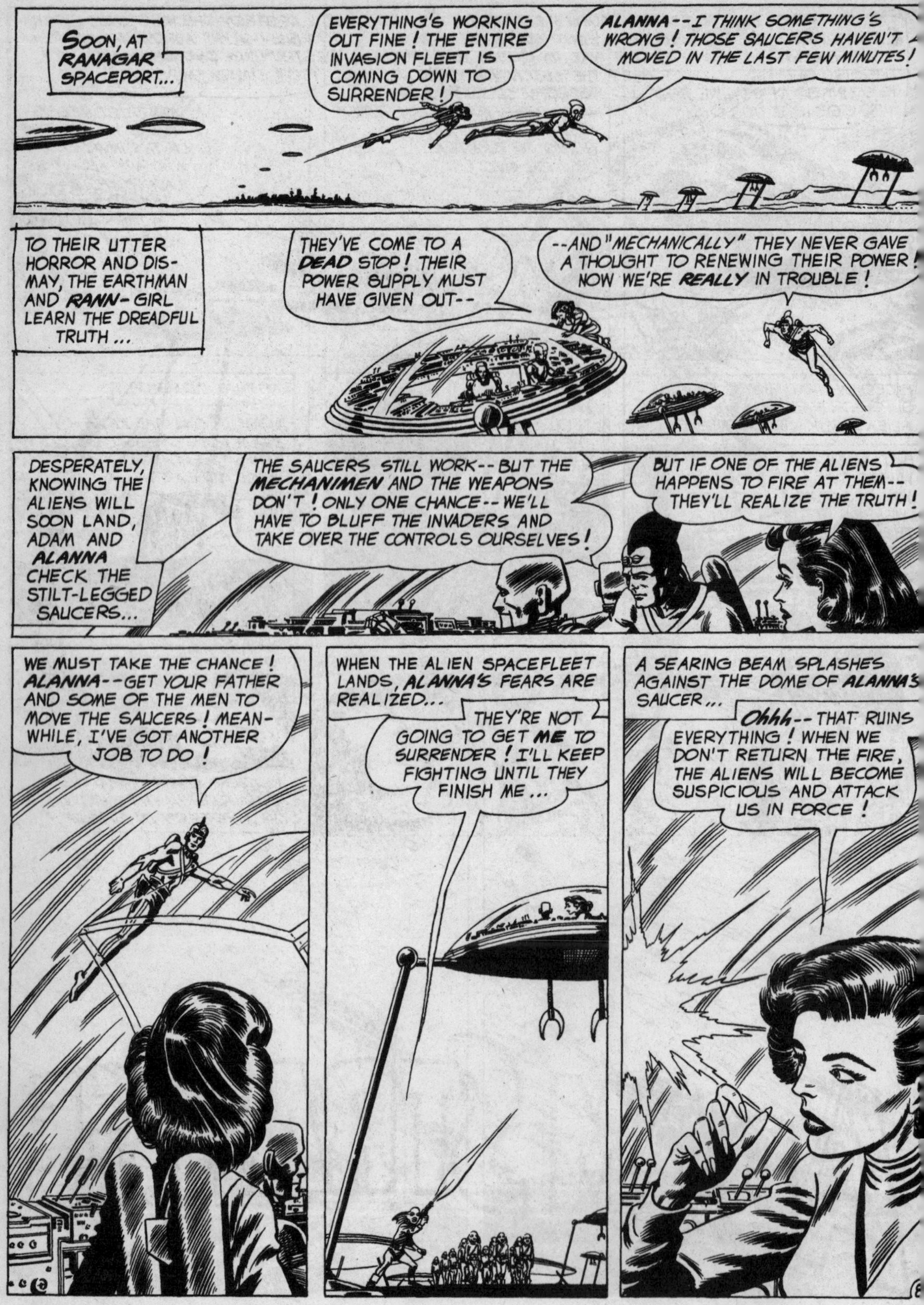
SOON, AT RANAGAR SPACEPORT...
EVERYTHING'S WORKING OUT FINE! THE ENTIRE INVASION FLEET IS COMING DOWN TO SURRENDER!
ALANNA--I THINK SOMETHING'S WRONG! THOSE SAUCERS HAVEN'T MOVED IN THE LAST FEW MINUTES!
TO THEIR UTTER HORROR AND DISMAY, THE EARTHMAN AND RANN-GIRL LEARN THE DREADFUL TRUTH...
THEY'VE COME TO A DEAD STOP! THEIR POWER SUPPLY MUST HAVE GIVEN OUT--
--AND "MECHANICALLY" THEY NEVER GAVE A THOUGHT TO RENEWING THEIR POWER! NOW WE'RE REALLY IN TROUBLE!
DESPERATELY, KNOWING THE ALIENS WILL SOON LAND, ADAM AND ALANNA CHECK THE STILT-LEGGED SAUCERS...
THE SAUCERS STILL WORK--BUT THE MECHANIMEN AND THE WEAPONS DON'T! ONLY ONE CHANCE--WE'LL HAVE TO BLUFF THE INVADERS AND TAKE OVER THE CONTROLS OURSELVES!
BUT IF ONE OF THE ALIENS HAPPENS TO FIRE AT THEM--THEY'LL REALIZE THE TRUTH!
WE MUST TAKE THE CHANCE! ALANNA--GET YOUR FATHER AND SOME OF THE MEN TO MOVE THE SAUCERS! MEANWHILE, I'VE GOT ANOTHER JOB TO DO!
WHEN THE ALIEN SPACEFLEET LANDS, ALANNA'S FEARS ARE REALIZED...
THEY'RE NOT GOING TO GET ME TO SURRENDER! I'LL KEEP FIGHTING UNTIL THEY FINISH ME...
A SEARING BEAM SPLASHES AGAINST THE DOME OF ALANNA'S SAUCER...
Ohhh--THAT RUINS EVERYTHING! WHEN WE DON'T RETURN THE FIRE, THE ALIENS WILL BECOME SUSPICIOUS AND ATTACK US IN FORCE!

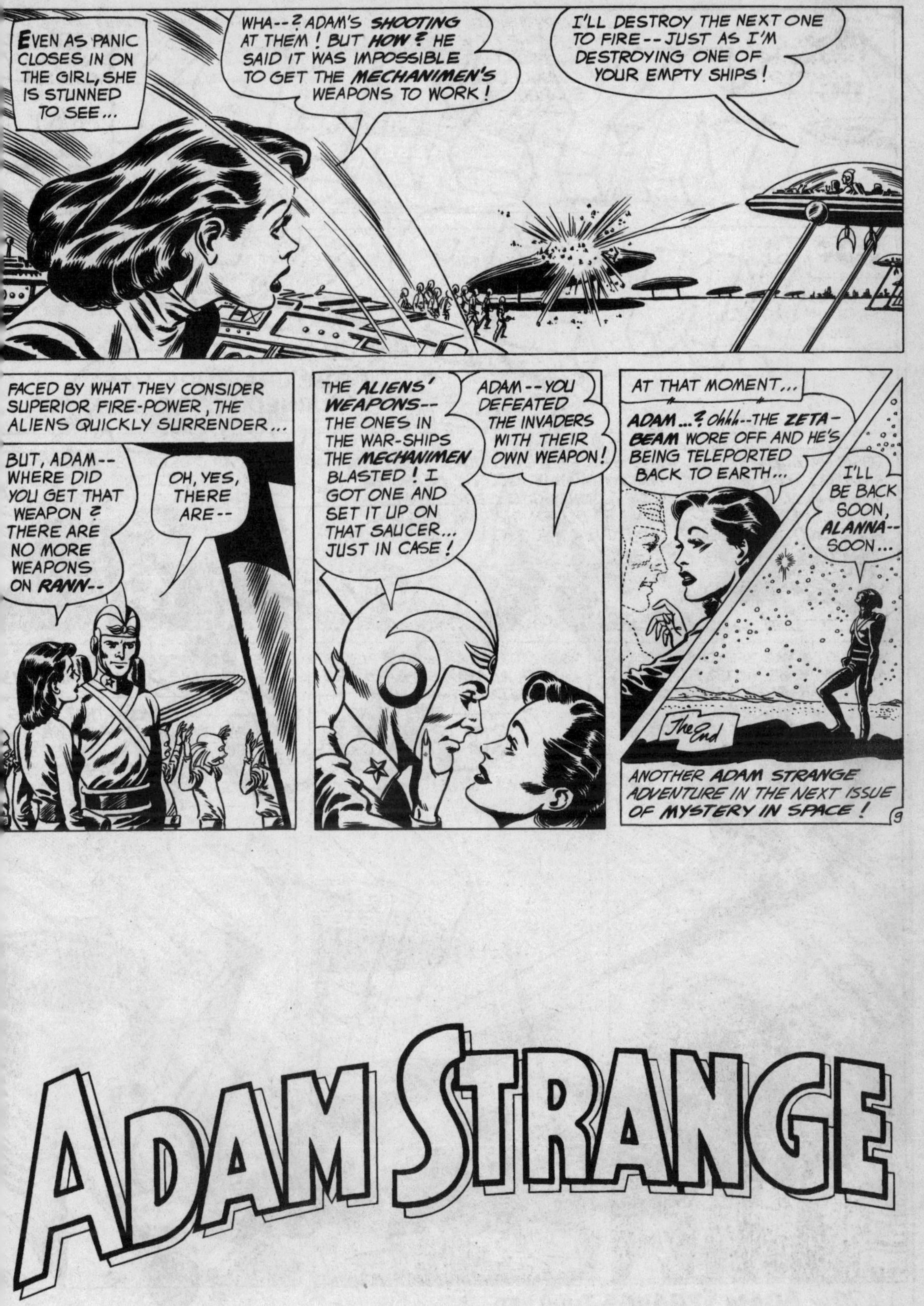
EVEN AS PANIC CLOSES IN ON THE GIRL, SHE IS STUNNED TO SEE...
WHA--? ADAM'S SHOOTING AT THEM! BUT HOW? HE SAID IT WAS IMPOSSIBLE TO GET THE MECHANIMEN'S WEAPONS TO WORK!
I'LL DESTROY THE NEXT ONE TO FIRE--JUST AS I'M DESTROYING ONE OF YOUR EMPTY SHIPS!
FACED BY WHAT THEY CONSIDER SUPERIOR FIRE-POWER, THE ALIENS QUICKLY SURRENDER...
BUT, ADAM--WHERE DID YOU GET THAT WEAPON? THERE ARE NO MORE WEAPONS ON RANN--
OH, YES, THERE ARE--
THE ALIENS' WEAPONS--THE ONES IN THE WAR-SHIPS THE MECHANIMEN BLASTED! I GOT ONE AND SET IT UP ON THAT SAUCER... JUST IN CASE!
ADAM--YOU DEFEATED THE INVADERS WITH THEIR OWN WEAPON!
AT THAT MOMENT...
ADAM...? Ohhh--THE ZETA-BEAM WORE OFF AND HE'S BEING TELEPORTED BACK TO EARTH...
I'LL BE BACK SOON, ALANNA--SOON...
The End
ANOTHER ADAM STRANGE ADVENTURE IN THE NEXT ISSUE OF MYSTERY IN SPACE!
9

ADAM STRANGE

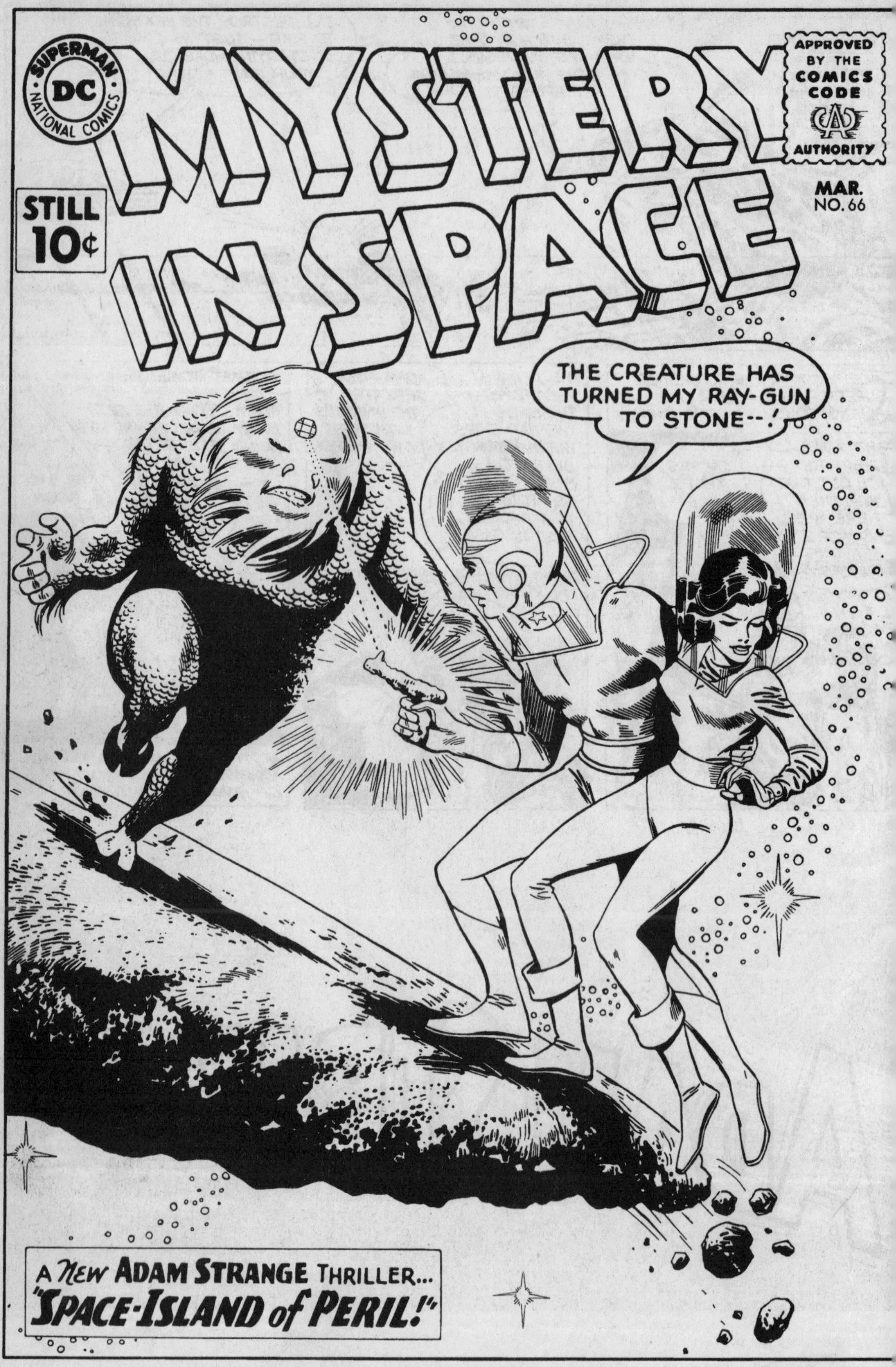
SUPERMAN DC NATIONAL COMICS
MYSTERY IN SPACE
APPROVED BY THE COMICS CODE AUTHORITY
STILL 10¢
MAR. NO. 66
THE CREATURE HAS TURNED MY RAY-GUN TO STONE--!
A NEW ADAM STRANGE THRILLER... "SPACE-ISLAND of PERIL!"

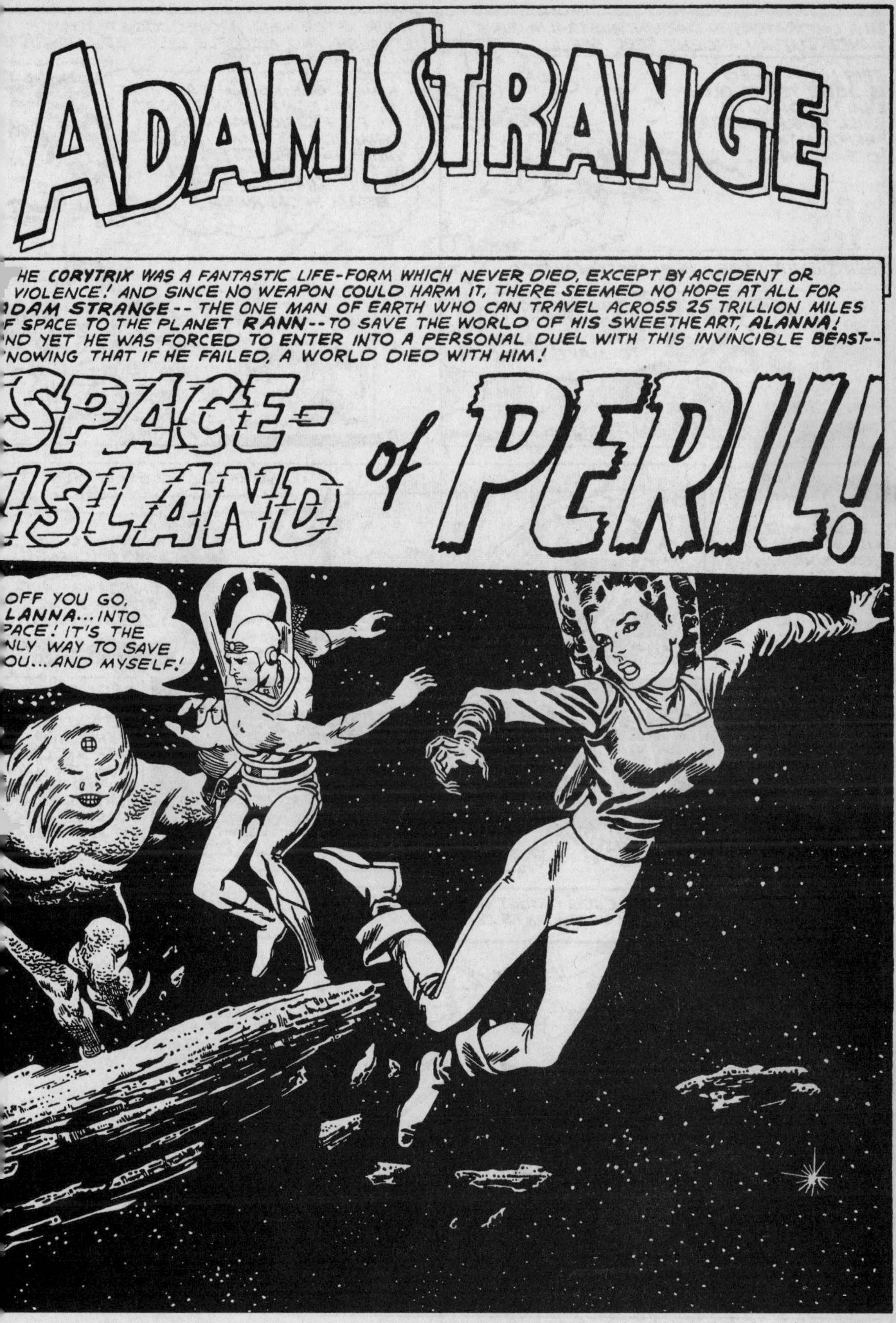
ADAM STRANGE
HE CORYTRIX WAS A FANTASTIC LIFE-FORM WHICH NEVER DIED, EXCEPT BY ACCIDENT OR VIOLENCE! AND SINCE NO WEAPON COULD HARM IT, THERE SEEMED NO HOPE AT ALL FOR DAM STRANGE -- THE ONE MAN OF EARTH WHO CAN TRAVEL ACROSS 25 TRILLION MILES F SPACE TO THE PLANET RANN -- TO SAVE THE WORLD OF HIS SWEETHEART, ALANNA! ND YET HE WAS FORCED TO ENTER INTO A PERSONAL DUEL WITH THIS INVINCIBLE BEAST-- NOWING THAT IF HE FAILED, A WORLD DIED WITH HIM!
SPACE-ISLAND of PERIL!
OFF YOU GO, LANNA... INTO PACE! IT'S THE NLY WAY TO SAVE OU... AND MYSELF!

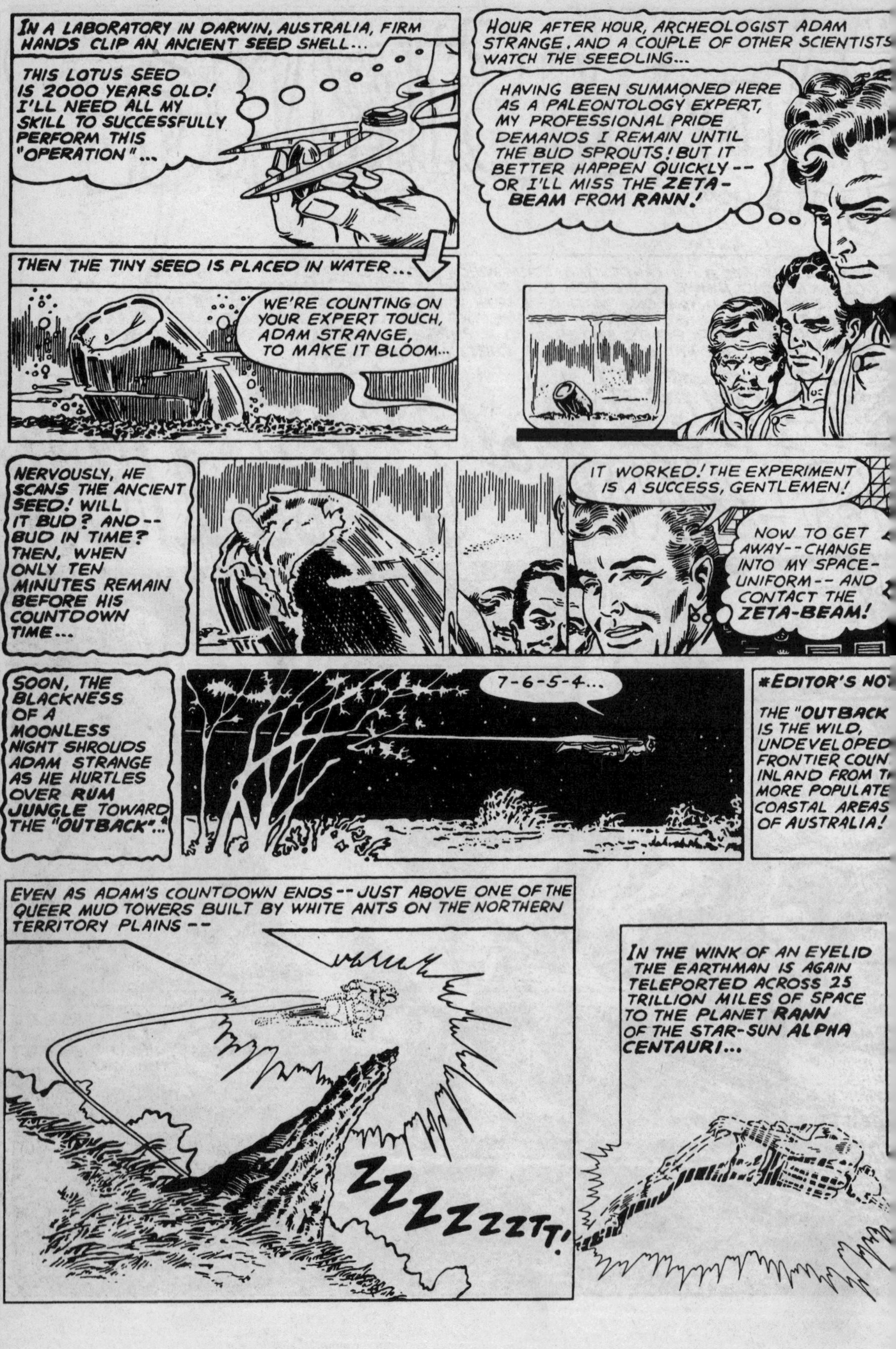
IN A LABORATORY IN DARWIN, AUSTRALIA, FIRM HANDS CLIP AN ANCIENT SEED SHELL...
THIS LOTUS SEED IS 2000 YEARS OLD! I'LL NEED ALL MY SKILL TO SUCCESSFULLY PERFORM THIS "OPERATION"...
HOUR AFTER HOUR, ARCHEOLOGIST ADAM STRANGE, AND A COUPLE OF OTHER SCIENTISTS WATCH THE SEEDLING...
HAVING BEEN SUMMONED HERE AS A PALEONTOLOGY EXPERT, MY PROFESSIONAL PRIDE DEMANDS I REMAIN UNTIL THE BUD SPROUTS! BUT IT BETTER HAPPEN QUICKLY -- OR I'LL MISS THE ZETA-BEAM FROM RANN!
THEN THE TINY SEED IS PLACED IN WATER...
WE'RE COUNTING ON YOUR EXPERT TOUCH, ADAM STRANGE, TO MAKE IT BLOOM...
NERVOUSLY, HE SCANS THE ANCIENT SEED! WILL IT BUD? AND -- BUD IN TIME? THEN, WHEN ONLY TEN MINUTES REMAIN BEFORE HIS COUNTDOWN TIME...
IT WORKED! THE EXPERIMENT IS A SUCCESS, GENTLEMEN!
NOW TO GET AWAY -- CHANGE INTO MY SPACE-UNIFORM -- AND CONTACT THE ZETA-BEAM!
SOON, THE BLACKNESS OF A MOONLESS NIGHT SHROUDS ADAM STRANGE AS HE HURTLES OVER RUM JUNGLE TOWARD THE "OUTBACK"*...
7-6-5-4...
*EDITOR'S NO
THE "OUTBACK IS THE WILD, UNDEVELOPED FRONTIER COUN INLAND FROM T MORE POPULATE COASTAL AREAS OF AUSTRALIA!
EVEN AS ADAM'S COUNTDOWN ENDS -- JUST ABOVE ONE OF THE QUEER MUD TOWERS BUILT BY WHITE ANTS ON THE NORTHERN TERRITORY PLAINS --
ZZZZZZZTTT!
IN THE WINK OF AN EYELID THE EARTHMAN IS AGAIN TELEPORTED ACROSS 25 TRILLION MILES OF SPACE TO THE PLANET RANN OF THE STAR-SUN ALPHA CENTAURI...

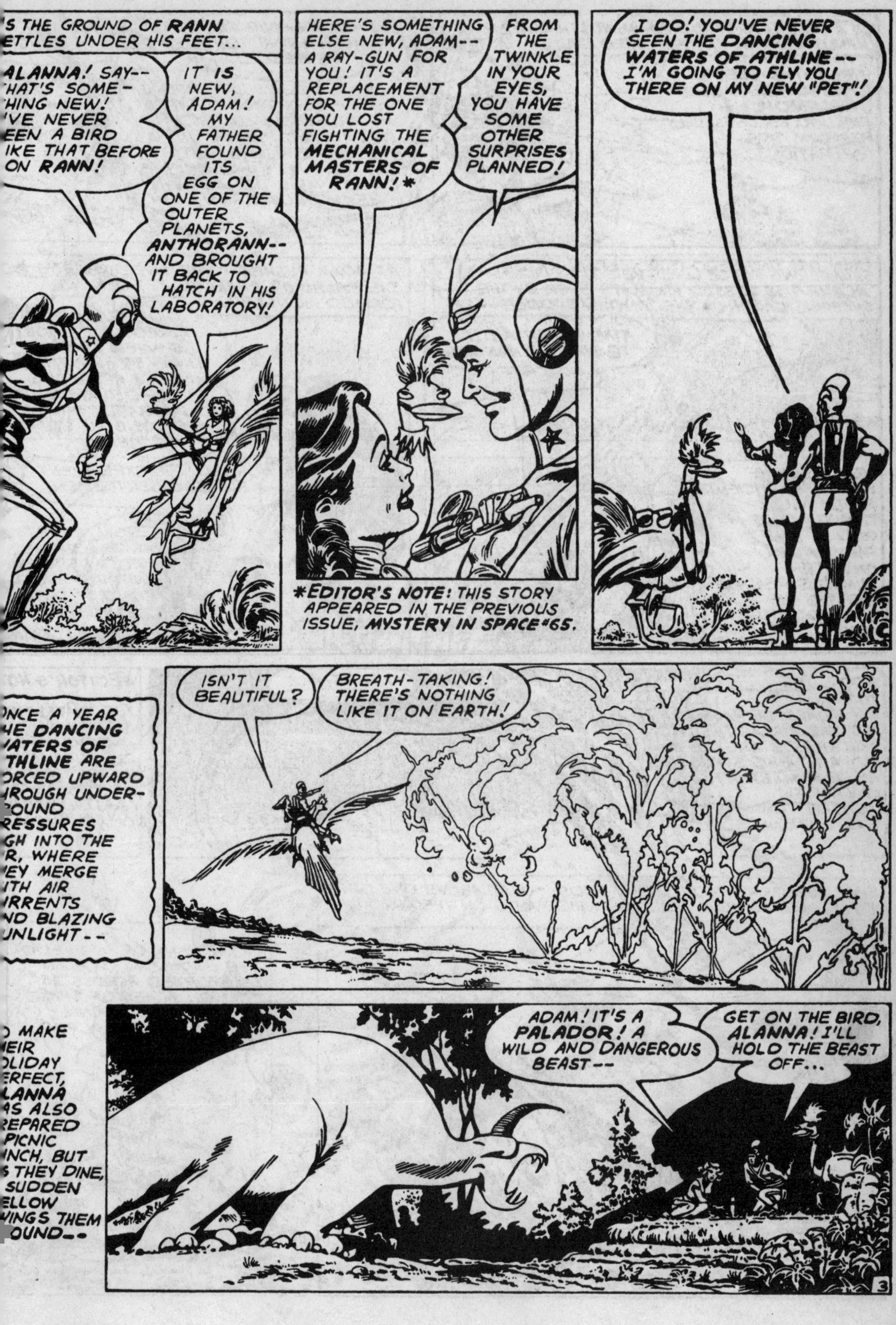
'S THE GROUND OF RANN
ETTLES UNDER HIS FEET...
ALANNA! SAY-- HAT'S SOME-THING NEW! VE NEVER EEN A BIRD IKE THAT BEFORE ON RANN!
IT IS NEW, ADAM! MY FATHER FOUND ITS EGG ON ONE OF THE OUTER PLANETS, ANTHORANN-- AND BROUGHT IT BACK TO HATCH IN HIS LABORATORY!
HERE'S SOMETHING ELSE NEW, ADAM-- A RAY-GUN FOR YOU! IT'S A REPLACEMENT FOR THE ONE YOU LOST FIGHTING THE MECHANICAL MASTERS OF RANN! *
FROM THE TWINKLE IN YOUR EYES, YOU HAVE SOME OTHER SURPRISES PLANNED!
*EDITOR'S NOTE: THIS STORY APPEARED IN THE PREVIOUS ISSUE, MYSTERY IN SPACE #65.
I DO! YOU'VE NEVER SEEN THE DANCING WATERS OF ATHLINE-- I'M GOING TO FLY YOU THERE ON MY NEW "PET"!
NCE A YEAR HE DANCING ATERS OF THLINE ARE ORCED UPWARD HROUGH UNDER-OUND RESSURES GH INTO THE R, WHERE EY MERGE TH AIR RRENTS ND BLAZING UNLIGHT--
ISN'T IT BEAUTIFUL?
BREATH-TAKING! THERE'S NOTHING LIKE IT ON EARTH!
MAKE EIR OLIDAY ERFECT, LANNA AS ALSO REPARED PICNIC NCH, BUT THEY DINE, SUDDEN ELLOW WINGS THEM OUND--
ADAM! IT'S A PALADOR! A WILD AND DANGEROUS BEAST--
GET ON THE BIRD, ALANNA! I'LL HOLD THE BEAST OFF...
3

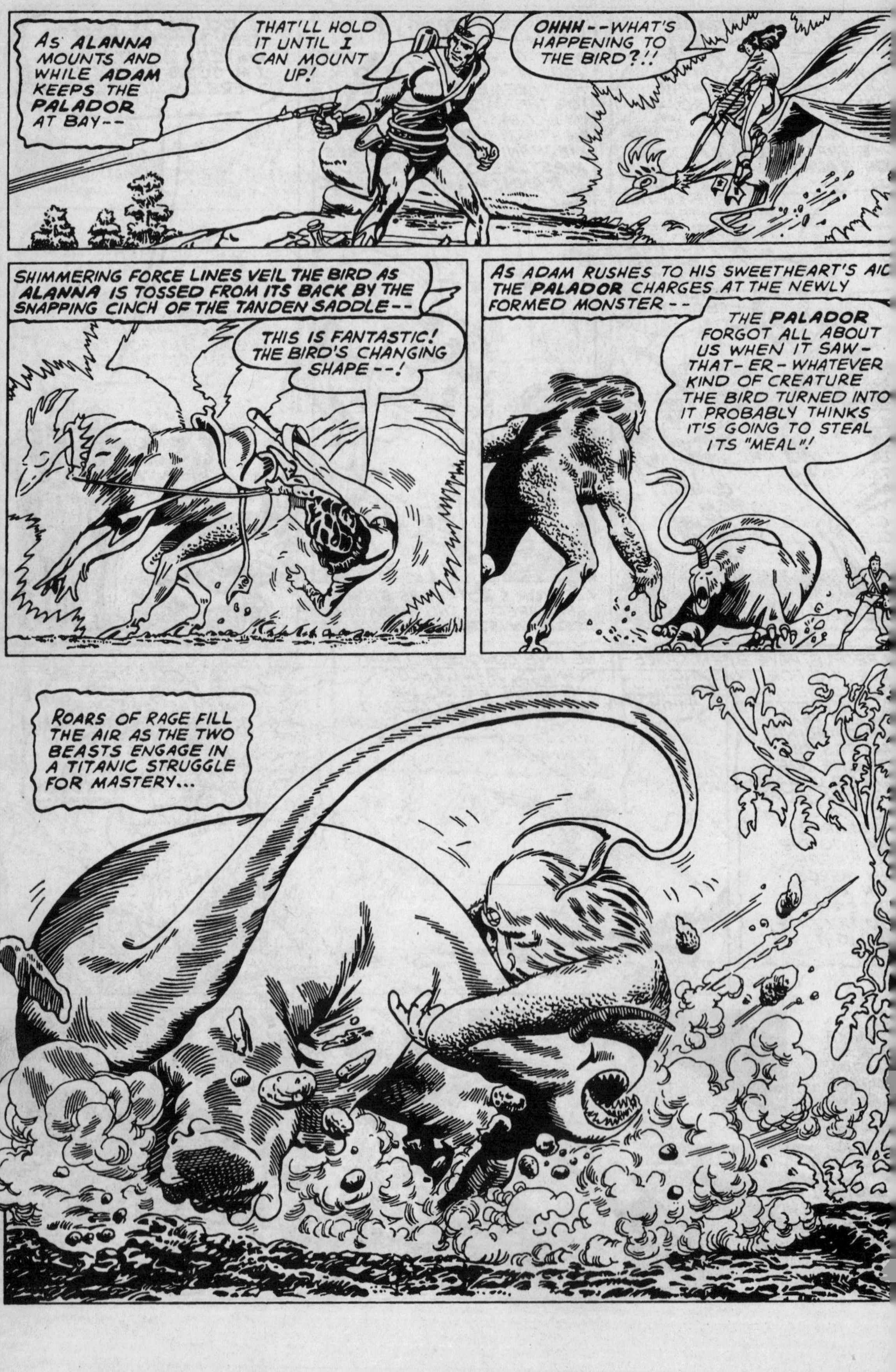

AS ALANNA MOUNTS AND WHILE ADAM KEEPS THE PALADOR AT BAY--
THAT'LL HOLD IT UNTIL I CAN MOUNT UP!
OHHH--WHAT'S HAPPENING TO THE BIRD?!!
SHIMMERING FORCE LINES VEIL THE BIRD AS ALANNA IS TOSSED FROM ITS BACK BY THE SNAPPING CINCH OF THE TANDEN SADDLE--
THIS IS FANTASTIC! THE BIRD'S CHANGING SHAPE--!
AS ADAM RUSHES TO HIS SWEETHEART'S AID THE PALADOR CHARGES AT THE NEWLY FORMED MONSTER--
THE PALADOR FORGOT ALL ABOUT US WHEN IT SAW-- THAT-- ER-- WHATEVER KIND OF CREATURE THE BIRD TURNED INTO IT PROBABLY THINKS IT'S GOING TO STEAL ITS "MEAL"!
ROARS OF RAGE FILL THE AIR AS THE TWO BEASTS ENGAGE IN A TITANIC STRUGGLE FOR MASTERY...

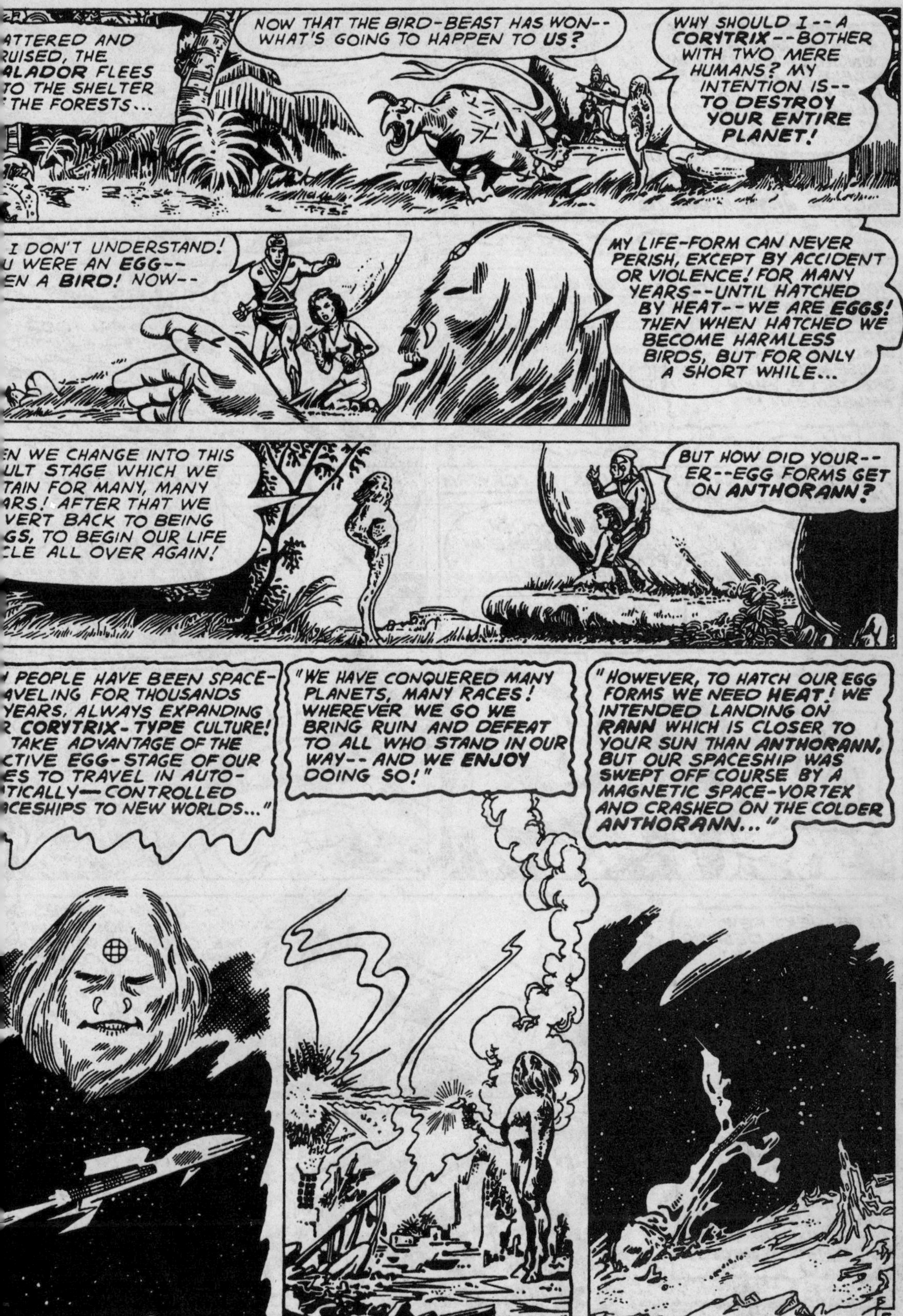
ATTERED AND
RUISED, THE
ALADOR FLEES
TO THE SHELTER
THE FORESTS...
NOW THAT THE BIRD-BEAST HAS WON-- WHAT'S GOING TO HAPPEN TO US?
WHY SHOULD I -- A CORYTRIX -- BOTHER WITH TWO MERE HUMANS? MY INTENTION IS -- TO DESTROY YOUR ENTIRE PLANET!
I DON'T UNDERSTAND! U WERE AN EGG-- EN A BIRD! NOW--
MY LIFE-FORM CAN NEVER PERISH, EXCEPT BY ACCIDENT OR VIOLENCE! FOR MANY YEARS--UNTIL HATCHED BY HEAT--WE ARE EGGS! THEN WHEN HATCHED WE BECOME HARMLESS BIRDS, BUT FOR ONLY A SHORT WHILE...
EN WE CHANGE INTO THIS ULT STAGE WHICH WE TAIN FOR MANY, MANY ARS! AFTER THAT WE VERT BACK TO BEING GS, TO BEGIN OUR LIFE CLE ALL OVER AGAIN!
BUT HOW DID YOUR-- ER--EGG FORMS GET ON ANTHORANN?
PEOPLE HAVE BEEN SPACE- AVELING FOR THOUSANDS YEARS, ALWAYS EXPANDING R CORYTRIX-TYPE CULTURE! TAKE ADVANTAGE OF THE CTIVE EGG-STAGE OF OUR ES TO TRAVEL IN AUTO- TICALLY—CONTROLLED ACESHIPS TO NEW WORLDS..."
"WE HAVE CONQUERED MANY PLANETS, MANY RACES! WHEREVER WE GO WE BRING RUIN AND DEFEAT TO ALL WHO STAND IN OUR WAY-- AND WE ENJOY DOING SO!"
"HOWEVER, TO HATCH OUR EGG FORMS WE NEED HEAT! WE INTENDED LANDING ON RANN WHICH IS CLOSER TO YOUR SUN THAN ANTHORANN, BUT OUR SPACESHIP WAS SWEPT OFF COURSE BY A MAGNETIC SPACE-VORTEX AND CRASHED ON THE COLDER ANTHORANN..."
5

"*ANTHORANN IS TOO FAR FROM THE SUN ALPHA CENTAURI TO HATCH MY PEOPLE! I COULD BRING THEM HERE TO HATCH -- BUT I'LL GET MORE ENJOYMENT OUT OF HURLING YOUR PLANET INTO THE SUN, THEREBY CAUSING THE SUN TO FLARE UP WITH SO MUCH HEAT THAT IT WILL CAUSE THE EGGS ON ANTHORANN TO HATCH!...*"

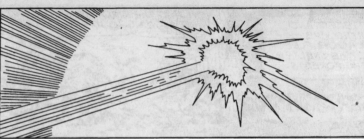

"*YOU WILL BE PLUNGED INTO DESPAIR, KNOWING YOUR FATE YET BEING UNABLE TO STOP IT! I SHALL GET MUCH AMUSEMENT FROM THE SPECTACLE, MUCH AMUSEMENT!*"

ADAM DRAWS HIS RAY-GUN EVEN AS THE CORYTRIX TELEPATHS ITS SCORN AT HIM...

YOU DON'T THINK WE'LL LET YOU GO AHEAD WITH YOUR PLANET-SHATTERING SCHEME, DO YOU?

LET ME? FOOLISH HUMAN--OBSERVE MY POWER AND BE WARNED! YOU ARE HELPLESS! YOU CANNOT EVEN FIGHT ME! WATCH!

ADAM! HE CHANGED YOUR RAY-GUN INTO -- STONE!

A CORYTRIX HAS THE POWER TO ALTER THE MOLECULAR STRUCTURE OF METAL INTO STONE, RENDERING YOUR WEAPONS USELESS! BUT I'VE WASTED ENOUGH TIME WITH YOU! I MUST PREPARE TO HURL RANN INTO THE SUN!

IN THE NEXT FEW DAYS, TO THE DESPAIR AND ANGUISH OF EVERY PERSON ON RANN, THE CORYTRIX GOES ABOUT ITS OPERATIONS...

IT'S FUSING A SERIES OF POWERFUL BOMBS INTO THE GROUND! WHEN THEY EXPLODE, THE CONCUSSION WILL HURL THE PLANET OUT OF ORBIT-- INWARD TO THE SUN!

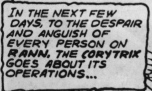

AGAIN AND AGAIN ADAM STRANGE LEADS A CHARGE OF RANAGAR WARRIORS AGAINST THE ALIEN CREATURE, BUT WITHOUT SUCCESS...

IT TURNS EVERY WEAPON WE POSSESS INTO STONE! WE'VE FAILED TO STOP IT ON THE GROUND -- AND IN THE AIR-- BUT MAYBE WE'LL HAVE BETTER SUCCESS UNDERGROUND!

OUT OF SIGHT OF THE *CORYTRIX*, THE EARTH-MAN BEGINS HIS SUBTERRANEAN OPERATION...

BY BORING UNDERNEATH THE LAND SECTION THE *CORYTRIX* IS MINING, WE'LL CUT IT OFF FROM *RANN*-- THEN SET OFF OUR OWN EXPLOSIVES TO SHOOT THE SEGMENT AND THE BEAST INTO SPACE... AND INTO THE SUN! THE COLLISION WON'T CAUSE ENOUGH HEAT TO HATCH THE EGGS ON *ANTHORANN!*

...UT JUST AS ADAM COMPLETES ...'S TASK, *ALANNA* BRINGS ...ORD OF DEFEAT!

...DAM! THE *CORYTRIX* ...S *LEAVING!* IT STOLE ... SPACESHIP AND ... GOING TO ...ETONATE ...HE BOMBS ...Y REMOTE ...ONTROL!

WE'VE GOT TO BRING IT BACK! IT'S OUR ONLY CHANCE!

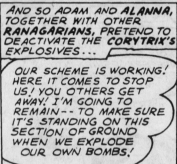

AND SO ADAM AND *ALANNA*, TOGETHER WITH OTHER *RANAGARIANS*, PRETEND TO DEACTIVATE THE *CORYTRIX'S* EXPLOSIVES...

OUR SCHEME IS WORKING! HERE IT COMES TO STOP US! YOU OTHERS GET AWAY! I'M GOING TO REMAIN-- TO MAKE SURE IT'S STANDING ON THIS SECTION OF GROUND WHEN WE EXPLODE OUR OWN BOMBS!

ALL BUT ADAM STRANGE FLEE AS THE ALIEN CREATURE APPROACHES...

GOOD! IT'S IN POSITION! NOW WHEN THEY FIRE OUR BOMBS, WE'LL *BOTH* BE THROWN SPACEWARD!

BELOW THE SURFACE OF THE PLANET A TERRIFIC EXPLOSION RIPS ROCK FROM ROCK AND SOIL FROM SOIL! UPWARD AND OUTWARD AWAY FROM *RANN* FLIES THE MINED SEGMENT OF THE PLANET...

THE TERRIFIC FORCE NEEDED TO FREE THIS CHUNK OF GROUND FROM *RANN'S* GRAVITY IS KNOCKING US OUT...

7

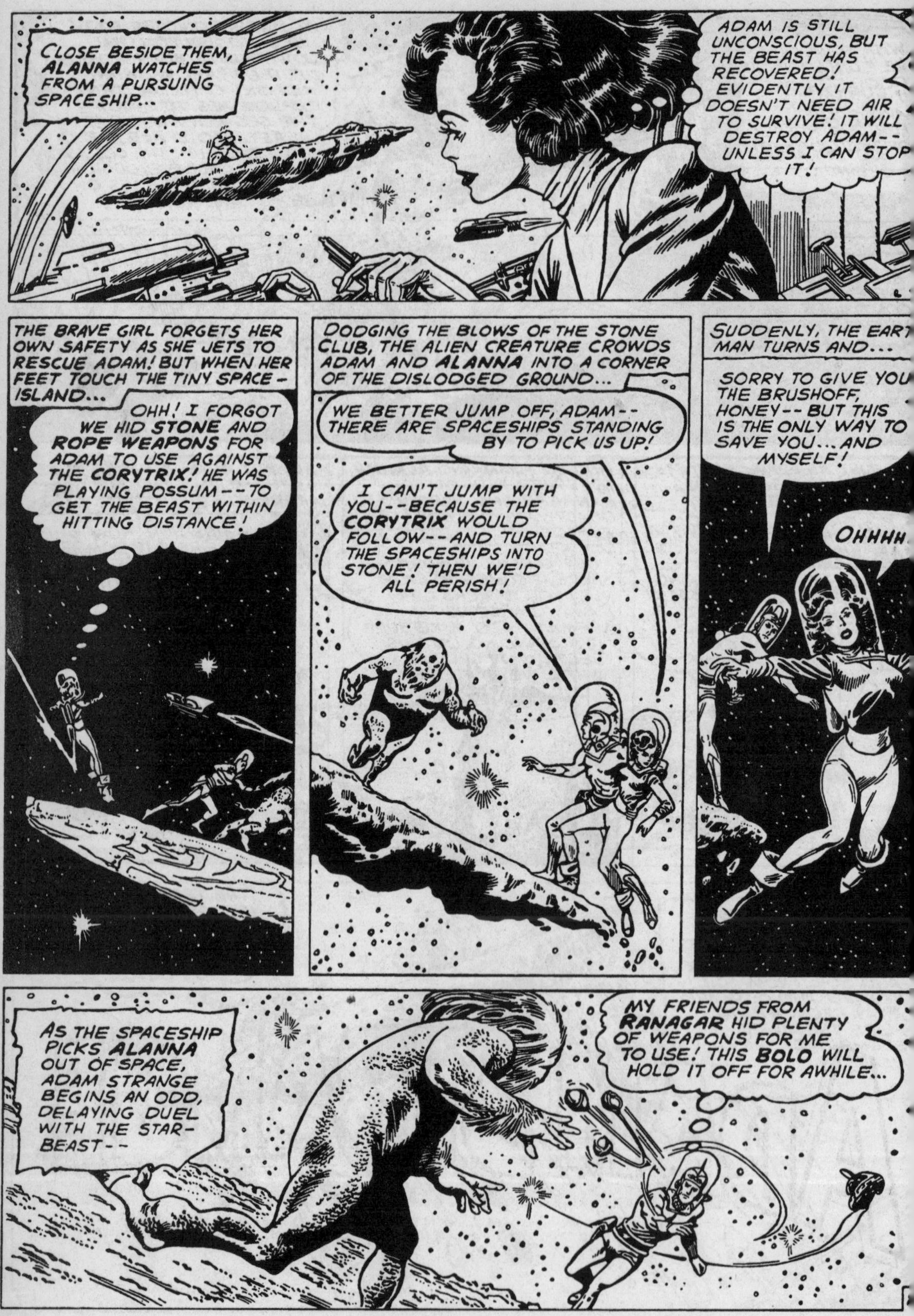
CLOSE BESIDE THEM, ALANNA WATCHES FROM A PURSUING SPACESHIP...
ADAM IS STILL UNCONSCIOUS, BUT THE BEAST HAS RECOVERED! EVIDENTLY IT DOESN'T NEED AIR TO SURVIVE! IT WILL DESTROY ADAM-- UNLESS I CAN STOP IT!
THE BRAVE GIRL FORGETS HER OWN SAFETY AS SHE JETS TO RESCUE ADAM! BUT WHEN HER FEET TOUCH THE TINY SPACE-ISLAND...
OHH! I FORGOT WE HID STONE AND ROPE WEAPONS FOR ADAM TO USE AGAINST THE CORYTRIX! HE WAS PLAYING POSSUM--TO GET THE BEAST WITHIN HITTING DISTANCE!
DODGING THE BLOWS OF THE STONE CLUB, THE ALIEN CREATURE CROWDS ADAM AND ALANNA INTO A CORNER OF THE DISLODGED GROUND...
WE BETTER JUMP OFF, ADAM-- THERE ARE SPACESHIPS STANDING BY TO PICK US UP!
I CAN'T JUMP WITH YOU--BECAUSE THE CORYTRIX WOULD FOLLOW--AND TURN THE SPACESHIPS INTO STONE! THEN WE'D ALL PERISH!
SUDDENLY, THE EART MAN TURNS AND...
SORRY TO GIVE YOU THE BRUSHOFF, HONEY-- BUT THIS IS THE ONLY WAY TO SAVE YOU...AND MYSELF!
OHHHH
AS THE SPACESHIP PICKS ALANNA OUT OF SPACE, ADAM STRANGE BEGINS AN ODD, DELAYING DUEL WITH THE STAR-BEAST--
MY FRIENDS FROM RANAGAR HID PLENTY OF WEAPONS FOR ME TO USE! THIS BOLO WILL HOLD IT OFF FOR AWHILE...

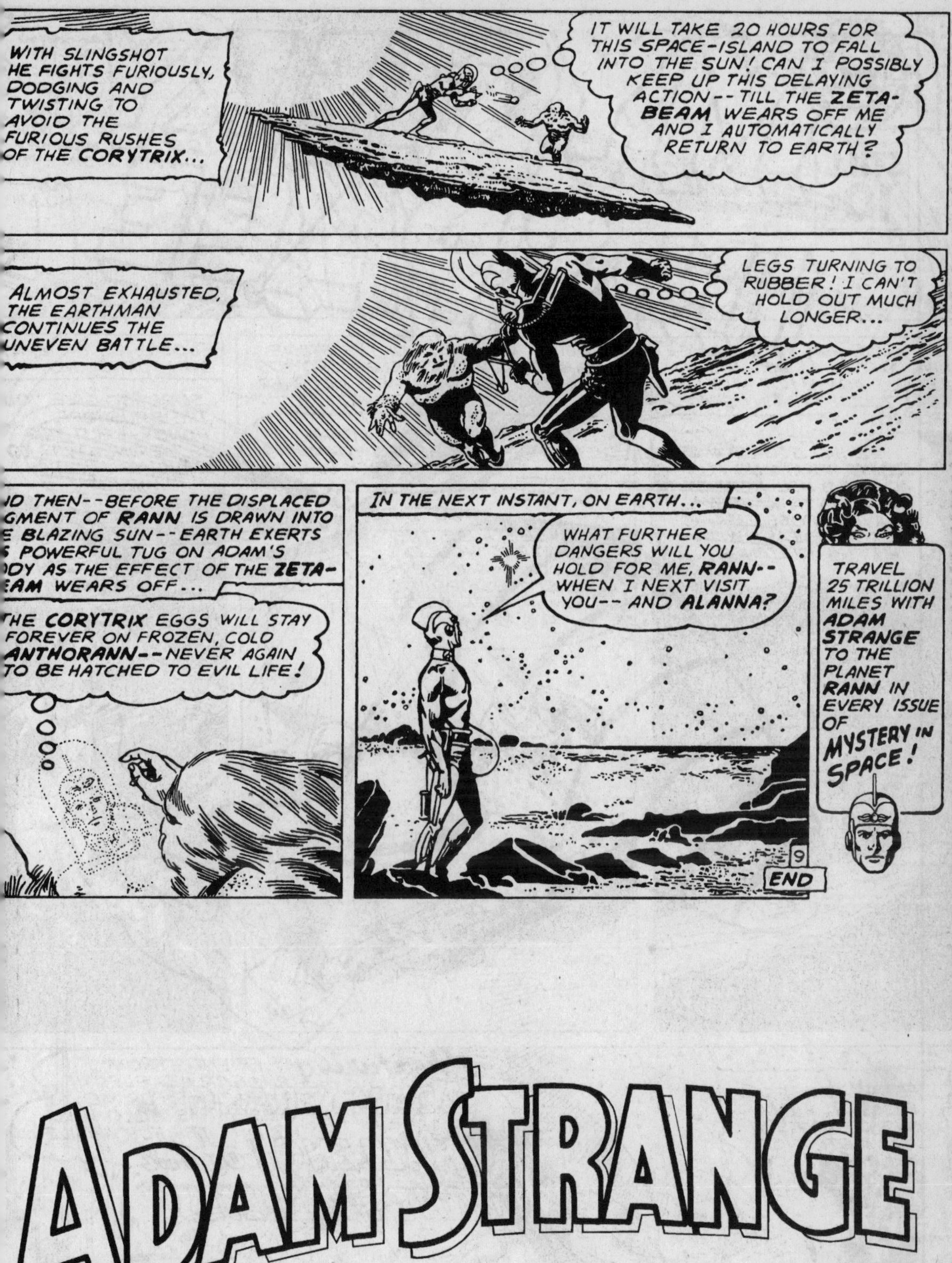
WITH SLINGSHOT HE FIGHTS FURIOUSLY, DODGING AND TWISTING TO AVOID THE FURIOUS RUSHES OF THE CORYTRIX...
IT WILL TAKE 20 HOURS FOR THIS SPACE-ISLAND TO FALL INTO THE SUN! CAN I POSSIBLY KEEP UP THIS DELAYING ACTION--TILL THE ZETA-BEAM WEARS OFF ME AND I AUTOMATICALLY RETURN TO EARTH?
ALMOST EXHAUSTED, THE EARTHMAN CONTINUES THE UNEVEN BATTLE...
LEGS TURNING TO RUBBER! I CAN'T HOLD OUT MUCH LONGER...
ID THEN--BEFORE THE DISPLACED GMENT OF RANN IS DRAWN INTO E BLAZING SUN--EARTH EXERTS S POWERFUL TUG ON ADAM'S DDY AS THE EFFECT OF THE ZETA-EAM WEARS OFF...
THE CORYTRIX EGGS WILL STAY FOREVER ON FROZEN, COLD ANTHORANN--NEVER AGAIN TO BE HATCHED TO EVIL LIFE!
IN THE NEXT INSTANT, ON EARTH...
WHAT FURTHER DANGERS WILL YOU HOLD FOR ME, RANN--WHEN I NEXT VISIT YOU--AND ALANNA?
9
END
TRAVEL 25 TRILLION MILES WITH ADAM STRANGE TO THE PLANET RANN IN EVERY ISSUE OF MYSTERY IN SPACE!

ADAM STRANGE

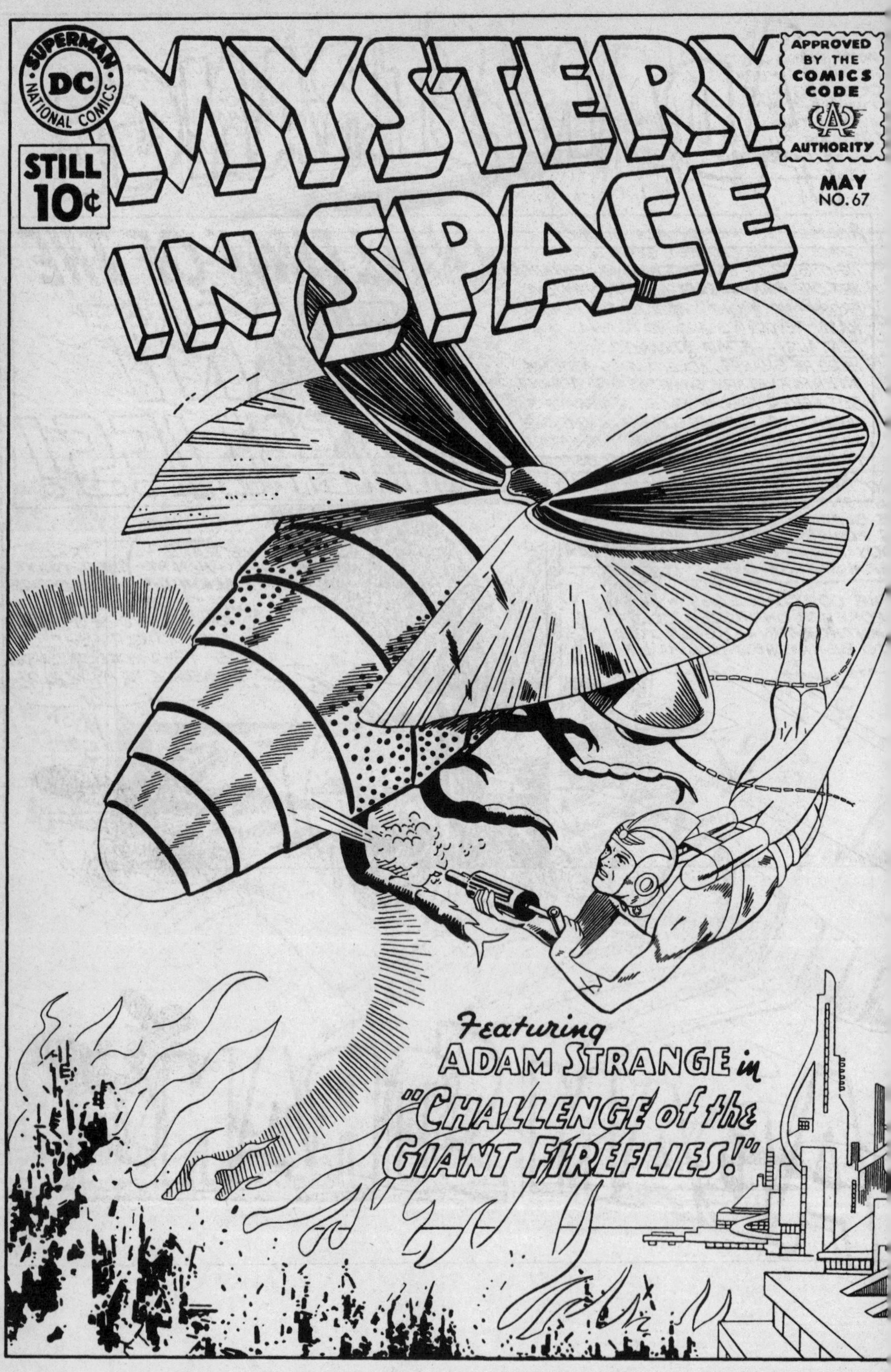
SUPERMAN
DC
NATIONAL COMICS
MYSTERY IN SPACE
APPROVED BY THE COMICS CODE AUTHORITY
STILL 10¢
MAY
NO. 67
Featuring
ADAM STRANGE in
"CHALLENGE of the GIANT FIREFLIES!"

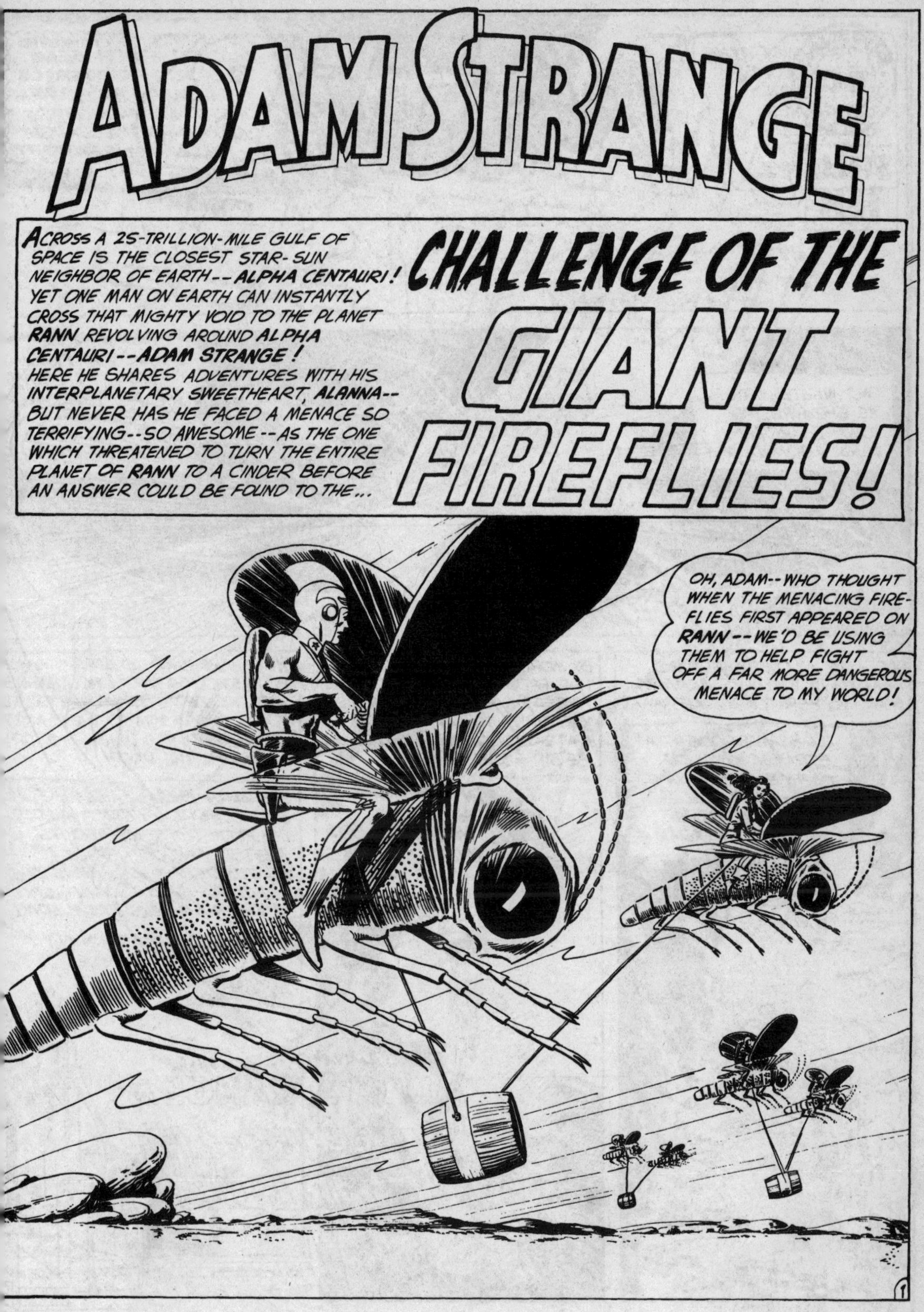
ADAM STRANGE
ACROSS A 25-TRILLION-MILE GULF OF SPACE IS THE CLOSEST STAR-SUN NEIGHBOR OF EARTH--ALPHA CENTAURI! YET ONE MAN ON EARTH CAN INSTANTLY CROSS THAT MIGHTY VOID TO THE PLANET RANN REVOLVING AROUND ALPHA CENTAURI--ADAM STRANGE! HERE HE SHARES ADVENTURES WITH HIS INTERPLANETARY SWEETHEART, ALANNA-- BUT NEVER HAS HE FACED A MENACE SO TERRIFYING--SO AWESOME--AS THE ONE WHICH THREATENED TO TURN THE ENTIRE PLANET OF RANN TO A CINDER BEFORE AN ANSWER COULD BE FOUND TO THE...
CHALLENGE OF THE GIANT FIREFLIES!
OH, ADAM--WHO THOUGHT WHEN THE MENACING FIRE-FLIES FIRST APPEARED ON RANN--WE'D BE USING THEM TO HELP FIGHT OFF A FAR MORE DANGEROUS MENACE TO MY WORLD!
1

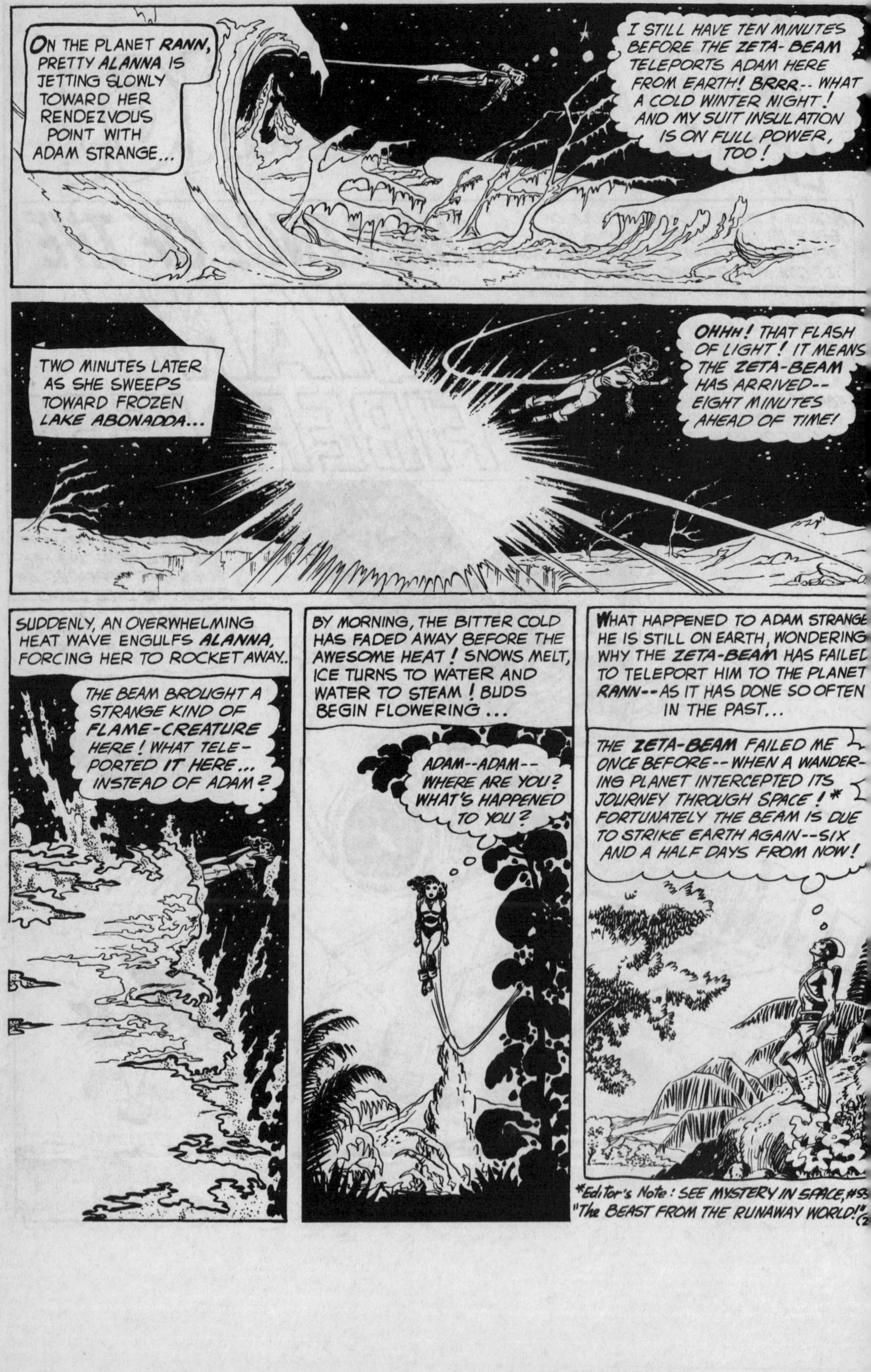
ON THE PLANET RANN, PRETTY ALANNA IS JETTING SLOWLY TOWARD HER RENDEZVOUS POINT WITH ADAM STRANGE...
I STILL HAVE TEN MINUTES BEFORE THE ZETA-BEAM TELEPORTS ADAM HERE FROM EARTH! BRRR-- WHAT A COLD WINTER NIGHT! AND MY SUIT INSULATION IS ON FULL POWER, TOO!
TWO MINUTES LATER AS SHE SWEEPS TOWARD FROZEN LAKE ABONADDA...
OHHH! THAT FLASH OF LIGHT! IT MEANS THE ZETA-BEAM HAS ARRIVED-- EIGHT MINUTES AHEAD OF TIME!
SUDDENLY, AN OVERWHELMING HEAT WAVE ENGULFS ALANNA, FORCING HER TO ROCKET AWAY..
THE BEAM BROUGHT A STRANGE KIND OF FLAME-CREATURE HERE! WHAT TELE-PORTED IT HERE... INSTEAD OF ADAM?
BY MORNING, THE BITTER COLD HAS FADED AWAY BEFORE THE AWESOME HEAT! SNOWS MELT, ICE TURNS TO WATER AND WATER TO STEAM! BUDS BEGIN FLOWERING...
ADAM--ADAM-- WHERE ARE YOU? WHAT'S HAPPENED TO YOU?
WHAT HAPPENED TO ADAM STRANGE HE IS STILL ON EARTH, WONDERING WHY THE ZETA-BEAM HAS FAILED TO TELEPORT HIM TO THE PLANET RANN--AS IT HAS DONE SO OFTEN IN THE PAST...
THE ZETA-BEAM FAILED ME ONCE BEFORE--WHEN A WANDER-ING PLANET INTERCEPTED ITS JOURNEY THROUGH SPACE!* FORTUNATELY THE BEAM IS DUE TO STRIKE EARTH AGAIN--SIX AND A HALF DAYS FROM NOW!
*Editor's Note: SEE MYSTERY IN SPACE, #5 "The BEAST FROM THE RUNAWAY WORLD!"

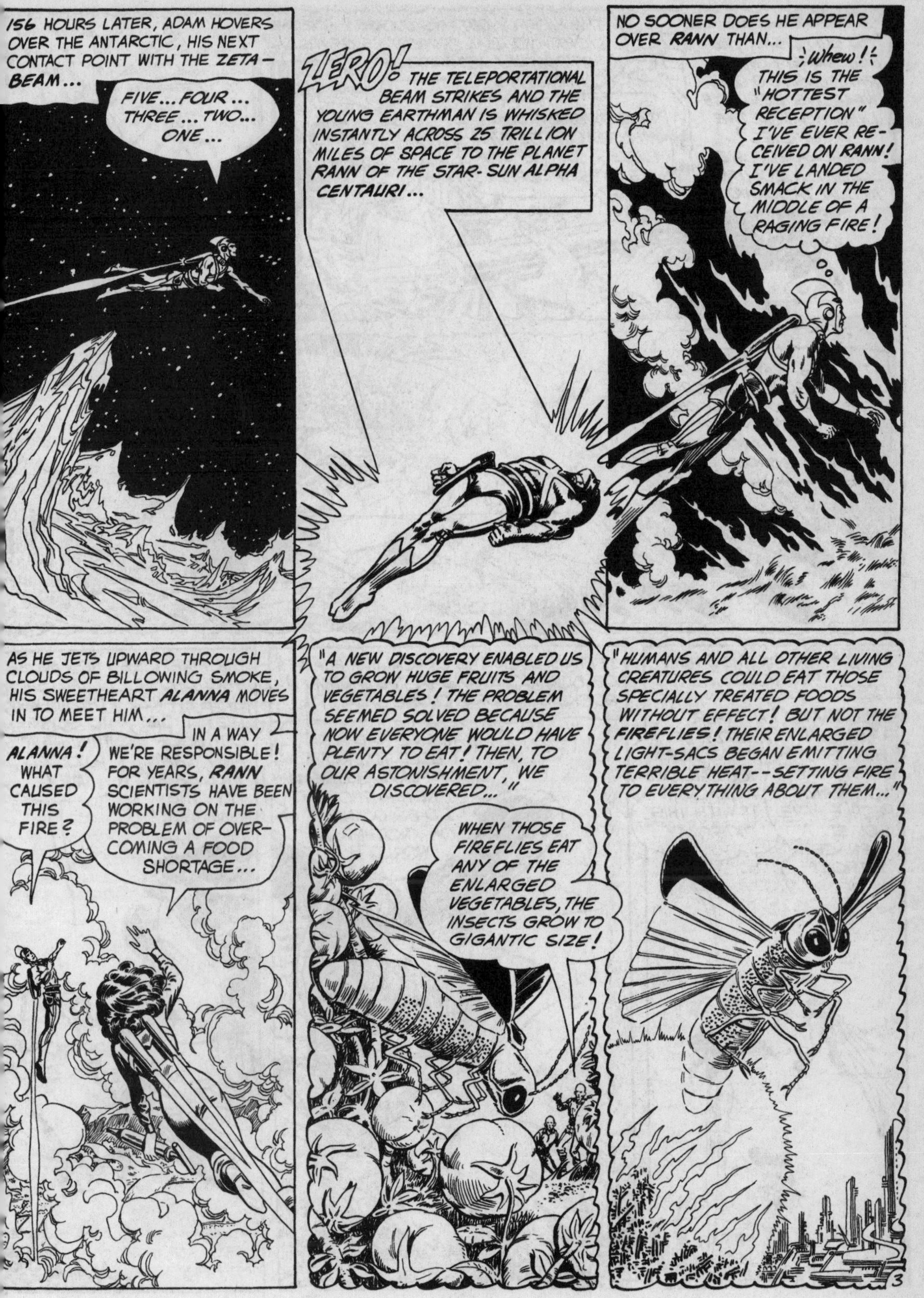
156 HOURS LATER, ADAM HOVERS OVER THE ANTARCTIC, HIS NEXT CONTACT POINT WITH THE ZETA-BEAM...
FIVE... FOUR... THREE... TWO... ONE...
ZERO!
THE TELEPORTATIONAL BEAM STRIKES AND THE YOUNG EARTHMAN IS WHISKED INSTANTLY ACROSS 25 TRILLION MILES OF SPACE TO THE PLANET RANN OF THE STAR-SUN ALPHA CENTAURI...
NO SOONER DOES HE APPEAR OVER RANN THAN...
Whew! THIS IS THE "HOTTEST RECEPTION" I'VE EVER RECEIVED ON RANN! I'VE LANDED SMACK IN THE MIDDLE OF A RAGING FIRE!
AS HE JETS UPWARD THROUGH CLOUDS OF BILLOWING SMOKE, HIS SWEETHEART ALANNA MOVES IN TO MEET HIM...
ALANNA! WHAT CAUSED THIS FIRE?
IN A WAY WE'RE RESPONSIBLE! FOR YEARS, RANN SCIENTISTS HAVE BEEN WORKING ON THE PROBLEM OF OVERCOMING A FOOD SHORTAGE...
"A NEW DISCOVERY ENABLED US TO GROW HUGE FRUITS AND VEGETABLES! THE PROBLEM SEEMED SOLVED BECAUSE NOW EVERYONE WOULD HAVE PLENTY TO EAT! THEN, TO OUR ASTONISHMENT, WE DISCOVERED..."
WHEN THOSE FIREFLIES EAT ANY OF THE ENLARGED VEGETABLES, THE INSECTS GROW TO GIGANTIC SIZE!
"HUMANS AND ALL OTHER LIVING CREATURES COULD EAT THOSE SPECIALLY TREATED FOODS WITHOUT EFFECT! BUT NOT THE FIREFLIES! THEIR ENLARGED LIGHT-SACS BEGAN EMITTING TERRIBLE HEAT--SETTING FIRE TO EVERYTHING ABOUT THEM..."
3

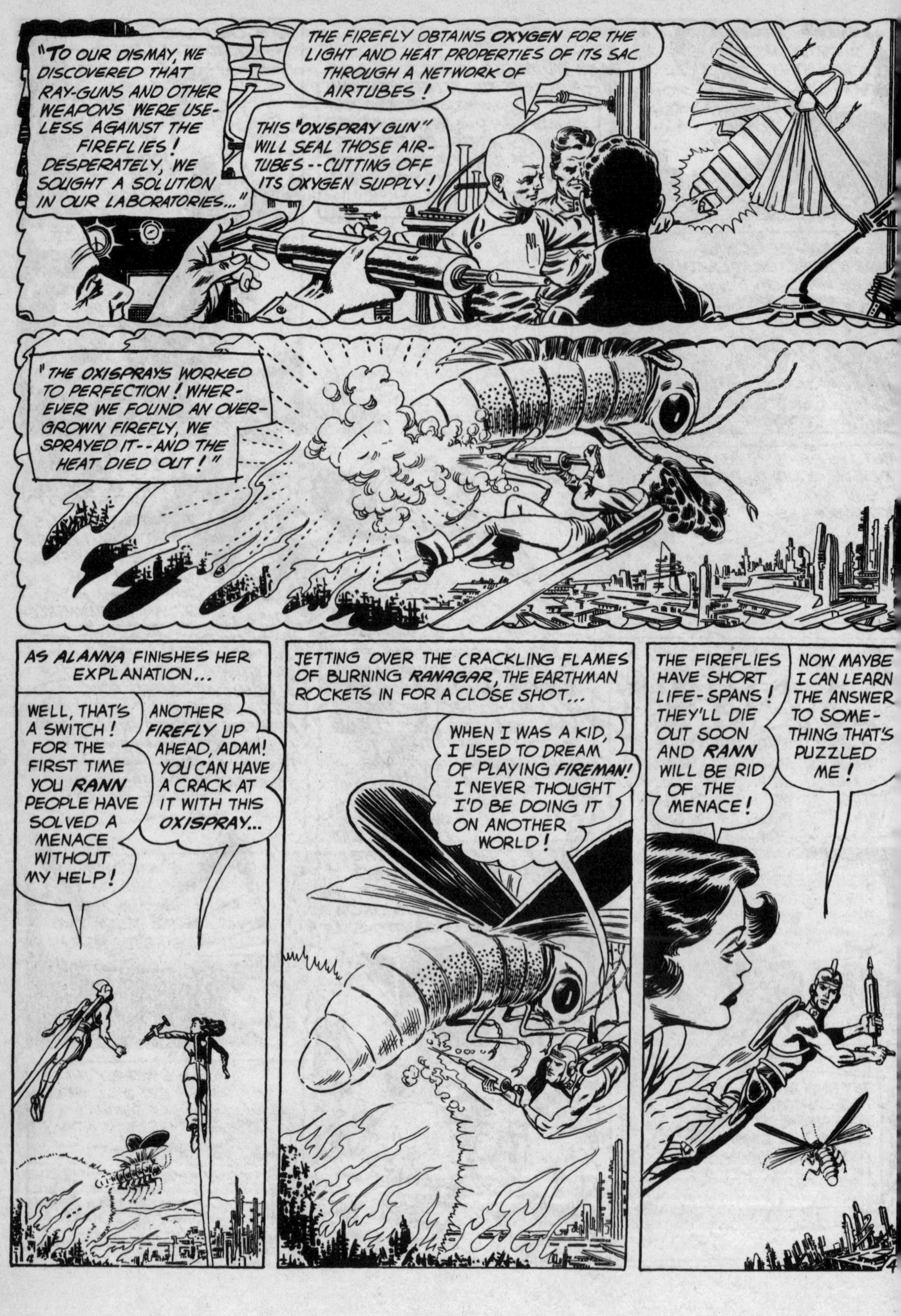
"TO OUR DISMAY, WE DISCOVERED THAT RAY-GUNS AND OTHER WEAPONS WERE USELESS AGAINST THE FIREFLIES! DESPERATELY, WE SOUGHT A SOLUTION IN OUR LABORATORIES..."
THE FIREFLY OBTAINS OXYGEN FOR THE LIGHT AND HEAT PROPERTIES OF ITS SAC THROUGH A NETWORK OF AIRTUBES!
THIS "OXISPRAY GUN" WILL SEAL THOSE AIR-TUBES--CUTTING OFF ITS OXYGEN SUPPLY!
"THE OXISPRAYS WORKED TO PERFECTION! WHEREVER WE FOUND AN OVERGROWN FIREFLY, WE SPRAYED IT--AND THE HEAT DIED OUT!"
AS ALANNA FINISHES HER EXPLANATION...
WELL, THAT'S A SWITCH! FOR THE FIRST TIME YOU RANN PEOPLE HAVE SOLVED A MENACE WITHOUT MY HELP!
ANOTHER FIREFLY UP AHEAD, ADAM! YOU CAN HAVE A CRACK AT IT WITH THIS OXISPRAY...
JETTING OVER THE CRACKLING FLAMES OF BURNING RANAGAR, THE EARTHMAN ROCKETS IN FOR A CLOSE SHOT...
WHEN I WAS A KID, I USED TO DREAM OF PLAYING FIREMAN! I NEVER THOUGHT I'D BE DOING IT ON ANOTHER WORLD!
THE FIREFLIES HAVE SHORT LIFE-SPANS! THEY'LL DIE OUT SOON AND RANN WILL BE RID OF THE MENACE!
NOW MAYBE I CAN LEARN THE ANSWER TO SOMETHING THAT'S PUZZLED ME!
4

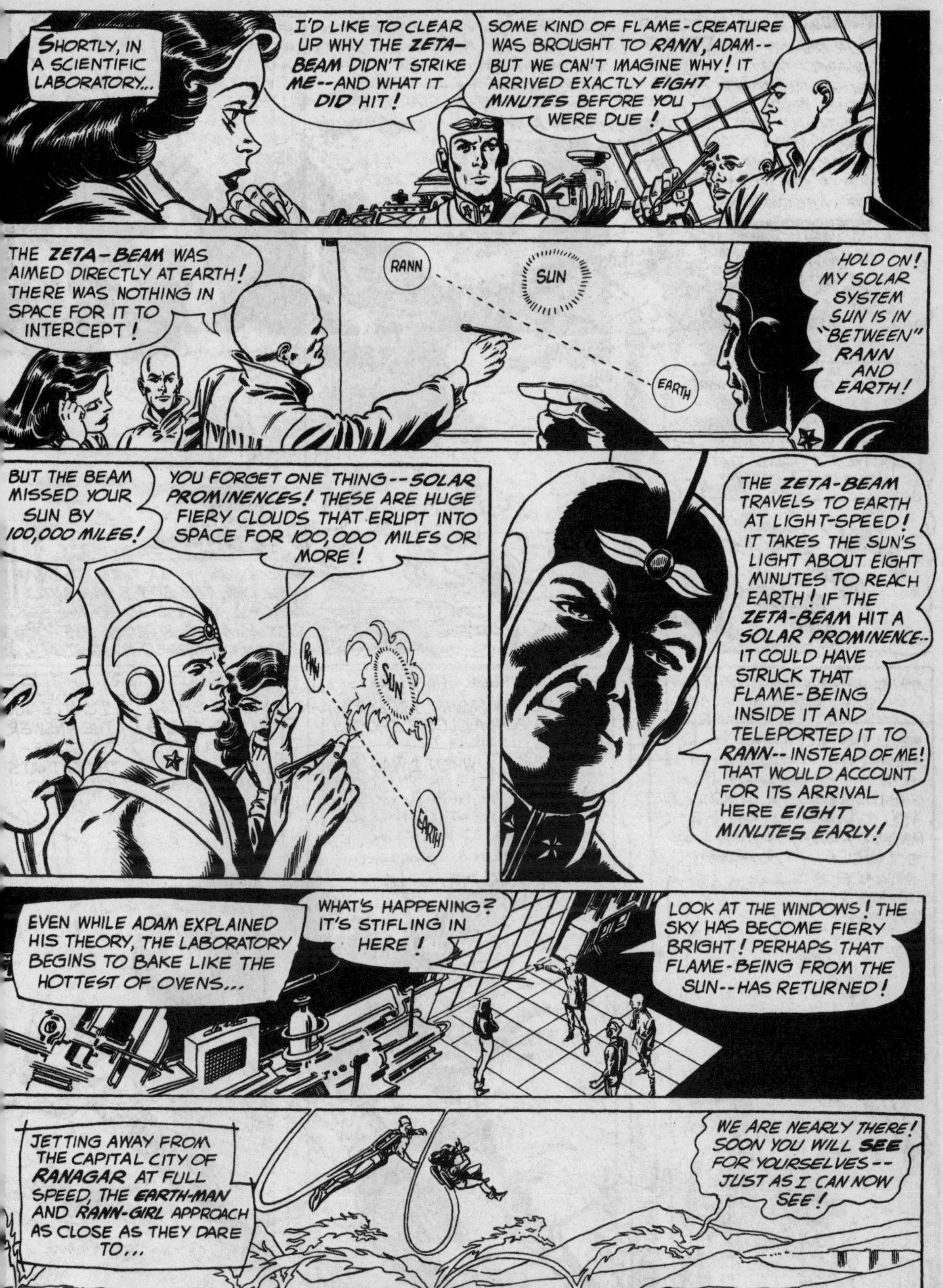
SHORTLY, IN A SCIENTIFIC LABORATORY...
I'D LIKE TO CLEAR UP WHY THE ZETA-BEAM DIDN'T STRIKE ME--AND WHAT IT DID HIT!
SOME KIND OF FLAME-CREATURE WAS BROUGHT TO RANN, ADAM--BUT WE CAN'T IMAGINE WHY! IT ARRIVED EXACTLY EIGHT MINUTES BEFORE YOU WERE DUE!
THE ZETA-BEAM WAS AIMED DIRECTLY AT EARTH! THERE WAS NOTHING IN SPACE FOR IT TO INTERCEPT!
RANN
SUN
EARTH
HOLD ON! MY SOLAR SYSTEM SUN IS IN "BETWEEN" RANN AND EARTH!
BUT THE BEAM MISSED YOUR SUN BY 100,000 MILES!
YOU FORGET ONE THING--SOLAR PROMINENCES! THESE ARE HUGE FIERY CLOUDS THAT ERUPT INTO SPACE FOR 100,000 MILES OR MORE!
RANN
SUN
EARTH
THE ZETA-BEAM TRAVELS TO EARTH AT LIGHT-SPEED! IT TAKES THE SUN'S LIGHT ABOUT EIGHT MINUTES TO REACH EARTH! IF THE ZETA-BEAM HIT A SOLAR PROMINENCE--IT COULD HAVE STRUCK THAT FLAME-BEING INSIDE IT AND TELEPORTED IT TO RANN--INSTEAD OF ME! THAT WOULD ACCOUNT FOR ITS ARRIVAL HERE EIGHT MINUTES EARLY!
EVEN WHILE ADAM EXPLAINED HIS THEORY, THE LABORATORY BEGINS TO BAKE LIKE THE HOTTEST OF OVENS...
WHAT'S HAPPENING? IT'S STIFLING IN HERE!
LOOK AT THE WINDOWS! THE SKY HAS BECOME FIERY BRIGHT! PERHAPS THAT FLAME-BEING FROM THE SUN--HAS RETURNED!
JETTING AWAY FROM THE CAPITAL CITY OF RANAGAR AT FULL SPEED, THE EARTH-MAN AND RANN-GIRL APPROACH AS CLOSE AS THEY DARE TO...
WE ARE NEARLY THERE! SOON YOU WILL SEE FOR YOURSELVES--JUST AS I CAN NOW SEE!
5

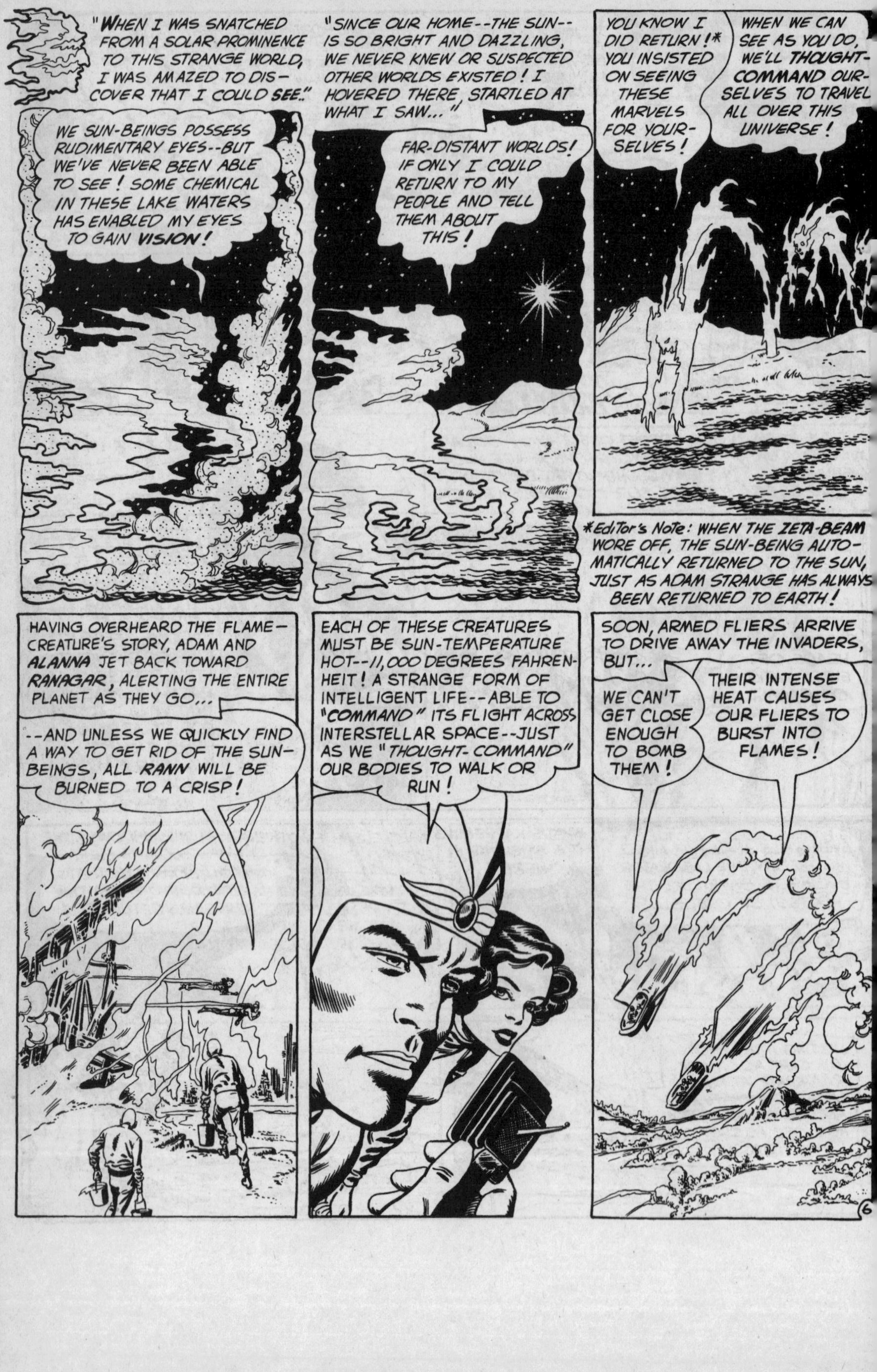
"WHEN I WAS SNATCHED FROM A SOLAR PROMINENCE TO THIS STRANGE WORLD, I WAS AMAZED TO DISCOVER THAT I COULD SEE."
WE SUN-BEINGS POSSESS RUDIMENTARY EYES--BUT WE'VE NEVER BEEN ABLE TO SEE! SOME CHEMICAL IN THESE LAKE WATERS HAS ENABLED MY EYES TO GAIN VISION!
"SINCE OUR HOME--THE SUN--IS SO BRIGHT AND DAZZLING, WE NEVER KNEW OR SUSPECTED OTHER WORLDS EXISTED! I HOVERED THERE, STARTLED AT WHAT I SAW..."
FAR-DISTANT WORLDS! IF ONLY I COULD RETURN TO MY PEOPLE AND TELL THEM ABOUT THIS!
YOU KNOW I DID RETURN!* YOU INSISTED ON SEEING THESE MARVELS FOR YOURSELVES!
WHEN WE CAN SEE AS YOU DO, WE'LL THOUGHT-COMMAND OURSELVES TO TRAVEL ALL OVER THIS UNIVERSE!
*Editor's Note: WHEN THE ZETA-BEAM WORE OFF, THE SUN-BEING AUTOMATICALLY RETURNED TO THE SUN, JUST AS ADAM STRANGE HAS ALWAYS BEEN RETURNED TO EARTH!
HAVING OVERHEARD THE FLAME-CREATURE'S STORY, ADAM AND ALANNA JET BACK TOWARD RANAGAR, ALERTING THE ENTIRE PLANET AS THEY GO...
--AND UNLESS WE QUICKLY FIND A WAY TO GET RID OF THE SUN-BEINGS, ALL RANN WILL BE BURNED TO A CRISP!
EACH OF THESE CREATURES MUST BE SUN-TEMPERATURE HOT--11,000 DEGREES FAHRENHEIT! A STRANGE FORM OF INTELLIGENT LIFE--ABLE TO "COMMAND" ITS FLIGHT ACROSS INTERSTELLAR SPACE--JUST AS WE "THOUGHT-COMMAND" OUR BODIES TO WALK OR RUN!
SOON, ARMED FLIERS ARRIVE TO DRIVE AWAY THE INVADERS, BUT...
WE CAN'T GET CLOSE ENOUGH TO BOMB THEM!
THEIR INTENSE HEAT CAUSES OUR FLIERS TO BURST INTO FLAMES!
6

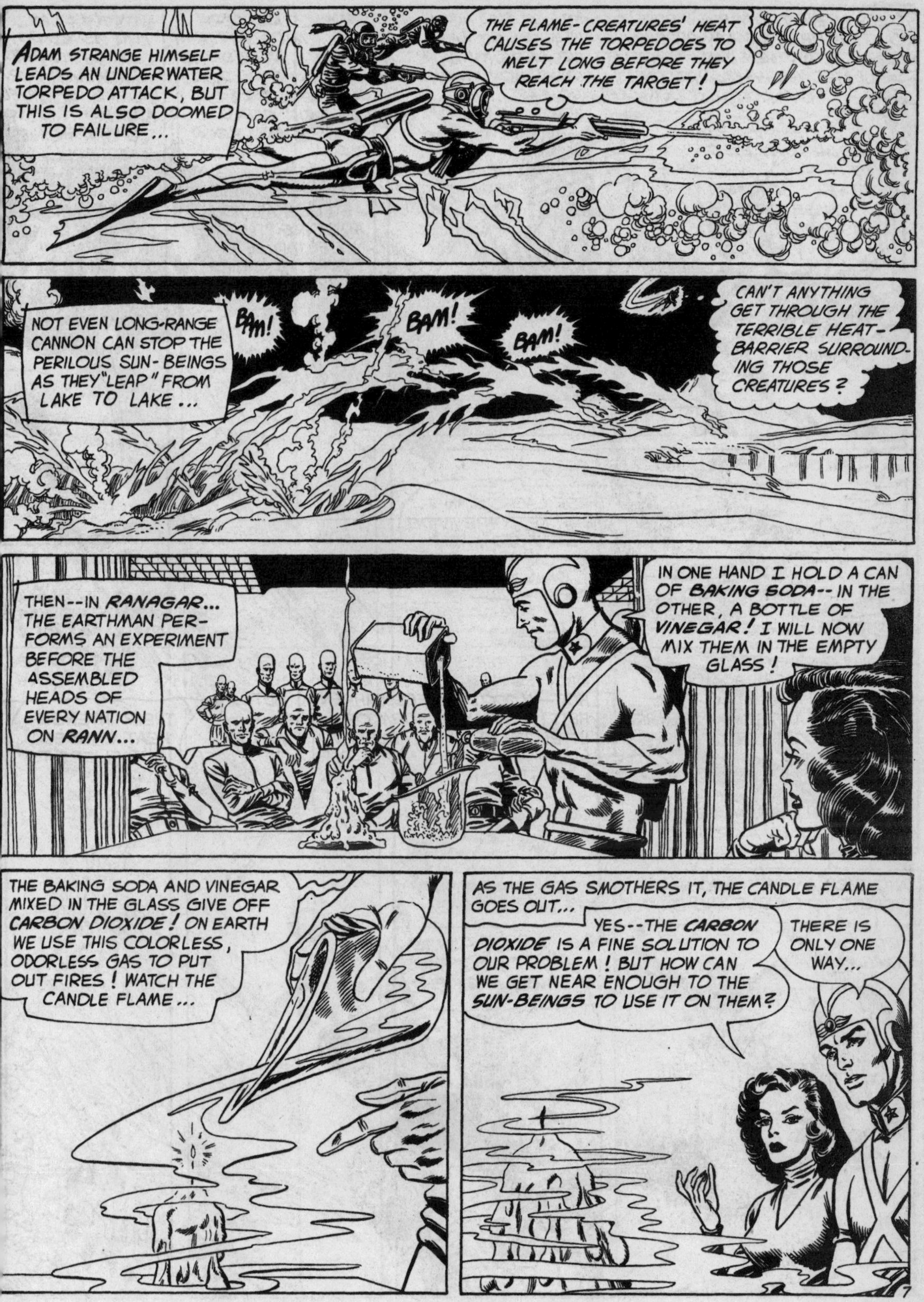

ADAM STRANGE HIMSELF LEADS AN UNDERWATER TORPEDO ATTACK, BUT THIS IS ALSO DOOMED TO FAILURE...
THE FLAME-CREATURES' HEAT CAUSES THE TORPEDOES TO MELT LONG BEFORE THEY REACH THE TARGET!
NOT EVEN LONG-RANGE CANNON CAN STOP THE PERILOUS SUN-BEINGS AS THEY "LEAP" FROM LAKE TO LAKE...
BAM!
BAM!
BAM!
CAN'T ANYTHING GET THROUGH THE TERRIBLE HEAT-BARRIER SURROUNDING THOSE CREATURES?
THEN--IN RANAGAR... THE EARTHMAN PERFORMS AN EXPERIMENT BEFORE THE ASSEMBLED HEADS OF EVERY NATION ON RANN...
IN ONE HAND I HOLD A CAN OF BAKING SODA-- IN THE OTHER, A BOTTLE OF VINEGAR! I WILL NOW MIX THEM IN THE EMPTY GLASS!
THE BAKING SODA AND VINEGAR MIXED IN THE GLASS GIVE OFF CARBON DIOXIDE! ON EARTH WE USE THIS COLORLESS, ODORLESS GAS TO PUT OUT FIRES! WATCH THE CANDLE FLAME...
AS THE GAS SMOTHERS IT, THE CANDLE FLAME GOES OUT...
YES--THE CARBON DIOXIDE IS A FINE SOLUTION TO OUR PROBLEM! BUT HOW CAN WE GET NEAR ENOUGH TO THE SUN-BEINGS TO USE IT ON THEM?
THERE IS ONLY ONE WAY...
7

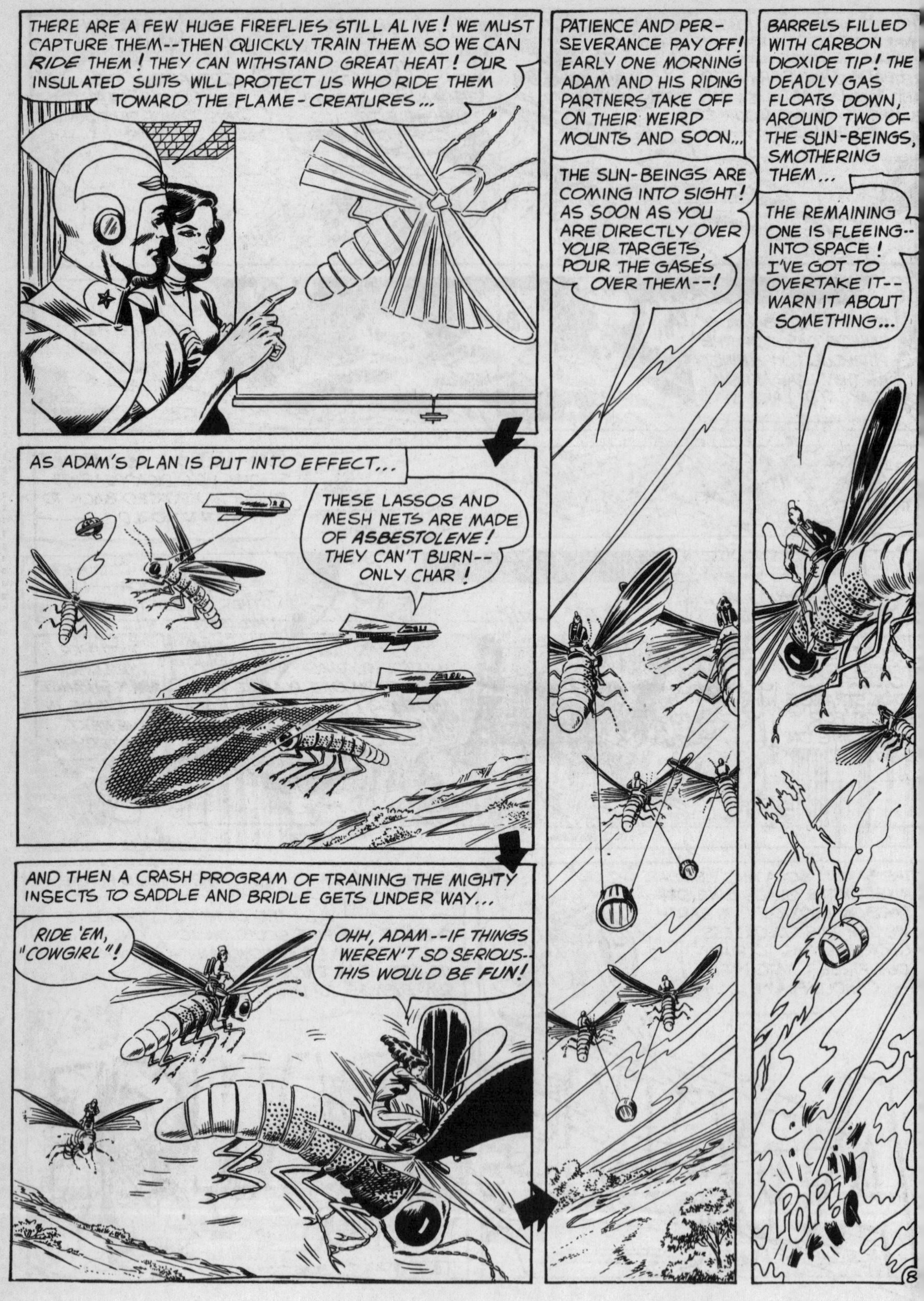
THERE ARE A FEW HUGE FIREFLIES STILL ALIVE! WE MUST CAPTURE THEM--THEN QUICKLY TRAIN THEM SO WE CAN RIDE THEM! THEY CAN WITHSTAND GREAT HEAT! OUR INSULATED SUITS WILL PROTECT US WHO RIDE THEM TOWARD THE FLAME-CREATURES...
AS ADAM'S PLAN IS PUT INTO EFFECT...
THESE LASSOS AND MESH NETS ARE MADE OF ASBESTOLENE! THEY CAN'T BURN--ONLY CHAR!
AND THEN A CRASH PROGRAM OF TRAINING THE MIGHTY INSECTS TO SADDLE AND BRIDLE GETS UNDER WAY...
RIDE 'EM, "COWGIRL"!
OHH, ADAM--IF THINGS WEREN'T SO SERIOUS--THIS WOULD BE FUN!
PATIENCE AND PERSEVERANCE PAY OFF! EARLY ONE MORNING ADAM AND HIS RIDING PARTNERS TAKE OFF ON THEIR WEIRD MOUNTS AND SOON...
THE SUN-BEINGS ARE COMING INTO SIGHT! AS SOON AS YOU ARE DIRECTLY OVER YOUR TARGETS, POUR THE GASES OVER THEM--!
BARRELS FILLED WITH CARBON DIOXIDE TIP! THE DEADLY GAS FLOATS DOWN, AROUND TWO OF THE SUN-BEINGS, SMOTHERING THEM...
THE REMAINING ONE IS FLEEING--INTO SPACE! I'VE GOT TO OVERTAKE IT--WARN IT ABOUT SOMETHING...
POP!
8

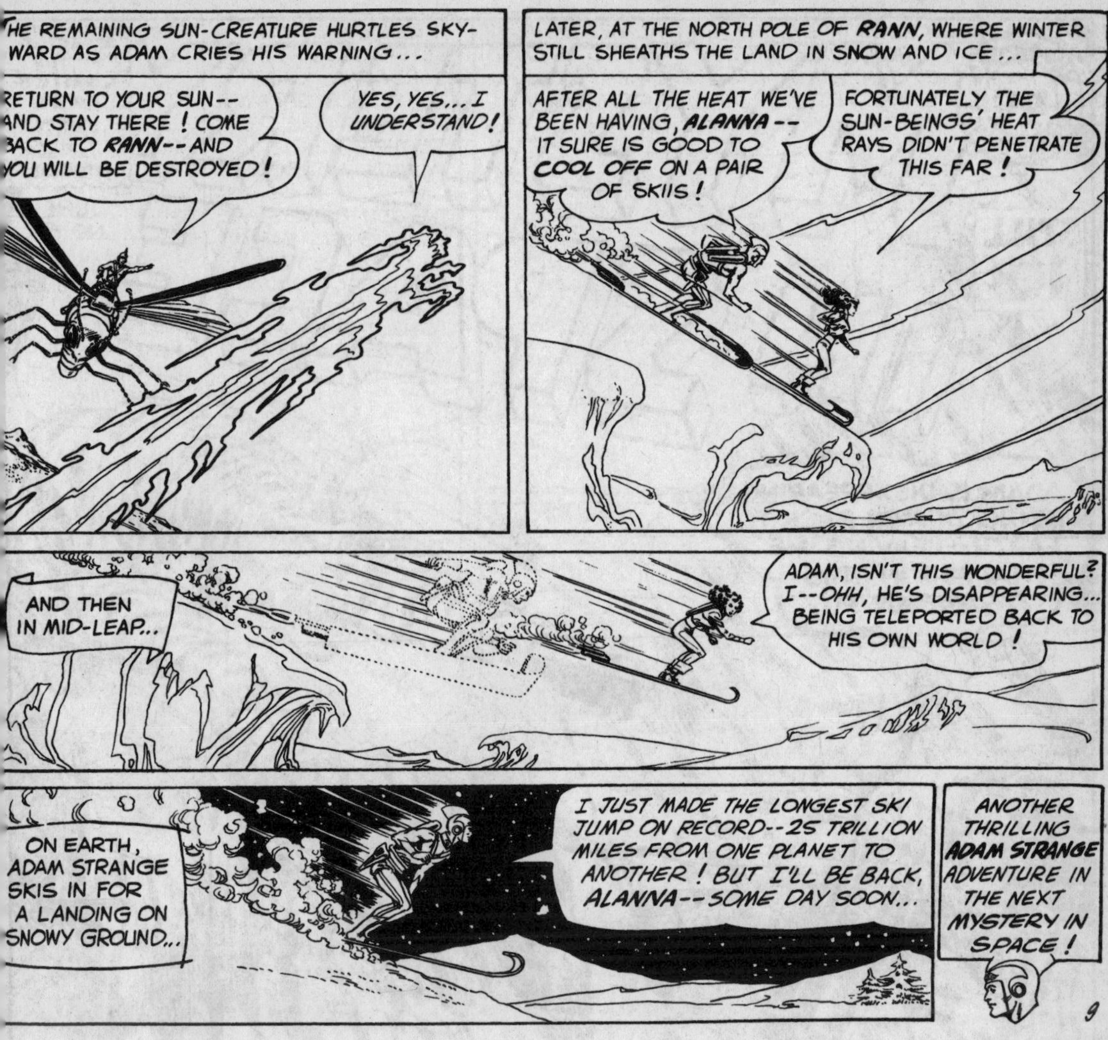
THE REMAINING SUN-CREATURE HURTLES SKYWARD AS ADAM CRIES HIS WARNING...
RETURN TO YOUR SUN--AND STAY THERE! COME BACK TO RANN--AND YOU WILL BE DESTROYED!
YES, YES... I UNDERSTAND!
LATER, AT THE NORTH POLE OF RANN, WHERE WINTER STILL SHEATHS THE LAND IN SNOW AND ICE...
AFTER ALL THE HEAT WE'VE BEEN HAVING, ALANNA--IT SURE IS GOOD TO COOL OFF ON A PAIR OF SKIIS!
FORTUNATELY THE SUN-BEINGS' HEAT RAYS DIDN'T PENETRATE THIS FAR!
AND THEN IN MID-LEAP...
ADAM, ISN'T THIS WONDERFUL? I--OHH, HE'S DISAPPEARING... BEING TELEPORTED BACK TO HIS OWN WORLD!
ON EARTH, ADAM STRANGE SKIS IN FOR A LANDING ON SNOWY GROUND...
I JUST MADE THE LONGEST SKI JUMP ON RECORD--25 TRILLION MILES FROM ONE PLANET TO ANOTHER! BUT I'LL BE BACK, ALANNA--SOME DAY SOON...
ANOTHER THRILLING ADAM STRANGE ADVENTURE IN THE NEXT MYSTERY IN SPACE!
9

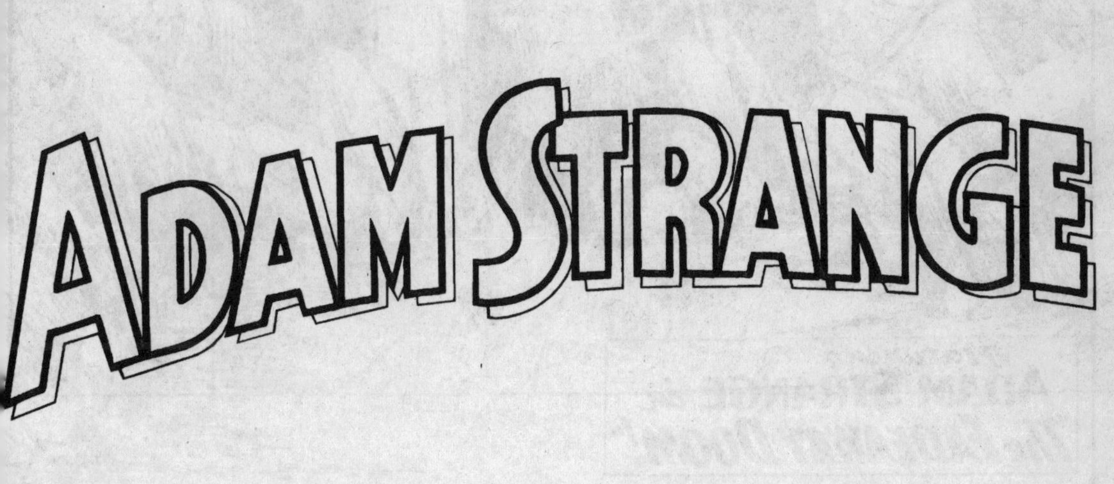
ADAM STRANGE

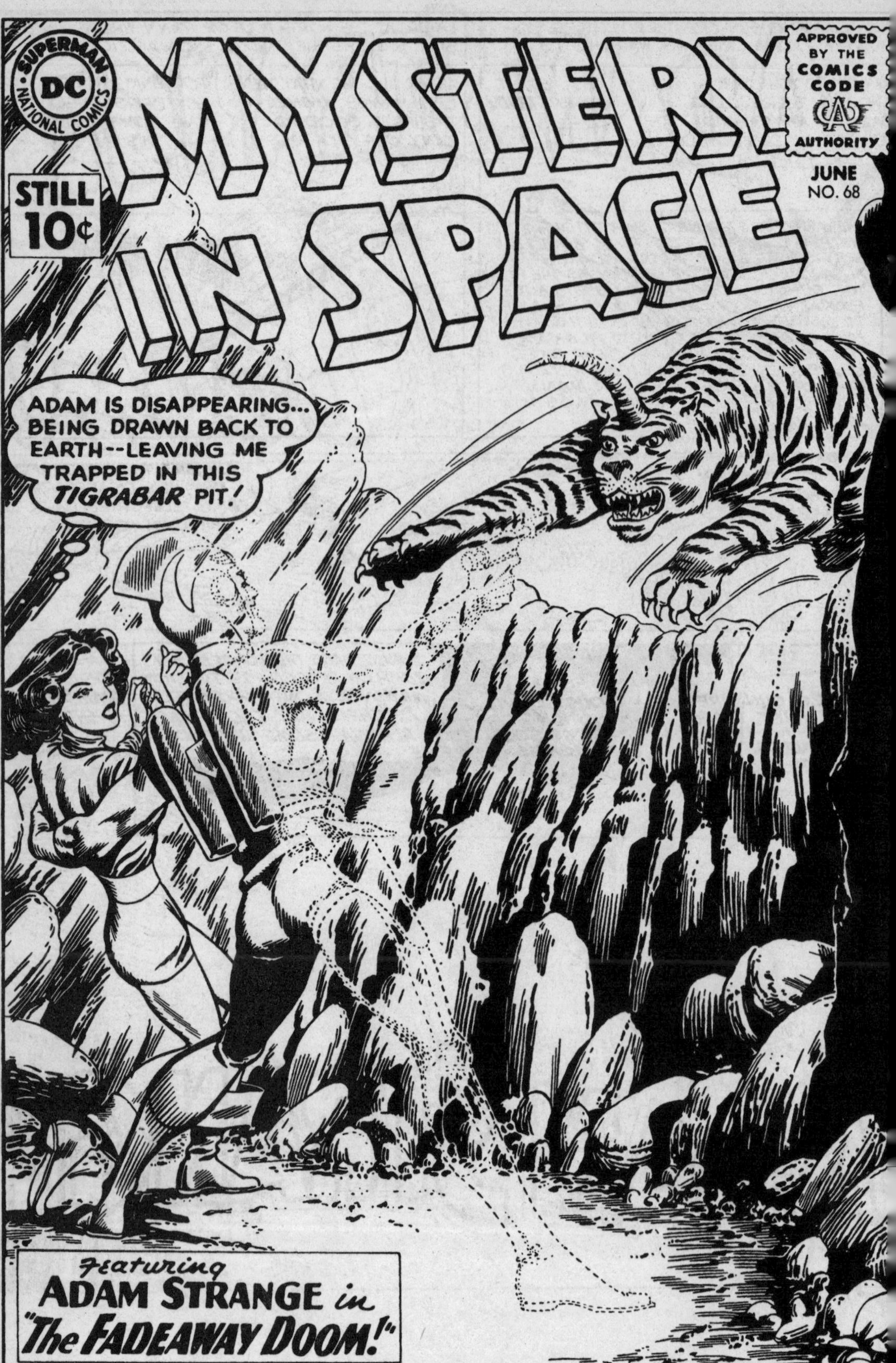
SUPERMAN DC NATIONAL COMICS
MYSTERY IN SPACE
APPROVED BY THE COMICS CODE AUTHORITY
STILL 10¢
JUNE NO. 68
ADAM IS DISAPPEARING... BEING DRAWN BACK TO EARTH--LEAVING ME TRAPPED IN THIS TIGRABAR PIT!
Featuring ADAM STRANGE in "The FADEAWAY DOOM!"

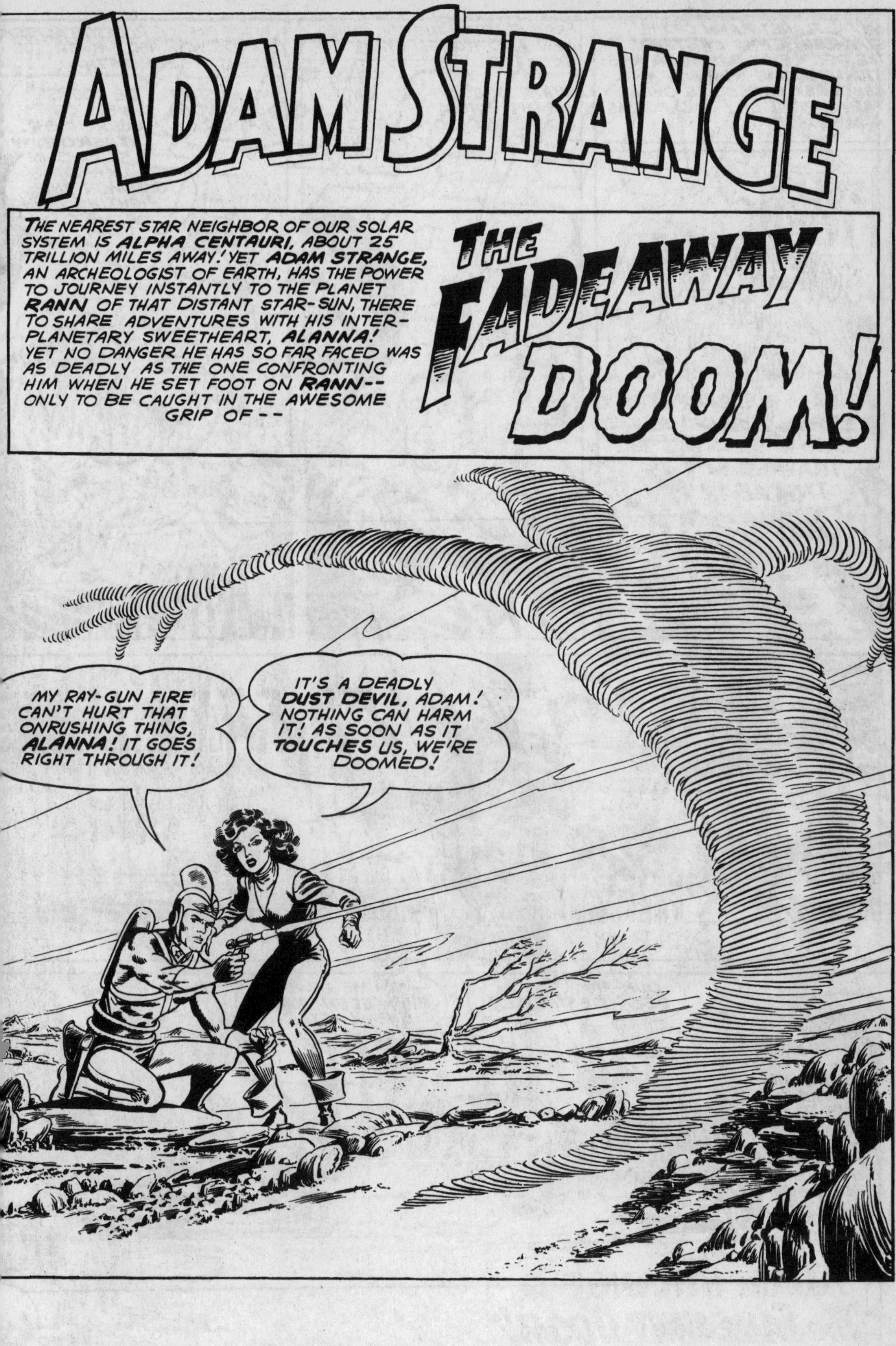
ADAM STRANGE
THE NEAREST STAR NEIGHBOR OF OUR SOLAR SYSTEM IS ALPHA CENTAURI, ABOUT 25 TRILLION MILES AWAY! YET ADAM STRANGE, AN ARCHEOLOGIST OF EARTH, HAS THE POWER TO JOURNEY INSTANTLY TO THE PLANET RANN OF THAT DISTANT STAR-SUN, THERE TO SHARE ADVENTURES WITH HIS INTER-PLANETARY SWEETHEART, ALANNA! YET NO DANGER HE HAS SO FAR FACED WAS AS DEADLY AS THE ONE CONFRONTING HIM WHEN HE SET FOOT ON RANN-- ONLY TO BE CAUGHT IN THE AWESOME GRIP OF --
THE FADEAWAY DOOM!
MY RAY-GUN FIRE CAN'T HURT THAT ONRUSHING THING, ALANNA! IT GOES RIGHT THROUGH IT!
IT'S A DEADLY DUST DEVIL, ADAM! NOTHING CAN HARM IT! AS SOON AS IT TOUCHES US, WE'RE DOOMED!

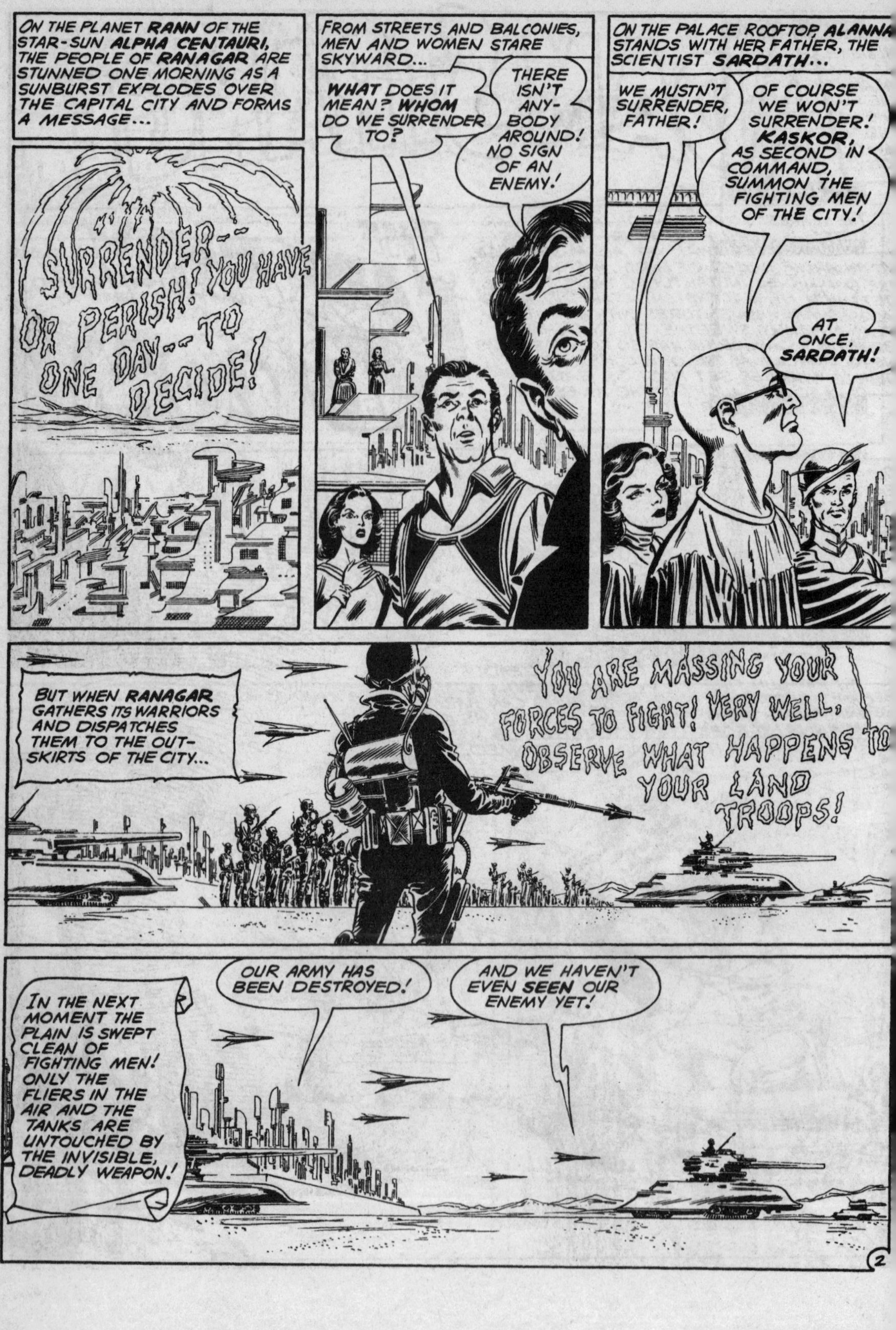
ON THE PLANET RANN OF THE STAR-SUN ALPHA CENTAURI, THE PEOPLE OF RANAGAR ARE STUNNED ONE MORNING AS A SUNBURST EXPLODES OVER THE CAPITAL CITY AND FORMS A MESSAGE...
"SURRENDER--OR PERISH! YOU HAVE ONE DAY--TO DECIDE!
FROM STREETS AND BALCONIES, MEN AND WOMEN STARE SKYWARD...
WHAT DOES IT MEAN? WHOM DO WE SURRENDER TO?
THERE ISN'T ANYBODY AROUND! NO SIGN OF AN ENEMY!
ON THE PALACE ROOFTOP, ALANNA STANDS WITH HER FATHER, THE SCIENTIST SARDATH...
WE MUSTN'T SURRENDER, FATHER!
OF COURSE WE WON'T SURRENDER! KASKOR, AS SECOND IN COMMAND, SUMMON THE FIGHTING MEN OF THE CITY!
AT ONCE, SARDATH!
BUT WHEN RANAGAR GATHERS ITS WARRIORS AND DISPATCHES THEM TO THE OUTSKIRTS OF THE CITY...
YOU ARE MASSING YOUR FORCES TO FIGHT! VERY WELL, OBSERVE WHAT HAPPENS TO YOUR LAND TROOPS!
IN THE NEXT MOMENT THE PLAIN IS SWEPT CLEAN OF FIGHTING MEN! ONLY THE FLIERS IN THE AIR AND THE TANKS ARE UNTOUCHED BY THE INVISIBLE, DEADLY WEAPON!
OUR ARMY HAS BEEN DESTROYED!
AND WE HAVEN'T EVEN SEEN OUR ENEMY YET!
2

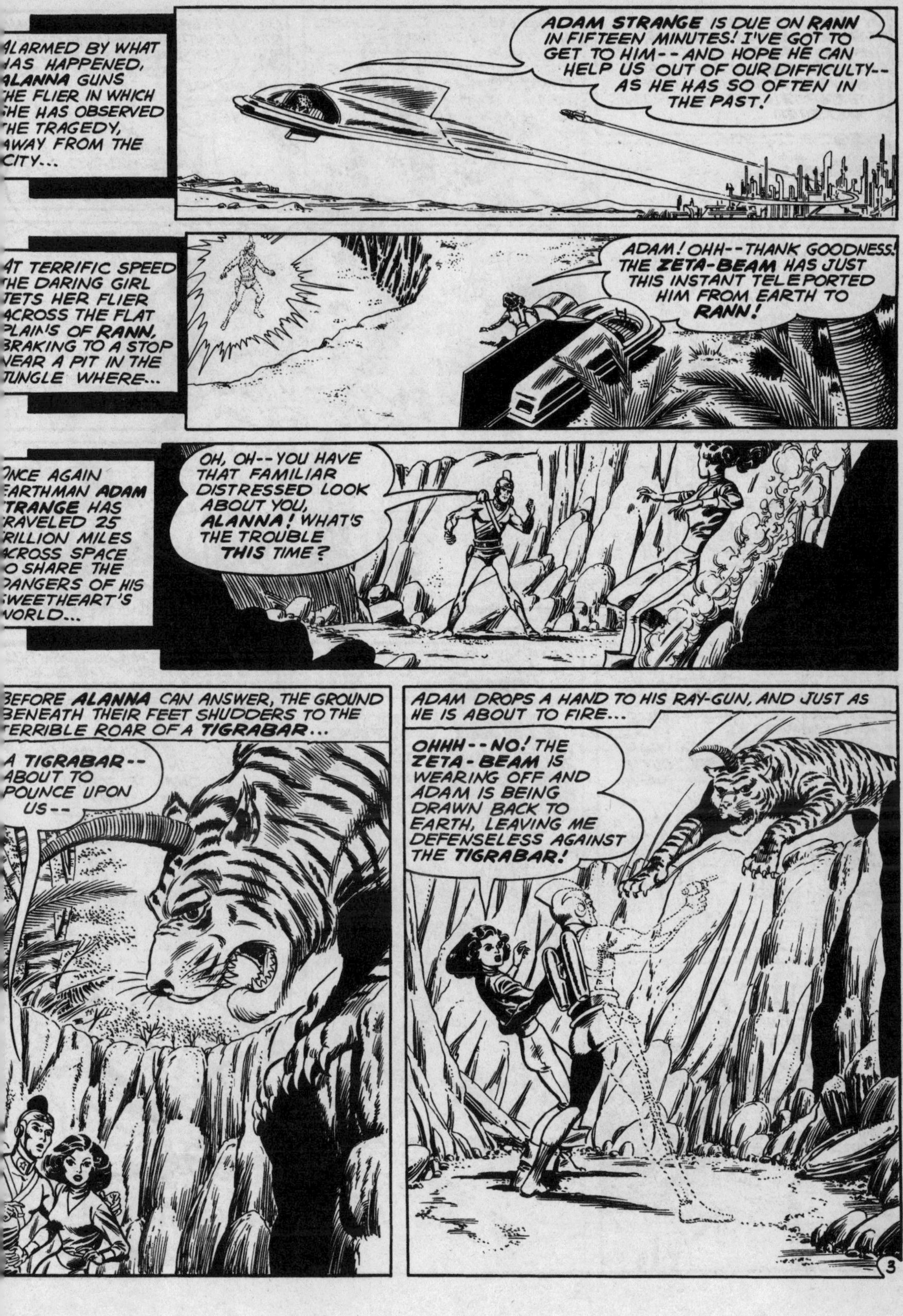
ALARMED BY WHAT HAS HAPPENED, ALANNA GUNS THE FLIER IN WHICH SHE HAS OBSERVED THE TRAGEDY, AWAY FROM THE CITY...
ADAM STRANGE IS DUE ON RANN IN FIFTEEN MINUTES! I'VE GOT TO GET TO HIM--AND HOPE HE CAN HELP US OUT OF OUR DIFFICULTY--AS HE HAS SO OFTEN IN THE PAST!
AT TERRIFIC SPEED THE DARING GIRL JETS HER FLIER ACROSS THE FLAT PLAINS OF RANN, BRAKING TO A STOP NEAR A PIT IN THE JUNGLE WHERE...
ADAM! OHH--THANK GOODNESS! THE ZETA-BEAM HAS JUST THIS INSTANT TELEPORTED HIM FROM EARTH TO RANN!
ONCE AGAIN EARTHMAN ADAM STRANGE HAS TRAVELED 25 TRILLION MILES ACROSS SPACE TO SHARE THE DANGERS OF HIS SWEETHEART'S WORLD...
OH, OH--YOU HAVE THAT FAMILIAR DISTRESSED LOOK ABOUT YOU, ALANNA! WHAT'S THE TROUBLE THIS TIME?
BEFORE ALANNA CAN ANSWER, THE GROUND BENEATH THEIR FEET SHUDDERS TO THE TERRIBLE ROAR OF A TIGRABAR...
A TIGRABAR--ABOUT TO POUNCE UPON US--
ADAM DROPS A HAND TO HIS RAY-GUN, AND JUST AS HE IS ABOUT TO FIRE...
OHHH--NO! THE ZETA-BEAM IS WEARING OFF AND ADAM IS BEING DRAWN BACK TO EARTH, LEAVING ME DEFENSELESS AGAINST THE TIGRABAR!
3

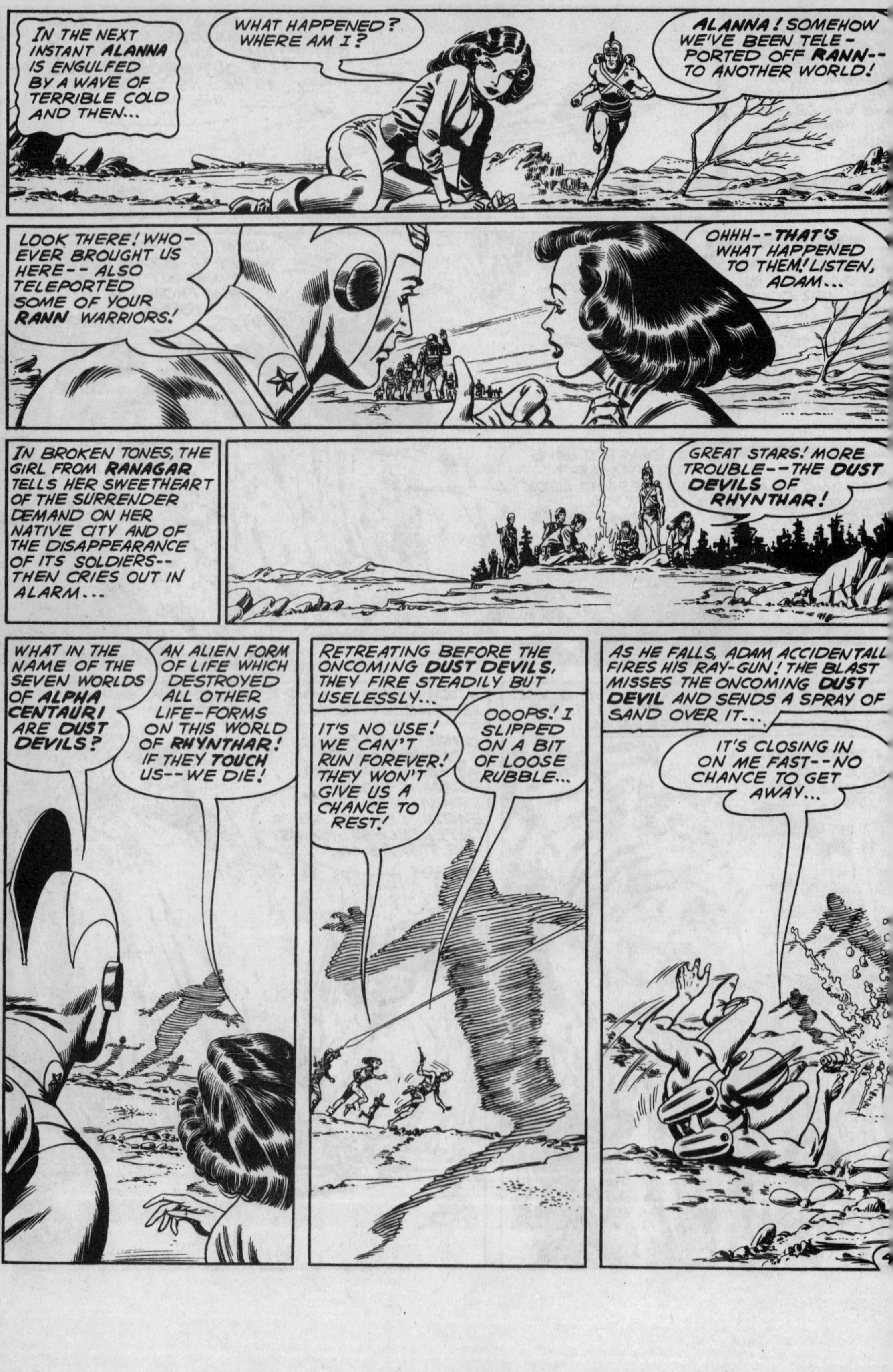
IN THE NEXT INSTANT ALANNA IS ENGULFED BY A WAVE OF TERRIBLE COLD AND THEN...
WHAT HAPPENED? WHERE AM I?
ALANNA! SOMEHOW WE'VE BEEN TELE-PORTED OFF RANN--TO ANOTHER WORLD!
LOOK THERE! WHO-EVER BROUGHT US HERE-- ALSO TELEPORTED SOME OF YOUR RANN WARRIORS!
OHHH--THAT'S WHAT HAPPENED TO THEM! LISTEN, ADAM...
IN BROKEN TONES, THE GIRL FROM RANAGAR TELLS HER SWEETHEART OF THE SURRENDER DEMAND ON HER NATIVE CITY AND OF THE DISAPPEARANCE OF ITS SOLDIERS--THEN CRIES OUT IN ALARM...
GREAT STARS! MORE TROUBLE--THE DUST DEVILS OF RHYNTHAR!
WHAT IN THE NAME OF THE SEVEN WORLDS OF ALPHA CENTAURI ARE DUST DEVILS?
AN ALIEN FORM OF LIFE WHICH DESTROYED ALL OTHER LIFE-FORMS ON THIS WORLD OF RHYNTHAR! IF THEY TOUCH US--WE DIE!
RETREATING BEFORE THE ONCOMING DUST DEVILS, THEY FIRE STEADILY BUT USELESSLY...
IT'S NO USE! WE CAN'T RUN FOREVER! THEY WON'T GIVE US A CHANCE TO REST!
OOOPS! I SLIPPED ON A BIT OF LOOSE RUBBLE...
AS HE FALLS, ADAM ACCIDENTALL FIRES HIS RAY-GUN! THE BLAST MISSES THE ONCOMING DUST DEVIL AND SENDS A SPRAY OF SAND OVER IT...
IT'S CLOSING IN ON ME FAST--NO CHANCE TO GET AWAY...

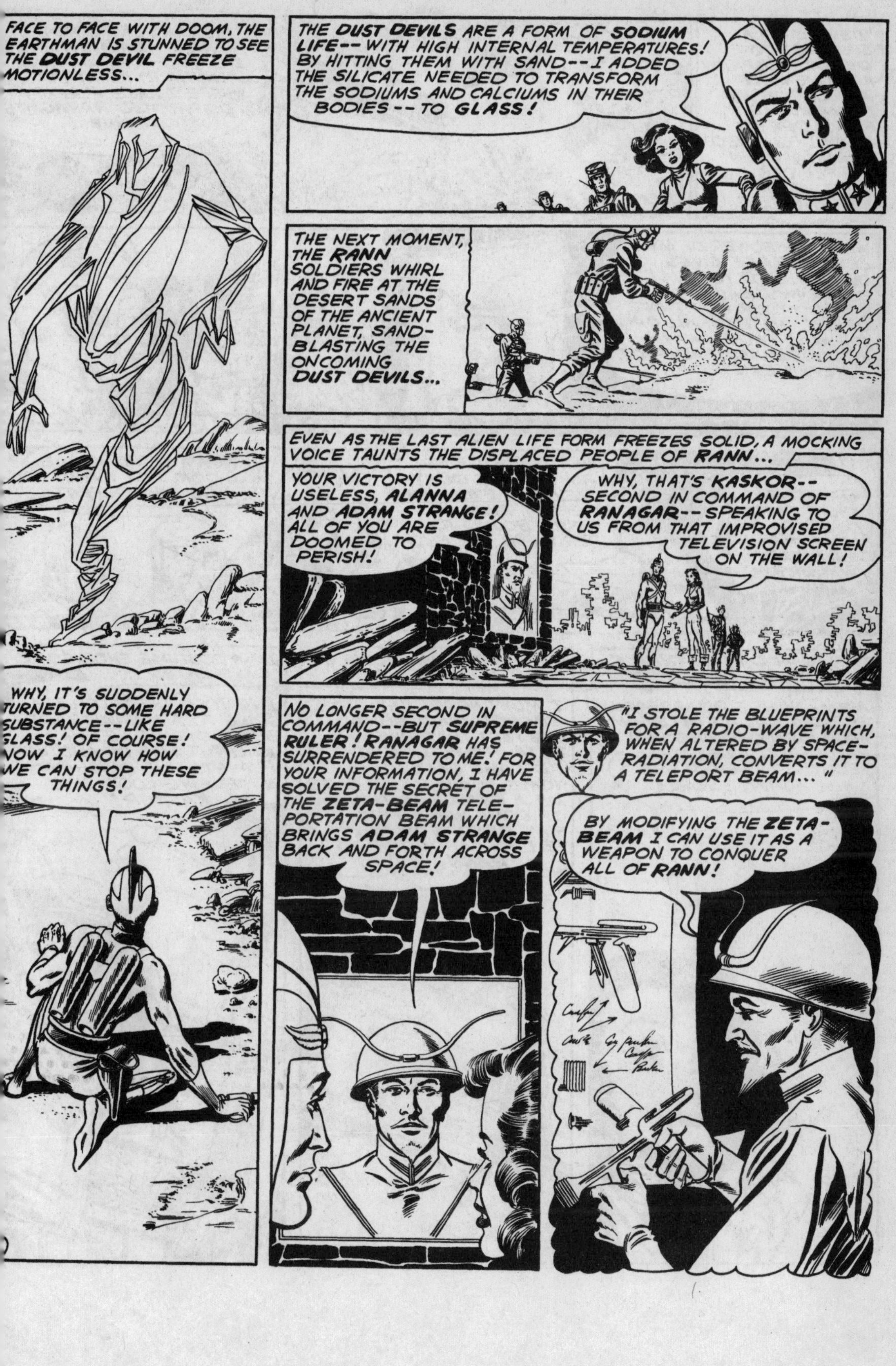
FACE TO FACE WITH DOOM, THE EARTHMAN IS STUNNED TO SEE THE DUST DEVIL FREEZE MOTIONLESS...
WHY, IT'S SUDDENLY TURNED TO SOME HARD SUBSTANCE--LIKE GLASS! OF COURSE! NOW I KNOW HOW WE CAN STOP THESE THINGS!
THE DUST DEVILS ARE A FORM OF SODIUM LIFE-- WITH HIGH INTERNAL TEMPERATURES! BY HITTING THEM WITH SAND--I ADDED THE SILICATE NEEDED TO TRANSFORM THE SODIUMS AND CALCIUMS IN THEIR BODIES--TO GLASS!
THE NEXT MOMENT, THE RANN SOLDIERS WHIRL AND FIRE AT THE DESERT SANDS OF THE ANCIENT PLANET, SAND-BLASTING THE ONCOMING DUST DEVILS...
EVEN AS THE LAST ALIEN LIFE FORM FREEZES SOLID, A MOCKING VOICE TAUNTS THE DISPLACED PEOPLE OF RANN...
YOUR VICTORY IS USELESS, ALANNA AND ADAM STRANGE! ALL OF YOU ARE DOOMED TO PERISH!
WHY, THAT'S KASKOR-- SECOND IN COMMAND OF RANAGAR-- SPEAKING TO US FROM THAT IMPROVISED TELEVISION SCREEN ON THE WALL!
NO LONGER SECOND IN COMMAND--BUT SUPREME RULER! RANAGAR HAS SURRENDERED TO ME! FOR YOUR INFORMATION, I HAVE SOLVED THE SECRET OF THE ZETA-BEAM TELE-PORTATION BEAM WHICH BRINGS ADAM STRANGE BACK AND FORTH ACROSS SPACE!
"I STOLE THE BLUEPRINTS FOR A RADIO-WAVE WHICH, WHEN ALTERED BY SPACE-RADIATION, CONVERTS IT TO A TELEPORT BEAM..."
BY MODIFYING THE ZETA-BEAM I CAN USE IT AS A WEAPON TO CONQUER ALL OF RANN!

"I EMPLOYED A SUNBURST TO DISTRACT SUSPICION FROM ME WHILE ANNOUNCING MY DEMAND FOR SURRENDER! LATER I FOLLOWED ALANNA WHEN SHE FLEW TO MEET ADAM STRANGE..."

THE ONLY ONE I REALLY FEAR IS ADAM STRANGE! I'LL TELEPORT HIM AND ALANNA TO RHYNTHAR-- WHERE I HAVE ALREADY DISPATCHED RANAGAR'S SOLDIERS!

WHEN THE POWER OF MY ZETA-CHARGE GIVES OUT, NONE OF YOU WILL BE DRAWN BACK TO RANN--YOUR POINT OF ORIGIN! INSTEAD, ALL OF YOU WILL FADE AWAY-- INTO OBLIVION! AS IF YOU NEVER EXISTED!

DAZED BY THEIR FATE, DESPAIR GRIPS THE RANAGAR WARRIORS...

WHAT'S THE USE OF FIGHTING THE DUST DEVILS? EVEN IF WE DEFEAT THEM ALL-- WE'RE BOUND TO PERISH IN THE END!

ADAM -- THIS IS ONE DOOM NOT EVEN YOU CAN DEFEAT...

THEN TO ADD TO ALANNA'S DEJECTION...

ADAM! OH, HE'S DISAPPEARING! HIS ORIGINAL ZETA-BEAM HAS WORN OFF AND HE'S RETURNING TO EARTH! ⸮SOB!⸮ I'LL NEVER SEE HIM AGAIN! ⸮SOB!⸮

ON EARTH, ADAM VOWS A FIGHT TO THE FINISH...

I MUST HOPE THAT KASKOR OVERLOOKED THE FACT THAT WHEN MY ZETA-POWER FADED, I'D COME BACK TO MY HOME PLANET! THIS GIVES ME A CHANCE TO THINK OF SOME WAY TO STOP HIM, BEFORE MY NEXT TELEPORTATION TRIP TO RANN...

IN A COSTUME SHOP SOME DAYS LATER...

I'VE TOLD THE TAILOR I'M GOING TO A MASQUERADE-- BUT I DIDN'T LET HIM KNOW IT WAS ON ANOTHER PLANET! I'VE DISGUISED MYSELF TO LOOK LIKE KASKOR!

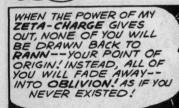

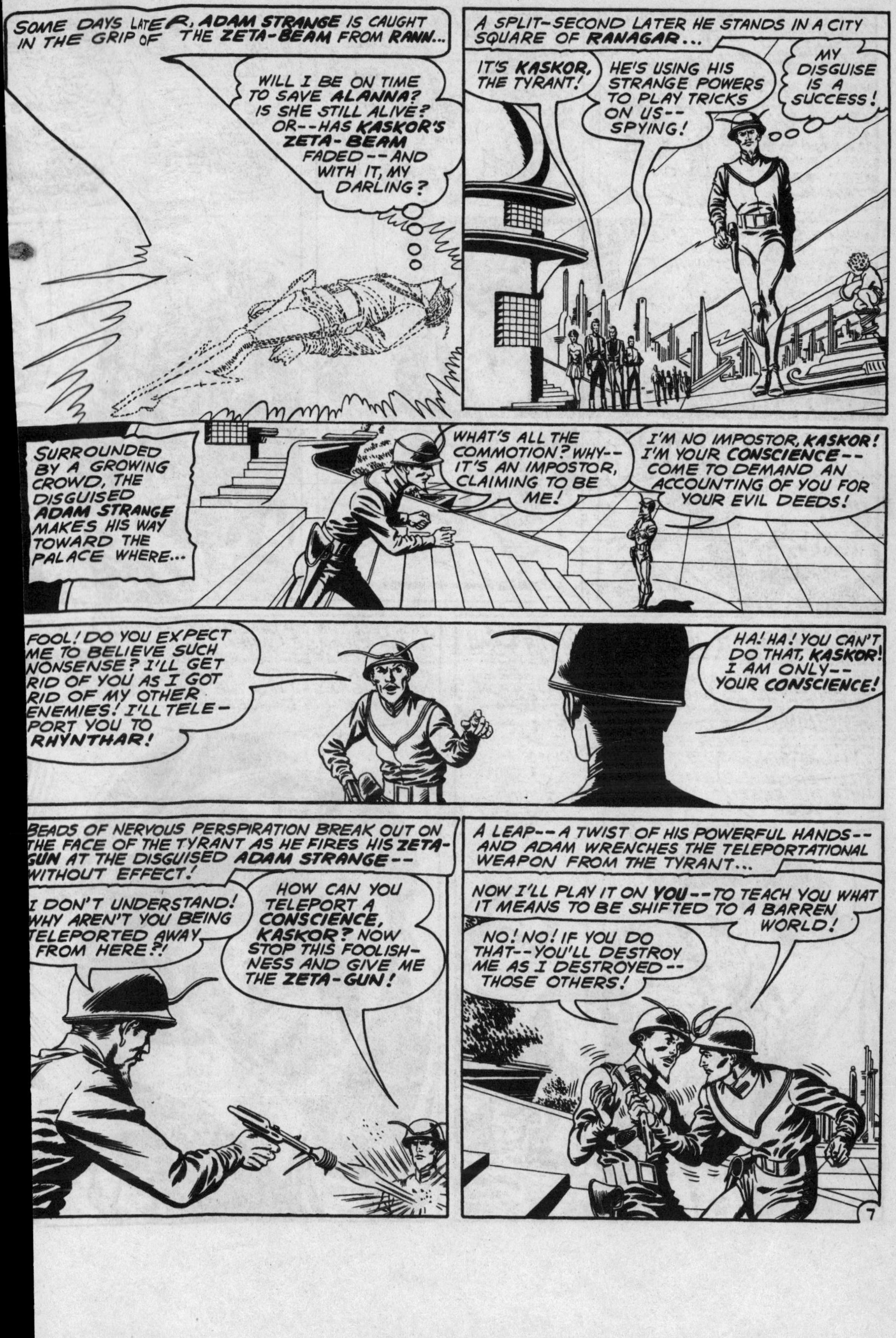
SOME DAYS LATER, ADAM STRANGE IS CAUGHT IN THE GRIP OF THE ZETA-BEAM FROM RANN...
WILL I BE ON TIME TO SAVE ALANNA? IS SHE STILL ALIVE? OR--HAS KASKOR'S ZETA-BEAM FADED--AND WITH IT, MY DARLING?
A SPLIT-SECOND LATER HE STANDS IN A CITY SQUARE OF RANAGAR...
IT'S KASKOR, THE TYRANT!
HE'S USING HIS STRANGE POWERS TO PLAY TRICKS ON US--SPYING!
MY DISGUISE IS A SUCCESS!
SURROUNDED BY A GROWING CROWD, THE DISGUISED ADAM STRANGE MAKES HIS WAY TOWARD THE PALACE WHERE...
WHAT'S ALL THE COMMOTION? WHY--IT'S AN IMPOSTOR, CLAIMING TO BE ME!
I'M NO IMPOSTOR, KASKOR! I'M YOUR CONSCIENCE--COME TO DEMAND AN ACCOUNTING OF YOU FOR YOUR EVIL DEEDS!
FOOL! DO YOU EXPECT ME TO BELIEVE SUCH NONSENSE? I'LL GET RID OF YOU AS I GOT RID OF MY OTHER ENEMIES! I'LL TELE-PORT YOU TO RHYNTHAR!
HA! HA! YOU CAN'T DO THAT, KASKOR! I AM ONLY--YOUR CONSCIENCE!
BEADS OF NERVOUS PERSPIRATION BREAK OUT ON THE FACE OF THE TYRANT AS HE FIRES HIS ZETA-GUN AT THE DISGUISED ADAM STRANGE--WITHOUT EFFECT!
I DON'T UNDERSTAND! WHY AREN'T YOU BEING TELEPORTED AWAY FROM HERE?!
HOW CAN YOU TELEPORT A CONSCIENCE, KASKOR? NOW STOP THIS FOOLISH-NESS AND GIVE ME THE ZETA-GUN!
A LEAP--A TWIST OF HIS POWERFUL HANDS--AND ADAM WRENCHES THE TELEPORTATIONAL WEAPON FROM THE TYRANT...
NOW I'LL PLAY IT ON YOU--TO TEACH YOU WHAT IT MEANS TO BE SHIFTED TO A BARREN WORLD!
NO! NO! IF YOU DO THAT--YOU'LL DESTROY ME AS I DESTROYED--THOSE OTHERS!
7

AS *KASKOR* FADES FROM VIEW, ADAM TURNS THE *ZETA-GUN* ON HIMSELF...

MY PLAN HAS WORKED SO FAR! BUT-- I MAY STILL BE TOO LATE TO SAVE *ALANNA!* IS SHE STILL ALIVE OR HAS SHE FADED TO-- OBLIVION?

THE NEXT INSTANT, HE STANDS ON THE DEAD WORLD OF *RHYNTHAR*...

TWO *KASKORS!* BUT HOW CAN THIS BE?

ALANNA, DON'T YOU KNOW ME? NO, YOU WOULDN'T SINCE I'M MADE UP TO LOOK LIKE OUR EVIL FRIEND...

REMOVING HIS MAKE-UP, ADAM FOLDS *ALANNA* IN HIS ARMS OUT EVEN AS *KASKOR* CRIES IN TERROR...

I WAS SO WORRIED! I THOUGHT YOU MIGHT HAVE DISAPPEARED-- FOREVER!

QUICK! YOU'VE GOT TO SAVE US FROM THE FADEAWAY DOOM

WHEN THE *ZETA-BEAM* CHARGE WEARS OFF, WE'LL ALL DISAPPEAR-- IF YOU DON'T DO SOMETHING ABOUT IT! CAN'T YOU UNDERSTAND? *I'LL* PERISH WITH THE REST OF YOU!

I THOUGHT YOU'D CRACK IF I PUT YOU IN THE SAME BOAT WITH THE REST OF US, *KASKOR!* IS THERE ANY COUNTER-WEAPON TO YOUR *ZETA-BEAM GUN?*

YES, YES! THE *ZETA-GUN* IS SET ONLY AT *HALF CHARGE!* WHEN THE EFFECT OF SUCH A CHARGE WEARS OFF, THE PERSON HAVING RECEIVED IT DISAPPEARS INTO NOTHINGNESS! IT'S THE *HALF CHARGE* WHICH IS DANGEROUS!

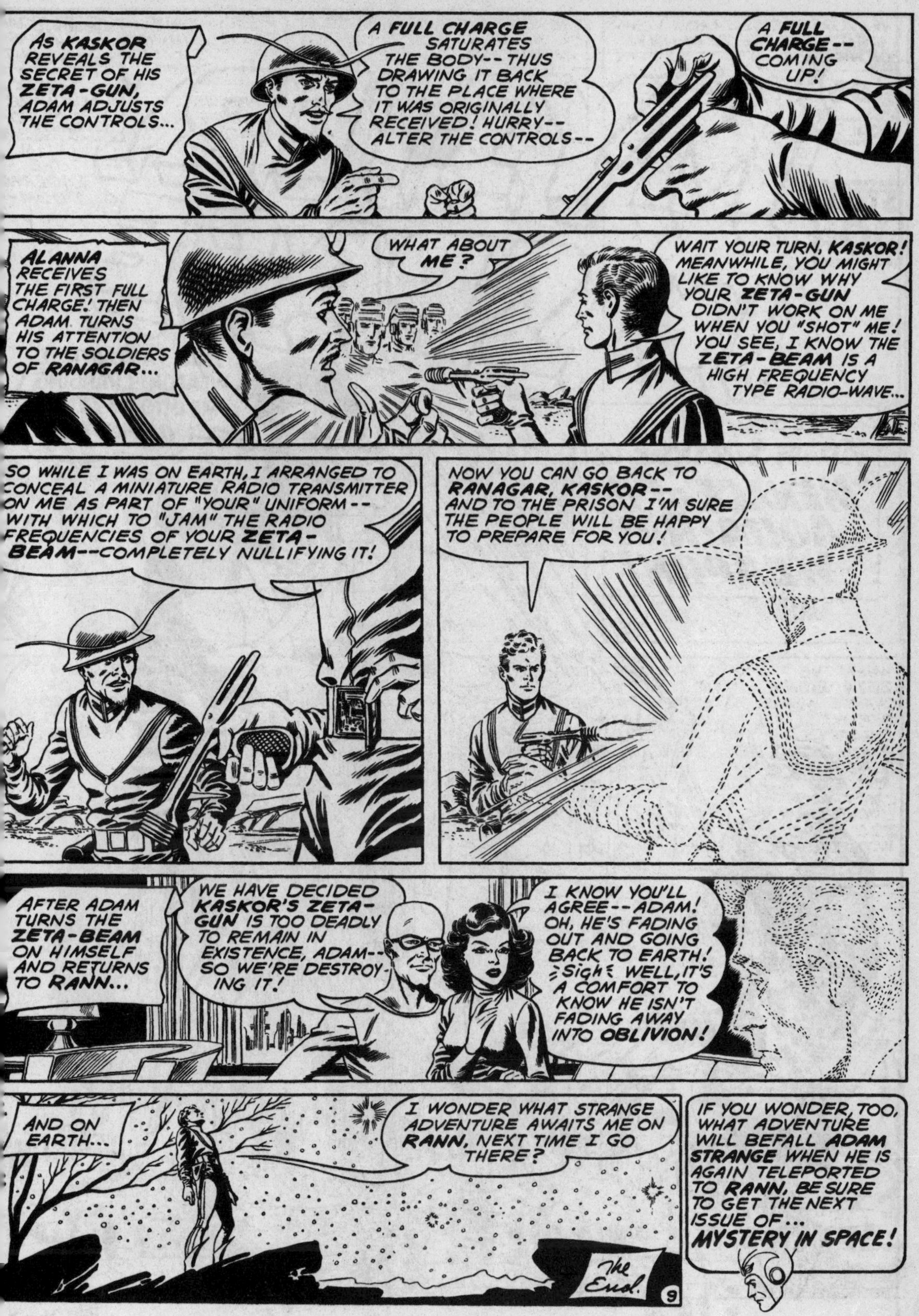
AS KASKOR REVEALS THE SECRET OF HIS ZETA-GUN, ADAM ADJUSTS THE CONTROLS...
A FULL CHARGE SATURATES THE BODY--THUS DRAWING IT BACK TO THE PLACE WHERE IT WAS ORIGINALLY RECEIVED! HURRY--ALTER THE CONTROLS--
A FULL CHARGE--COMING UP!
ALANNA RECEIVES THE FIRST FULL CHARGE! THEN ADAM TURNS HIS ATTENTION TO THE SOLDIERS OF RANAGAR...
WHAT ABOUT ME?
WAIT YOUR TURN, KASKOR! MEANWHILE, YOU MIGHT LIKE TO KNOW WHY YOUR ZETA-GUN DIDN'T WORK ON ME WHEN YOU "SHOT" ME! YOU SEE, I KNOW THE ZETA-BEAM IS A HIGH FREQUENCY TYPE RADIO-WAVE...
SO WHILE I WAS ON EARTH, I ARRANGED TO CONCEAL A MINIATURE RADIO TRANSMITTER ON ME AS PART OF "YOUR" UNIFORM--WITH WHICH TO "JAM" THE RADIO FREQUENCIES OF YOUR ZETA-BEAM--COMPLETELY NULLIFYING IT!
NOW YOU CAN GO BACK TO RANAGAR, KASKOR--AND TO THE PRISON I'M SURE THE PEOPLE WILL BE HAPPY TO PREPARE FOR YOU!
AFTER ADAM TURNS THE ZETA-BEAM ON HIMSELF AND RETURNS TO RANN...
WE HAVE DECIDED KASKOR'S ZETA-GUN IS TOO DEADLY TO REMAIN IN EXISTENCE, ADAM--SO WE'RE DESTROYING IT!
I KNOW YOU'LL AGREE--ADAM! OH, HE'S FADING OUT AND GOING BACK TO EARTH! Sigh WELL, IT'S A COMFORT TO KNOW HE ISN'T FADING AWAY INTO OBLIVION!
AND ON EARTH...
I WONDER WHAT STRANGE ADVENTURE AWAITS ME ON RANN, NEXT TIME I GO THERE?
The End.
9
IF YOU WONDER, TOO, WHAT ADVENTURE WILL BEFALL ADAM STRANGE WHEN HE IS AGAIN TELEPORTED TO RANN, BE SURE TO GET THE NEXT ISSUE OF... MYSTERY IN SPACE!

SUPERMAN
DC
NATIONAL COMICS
AUG.
NO. 69
APPROVED BY THE COMICS CODE AUTHORITY
MYSTERY IN SPACE
STILL 10¢
Featuring ADAM STRANGE in "MENACE of the AQUA-RAY WEAPON!"
THAT FANTASTIC WEAPON--CHANGING ME INTO A PUDDLE OF WATER!

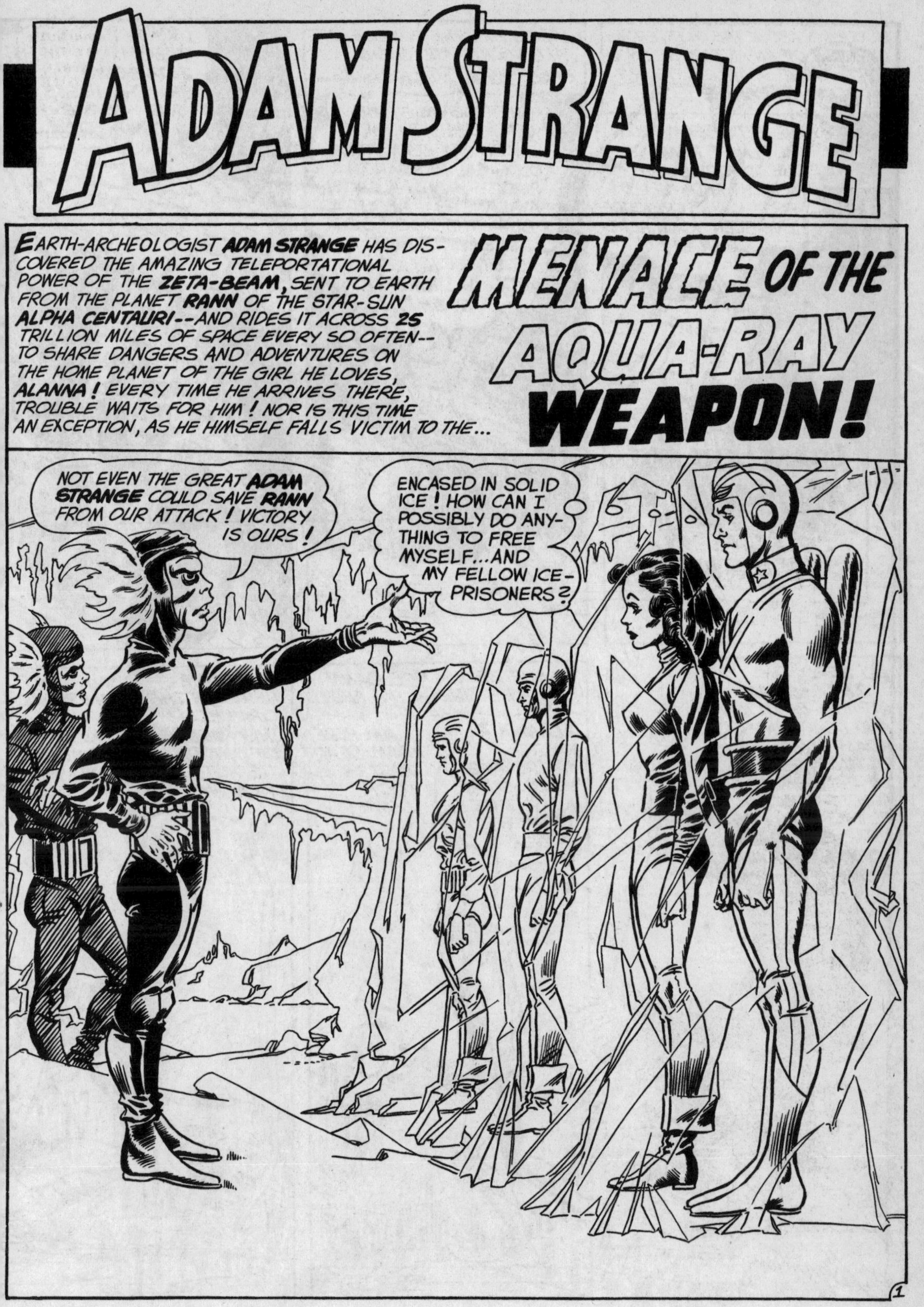
ADAM STRANGE
EARTH-ARCHEOLOGIST ADAM STRANGE HAS DISCOVERED THE AMAZING TELEPORTATIONAL POWER OF THE ZETA-BEAM, SENT TO EARTH FROM THE PLANET RANN OF THE STAR-SUN ALPHA CENTAURI--AND RIDES IT ACROSS 25 TRILLION MILES OF SPACE EVERY SO OFTEN--TO SHARE DANGERS AND ADVENTURES ON THE HOME PLANET OF THE GIRL HE LOVES, ALANNA! EVERY TIME HE ARRIVES THERE, TROUBLE WAITS FOR HIM! NOR IS THIS TIME AN EXCEPTION, AS HE HIMSELF FALLS VICTIM TO THE...
MENACE OF THE AQUA-RAY WEAPON!
NOT EVEN THE GREAT ADAM STRANGE COULD SAVE RANN FROM OUR ATTACK! VICTORY IS OURS!
ENCASED IN SOLID ICE! HOW CAN I POSSIBLY DO ANYTHING TO FREE MYSELF...AND MY FELLOW ICE-PRISONERS?
1

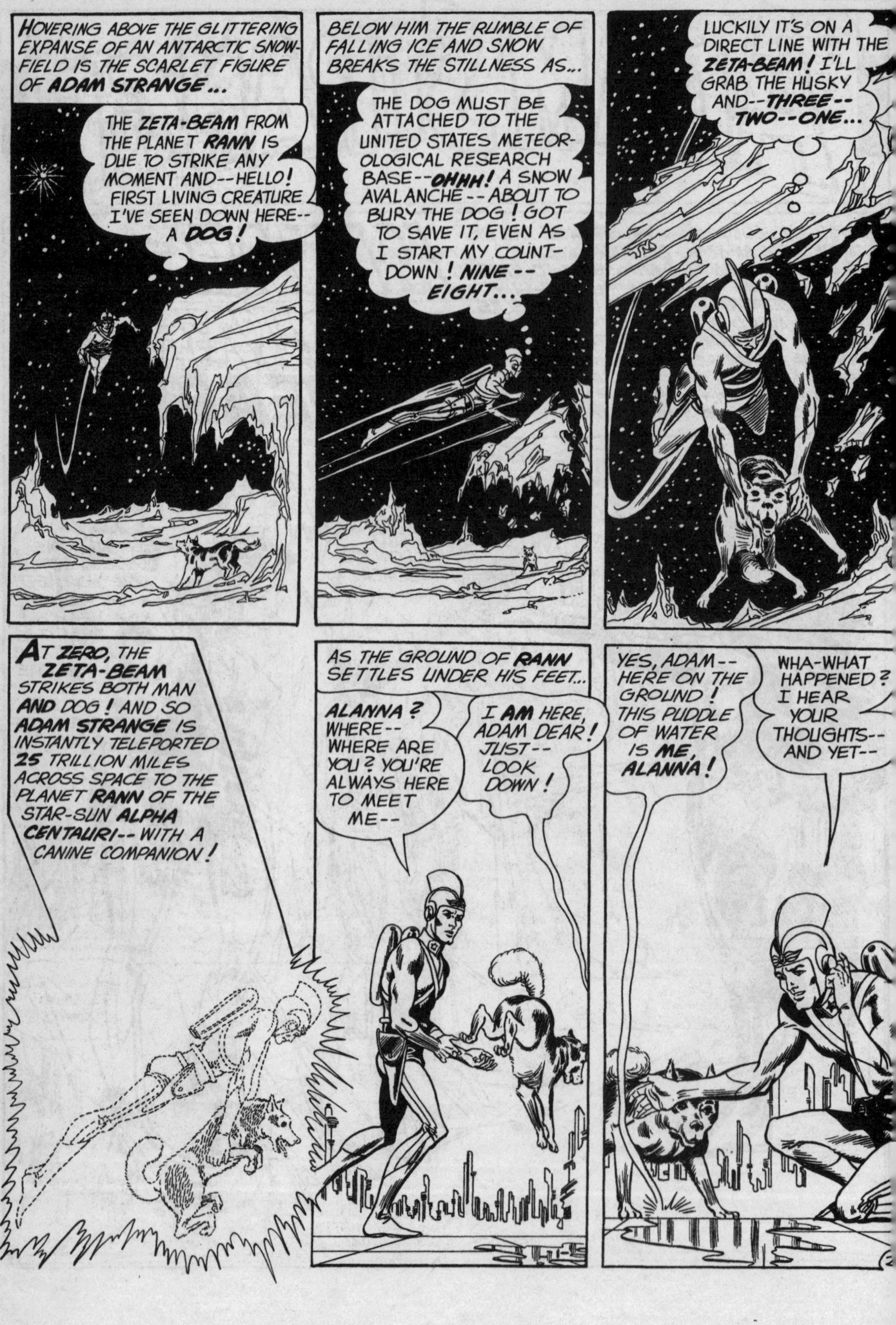
HOVERING ABOVE THE GLITTERING EXPANSE OF AN ANTARCTIC SNOW-FIELD IS THE SCARLET FIGURE OF ADAM STRANGE...
THE ZETA-BEAM FROM THE PLANET RANN IS DUE TO STRIKE ANY MOMENT AND--HELLO! FIRST LIVING CREATURE I'VE SEEN DOWN HERE--A DOG!
BELOW HIM THE RUMBLE OF FALLING ICE AND SNOW BREAKS THE STILLNESS AS...
THE DOG MUST BE ATTACHED TO THE UNITED STATES METEOROLOGICAL RESEARCH BASE--OHHH! A SNOW AVALANCHE--ABOUT TO BURY THE DOG! GOT TO SAVE IT, EVEN AS I START MY COUNT-DOWN! NINE--EIGHT...
LUCKILY IT'S ON A DIRECT LINE WITH THE ZETA-BEAM! I'LL GRAB THE HUSKY AND--THREE--TWO--ONE...
AT ZERO, THE ZETA-BEAM STRIKES BOTH MAN AND DOG! AND SO ADAM STRANGE IS INSTANTLY TELEPORTED 25 TRILLION MILES ACROSS SPACE TO THE PLANET RANN OF THE STAR-SUN ALPHA CENTAURI--WITH A CANINE COMPANION!
AS THE GROUND OF RANN SETTLES UNDER HIS FEET...
ALANNA? WHERE--WHERE ARE YOU? YOU'RE ALWAYS HERE TO MEET ME--
I AM HERE, ADAM DEAR! JUST--LOOK DOWN!
YES, ADAM--HERE ON THE GROUND! THIS PUDDLE OF WATER IS ME, ALANNA!
WHA-WHAT HAPPENED? I HEAR YOUR THOUGHTS--AND YET--

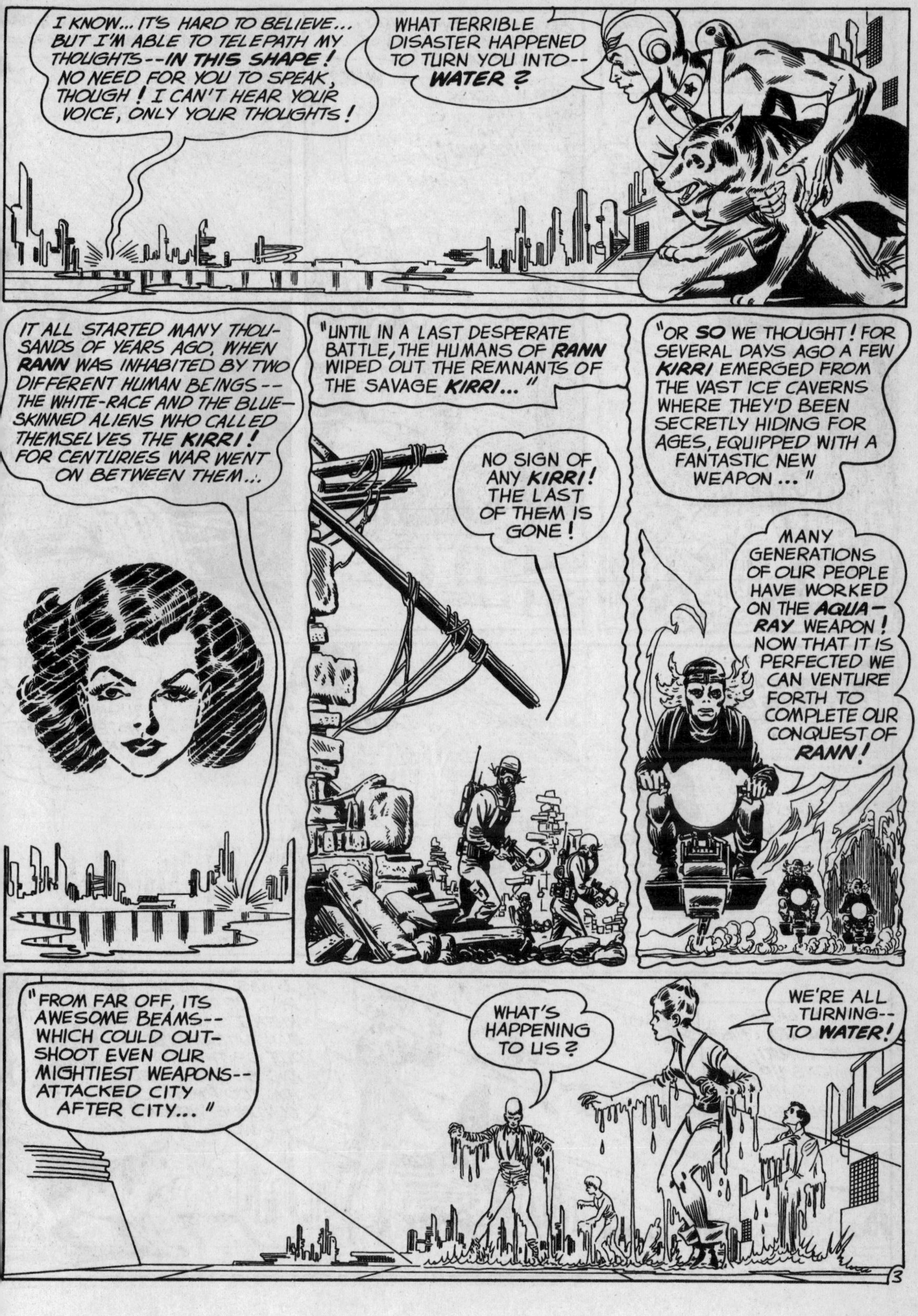
I KNOW... IT'S HARD TO BELIEVE... BUT I'M ABLE TO TELEPATH MY THOUGHTS--IN THIS SHAPE! NO NEED FOR YOU TO SPEAK, THOUGH! I CAN'T HEAR YOUR VOICE, ONLY YOUR THOUGHTS!
WHAT TERRIBLE DISASTER HAPPENED TO TURN YOU INTO--WATER?
IT ALL STARTED MANY THOUSANDS OF YEARS AGO, WHEN RANN WAS INHABITED BY TWO DIFFERENT HUMAN BEINGS--THE WHITE-RACE AND THE BLUE-SKINNED ALIENS WHO CALLED THEMSELVES THE KIRRI! FOR CENTURIES WAR WENT ON BETWEEN THEM...
"UNTIL IN A LAST DESPERATE BATTLE, THE HUMANS OF RANN WIPED OUT THE REMNANTS OF THE SAVAGE KIRRI..."
NO SIGN OF ANY KIRRI! THE LAST OF THEM IS GONE!
"OR SO WE THOUGHT! FOR SEVERAL DAYS AGO A FEW KIRRI EMERGED FROM THE VAST ICE CAVERNS WHERE THEY'D BEEN SECRETLY HIDING FOR AGES, EQUIPPED WITH A FANTASTIC NEW WEAPON..."
MANY GENERATIONS OF OUR PEOPLE HAVE WORKED ON THE AQUA-RAY WEAPON! NOW THAT IT IS PERFECTED WE CAN VENTURE FORTH TO COMPLETE OUR CONQUEST OF RANN!
"FROM FAR OFF, ITS AWESOME BEAMS--WHICH COULD OUT-SHOOT EVEN OUR MIGHTIEST WEAPONS--ATTACKED CITY AFTER CITY..."
WHAT'S HAPPENING TO US?
WE'RE ALL TURNING--TO WATER!
3

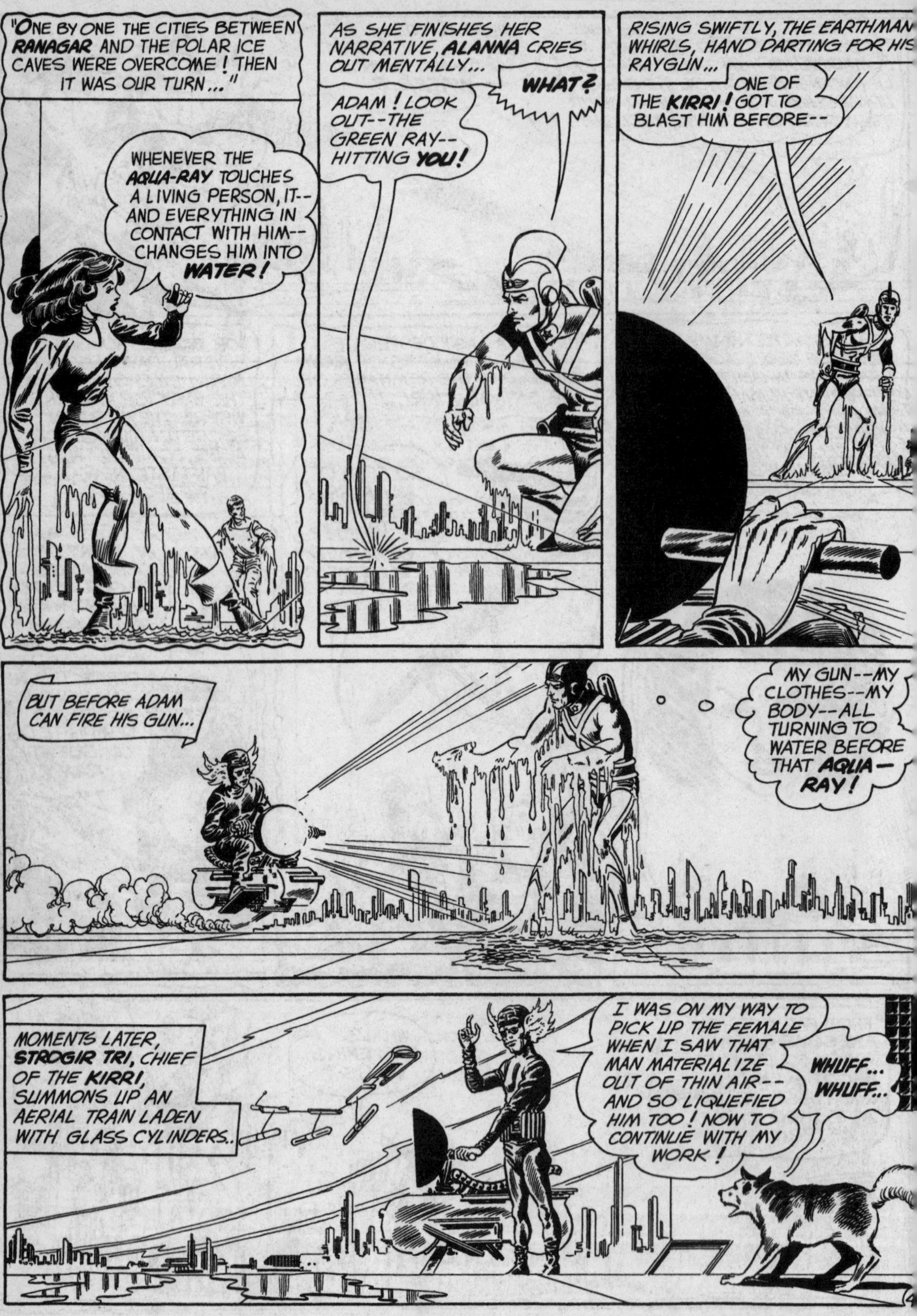
"ONE BY ONE THE CITIES BETWEEN RANAGAR AND THE POLAR ICE CAVES WERE OVERCOME! THEN IT WAS OUR TURN..."
WHENEVER THE AQUA-RAY TOUCHES A LIVING PERSON, IT--AND EVERYTHING IN CONTACT WITH HIM--CHANGES HIM INTO WATER!
AS SHE FINISHES HER NARRATIVE, ALANNA CRIES OUT MENTALLY...
ADAM! LOOK OUT--THE GREEN RAY--HITTING YOU!
WHAT?
RISING SWIFTLY, THE EARTHMAN WHIRLS, HAND DARTING FOR HIS RAYGUN...
ONE OF THE KIRRI! GOT TO BLAST HIM BEFORE--
BUT BEFORE ADAM CAN FIRE HIS GUN...
MY GUN--MY CLOTHES--MY BODY--ALL TURNING TO WATER BEFORE THAT AQUA-RAY!
MOMENTS LATER, STROGIR TRI, CHIEF OF THE KIRRI, SUMMONS UP AN AERIAL TRAIN LADEN WITH GLASS CYLINDERS..
I WAS ON MY WAY TO PICK UP THE FEMALE WHEN I SAW THAT MAN MATERIALIZE OUT OF THIN AIR--AND SO LIQUEFIED HIM TOO! NOW TO CONTINUE WITH MY WORK!
WHUFF... WHUFF...

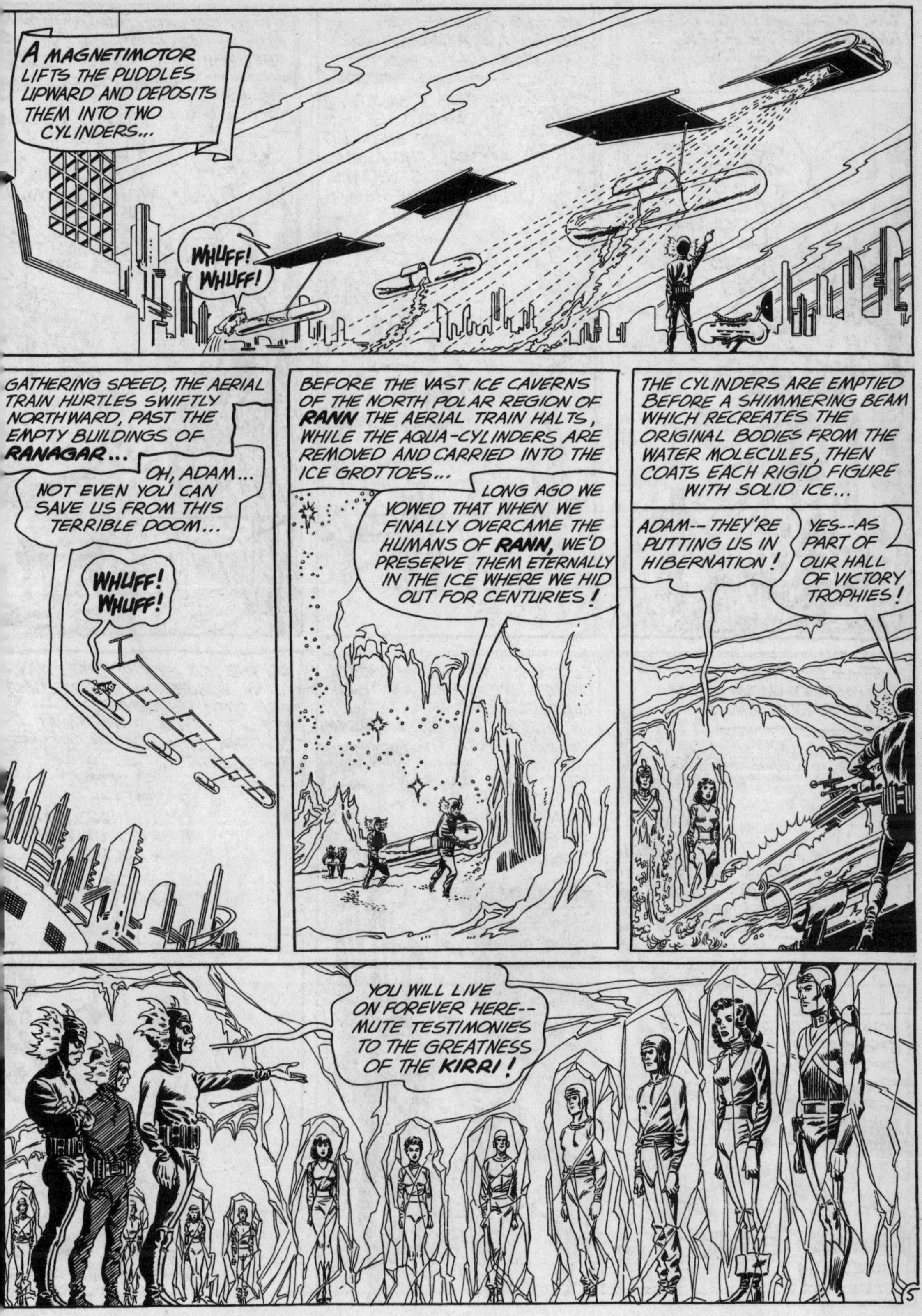
A MAGNETIMOTOR LIFTS THE PUDDLES UPWARD AND DEPOSITS THEM INTO TWO CYLINDERS...
WHUFF! WHUFF!
GATHERING SPEED, THE AERIAL TRAIN HURTLES SWIFTLY NORTHWARD, PAST THE EMPTY BUILDINGS OF RANAGAR...
OH, ADAM... NOT EVEN YOU CAN SAVE US FROM THIS TERRIBLE DOOM...
WHUFF! WHUFF!
BEFORE THE VAST ICE CAVERNS OF THE NORTH POLAR REGION OF RANN THE AERIAL TRAIN HALTS, WHILE THE AQUA-CYLINDERS ARE REMOVED AND CARRIED INTO THE ICE GROTTOES...
LONG AGO WE VOWED THAT WHEN WE FINALLY OVERCAME THE HUMANS OF RANN, WE'D PRESERVE THEM ETERNALLY IN THE ICE WHERE WE HID OUT FOR CENTURIES!
THE CYLINDERS ARE EMPTIED BEFORE A SHIMMERING BEAM WHICH RECREATES THE ORIGINAL BODIES FROM THE WATER MOLECULES, THEN COATS EACH RIGID FIGURE WITH SOLID ICE...
ADAM--THEY'RE PUTTING US IN HIBERNATION!
YES--AS PART OF OUR HALL OF VICTORY TROPHIES!
YOU WILL LIVE ON FOREVER HERE--MUTE TESTIMONIES TO THE GREATNESS OF THE KIRRI!
5

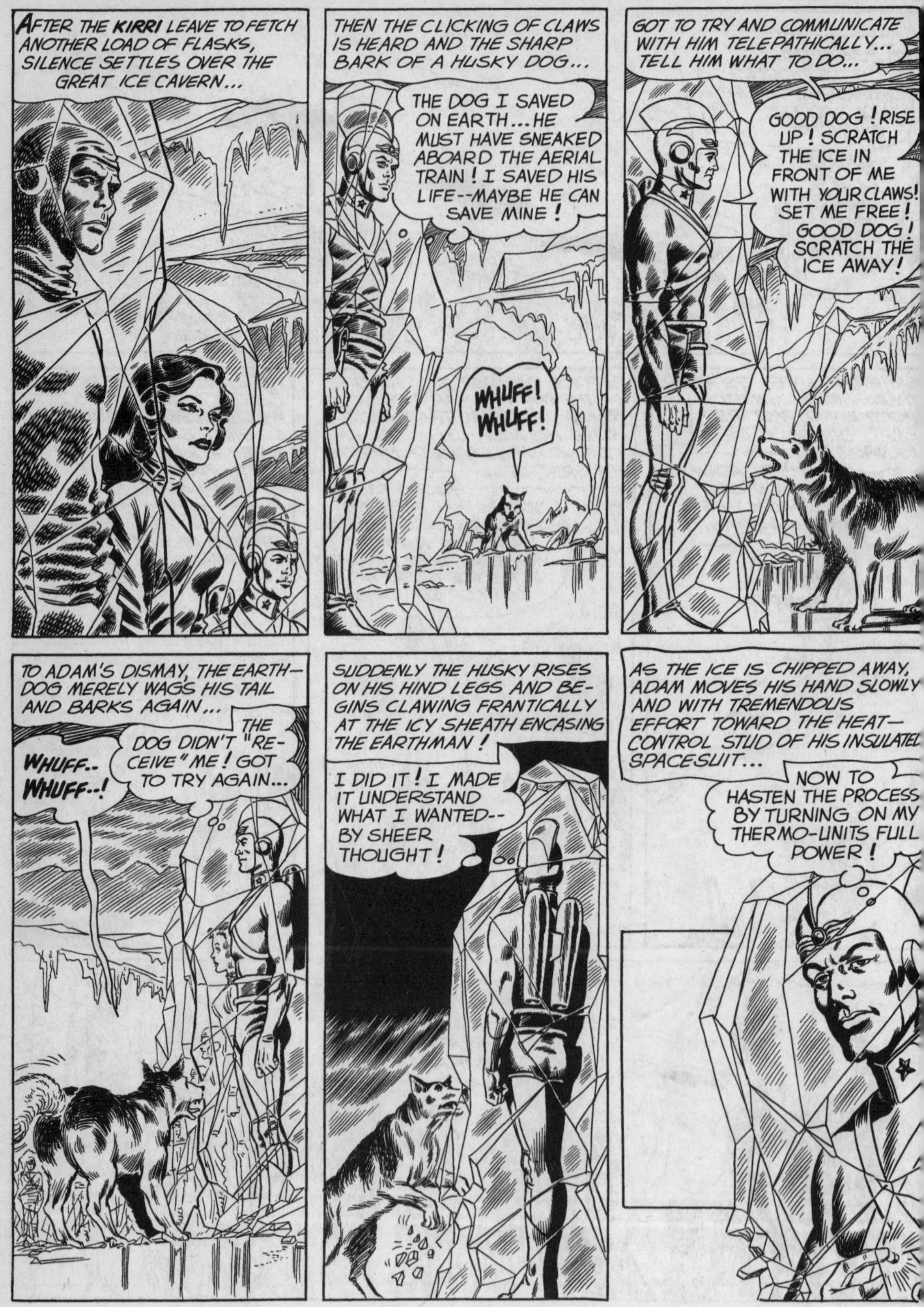
AFTER THE KIRRI LEAVE TO FETCH ANOTHER LOAD OF FLASKS, SILENCE SETTLES OVER THE GREAT ICE CAVERN...
THEN THE CLICKING OF CLAWS IS HEARD AND THE SHARP BARK OF A HUSKY DOG...
THE DOG I SAVED ON EARTH...HE MUST HAVE SNEAKED ABOARD THE AERIAL TRAIN! I SAVED HIS LIFE--MAYBE HE CAN SAVE MINE!
WHUFF! WHUFF!
GOT TO TRY AND COMMUNICATE WITH HIM TELEPATHICALLY... TELL HIM WHAT TO DO...
GOOD DOG! RISE UP! SCRATCH THE ICE IN FRONT OF ME WITH YOUR CLAWS! SET ME FREE! GOOD DOG! SCRATCH THE ICE AWAY!
TO ADAM'S DISMAY, THE EARTH-DOG MERELY WAGS HIS TAIL AND BARKS AGAIN...
WHUFF-- WHUFF--!
THE DOG DIDN'T "RECEIVE" ME! GOT TO TRY AGAIN...
SUDDENLY THE HUSKY RISES ON HIS HIND LEGS AND BEGINS CLAWING FRANTICALLY AT THE ICY SHEATH ENCASING THE EARTHMAN!
I DID IT! I MADE IT UNDERSTAND WHAT I WANTED-- BY SHEER THOUGHT!
AS THE ICE IS CHIPPED AWAY, ADAM MOVES HIS HAND SLOWLY AND WITH TREMENDOUS EFFORT TOWARD THE HEAT-CONTROL STUD OF HIS INSULATED SPACESUIT...
NOW TO HASTEN THE PROCESS BY TURNING ON MY THERMO-UNITS FULL POWER!

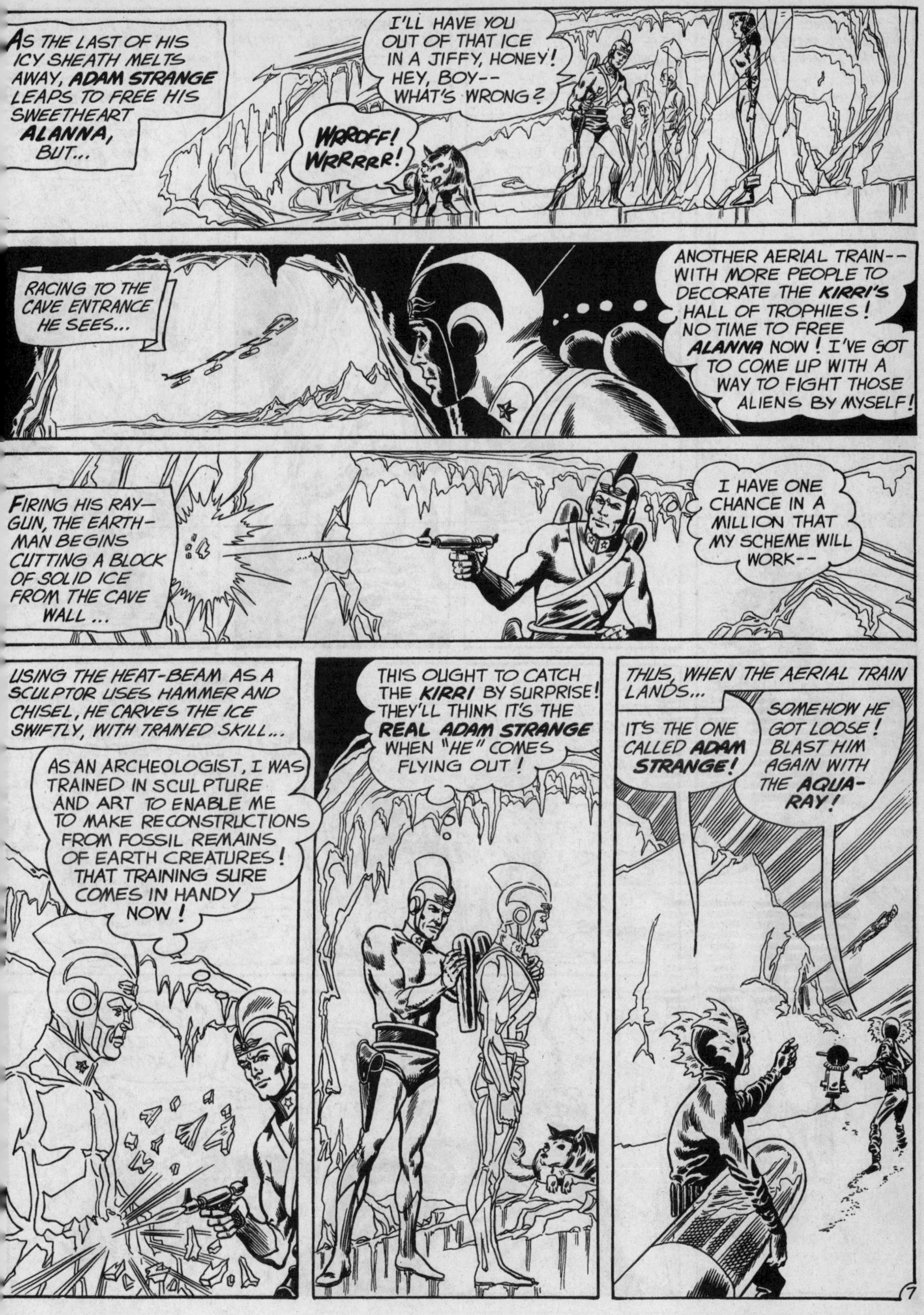

AS THE LAST OF HIS ICY SHEATH MELTS AWAY, ADAM STRANGE LEAPS TO FREE HIS SWEETHEART ALANNA, BUT...
I'LL HAVE YOU OUT OF THAT ICE IN A JIFFY, HONEY! HEY, BOY-- WHAT'S WRONG?
WRROFF! WRRRRR!
RACING TO THE CAVE ENTRANCE HE SEES...
ANOTHER AERIAL TRAIN-- WITH MORE PEOPLE TO DECORATE THE KIRRI'S HALL OF TROPHIES! NO TIME TO FREE ALANNA NOW! I'VE GOT TO COME UP WITH A WAY TO FIGHT THOSE ALIENS BY MYSELF!
FIRING HIS RAY-GUN, THE EARTH-MAN BEGINS CUTTING A BLOCK OF SOLID ICE FROM THE CAVE WALL...
I HAVE ONE CHANCE IN A MILLION THAT MY SCHEME WILL WORK--
USING THE HEAT-BEAM AS A SCULPTOR USES HAMMER AND CHISEL, HE CARVES THE ICE SWIFTLY, WITH TRAINED SKILL...
AS AN ARCHEOLOGIST, I WAS TRAINED IN SCULPTURE AND ART TO ENABLE ME TO MAKE RECONSTRUCTIONS FROM FOSSIL REMAINS OF EARTH CREATURES! THAT TRAINING SURE COMES IN HANDY NOW!
THIS OUGHT TO CATCH THE KIRRI BY SURPRISE! THEY'LL THINK IT'S THE REAL ADAM STRANGE WHEN "HE" COMES FLYING OUT!
THUS, WHEN THE AERIAL TRAIN LANDS...
IT'S THE ONE CALLED ADAM STRANGE!
SOMEHOW HE GOT LOOSE! BLAST HIM AGAIN WITH THE AQUA-RAY!
7

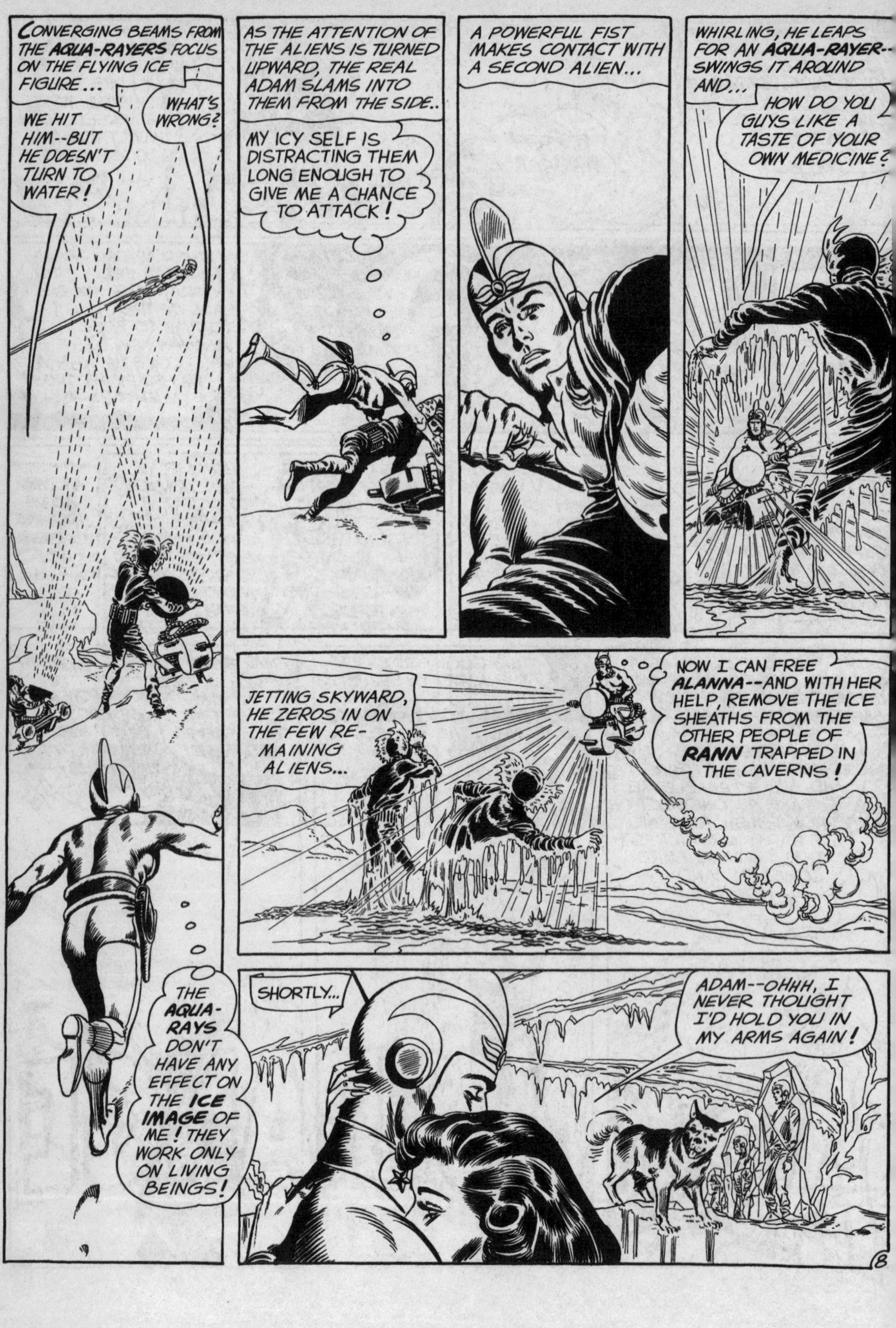
CONVERGING BEAMS FROM THE AQUA-RAYERS FOCUS ON THE FLYING ICE FIGURE...
WE HIT HIM--BUT HE DOESN'T TURN TO WATER!
WHAT'S WRONG?
THE AQUA-RAYS DON'T HAVE ANY EFFECT ON THE ICE IMAGE OF ME! THEY WORK ONLY ON LIVING BEINGS!
AS THE ATTENTION OF THE ALIENS IS TURNED UPWARD, THE REAL ADAM SLAMS INTO THEM FROM THE SIDE..
MY ICY SELF IS DISTRACTING THEM LONG ENOUGH TO GIVE ME A CHANCE TO ATTACK!
A POWERFUL FIST MAKES CONTACT WITH A SECOND ALIEN...
WHIRLING, HE LEAPS FOR AN AQUA-RAYER--SWINGS IT AROUND AND...
HOW DO YOU GUYS LIKE A TASTE OF YOUR OWN MEDICINE?
JETTING SKYWARD, HE ZEROS IN ON THE FEW RE-MAINING ALIENS...
NOW I CAN FREE ALANNA--AND WITH HER HELP, REMOVE THE ICE SHEATHS FROM THE OTHER PEOPLE OF RANN TRAPPED IN THE CAVERNS!
SHORTLY...
ADAM--OHHH, I NEVER THOUGHT I'D HOLD YOU IN MY ARMS AGAIN!
8

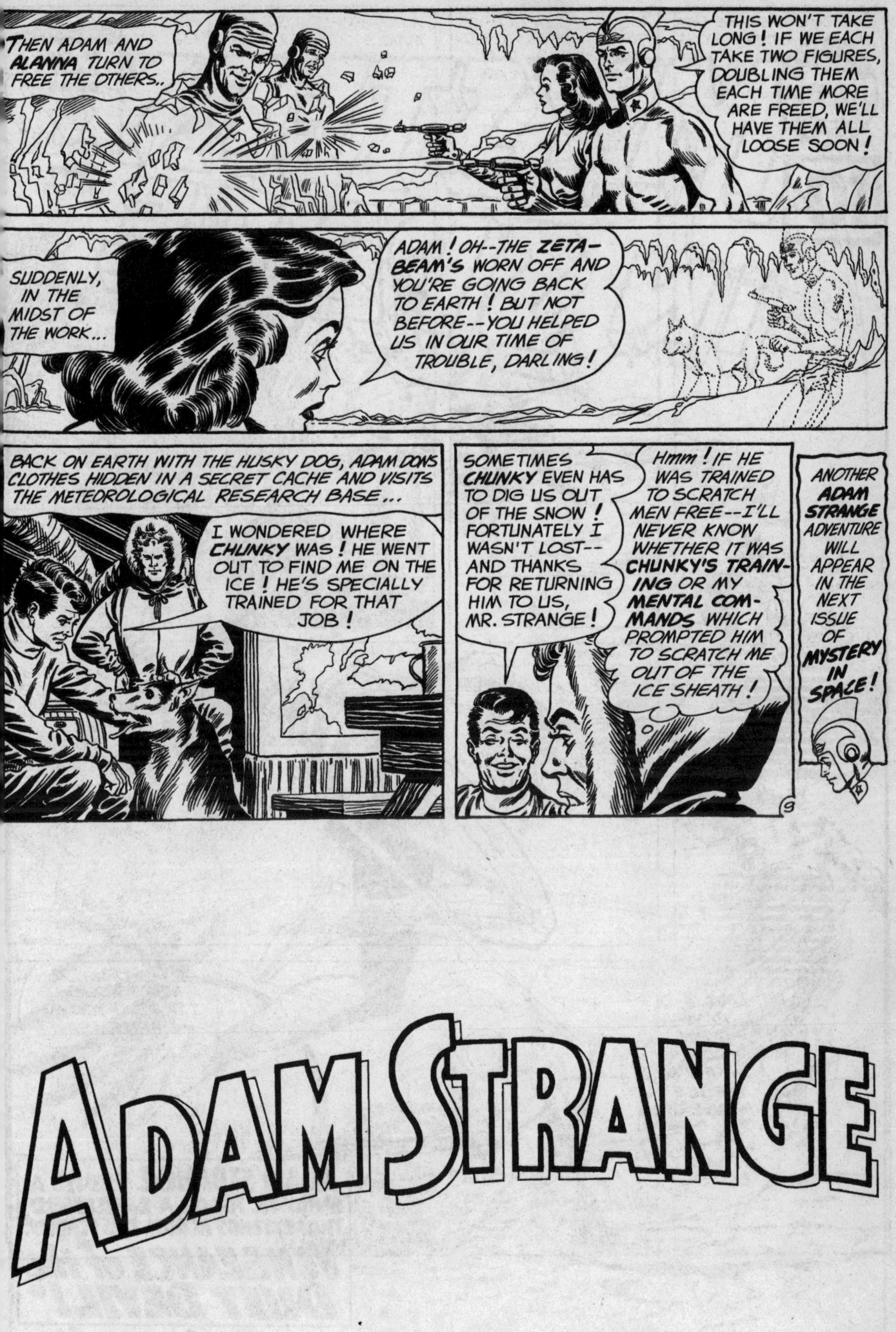
THEN ADAM AND ALANNA TURN TO FREE THE OTHERS..
THIS WON'T TAKE LONG! IF WE EACH TAKE TWO FIGURES, DOUBLING THEM EACH TIME MORE ARE FREED, WE'LL HAVE THEM ALL LOOSE SOON!
SUDDENLY, IN THE MIDST OF THE WORK...
ADAM! OH--THE ZETA-BEAM'S WORN OFF AND YOU'RE GOING BACK TO EARTH! BUT NOT BEFORE--YOU HELPED US IN OUR TIME OF TROUBLE, DARLING!
BACK ON EARTH WITH THE HUSKY DOG, ADAM DONS CLOTHES HIDDEN IN A SECRET CACHE AND VISITS THE METEOROLOGICAL RESEARCH BASE...
I WONDERED WHERE CHUNKY WAS! HE WENT OUT TO FIND ME ON THE ICE! HE'S SPECIALLY TRAINED FOR THAT JOB!
SOMETIMES CHUNKY EVEN HAS TO DIG US OUT OF THE SNOW! FORTUNATELY I WASN'T LOST--AND THANKS FOR RETURNING HIM TO US, MR. STRANGE!
Hmm! IF HE WAS TRAINED TO SCRATCH MEN FREE--I'LL NEVER KNOW WHETHER IT WAS CHUNKY'S TRAINING OR MY MENTAL COMMANDS WHICH PROMPTED HIM TO SCRATCH ME OUT OF THE ICE SHEATH!
ANOTHER ADAM STRANGE ADVENTURE WILL APPEAR IN THE NEXT ISSUE OF MYSTERY IN SPACE!
9

ADAM STRANGE

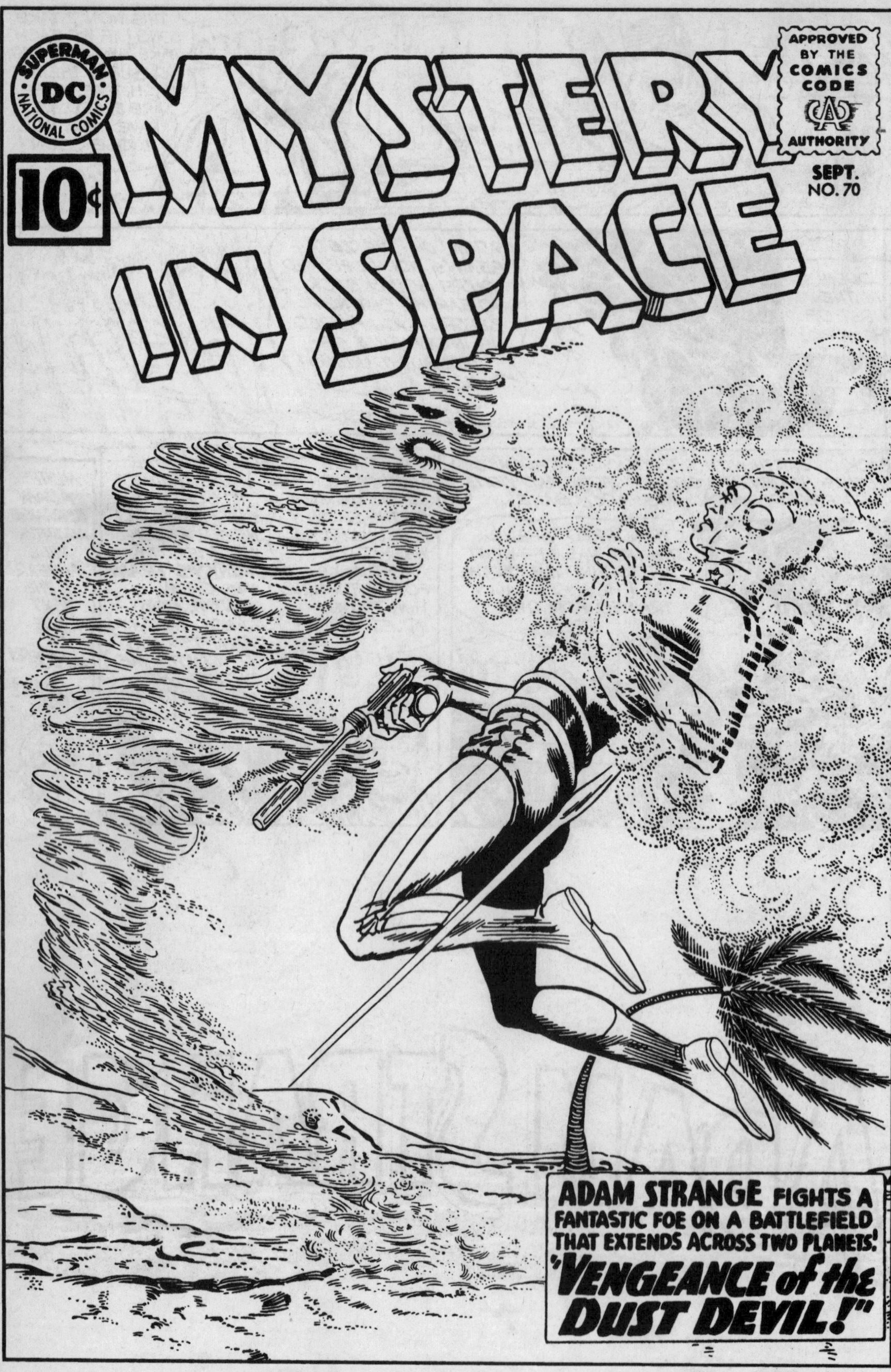
SUPERMAN DC NATIONAL COMICS
10¢
MYSTERY IN SPACE
APPROVED BY THE COMICS CODE AUTHORITY
SEPT. NO. 70
ADAM STRANGE FIGHTS A FANTASTIC FOE ON A BATTLEFIELD THAT EXTENDS ACROSS TWO PLANETS!
"VENGEANCE of the DUST DEVIL!"

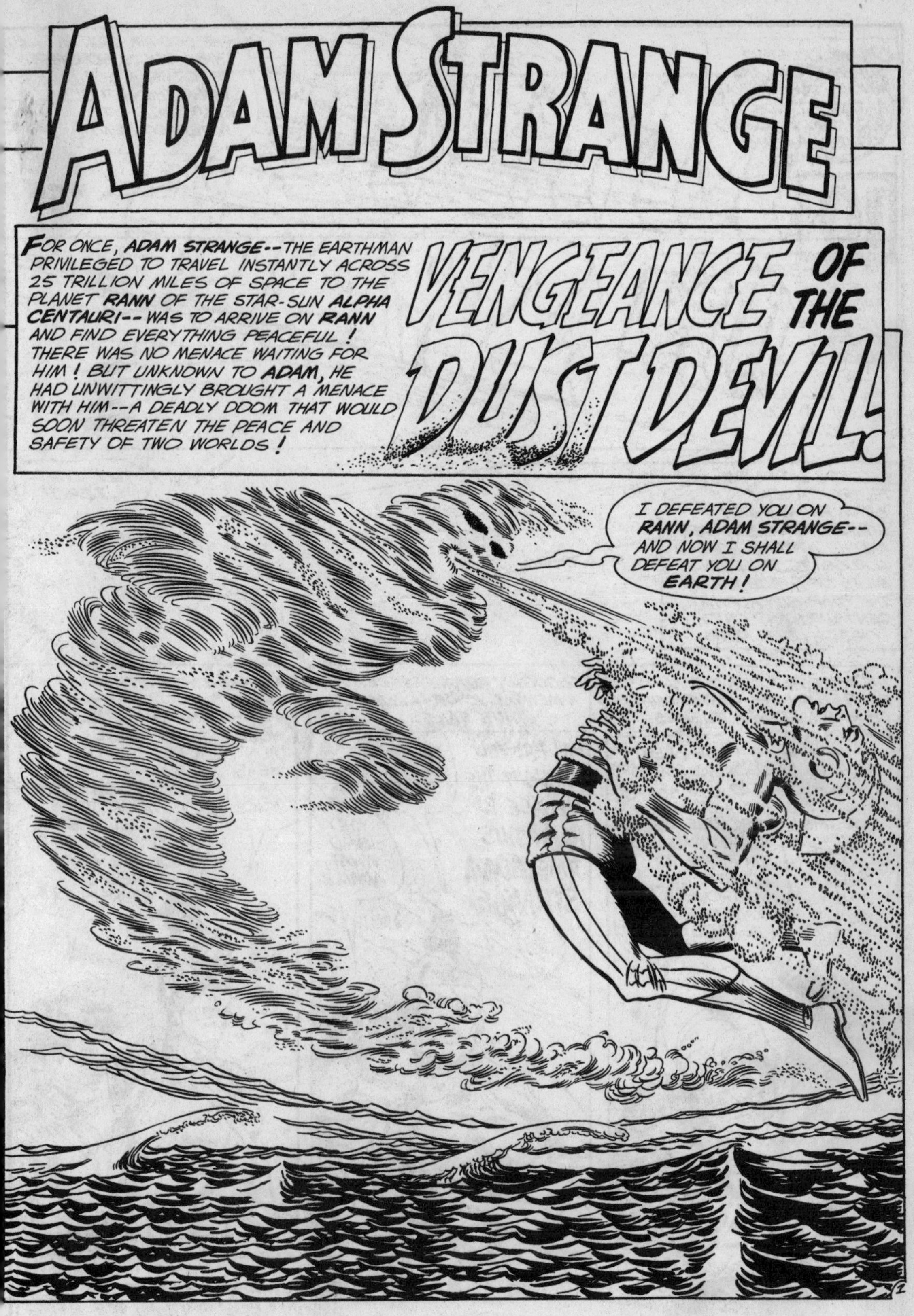
ADAM STRANGE
FOR ONCE, ADAM STRANGE--THE EARTHMAN PRIVILEGED TO TRAVEL INSTANTLY ACROSS 25 TRILLION MILES OF SPACE TO THE PLANET RANN OF THE STAR-SUN ALPHA CENTAURI--WAS TO ARRIVE ON RANN AND FIND EVERYTHING PEACEFUL! THERE WAS NO MENACE WAITING FOR HIM! BUT UNKNOWN TO ADAM, HE HAD UNWITTINGLY BROUGHT A MENACE WITH HIM--A DEADLY DOOM THAT WOULD SOON THREATEN THE PEACE AND SAFETY OF TWO WORLDS!
VENGEANCE OF THE DUST DEVIL!
I DEFEATED YOU ON RANN, ADAM STRANGE--AND NOW I SHALL DEFEAT YOU ON EARTH!

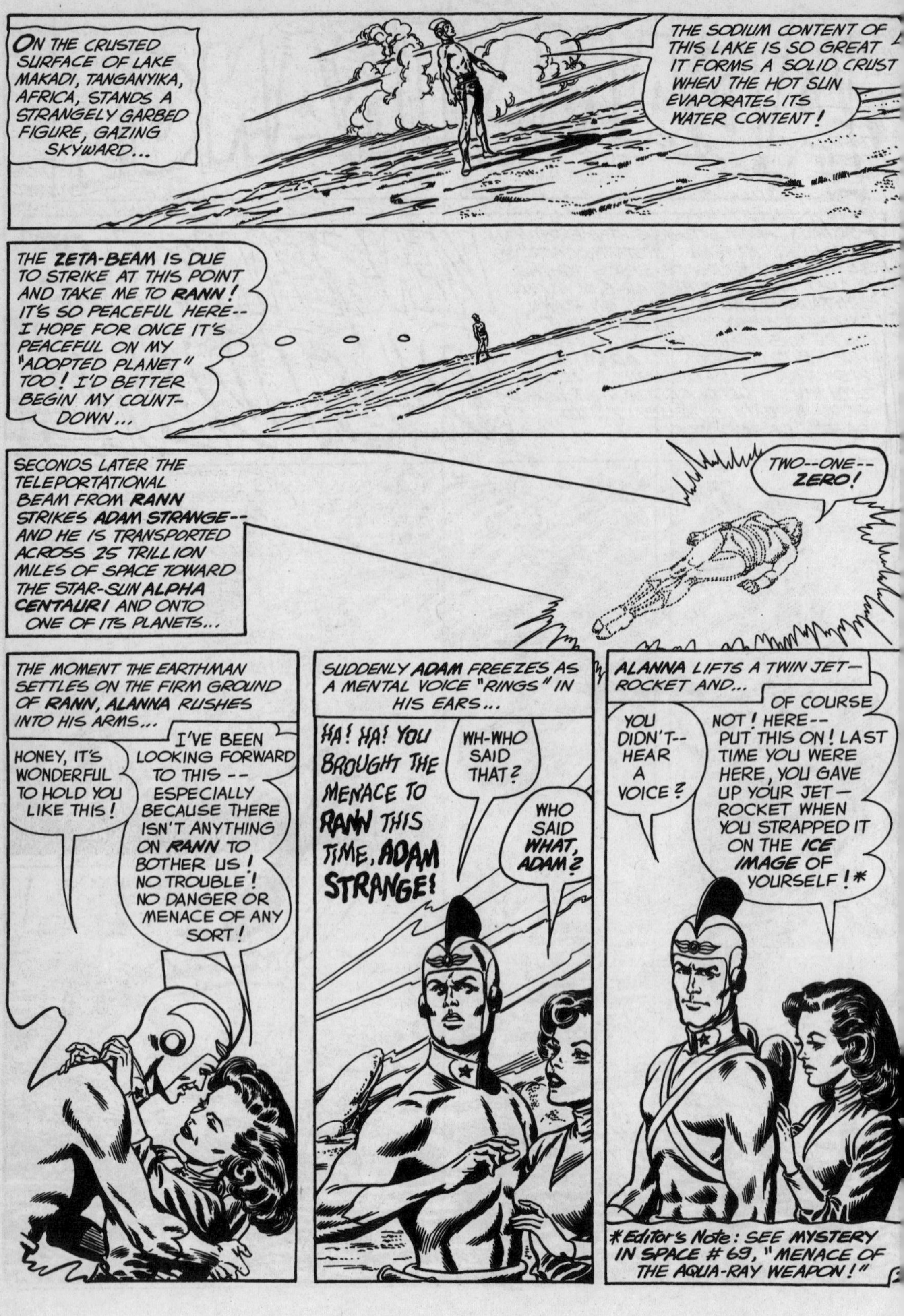
ON THE CRUSTED SURFACE OF LAKE MAKADI, TANGANYIKA, AFRICA, STANDS A STRANGELY GARBED FIGURE, GAZING SKYWARD...
THE SODIUM CONTENT OF THIS LAKE IS SO GREAT IT FORMS A SOLID CRUST WHEN THE HOT SUN EVAPORATES ITS WATER CONTENT!
THE ZETA-BEAM IS DUE TO STRIKE AT THIS POINT AND TAKE ME TO RANN! IT'S SO PEACEFUL HERE-- I HOPE FOR ONCE IT'S PEACEFUL ON MY "ADOPTED PLANET" TOO! I'D BETTER BEGIN MY COUNT-DOWN...
SECONDS LATER THE TELEPORTATIONAL BEAM FROM RANN STRIKES ADAM STRANGE-- AND HE IS TRANSPORTED ACROSS 25 TRILLION MILES OF SPACE TOWARD THE STAR-SUN ALPHA CENTAURI AND ONTO ONE OF ITS PLANETS...
TWO--ONE-- ZERO!
THE MOMENT THE EARTHMAN SETTLES ON THE FIRM GROUND OF RANN, ALANNA RUSHES INTO HIS ARMS...
HONEY, IT'S WONDERFUL TO HOLD YOU LIKE THIS!
I'VE BEEN LOOKING FORWARD TO THIS -- ESPECIALLY BECAUSE THERE ISN'T ANYTHING ON RANN TO BOTHER US! NO TROUBLE! NO DANGER OR MENACE OF ANY SORT!
SUDDENLY ADAM FREEZES AS A MENTAL VOICE "RINGS" IN HIS EARS...
HA! HA! YOU BROUGHT THE MENACE TO RANN THIS TIME, ADAM STRANGE!
WH-WHO SAID THAT?
WHO SAID WHAT, ADAM?
ALANNA LIFTS A TWIN JET-ROCKET AND...
YOU DIDN'T-- HEAR A VOICE?
OF COURSE NOT! HERE-- PUT THIS ON! LAST TIME YOU WERE HERE, YOU GAVE UP YOUR JET-ROCKET WHEN YOU STRAPPED IT ON THE ICE IMAGE OF YOURSELF!*
*Editor's Note: SEE MYSTERY IN SPACE #69, "MENACE OF THE AQUA-RAY WEAPON!"

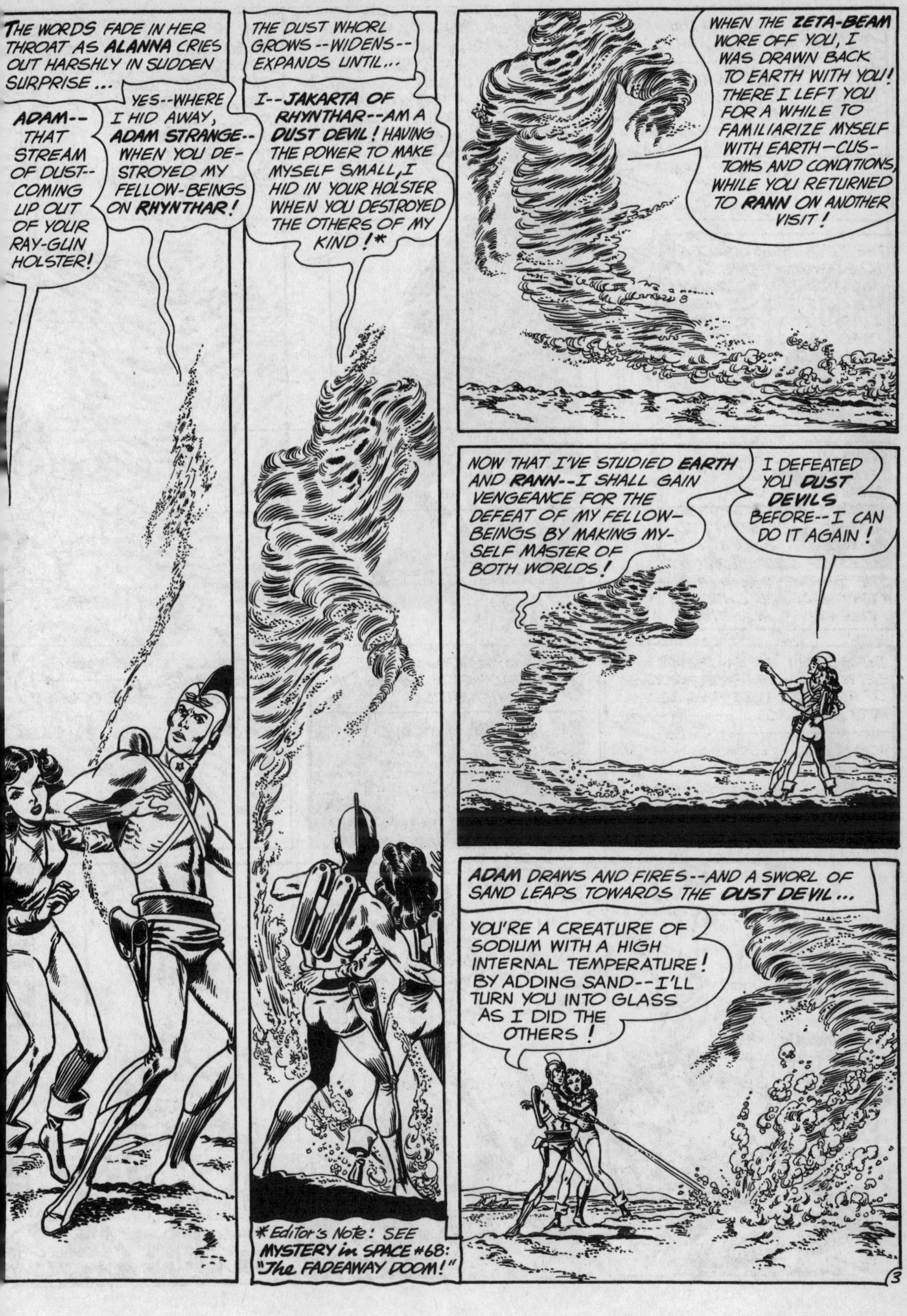
THE WORDS FADE IN HER THROAT AS ALANNA CRIES OUT HARSHLY IN SUDDEN SURPRISE ...
ADAM-- THAT STREAM OF DUST--COMING UP OUT OF YOUR RAY-GUN HOLSTER!
YES--WHERE I HID AWAY, ADAM STRANGE--WHEN YOU DESTROYED MY FELLOW-BEINGS ON RHYNTHAR!
THE DUST WHORL GROWS--WIDENS--EXPANDS UNTIL...
I--JAKARTA OF RHYNTHAR--AM A DUST DEVIL! HAVING THE POWER TO MAKE MYSELF SMALL, I HID IN YOUR HOLSTER WHEN YOU DESTROYED THE OTHERS OF MY KIND!*
*Editor's Note: SEE MYSTERY in SPACE #68: "The FADEAWAY DOOM!"
WHEN THE ZETA-BEAM WORE OFF YOU, I WAS DRAWN BACK TO EARTH WITH YOU! THERE I LEFT YOU FOR A WHILE TO FAMILIARIZE MYSELF WITH EARTH—CUSTOMS AND CONDITIONS, WHILE YOU RETURNED TO RANN ON ANOTHER VISIT!
NOW THAT I'VE STUDIED EARTH AND RANN--I SHALL GAIN VENGEANCE FOR THE DEFEAT OF MY FELLOW-BEINGS BY MAKING MYSELF MASTER OF BOTH WORLDS!
I DEFEATED YOU DUST DEVILS BEFORE--I CAN DO IT AGAIN!
ADAM DRAWS AND FIRES--AND A SWORL OF SAND LEAPS TOWARDS THE DUST DEVIL...
YOU'RE A CREATURE OF SODIUM WITH A HIGH INTERNAL TEMPERATURE! BY ADDING SAND--I'LL TURN YOU INTO GLASS AS I DID THE OTHERS!
3

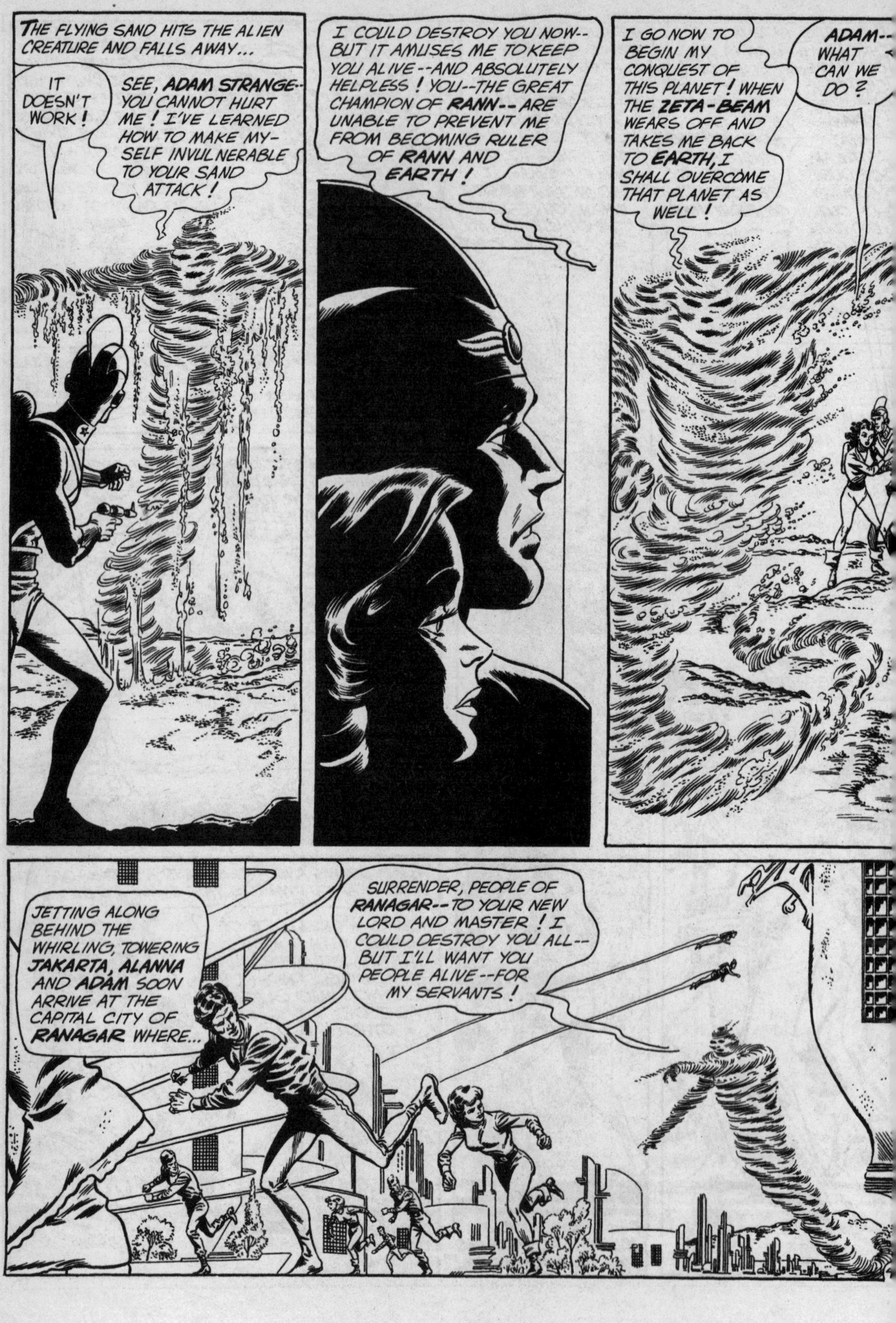
THE FLYING SAND HITS THE ALIEN CREATURE AND FALLS AWAY...
IT DOESN'T WORK!
SEE, ADAM STRANGE--YOU CANNOT HURT ME! I'VE LEARNED HOW TO MAKE MYSELF INVULNERABLE TO YOUR SAND ATTACK!
I COULD DESTROY YOU NOW--BUT IT AMUSES ME TO KEEP YOU ALIVE--AND ABSOLUTELY HELPLESS! YOU--THE GREAT CHAMPION OF RANN--ARE UNABLE TO PREVENT ME FROM BECOMING RULER OF RANN AND EARTH!
I GO NOW TO BEGIN MY CONQUEST OF THIS PLANET! WHEN THE ZETA-BEAM WEARS OFF AND TAKES ME BACK TO EARTH, I SHALL OVERCOME THAT PLANET AS WELL!
ADAM--WHAT CAN WE DO?
JETTING ALONG BEHIND THE WHIRLING, TOWERING JAKARTA, ALANNA AND ADAM SOON ARRIVE AT THE CAPITAL CITY OF RANAGAR WHERE...
SURRENDER, PEOPLE OF RANAGAR--TO YOUR NEW LORD AND MASTER! I COULD DESTROY YOU ALL--BUT I'LL WANT YOU PEOPLE ALIVE--FOR MY SERVANTS!

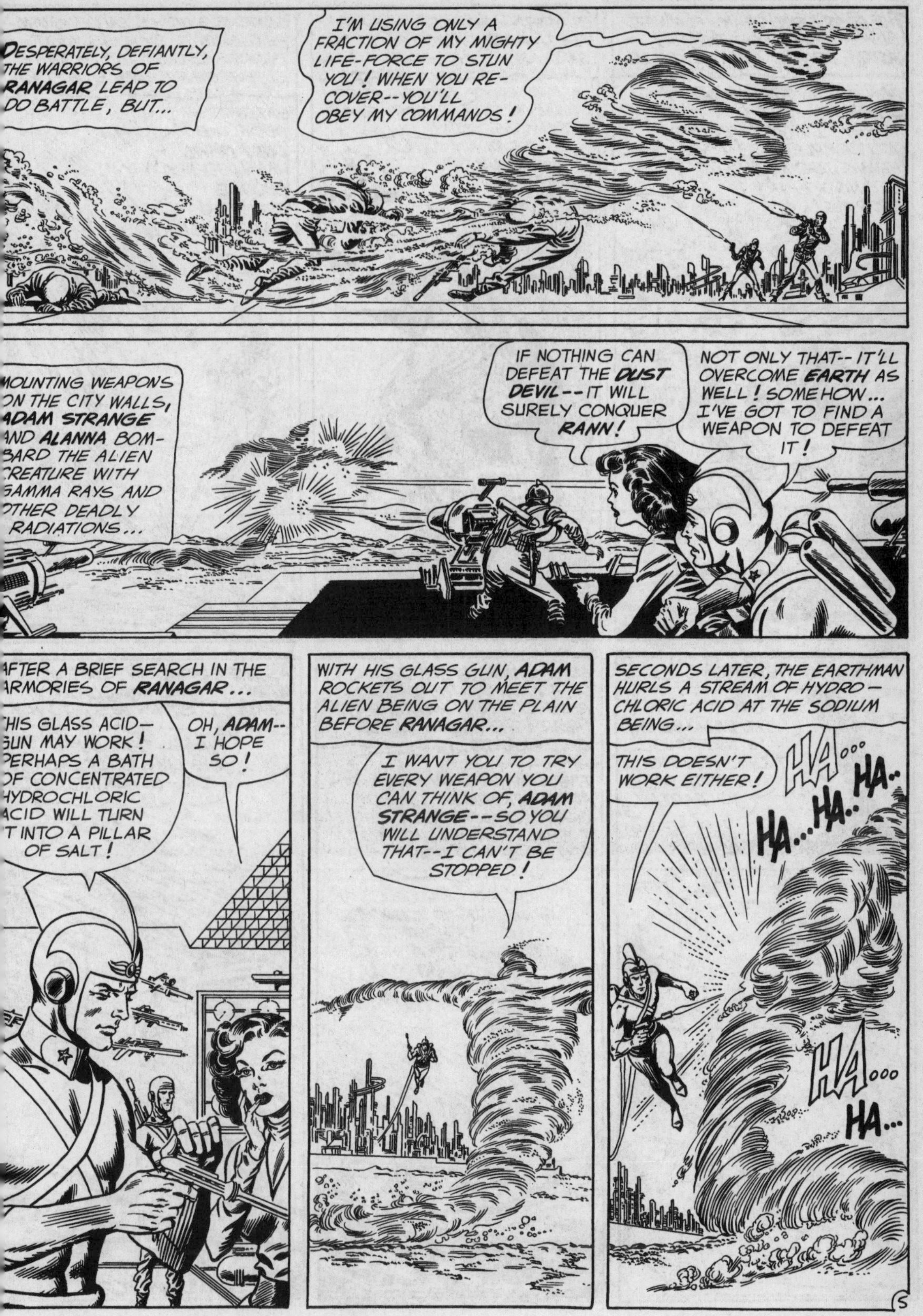
DESPERATELY, DEFIANTLY, THE WARRIORS OF RANAGAR LEAP TO DO BATTLE, BUT...
I'M USING ONLY A FRACTION OF MY MIGHTY LIFE-FORCE TO STUN YOU! WHEN YOU RE-COVER--YOU'LL OBEY MY COMMANDS!
MOUNTING WEAPONS ON THE CITY WALLS, ADAM STRANGE AND ALANNA BOMBARD THE ALIEN CREATURE WITH GAMMA RAYS AND OTHER DEADLY RADIATIONS...
IF NOTHING CAN DEFEAT THE DUST DEVIL--IT WILL SURELY CONQUER RANN!
NOT ONLY THAT--IT'LL OVERCOME EARTH AS WELL! SOMEHOW... I'VE GOT TO FIND A WEAPON TO DEFEAT IT!
AFTER A BRIEF SEARCH IN THE ARMORIES OF RANAGAR...
THIS GLASS ACID-GUN MAY WORK! PERHAPS A BATH OF CONCENTRATED HYDROCHLORIC ACID WILL TURN IT INTO A PILLAR OF SALT!
OH, ADAM-- I HOPE SO!
WITH HIS GLASS GUN, ADAM ROCKETS OUT TO MEET THE ALIEN BEING ON THE PLAIN BEFORE RANAGAR...
I WANT YOU TO TRY EVERY WEAPON YOU CAN THINK OF, ADAM STRANGE--SO YOU WILL UNDERSTAND THAT--I CAN'T BE STOPPED!
SECONDS LATER, THE EARTHMAN HURLS A STREAM OF HYDRO-CHLORIC ACID AT THE SODIUM BEING...
THIS DOESN'T WORK EITHER!
HA... HA.. HA.. HA...
HA... HA...
5

THE **DUST DEVIL** LEANS FORWARD, BLOWS A SPRAY OF DUST AT **ADAM**, DRIVING HIM BACKWARD...

NOW IT'S MY TURN, **ADAM STRANGE**--BUT DON'T WORRY! I WON'T DESTROY YOU COMPLETELY! I'M HAVING TOO MUCH FUN SEEING YOU TRY TO STOP ME!

OHH!

BLINDED--KNOCKED OFF HIS FEET--**ADAM** CRUMPLES TO THE SANDY SOIL...

GOT TO--TRY AGAIN--KEEP TRYING...

SNATCHING UP HIS FALLEN GUN, HE CLEANS IT BY RUBBING ITS BARREL AGAINST THE SILKEN SLEEVE OF HIS SPACE LINIFORM...

SAY, THAT'S ODD! THE **DUST DEVIL** HAS SUDDENLY BECOME RIGID--AS IF PARALYZED!

IN THE NEXT INSTANT...

GREAT STARS! THE **ZETA-BEAM** IS WEARING OFF--TAKING US BOTH BACK TO **EARTH!**

ADAM LANDS IN THE TROUGH OF A WAVE OF THE VAST PACIFIC OCEAN--IN TIME TO "HEAR" THE ANGRY "VOICE" OF **JAKARTA**...

I'VE CHANGED MY MIND, **ADAM STRANGE**! I'M NOT GOING TO LET YOU LIVE! I SHALL PUT AN END TO YOU HERE AND NOW!

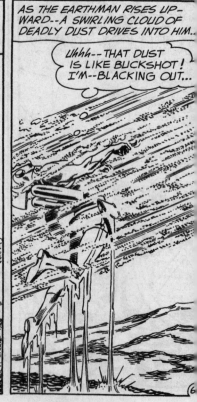

AS THE EARTHMAN RISES UP-WARD--A SWIRLING CLOUD OF DEADLY DUST DRIVES INTO HIM...

UHHH--THAT DUST IS LIKE BUCKSHOT! I'M--BLACKING OUT...

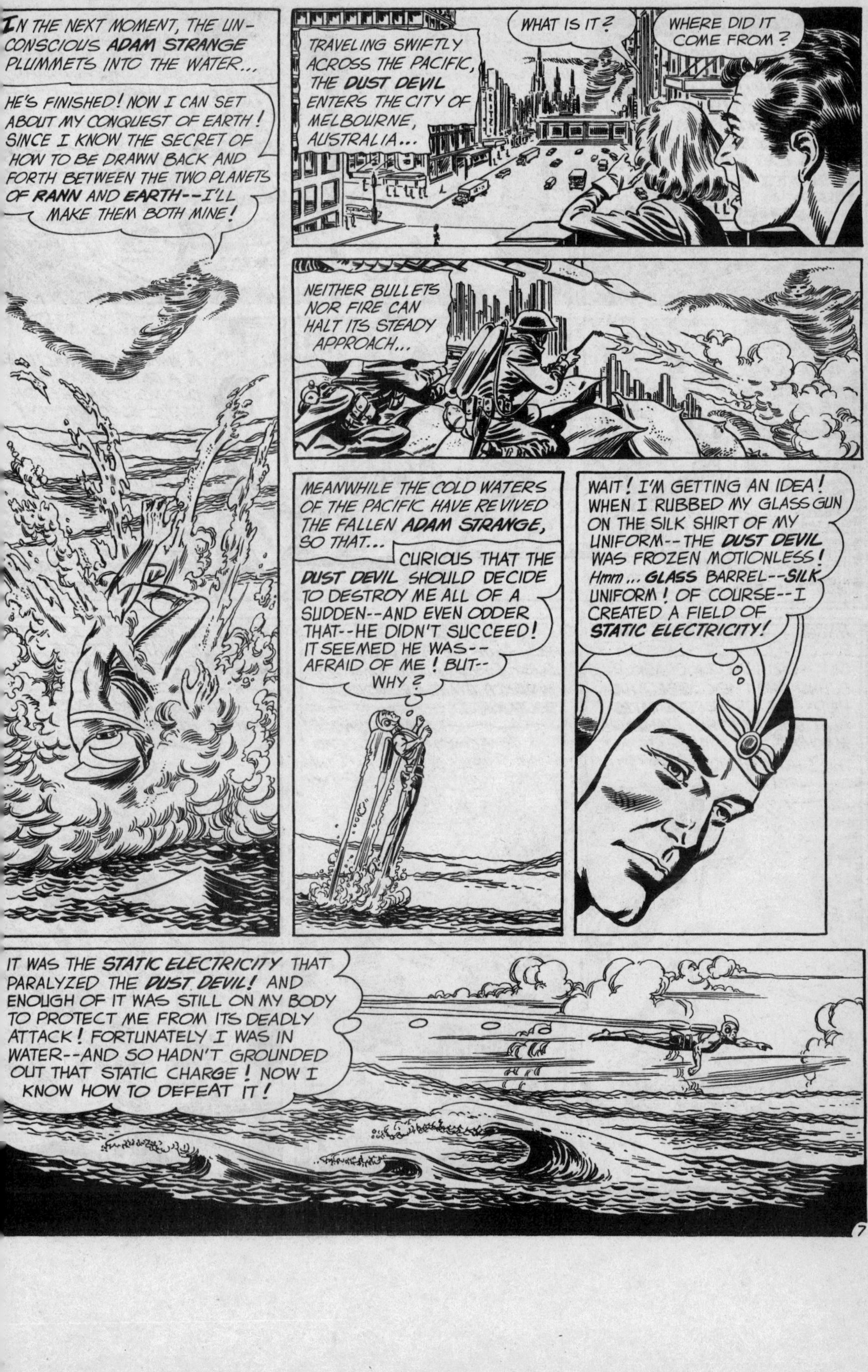
IN THE NEXT MOMENT, THE UNCONSCIOUS ADAM STRANGE PLUMMETS INTO THE WATER...
HE'S FINISHED! NOW I CAN SET ABOUT MY CONQUEST OF EARTH! SINCE I KNOW THE SECRET OF HOW TO BE DRAWN BACK AND FORTH BETWEEN THE TWO PLANETS OF RANN AND EARTH--I'LL MAKE THEM BOTH MINE!
TRAVELING SWIFTLY ACROSS THE PACIFIC, THE DUST DEVIL ENTERS THE CITY OF MELBOURNE, AUSTRALIA...
WHAT IS IT?
WHERE DID IT COME FROM?
NEITHER BULLETS NOR FIRE CAN HALT ITS STEADY APPROACH...
MEANWHILE THE COLD WATERS OF THE PACIFIC HAVE REVIVED THE FALLEN ADAM STRANGE, SO THAT...
CURIOUS THAT THE DUST DEVIL SHOULD DECIDE TO DESTROY ME ALL OF A SUDDEN--AND EVEN ODDER THAT--HE DIDN'T SUCCEED! IT SEEMED HE WAS--AFRAID OF ME! BUT--WHY?
WAIT! I'M GETTING AN IDEA! WHEN I RUBBED MY GLASS GUN ON THE SILK SHIRT OF MY UNIFORM--THE DUST DEVIL WAS FROZEN MOTIONLESS! Hmm... GLASS BARREL--SILK UNIFORM! OF COURSE--I CREATED A FIELD OF STATIC ELECTRICITY!
IT WAS THE STATIC ELECTRICITY THAT PARALYZED THE DUST DEVIL! AND ENOUGH OF IT WAS STILL ON MY BODY TO PROTECT ME FROM ITS DEADLY ATTACK! FORTUNATELY I WAS IN WATER--AND SO HADN'T GROUNDED OUT THAT STATIC CHARGE! NOW I KNOW HOW TO DEFEAT IT!
7

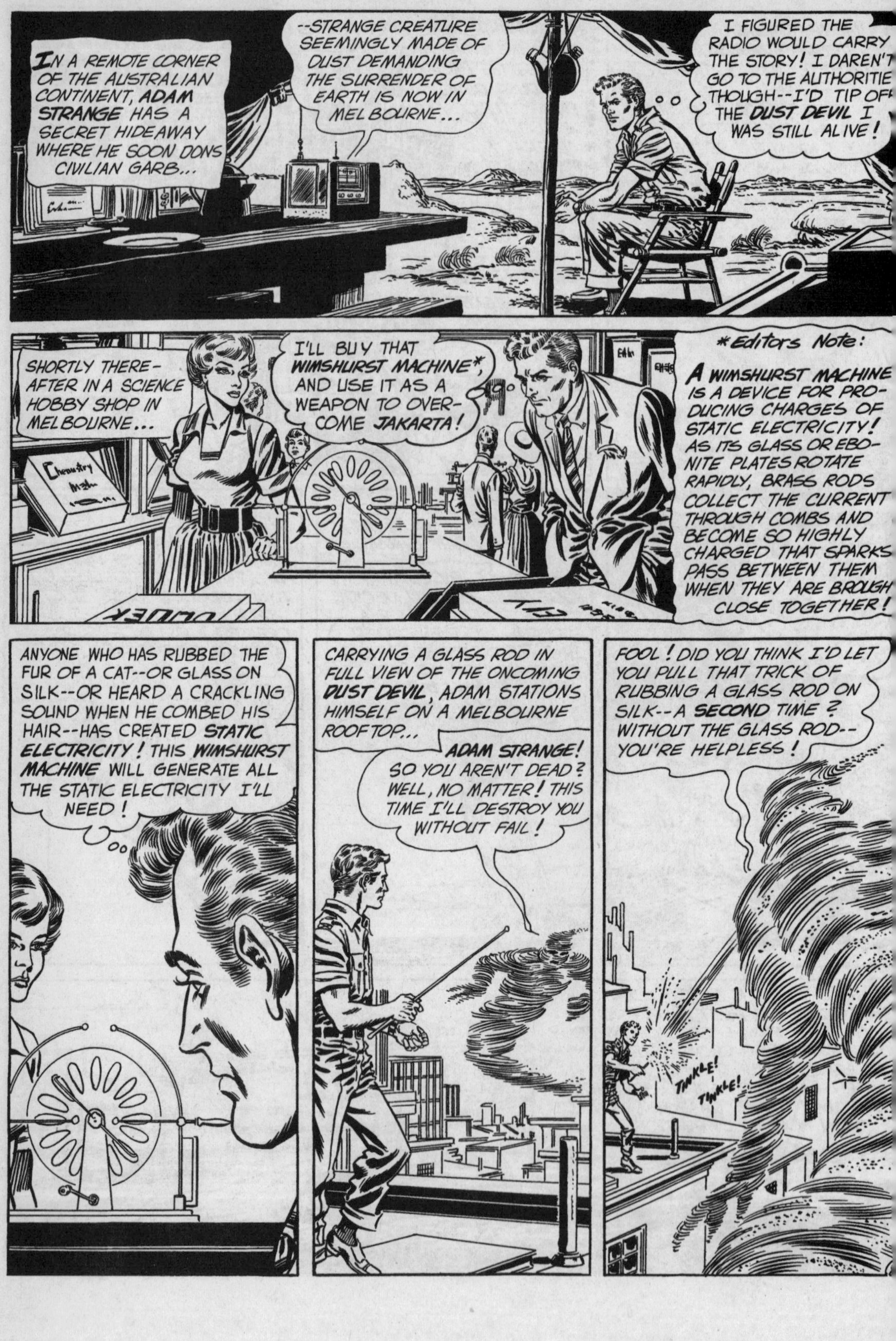
IN A REMOTE CORNER OF THE AUSTRALIAN CONTINENT, ADAM STRANGE HAS A SECRET HIDEAWAY WHERE HE SOON DONS CIVILIAN GARB...
--STRANGE CREATURE SEEMINGLY MADE OF DUST DEMANDING THE SURRENDER OF EARTH IS NOW IN MELBOURNE...
I FIGURED THE RADIO WOULD CARRY THE STORY! I DAREN'T GO TO THE AUTHORITIE THOUGH--I'D TIP OFF THE DUST DEVIL I WAS STILL ALIVE!
SHORTLY THERE-AFTER IN A SCIENCE HOBBY SHOP IN MELBOURNE...
I'LL BUY THAT WIMSHURST MACHINE*, AND USE IT AS A WEAPON TO OVER-COME JAKARTA!
*Editors Note:
A WIMSHURST MACHINE IS A DEVICE FOR PRO-DUCING CHARGES OF STATIC ELECTRICITY! AS ITS GLASS OR EBO-NITE PLATES ROTATE RAPIDLY, BRASS RODS COLLECT THE CURRENT THROUGH COMBS AND BECOME SO HIGHLY CHARGED THAT SPARKS PASS BETWEEN THEM WHEN THEY ARE BROUGH CLOSE TOGETHER!
ANYONE WHO HAS RUBBED THE FUR OF A CAT--OR GLASS ON SILK--OR HEARD A CRACKLING SOUND WHEN HE COMBED HIS HAIR--HAS CREATED STATIC ELECTRICITY! THIS WIMSHURST MACHINE WILL GENERATE ALL THE STATIC ELECTRICITY I'LL NEED!
CARRYING A GLASS ROD IN FULL VIEW OF THE ONCOMING DUST DEVIL, ADAM STATIONS HIMSELF ON A MELBOURNE ROOFTOP...
ADAM STRANGE! SO YOU AREN'T DEAD? WELL, NO MATTER! THIS TIME I'LL DESTROY YOU WITHOUT FAIL!
FOOL! DID YOU THINK I'D LET YOU PULL THAT TRICK OF RUBBING A GLASS ROD ON SILK--A SECOND TIME? WITHOUT THE GLASS ROD--YOU'RE HELPLESS!
TINKLE! TINKLE!

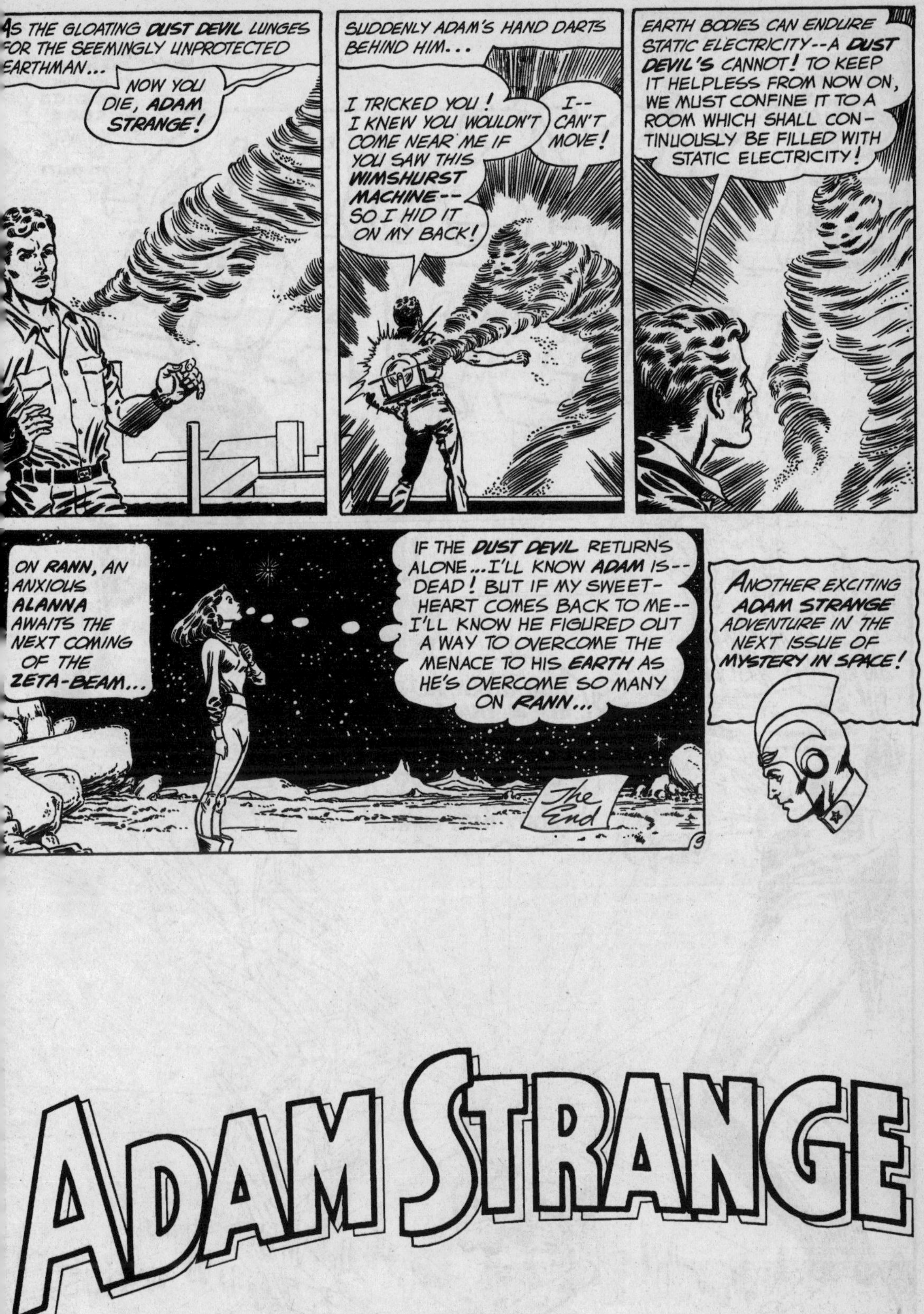
AS THE GLOATING DUST DEVIL LUNGES FOR THE SEEMINGLY UNPROTECTED EARTHMAN...
NOW YOU DIE, ADAM STRANGE!
SUDDENLY ADAM'S HAND DARTS BEHIND HIM...
I TRICKED YOU! I KNEW YOU WOULDN'T COME NEAR ME IF YOU SAW THIS WIMSHURST MACHINE-- SO I HID IT ON MY BACK!
I-- CAN'T MOVE!
EARTH BODIES CAN ENDURE STATIC ELECTRICITY--A DUST DEVIL'S CANNOT! TO KEEP IT HELPLESS FROM NOW ON, WE MUST CONFINE IT TO A ROOM WHICH SHALL CONTINUOUSLY BE FILLED WITH STATIC ELECTRICITY!
ON RANN, AN ANXIOUS ALANNA AWAITS THE NEXT COMING OF THE ZETA-BEAM...
IF THE DUST DEVIL RETURNS ALONE...I'LL KNOW ADAM IS--DEAD! BUT IF MY SWEETHEART COMES BACK TO ME--I'LL KNOW HE FIGURED OUT A WAY TO OVERCOME THE MENACE TO HIS EARTH AS HE'S OVERCOME SO MANY ON RANN...
The End
9
ANOTHER EXCITING ADAM STRANGE ADVENTURE IN THE NEXT ISSUE OF MYSTERY IN SPACE!

ADAM STRANGE

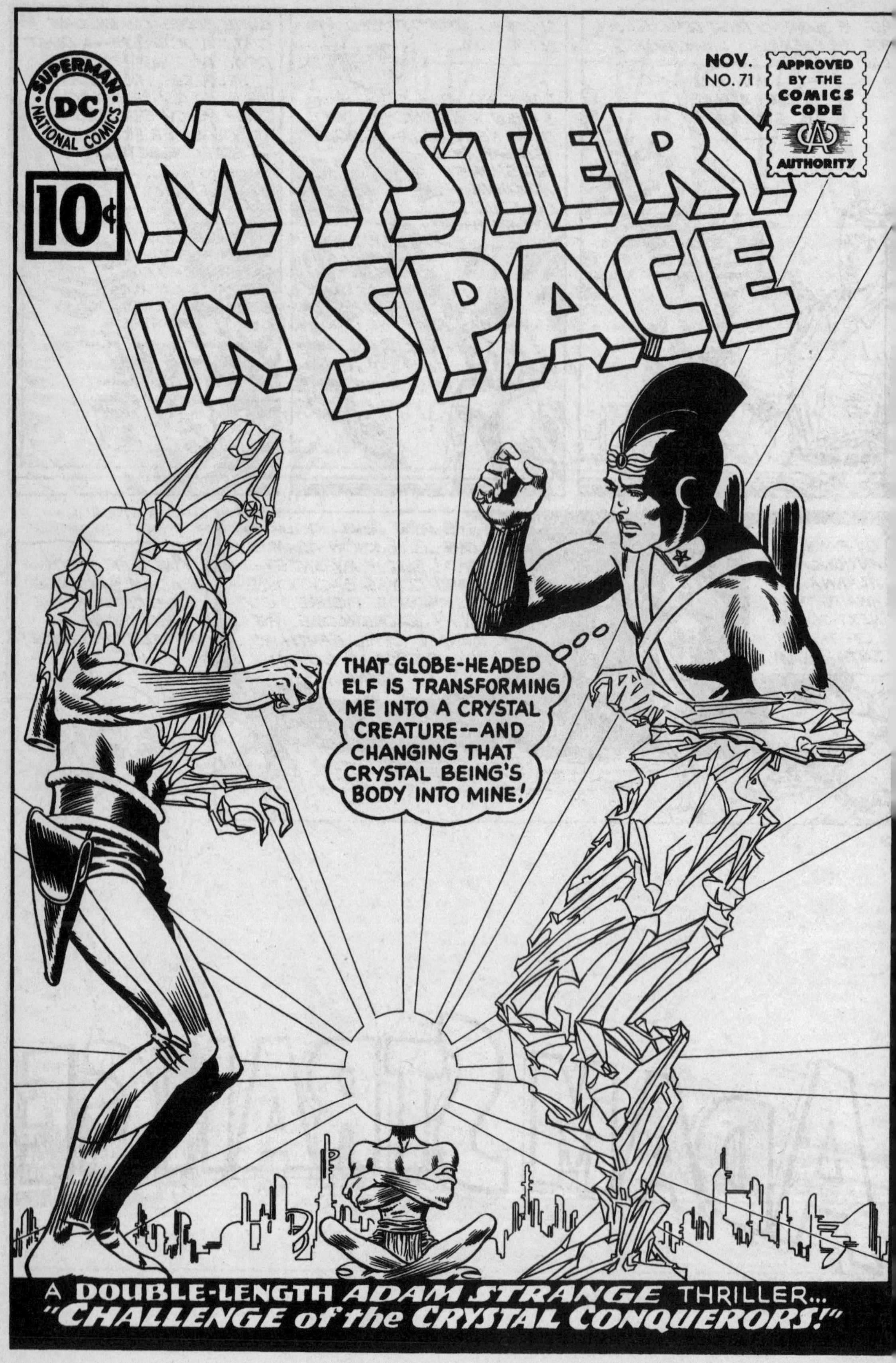

SUPERMAN DC NATIONAL COMICS
NOV. NO. 71
APPROVED BY THE COMICS CODE AUTHORITY
10¢
MYSTERY IN SPACE
THAT GLOBE-HEADED ELF IS TRANSFORMING ME INTO A CRYSTAL CREATURE--AND CHANGING THAT CRYSTAL BEING'S BODY INTO MINE!
A DOUBLE-LENGTH ADAM STRANGE THRILLER...
"CHALLENGE of the CRYSTAL CONQUERORS!"

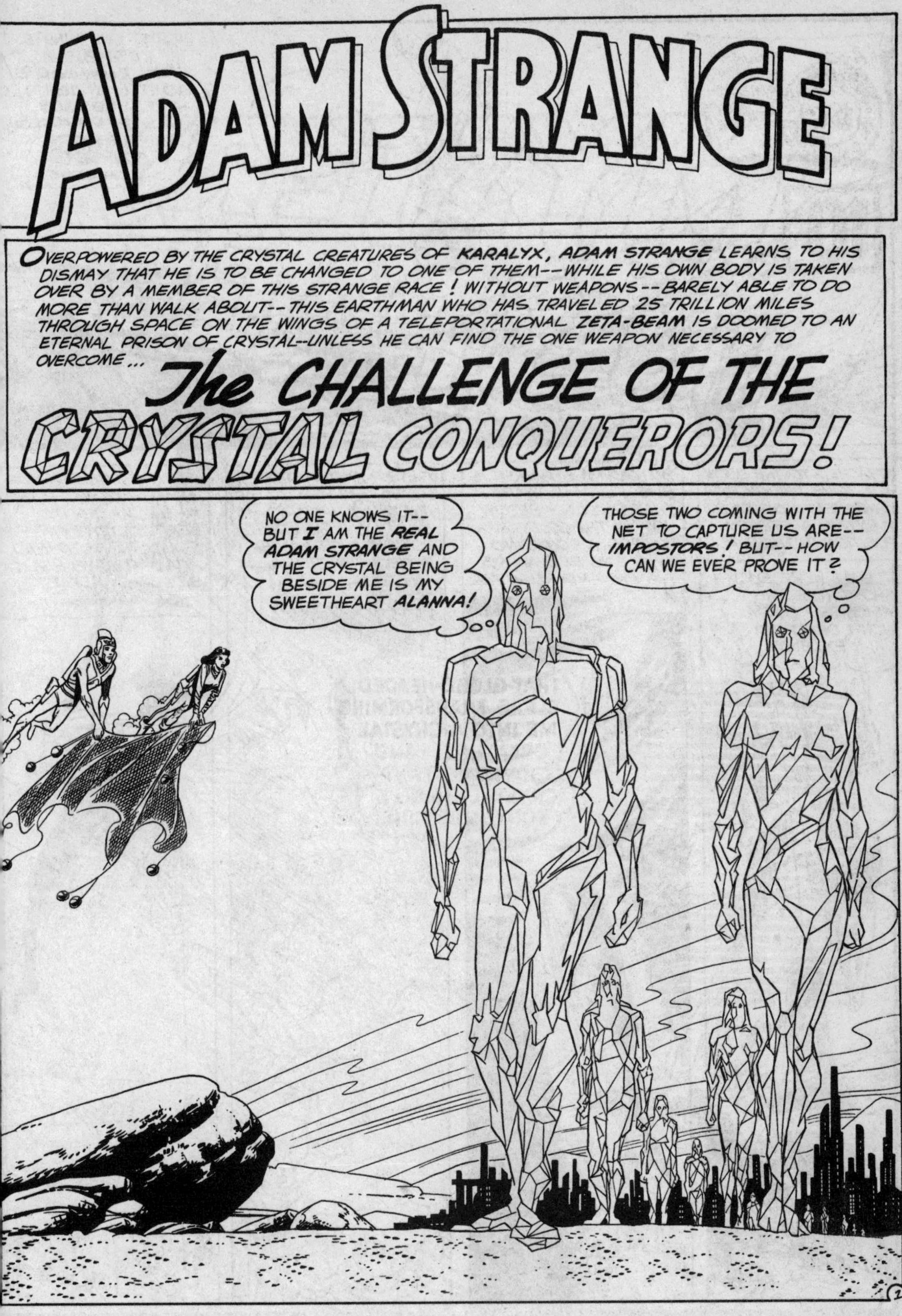
ADAM STRANGE
OVERPOWERED BY THE CRYSTAL CREATURES OF KARALYX, ADAM STRANGE LEARNS TO HIS DISMAY THAT HE IS TO BE CHANGED TO ONE OF THEM--WHILE HIS OWN BODY IS TAKEN OVER BY A MEMBER OF THIS STRANGE RACE! WITHOUT WEAPONS--BARELY ABLE TO DO MORE THAN WALK ABOUT--THIS EARTHMAN WHO HAS TRAVELED 25 TRILLION MILES THROUGH SPACE ON THE WINGS OF A TELEPORTATIONAL ZETA-BEAM IS DOOMED TO AN ETERNAL PRISON OF CRYSTAL--UNLESS HE CAN FIND THE ONE WEAPON NECESSARY TO OVERCOME...
The CHALLENGE OF THE CRYSTAL CONQUERORS!
NO ONE KNOWS IT--BUT I AM THE REAL ADAM STRANGE AND THE CRYSTAL BEING BESIDE ME IS MY SWEETHEART ALANNA!
THOSE TWO COMING WITH THE NET TO CAPTURE US ARE--IMPOSTORS! BUT--HOW CAN WE EVER PROVE IT?

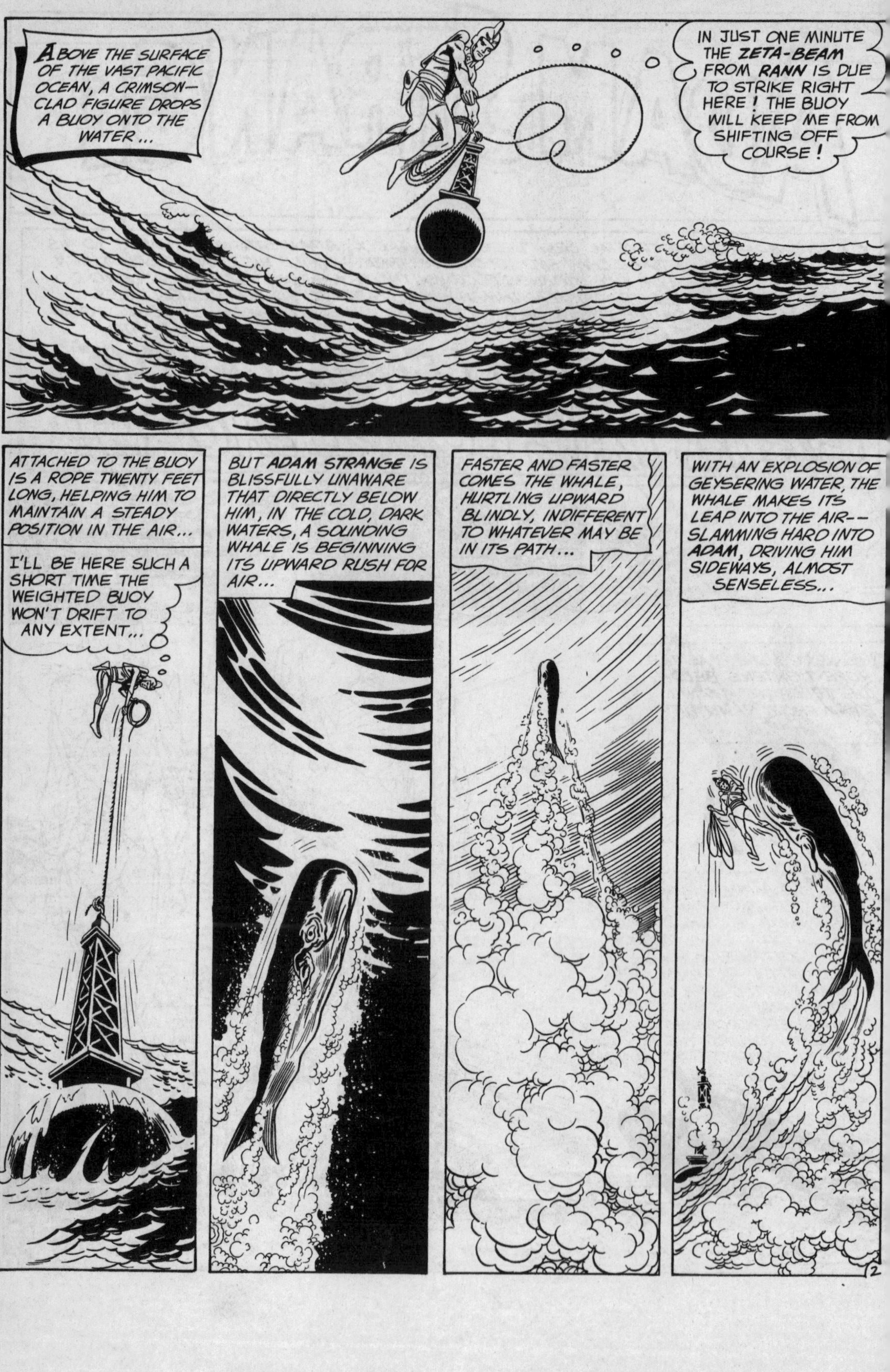
ABOVE THE SURFACE OF THE VAST PACIFIC OCEAN, A CRIMSON-CLAD FIGURE DROPS A BUOY ONTO THE WATER...
IN JUST ONE MINUTE THE ZETA-BEAM FROM RANN IS DUE TO STRIKE RIGHT HERE! THE BUOY WILL KEEP ME FROM SHIFTING OFF COURSE!
ATTACHED TO THE BUOY IS A ROPE TWENTY FEET LONG, HELPING HIM TO MAINTAIN A STEADY POSITION IN THE AIR...
I'LL BE HERE SUCH A SHORT TIME THE WEIGHTED BUOY WON'T DRIFT TO ANY EXTENT...
BUT ADAM STRANGE IS BLISSFULLY UNAWARE THAT DIRECTLY BELOW HIM, IN THE COLD, DARK WATERS, A SOUNDING WHALE IS BEGINNING ITS UPWARD RUSH FOR AIR...
FASTER AND FASTER COMES THE WHALE, HURTLING UPWARD BLINDLY, INDIFFERENT TO WHATEVER MAY BE IN ITS PATH...
WITH AN EXPLOSION OF GEYSERING WATER, THE WHALE MAKES ITS LEAP INTO THE AIR--SLAMMING HARD INTO ADAM, DRIVING HIM SIDEWAYS, ALMOST SENSELESS...
2

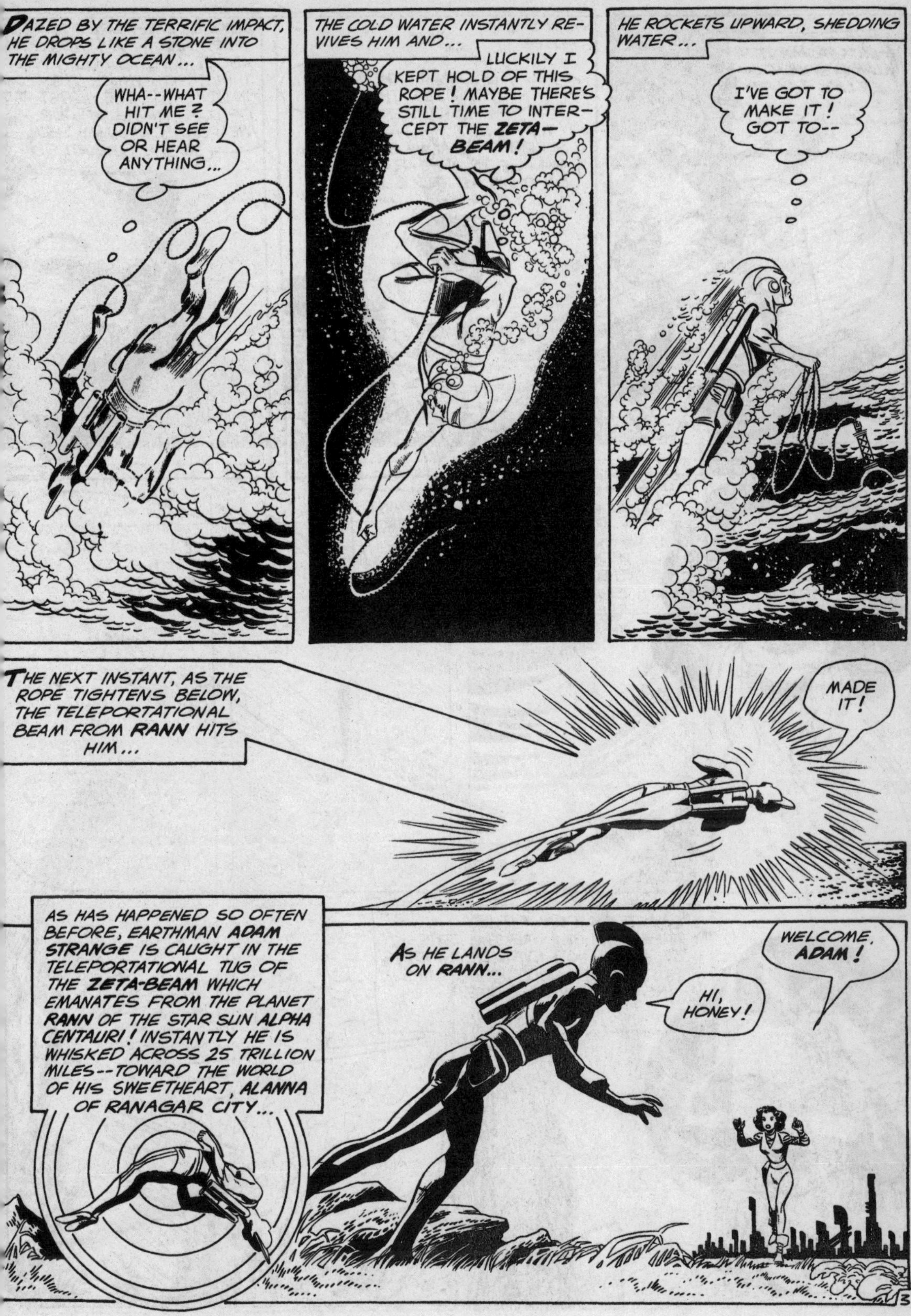
DAZED BY THE TERRIFIC IMPACT, HE DROPS LIKE A STONE INTO THE MIGHTY OCEAN...
WHA--WHAT HIT ME? DIDN'T SEE OR HEAR ANYTHING...
THE COLD WATER INSTANTLY REVIVES HIM AND...
LUCKILY I KEPT HOLD OF THIS ROPE! MAYBE THERE'S STILL TIME TO INTERCEPT THE ZETA-BEAM!
HE ROCKETS UPWARD, SHEDDING WATER...
I'VE GOT TO MAKE IT! GOT TO--
THE NEXT INSTANT, AS THE ROPE TIGHTENS BELOW, THE TELEPORTATIONAL BEAM FROM RANN HITS HIM...
MADE IT!
AS HAS HAPPENED SO OFTEN BEFORE, EARTHMAN ADAM STRANGE IS CAUGHT IN THE TELEPORTATIONAL TUG OF THE ZETA-BEAM WHICH EMANATES FROM THE PLANET RANN OF THE STAR SUN ALPHA CENTAURI! INSTANTLY HE IS WHISKED ACROSS 25 TRILLION MILES--TOWARD THE WORLD OF HIS SWEETHEART, ALANNA OF RANAGAR CITY...
AS HE LANDS ON RANN...
WELCOME, ADAM!
HI, HONEY!
3

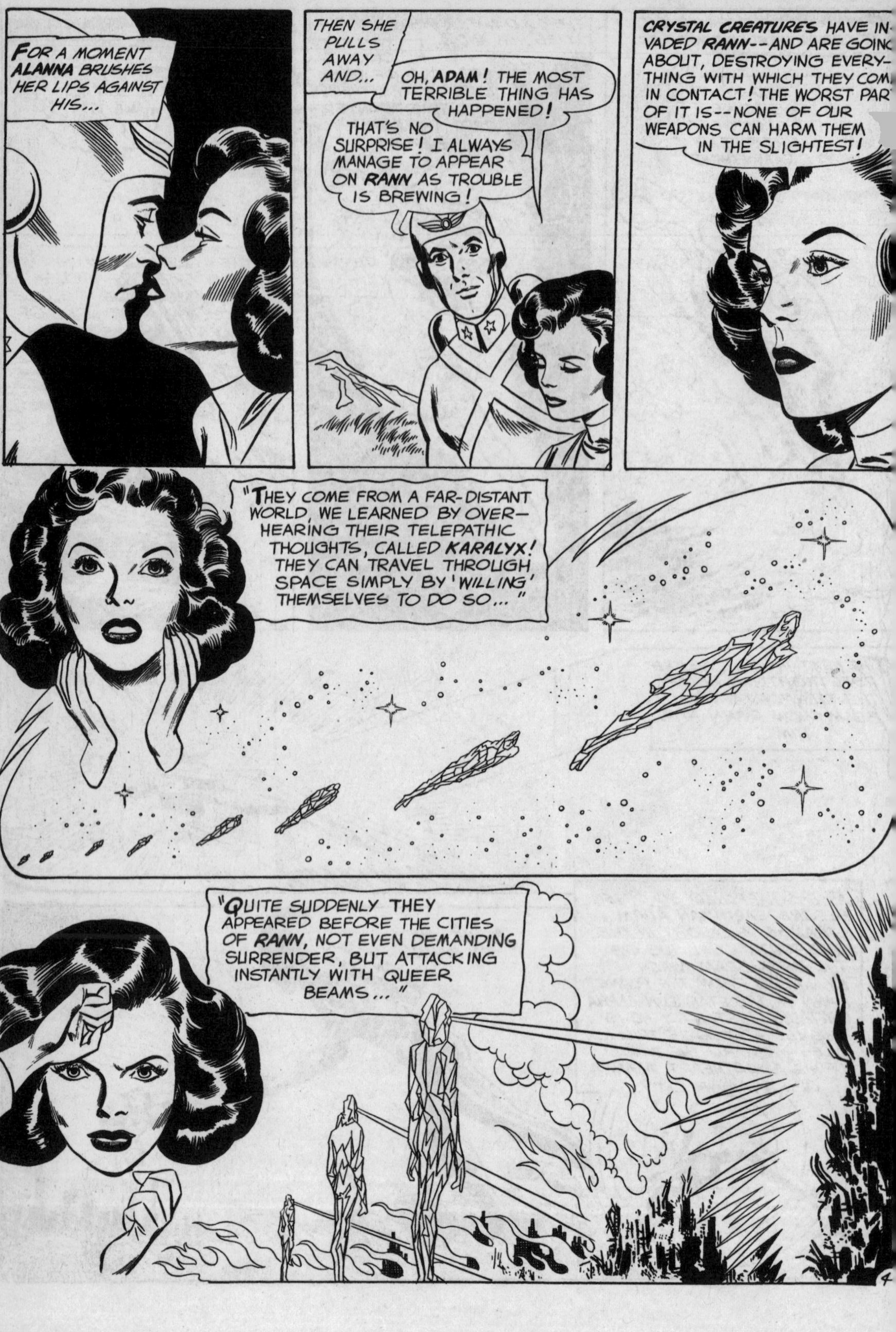
FOR A MOMENT ALANNA BRUSHES HER LIPS AGAINST HIS...
THEN SHE PULLS AWAY AND...
OH, ADAM! THE MOST TERRIBLE THING HAS HAPPENED!
THAT'S NO SURPRISE! I ALWAYS MANAGE TO APPEAR ON RANN AS TROUBLE IS BREWING!
CRYSTAL CREATURES HAVE INVADED RANN--AND ARE GOING ABOUT, DESTROYING EVERYTHING WITH WHICH THEY COME IN CONTACT! THE WORST PART OF IT IS--NONE OF OUR WEAPONS CAN HARM THEM IN THE SLIGHTEST!
"THEY COME FROM A FAR-DISTANT WORLD, WE LEARNED BY OVERHEARING THEIR TELEPATHIC THOUGHTS, CALLED KARALYX! THEY CAN TRAVEL THROUGH SPACE SIMPLY BY 'WILLING' THEMSELVES TO DO SO..."
"QUITE SUDDENLY THEY APPEARED BEFORE THE CITIES OF RANN, NOT EVEN DEMANDING SURRENDER, BUT ATTACKING INSTANTLY WITH QUEER BEAMS..."
4

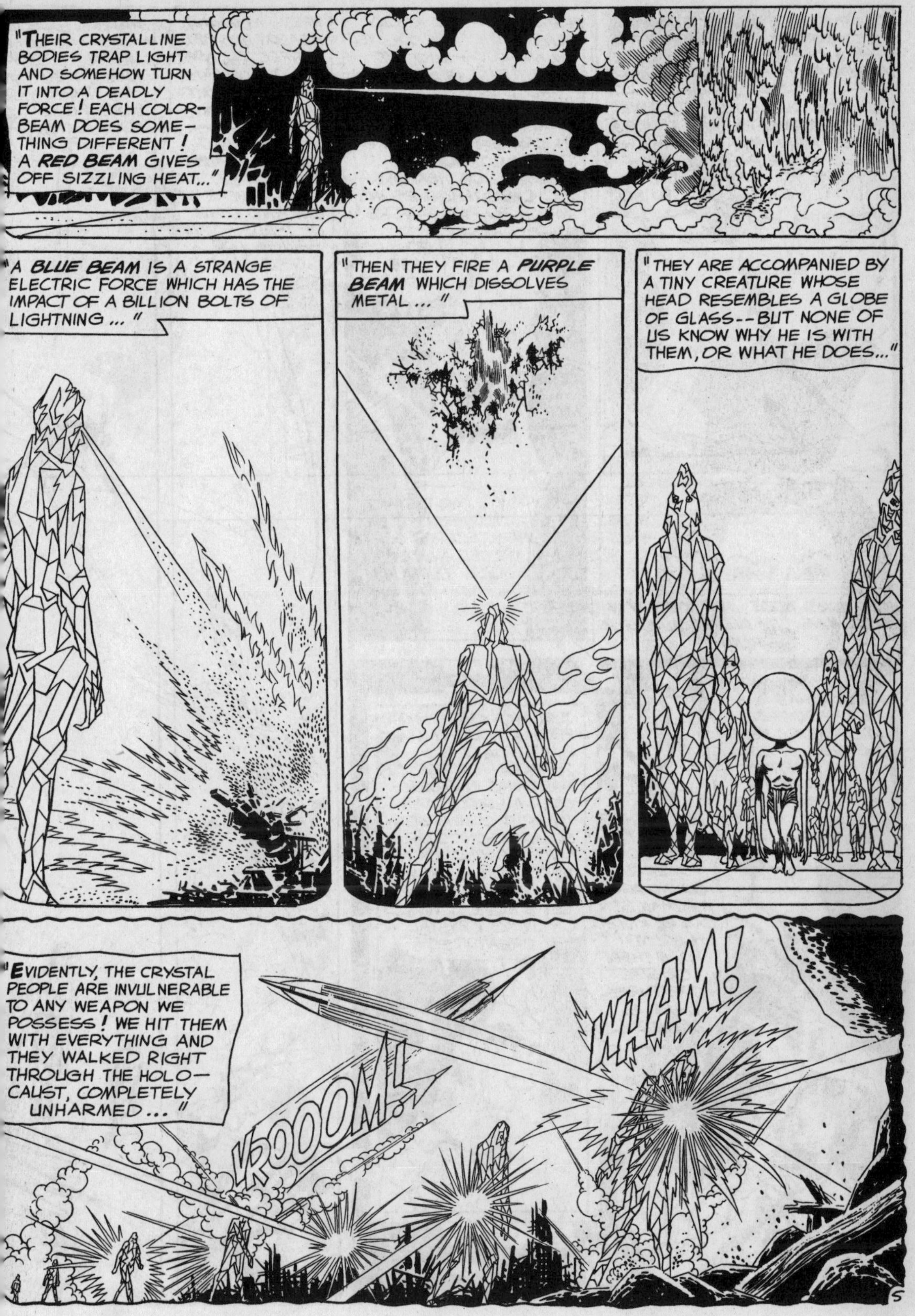
"THEIR CRYSTALLINE BODIES TRAP LIGHT AND SOMEHOW TURN IT INTO A DEADLY FORCE! EACH COLOR-BEAM DOES SOMETHING DIFFERENT! A RED BEAM GIVES OFF SIZZLING HEAT..."
"A BLUE BEAM IS A STRANGE ELECTRIC FORCE WHICH HAS THE IMPACT OF A BILLION BOLTS OF LIGHTNING ..."
"THEN THEY FIRE A PURPLE BEAM WHICH DISSOLVES METAL ..."
"THEY ARE ACCOMPANIED BY A TINY CREATURE WHOSE HEAD RESEMBLES A GLOBE OF GLASS--BUT NONE OF US KNOW WHY HE IS WITH THEM, OR WHAT HE DOES..."
"EVIDENTLY, THE CRYSTAL PEOPLE ARE INVULNERABLE TO ANY WEAPON WE POSSESS! WE HIT THEM WITH EVERYTHING AND THEY WALKED RIGHT THROUGH THE HOLOCAUST, COMPLETELY UNHARMED ..."
WHAM!
VROOOM!
5

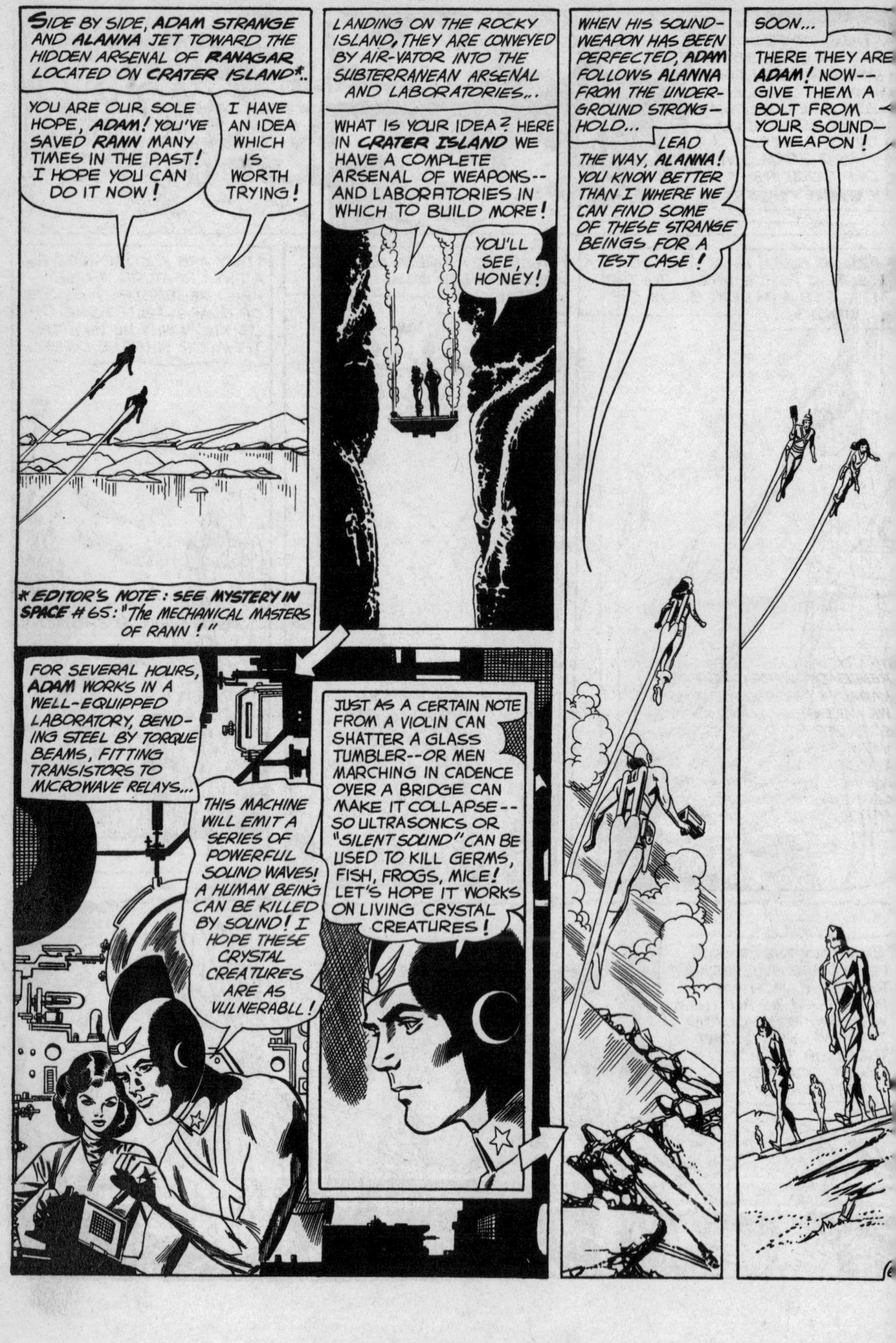
SIDE BY SIDE, ADAM STRANGE AND ALANNA JET TOWARD THE HIDDEN ARSENAL OF RANAGAR LOCATED ON CRATER ISLAND*.
YOU ARE OUR SOLE HOPE, ADAM! YOU'VE SAVED RANN MANY TIMES IN THE PAST! I HOPE YOU CAN DO IT NOW!
I HAVE AN IDEA WHICH IS WORTH TRYING!
*EDITOR'S NOTE: SEE MYSTERY IN SPACE #65: "The MECHANICAL MASTERS OF RANN!"
LANDING ON THE ROCKY ISLAND, THEY ARE CONVEYED BY AIR-VATOR INTO THE SUBTERRANEAN ARSENAL AND LABORATORIES...
WHAT IS YOUR IDEA? HERE IN CRATER ISLAND WE HAVE A COMPLETE ARSENAL OF WEAPONS--AND LABORATORIES IN WHICH TO BUILD MORE!
YOU'LL SEE, HONEY!
FOR SEVERAL HOURS, ADAM WORKS IN A WELL-EQUIPPED LABORATORY, BENDING STEEL BY TORQUE BEAMS, FITTING TRANSISTORS TO MICROWAVE RELAYS...
THIS MACHINE WILL EMIT A SERIES OF POWERFUL SOUND WAVES! A HUMAN BEING CAN BE KILLED BY SOUND! I HOPE THESE CRYSTAL CREATURES ARE AS VULNERABLL!
JUST AS A CERTAIN NOTE FROM A VIOLIN CAN SHATTER A GLASS TUMBLER--OR MEN MARCHING IN CADENCE OVER A BRIDGE CAN MAKE IT COLLAPSE--SO ULTRASONICS OR "SILENT SOUND" CAN BE USED TO KILL GERMS, FISH, FROGS, MICE! LET'S HOPE IT WORKS ON LIVING CRYSTAL CREATURES!
WHEN HIS SOUND-WEAPON HAS BEEN PERFECTED, ADAM FOLLOWS ALANNA FROM THE UNDERGROUND STRONGHOLD...
LEAD THE WAY, ALANNA! YOU KNOW BETTER THAN I WHERE WE CAN FIND SOME OF THESE STRANGE BEINGS FOR A TEST CASE!
SOON...
THERE THEY ARE ADAM! NOW--GIVE THEM A BOLT FROM YOUR SOUND-WEAPON!

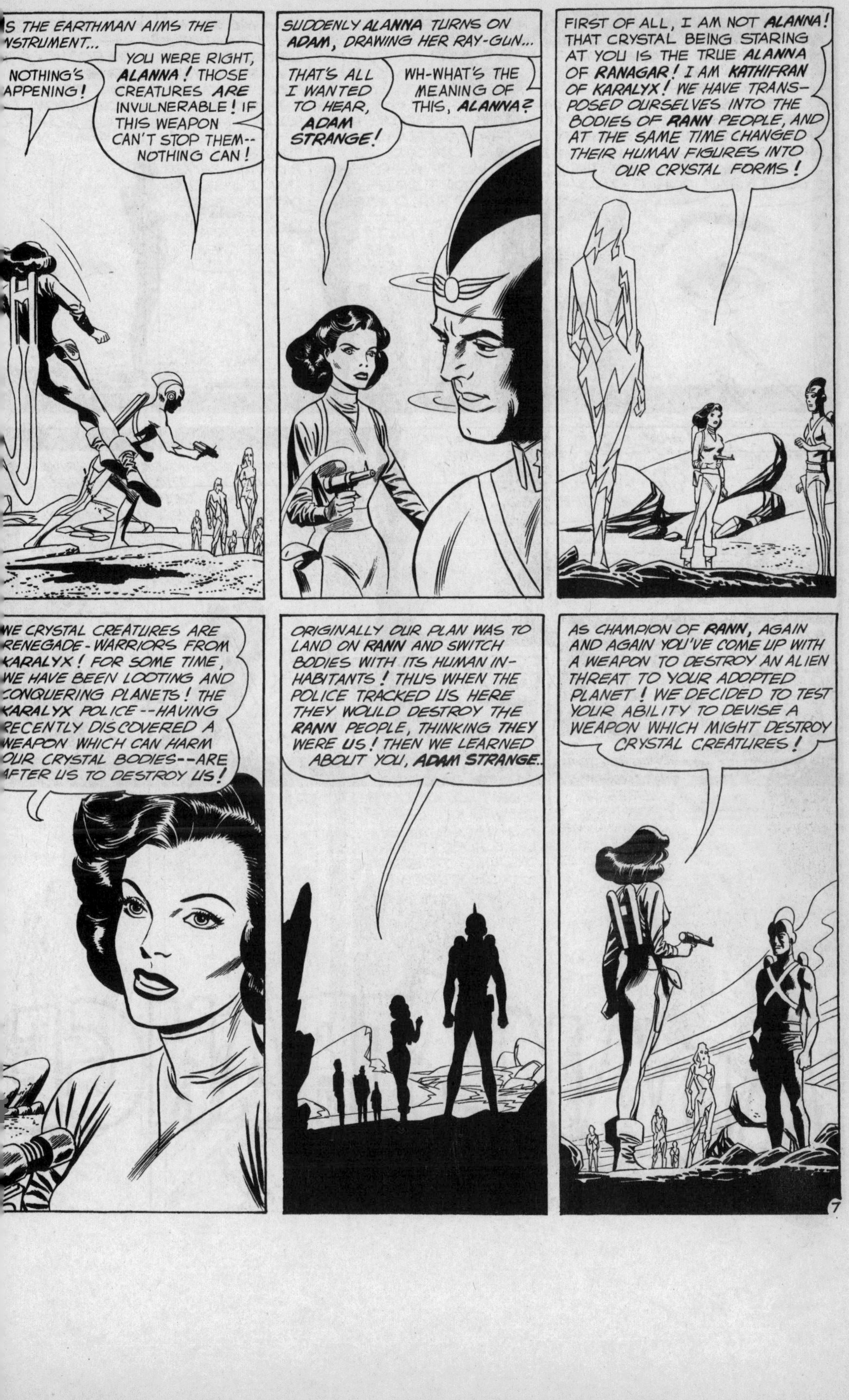
S THE EARTHMAN AIMS THE NSTRUMENT...
NOTHING'S APPENING!
YOU WERE RIGHT, ALANNA! THOSE CREATURES ARE INVULNERABLE! IF THIS WEAPON CAN'T STOP THEM-- NOTHING CAN!
SUDDENLY ALANNA TURNS ON ADAM, DRAWING HER RAY-GUN...
THAT'S ALL I WANTED TO HEAR, ADAM STRANGE!
WH-WHAT'S THE MEANING OF THIS, ALANNA?
FIRST OF ALL, I AM NOT ALANNA! THAT CRYSTAL BEING STARING AT YOU IS THE TRUE ALANNA OF RANAGAR! I AM KATHIFRAN OF KARALYX! WE HAVE TRANS-POSED OURSELVES INTO THE BODIES OF RANN PEOPLE, AND AT THE SAME TIME CHANGED THEIR HUMAN FIGURES INTO OUR CRYSTAL FORMS!
WE CRYSTAL CREATURES ARE RENEGADE-WARRIORS FROM KARALYX! FOR SOME TIME, WE HAVE BEEN LOOTING AND CONQUERING PLANETS! THE KARALYX POLICE--HAVING RECENTLY DISCOVERED A WEAPON WHICH CAN HARM OUR CRYSTAL BODIES--ARE AFTER US TO DESTROY US!
ORIGINALLY OUR PLAN WAS TO LAND ON RANN AND SWITCH BODIES WITH ITS HUMAN IN-HABITANTS! THUS WHEN THE POLICE TRACKED US HERE THEY WOULD DESTROY THE RANN PEOPLE, THINKING THEY WERE US! THEN WE LEARNED ABOUT YOU, ADAM STRANGE...
AS CHAMPION OF RANN, AGAIN AND AGAIN YOU'VE COME UP WITH A WEAPON TO DESTROY AN ALIEN THREAT TO YOUR ADOPTED PLANET! WE DECIDED TO TEST YOUR ABILITY TO DEVISE A WEAPON WHICH MIGHT DESTROY CRYSTAL CREATURES!
7

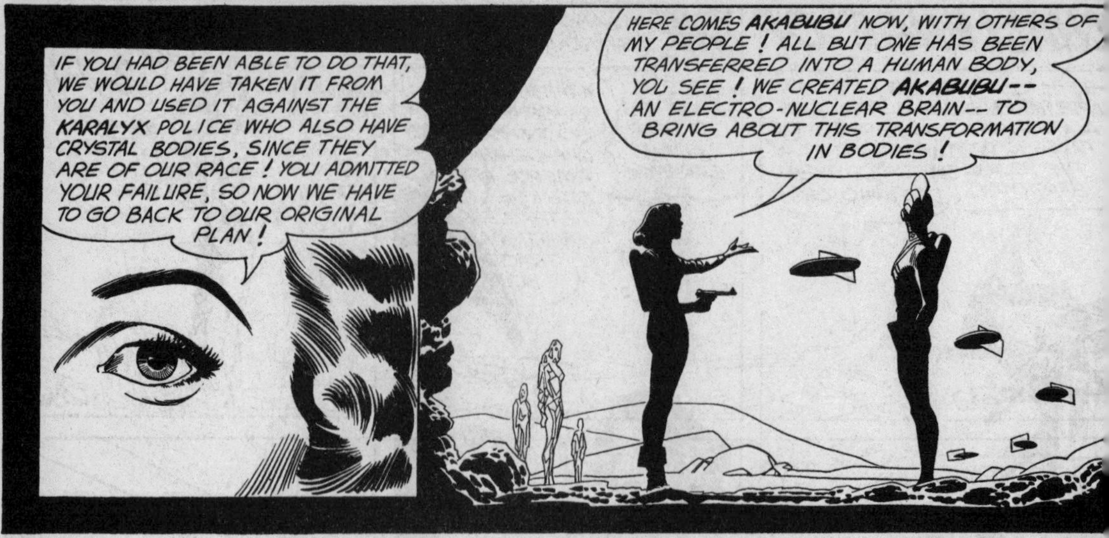
IF YOU HAD BEEN ABLE TO DO THAT, WE WOULD HAVE TAKEN IT FROM YOU AND USED IT AGAINST THE KARALYX POLICE WHO ALSO HAVE CRYSTAL BODIES, SINCE THEY ARE OF OUR RACE! YOU ADMITTED YOUR FAILURE, SO NOW WE HAVE TO GO BACK TO OUR ORIGINAL PLAN!
HERE COMES AKABUBU NOW, WITH OTHERS OF MY PEOPLE! ALL BUT ONE HAS BEEN TRANSFERRED INTO A HUMAN BODY, YOU SEE! WE CREATED AKABUBU-- AN ELECTRO-NUCLEAR BRAIN-- TO BRING ABOUT THIS TRANSFORMATION IN BODIES!

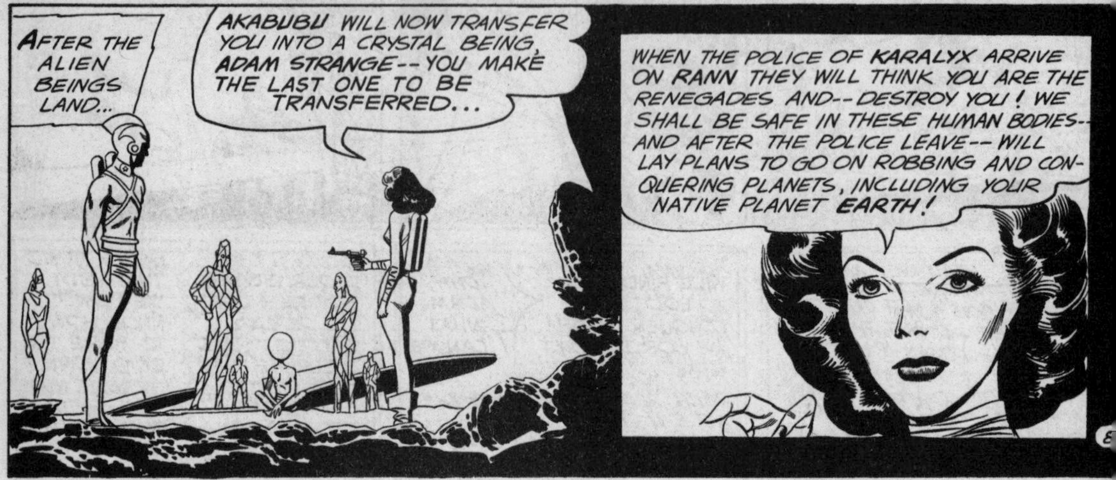
AFTER THE ALIEN BEINGS LAND...
AKABUBU WILL NOW TRANSFER YOU INTO A CRYSTAL BEING, ADAM STRANGE--YOU MAKE THE LAST ONE TO BE TRANSFERRED...
WHEN THE POLICE OF KARALYX ARRIVE ON RANN THEY WILL THINK YOU ARE THE RENEGADES AND--DESTROY YOU! WE SHALL BE SAFE IN THESE HUMAN BODIES-- AND AFTER THE POLICE LEAVE--WILL LAY PLANS TO GO ON ROBBING AND CONQUERING PLANETS, INCLUDING YOUR NATIVE PLANET EARTH!

ADAM STRANGE

CHALLENGE OF THE CRYSTAL CONQUERORS CHAPTER 2

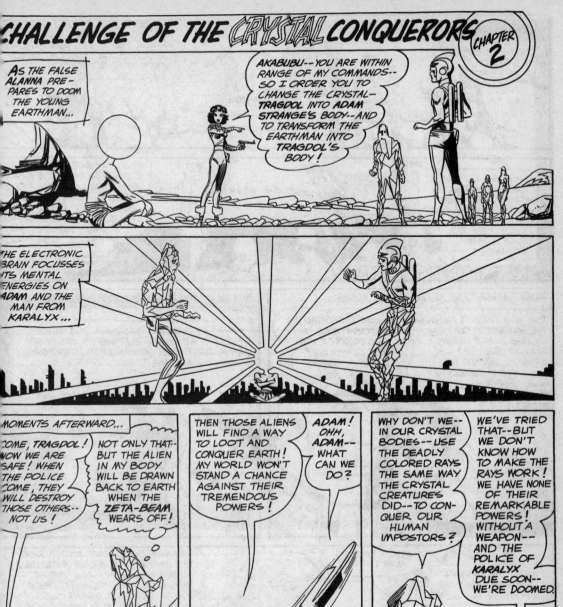

AS THE FALSE ALANNA PREPARES TO DOOM THE YOUNG EARTHMAN...

AKABUBU--YOU ARE WITHIN RANGE OF MY COMMANDS--SO I ORDER YOU TO CHANGE THE CRYSTAL-TRAGDOL INTO ADAM STRANGE'S BODY--AND TO TRANSFORM THE EARTHMAN INTO TRAGDOL'S BODY!

THE ELECTRONIC BRAIN FOCUSSES ITS MENTAL ENERGIES ON ADAM AND THE MAN FROM KARALYX...

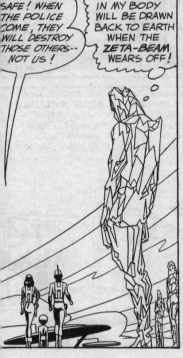

MOMENTS AFTERWARD...

COME, TRAGDOL! NOW WE ARE SAFE! WHEN THE POLICE COME, THEY WILL DESTROY THOSE OTHERS-- NOT US!

NOT ONLY THAT--BUT THE ALIEN IN MY BODY WILL BE DRAWN BACK TO EARTH WHEN THE ZETA-BEAM WEARS OFF!

THEN THOSE ALIENS WILL FIND A WAY TO LOOT AND CONQUER EARTH! MY WORLD WON'T STAND A CHANCE AGAINST THEIR TREMENDOUS POWERS!

ADAM! OHH, ADAM-- WHAT CAN WE DO?

WHY DON'T WE--IN OUR CRYSTAL BODIES--USE THE DEADLY COLORED RAYS THE SAME WAY THE CRYSTAL CREATURES DID--TO CONQUER OUR HUMAN IMPOSTORS?

WE'VE TRIED THAT--BUT WE DON'T KNOW HOW TO MAKE THE RAYS WORK! WE HAVE NONE OF THEIR REMARKABLE POWERS! WITHOUT A WEAPON-- AND THE POLICE OF KARALYX DUE SOON-- WE'RE DOOMED.

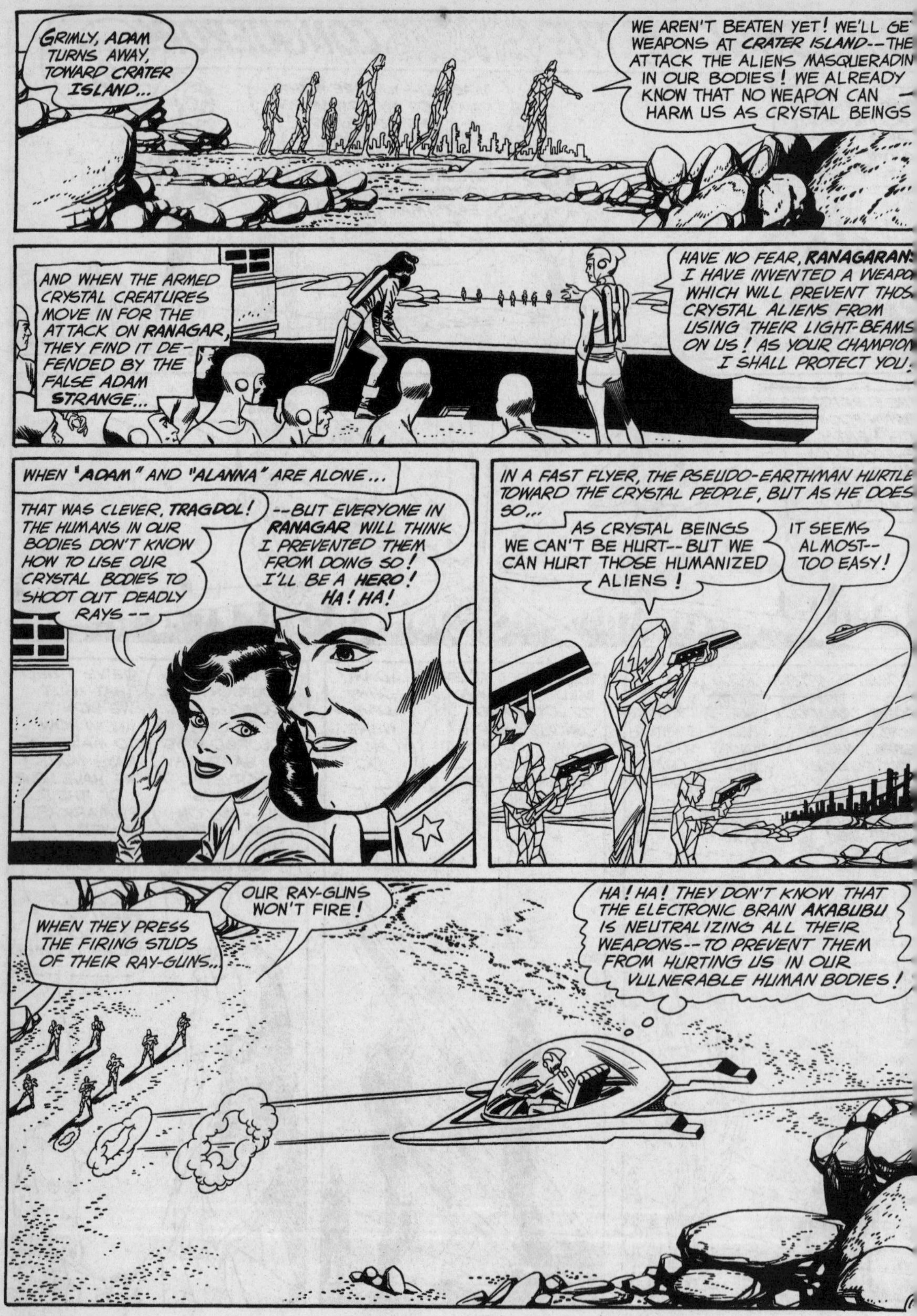
GRIMLY, ADAM TURNS AWAY, TOWARD CRATER ISLAND...
WE AREN'T BEATEN YET! WE'LL GE WEAPONS AT CRATER ISLAND--THE ATTACK THE ALIENS MASQUERADIN IN OUR BODIES! WE ALREADY KNOW THAT NO WEAPON CAN HARM US AS CRYSTAL BEINGS
AND WHEN THE ARMED CRYSTAL CREATURES MOVE IN FOR THE ATTACK ON RANAGAR, THEY FIND IT DEFENDED BY THE FALSE ADAM STRANGE...
HAVE NO FEAR, RANAGARAN I HAVE INVENTED A WEAPO WHICH WILL PREVENT THOS CRYSTAL ALIENS FROM USING THEIR LIGHT-BEAMS ON US! AS YOUR CHAMPIO I SHALL PROTECT YOU
WHEN "ADAM" AND "ALANNA" ARE ALONE...
THAT WAS CLEVER, TRAGDOL! THE HUMANS IN OUR BODIES DON'T KNOW HOW TO USE OUR CRYSTAL BODIES TO SHOOT OUT DEADLY RAYS --
--BUT EVERYONE IN RANAGAR WILL THINK I PREVENTED THEM FROM DOING SO! I'LL BE A HERO! HA! HA!
IN A FAST FLYER, THE PSEUDO-EARTHMAN HURTLE TOWARD THE CRYSTAL PEOPLE, BUT AS HE DOES SO...
AS CRYSTAL BEINGS WE CAN'T BE HURT-- BUT WE CAN HURT THOSE HUMANIZED ALIENS!
IT SEEMS ALMOST-- TOO EASY!
WHEN THEY PRESS THE FIRING STUDS OF THEIR RAY-GUNS...
OUR RAY-GUNS WON'T FIRE!
HA! HA! THEY DON'T KNOW THAT THE ELECTRONIC BRAIN AKABUBU IS NEUTRALIZING ALL THEIR WEAPONS--TO PREVENT THEM FROM HURTING US IN OUR VULNERABLE HUMAN BODIES!

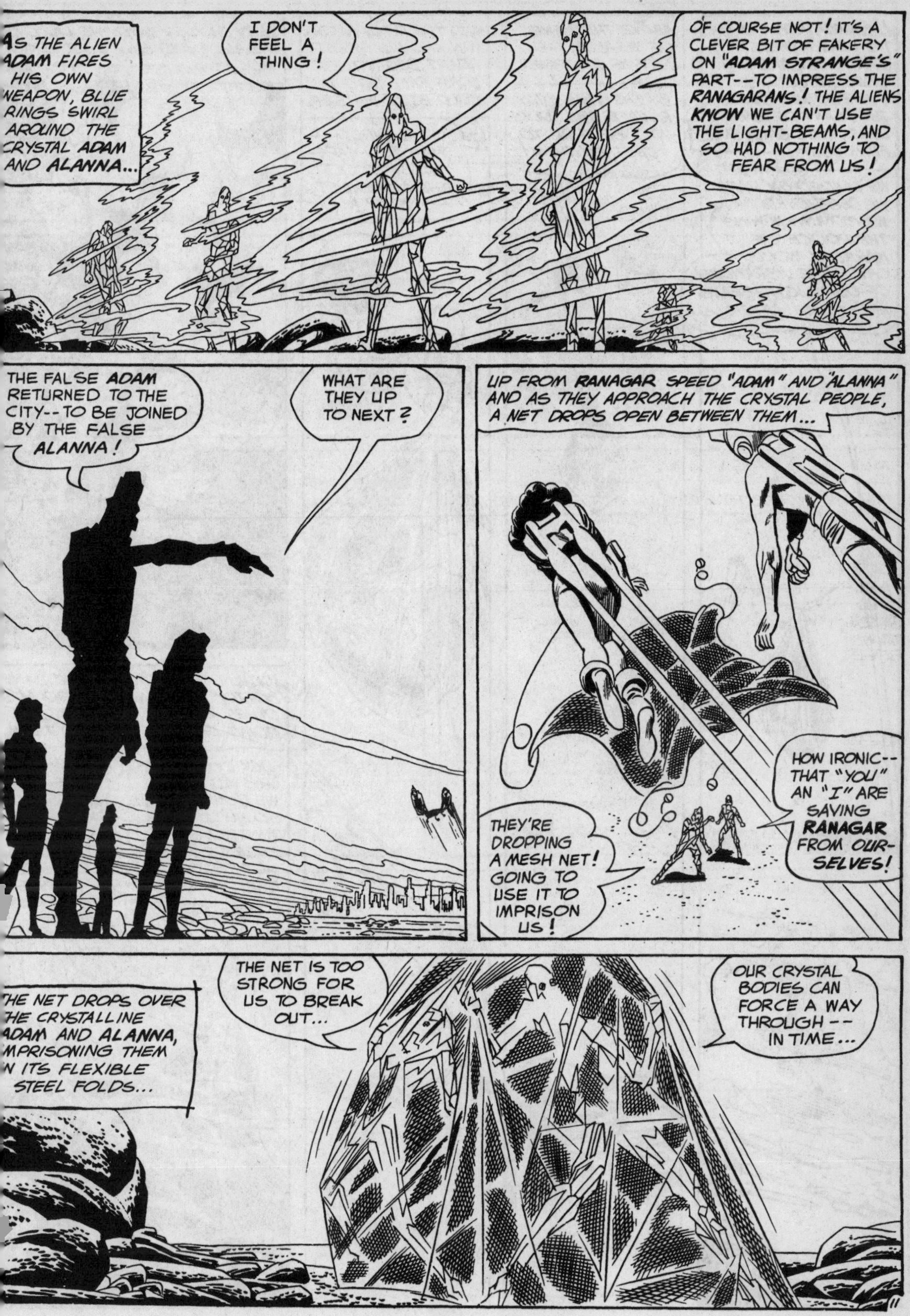
AS THE ALIEN ADAM FIRES HIS OWN WEAPON, BLUE RINGS SWIRL AROUND THE CRYSTAL ADAM AND ALANNA...
I DON'T FEEL A THING!
OF COURSE NOT! IT'S A CLEVER BIT OF FAKERY ON "ADAM STRANGE'S" PART--TO IMPRESS THE RANAGARANS! THE ALIENS KNOW WE CAN'T USE THE LIGHT-BEAMS, AND SO HAD NOTHING TO FEAR FROM US!
THE FALSE ADAM RETURNED TO THE CITY--TO BE JOINED BY THE FALSE ALANNA!
WHAT ARE THEY UP TO NEXT?
UP FROM RANAGAR SPEED "ADAM" AND "ALANNA" AND AS THEY APPROACH THE CRYSTAL PEOPLE, A NET DROPS OPEN BETWEEN THEM...
THEY'RE DROPPING A MESH NET! GOING TO USE IT TO IMPRISON US!
HOW IRONIC--THAT "YOU" AN "I" ARE SAVING RANAGAR FROM OUR-SELVES!
THE NET DROPS OVER THE CRYSTALLINE ADAM AND ALANNA, IMPRISONING THEM IN ITS FLEXIBLE STEEL FOLDS...
THE NET IS TOO STRONG FOR US TO BREAK OUT...
OUR CRYSTAL BODIES CAN FORCE A WAY THROUGH--IN TIME...
11

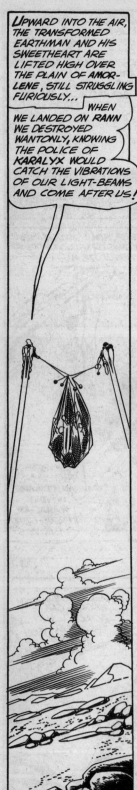

UPWARD INTO THE AIR, THE TRANSFORMED EARTHMAN AND HIS SWEETHEART ARE LIFTED HIGH OVER THE PLAIN OF AMOR-LENE, STILL STRUGGLING FURIOUSLY...

WHEN WE LANDED ON *RANN* WE DESTROYED WANTONLY, KNOWING THE POLICE OF *KARALYX* WOULD CATCH THE VIBRATIONS OF OUR LIGHT-BEAMS AND COME AFTER US!

ABOVE THE *LAKE OF INSALLA*, THE NET IS DROPPED...

BY THE TIME THEY ESCAPE, THE POLICE WILL BE HERE TO DESTROY THEM!

AND THE REAL EARTH-MAN AND HIS SWEET-HEART BEGIN THEIR LONG FALL INTO THE COLD BLUE WATERS..

WE PLANNED THIS TOO CARE-FULLY TO LET THEM SPOIL IT NOW!

THEY GEYSER INTO THE *LAKE OF INSALLA* AND SINK LIKE HEAVY ROCKS...

UNTIL THEY STAND ON THE LAKE BOTTOM, STARING UPWARD AS OTHER CRYSTALLIZED HUMANS COME FALLING TOWARD THEM..

LUCKILY, AS CRYSTAL BEINGS WE DON'T BREATHE-- SO WE'LL HAVE TIME TO BREAK FREE OF THIS NET! BUT THEN WHAT--

ALANNA, WE'RE IN THE *LAKE OF INSALLA* RIGHT? DOESN'T *RANAGAR* GET ITS DRINKING WATER FROM THIS LAKE?

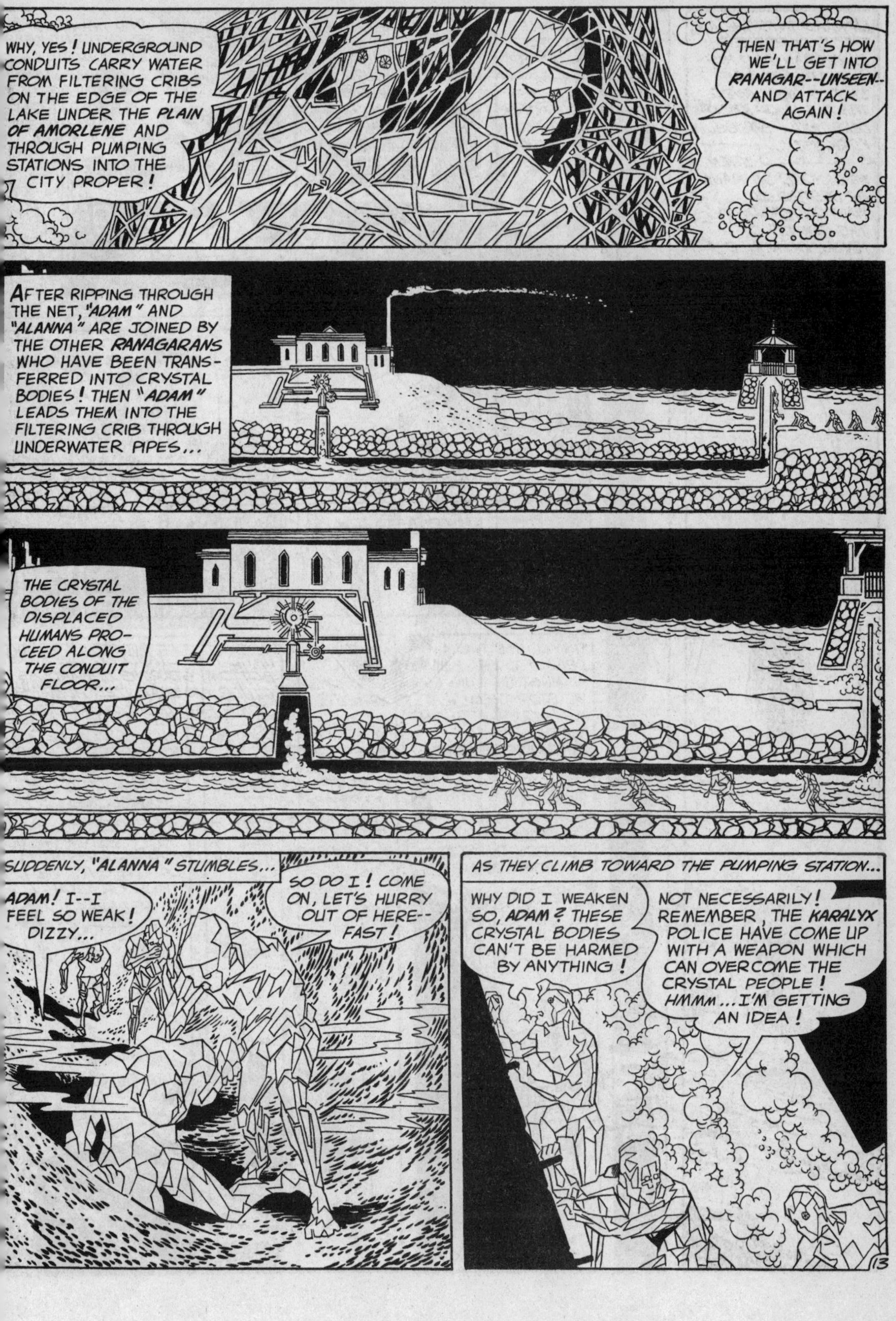
WHY, YES! UNDERGROUND CONDUITS CARRY WATER FROM FILTERING CRIBS ON THE EDGE OF THE LAKE UNDER THE PLAIN OF AMORLENE AND THROUGH PUMPING STATIONS INTO THE CITY PROPER!
THEN THAT'S HOW WE'LL GET INTO RANAGAR--UNSEEN-- AND ATTACK AGAIN!
AFTER RIPPING THROUGH THE NET, "ADAM" AND "ALANNA" ARE JOINED BY THE OTHER RANAGARANS WHO HAVE BEEN TRANSFERRED INTO CRYSTAL BODIES! THEN "ADAM" LEADS THEM INTO THE FILTERING CRIB THROUGH UNDERWATER PIPES...
THE CRYSTAL BODIES OF THE DISPLACED HUMANS PROCEED ALONG THE CONDUIT FLOOR...
SUDDENLY, "ALANNA" STUMBLES...
ADAM! I--I FEEL SO WEAK! DIZZY...
SO DO I! COME ON, LET'S HURRY OUT OF HERE-- FAST!
AS THEY CLIMB TOWARD THE PUMPING STATION...
WHY DID I WEAKEN SO, ADAM? THESE CRYSTAL BODIES CAN'T BE HARMED BY ANYTHING!
NOT NECESSARILY! REMEMBER, THE KARALYX POLICE HAVE COME UP WITH A WEAPON WHICH CAN OVERCOME THE CRYSTAL PEOPLE! HMMM... I'M GETTING AN IDEA!
13

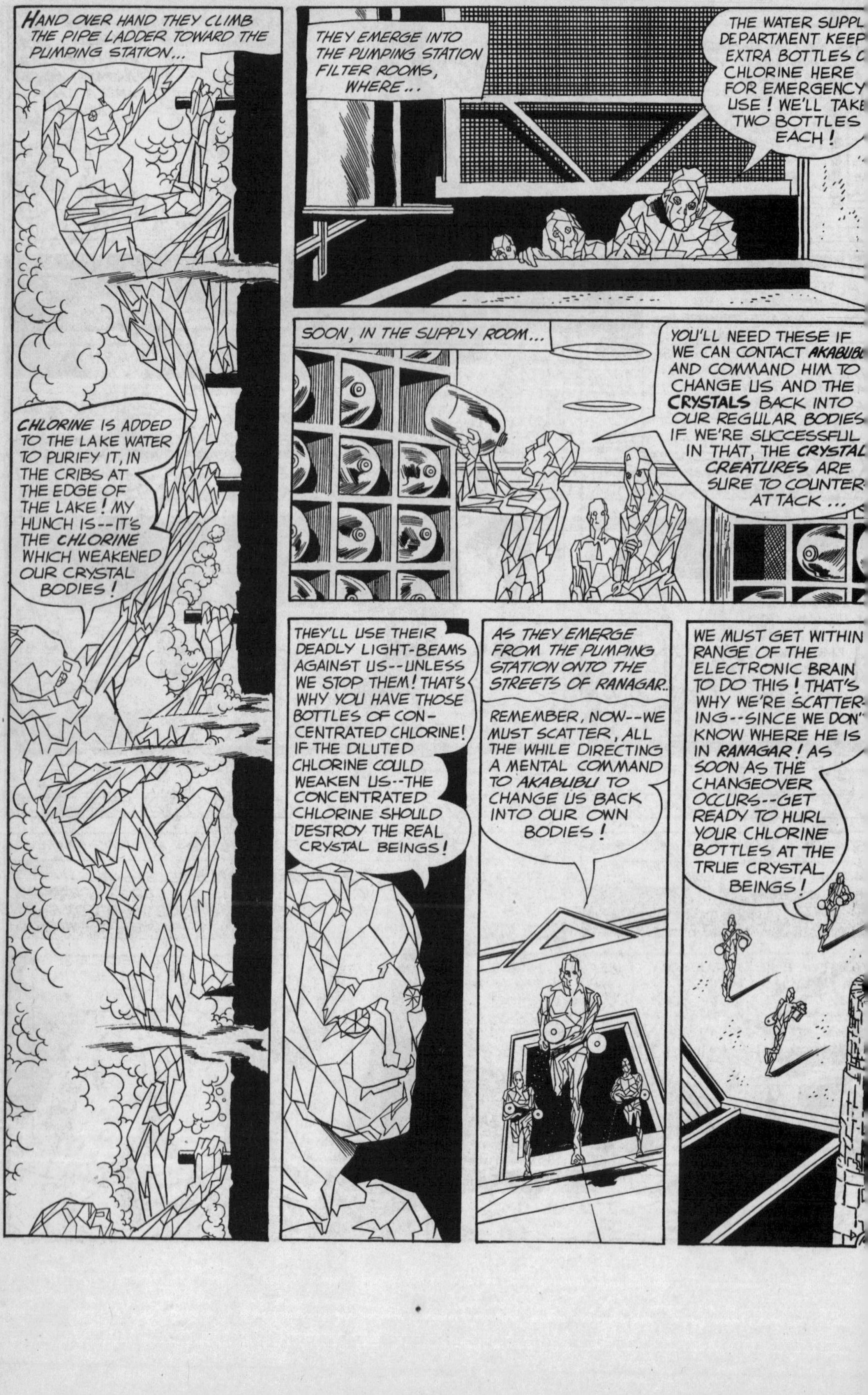
HAND OVER HAND THEY CLIMB THE PIPE LADDER TOWARD THE PUMPING STATION...
CHLORINE IS ADDED TO THE LAKE WATER TO PURIFY IT, IN THE CRIBS AT THE EDGE OF THE LAKE! MY HUNCH IS--IT'S THE CHLORINE WHICH WEAKENED OUR CRYSTAL BODIES!
THEY EMERGE INTO THE PUMPING STATION FILTER ROOMS, WHERE...
THE WATER SUPPL DEPARTMENT KEEP EXTRA BOTTLES C CHLORINE HERE FOR EMERGENCY USE! WE'LL TAKE TWO BOTTLES EACH!
SOON, IN THE SUPPLY ROOM...
YOU'LL NEED THESE IF WE CAN CONTACT AKABUBU AND COMMAND HIM TO CHANGE US AND THE CRYSTALS BACK INTO OUR REGULAR BODIES IF WE'RE SUCCESSFUL IN THAT, THE CRYSTAL CREATURES ARE SURE TO COUNTER-ATTACK...
THEY'LL USE THEIR DEADLY LIGHT-BEAMS AGAINST US--UNLESS WE STOP THEM! THAT'S WHY YOU HAVE THOSE BOTTLES OF CONCENTRATED CHLORINE! IF THE DILUTED CHLORINE COULD WEAKEN US--THE CONCENTRATED CHLORINE SHOULD DESTROY THE REAL CRYSTAL BEINGS!
AS THEY EMERGE FROM THE PUMPING STATION ONTO THE STREETS OF RANAGAR..
REMEMBER, NOW--WE MUST SCATTER, ALL THE WHILE DIRECTING A MENTAL COMMAND TO AKABUBU TO CHANGE US BACK INTO OUR OWN BODIES!
WE MUST GET WITHIN RANGE OF THE ELECTRONIC BRAIN TO DO THIS! THAT'S WHY WE'RE SCATTERING--SINCE WE DON'T KNOW WHERE HE IS IN RANAGAR! AS SOON AS THE CHANGEOVER OCCURS--GET READY TO HURL YOUR CHLORINE BOTTLES AT THE TRUE CRYSTAL BEINGS!

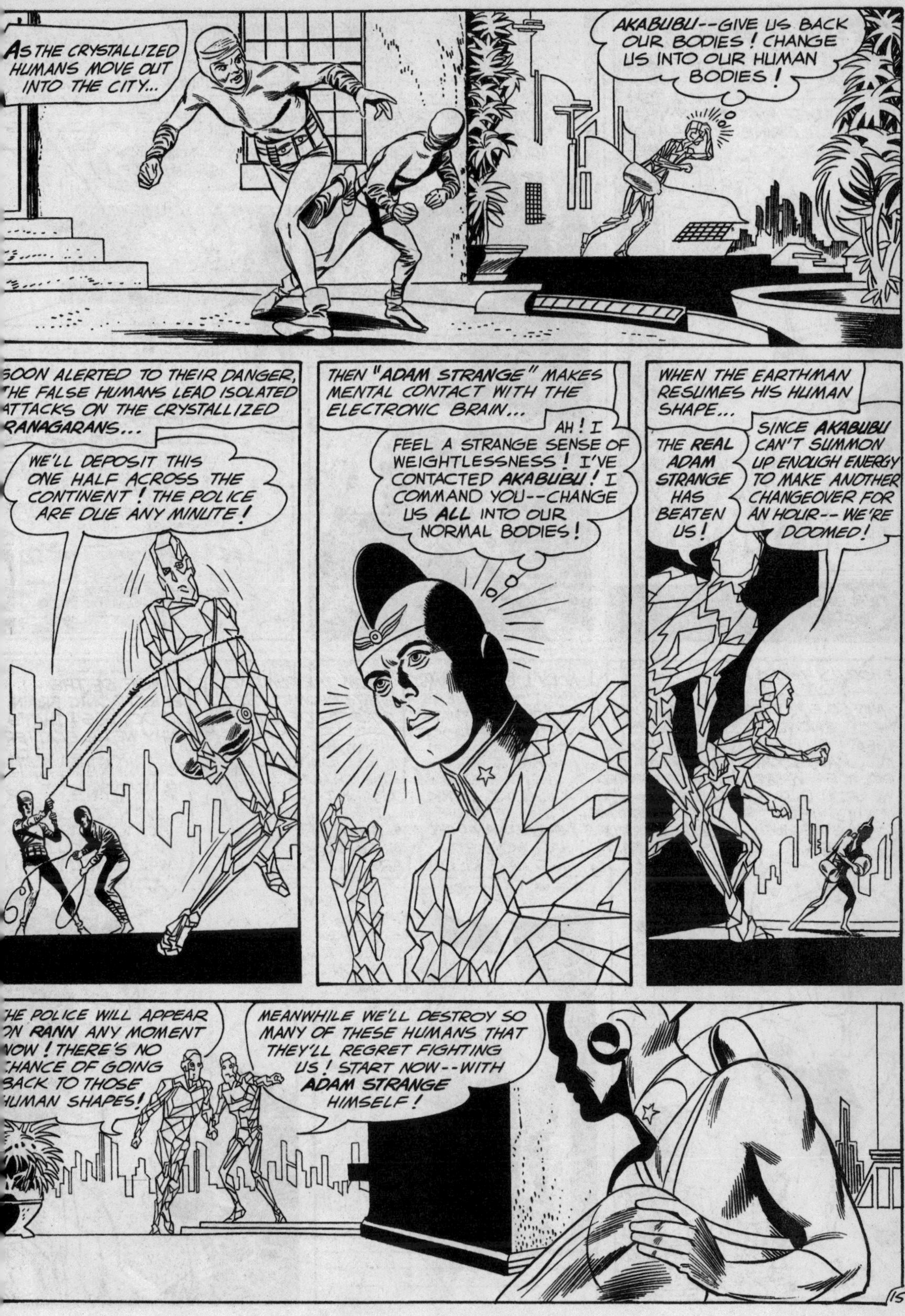
AS THE CRYSTALLIZED HUMANS MOVE OUT INTO THE CITY...
AKABUBU--GIVE US BACK OUR BODIES! CHANGE US INTO OUR HUMAN BODIES!
SOON ALERTED TO THEIR DANGER, THE FALSE HUMANS LEAD ISOLATED ATTACKS ON THE CRYSTALLIZED RANAGARANS...
WE'LL DEPOSIT THIS ONE HALF ACROSS THE CONTINENT! THE POLICE ARE DUE ANY MINUTE!
THEN "ADAM STRANGE" MAKES MENTAL CONTACT WITH THE ELECTRONIC BRAIN...
AH! I FEEL A STRANGE SENSE OF WEIGHTLESSNESS! I'VE CONTACTED AKABUBU! I COMMAND YOU--CHANGE US ALL INTO OUR NORMAL BODIES!
WHEN THE EARTHMAN RESUMES HIS HUMAN SHAPE...
THE REAL ADAM STRANGE HAS BEATEN US!
SINCE AKABUBU CAN'T SUMMON UP ENOUGH ENERGY TO MAKE ANOTHER CHANGEOVER FOR AN HOUR-- WE'RE DOOMED!
HE POLICE WILL APPEAR ON RANN ANY MOMENT NOW! THERE'S NO CHANCE OF GOING BACK TO THOSE HUMAN SHAPES!
MEANWHILE WE'LL DESTROY SO MANY OF THESE HUMANS THAT THEY'LL REGRET FIGHTING US! START NOW--WITH ADAM STRANGE HIMSELF!
15

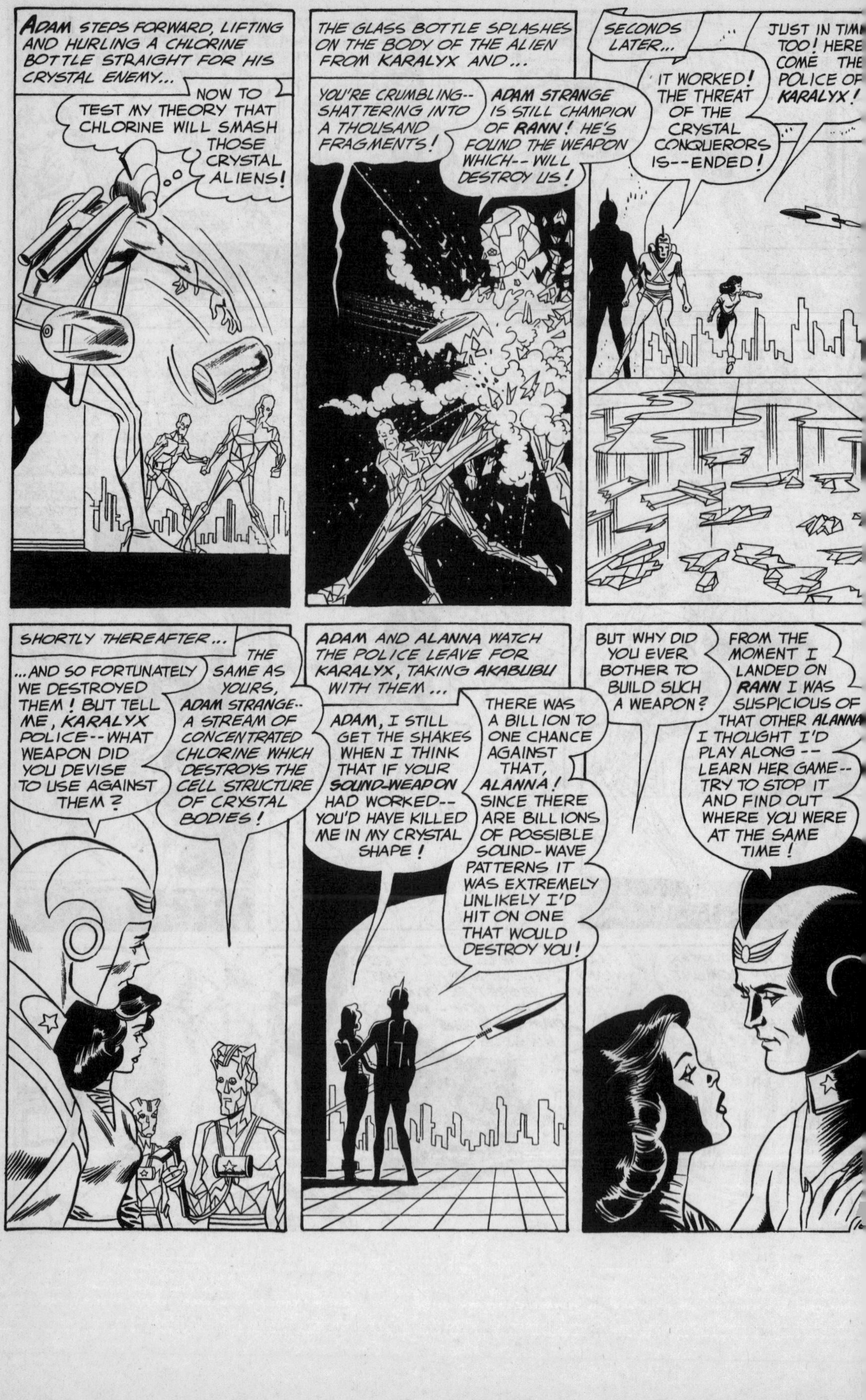
ADAM STEPS FORWARD, LIFTING AND HURLING A CHLORINE BOTTLE STRAIGHT FOR HIS CRYSTAL ENEMY...
NOW TO TEST MY THEORY THAT CHLORINE WILL SMASH THOSE CRYSTAL ALIENS!
THE GLASS BOTTLE SPLASHES ON THE BODY OF THE ALIEN FROM KARALYX AND...
YOU'RE CRUMBLING-- SHATTERING INTO A THOUSAND FRAGMENTS!
ADAM STRANGE IS STILL CHAMPION OF RANN! HE'S FOUND THE WEAPON WHICH-- WILL DESTROY US!
SECONDS LATER...
IT WORKED! THE THREAT OF THE CRYSTAL CONQUERORS IS--ENDED!
JUST IN TIM TOO! HERE COME THE POLICE OF KARALYX!
SHORTLY THEREAFTER...
...AND SO FORTUNATELY WE DESTROYED THEM! BUT TELL ME, KARALYX POLICE--WHAT WEAPON DID YOU DEVISE TO USE AGAINST THEM?
THE SAME AS YOURS, ADAM STRANGE.. A STREAM OF CONCENTRATED CHLORINE WHICH DESTROYS THE CELL STRUCTURE OF CRYSTAL BODIES!
ADAM AND ALANNA WATCH THE POLICE LEAVE FOR KARALYX, TAKING AKABUBU WITH THEM...
ADAM, I STILL GET THE SHAKES WHEN I THINK THAT IF YOUR SOUND-WEAPON HAD WORKED-- YOU'D HAVE KILLED ME IN MY CRYSTAL SHAPE!
THERE WAS A BILLION TO ONE CHANCE AGAINST THAT, ALANNA! SINCE THERE ARE BILLIONS OF POSSIBLE SOUND-WAVE PATTERNS IT WAS EXTREMELY UNLIKELY I'D HIT ON ONE THAT WOULD DESTROY YOU!
BUT WHY DID YOU EVER BOTHER TO BUILD SUCH A WEAPON?
FROM THE MOMENT I LANDED ON RANN I WAS SUSPICIOUS OF THAT OTHER ALANNA I THOUGHT I'D PLAY ALONG -- LEARN HER GAME-- TRY TO STOP IT AND FIND OUT WHERE YOU WERE AT THE SAME TIME!

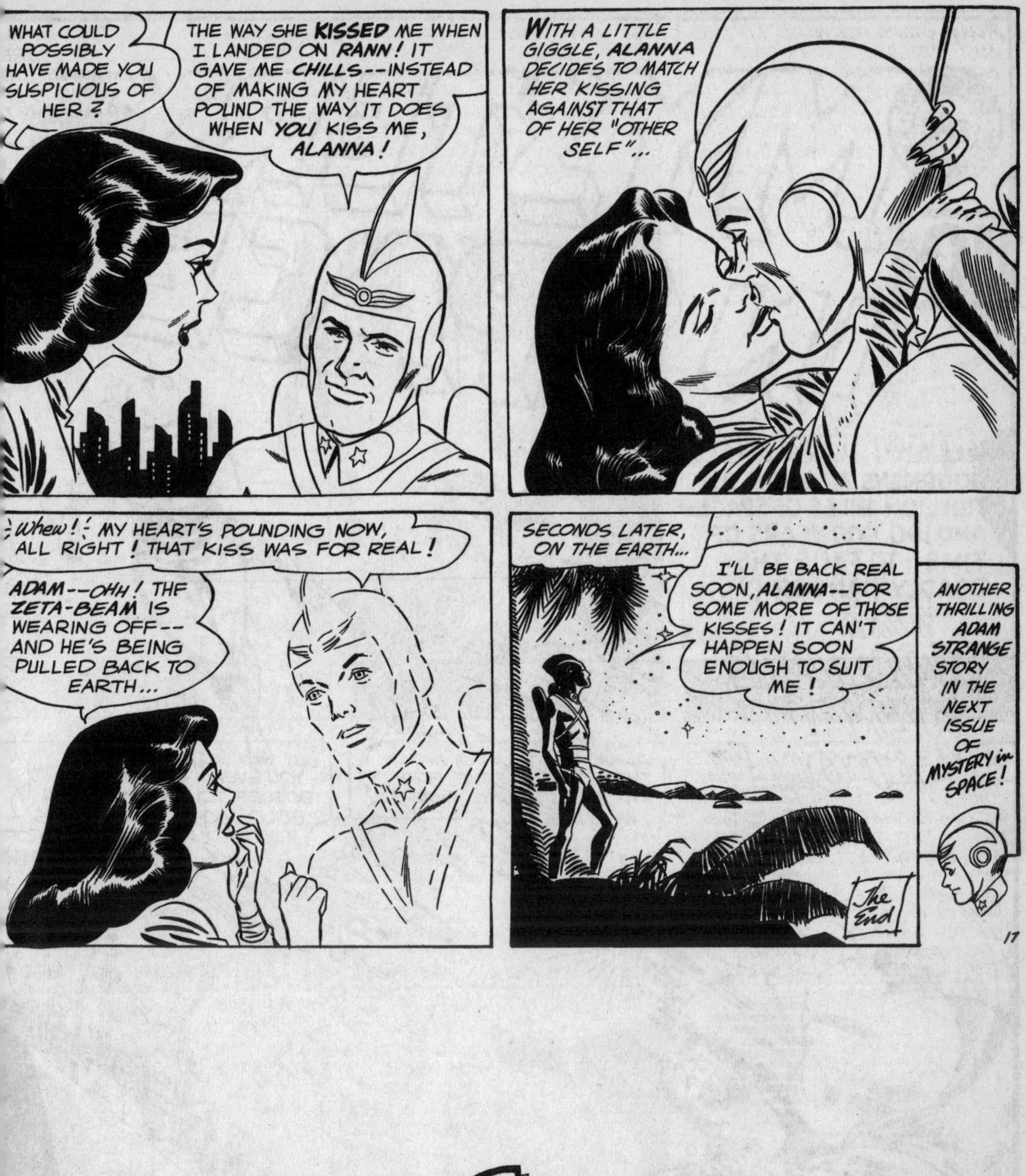
WHAT COULD POSSIBLY HAVE MADE YOU SUSPICIOUS OF HER?
THE WAY SHE KISSED ME WHEN I LANDED ON RANN! IT GAVE ME CHILLS--INSTEAD OF MAKING MY HEART POUND THE WAY IT DOES WHEN YOU KISS ME, ALANNA!
WITH A LITTLE GIGGLE, ALANNA DECIDES TO MATCH HER KISSING AGAINST THAT OF HER "OTHER SELF"...
Whew! MY HEART'S POUNDING NOW, ALL RIGHT! THAT KISS WAS FOR REAL!
ADAM--OHH! THE ZETA-BEAM IS WEARING OFF--AND HE'S BEING PULLED BACK TO EARTH...
SECONDS LATER, ON THE EARTH...
I'LL BE BACK REAL SOON, ALANNA--FOR SOME MORE OF THOSE KISSES! IT CAN'T HAPPEN SOON ENOUGH TO SUIT ME!
ANOTHER THRILLING ADAM STRANGE STORY IN THE NEXT ISSUE OF MYSTERY in SPACE!
The End
17

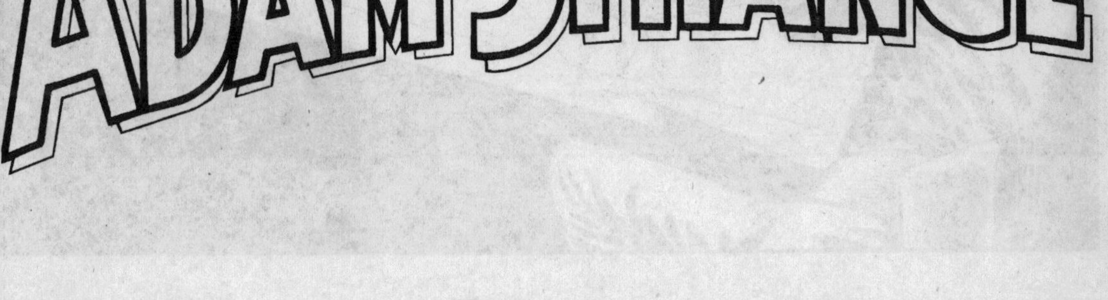
ADAM STRANGE

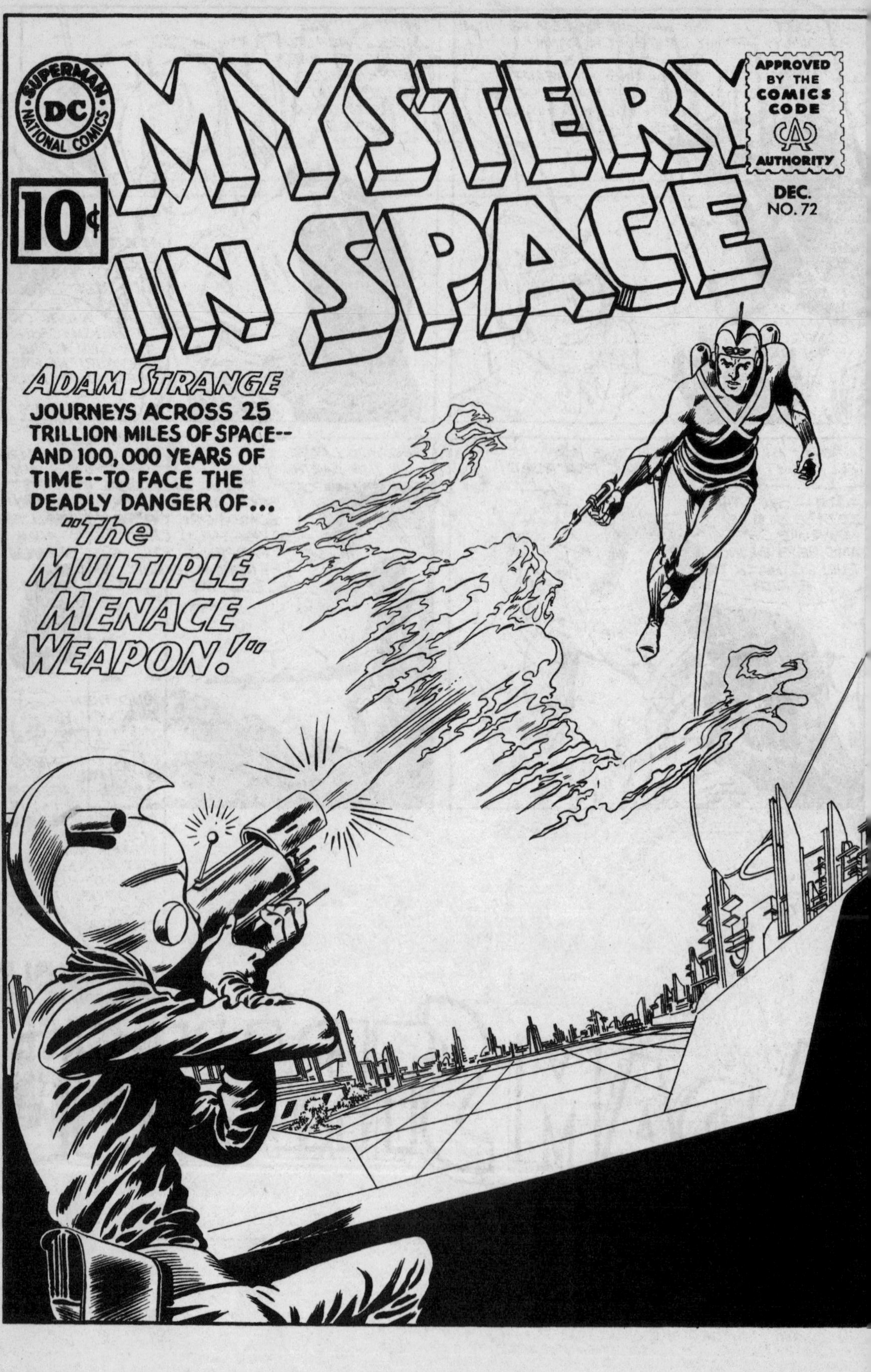
SUPERMAN
DC
NATIONAL COMICS
MYSTERY IN SPACE
APPROVED BY THE COMICS CODE AUTHORITY
10¢
DEC.
NO. 72
ADAM STRANGE
JOURNEYS ACROSS 25 TRILLION MILES OF SPACE--AND 100,000 YEARS OF TIME--TO FACE THE DEADLY DANGER OF...
"The MULTIPLE MENACE WEAPON!"

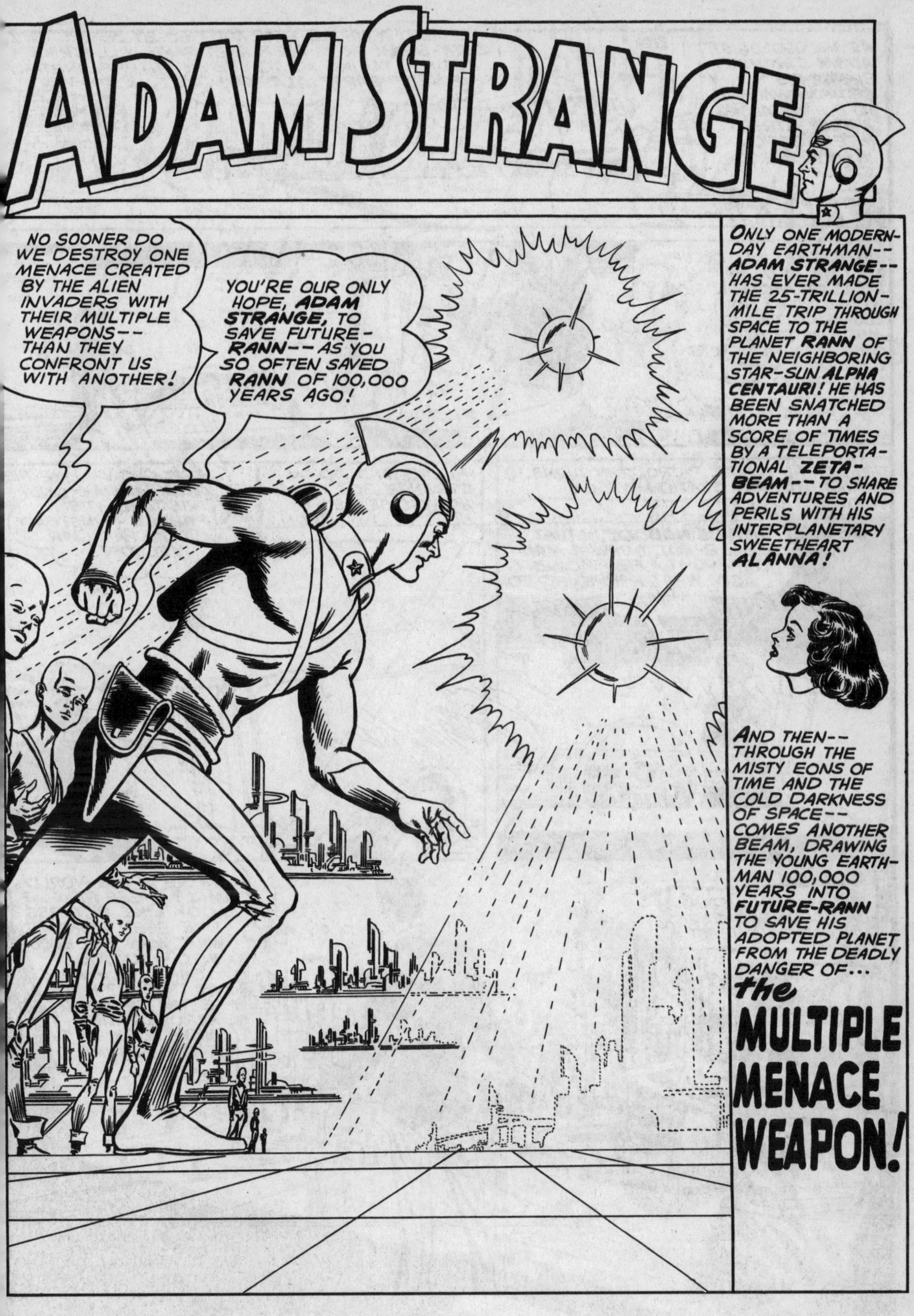
ADAM STRANGE
NO SOONER DO WE DESTROY ONE MENACE CREATED BY THE ALIEN INVADERS WITH THEIR MULTIPLE WEAPONS-- THAN THEY CONFRONT US WITH ANOTHER!
YOU'RE OUR ONLY HOPE, ADAM STRANGE, TO SAVE FUTURE-RANN--AS YOU SO OFTEN SAVED RANN OF 100,000 YEARS AGO!
ONLY ONE MODERN-DAY EARTHMAN--ADAM STRANGE--HAS EVER MADE THE 25-TRILLION-MILE TRIP THROUGH SPACE TO THE PLANET RANN OF THE NEIGHBORING STAR-SUN ALPHA CENTAURI! HE HAS BEEN SNATCHED MORE THAN A SCORE OF TIMES BY A TELEPORTATIONAL ZETA-BEAM--TO SHARE ADVENTURES AND PERILS WITH HIS INTERPLANETARY SWEETHEART ALANNA!
AND THEN--THROUGH THE MISTY EONS OF TIME AND THE COLD DARKNESS OF SPACE--COMES ANOTHER BEAM, DRAWING THE YOUNG EARTHMAN 100,000 YEARS INTO FUTURE-RANN TO SAVE HIS ADOPTED PLANET FROM THE DEADLY DANGER OF...
the MULTIPLE MENACE WEAPON!

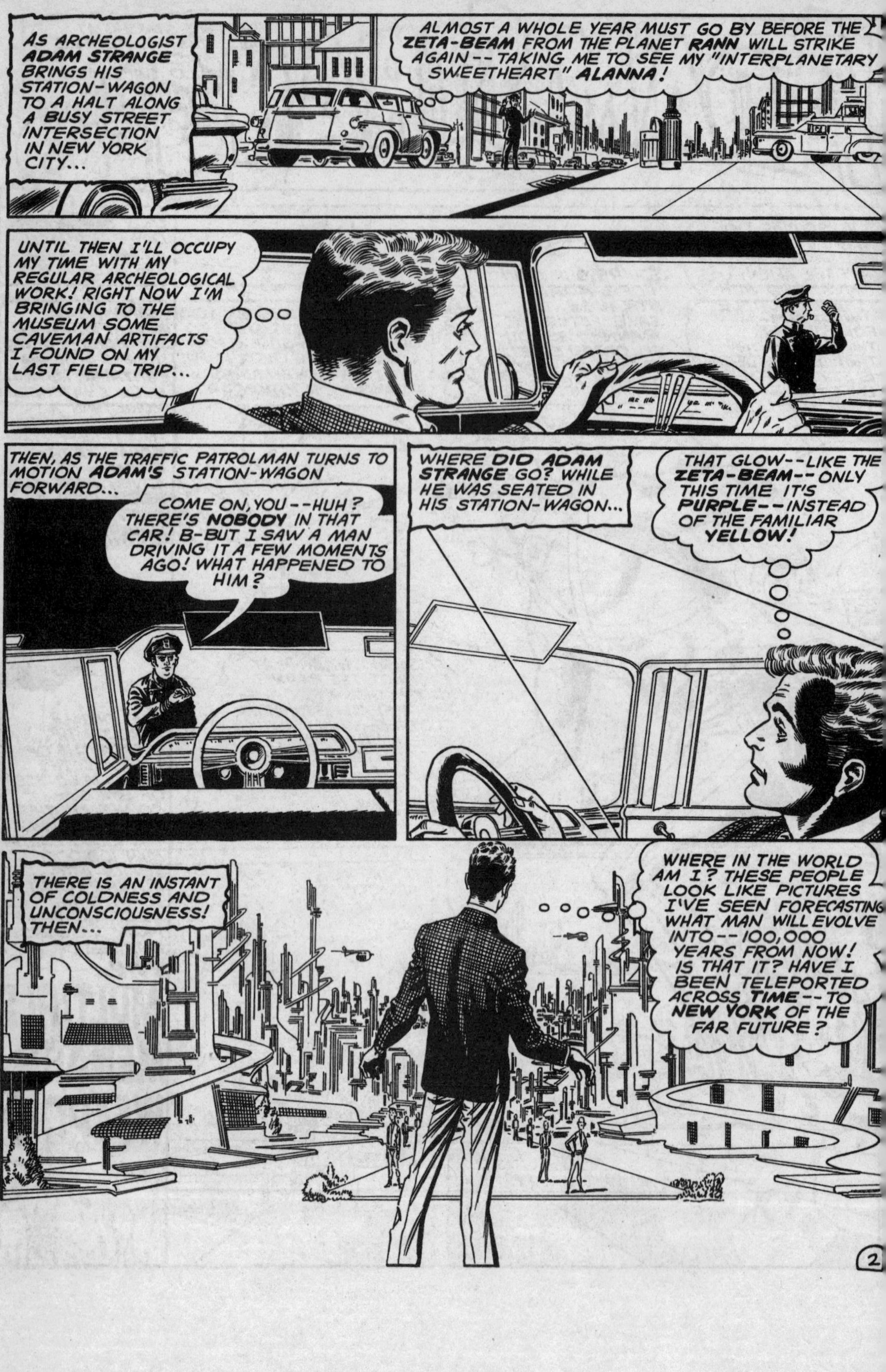
AS ARCHEOLOGIST ADAM STRANGE BRINGS HIS STATION-WAGON TO A HALT ALONG A BUSY STREET INTERSECTION IN NEW YORK CITY...
ALMOST A WHOLE YEAR MUST GO BY BEFORE THE ZETA-BEAM FROM THE PLANET RANN WILL STRIKE AGAIN--TAKING ME TO SEE MY "INTERPLANETARY SWEETHEART" ALANNA!
UNTIL THEN I'LL OCCUPY MY TIME WITH MY REGULAR ARCHEOLOGICAL WORK! RIGHT NOW I'M BRINGING TO THE MUSEUM SOME CAVEMAN ARTIFACTS I FOUND ON MY LAST FIELD TRIP...
THEN, AS THE TRAFFIC PATROLMAN TURNS TO MOTION ADAM'S STATION-WAGON FORWARD...
COME ON, YOU--HUH? THERE'S NOBODY IN THAT CAR! B-BUT I SAW A MAN DRIVING IT A FEW MOMENTS AGO! WHAT HAPPENED TO HIM?
WHERE DID ADAM STRANGE GO? WHILE HE WAS SEATED IN HIS STATION-WAGON...
THAT GLOW--LIKE THE ZETA-BEAM--ONLY THIS TIME IT'S PURPLE--INSTEAD OF THE FAMILIAR YELLOW!
THERE IS AN INSTANT OF COLDNESS AND UNCONSCIOUSNESS! THEN...
WHERE IN THE WORLD AM I? THESE PEOPLE LOOK LIKE PICTURES I'VE SEEN FORECASTING WHAT MAN WILL EVOLVE INTO--100,000 YEARS FROM NOW! IS THAT IT? HAVE I BEEN TELEPORTED ACROSS TIME--TO NEW YORK OF THE FAR FUTURE?
2

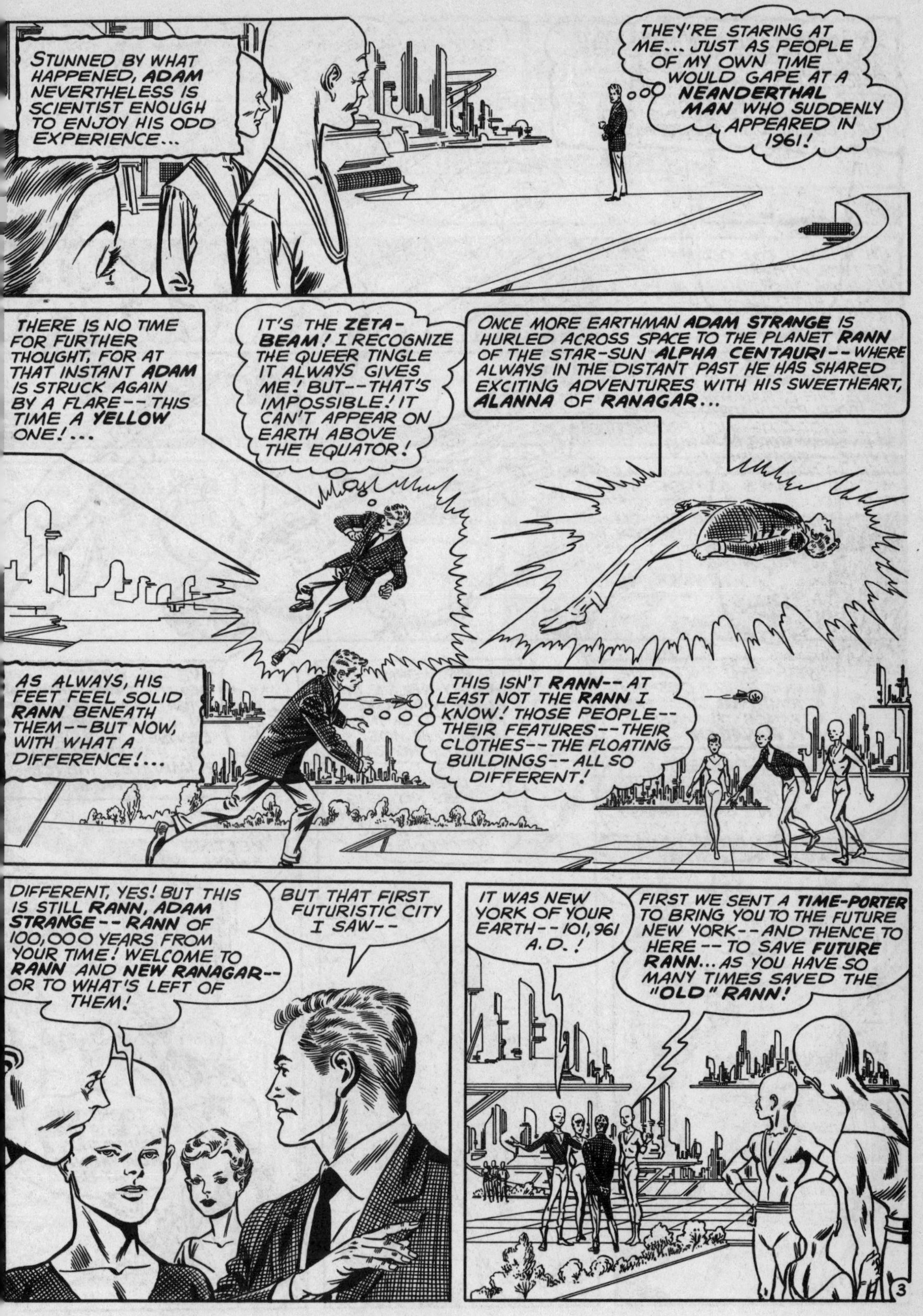
STUNNED BY WHAT HAPPENED, ADAM NEVERTHELESS IS SCIENTIST ENOUGH TO ENJOY HIS ODD EXPERIENCE...
THEY'RE STARING AT ME... JUST AS PEOPLE OF MY OWN TIME WOULD GAPE AT A NEANDERTHAL MAN WHO SUDDENLY APPEARED IN 1961!
THERE IS NO TIME FOR FURTHER THOUGHT, FOR AT THAT INSTANT ADAM IS STRUCK AGAIN BY A FLARE--THIS TIME A YELLOW ONE!...
IT'S THE ZETA-BEAM! I RECOGNIZE THE QUEER TINGLE IT ALWAYS GIVES ME! BUT--THAT'S IMPOSSIBLE! IT CAN'T APPEAR ON EARTH ABOVE THE EQUATOR!
ONCE MORE EARTHMAN ADAM STRANGE IS HURLED ACROSS SPACE TO THE PLANET RANN OF THE STAR-SUN ALPHA CENTAURI--WHERE ALWAYS IN THE DISTANT PAST HE HAS SHARED EXCITING ADVENTURES WITH HIS SWEETHEART, ALANNA OF RANAGAR...
AS ALWAYS, HIS FEET FEEL SOLID RANN BENEATH THEM--BUT NOW, WITH WHAT A DIFFERENCE!...
THIS ISN'T RANN--AT LEAST NOT THE RANN I KNOW! THOSE PEOPLE--THEIR FEATURES--THEIR CLOTHES--THE FLOATING BUILDINGS--ALL SO DIFFERENT!
DIFFERENT, YES! BUT THIS IS STILL RANN, ADAM STRANGE--RANN OF 100,000 YEARS FROM YOUR TIME! WELCOME TO RANN AND NEW RANAGAR--OR TO WHAT'S LEFT OF THEM!
BUT THAT FIRST FUTURISTIC CITY I SAW--
IT WAS NEW YORK OF YOUR EARTH--101,961 A.D.!
FIRST WE SENT A TIME-PORTER TO BRING YOU TO THE FUTURE NEW YORK--AND THENCE TO HERE--TO SAVE FUTURE RANN...AS YOU HAVE SO MANY TIMES SAVED THE "OLD" RANN!
3

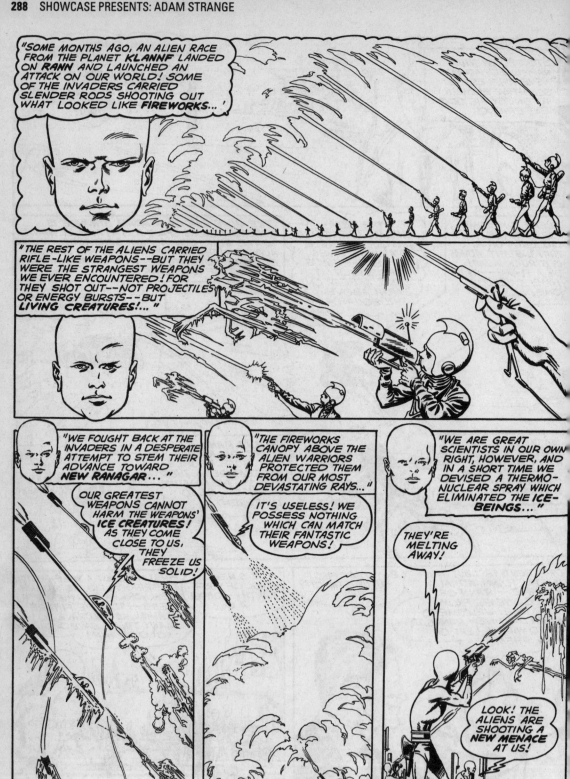

"SOME MONTHS AGO, AN ALIEN RACE FROM THE PLANET *KLANNF* LANDED ON *RANN* AND LAUNCHED AN ATTACK ON OUR WORLD! SOME OF THE INVADERS CARRIED SLENDER RODS SHOOTING OUT WHAT LOOKED LIKE *FIREWORKS...*'

"THE REST OF THE ALIENS CARRIED RIFLE-LIKE WEAPONS--BUT THEY WERE THE STRANGEST WEAPONS WE EVER ENCOUNTERED! FOR THEY SHOT OUT--NOT PROJECTILES OR ENERGY BURSTS--BUT *LIVING CREATURES!...* "

"WE FOUGHT BACK AT THE INVADERS IN A DESPERATE ATTEMPT TO STEM THEIR ADVANCE TOWARD *NEW RANAGAR...* "

OUR GREATEST WEAPONS CANNOT HARM THE WEAPONS' *ICE CREATURES!* AS THEY COME CLOSE TO US, THEY FREEZE US SOLID!

"THE FIREWORKS CANOPY ABOVE THE ALIEN WARRIORS PROTECTED THEM FROM OUR MOST DEVASTATING RAYS..." "

IT'S USELESS! WE POSSESS NOTHING WHICH CAN MATCH THEIR FANTASTIC WEAPONS!

"WE ARE GREAT SCIENTISTS IN OUR OWN RIGHT, HOWEVER, AND IN A SHORT TIME WE DEVISED A THERMO-NUCLEAR SPRAY WHICH ELIMINATED THE *ICE-BEINGS...* "

THEY'RE MELTING AWAY!

LOOK! THE ALIENS ARE SHOOTING A *NEW MENACE* AT US!

4

"SURE ENOUGH-- EVEN AS THE *ICE-BEINGS* MELTED AWAY, THE SUPER-RIFLES OF THE INVADERS BEGAN FIRING *STONE CREATURES* AT US..."

PEOPLE OF *RANN!* NOTHING CAN WITHSTAND OUR *SPATIAL RIFLES!* AND WHEN WE CONQUER YOU, WE SHALL LAUNCH AN ATTACK ON *EARTH,* YOUR PLANETARY ALLY!

OUR *WONDER WEAPONS* REACH OUT INTO SPACE-- LIFTING STRANGE LIFE-FORMS FROM THEIR OWN WORLDS-- BRINGING THEM HERE BEFORE YOU, TO DO OUR BIDDING!

OURS IS A *MULTIPLE-THREAT WEAPON!* NO SOONER DO YOU DESTROY ONE LIFE-FORM THAN WE HURL ANOTHER AT YOU! IN TIME YOU WILL BE COMPLETELY ANNIHILATED!

"WE WERE FORCED TO RETREAT--AND BY THE TIME WE DISCOVERED A WAY TO DESTROY THE *STONE MEN,* OUR BATTLE-LINES HAD SHRUNK CLOSER TO *NEW RANAGAR...* "

OUR *SPARKLE ARROWS* CAUSE THE *STONE CREATURES* TO CRUMBLE--BUT WHAT QUEER NEW LIFE-FORM WILL THEY SHOOT AT US NEXT?

WE CAN'T HOLD OUT MUCH LONGER!

"OUR NEXT OPPONENTS WERE *SMOKE-DRAGONS* WHOSE BREATHS TURNED EVERY-THING INTO SOLID GLASS..."

OUR CAUSE IS HOPELESS, JANNA!

WE'RE NOT DEFEATED YET, *JULAN!* THERE MUST BE SOME WAY TO STOP THEM-- THERE'S GOT TO BE ---

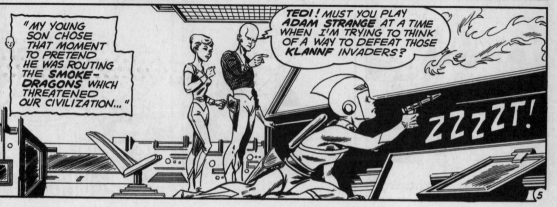

"MY YOUNG SON CHOSE THAT MOMENT TO PRETEND HE WAS ROUTING THE *SMOKE-DRAGONS* WHICH THREATENED OUR CIVILIZATION..."

TEDI! MUST YOU PLAY *ADAM STRANGE* AT A TIME WHEN I'M TRYING TO THINK OF A WAY TO DEFEAT THOSE *KLANNF* INVADERS?

ZZZZT!

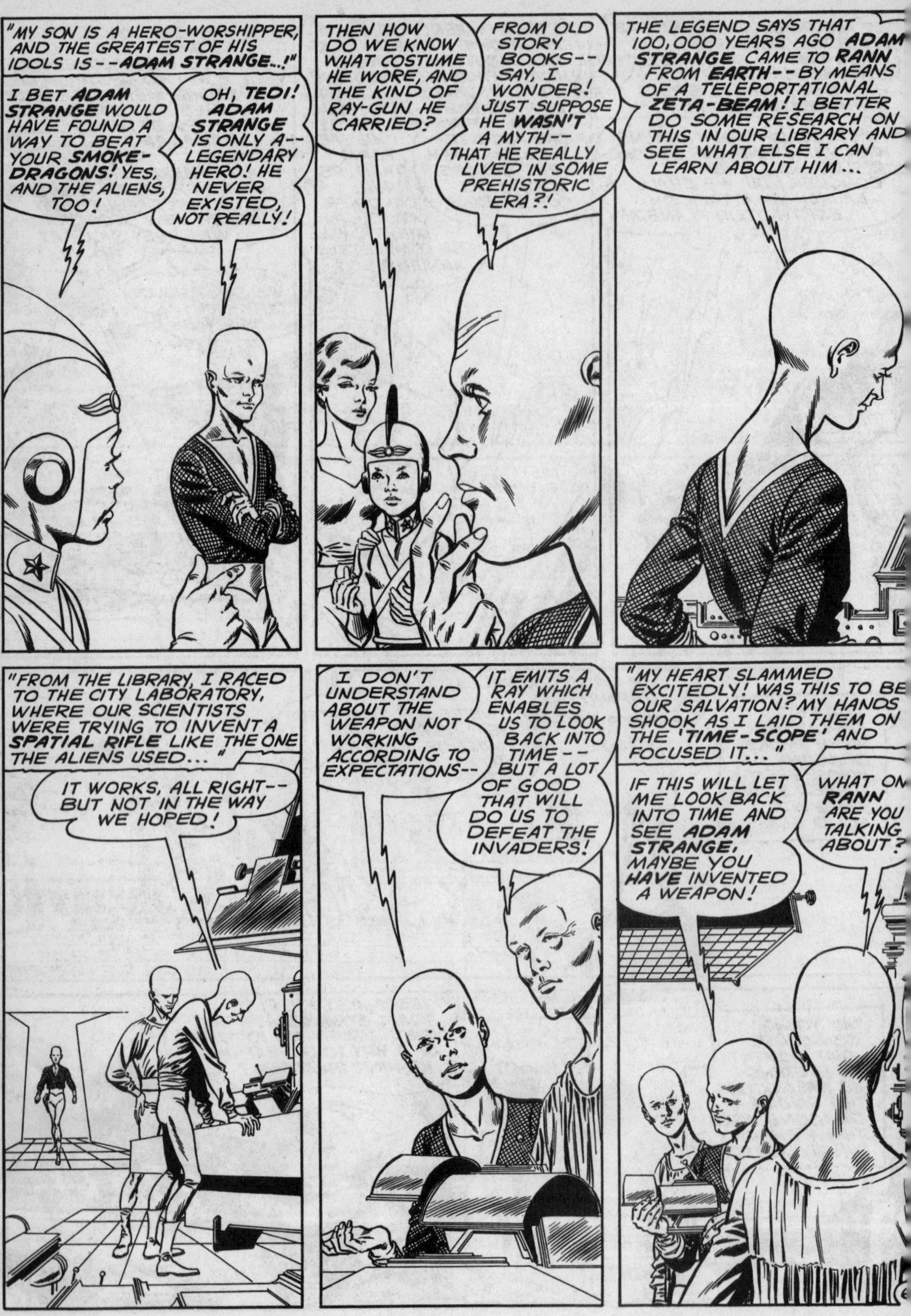
"MY SON IS A HERO-WORSHIPPER, AND THE GREATEST OF HIS IDOLS IS--ADAM STRANGE...!"
I BET ADAM STRANGE WOULD HAVE FOUND A WAY TO BEAT YOUR SMOKE-DRAGONS! YES, AND THE ALIENS, TOO!
OH, TEOI! ADAM STRANGE IS ONLY A--LEGENDARY HERO! HE NEVER EXISTED, NOT REALLY!
THEN HOW DO WE KNOW WHAT COSTUME HE WORE, AND THE KIND OF RAY-GUN HE CARRIED?
FROM OLD STORY BOOKS--SAY, I WONDER! JUST SUPPOSE HE WASN'T A MYTH--THAT HE REALLY LIVED IN SOME PREHISTORIC ERA?!
THE LEGEND SAYS THAT 100,000 YEARS AGO ADAM STRANGE CAME TO RANN FROM EARTH--BY MEANS OF A TELEPORTATIONAL ZETA-BEAM! I BETTER DO SOME RESEARCH ON THIS IN OUR LIBRARY AND SEE WHAT ELSE I CAN LEARN ABOUT HIM...
"FROM THE LIBRARY, I RACED TO THE CITY LABORATORY, WHERE OUR SCIENTISTS WERE TRYING TO INVENT A SPATIAL RIFLE LIKE THE ONE THE ALIENS USED..."
IT WORKS, ALL RIGHT--BUT NOT IN THE WAY WE HOPED!
I DON'T UNDERSTAND ABOUT THE WEAPON NOT WORKING ACCORDING TO EXPECTATIONS--
IT EMITS A RAY WHICH ENABLES US TO LOOK BACK INTO TIME--BUT A LOT OF GOOD THAT WILL DO US TO DEFEAT THE INVADERS!
"MY HEART SLAMMED EXCITEDLY! WAS THIS TO BE OUR SALVATION? MY HANDS SHOOK AS I LAID THEM ON THE 'TIME-SCOPE' AND FOCUSED IT..."
IF THIS WILL LET ME LOOK BACK INTO TIME AND SEE ADAM STRANGE, MAYBE YOU HAVE INVENTED A WEAPON!
WHAT ON RANN ARE YOU TALKING ABOUT?

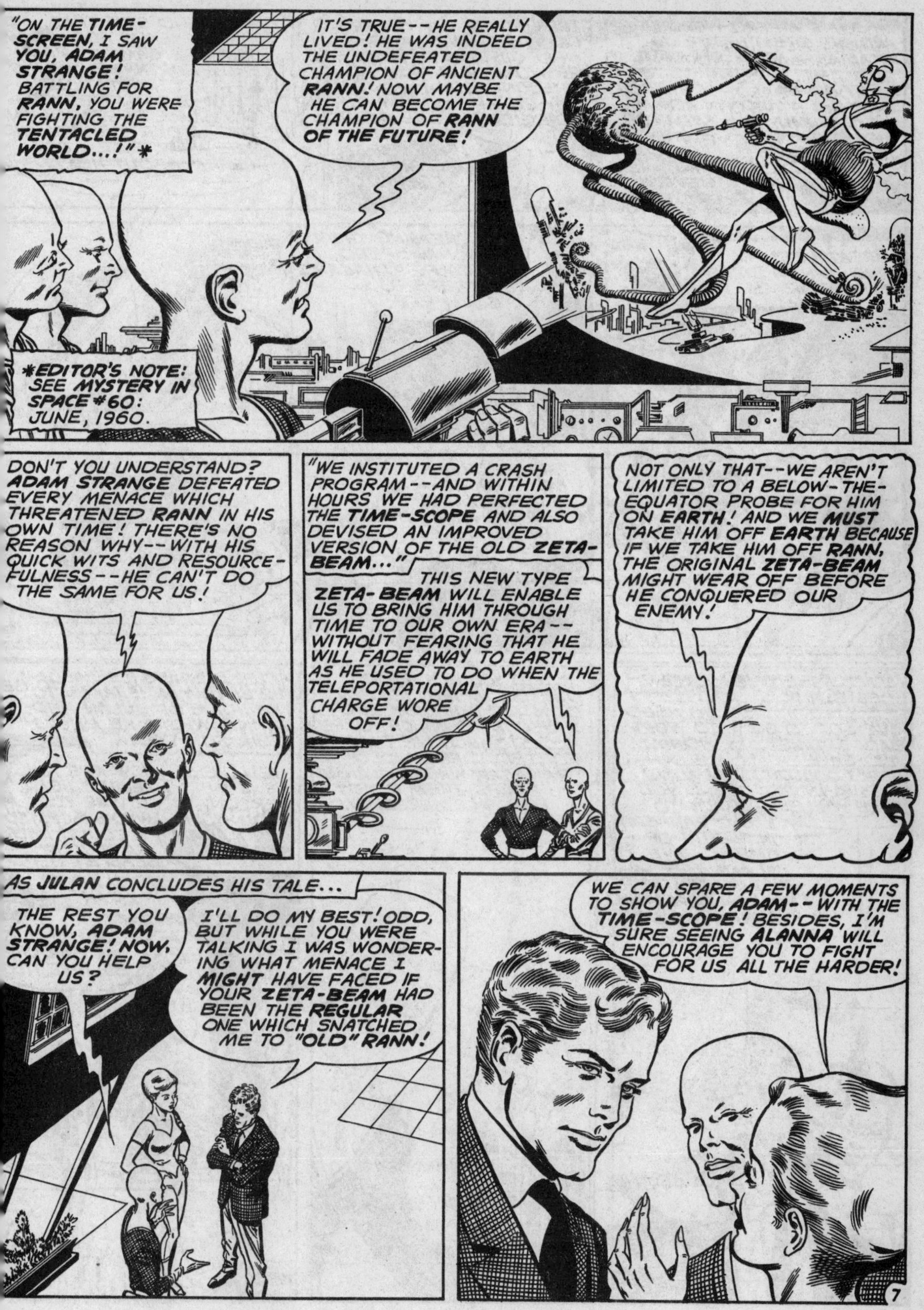
"ON THE TIME-SCREEN, I SAW YOU, ADAM STRANGE! BATTLING FOR RANN, YOU WERE FIGHTING THE TENTACLED WORLD...!"*
IT'S TRUE--HE REALLY LIVED! HE WAS INDEED THE UNDEFEATED CHAMPION OF ANCIENT RANN! NOW MAYBE HE CAN BECOME THE CHAMPION OF RANN OF THE FUTURE!
*EDITOR'S NOTE: SEE MYSTERY IN SPACE #60: JUNE, 1960.
DON'T YOU UNDERSTAND? ADAM STRANGE DEFEATED EVERY MENACE WHICH THREATENED RANN IN HIS OWN TIME! THERE'S NO REASON WHY--WITH HIS QUICK WITS AND RESOURCE-FULNESS--HE CAN'T DO THE SAME FOR US!
"WE INSTITUTED A CRASH PROGRAM--AND WITHIN HOURS WE HAD PERFECTED THE TIME-SCOPE AND ALSO DEVISED AN IMPROVED VERSION OF THE OLD ZETA-BEAM..."
THIS NEW TYPE ZETA-BEAM WILL ENABLE US TO BRING HIM THROUGH TIME TO OUR OWN ERA--WITHOUT FEARING THAT HE WILL FADE AWAY TO EARTH AS HE USED TO DO WHEN THE TELEPORTATIONAL CHARGE WORE OFF!
NOT ONLY THAT--WE AREN'T LIMITED TO A BELOW-THE-EQUATOR PROBE FOR HIM ON EARTH! AND WE MUST TAKE HIM OFF EARTH BECAUSE IF WE TAKE HIM OFF RANN, THE ORIGINAL ZETA-BEAM MIGHT WEAR OFF BEFORE HE CONQUERED OUR ENEMY!
AS JULAN CONCLUDES HIS TALE...
THE REST YOU KNOW, ADAM STRANGE! NOW, CAN YOU HELP US?
I'LL DO MY BEST! ODD, BUT WHILE YOU WERE TALKING I WAS WONDERING WHAT MENACE I MIGHT HAVE FACED IF YOUR ZETA-BEAM HAD BEEN THE REGULAR ONE WHICH SNATCHED ME TO "OLD" RANN!
WE CAN SPARE A FEW MOMENTS TO SHOW YOU, ADAM--WITH THE TIME-SCOPE! BESIDES, I'M SURE SEEING ALANNA WILL ENCOURAGE YOU TO FIGHT FOR US ALL THE HARDER!
7

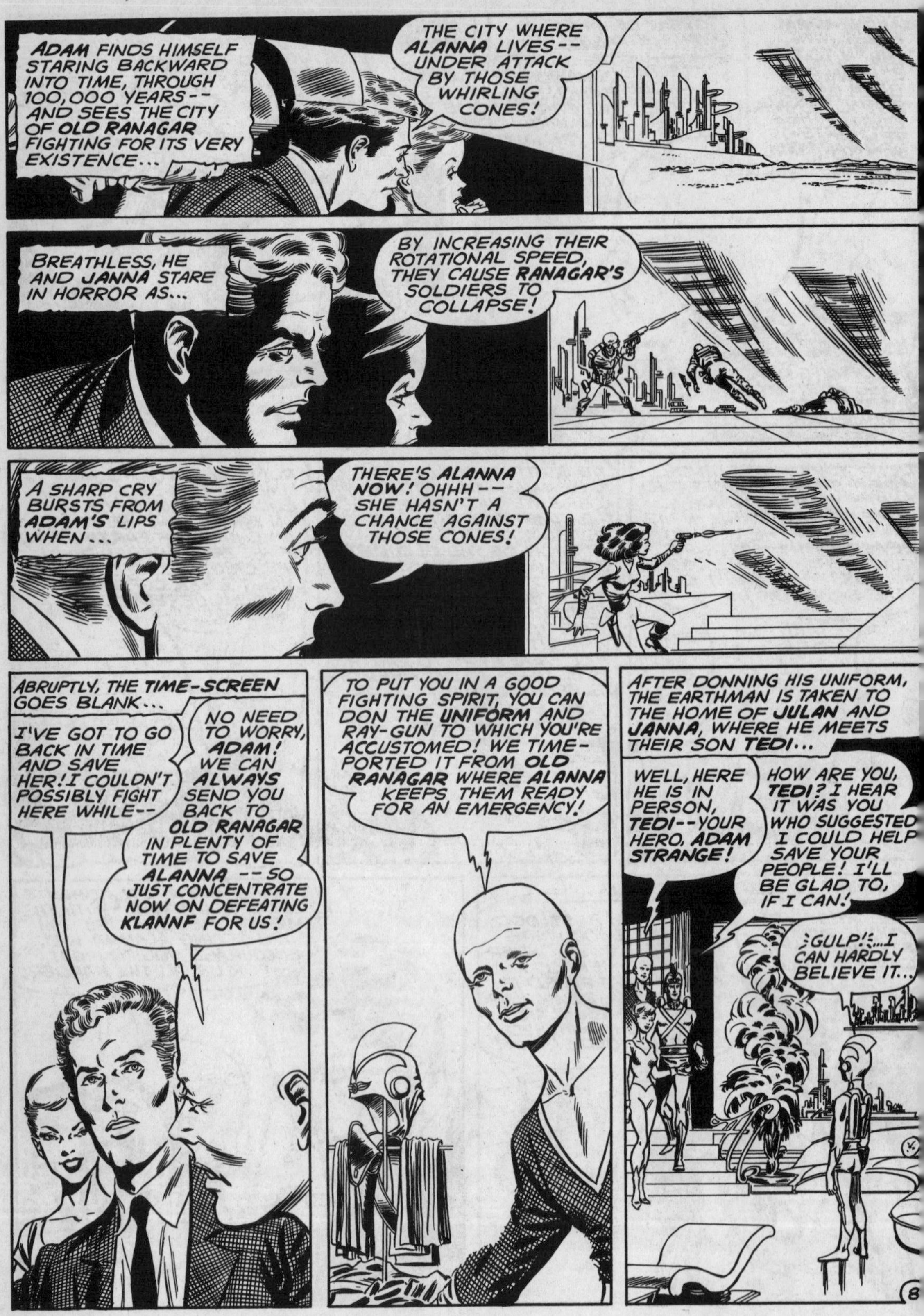
ADAM FINDS HIMSELF STARING BACKWARD INTO TIME, THROUGH 100,000 YEARS-- AND SEES THE CITY OF OLD RANAGAR FIGHTING FOR ITS VERY EXISTENCE...
THE CITY WHERE ALANNA LIVES-- UNDER ATTACK BY THOSE WHIRLING CONES!
BREATHLESS, HE AND JANNA STARE IN HORROR AS...
BY INCREASING THEIR ROTATIONAL SPEED, THEY CAUSE RANAGAR'S SOLDIERS TO COLLAPSE!
A SHARP CRY BURSTS FROM ADAM'S LIPS WHEN...
THERE'S ALANNA NOW! OHHH-- SHE HASN'T A CHANCE AGAINST THOSE CONES!
ABRUPTLY, THE TIME-SCREEN GOES BLANK...
I'VE GOT TO GO BACK IN TIME AND SAVE HER! I COULDN'T POSSIBLY FIGHT HERE WHILE--
NO NEED TO WORRY, ADAM! WE CAN ALWAYS SEND YOU BACK TO OLD RANAGAR IN PLENTY OF TIME TO SAVE ALANNA -- SO JUST CONCENTRATE NOW ON DEFEATING KLANNF FOR US!
TO PUT YOU IN A GOOD FIGHTING SPIRIT, YOU CAN DON THE UNIFORM AND RAY-GUN TO WHICH YOU'RE ACCUSTOMED! WE TIME-PORTED IT FROM OLD RANAGAR WHERE ALANNA KEEPS THEM READY FOR AN EMERGENCY!
AFTER DONNING HIS UNIFORM, THE EARTHMAN IS TAKEN TO THE HOME OF JULAN AND JANNA, WHERE HE MEETS THEIR SON TEDI...
WELL, HERE HE IS IN PERSON, TEDI--YOUR HERO, ADAM STRANGE!
HOW ARE YOU, TEDI? I HEAR IT WAS YOU WHO SUGGESTED I COULD HELP SAVE YOUR PEOPLE! I'LL BE GLAD TO, IF I CAN!
GULP!...I CAN HARDLY BELIEVE IT...
8

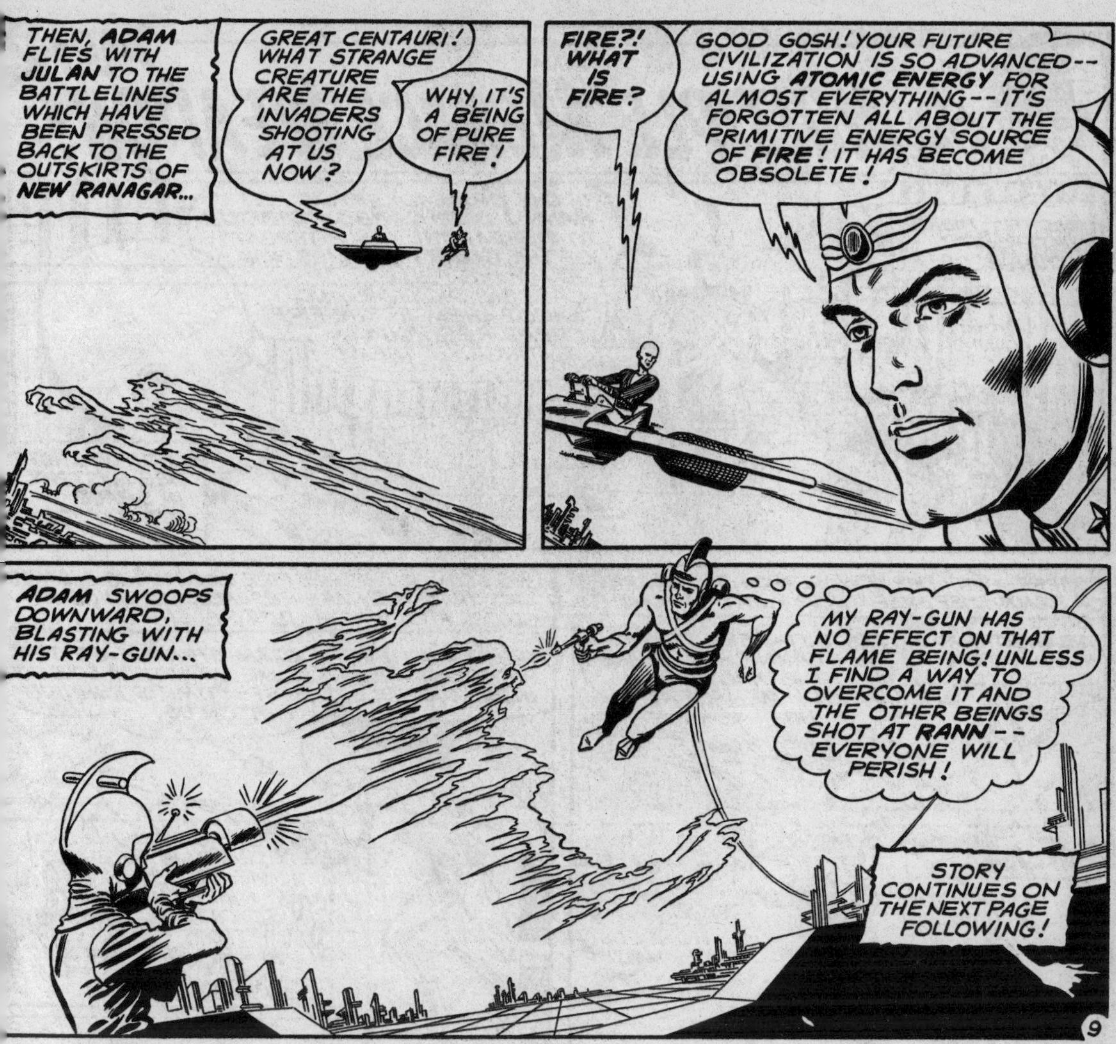
THEN, ADAM FLIES WITH JULAN TO THE BATTLELINES WHICH HAVE BEEN PRESSED BACK TO THE OUTSKIRTS OF NEW RANAGAR...
GREAT CENTAURI! WHAT STRANGE CREATURE ARE THE INVADERS SHOOTING AT US NOW?
WHY, IT'S A BEING OF PURE FIRE!
FIRE?! WHAT IS FIRE?
GOOD GOSH! YOUR FUTURE CIVILIZATION IS SO ADVANCED-- USING ATOMIC ENERGY FOR ALMOST EVERYTHING--IT'S FORGOTTEN ALL ABOUT THE PRIMITIVE ENERGY SOURCE OF FIRE! IT HAS BECOME OBSOLETE!
ADAM SWOOPS DOWNWARD, BLASTING WITH HIS RAY-GUN...
MY RAY-GUN HAS NO EFFECT ON THAT FLAME BEING! UNLESS I FIND A WAY TO OVERCOME IT AND THE OTHER BEINGS SHOT AT RANN-- EVERYONE WILL PERISH!
STORY CONTINUES ON THE NEXT PAGE FOLLOWING!
9

ADAM STRANGE

the MULTIPLE MENACE WEAPON! PART 2

SHORTLY THERE-AFTER, AT A COUNCIL OF WAR...

IN ONE OF MY ADVENTURES ON RANN I USED CARBON DIOXIDE TO DEFEAT THE "FIRE THREAT" OF THE GIANT FIREFLIES!* IF YOU MAKE PELLETS OF CARBON DIOXIDE AND SHOOT THEM AT THE FIRE CREATURES, YOU'LL EXTINGUISH THEM!

*EDITOR'S NOTE: SEE MYSTERY IN SPACE #67 MAY, 1961.

EQUIPPED WITH THIS NEW WEAPON, THE WARRIORS OF RANN DISPERSE THEIR FIERY OPPONENTS...

THE EARTHMAN'S PLAN WORKS PERFECTLY!

YES, BUT--SEE THERE! THE KLANNF ALIENS ARE SHOOTING ANOTHER DEADLY MENACE AT US!

NO SOONER ARE THE FIRE CREATURES SNUFFED OUT THAN THEY ARE REPLACED BY SHINING GLOBES FITTED WITH JUTTING SPIKES...

THOSE MULTIPLE WEAPONS ARE INEXHAUSTIBLE!

ADAM STRANGE BETTER COME UP WITH A SOLUTION FAST--TIME'S RUNNING OUT ON US!

HELPLESS BEFORE THIS NEW THREAT, THE NEW RANAGARANS ARE DRIVEN BACK INTO THE CITY PROPER...

WHAT'LL WE DO, ADAM? THOSE SHINING GLOBES ARE EMITTING A RADIATION THAT CAUSES OUR BUILDING TO DISAPPEAR!

TO THE LABORATORY, JULAN-- HURRY!

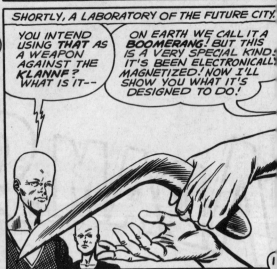

SHORTLY, A LABORATORY OF THE FUTURE CITY.

YOU INTEND USING THAT AS A WEAPON AGAINST THE KLANNF? WHAT IS IT--

ON EARTH WE CALL IT A BOOMERANG! BUT THIS IS A VERY SPECIAL KIND! IT'S BEEN ELECTRONICALLY MAGNETIZED! NOW I'LL SHOW YOU WHAT IT'S DESIGNED TO DO!

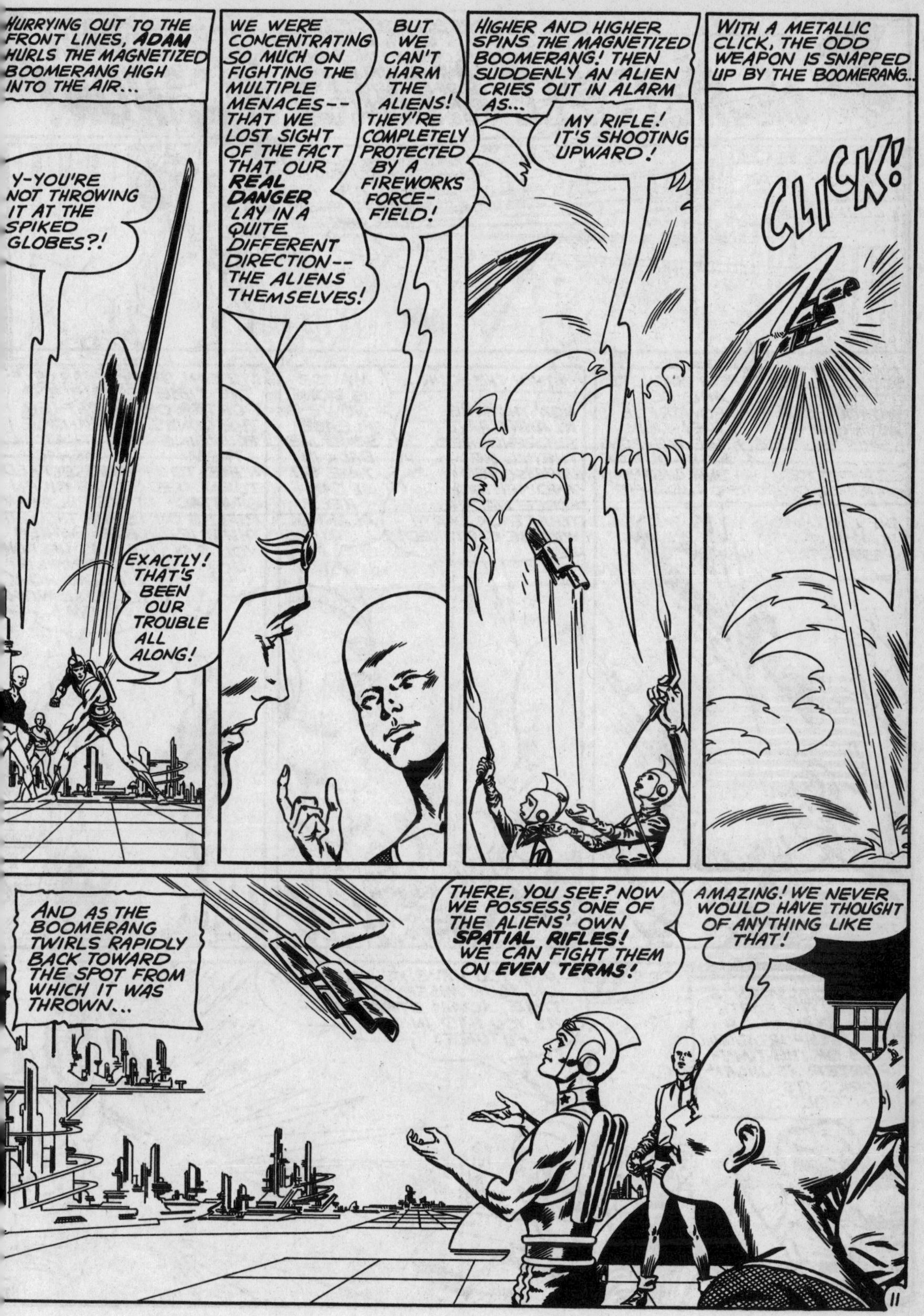
HURRYING OUT TO THE FRONT LINES, ADAM HURLS THE MAGNETIZED BOOMERANG HIGH INTO THE AIR...
Y-YOU'RE NOT THROWING IT AT THE SPIKED GLOBES?!
EXACTLY! THAT'S BEEN OUR TROUBLE ALL ALONG!
WE WERE CONCENTRATING SO MUCH ON FIGHTING THE MULTIPLE MENACES-- THAT WE LOST SIGHT OF THE FACT THAT OUR REAL DANGER LAY IN A QUITE DIFFERENT DIRECTION-- THE ALIENS THEMSELVES!
BUT WE CAN'T HARM THE ALIENS! THEY'RE COMPLETELY PROTECTED BY A FIREWORKS FORCE-FIELD!
HIGHER AND HIGHER SPINS THE MAGNETIZED BOOMERANG! THEN SUDDENLY AN ALIEN CRIES OUT IN ALARM AS...
MY RIFLE! IT'S SHOOTING UPWARD!
WITH A METALLIC CLICK, THE ODD WEAPON IS SNAPPED UP BY THE BOOMERANG...
CLICK!
AND AS THE BOOMERANG TWIRLS RAPIDLY BACK TOWARD THE SPOT FROM WHICH IT WAS THROWN...
THERE, YOU SEE? NOW WE POSSESS ONE OF THE ALIENS' OWN SPATIAL RIFLES! WE CAN FIGHT THEM ON EVEN TERMS!
AMAZING! WE NEVER WOULD HAVE THOUGHT OF ANYTHING LIKE THAT!
11

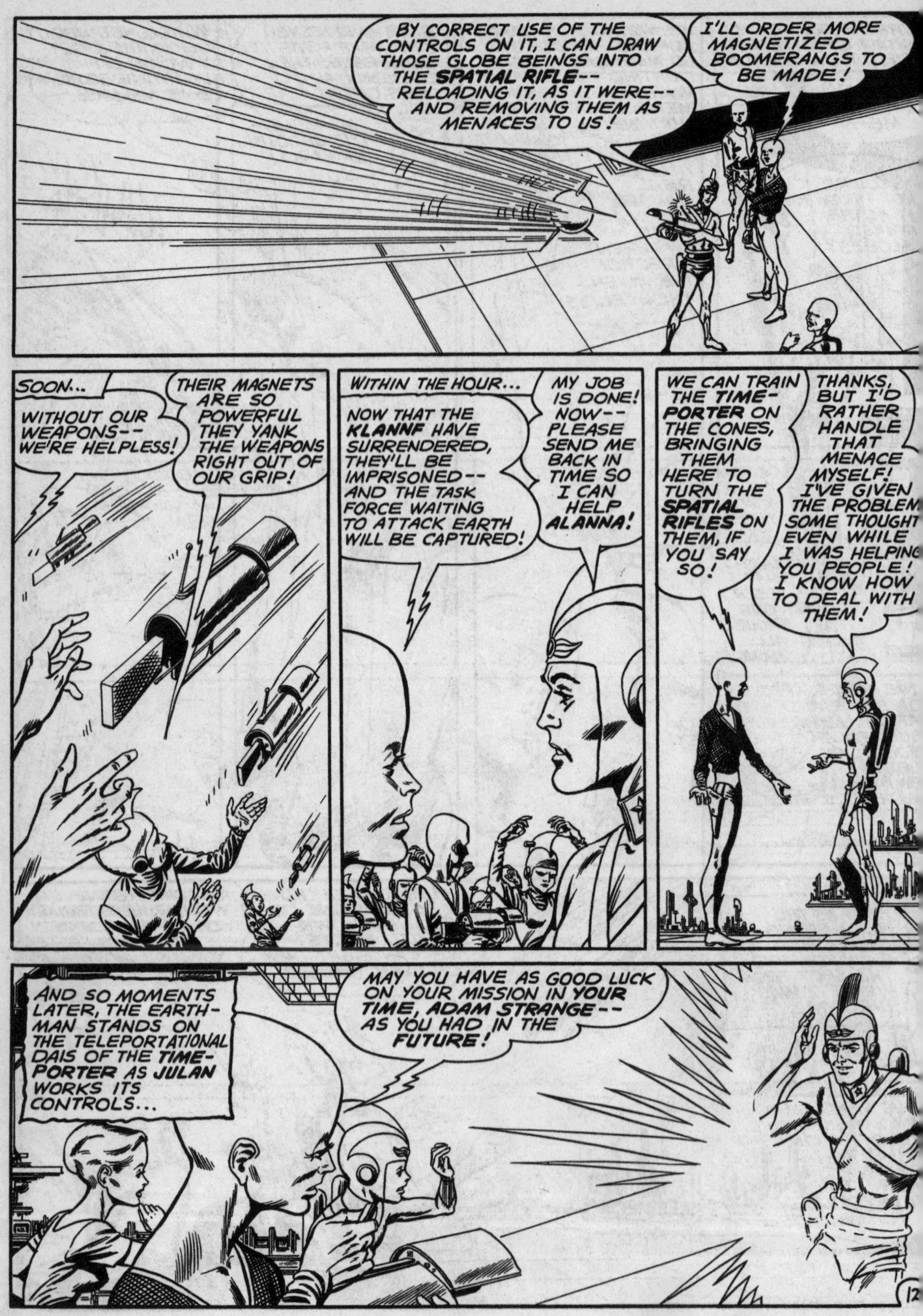
BY CORRECT USE OF THE CONTROLS ON IT, I CAN DRAW THOSE GLOBE BEINGS INTO THE SPATIAL RIFLE-- RELOADING IT, AS IT WERE-- AND REMOVING THEM AS MENACES TO US!
I'LL ORDER MORE MAGNETIZED BOOMERANGS TO BE MADE!
SOON...
WITHOUT OUR WEAPONS-- WE'RE HELPLESS!
THEIR MAGNETS ARE SO POWERFUL THEY YANK THE WEAPONS RIGHT OUT OF OUR GRIP!
WITHIN THE HOUR...
NOW THAT THE KLANNF HAVE SURRENDERED, THEY'LL BE IMPRISONED-- AND THE TASK FORCE WAITING TO ATTACK EARTH WILL BE CAPTURED!
MY JOB IS DONE! NOW-- PLEASE SEND ME BACK IN TIME SO I CAN HELP ALANNA!
WE CAN TRAIN THE TIME-PORTER ON THE CONES, BRINGING THEM HERE TO TURN THE SPATIAL RIFLES ON THEM, IF YOU SAY SO!
THANKS, BUT I'D RATHER HANDLE THAT MENACE MYSELF! I'VE GIVEN THE PROBLEM SOME THOUGHT EVEN WHILE I WAS HELPING YOU PEOPLE! I KNOW HOW TO DEAL WITH THEM!
AND SO MOMENTS LATER, THE EARTH-MAN STANDS ON THE TELEPORTATIONAL DAIS OF THE TIME-PORTER AS JULAN WORKS ITS CONTROLS...
MAY YOU HAVE AS GOOD LUCK ON YOUR MISSION IN YOUR TIME, ADAM STRANGE-- AS YOU HAD IN THE FUTURE!
12

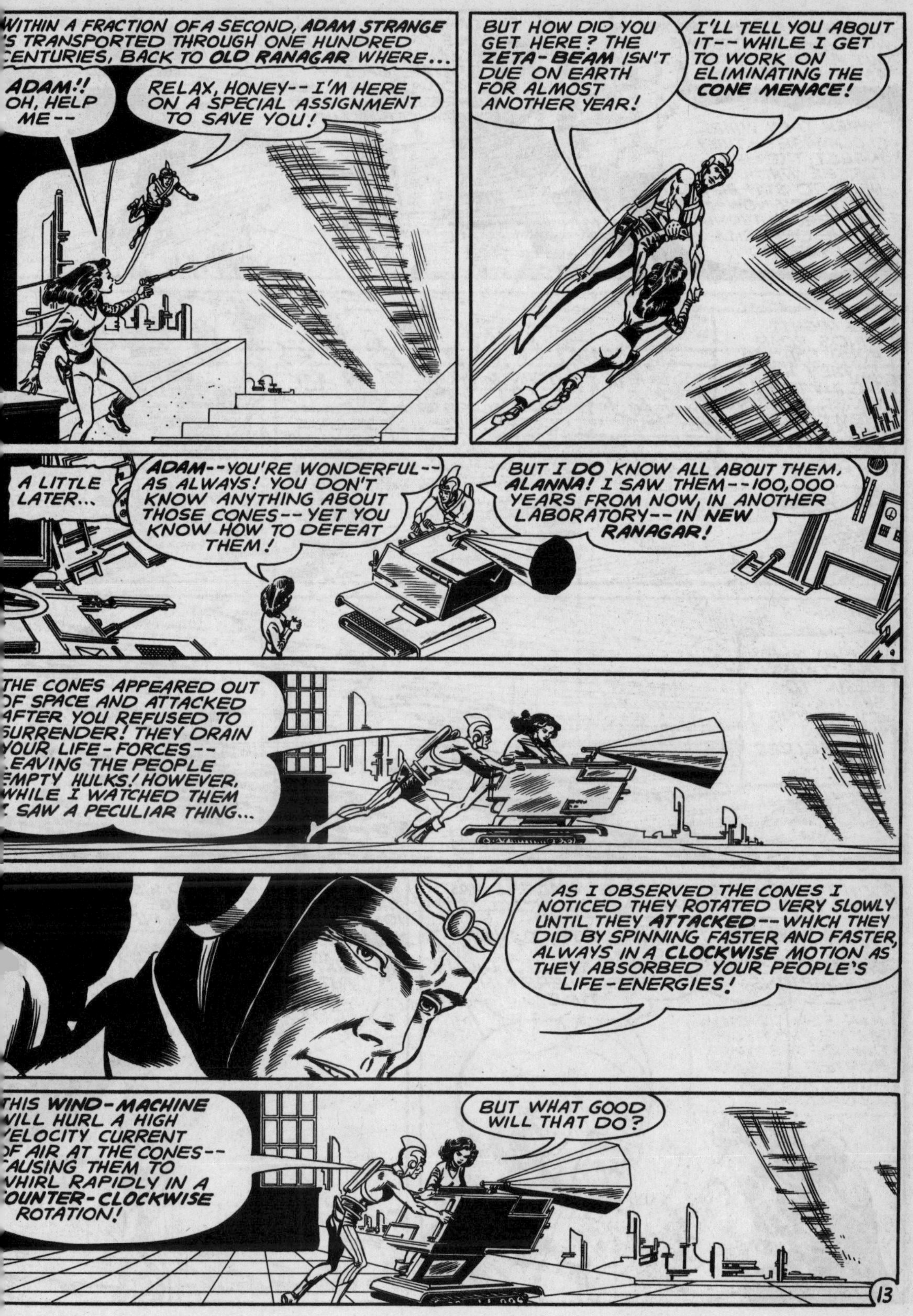
WITHIN A FRACTION OF A SECOND, ADAM STRANGE IS TRANSPORTED THROUGH ONE HUNDRED CENTURIES, BACK TO OLD RANAGAR WHERE...
ADAM!! OH, HELP ME--
RELAX, HONEY--I'M HERE ON A SPECIAL ASSIGNMENT TO SAVE YOU!
BUT HOW DID YOU GET HERE? THE ZETA-BEAM ISN'T DUE ON EARTH FOR ALMOST ANOTHER YEAR!
I'LL TELL YOU ABOUT IT--WHILE I GET TO WORK ON ELIMINATING THE CONE MENACE!
A LITTLE LATER...
ADAM--YOU'RE WONDERFUL--AS ALWAYS! YOU DON'T KNOW ANYTHING ABOUT THOSE CONES--YET YOU KNOW HOW TO DEFEAT THEM!
BUT I DO KNOW ALL ABOUT THEM, ALANNA! I SAW THEM--100,000 YEARS FROM NOW, IN ANOTHER LABORATORY--IN NEW RANAGAR!
THE CONES APPEARED OUT OF SPACE AND ATTACKED AFTER YOU REFUSED TO SURRENDER! THEY DRAIN YOUR LIFE-FORCES--LEAVING THE PEOPLE EMPTY HULKS! HOWEVER, WHILE I WATCHED THEM I SAW A PECULIAR THING...
AS I OBSERVED THE CONES I NOTICED THEY ROTATED VERY SLOWLY UNTIL THEY ATTACKED--WHICH THEY DID BY SPINNING FASTER AND FASTER, ALWAYS IN A CLOCKWISE MOTION AS THEY ABSORBED YOUR PEOPLE'S LIFE-ENERGIES!
THIS WIND-MACHINE WILL HURL A HIGH VELOCITY CURRENT OF AIR AT THE CONES--CAUSING THEM TO WHIRL RAPIDLY IN A COUNTER-CLOCKWISE ROTATION!
BUT WHAT GOOD WILL THAT DO?
13

THE SHRILL MOAN OF RACING WIND ALMOST DROWNS OUT *ADAM'S* WORDS AS HE EXPLAINS...

WHEN THEY WHIRL CLOCKWISE-- THEY INGEST THE LIFE- FORCES WHICH THEY NEED TO STAY ALIVE! BUT WATCH NOW--AS THEY BEGIN TURNING IN THE OPPOSITE DIRECTION!

THE MIGHTY WINDS ROAR EVEN LOUDER AS THEY HIT THE INVADER CONES, TWIRLING THEM COUNTER- CLOCKWISE, FASTER AND FASTER...

WHOOOO

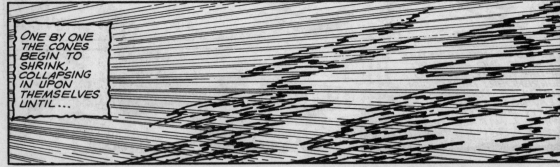

ONE BY ONE THE CONES BEGIN TO SHRINK, COLLAPSING IN UPON THEMSELVES UNTIL...

SOON THE GRIM THREAT OF THE INVADERS HAS EVAPORATED TO NOTHINGNESS...

ADAM, YOU DID IT AGAIN! YOU'RE THE CHAMPION OF CHAMPIONS!

I SHUDDER TO THINK OF WHAT WOULD HAVE HAPPENED, IF I DIDN'T APPEAR HERE "IN TIME"...

AFTER *ADAM* HAS TOLD HIS SWEETHEART THE REST OF HIS STRANGE ADVENTURE 100,000 YEARS IN THE FUTURE...

...AND SO THE STRANGE FATE THAT BROUGHT ME INTO THE FUTURE TO SAVE *NEW RANN*, ALSO GAVE ME THE FREAK OPPORTUNITY TO SAVE "OLD" RANN!

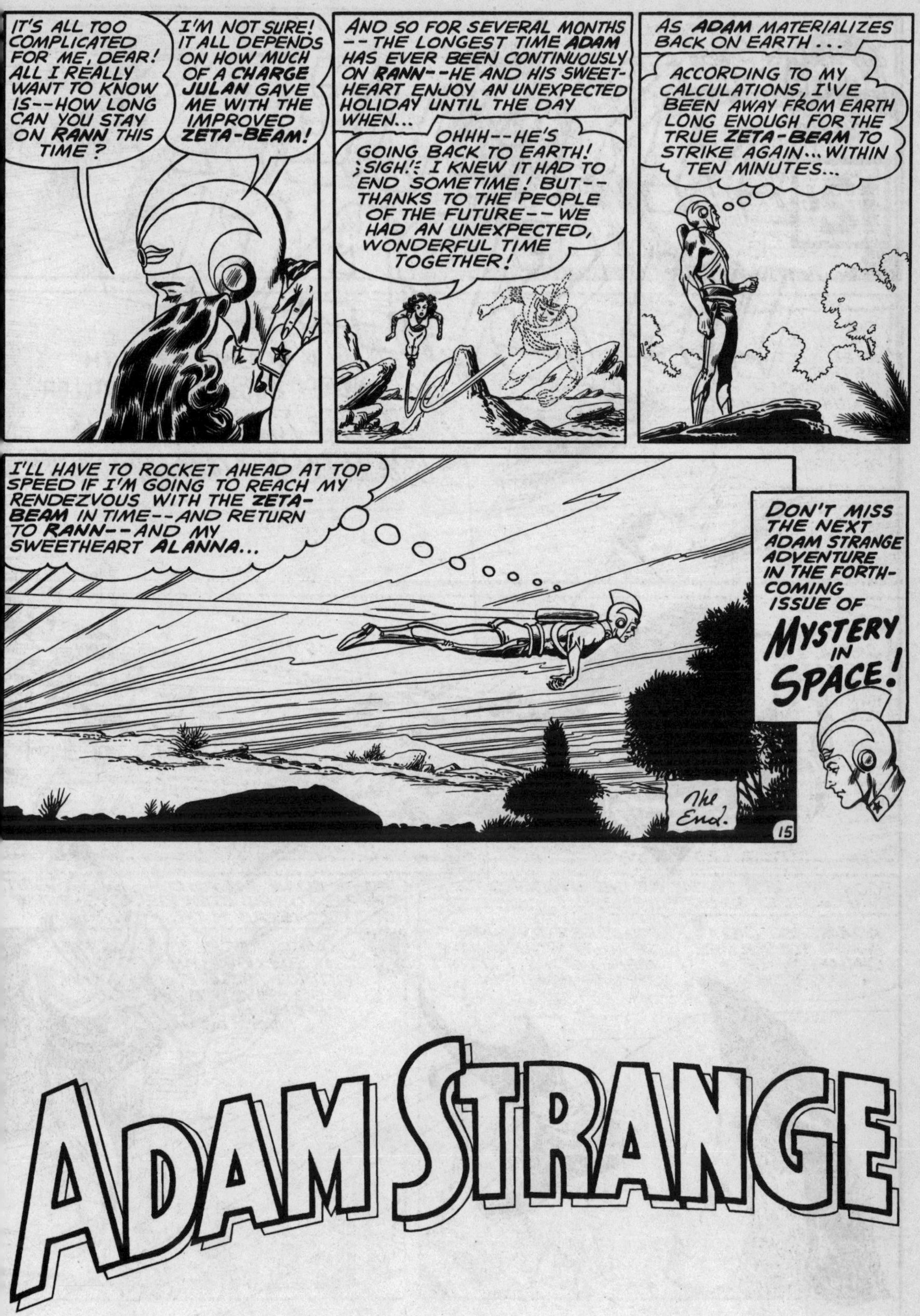
IT'S ALL TOO COMPLICATED FOR ME, DEAR! ALL I REALLY WANT TO KNOW IS--HOW LONG CAN YOU STAY ON RANN THIS TIME?
I'M NOT SURE! IT ALL DEPENDS ON HOW MUCH OF A CHARGE JULAN GAVE ME WITH THE IMPROVED ZETA-BEAM!
AND SO FOR SEVERAL MONTHS--THE LONGEST TIME ADAM HAS EVER BEEN CONTINUOUSLY ON RANN--HE AND HIS SWEETHEART ENJOY AN UNEXPECTED HOLIDAY UNTIL THE DAY WHEN...
OHHH--HE'S GOING BACK TO EARTH! *SIGH!* I KNEW IT HAD TO END SOMETIME! BUT--THANKS TO THE PEOPLE OF THE FUTURE--WE HAD AN UNEXPECTED, WONDERFUL TIME TOGETHER!
AS ADAM MATERIALIZES BACK ON EARTH...
ACCORDING TO MY CALCULATIONS, I'VE BEEN AWAY FROM EARTH LONG ENOUGH FOR THE TRUE ZETA-BEAM TO STRIKE AGAIN...WITHIN TEN MINUTES...
I'LL HAVE TO ROCKET AHEAD AT TOP SPEED IF I'M GOING TO REACH MY RENDEZVOUS WITH THE ZETA-BEAM IN TIME--AND RETURN TO RANN--AND MY SWEETHEART ALANNA...
DON'T MISS THE NEXT ADAM STRANGE ADVENTURE IN THE FORTHCOMING ISSUE OF MYSTERY IN SPACE!
The End.
15

ADAM STRANGE

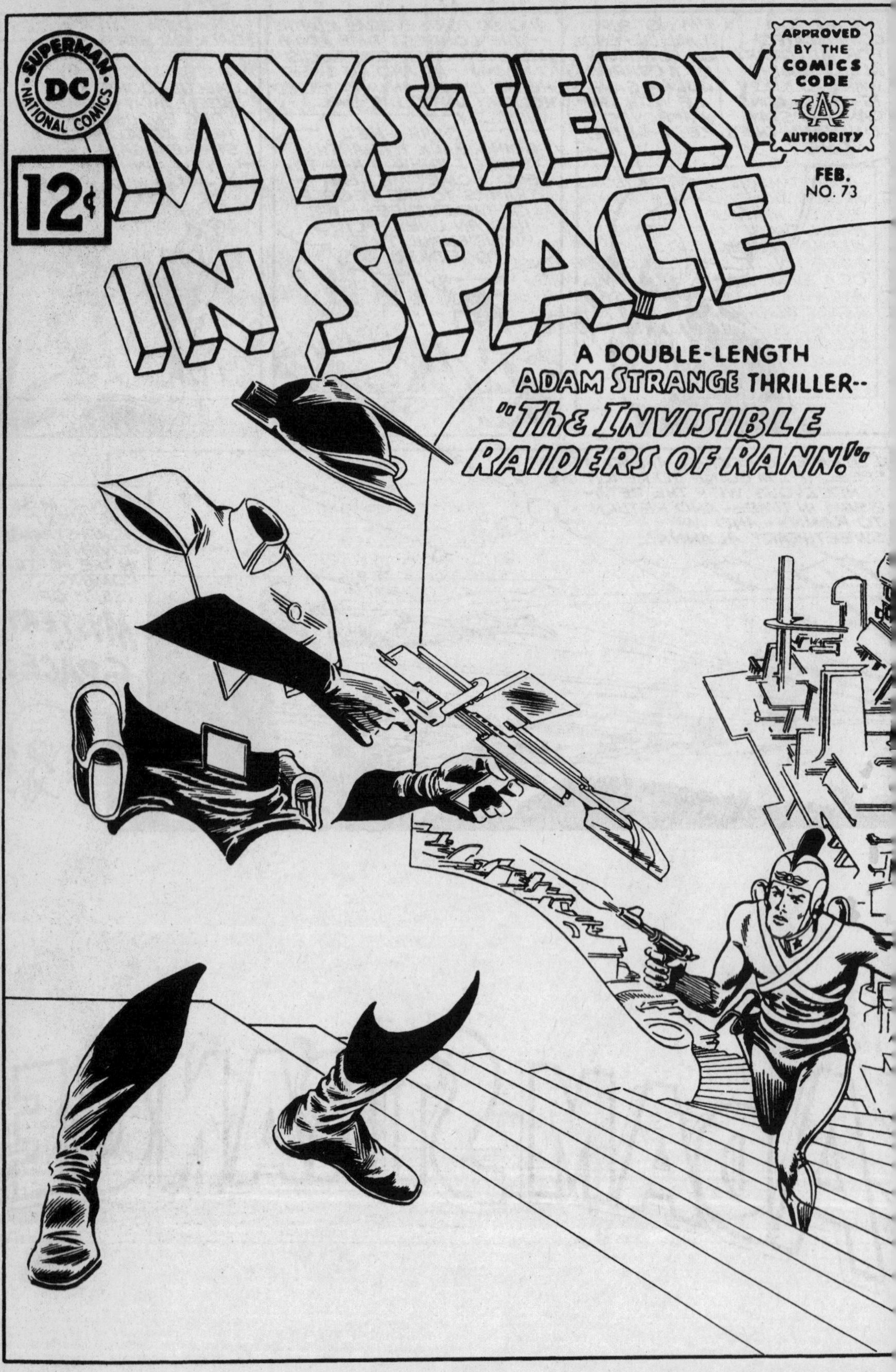
SUPERMAN DC NATIONAL COMICS
12¢
MYSTERY IN SPACE
APPROVED BY THE COMICS CODE AUTHORITY
FEB. NO. 73
A DOUBLE-LENGTH ADAM STRANGE THRILLER--
"The INVISIBLE RAIDERS OF RANN!"

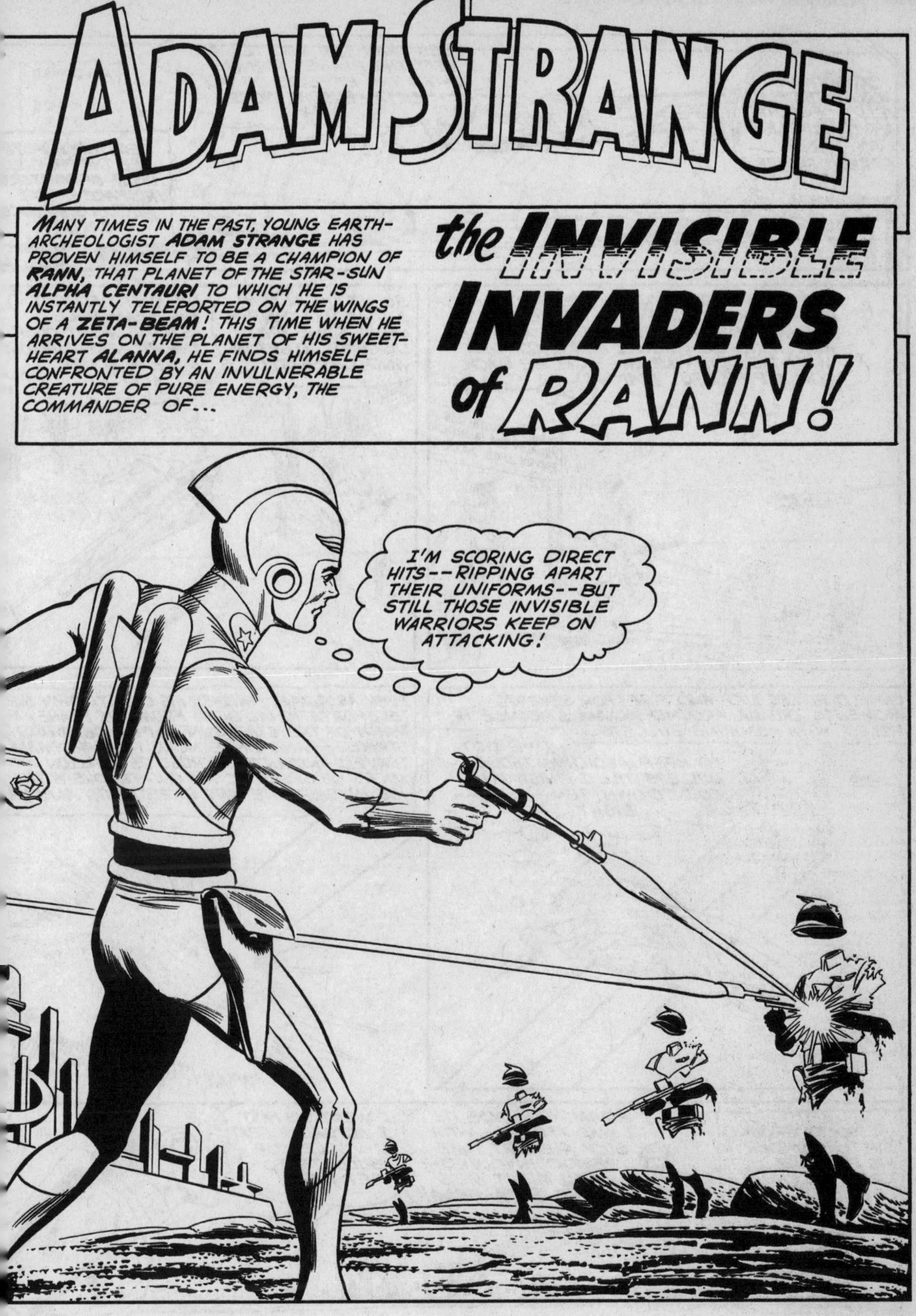
ADAM STRANGE
MANY TIMES IN THE PAST, YOUNG EARTH-ARCHEOLOGIST ADAM STRANGE HAS PROVEN HIMSELF TO BE A CHAMPION OF RANN, THAT PLANET OF THE STAR-SUN ALPHA CENTAURI TO WHICH HE IS INSTANTLY TELEPORTED ON THE WINGS OF A ZETA-BEAM! THIS TIME WHEN HE ARRIVES ON THE PLANET OF HIS SWEETHEART ALANNA, HE FINDS HIMSELF CONFRONTED BY AN INVULNERABLE CREATURE OF PURE ENERGY, THE COMMANDER OF...
the INVISIBLE INVADERS of RANN!
I'M SCORING DIRECT HITS--RIPPING APART THEIR UNIFORMS--BUT STILL THOSE INVISIBLE WARRIORS KEEP ON ATTACKING!

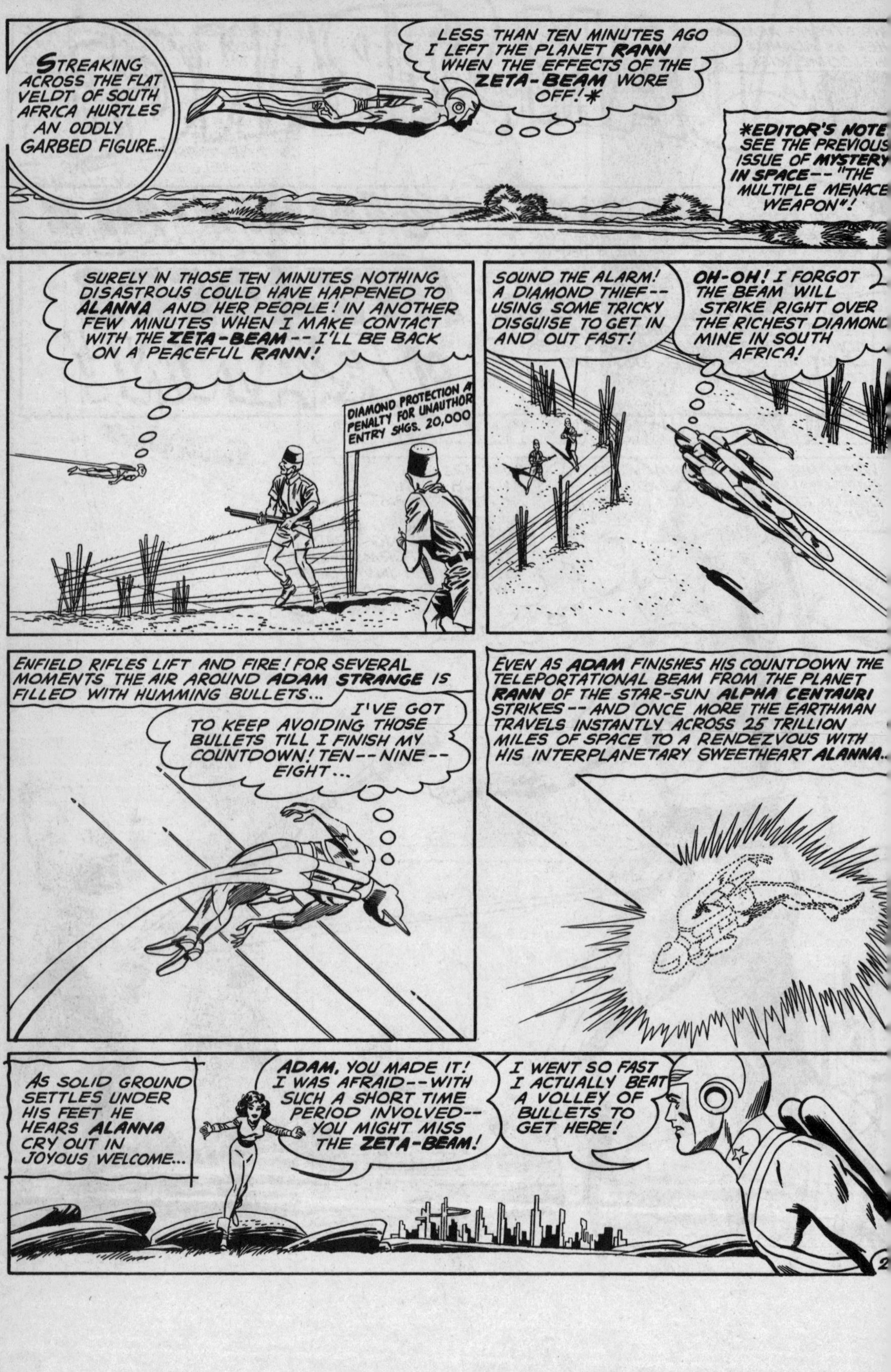
STREAKING ACROSS THE FLAT VELDT OF SOUTH AFRICA HURTLES AN ODDLY GARBED FIGURE...
LESS THAN TEN MINUTES AGO I LEFT THE PLANET RANN WHEN THE EFFECTS OF THE ZETA-BEAM WORE OFF!*
*EDITOR'S NOTE SEE THE PREVIOUS ISSUE OF MYSTERY IN SPACE--"THE MULTIPLE MENACE WEAPON"!
SURELY IN THOSE TEN MINUTES NOTHING DISASTROUS COULD HAVE HAPPENED TO ALANNA AND HER PEOPLE! IN ANOTHER FEW MINUTES WHEN I MAKE CONTACT WITH THE ZETA-BEAM--I'LL BE BACK ON A PEACEFUL RANN!
DIAMOND PROTECTION A PENALTY FOR UNAUTHOR ENTRY SHGS. 20,000
SOUND THE ALARM! A DIAMOND THIEF--USING SOME TRICKY DISGUISE TO GET IN AND OUT FAST!
OH-OH! I FORGOT THE BEAM WILL STRIKE RIGHT OVER THE RICHEST DIAMOND MINE IN SOUTH AFRICA!
ENFIELD RIFLES LIFT AND FIRE! FOR SEVERAL MOMENTS THE AIR AROUND ADAM STRANGE IS FILLED WITH HUMMING BULLETS...
I'VE GOT TO KEEP AVOIDING THOSE BULLETS TILL I FINISH MY COUNTDOWN! TEN--NINE--EIGHT...
EVEN AS ADAM FINISHES HIS COUNTDOWN THE TELEPORTATIONAL BEAM FROM THE PLANET RANN OF THE STAR-SUN ALPHA CENTAURI STRIKES--AND ONCE MORE THE EARTHMAN TRAVELS INSTANTLY ACROSS 25 TRILLION MILES OF SPACE TO A RENDEZVOUS WITH HIS INTERPLANETARY SWEETHEART ALANNA...
AS SOLID GROUND SETTLES UNDER HIS FEET HE HEARS ALANNA CRY OUT IN JOYOUS WELCOME...
ADAM, YOU MADE IT! I WAS AFRAID--WITH SUCH A SHORT TIME PERIOD INVOLVED--YOU MIGHT MISS THE ZETA-BEAM!
I WENT SO FAST I ACTUALLY BEAT A VOLLEY OF BULLETS TO GET HERE!

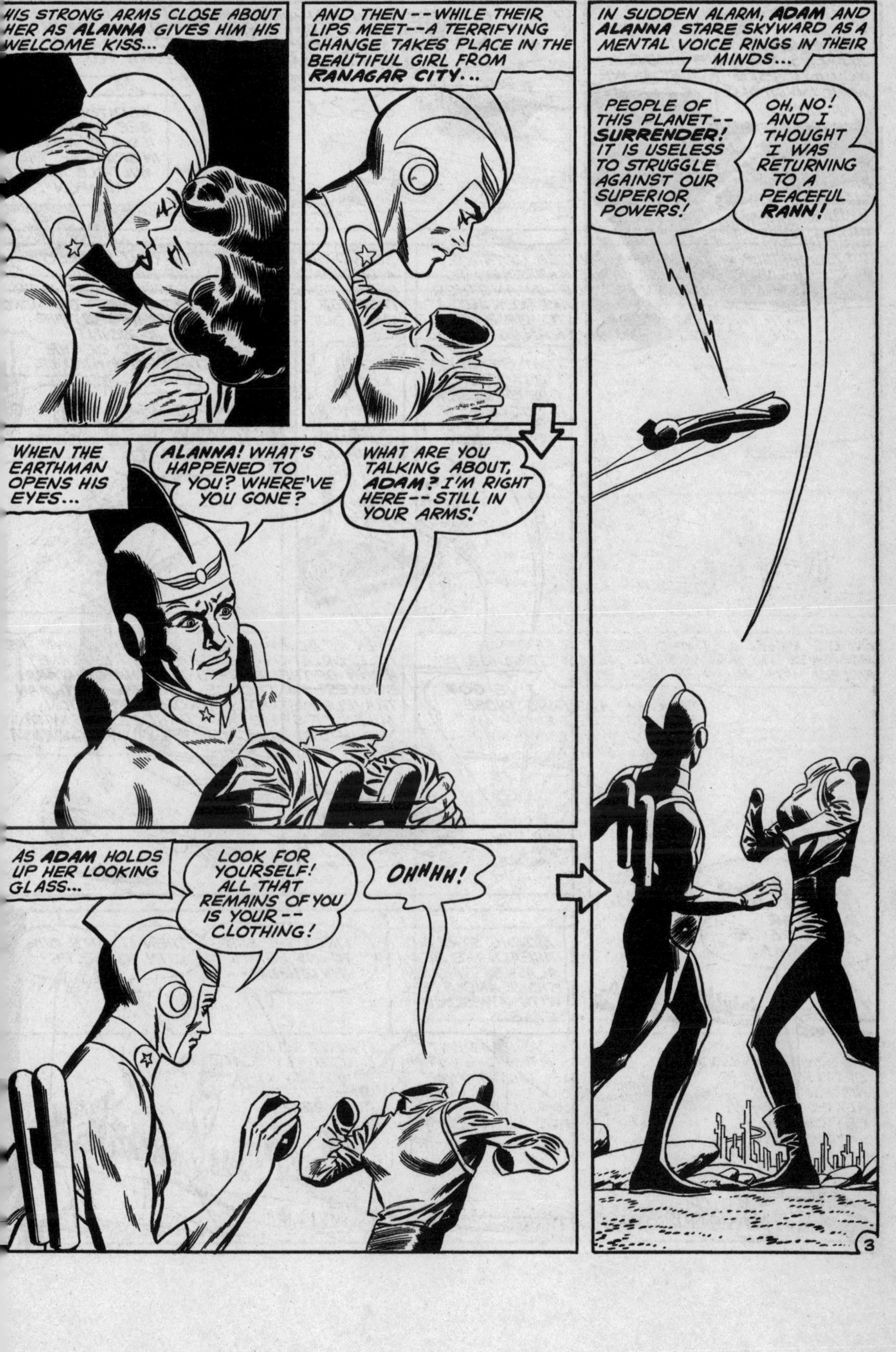
HIS STRONG ARMS CLOSE ABOUT HER AS ALANNA GIVES HIM HIS WELCOME KISS...
AND THEN--WHILE THEIR LIPS MEET--A TERRIFYING CHANGE TAKES PLACE IN THE BEAUTIFUL GIRL FROM RANAGAR CITY...
WHEN THE EARTHMAN OPENS HIS EYES...
ALANNA! WHAT'S HAPPENED TO YOU? WHERE'VE YOU GONE?
WHAT ARE YOU TALKING ABOUT, ADAM? I'M RIGHT HERE--STILL IN YOUR ARMS!
AS ADAM HOLDS UP HER LOOKING GLASS...
LOOK FOR YOURSELF! ALL THAT REMAINS OF YOU IS YOUR--CLOTHING!
OHHHH!
IN SUDDEN ALARM, ADAM AND ALANNA STARE SKYWARD AS A MENTAL VOICE RINGS IN THEIR MINDS...
PEOPLE OF THIS PLANET--SURRENDER! IT IS USELESS TO STRUGGLE AGAINST OUR SUPERIOR POWERS!
OH, NO! AND I THOUGHT I WAS RETURNING TO A PEACEFUL RANN!
3

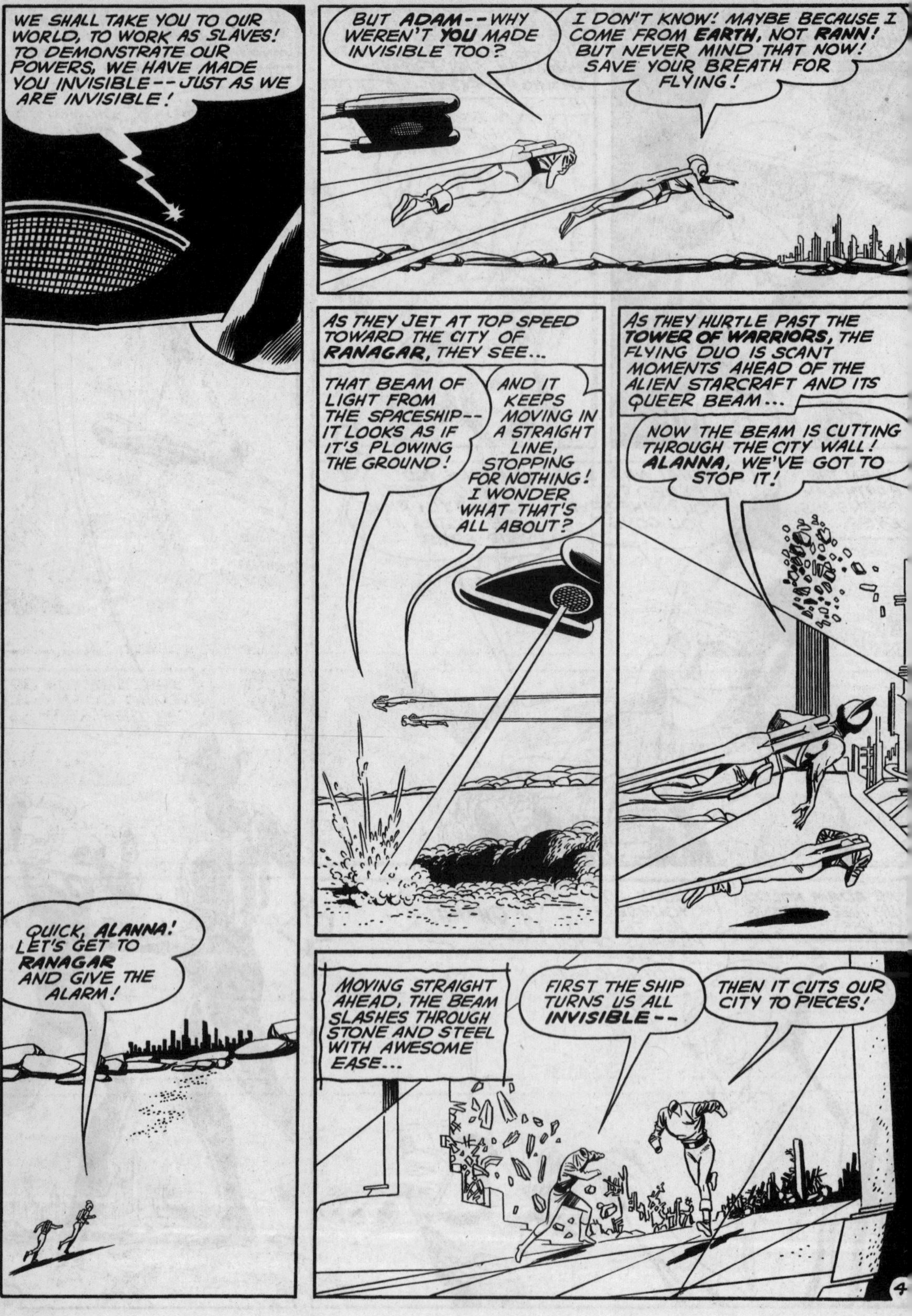
WE SHALL TAKE YOU TO OUR WORLD, TO WORK AS SLAVES! TO DEMONSTRATE OUR POWERS, WE HAVE MADE YOU INVISIBLE--JUST AS WE ARE INVISIBLE!
QUICK, ALANNA! LET'S GET TO RANAGAR AND GIVE THE ALARM!
BUT ADAM--WHY WEREN'T YOU MADE INVISIBLE TOO?
I DON'T KNOW! MAYBE BECAUSE I COME FROM EARTH, NOT RANN! BUT NEVER MIND THAT NOW! SAVE YOUR BREATH FOR FLYING!
AS THEY JET AT TOP SPEED TOWARD THE CITY OF RANAGAR, THEY SEE...
THAT BEAM OF LIGHT FROM THE SPACESHIP--IT LOOKS AS IF IT'S PLOWING THE GROUND!
AND IT KEEPS MOVING IN A STRAIGHT LINE, STOPPING FOR NOTHING! I WONDER WHAT THAT'S ALL ABOUT?
AS THEY HURTLE PAST THE TOWER OF WARRIORS, THE FLYING DUO IS SCANT MOMENTS AHEAD OF THE ALIEN STARCRAFT AND ITS QUEER BEAM...
NOW THE BEAM IS CUTTING THROUGH THE CITY WALL! ALANNA, WE'VE GOT TO STOP IT!
MOVING STRAIGHT AHEAD, THE BEAM SLASHES THROUGH STONE AND STEEL WITH AWESOME EASE...
FIRST THE SHIP TURNS US ALL INVISIBLE--
THEN IT CUTS OUR CITY TO PIECES!
4

UPWARD TO MEET THIS STRANGE MENACE COME THE ARMED FLIERS OF *RANAGAR*...

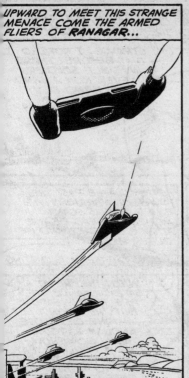

DARTING HERE AND THERE TO AVOID THE RETURN FIRE OF THE STARSHIP, *ADAM STRANGE* JOINS IN THE ATTACK, SCORING HIT AFTER HIT...

WE'RE DAMAGING THE SHIP! KEEP UP THE ATTACK!

MOMENTS LATER, WITH A SCREAM OF TORTURED METAL THE CRIPPLED ALIEN CRAFT CRASH-LANDS A FEW MILES BEYOND *RANAGAR*...

SHE'S DOWN! NOW THE INVADERS WILL SURRENDER TO US!

BUT INSTEAD OF SURRENDERING, THE GREAT VESSEL POURS OUT PLATOON AFTER PLATOON OF INVISIBLE WARRIORS...

IF THEIR SHIP CAN BE BROUGHT DOWN--SO CAN THEY! KEEP FIRING!

BUT AS THE UNSEEN HORDE ADVANCES, FIRING STEADILY, THEY SEEM INVULNERABLE TO ALL TYPES OF WEAPONS...

I'M SCORING DIRECT HITS--RIPPING APART THEIR UNIFORMS--BUT THEY KEEP ON COMING!

AGAIN AND AGAIN A RAIN OF DEADLY RAY-BEAMS CUTS INTO THE INVISIBLE ATTACKERS, WITHOUT EFFECT...

5

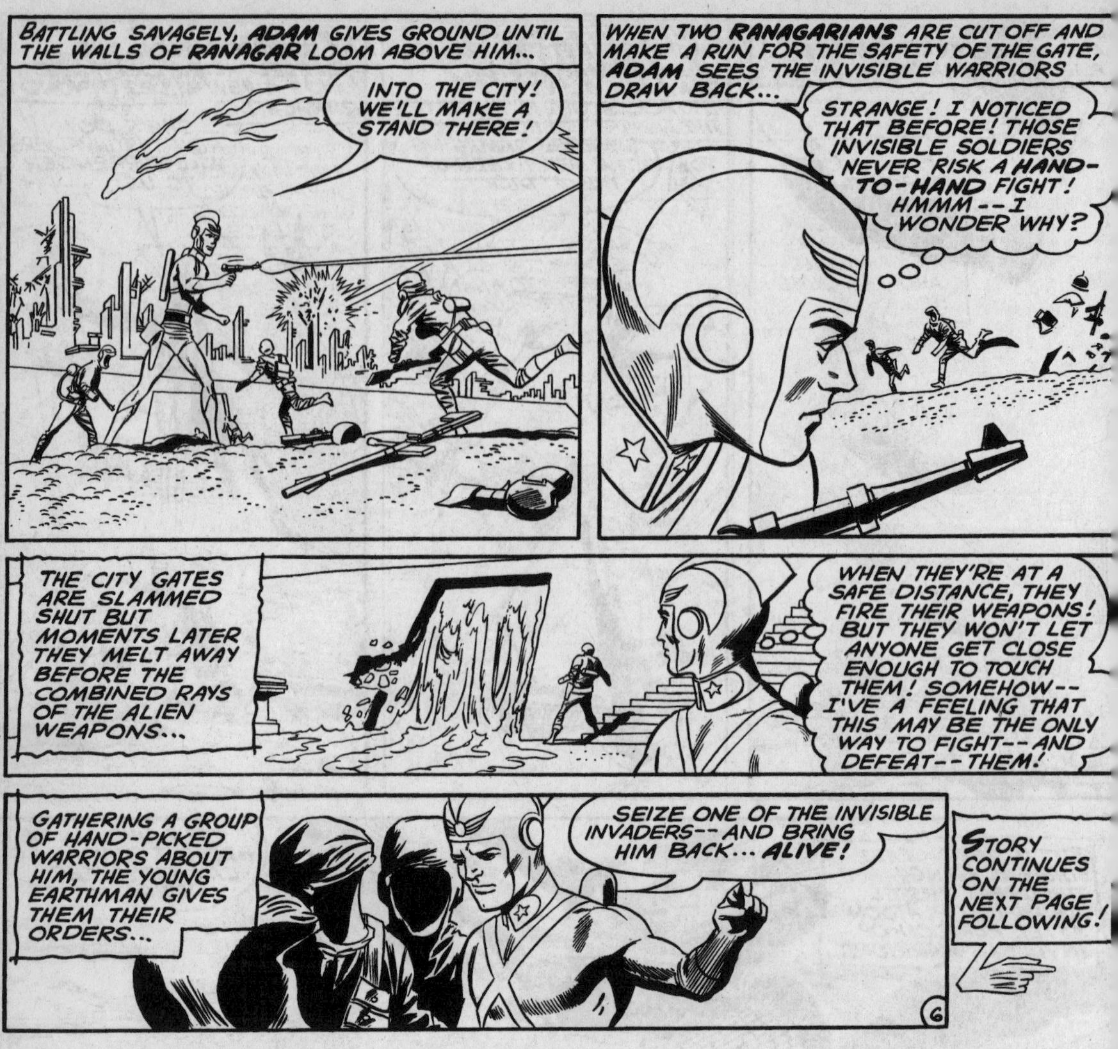
BATTLING SAVAGELY, ADAM GIVES GROUND UNTIL THE WALLS OF RANAGAR LOOM ABOVE HIM...
INTO THE CITY! WE'LL MAKE A STAND THERE!
WHEN TWO RANAGARIANS ARE CUT OFF AND MAKE A RUN FOR THE SAFETY OF THE GATE, ADAM SEES THE INVISIBLE WARRIORS DRAW BACK...
STRANGE! I NOTICED THAT BEFORE! THOSE INVISIBLE SOLDIERS NEVER RISK A HAND-TO-HAND FIGHT! HMMM--I WONDER WHY?
THE CITY GATES ARE SLAMMED SHUT BUT MOMENTS LATER THEY MELT AWAY BEFORE THE COMBINED RAYS OF THE ALIEN WEAPONS...
WHEN THEY'RE AT A SAFE DISTANCE, THEY FIRE THEIR WEAPONS! BUT THEY WON'T LET ANYONE GET CLOSE ENOUGH TO TOUCH THEM! SOMEHOW--I'VE A FEELING THAT THIS MAY BE THE ONLY WAY TO FIGHT--AND DEFEAT--THEM!
GATHERING A GROUP OF HAND-PICKED WARRIORS ABOUT HIM, THE YOUNG EARTHMAN GIVES THEM THEIR ORDERS...
SEIZE ONE OF THE INVISIBLE INVADERS--AND BRING HIM BACK... ALIVE!
STORY CONTINUES ON THE NEXT PAGE FOLLOWING!
6

ADAM STRANGE

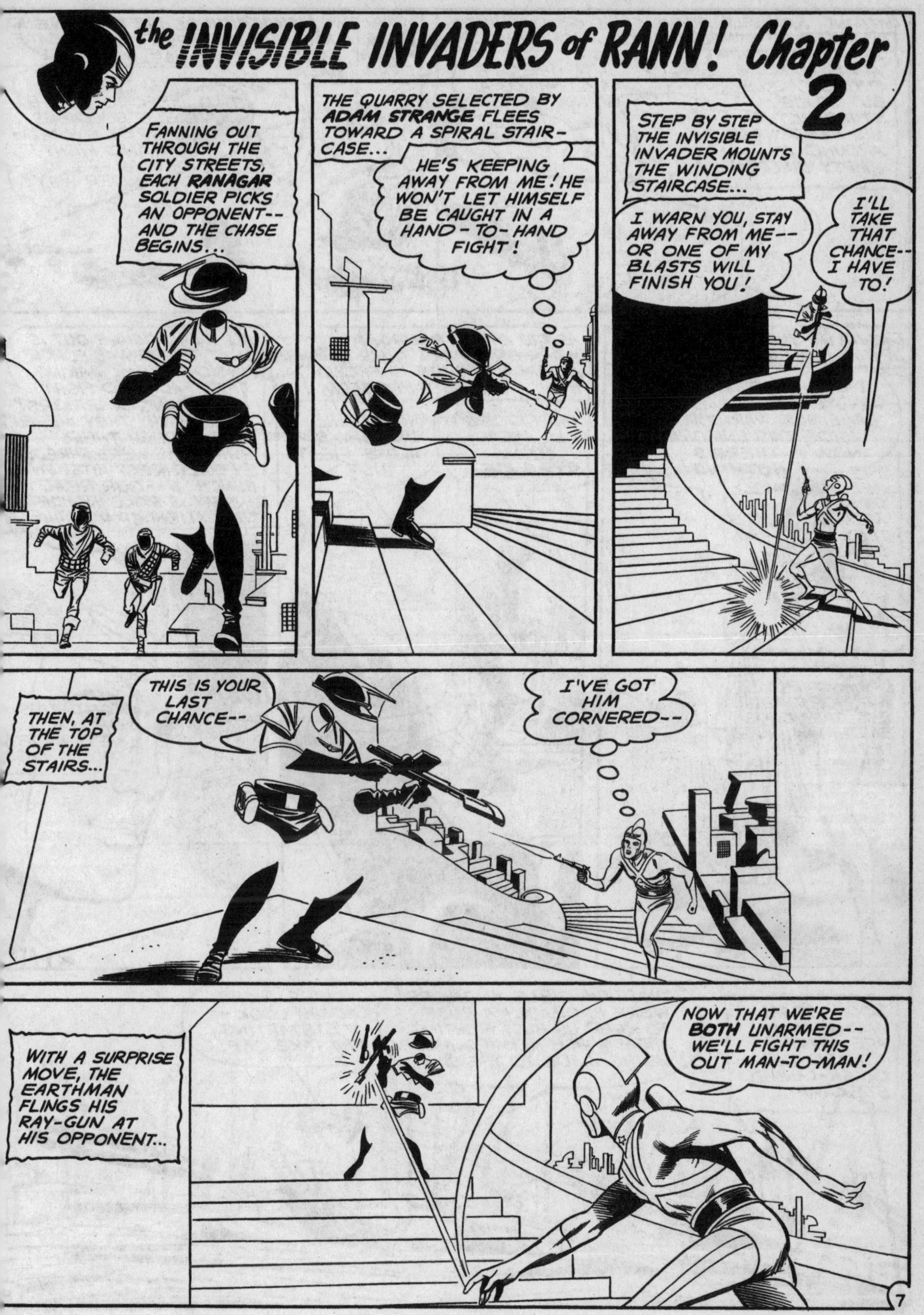
the INVISIBLE INVADERS of RANN! Chapter 2
FANNING OUT THROUGH THE CITY STREETS, EACH RANAGAR SOLDIER PICKS AN OPPONENT-- AND THE CHASE BEGINS...
THE QUARRY SELECTED BY ADAM STRANGE FLEES TOWARD A SPIRAL STAIR-CASE...
HE'S KEEPING AWAY FROM ME! HE WON'T LET HIMSELF BE CAUGHT IN A HAND-TO-HAND FIGHT!
STEP BY STEP THE INVISIBLE INVADER MOUNTS THE WINDING STAIRCASE...
I WARN YOU, STAY AWAY FROM ME-- OR ONE OF MY BLASTS WILL FINISH YOU!
I'LL TAKE THAT CHANCE-- I HAVE TO!
THEN, AT THE TOP OF THE STAIRS...
THIS IS YOUR LAST CHANCE--
I'VE GOT HIM CORNERED--
WITH A SURPRISE MOVE, THE EARTHMAN FLINGS HIS RAY-GUN AT HIS OPPONENT...
NOW THAT WE'RE BOTH UNARMED-- WE'LL FIGHT THIS OUT MAN-TO-MAN!
7

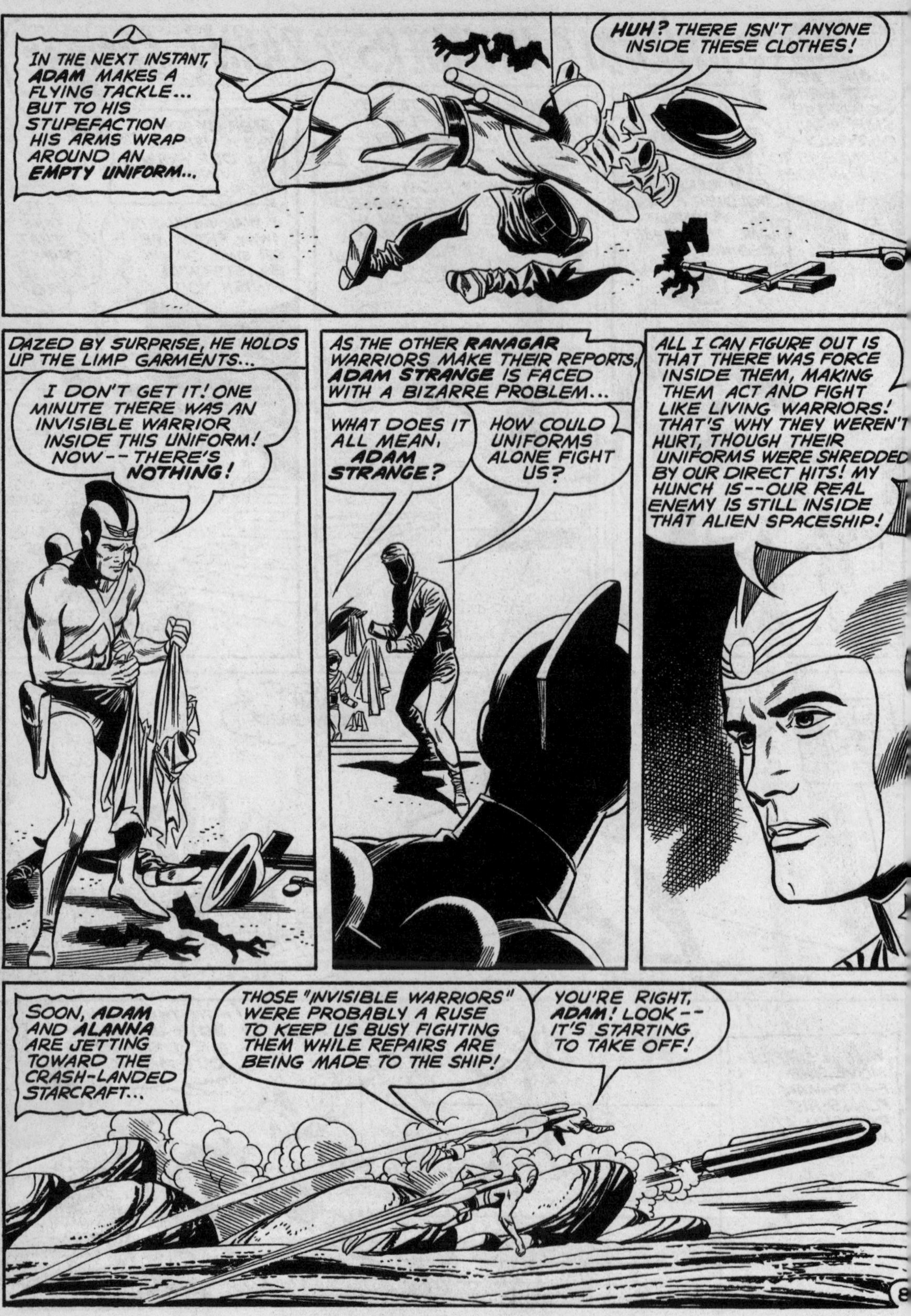
IN THE NEXT INSTANT, ADAM MAKES A FLYING TACKLE... BUT TO HIS STUPEFACTION HIS ARMS WRAP AROUND AN EMPTY UNIFORM...
HUH? THERE ISN'T ANYONE INSIDE THESE CLOTHES!
DAZED BY SURPRISE, HE HOLDS UP THE LIMP GARMENTS...
I DON'T GET IT! ONE MINUTE THERE WAS AN INVISIBLE WARRIOR INSIDE THIS UNIFORM! NOW--THERE'S NOTHING!
AS THE OTHER RANAGAR WARRIORS MAKE THEIR REPORTS, ADAM STRANGE IS FACED WITH A BIZARRE PROBLEM...
WHAT DOES IT ALL MEAN, ADAM STRANGE?
HOW COULD UNIFORMS ALONE FIGHT US?
ALL I CAN FIGURE OUT IS THAT THERE WAS FORCE INSIDE THEM, MAKING THEM ACT AND FIGHT LIKE LIVING WARRIORS! THAT'S WHY THEY WEREN'T HURT, THOUGH THEIR UNIFORMS WERE SHREDDED BY OUR DIRECT HITS! MY HUNCH IS--OUR REAL ENEMY IS STILL INSIDE THAT ALIEN SPACESHIP!
SOON, ADAM AND ALANNA ARE JETTING TOWARD THE CRASH-LANDED STARCRAFT...
THOSE "INVISIBLE WARRIORS" WERE PROBABLY A RUSE TO KEEP US BUSY FIGHTING THEM WHILE REPAIRS ARE BEING MADE TO THE SHIP!
YOU'RE RIGHT, ADAM! LOOK--IT'S STARTING TO TAKE OFF!
8

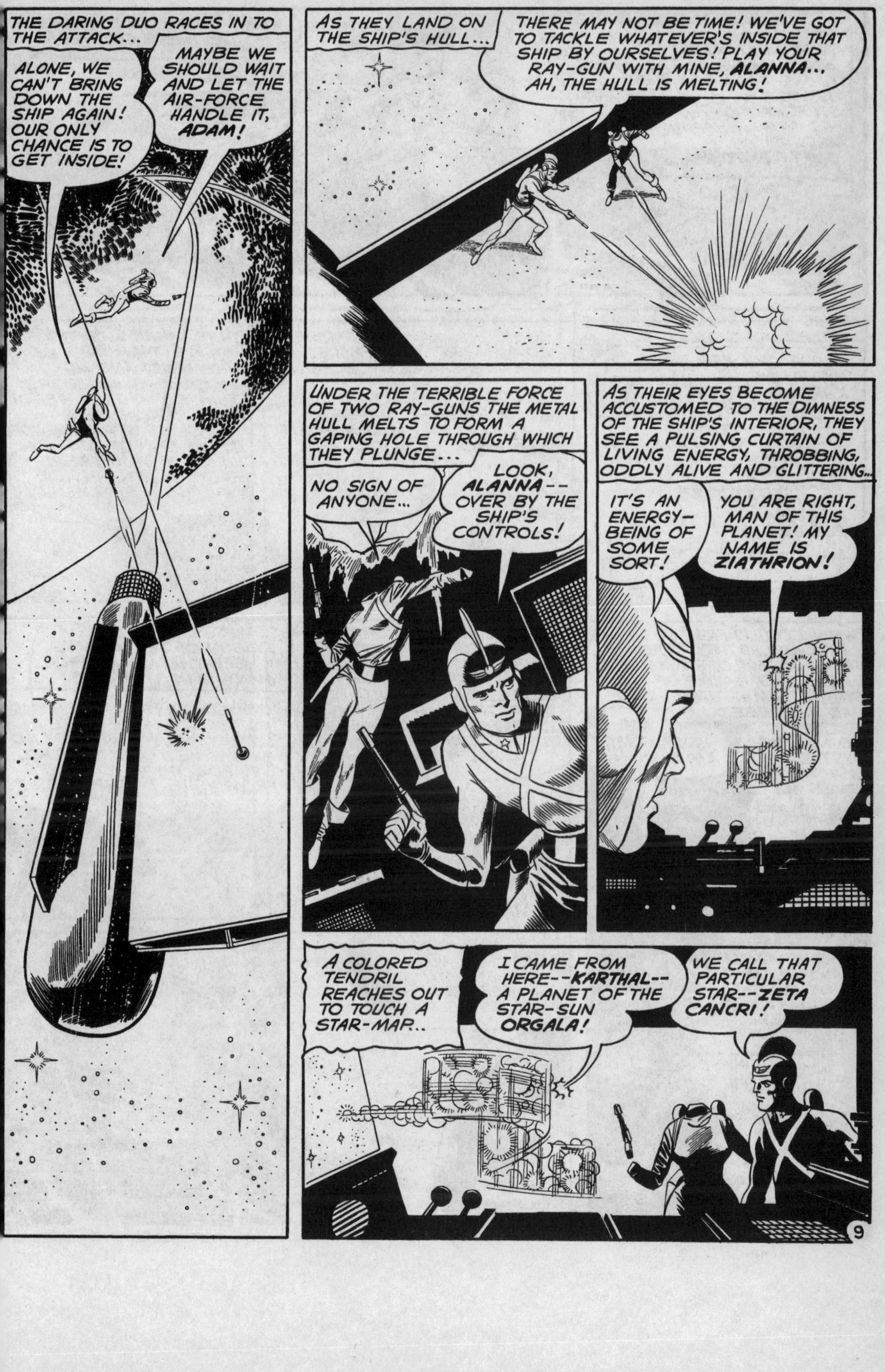
THE DARING DUO RACES IN TO THE ATTACK...
ALONE, WE CAN'T BRING DOWN THE SHIP AGAIN! OUR ONLY CHANCE IS TO GET INSIDE!
MAYBE WE SHOULD WAIT AND LET THE AIR-FORCE HANDLE IT, ADAM!
AS THEY LAND ON THE SHIP'S HULL...
THERE MAY NOT BE TIME! WE'VE GOT TO TACKLE WHATEVER'S INSIDE THAT SHIP BY OURSELVES! PLAY YOUR RAY-GUN WITH MINE, ALANNA... AH, THE HULL IS MELTING!
UNDER THE TERRIBLE FORCE OF TWO RAY-GUNS THE METAL HULL MELTS TO FORM A GAPING HOLE THROUGH WHICH THEY PLUNGE...
NO SIGN OF ANYONE...
LOOK, ALANNA-- OVER BY THE SHIP'S CONTROLS!
AS THEIR EYES BECOME ACCUSTOMED TO THE DIMNESS OF THE SHIP'S INTERIOR, THEY SEE A PULSING CURTAIN OF LIVING ENERGY, THROBBING, ODDLY ALIVE AND GLITTERING...
IT'S AN ENERGY-BEING OF SOME SORT!
YOU ARE RIGHT, MAN OF THIS PLANET! MY NAME IS ZIATHRION!
A COLORED TENDRIL REACHES OUT TO TOUCH A STAR-MAP..
I CAME FROM HERE--KARTHAL--A PLANET OF THE STAR-SUN ORGALA!
WE CALL THAT PARTICULAR STAR--ZETA CANCRI!
9

"MANY YEARS AGO I WAS ACCLAIMED THE GREATEST SCIENTIST OF MY RACE! IN MY PRIDE I SOUGHT TO DOMINATE MY FELLOW-BEINGS SO AS TO RULE THEM..."

YOU WILL OBEY ME -- OR PERISH!

"ALONE OR A FEW, MY FELLOW KARTHALS WERE NO MATCH FOR ME! ONLY WHEN THEY ALL BANDED TOGETHER WERE THEY ABLE TO OVERCOME MY GREAT POWERS... "

I'M HELPLESS AGAINST THEIR COMBINED ENERGIES!

"WHEN I COULD FIGHT NO LONGER I WATCHED AS THEY REMOVED THE GREATEST OF MY MANY INVENTIONS, A CORE OF SYNTHETI-MATTER WHICH I HAD ABSORBED..."

NO, NO! THE SYNTHETI-MATTER GIVES ME ALL MY GREAT POWERS!

WE KNOW THAT, ZIATHRION!

WE SHALL HIDE YOUR SYNTHETI-MATTER CORE ON A FAR-OFF PLANET WHILE YOU REMAIN HERE AS OUR PRISONER -- FOREVER! WE CANNOT DESTROY YOU, SINCE YOU CONSIST OF LIVING ENERGY, BUT WE CAN KEEP YOU HELPLESS!

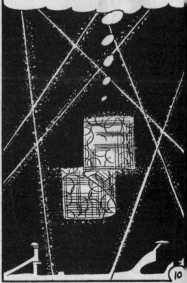

"I WAS PLACED INSIDE A PRISON OF THETA-RAYS WHERE I REMAINED FOR MANY, MANY YEARS... "

I'M NOT QUITE AS HELPLESS AS THEY IMAGINE! ONCE I DETERMINE WHERE THEY HID MY SYNTHETI-MATTER CORE, I'LL FIND A WAY TO ESCAPE FROM HERE AND RECOVER IT!

10

"AT LONG LAST I LEARNED MY INVENTION HAD BEEN HIDDEN ON THE PLANET *RANN* OF THE STAR-SUN *ALPHA CENTAURI*..."

WE SELECTED THIS PLANET BECAUSE ITS STAR-SUN IS SIMILAR TO OUR OWN!

DIFFERENT TYPE STAR-SUNS MAKE US *INERT!* WE COULDN'T HIDE THE CORE ON PLANETS OF SUCH SUNS WITHOUT BEING MADE MOTIONLESS!

"HAVING LEARNED THIS, I CREATED A DUPLICATE OF MYSELF AND LEFT IT IN PRISON IN MY PLACE WHILE I FLED AWAY FROM MY HOME PLANET..."

I STILL HAVE ENOUGH POWER TO ESCAPE! BY KEEPING MY "DOUBLE" HERE, MY CAPTORS WON'T REALIZE I'M GONE-- AND WON'T INTERFERE AS I JOURNEY TO *RANN* TO REGAIN MY ENERGY CORE!

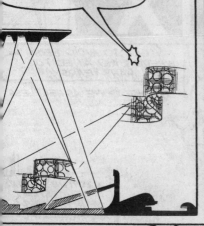

"AS SOON AS I ARRIVED OVER *RANN* I TURNED EVERYONE INVISIBLE TO DEMONSTRATE MY POWERS--EXPECTING YOUR PEOPLE TO SURRENDER..."

I REALLY DON'T WANT THEM AS MY SLAVES-- I'M ONLY PLAYING FOR TIME WHILE I SEARCH FOR MY SYNTHETI-MATTER CORE WHICH IS HIDDEN SOME-WHERE ON THIS PLANET!

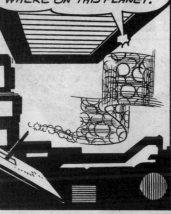

"WHILE I WAS USING A *PLOW-RAY* TO HUNT FOR THE CORE, YOU AND YOUR PEOPLE ATTACKED ME..."

I'M VULNERABLE TO ATTACK UNTIL I CAN MERGE MYSELF WITH MY SYNTHETI-MATTER CORE! I'VE GOT TO--CRASH-LAND!

THE REST YOU KNOW! MY MENTAL POWERS WERE STILL GREAT ENOUGH TO FILL OUT THOSE UNIFORMS WITH "INVISIBLE" WARRIORS AND FIGHT YOU, STALLING FOR TIME TO REPAIR MY SHIP!

IT WAS A GOOD TRY, *ZIATHRION* --BUT I'VE GOT TO OVERCOME YOU TO PROTECT *RANN!* SINCE YOU ADMITTED YOU'RE VULNERABLE, THAT SHOULDN'T BE VERY HARD!

FOOL! IT'S *TOO LATE* TO OVERCOME ME *NOW!*

11

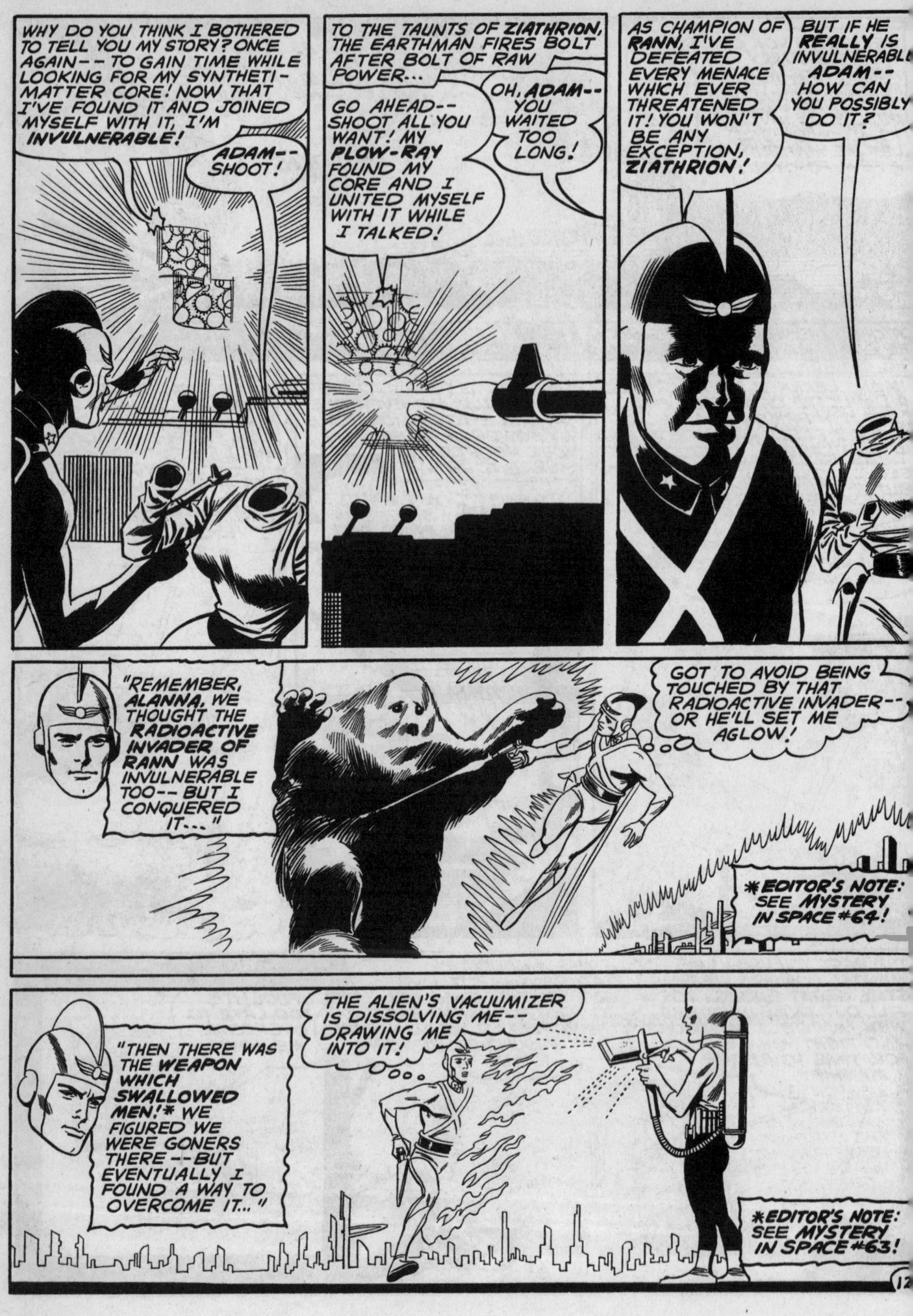
WHY DO YOU THINK I BOTHERED TO TELL YOU MY STORY? ONCE AGAIN-- TO GAIN TIME WHILE LOOKING FOR MY SYNTHETI-MATTER CORE! NOW THAT I'VE FOUND IT AND JOINED MYSELF WITH IT, I'M INVULNERABLE!
ADAM-- SHOOT!
TO THE TAUNTS OF ZIATHRION, THE EARTHMAN FIRES BOLT AFTER BOLT OF RAW POWER...
GO AHEAD-- SHOOT ALL YOU WANT! MY PLOW-RAY FOUND MY CORE AND I UNITED MYSELF WITH IT WHILE I TALKED!
OH, ADAM-- YOU WAITED TOO LONG!
AS CHAMPION OF RANN, I'VE DEFEATED EVERY MENACE WHICH EVER THREATENED IT! YOU WON'T BE ANY EXCEPTION, ZIATHRION!
BUT IF HE REALLY IS INVULNERABLE ADAM-- HOW CAN YOU POSSIBLY DO IT?
"REMEMBER, ALANNA, WE THOUGHT THE RADIOACTIVE INVADER OF RANN WAS INVULNERABLE TOO-- BUT I CONQUERED IT..."
GOT TO AVOID BEING TOUCHED BY THAT RADIOACTIVE INVADER-- OR HE'LL SET ME AGLOW!
*EDITOR'S NOTE: SEE MYSTERY IN SPACE #64!
"THEN THERE WAS THE WEAPON WHICH SWALLOWED MEN!* WE FIGURED WE WERE GONERS THERE--BUT EVENTUALLY I FOUND A WAY TO OVERCOME IT..."
THE ALIEN'S VACUUMIZER IS DISSOLVING ME-- DRAWING ME INTO IT!
*EDITOR'S NOTE: SEE MYSTERY IN SPACE #63!
12

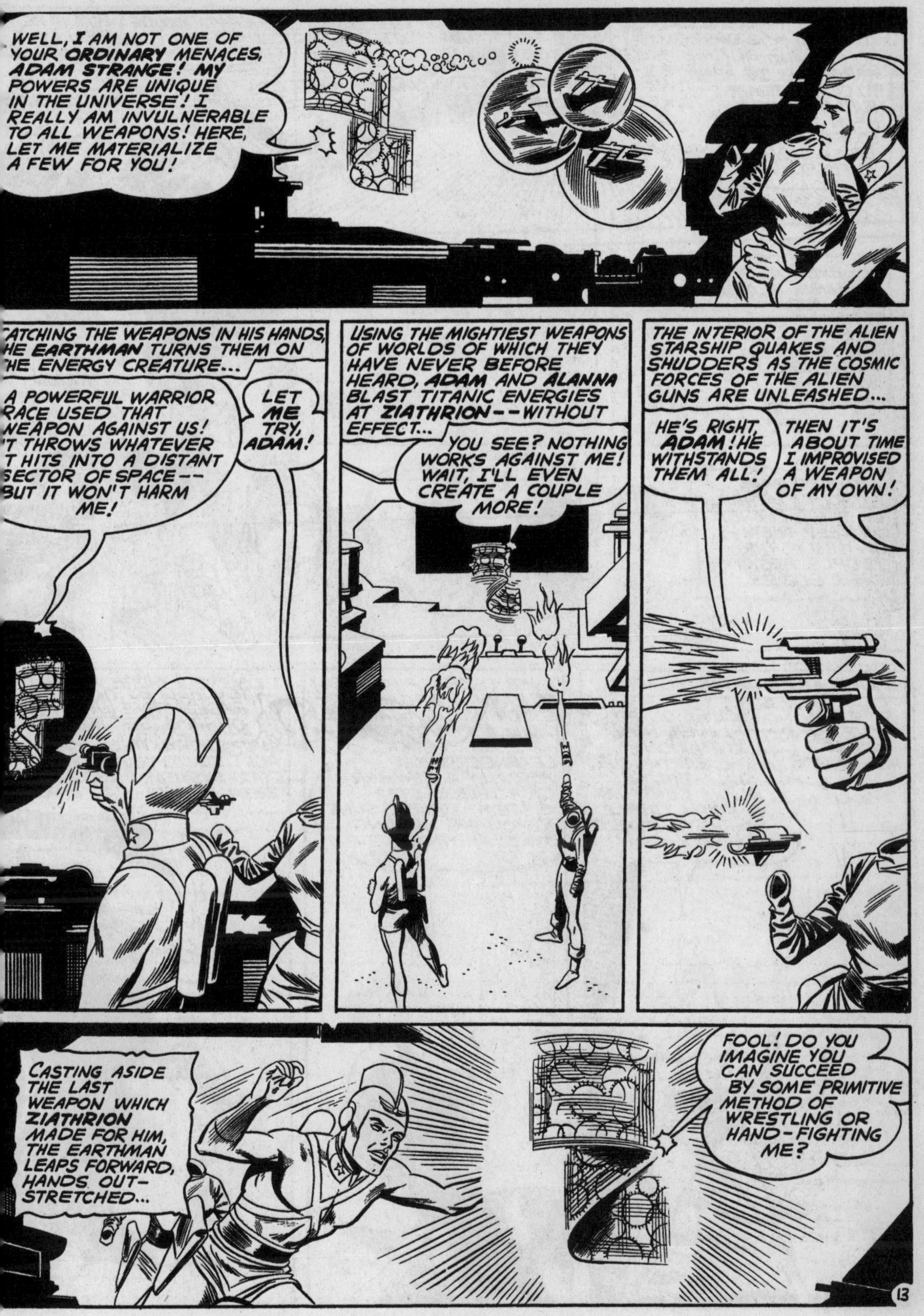
WELL, I AM NOT ONE OF YOUR ORDINARY MENACES, ADAM STRANGE! MY POWERS ARE UNIQUE IN THE UNIVERSE! I REALLY AM INVULNERABLE TO ALL WEAPONS! HERE, LET ME MATERIALIZE A FEW FOR YOU!
CATCHING THE WEAPONS IN HIS HANDS, THE EARTHMAN TURNS THEM ON THE ENERGY CREATURE...
A POWERFUL WARRIOR RACE USED THAT WEAPON AGAINST US! IT THROWS WHATEVER IT HITS INTO A DISTANT SECTOR OF SPACE-- BUT IT WON'T HARM ME!
LET ME TRY, ADAM!
USING THE MIGHTIEST WEAPONS OF WORLDS OF WHICH THEY HAVE NEVER BEFORE HEARD, ADAM AND ALANNA BLAST TITANIC ENERGIES AT ZIATHRION--WITHOUT EFFECT...
YOU SEE? NOTHING WORKS AGAINST ME! WAIT, I'LL EVEN CREATE A COUPLE MORE!
THE INTERIOR OF THE ALIEN STARSHIP QUAKES AND SHUDDERS AS THE COSMIC FORCES OF THE ALIEN GUNS ARE UNLEASHED...
HE'S RIGHT, ADAM! HE WITHSTANDS THEM ALL!
THEN IT'S ABOUT TIME I IMPROVISED A WEAPON OF MY OWN!
CASTING ASIDE THE LAST WEAPON WHICH ZIATHRION MADE FOR HIM, THE EARTHMAN LEAPS FORWARD, HANDS OUT-STRETCHED...
FOOL! DO YOU IMAGINE YOU CAN SUCCEED BY SOME PRIMITIVE METHOD OF WRESTLING OR HAND-FIGHTING ME?
13

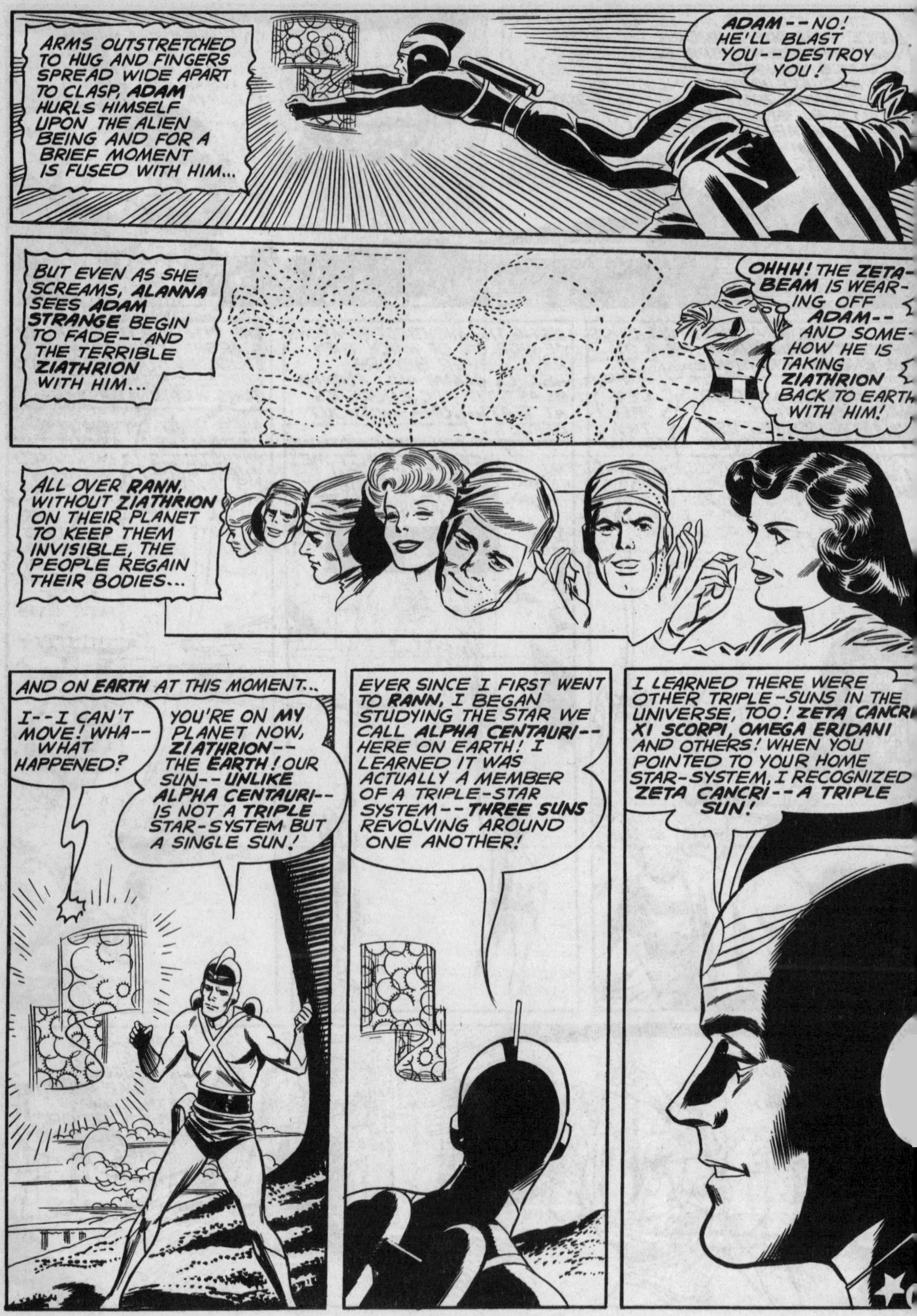
ARMS OUTSTRETCHED TO HUG AND FINGERS SPREAD WIDE APART TO CLASP, ADAM HURLS HIMSELF UPON THE ALIEN BEING AND FOR A BRIEF MOMENT IS FUSED WITH HIM...
ADAM--NO! HE'LL BLAST YOU--DESTROY YOU!
BUT EVEN AS SHE SCREAMS, ALANNA SEES ADAM STRANGE BEGIN TO FADE--AND THE TERRIBLE ZIATHRION WITH HIM...
OHHH! THE ZETA-BEAM IS WEARING OFF ADAM--AND SOMEHOW HE IS TAKING ZIATHRION BACK TO EARTH WITH HIM!
ALL OVER RANN, WITHOUT ZIATHRION ON THEIR PLANET TO KEEP THEM INVISIBLE, THE PEOPLE REGAIN THEIR BODIES...
AND ON EARTH AT THIS MOMENT...
I--I CAN'T MOVE! WHA--WHAT HAPPENED?
YOU'RE ON MY PLANET NOW, ZIATHRION--THE EARTH! OUR SUN--UNLIKE ALPHA CENTAURI--IS NOT A TRIPLE STAR-SYSTEM BUT A SINGLE SUN!
EVER SINCE I FIRST WENT TO RANN, I BEGAN STUDYING THE STAR WE CALL ALPHA CENTAURI--HERE ON EARTH! I LEARNED IT WAS ACTUALLY A MEMBER OF A TRIPLE-STAR SYSTEM--THREE SUNS REVOLVING AROUND ONE ANOTHER!
I LEARNED THERE WERE OTHER TRIPLE-SUNS IN THE UNIVERSE, TOO! ZETA CANCRI XI SCORPI, OMEGA ERIDANI AND OTHERS! WHEN YOU POINTED TO YOUR HOME STAR-SYSTEM, I RECOGNIZED ZETA CANCRI--A TRIPLE SUN!

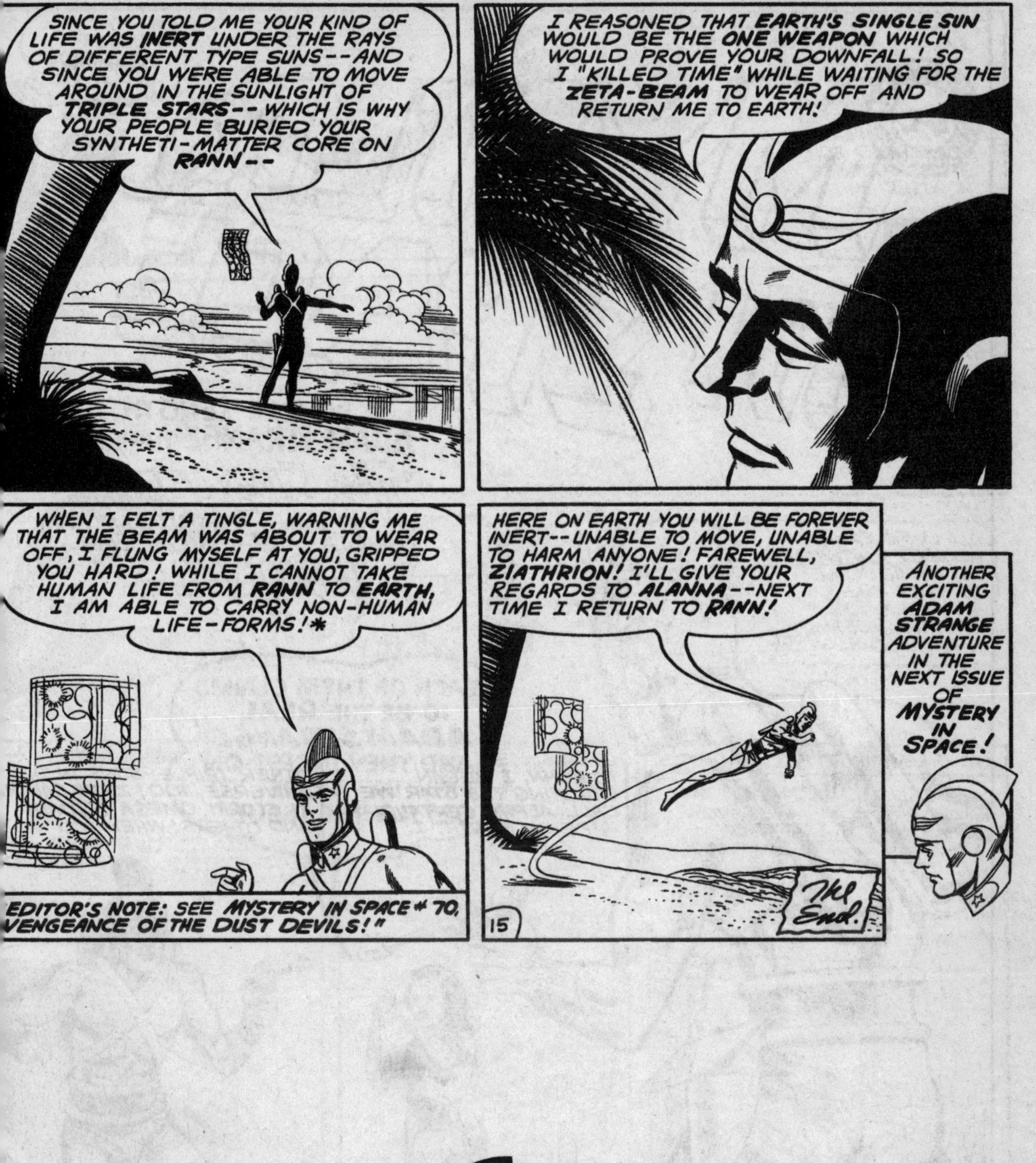
SINCE YOU TOLD ME YOUR KIND OF LIFE WAS INERT UNDER THE RAYS OF DIFFERENT TYPE SUNS--AND SINCE YOU WERE ABLE TO MOVE AROUND IN THE SUNLIGHT OF TRIPLE STARS--WHICH IS WHY YOUR PEOPLE BURIED YOUR SYNTHETI-MATTER CORE ON RANN--
I REASONED THAT EARTH'S SINGLE SUN WOULD BE THE ONE WEAPON WHICH WOULD PROVE YOUR DOWNFALL! SO I "KILLED TIME" WHILE WAITING FOR THE ZETA-BEAM TO WEAR OFF AND RETURN ME TO EARTH!
WHEN I FELT A TINGLE, WARNING ME THAT THE BEAM WAS ABOUT TO WEAR OFF, I FLUNG MYSELF AT YOU, GRIPPED YOU HARD! WHILE I CANNOT TAKE HUMAN LIFE FROM RANN TO EARTH, I AM ABLE TO CARRY NON-HUMAN LIFE-FORMS!*
EDITOR'S NOTE: SEE MYSTERY IN SPACE #70, VENGEANCE OF THE DUST DEVILS!"
HERE ON EARTH YOU WILL BE FOREVER INERT--UNABLE TO MOVE, UNABLE TO HARM ANYONE! FAREWELL, ZIATHRION! I'LL GIVE YOUR REGARDS TO ALANNA--NEXT TIME I RETURN TO RANN!
15
The End.
ANOTHER EXCITING ADAM STRANGE ADVENTURE IN THE NEXT ISSUE OF MYSTERY IN SPACE!

ADAM STRANGE

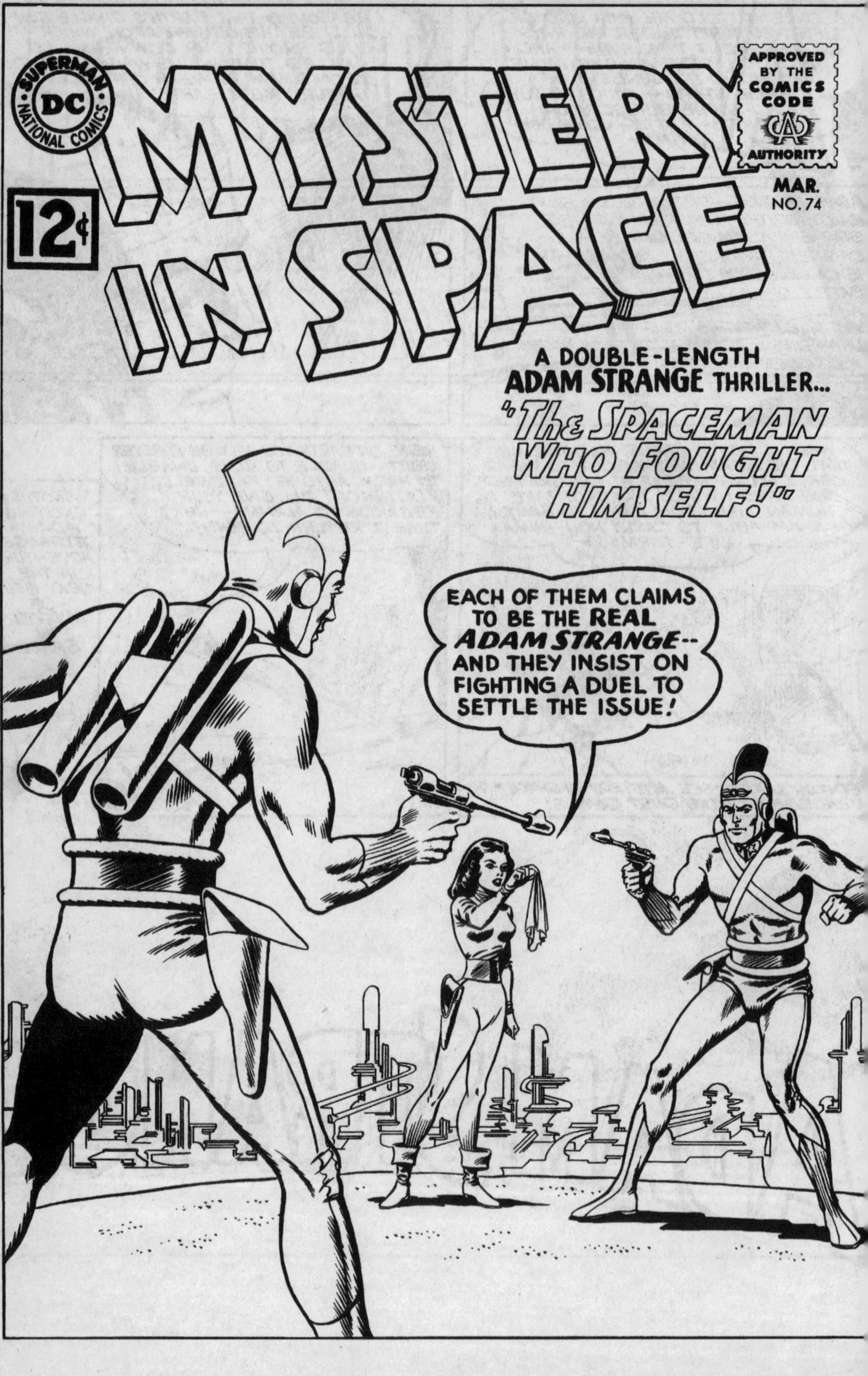
SUPERMAN DC NATIONAL COMICS
MYSTERY IN SPACE
12¢
APPROVED BY THE COMICS CODE AUTHORITY
MAR. NO. 74
A DOUBLE-LENGTH ADAM STRANGE THRILLER...
"The Spaceman Who Fought Himself!"
EACH OF THEM CLAIMS TO BE THE REAL ADAM STRANGE-- AND THEY INSIST ON FIGHTING A DUEL TO SETTLE THE ISSUE!

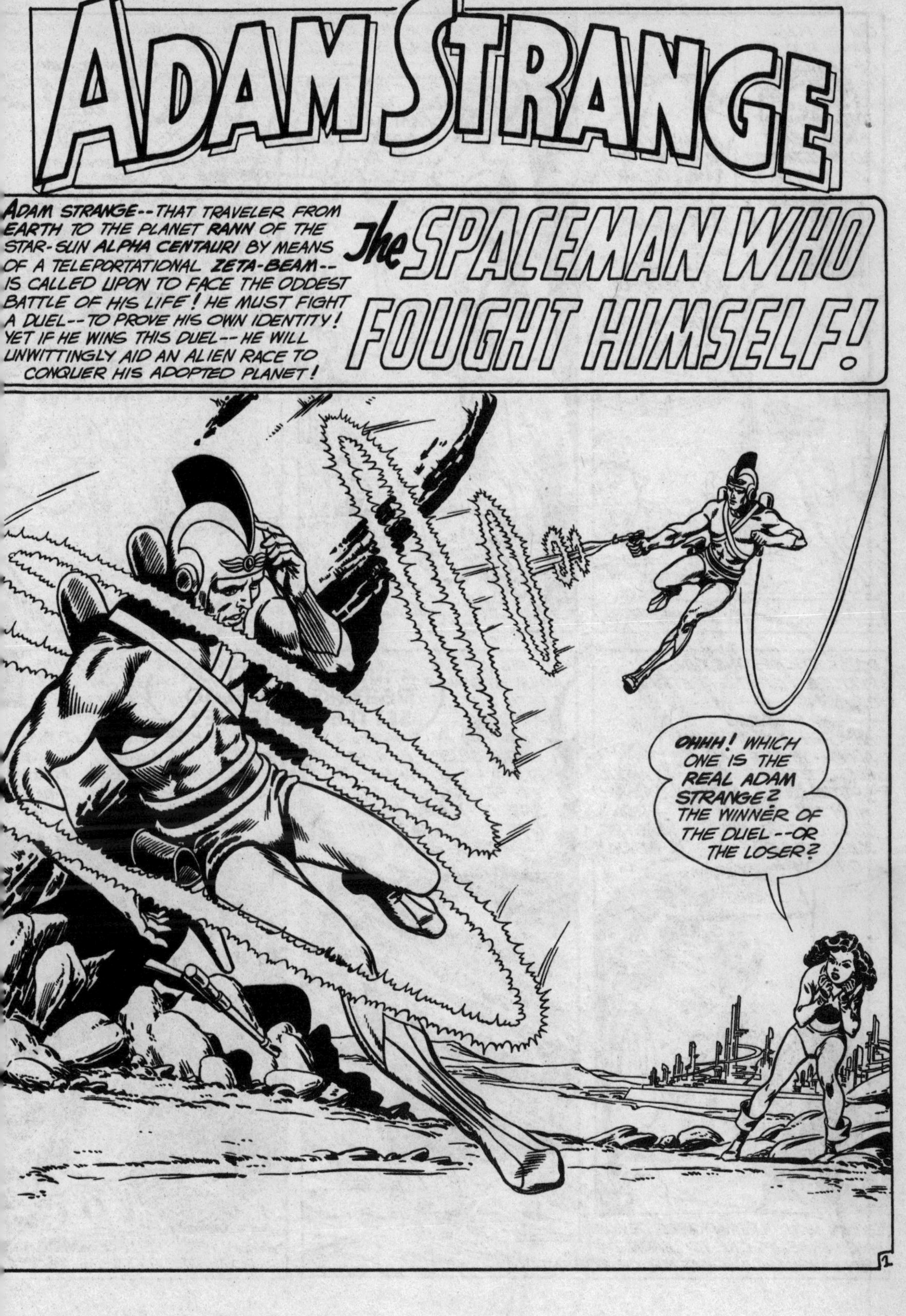
ADAM STRANGE
ADAM STRANGE--THAT TRAVELER FROM EARTH TO THE PLANET RANN OF THE STAR-SUN ALPHA CENTAURI BY MEANS OF A TELEPORTATIONAL ZETA-BEAM--IS CALLED UPON TO FACE THE ODDEST BATTLE OF HIS LIFE! HE MUST FIGHT A DUEL--TO PROVE HIS OWN IDENTITY! YET IF HE WINS THIS DUEL--HE WILL UNWITTINGLY AID AN ALIEN RACE TO CONQUER HIS ADOPTED PLANET!
The SPACEMAN WHO FOUGHT HIMSELF!
OHHH! WHICH ONE IS THE REAL ADAM STRANGE? THE WINNER OF THE DUEL--OR THE LOSER?

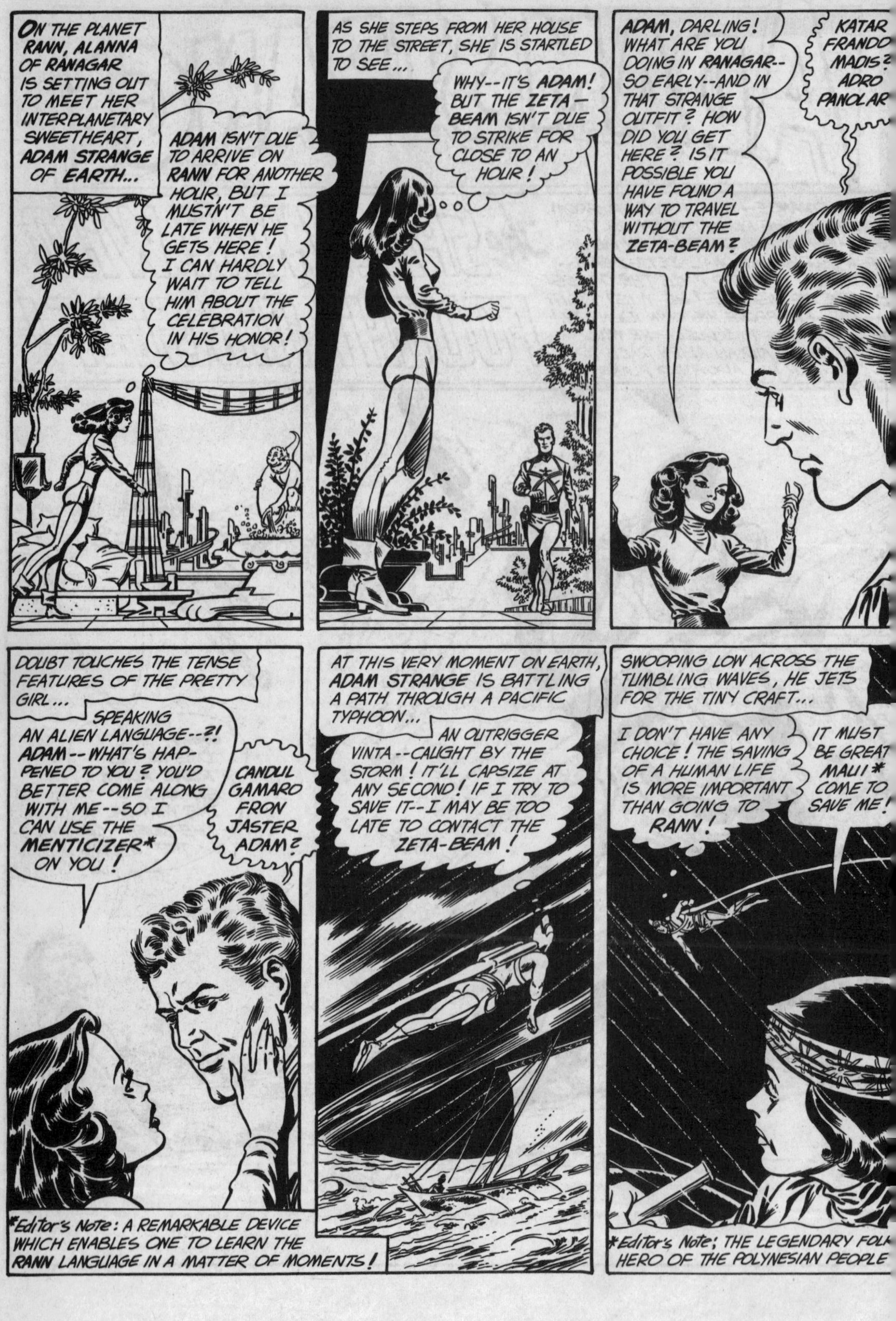
ON THE PLANET RANN, ALANNA OF RANAGAR IS SETTING OUT TO MEET HER INTERPLANETARY SWEETHEART, ADAM STRANGE OF EARTH...
ADAM ISN'T DUE TO ARRIVE ON RANN FOR ANOTHER HOUR, BUT I MUSTN'T BE LATE WHEN HE GETS HERE! I CAN HARDLY WAIT TO TELL HIM ABOUT THE CELEBRATION IN HIS HONOR!
AS SHE STEPS FROM HER HOUSE TO THE STREET, SHE IS STARTLED TO SEE...
WHY--IT'S ADAM! BUT THE ZETA-BEAM ISN'T DUE TO STRIKE FOR CLOSE TO AN HOUR!
ADAM, DARLING! WHAT ARE YOU DOING IN RANAGAR--SO EARLY--AND IN THAT STRANGE OUTFIT? HOW DID YOU GET HERE? IS IT POSSIBLE YOU HAVE FOUND A WAY TO TRAVEL WITHOUT THE ZETA-BEAM?
KATAR FRANDO MADIS? ADRO PANOLAR
DOUBT TOUCHES THE TENSE FEATURES OF THE PRETTY GIRL...
SPEAKING AN ALIEN LANGUAGE--?! ADAM--WHAT'S HAPPENED TO YOU? YOU'D BETTER COME ALONG WITH ME--SO I CAN USE THE MENTICIZER* ON YOU!
CANDUL GAMARO FRON JASTER ADAM?
*Editor's Note: A REMARKABLE DEVICE WHICH ENABLES ONE TO LEARN THE RANN LANGUAGE IN A MATTER OF MOMENTS!
AT THIS VERY MOMENT ON EARTH, ADAM STRANGE IS BATTLING A PATH THROUGH A PACIFIC TYPHOON...
AN OUTRIGGER VINTA--CAUGHT BY THE STORM! IT'LL CAPSIZE AT ANY SECOND! IF I TRY TO SAVE IT--I MAY BE TOO LATE TO CONTACT THE ZETA-BEAM!
SWOOPING LOW ACROSS THE TUMBLING WAVES, HE JETS FOR THE TINY CRAFT...
I DON'T HAVE ANY CHOICE! THE SAVING OF A HUMAN LIFE IS MORE IMPORTANT THAN GOING TO RANN!
IT MUST BE GREAT MAUI* COME TO SAVE ME!
*Editor's Note: THE LEGENDARY FOLK HERO OF THE POLYNESIAN PEOPLE

JETTING A COURSE THROUGH THE STORM AT TOP SPEED, HE SOON PUSHES THE VINTA UP ON THE SANDS OF A PACIFIC ISLAND...

IF THE GIRL CLAIMS MAUI SAVED HER-- NOBODY WILL PAY SERIOUS ATTENTION TO HER DESCRIPTION OF A FLYING HUMAN WHO SAVED HER-- AND MY SECRET IDENTITY WILL BE SAFE!

TURNING, HE HURTLES AT FULL SPEED THROUGH THE MIGHTY TYPHOON...

MAYBE IF I GO FAST ENOUGH-- I CAN STILL KEEP MY RENDEZVOUS WITH THE ZETA-BEAM!

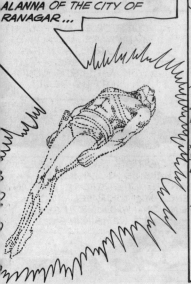

AND THEN, AS HE HAS SO OFTEN IN THE PAST, THE YOUNG EARTH ARCHEOLOGIST MAKES CONTACT WITH THE TELEPORTATIONAL BEAM FROM THE PLANET RANN-- TO BE HURLED ACROSS 25 TRILLION MILES OF SPACE TO THE THIRD PLANET OF THE STAR-SUN ALPHA CENTAURI-- WHERE LIVES HIS SWEETHEART ALANNA OF THE CITY OF RANAGAR...

BUT THIS TIME AS HE SETS FOOT ON HIS ADOPTED PLANET, THERE IS NO ALANNA TO WELCOME HIM...

SHE'D SURELY BE HERE TO MEET ME--UNLESS--GREAT CENTAURI! DON'T TELL ME ANOTHER MENACE HAS STRUCK RANN WHILE I WAS GONE?!

SOMEWHAT LATER, AS ALANNA IS FITTING THE MENTICIZER ABOUT THE HEAD OF THE MAN SHE BELIEVES TO BE ADAM STRANGE...

WHILE YOU WEAR THIS YOU NOT ONLY CAN LEARN OUR LANGUAGE BUT--ADAM! OH MY GOODNESS! ARE THERE TWO OF YOU?

ALANNA! WHO IS HE?

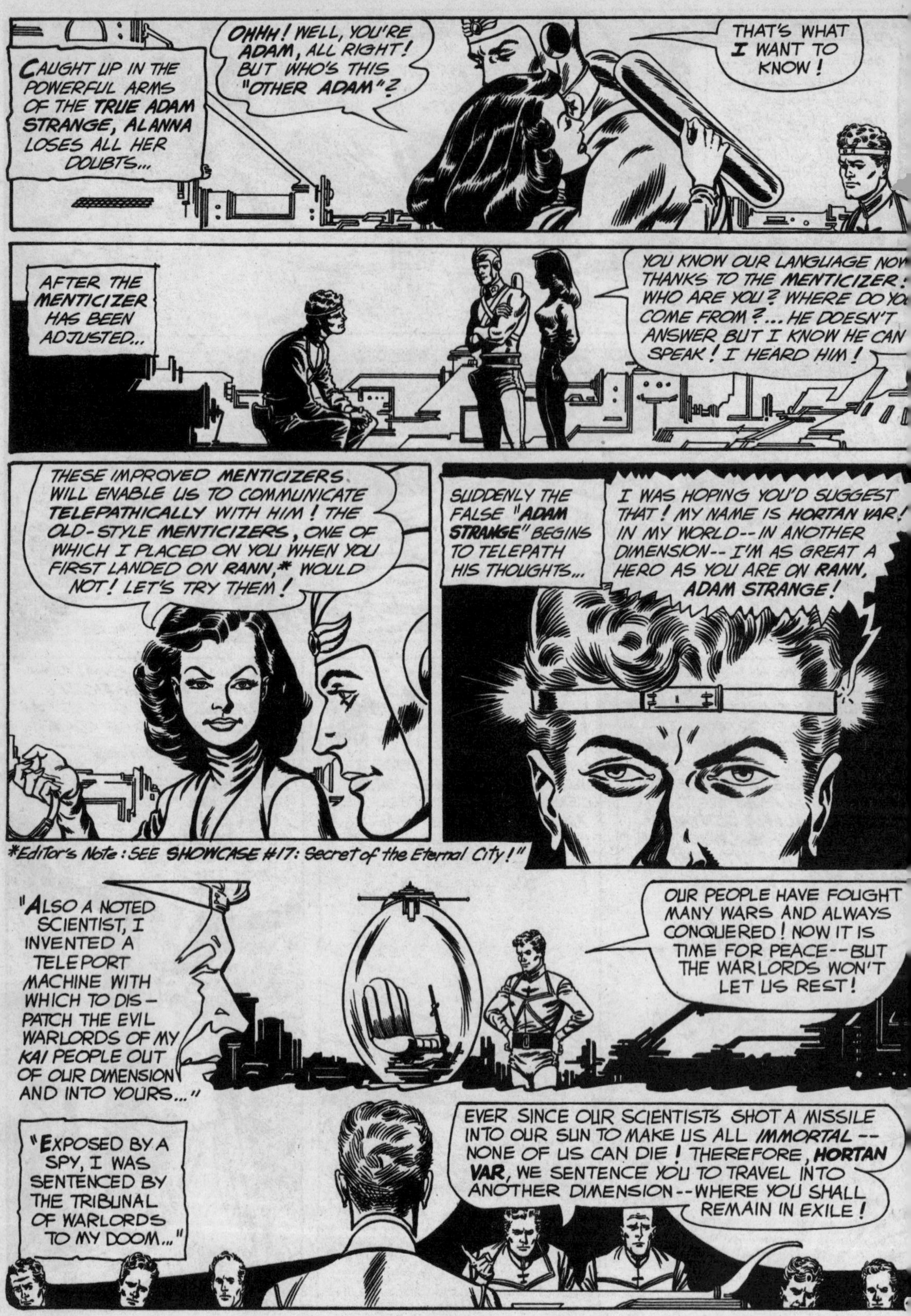
CAUGHT UP IN THE POWERFUL ARMS OF THE TRUE ADAM STRANGE, ALANNA LOSES ALL HER DOUBTS...
OHHH! WELL, YOU'RE ADAM, ALL RIGHT! BUT WHO'S THIS "OTHER ADAM"?
THAT'S WHAT I WANT TO KNOW!
AFTER THE MENTICIZER HAS BEEN ADJUSTED...
YOU KNOW OUR LANGUAGE NOW THANKS TO THE MENTICIZER: WHO ARE YOU? WHERE DO YOU COME FROM?... HE DOESN'T ANSWER BUT I KNOW HE CAN SPEAK! I HEARD HIM!
THESE IMPROVED MENTICIZERS WILL ENABLE US TO COMMUNICATE TELEPATHICALLY WITH HIM! THE OLD-STYLE MENTICIZERS, ONE OF WHICH I PLACED ON YOU WHEN YOU FIRST LANDED ON RANN,* WOULD NOT! LET'S TRY THEM!
SUDDENLY THE FALSE "ADAM STRANGE" BEGINS TO TELEPATH HIS THOUGHTS...
I WAS HOPING YOU'D SUGGEST THAT! MY NAME IS HORTAN VAR! IN MY WORLD--IN ANOTHER DIMENSION--I'M AS GREAT A HERO AS YOU ARE ON RANN, ADAM STRANGE!
*Editor's Note: SEE SHOWCASE #17: Secret of the Eternal City!"
"ALSO A NOTED SCIENTIST, I INVENTED A TELEPORT MACHINE WITH WHICH TO DIS-PATCH THE EVIL WARLORDS OF MY KAI PEOPLE OUT OF OUR DIMENSION AND INTO YOURS..."
OUR PEOPLE HAVE FOUGHT MANY WARS AND ALWAYS CONQUERED! NOW IT IS TIME FOR PEACE--BUT THE WARLORDS WON'T LET US REST!
"EXPOSED BY A SPY, I WAS SENTENCED BY THE TRIBUNAL OF WARLORDS TO MY DOOM..."
EVER SINCE OUR SCIENTISTS SHOT A MISSILE INTO OUR SUN TO MAKE US ALL IMMORTAL -- NONE OF US CAN DIE! THEREFORE, HORTAN VAR, WE SENTENCE YOU TO TRAVEL INTO ANOTHER DIMENSION--WHERE YOU SHALL REMAIN IN EXILE!

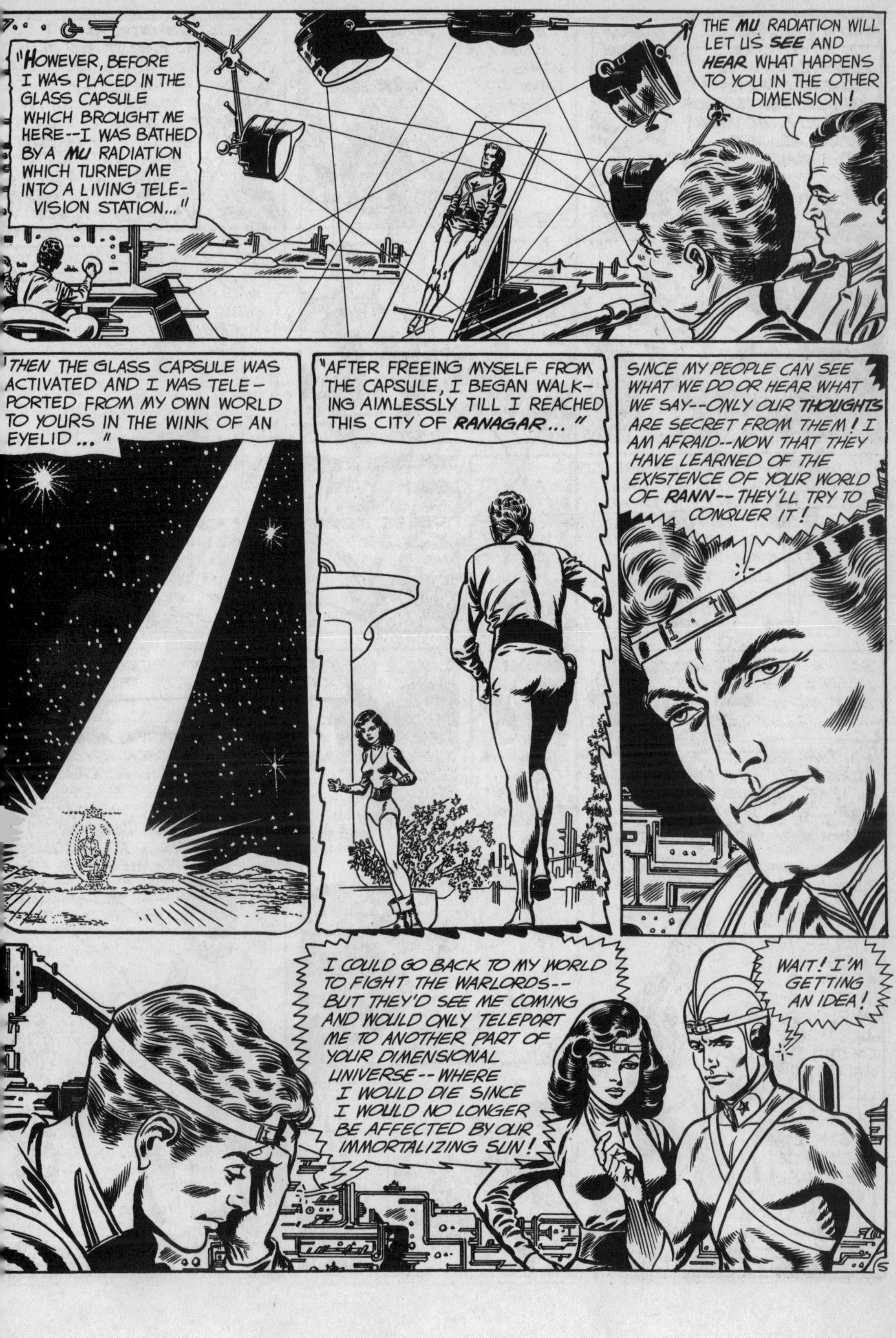
"HOWEVER, BEFORE I WAS PLACED IN THE GLASS CAPSULE WHICH BROUGHT ME HERE--I WAS BATHED BY A MU RADIATION WHICH TURNED ME INTO A LIVING TELE-VISION STATION..."
THE MU RADIATION WILL LET US SEE AND HEAR WHAT HAPPENS TO YOU IN THE OTHER DIMENSION!
"THEN THE GLASS CAPSULE WAS ACTIVATED AND I WAS TELE-PORTED FROM MY OWN WORLD TO YOURS IN THE WINK OF AN EYELID..."
"AFTER FREEING MYSELF FROM THE CAPSULE, I BEGAN WALK-ING AIMLESSLY TILL I REACHED THIS CITY OF RANAGAR..."
SINCE MY PEOPLE CAN SEE WHAT WE DO OR HEAR WHAT WE SAY--ONLY OUR THOUGHTS ARE SECRET FROM THEM! I AM AFRAID--NOW THAT THEY HAVE LEARNED OF THE EXISTENCE OF YOUR WORLD OF RANN--THEY'LL TRY TO CONQUER IT!
I COULD GO BACK TO MY WORLD TO FIGHT THE WARLORDS--BUT THEY'D SEE ME COMING AND WOULD ONLY TELEPORT ME TO ANOTHER PART OF YOUR DIMENSIONAL UNIVERSE--WHERE I WOULD DIE SINCE I WOULD NO LONGER BE AFFECTED BY OUR IMMORTALIZING SUN!
WAIT! I'M GETTING AN IDEA!

I LOOK ENOUGH LIKE YOU TO BE YOUR *TWIN!* SUPPOSE *I* WERE TO GO TO YOUR KAI WORLD INSTEAD OF YOU? TO FIGHT YOUR BATTLE AGAINST THOSE WARLORDS?

IF ONLY YOU COULD, I'M SURE YOU'D WIN!

BUT BEFORE I DO, HORTAN VAR--YOU HAVE TO *DIE!*

ADAM! HOW CAN YOU EVEN SAY--I MEAN THINK SUCH A THING!

OUR FIRST JOB IS TO FOOL THE KAI WARLORDS INTO THINKING HORTAN VAR IS NO LONGER A THREAT TO THEM! IF THEY SEE ME "KILL" HIM--SAY, IN A DUEL--THEY WON'T BE EXPECTING ME IN HIS PLACE!

GREAT IDEA! AND TO MAKE SURE OUR ENEMIES *KNOW* WHAT'S HAPPENING I'LL OCCASIONALL THROW IN A FEW WORDS OF MY OWN LANGUAGE SO IN TIME THEY'L COMPREHEND THE *RANN* LANGUAGE

SOON AFTER, IN ORDER TO DECEIVE THE KAI WARLORDS, *ADAM* AND *HORTAN VAR* ENGAGE IN A LITTLE BIT OF PLAY-ACTING..

NOW THAT THE TWO OF US ARE ALONE--I'LL CONFESS MY SCHEME, *ADAM STRANGE!* I'VE LOST MY OWN WORLD-- SO I MEAN TO TAKE YOUR PLACE HERE!

YOU SCOUNDREL!

ALANNA GAVE ME THIS UNIFORM BECAUSE *SHE* KNOWS I'M THE REAL *ADAM STRANGE!*

YOU'RE A WEAK IMITATION OF THE REAL THING AND I'LL PROVE IT!

STOP, BOTH OF YOU! THIS IS DREAD- FUL!

STILL ACTING, STILL PRETENDING, SO AS TO FOOL THE WATCHING, LISTENING KAI WARLORDS...

THE CELEBRATION IN *ADAM STRANGE'S* HONOR TONIGHT CAN'T HAVE *TWO* HONORED GUESTS! ; SIGH! THERE'S ONLY ONE THING TO DO! IT'S OUR CUSTOM WHEN ANY DISPUTE ARISES TO--DUEL TO THE DEATH OVER IT!

THAT SUITS ME FINE!

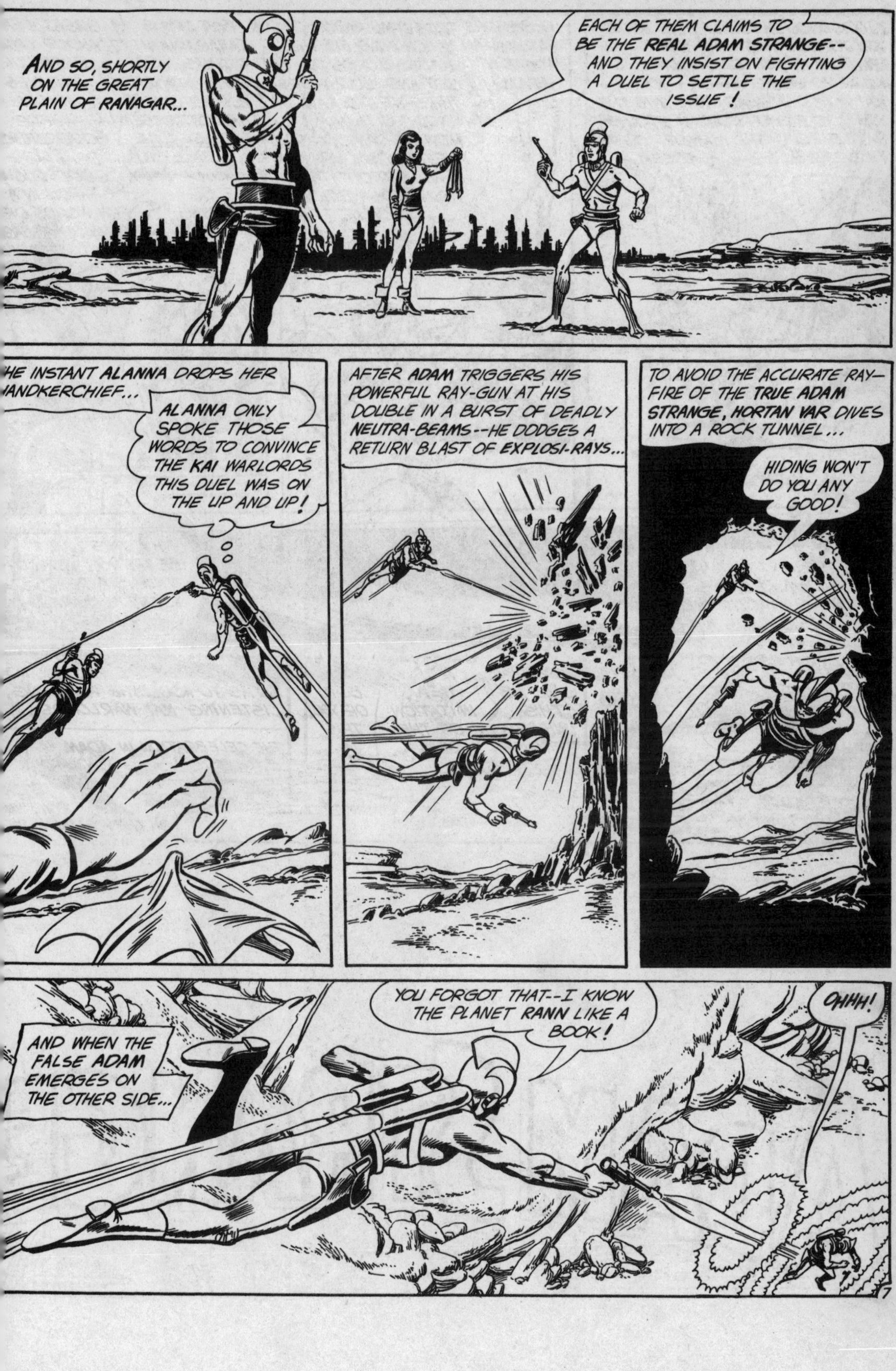
AND SO, SHORTLY ON THE GREAT PLAIN OF RANAGAR...
EACH OF THEM CLAIMS TO BE THE REAL ADAM STRANGE-- AND THEY INSIST ON FIGHTING A DUEL TO SETTLE THE ISSUE!
HE INSTANT ALANNA DROPS HER HANDKERCHIEF...
ALANNA ONLY SPOKE THOSE WORDS TO CONVINCE THE KAI WARLORDS THIS DUEL WAS ON THE UP AND UP!
AFTER ADAM TRIGGERS HIS POWERFUL RAY-GUN AT HIS DOUBLE IN A BURST OF DEADLY NEUTRA-BEAMS--HE DODGES A RETURN BLAST OF EXPLOSI-RAYS...
TO AVOID THE ACCURATE RAY-FIRE OF THE TRUE ADAM STRANGE, HORTAN VAR DIVES INTO A ROCK TUNNEL...
HIDING WON'T DO YOU ANY GOOD!
AND WHEN THE FALSE ADAM EMERGES ON THE OTHER SIDE...
YOU FORGOT THAT--I KNOW THE PLANET RANN LIKE A BOOK!
OHHH!
7

CAUGHT BY THOSE LETHAL BLUE RADI-RINGS, HORTAN VAR PLUMMETS TO THE GROUND...

OHHH! WHICH IS THE REAL *ADAM STRANGE?* THE WINNER--OR THE LOSER?

HORTAN VAR IS "DEAD", ADAM!

THOSE MU RADIATIONS WHICH ENABLED THE *KAI* WARLORDS TO SEE AND HEAR EVERYTHING WE DID HAVE "DIED" WITH HIM! NOW WE CAN GO AHEAD WITH OUR PLAN, WITHOUT THE WARLORDS "TUNING" IN ON US!

SOON AFTER, IN A SMALL RANAGARIAN LABORATORY, ADAM STRANGE STEPS INTO THE DIMENSI-PORTER INVENTED BY HORTAN VAR AND MANIPULATES ITS CONTROLS...

GOOD LUCK, DARLING-- GOOD LUCK

IN THE NEXT INSTANT, AS *ADAM* PRESSES DOWN THE ACTIVATING LEVER HE FINDS HIMSELF TRANSPORTED THROUGH SPACE TO...

WHY, THIS CAN'T BE THE KAI WORLD! THIS IS A DEAD PLANET! BARREN! LIFELESS!

STOR CONTINUE ON THE FOLLOWING PAG

ADAM STRANGE

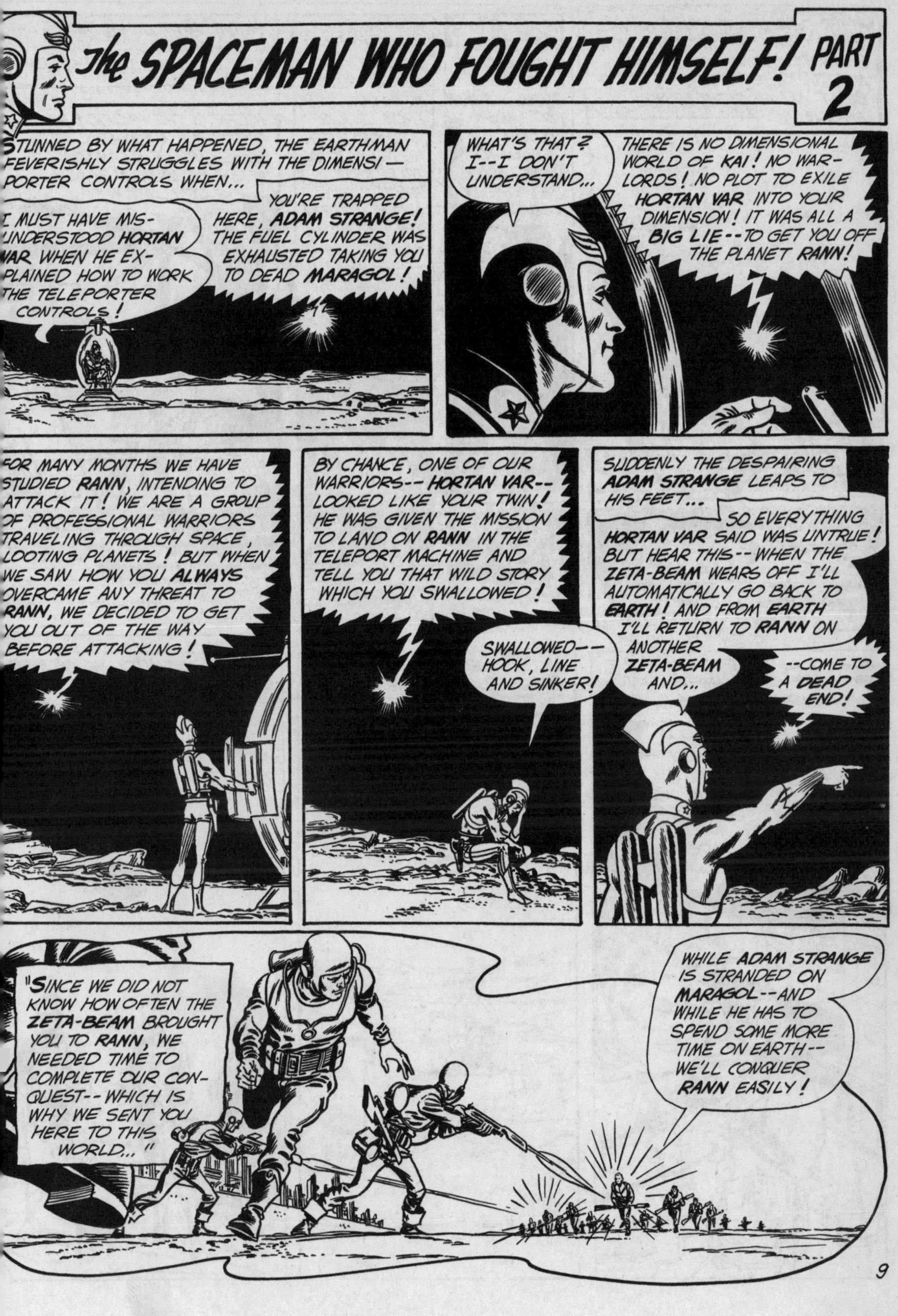
The SPACEMAN WHO FOUGHT HIMSELF! PART 2
STUNNED BY WHAT HAPPENED, THE EARTHMAN FEVERISHLY STRUGGLES WITH THE DIMENSI-PORTER CONTROLS WHEN...
I MUST HAVE MIS-UNDERSTOOD HORTAN VAR WHEN HE EX-PLAINED HOW TO WORK THE TELEPORTER CONTROLS!
YOU'RE TRAPPED HERE, ADAM STRANGE! THE FUEL CYLINDER WAS EXHAUSTED TAKING YOU TO DEAD MARAGOL!
WHAT'S THAT? I--I DON'T UNDERSTAND...
THERE IS NO DIMENSIONAL WORLD OF KAI! NO WAR-LORDS! NO PLOT TO EXILE HORTAN VAR INTO YOUR DIMENSION! IT WAS ALL A BIG LIE--TO GET YOU OFF THE PLANET RANN!
FOR MANY MONTHS WE HAVE STUDIED RANN, INTENDING TO ATTACK IT! WE ARE A GROUP OF PROFESSIONAL WARRIORS TRAVELING THROUGH SPACE, LOOTING PLANETS! BUT WHEN WE SAW HOW YOU ALWAYS OVERCAME ANY THREAT TO RANN, WE DECIDED TO GET YOU OUT OF THE WAY BEFORE ATTACKING!
BY CHANCE, ONE OF OUR WARRIORS--HORTAN VAR--LOOKED LIKE YOUR TWIN! HE WAS GIVEN THE MISSION TO LAND ON RANN IN THE TELEPORT MACHINE AND TELL YOU THAT WILD STORY WHICH YOU SWALLOWED!
SWALLOWED--HOOK, LINE AND SINKER!
SUDDENLY THE DESPAIRING ADAM STRANGE LEAPS TO HIS FEET...
SO EVERYTHING HORTAN VAR SAID WAS UNTRUE! BUT HEAR THIS--WHEN THE ZETA-BEAM WEARS OFF I'LL AUTOMATICALLY GO BACK TO EARTH! AND FROM EARTH I'LL RETURN TO RANN ON ANOTHER ZETA-BEAM AND...
--COME TO A DEAD END!
"SINCE WE DID NOT KNOW HOW OFTEN THE ZETA-BEAM BROUGHT YOU TO RANN, WE NEEDED TIME TO COMPLETE OUR CON-QUEST--WHICH IS WHY WE SENT YOU HERE TO THIS WORLD..."
WHILE ADAM STRANGE IS STRANDED ON MARAGOL--AND WHILE HE HAS TO SPEND SOME MORE TIME ON EARTH--WE'LL CONQUER RANN EASILY!
9

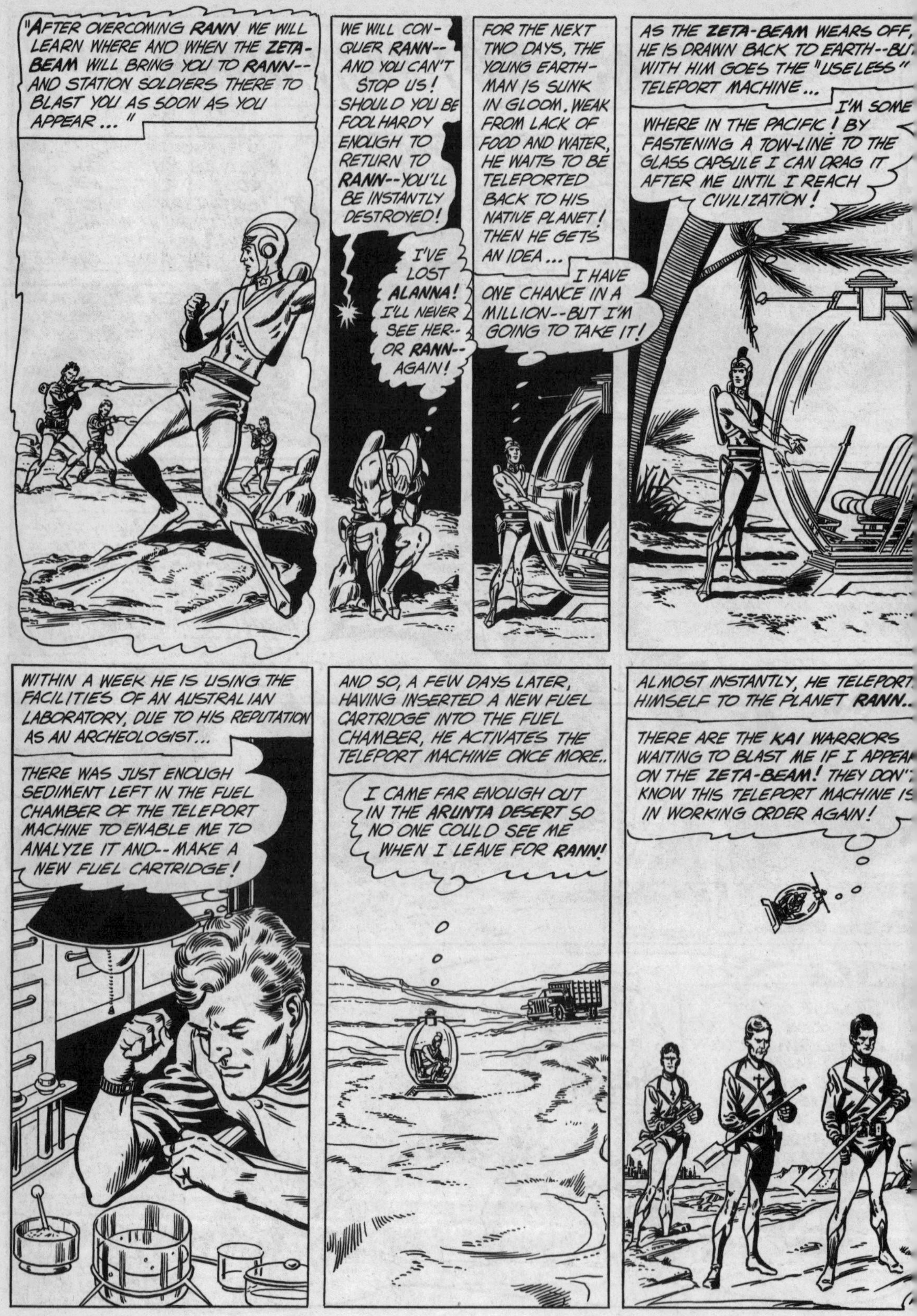
"AFTER OVERCOMING RANN WE WILL LEARN WHERE AND WHEN THE ZETA-BEAM WILL BRING YOU TO RANN--AND STATION SOLDIERS THERE TO BLAST YOU AS SOON AS YOU APPEAR ..."
WE WILL CONQUER RANN--AND YOU CAN'T STOP US! SHOULD YOU BE FOOLHARDY ENOUGH TO RETURN TO RANN--YOU'LL BE INSTANTLY DESTROYED!
I'VE LOST ALANNA! I'LL NEVER SEE HER--OR RANN--AGAIN!
FOR THE NEXT TWO DAYS, THE YOUNG EARTH-MAN IS SUNK IN GLOOM. WEAK FROM LACK OF FOOD AND WATER, HE WAITS TO BE TELEPORTED BACK TO HIS NATIVE PLANET! THEN HE GETS AN IDEA ...
I HAVE ONE CHANCE IN A MILLION--BUT I'M GOING TO TAKE IT!
AS THE ZETA-BEAM WEARS OFF, HE IS DRAWN BACK TO EARTH--BU WITH HIM GOES THE "USELESS" TELEPORT MACHINE ...
I'M SOME WHERE IN THE PACIFIC! BY FASTENING A TOW-LINE TO THE GLASS CAPSULE I CAN DRAG IT AFTER ME UNTIL I REACH CIVILIZATION!
WITHIN A WEEK HE IS USING THE FACILITIES OF AN AUSTRALIAN LABORATORY, DUE TO HIS REPUTATION AS AN ARCHEOLOGIST...
THERE WAS JUST ENOUGH SEDIMENT LEFT IN THE FUEL CHAMBER OF THE TELEPORT MACHINE TO ENABLE ME TO ANALYZE IT AND--MAKE A NEW FUEL CARTRIDGE!
AND SO, A FEW DAYS LATER, HAVING INSERTED A NEW FUEL CARTRIDGE INTO THE FUEL CHAMBER, HE ACTIVATES THE TELEPORT MACHINE ONCE MORE..
I CAME FAR ENOUGH OUT IN THE ARUNTA DESERT SO NO ONE COULD SEE ME WHEN I LEAVE FOR RANN!
ALMOST INSTANTLY, HE TELEPORT HIMSELF TO THE PLANET RANN..
THERE ARE THE KAI WARRIORS WAITING TO BLAST ME IF I APPEA ON THE ZETA-BEAM! THEY DON' KNOW THIS TELEPORT MACHINE IS IN WORKING ORDER AGAIN!

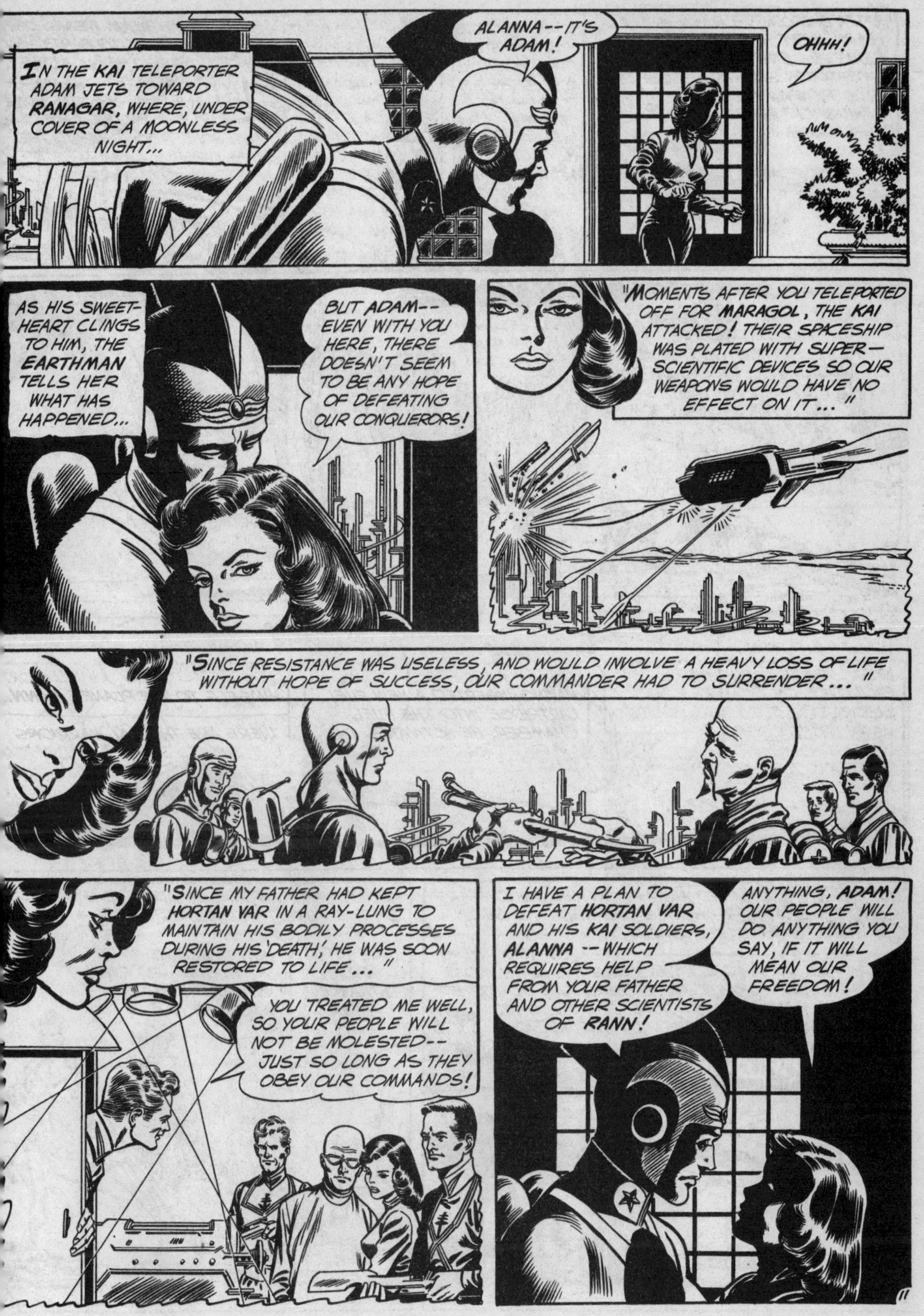
IN THE KAI TELEPORTER ADAM JETS TOWARD RANAGAR, WHERE, UNDER COVER OF A MOONLESS NIGHT...
ALANNA--IT'S ADAM!
OHHH!
AS HIS SWEET-HEART CLINGS TO HIM, THE EARTHMAN TELLS HER WHAT HAS HAPPENED...
BUT ADAM--EVEN WITH YOU HERE, THERE DOESN'T SEEM TO BE ANY HOPE OF DEFEATING OUR CONQUERORS!
"MOMENTS AFTER YOU TELEPORTED OFF FOR MARAGOL, THE KAI ATTACKED! THEIR SPACESHIP WAS PLATED WITH SUPER-SCIENTIFIC DEVICES SO OUR WEAPONS WOULD HAVE NO EFFECT ON IT..."
"SINCE RESISTANCE WAS USELESS, AND WOULD INVOLVE A HEAVY LOSS OF LIFE WITHOUT HOPE OF SUCCESS, OUR COMMANDER HAD TO SURRENDER..."
"SINCE MY FATHER HAD KEPT HORTAN VAR IN A RAY-LUNG TO MAINTAIN HIS BODILY PROCESSES DURING HIS 'DEATH,' HE WAS SOON RESTORED TO LIFE..."
YOU TREATED ME WELL, SO YOUR PEOPLE WILL NOT BE MOLESTED--JUST SO LONG AS THEY OBEY OUR COMMANDS!
I HAVE A PLAN TO DEFEAT HORTAN VAR AND HIS KAI SOLDIERS, ALANNA--WHICH REQUIRES HELP FROM YOUR FATHER AND OTHER SCIENTISTS OF RANN!
ANYTHING, ADAM! OUR PEOPLE WILL DO ANYTHING YOU SAY, IF IT WILL MEAN OUR FREEDOM!
11

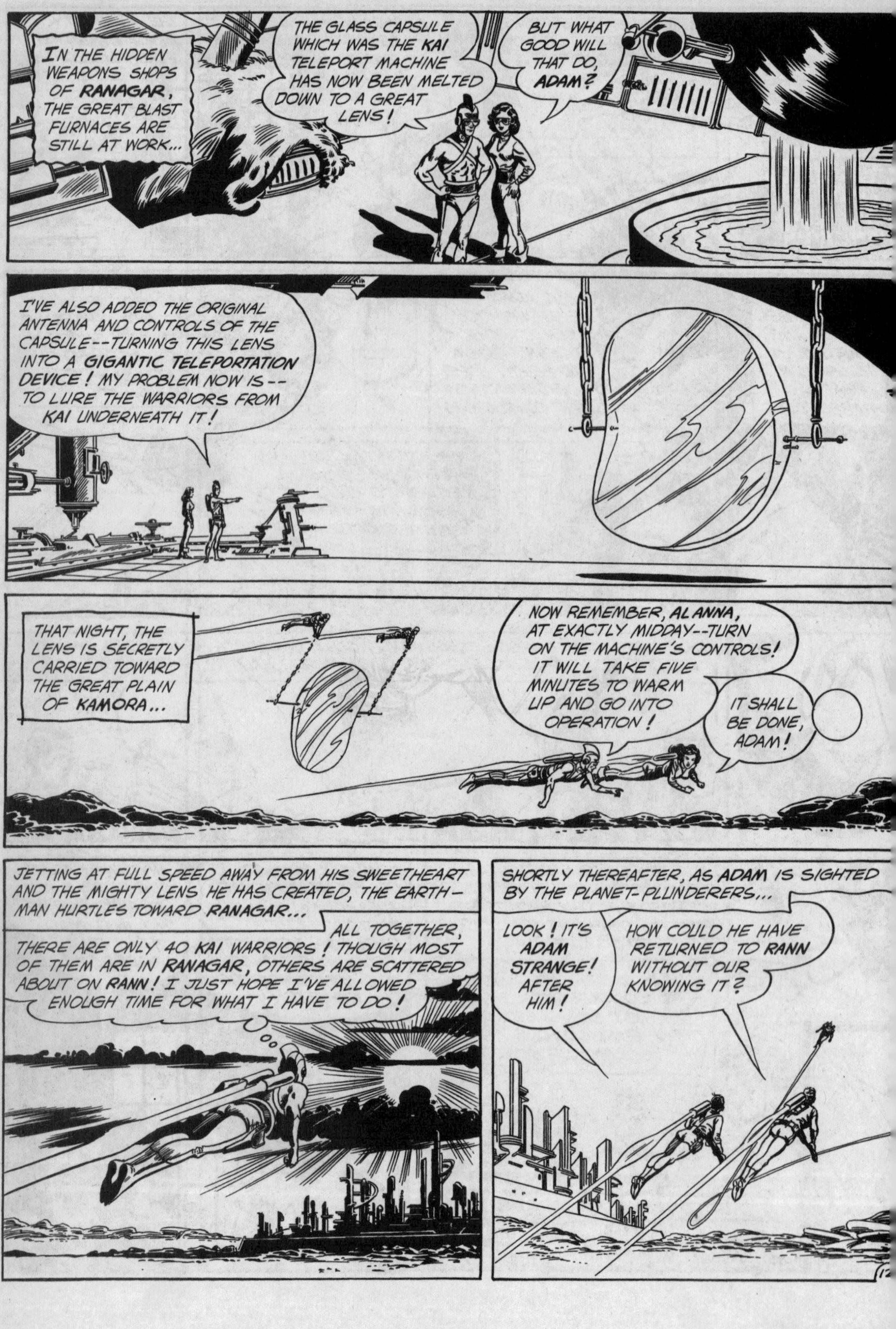
IN THE HIDDEN WEAPONS SHOPS OF RANAGAR, THE GREAT BLAST FURNACES ARE STILL AT WORK...
THE GLASS CAPSULE WHICH WAS THE KAI TELEPORT MACHINE HAS NOW BEEN MELTED DOWN TO A GREAT LENS!
BUT WHAT GOOD WILL THAT DO, ADAM?
I'VE ALSO ADDED THE ORIGINAL ANTENNA AND CONTROLS OF THE CAPSULE--TURNING THIS LENS INTO A GIGANTIC TELEPORTATION DEVICE! MY PROBLEM NOW IS--TO LURE THE WARRIORS FROM KAI UNDERNEATH IT!
THAT NIGHT, THE LENS IS SECRETLY CARRIED TOWARD THE GREAT PLAIN OF KAMORA...
NOW REMEMBER, ALANNA, AT EXACTLY MIDDAY--TURN ON THE MACHINE'S CONTROLS! IT WILL TAKE FIVE MINUTES TO WARM UP AND GO INTO OPERATION!
IT SHALL BE DONE, ADAM!
JETTING AT FULL SPEED AWAY FROM HIS SWEETHEART AND THE MIGHTY LENS HE HAS CREATED, THE EARTH-MAN HURTLES TOWARD RANAGAR...
ALL TOGETHER, THERE ARE ONLY 40 KAI WARRIORS! THOUGH MOST OF THEM ARE IN RANAGAR, OTHERS ARE SCATTERED ABOUT ON RANN! I JUST HOPE I'VE ALLOWED ENOUGH TIME FOR WHAT I HAVE TO DO!
SHORTLY THEREAFTER, AS ADAM IS SIGHTED BY THE PLANET-PLUNDERERS...
LOOK! IT'S ADAM STRANGE! AFTER HIM!
HOW COULD HE HAVE RETURNED TO RANN WITHOUT OUR KNOWING IT?

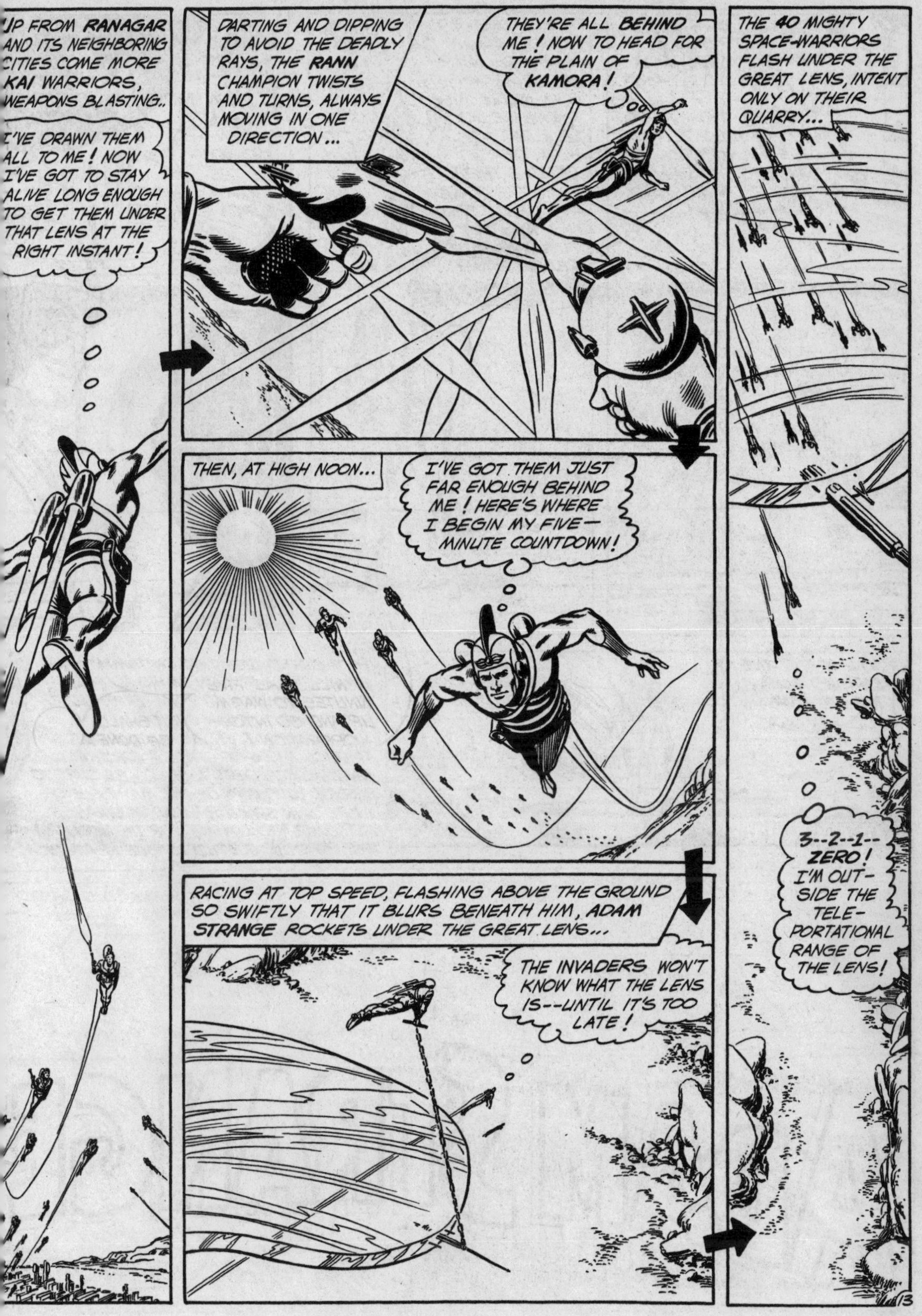
UP FROM RANAGAR AND ITS NEIGHBORING CITIES COME MORE KAI WARRIORS, WEAPONS BLASTING..
I'VE DRAWN THEM ALL TO ME! NOW I'VE GOT TO STAY ALIVE LONG ENOUGH TO GET THEM UNDER THAT LENS AT THE RIGHT INSTANT!
DARTING AND DIPPING TO AVOID THE DEADLY RAYS, THE RANN CHAMPION TWISTS AND TURNS, ALWAYS MOVING IN ONE DIRECTION...
THEY'RE ALL BEHIND ME! NOW TO HEAD FOR THE PLAIN OF KAMORA!
THE 40 MIGHTY SPACE-WARRIORS FLASH UNDER THE GREAT LENS, INTENT ONLY ON THEIR QUARRY...
THEN, AT HIGH NOON...
I'VE GOT THEM JUST FAR ENOUGH BEHIND ME! HERE'S WHERE I BEGIN MY FIVE-MINUTE COUNTDOWN!
RACING AT TOP SPEED, FLASHING ABOVE THE GROUND SO SWIFTLY THAT IT BLURS BENEATH HIM, ADAM STRANGE ROCKETS UNDER THE GREAT LENS...
THE INVADERS WON'T KNOW WHAT THE LENS IS--UNTIL IT'S TOO LATE!
3--2--1--ZERO! I'M OUTSIDE THE TELEPORTATIONAL RANGE OF THE LENS!
13

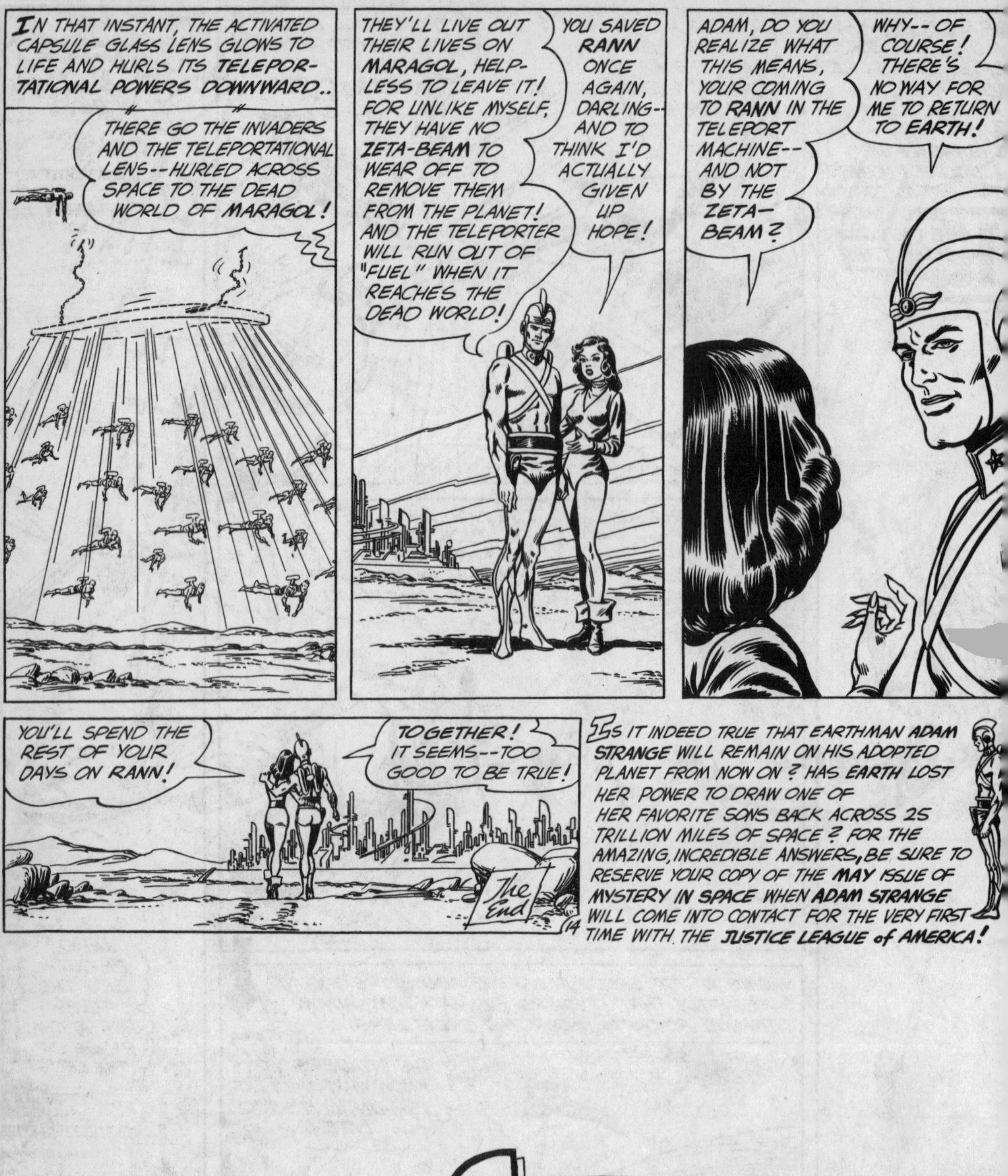
IN THAT INSTANT, THE ACTIVATED CAPSULE GLASS LENS GLOWS TO LIFE AND HURLS ITS TELEPORTATIONAL POWERS DOWNWARD..
THERE GO THE INVADERS AND THE TELEPORTATIONAL LENS--HURLED ACROSS SPACE TO THE DEAD WORLD OF MARAGOL!
THEY'LL LIVE OUT THEIR LIVES ON MARAGOL, HELPLESS TO LEAVE IT! FOR UNLIKE MYSELF, THEY HAVE NO ZETA-BEAM TO WEAR OFF TO REMOVE THEM FROM THE PLANET! AND THE TELEPORTER WILL RUN OUT OF "FUEL" WHEN IT REACHES THE DEAD WORLD!
YOU SAVED RANN ONCE AGAIN, DARLING--AND TO THINK I'D ACTUALLY GIVEN UP HOPE!
ADAM, DO YOU REALIZE WHAT THIS MEANS, YOUR COMING TO RANN IN THE TELEPORT MACHINE--AND NOT BY THE ZETA-BEAM?
WHY--OF COURSE! THERE'S NO WAY FOR ME TO RETURN TO EARTH!
YOU'LL SPEND THE REST OF YOUR DAYS ON RANN!
TOGETHER! IT SEEMS--TOO GOOD TO BE TRUE!
The End
14
IS IT INDEED TRUE THAT EARTHMAN ADAM STRANGE WILL REMAIN ON HIS ADOPTED PLANET FROM NOW ON? HAS EARTH LOST HER POWER TO DRAW ONE OF HER FAVORITE SONS BACK ACROSS 25 TRILLION MILES OF SPACE? FOR THE AMAZING, INCREDIBLE ANSWERS, BE SURE TO RESERVE YOUR COPY OF THE MAY ISSUE OF MYSTERY IN SPACE WHEN ADAM STRANGE WILL COME INTO CONTACT FOR THE VERY FIRST TIME WITH THE JUSTICE LEAGUE of AMERICA!

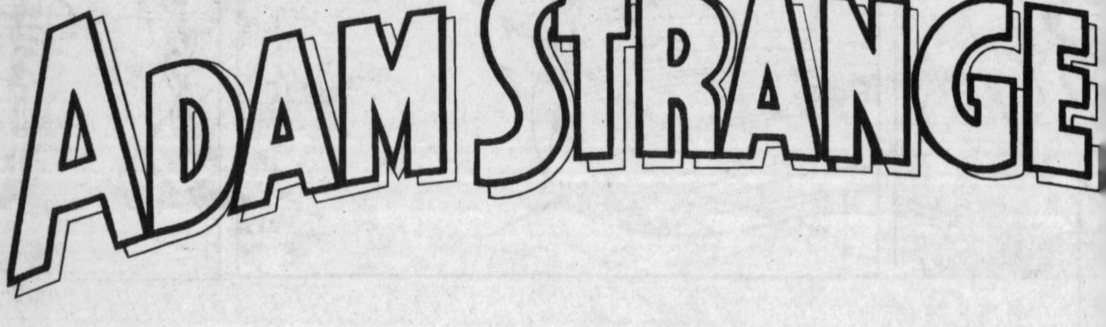
ADAM STRANGE

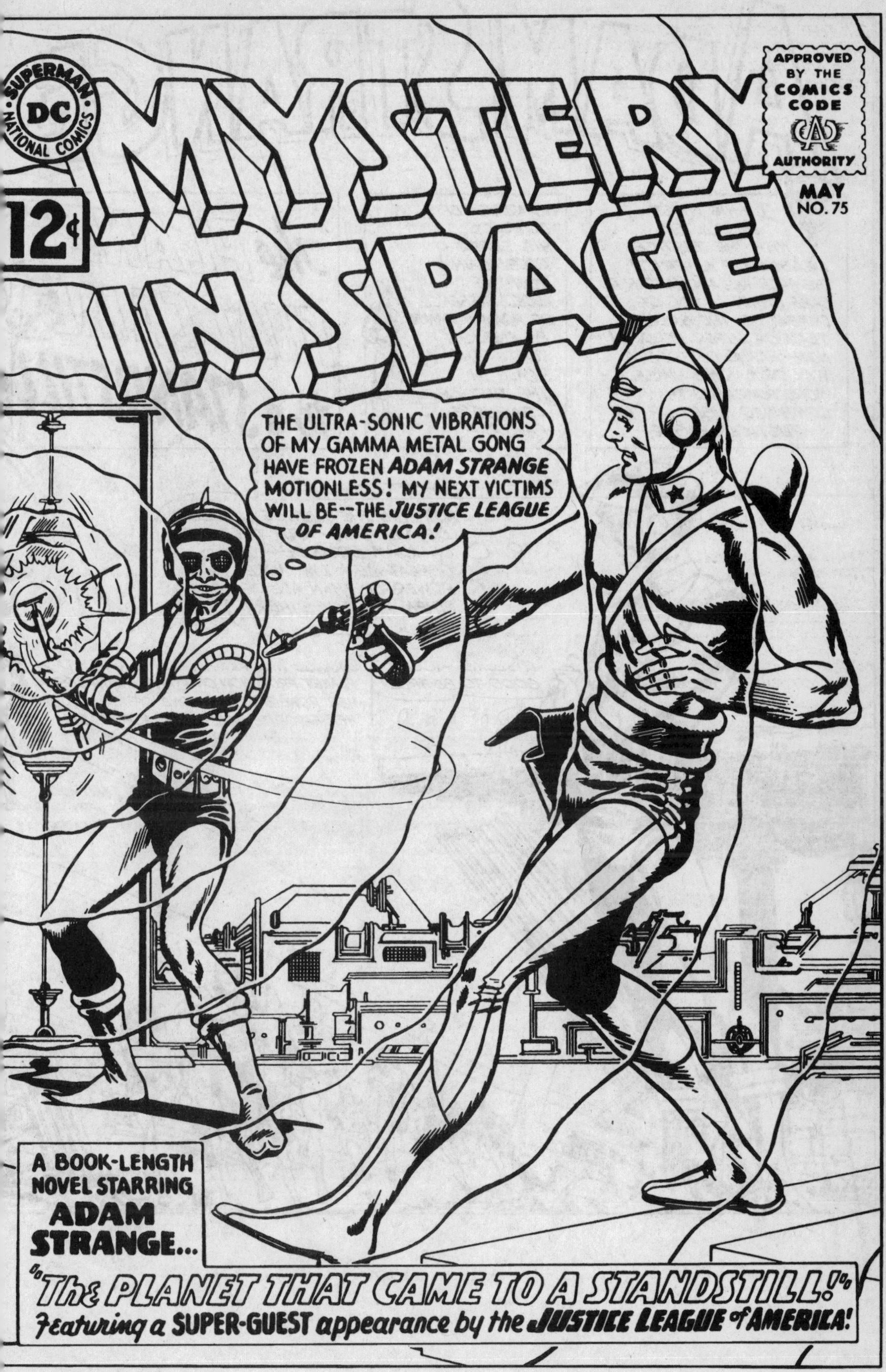
SUPERMAN DC NATIONAL COMICS
MYSTERY IN SPACE
APPROVED BY THE COMICS CODE AUTHORITY
12¢
MAY NO. 75
THE ULTRA-SONIC VIBRATIONS OF MY GAMMA METAL GONG HAVE FROZEN ADAM STRANGE MOTIONLESS! MY NEXT VICTIMS WILL BE--THE JUSTICE LEAGUE OF AMERICA!
A BOOK-LENGTH NOVEL STARRING ADAM STRANGE...
"The PLANET THAT CAME TO A STANDSTILL!"
Featuring a SUPER-GUEST appearance by the JUSTICE LEAGUE of AMERICA!

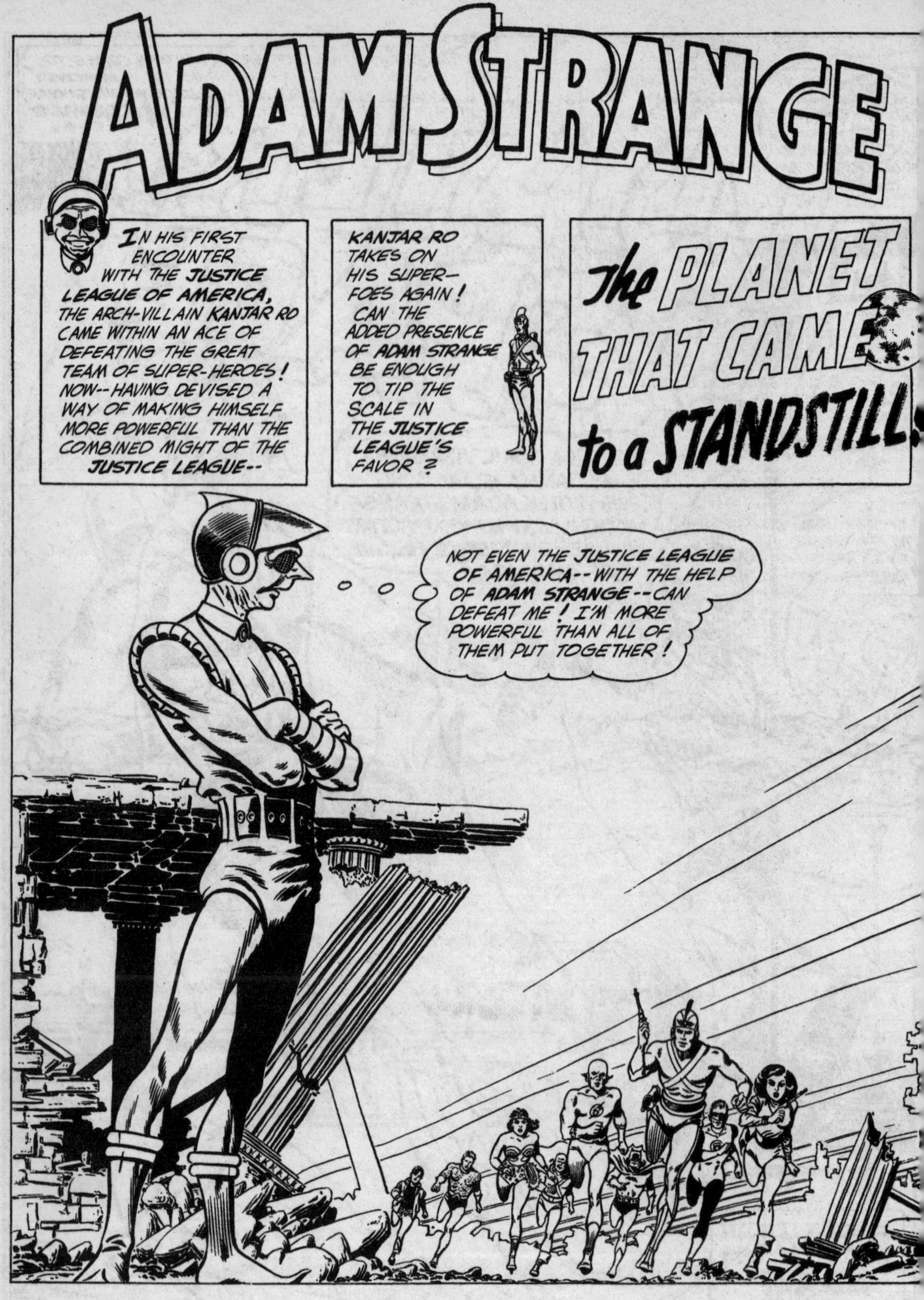
ADAM STRANGE
IN HIS FIRST ENCOUNTER WITH THE JUSTICE LEAGUE OF AMERICA, THE ARCH-VILLAIN KANJAR RO CAME WITHIN AN ACE OF DEFEATING THE GREAT TEAM OF SUPER-HEROES! NOW--HAVING DEVISED A WAY OF MAKING HIMSELF MORE POWERFUL THAN THE COMBINED MIGHT OF THE JUSTICE LEAGUE--
KANJAR RO TAKES ON HIS SUPER-FOES AGAIN! CAN THE ADDED PRESENCE OF ADAM STRANGE BE ENOUGH TO TIP THE SCALE IN THE JUSTICE LEAGUE'S FAVOR?
The PLANET THAT CAME to a STANDSTILL!
NOT EVEN THE JUSTICE LEAGUE OF AMERICA--WITH THE HELP OF ADAM STRANGE--CAN DEFEAT ME! I'M MORE POWERFUL THAN ALL OF THEM PUT TOGETHER!

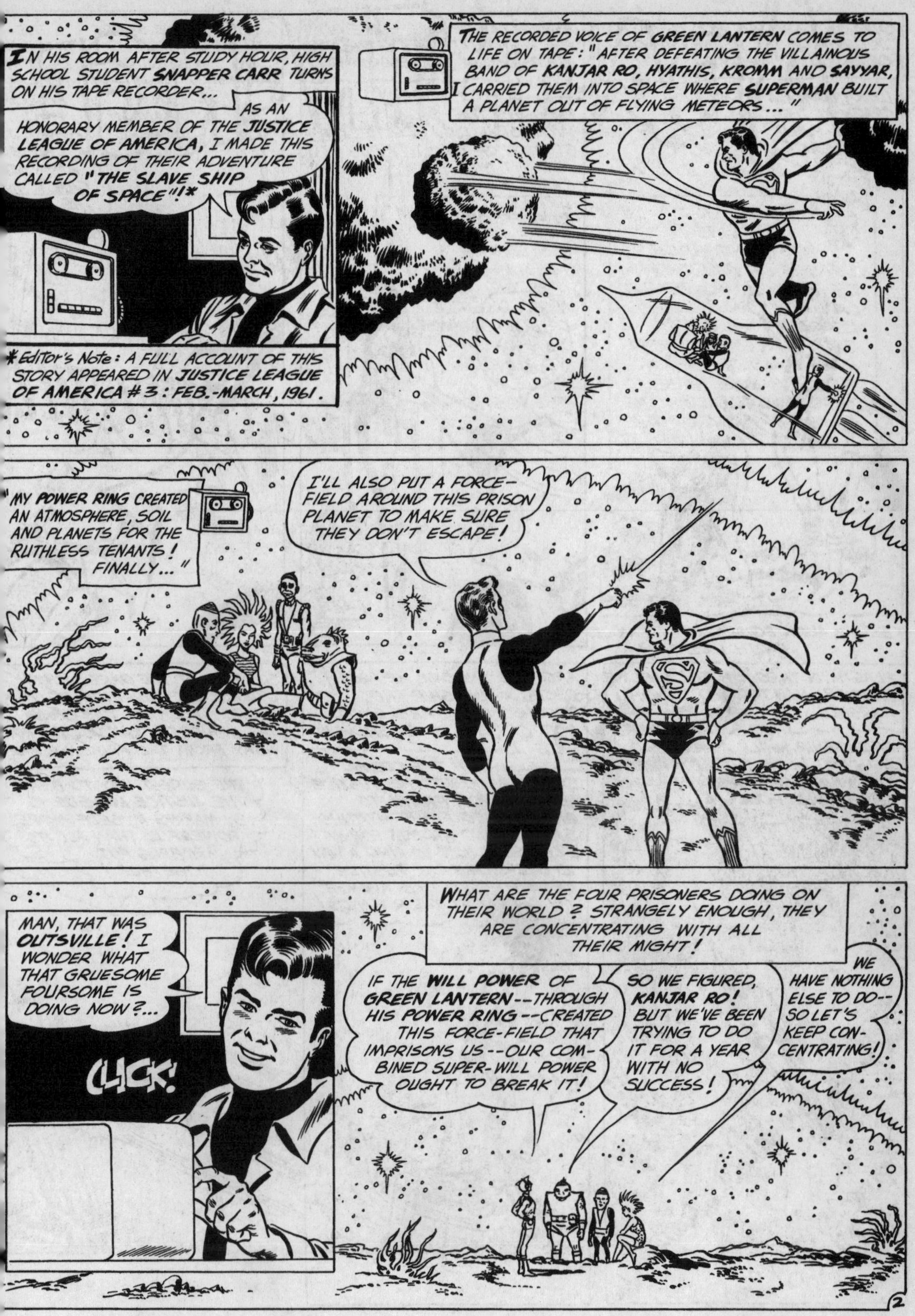
IN HIS ROOM AFTER STUDY HOUR, HIGH SCHOOL STUDENT SNAPPER CARR TURNS ON HIS TAPE RECORDER...
AS AN HONORARY MEMBER OF THE JUSTICE LEAGUE OF AMERICA, I MADE THIS RECORDING OF THEIR ADVENTURE CALLED "THE SLAVE SHIP OF SPACE"!*
*Editor's Note: A FULL ACCOUNT OF THIS STORY APPEARED IN JUSTICE LEAGUE OF AMERICA #3: FEB.-MARCH, 1961.
THE RECORDED VOICE OF GREEN LANTERN COMES TO LIFE ON TAPE: "AFTER DEFEATING THE VILLAINOUS BAND OF KANJAR RO, HYATHIS, KROMM AND SAYYAR, I CARRIED THEM INTO SPACE WHERE SUPERMAN BUILT A PLANET OUT OF FLYING METEORS..."
"MY POWER RING CREATED AN ATMOSPHERE, SOIL AND PLANETS FOR THE RUTHLESS TENANTS! FINALLY..."
I'LL ALSO PUT A FORCE-FIELD AROUND THIS PRISON PLANET TO MAKE SURE THEY DON'T ESCAPE!
MAN, THAT WAS OUTSVILLE! I WONDER WHAT THAT GRUESOME FOURSOME IS DOING NOW?...
CLICK!
WHAT ARE THE FOUR PRISONERS DOING ON THEIR WORLD? STRANGELY ENOUGH, THEY ARE CONCENTRATING WITH ALL THEIR MIGHT!
IF THE WILL POWER OF GREEN LANTERN--THROUGH HIS POWER RING--CREATED THIS FORCE-FIELD THAT IMPRISONS US--OUR COMBINED SUPER-WILL POWER OUGHT TO BREAK IT!
SO WE FIGURED, KANJAR RO! BUT WE'VE BEEN TRYING TO DO IT FOR A YEAR WITH NO SUCCESS!
WE HAVE NOTHING ELSE TO DO--SO LET'S KEEP CONCENTRATING!
2

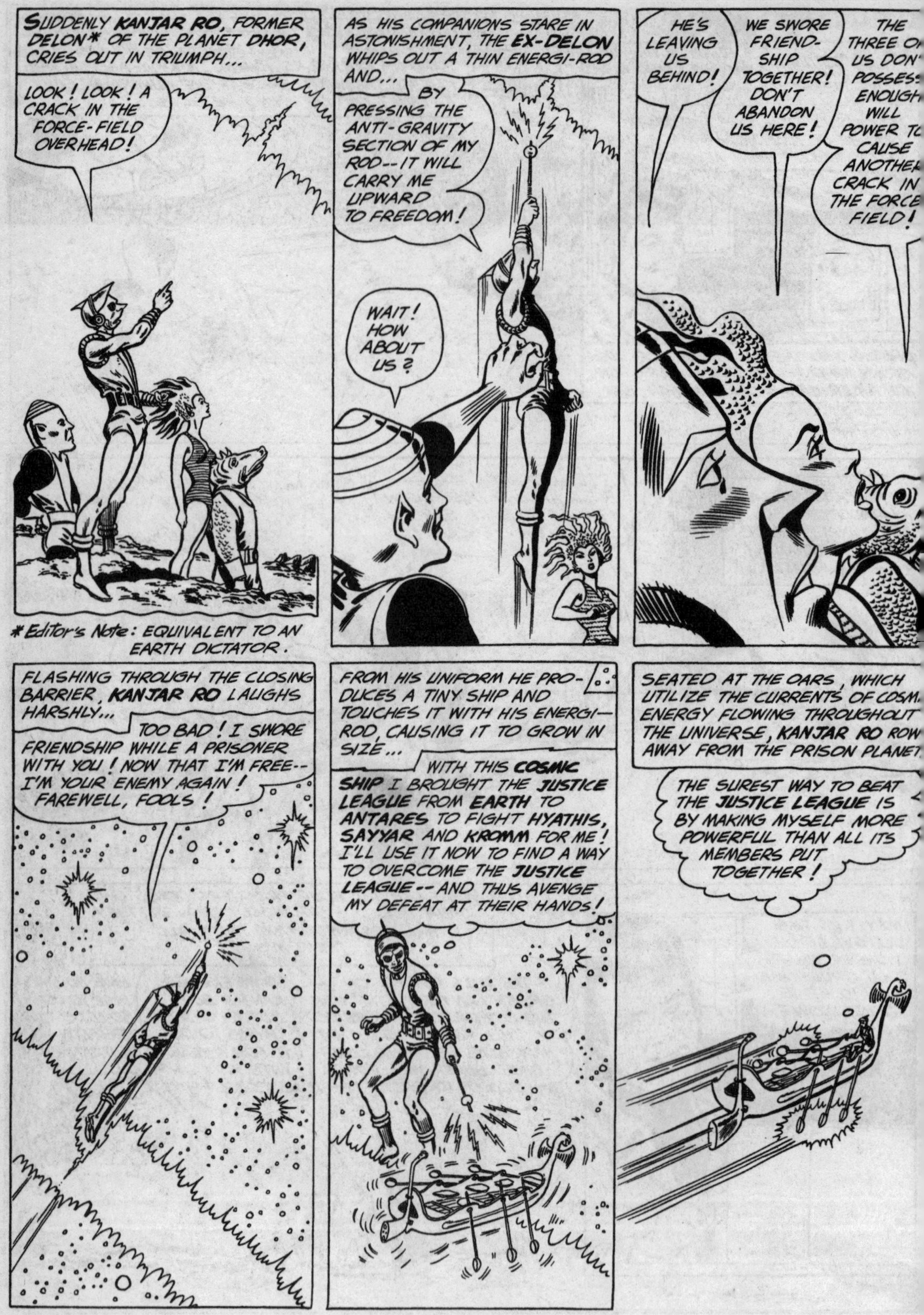
SUDDENLY KANJAR RO, FORMER DELON* OF THE PLANET DHOR, CRIES OUT IN TRIUMPH...
LOOK! LOOK! A CRACK IN THE FORCE-FIELD OVERHEAD!
*Editor's Note: EQUIVALENT TO AN EARTH DICTATOR.
AS HIS COMPANIONS STARE IN ASTONISHMENT, THE EX-DELON WHIPS OUT A THIN ENERGI-ROD AND...
BY PRESSING THE ANTI-GRAVITY SECTION OF MY ROD--IT WILL CARRY ME UPWARD TO FREEDOM!
WAIT! HOW ABOUT US?
HE'S LEAVING US BEHIND!
WE SWORE FRIENDSHIP TOGETHER! DON'T ABANDON US HERE!
FLASHING THROUGH THE CLOSING BARRIER, KANJAR RO LAUGHS HARSHLY...
TOO BAD! I SWORE FRIENDSHIP WHILE A PRISONER WITH YOU! NOW THAT I'M FREE--I'M YOUR ENEMY AGAIN! FAREWELL, FOOLS!
FROM HIS UNIFORM HE PRODUCES A TINY SHIP AND TOUCHES IT WITH HIS ENERGI-ROD, CAUSING IT TO GROW IN SIZE...
WITH THIS COSMIC SHIP I BROUGHT THE JUSTICE LEAGUE FROM EARTH TO ANTARES TO FIGHT HYATHIS, SAYYAR AND KROMM FOR ME! I'LL USE IT NOW TO FIND A WAY TO OVERCOME THE JUSTICE LEAGUE--AND THUS AVENGE MY DEFEAT AT THEIR HANDS!
THE SUREST WAY TO BEAT THE JUSTICE LEAGUE IS BY MAKING MYSELF MORE POWERFUL THAN ALL ITS MEMBERS PUT TOGETHER!

WITH HEAT AND OXYGEN FURNISHED BY HIS ROD, HE IS SOON HURTLING THROUGH SPACE AT BETTER THAN LIGHT-SPEED...

DURING THE TIME OF MY IMPRISONMENT, I DID PLENTY OF THINKING! *SUPERMAN*--A NATIVE OF *KRYPTON*--DERIVES HIS SUPER-POWERS FROM THE LESSER GRAVITY OF EARTH AND ITS YELLOW SUN! MY PLAN IS TO SEEK OUT A PLANET SIMILAR TO EARTH--BATHED BY A *TRIPLE SUN!*

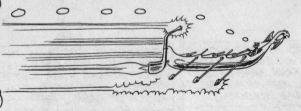

THERE--AS CLOSE TO EARTH AS I CAN FIND SUCH A PLANET--I'LL EXPERIMENT UNTIL THE LESSER GRAVITY OF THAT PLANET COMPARED TO MY NATIVE WORLD OF *DHOR*--AND THE RADIATIONS OF ITS TRIPLE SUNS--MAKES ME THREE TIMES AS STRONG AS *SUPERMAN*--THREE TIMES FASTER THAN *THE FLASH!*

I'LL NEED MEN TO BUILD A LABORATORY AND WORK FOR ME WHILE I PERFORM MY TESTS! WELL, IT SHOULDN'T BE TOO HARD TO GET THEM, WITH MY GREAT SCIENTIFIC POWERS...

ISN'T IT WONDERFUL, *ADAM?* SINCE YOU DIDN'T JOURNEY TO *RANN* ON A *ZETA-BEAM* LAST TIME *--IT WON'T WEAR OFF TO DRAW YOU BACK TO EARTH! YOU CAN STAY ON *RANN* THE REST OF YOUR LIFE!

I WAS NEVER HAPPIER, ANGEL!

SOME WEEKS LATER ON THE PLANET *RANN* OF THE TRIPLE STAR-SUN SYSTEM OF *ALPHA CENTAURI*, A YOUNG EARTH ARCHEOLOGIST AND HIS INTERPLANETARY SWEETHEART, *ALANNA OF RANAGAR*, ARE ENGAGED IN SCIENTIFIC RESEARCH...

THERE THEY ARE, HONEY-- THE "AURORA BOREALIS" OF RANN!

*Editor's Note: SEE "THE SPACEMAN WHO FOUGHT HIMSELF" IN PREVIOUS ISSUE OF MYSTERY IN SPACE!

(4)

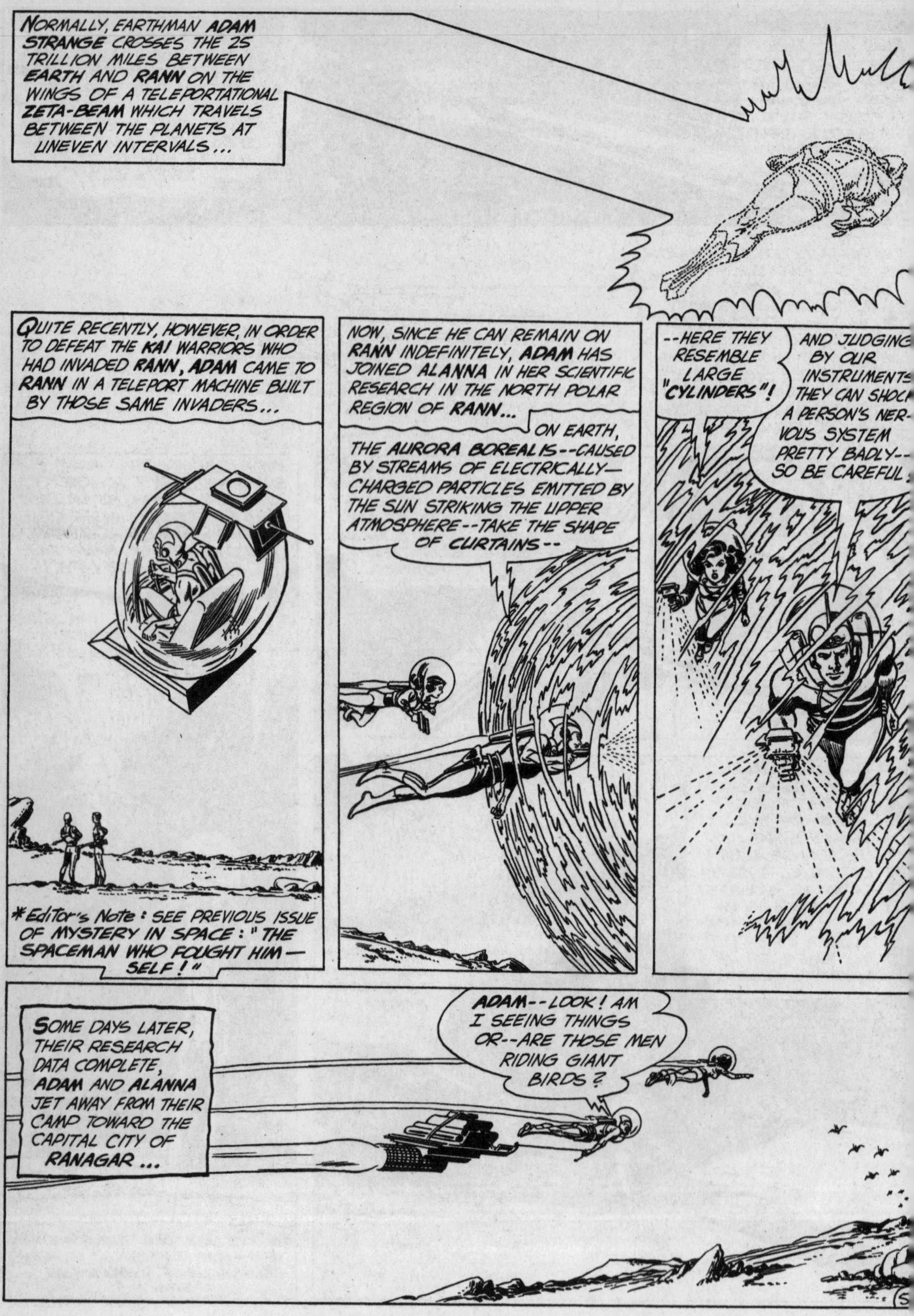
NORMALLY, EARTHMAN ADAM STRANGE CROSSES THE 25 TRILLION MILES BETWEEN EARTH AND RANN ON THE WINGS OF A TELEPORTATIONAL ZETA-BEAM WHICH TRAVELS BETWEEN THE PLANETS AT UNEVEN INTERVALS...
QUITE RECENTLY, HOWEVER, IN ORDER TO DEFEAT THE KAI WARRIORS WHO HAD INVADED RANN, ADAM CAME TO RANN IN A TELEPORT MACHINE BUILT BY THOSE SAME INVADERS...
*Editor's Note: SEE PREVIOUS ISSUE OF MYSTERY IN SPACE: "THE SPACEMAN WHO FOUGHT HIMSELF!"
NOW, SINCE HE CAN REMAIN ON RANN INDEFINITELY, ADAM HAS JOINED ALANNA IN HER SCIENTIFIC RESEARCH IN THE NORTH POLAR REGION OF RANN...
ON EARTH, THE AURORA BOREALIS--CAUSED BY STREAMS OF ELECTRICALLY-CHARGED PARTICLES EMITTED BY THE SUN STRIKING THE UPPER ATMOSPHERE--TAKE THE SHAPE OF CURTAINS--
--HERE THEY RESEMBLE LARGE "CYLINDERS"!
AND JUDGING BY OUR INSTRUMENTS THEY CAN SHOCK A PERSON'S NERVOUS SYSTEM PRETTY BADLY--SO BE CAREFUL
SOME DAYS LATER, THEIR RESEARCH DATA COMPLETE, ADAM AND ALANNA JET AWAY FROM THEIR CAMP TOWARD THE CAPITAL CITY OF RANAGAR...
ADAM--LOOK! AM I SEEING THINGS OR--ARE THOSE MEN RIDING GIANT BIRDS?

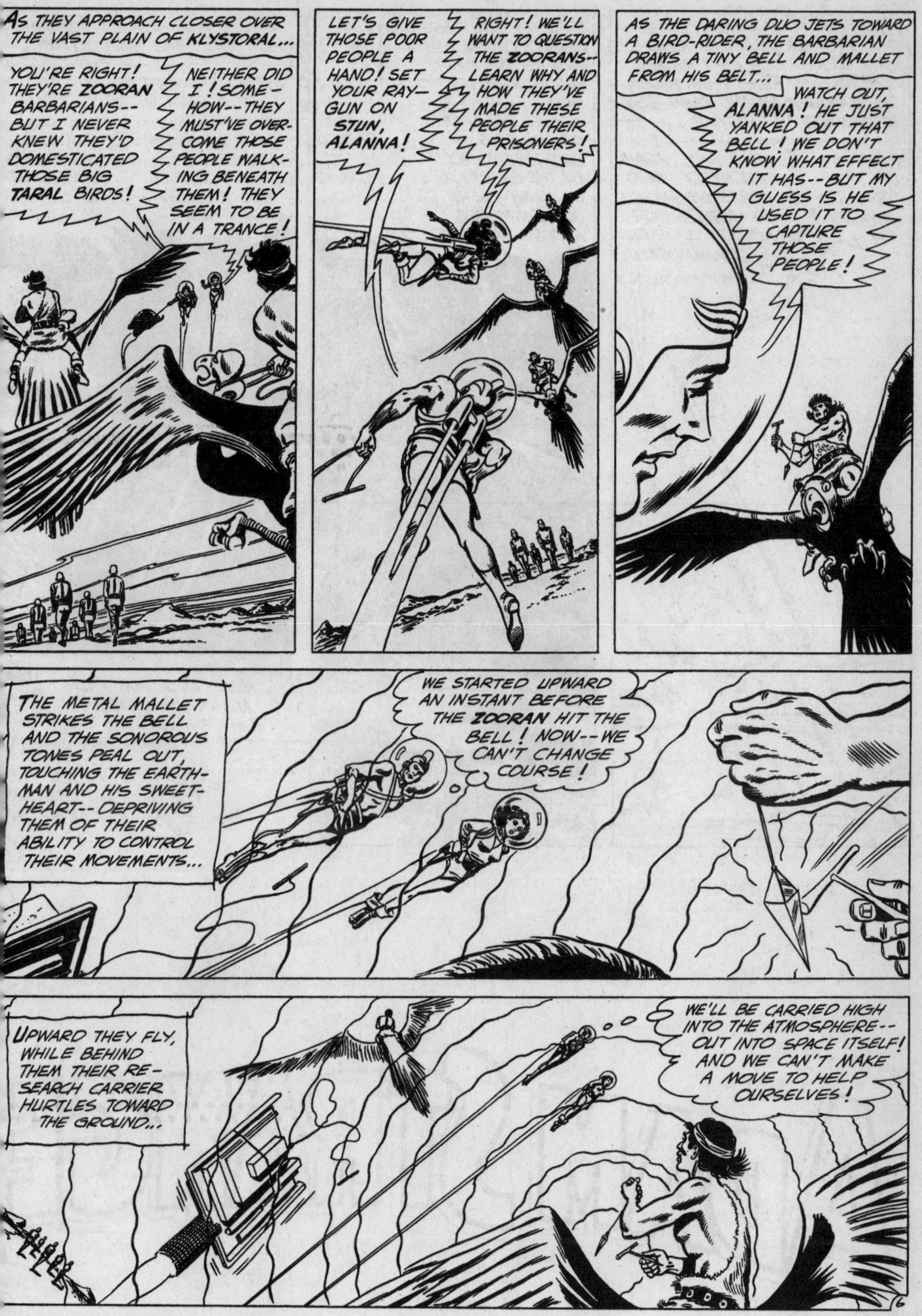
AS THEY APPROACH CLOSER OVER THE VAST PLAIN OF KLYSTORAL...
YOU'RE RIGHT! THEY'RE ZOORAN BARBARIANS-- BUT I NEVER KNEW THEY'D DOMESTICATED THOSE BIG TARAL BIRDS!
NEITHER DID I! SOMEHOW--THEY MUST'VE OVERCOME THOSE PEOPLE WALKING BENEATH THEM! THEY SEEM TO BE IN A TRANCE!
LET'S GIVE THOSE POOR PEOPLE A HAND! SET YOUR RAY-GUN ON STUN, ALANNA!
RIGHT! WE'LL WANT TO QUESTION THE ZOORANS--LEARN WHY AND HOW THEY'VE MADE THESE PEOPLE THEIR PRISONERS!
AS THE DARING DUO JETS TOWARD A BIRD-RIDER, THE BARBARIAN DRAWS A TINY BELL AND MALLET FROM HIS BELT...
WATCH OUT, ALANNA! HE JUST YANKED OUT THAT BELL! WE DON'T KNOW WHAT EFFECT IT HAS--BUT MY GUESS IS HE USED IT TO CAPTURE THOSE PEOPLE!
THE METAL MALLET STRIKES THE BELL AND THE SONOROUS TONES PEAL OUT, TOUCHING THE EARTHMAN AND HIS SWEETHEART--DEPRIVING THEM OF THEIR ABILITY TO CONTROL THEIR MOVEMENTS...
WE STARTED UPWARD AN INSTANT BEFORE THE ZOORAN HIT THE BELL! NOW--WE CAN'T CHANGE COURSE!
UPWARD THEY FLY, WHILE BEHIND THEM THEIR RESEARCH CARRIER HURTLES TOWARD THE GROUND...
WE'LL BE CARRIED HIGH INTO THE ATMOSPHERE--OUT INTO SPACE ITSELF! AND WE CAN'T MAKE A MOVE TO HELP OURSELVES!
6

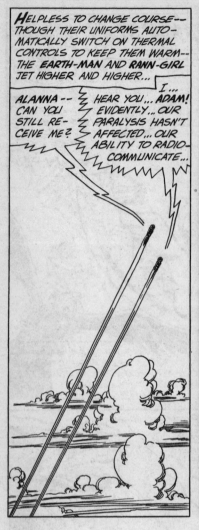

HELPLESS TO CHANGE COURSE--THOUGH THEIR UNIFORMS AUTO-MATICALLY SWITCH ON THERMAL CONTROLS TO KEEP THEM WARM--THE *EARTH-MAN* AND *RANN-GIRL* JET HIGHER AND HIGHER...

ALANNA-- CAN YOU STILL RE-CEIVE ME?

I... HEAR YOU... *ADAM!* EVIDENTLY... OUR PARALYSIS HASN'T AFFECTED... OUR ABILITY TO RADIO-COMMUNICATE...

THEN THE INEXORABLE DRAG OF GRAVITY CATCHES THEM IN ITS GRIP AS THE MIGHTY PLANET BELOW REFUSES TO LET THEM GO...

THE SPEED OF OUR JETS IS COUNTERBALANCED BY THE GRAVITY PULL OF *RANN*--WE'RE GOING INTO ORBIT AROUND THE PLANET!

IF ONLY *RADAR* CAN SPOT US--AND SEND HELP...

AROUND AND AROUND THE PLANET GO THE LIVING SATELLITES...

EVEN IF THEY SEE US FROM A *RANAGARAN* OBSERVATORY--BY THE TIME ANYONE CAN REACH US-- OUR JETS WILL HAVE RUN OUT OF FUEL!

AND THEN *SOB* WE'LL HURTLE DOWNWARD TO CRASH AND DIE!

HOW CAN *ADAM* AND *ALANNA* POSSIBLY SAVE THEMSELVES FROM THIS FANTASTIC TRAP?

TURN TO CHAPTER TWO-- AND READ ON!

ADAM STRANGE

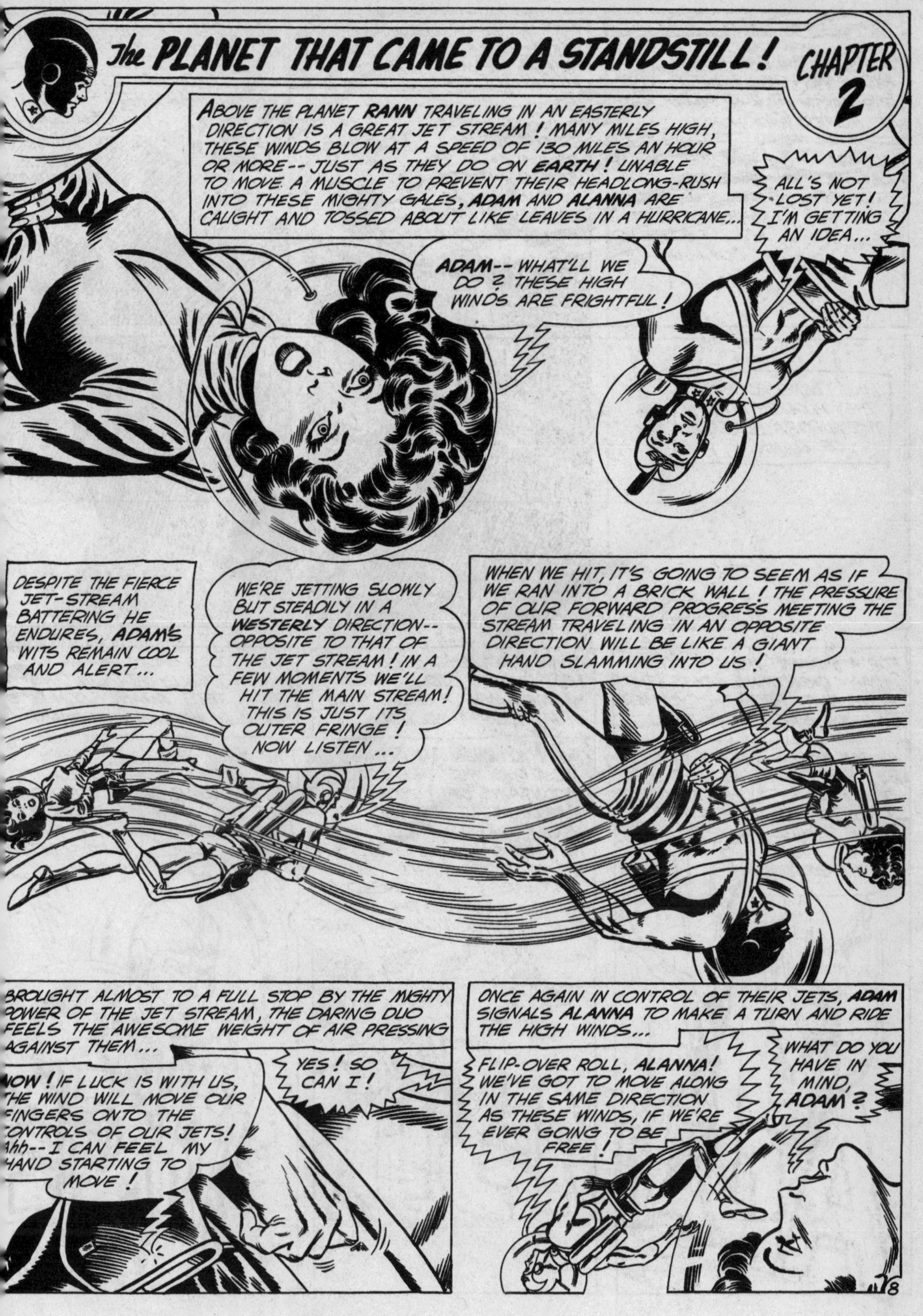
The PLANET THAT CAME TO A STANDSTILL!
CHAPTER 2
ABOVE THE PLANET RANN TRAVELING IN AN EASTERLY DIRECTION IS A GREAT JET STREAM! MANY MILES HIGH, THESE WINDS BLOW AT A SPEED OF 130 MILES AN HOUR OR MORE-- JUST AS THEY DO ON EARTH! UNABLE TO MOVE A MUSCLE TO PREVENT THEIR HEADLONG-RUSH INTO THESE MIGHTY GALES, ADAM AND ALANNA ARE CAUGHT AND TOSSED ABOUT LIKE LEAVES IN A HURRICANE...
ADAM-- WHAT'LL WE DO? THESE HIGH WINDS ARE FRIGHTFUL!
ALL'S NOT LOST YET! I'M GETTING AN IDEA...
DESPITE THE FIERCE JET-STREAM BATTERING HE ENDURES, ADAM'S WITS REMAIN COOL AND ALERT...
WE'RE JETTING SLOWLY BUT STEADILY IN A WESTERLY DIRECTION-- OPPOSITE TO THAT OF THE JET STREAM! IN A FEW MOMENTS WE'LL HIT THE MAIN STREAM! THIS IS JUST ITS OUTER FRINGE! NOW LISTEN...
WHEN WE HIT, IT'S GOING TO SEEM AS IF WE RAN INTO A BRICK WALL! THE PRESSURE OF OUR FORWARD PROGRESS MEETING THE STREAM TRAVELING IN AN OPPOSITE DIRECTION WILL BE LIKE A GIANT HAND SLAMMING INTO US!
BROUGHT ALMOST TO A FULL STOP BY THE MIGHTY POWER OF THE JET STREAM, THE DARING DUO FEELS THE AWESOME WEIGHT OF AIR PRESSING AGAINST THEM...
NOW! IF LUCK IS WITH US, THE WIND WILL MOVE OUR FINGERS ONTO THE CONTROLS OF OUR JETS! Ahh-- I CAN FEEL MY HAND STARTING TO MOVE!
YES! SO CAN I!
ONCE AGAIN IN CONTROL OF THEIR JETS, ADAM SIGNALS ALANNA TO MAKE A TURN AND RIDE THE HIGH WINDS...
FLIP-OVER ROLL, ALANNA! WE'VE GOT TO MOVE ALONG IN THE SAME DIRECTION AS THESE WINDS, IF WE'RE EVER GOING TO BE FREE!
WHAT DO YOU HAVE IN MIND, ADAM?
8

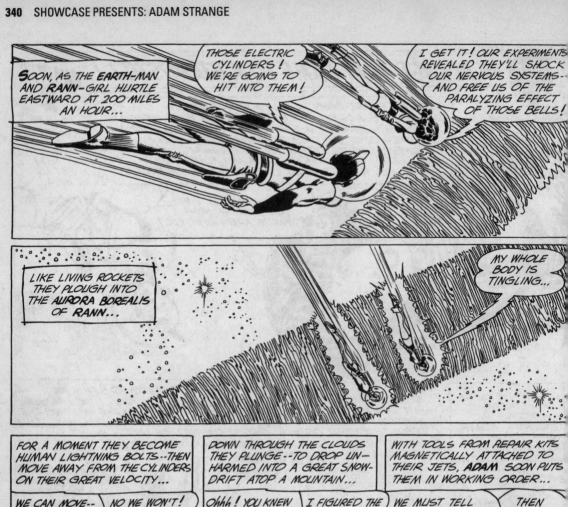

SOON, AS THE **EARTH-MAN** AND **RANN**-GIRL HURTLE EASTWARD AT 200 MILES AN HOUR...

THOSE ELECTRIC CYLINDERS! WE'RE GOING TO HIT INTO THEM!

I GET IT! OUR EXPERIMENTS REVEALED THEY'LL SHOCK OUR NERVOUS SYSTEMS-- AND FREE US OF THE PARALYZING EFFECT OF THOSE BELLS!

LIKE LIVING ROCKETS THEY PLOUGH INTO THE **AURORA BOREALIS** OF **RANN**...

MY WHOLE BODY IS TINGLING...

FOR A MOMENT THEY BECOME HUMAN LIGHTNING BOLTS--THEN MOVE AWAY FROM THE CYLINDERS ON THEIR GREAT VELOCITY...

WE CAN MOVE-- BUT NOW OUR JETS HAVE CONKED OUT! WE'RE GOING TO FALL MILES TO THE GROUND!

NO WE WON'T! WE HAVE LESS THAN A QUARTER OF A MILE TO FALL!

DOWN THROUGH THE CLOUDS THEY PLUNGE--TO DROP UN-HARMED INTO A GREAT SNOW-DRIFT ATOP A MOUNTAIN...

Ohhh! YOU KNEW ALL ALONG THE **MOUNTAINS OF MARLE** WERE HERE! THAT'S WHY YOU SAID WE MUST GO EASTWARD!

I FIGURED THE ELECTRIC CYLINDERS WOULD SHORT-CIRCUIT OUR JETS AND WE'D FALL-- BUT I ARRANGED IT SO THE FALL WOULDN'T HURT US!

WITH TOOLS FROM REPAIR KITS MAGNETICALLY ATTACHED TO THEIR JETS, **ADAM** SOON PUTS THEM IN WORKING ORDER...

WE MUST TELL THE AUTHORITIES IN **RANAGAR** OF THE BIRD-MEN OF **ZOORA**--

THEN ORGANIZE A RESCUE PARTY TO FREE THEIR PRISONERS!

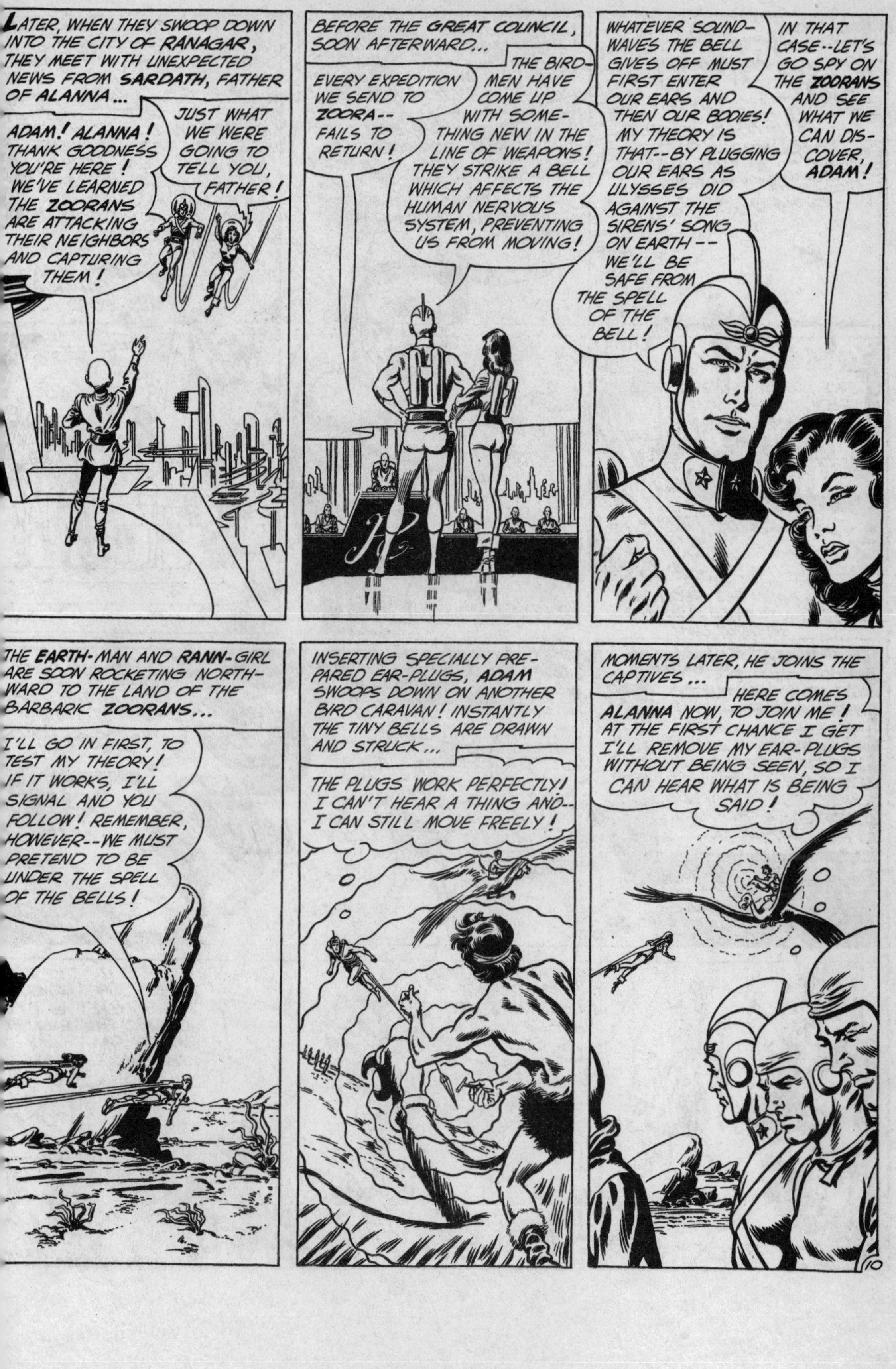
LATER, WHEN THEY SWOOP DOWN INTO THE CITY OF RANAGAR, THEY MEET WITH UNEXPECTED NEWS FROM SARDATH, FATHER OF ALANNA...
JUST WHAT WE WERE GOING TO TELL YOU, FATHER!
ADAM! ALANNA! THANK GOODNESS YOU'RE HERE! WE'VE LEARNED THE ZOORANS ARE ATTACKING THEIR NEIGHBORS AND CAPTURING THEM!
BEFORE THE GREAT COUNCIL, SOON AFTERWARD...
EVERY EXPEDITION WE SEND TO ZOORA-- FAILS TO RETURN!
THE BIRD-MEN HAVE COME UP WITH SOME-THING NEW IN THE LINE OF WEAPONS! THEY STRIKE A BELL WHICH AFFECTS THE HUMAN NERVOUS SYSTEM, PREVENTING US FROM MOVING!
WHATEVER SOUND-WAVES THE BELL GIVES OFF MUST FIRST ENTER OUR EARS AND THEN OUR BODIES! MY THEORY IS THAT--BY PLUGGING OUR EARS AS ULYSSES DID AGAINST THE SIRENS' SONG ON EARTH -- WE'LL BE SAFE FROM THE SPELL OF THE BELL!
IN THAT CASE--LET'S GO SPY ON THE ZOORANS AND SEE WHAT WE CAN DIS-COVER, ADAM!
THE EARTH-MAN AND RANN-GIRL ARE SOON ROCKETING NORTH-WARD TO THE LAND OF THE BARBARIC ZOORANS...
I'LL GO IN FIRST, TO TEST MY THEORY! IF IT WORKS, I'LL SIGNAL AND YOU FOLLOW! REMEMBER, HOWEVER--WE MUST PRETEND TO BE UNDER THE SPELL OF THE BELLS!
INSERTING SPECIALLY PRE-PARED EAR-PLUGS, ADAM SWOOPS DOWN ON ANOTHER BIRD CARAVAN! INSTANTLY THE TINY BELLS ARE DRAWN AND STRUCK...
THE PLUGS WORK PERFECTLY! I CAN'T HEAR A THING AND-- I CAN STILL MOVE FREELY!
MOMENTS LATER, HE JOINS THE CAPTIVES...
HERE COMES ALANNA NOW, TO JOIN ME! AT THE FIRST CHANCE I GET I'LL REMOVE MY EAR-PLUGS WITHOUT BEING SEEN, SO I CAN HEAR WHAT IS BEING SAID!
10

ADOPTING THE SHUFFLING WALK OF THE HELPLESS CAPTIVES, ADAM AND ALANNA COME AT LAST TO THE ANCIENT RUINS OF VARDANA...

I WAS HERE ONCE BEFORE-- WHEN THE ZOORANS TELEPORTED ME TO ANTHORANN!* BUT-- WHO'S THAT ODD-LOOKING CHARACTER?

*Editor's Note: SEE SHOWCASE #17: "The PLANET AND THE PENDULUM"

KANJAR RO HAS FOUND HIS EARTH-LIKE PLANET WITH A TRIPLE SUN--AND A SOURCE OF MANPOWER TO HELP HIM IN HIS RADIATION RESEARCH...

HURRY THIS BATCH TO MY LABORATORY! I STILL HAVE MUCH WORK TO DO BEFORE I CAN GIVE MYSELF SUPER-POWERS!

FOLLOWING THE FORMER ENEMY OF THE JUSTICE LEAGUE OF AMERICA, ADAM AND ALANNA PROCEED TO AN UNDERGROUND LABORATORY WHERE...

TOMORROW I SHALL FLOOD THE GENERATO-SCREENS WITH RADIATION-- THEN BATHE MYSELF IN THEIR GLOW! AFTER THAT-- I SHALL BE MORE SUPER THAN SUPERMAN HIMSELF!

GREATER THAN SUPERMAN GOOD GOSH!

NEXT DAY, KANJAR RO SETS THE MIGHTY GENERATOR SCREENS IN ACTION AND STANDS BEFORE THEM, BATHING IN THE RADIATION OF THE TRIPLE STAR-SUN SYSTEM OF ALPHA CENTAURI...

ACCORDING TO MY CALCULATIONS -- FIVE MINUTES OF SUCH INTENSITY WILL BE ENOUGH FOR NOW!

*:Whew!!: THOSE BARS HE'S SNAPPED LIKE MATCHSTICKS ARE MADE OF--SOLID STEEL!

I DID IT! I'VE MADE MYSELF SUPER-POWERFUL! I KNEW--EVEN AS MY COSMIC SHIP BROUGHT ME TO RANN--MY THEORY WAS CORRECT!

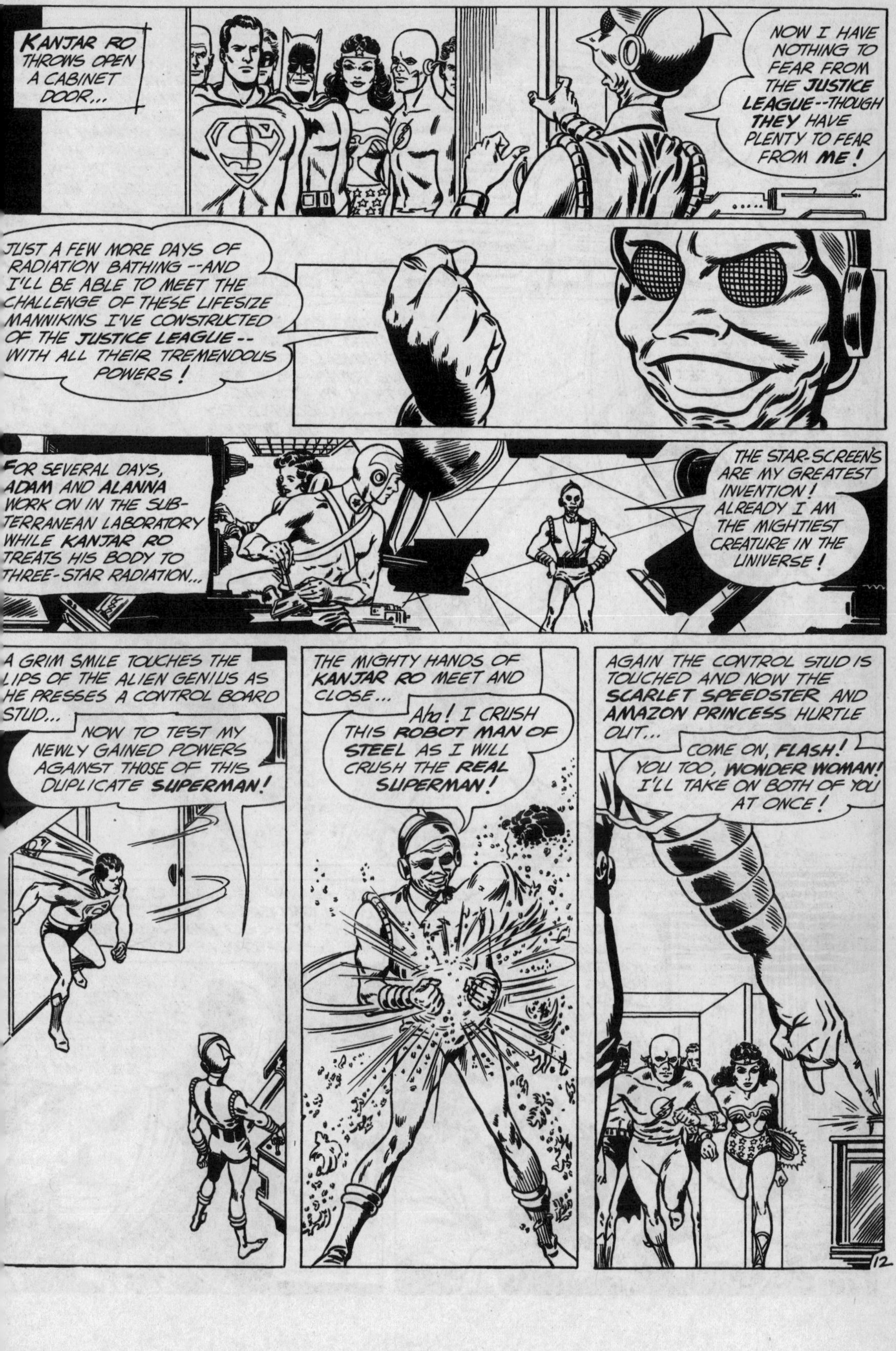
KANJAR RO THROWS OPEN A CABINET DOOR...
NOW I HAVE NOTHING TO FEAR FROM THE JUSTICE LEAGUE--THOUGH THEY HAVE PLENTY TO FEAR FROM ME!
JUST A FEW MORE DAYS OF RADIATION BATHING --AND I'LL BE ABLE TO MEET THE CHALLENGE OF THESE LIFESIZE MANNIKINS I'VE CONSTRUCTED OF THE JUSTICE LEAGUE -- WITH ALL THEIR TREMENDOUS POWERS!
FOR SEVERAL DAYS, ADAM AND ALANNA WORK ON IN THE SUB-TERRANEAN LABORATORY WHILE KANJAR RO TREATS HIS BODY TO THREE-STAR RADIATION...
THE STAR-SCREENS ARE MY GREATEST INVENTION! ALREADY I AM THE MIGHTIEST CREATURE IN THE UNIVERSE!
A GRIM SMILE TOUCHES THE LIPS OF THE ALIEN GENIUS AS HE PRESSES A CONTROL BOARD STUD...
NOW TO TEST MY NEWLY GAINED POWERS AGAINST THOSE OF THIS DUPLICATE SUPERMAN!
THE MIGHTY HANDS OF KANJAR RO MEET AND CLOSE...
Aha! I CRUSH THIS ROBOT MAN OF STEEL AS I WILL CRUSH THE REAL SUPERMAN!
AGAIN THE CONTROL STUD IS TOUCHED AND NOW THE SCARLET SPEEDSTER AND AMAZON PRINCESS HURTLE OUT...
COME ON, FLASH! YOU TOO, WONDER WOMAN! I'LL TAKE ON BOTH OF YOU AT ONCE!
12

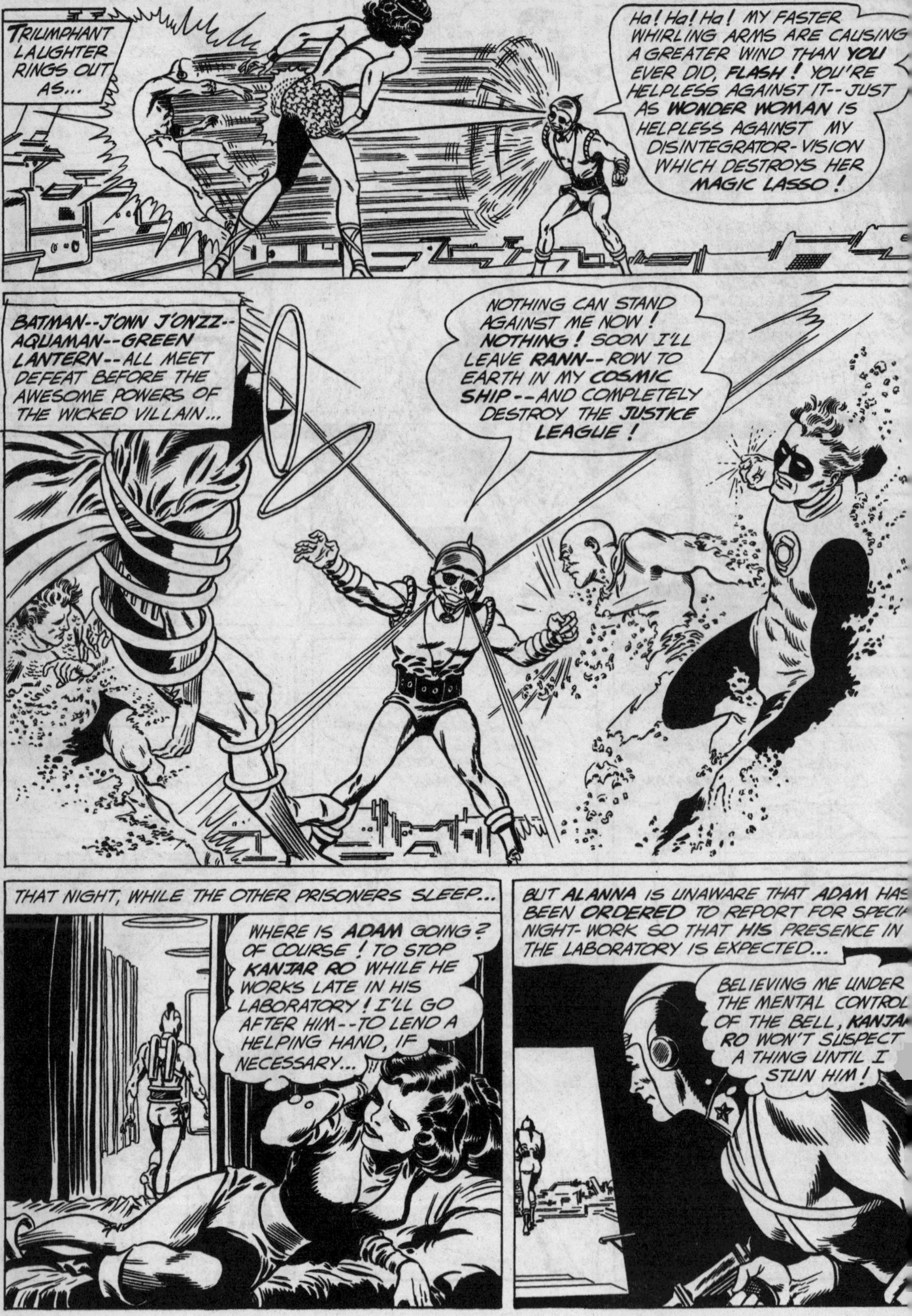
TRIUMPHANT LAUGHTER RINGS OUT AS...
HA! HA! HA! MY FASTER WHIRLING ARMS ARE CAUSING A GREATER WIND THAN YOU EVER DID, FLASH! YOU'RE HELPLESS AGAINST IT--JUST AS WONDER WOMAN IS HELPLESS AGAINST MY DISINTEGRATOR-VISION WHICH DESTROYS HER MAGIC LASSO!
BATMAN--J'ONN J'ONZZ--AQUAMAN--GREEN LANTERN--ALL MEET DEFEAT BEFORE THE AWESOME POWERS OF THE WICKED VILLAIN...
NOTHING CAN STAND AGAINST ME NOW! NOTHING! SOON I'LL LEAVE RANN--ROW TO EARTH IN MY COSMIC SHIP--AND COMPLETELY DESTROY THE JUSTICE LEAGUE!
THAT NIGHT, WHILE THE OTHER PRISONERS SLEEP...
WHERE IS ADAM GOING? OF COURSE! TO STOP KANJAR RO WHILE HE WORKS LATE IN HIS LABORATORY! I'LL GO AFTER HIM--TO LEND A HELPING HAND, IF NECESSARY...
BUT ALANNA IS UNAWARE THAT ADAM HAS BEEN ORDERED TO REPORT FOR SPECI NIGHT-WORK SO THAT HIS PRESENCE IN THE LABORATORY IS EXPECTED...
BELIEVING ME UNDER THE MENTAL CONTROL OF THE BELL, KANJA RO WON'T SUSPECT A THING UNTIL I STUN HIM!

AND WHAT **ALANNA** DOES NOT SUSPECT IS--AN ALARM HAS BEEN PREPARED TO RING IF ANY INTRUDER SHOULD ATTEMPT TO ENTER THE LABORATORY...

WHO GOES THERE?

OHHH--NO! WHAT HAVE I DONE?

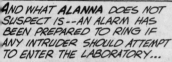

CLAANG!

ALERTED BY THE ALARM, KANJAR RO MOVES WITH BLINDING SPEED TOWARD HIS **GAMMA GONG**...

YOU DREW A RAY-GUN ON ME! THAT MEANS YOU'RE NOT UNDER THE CONTROL OF THE TINKLE BELL! WELL, I'LL FIX THAT...

HE STRIKES THE GONG AND...

THE GAMMA VIBRATIONS OF MY GONG HAVE FROZEN HIM MOTIONLESS!

A STRUGGLING **ALANNA** IS BROUGHT FORWARD BY THE GUARDS...

ANOTHER ONE! IF I'D KNOWN THERE WERE MORE THAN ONE I'D HAVE IN-CREASED THE RANGE OF THE GONG VIBRATIONS BY HITTING IT HARDER! I MUST LEARN HOW THESE TWO EVADED THE DOMI-NATION OF THE BELL--BUT I CAN'T SPARE THE TIME RIGHT NOW!

FROM A COMPARTMENT IN A LABORATORY CABINET **KANJAR RO** LIFTS A SUPER-SONIC WHISTLE AND BLOWS IT, FREEING **ADAM** FROM THE SPELL OF THE GAMMA GONG...

I CAN MOVE AGAIN--BUT IT WON'T DO ME ANY GOOD! I'M REALLY HIS PRISONER NOW!

ADAM AND ALANNA ARE TAKEN TO A LARGE ROOM AND PLACED IN DUPLICATE CHAIRS AS KANJAR RO THROWS A SWITCH...

MY GRAVITY-PRISON WILL KEEP YOU ROOTED TO THESE CHAIRS UNTIL I CAN QUESTION YOU! EXCEPT WHEN IT COMES TIME TO EAT--YOU WON'T BE ABLE TO MOVE A FINGER!

4

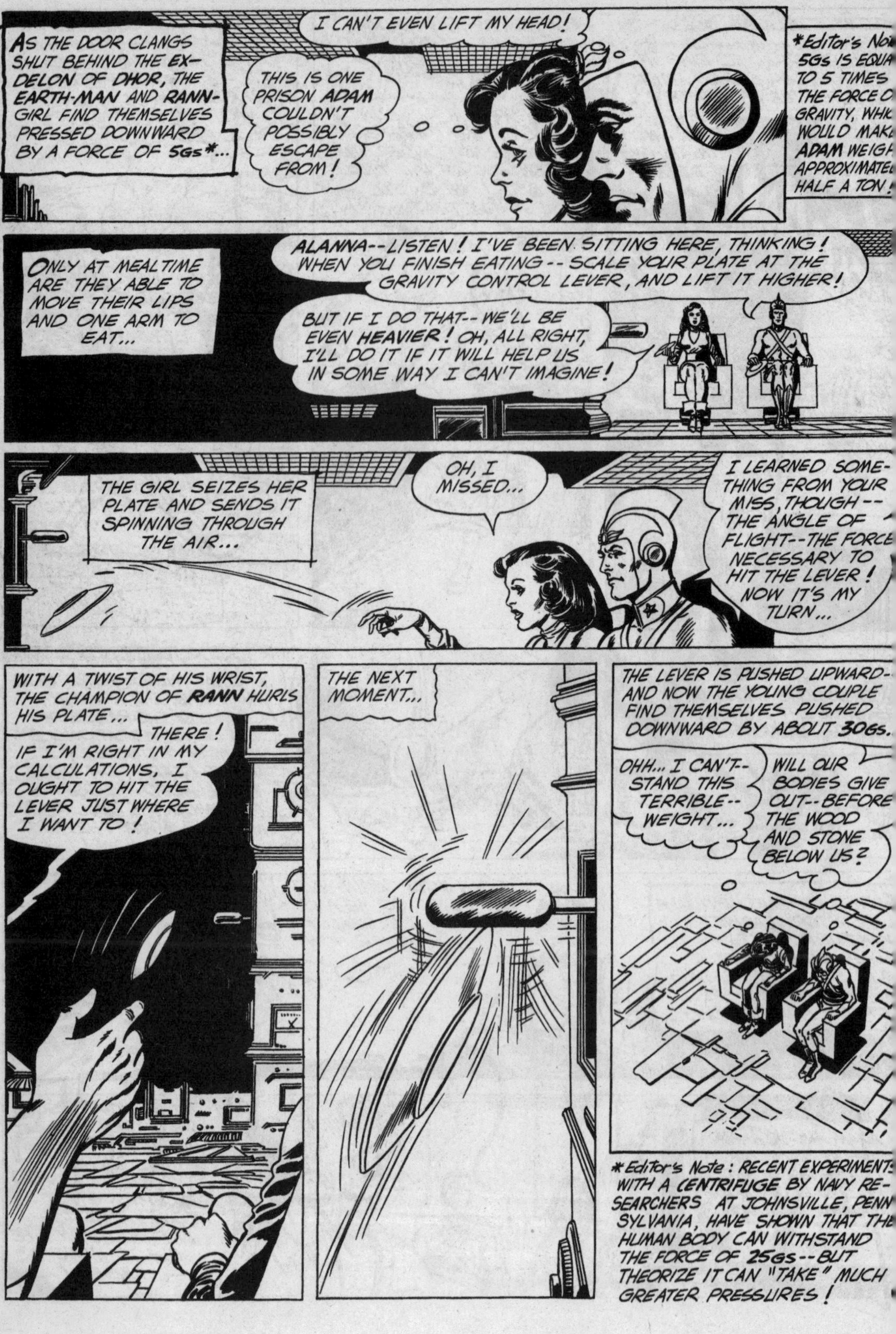
AS THE DOOR CLANGS SHUT BEHIND THE EX-DELON OF DHOR, THE EARTH-MAN AND RANN-GIRL FIND THEMSELVES PRESSED DOWNWARD BY A FORCE OF 5Gs*...
I CAN'T EVEN LIFT MY HEAD!
THIS IS ONE PRISON ADAM COULDN'T POSSIBLY ESCAPE FROM!
ONLY AT MEALTIME ARE THEY ABLE TO MOVE THEIR LIPS AND ONE ARM TO EAT...
ALANNA--LISTEN! I'VE BEEN SITTING HERE, THINKING! WHEN YOU FINISH EATING--SCALE YOUR PLATE AT THE GRAVITY CONTROL LEVER, AND LIFT IT HIGHER!
BUT IF I DO THAT--WE'LL BE EVEN HEAVIER! OH, ALL RIGHT, I'LL DO IT IF IT WILL HELP US IN SOME WAY I CAN'T IMAGINE!
THE GIRL SEIZES HER PLATE AND SENDS IT SPINNING THROUGH THE AIR...
OH, I MISSED...
I LEARNED SOMETHING FROM YOUR MISS, THOUGH--THE ANGLE OF FLIGHT--THE FORCE NECESSARY TO HIT THE LEVER! NOW IT'S MY TURN...
WITH A TWIST OF HIS WRIST, THE CHAMPION OF RANN HURLS HIS PLATE...
THERE! IF I'M RIGHT IN MY CALCULATIONS, I OUGHT TO HIT THE LEVER JUST WHERE I WANT TO!
THE NEXT MOMENT...
THE LEVER IS PUSHED UPWARD--AND NOW THE YOUNG COUPLE FIND THEMSELVES PUSHED DOWNWARD BY ABOUT 30Gs...
OHH... I CAN'T-STAND THIS TERRIBLE--WEIGHT...
WILL OUR BODIES GIVE OUT--BEFORE THE WOOD AND STONE BELOW US?

*Editor's Note: 5Gs IS EQUA[L] TO 5 TIMES THE FORCE O[F] GRAVITY, WHIC[H] WOULD MAK[E] ADAM WEIGH APPROXIMATE[LY] HALF A TON!

*Editor's Note: RECENT EXPERIMENTS WITH A CENTRIFUGE BY NAVY RESEARCHERS AT JOHNSVILLE, PENNSYLVANIA, HAVE SHOWN THAT THE HUMAN BODY CAN WITHSTAND THE FORCE OF 25Gs--BUT THEORIZE IT CAN "TAKE" MUCH GREATER PRESSURES!

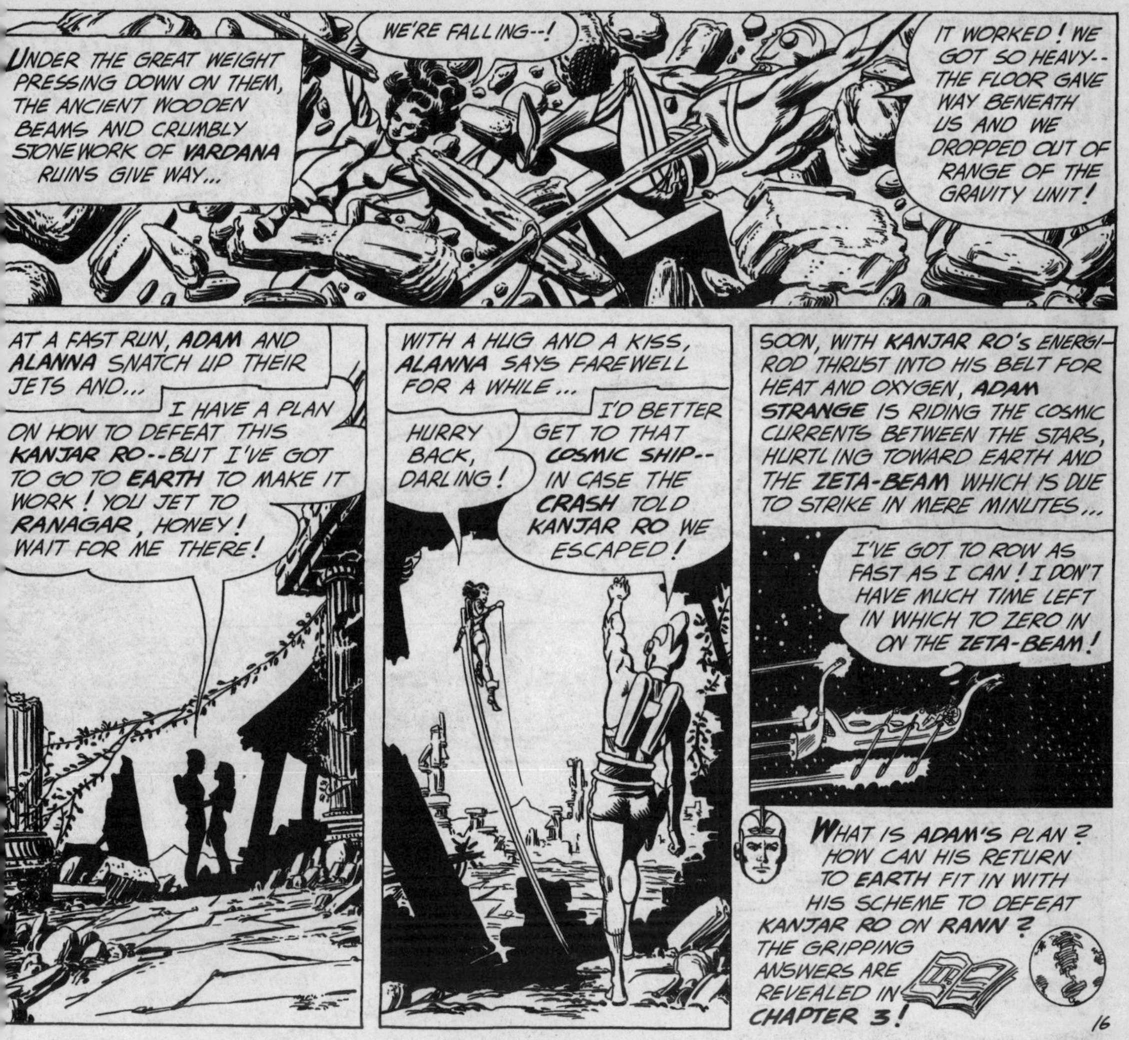
UNDER THE GREAT WEIGHT PRESSING DOWN ON THEM, THE ANCIENT WOODEN BEAMS AND CRUMBLY STONEWORK OF VARDANA RUINS GIVE WAY...
WE'RE FALLING--!
IT WORKED! WE GOT SO HEAVY-- THE FLOOR GAVE WAY BENEATH US AND WE DROPPED OUT OF RANGE OF THE GRAVITY UNIT!
AT A FAST RUN, ADAM AND ALANNA SNATCH UP THEIR JETS AND...
I HAVE A PLAN ON HOW TO DEFEAT THIS KANJAR RO--BUT I'VE GOT TO GO TO EARTH TO MAKE IT WORK! YOU JET TO RANAGAR, HONEY! WAIT FOR ME THERE!
WITH A HUG AND A KISS, ALANNA SAYS FAREWELL FOR A WHILE...
HURRY BACK, DARLING!
I'D BETTER GET TO THAT COSMIC SHIP-- IN CASE THE CRASH TOLD KANJAR RO WE ESCAPED!
SOON, WITH KANJAR RO'S ENERGI-ROD THRUST INTO HIS BELT FOR HEAT AND OXYGEN, ADAM STRANGE IS RIDING THE COSMIC CURRENTS BETWEEN THE STARS, HURTLING TOWARD EARTH AND THE ZETA-BEAM WHICH IS DUE TO STRIKE IN MERE MINUTES...
I'VE GOT TO ROW AS FAST AS I CAN! I DON'T HAVE MUCH TIME LEFT IN WHICH TO ZERO IN ON THE ZETA-BEAM!
WHAT IS ADAM'S PLAN? HOW CAN HIS RETURN TO EARTH FIT IN WITH HIS SCHEME TO DEFEAT KANJAR RO ON RANN? THE GRIPPING ANSWERS ARE REVEALED IN CHAPTER 3!
16

ADAM STRANGE

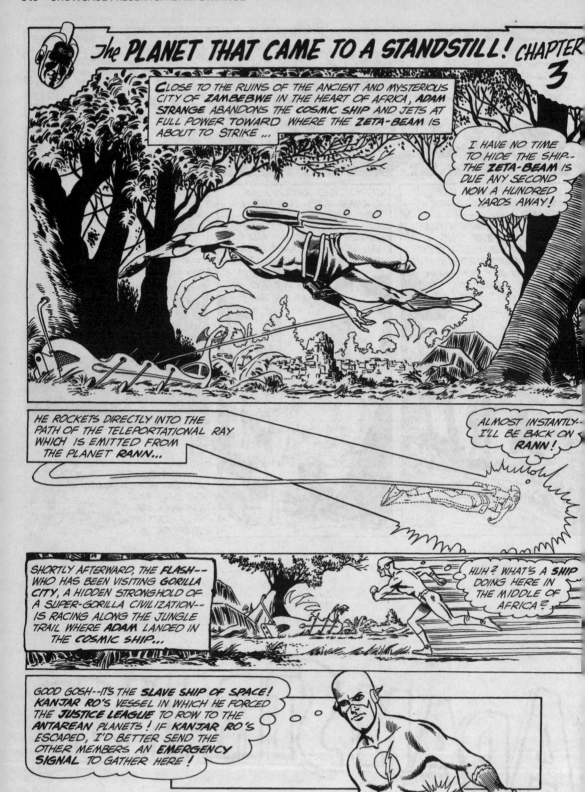

The PLANET THAT CAME TO A STANDSTILL! CHAPTER 3

CLOSE TO THE RUINS OF THE ANCIENT AND MYSTERIOUS CITY OF *ZAMBEBWE* IN THE HEART OF AFRICA, *ADAM STRANGE* ABANDONS THE *COSMIC SHIP* AND JETS AT FULL POWER TOWARD WHERE THE *ZETA-BEAM* IS ABOUT TO STRIKE...

I HAVE NO TIME TO HIDE THE SHIP.-- THE *ZETA-BEAM* IS DUE ANY SECOND NOW A HUNDRED YARDS AWAY!

HE ROCKETS DIRECTLY INTO THE PATH OF THE TELEPORTATIONAL RAY WHICH IS EMITTED FROM THE PLANET *RANN*...

ALMOST INSTANTLY-- I'LL BE BACK ON *RANN*!

SHORTLY AFTERWARD, THE *FLASH*-- WHO HAS BEEN VISITING *GORILLA CITY*, A HIDDEN STRONGHOLD OF A SUPER-GORILLA CIVILIZATION-- IS RACING ALONG THE JUNGLE TRAIL WHERE *ADAM* LANDED IN THE *COSMIC SHIP*...

HUH? WHAT'S A *SHIP* DOING HERE IN THE MIDDLE OF AFRICA?

GOOD GOSH--IT'S THE *SLAVE SHIP OF SPACE!* KANJAR RO'S VESSEL IN WHICH HE FORCED THE *JUSTICE LEAGUE* TO ROW TO THE *ANTAREAN PLANETS*! IF KANJAR RO'S ESCAPED, I'D BETTER SEND THE OTHER MEMBERS AN *EMERGENCY SIGNAL* TO GATHER HERE !

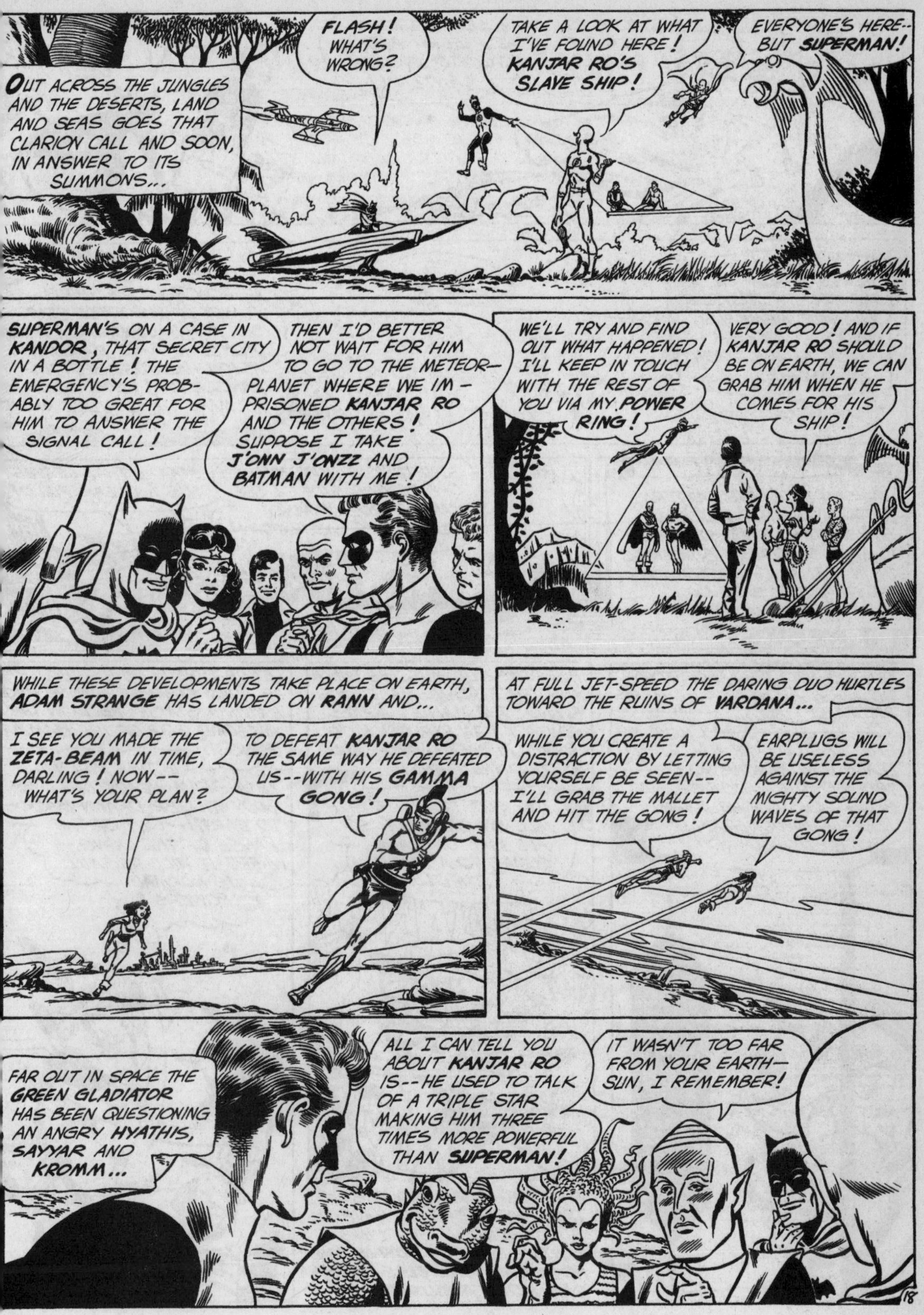
OUT ACROSS THE JUNGLES AND THE DESERTS, LAND AND SEAS GOES THAT CLARION CALL AND SOON, IN ANSWER TO ITS SUMMONS...
FLASH! WHAT'S WRONG?
TAKE A LOOK AT WHAT I'VE FOUND HERE! KANJAR RO'S SLAVE SHIP!
EVERYONE'S HERE-- BUT SUPERMAN!
SUPERMAN'S ON A CASE IN KANDOR, THAT SECRET CITY IN A BOTTLE! THE EMERGENCY'S PROBABLY TOO GREAT FOR HIM TO ANSWER THE SIGNAL CALL!
THEN I'D BETTER NOT WAIT FOR HIM TO GO TO THE METEOR-PLANET WHERE WE IMPRISONED KANJAR RO AND THE OTHERS! SUPPOSE I TAKE J'ONN J'ONZZ AND BATMAN WITH ME!
WE'LL TRY AND FIND OUT WHAT HAPPENED! I'LL KEEP IN TOUCH WITH THE REST OF YOU VIA MY POWER RING!
VERY GOOD! AND IF KANJAR RO SHOULD BE ON EARTH, WE CAN GRAB HIM WHEN HE COMES FOR HIS SHIP!
WHILE THESE DEVELOPMENTS TAKE PLACE ON EARTH, ADAM STRANGE HAS LANDED ON RANN AND...
I SEE YOU MADE THE ZETA-BEAM IN TIME, DARLING! NOW-- WHAT'S YOUR PLAN?
TO DEFEAT KANJAR RO THE SAME WAY HE DEFEATED US--WITH HIS GAMMA GONG!
AT FULL JET-SPEED THE DARING DUO HURTLES TOWARD THE RUINS OF VARDANA...
WHILE YOU CREATE A DISTRACTION BY LETTING YOURSELF BE SEEN-- I'LL GRAB THE MALLET AND HIT THE GONG!
EARPLUGS WILL BE USELESS AGAINST THE MIGHTY SOUND WAVES OF THAT GONG!
FAR OUT IN SPACE THE GREEN GLADIATOR HAS BEEN QUESTIONING AN ANGRY HYATHIS, SAYYAR AND KROMM...
ALL I CAN TELL YOU ABOUT KANJAR RO IS--HE USED TO TALK OF A TRIPLE STAR MAKING HIM THREE TIMES MORE POWERFUL THAN SUPERMAN!
IT WASN'T TOO FAR FROM YOUR EARTH-SUN, I REMEMBER!
18

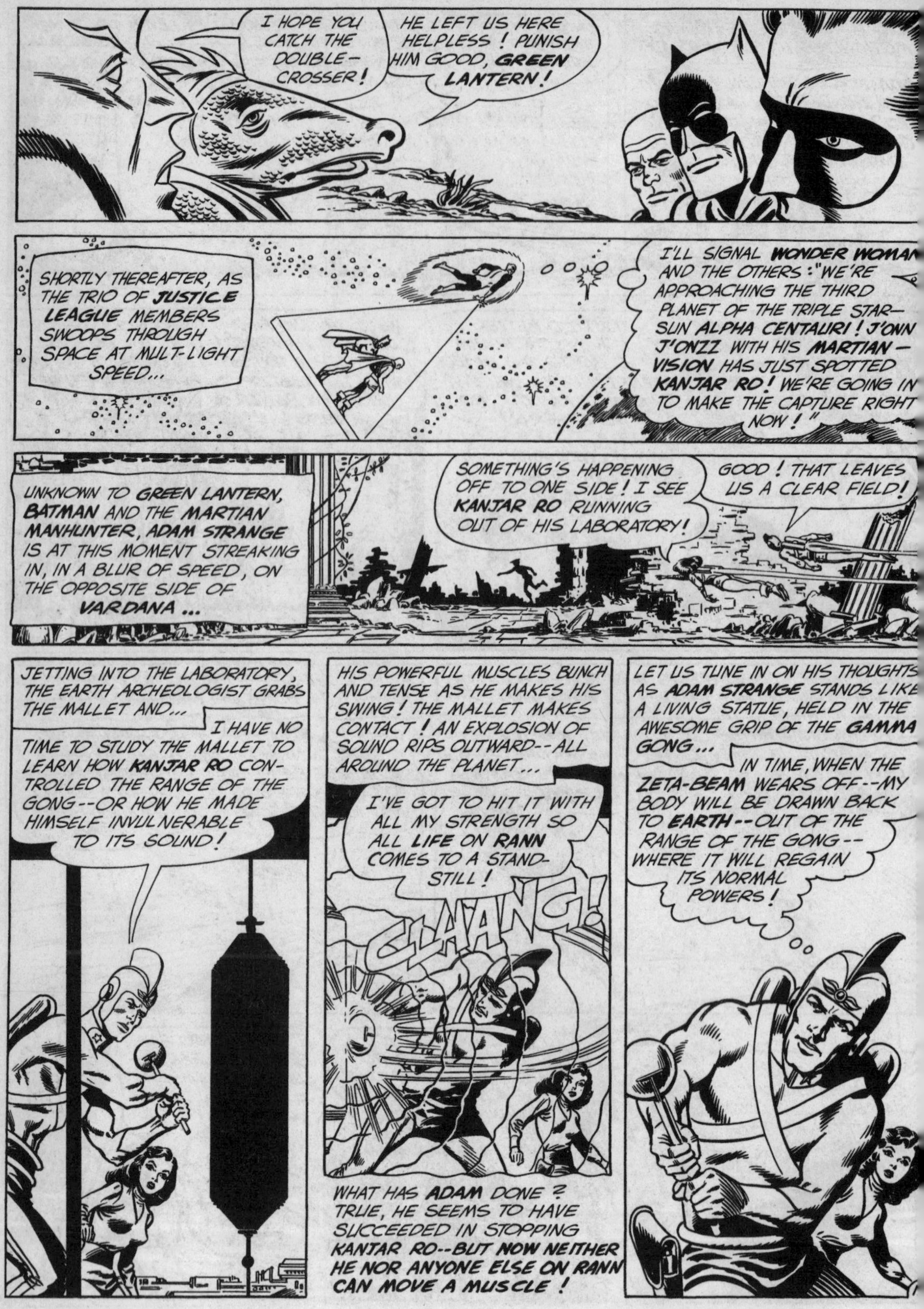
I HOPE YOU CATCH THE DOUBLE-CROSSER!
HE LEFT US HERE HELPLESS! PUNISH HIM GOOD, GREEN LANTERN!
SHORTLY THEREAFTER, AS THE TRIO OF JUSTICE LEAGUE MEMBERS SWOOPS THROUGH SPACE AT MULT-LIGHT SPEED...
I'LL SIGNAL WONDER WOMAN AND THE OTHERS: "WE'RE APPROACHING THE THIRD PLANET OF THE TRIPLE STAR-SUN ALPHA CENTAURI! J'ONN J'ONZZ WITH HIS MARTIAN-VISION HAS JUST SPOTTED KANJAR RO! WE'RE GOING IN TO MAKE THE CAPTURE RIGHT NOW!"
UNKNOWN TO GREEN LANTERN, BATMAN AND THE MARTIAN MANHUNTER, ADAM STRANGE IS AT THIS MOMENT STREAKING IN, IN A BLUR OF SPEED, ON THE OPPOSITE SIDE OF VARDANA...
SOMETHING'S HAPPENING OFF TO ONE SIDE! I SEE KANJAR RO RUNNING OUT OF HIS LABORATORY!
GOOD! THAT LEAVES US A CLEAR FIELD!
JETTING INTO THE LABORATORY, THE EARTH ARCHEOLOGIST GRABS THE MALLET AND...
I HAVE NO TIME TO STUDY THE MALLET TO LEARN HOW KANJAR RO CONTROLLED THE RANGE OF THE GONG--OR HOW HE MADE HIMSELF INVULNERABLE TO ITS SOUND!
HIS POWERFUL MUSCLES BUNCH AND TENSE AS HE MAKES HIS SWING! THE MALLET MAKES CONTACT! AN EXPLOSION OF SOUND RIPS OUTWARD--ALL AROUND THE PLANET...
I'VE GOT TO HIT IT WITH ALL MY STRENGTH SO ALL LIFE ON RANN COMES TO A STANDSTILL!
CLLANG!
WHAT HAS ADAM DONE? TRUE, HE SEEMS TO HAVE SUCCEEDED IN STOPPING KANJAR RO--BUT NOW NEITHER HE NOR ANYONE ELSE ON RANN CAN MOVE A MUSCLE!
LET US TUNE IN ON HIS THOUGHTS AS ADAM STRANGE STANDS LIKE A LIVING STATUE, HELD IN THE AWESOME GRIP OF THE GAMMA GONG...
IN TIME, WHEN THE ZETA-BEAM WEARS OFF--MY BODY WILL BE DRAWN BACK TO EARTH--OUT OF THE RANGE OF THE GONG--WHERE IT WILL REGAIN ITS NORMAL POWERS!

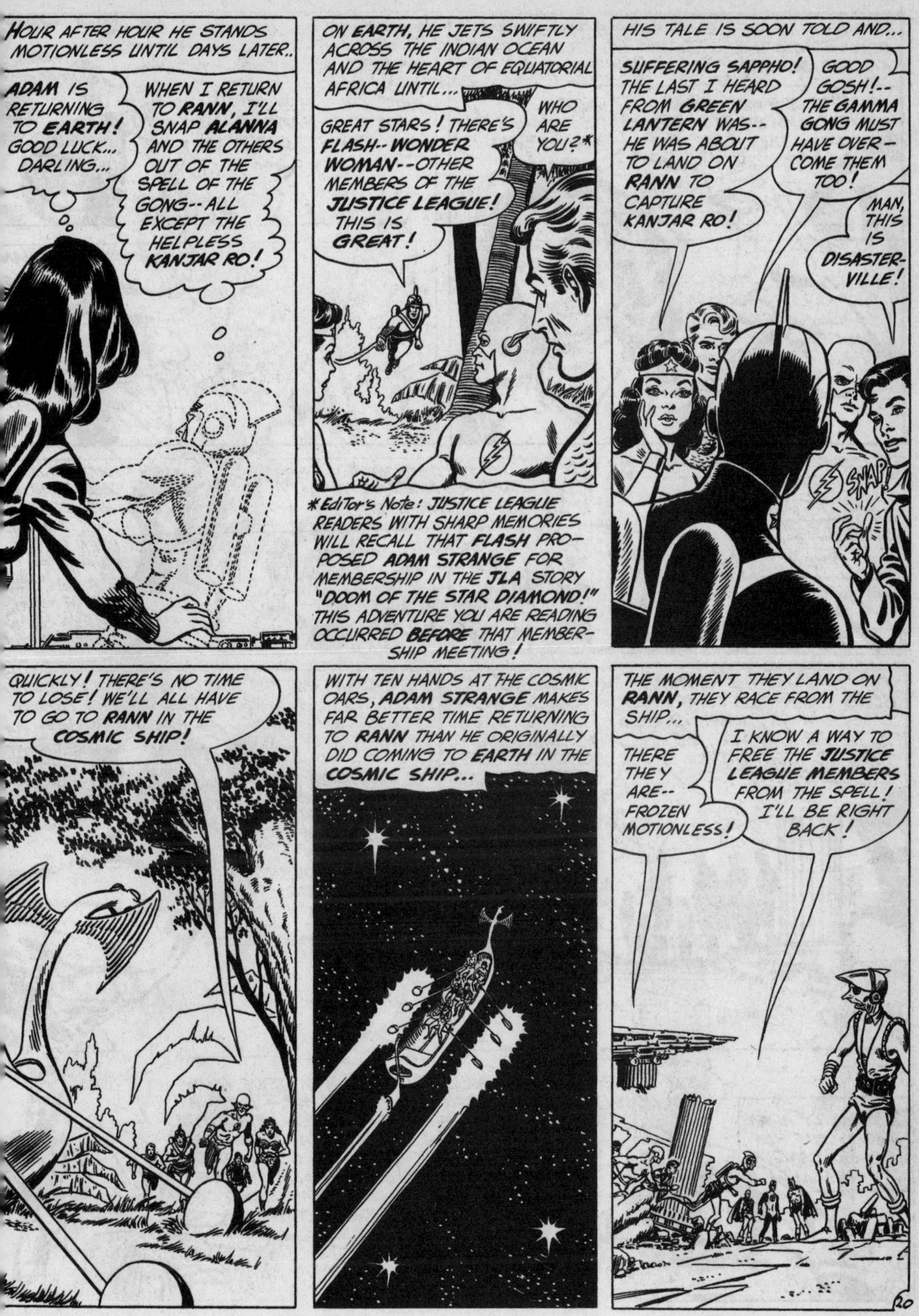
HOUR AFTER HOUR HE STANDS MOTIONLESS UNTIL DAYS LATER..
ADAM IS RETURNING TO EARTH! GOOD LUCK... DARLING...
WHEN I RETURN TO RANN, I'LL SNAP ALANNA AND THE OTHERS OUT OF THE SPELL OF THE GONG--ALL EXCEPT THE HELPLESS KANJAR RO!
ON EARTH, HE JETS SWIFTLY ACROSS THE INDIAN OCEAN AND THE HEART OF EQUATORIAL AFRICA UNTIL...
GREAT STARS! THERE'S FLASH--WONDER WOMAN--OTHER MEMBERS OF THE JUSTICE LEAGUE! THIS IS GREAT!
WHO ARE YOU?*
*Editor's Note: JUSTICE LEAGUE READERS WITH SHARP MEMORIES WILL RECALL THAT FLASH PROPOSED ADAM STRANGE FOR MEMBERSHIP IN THE JLA STORY "DOOM OF THE STAR DIAMOND!" THIS ADVENTURE YOU ARE READING OCCURRED BEFORE THAT MEMBERSHIP MEETING!
HIS TALE IS SOON TOLD AND...
SUFFERING SAPPHO! THE LAST I HEARD FROM GREEN LANTERN WAS--HE WAS ABOUT TO LAND ON RANN TO CAPTURE KANJAR RO!
GOOD GOSH!--THE GAMMA GONG MUST HAVE OVERCOME THEM TOO!
MAN, THIS IS DISASTER-VILLE!
SNAP!
QUICKLY! THERE'S NO TIME TO LOSE! WE'LL ALL HAVE TO GO TO RANN IN THE COSMIC SHIP!
WITH TEN HANDS AT THE COSMIC OARS, ADAM STRANGE MAKES FAR BETTER TIME RETURNING TO RANN THAN HE ORIGINALLY DID COMING TO EARTH IN THE COSMIC SHIP...
THE MOMENT THEY LAND ON RANN, THEY RACE FROM THE SHIP...
THERE THEY ARE--FROZEN MOTIONLESS!
I KNOW A WAY TO FREE THE JUSTICE LEAGUE MEMBERS FROM THE SPELL! I'LL BE RIGHT BACK!
20

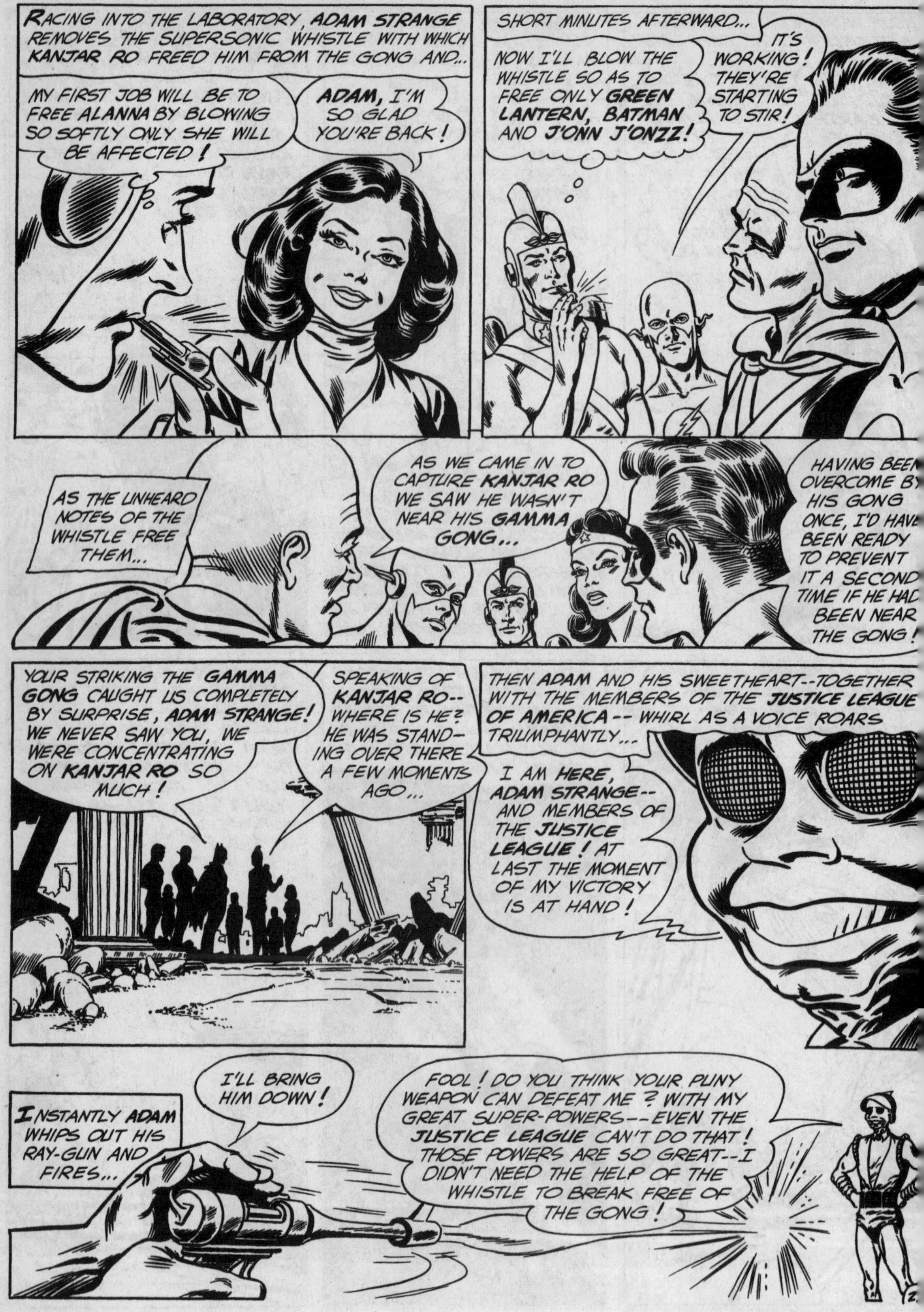
RACING INTO THE LABORATORY, ADAM STRANGE REMOVES THE SUPERSONIC WHISTLE WITH WHICH KANJAR RO FREED HIM FROM THE GONG AND...
MY FIRST JOB WILL BE TO FREE ALANNA BY BLOWING SO SOFTLY ONLY SHE WILL BE AFFECTED!
ADAM, I'M SO GLAD YOU'RE BACK!
SHORT MINUTES AFTERWARD...
NOW I'LL BLOW THE WHISTLE SO AS TO FREE ONLY GREEN LANTERN, BATMAN AND J'ONN J'ONZZ!
IT'S WORKING! THEY'RE STARTING TO STIR!
AS THE UNHEARD NOTES OF THE WHISTLE FREE THEM...
AS WE CAME IN TO CAPTURE KANJAR RO WE SAW HE WASN'T NEAR HIS GAMMA GONG...
HAVING BEEN OVERCOME BY HIS GONG ONCE, I'D HAVE BEEN READY TO PREVENT IT A SECOND TIME IF HE HAD BEEN NEAR THE GONG!
YOUR STRIKING THE GAMMA GONG CAUGHT US COMPLETELY BY SURPRISE, ADAM STRANGE! WE NEVER SAW YOU, WE WERE CONCENTRATING ON KANJAR RO SO MUCH!
SPEAKING OF KANJAR RO-- WHERE IS HE? HE WAS STANDING OVER THERE A FEW MOMENTS AGO...
THEN ADAM AND HIS SWEETHEART--TOGETHER WITH THE MEMBERS OF THE JUSTICE LEAGUE OF AMERICA-- WHIRL AS A VOICE ROARS TRIUMPHANTLY...
I AM HERE, ADAM STRANGE-- AND MEMBERS OF THE JUSTICE LEAGUE! AT LAST THE MOMENT OF MY VICTORY IS AT HAND!
INSTANTLY ADAM WHIPS OUT HIS RAY-GUN AND FIRES...
I'LL BRING HIM DOWN!
FOOL! DO YOU THINK YOUR PUNY WEAPON CAN DEFEAT ME? WITH MY GREAT SUPER-POWERS--EVEN THE JUSTICE LEAGUE CAN'T DO THAT! THOSE POWERS ARE SO GREAT--I DIDN'T NEED THE HELP OF THE WHISTLE TO BREAK FREE OF THE GONG!

THE SCARLET SPEEDSTER LEAPS FORWARD IN ANSWER TO THAT CHALLENGE...

WE'LL SOON SEE ABOUT THAT!

YOU THINK YOU'RE FAST, FLASH? WELL-- JUST WATCH ME IN FLASHY ACTION!

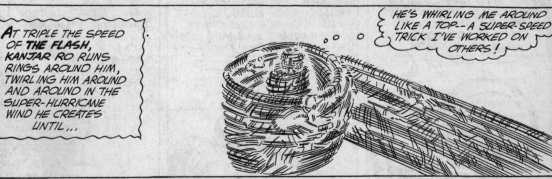

AT TRIPLE THE SPEED OF THE FLASH, KANJAR RO RUNS RINGS AROUND HIM, TWIRLING HIM AROUND AND AROUND IN THE SUPER-HURRICANE WIND HE CREATES UNTIL...

HE'S WHIRLING ME AROUND LIKE A TOP-- A SUPER-SPEED TRICK I'VE WORKED ON OTHERS!

AS A DETERMINED GREEN LANTERN STABS OUT WITH HIS POWER RING...

HA! HA! HA! SINCE MY WILL POWER IS THREE TIMES AS STRONG AS YOURS-- I CAN PREVENT YOU FROM USING YOUR RING!

I ALMOST FEEL SORRY FOR ADAM STRANGE-- JUST STANDING THERE HELPLESS-- UNABLE TO DO ANYTHING!

NOW, J'ONN J'ONZZ-- I'LL START A FIRE WITH MY HEAT VISION-- TO KEEP YOU OUT OF ACTION!

OHHH! HE KNOWS FIRE IS MY WEAKNESS!

POOR ADAM STRANGE! JUST STANDING THERE--OVER- COME BY DESPAIR! MAYBE HE'LL CHEER UP WHEN I ROPE KANJAR RO!

WONDER WOMAN-- IT'S YOUR TURN TO EXPERIENCE MY MIGHTY POWER!

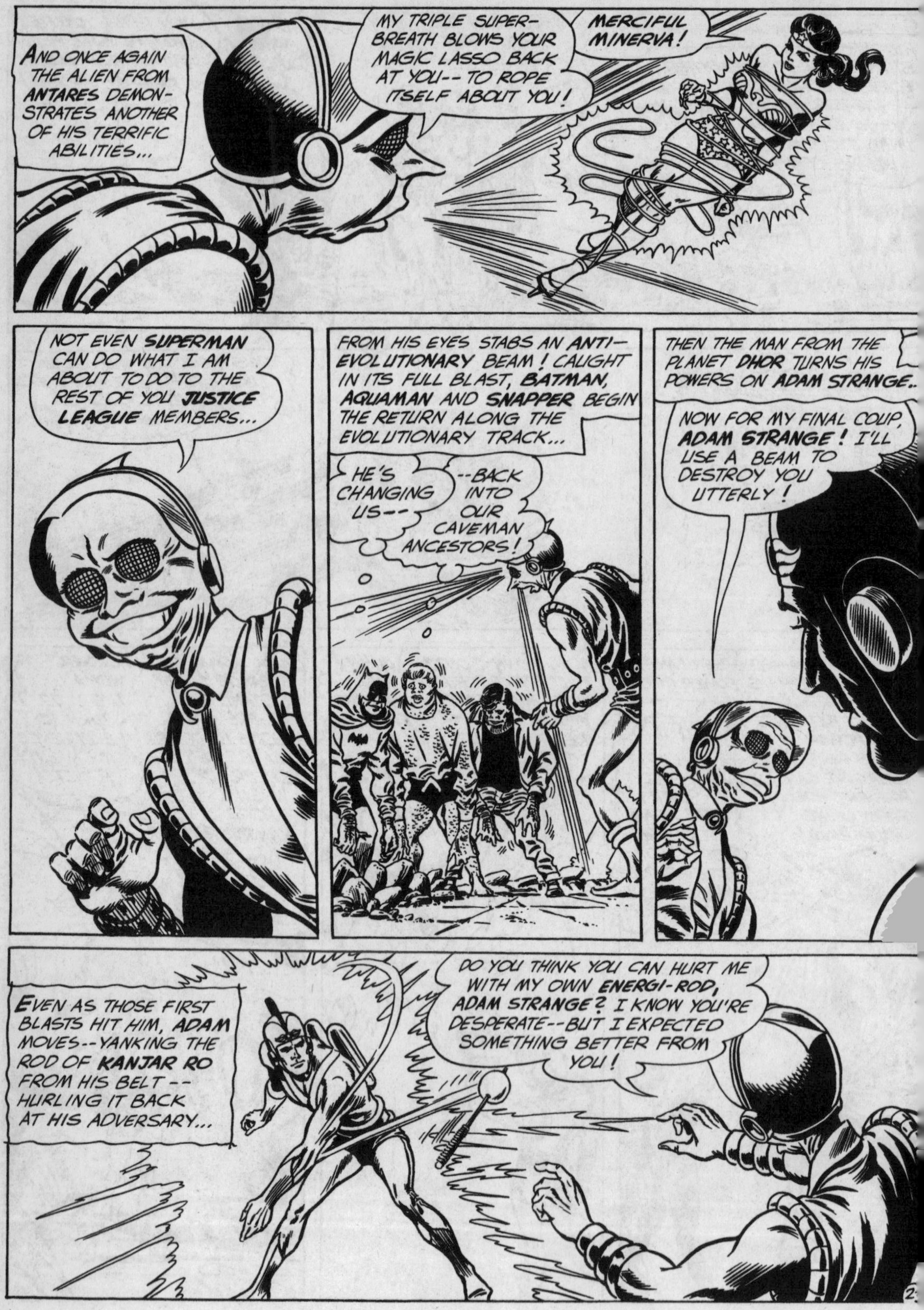
AND ONCE AGAIN THE ALIEN FROM ANTARES DEMON-STRATES ANOTHER OF HIS TERRIFIC ABILITIES...
MY TRIPLE SUPER-BREATH BLOWS YOUR MAGIC LASSO BACK AT YOU-- TO ROPE ITSELF ABOUT YOU!
MERCIFUL MINERVA!
NOT EVEN SUPERMAN CAN DO WHAT I AM ABOUT TO DO TO THE REST OF YOU JUSTICE LEAGUE MEMBERS...
FROM HIS EYES STABS AN ANTI-EVOLUTIONARY BEAM! CAUGHT IN ITS FULL BLAST, BATMAN, AQUAMAN AND SNAPPER BEGIN THE RETURN ALONG THE EVOLUTIONARY TRACK...
HE'S CHANGING US--
--BACK INTO OUR CAVEMAN ANCESTORS!
THEN THE MAN FROM THE PLANET DHOR TURNS HIS POWERS ON ADAM STRANGE...
NOW FOR MY FINAL COUP, ADAM STRANGE! I'LL USE A BEAM TO DESTROY YOU UTTERLY!
EVEN AS THOSE FIRST BLASTS HIT HIM, ADAM MOVES--YANKING THE ROD OF KANJAR RO FROM HIS BELT--HURLING IT BACK AT HIS ADVERSARY...
DO YOU THINK YOU CAN HURT ME WITH MY OWN ENERGI-ROD, ADAM STRANGE? I KNOW YOU'RE DESPERATE--BUT I EXPECTED SOMETHING BETTER FROM YOU!

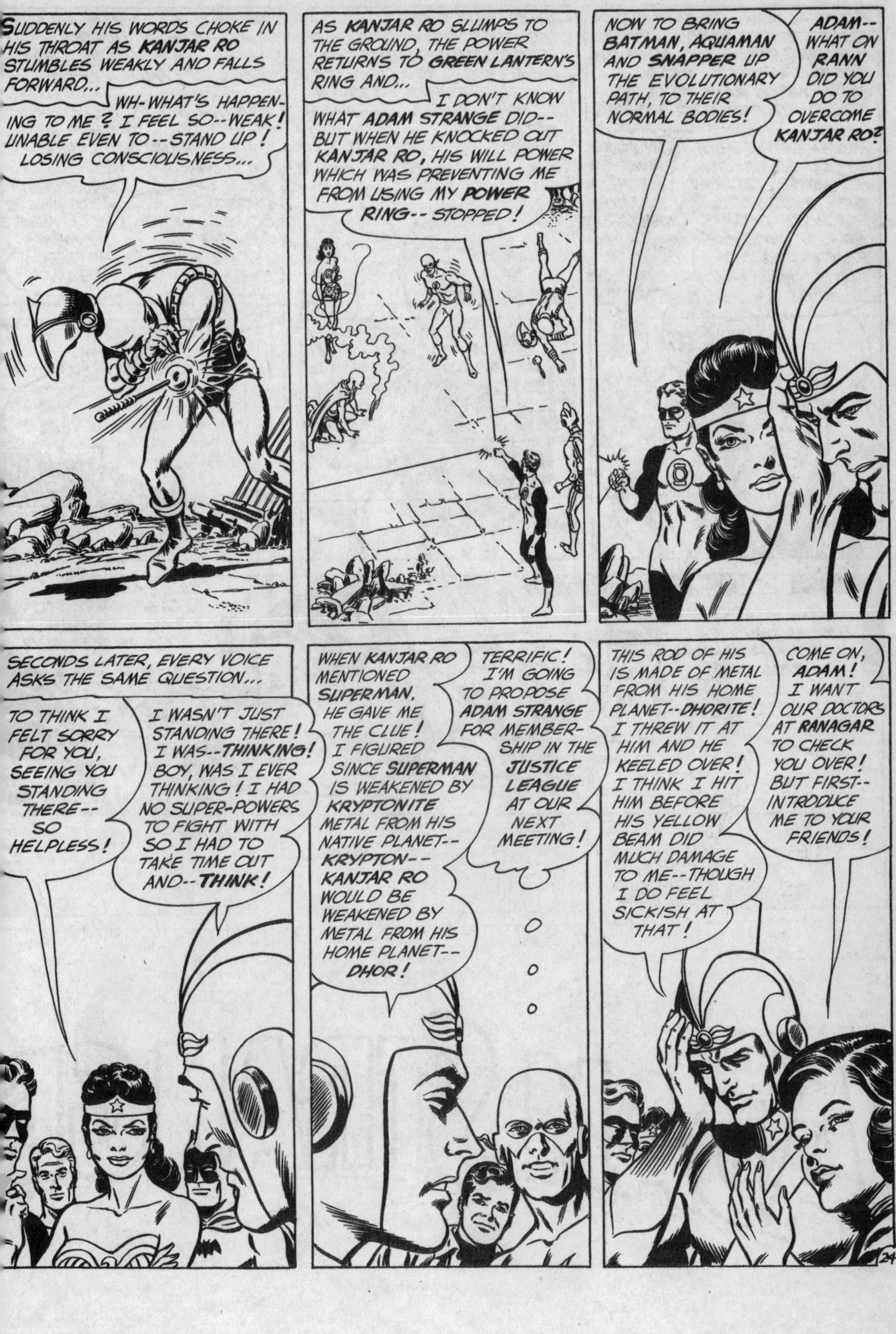
SUDDENLY HIS WORDS CHOKE IN HIS THROAT AS KANJAR RO STUMBLES WEAKLY AND FALLS FORWARD...
WH-WHAT'S HAPPENING TO ME? I FEEL SO--WEAK! UNABLE EVEN TO--STAND UP! LOSING CONSCIOUSNESS...
AS KANJAR RO SLUMPS TO THE GROUND, THE POWER RETURNS TO GREEN LANTERN'S RING AND...
I DON'T KNOW WHAT ADAM STRANGE DID--BUT WHEN HE KNOCKED OUT KANJAR RO, HIS WILL POWER WHICH WAS PREVENTING ME FROM USING MY POWER RING--STOPPED!
NOW TO BRING BATMAN, AQUAMAN AND SNAPPER UP THE EVOLUTIONARY PATH, TO THEIR NORMAL BODIES!
ADAM--WHAT ON RANN DID YOU DO TO OVERCOME KANJAR RO?
SECONDS LATER, EVERY VOICE ASKS THE SAME QUESTION...
TO THINK I FELT SORRY FOR YOU, SEEING YOU STANDING THERE--SO HELPLESS!
I WASN'T JUST STANDING THERE! I WAS--THINKING! BOY, WAS I EVER THINKING! I HAD NO SUPER-POWERS TO FIGHT WITH SO I HAD TO TAKE TIME OUT AND--THINK!
WHEN KANJAR RO MENTIONED SUPERMAN, HE GAVE ME THE CLUE! I FIGURED SINCE SUPERMAN IS WEAKENED BY KRYPTONITE METAL FROM HIS NATIVE PLANET--KRYPTON--KANJAR RO WOULD BE WEAKENED BY METAL FROM HIS HOME PLANET--DHOR!
TERRIFIC! I'M GOING TO PROPOSE ADAM STRANGE FOR MEMBERSHIP IN THE JUSTICE LEAGUE AT OUR NEXT MEETING!
THIS ROD OF HIS IS MADE OF METAL FROM HIS HOME PLANET--DHORITE! I THREW IT AT HIM AND HE KEELED OVER! I THINK I HIT HIM BEFORE HIS YELLOW BEAM DID MUCH DAMAGE TO ME--THOUGH I DO FEEL SICKISH AT THAT!
COME ON, ADAM! I WANT OUR DOCTORS AT RANAGAR TO CHECK YOU OVER! BUT FIRST--INTRODUCE ME TO YOUR FRIENDS!
24

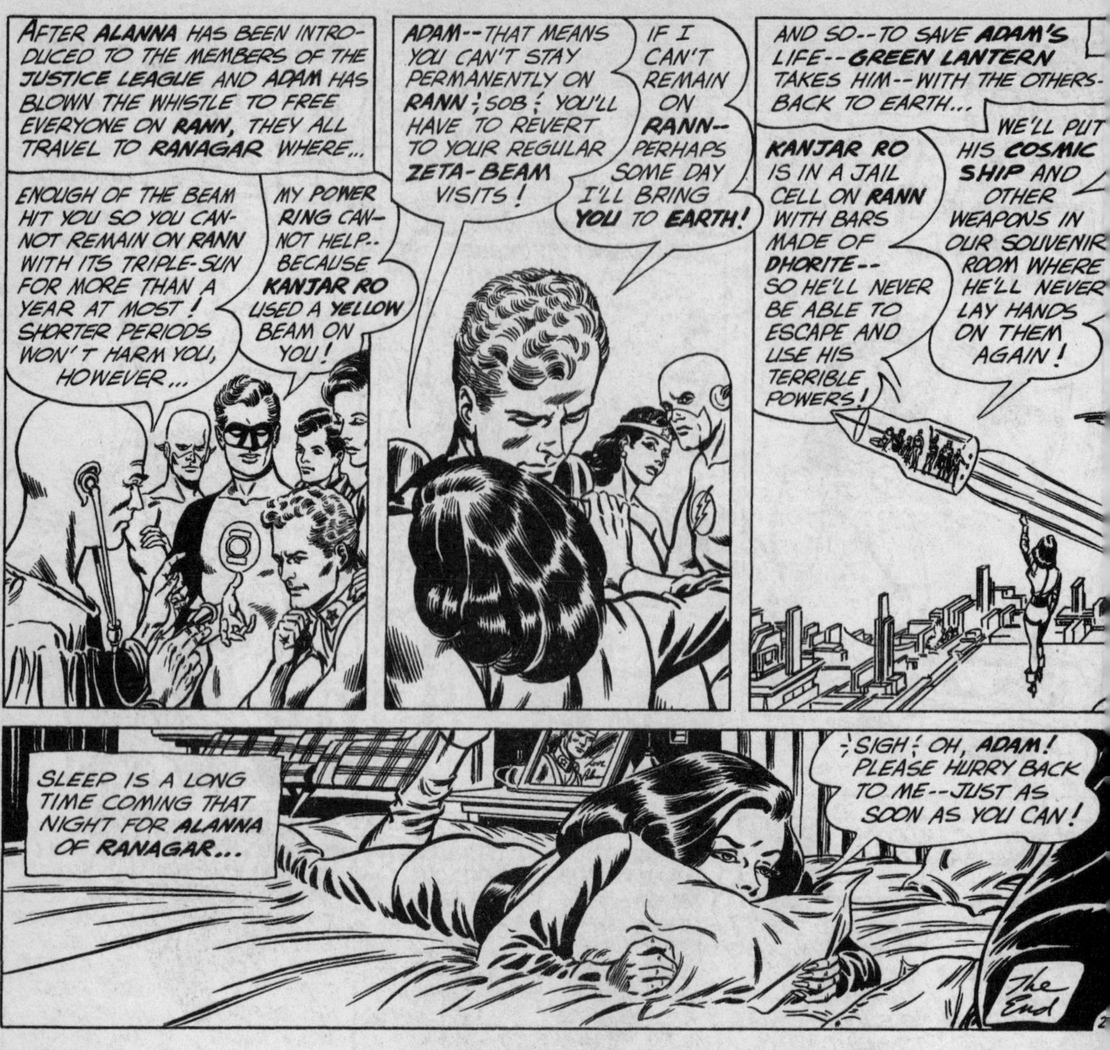
AFTER ALANNA HAS BEEN INTRODUCED TO THE MEMBERS OF THE JUSTICE LEAGUE AND ADAM HAS BLOWN THE WHISTLE TO FREE EVERYONE ON RANN, THEY ALL TRAVEL TO RANAGAR WHERE...
ENOUGH OF THE BEAM HIT YOU SO YOU CANNOT REMAIN ON RANN WITH ITS TRIPLE-SUN FOR MORE THAN A YEAR AT MOST! SHORTER PERIODS WON'T HARM YOU, HOWEVER...
MY POWER RING CANNOT HELP.. BECAUSE KANJAR RO USED A YELLOW BEAM ON YOU!
ADAM--THAT MEANS YOU CAN'T STAY PERMANENTLY ON RANN ;SOB; YOU'LL HAVE TO REVERT TO YOUR REGULAR ZETA-BEAM VISITS!
IF I CAN'T REMAIN ON RANN-- PERHAPS SOME DAY I'LL BRING YOU TO EARTH!
AND SO--TO SAVE ADAM'S LIFE--GREEN LANTERN TAKES HIM--WITH THE OTHERS-BACK TO EARTH...
KANJAR RO IS IN A JAIL CELL ON RANN WITH BARS MADE OF DHORITE-- SO HE'LL NEVER BE ABLE TO ESCAPE AND USE HIS TERRIBLE POWERS!
WE'LL PUT HIS COSMIC SHIP AND OTHER WEAPONS IN OUR SOUVENIR ROOM WHERE HE'LL NEVER LAY HANDS ON THEM AGAIN!
SLEEP IS A LONG TIME COMING THAT NIGHT FOR ALANNA OF RANAGAR...
;SIGH; OH, ADAM! PLEASE HURRY BACK TO ME--JUST AS SOON AS YOU CAN!
The End

ADAM STRANGE

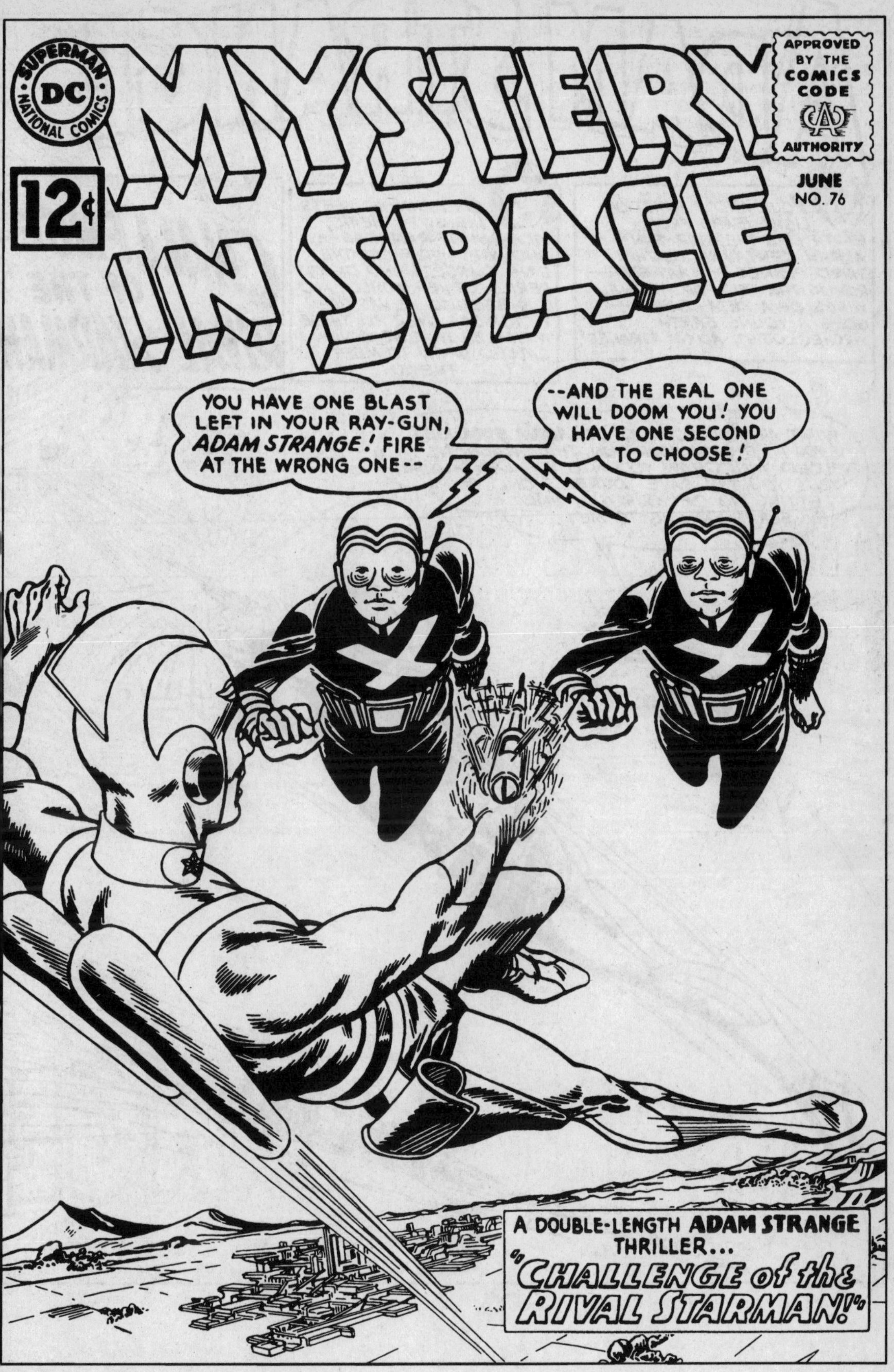
SUPERMAN DC NATIONAL COMICS
MYSTERY IN SPACE
12¢
APPROVED BY THE COMICS CODE AUTHORITY
JUNE NO. 76
YOU HAVE ONE BLAST LEFT IN YOUR RAY-GUN, ADAM STRANGE! FIRE AT THE WRONG ONE--
--AND THE REAL ONE WILL DOOM YOU! YOU HAVE ONE SECOND TO CHOOSE!
A DOUBLE-LENGTH ADAM STRANGE THRILLER...
"CHALLENGE of the RIVAL STARMAN!"

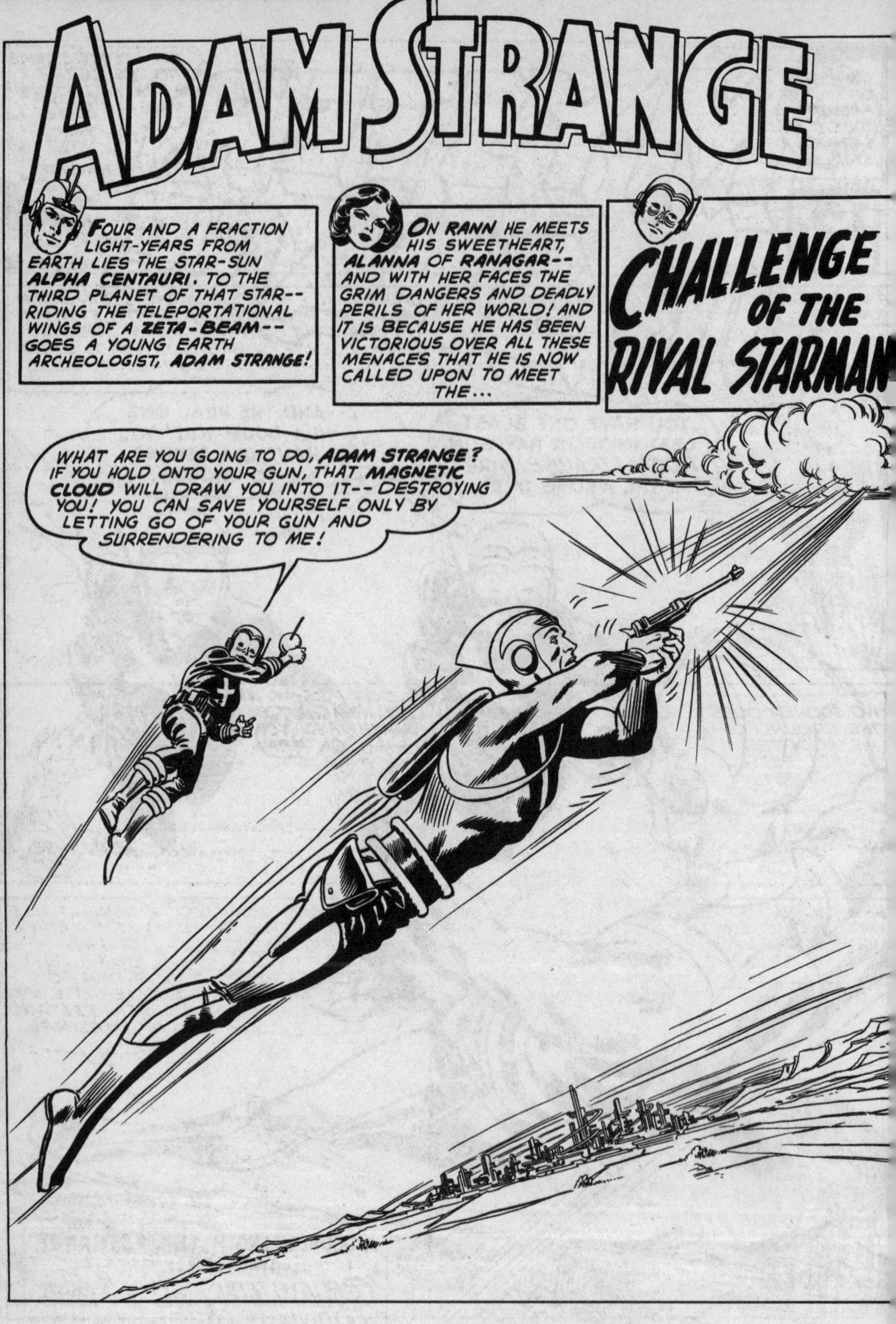
ADAM STRANGE
FOUR AND A FRACTION LIGHT-YEARS FROM EARTH LIES THE STAR-SUN ALPHA CENTAURI. TO THE THIRD PLANET OF THAT STAR--RIDING THE TELEPORTATIONAL WINGS OF A ZETA-BEAM--GOES A YOUNG EARTH ARCHEOLOGIST, ADAM STRANGE!
ON RANN HE MEETS HIS SWEETHEART, ALANNA OF RANAGAR--AND WITH HER FACES THE GRIM DANGERS AND DEADLY PERILS OF HER WORLD! AND IT IS BECAUSE HE HAS BEEN VICTORIOUS OVER ALL THESE MENACES THAT HE IS NOW CALLED UPON TO MEET THE...
CHALLENGE OF THE RIVAL STARMAN
WHAT ARE YOU GOING TO DO, ADAM STRANGE? IF YOU HOLD ONTO YOUR GUN, THAT MAGNETIC CLOUD WILL DRAW YOU INTO IT-- DESTROYING YOU! YOU CAN SAVE YOURSELF ONLY BY LETTING GO OF YOUR GUN AND SURRENDERING TO ME!

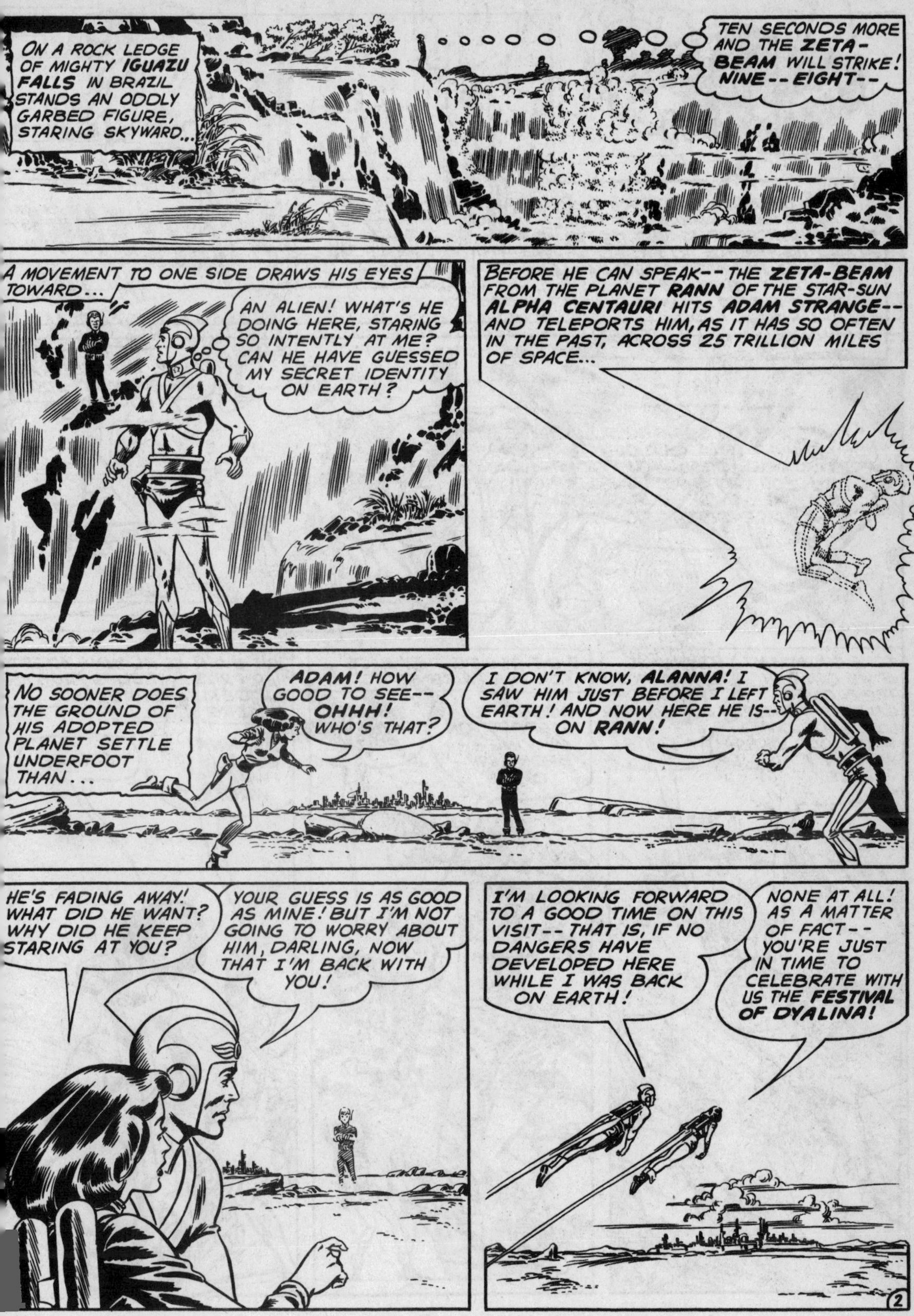
ON A ROCK LEDGE OF MIGHTY IGUAZU FALLS IN BRAZIL STANDS AN ODDLY GARBED FIGURE, STARING SKYWARD...
TEN SECONDS MORE AND THE ZETA-BEAM WILL STRIKE! NINE--EIGHT--
A MOVEMENT TO ONE SIDE DRAWS HIS EYES TOWARD...
AN ALIEN! WHAT'S HE DOING HERE, STARING SO INTENTLY AT ME? CAN HE HAVE GUESSED MY SECRET IDENTITY ON EARTH?
BEFORE HE CAN SPEAK--THE ZETA-BEAM FROM THE PLANET RANN OF THE STAR-SUN ALPHA CENTAURI HITS ADAM STRANGE--AND TELEPORTS HIM, AS IT HAS SO OFTEN IN THE PAST, ACROSS 25 TRILLION MILES OF SPACE...
NO SOONER DOES THE GROUND OF HIS ADOPTED PLANET SETTLE UNDERFOOT THAN...
ADAM! HOW GOOD TO SEE--OHHH! WHO'S THAT?
I DON'T KNOW, ALANNA! I SAW HIM JUST BEFORE I LEFT EARTH! AND NOW HERE HE IS--ON RANN!
HE'S FADING AWAY! WHAT DID HE WANT? WHY DID HE KEEP STARING AT YOU?
YOUR GUESS IS AS GOOD AS MINE! BUT I'M NOT GOING TO WORRY ABOUT HIM, DARLING, NOW THAT I'M BACK WITH YOU!
I'M LOOKING FORWARD TO A GOOD TIME ON THIS VISIT--THAT IS, IF NO DANGERS HAVE DEVELOPED HERE WHILE I WAS BACK ON EARTH!
NONE AT ALL! AS A MATTER OF FACT--YOU'RE JUST IN TIME TO CELEBRATE WITH US THE FESTIVAL OF DYALINA!
2

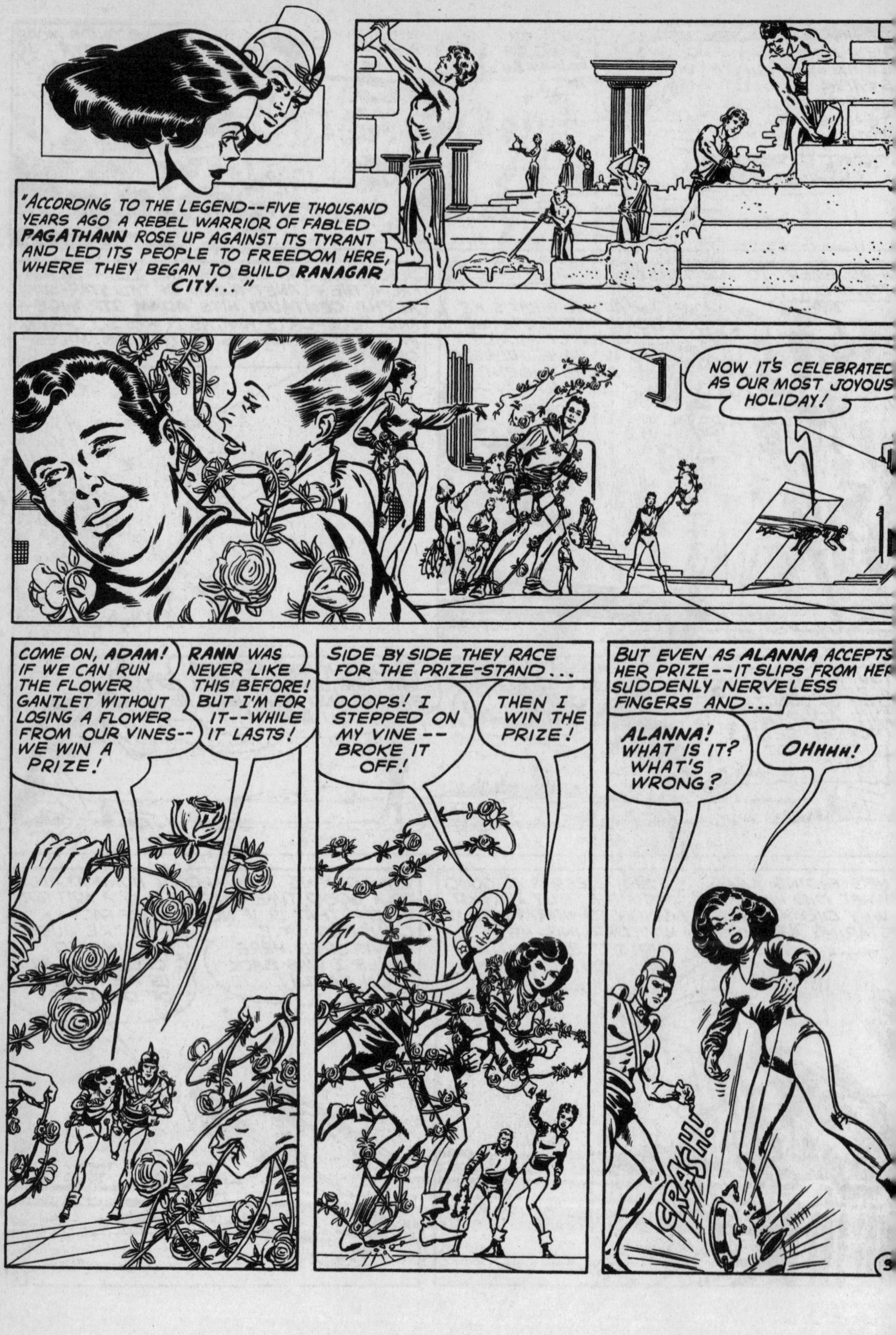
"ACCORDING TO THE LEGEND--FIVE THOUSAND YEARS AGO A REBEL WARRIOR OF FABLED PAGATHANN ROSE UP AGAINST ITS TYRANT AND LED ITS PEOPLE TO FREEDOM HERE, WHERE THEY BEGAN TO BUILD RANAGAR CITY..."
NOW IT'S CELEBRATED AS OUR MOST JOYOUS HOLIDAY!
COME ON, ADAM! IF WE CAN RUN THE FLOWER GANTLET WITHOUT LOSING A FLOWER FROM OUR VINES--WE WIN A PRIZE!
RANN WAS NEVER LIKE THIS BEFORE! BUT I'M FOR IT--WHILE IT LASTS!
SIDE BY SIDE THEY RACE FOR THE PRIZE-STAND...
OOOPS! I STEPPED ON MY VINE--BROKE IT OFF!
THEN I WIN THE PRIZE!
BUT EVEN AS ALANNA ACCEPTS HER PRIZE--IT SLIPS FROM HER SUDDENLY NERVELESS FINGERS AND...
ALANNA! WHAT IS IT? WHAT'S WRONG?
OHHHH!
CRASH!

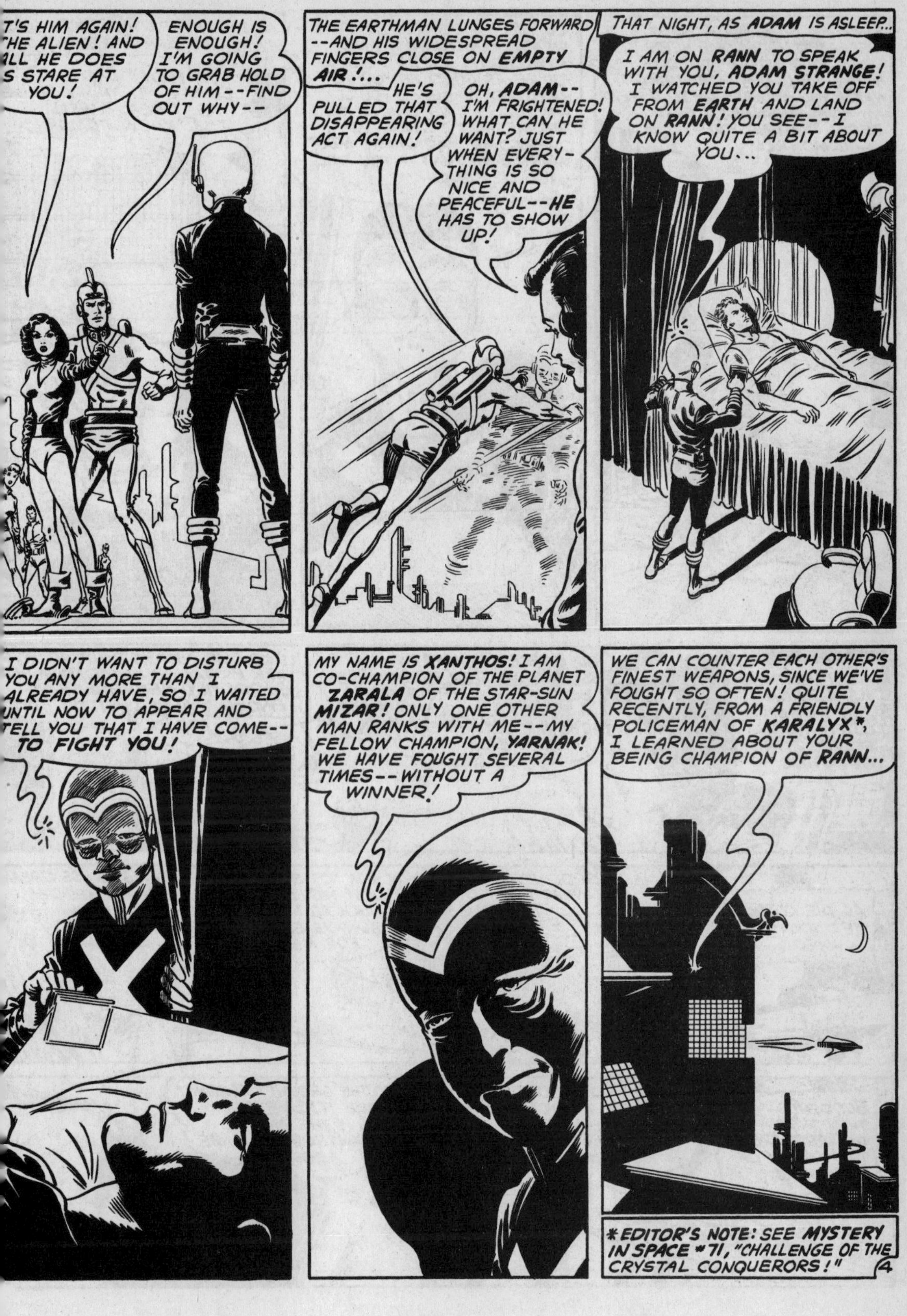
T'S HIM AGAIN! THE ALIEN! AND ALL HE DOES S STARE AT YOU!
ENOUGH IS ENOUGH! I'M GOING TO GRAB HOLD OF HIM--FIND OUT WHY--
THE EARTHMAN LUNGES FORWARD --AND HIS WIDESPREAD FINGERS CLOSE ON EMPTY AIR!...
HE'S PULLED THAT DISAPPEARING ACT AGAIN!
OH, ADAM-- I'M FRIGHTENED! WHAT CAN HE WANT? JUST WHEN EVERYTHING IS SO NICE AND PEACEFUL--HE HAS TO SHOW UP!
THAT NIGHT, AS ADAM IS ASLEEP...
I AM ON RANN TO SPEAK WITH YOU, ADAM STRANGE! I WATCHED YOU TAKE OFF FROM EARTH AND LAND ON RANN! YOU SEE--I KNOW QUITE A BIT ABOUT YOU...
I DIDN'T WANT TO DISTURB YOU ANY MORE THAN I ALREADY HAVE, SO I WAITED UNTIL NOW TO APPEAR AND TELL YOU THAT I HAVE COME-- TO FIGHT YOU!
MY NAME IS XANTHOS! I AM CO-CHAMPION OF THE PLANET ZARALA OF THE STAR-SUN MIZAR! ONLY ONE OTHER MAN RANKS WITH ME--MY FELLOW CHAMPION, YARNAK! WE HAVE FOUGHT SEVERAL TIMES--WITHOUT A WINNER!
WE CAN COUNTER EACH OTHER'S FINEST WEAPONS, SINCE WE'VE FOUGHT SO OFTEN! QUITE RECENTLY, FROM A FRIENDLY POLICEMAN OF KARALYX*, I LEARNED ABOUT YOUR BEING CHAMPION OF RANN...
*EDITOR'S NOTE: SEE MYSTERY IN SPACE #71, "CHALLENGE OF THE CRYSTAL CONQUERORS!"
4

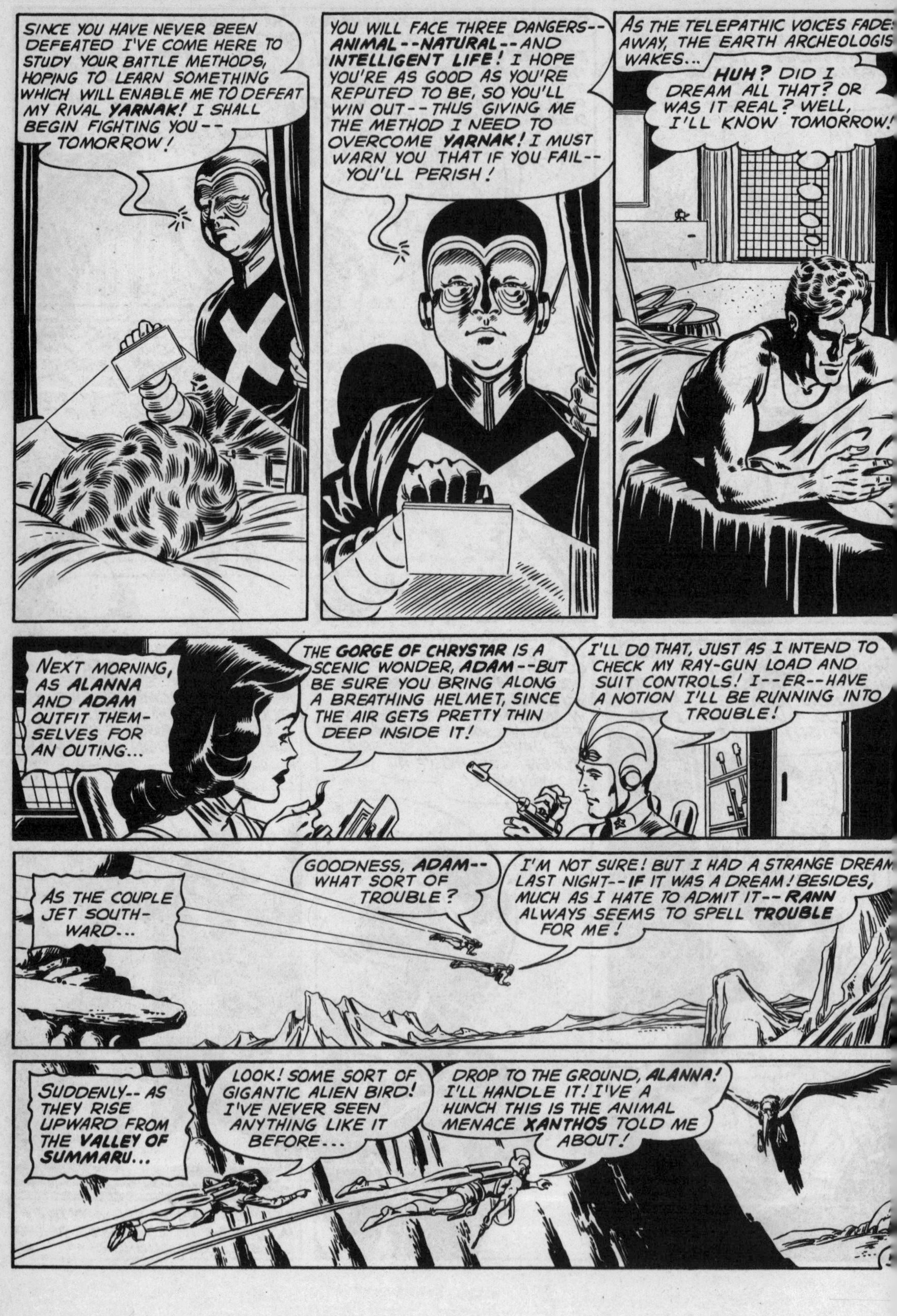
SINCE YOU HAVE NEVER BEEN DEFEATED I'VE COME HERE TO STUDY YOUR BATTLE METHODS, HOPING TO LEARN SOMETHING WHICH WILL ENABLE ME TO DEFEAT MY RIVAL YARNAK! I SHALL BEGIN FIGHTING YOU-- TOMORROW!
YOU WILL FACE THREE DANGERS-- ANIMAL--NATURAL--AND INTELLIGENT LIFE! I HOPE YOU'RE AS GOOD AS YOU'RE REPUTED TO BE, SO YOU'LL WIN OUT--THUS GIVING ME THE METHOD I NEED TO OVERCOME YARNAK! I MUST WARN YOU THAT IF YOU FAIL-- YOU'LL PERISH!
AS THE TELEPATHIC VOICES FADE AWAY, THE EARTH ARCHEOLOGIS WAKES...
HUH? DID I DREAM ALL THAT? OR WAS IT REAL? WELL, I'LL KNOW TOMORROW!
NEXT MORNING, AS ALANNA AND ADAM OUTFIT THEMSELVES FOR AN OUTING...
THE GORGE OF CHRYSTAR IS A SCENIC WONDER, ADAM--BUT BE SURE YOU BRING ALONG A BREATHING HELMET, SINCE THE AIR GETS PRETTY THIN DEEP INSIDE IT!
I'LL DO THAT, JUST AS I INTEND TO CHECK MY RAY-GUN LOAD AND SUIT CONTROLS! I--ER--HAVE A NOTION I'LL BE RUNNING INTO TROUBLE!
AS THE COUPLE JET SOUTHWARD...
GOODNESS, ADAM-- WHAT SORT OF TROUBLE?
I'M NOT SURE! BUT I HAD A STRANGE DREAM LAST NIGHT--IF IT WAS A DREAM! BESIDES, MUCH AS I HATE TO ADMIT IT--RANN ALWAYS SEEMS TO SPELL TROUBLE FOR ME!
SUDDENLY--AS THEY RISE UPWARD FROM THE VALLEY OF SUMMARU...
LOOK! SOME SORT OF GIGANTIC ALIEN BIRD! I'VE NEVER SEEN ANYTHING LIKE IT BEFORE...
DROP TO THE GROUND, ALANNA! I'LL HANDLE IT! I'VE A HUNCH THIS IS THE ANIMAL MENACE XANTHOS TOLD ME ABOUT!

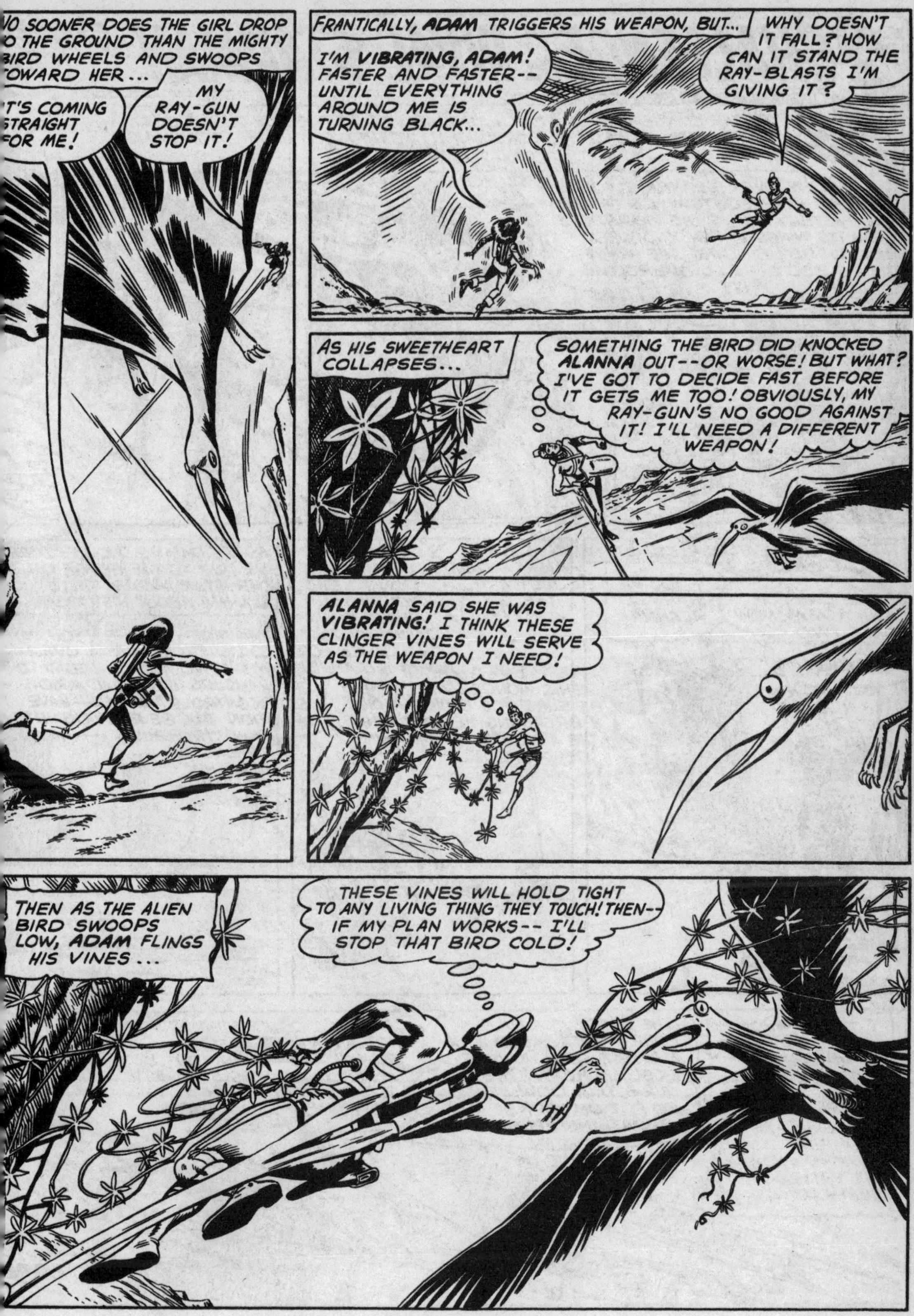
NO SOONER DOES THE GIRL DROP TO THE GROUND THAN THE MIGHTY BIRD WHEELS AND SWOOPS TOWARD HER...
IT'S COMING STRAIGHT FOR ME!
MY RAY-GUN DOESN'T STOP IT!
FRANTICALLY, ADAM TRIGGERS HIS WEAPON, BUT...
I'M VIBRATING, ADAM! FASTER AND FASTER-- UNTIL EVERYTHING AROUND ME IS TURNING BLACK...
WHY DOESN'T IT FALL? HOW CAN IT STAND THE RAY-BLASTS I'M GIVING IT?
AS HIS SWEETHEART COLLAPSES...
SOMETHING THE BIRD DID KNOCKED ALANNA OUT--OR WORSE! BUT WHAT? I'VE GOT TO DECIDE FAST BEFORE IT GETS ME TOO! OBVIOUSLY, MY RAY-GUN'S NO GOOD AGAINST IT! I'LL NEED A DIFFERENT WEAPON!
ALANNA SAID SHE WAS VIBRATING! I THINK THESE CLINGER VINES WILL SERVE AS THE WEAPON I NEED!
THEN AS THE ALIEN BIRD SWOOPS LOW, ADAM FLINGS HIS VINES...
THESE VINES WILL HOLD TIGHT TO ANY LIVING THING THEY TOUCH! THEN-- IF MY PLAN WORKS-- I'LL STOP THAT BIRD COLD!

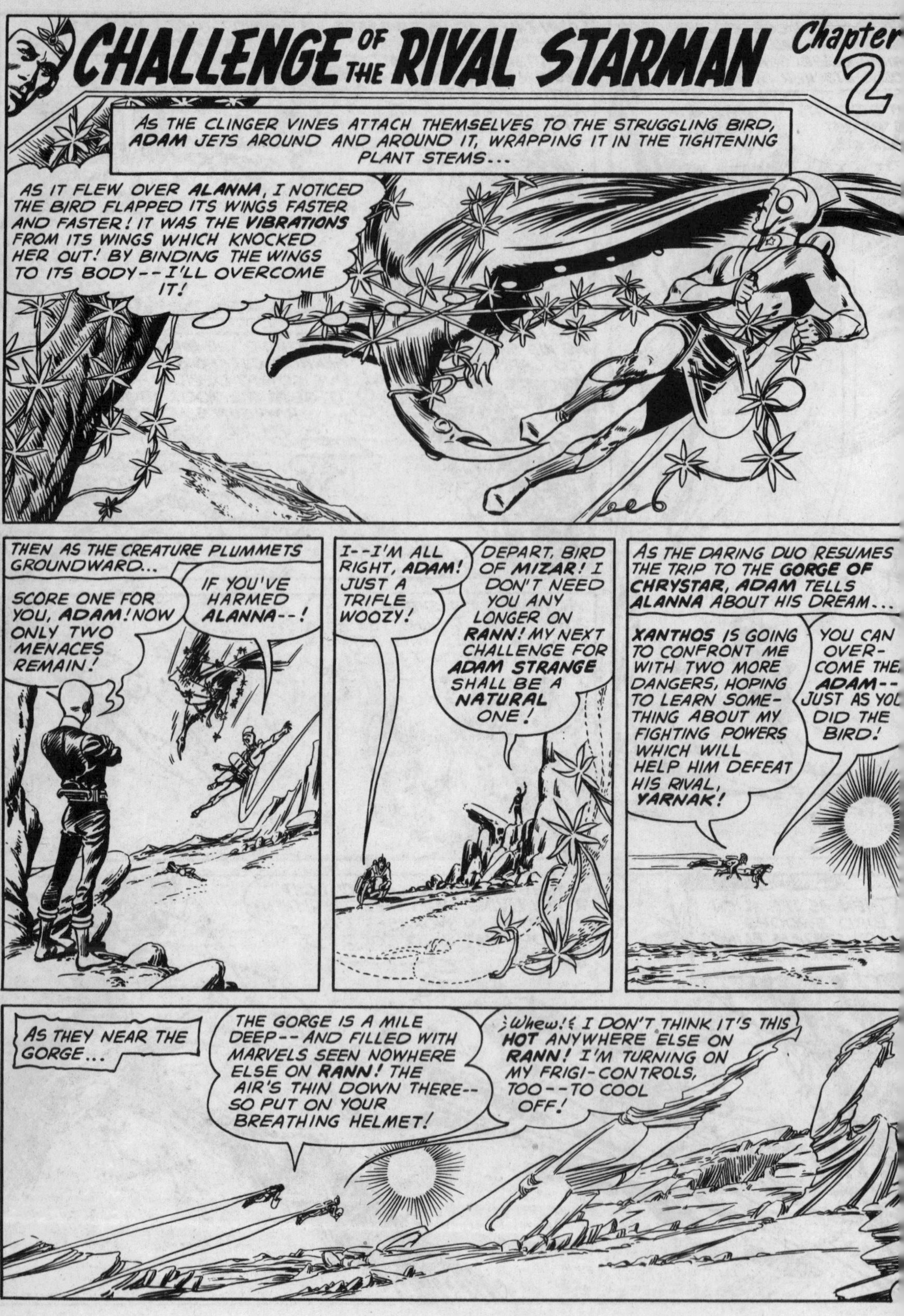
CHALLENGE OF THE RIVAL STARMAN
Chapter 2
AS THE CLINGER VINES ATTACH THEMSELVES TO THE STRUGGLING BIRD, ADAM JETS AROUND AND AROUND IT, WRAPPING IT IN THE TIGHTENING PLANT STEMS...
AS IT FLEW OVER ALANNA, I NOTICED THE BIRD FLAPPED ITS WINGS FASTER AND FASTER! IT WAS THE VIBRATIONS FROM ITS WINGS WHICH KNOCKED HER OUT! BY BINDING THE WINGS TO ITS BODY--I'LL OVERCOME IT!
THEN AS THE CREATURE PLUMMETS GROUNDWARD...
SCORE ONE FOR YOU, ADAM! NOW ONLY TWO MENACES REMAIN!
IF YOU'VE HARMED ALANNA--!
I--I'M ALL RIGHT, ADAM! JUST A TRIFLE WOOZY!
DEPART, BIRD OF MIZAR! I DON'T NEED YOU ANY LONGER ON RANN! MY NEXT CHALLENGE FOR ADAM STRANGE SHALL BE A NATURAL ONE!
AS THE DARING DUO RESUMES THE TRIP TO THE GORGE OF CHRYSTAR, ADAM TELLS ALANNA ABOUT HIS DREAM...
XANTHOS IS GOING TO CONFRONT ME WITH TWO MORE DANGERS, HOPING TO LEARN SOMETHING ABOUT MY FIGHTING POWERS WHICH WILL HELP HIM DEFEAT HIS RIVAL, YARNAK!
YOU CAN OVERCOME THE ADAM--JUST AS YOU DID THE BIRD!
AS THEY NEAR THE GORGE...
THE GORGE IS A MILE DEEP--AND FILLED WITH MARVELS SEEN NOWHERE ELSE ON RANN! THE AIR'S THIN DOWN THERE--SO PUT ON YOUR BREATHING HELMET!
Whew! I DON'T THINK IT'S THIS HOT ANYWHERE ELSE ON RANN! I'M TURNING ON MY FRIGI-CONTROLS, TOO--TO COOL OFF!

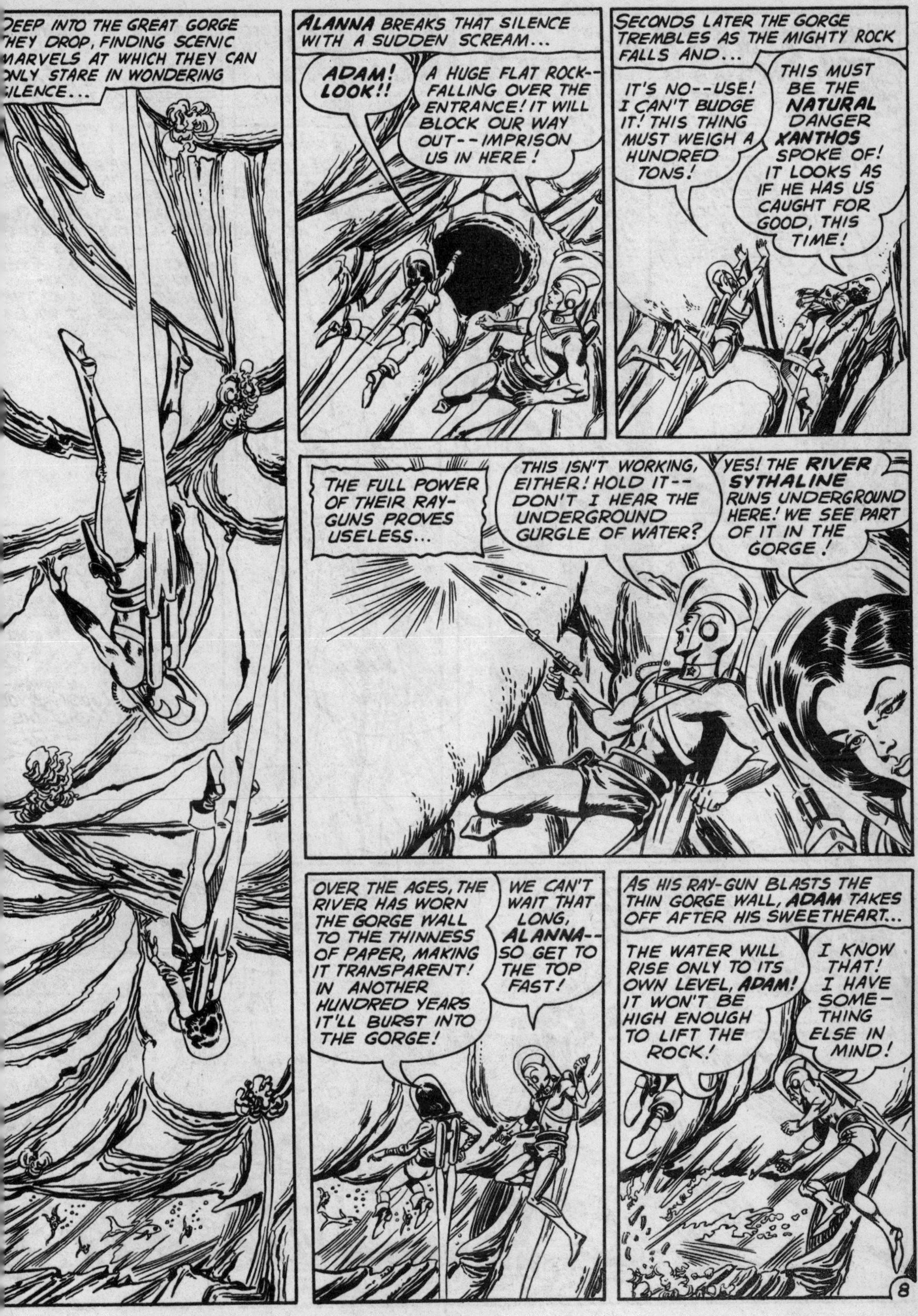
DEEP INTO THE GREAT GORGE THEY DROP, FINDING SCENIC MARVELS AT WHICH THEY CAN ONLY STARE IN WONDERING SILENCE...
ALANNA BREAKS THAT SILENCE WITH A SUDDEN SCREAM...
ADAM! LOOK!!
A HUGE FLAT ROCK--FALLING OVER THE ENTRANCE! IT WILL BLOCK OUR WAY OUT--IMPRISON US IN HERE!
SECONDS LATER THE GORGE TREMBLES AS THE MIGHTY ROCK FALLS AND...
IT'S NO--USE! I CAN'T BUDGE IT! THIS THING MUST WEIGH A HUNDRED TONS!
THIS MUST BE THE NATURAL DANGER XANTHOS SPOKE OF! IT LOOKS AS IF HE HAS US CAUGHT FOR GOOD, THIS TIME!
THE FULL POWER OF THEIR RAY-GUNS PROVES USELESS...
THIS ISN'T WORKING, EITHER! HOLD IT--DON'T I HEAR THE UNDERGROUND GURGLE OF WATER?
YES! THE RIVER SYTHALINE RUNS UNDERGROUND HERE! WE SEE PART OF IT IN THE GORGE!
OVER THE AGES, THE RIVER HAS WORN THE GORGE WALL TO THE THINNESS OF PAPER, MAKING IT TRANSPARENT! IN ANOTHER HUNDRED YEARS IT'LL BURST INTO THE GORGE!
WE CAN'T WAIT THAT LONG, ALANNA--SO GET TO THE TOP FAST!
AS HIS RAY-GUN BLASTS THE THIN GORGE WALL, ADAM TAKES OFF AFTER HIS SWEETHEART...
THE WATER WILL RISE ONLY TO ITS OWN LEVEL, ADAM! IT WON'T BE HIGH ENOUGH TO LIFT THE ROCK!
I KNOW THAT! I HAVE SOMETHING ELSE IN MIND!
8

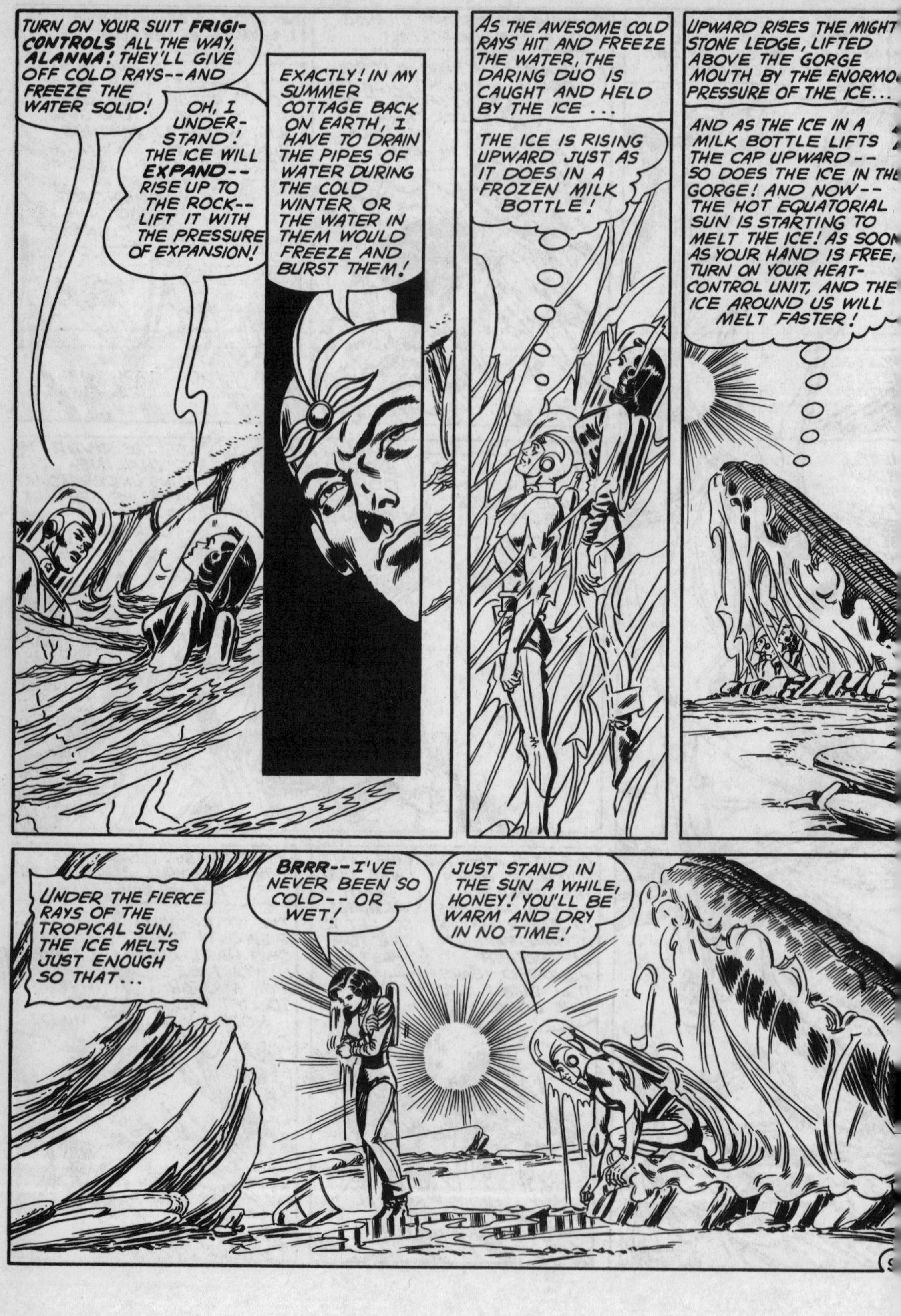
TURN ON YOUR SUIT FRIGI-CONTROLS ALL THE WAY, ALANNA! THEY'LL GIVE OFF COLD RAYS--AND FREEZE THE WATER SOLID!
OH, I UNDER-STAND! THE ICE WILL EXPAND--RISE UP TO THE ROCK--LIFT IT WITH THE PRESSURE OF EXPANSION!
EXACTLY! IN MY SUMMER COTTAGE BACK ON EARTH, I HAVE TO DRAIN THE PIPES OF WATER DURING THE COLD WINTER OR THE WATER IN THEM WOULD FREEZE AND BURST THEM!
AS THE AWESOME COLD RAYS HIT AND FREEZE THE WATER, THE DARING DUO IS CAUGHT AND HELD BY THE ICE ...
THE ICE IS RISING UPWARD JUST AS IT DOES IN A FROZEN MILK BOTTLE!
UPWARD RISES THE MIGHT STONE LEDGE, LIFTED ABOVE THE GORGE MOUTH BY THE ENORMO PRESSURE OF THE ICE...
AND AS THE ICE IN A MILK BOTTLE LIFTS THE CAP UPWARD--SO DOES THE ICE IN THE GORGE! AND NOW--THE HOT EQUATORIAL SUN IS STARTING TO MELT THE ICE! AS SOON AS YOUR HAND IS FREE, TURN ON YOUR HEAT-CONTROL UNIT, AND THE ICE AROUND US WILL MELT FASTER!
UNDER THE FIERCE RAYS OF THE TROPICAL SUN, THE ICE MELTS JUST ENOUGH SO THAT...
BRRR--I'VE NEVER BEEN SO COLD--OR WET!
JUST STAND IN THE SUN A WHILE, HONEY! YOU'LL BE WARM AND DRY IN NO TIME!

AS THEY STAND DRYING OUT...

SCORE TWO FOR YOU, **ADAM STRANGE!** NOW TO SEE HOW YOU DO AGAINST AN **INTELLIGENT** MENACE--IN A PERSONAL DUEL WITH ME!

YOU STAY HERE, **ALANNA!** I DON'T WANT ANY HARM TO COME TO YOU!

MOMENTS LATER, THE EARTHMAN JETS SKYWARD TO MEET HIS ANTAGONIST, WHO HAS RISEN INTO THE AIR WITH THE AID OF HIS ANTI-GRAVITY BELT...

HERE I COME, ADAM--FIRING MY FIRST WEAPON! IF ONE OF THOSE EXPANDING BLACK GLOBES HITS YOU-- YOU'RE FINISHED!

THEY'RE MOVING SO FAST-- I HAVE TIME FOR ONLY ONE SHOT! AND THEY'RE SO FAR APART-- I'LL NEVER HIT THEM ALL WITH JUST ONE BLAST!

TREMBLING WITH ANXIETY, **ALANNA** STARES SKYWARD...

¡OH! **ADAM** ALMOST MISSED HIS SHOT--BARELY HIT THE FIRST GLOBE A GLANCING BLOW! AND NOW--HE HAS NO TIME FOR ANOTHER SHOT!

BUT **ADAM** HAD NO INTENTION OF MAKING A DIRECT HIT! FOR EVEN AS HE WAS FIRING...

MY ONLY CHANCE IS TO MAKE CONTACT--BY APPLYING "ENGLISH" TO THE FIRST GLOBE!

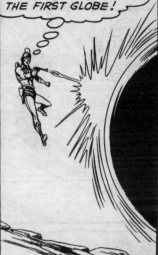

HIS RAKING SHOT HITS THE FIRST GLOBE-- DRIVES IT INTO THE SECOND AT AN ANGLE...

THE FACT THAT THEY **LOOK** LIKE **CUEBALLS**--GAVE ME THE INSPIRATION TO TRY STOPPING THEM--BY BOUNCING THEM OFF ONE ANOTHER!

10

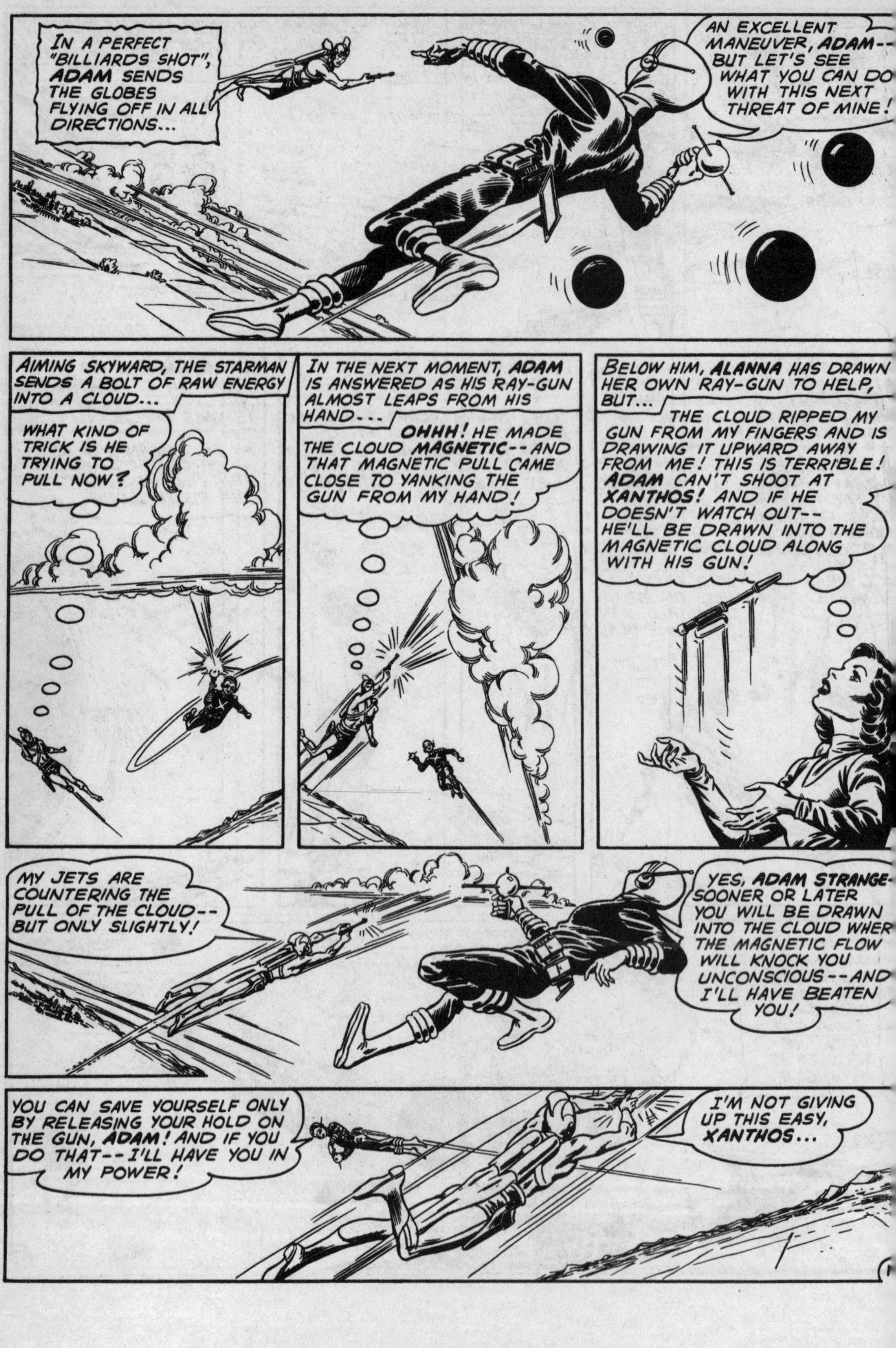
IN A PERFECT "BILLIARDS SHOT", ADAM SENDS THE GLOBES FLYING OFF IN ALL DIRECTIONS...
AN EXCELLENT MANEUVER, ADAM-- BUT LET'S SEE WHAT YOU CAN DO WITH THIS NEXT THREAT OF MINE!
AIMING SKYWARD, THE STARMAN SENDS A BOLT OF RAW ENERGY INTO A CLOUD...
WHAT KIND OF TRICK IS HE TRYING TO PULL NOW?
IN THE NEXT MOMENT, ADAM IS ANSWERED AS HIS RAY-GUN ALMOST LEAPS FROM HIS HAND...
OHHH! HE MADE THE CLOUD MAGNETIC--AND THAT MAGNETIC PULL CAME CLOSE TO YANKING THE GUN FROM MY HAND!
BELOW HIM, ALANNA HAS DRAWN HER OWN RAY-GUN TO HELP, BUT...
THE CLOUD RIPPED MY GUN FROM MY FINGERS AND IS DRAWING IT UPWARD AWAY FROM ME! THIS IS TERRIBLE! ADAM CAN'T SHOOT AT XANTHOS! AND IF HE DOESN'T WATCH OUT-- HE'LL BE DRAWN INTO THE MAGNETIC CLOUD ALONG WITH HIS GUN!
MY JETS ARE COUNTERING THE PULL OF THE CLOUD-- BUT ONLY SLIGHTLY!
YES, ADAM STRANGE- SOONER OR LATER YOU WILL BE DRAWN INTO THE CLOUD WHER THE MAGNETIC FLOW WILL KNOCK YOU UNCONSCIOUS--AND I'LL HAVE BEATEN YOU!
YOU CAN SAVE YOURSELF ONLY BY RELEASING YOUR HOLD ON THE GUN, ADAM! AND IF YOU DO THAT--I'LL HAVE YOU IN MY POWER!
I'M NOT GIVING UP THIS EASY, XANTHOS...

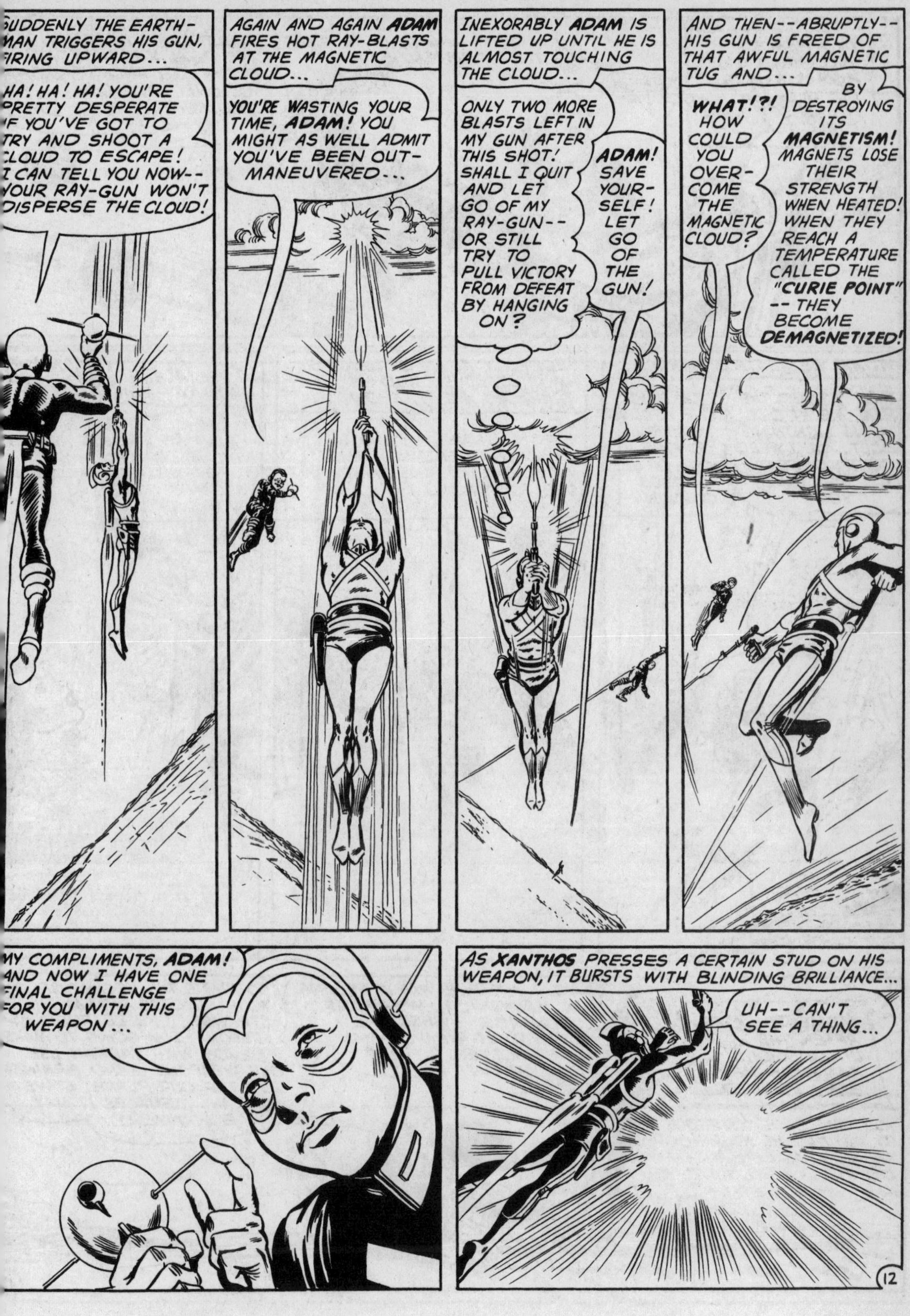
SUDDENLY THE EARTH-MAN TRIGGERS HIS GUN, FIRING UPWARD...
HA! HA! HA! YOU'RE PRETTY DESPERATE IF YOU'VE GOT TO TRY AND SHOOT A CLOUD TO ESCAPE! I CAN TELL YOU NOW--YOUR RAY-GUN WON'T DISPERSE THE CLOUD!
AGAIN AND AGAIN ADAM FIRES HOT RAY-BLASTS AT THE MAGNETIC CLOUD...
YOU'RE WASTING YOUR TIME, ADAM! YOU MIGHT AS WELL ADMIT YOU'VE BEEN OUT-MANEUVERED...
INEXORABLY ADAM IS LIFTED UP UNTIL HE IS ALMOST TOUCHING THE CLOUD...
ONLY TWO MORE BLASTS LEFT IN MY GUN AFTER THIS SHOT! SHALL I QUIT AND LET GO OF MY RAY-GUN--OR STILL TRY TO PULL VICTORY FROM DEFEAT BY HANGING ON?
ADAM! SAVE YOURSELF! LET GO OF THE GUN!
AND THEN--ABRUPTLY--HIS GUN IS FREED OF THAT AWFUL MAGNETIC TUG AND...
WHAT!?! HOW COULD YOU OVERCOME THE MAGNETIC CLOUD?
BY DESTROYING ITS MAGNETISM! MAGNETS LOSE THEIR STRENGTH WHEN HEATED! WHEN THEY REACH A TEMPERATURE CALLED THE "CURIE POINT" -- THEY BECOME DEMAGNETIZED!
MY COMPLIMENTS, ADAM! AND NOW I HAVE ONE FINAL CHALLENGE FOR YOU WITH THIS WEAPON...
AS XANTHOS PRESSES A CERTAIN STUD ON HIS WEAPON, IT BURSTS WITH BLINDING BRILLIANCE...
UH--CAN'T SEE A THING...
12

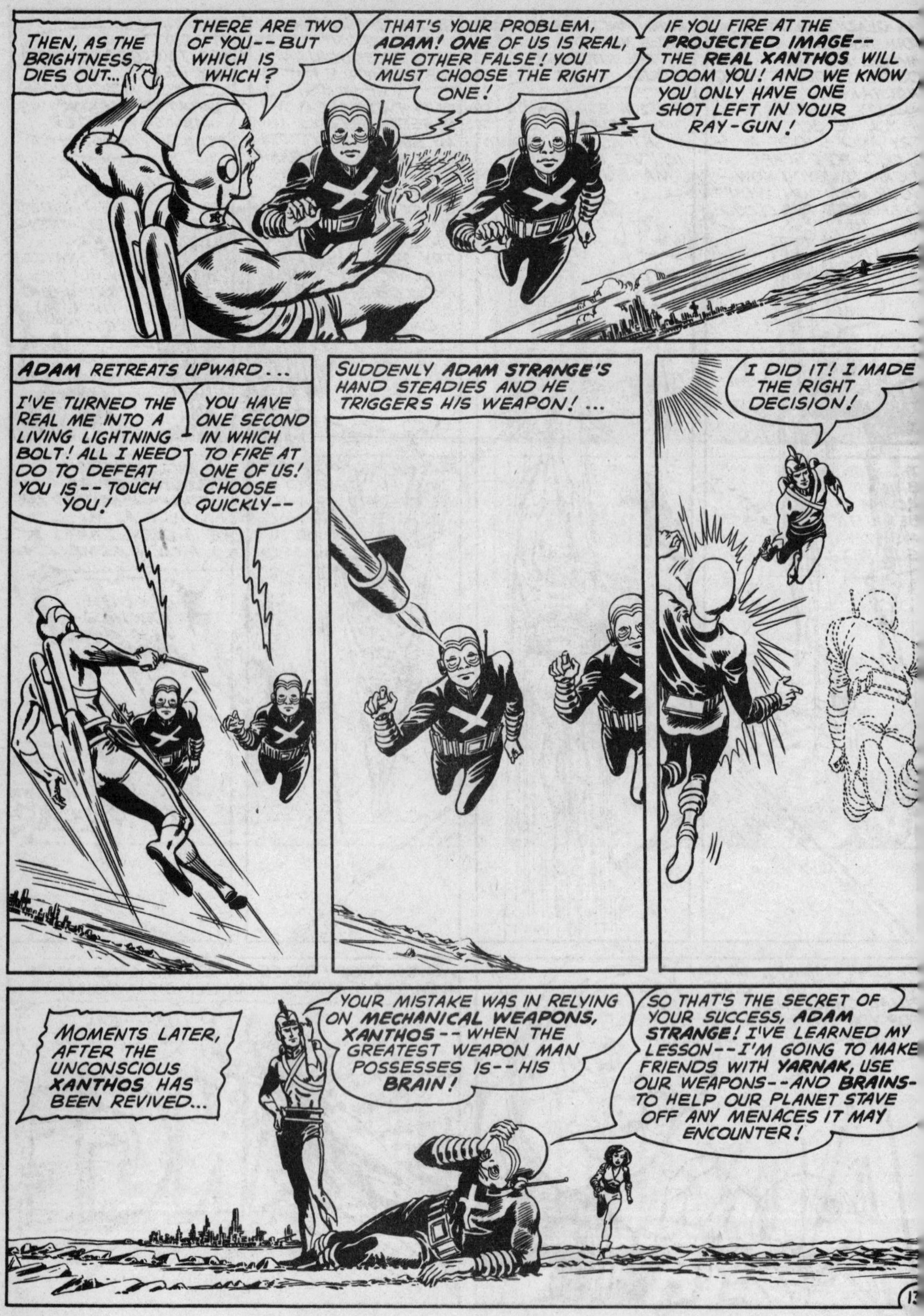
THEN, AS THE BRIGHTNESS DIES OUT...
THERE ARE TWO OF YOU--BUT WHICH IS WHICH?
THAT'S YOUR PROBLEM, ADAM! ONE OF US IS REAL, THE OTHER FALSE! YOU MUST CHOOSE THE RIGHT ONE!
IF YOU FIRE AT THE PROJECTED IMAGE--THE REAL XANTHOS WILL DOOM YOU! AND WE KNOW YOU ONLY HAVE ONE SHOT LEFT IN YOUR RAY-GUN!
ADAM RETREATS UPWARD...
I'VE TURNED THE REAL ME INTO A LIVING LIGHTNING BOLT! ALL I NEED DO TO DEFEAT YOU IS--TOUCH YOU!
YOU HAVE ONE SECOND IN WHICH TO FIRE AT ONE OF US! CHOOSE QUICKLY--
SUDDENLY ADAM STRANGE'S HAND STEADIES AND HE TRIGGERS HIS WEAPON! ...
I DID IT! I MADE THE RIGHT DECISION!
MOMENTS LATER, AFTER THE UNCONSCIOUS XANTHOS HAS BEEN REVIVED...
YOUR MISTAKE WAS IN RELYING ON MECHANICAL WEAPONS, XANTHOS--WHEN THE GREATEST WEAPON MAN POSSESSES IS--HIS BRAIN!
SO THAT'S THE SECRET OF YOUR SUCCESS, ADAM STRANGE! I'VE LEARNED MY LESSON--I'M GOING TO MAKE FRIENDS WITH YARNAK, USE OUR WEAPONS--AND BRAINS--TO HELP OUR PLANET STAVE OFF ANY MENACES IT MAY ENCOUNTER!

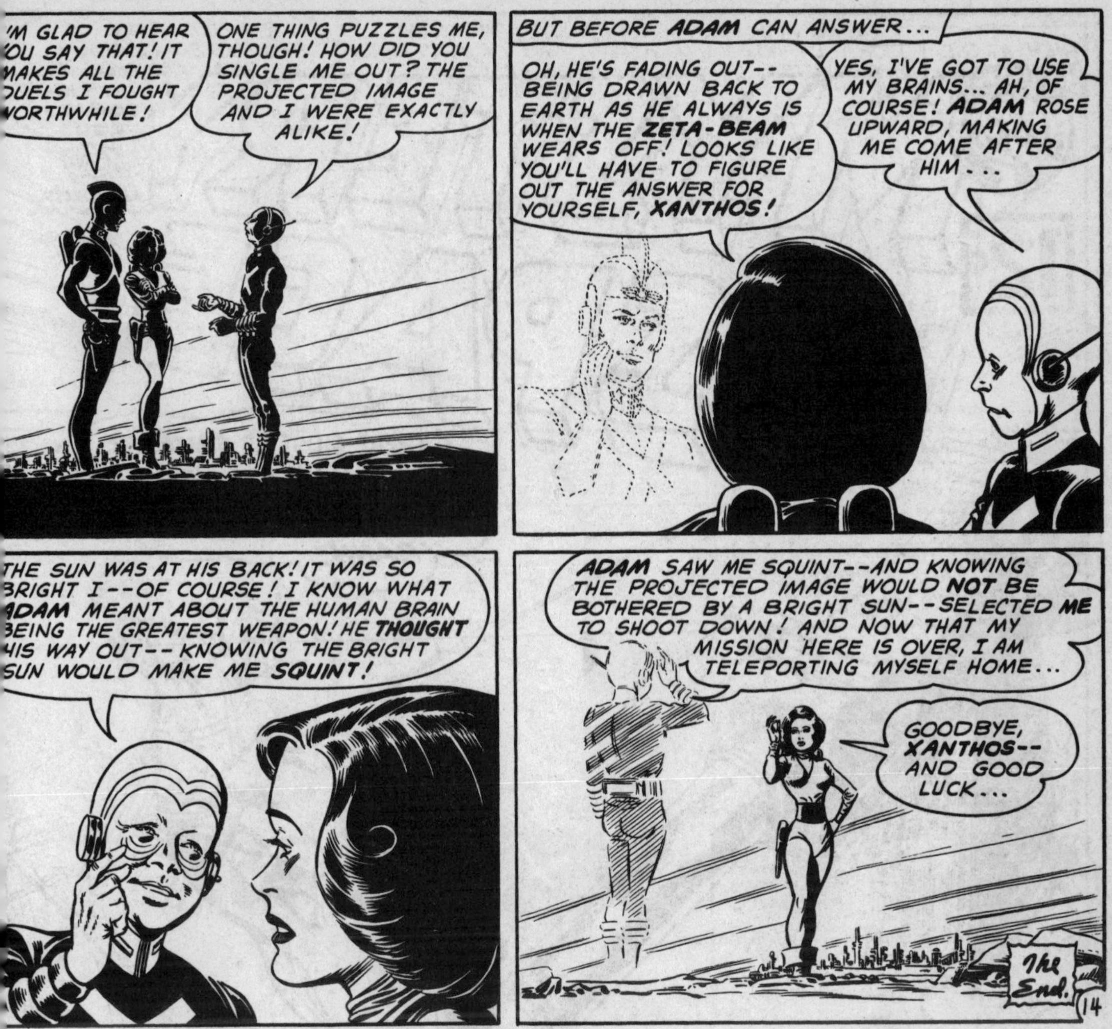

I'M GLAD TO HEAR YOU SAY THAT! IT MAKES ALL THE DUELS I FOUGHT WORTHWHILE!
ONE THING PUZZLES ME, THOUGH! HOW DID YOU SINGLE ME OUT? THE PROJECTED IMAGE AND I WERE EXACTLY ALIKE!
BUT BEFORE ADAM CAN ANSWER...
OH, HE'S FADING OUT-- BEING DRAWN BACK TO EARTH AS HE ALWAYS IS WHEN THE ZETA-BEAM WEARS OFF! LOOKS LIKE YOU'LL HAVE TO FIGURE OUT THE ANSWER FOR YOURSELF, XANTHOS!
YES, I'VE GOT TO USE MY BRAINS... AH, OF COURSE! ADAM ROSE UPWARD, MAKING ME COME AFTER HIM...
THE SUN WAS AT HIS BACK! IT WAS SO BRIGHT I--OF COURSE! I KNOW WHAT ADAM MEANT ABOUT THE HUMAN BRAIN BEING THE GREATEST WEAPON! HE THOUGHT HIS WAY OUT-- KNOWING THE BRIGHT SUN WOULD MAKE ME SQUINT!
ADAM SAW ME SQUINT--AND KNOWING THE PROJECTED IMAGE WOULD NOT BE BOTHERED BY A BRIGHT SUN--SELECTED ME TO SHOOT DOWN! AND NOW THAT MY MISSION HERE IS OVER, I AM TELEPORTING MYSELF HOME...
GOODBYE, XANTHOS-- AND GOOD LUCK...
The End.
14

ADAM STRANGE

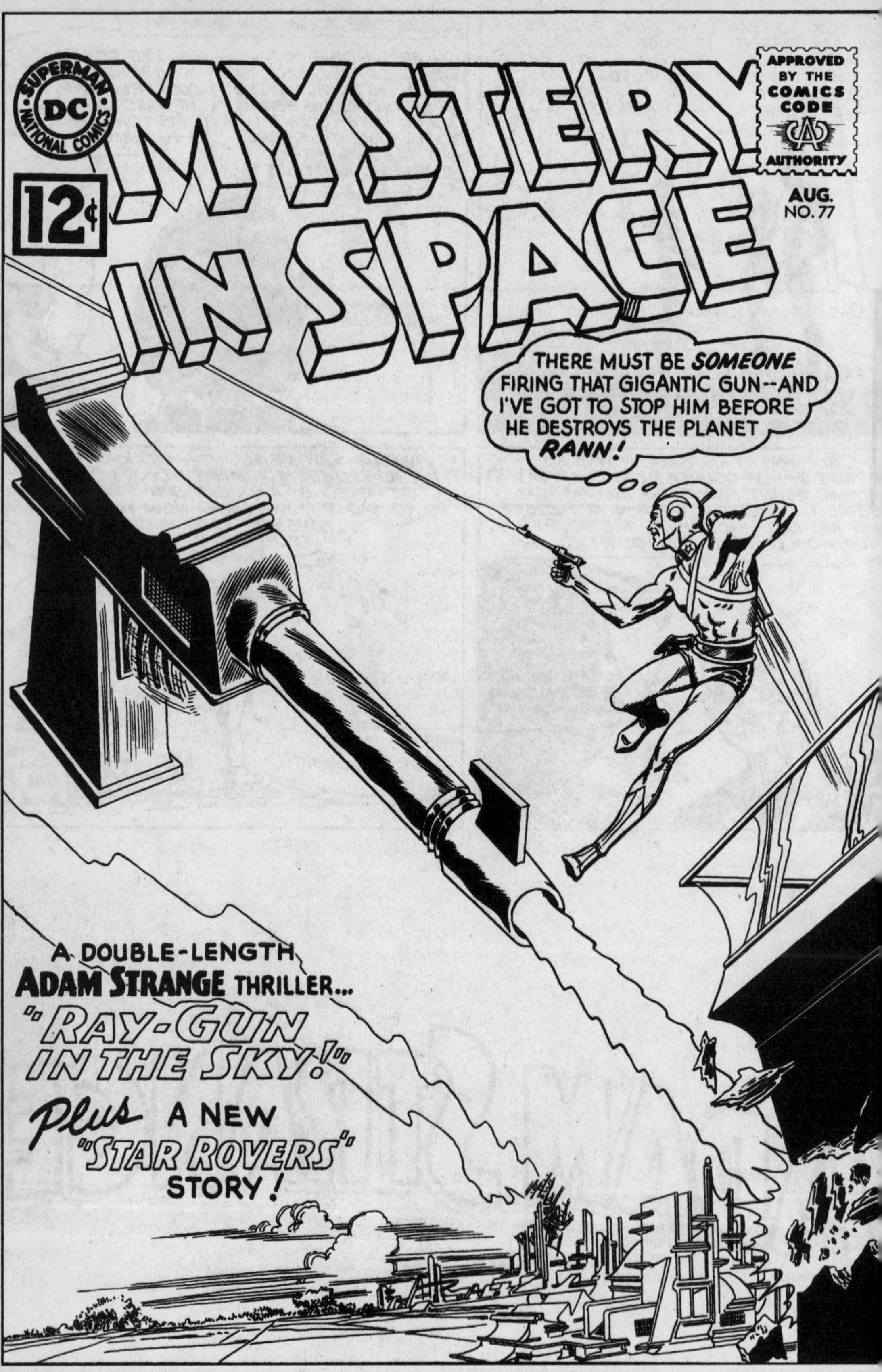
SUPERMAN DC NATIONAL COMICS
MYSTERY IN SPACE
APPROVED BY THE COMICS CODE AUTHORITY
12¢
AUG. NO. 77
THERE MUST BE SOMEONE FIRING THAT GIGANTIC GUN--AND I'VE GOT TO STOP HIM BEFORE HE DESTROYS THE PLANET RANN!
A DOUBLE-LENGTH ADAM STRANGE THRILLER...
"RAY-GUN IN THE SKY!"
Plus A NEW "STAR ROVERS" STORY!

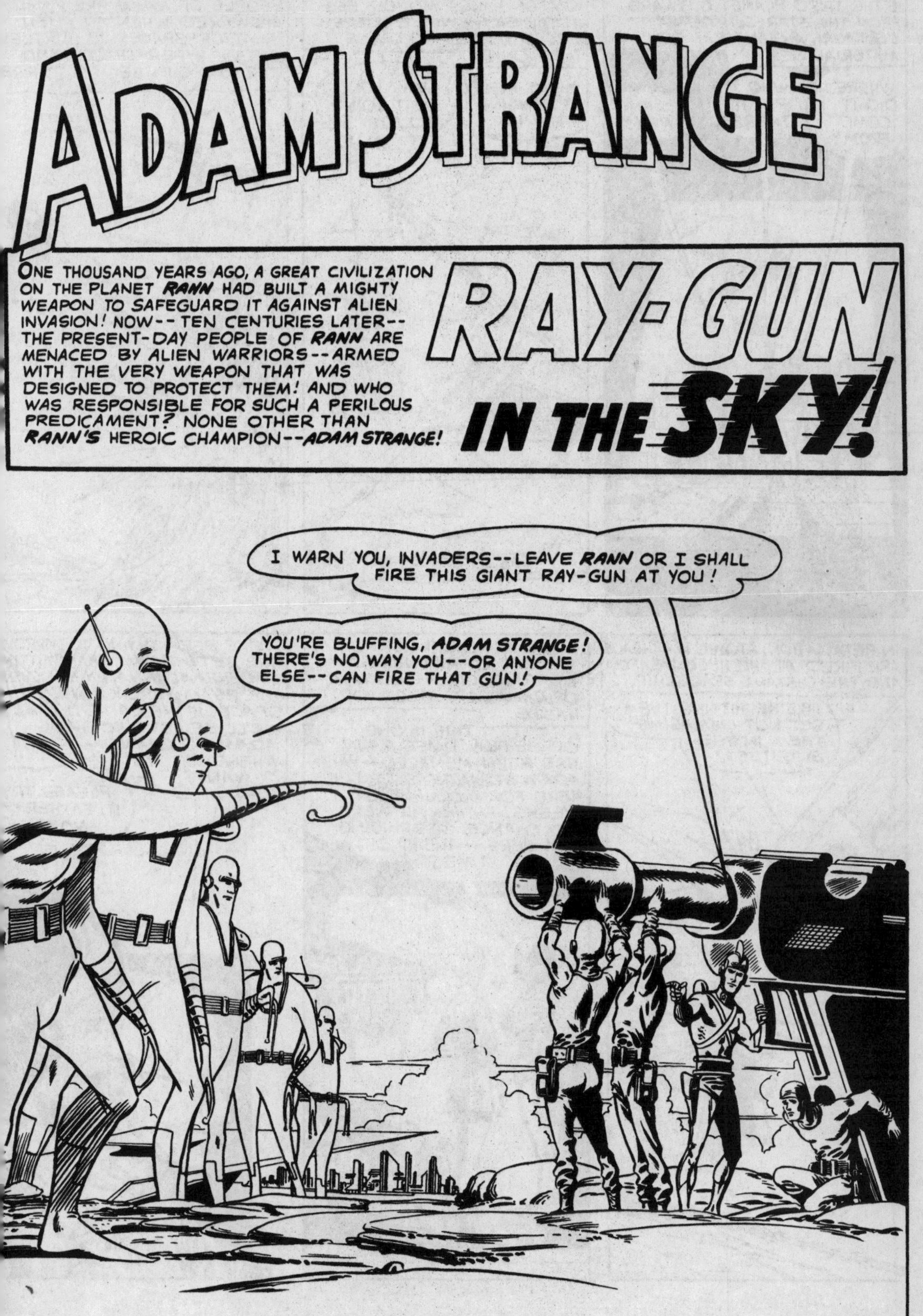
ADAM STRANGE
ONE THOUSAND YEARS AGO, A GREAT CIVILIZATION ON THE PLANET RANN HAD BUILT A MIGHTY WEAPON TO SAFEGUARD IT AGAINST ALIEN INVASION! NOW--TEN CENTURIES LATER--THE PRESENT-DAY PEOPLE OF RANN ARE MENACED BY ALIEN WARRIORS--ARMED WITH THE VERY WEAPON THAT WAS DESIGNED TO PROTECT THEM! AND WHO WAS RESPONSIBLE FOR SUCH A PERILOUS PREDICAMENT? NONE OTHER THAN RANN'S HEROIC CHAMPION--ADAM STRANGE!
RAY-GUN IN THE SKY!
I WARN YOU, INVADERS--LEAVE RANN OR I SHALL FIRE THIS GIANT RAY-GUN AT YOU!
YOU'RE BLUFFING, ADAM STRANGE! THERE'S NO WAY YOU--OR ANYONE ELSE--CAN FIRE THAT GUN!

ABOVE THE PLANET *RANN*, WHICH IS THE THIRD PLANET OUTWARD FROM THE STAR-SUN *ALPHA CENTAURI*, A GIANT RAY-GUN MATERIALIZES...

WHERE DID IT COME FROM?

WHO PUT IT THERE?

--AND WHY?

FOR SEVERAL DAYS THE GREAT WEAPON HANGS MOTIONLESS IN THE SKY-- WHILE FLIERS CIRCLE IT, KEEPING CLOSE TABS ON IT...

WHAT KEEPS IT HANGING THERE?

HOW LONG IS IT GOING TO STAY?

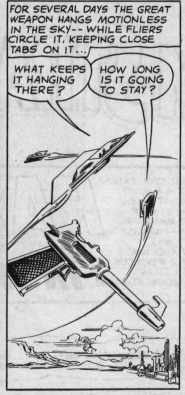

THE QUESTIONS OF THE PUZZLED PEOPLE OF *RANN* ARE FINALLY ANSWERED WHEN AN ALIEN "FLATTOP" SPACESHIP HURTLES OUT OF HYPER-SPACE--AND THE RAY-GUN BEGINS TO FIRE!

IN RETALIATION, ATOMIC WARHEADS ARE FIRED AT THE HUGE WEAPON AND THE DISTANT SPACESHIP...

WE'RE HITTING THEM-- BUT NOT DAMAGING THEM IN THE SLIGHTEST!

WHILE IN A LABORATORY OF THE CITY OF *RANAGAR*, A WORRIED GIRL-- *ALANNA OF RANAGAR*--BEGS FOR HASTE...

THIS IS ONE OF THE FEW TIMES *RANN* HAS BEEN MENACED--WHEN *ADAM STRANGE* ISN'T DUE HERE FOR A COUPLE OF WEEKS! FATHER, IS THERE ANY CHANCE OF BRINGING HIM HERE-- AHEAD OF TIME?

WE'VE BEEN TRYING TO IMPROVE THE *ZETA-BEAM* TRANSMITTING MACHINE, *ALANNA*, BY SENDING THE BEAM THROUGH HYPER-SPACE! IF WE CAN DO THAT, WE'LL BE ABLE TO BRING *ADAM* TO *RANN* WHENEVER WE WANT!

PLEASE TRY IT, FATHER-- NOW!

WE MUST GET *ADAM* HERE AT ONCE TO STOP THAT GREAT RAY-GUN! OTHERWISE THE ALIENS WILL DESTROY ALL *RANN!* ALREADY THEY'VE DEMOLISHED THE *ALDAVIAN HILLS!*

I AGREE! WE MUST MAKE THE ATTEMPT!

OUR MAIN CONCERN IS THAT RADIATION WHICH EXISTS IN *NORMAL SPACE* AND WHICH TRANSFORMS THE *ZETA-BEAM*--MAY NOT EXIST IN *HYPER-SPACE!* WE'LL SOON KNOW...

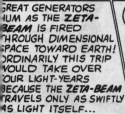

GREAT GENERATORS HUM AS THE *ZETA-BEAM* IS FIRED THROUGH DIMENSIONAL SPACE TOWARD EARTH! ORDINARILY THIS TRIP WOULD TAKE OVER FOUR LIGHT-YEARS BECAUSE THE *ZETA-BEAM* TRAVELS ONLY AS SWIFTLY AS LIGHT ITSELF...

WE EXAMINED *ADAM* WHEN HE WAS ON *RANN* TO FIGHT *KANJAR-RO** AND GEARED THE *ZETA-BEAM* TO SEEK HIM OUT NO MATTER WHERE HE IS ON EARTH!

OHH, I JUST HOPE IT WORKS!

**EDITOR'S NOTE:* SEE *MYSTERY IN SPACE #75* "PLANET THAT CAME TO A STANDSTILL!"

AT THIS MOMENT ON A NEW YORK CITY STREET...

OH-OH! THERE'S THAT SAME OFFICER I SAW JUST BEFORE THE FUTURE PEOPLE OF *RANN* TELEPORTED ME TO HELP FIGHT THE *MULTIPLE MENACE WEAPON!**

**EDITOR'S NOTE:* SEE *MYSTERY IN SPACE #72.*

SAY, HAVEN'T I SEEN YOU BEFORE? OF COURSE, YOU'RE THE MAN WHO SUDDENLY DISAPPEARED, LEAVING YOUR CAR STANDING HERE! HOW IN THUNDER DID YOU DO IT?

I'M AN ARCHEOLOGIST, OFFICER! IT'S A LONG STORY BUT--ER--I WAS TRANSPORTING SOME ANCIENT CHALDEAN MAGICIANS' ARTIFACTS AND--ER--ONE OF THEM MUST'VE WORKED THEIR MAGIC ON ME...

I MUST KEEP MY TELEPORTATION TRAVEL TO *RANN* A SECRET...

WELL, SEE THAT YOU DON'T LET IT HAPPEN--*HUH?* FOR PETE'S SAKE--HE'S GONE--PULLED THAT DISAPPEARING ACT AGAIN!

3

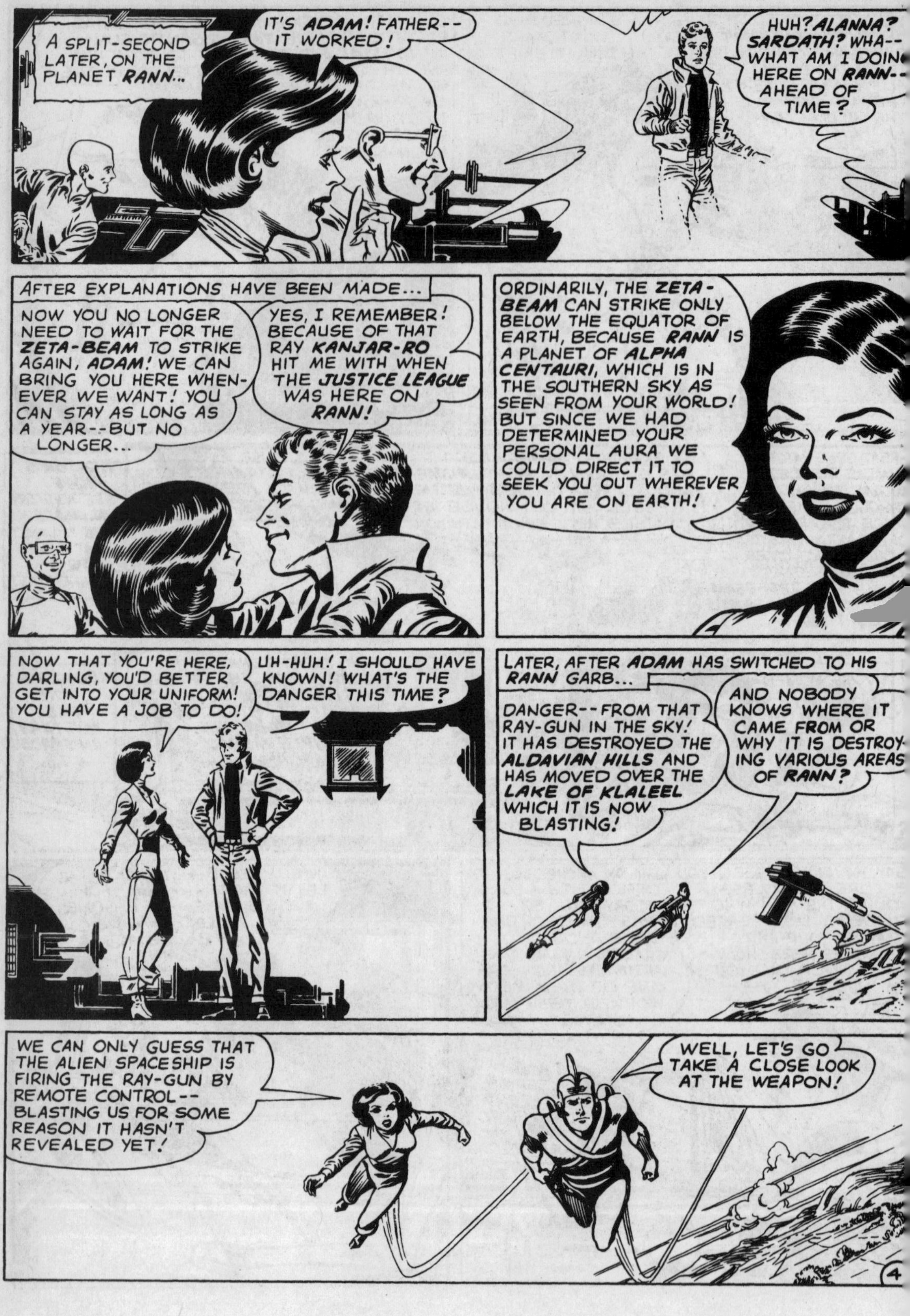
A SPLIT-SECOND LATER, ON THE PLANET RANN...
IT'S ADAM! FATHER-- IT WORKED!
HUH? ALANNA? SARDATH? WHA-- WHAT AM I DOING HERE ON RANN-- AHEAD OF TIME?
AFTER EXPLANATIONS HAVE BEEN MADE...
NOW YOU NO LONGER NEED TO WAIT FOR THE ZETA-BEAM TO STRIKE AGAIN, ADAM! WE CAN BRING YOU HERE WHENEVER WE WANT! YOU CAN STAY AS LONG AS A YEAR--BUT NO LONGER...
YES, I REMEMBER! BECAUSE OF THAT RAY KANJAR-RO HIT ME WITH WHEN THE JUSTICE LEAGUE WAS HERE ON RANN!
ORDINARILY, THE ZETA-BEAM CAN STRIKE ONLY BELOW THE EQUATOR OF EARTH, BECAUSE RANN IS A PLANET OF ALPHA CENTAURI, WHICH IS IN THE SOUTHERN SKY AS SEEN FROM YOUR WORLD! BUT SINCE WE HAD DETERMINED YOUR PERSONAL AURA WE COULD DIRECT IT TO SEEK YOU OUT WHEREVER YOU ARE ON EARTH!
NOW THAT YOU'RE HERE, DARLING, YOU'D BETTER GET INTO YOUR UNIFORM! YOU HAVE A JOB TO DO!
UH-HUH! I SHOULD HAVE KNOWN! WHAT'S THE DANGER THIS TIME?
LATER, AFTER ADAM HAS SWITCHED TO HIS RANN GARB...
DANGER--FROM THAT RAY-GUN IN THE SKY! IT HAS DESTROYED THE ALDAVIAN HILLS AND HAS MOVED OVER THE LAKE OF KLALEEL WHICH IT IS NOW BLASTING!
AND NOBODY KNOWS WHERE IT CAME FROM OR WHY IT IS DESTROYING VARIOUS AREAS OF RANN?
WE CAN ONLY GUESS THAT THE ALIEN SPACESHIP IS FIRING THE RAY-GUN BY REMOTE CONTROL-- BLASTING US FOR SOME REASON IT HASN'T REVEALED YET!
WELL, LET'S GO TAKE A CLOSE LOOK AT THE WEAPON!
4

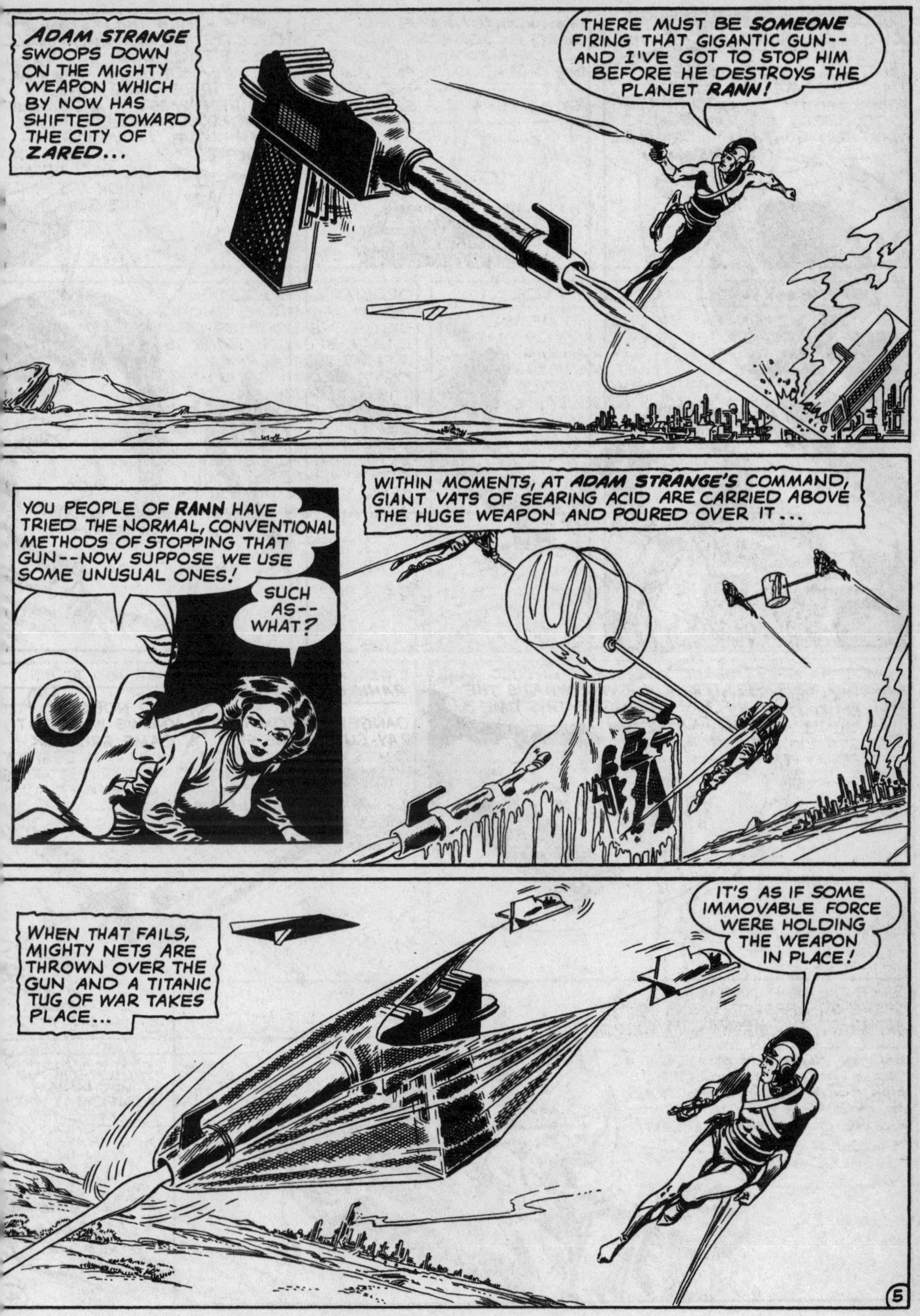
ADAM STRANGE SWOOPS DOWN ON THE MIGHTY WEAPON WHICH BY NOW HAS SHIFTED TOWARD THE CITY OF ZARED...
THERE MUST BE SOMEONE FIRING THAT GIGANTIC GUN--AND I'VE GOT TO STOP HIM BEFORE HE DESTROYS THE PLANET RANN!
YOU PEOPLE OF RANN HAVE TRIED THE NORMAL, CONVENTIONAL METHODS OF STOPPING THAT GUN--NOW SUPPOSE WE USE SOME UNUSUAL ONES!
SUCH AS--WHAT?
WITHIN MOMENTS, AT ADAM STRANGE'S COMMAND, GIANT VATS OF SEARING ACID ARE CARRIED ABOVE THE HUGE WEAPON AND POURED OVER IT...
WHEN THAT FAILS, MIGHTY NETS ARE THROWN OVER THE GUN AND A TITANIC TUG OF WAR TAKES PLACE...
IT'S AS IF SOME IMMOVABLE FORCE WERE HOLDING THE WEAPON IN PLACE!
5

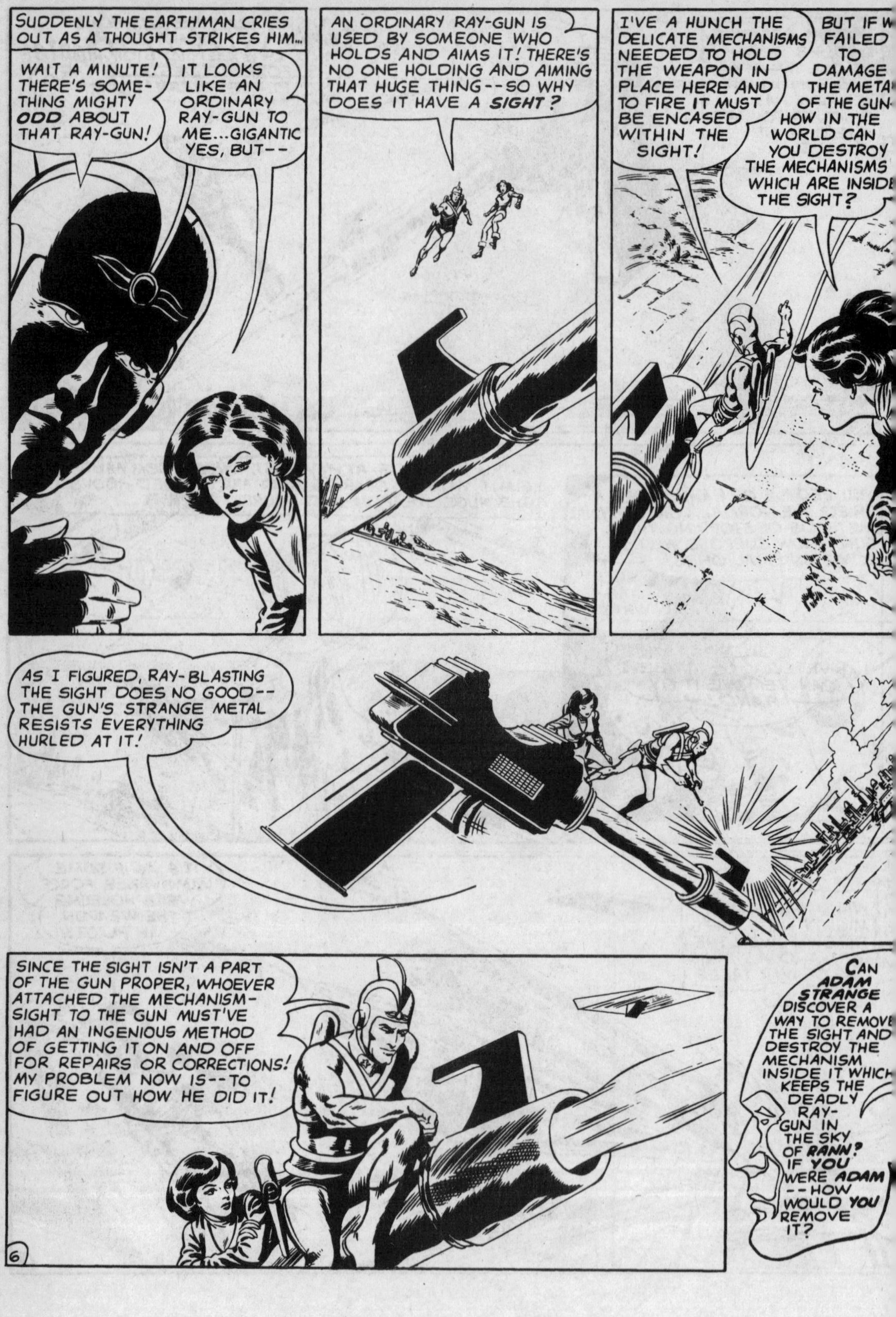
SUDDENLY THE EARTHMAN CRIES OUT AS A THOUGHT STRIKES HIM...
WAIT A MINUTE! THERE'S SOMETHING MIGHTY ODD ABOUT THAT RAY-GUN!
IT LOOKS LIKE AN ORDINARY RAY-GUN TO ME...GIGANTIC YES, BUT--
AN ORDINARY RAY-GUN IS USED BY SOMEONE WHO HOLDS AND AIMS IT! THERE'S NO ONE HOLDING AND AIMING THAT HUGE THING--SO WHY DOES IT HAVE A SIGHT?
I'VE A HUNCH THE DELICATE MECHANISMS NEEDED TO HOLD THE WEAPON IN PLACE HERE AND TO FIRE IT MUST BE ENCASED WITHIN THE SIGHT!
BUT IF W FAILED TO DAMAGE THE META OF THE GUN HOW IN THE WORLD CAN YOU DESTROY THE MECHANISMS WHICH ARE INSID THE SIGHT?
AS I FIGURED, RAY-BLASTING THE SIGHT DOES NO GOOD--THE GUN'S STRANGE METAL RESISTS EVERYTHING HURLED AT IT!
SINCE THE SIGHT ISN'T A PART OF THE GUN PROPER, WHOEVER ATTACHED THE MECHANISM-SIGHT TO THE GUN MUST'VE HAD AN INGENIOUS METHOD OF GETTING IT ON AND OFF FOR REPAIRS OR CORRECTIONS! MY PROBLEM NOW IS--TO FIGURE OUT HOW HE DID IT!
6
CAN ADAM STRANGE DISCOVER A WAY TO REMOVE THE SIGHT AND DESTROY THE MECHANISM INSIDE IT WHICH KEEPS THE DEADLY RAY-GUN IN THE SKY OF RANN? IF YOU WERE ADAM--HOW WOULD YOU REMOVE IT?

RAY-GUN IN THE SKY

Chapter 2

FIRST I'LL TRY BRUTE FORCE TO TRY AND KNOCK THE SIGHT OUT OF THE SLOT INTO WHICH IT FITS SO TIGHTLY!

IT DOESN'T WORK, ADAM! YOU'LL HAVE TO TRY SOMETHING ELSE!

SINCE THE SIGHT ISN'T RIVETED ON--MAYBE I CAN REMOVE IT BY HAND!

HE CAN'T BE SERIOUS-- YET WHY IS HE TAKING OFF HIS GLOVES?!

NOW WATCH AS I PLACE MY BARE HANDS ON THE MUZZLE OF THE GUN ON EITHER SIDE OF THE SIGHT! IF I'VE FIGURED THIS RIGHT, THE HEAT FROM MY HANDS WILL EXPAND THE METAL OF THE MUZZLE...

AT THE SAME TIME I'LL BLOW COLD AIR ON THE SIGHT ITSELF--TO MAKE ITS METAL CONTRACT!

THEN I REACH OUT SWIFTLY WHILE THE BARREL IS EXPANDED AND THE SIGHT CONTRACTED--AND YANK THE SIGHT FROM THE SLOT INTO WHICH IT FITS!

7

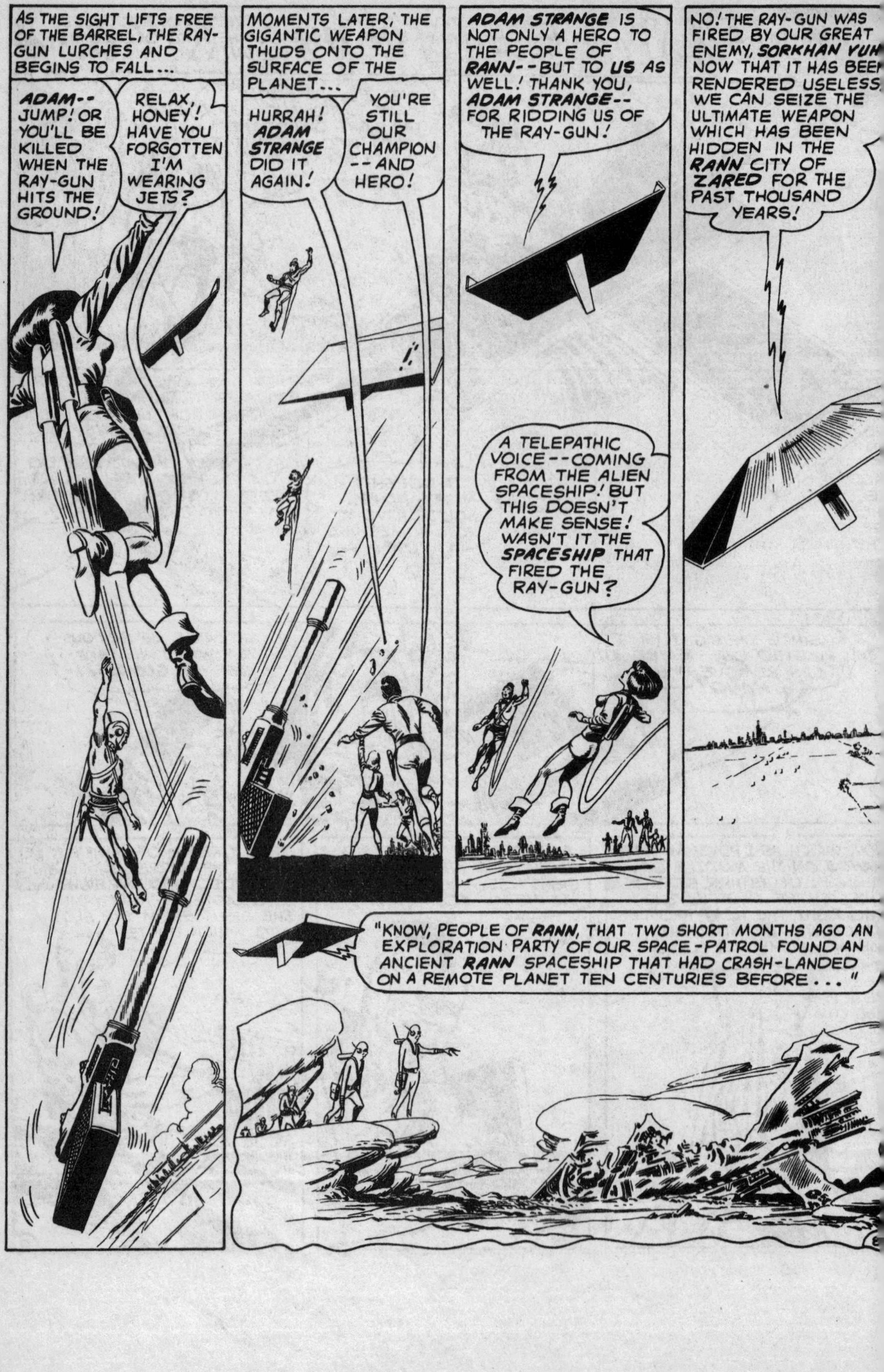
AS THE SIGHT LIFTS FREE OF THE BARREL, THE RAY-GUN LURCHES AND BEGINS TO FALL...
ADAM--JUMP! OR YOU'LL BE KILLED WHEN THE RAY-GUN HITS THE GROUND!
RELAX, HONEY! HAVE YOU FORGOTTEN I'M WEARING JETS?
MOMENTS LATER, THE GIGANTIC WEAPON THUDS ONTO THE SURFACE OF THE PLANET...
HURRAH! ADAM STRANGE DID IT AGAIN!
YOU'RE STILL OUR CHAMPION--AND HERO!
ADAM STRANGE IS NOT ONLY A HERO TO THE PEOPLE OF RANN--BUT TO US AS WELL! THANK YOU, ADAM STRANGE--FOR RIDDING US OF THE RAY-GUN!
A TELEPATHIC VOICE--COMING FROM THE ALIEN SPACESHIP! BUT THIS DOESN'T MAKE SENSE! WASN'T IT THE SPACESHIP THAT FIRED THE RAY-GUN?
NO! THE RAY-GUN WAS FIRED BY OUR GREAT ENEMY, SORKHAN YUH NOW THAT IT HAS BEEN RENDERED USELESS, WE CAN SEIZE THE ULTIMATE WEAPON WHICH HAS BEEN HIDDEN IN THE RANN CITY OF ZARED FOR THE PAST THOUSAND YEARS!
"KNOW, PEOPLE OF RANN, THAT TWO SHORT MONTHS AGO AN EXPLORATION PARTY OF OUR SPACE-PATROL FOUND AN ANCIENT RANN SPACESHIP THAT HAD CRASH-LANDED ON A REMOTE PLANET TEN CENTURIES BEFORE..."

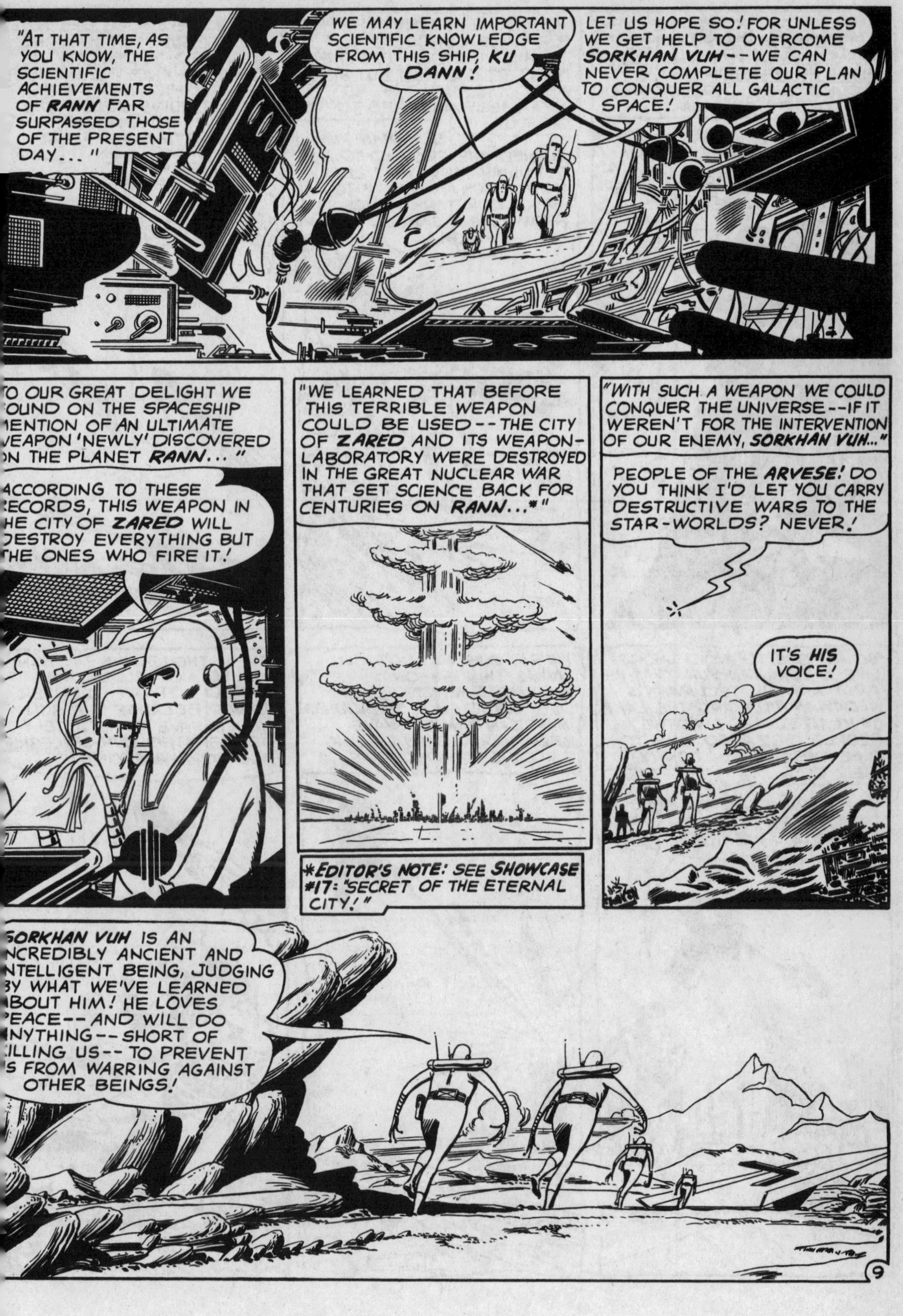
"AT THAT TIME, AS YOU KNOW, THE SCIENTIFIC ACHIEVEMENTS OF RANN FAR SURPASSED THOSE OF THE PRESENT DAY..."
WE MAY LEARN IMPORTANT SCIENTIFIC KNOWLEDGE FROM THIS SHIP, KU DANN!
LET US HOPE SO! FOR UNLESS WE GET HELP TO OVERCOME SORKHAN VUH--WE CAN NEVER COMPLETE OUR PLAN TO CONQUER ALL GALACTIC SPACE!
TO OUR GREAT DELIGHT WE FOUND ON THE SPACESHIP MENTION OF AN ULTIMATE WEAPON 'NEWLY' DISCOVERED ON THE PLANET RANN..."
ACCORDING TO THESE RECORDS, THIS WEAPON IN THE CITY OF ZARED WILL DESTROY EVERYTHING BUT THE ONES WHO FIRE IT!
"WE LEARNED THAT BEFORE THIS TERRIBLE WEAPON COULD BE USED--THE CITY OF ZARED AND ITS WEAPON-LABORATORY WERE DESTROYED IN THE GREAT NUCLEAR WAR THAT SET SCIENCE BACK FOR CENTURIES ON RANN...*"
*EDITOR'S NOTE: SEE SHOWCASE #17: "SECRET OF THE ETERNAL CITY!"
"WITH SUCH A WEAPON WE COULD CONQUER THE UNIVERSE--IF IT WEREN'T FOR THE INTERVENTION OF OUR ENEMY, SORKHAN VUH..."
PEOPLE OF THE ARVESE! DO YOU THINK I'D LET YOU CARRY DESTRUCTIVE WARS TO THE STAR-WORLDS? NEVER!
IT'S HIS VOICE!
SORKHAN VUH IS AN INCREDIBLY ANCIENT AND INTELLIGENT BEING, JUDGING BY WHAT WE'VE LEARNED ABOUT HIM! HE LOVES PEACE--AND WILL DO ANYTHING--SHORT OF KILLING US--TO PREVENT US FROM WARRING AGAINST OTHER BEINGS!
9

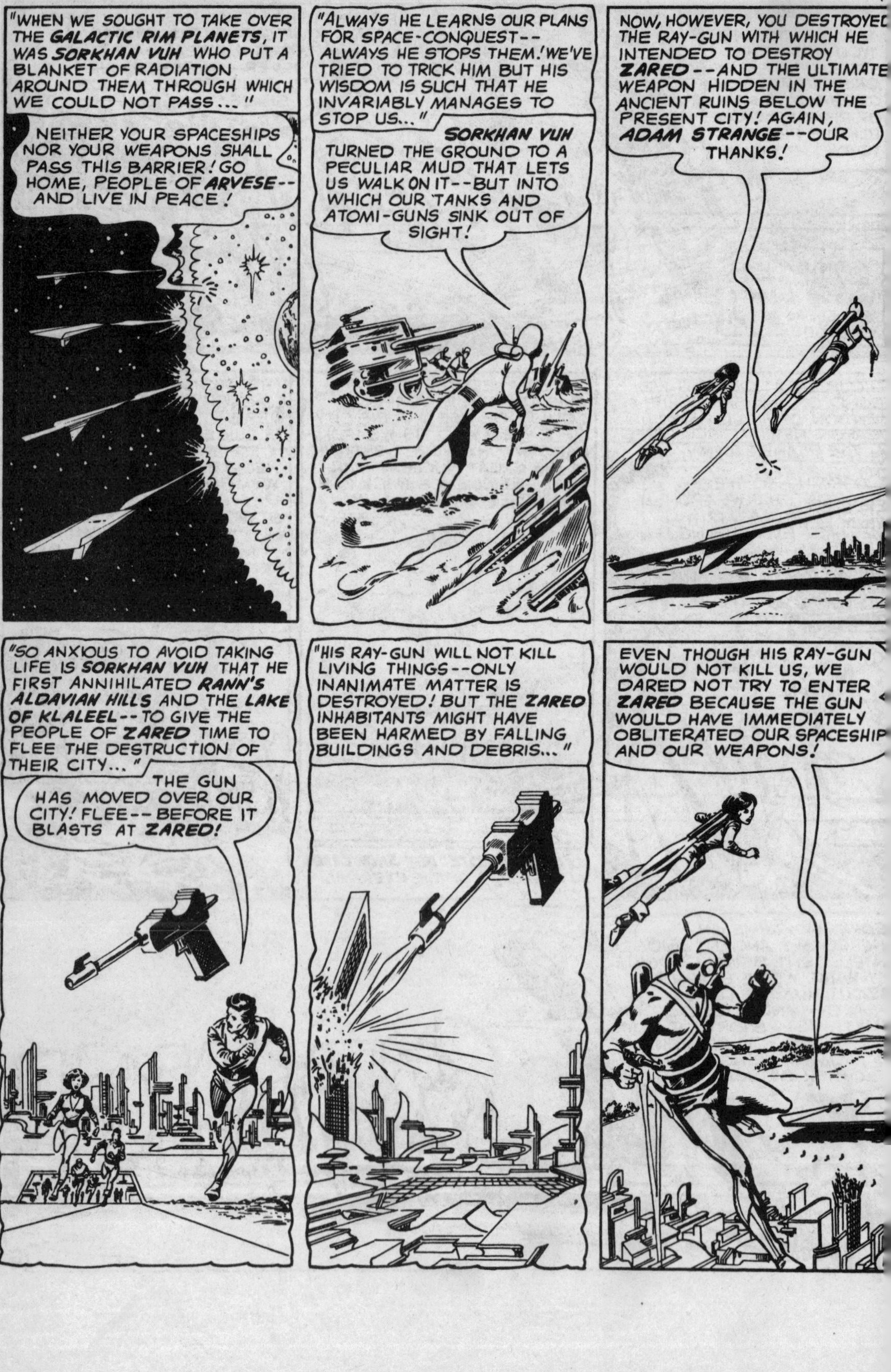
"WHEN WE SOUGHT TO TAKE OVER THE GALACTIC RIM PLANETS, IT WAS SORKHAN VUH WHO PUT A BLANKET OF RADIATION AROUND THEM THROUGH WHICH WE COULD NOT PASS..."
NEITHER YOUR SPACESHIPS NOR YOUR WEAPONS SHALL PASS THIS BARRIER! GO HOME, PEOPLE OF ARVESE--AND LIVE IN PEACE!
"ALWAYS HE LEARNS OUR PLANS FOR SPACE-CONQUEST--ALWAYS HE STOPS THEM! WE'VE TRIED TO TRICK HIM BUT HIS WISDOM IS SUCH THAT HE INVARIABLY MANAGES TO STOP US..."
SORKHAN VUH TURNED THE GROUND TO A PECULIAR MUD THAT LETS US WALK ON IT--BUT INTO WHICH OUR TANKS AND ATOMI-GUNS SINK OUT OF SIGHT!
NOW, HOWEVER, YOU DESTROYED THE RAY-GUN WITH WHICH HE INTENDED TO DESTROY ZARED--AND THE ULTIMATE WEAPON HIDDEN IN THE ANCIENT RUINS BELOW THE PRESENT CITY! AGAIN, ADAM STRANGE--OUR THANKS!
"SO ANXIOUS TO AVOID TAKING LIFE IS SORKHAN VUH THAT HE FIRST ANNIHILATED RANN'S ALDAVIAN HILLS AND THE LAKE OF KLALEEL--TO GIVE THE PEOPLE OF ZARED TIME TO FLEE THE DESTRUCTION OF THEIR CITY..."
THE GUN HAS MOVED OVER OUR CITY! FLEE--BEFORE IT BLASTS AT ZARED!
"HIS RAY-GUN WILL NOT KILL LIVING THINGS--ONLY INANIMATE MATTER IS DESTROYED! BUT THE ZARED INHABITANTS MIGHT HAVE BEEN HARMED BY FALLING BUILDINGS AND DEBRIS..."
EVEN THOUGH HIS RAY-GUN WOULD NOT KILL US, WE DARED NOT TRY TO ENTER ZARED BECAUSE THE GUN WOULD HAVE IMMEDIATELY OBLITERATED OUR SPACESHIP AND OUR WEAPONS!

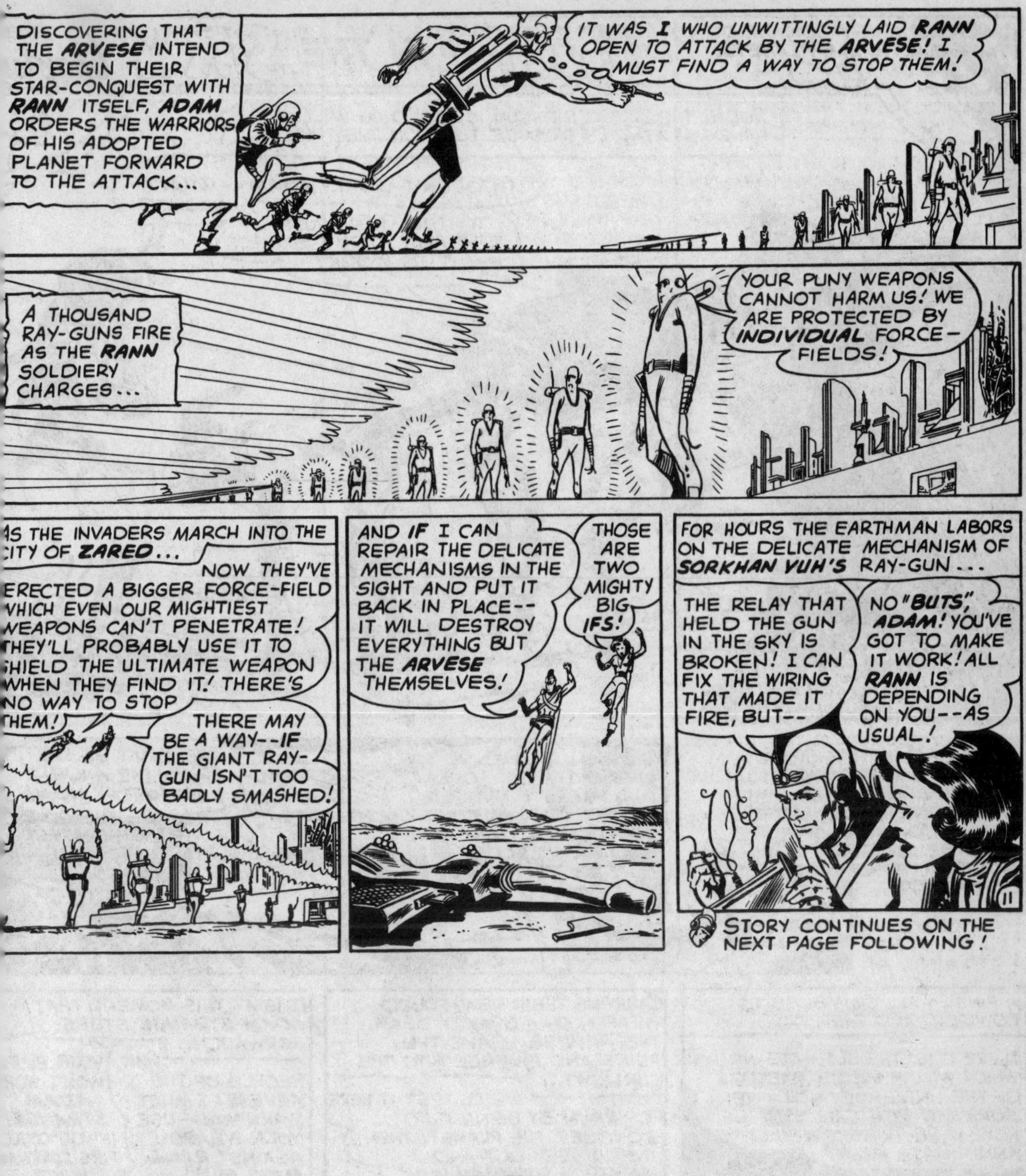
DISCOVERING THAT THE ARVESE INTEND TO BEGIN THEIR STAR-CONQUEST WITH RANN ITSELF, ADAM ORDERS THE WARRIORS OF HIS ADOPTED PLANET FORWARD TO THE ATTACK...
IT WAS I WHO UNWITTINGLY LAID RANN OPEN TO ATTACK BY THE ARVESE! I MUST FIND A WAY TO STOP THEM!
A THOUSAND RAY-GUNS FIRE AS THE RANN SOLDIERY CHARGES...
YOUR PUNY WEAPONS CANNOT HARM US! WE ARE PROTECTED BY INDIVIDUAL FORCE-FIELDS!
AS THE INVADERS MARCH INTO THE CITY OF ZARED...
NOW THEY'VE ERECTED A BIGGER FORCE-FIELD WHICH EVEN OUR MIGHTIEST WEAPONS CAN'T PENETRATE! THEY'LL PROBABLY USE IT TO SHIELD THE ULTIMATE WEAPON WHEN THEY FIND IT! THERE'S NO WAY TO STOP THEM!
THERE MAY BE A WAY--IF THE GIANT RAY-GUN ISN'T TOO BADLY SMASHED!
AND IF I CAN REPAIR THE DELICATE MECHANISMS IN THE SIGHT AND PUT IT BACK IN PLACE-- IT WILL DESTROY EVERYTHING BUT THE ARVESE THEMSELVES!
THOSE ARE TWO MIGHTY BIG IFS!
FOR HOURS THE EARTHMAN LABORS ON THE DELICATE MECHANISM OF SORKHAN VUH'S RAY-GUN...
THE RELAY THAT HELD THE GUN IN THE SKY IS BROKEN! I CAN FIX THE WIRING THAT MADE IT FIRE, BUT--
NO "BUTS," ADAM! YOU'VE GOT TO MAKE IT WORK! ALL RANN IS DEPENDING ON YOU--AS USUAL!
11

STORY CONTINUES ON THE NEXT PAGE FOLLOWING!

ADAM STRANGE

RAY-GUN IN THE SKY Chapter 3

SOON, THE GREAT RAY-GUN IS RAISED BY WILLING HANDS AS *ADAM STRANGE* TUGS ON THE TRIGGER...

IT DOESN'T WORK! *ADAM* -- WHAT'S WRONG?

TO TELL THE TRUTH, I REALLY DIDN'T EXPECT IT TO WORK!

WHILE *ADAM* HAS BEEN REPAIRING THE SIGHT, THE *ARVESE* ALIENS HAVE PENETRATED DEEP INTO THE OLD RUINS BELOW THE MODERN DAY CITY OF *ZARED*...

WE CAN'T BE FAR FROM THE ANCIENT LABORATORY NOW!

A FINAL WALL CRUMBLES TO POWDER, AND THEN...

THERE IT IS! THE ULTIMATE WEAPON WHICH WILL MAKE US MASTERS OF THE UNIVERSE! NOT EVEN *SORKHAN VUH* CAN STOP US NOW! IF HE TRIES -- WE'LL ANNIHILATE *RANN!*

CARRYING THEIR NEW-FOUND WEAPON ON A GRAVITY BEAM, THE *ARVESE* LEAVE THE RUINS AND EMERGE INTO THE SUNLIGHT...

WE'LL TEST IT HERE ON *RANN* BY USING IT TO CONQUER THE PLANET! THEN WE'LL SEEK OUT AND DESTROY *SORKHAN VUH!*

IT IS AT THIS MOMENT THAT *ADAM STRANGE* STEPS FORWARD...

PEOPLE OF THE *ARVESE!* I MUST WARN YOU -- USE YOUR WEAPON AGAINST *RANN,* AND I SHALL DESTROY YOUR SPACESHIP, LEAVING YOU STRANDED HERE!

WAIT, YOUR BLUFF WON'T WORK *ADAM STRANGE!* IF YOU COULD FIRE *SORKHAN-VUH'S* RAY-GUN, YOU WOULD HAVE DONE SO BY NOW!

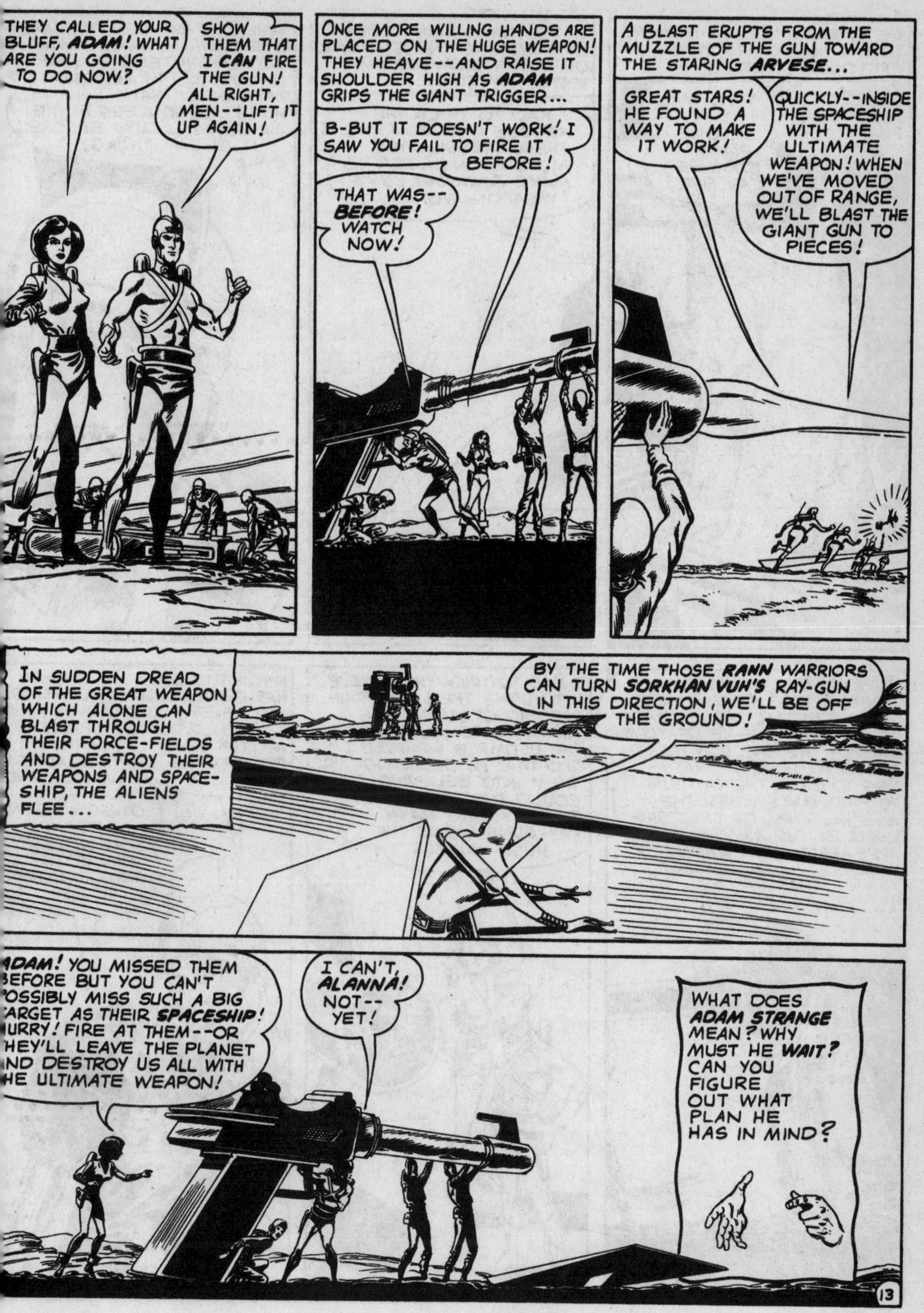
THEY CALLED YOUR BLUFF, ADAM! WHAT ARE YOU GOING TO DO NOW?
SHOW THEM THAT I CAN FIRE THE GUN! ALL RIGHT, MEN--LIFT IT UP AGAIN!
ONCE MORE WILLING HANDS ARE PLACED ON THE HUGE WEAPON! THEY HEAVE--AND RAISE IT SHOULDER HIGH AS ADAM GRIPS THE GIANT TRIGGER...
B-BUT IT DOESN'T WORK! I SAW YOU FAIL TO FIRE IT BEFORE!
THAT WAS--BEFORE! WATCH NOW!
A BLAST ERUPTS FROM THE MUZZLE OF THE GUN TOWARD THE STARING ARVESE...
GREAT STARS! HE FOUND A WAY TO MAKE IT WORK!
QUICKLY--INSIDE THE SPACESHIP WITH THE ULTIMATE WEAPON! WHEN WE'VE MOVED OUT OF RANGE, WE'LL BLAST THE GIANT GUN TO PIECES!
IN SUDDEN DREAD OF THE GREAT WEAPON WHICH ALONE CAN BLAST THROUGH THEIR FORCE-FIELDS AND DESTROY THEIR WEAPONS AND SPACESHIP, THE ALIENS FLEE...
BY THE TIME THOSE RANN WARRIORS CAN TURN SORKHAN VUH'S RAY-GUN IN THIS DIRECTION, WE'LL BE OFF THE GROUND!
ADAM! YOU MISSED THEM BEFORE BUT YOU CAN'T POSSIBLY MISS SUCH A BIG TARGET AS THEIR SPACESHIP! HURRY! FIRE AT THEM--OR THEY'LL LEAVE THE PLANET AND DESTROY US ALL WITH THE ULTIMATE WEAPON!
I CAN'T, ALANNA! NOT--YET!
WHAT DOES ADAM STRANGE MEAN? WHY MUST HE WAIT? CAN YOU FIGURE OUT WHAT PLAN HE HAS IN MIND?
13

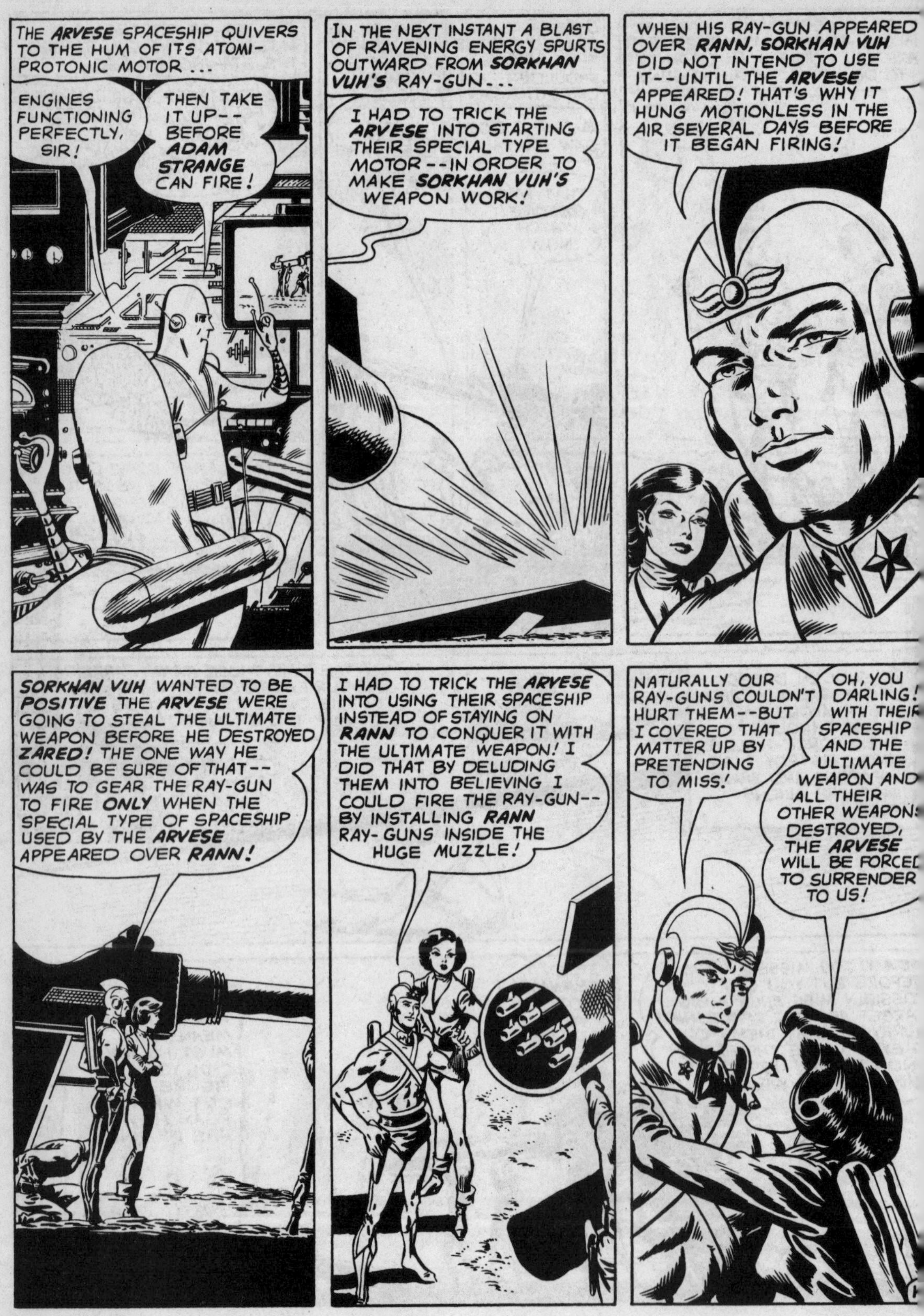
THE ARVESE SPACESHIP QUIVERS TO THE HUM OF ITS ATOMI-PROTONIC MOTOR ...
ENGINES FUNCTIONING PERFECTLY, SIR!
THEN TAKE IT UP-- BEFORE ADAM STRANGE CAN FIRE!
IN THE NEXT INSTANT A BLAST OF RAVENING ENERGY SPURTS OUTWARD FROM SORKHAN VUH'S RAY-GUN...
I HAD TO TRICK THE ARVESE INTO STARTING THEIR SPECIAL TYPE MOTOR--IN ORDER TO MAKE SORKHAN VUH'S WEAPON WORK!
WHEN HIS RAY-GUN APPEARED OVER RANN, SORKHAN VUH DID NOT INTEND TO USE IT--UNTIL THE ARVESE APPEARED! THAT'S WHY IT HUNG MOTIONLESS IN THE AIR SEVERAL DAYS BEFORE IT BEGAN FIRING!
SORKHAN VUH WANTED TO BE POSITIVE THE ARVESE WERE GOING TO STEAL THE ULTIMATE WEAPON BEFORE HE DESTROYED ZARED! THE ONE WAY HE COULD BE SURE OF THAT--WAS TO GEAR THE RAY-GUN TO FIRE ONLY WHEN THE SPECIAL TYPE OF SPACESHIP USED BY THE ARVESE APPEARED OVER RANN!
I HAD TO TRICK THE ARVESE INTO USING THEIR SPACESHIP INSTEAD OF STAYING ON RANN TO CONQUER IT WITH THE ULTIMATE WEAPON! I DID THAT BY DELUDING THEM INTO BELIEVING I COULD FIRE THE RAY-GUN--BY INSTALLING RANN RAY-GUNS INSIDE THE HUGE MUZZLE!
NATURALLY OUR RAY-GUNS COULDN'T HURT THEM--BUT I COVERED THAT MATTER UP BY PRETENDING TO MISS!
OH, YOU DARLING! WITH THEIR SPACESHIP AND THE ULTIMATE WEAPON AND ALL THEIR OTHER WEAPONS DESTROYED, THE ARVESE WILL BE FORCED TO SURRENDER TO US!

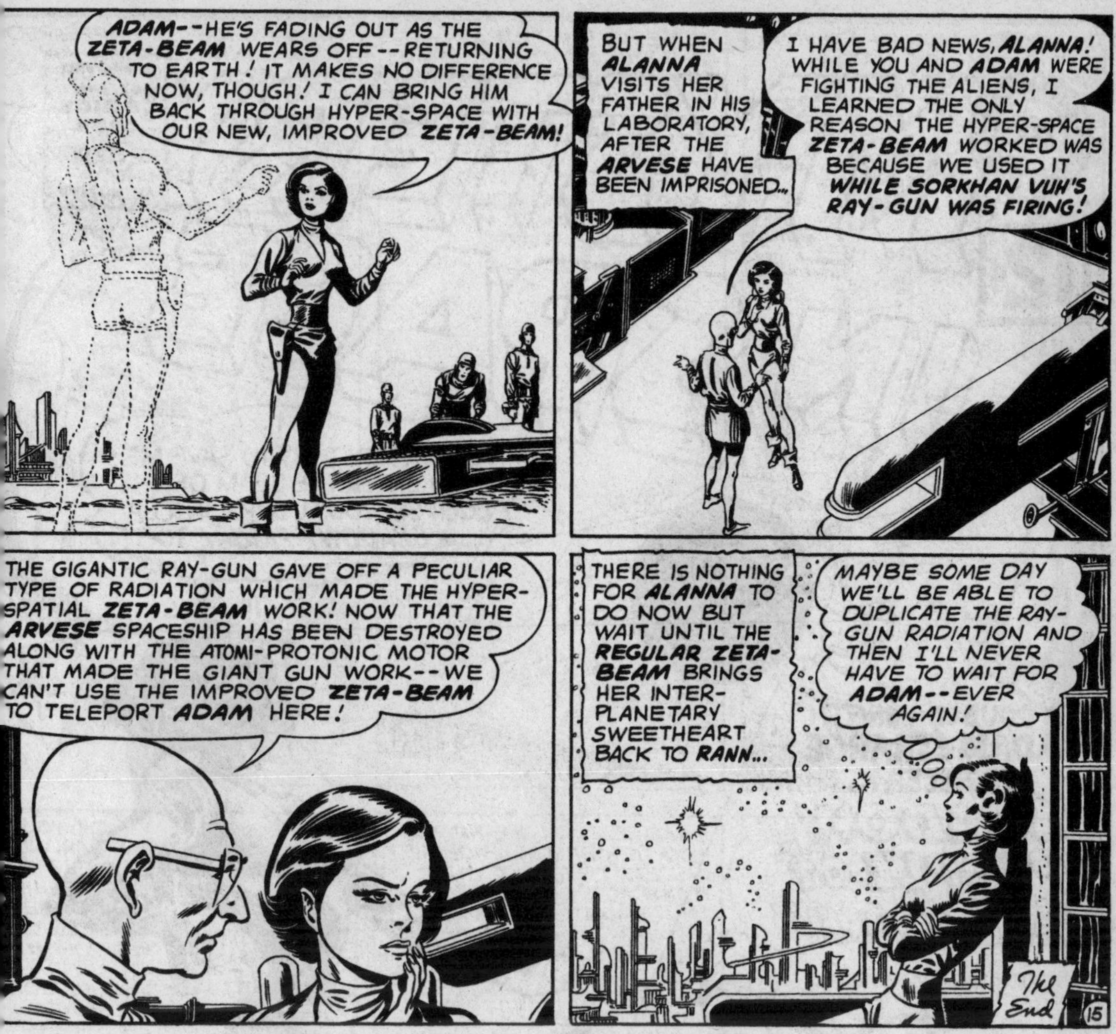
ADAM--HE'S FADING OUT AS THE ZETA-BEAM WEARS OFF--RETURNING TO EARTH! IT MAKES NO DIFFERENCE NOW, THOUGH! I CAN BRING HIM BACK THROUGH HYPER-SPACE WITH OUR NEW, IMPROVED ZETA-BEAM!
BUT WHEN ALANNA VISITS HER FATHER IN HIS LABORATORY, AFTER THE ARVESE HAVE BEEN IMPRISONED...
I HAVE BAD NEWS, ALANNA! WHILE YOU AND ADAM WERE FIGHTING THE ALIENS, I LEARNED THE ONLY REASON THE HYPER-SPACE ZETA-BEAM WORKED WAS BECAUSE WE USED IT WHILE SORKHAN VUH'S RAY-GUN WAS FIRING!
THE GIGANTIC RAY-GUN GAVE OFF A PECULIAR TYPE OF RADIATION WHICH MADE THE HYPER-SPATIAL ZETA-BEAM WORK! NOW THAT THE ARVESE SPACESHIP HAS BEEN DESTROYED ALONG WITH THE ATOMI-PROTONIC MOTOR THAT MADE THE GIANT GUN WORK--WE CAN'T USE THE IMPROVED ZETA-BEAM TO TELEPORT ADAM HERE!
THERE IS NOTHING FOR ALANNA TO DO NOW BUT WAIT UNTIL THE REGULAR ZETA-BEAM BRINGS HER INTER-PLANETARY SWEETHEART BACK TO RANN...
MAYBE SOME DAY WE'LL BE ABLE TO DUPLICATE THE RAY-GUN RADIATION AND THEN I'LL NEVER HAVE TO WAIT FOR ADAM--EVER AGAIN!
The End
15

ADAM STRANGE

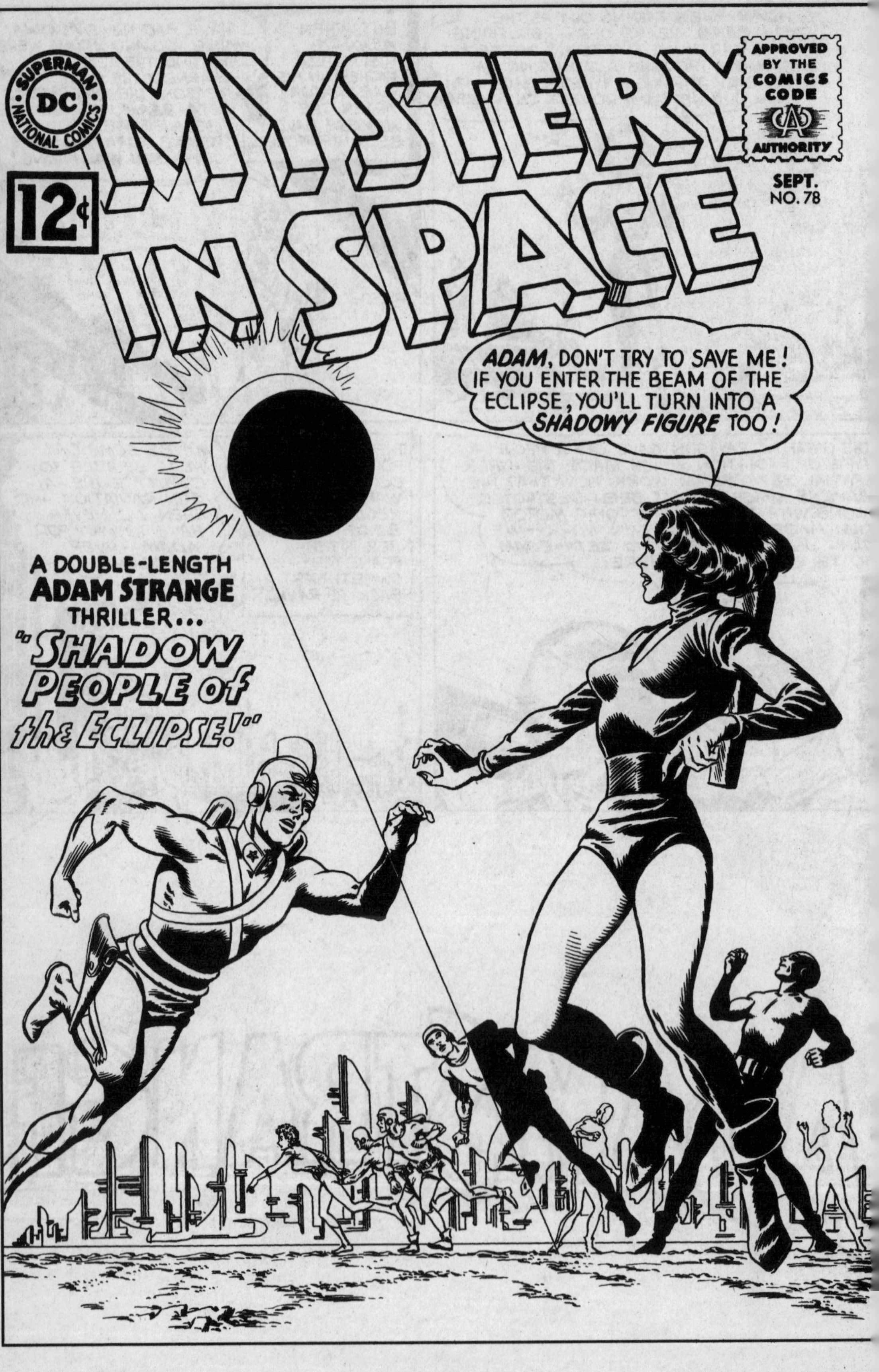
SUPERMAN DC NATIONAL COMICS
12¢
MYSTERY IN SPACE
APPROVED BY THE COMICS CODE AUTHORITY
SEPT. NO. 78
ADAM, DON'T TRY TO SAVE ME! IF YOU ENTER THE BEAM OF THE ECLIPSE, YOU'LL TURN INTO A SHADOWY FIGURE TOO!
A DOUBLE-LENGTH ADAM STRANGE THRILLER... "SHADOW PEOPLE of the ECLIPSE!"

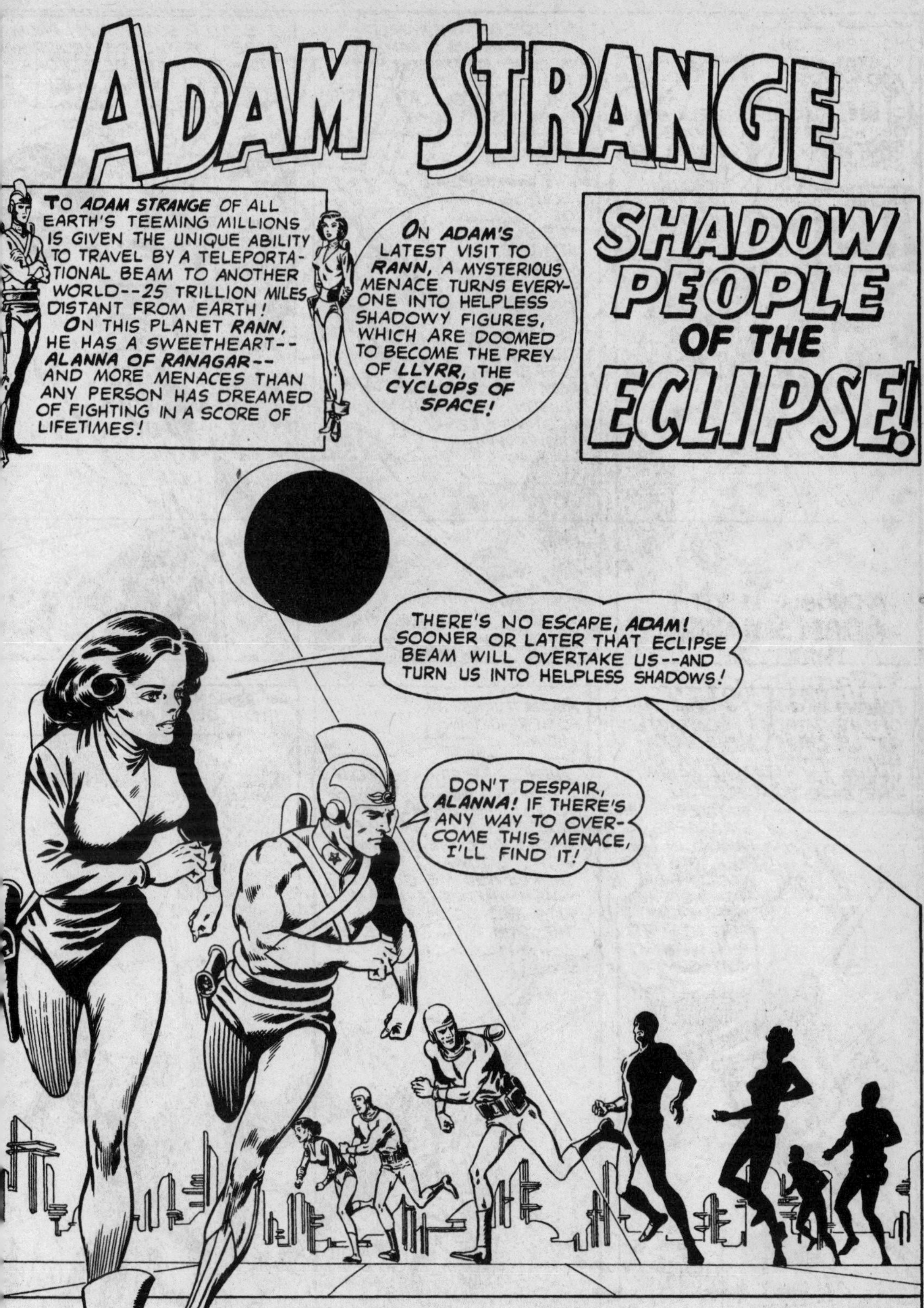
ADAM STRANGE
TO ADAM STRANGE OF ALL EARTH'S TEEMING MILLIONS IS GIVEN THE UNIQUE ABILITY TO TRAVEL BY A TELEPORTATIONAL BEAM TO ANOTHER WORLD--25 TRILLION MILES DISTANT FROM EARTH! ON THIS PLANET RANN, HE HAS A SWEETHEART--ALANNA OF RANAGAR--AND MORE MENACES THAN ANY PERSON HAS DREAMED OF FIGHTING IN A SCORE OF LIFETIMES!
ON ADAM'S LATEST VISIT TO RANN, A MYSTERIOUS MENACE TURNS EVERYONE INTO HELPLESS SHADOWY FIGURES, WHICH ARE DOOMED TO BECOME THE PREY OF LLYRR, THE CYCLOPS OF SPACE!
SHADOW PEOPLE OF THE ECLIPSE!
THERE'S NO ESCAPE, ADAM! SOONER OR LATER THAT ECLIPSE BEAM WILL OVERTAKE US--AND TURN US INTO HELPLESS SHADOWS!
DON'T DESPAIR, ALANNA! IF THERE'S ANY WAY TO OVERCOME THIS MENACE, I'LL FIND IT!

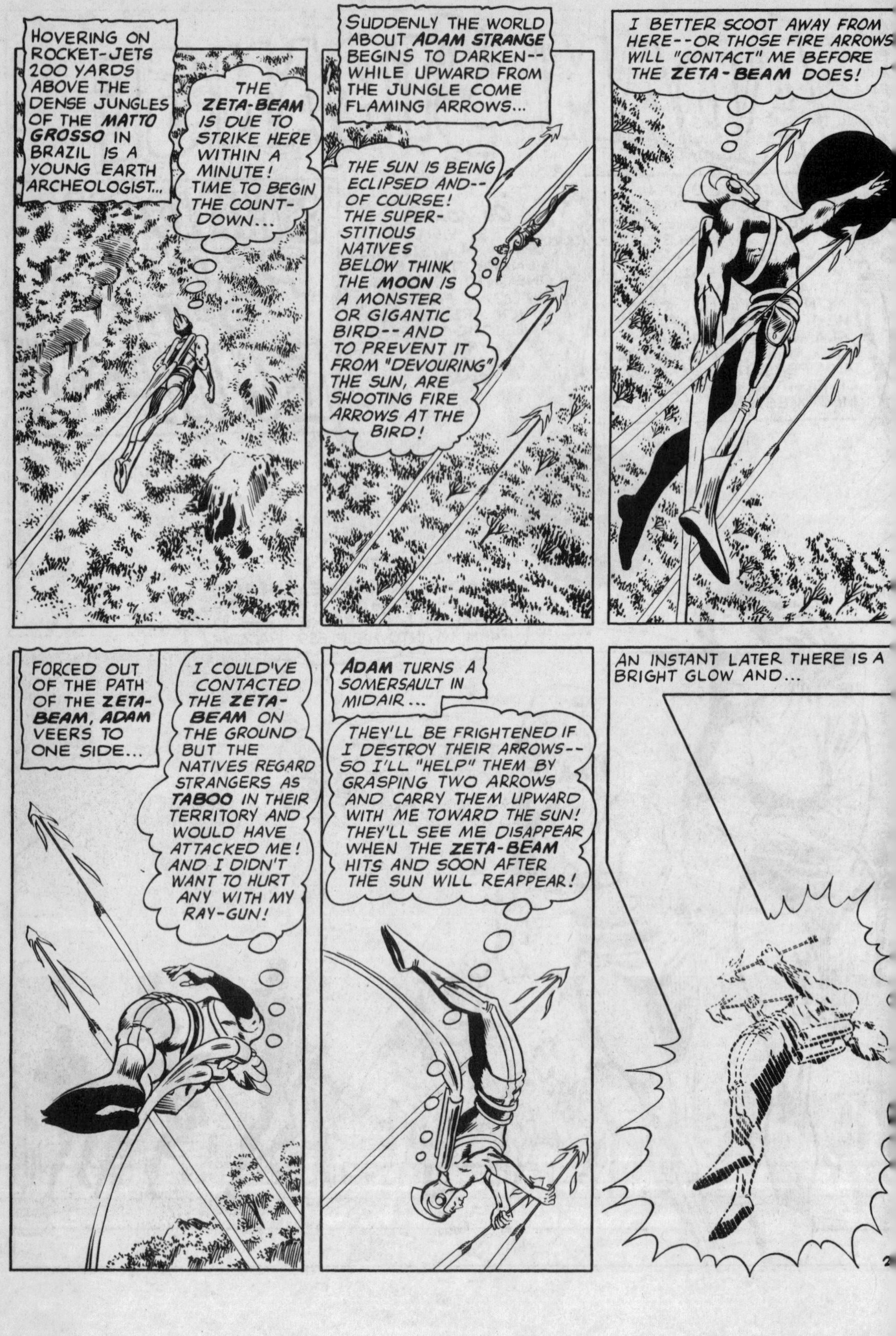
HOVERING ON ROCKET-JETS 200 YARDS ABOVE THE DENSE JUNGLES OF THE MATTO GROSSO IN BRAZIL IS A YOUNG EARTH ARCHEOLOGIST...
THE ZETA-BEAM IS DUE TO STRIKE HERE WITHIN A MINUTE! TIME TO BEGIN THE COUNT-DOWN...
SUDDENLY THE WORLD ABOUT ADAM STRANGE BEGINS TO DARKEN--WHILE UPWARD FROM THE JUNGLE COME FLAMING ARROWS...
THE SUN IS BEING ECLIPSED AND--OF COURSE! THE SUPER-STITIOUS NATIVES BELOW THINK THE MOON IS A MONSTER OR GIGANTIC BIRD--AND TO PREVENT IT FROM "DEVOURING" THE SUN, ARE SHOOTING FIRE ARROWS AT THE BIRD!
I BETTER SCOOT AWAY FROM HERE--OR THOSE FIRE ARROWS WILL "CONTACT" ME BEFORE THE ZETA-BEAM DOES!
FORCED OUT OF THE PATH OF THE ZETA-BEAM, ADAM VEERS TO ONE SIDE...
I COULD'VE CONTACTED THE ZETA-BEAM ON THE GROUND BUT THE NATIVES REGARD STRANGERS AS TABOO IN THEIR TERRITORY AND WOULD HAVE ATTACKED ME! AND I DIDN'T WANT TO HURT ANY WITH MY RAY-GUN!
ADAM TURNS A SOMERSAULT IN MIDAIR...
THEY'LL BE FRIGHTENED IF I DESTROY THEIR ARROWS--SO I'LL "HELP" THEM BY GRASPING TWO ARROWS AND CARRY THEM UPWARD WITH ME TOWARD THE SUN! THEY'LL SEE ME DISAPPEAR WHEN THE ZETA-BEAM HITS AND SOON AFTER THE SUN WILL REAPPEAR!
AN INSTANT LATER THERE IS A BRIGHT GLOW AND...

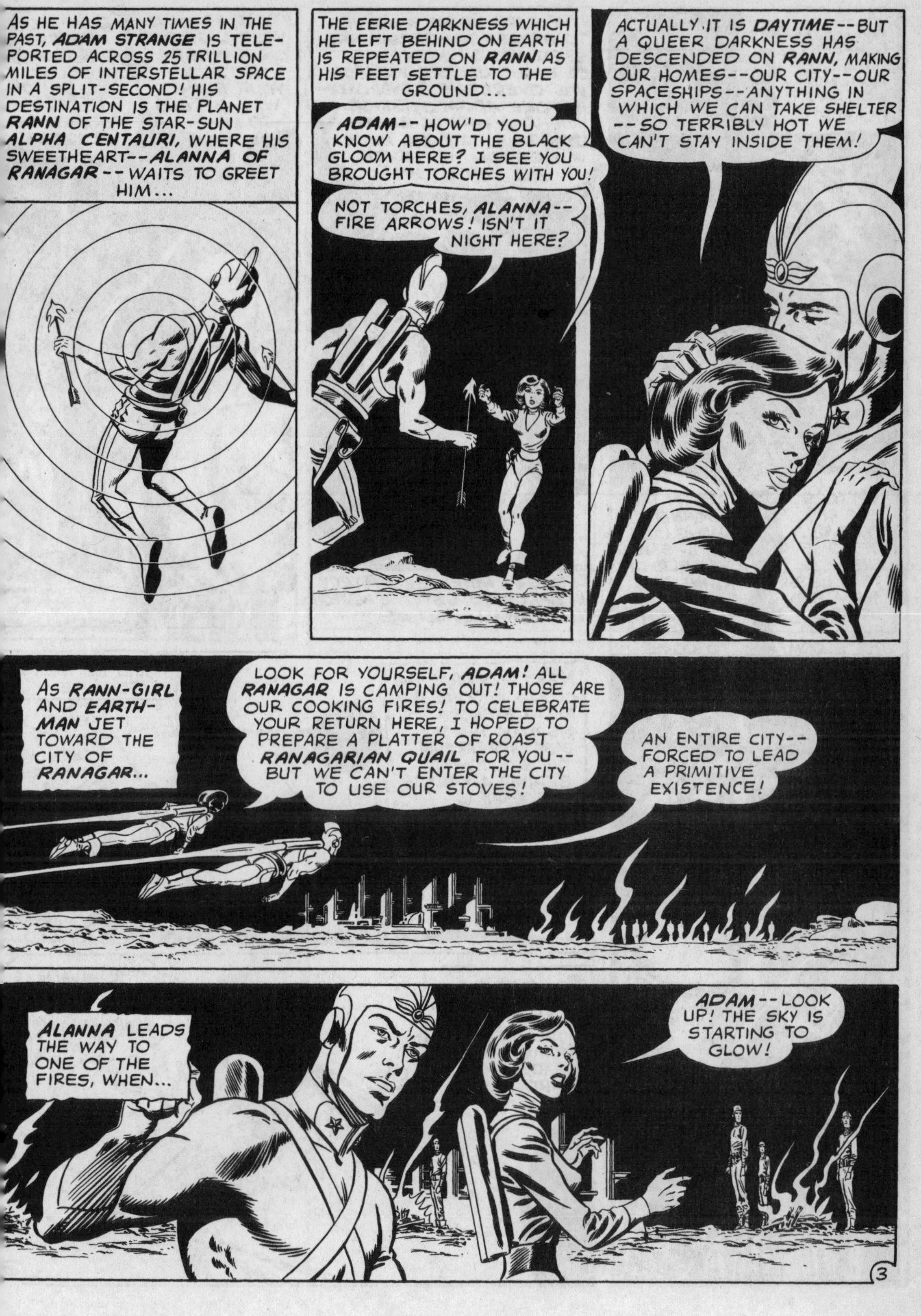
AS HE HAS MANY TIMES IN THE PAST, ADAM STRANGE IS TELEPORTED ACROSS 25 TRILLION MILES OF INTERSTELLAR SPACE IN A SPLIT-SECOND! HIS DESTINATION IS THE PLANET RANN OF THE STAR-SUN ALPHA CENTAURI, WHERE HIS SWEETHEART--ALANNA OF RANAGAR--WAITS TO GREET HIM...
THE EERIE DARKNESS WHICH HE LEFT BEHIND ON EARTH IS REPEATED ON RANN AS HIS FEET SETTLE TO THE GROUND...
ADAM--HOW'D YOU KNOW ABOUT THE BLACK GLOOM HERE? I SEE YOU BROUGHT TORCHES WITH YOU!
NOT TORCHES, ALANNA--FIRE ARROWS! ISN'T IT NIGHT HERE?
ACTUALLY IT IS DAYTIME--BUT A QUEER DARKNESS HAS DESCENDED ON RANN, MAKING OUR HOMES--OUR CITY--OUR SPACESHIPS--ANYTHING IN WHICH WE CAN TAKE SHELTER--SO TERRIBLY HOT WE CAN'T STAY INSIDE THEM!
AS RANN-GIRL AND EARTH-MAN JET TOWARD THE CITY OF RANAGAR...
LOOK FOR YOURSELF, ADAM! ALL RANAGAR IS CAMPING OUT! THOSE ARE OUR COOKING FIRES! TO CELEBRATE YOUR RETURN HERE, I HOPED TO PREPARE A PLATTER OF ROAST RANAGARIAN QUAIL FOR YOU--BUT WE CAN'T ENTER THE CITY TO USE OUR STOVES!
AN ENTIRE CITY--FORCED TO LEAD A PRIMITIVE EXISTENCE!
ALANNA LEADS THE WAY TO ONE OF THE FIRES, WHEN...
ADAM--LOOK UP! THE SKY IS STARTING TO GLOW!
3

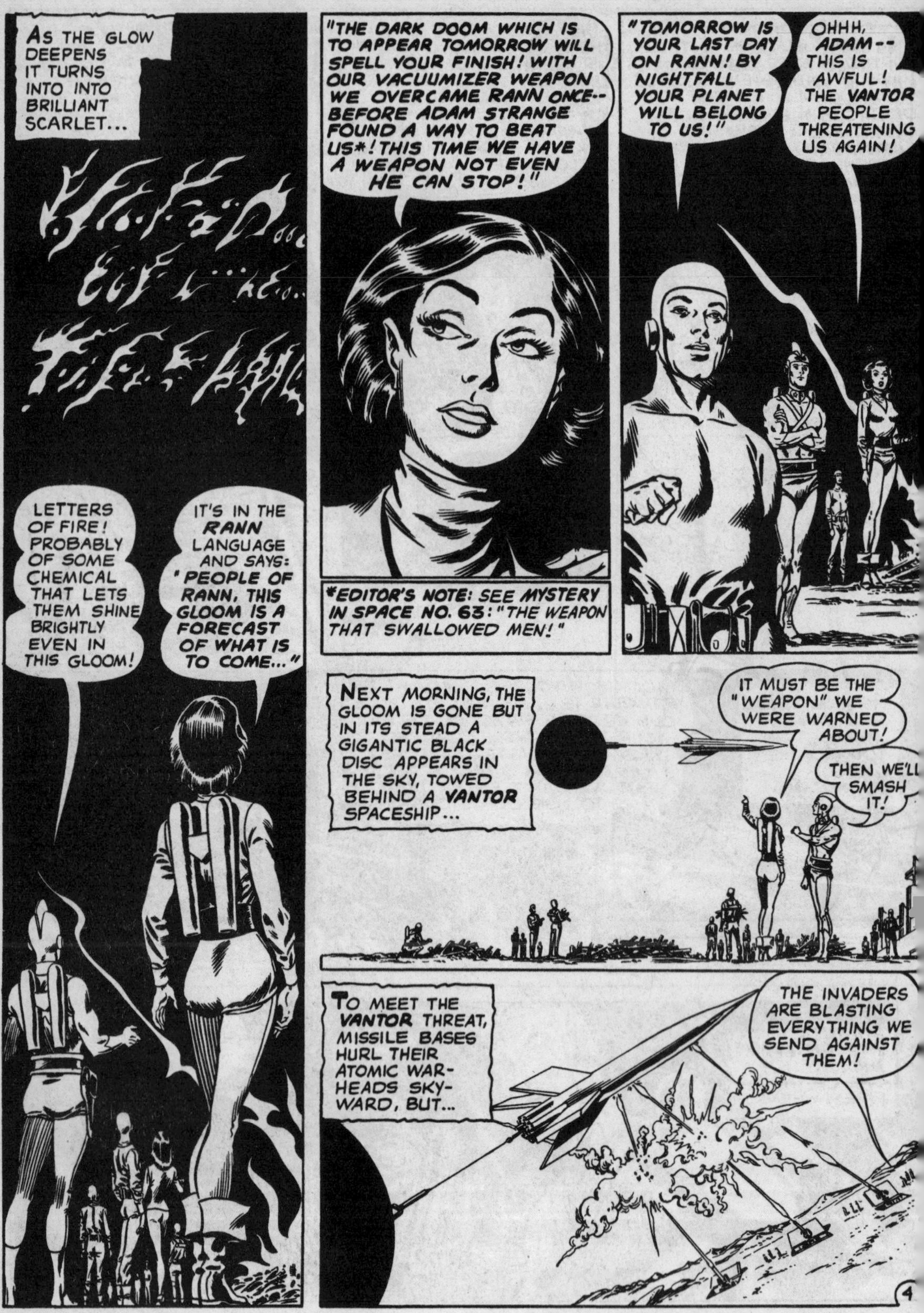
AS THE GLOW DEEPENS IT TURNS INTO INTO BRILLIANT SCARLET...
LETTERS OF FIRE! PROBABLY OF SOME CHEMICAL THAT LETS THEM SHINE BRIGHTLY EVEN IN THIS GLOOM!
IT'S IN THE RANN LANGUAGE AND SAYS: 'PEOPLE OF RANN, THIS GLOOM IS A FORECAST OF WHAT IS TO COME..."
"THE DARK DOOM WHICH IS TO APPEAR TOMORROW WILL SPELL YOUR FINISH! WITH OUR VACUUMIZER WEAPON WE OVERCAME RANN ONCE--BEFORE ADAM STRANGE FOUND A WAY TO BEAT US*! THIS TIME WE HAVE A WEAPON NOT EVEN HE CAN STOP!"
*EDITOR'S NOTE: SEE MYSTERY IN SPACE NO. 63: "THE WEAPON THAT SWALLOWED MEN!"
"TOMORROW IS YOUR LAST DAY ON RANN! BY NIGHTFALL YOUR PLANET WILL BELONG TO US!"
OHHH, ADAM-- THIS IS AWFUL! THE VANTOR PEOPLE THREATENING US AGAIN!
NEXT MORNING, THE GLOOM IS GONE BUT IN ITS STEAD A GIGANTIC BLACK DISC APPEARS IN THE SKY, TOWED BEHIND A VANTOR SPACESHIP...
IT MUST BE THE "WEAPON" WE WERE WARNED ABOUT!
THEN WE'LL SMASH IT!
TO MEET THE VANTOR THREAT, MISSILE BASES HURL THEIR ATOMIC WAR-HEADS SKY-WARD, BUT...
THE INVADERS ARE BLASTING EVERYTHING WE SEND AGAINST THEM!
4

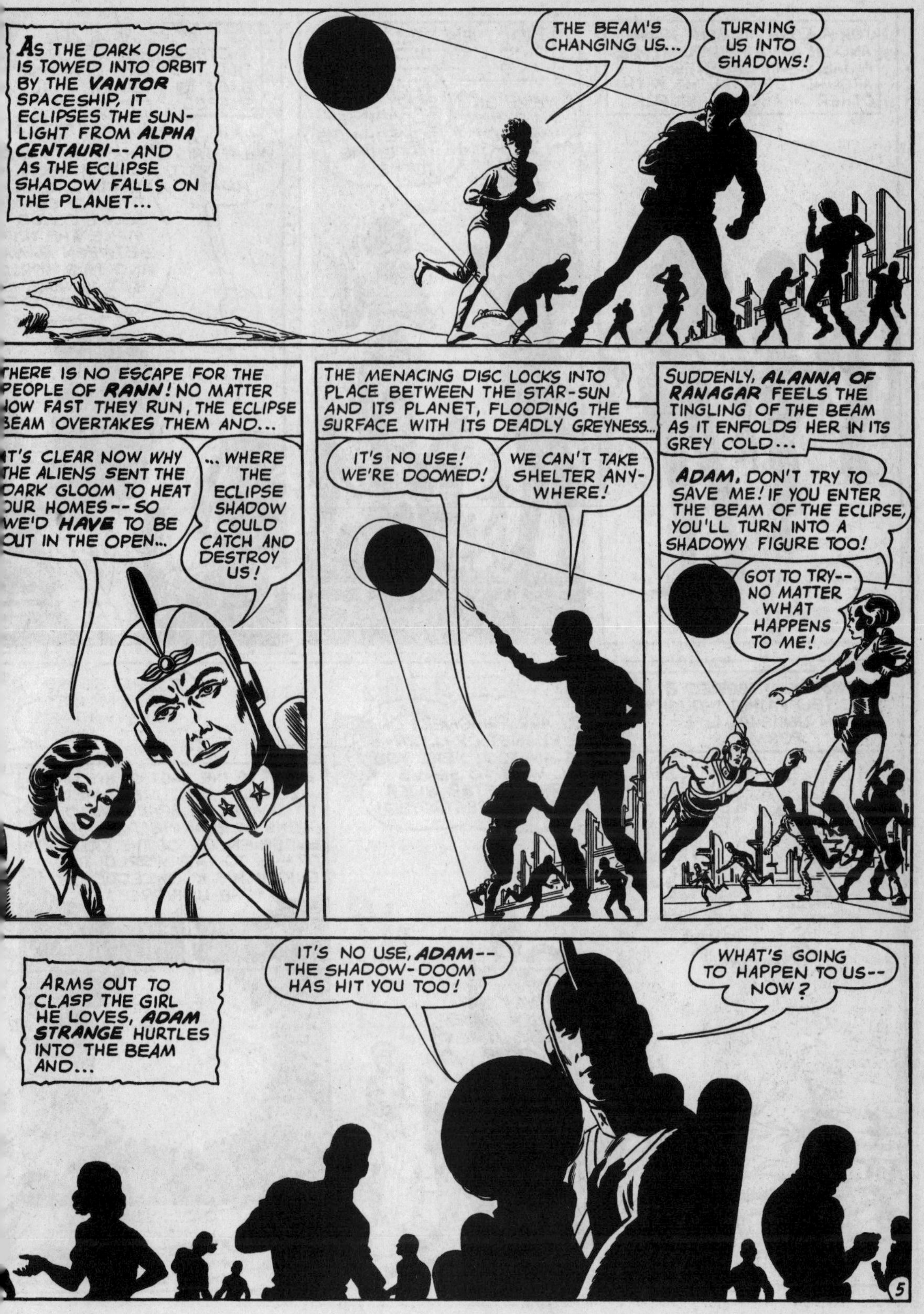

AS THE DARK DISC IS TOWED INTO ORBIT BY THE VANTOR SPACESHIP, IT ECLIPSES THE SUN-LIGHT FROM ALPHA CENTAURI--AND AS THE ECLIPSE SHADOW FALLS ON THE PLANET...
THE BEAM'S CHANGING US...
TURNING US INTO SHADOWS!
THERE IS NO ESCAPE FOR THE PEOPLE OF RANN! NO MATTER HOW FAST THEY RUN, THE ECLIPSE BEAM OVERTAKES THEM AND...
IT'S CLEAR NOW WHY THE ALIENS SENT THE DARK GLOOM TO HEAT OUR HOMES--SO WE'D HAVE TO BE OUT IN THE OPEN...
... WHERE THE ECLIPSE SHADOW COULD CATCH AND DESTROY US!
THE MENACING DISC LOCKS INTO PLACE BETWEEN THE STAR-SUN AND ITS PLANET, FLOODING THE SURFACE WITH ITS DEADLY GREYNESS...
IT'S NO USE! WE'RE DOOMED!
WE CAN'T TAKE SHELTER ANY-WHERE!
SUDDENLY, ALANNA OF RANAGAR FEELS THE TINGLING OF THE BEAM AS IT ENFOLDS HER IN ITS GREY COLD...
ADAM, DON'T TRY TO SAVE ME! IF YOU ENTER THE BEAM OF THE ECLIPSE, YOU'LL TURN INTO A SHADOWY FIGURE TOO!
GOT TO TRY--NO MATTER WHAT HAPPENS TO ME!
ARMS OUT TO CLASP THE GIRL HE LOVES, ADAM STRANGE HURTLES INTO THE BEAM AND...
IT'S NO USE, ADAM--THE SHADOW-DOOM HAS HIT YOU TOO!
WHAT'S GOING TO HAPPEN TO US--NOW?
5

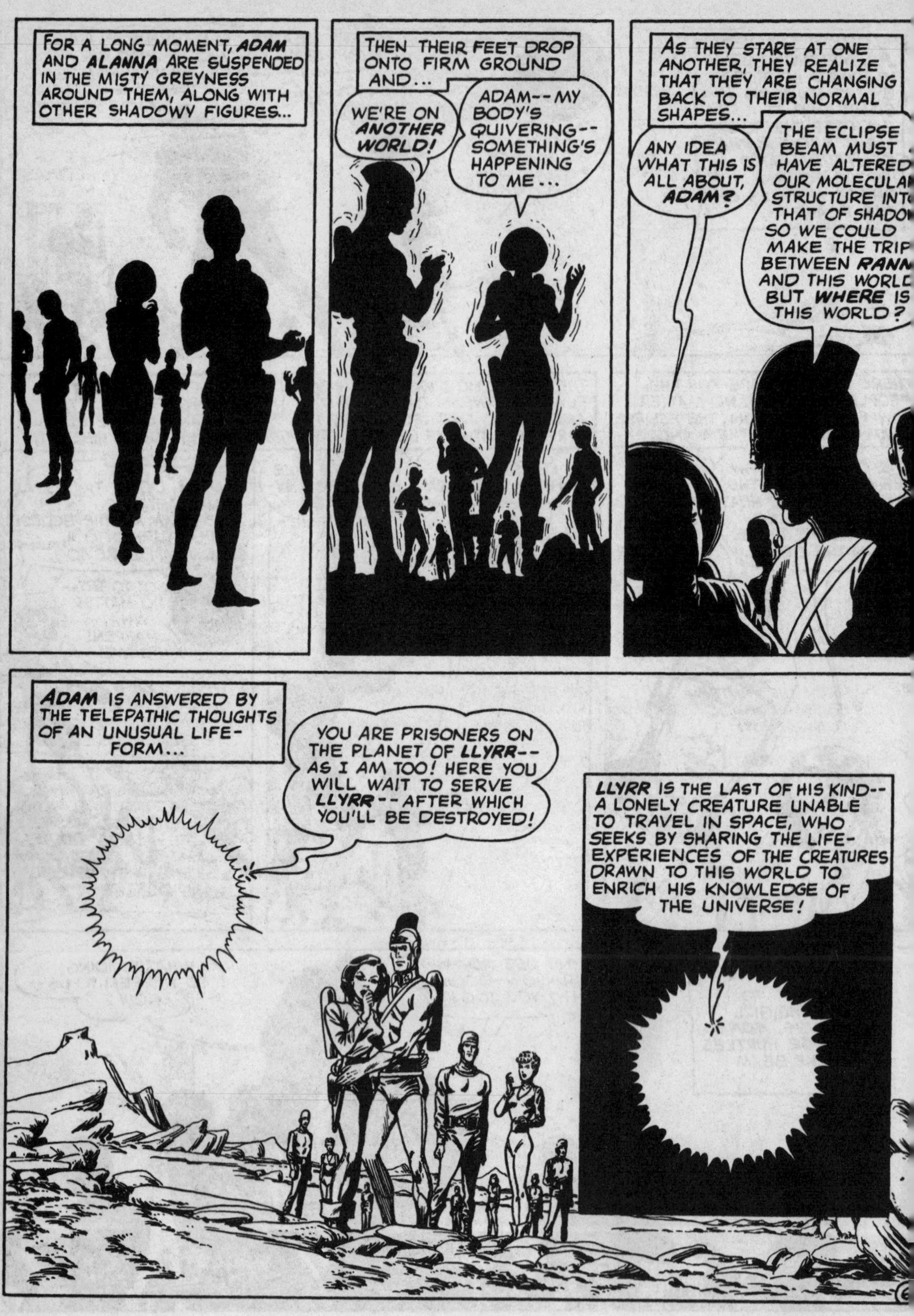
FOR A LONG MOMENT, ADAM AND ALANNA ARE SUSPENDED IN THE MISTY GREYNESS AROUND THEM, ALONG WITH OTHER SHADOWY FIGURES...
THEN THEIR FEET DROP ONTO FIRM GROUND AND...
WE'RE ON ANOTHER WORLD!
ADAM-- MY BODY'S QUIVERING-- SOMETHING'S HAPPENING TO ME...
AS THEY STARE AT ONE ANOTHER, THEY REALIZE THAT THEY ARE CHANGING BACK TO THEIR NORMAL SHAPES...
ANY IDEA WHAT THIS IS ALL ABOUT, ADAM?
THE ECLIPSE BEAM MUST HAVE ALTERED OUR MOLECULA STRUCTURE INT THAT OF SHADO SO WE COULD MAKE THE TRIP BETWEEN RANN AND THIS WORLD BUT WHERE IS THIS WORLD?
ADAM IS ANSWERED BY THE TELEPATHIC THOUGHTS OF AN UNUSUAL LIFE-FORM...
YOU ARE PRISONERS ON THE PLANET OF LLYRR-- AS I AM TOO! HERE YOU WILL WAIT TO SERVE LLYRR-- AFTER WHICH YOU'LL BE DESTROYED!
LLYRR IS THE LAST OF HIS KIND-- A LONELY CREATURE UNABLE TO TRAVEL IN SPACE, WHO SEEKS BY SHARING THE LIFE-EXPERIENCES OF THE CREATURES DRAWN TO THIS WORLD TO ENRICH HIS KNOWLEDGE OF THE UNIVERSE!

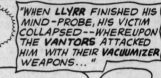

"LLYRR HAS TREMENDOUS MENTAL POWERS! HE IS ABLE TO ENTER INTO THE MIND OF ANOTHER CREATURE, RELIVING ITS ADVENTURES, ITS HOPES AND SORROWS, ITS JOYS AND FAILURES..."

BY PENETRATING THE MINDS OF THESE CRYSTAL CREATURES, I CAN SHARE THEIR LIFE-EXPERIENCES!

"VERY FEW TRAVELERS IN SPACE EVER CAME THIS WAY, HOWEVER--UNTIL A VANTOR SHIP LANDED HERE A SHORT TIME AGO..."

A NEW FORM OF INTELLIGENT LIFE! I SHALL JOIN MY MIND WITH ONE OF THEIRS!

"WHEN LLYRR FINISHED HIS MIND-PROBE, HIS VICTIM COLLAPSED--WHEREUPON THE VANTORS ATTACKED HIM WITH THEIR VACUUMIZER WEAPONS..."

OUR VACUUMIZERS HAVE NO EFFECT ON HIM!

WE'RE HELPLESS! HE'LL DESTROY US ALL-- UNLESS--

"THEN THE VANTOR COMMANDER LEAPED FORWARD..."

HEAR ME, O MIGHTY ONE! SPARE ME AND MY PEOPLE--AND WE'LL BRING MANY VARIETIES OF INTELLIGENT LIFE HERE TO YOU--SO YOU CAN ENJOY THEIR EXPERIENCES!

WE ARE FEW IN NUMBER-- BUT WE CAN POPULATE YOUR PLANET WITH SO MANY LIFE-FORMS THAT YOU'LL NEVER BE LONELY AGAIN!

HALF OF YOU MAY GO-- TO SEND ME THE FIRST OF THESE LIFE-FORMS! WHEN THEY COME, I'LL RELEASE THE OTHERS!

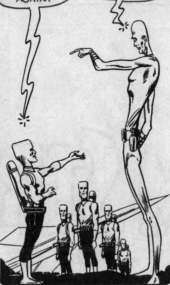

"TO HELP THEM ENTRAP THESE 'EXCHANGE-PRISONERS,' LLYRR GAVE THE VANTORS THE BLACK DISC..."

STAR-SUN LIGHT TRAVELING THROUGH THE DISC WILL ALTER THE MOLECULAR STRUCTURE OF THE LIFE-FORMS' BODIES-- CHANGING THEM TO SHADOWS-- TRANSMITTING THEM HERE TO MY WORLD!

7

"THE VANTORS WENT TO MANY PLANETS AND WITH THE BLACK DISC AND ITS ECLIPSE BEAM, DREW OFF THEIR PEOPLE AND SENT THEM TO LLYRR'S WORLD..."
THERE ARE ENOUGH LIFE-FORMS HERE TO LAST ME A LIFETIME!
AS THE ENERGY-BEING FINISHES TELEPATHING ITS THOUGHTS...
HERE COMES LLYRR NOW! ADAM--IF HE CHOOSES ONE OF US AS HIS MIND-VICTIM, IT'LL MEAN THAT PERSON'S DOOM--
PUT YOUR GUN AWAY, HUMAN! IT'S TOO PUNY A WEAPON TO HAVE ANY EFFECT ON LLYRR!
THERE! LLYRR HAS CHOSEN HIS LATEST VICTIM! WE ALL HAVE A LITTLE WHILE YET TO LIVE...
THERE'S GOT TO BE A WAY TO DEFEAT HIM!
THERE IS NO WAY! WE HAVE ALL TRIED! MANY LIFE-FORMS HERE HAVE TREMENDOUS MENTAL AND OTHER FORMS OF ENERGY--YET LLYRR IS SO MUCH SUPERIOR TO US THAT WE CANNOT EVEN DENT HIS MIND!
ADAM, IT'S HOPELESS! NOT EVEN YOU CAN VANQUISH LLYRR!
STORY CONTINUED ON THE NEXT PAGE FOLLOWING!
8

ADAM STRANGE

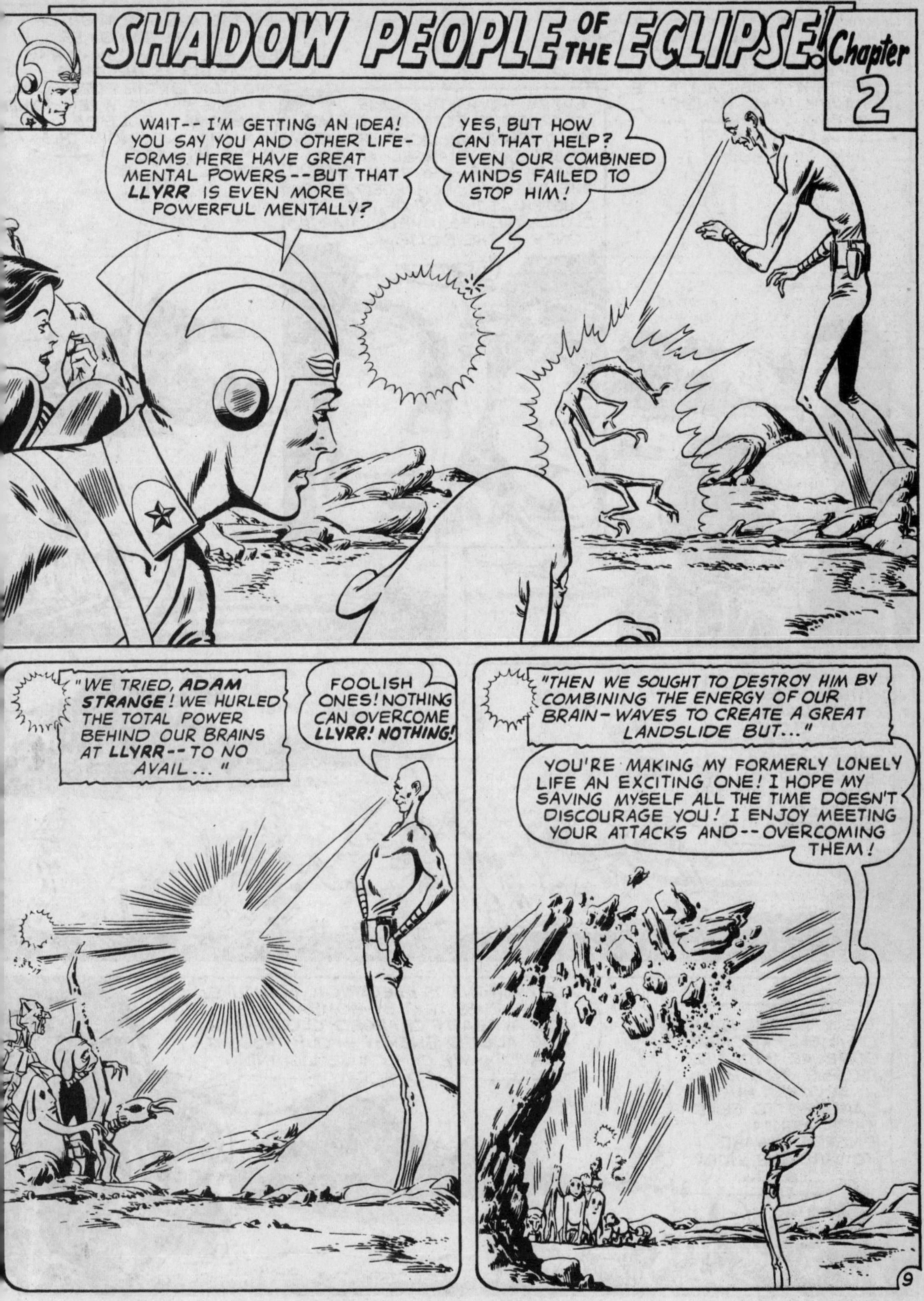
SHADOW PEOPLE OF THE ECLIPSE! Chapter 2
WAIT-- I'M GETTING AN IDEA! YOU SAY YOU AND OTHER LIFE-FORMS HERE HAVE GREAT MENTAL POWERS--BUT THAT LLYRR IS EVEN MORE POWERFUL MENTALLY?
YES, BUT HOW CAN THAT HELP? EVEN OUR COMBINED MINDS FAILED TO STOP HIM!
"WE TRIED, ADAM STRANGE! WE HURLED THE TOTAL POWER BEHIND OUR BRAINS AT LLYRR--TO NO AVAIL..."
FOOLISH ONES! NOTHING CAN OVERCOME LLYRR! NOTHING!
"THEN WE SOUGHT TO DESTROY HIM BY COMBINING THE ENERGY OF OUR BRAIN-WAVES TO CREATE A GREAT LANDSLIDE BUT..."
YOU'RE MAKING MY FORMERLY LONELY LIFE AN EXCITING ONE! I HOPE MY SAVING MYSELF ALL THE TIME DOESN'T DISCOURAGE YOU! I ENJOY MEETING YOUR ATTACKS AND--OVERCOMING THEM!
9

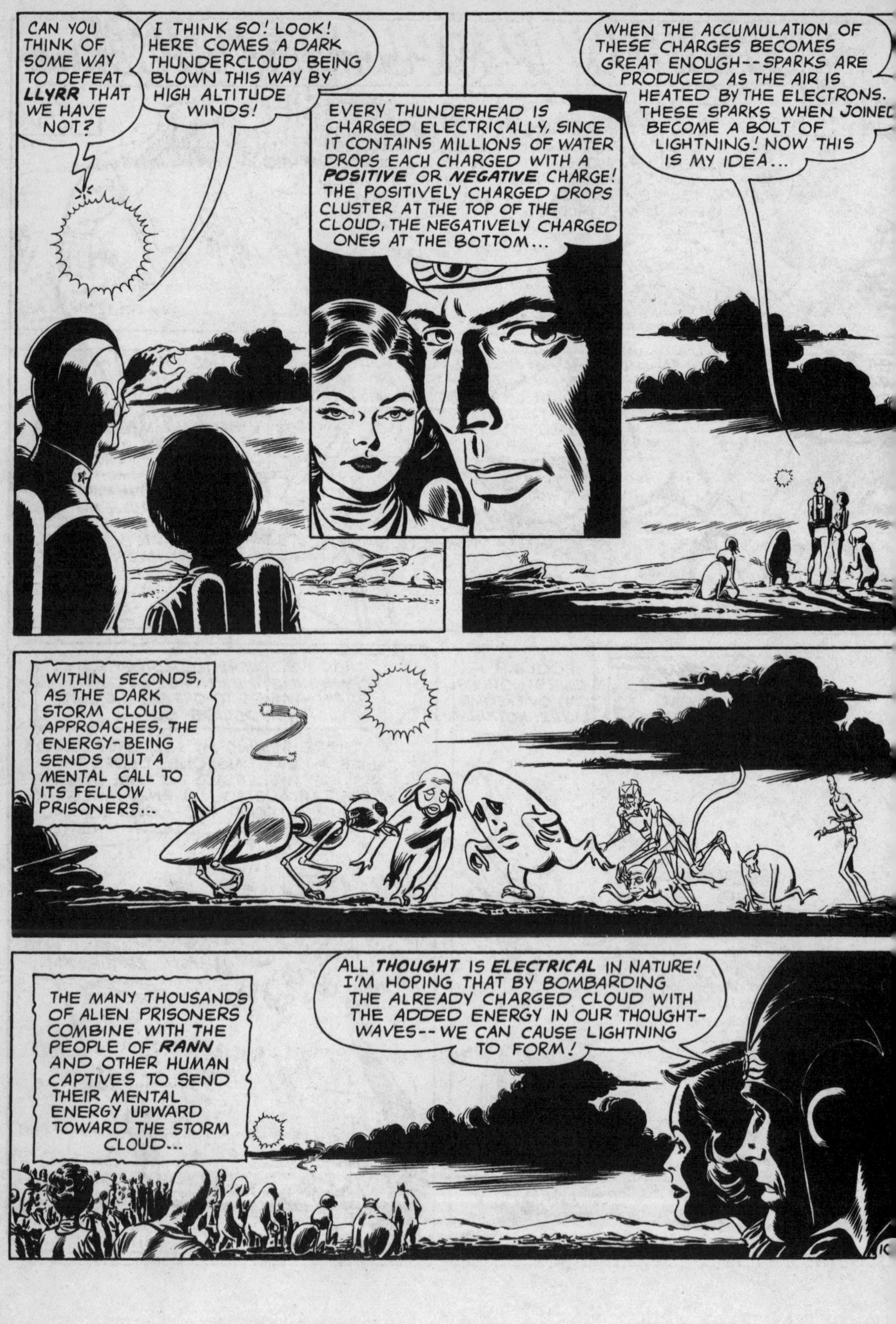
CAN YOU THINK OF SOME WAY TO DEFEAT LLYRR THAT WE HAVE NOT?
I THINK SO! LOOK! HERE COMES A DARK THUNDERCLOUD BEING BLOWN THIS WAY BY HIGH ALTITUDE WINDS!
EVERY THUNDERHEAD IS CHARGED ELECTRICALLY, SINCE IT CONTAINS MILLIONS OF WATER DROPS EACH CHARGED WITH A POSITIVE OR NEGATIVE CHARGE! THE POSITIVELY CHARGED DROPS CLUSTER AT THE TOP OF THE CLOUD, THE NEGATIVELY CHARGED ONES AT THE BOTTOM...
WHEN THE ACCUMULATION OF THESE CHARGES BECOMES GREAT ENOUGH--SPARKS ARE PRODUCED AS THE AIR IS HEATED BY THE ELECTRONS. THESE SPARKS WHEN JOINED BECOME A BOLT OF LIGHTNING! NOW THIS IS MY IDEA...
WITHIN SECONDS, AS THE DARK STORM CLOUD APPROACHES, THE ENERGY-BEING SENDS OUT A MENTAL CALL TO ITS FELLOW PRISONERS...
THE MANY THOUSANDS OF ALIEN PRISONERS COMBINE WITH THE PEOPLE OF RANN AND OTHER HUMAN CAPTIVES TO SEND THEIR MENTAL ENERGY UPWARD TOWARD THE STORM CLOUD...
ALL THOUGHT IS ELECTRICAL IN NATURE! I'M HOPING THAT BY BOMBARDING THE ALREADY CHARGED CLOUD WITH THE ADDED ENERGY IN OUR THOUGHT-WAVES--WE CAN CAUSE LIGHTNING TO FORM!

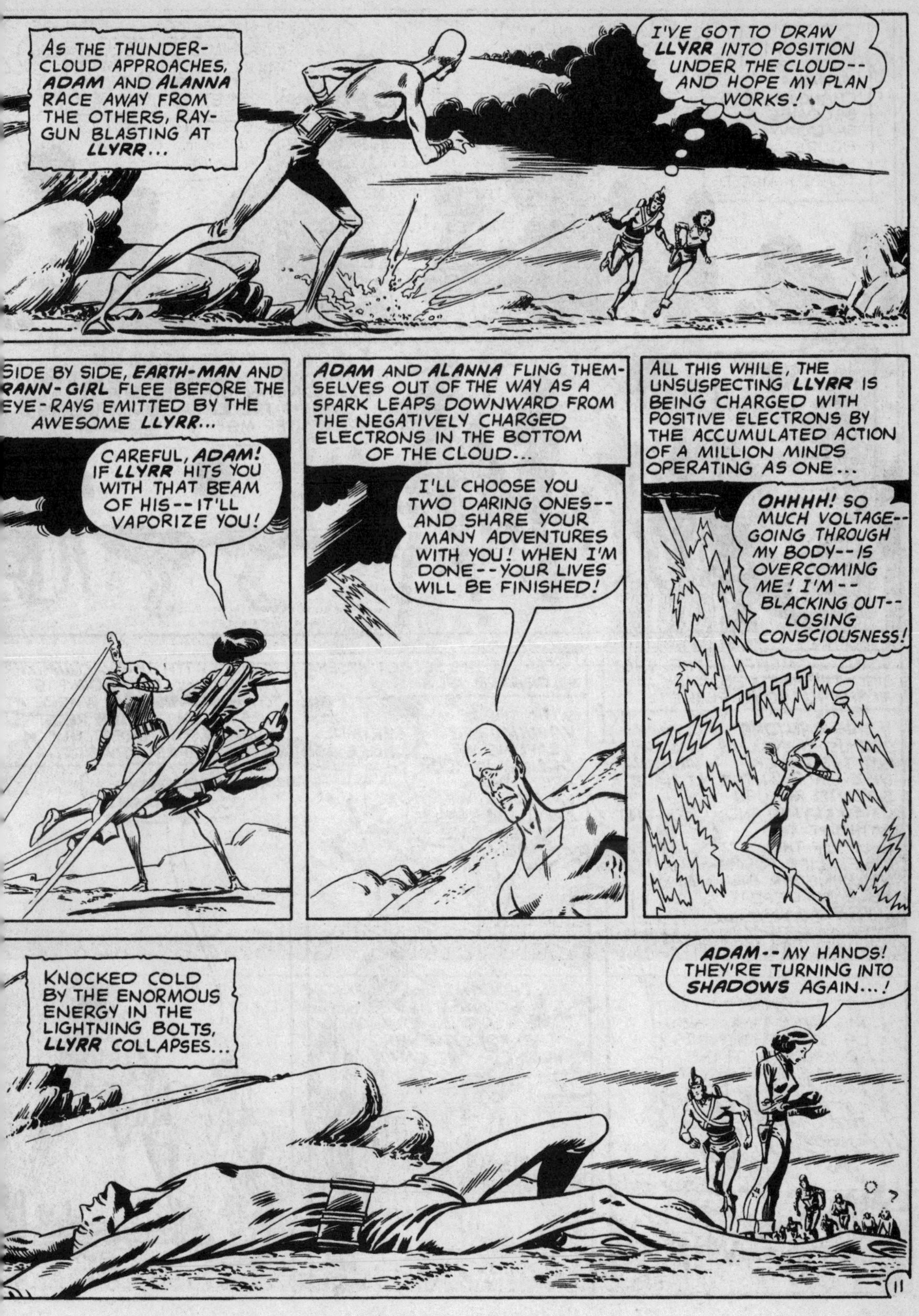
AS THE THUNDER-CLOUD APPROACHES, ADAM AND ALANNA RACE AWAY FROM THE OTHERS, RAY-GUN BLASTING AT LLYRR...
I'VE GOT TO DRAW LLYRR INTO POSITION UNDER THE CLOUD-- AND HOPE MY PLAN WORKS!
SIDE BY SIDE, EARTH-MAN AND RANN-GIRL FLEE BEFORE THE EYE-RAYS EMITTED BY THE AWESOME LLYRR...
CAREFUL, ADAM! IF LLYRR HITS YOU WITH THAT BEAM OF HIS--IT'LL VAPORIZE YOU!
ADAM AND ALANNA FLING THEMSELVES OUT OF THE WAY AS A SPARK LEAPS DOWNWARD FROM THE NEGATIVELY CHARGED ELECTRONS IN THE BOTTOM OF THE CLOUD...
I'LL CHOOSE YOU TWO DARING ONES-- AND SHARE YOUR MANY ADVENTURES WITH YOU! WHEN I'M DONE--YOUR LIVES WILL BE FINISHED!
ALL THIS WHILE, THE UNSUSPECTING LLYRR IS BEING CHARGED WITH POSITIVE ELECTRONS BY THE ACCUMULATED ACTION OF A MILLION MINDS OPERATING AS ONE...
OHHHH! SO MUCH VOLTAGE-- GOING THROUGH MY BODY--IS OVERCOMING ME! I'M-- BLACKING OUT-- LOSING CONSCIOUSNESS!
ZZZTTTTT
KNOCKED COLD BY THE ENORMOUS ENERGY IN THE LIGHTNING BOLTS, LLYRR COLLAPSES...
ADAM--MY HANDS! THEY'RE TURNING INTO SHADOWS AGAIN...!
11

As *ADAM* watches, *ALANNA* changes shape— becomes a shadowy figure again, even as he does himself..

WHAT'S CAUSING THIS TO HAPPEN TO US?

I THINK I UNDERSTAND! WHEN *LLYRR* LOST CONSCIOUSNESS, HIS GREAT MENTAL POWERS WHICH KEPT US HERE ON THIS PLANET--FADED OUT!

All around them the many life-forms of the prisoners of *LLYRR* also become shadowy creatures-- then fade away...

NOW I EXPECT WE WILL BE DRAWN BACK TO *RANN*--JUST AS I'M DRAWN BACK TO *EARTH* WHEN THE *ZETA-BEAM* WEARS OFF ME!

Scant moments later, they find themselves back on *ALANNA'S* home planet...

IF THE *VANTORS* SEE US THEY'LL PUT THE BLACK DISC BACK IN THE SKY AND RETURN US TO *LLYRR*! AND WITHOUT THE HELP OF THE OTHER LIFE-FORMS-- WE'LL NEVER BE ABLE TO DEFEAT *LLYRR* AGAIN!

DON'T WORRY, *ALANNA*-- I HAVE A PLAN TO PREVENT *THAT* FROM HAPPENING!

Later, at the secret arsenal at *CRATER ISLAND*...

WITH THESE *VACUUMIZER* WEAPONS WE ORGINALLY TOOK FROM THE *VANTORS*, WE SHOULD BE ABLE TO OVERCOME THEM!

I CERTAINLY HOPE SO!

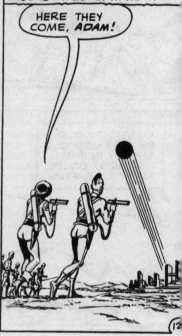

Armed with the *VACUUMIZER* the daring duo rockets toward *RANAGAR* where at first sight of the returned humans, the great black disc is fired upward...

HERE THEY COME, *ADAM*!

12

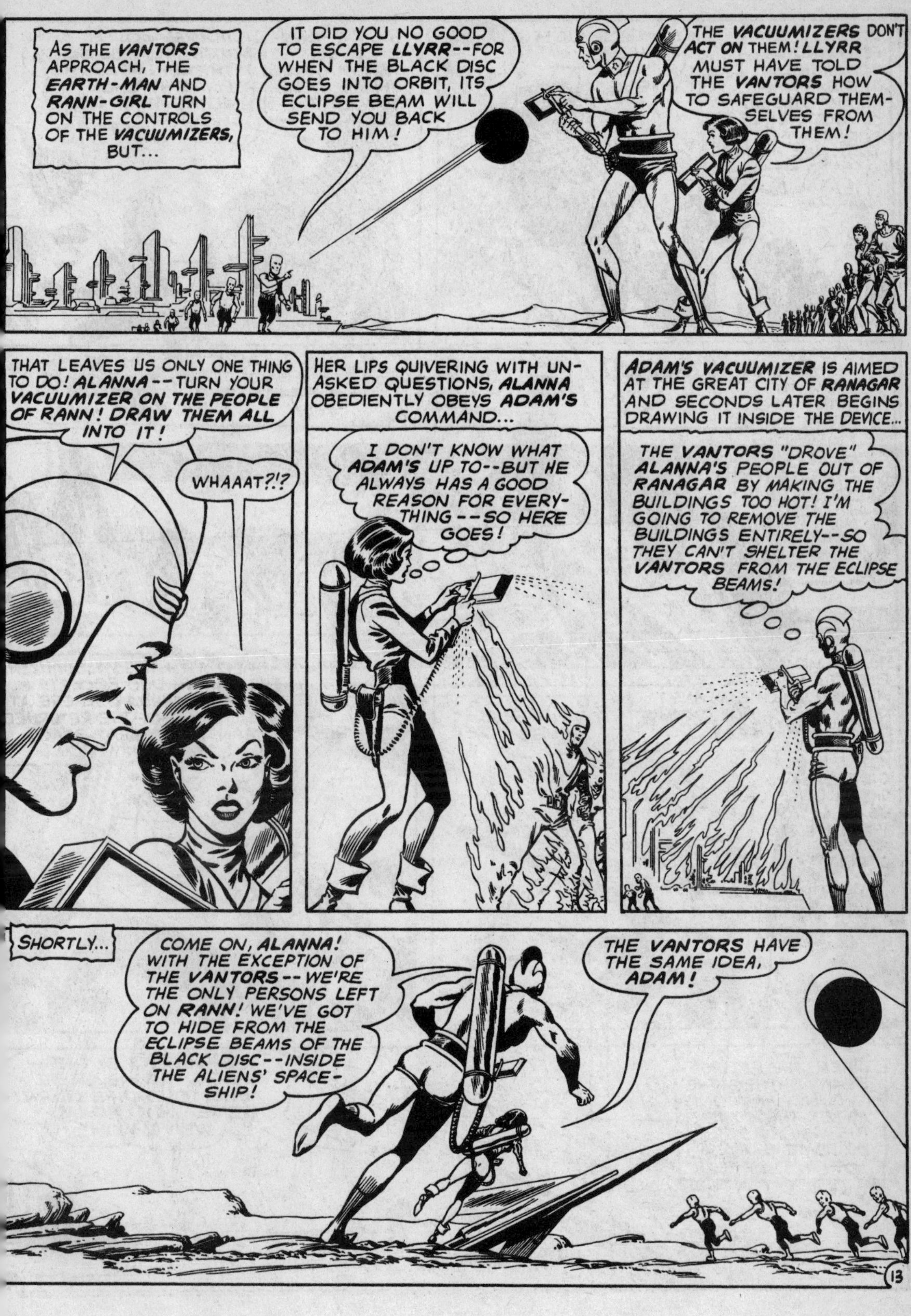

AS THE VANTORS APPROACH, THE EARTH-MAN AND RANN-GIRL TURN ON THE CONTROLS OF THE VACUUMIZERS, BUT...
IT DID YOU NO GOOD TO ESCAPE LLYRR--FOR WHEN THE BLACK DISC GOES INTO ORBIT, ITS ECLIPSE BEAM WILL SEND YOU BACK TO HIM!
THE VACUUMIZERS DON'T ACT ON THEM! LLYRR MUST HAVE TOLD THE VANTORS HOW TO SAFEGUARD THEMSELVES FROM THEM!
THAT LEAVES US ONLY ONE THING TO DO! ALANNA--TURN YOUR VACUUMIZER ON THE PEOPLE OF RANN! DRAW THEM ALL INTO IT!
WHAAAT?!?
HER LIPS QUIVERING WITH UNASKED QUESTIONS, ALANNA OBEDIENTLY OBEYS ADAM'S COMMAND...
I DON'T KNOW WHAT ADAM'S UP TO--BUT HE ALWAYS HAS A GOOD REASON FOR EVERYTHING--SO HERE GOES!
ADAM'S VACUUMIZER IS AIMED AT THE GREAT CITY OF RANAGAR AND SECONDS LATER BEGINS DRAWING IT INSIDE THE DEVICE...
THE VANTORS "DROVE" ALANNA'S PEOPLE OUT OF RANAGAR BY MAKING THE BUILDINGS TOO HOT! I'M GOING TO REMOVE THE BUILDINGS ENTIRELY--SO THEY CAN'T SHELTER THE VANTORS FROM THE ECLIPSE BEAMS!
SHORTLY...
COME ON, ALANNA! WITH THE EXCEPTION OF THE VANTORS--WE'RE THE ONLY PERSONS LEFT ON RANN! WE'VE GOT TO HIDE FROM THE ECLIPSE BEAMS OF THE BLACK DISC--INSIDE THE ALIENS' SPACESHIP!
THE VANTORS HAVE THE SAME IDEA, ADAM!
13

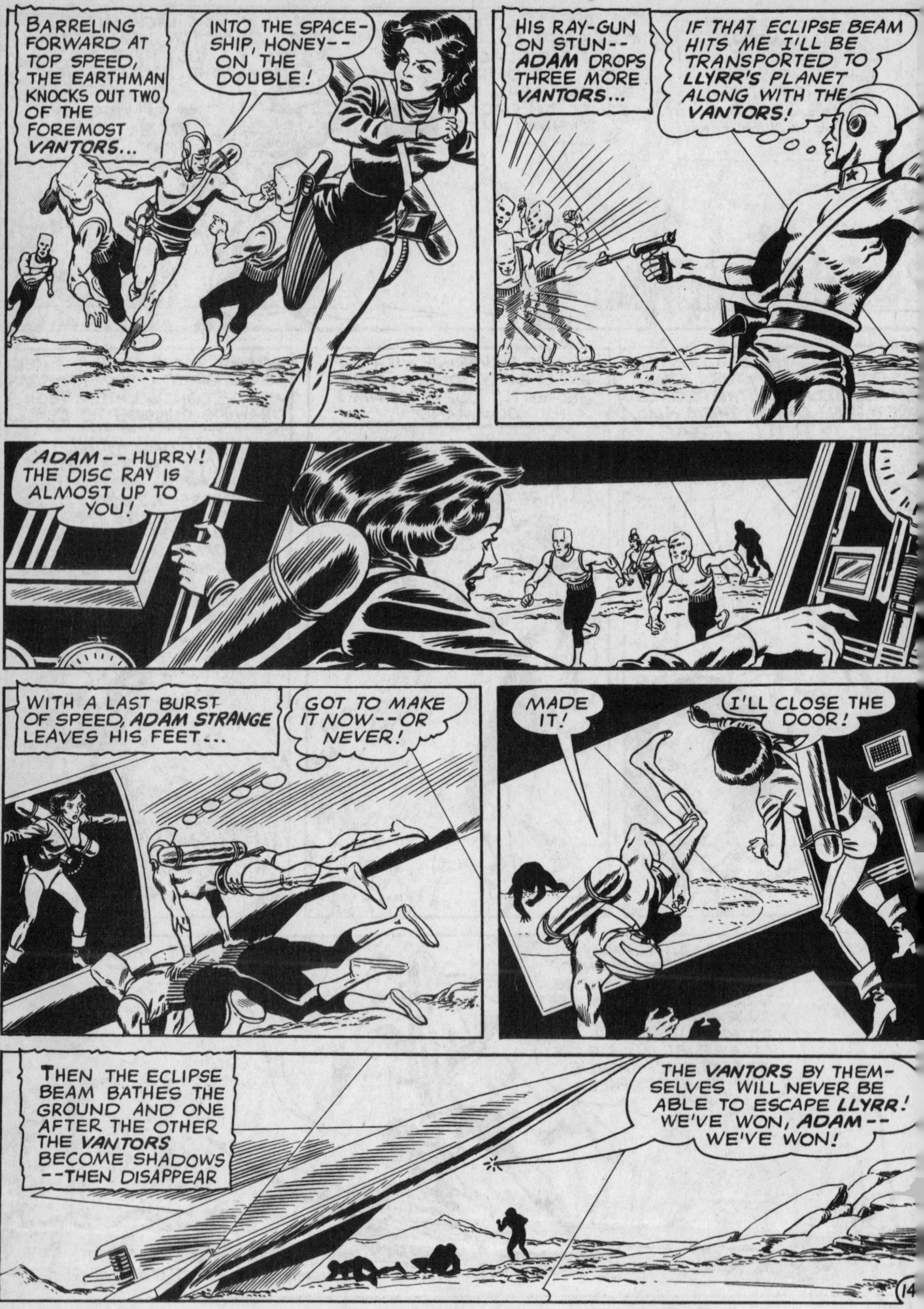
BARRELING FORWARD AT TOP SPEED, THE EARTHMAN KNOCKS OUT TWO OF THE FOREMOST VANTORS...
INTO THE SPACE-SHIP, HONEY-- ON THE DOUBLE!
HIS RAY-GUN ON STUN-- ADAM DROPS THREE MORE VANTORS...
IF THAT ECLIPSE BEAM HITS ME I'LL BE TRANSPORTED TO LLYRR'S PLANET ALONG WITH THE VANTORS!
ADAM--HURRY! THE DISC RAY IS ALMOST UP TO YOU!
WITH A LAST BURST OF SPEED, ADAM STRANGE LEAVES HIS FEET...
GOT TO MAKE IT NOW--OR NEVER!
MADE IT!
I'LL CLOSE THE DOOR!
THEN THE ECLIPSE BEAM BATHES THE GROUND AND ONE AFTER THE OTHER THE VANTORS BECOME SHADOWS --THEN DISAPPEAR
THE VANTORS BY THEM-SELVES WILL NEVER BE ABLE TO ESCAPE LLYRR! WE'VE WON, ADAM-- WE'VE WON!
14

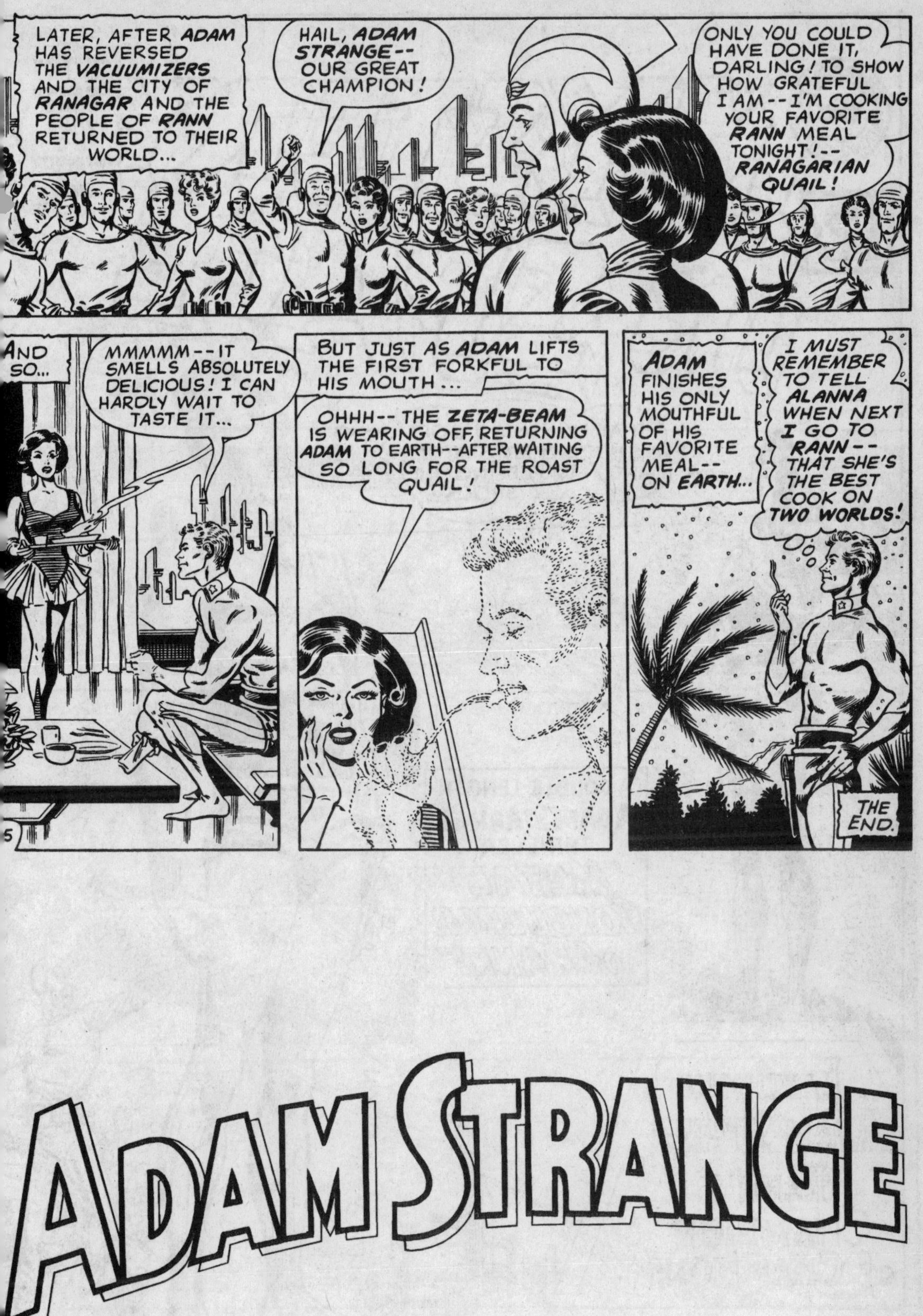
LATER, AFTER ADAM HAS REVERSED THE VACUUMIZERS AND THE CITY OF RANAGAR AND THE PEOPLE OF RANN RETURNED TO THEIR WORLD...
HAIL, ADAM STRANGE-- OUR GREAT CHAMPION!
ONLY YOU COULD HAVE DONE IT, DARLING! TO SHOW HOW GRATEFUL I AM--I'M COOKING YOUR FAVORITE RANN MEAL TONIGHT!-- RANAGARIAN QUAIL!
AND SO...
MMMMM--IT SMELLS ABSOLUTELY DELICIOUS! I CAN HARDLY WAIT TO TASTE IT...
BUT JUST AS ADAM LIFTS THE FIRST FORKFUL TO HIS MOUTH...
OHHH-- THE ZETA-BEAM IS WEARING OFF, RETURNING ADAM TO EARTH--AFTER WAITING SO LONG FOR THE ROAST QUAIL!
ADAM FINISHES HIS ONLY MOUTHFUL OF HIS FAVORITE MEAL-- ON EARTH...
I MUST REMEMBER TO TELL ALANNA WHEN NEXT I GO TO RANN-- THAT SHE'S THE BEST COOK ON TWO WORLDS!
THE END.

ADAM STRANGE

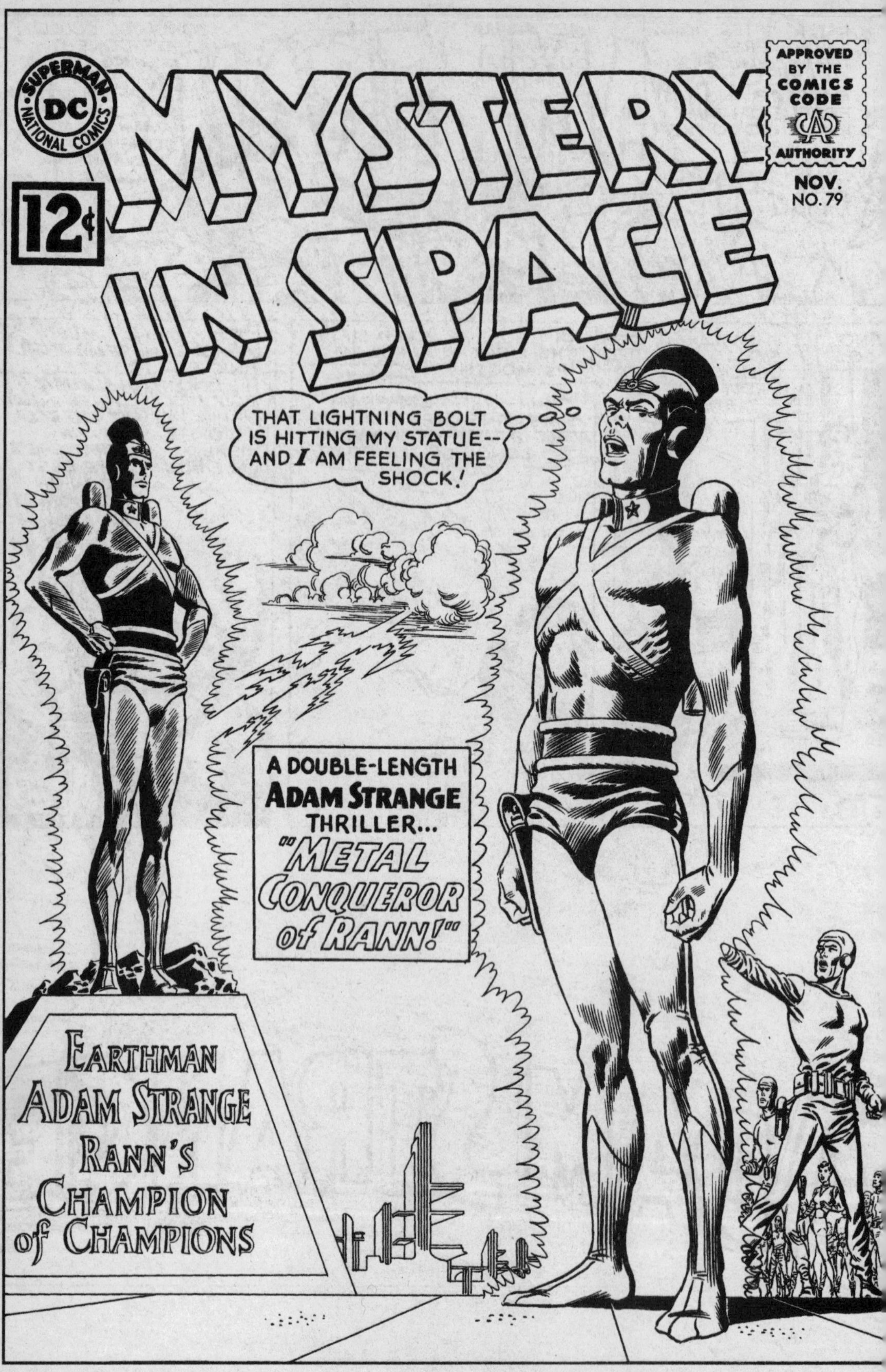
SUPERMAN DC NATIONAL COMICS
MYSTERY IN SPACE
12¢
APPROVED BY THE COMICS CODE AUTHORITY
NOV. NO. 79
THAT LIGHTNING BOLT IS HITTING MY STATUE-- AND I AM FEELING THE SHOCK!
A DOUBLE-LENGTH ADAM STRANGE THRILLER... "METAL CONQUEROR of RANN!"
EARTHMAN ADAM STRANGE RANN'S CHAMPION of CHAMPIONS

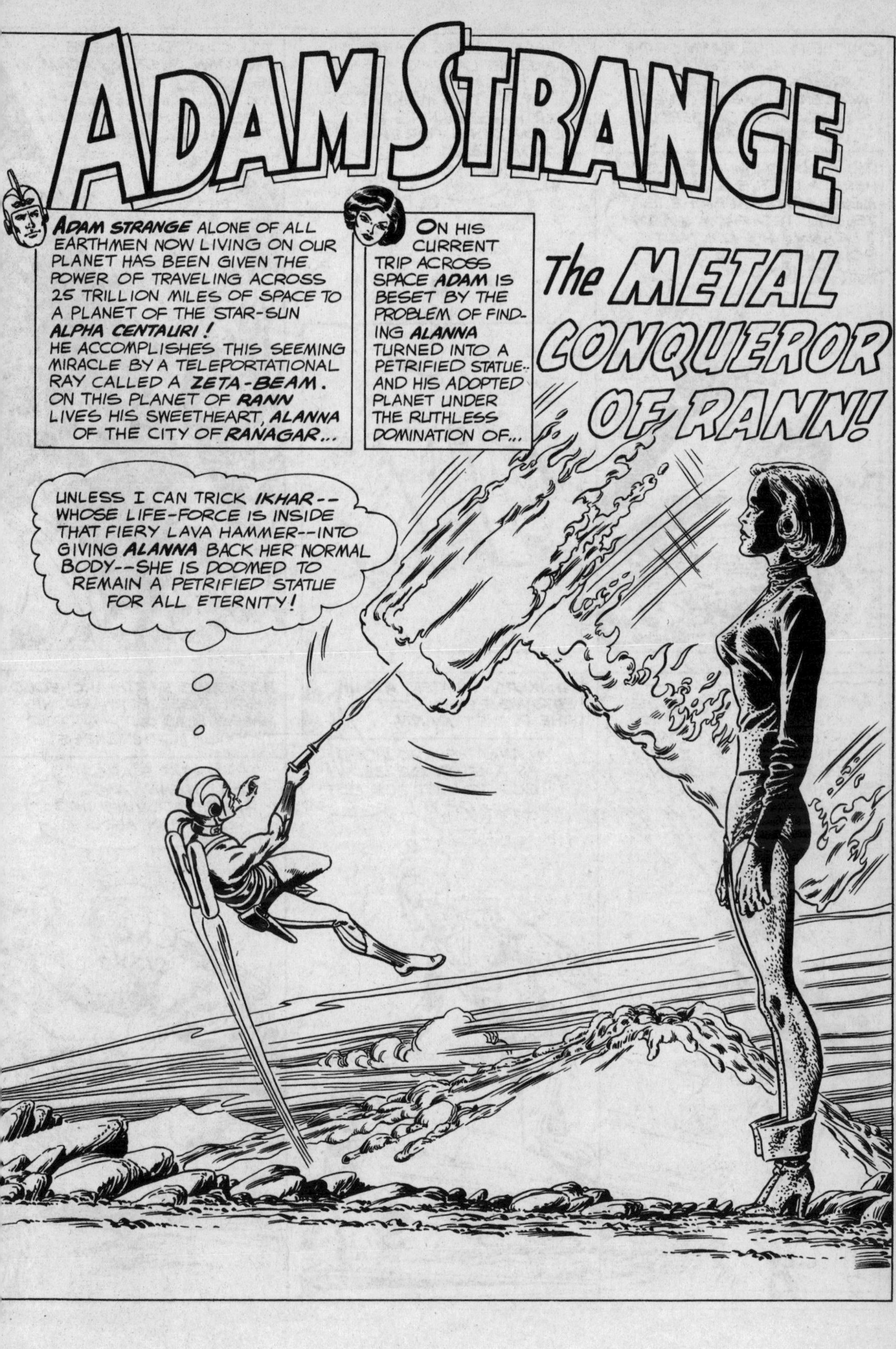
ADAM STRANGE
ADAM STRANGE ALONE OF ALL EARTHMEN NOW LIVING ON OUR PLANET HAS BEEN GIVEN THE POWER OF TRAVELING ACROSS 25 TRILLION MILES OF SPACE TO A PLANET OF THE STAR-SUN ALPHA CENTAURI! HE ACCOMPLISHES THIS SEEMING MIRACLE BY A TELEPORTATIONAL RAY CALLED A ZETA-BEAM. ON THIS PLANET OF RANN LIVES HIS SWEETHEART, ALANNA OF THE CITY OF RANAGAR...
ON HIS CURRENT TRIP ACROSS SPACE ADAM IS BESET BY THE PROBLEM OF FINDING ALANNA TURNED INTO A PETRIFIED STATUE.. AND HIS ADOPTED PLANET UNDER THE RUTHLESS DOMINATION OF...
The METAL CONQUEROR OF RANN!
UNLESS I CAN TRICK IKHAR--WHOSE LIFE-FORCE IS INSIDE THAT FIERY LAVA HAMMER--INTO GIVING ALANNA BACK HER NORMAL BODY--SHE IS DOOMED TO REMAIN A PETRIFIED STATUE FOR ALL ETERNITY!

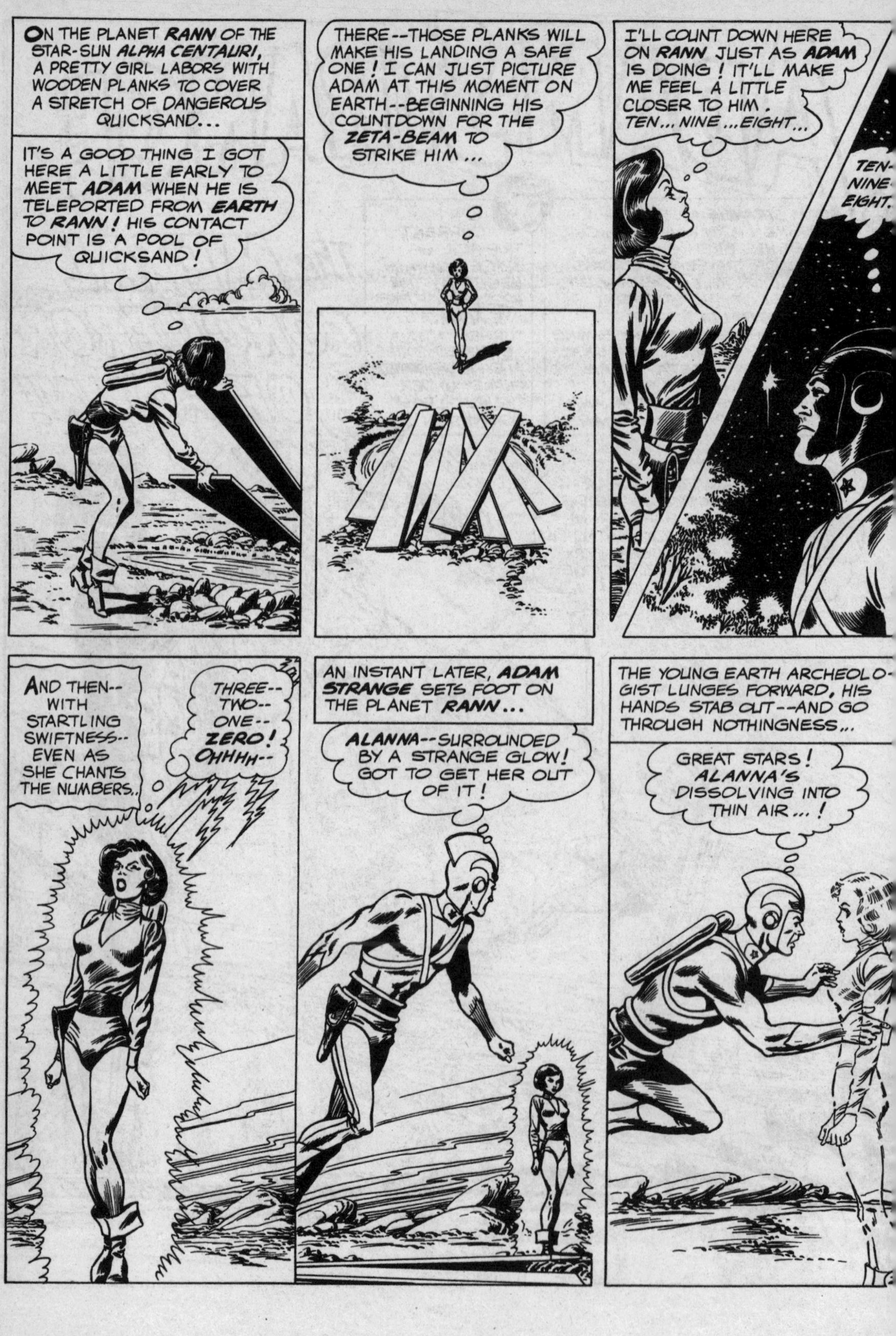

ON THE PLANET RANN OF THE STAR-SUN ALPHA CENTAURI, A PRETTY GIRL LABORS WITH WOODEN PLANKS TO COVER A STRETCH OF DANGEROUS QUICKSAND...
IT'S A GOOD THING I GOT HERE A LITTLE EARLY TO MEET ADAM WHEN HE IS TELEPORTED FROM EARTH TO RANN! HIS CONTACT POINT IS A POOL OF QUICKSAND!
THERE--THOSE PLANKS WILL MAKE HIS LANDING A SAFE ONE! I CAN JUST PICTURE ADAM AT THIS MOMENT ON EARTH--BEGINNING HIS COUNTDOWN FOR THE ZETA-BEAM TO STRIKE HIM...
I'LL COUNT DOWN HERE ON RANN JUST AS ADAM IS DOING! IT'LL MAKE ME FEEL A LITTLE CLOSER TO HIM. TEN... NINE ...EIGHT...
TEN-NINE-EIGHT.
AND THEN--WITH STARTLING SWIFTNESS--EVEN AS SHE CHANTS THE NUMBERS...
THREE--TWO--ONE--ZERO! OHHHH--
AN INSTANT LATER, ADAM STRANGE SETS FOOT ON THE PLANET RANN...
ALANNA--SURROUNDED BY A STRANGE GLOW! GOT TO GET HER OUT OF IT!
THE YOUNG EARTH ARCHEOLOGIST LUNGES FORWARD, HIS HANDS STAB OUT--AND GO THROUGH NOTHINGNESS...
GREAT STARS! ALANNA'S DISSOLVING INTO THIN AIR...!

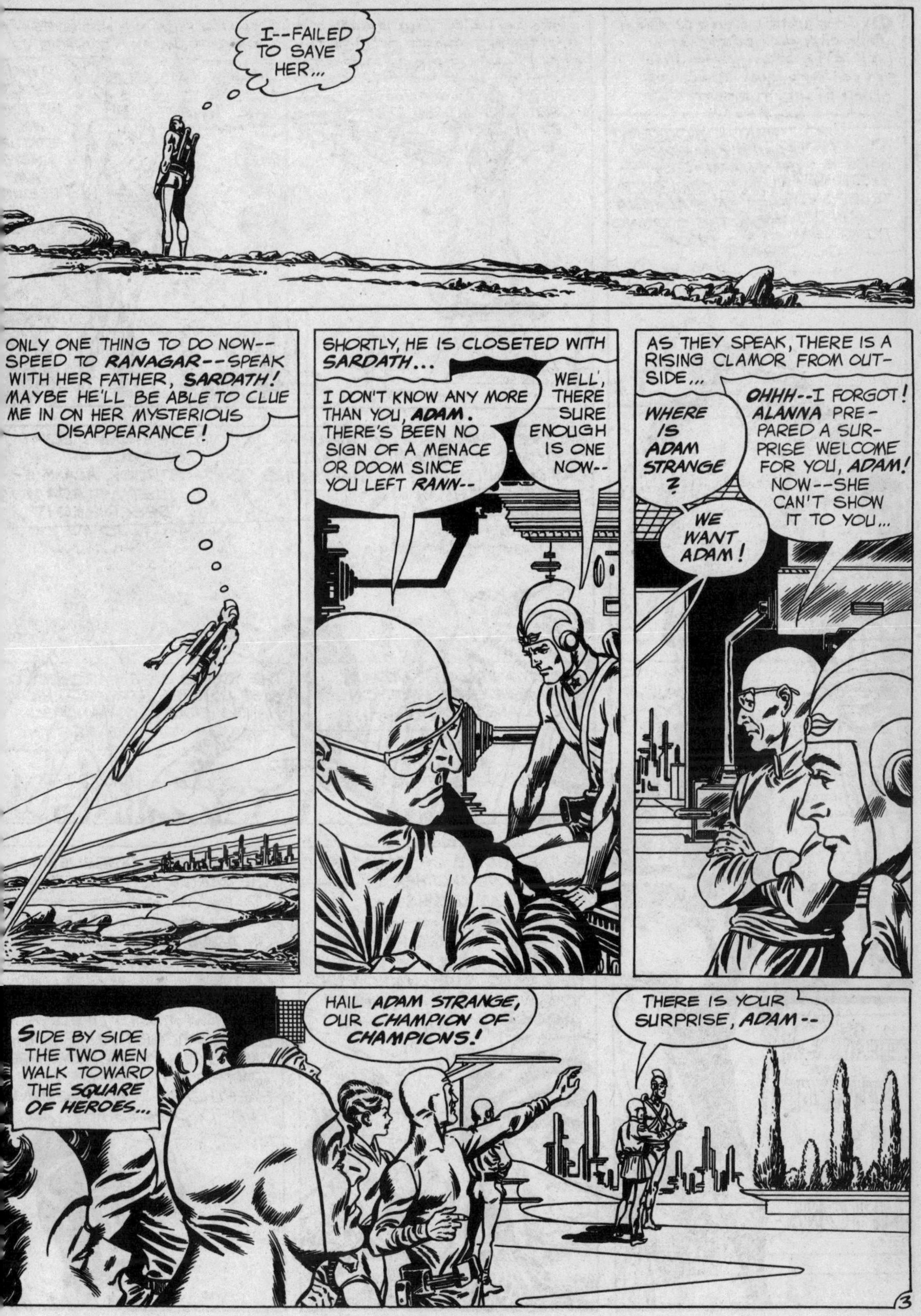
I--FAILED TO SAVE HER...
ONLY ONE THING TO DO NOW--SPEED TO RANAGAR--SPEAK WITH HER FATHER, SARDATH! MAYBE HE'LL BE ABLE TO CLUE ME IN ON HER MYSTERIOUS DISAPPEARANCE!
SHORTLY, HE IS CLOSETED WITH SARDATH...
I DON'T KNOW ANY MORE THAN YOU, ADAM. THERE'S BEEN NO SIGN OF A MENACE OR DOOM SINCE YOU LEFT RANN--
WELL, THERE SURE ENOUGH IS ONE NOW--
AS THEY SPEAK, THERE IS A RISING CLAMOR FROM OUTSIDE...
WHERE IS ADAM STRANGE?
WE WANT ADAM!
OHHH--I FORGOT! ALANNA PREPARED A SURPRISE WELCOME FOR YOU, ADAM! NOW--SHE CAN'T SHOW IT TO YOU...
SIDE BY SIDE THE TWO MEN WALK TOWARD THE SQUARE OF HEROES...
HAIL ADAM STRANGE, OUR CHAMPION OF CHAMPIONS!
THERE IS YOUR SURPRISE, ADAM--
3

MIXED EMOTIONS WAR IN *ADAM* AS HE STARES UPWARD AT A LIFE-SIZE STATUE OF HIMSELF--AND SWALLOWS THE LUMP IN HIS THROAT...

WHAT A MOCKERY! "RANN'S CHAMPION OF CHAMPIONS"-- WHEN I COULDN'T EVEN SAVE *ALANNA* FROM THE GLOWING DOOM...!

EARTHMAN STRANGE NN'S MPION AMPIONS

EVEN AS HE BLINKS AGAINST THE TEARS FILMING HIS EYES--A GLITTERING SHAFT OF LIGHTNING RIPS FROM AN OVERHEAD CLOUD AND STRIKES THE STATUE...

THAT BOLT HITTING MY STATUE AND I AM FEELING THE SHOCK

EARTHMAN ADAM STRANGE RANN'S CHAMPION OF CHAMPIONS

SHOCKED THROATS GASP AND TONGUES CRY OUT IN DISMAY AS THE EARTHMAN SHIMMERS OUT OF SIGHT...

ADAM-- WHAT'S HAPPENING TO YOU?!

THE SAME SORT OF BOLT WHICH STRUCK ALANNA-- JUST AS *ADAM* DESCRIBED IT TO ME!

AS THE PEOPLE OF *RANAGAR* TURN TO ONE ANOTHER IN STUNNED AMAZEMENT...

IS THERE ANYTHING WE CAN DO TO SAVE *ADAM*?

SAVE HIM FROM-- WHAT? WE DON'T EVEN KNOW WHO-- OR WHAT--

I MADE ADAM DISAPPEAR!

EYES WIDEN IN DISBELIEF AS THE STATUE OF *ADAM STRANGE* "TALKS"...

YES! I DISPOSED OF *ADAM STRANGE*! I-- *IKHAR THE UNDYING!* MASTER OF THE MINERAL WORLD--AND THE NEW MASTER OF *RANN!* EVEN NOW ADAM'S LIFELESS BODY IS MORE THAN A THOUSAND LIGHT-YEARS FROM HERE-- TRAPPED WITH THAT OF HIS SWEETHEART IN AN OTHERWISE EMPTY SPACESHIP!

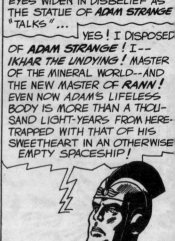

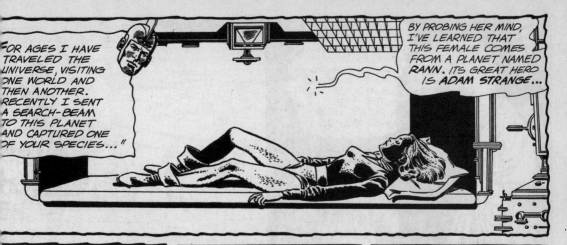

"FOR AGES I HAVE TRAVELED THE UNIVERSE, VISITING ONE WORLD AND THEN ANOTHER. RECENTLY I SENT A SEARCH-BEAM TO THIS PLANET AND CAPTURED ONE OF YOUR SPECIES..."

BY PROBING HER MIND, I'VE LEARNED THAT THIS FEMALE COMES FROM A PLANET NAMED *RANN*. ITS GREAT HERO IS *ADAM STRANGE*...

SHE HAS BEEN PETRIFIED BY MY ELECTOLONIS BEAM. I SHALL NOW BRING *ADAM STRANGE* HERE THE SAME WAY--SO THAT HE TOO SHALL LIE PETRIFIED IN MY SPACESHIP!

THE GLOATING THOUGHTS OF *IKHAR THE UNDYING* FLOAT OUT OVER THE HEADS OF THE PEOPLE OF *RANAGAR*...

SINCE I CAN LIVE IN INANIMATE MATTER--YOU CANNOT HARM ME! YOU MAY DESTROY THIS STATUE IN AN EFFORT TO DESTROY ME--BUT I SHALL SIMPLY TRANSFER MYSELF TO ANOTHER MINERAL OBJECT!*

EEYAH--THE STATUE IS MOVING--

*Editor's Note: A MINERAL IS ANY INORGANIC SUBSTANCE. IT MAY EXIST IN A SOLID, GASEOUS OR LIQUID STATE.

YOUR HERO AND HIS SWEET-HEART ARE NOW PETRIFIED STATUES --COMPLETELY UN-ABLE TO HELP YOU! IT AMUSES ME TO APPEAR IN HIS STATUE-IMAGE AS I BECOME YOUR RULER! YOUR *NEW*-- HA-HA--CHAMPION OF CHAMPIONS!

IF THE *ZETA-BEAM* FAILS TO BRING *ADAM STRANGE* BACK TO EARTH WHEN IT WEARS OFF--HE'LL TRAVEL FOREVER IN INTER-STELLAR SPACE! BUT IF IT DOES TAKE HIM BACK TO EARTH--HE'LL ONLY BE A LIFELESS STATUE! I HAVE NOTHING TO FEAR FROM YOUR EX-CHAMPION NOW!

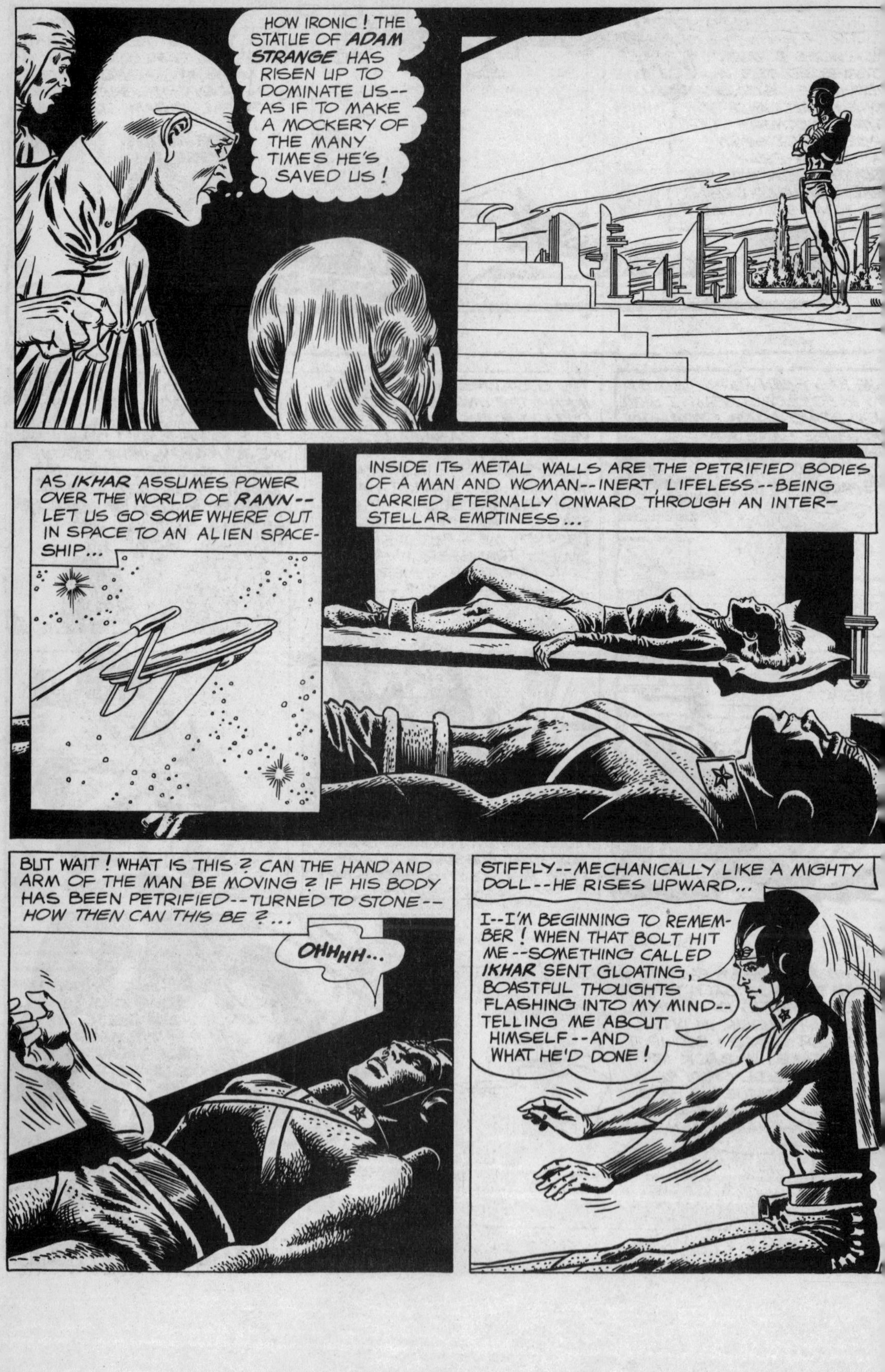
HOW IRONIC! THE STATUE OF ADAM STRANGE HAS RISEN UP TO DOMINATE US-- AS IF TO MAKE A MOCKERY OF THE MANY TIMES HE'S SAVED US!
AS IKHAR ASSUMES POWER OVER THE WORLD OF RANN-- LET US GO SOMEWHERE OUT IN SPACE TO AN ALIEN SPACE-SHIP...
INSIDE ITS METAL WALLS ARE THE PETRIFIED BODIES OF A MAN AND WOMAN--INERT, LIFELESS--BEING CARRIED ETERNALLY ONWARD THROUGH AN INTER-STELLAR EMPTINESS...
BUT WAIT! WHAT IS THIS? CAN THE HAND AND ARM OF THE MAN BE MOVING? IF HIS BODY HAS BEEN PETRIFIED--TURNED TO STONE-- HOW THEN CAN THIS BE?...
OHHHH...
STIFFLY--MECHANICALLY LIKE A MIGHTY DOLL--HE RISES UPWARD...
I--I'M BEGINNING TO REMEMBER! WHEN THAT BOLT HIT ME--SOMETHING CALLED IKHAR SENT GLOATING, BOASTFUL THOUGHTS FLASHING INTO MY MIND-- TELLING ME ABOUT HIMSELF--AND WHAT HE'D DONE!

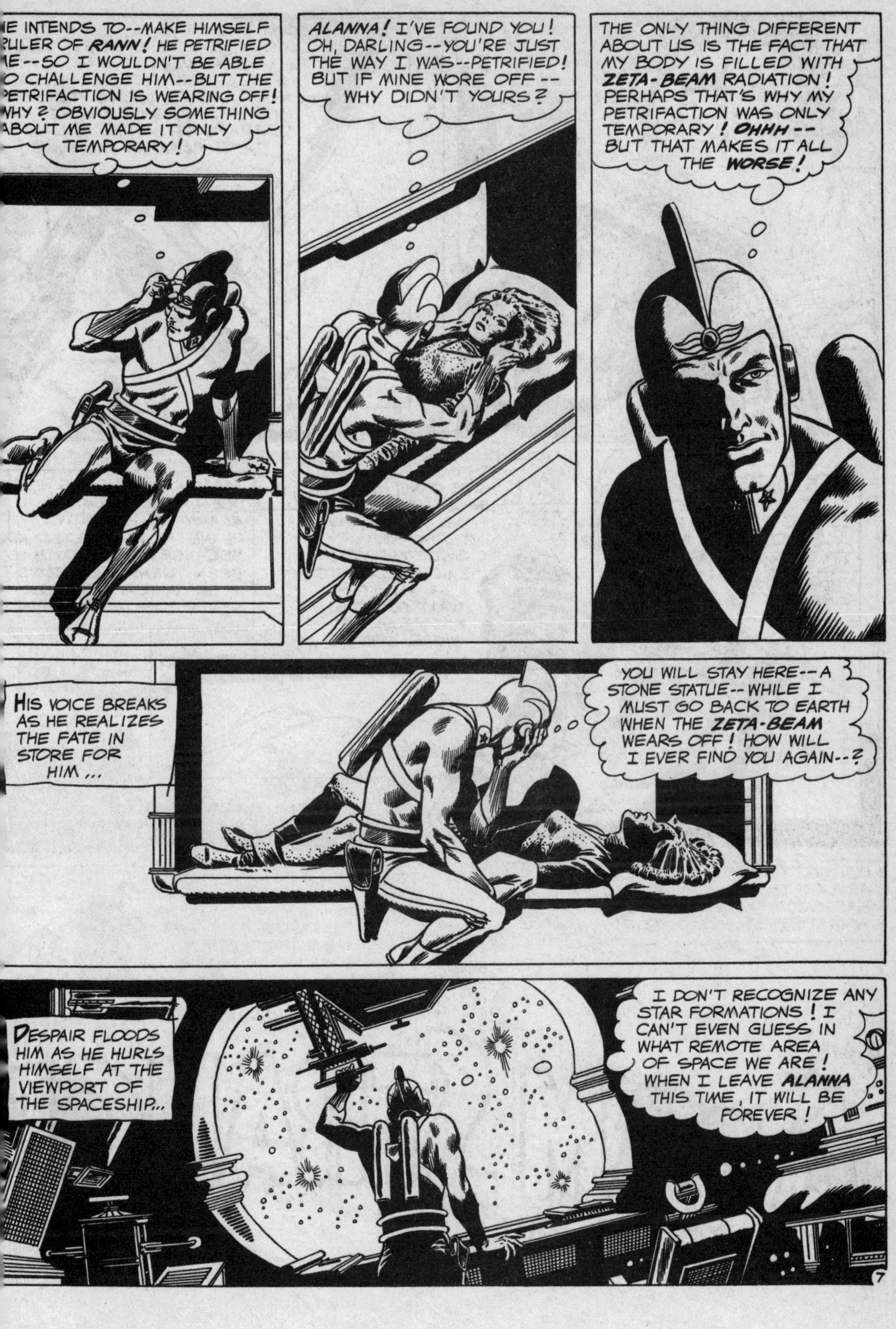
HE INTENDS TO--MAKE HIMSELF RULER OF RANN! HE PETRIFIED ME--SO I WOULDN'T BE ABLE TO CHALLENGE HIM--BUT THE PETRIFACTION IS WEARING OFF! WHY? OBVIOUSLY SOMETHING ABOUT ME MADE IT ONLY TEMPORARY!
ALANNA! I'VE FOUND YOU! OH, DARLING--YOU'RE JUST THE WAY I WAS--PETRIFIED! BUT IF MINE WORE OFF--WHY DIDN'T YOURS?
THE ONLY THING DIFFERENT ABOUT US IS THE FACT THAT MY BODY IS FILLED WITH ZETA-BEAM RADIATION! PERHAPS THAT'S WHY MY PETRIFACTION WAS ONLY TEMPORARY! OHHH--BUT THAT MAKES IT ALL THE WORSE!
HIS VOICE BREAKS AS HE REALIZES THE FATE IN STORE FOR HIM...
YOU WILL STAY HERE--A STONE STATUE--WHILE I MUST GO BACK TO EARTH WHEN THE ZETA-BEAM WEARS OFF! HOW WILL I EVER FIND YOU AGAIN--?
DESPAIR FLOODS HIM AS HE HURLS HIMSELF AT THE VIEWPORT OF THE SPACESHIP...
I DON'T RECOGNIZE ANY STAR FORMATIONS! I CAN'T EVEN GUESS IN WHAT REMOTE AREA OF SPACE WE ARE! WHEN I LEAVE ALANNA THIS TIME, IT WILL BE FOREVER!
7

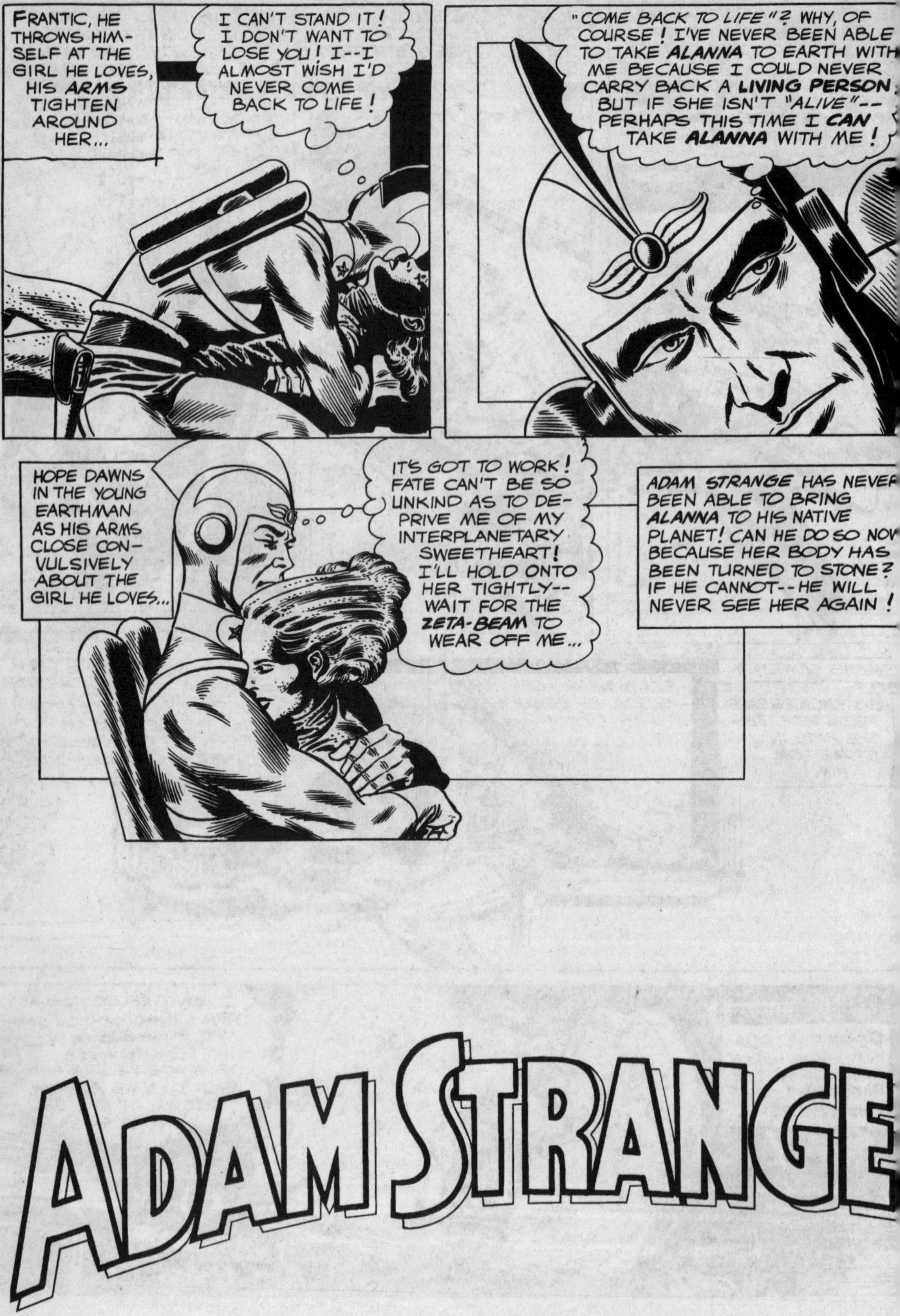
FRANTIC, HE THROWS HIMSELF AT THE GIRL HE LOVES, HIS ARMS TIGHTEN AROUND HER...
I CAN'T STAND IT! I DON'T WANT TO LOSE YOU! I--I ALMOST WISH I'D NEVER COME BACK TO LIFE!
"COME BACK TO LIFE"? WHY, OF COURSE! I'VE NEVER BEEN ABLE TO TAKE ALANNA TO EARTH WITH ME BECAUSE I COULD NEVER CARRY BACK A LIVING PERSON! BUT IF SHE ISN'T "ALIVE"-- PERHAPS THIS TIME I CAN TAKE ALANNA WITH ME!
HOPE DAWNS IN THE YOUNG EARTHMAN AS HIS ARMS CLOSE CONVULSIVELY ABOUT THE GIRL HE LOVES...
IT'S GOT TO WORK! FATE CAN'T BE SO UNKIND AS TO DEPRIVE ME OF MY INTERPLANETARY SWEETHEART! I'LL HOLD ONTO HER TIGHTLY-- WAIT FOR THE ZETA-BEAM TO WEAR OFF ME...
ADAM STRANGE HAS NEVER BEEN ABLE TO BRING ALANNA TO HIS NATIVE PLANET! CAN HE DO SO NOW BECAUSE HER BODY HAS BEEN TURNED TO STONE? IF HE CANNOT--HE WILL NEVER SEE HER AGAIN!
ADAM STRANGE

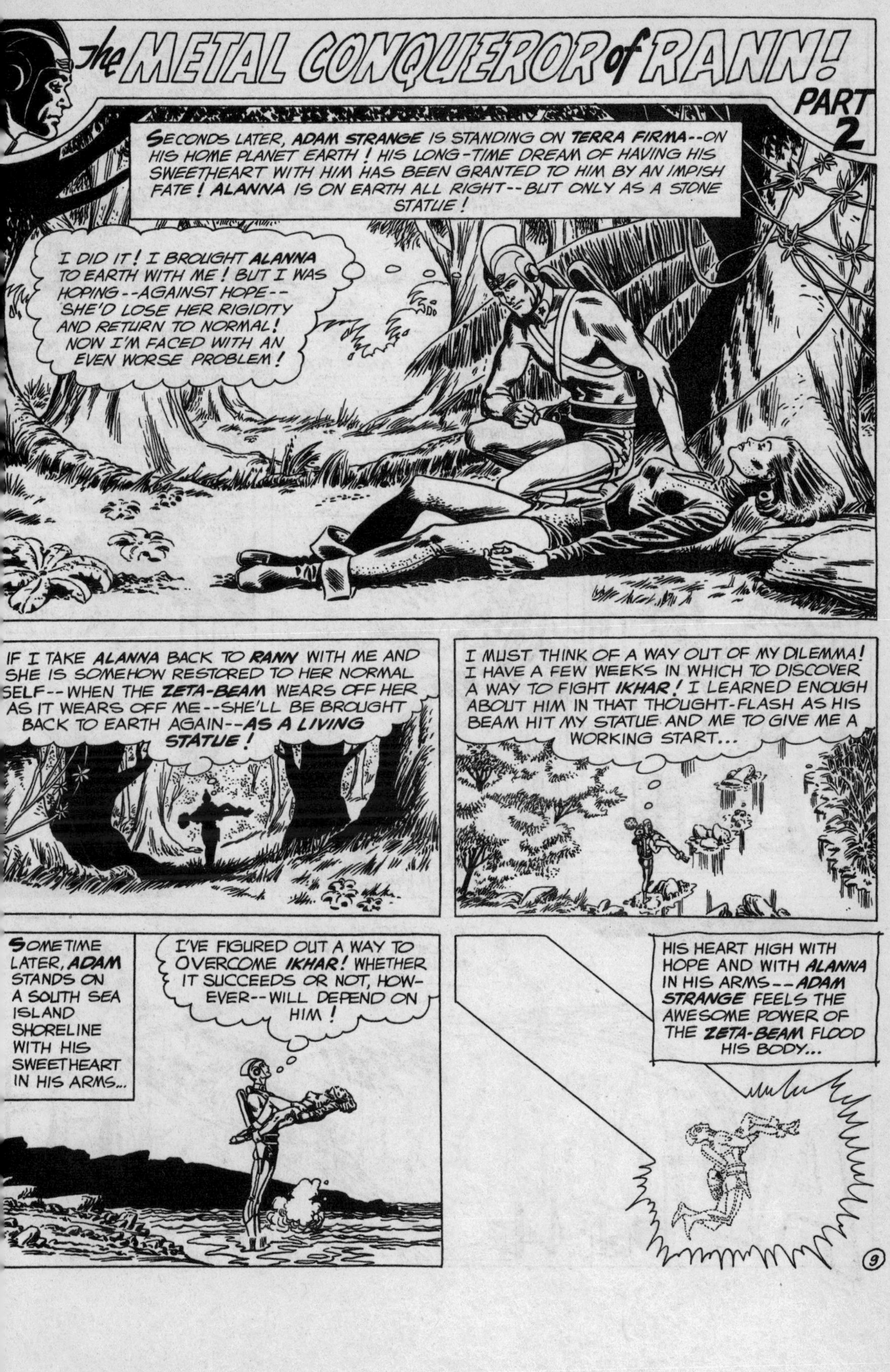

The METAL CONQUEROR of RANN! PART 2
SECONDS LATER, ADAM STRANGE IS STANDING ON TERRA FIRMA--ON HIS HOME PLANET EARTH! HIS LONG-TIME DREAM OF HAVING HIS SWEETHEART WITH HIM HAS BEEN GRANTED TO HIM BY AN IMPISH FATE! ALANNA IS ON EARTH ALL RIGHT--BUT ONLY AS A STONE STATUE!
I DID IT! I BROUGHT ALANNA TO EARTH WITH ME! BUT I WAS HOPING--AGAINST HOPE--SHE'D LOSE HER RIGIDITY AND RETURN TO NORMAL! NOW I'M FACED WITH AN EVEN WORSE PROBLEM!
IF I TAKE ALANNA BACK TO RANN WITH ME AND SHE IS SOMEHOW RESTORED TO HER NORMAL SELF--WHEN THE ZETA-BEAM WEARS OFF HER AS IT WEARS OFF ME--SHE'LL BE BROUGHT BACK TO EARTH AGAIN--AS A LIVING STATUE!
I MUST THINK OF A WAY OUT OF MY DILEMMA! I HAVE A FEW WEEKS IN WHICH TO DISCOVER A WAY TO FIGHT IKHAR! I LEARNED ENOUGH ABOUT HIM IN THAT THOUGHT-FLASH AS HIS BEAM HIT MY STATUE AND ME TO GIVE ME A WORKING START...
SOMETIME LATER, ADAM STANDS ON A SOUTH SEA ISLAND SHORELINE WITH HIS SWEETHEART IN HIS ARMS...
I'VE FIGURED OUT A WAY TO OVERCOME IKHAR! WHETHER IT SUCCEEDS OR NOT, HOWEVER--WILL DEPEND ON HIM!
HIS HEART HIGH WITH HOPE AND WITH ALANNA IN HIS ARMS--ADAM STRANGE FEELS THE AWESOME POWER OF THE ZETA-BEAM FLOOD HIS BODY...
9

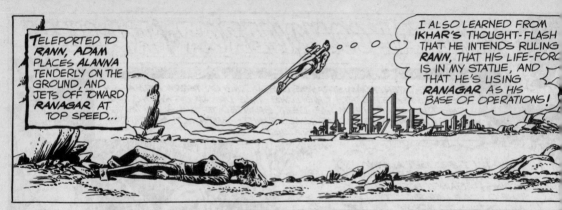

TELEPORTED TO RANN, ADAM PLACES ALANNA TENDERLY ON THE GROUND, AND JETS OFF TOWARD RANAGAR AT TOP SPEED...

I ALSO LEARNED FROM IKHAR'S THOUGHT-FLASH THAT HE INTENDS RULING RANN, THAT HIS LIFE-FORCE IS IN MY STATUE, AND THAT HE'S USING RANAGAR AS HIS BASE OF OPERATIONS!

IN THE CAPITAL CITY OF RANAGAR...

ADAM STRANGE? THIS IS IMPOSSIBLE! THERE WAS NO WAY FOR YOU TO COME HERE!

NO? LET ME PROVE IT TO YOU!

HIS RAY-GUN BLASTS THE STATUE FORM OF IKHAR WITH SUCH TERRIFIC HEAT THAT...

I'VE TURNED YOU INTO MOLTEN METAL!

FOOL! I CAN INHABIT ANY MINERAL FORM I DESIRE! YOU'VE MELTED YOUR STATUE -- BUT YOU HAVEN'T HARMED ME!

BZZZt!

EVEN AS HE SPEAKS, IKHAR ENTERS INTO THE STONY STRUCTURE OF A GREAT BUILDING AND...

YOU SEE? YOU CAN'T DEFEAT ME AND I'LL NEVER SURRENDER TO YOU! SO WHY NOT BE SENSIBLE AND GIVE UP?

NEVER! SO LONG AS I HAVE MY RAY-GUN I'LL FIGHT ON AND ON!

THE STONE HANDS DISINTEGRATE -- BUT IN THEIR PLACE...

I SWITCHED TO THE GLASS WINDOWS -- AND ANIMATED THEM INTO A GLASSY SPEAR!

I'M READY FOR YOU!

BZZZt!

THE GLASS SPEAR CRACKS TO PIECES, BUT...

DON'T GO AWAY, ADAM. I'LL RETURN SHORTLY TO CONTINUE OUR BATTLE!

I DON'T TRUST YOU, IKHAR! I'LL GO BACK TO ALANNA-- SO I'LL KNOW YOU CAN'T HARM ME THROUGH HER!

BZZT!

SHORTLY THEREAFTER, AS THE YOUNG EARTH ARCHEOLOGIST STANDS GUARD OVER HIS PETRIFIED SWEETHEART...

AN EXTINCT VOLCANO-- COMING TO LIFE! IKHAR MUST HAVE ACTIVATED IT FOR SOME DREAD PURPOSE OF HIS OWN!

HIS EYES WIDEN AS HE SEES...

A GIGANTIC CREATURE OF LIVING LAVA!

TRY AND STOP ME NOW, ADAM STRANGE!

AS LONG AS I CAN FIRE MY RAY-GUN-- I'LL KEEP FIGHTING!

BZZZT!

SWIFTLY IKHAR AGAIN CHANGES SHAPE--THIS TIME TO A FIERY LAVA HAMMER...

YOU SEE? MY RAY-GUN MAY NOT HURT YOU--BUT IT DESTROYS THE THINGS YOU HIDE IN! SOONER OR LATER YOU'LL RUN OUT OF HIDING PLACES!

I'LL GET YOU YET!

BZZZT!

11

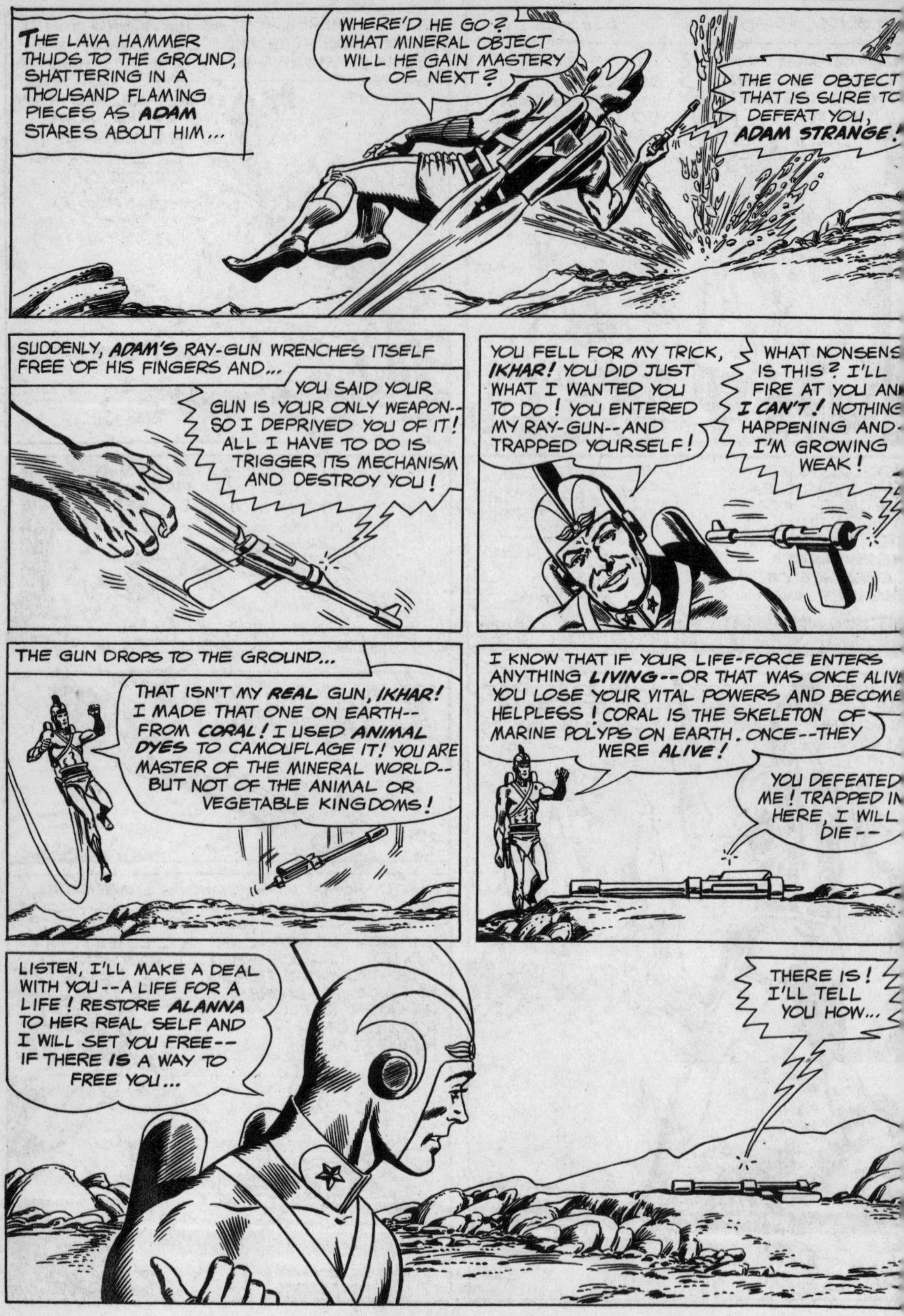
THE LAVA HAMMER THUDS TO THE GROUND, SHATTERING IN A THOUSAND FLAMING PIECES AS ADAM STARES ABOUT HIM...
WHERE'D HE GO? WHAT MINERAL OBJECT WILL HE GAIN MASTERY OF NEXT?
THE ONE OBJECT THAT IS SURE TO DEFEAT YOU, ADAM STRANGE!
SUDDENLY, ADAM'S RAY-GUN WRENCHES ITSELF FREE OF HIS FINGERS AND...
YOU SAID YOUR GUN IS YOUR ONLY WEAPON--SO I DEPRIVED YOU OF IT! ALL I HAVE TO DO IS TRIGGER ITS MECHANISM AND DESTROY YOU!
YOU FELL FOR MY TRICK, IKHAR! YOU DID JUST WHAT I WANTED YOU TO DO! YOU ENTERED MY RAY-GUN--AND TRAPPED YOURSELF!
WHAT NONSENS IS THIS? I'LL FIRE AT YOU AN I CAN'T! NOTHING HAPPENING AND- I'M GROWING WEAK!
THE GUN DROPS TO THE GROUND...
THAT ISN'T MY REAL GUN, IKHAR! I MADE THAT ONE ON EARTH--FROM CORAL! I USED ANIMAL DYES TO CAMOUFLAGE IT! YOU ARE MASTER OF THE MINERAL WORLD--BUT NOT OF THE ANIMAL OR VEGETABLE KINGDOMS!
I KNOW THAT IF YOUR LIFE-FORCE ENTERS ANYTHING LIVING--OR THAT WAS ONCE ALIVE YOU LOSE YOUR VITAL POWERS AND BECOME HELPLESS! CORAL IS THE SKELETON OF MARINE POLYPS ON EARTH. ONCE--THEY WERE ALIVE!
YOU DEFEATED ME! TRAPPED IN HERE, I WILL DIE--
LISTEN, I'LL MAKE A DEAL WITH YOU--A LIFE FOR A LIFE! RESTORE ALANNA TO HER REAL SELF AND I WILL SET YOU FREE--IF THERE IS A WAY TO FREE YOU...
THERE IS! I'LL TELL YOU HOW...

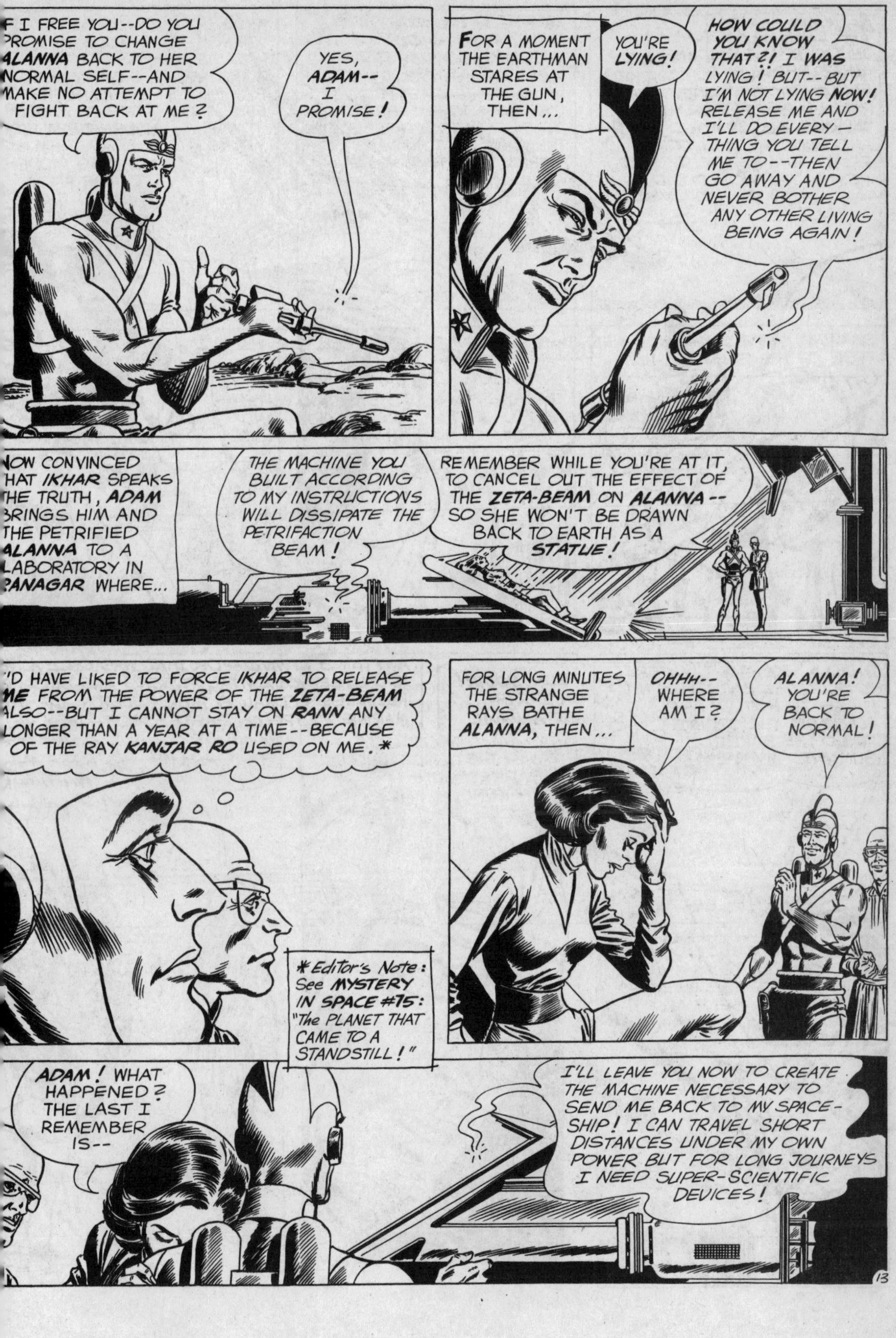
F I FREE YOU--DO YOU PROMISE TO CHANGE ALANNA BACK TO HER NORMAL SELF--AND MAKE NO ATTEMPT TO FIGHT BACK AT ME?
YES, ADAM-- I PROMISE!
FOR A MOMENT THE EARTHMAN STARES AT THE GUN, THEN...
YOU'RE LYING!
HOW COULD YOU KNOW THAT?! I WAS LYING! BUT--BUT I'M NOT LYING NOW! RELEASE ME AND I'LL DO EVERY-THING YOU TELL ME TO--THEN GO AWAY AND NEVER BOTHER ANY OTHER LIVING BEING AGAIN!
NOW CONVINCED THAT IKHAR SPEAKS THE TRUTH, ADAM BRINGS HIM AND THE PETRIFIED ALANNA TO A LABORATORY IN RANAGAR WHERE...
THE MACHINE YOU BUILT ACCORDING TO MY INSTRUCTIONS WILL DISSIPATE THE PETRIFACTION BEAM!
REMEMBER WHILE YOU'RE AT IT, TO CANCEL OUT THE EFFECT OF THE ZETA-BEAM ON ALANNA--SO SHE WON'T BE DRAWN BACK TO EARTH AS A STATUE!
I'D HAVE LIKED TO FORCE IKHAR TO RELEASE ME FROM THE POWER OF THE ZETA-BEAM ALSO--BUT I CANNOT STAY ON RANN ANY LONGER THAN A YEAR AT A TIME--BECAUSE OF THE RAY KANJAR RO USED ON ME.*
*Editor's Note: See MYSTERY IN SPACE #75: "The PLANET THAT CAME TO A STANDSTILL!"
FOR LONG MINUTES THE STRANGE RAYS BATHE ALANNA, THEN...
OHHH--WHERE AM I?
ALANNA! YOU'RE BACK TO NORMAL!
ADAM! WHAT HAPPENED? THE LAST I REMEMBER IS--
I'LL LEAVE YOU NOW TO CREATE THE MACHINE NECESSARY TO SEND ME BACK TO MY SPACE-SHIP! I CAN TRAVEL SHORT DISTANCES UNDER MY OWN POWER BUT FOR LONG JOURNEYS I NEED SUPER-SCIENTIFIC DEVICES!
13

As IKHAR leaves the laboratory...

ADAM, I UNDERSTAND HOW YOU TRICKED IKHAR INTO ENTERING YOUR RAY-GUN BY DELIBERATELY TALKING ABOUT IT SO MUCH-- AND HOW THE LIFE-CORAL FROZE HIM INSIDE IT--BUT HOW IN THE WORLD DID YOU KNOW HE WAS *LYING*?

AS I HELD THE RAY-GUN I COULD FEEL *IKHAR'S* PULSATIONS INSIDE IT--LIKE HUMAN HEARTBEATS! WHEN HE MADE HIS FIRST PROMISE, HIS PULSATIONS SPEEDED UP-- AS A LIE-DETECTOR RECORDS THE FACT THAT HUMANS DO-- WHEN THEY TELL A LIE!

ADAM, I--

ANOTHER THING! HOW DID YOU MAKE YOUR RAY-GUN FIRE WHEN IT WAS A FAKE?

BY USING A "HOLD-OUT" STRAPPED TO MY ARM. GAMBLERS ON MY WORLD USE THEM TO FEED THEM-- SELVES HIDDEN CARDS FROM UNDER THEIR SLEEVES!

I HAD A "HOLD-OUT" ALTERED TO CLIP THIS BARREL GUN TO IT! AS I SHOT MY ARM FORWARD, THE SPRING FIRED THE BARREL GUN INTO MY PALM!

IT HAPPENED IN A SPLIT— SECOND, TOO FAST FOR IKHAR TO NOTICE IT! WHEN I FIRED MY "RAY-GUN"--ACTUALLY IT WAS THE CONCEALED BARREL GUN FIRING!

ONLY A *CHAMPION OF CHAMPIONS* COULD HAVE THOUGHT UP A STUNT LIKE THAT, *ADAM*!

ADAM STRANGE HOW LONG ARE YOU GOING TO KEEP ME WAITING?

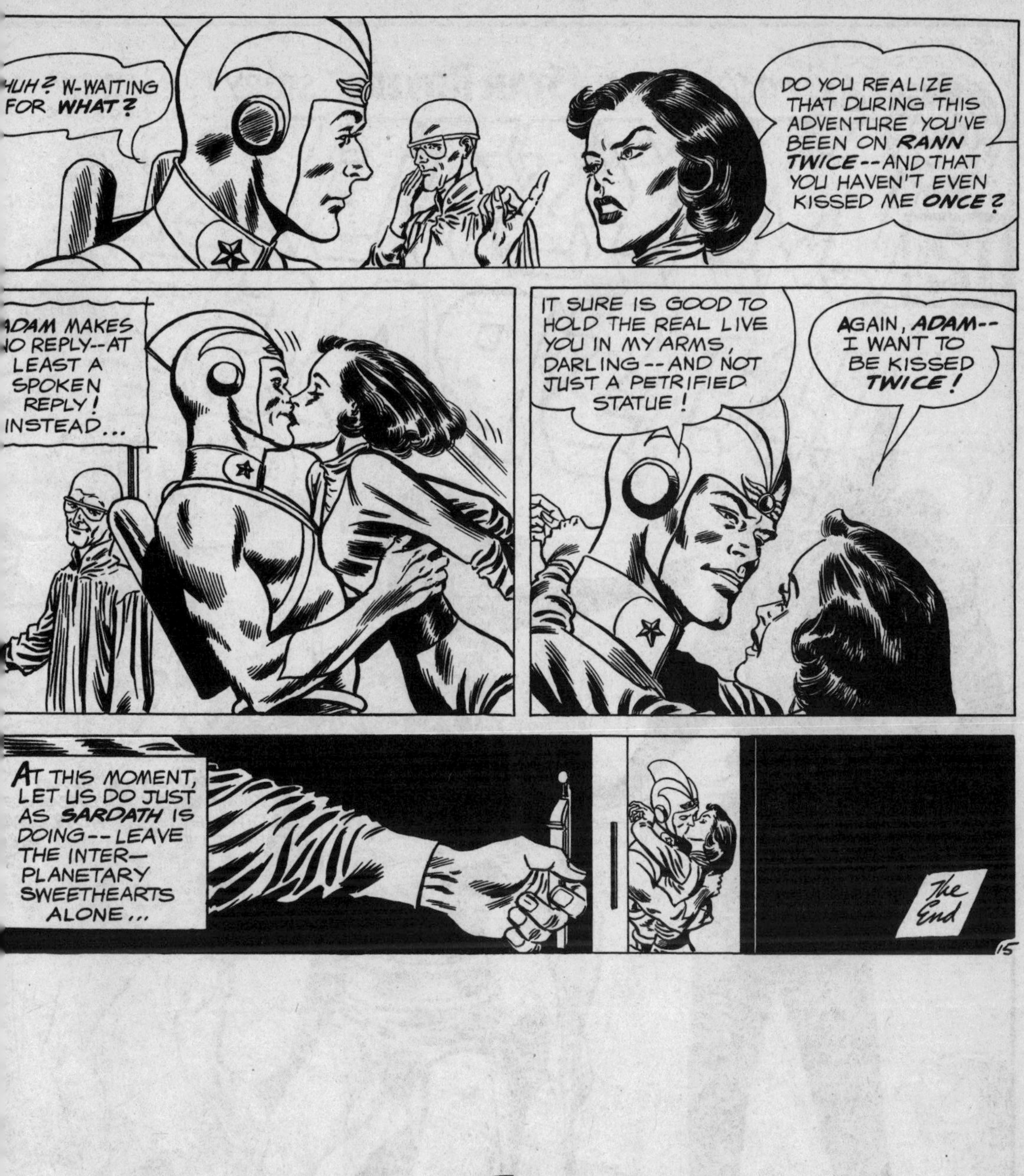
HUH? W-WAITING FOR WHAT?
DO YOU REALIZE THAT DURING THIS ADVENTURE YOU'VE BEEN ON RANN TWICE--AND THAT YOU HAVEN'T EVEN KISSED ME ONCE?
ADAM MAKES NO REPLY--AT LEAST A SPOKEN REPLY! INSTEAD...
IT SURE IS GOOD TO HOLD THE REAL LIVE YOU IN MY ARMS, DARLING--AND NOT JUST A PETRIFIED STATUE!
AGAIN, ADAM--I WANT TO BE KISSED TWICE!
AT THIS MOMENT, LET US DO JUST AS SARDATH IS DOING--LEAVE THE INTER-PLANETARY SWEETHEARTS ALONE...
The End
15

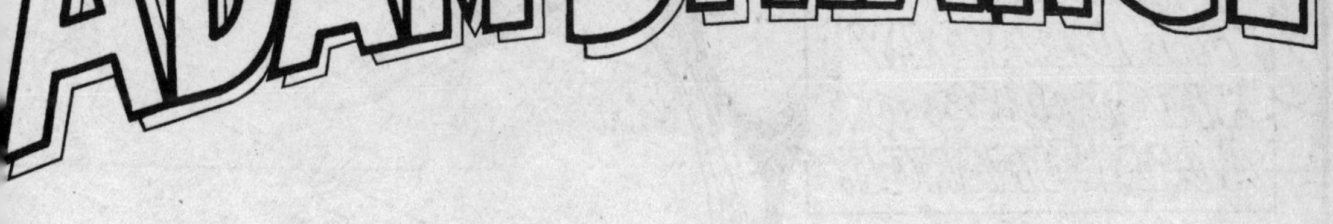
ADAM STRANGE

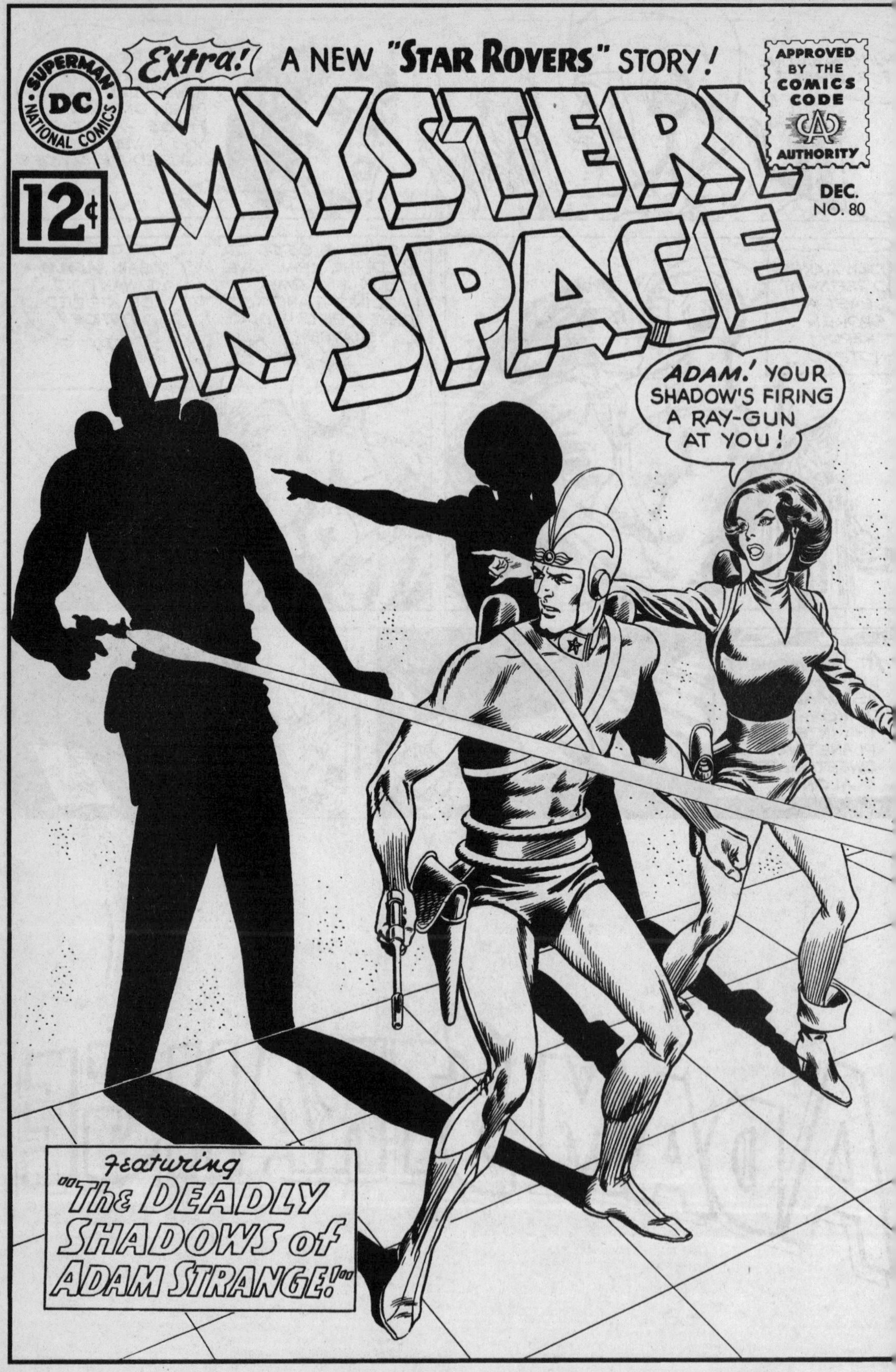
SUPERMAN DC NATIONAL COMICS
Extra! A NEW "STAR ROVERS" STORY!
APPROVED BY THE COMICS CODE AUTHORITY
MYSTERY IN SPACE
12¢
DEC. NO. 80
ADAM! YOUR SHADOW'S FIRING A RAY-GUN AT YOU!
Featuring "The DEADLY SHADOWS of ADAM STRANGE!"

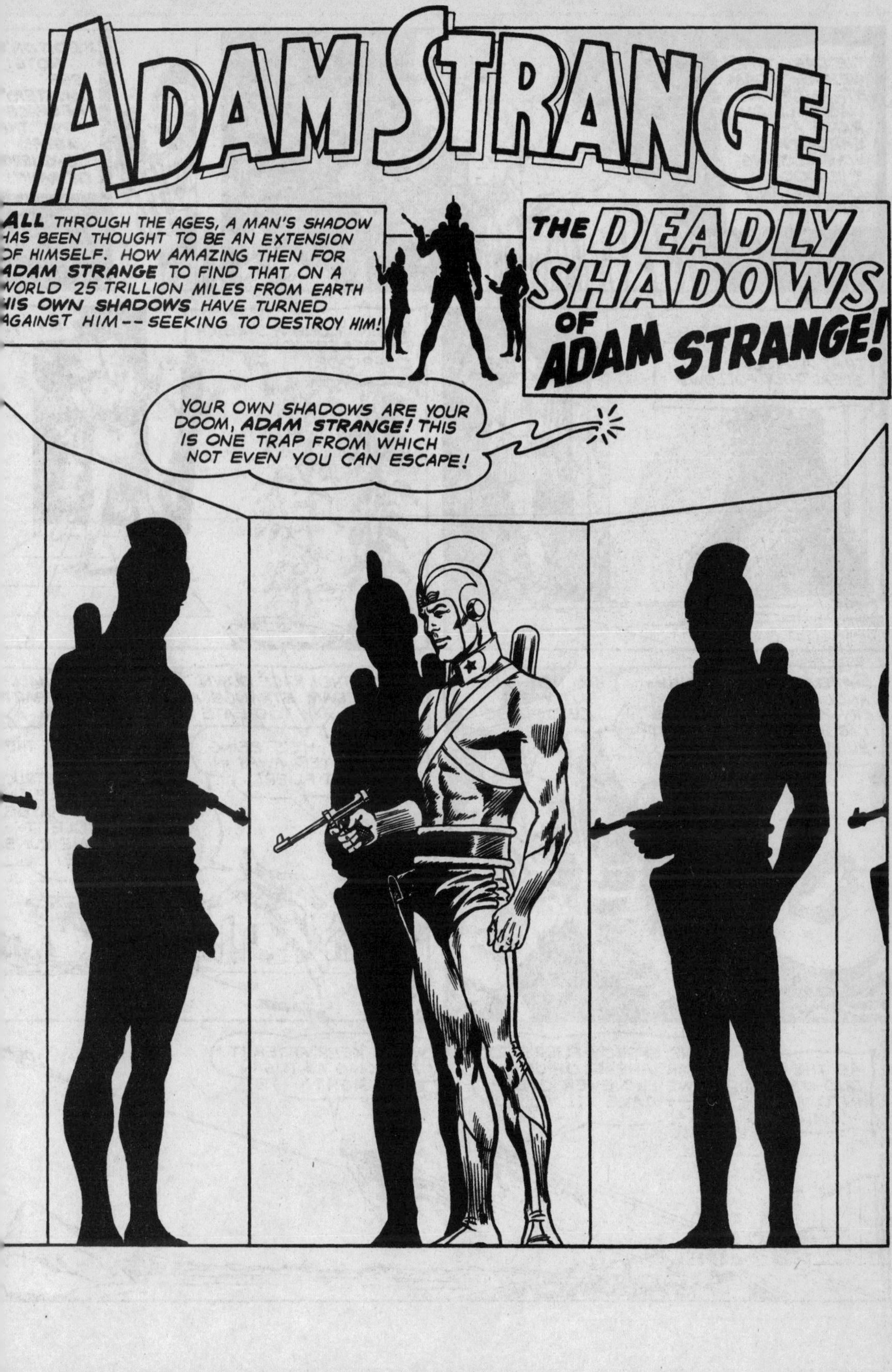
ADAM STRANGE
ALL THROUGH THE AGES, A MAN'S SHADOW HAS BEEN THOUGHT TO BE AN EXTENSION OF HIMSELF. HOW AMAZING THEN FOR ADAM STRANGE TO FIND THAT ON A WORLD 25 TRILLION MILES FROM EARTH HIS OWN SHADOWS HAVE TURNED AGAINST HIM -- SEEKING TO DESTROY HIM!
THE DEADLY SHADOWS OF ADAM STRANGE!
YOUR OWN SHADOWS ARE YOUR DOOM, ADAM STRANGE! THIS IS ONE TRAP FROM WHICH NOT EVEN YOU CAN ESCAPE!

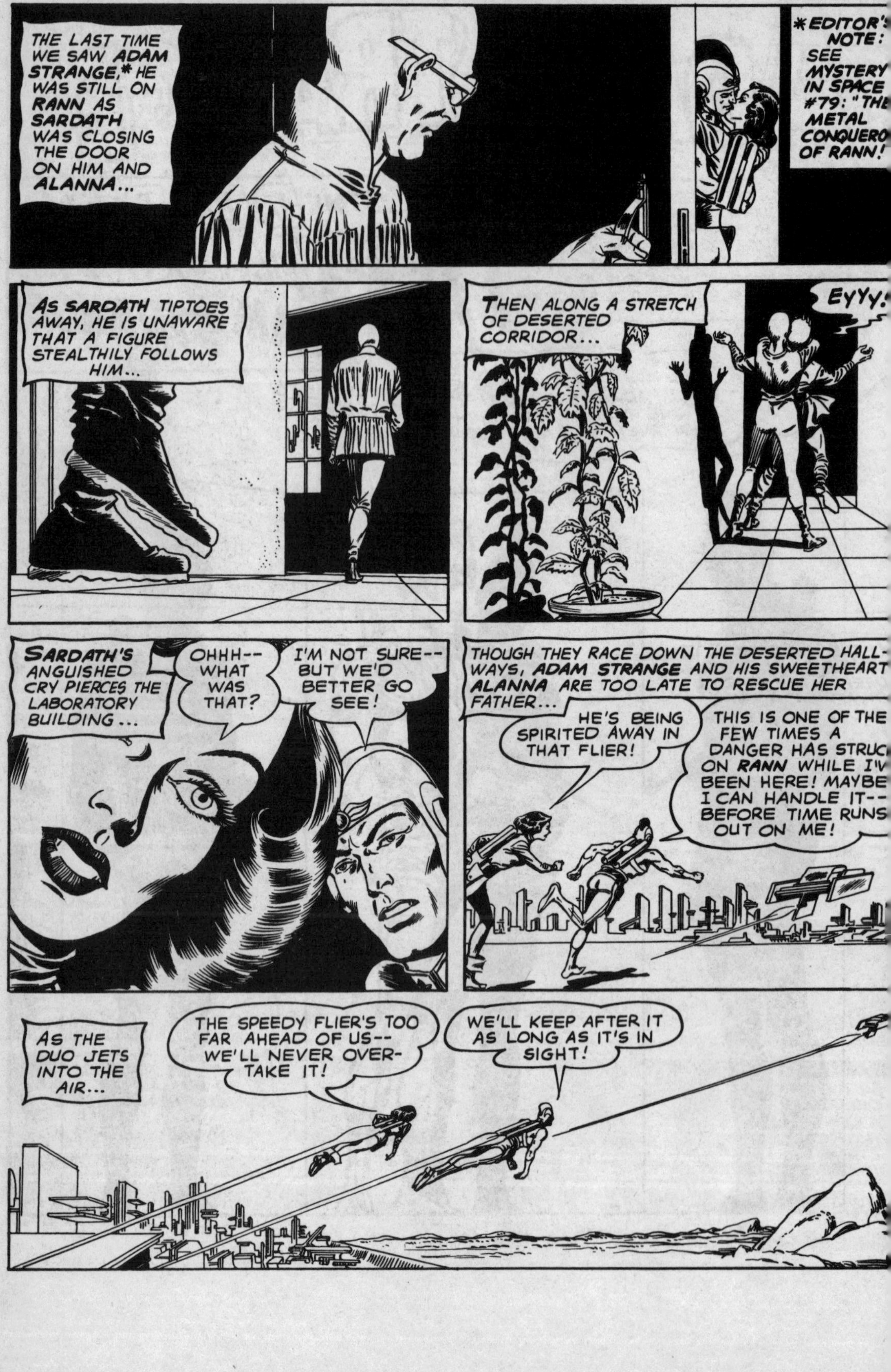
THE LAST TIME WE SAW ADAM STRANGE,* HE WAS STILL ON RANN AS SARDATH WAS CLOSING THE DOOR ON HIM AND ALANNA...
*EDITOR' NOTE: SEE MYSTERY IN SPACE #79: "THI METAL CONQUERO OF RANN!
AS SARDATH TIPTOES AWAY, HE IS UNAWARE THAT A FIGURE STEALTHILY FOLLOWS HIM...
THEN ALONG A STRETCH OF DESERTED CORRIDOR...
EyYy
SARDATH'S ANGUISHED CRY PIERCES THE LABORATORY BUILDING...
OHHH-- WHAT WAS THAT?
I'M NOT SURE-- BUT WE'D BETTER GO SEE!
THOUGH THEY RACE DOWN THE DESERTED HALL-WAYS, ADAM STRANGE AND HIS SWEETHEART ALANNA ARE TOO LATE TO RESCUE HER FATHER...
HE'S BEING SPIRITED AWAY IN THAT FLIER!
THIS IS ONE OF THE FEW TIMES A DANGER HAS STRUC ON RANN WHILE I'V BEEN HERE! MAYBE I CAN HANDLE IT-- BEFORE TIME RUNS OUT ON ME!
AS THE DUO JETS INTO THE AIR...
THE SPEEDY FLIER'S TOO FAR AHEAD OF US-- WE'LL NEVER OVER-TAKE IT!
WE'LL KEEP AFTER IT AS LONG AS IT'S IN SIGHT!

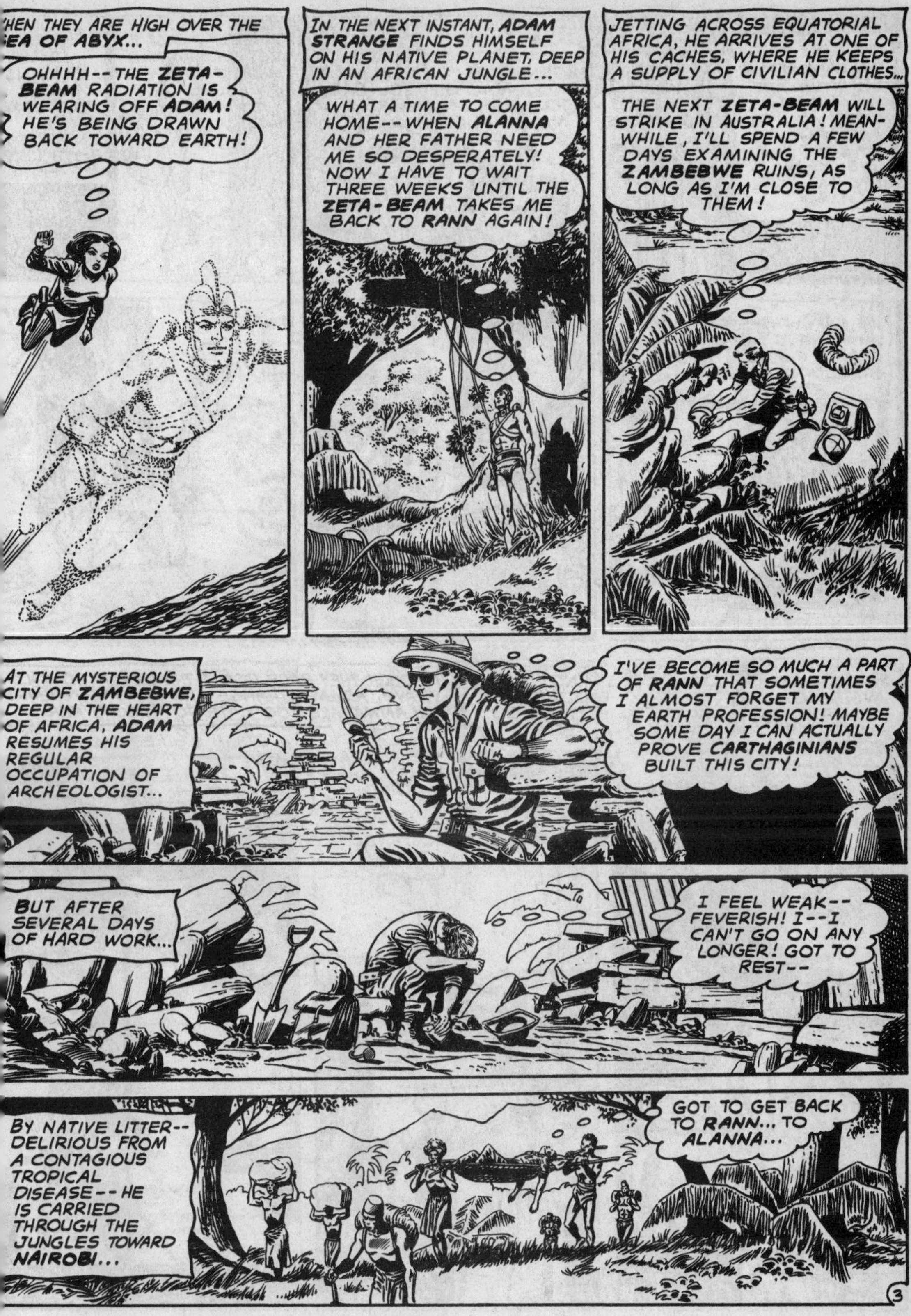
WHEN THEY ARE HIGH OVER THE SEA OF ABYX...
OHHHH--THE ZETA-BEAM RADIATION IS WEARING OFF ADAM! HE'S BEING DRAWN BACK TOWARD EARTH!
IN THE NEXT INSTANT, ADAM STRANGE FINDS HIMSELF ON HIS NATIVE PLANET, DEEP IN AN AFRICAN JUNGLE...
WHAT A TIME TO COME HOME--WHEN ALANNA AND HER FATHER NEED ME SO DESPERATELY! NOW I HAVE TO WAIT THREE WEEKS UNTIL THE ZETA-BEAM TAKES ME BACK TO RANN AGAIN!
JETTING ACROSS EQUATORIAL AFRICA, HE ARRIVES AT ONE OF HIS CACHES, WHERE HE KEEPS A SUPPLY OF CIVILIAN CLOTHES...
THE NEXT ZETA-BEAM WILL STRIKE IN AUSTRALIA! MEANWHILE, I'LL SPEND A FEW DAYS EXAMINING THE ZAMBEBWE RUINS, AS LONG AS I'M CLOSE TO THEM!
AT THE MYSTERIOUS CITY OF ZAMBEBWE, DEEP IN THE HEART OF AFRICA, ADAM RESUMES HIS REGULAR OCCUPATION OF ARCHEOLOGIST...
I'VE BECOME SO MUCH A PART OF RANN THAT SOMETIMES I ALMOST FORGET MY EARTH PROFESSION! MAYBE SOME DAY I CAN ACTUALLY PROVE CARTHAGINIANS BUILT THIS CITY!
BUT AFTER SEVERAL DAYS OF HARD WORK...
I FEEL WEAK--FEVERISH! I--I CAN'T GO ON ANY LONGER! GOT TO REST--
BY NATIVE LITTER--DELIRIOUS FROM A CONTAGIOUS TROPICAL DISEASE--HE IS CARRIED THROUGH THE JUNGLES TOWARD NAIROBI...
GOT TO GET BACK TO RANN... TO ALANNA...
3

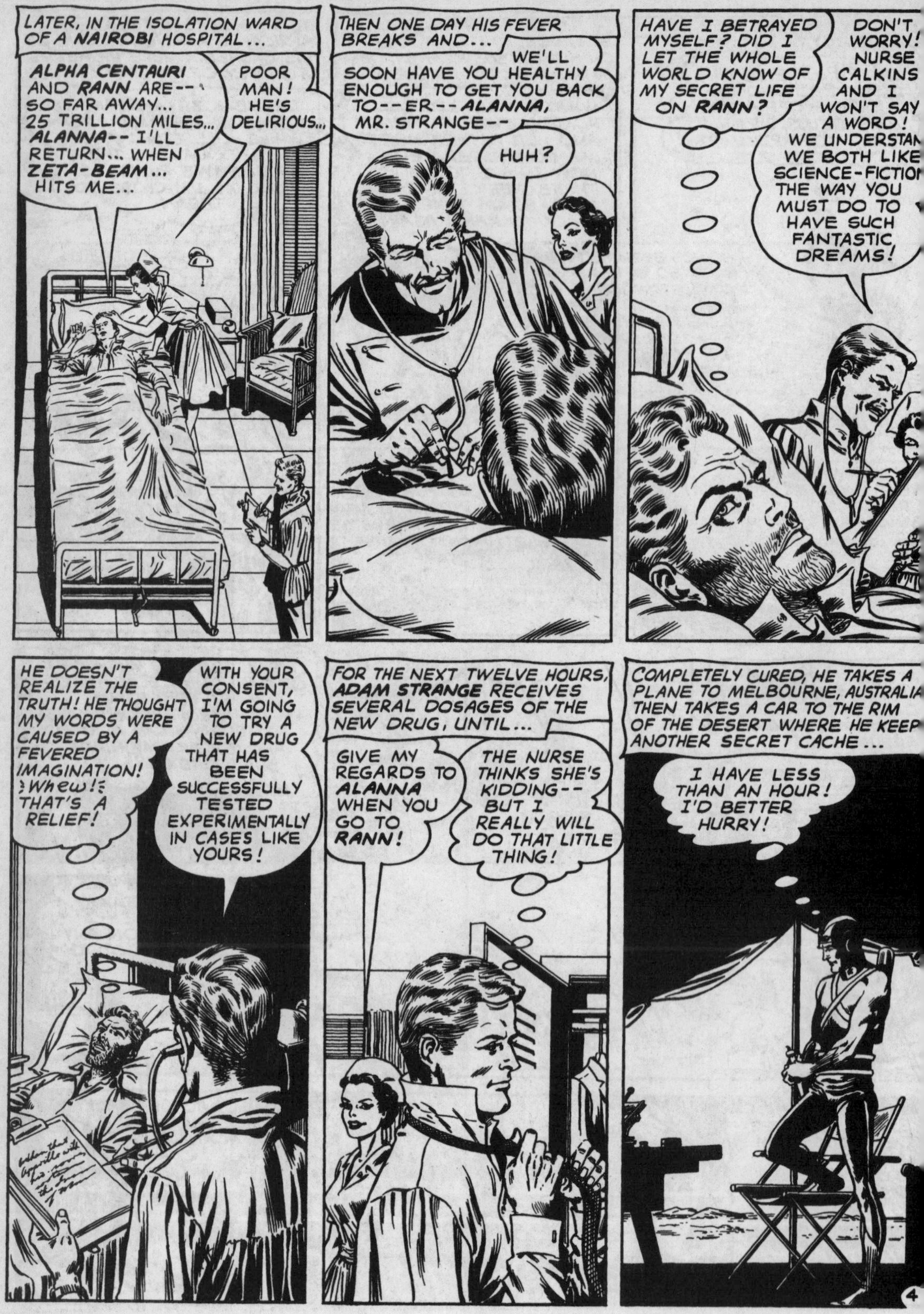
LATER, IN THE ISOLATION WARD OF A NAIROBI HOSPITAL...
ALPHA CENTAURI AND RANN ARE-- SO FAR AWAY... 25 TRILLION MILES... ALANNA-- I'LL RETURN... WHEN ZETA-BEAM... HITS ME...
POOR MAN! HE'S DELIRIOUS...
THEN ONE DAY HIS FEVER BREAKS AND...
WE'LL SOON HAVE YOU HEALTHY ENOUGH TO GET YOU BACK TO--ER--ALANNA, MR. STRANGE--
HUH?
HAVE I BETRAYED MYSELF? DID I LET THE WHOLE WORLD KNOW OF MY SECRET LIFE ON RANN?
DON'T WORRY! NURSE CALKINS AND I WON'T SAY A WORD! WE UNDERSTAN WE BOTH LIKE SCIENCE-FICTIO THE WAY YOU MUST DO TO HAVE SUCH FANTASTIC DREAMS!
HE DOESN'T REALIZE THE TRUTH! HE THOUGHT MY WORDS WERE CAUSED BY A FEVERED IMAGINATION! WHEW! THAT'S A RELIEF!
WITH YOUR CONSENT, I'M GOING TO TRY A NEW DRUG THAT HAS BEEN SUCCESSFULLY TESTED EXPERIMENTALLY IN CASES LIKE YOURS!
FOR THE NEXT TWELVE HOURS, ADAM STRANGE RECEIVES SEVERAL DOSAGES OF THE NEW DRUG, UNTIL...
GIVE MY REGARDS TO ALANNA WHEN YOU GO TO RANN!
THE NURSE THINKS SHE'S KIDDING-- BUT I REALLY WILL DO THAT LITTLE THING!
COMPLETELY CURED, HE TAKES A PLANE TO MELBOURNE, AUSTRALIA THEN TAKES A CAR TO THE RIM OF THE DESERT WHERE HE KEEP ANOTHER SECRET CACHE...
I HAVE LESS THAN AN HOUR! I'D BETTER HURRY!
4

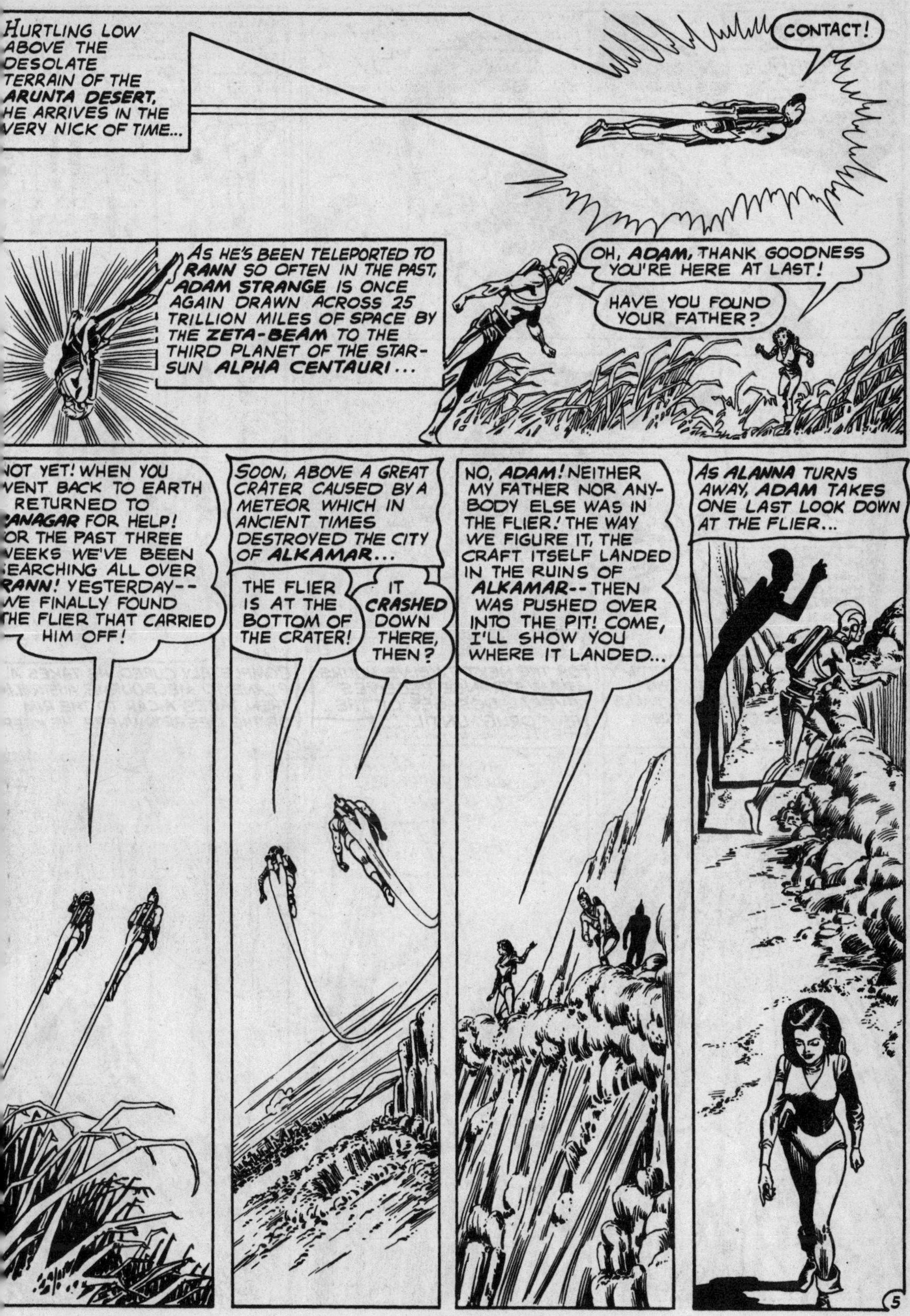
HURTLING LOW ABOVE THE DESOLATE TERRAIN OF THE ARUNTA DESERT, HE ARRIVES IN THE VERY NICK OF TIME...
CONTACT!
AS HE'S BEEN TELEPORTED TO RANN SO OFTEN IN THE PAST, ADAM STRANGE IS ONCE AGAIN DRAWN ACROSS 25 TRILLION MILES OF SPACE BY THE ZETA-BEAM TO THE THIRD PLANET OF THE STAR-SUN ALPHA CENTAURI...
OH, ADAM, THANK GOODNESS YOU'RE HERE AT LAST!
HAVE YOU FOUND YOUR FATHER?
NOT YET! WHEN YOU WENT BACK TO EARTH I RETURNED TO RANAGAR FOR HELP! FOR THE PAST THREE WEEKS WE'VE BEEN SEARCHING ALL OVER RANN! YESTERDAY-- WE FINALLY FOUND THE FLIER THAT CARRIED HIM OFF!
SOON, ABOVE A GREAT CRATER CAUSED BY A METEOR WHICH IN ANCIENT TIMES DESTROYED THE CITY OF ALKAMAR...
THE FLIER IS AT THE BOTTOM OF THE CRATER!
IT CRASHED DOWN THERE, THEN?
NO, ADAM! NEITHER MY FATHER NOR ANYBODY ELSE WAS IN THE FLIER! THE WAY WE FIGURE IT, THE CRAFT ITSELF LANDED IN THE RUINS OF ALKAMAR-- THEN WAS PUSHED OVER INTO THE PIT! COME, I'LL SHOW YOU WHERE IT LANDED...
AS ALANNA TURNS AWAY, ADAM TAKES ONE LAST LOOK DOWN AT THE FLIER...
5

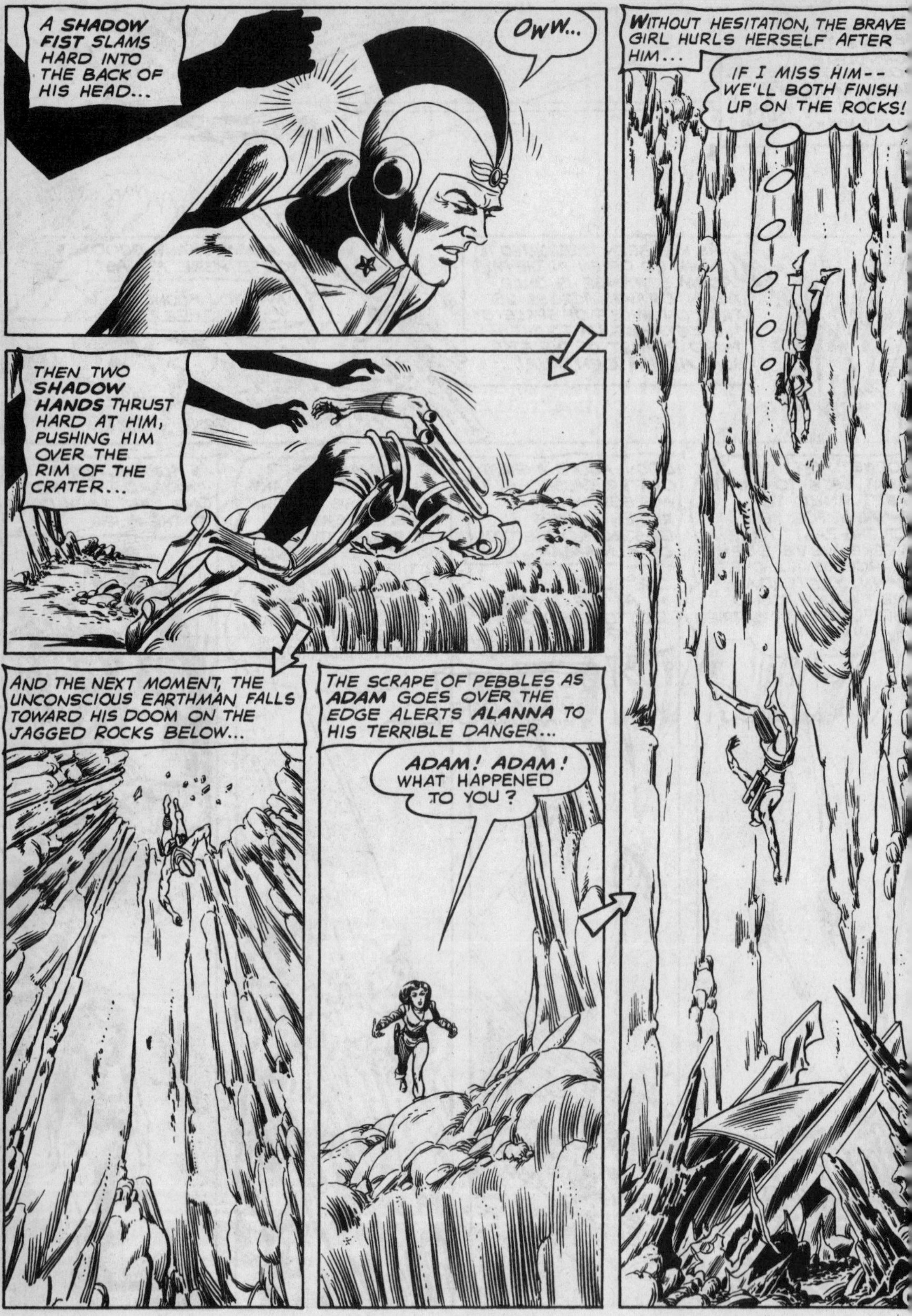
A SHADOW FIST SLAMS HARD INTO THE BACK OF HIS HEAD...
OWW...
THEN TWO SHADOW HANDS THRUST HARD AT HIM, PUSHING HIM OVER THE RIM OF THE CRATER...
AND THE NEXT MOMENT, THE UNCONSCIOUS EARTHMAN FALLS TOWARD HIS DOOM ON THE JAGGED ROCKS BELOW...
THE SCRAPE OF PEBBLES AS ADAM GOES OVER THE EDGE ALERTS ALANNA TO HIS TERRIBLE DANGER...
ADAM! ADAM! WHAT HAPPENED TO YOU?
WITHOUT HESITATION, THE BRAVE GIRL HURLS HERSELF AFTER HIM...
IF I MISS HIM-- WE'LL BOTH FINISH UP ON THE ROCKS!

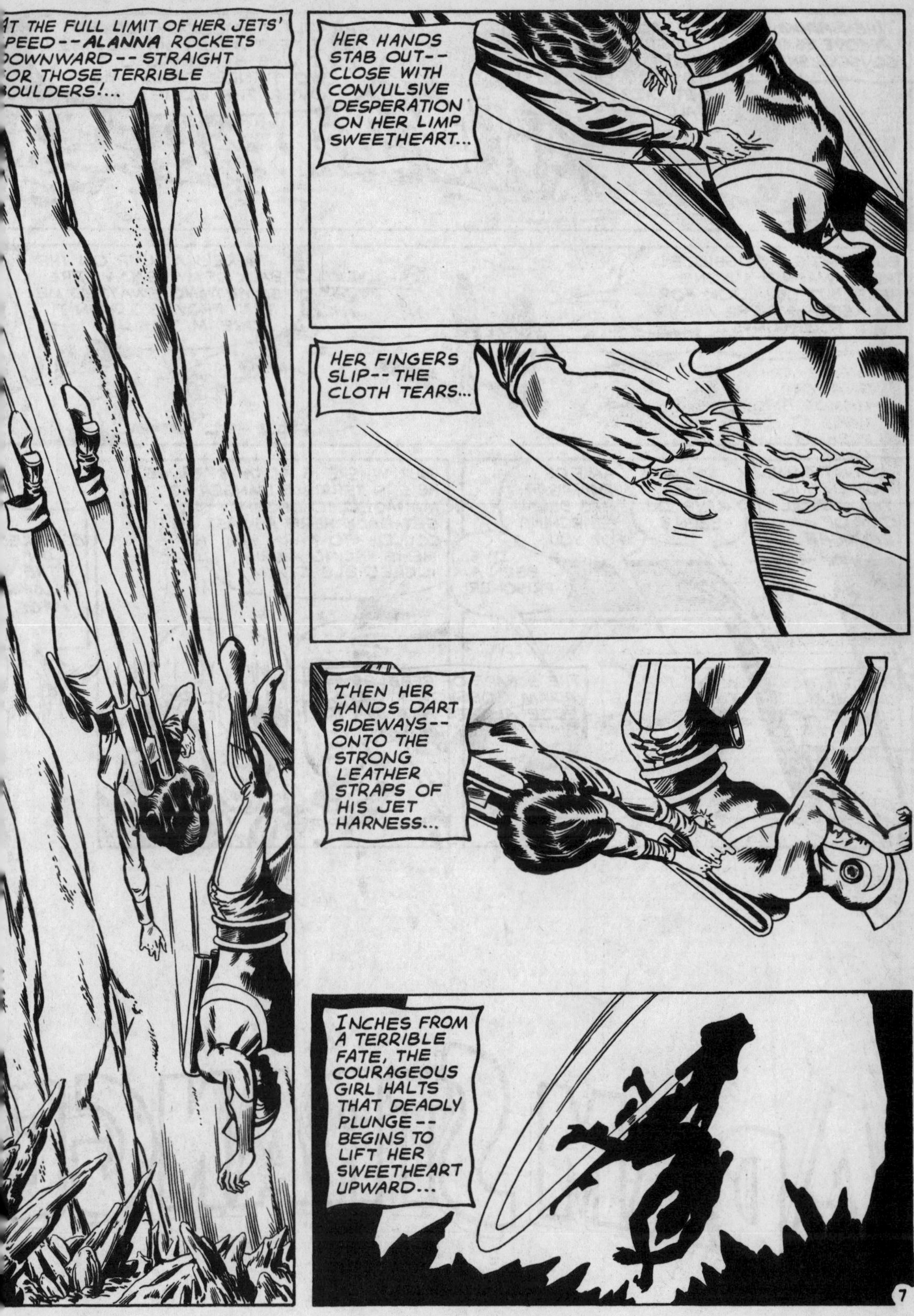
AT THE FULL LIMIT OF HER JETS' SPEED--ALANNA ROCKETS DOWNWARD--STRAIGHT FOR THOSE TERRIBLE BOULDERS!...
HER HANDS STAB OUT--CLOSE WITH CONVULSIVE DESPERATION ON HER LIMP SWEETHEART...
HER FINGERS SLIP--THE CLOTH TEARS...
THEN HER HANDS DART SIDEWAYS--ONTO THE STRONG LEATHER STRAPS OF HIS JET HARNESS...
INCHES FROM A TERRIBLE FATE, THE COURAGEOUS GIRL HALTS THAT DEADLY PLUNGE--BEGINS TO LIFT HER SWEETHEART UPWARD...
7

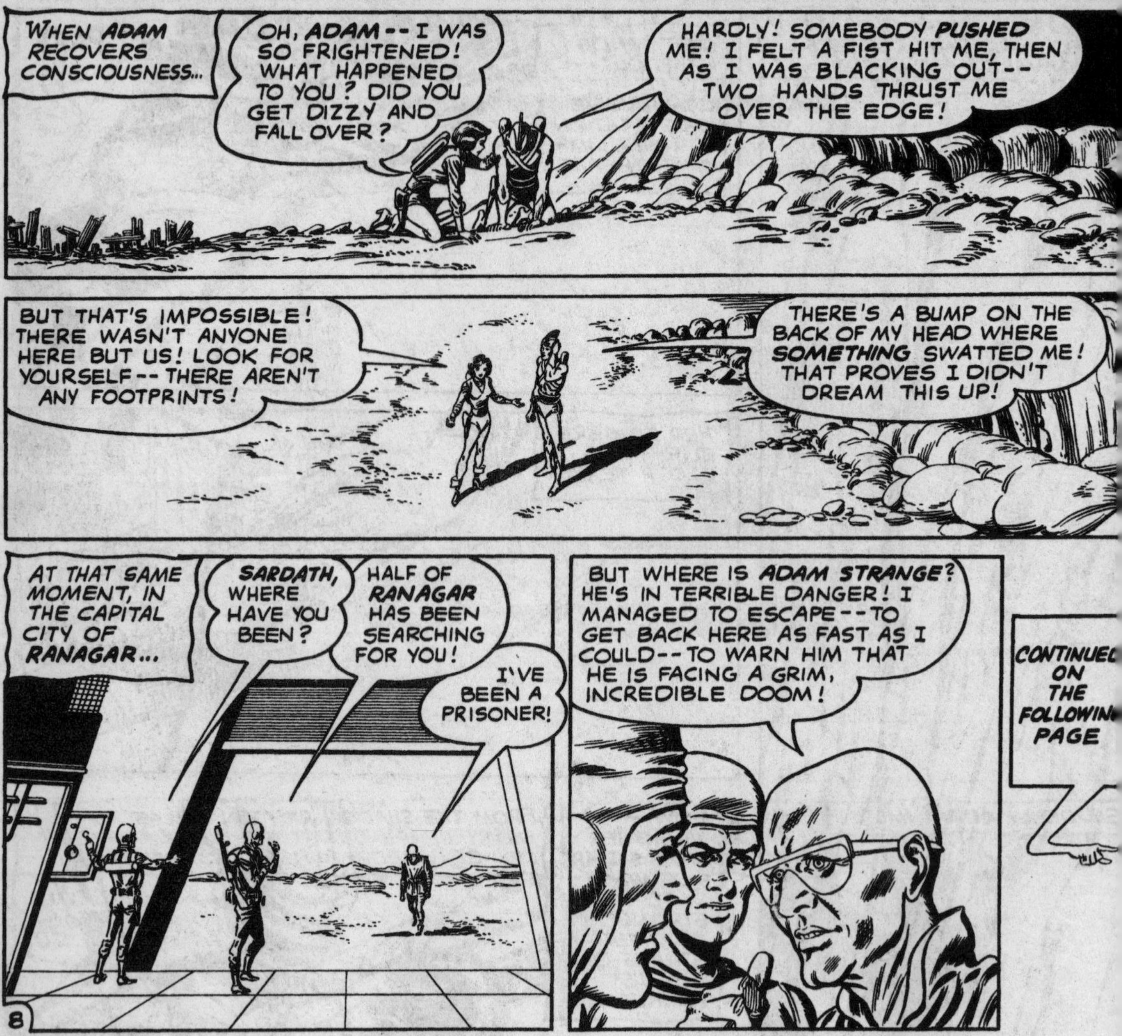
WHEN ADAM RECOVERS CONSCIOUSNESS...
OH, ADAM -- I WAS SO FRIGHTENED! WHAT HAPPENED TO YOU? DID YOU GET DIZZY AND FALL OVER?
HARDLY! SOMEBODY PUSHED ME! I FELT A FIST HIT ME, THEN AS I WAS BLACKING OUT-- TWO HANDS THRUST ME OVER THE EDGE!
BUT THAT'S IMPOSSIBLE! THERE WASN'T ANYONE HERE BUT US! LOOK FOR YOURSELF -- THERE AREN'T ANY FOOTPRINTS!
THERE'S A BUMP ON THE BACK OF MY HEAD WHERE SOMETHING SWATTED ME! THAT PROVES I DIDN'T DREAM THIS UP!
AT THAT SAME MOMENT, IN THE CAPITAL CITY OF RANAGAR...
SARDATH, WHERE HAVE YOU BEEN?
HALF OF RANAGAR HAS BEEN SEARCHING FOR YOU!
I'VE BEEN A PRISONER!
8
BUT WHERE IS ADAM STRANGE? HE'S IN TERRIBLE DANGER! I MANAGED TO ESCAPE--TO GET BACK HERE AS FAST AS I COULD--TO WARN HIM THAT HE IS FACING A GRIM, INCREDIBLE DOOM!
CONTINUED ON THE FOLLOWING PAGE

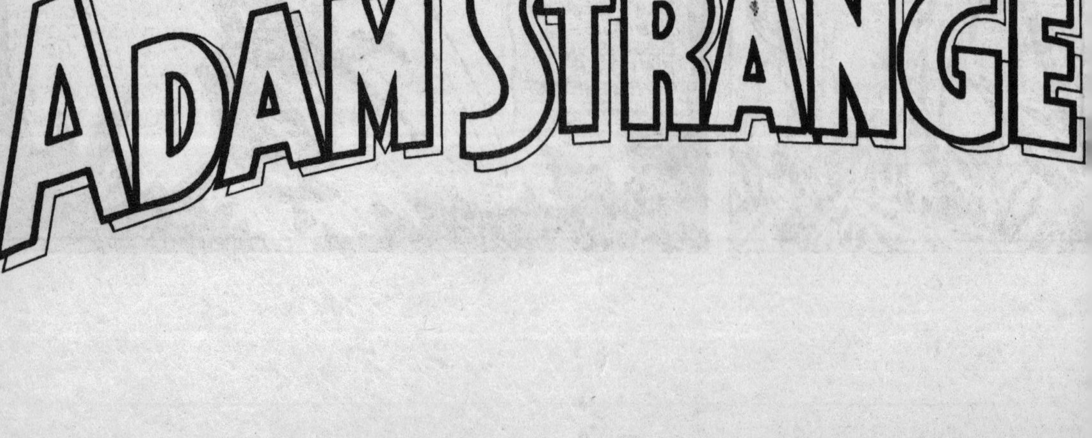
ADAM STRANGE

THE DEADLY SHADOWS OF ADAM STRANGE PART 2

IN THE RUINED CITY OF ALKAMAR, ALANNA AND ADAM MOVE FORWARD CAUTIOUSLY...

THE FLIER CARRYING MY FATHER LANDED JUST AHEAD, ADAM!

WHAT PUZZLES ME IS-- WHY THE FLIER WAS LATER PUSHED INTO THE CRATER?

SUDDENLY ADAM HALTS...

MY SHADOW-- MAKING A MOVE I'M NOT MAKING!

FROM THE SHADOW RAY-GUN A BLAST OF ENERGY LEAPS OUT AT THE EARTHMAN AS A CRY OF HORROR BURSTS FROM ALANNA...

ADAM-- YOUR OWN SHADOW IS FIRING A RAY-GUN AT YOU!

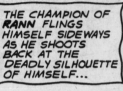

THE CHAMPION OF RANN FLINGS HIMSELF SIDEWAYS AS HE SHOOTS BACK AT THE DEADLY SILHOUETTE OF HIMSELF...

I WONDER IF-- IT WAS ANOTHER OF MY SHADOWS THAT HIT ME AND PUSHED ME OVER THE CLIFF?

9

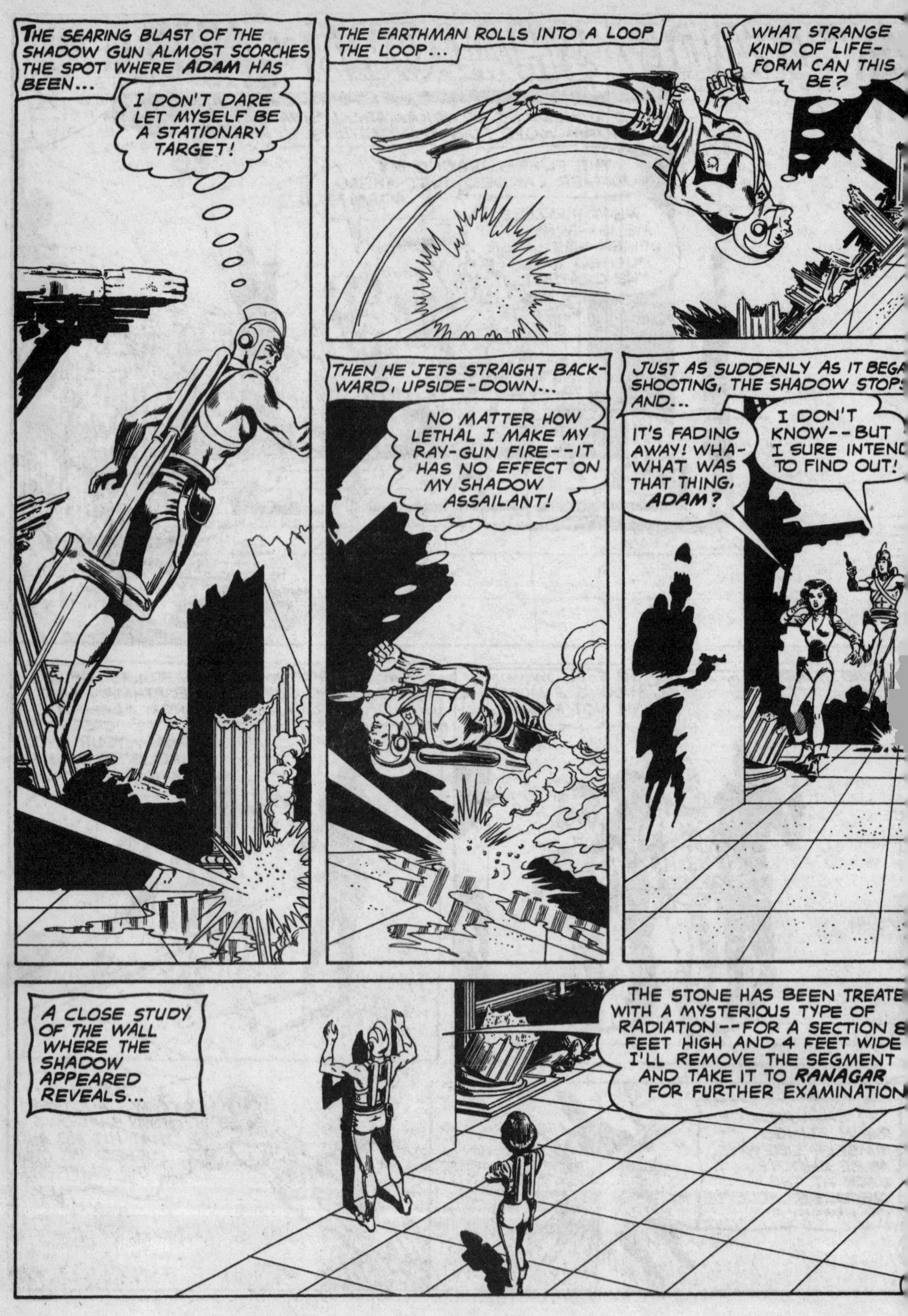
THE SEARING BLAST OF THE SHADOW GUN ALMOST SCORCHES THE SPOT WHERE ADAM HAS BEEN...
I DON'T DARE LET MYSELF BE A STATIONARY TARGET!
THE EARTHMAN ROLLS INTO A LOOP THE LOOP...
WHAT STRANGE KIND OF LIFE-FORM CAN THIS BE?
THEN HE JETS STRAIGHT BACKWARD, UPSIDE-DOWN...
NO MATTER HOW LETHAL I MAKE MY RAY-GUN FIRE--IT HAS NO EFFECT ON MY SHADOW ASSAILANT!
JUST AS SUDDENLY AS IT BEGA SHOOTING, THE SHADOW STOPS AND...
IT'S FADING AWAY! WHA-WHAT WAS THAT THING, ADAM?
I DON'T KNOW--BUT I SURE INTEND TO FIND OUT!
A CLOSE STUDY OF THE WALL WHERE THE SHADOW APPEARED REVEALS...
THE STONE HAS BEEN TREATE WITH A MYSTERIOUS TYPE OF RADIATION--FOR A SECTION 8 FEET HIGH AND 4 FEET WIDE I'LL REMOVE THE SEGMENT AND TAKE IT TO RANAGAR FOR FURTHER EXAMINATION

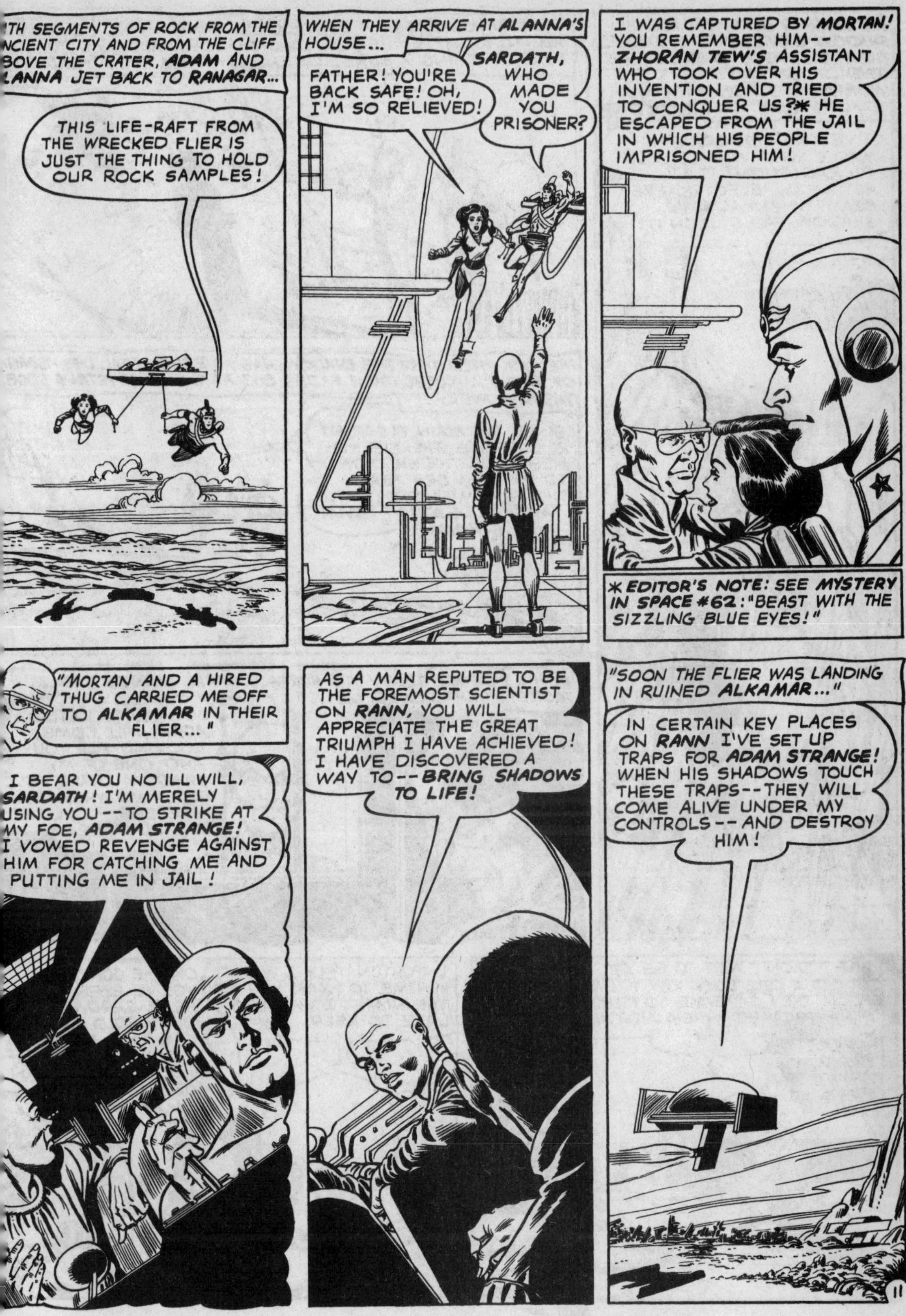
ITH SEGMENTS OF ROCK FROM THE NCIENT CITY AND FROM THE CLIFF BOVE THE CRATER, ADAM AND LANNA JET BACK TO RANAGAR...
THIS LIFE-RAFT FROM THE WRECKED FLIER IS JUST THE THING TO HOLD OUR ROCK SAMPLES!
WHEN THEY ARRIVE AT ALANNA'S HOUSE...
FATHER! YOU'RE BACK SAFE! OH, I'M SO RELIEVED!
SARDATH, WHO MADE YOU PRISONER?
I WAS CAPTURED BY MORTAN! YOU REMEMBER HIM-- ZHORAN TEW'S ASSISTANT WHO TOOK OVER HIS INVENTION AND TRIED TO CONQUER US?* HE ESCAPED FROM THE JAIL IN WHICH HIS PEOPLE IMPRISONED HIM!
*EDITOR'S NOTE: SEE MYSTERY IN SPACE #62: "BEAST WITH THE SIZZLING BLUE EYES!"
"MORTAN AND A HIRED THUG CARRIED ME OFF TO ALKAMAR IN THEIR FLIER..."
I BEAR YOU NO ILL WILL, SARDATH! I'M MERELY USING YOU--TO STRIKE AT MY FOE, ADAM STRANGE! I VOWED REVENGE AGAINST HIM FOR CATCHING ME AND PUTTING ME IN JAIL!
AS A MAN REPUTED TO BE THE FOREMOST SCIENTIST ON RANN, YOU WILL APPRECIATE THE GREAT TRIUMPH I HAVE ACHIEVED! I HAVE DISCOVERED A WAY TO--BRING SHADOWS TO LIFE!
"SOON THE FLIER WAS LANDING IN RUINED ALKAMAR..."
IN CERTAIN KEY PLACES ON RANN I'VE SET UP TRAPS FOR ADAM STRANGE! WHEN HIS SHADOWS TOUCH THESE TRAPS--THEY WILL COME ALIVE UNDER MY CONTROLS--AND DESTROY HIM!
11

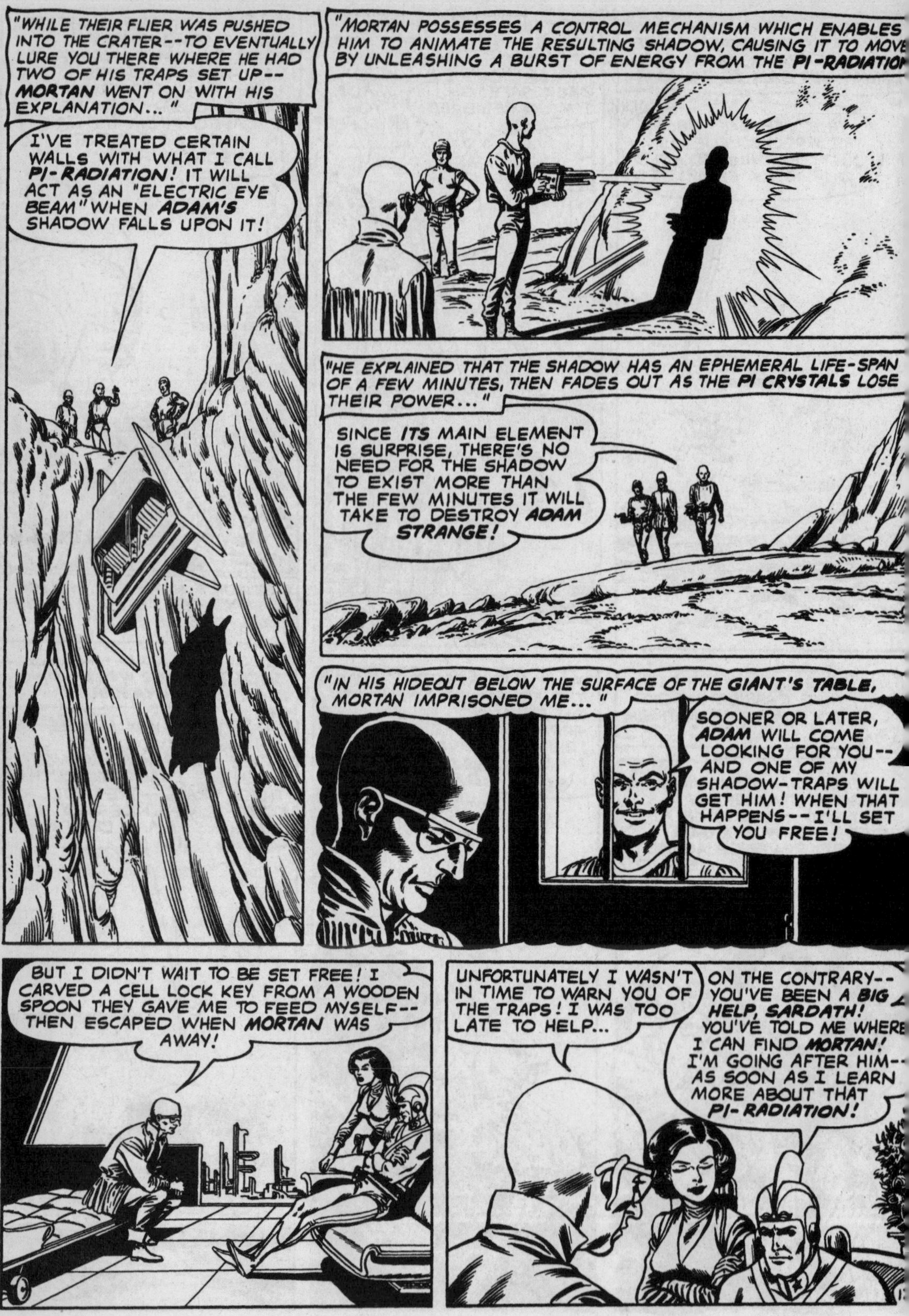
"WHILE THEIR FLIER WAS PUSHED INTO THE CRATER--TO EVENTUALLY LURE YOU THERE WHERE HE HAD TWO OF HIS TRAPS SET UP--MORTAN WENT ON WITH HIS EXPLANATION..."
I'VE TREATED CERTAIN WALLS WITH WHAT I CALL PI-RADIATION! IT WILL ACT AS AN "ELECTRIC EYE BEAM" WHEN ADAM'S SHADOW FALLS UPON IT!
"MORTAN POSSESSES A CONTROL MECHANISM WHICH ENABLES HIM TO ANIMATE THE RESULTING SHADOW, CAUSING IT TO MOVE BY UNLEASHING A BURST OF ENERGY FROM THE PI-RADIATION
"HE EXPLAINED THAT THE SHADOW HAS AN EPHEMERAL LIFE-SPAN OF A FEW MINUTES, THEN FADES OUT AS THE PI CRYSTALS LOSE THEIR POWER..."
SINCE ITS MAIN ELEMENT IS SURPRISE, THERE'S NO NEED FOR THE SHADOW TO EXIST MORE THAN THE FEW MINUTES IT WILL TAKE TO DESTROY ADAM STRANGE!
"IN HIS HIDEOUT BELOW THE SURFACE OF THE GIANT'S TABLE, MORTAN IMPRISONED ME..."
SOONER OR LATER, ADAM WILL COME LOOKING FOR YOU--AND ONE OF MY SHADOW-TRAPS WILL GET HIM! WHEN THAT HAPPENS--I'LL SET YOU FREE!
BUT I DIDN'T WAIT TO BE SET FREE! I CARVED A CELL LOCK KEY FROM A WOODEN SPOON THEY GAVE ME TO FEED MYSELF--THEN ESCAPED WHEN MORTAN WAS AWAY!
UNFORTUNATELY I WASN'T IN TIME TO WARN YOU OF THE TRAPS! I WAS TOO LATE TO HELP...
ON THE CONTRARY--YOU'VE BEEN A BIG HELP, SARDATH! YOU'VE TOLD ME WHERE I CAN FIND MORTAN! I'M GOING AFTER HIM--AS SOON AS I LEARN MORE ABOUT THAT PI-RADIATION!

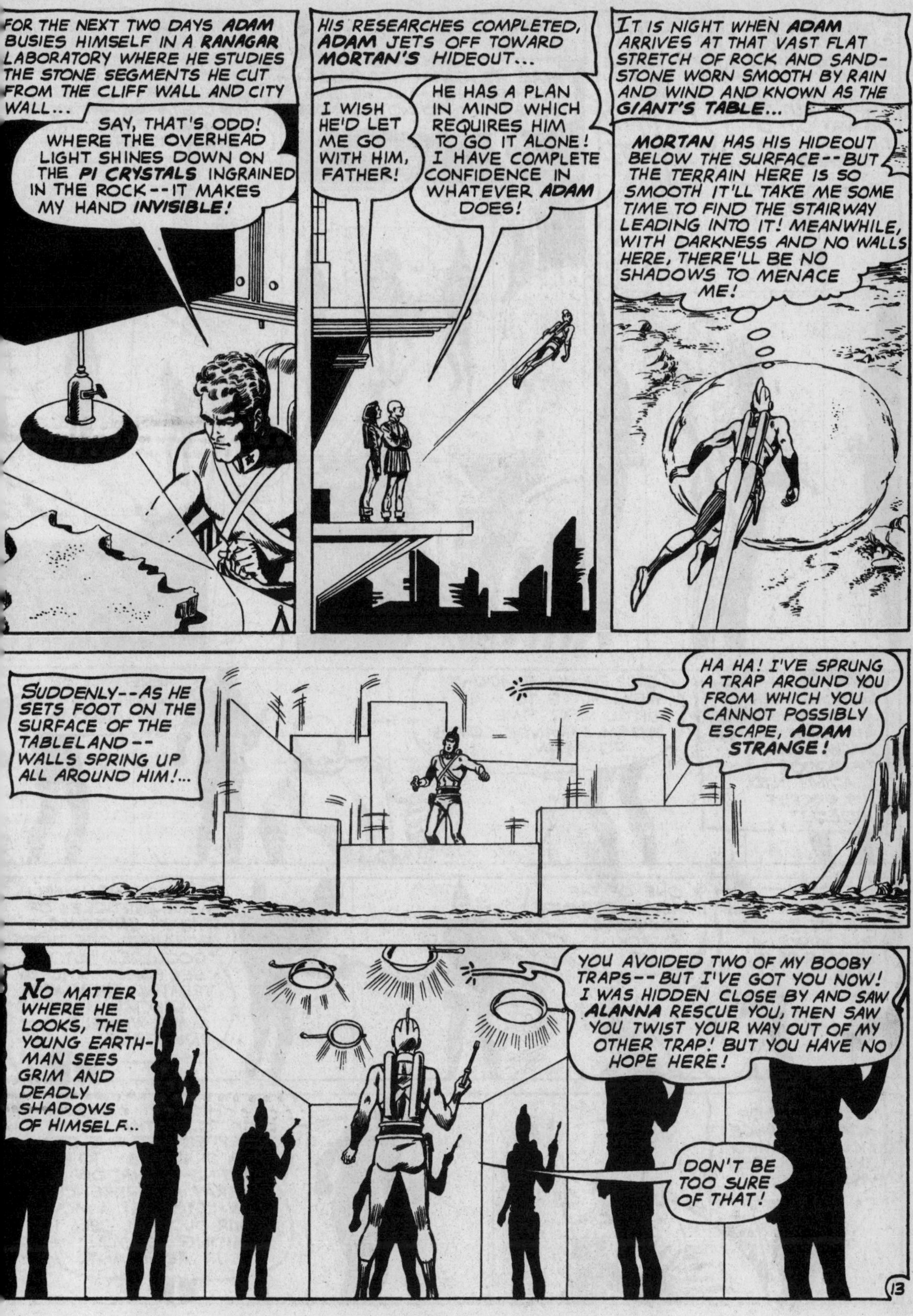
FOR THE NEXT TWO DAYS ADAM BUSIES HIMSELF IN A RANAGAR LABORATORY WHERE HE STUDIES THE STONE SEGMENTS HE CUT FROM THE CLIFF WALL AND CITY WALL...
SAY, THAT'S ODD! WHERE THE OVERHEAD LIGHT SHINES DOWN ON THE PI CRYSTALS INGRAINED IN THE ROCK--IT MAKES MY HAND INVISIBLE!
HIS RESEARCHES COMPLETED, ADAM JETS OFF TOWARD MORTAN'S HIDEOUT...
I WISH HE'D LET ME GO WITH HIM, FATHER!
HE HAS A PLAN IN MIND WHICH REQUIRES HIM TO GO IT ALONE! I HAVE COMPLETE CONFIDENCE IN WHATEVER ADAM DOES!
IT IS NIGHT WHEN ADAM ARRIVES AT THAT VAST FLAT STRETCH OF ROCK AND SANDSTONE WORN SMOOTH BY RAIN AND WIND AND KNOWN AS THE GIANT'S TABLE...
MORTAN HAS HIS HIDEOUT BELOW THE SURFACE--BUT THE TERRAIN HERE IS SO SMOOTH IT'LL TAKE ME SOME TIME TO FIND THE STAIRWAY LEADING INTO IT! MEANWHILE, WITH DARKNESS AND NO WALLS HERE, THERE'LL BE NO SHADOWS TO MENACE ME!
SUDDENLY--AS HE SETS FOOT ON THE SURFACE OF THE TABLELAND--WALLS SPRING UP ALL AROUND HIM!...
HA HA! I'VE SPRUNG A TRAP AROUND YOU FROM WHICH YOU CANNOT POSSIBLY ESCAPE, ADAM STRANGE!
NO MATTER WHERE HE LOOKS, THE YOUNG EARTH-MAN SEES GRIM AND DEADLY SHADOWS OF HIMSELF..
YOU AVOIDED TWO OF MY BOOBY TRAPS--BUT I'VE GOT YOU NOW! I WAS HIDDEN CLOSE BY AND SAW ALANNA RESCUE YOU, THEN SAW YOU TWIST YOUR WAY OUT OF MY OTHER TRAP! BUT YOU HAVE NO HOPE HERE!
DON'T BE TOO SURE OF THAT!
13

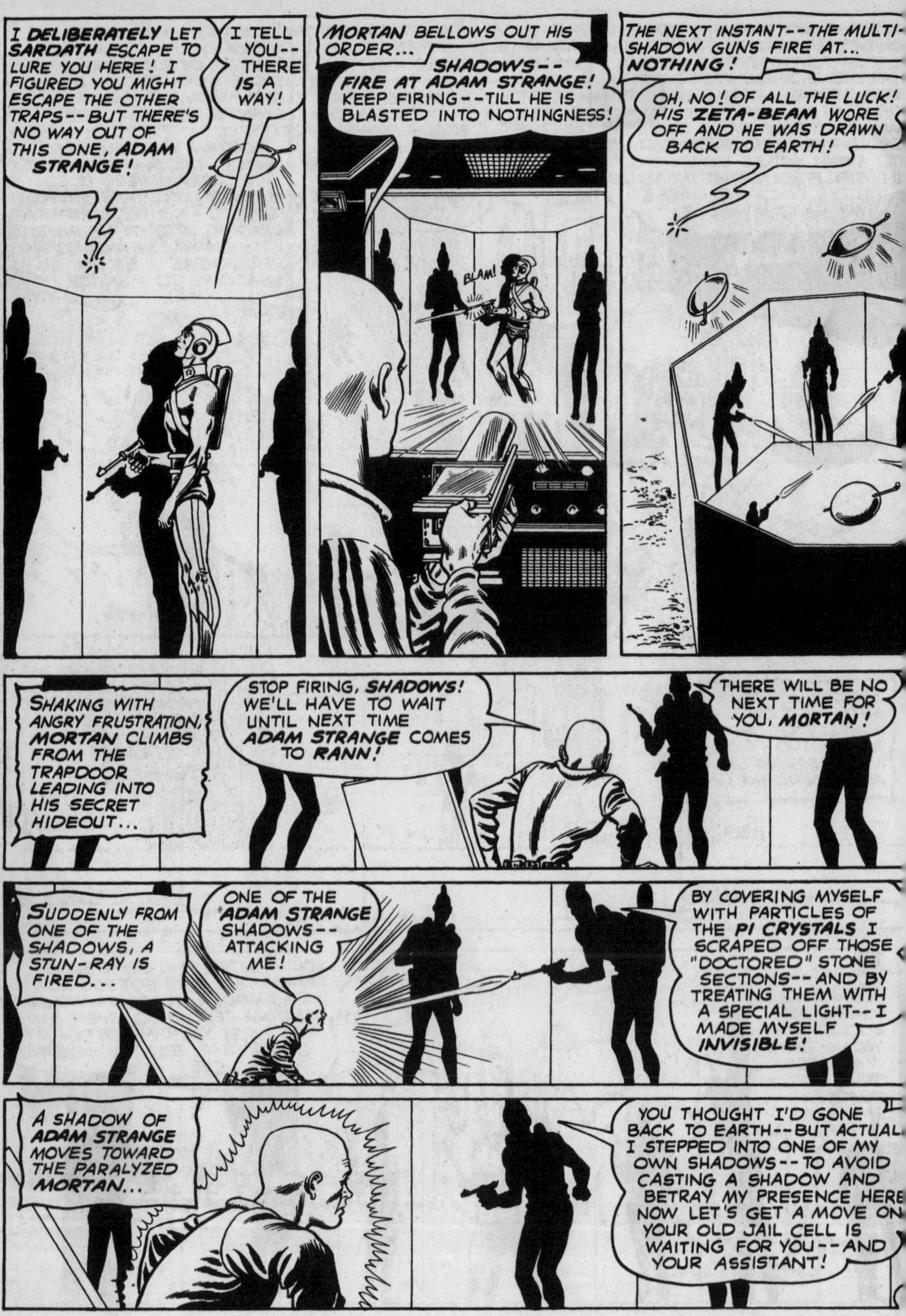
I DELIBERATELY LET SARDATH ESCAPE TO LURE YOU HERE! I FIGURED YOU MIGHT ESCAPE THE OTHER TRAPS--BUT THERE'S NO WAY OUT OF THIS ONE, ADAM STRANGE!
I TELL YOU--THERE IS A WAY!
MORTAN BELLOWS OUT HIS ORDER...
SHADOWS--FIRE AT ADAM STRANGE! KEEP FIRING--TILL HE IS BLASTED INTO NOTHINGNESS!
BLAM!
THE NEXT INSTANT--THE MULTI-SHADOW GUNS FIRE AT... NOTHING!
OH, NO! OF ALL THE LUCK! HIS ZETA-BEAM WORE OFF AND HE WAS DRAWN BACK TO EARTH!
SHAKING WITH ANGRY FRUSTRATION, MORTAN CLIMBS FROM THE TRAPDOOR LEADING INTO HIS SECRET HIDEOUT...
STOP FIRING, SHADOWS! WE'LL HAVE TO WAIT UNTIL NEXT TIME ADAM STRANGE COMES TO RANN!
THERE WILL BE NO NEXT TIME FOR YOU, MORTAN!
SUDDENLY FROM ONE OF THE SHADOWS, A STUN-RAY IS FIRED...
ONE OF THE ADAM STRANGE SHADOWS--ATTACKING ME!
BY COVERING MYSELF WITH PARTICLES OF THE PI CRYSTALS I SCRAPED OFF THOSE "DOCTORED" STONE SECTIONS--AND BY TREATING THEM WITH A SPECIAL LIGHT--I MADE MYSELF INVISIBLE!
A SHADOW OF ADAM STRANGE MOVES TOWARD THE PARALYZED MORTAN...
YOU THOUGHT I'D GONE BACK TO EARTH--BUT ACTUAL I STEPPED INTO ONE OF MY OWN SHADOWS--TO AVOID CASTING A SHADOW AND BETRAY MY PRESENCE HERE NOW LET'S GET A MOVE ON YOUR OLD JAIL CELL IS WAITING FOR YOU--AND YOUR ASSISTANT!

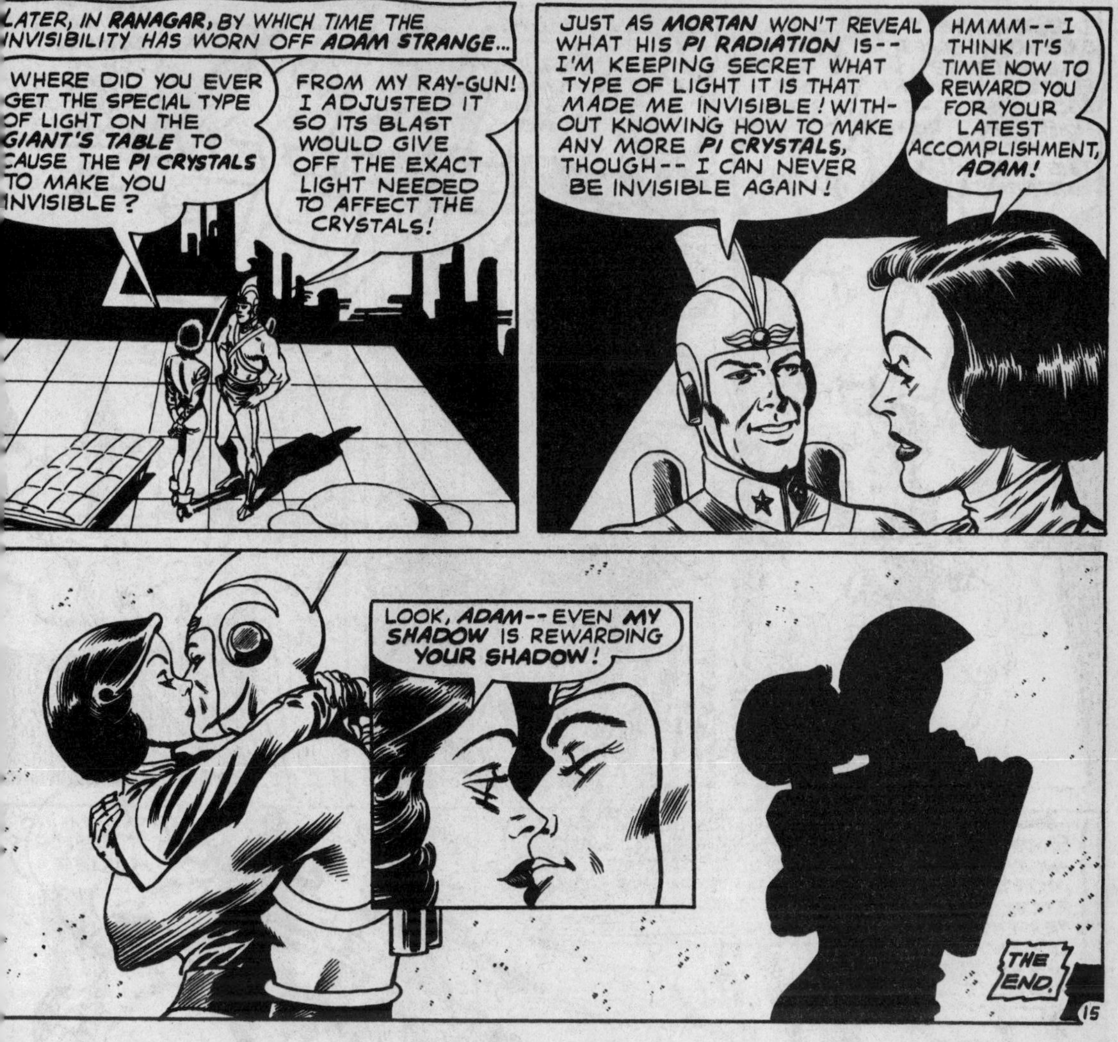
LATER, IN RANAGAR, BY WHICH TIME THE INVISIBILITY HAS WORN OFF ADAM STRANGE...
WHERE DID YOU EVER GET THE SPECIAL TYPE OF LIGHT ON THE GIANT'S TABLE TO CAUSE THE PI CRYSTALS TO MAKE YOU INVISIBLE?
FROM MY RAY-GUN! I ADJUSTED IT SO ITS BLAST WOULD GIVE OFF THE EXACT LIGHT NEEDED TO AFFECT THE CRYSTALS!
JUST AS MORTAN WON'T REVEAL WHAT HIS PI RADIATION IS-- I'M KEEPING SECRET WHAT TYPE OF LIGHT IT IS THAT MADE ME INVISIBLE! WITHOUT KNOWING HOW TO MAKE ANY MORE PI CRYSTALS, THOUGH-- I CAN NEVER BE INVISIBLE AGAIN!
HMMM-- I THINK IT'S TIME NOW TO REWARD YOU FOR YOUR LATEST ACCOMPLISHMENT, ADAM!
LOOK, ADAM-- EVEN MY SHADOW IS REWARDING YOUR SHADOW!
THE END.
15

ADAM STRANGE

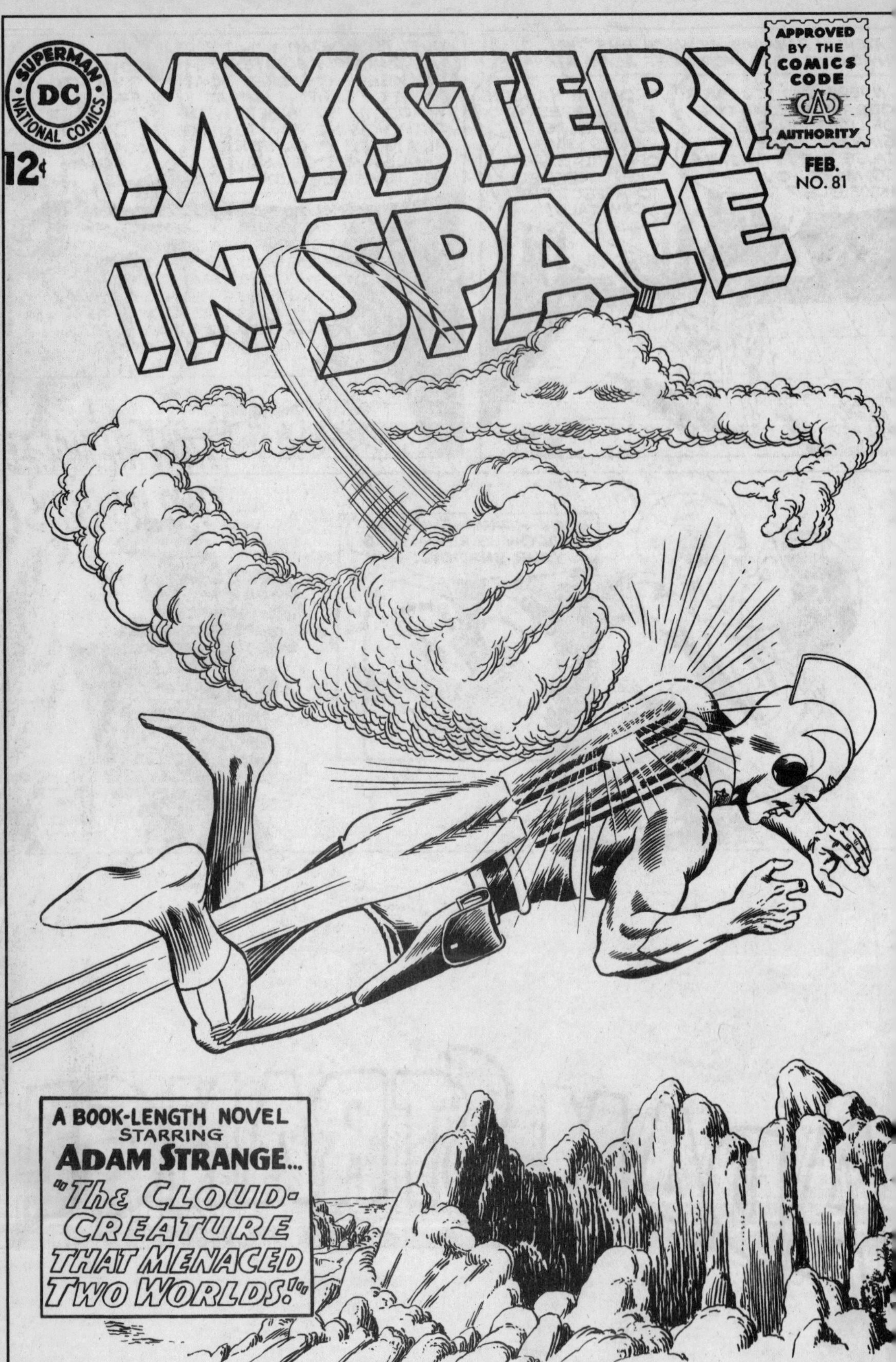
MYSTERY IN SPACE
SUPERMAN DC NATIONAL COMICS
12¢
APPROVED BY THE COMICS CODE AUTHORITY
FEB. NO. 81
A BOOK-LENGTH NOVEL STARRING ADAM STRANGE...
"The CLOUD-CREATURE THAT MENACED TWO WORLDS!"

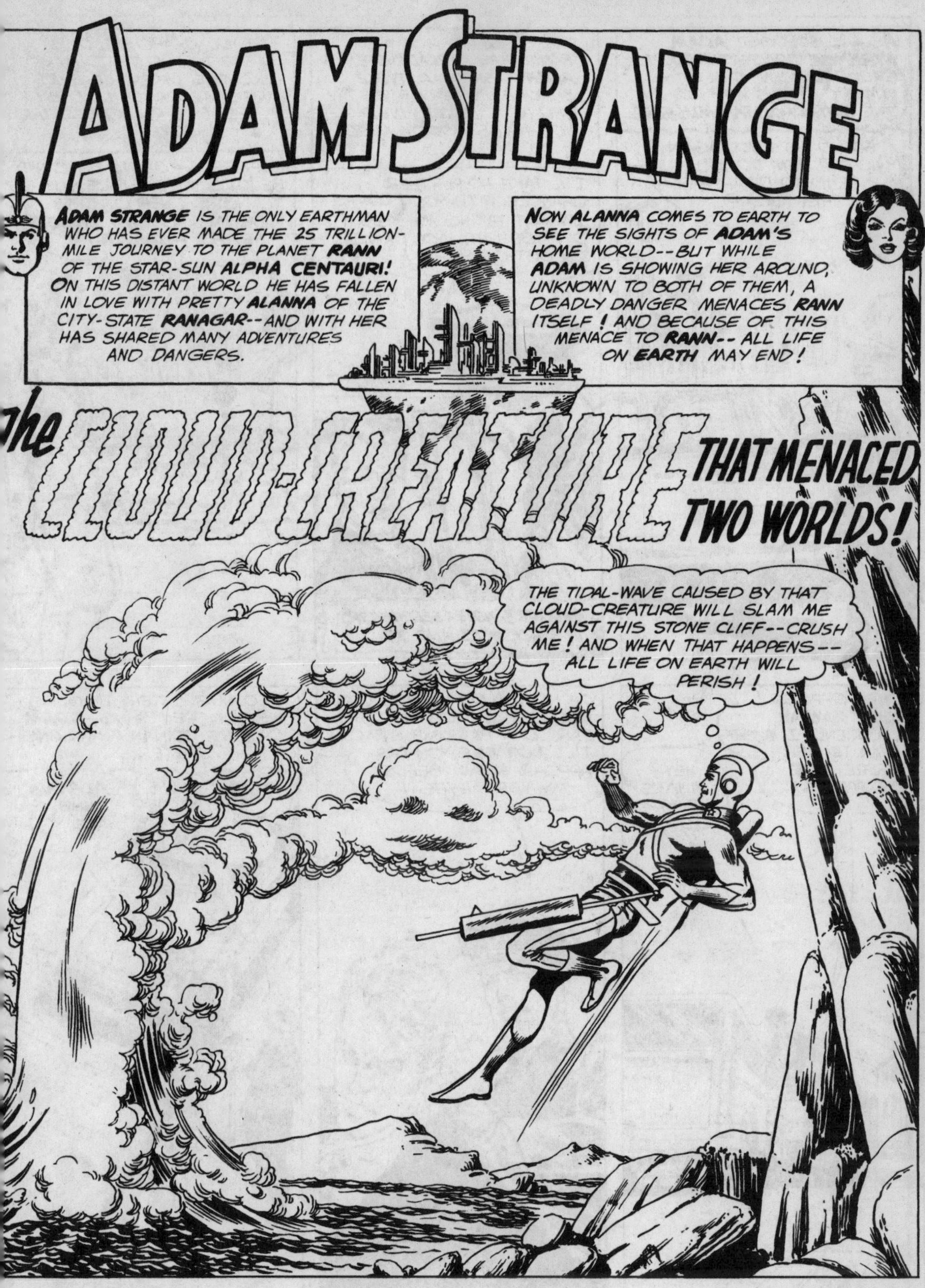
ADAM STRANGE
ADAM STRANGE IS THE ONLY EARTHMAN WHO HAS EVER MADE THE 25 TRILLION-MILE JOURNEY TO THE PLANET RANN OF THE STAR-SUN ALPHA CENTAURI! ON THIS DISTANT WORLD HE HAS FALLEN IN LOVE WITH PRETTY ALANNA OF THE CITY-STATE RANAGAR--AND WITH HER HAS SHARED MANY ADVENTURES AND DANGERS.
NOW ALANNA COMES TO EARTH TO SEE THE SIGHTS OF ADAM'S HOME WORLD--BUT WHILE ADAM IS SHOWING HER AROUND, UNKNOWN TO BOTH OF THEM, A DEADLY DANGER MENACES RANN ITSELF! AND BECAUSE OF THIS MENACE TO RANN-- ALL LIFE ON EARTH MAY END!
the CLOUD-CREATURE THAT MENACED TWO WORLDS!
THE TIDAL-WAVE CAUSED BY THAT CLOUD-CREATURE WILL SLAM ME AGAINST THIS STONE CLIFF--CRUSH ME! AND WHEN THAT HAPPENS-- ALL LIFE ON EARTH WILL PERISH!

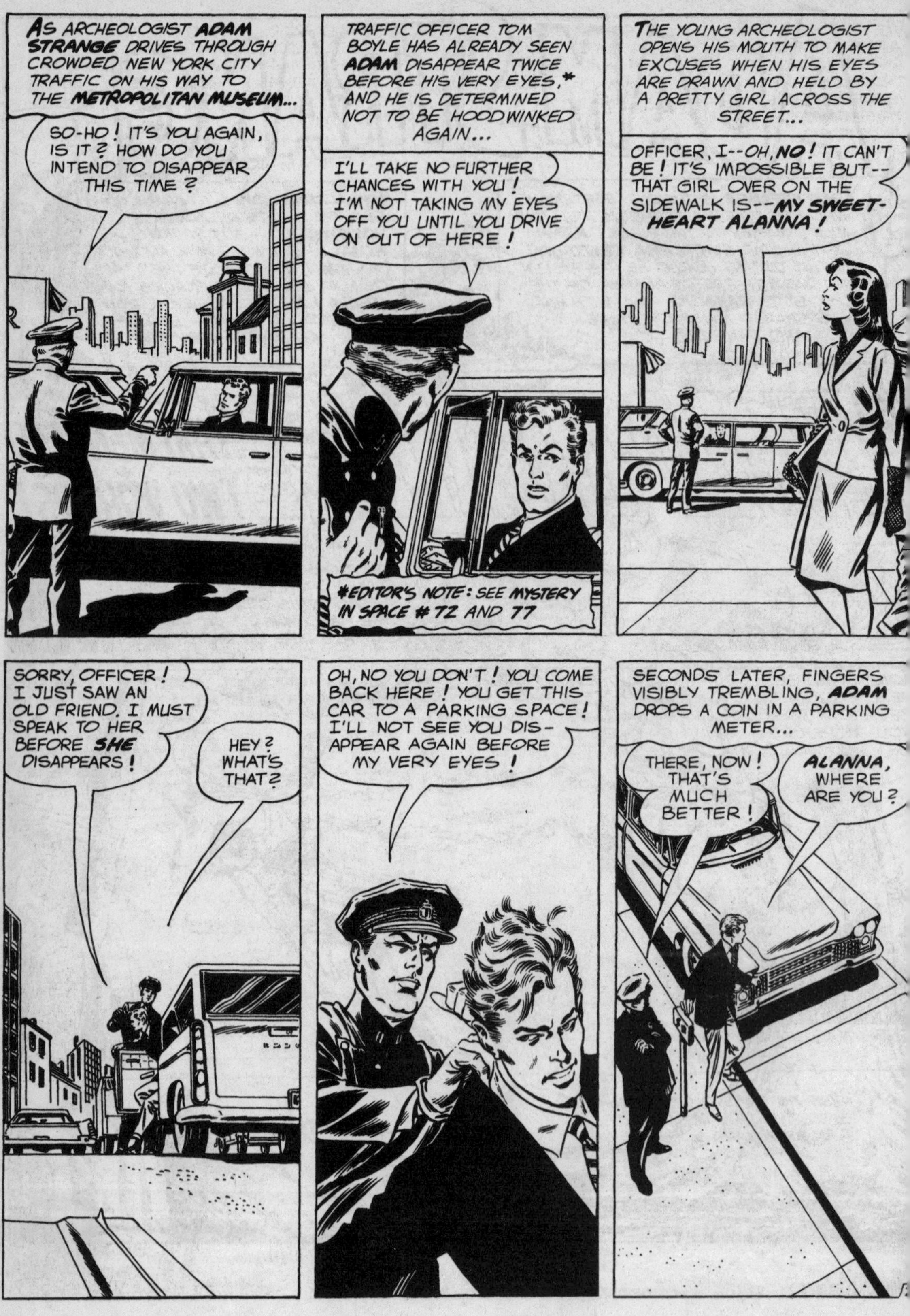
AS ARCHEOLOGIST ADAM STRANGE DRIVES THROUGH CROWDED NEW YORK CITY TRAFFIC ON HIS WAY TO THE METROPOLITAN MUSEUM...
SO-HO! IT'S YOU AGAIN, IS IT? HOW DO YOU INTEND TO DISAPPEAR THIS TIME?
TRAFFIC OFFICER TOM BOYLE HAS ALREADY SEEN ADAM DISAPPEAR TWICE BEFORE HIS VERY EYES,* AND HE IS DETERMINED NOT TO BE HOODWINKED AGAIN...
I'LL TAKE NO FURTHER CHANCES WITH YOU! I'M NOT TAKING MY EYES OFF YOU UNTIL YOU DRIVE ON OUT OF HERE!
*EDITOR'S NOTE: SEE MYSTERY IN SPACE #72 AND 77
THE YOUNG ARCHEOLOGIST OPENS HIS MOUTH TO MAKE EXCUSES WHEN HIS EYES ARE DRAWN AND HELD BY A PRETTY GIRL ACROSS THE STREET...
OFFICER, I--OH, NO! IT CAN'T BE! IT'S IMPOSSIBLE BUT--THAT GIRL OVER ON THE SIDEWALK IS--MY SWEETHEART ALANNA!
SORRY, OFFICER! I JUST SAW AN OLD FRIEND. I MUST SPEAK TO HER BEFORE SHE DISAPPEARS!
HEY? WHAT'S THAT?
OH, NO YOU DON'T! YOU COME BACK HERE! YOU GET THIS CAR TO A PARKING SPACE! I'LL NOT SEE YOU DISAPPEAR AGAIN BEFORE MY VERY EYES!
SECONDS LATER, FINGERS VISIBLY TREMBLING, ADAM DROPS A COIN IN A PARKING METER...
THERE, NOW! THAT'S MUCH BETTER!
ALANNA, WHERE ARE YOU?

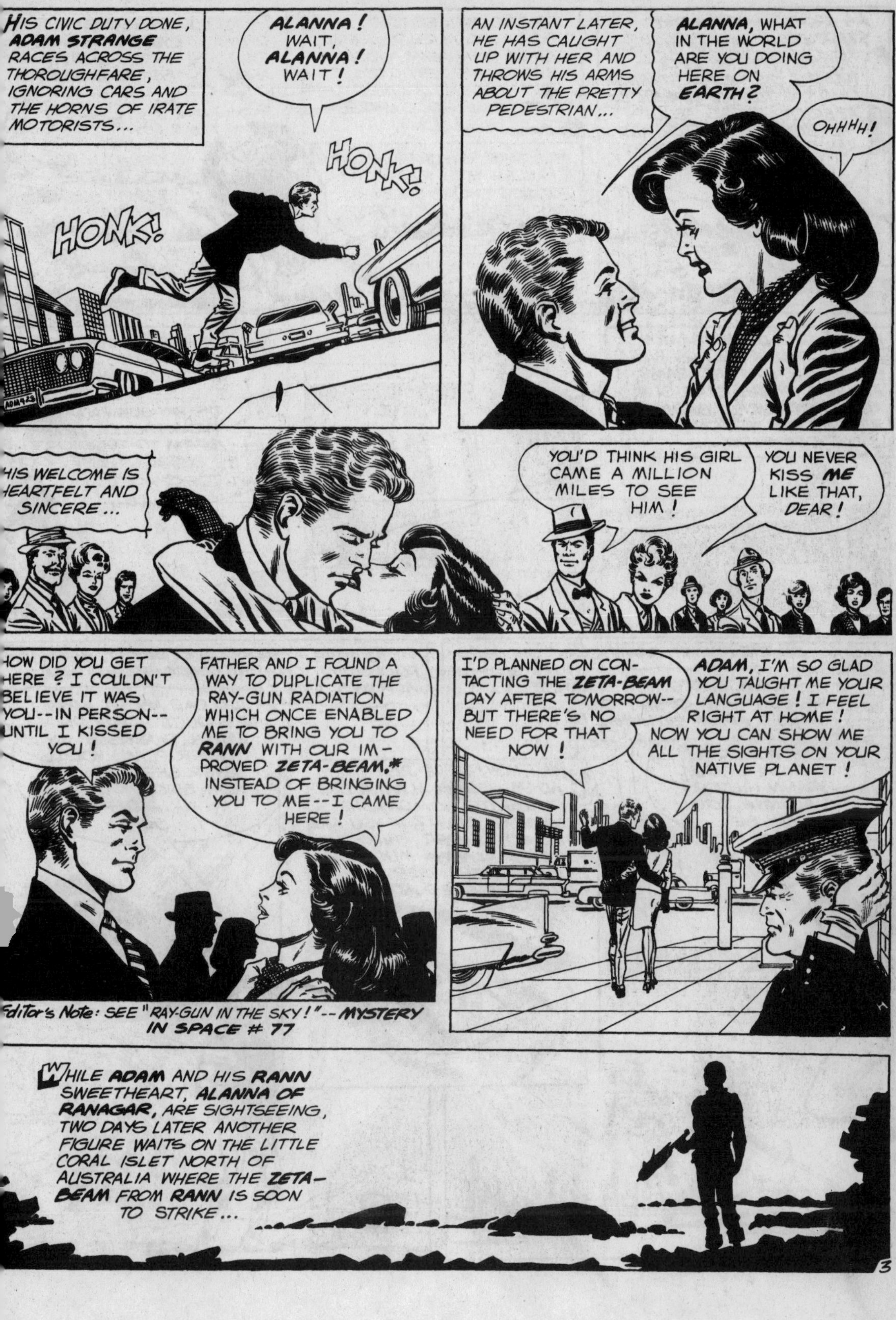
HIS CIVIC DUTY DONE, ADAM STRANGE RACES ACROSS THE THOROUGHFARE, IGNORING CARS AND THE HORNS OF IRATE MOTORISTS...
ALANNA! WAIT, ALANNA! WAIT!
HONK!
HONK!
AN INSTANT LATER, HE HAS CAUGHT UP WITH HER AND THROWS HIS ARMS ABOUT THE PRETTY PEDESTRIAN...
ALANNA, WHAT IN THE WORLD ARE YOU DOING HERE ON EARTH?
OHHHH!
HIS WELCOME IS HEARTFELT AND SINCERE...
YOU'D THINK HIS GIRL CAME A MILLION MILES TO SEE HIM!
YOU NEVER KISS ME LIKE THAT, DEAR!
HOW DID YOU GET HERE? I COULDN'T BELIEVE IT WAS YOU--IN PERSON--UNTIL I KISSED YOU!
FATHER AND I FOUND A WAY TO DUPLICATE THE RAY-GUN RADIATION WHICH ONCE ENABLED ME TO BRING YOU TO RANN WITH OUR IMPROVED ZETA-BEAM.* INSTEAD OF BRINGING YOU TO ME--I CAME HERE!
Editor's Note: SEE "RAY-GUN IN THE SKY!"--MYSTERY IN SPACE # 77
I'D PLANNED ON CONTACTING THE ZETA-BEAM DAY AFTER TOMORROW--BUT THERE'S NO NEED FOR THAT NOW!
ADAM, I'M SO GLAD YOU TAUGHT ME YOUR LANGUAGE! I FEEL RIGHT AT HOME! NOW YOU CAN SHOW ME ALL THE SIGHTS ON YOUR NATIVE PLANET!
WHILE ADAM AND HIS RANN SWEETHEART, ALANNA OF RANAGAR, ARE SIGHTSEEING, TWO DAYS LATER ANOTHER FIGURE WAITS ON THE LITTLE CORAL ISLET NORTH OF AUSTRALIA WHERE THE ZETA-BEAM FROM RANN IS SOON TO STRIKE...
3

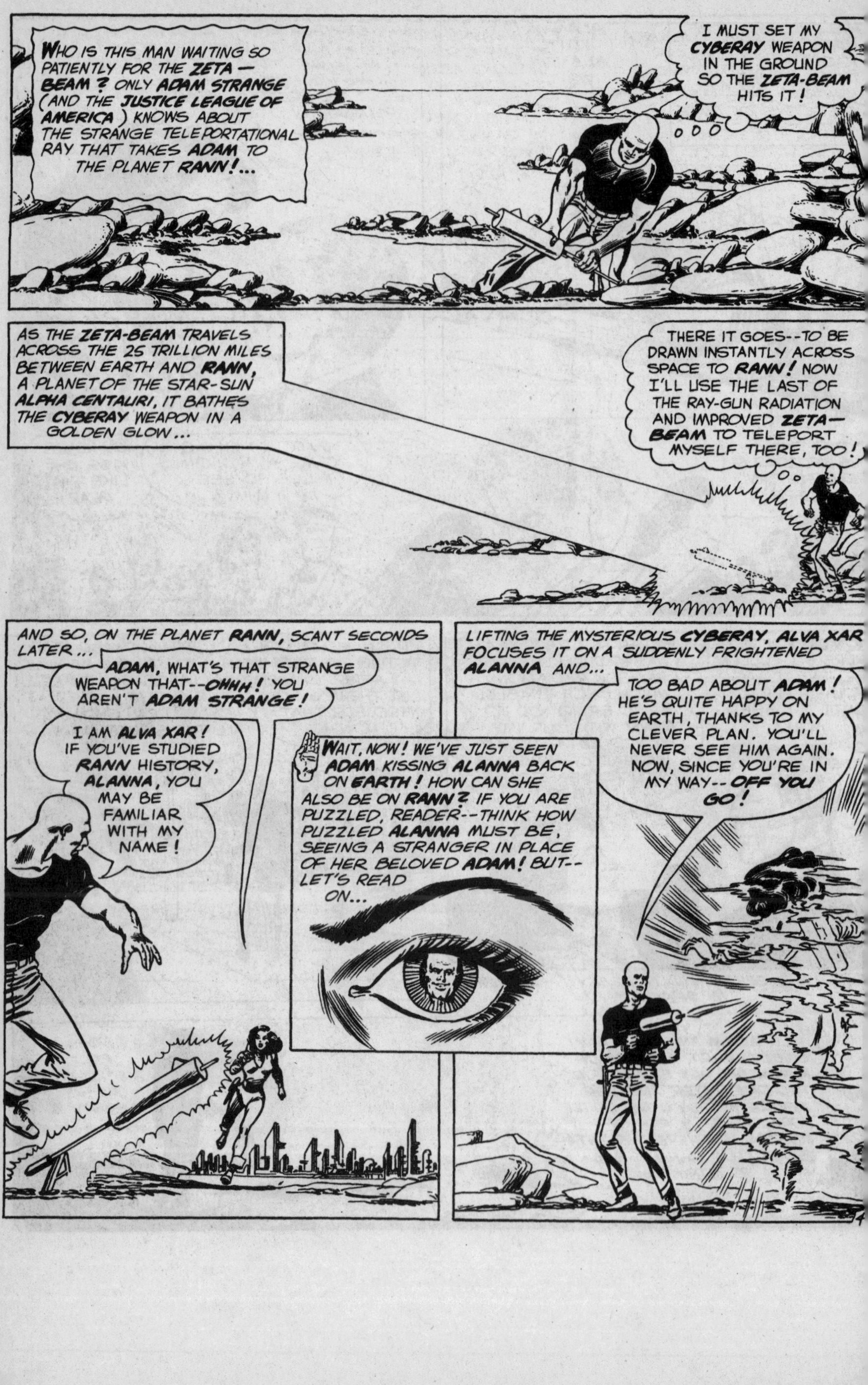
WHO IS THIS MAN WAITING SO PATIENTLY FOR THE ZETA-BEAM? ONLY ADAM STRANGE (AND THE JUSTICE LEAGUE OF AMERICA) KNOWS ABOUT THE STRANGE TELEPORTATIONAL RAY THAT TAKES ADAM TO THE PLANET RANN!...
I MUST SET MY CYBERAY WEAPON IN THE GROUND SO THE ZETA-BEAM HITS IT!
AS THE ZETA-BEAM TRAVELS ACROSS THE 25 TRILLION MILES BETWEEN EARTH AND RANN, A PLANET OF THE STAR-SUN ALPHA CENTAURI, IT BATHES THE CYBERAY WEAPON IN A GOLDEN GLOW...
THERE IT GOES--TO BE DRAWN INSTANTLY ACROSS SPACE TO RANN! NOW I'LL USE THE LAST OF THE RAY-GUN RADIATION AND IMPROVED ZETA-BEAM TO TELEPORT MYSELF THERE, TOO!
AND SO, ON THE PLANET RANN, SCANT SECONDS LATER...
ADAM, WHAT'S THAT STRANGE WEAPON THAT--OHHH! YOU AREN'T ADAM STRANGE!
I AM ALVA XAR! IF YOU'VE STUDIED RANN HISTORY, ALANNA, YOU MAY BE FAMILIAR WITH MY NAME!
WAIT, NOW! WE'VE JUST SEEN ADAM KISSING ALANNA BACK ON EARTH! HOW CAN SHE ALSO BE ON RANN? IF YOU ARE PUZZLED, READER--THINK HOW PUZZLED ALANNA MUST BE, SEEING A STRANGER IN PLACE OF HER BELOVED ADAM! BUT--LET'S READ ON...
LIFTING THE MYSTERIOUS CYBERAY, ALVA XAR FOCUSES IT ON A SUDDENLY FRIGHTENED ALANNA AND...
TOO BAD ABOUT ADAM! HE'S QUITE HAPPY ON EARTH, THANKS TO MY CLEVER PLAN. YOU'LL NEVER SEE HIM AGAIN. NOW, SINCE YOU'RE IN MY WAY--OFF YOU GO!

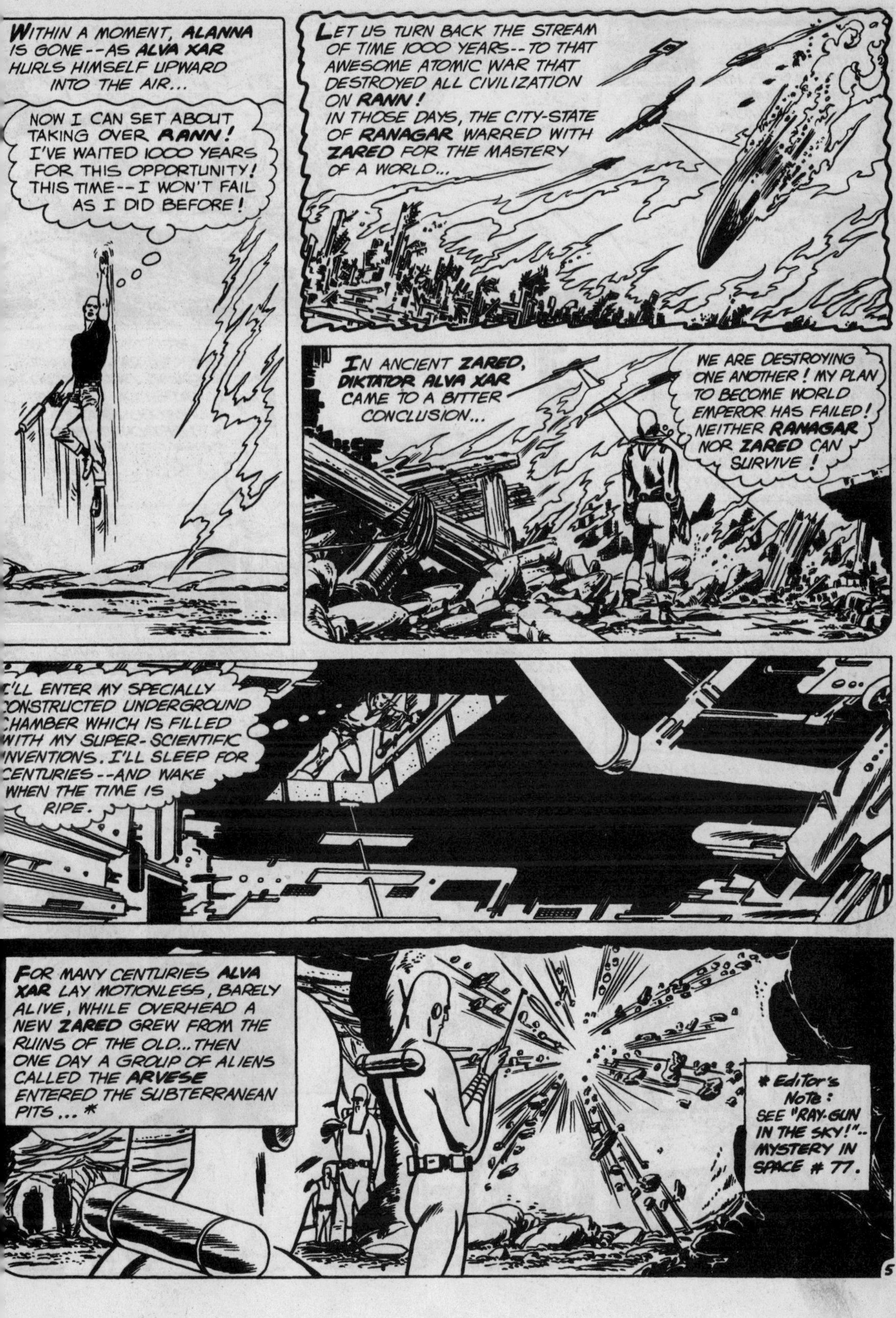

WITHIN A MOMENT, ALANNA IS GONE--AS ALVA XAR HURLS HIMSELF UPWARD INTO THE AIR...
NOW I CAN SET ABOUT TAKING OVER RANN! I'VE WAITED 1000 YEARS FOR THIS OPPORTUNITY! THIS TIME--I WON'T FAIL AS I DID BEFORE!
LET US TURN BACK THE STREAM OF TIME 1000 YEARS--TO THAT AWESOME ATOMIC WAR THAT DESTROYED ALL CIVILIZATION ON RANN! IN THOSE DAYS, THE CITY-STATE OF RANAGAR WARRED WITH ZARED FOR THE MASTERY OF A WORLD...
IN ANCIENT ZARED, DIKTATOR ALVA XAR CAME TO A BITTER CONCLUSION...
WE ARE DESTROYING ONE ANOTHER! MY PLAN TO BECOME WORLD EMPEROR HAS FAILED! NEITHER RANAGAR NOR ZARED CAN SURVIVE!
I'LL ENTER MY SPECIALLY CONSTRUCTED UNDERGROUND CHAMBER WHICH IS FILLED WITH MY SUPER-SCIENTIFIC INVENTIONS. I'LL SLEEP FOR CENTURIES--AND WAKE WHEN THE TIME IS RIPE.
FOR MANY CENTURIES ALVA XAR LAY MOTIONLESS, BARELY ALIVE, WHILE OVERHEAD A NEW ZARED GREW FROM THE RUINS OF THE OLD...THEN ONE DAY A GROUP OF ALIENS CALLED THE ARVESE ENTERED THE SUBTERRANEAN PITS...*
* Editor's Note: SEE "RAY-GUN IN THE SKY!"-- MYSTERY IN SPACE # 77.
5

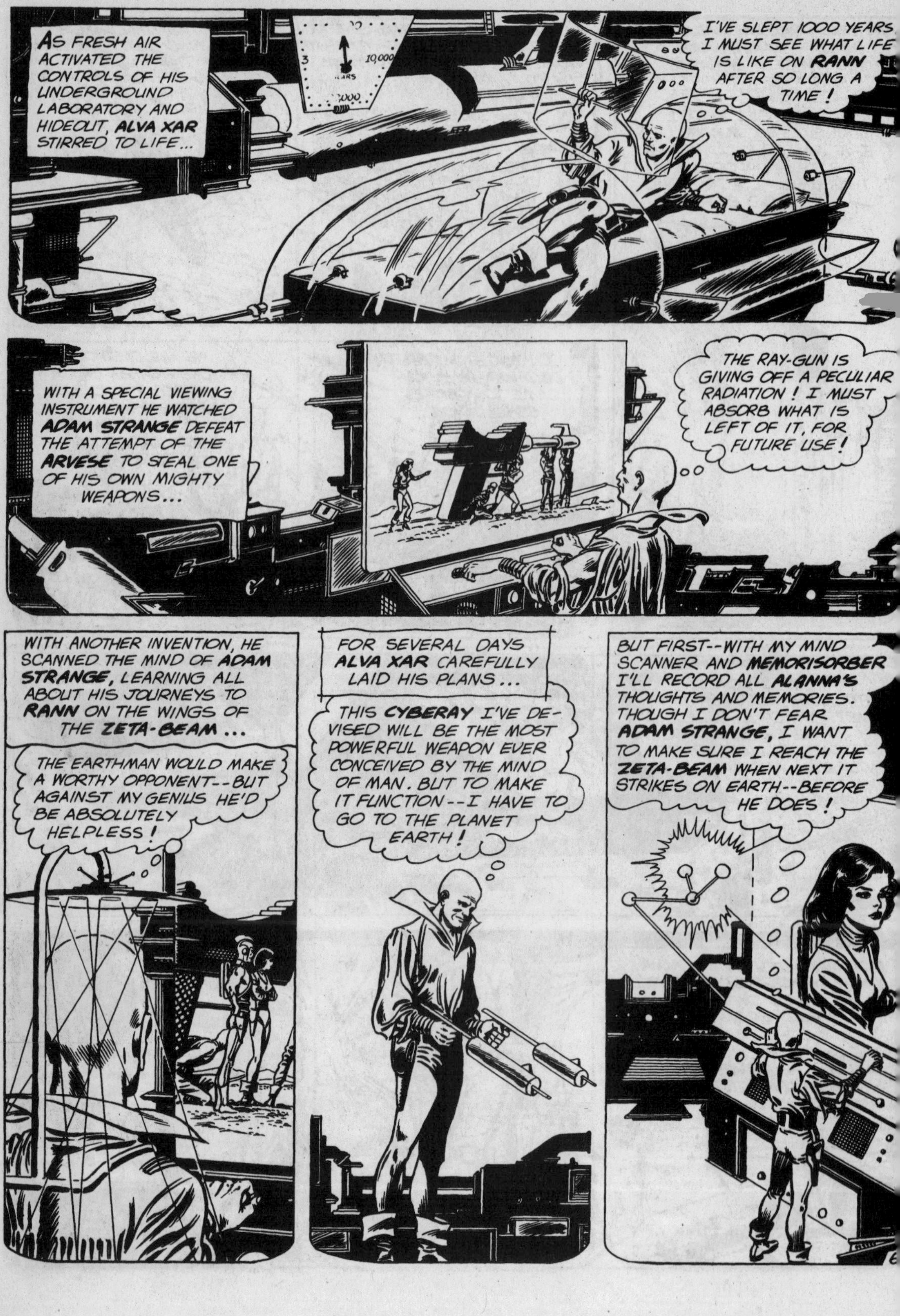
AS FRESH AIR ACTIVATED THE CONTROLS OF HIS UNDERGROUND LABORATORY AND HIDEOUT, ALVA XAR STIRRED TO LIFE...
I'VE SLEPT 1000 YEARS. I MUST SEE WHAT LIFE IS LIKE ON RANN AFTER SO LONG A TIME!
WITH A SPECIAL VIEWING INSTRUMENT HE WATCHED ADAM STRANGE DEFEAT THE ATTEMPT OF THE ARVESE TO STEAL ONE OF HIS OWN MIGHTY WEAPONS...
THE RAY-GUN IS GIVING OFF A PECULIAR RADIATION! I MUST ABSORB WHAT IS LEFT OF IT, FOR FUTURE USE!
WITH ANOTHER INVENTION, HE SCANNED THE MIND OF ADAM STRANGE, LEARNING ALL ABOUT HIS JOURNEYS TO RANN ON THE WINGS OF THE ZETA-BEAM...
THE EARTHMAN WOULD MAKE A WORTHY OPPONENT--BUT AGAINST MY GENIUS HE'D BE ABSOLUTELY HELPLESS!
FOR SEVERAL DAYS ALVA XAR CAREFULLY LAID HIS PLANS...
THIS CYBERAY I'VE DEVISED WILL BE THE MOST POWERFUL WEAPON EVER CONCEIVED BY THE MIND OF MAN. BUT TO MAKE IT FUNCTION--I HAVE TO GO TO THE PLANET EARTH!
BUT FIRST--WITH MY MIND SCANNER AND MEMORISORBER I'LL RECORD ALL ALANNA'S THOUGHTS AND MEMORIES. THOUGH I DON'T FEAR ADAM STRANGE, I WANT TO MAKE SURE I REACH THE ZETA-BEAM WHEN NEXT IT STRIKES ON EARTH--BEFORE HE DOES!

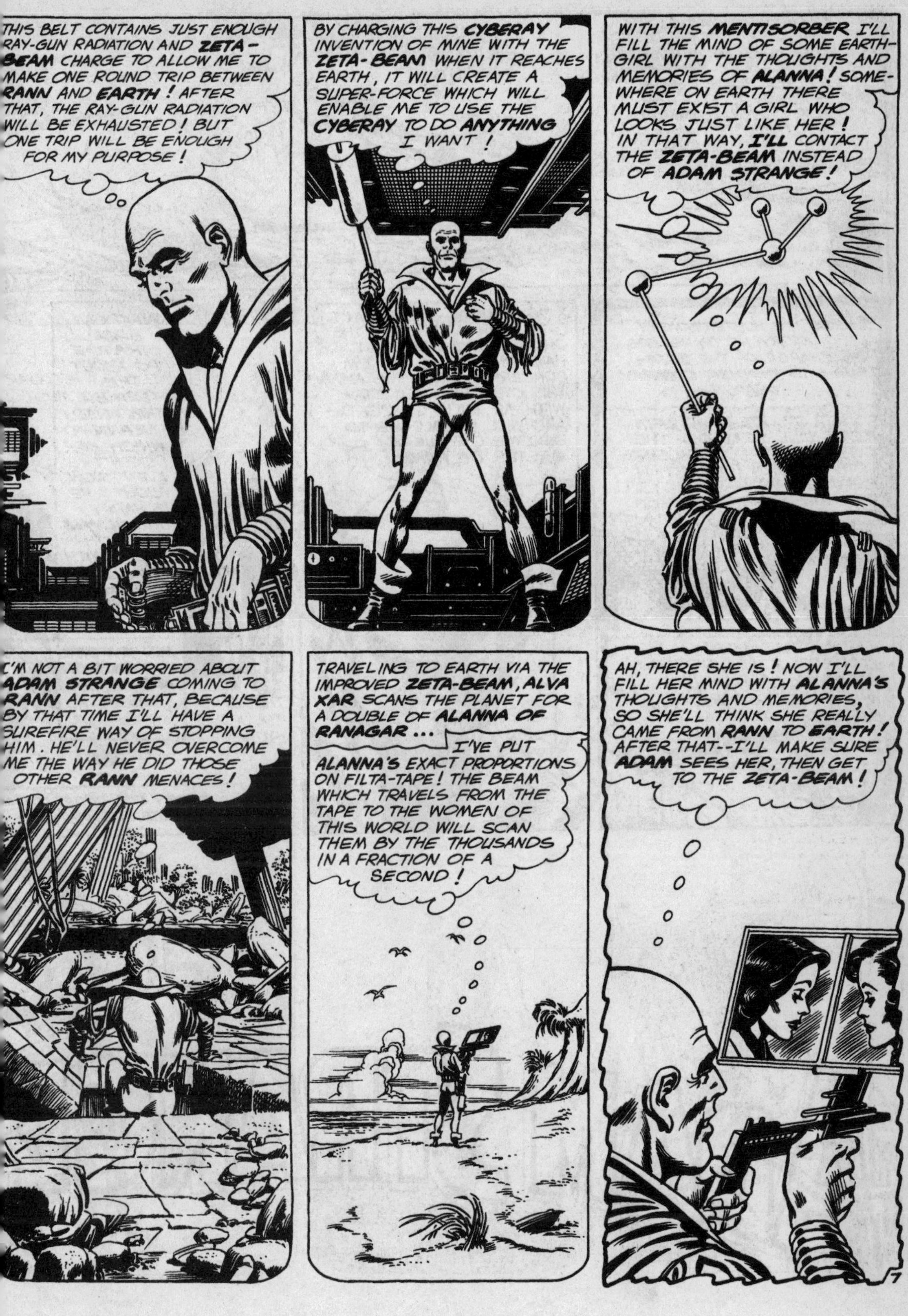
THIS BELT CONTAINS JUST ENOUGH RAY-GUN RADIATION AND ZETA-BEAM CHARGE TO ALLOW ME TO MAKE ONE ROUND TRIP BETWEEN RANN AND EARTH! AFTER THAT, THE RAY-GUN RADIATION WILL BE EXHAUSTED! BUT ONE TRIP WILL BE ENOUGH FOR MY PURPOSE!
BY CHARGING THIS CYBERAY INVENTION OF MINE WITH THE ZETA-BEAM WHEN IT REACHES EARTH, IT WILL CREATE A SUPER-FORCE WHICH WILL ENABLE ME TO USE THE CYBERAY TO DO ANYTHING I WANT!
WITH THIS MENTISORBER I'LL FILL THE MIND OF SOME EARTH-GIRL WITH THE THOUGHTS AND MEMORIES OF ALANNA! SOMEWHERE ON EARTH THERE MUST EXIST A GIRL WHO LOOKS JUST LIKE HER! IN THAT WAY, I'LL CONTACT THE ZETA-BEAM INSTEAD OF ADAM STRANGE!
I'M NOT A BIT WORRIED ABOUT ADAM STRANGE COMING TO RANN AFTER THAT, BECAUSE BY THAT TIME I'LL HAVE A SUREFIRE WAY OF STOPPING HIM. HE'LL NEVER OVERCOME ME THE WAY HE DID THOSE OTHER RANN MENACES!
TRAVELING TO EARTH VIA THE IMPROVED ZETA-BEAM, ALVA XAR SCANS THE PLANET FOR A DOUBLE OF ALANNA OF RANAGAR...
I'VE PUT ALANNA'S EXACT PROPORTIONS ON FILTA-TAPE! THE BEAM WHICH TRAVELS FROM THE TAPE TO THE WOMEN OF THIS WORLD WILL SCAN THEM BY THE THOUSANDS IN A FRACTION OF A SECOND!
AH, THERE SHE IS! NOW I'LL FILL HER MIND WITH ALANNA'S THOUGHTS AND MEMORIES, SO SHE'LL THINK SHE REALLY CAME FROM RANN TO EARTH! AFTER THAT--I'LL MAKE SURE ADAM SEES HER, THEN GET TO THE ZETA-BEAM!
7

NOW AS HE HURTLES ACROSS THE ARID PLAIN OF *SAREEL* ON HIS HOME PLANET, *ALVA XAR* IS READY TO PUT HIS PLAN FOR CONQUEST INTO ACTION...

*I*NSIDE HIS SUBTERRANEAN LABORATORY, HE TRANSFERS THE CHARGE OF THE *ZETA-BEAM* TO ANOTHER *CYBERAY* WEAPON...

SOONER OR LATER, THE *ZETA-BEAM* WILL WEAR OFF THE *CYBERAY* WEAPON, CAUSING IT TO RETURN TO EARTH! BEFORE THAT HAPPENS, I'LL TRANSFER THE CHARGE IN THE FIRST *CYBERAY* TO A DUPLICATE SECOND ONE!

I DON'T KNOW--AND I DON'T CARE-- WHAT EFFECTS THE ORIGINAL *CYBERAY* WILL HAVE ON EARTH! ALL I'M CONCERNED ABOUT IS *RANN!* THIS *CYBERAY* WILL STAY WITH ME, FULLY CHARGED-- AND WILL ENABLE ME TO BECOME COMPLETE MASTER OF *RANN!*

WHAT CAN *ADAM STRANGE* DO ABOUT THIS TERRIBLE THREAT TO *RANN*-- WHICH HE DOESN'T EVEN KNOW ABOUT? HE IS HAPPY WITH *ALANNA* ON EARTH-- THAT IS, WITH SOME GIRL BOTH HE AND SHE *THINK* IS *ALANNA!*

AND WHATEVER HAPPENED TO *ALANNA*, BY THE WAY?

STORY CONTINUES ON NEXT PAGE FOLLOWING!

ADAM STRANGE

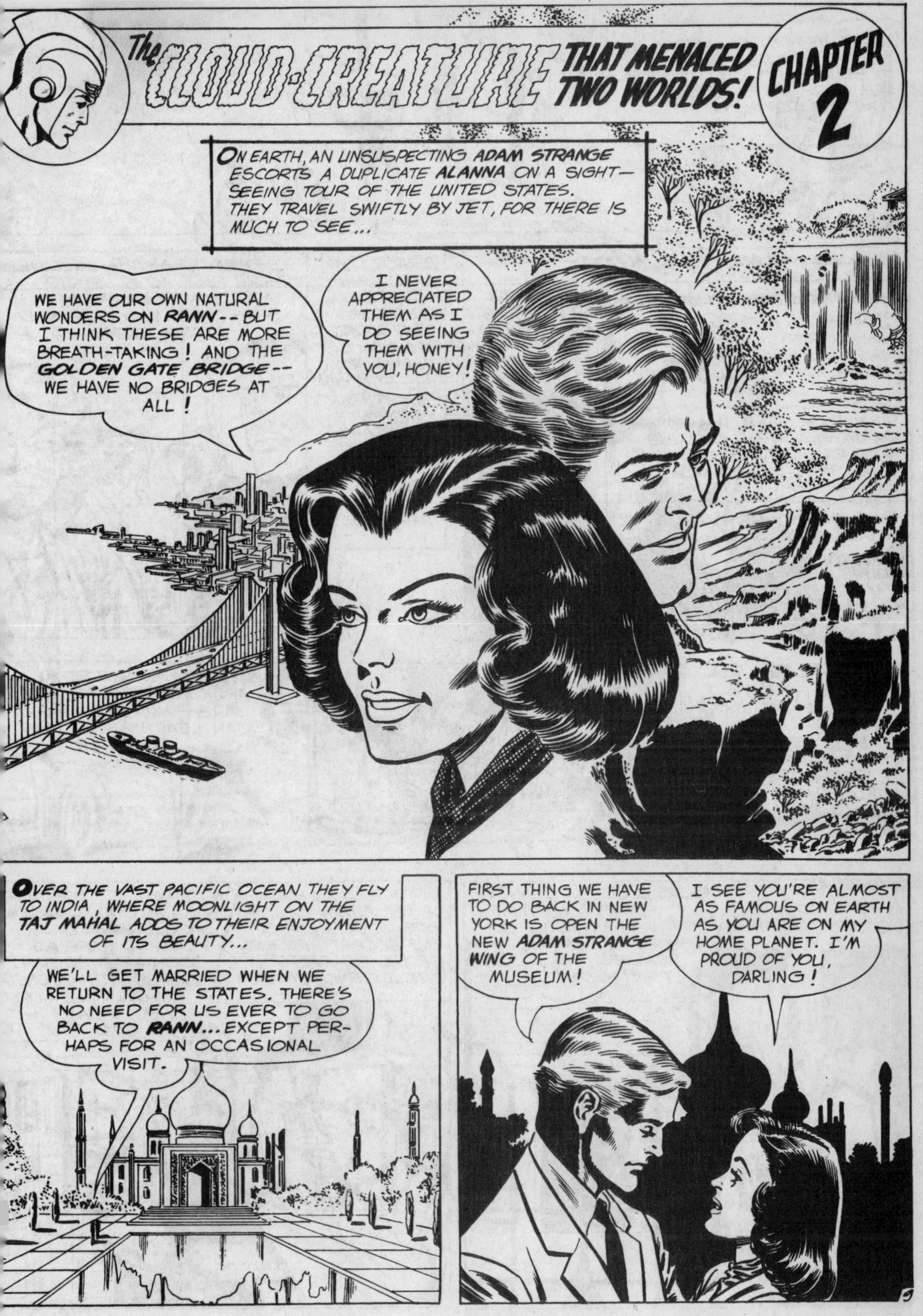
The CLOUD-CREATURE THAT MENACED TWO WORLDS!
CHAPTER 2
ON EARTH, AN UNSUSPECTING ADAM STRANGE ESCORTS A DUPLICATE ALANNA ON A SIGHT-SEEING TOUR OF THE UNITED STATES. THEY TRAVEL SWIFTLY BY JET, FOR THERE IS MUCH TO SEE...
WE HAVE OUR OWN NATURAL WONDERS ON RANN--BUT I THINK THESE ARE MORE BREATH-TAKING! AND THE GOLDEN GATE BRIDGE--WE HAVE NO BRIDGES AT ALL!
I NEVER APPRECIATED THEM AS I DO SEEING THEM WITH YOU, HONEY!
OVER THE VAST PACIFIC OCEAN THEY FLY TO INDIA, WHERE MOONLIGHT ON THE TAJ MAHAL ADDS TO THEIR ENJOYMENT OF ITS BEAUTY...
WE'LL GET MARRIED WHEN WE RETURN TO THE STATES. THERE'S NO NEED FOR US EVER TO GO BACK TO RANN... EXCEPT PERHAPS FOR AN OCCASIONAL VISIT.
FIRST THING WE HAVE TO DO BACK IN NEW YORK IS OPEN THE NEW ADAM STRANGE WING OF THE MUSEUM!
I SEE YOU'RE ALMOST AS FAMOUS ON EARTH AS YOU ARE ON MY HOME PLANET. I'M PROUD OF YOU, DARLING!

IN NEW YORK, TWO DAYS LATER...

THE NEW WING IS JUST UP AHEAD. I'M SCHEDULED TO MAKE A LITTLE SPEECH BUT I HAVE TIME TO SHOW YOU AROUND FIRST!

SUDDENLY, ALANNA STOPS ABSOLUTELY MOTIONLESS...

ALANNA-- WHAT'S WRONG? YOU-- YOU'RE AS HARD AND AS RIGID AS MARBLE!

TERROR LAYS AN ICY HAND OVER HIS HEART AS THE YOUNG ARCHEOLOGIST TURNS FROM HIS STRICKEN SWEETHEART AND SEES THAT SHE IS NOT THE ONLY PERSON SO AFFECTED...

I SEEM TO BE THE ONLY ONE HERE ABLE TO MOVE AND TALK! I WONDER IF THE SAME THING HAS HAPPENED ON THE OUTSIDE?

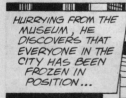

HURRYING FROM THE MUSEUM, HE DISCOVERS THAT EVERYONE IN THE CITY HAS BEEN FROZEN IN POSITION...

I'VE GOT TO GET TO MY APARTMENT-- DON MY RAN GARB-- AND SEE WHAT I CAN LEARN ABOUT THIS DISASTER!

IN HIS APARTMENT SOON AFTERWARD...

THERE'S JUST A CHANCE THAT ADVANCE WARNING OF THIS FANTASTIC HAPPENING MAY HAVE REACHED THE *PENTAGON!*

LESS THAN AN HOUR LATER, ADAM IS BUSILY SEARCHING THE SECRET RECORDS OF THE GOVERNMENT INTELLIGENCE AGENCY...

NOTHING! YET WORD OF SUCH AN ODD OCCURRENC SHOULD HAVE BEEN FLASHED HERE AS SOON AS IT BEGAN. UNLESS-- IT HAPPENED ALL OVER THE WORLD AT THE SAME TIME!

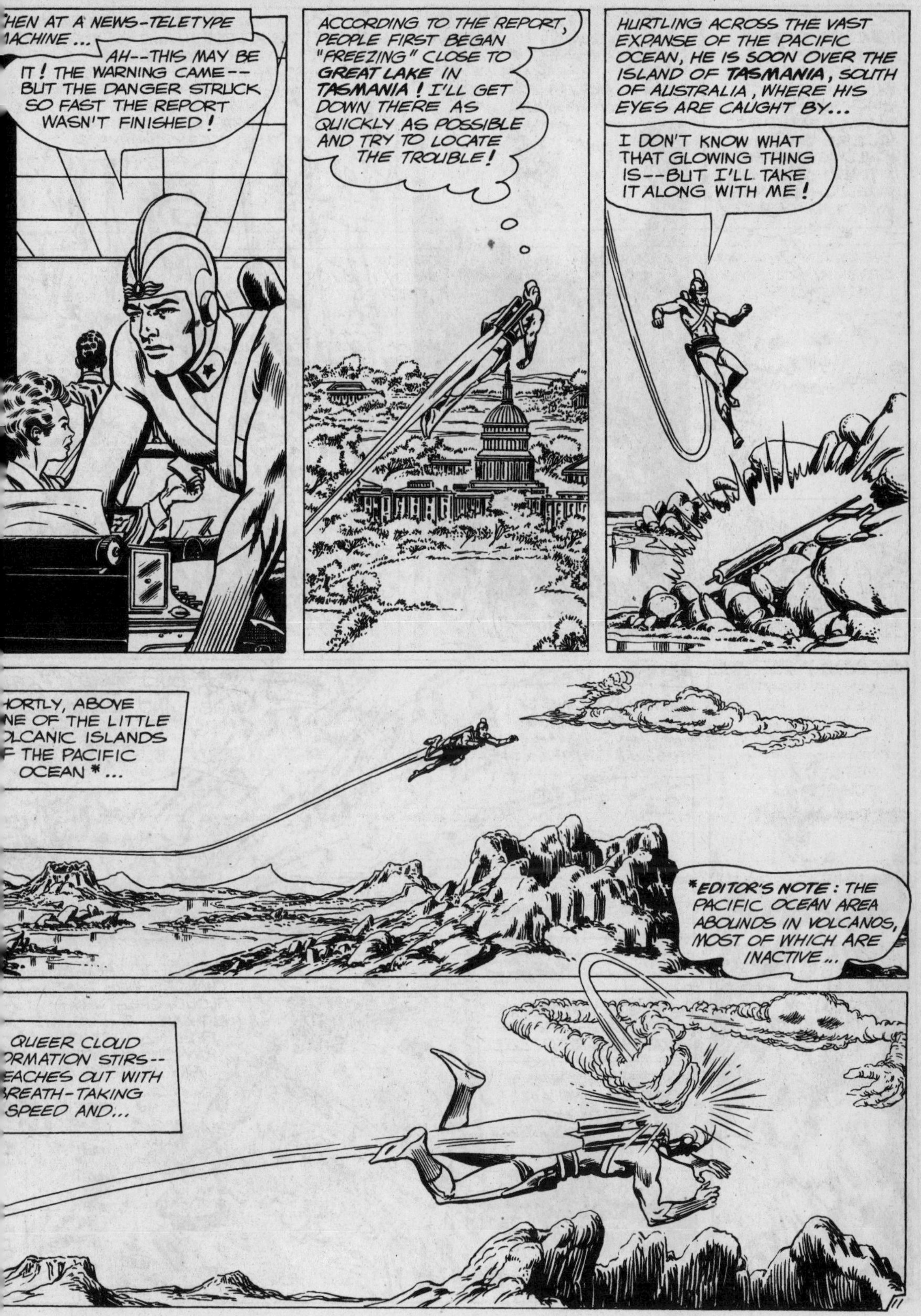
HEN AT A NEWS-TELETYPE MACHINE...
AH--THIS MAY BE IT! THE WARNING CAME--BUT THE DANGER STRUCK SO FAST THE REPORT WASN'T FINISHED!
ACCORDING TO THE REPORT, PEOPLE FIRST BEGAN "FREEZING" CLOSE TO GREAT LAKE IN TASMANIA! I'LL GET DOWN THERE AS QUICKLY AS POSSIBLE AND TRY TO LOCATE THE TROUBLE!
HURTLING ACROSS THE VAST EXPANSE OF THE PACIFIC OCEAN, HE IS SOON OVER THE ISLAND OF TASMANIA, SOUTH OF AUSTRALIA, WHERE HIS EYES ARE CAUGHT BY...
I DON'T KNOW WHAT THAT GLOWING THING IS--BUT I'LL TAKE IT ALONG WITH ME!
HORTLY, ABOVE NE OF THE LITTLE OLCANIC ISLANDS F THE PACIFIC OCEAN*...
*EDITOR'S NOTE: THE PACIFIC OCEAN AREA ABOUNDS IN VOLCANOS, MOST OF WHICH ARE INACTIVE...
QUEER CLOUD ORMATION STIRS--EACHES OUT WITH BREATH-TAKING SPEED AND...
11

DAZED BY THAT TREACHEROUS BLOW, **ADAM** DROPS LIKE A PLUMMET INTO THE MAW OF A VOLCANO...

RASH CREATURE! ALL LIFE ON THIS WORLD IS SUSPENDED IN TIME! ONLY YOU DARED CHALLENGE MY SOLITARY RULE!

FAR BELOW THE FALLING ARCHEOLOGIST, LAVA BUBBLES UPWARD IN GREAT MOLTEN SPOUTS. THE EARTH'S CRUST SHIFTS AND ITS HOT LIQUIDS REACT BY RISING...

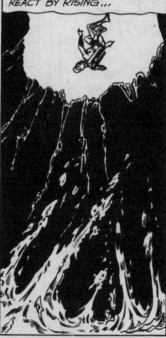

WITH A CRUNCHING OF STONE AND A GIGANTIC SHUDDER, THE VOLCANO ERUPTS! A SEA OF STEAMING MAGMA RISES UPWARD, SENDING GOUTS OF LAVA SKYWARD...

OHHH-- WHERE AM I? WHA--WHAT ARE THOSE FIERY CHUNKS?

UNDERSTANDING OF HIS DANGER DRIVES HIS HAND TOWARD HIS JET CONTROLS...

CAN I MAKE IT? OR WILL THE LAVA ENGULF ME BEFORE MY JETS GET ME INTO THE OPEN AIR?

HIS JETS THROBBING WITH POWER, **ADAM STRANGE** RISES OUT OF THE ERUPTING CRATER SECONDS BEFORE THE AIR FILLS WITH HOT ASHES AND BURNING LAVA...

I'VE GOT TO TAKE MY CHANCES WITH THAT CLOUD-CREATURE-- ALTHOUGH I HAVE THE FEELING THAT MY RAY-GUN WON'T BE ANY HELP TO ME!

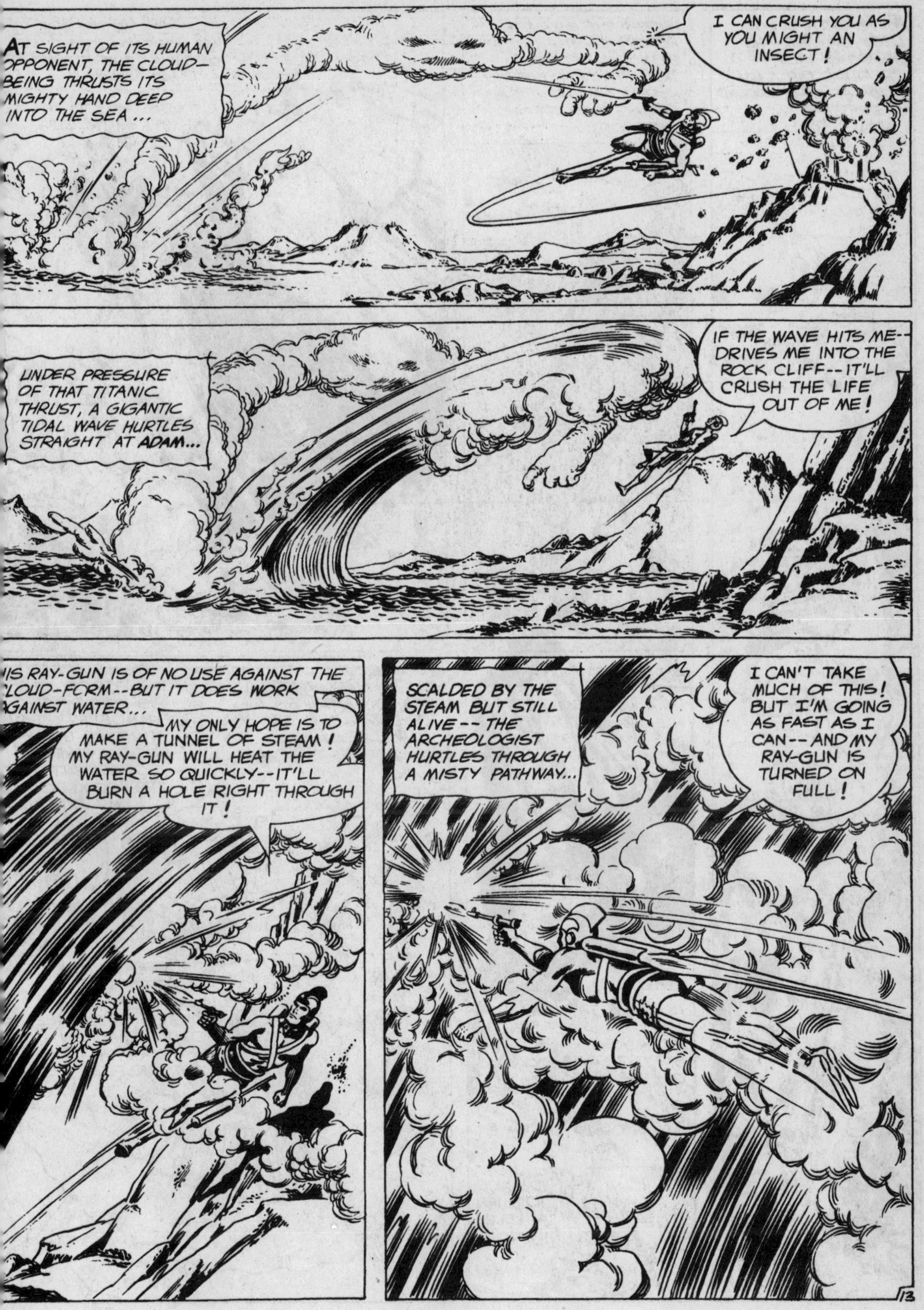
AT SIGHT OF ITS HUMAN OPPONENT, THE CLOUD-BEING THRUSTS ITS MIGHTY HAND DEEP INTO THE SEA ...
I CAN CRUSH YOU AS YOU MIGHT AN INSECT!
UNDER PRESSURE OF THAT TITANIC THRUST, A GIGANTIC TIDAL WAVE HURTLES STRAIGHT AT ADAM...
IF THE WAVE HITS ME-- DRIVES ME INTO THE ROCK CLIFF--IT'LL CRUSH THE LIFE OUT OF ME!
HIS RAY-GUN IS OF NO USE AGAINST THE CLOUD-FORM--BUT IT DOES WORK AGAINST WATER...
MY ONLY HOPE IS TO MAKE A TUNNEL OF STEAM! MY RAY-GUN WILL HEAT THE WATER SO QUICKLY--IT'LL BURN A HOLE RIGHT THROUGH IT!
SCALDED BY THE STEAM BUT STILL ALIVE -- THE ARCHEOLOGIST HURTLES THROUGH A MISTY PATHWAY...
I CAN'T TAKE MUCH OF THIS! BUT I'M GOING AS FAST AS I CAN-- AND MY RAY-GUN IS TURNED ON FULL!
13

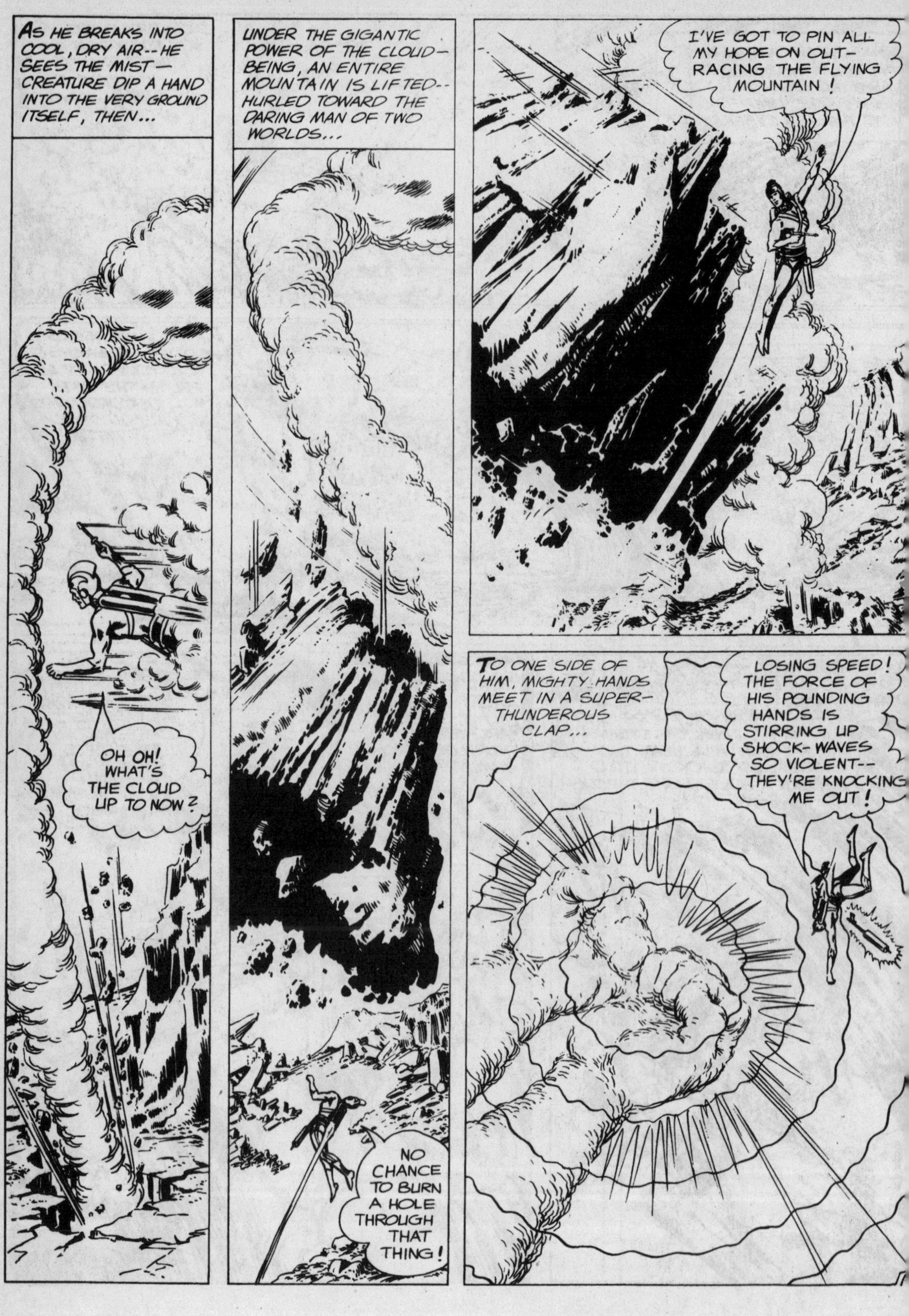
AS HE BREAKS INTO COOL, DRY AIR-- HE SEES THE MIST-CREATURE DIP A HAND INTO THE VERY GROUND ITSELF, THEN...
OH OH! WHAT'S THE CLOUD UP TO NOW?
UNDER THE GIGANTIC POWER OF THE CLOUD-BEING, AN ENTIRE MOUNTAIN IS LIFTED-- HURLED TOWARD THE DARING MAN OF TWO WORLDS...
NO CHANCE TO BURN A HOLE THROUGH THAT THING!
I'VE GOT TO PIN ALL MY HOPE ON OUT-RACING THE FLYING MOUNTAIN!
TO ONE SIDE OF HIM, MIGHTY HANDS MEET IN A SUPER-THUNDEROUS CLAP...
LOSING SPEED! THE FORCE OF HIS POUNDING HANDS IS STIRRING UP SHOCK-WAVES SO VIOLENT-- THEY'RE KNOCKING ME OUT!

GRIMLY BATTLING AGAINST THE AWESOME SHOCK-WAVES, **ADAM** REACHES OUT A DESPERATE HAND FOR THE FALLING **CYBERAY**...

THAT THING-- FELL FROM MY BELT. DON'T KNOW WHAT IT IS BUT--MAYBE IT CAN HELP ME-- IN-- SOME WAY...

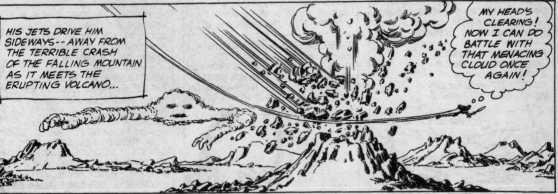

HIS JETS DRIVE HIM SIDEWAYS--AWAY FROM THE TERRIBLE CRASH OF THE FALLING MOUNTAIN AS IT MEETS THE ERUPTING VOLCANO...

MY HEAD'S CLEARING! NOW I CAN DO BATTLE WITH THAT MENACING CLOUD ONCE AGAIN!

IN A BACKWASH OF QUIET AIR, HE MOVES THE CONTROLS OF THE CYBERAY--BUT WITH HIS ATTENTION FOCUSED ON THE ODD WEAPON HE DOES NOT SEE ...

THERE'S NO "FIRING TRIGGER" ON IT! BUT IT MUST DO **SOME-THING!**

MIGHTY FINGERS TIGHTEN ON THE ARCHEOLOGIST--HOLD HIM FIRMLY...

I'LL TELL YOU WHAT IT DOES. **IT MADE ME!** I EVOLVED FROM THE RAW POWER IT CONTAINS! AND I FEED ON TIME ITSELF!

SQUEEZED SO TIGHTLY, HIS SENSES REEL, **ADAM** IS BUOYED BY ONE THOUGHT...

THE HAND-- GOING TO PUSH ME INTO THE OCEAN-- HOLD ME THERE. BUT I CAN'T LET IT HAPPEN! EVERYONE ON EARTH BUT ME-HELPLESS! EVEN **ALANNA!** GOT TO STOP THIS THING SOMEHOW...

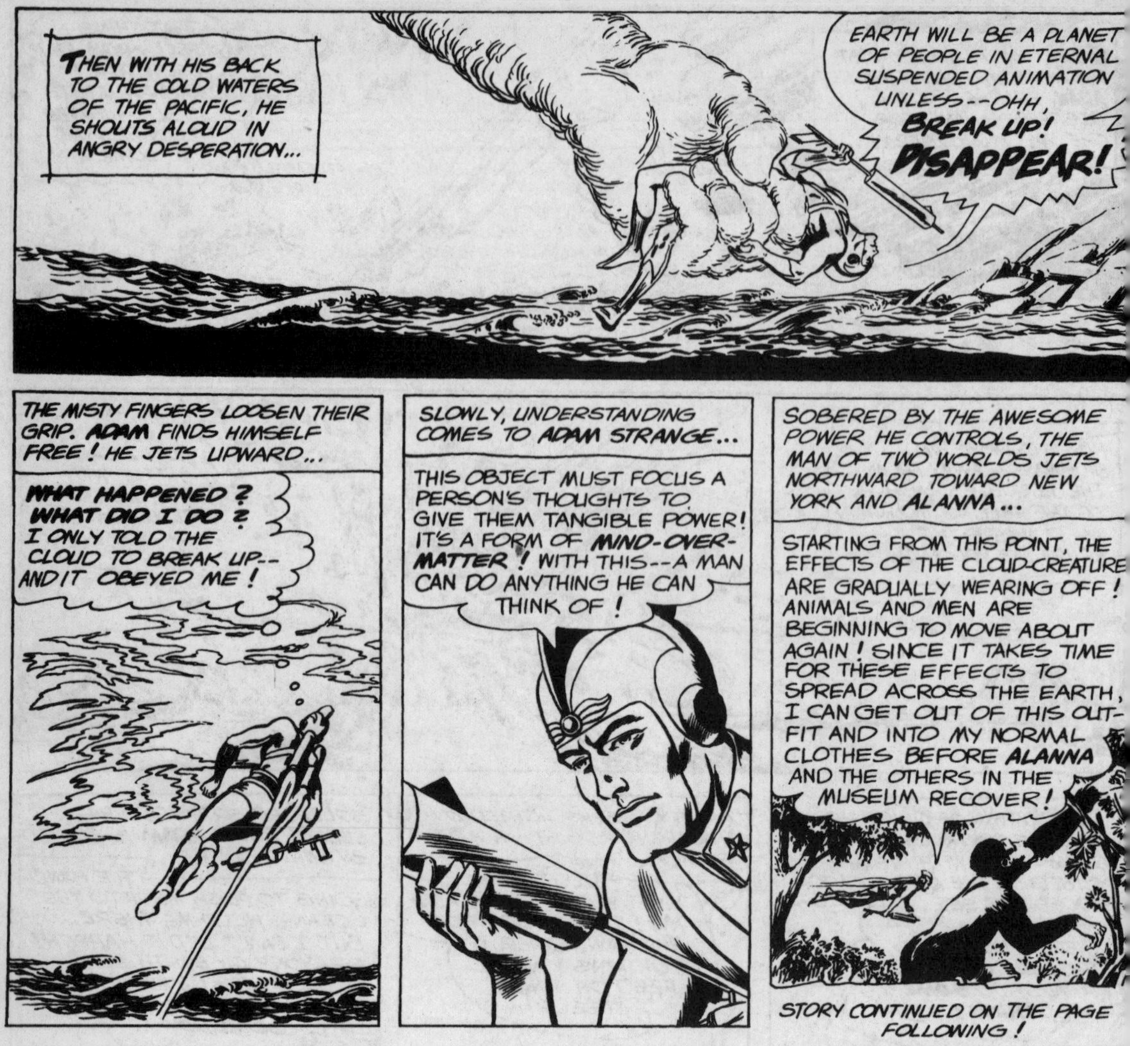
THEN WITH HIS BACK TO THE COLD WATERS OF THE PACIFIC, HE SHOUTS ALOUD IN ANGRY DESPERATION...
EARTH WILL BE A PLANET OF PEOPLE IN ETERNAL SUSPENDED ANIMATION UNLESS--OHH, BREAK UP! DISAPPEAR!
THE MISTY FINGERS LOOSEN THEIR GRIP. ADAM FINDS HIMSELF FREE! HE JETS UPWARD...
WHAT HAPPENED? WHAT DID I DO? I ONLY TOLD THE CLOUD TO BREAK UP--AND IT OBEYED ME!
SLOWLY, UNDERSTANDING COMES TO ADAM STRANGE...
THIS OBJECT MUST FOCUS A PERSON'S THOUGHTS TO GIVE THEM TANGIBLE POWER! IT'S A FORM OF MIND-OVER-MATTER! WITH THIS--A MAN CAN DO ANYTHING HE CAN THINK OF!
SOBERED BY THE AWESOME POWER HE CONTROLS, THE MAN OF TWO WORLDS JETS NORTHWARD TOWARD NEW YORK AND ALANNA...
STARTING FROM THIS POINT, THE EFFECTS OF THE CLOUD-CREATURE ARE GRADUALLY WEARING OFF! ANIMALS AND MEN ARE BEGINNING TO MOVE ABOUT AGAIN! SINCE IT TAKES TIME FOR THESE EFFECTS TO SPREAD ACROSS THE EARTH, I CAN GET OUT OF THIS OUT-FIT AND INTO MY NORMAL CLOTHES BEFORE ALANNA AND THE OTHERS IN THE MUSEUM RECOVER!
STORY CONTINUED ON THE PAGE FOLLOWING!

ADAM STRANGE

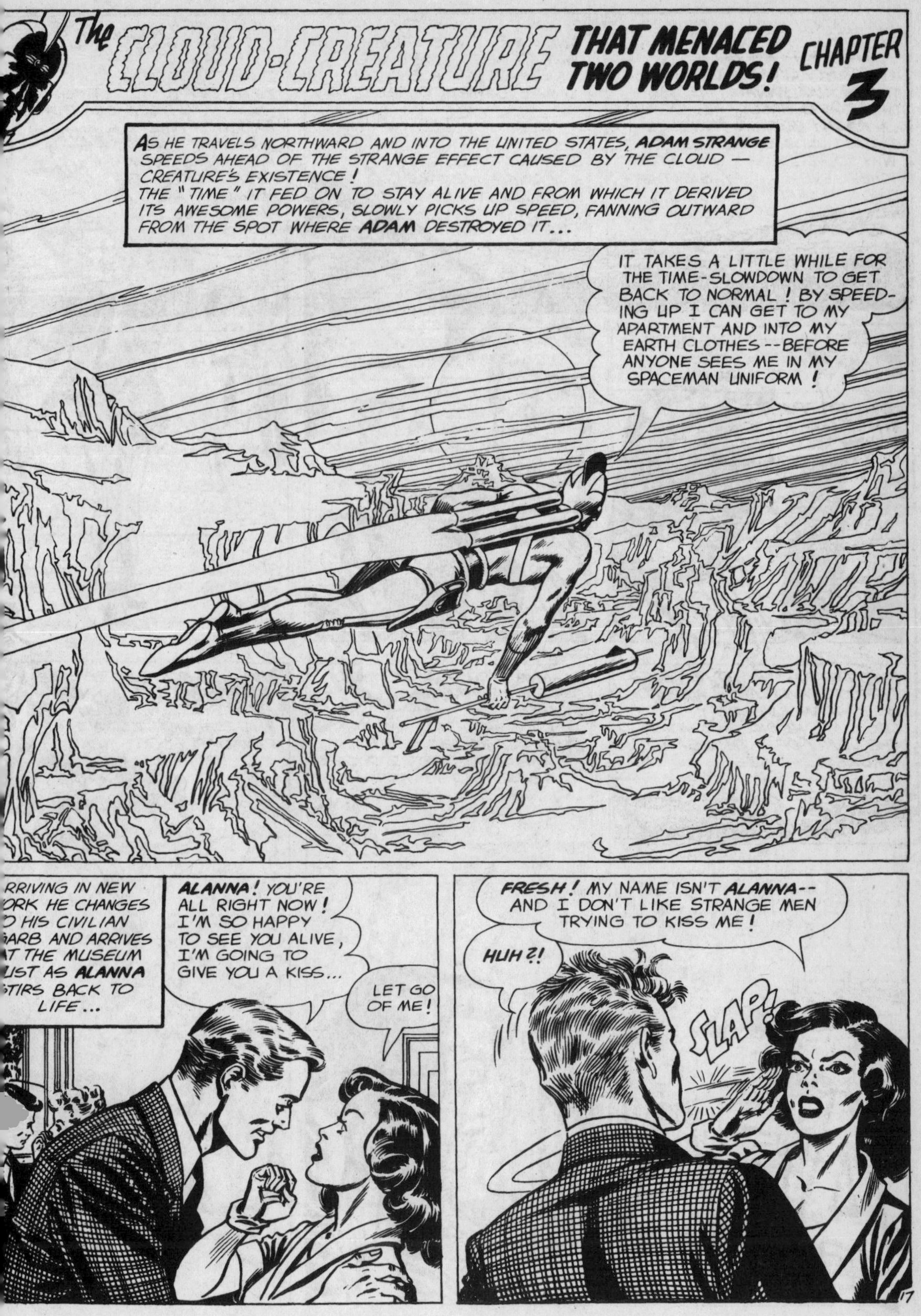
The CLOUD-CREATURE THAT MENACED TWO WORLDS!
CHAPTER 3
AS HE TRAVELS NORTHWARD AND INTO THE UNITED STATES, ADAM STRANGE SPEEDS AHEAD OF THE STRANGE EFFECT CAUSED BY THE CLOUD — CREATURE'S EXISTENCE! THE "TIME" IT FED ON TO STAY ALIVE AND FROM WHICH IT DERIVED ITS AWESOME POWERS, SLOWLY PICKS UP SPEED, FANNING OUTWARD FROM THE SPOT WHERE ADAM DESTROYED IT...
IT TAKES A LITTLE WHILE FOR THE TIME-SLOWDOWN TO GET BACK TO NORMAL! BY SPEEDING UP I CAN GET TO MY APARTMENT AND INTO MY EARTH CLOTHES --BEFORE ANYONE SEES ME IN MY SPACEMAN UNIFORM!
RRIVING IN NEW ORK HE CHANGES O HIS CIVILIAN GARB AND ARRIVES T THE MUSEUM UST AS ALANNA STIRS BACK TO LIFE...
ALANNA! YOU'RE ALL RIGHT NOW! I'M SO HAPPY TO SEE YOU ALIVE, I'M GOING TO GIVE YOU A KISS...
LET GO OF ME!
FRESH! MY NAME ISN'T ALANNA-- AND I DON'T LIKE STRANGE MEN TRYING TO KISS ME!
HUH?!
SLAP!
17

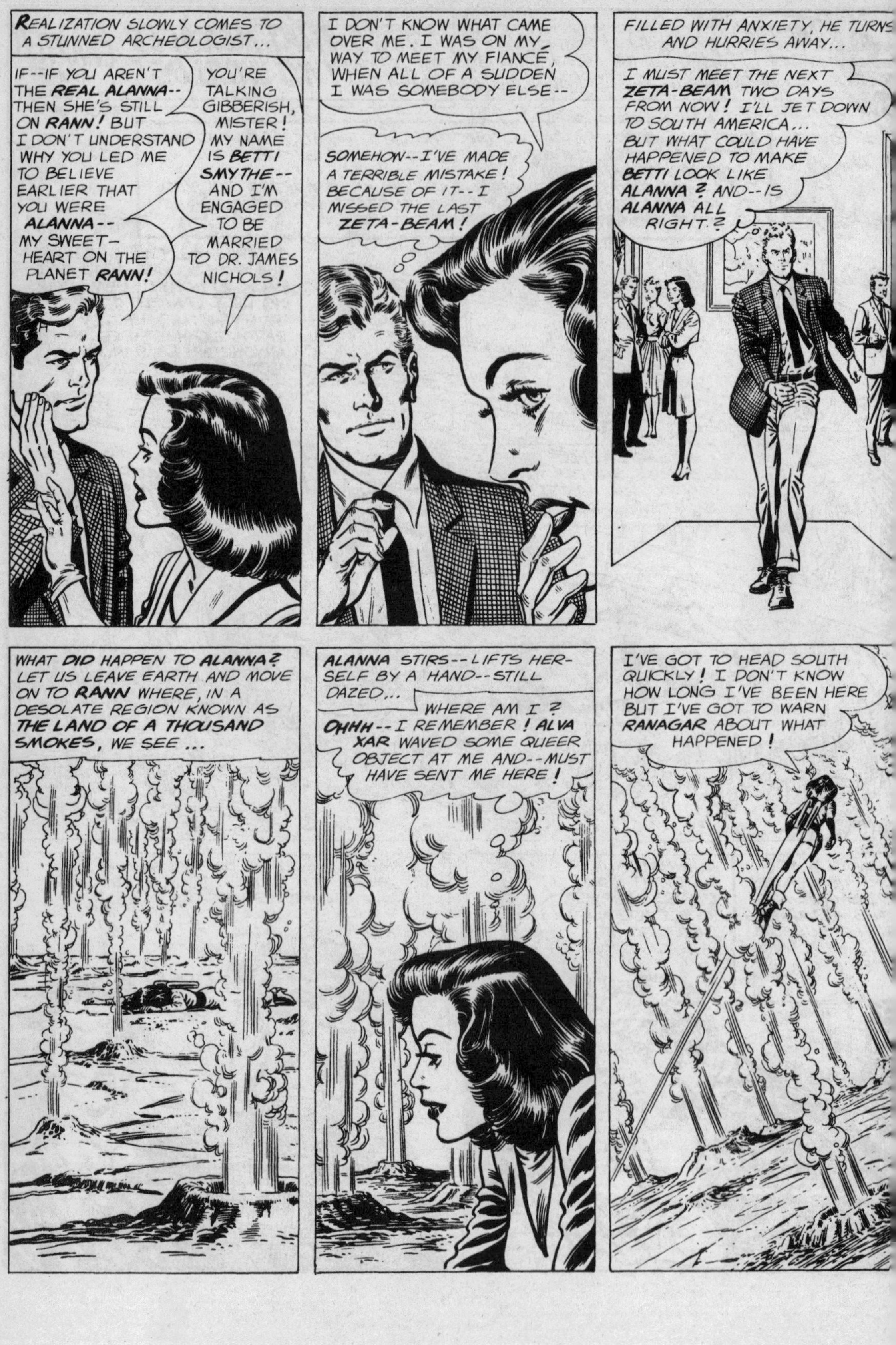
REALIZATION SLOWLY COMES TO A STUNNED ARCHEOLOGIST...
IF--IF YOU AREN'T THE REAL ALANNA-- THEN SHE'S STILL ON RANN! BUT I DON'T UNDERSTAND WHY YOU LED ME TO BELIEVE EARLIER THAT YOU WERE ALANNA-- MY SWEETHEART ON THE PLANET RANN!
YOU'RE TALKING GIBBERISH, MISTER! MY NAME IS BETTI SMYTHE-- AND I'M ENGAGED TO BE MARRIED TO DR. JAMES NICHOLS!
I DON'T KNOW WHAT CAME OVER ME. I WAS ON MY WAY TO MEET MY FIANCÉ, WHEN ALL OF A SUDDEN I WAS SOMEBODY ELSE--
SOMEHOW--I'VE MADE A TERRIBLE MISTAKE! BECAUSE OF IT--I MISSED THE LAST ZETA-BEAM!
FILLED WITH ANXIETY, HE TURNS AND HURRIES AWAY...
I MUST MEET THE NEXT ZETA-BEAM TWO DAYS FROM NOW! I'LL JET DOWN TO SOUTH AMERICA... BUT WHAT COULD HAVE HAPPENED TO MAKE BETTI LOOK LIKE ALANNA? AND--IS ALANNA ALL RIGHT?
WHAT DID HAPPEN TO ALANNA? LET US LEAVE EARTH AND MOVE ON TO RANN WHERE, IN A DESOLATE REGION KNOWN AS THE LAND OF A THOUSAND SMOKES, WE SEE...
ALANNA STIRS--LIFTS HERSELF BY A HAND--STILL DAZED...
WHERE AM I?
OHHH--I REMEMBER! ALVA XAR WAVED SOME QUEER OBJECT AT ME AND--MUST HAVE SENT ME HERE!
I'VE GOT TO HEAD SOUTH QUICKLY! I DON'T KNOW HOW LONG I'VE BEEN HERE BUT I'VE GOT TO WARN RANAGAR ABOUT WHAT HAPPENED!

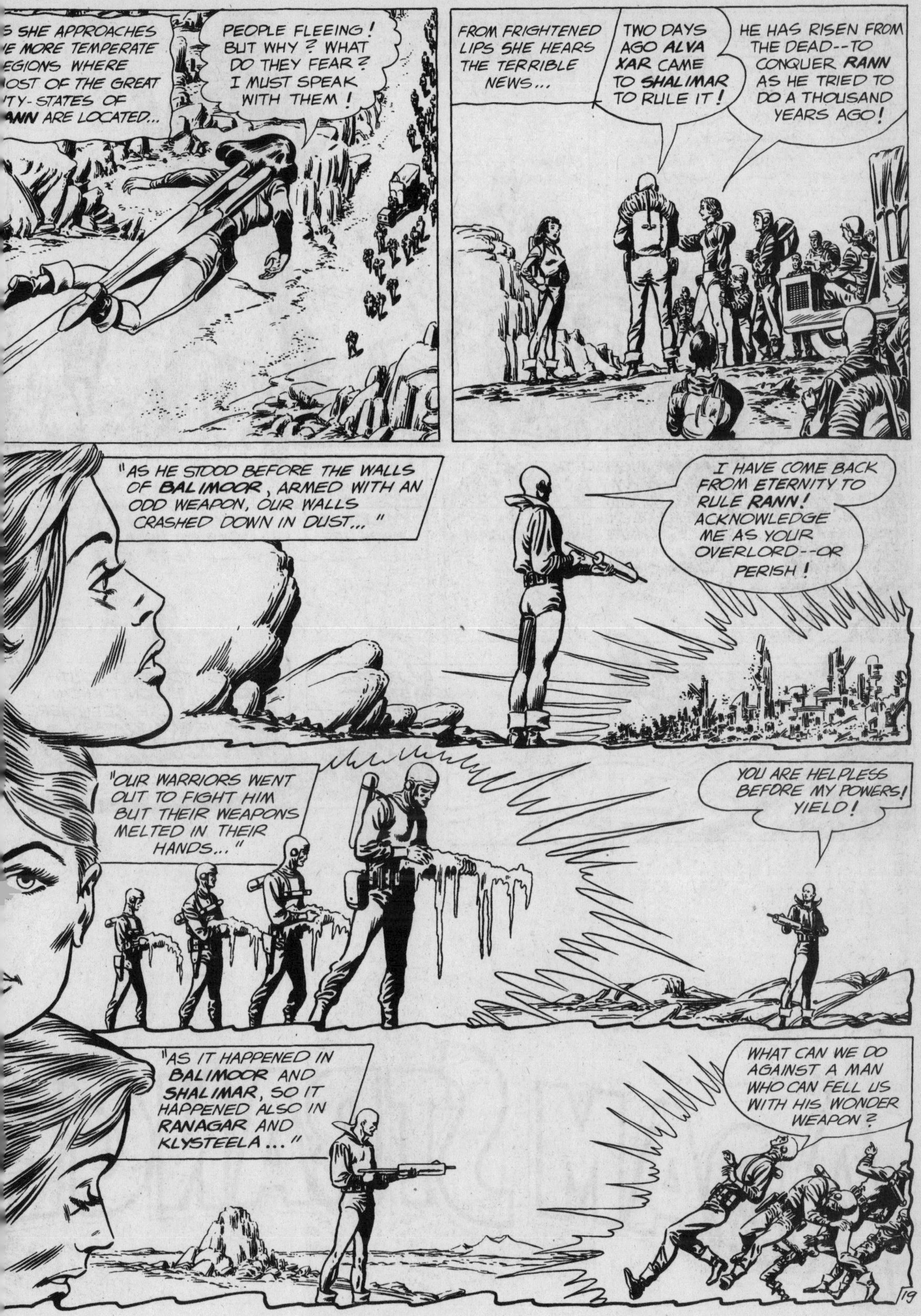
S SHE APPROACHES
IE MORE TEMPERATE
EGIONS WHERE
OST OF THE GREAT
ITY-STATES OF
ANN ARE LOCATED...
PEOPLE FLEEING! BUT WHY? WHAT DO THEY FEAR? I MUST SPEAK WITH THEM!
FROM FRIGHTENED LIPS SHE HEARS THE TERRIBLE NEWS...
TWO DAYS AGO ALVA XAR CAME TO SHALIMAR TO RULE IT!
HE HAS RISEN FROM THE DEAD--TO CONQUER RANN AS HE TRIED TO DO A THOUSAND YEARS AGO!
"AS HE STOOD BEFORE THE WALLS OF BALIMOOR, ARMED WITH AN ODD WEAPON, OUR WALLS CRASHED DOWN IN DUST..."
I HAVE COME BACK FROM ETERNITY TO RULE RANN! ACKNOWLEDGE ME AS YOUR OVERLORD--OR PERISH!
"OUR WARRIORS WENT OUT TO FIGHT HIM BUT THEIR WEAPONS MELTED IN THEIR HANDS..."
YOU ARE HELPLESS BEFORE MY POWERS! YIELD!
"AS IT HAPPENED IN BALIMOOR AND SHALIMAR, SO IT HAPPENED ALSO IN RANAGAR AND KLYSTEELA..."
WHAT CAN WE DO AGAINST A MAN WHO CAN FELL US WITH HIS WONDER WEAPON?
19

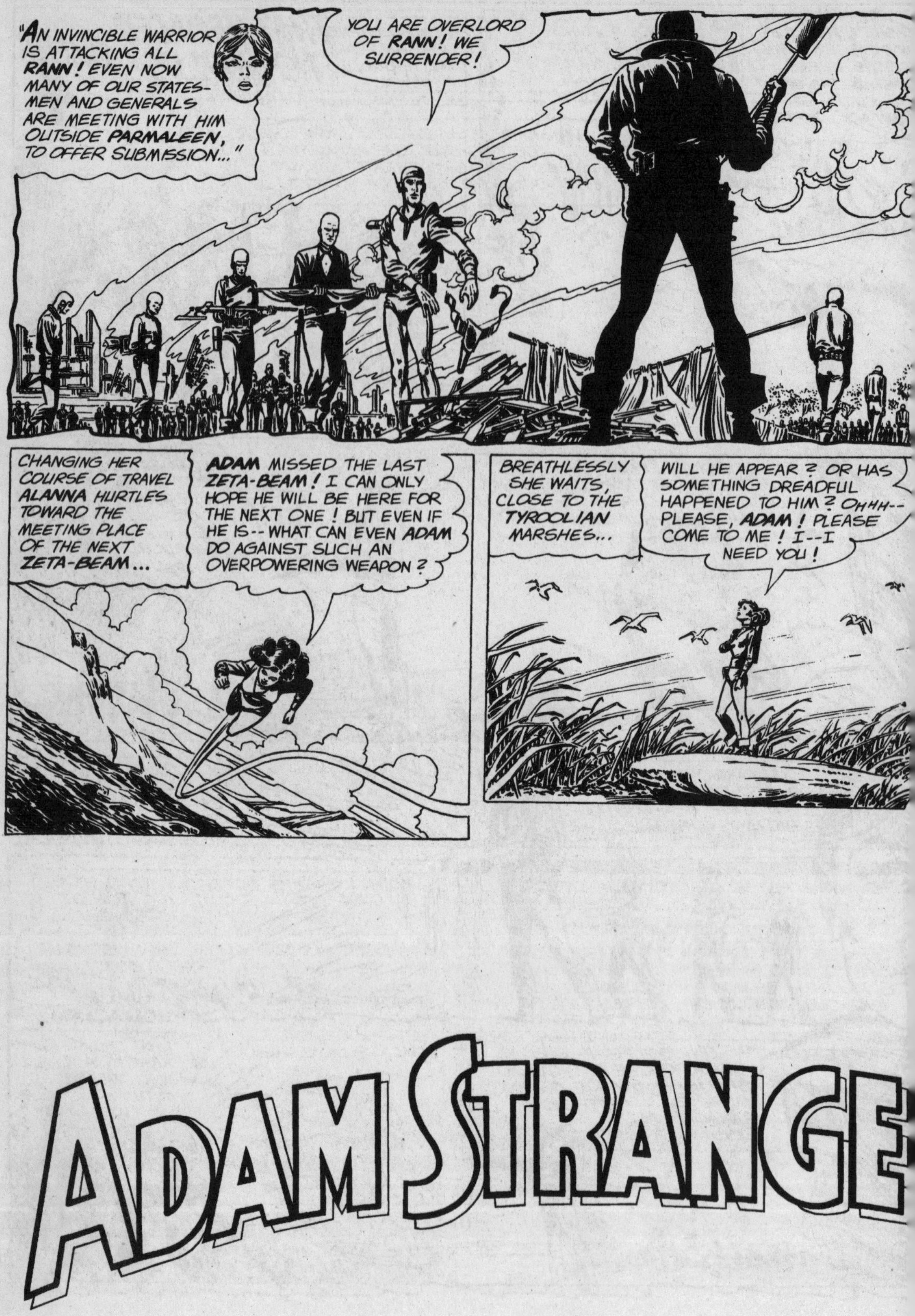
"AN INVINCIBLE WARRIOR IS ATTACKING ALL RANN! EVEN NOW MANY OF OUR STATES-MEN AND GENERALS ARE MEETING WITH HIM OUTSIDE PARMALEEN, TO OFFER SUBMISSION..."
YOU ARE OVERLORD OF RANN! WE SURRENDER!
CHANGING HER COURSE OF TRAVEL ALANNA HURTLES TOWARD THE MEETING PLACE OF THE NEXT ZETA-BEAM...
ADAM MISSED THE LAST ZETA-BEAM! I CAN ONLY HOPE HE WILL BE HERE FOR THE NEXT ONE! BUT EVEN IF HE IS--WHAT CAN EVEN ADAM DO AGAINST SUCH AN OVERPOWERING WEAPON?
BREATHLESSLY SHE WAITS, CLOSE TO THE TYROOLIAN MARSHES...
WILL HE APPEAR? OR HAS SOMETHING DREADFUL HAPPENED TO HIM? OHHH-- PLEASE, ADAM! PLEASE COME TO ME! I--I NEED YOU!

ADAM STRANGE

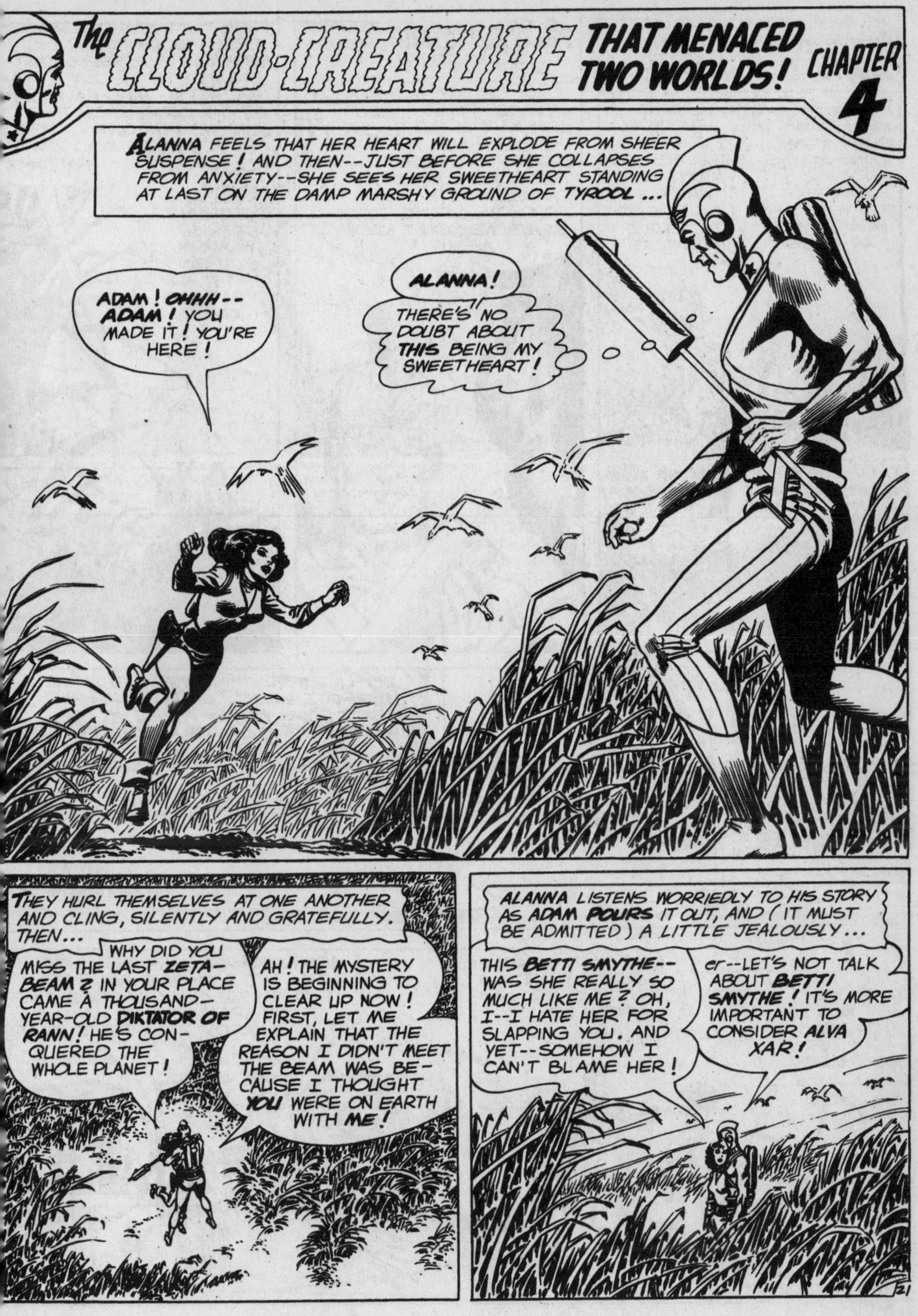
The CLOUD-CREATURE THAT MENACED TWO WORLDS! CHAPTER 4
ALANNA FEELS THAT HER HEART WILL EXPLODE FROM SHEER SUSPENSE! AND THEN--JUST BEFORE SHE COLLAPSES FROM ANXIETY--SHE SEES HER SWEETHEART STANDING AT LAST ON THE DAMP MARSHY GROUND OF TYROOL...
ADAM! OHHH--ADAM! YOU MADE IT! YOU'RE HERE!
ALANNA!
THERE'S NO DOUBT ABOUT THIS BEING MY SWEETHEART!
THEY HURL THEMSELVES AT ONE ANOTHER AND CLING, SILENTLY AND GRATEFULLY. THEN...
WHY DID YOU MISS THE LAST ZETA-BEAM? IN YOUR PLACE CAME A THOUSAND-YEAR-OLD DIKTATOR OF RANN! HE'S CONQUERED THE WHOLE PLANET!
AH! THE MYSTERY IS BEGINNING TO CLEAR UP NOW! FIRST, LET ME EXPLAIN THAT THE REASON I DIDN'T MEET THE BEAM WAS BECAUSE I THOUGHT YOU WERE ON EARTH WITH ME!
ALANNA LISTENS WORRIEDLY TO HIS STORY AS ADAM POURS IT OUT, AND (IT MUST BE ADMITTED) A LITTLE JEALOUSLY...
THIS BETTI SMYTHE--WAS SHE REALLY SO MUCH LIKE ME? OH, I--I HATE HER FOR SLAPPING YOU. AND YET--SOMEHOW I CAN'T BLAME HER!
er--LET'S NOT TALK ABOUT BETTI SMYTHE! IT'S MORE IMPORTANT TO CONSIDER ALVA XAR!
21

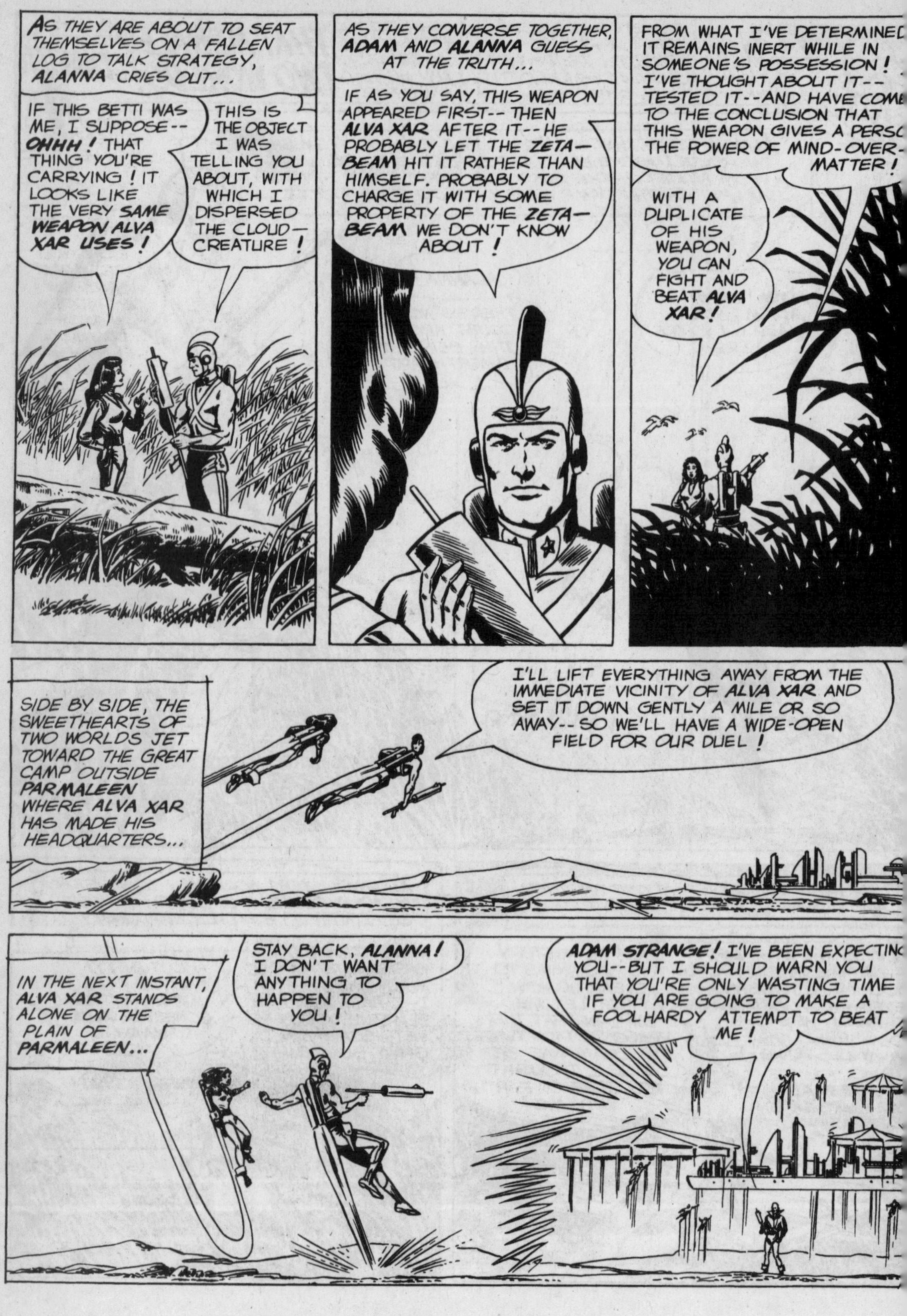
AS THEY ARE ABOUT TO SEAT THEMSELVES ON A FALLEN LOG TO TALK STRATEGY, ALANNA CRIES OUT...
IF THIS BETTI WAS ME, I SUPPOSE-- OHHH! THAT THING YOU'RE CARRYING! IT LOOKS LIKE THE VERY SAME WEAPON ALVA XAR USES!
THIS IS THE OBJECT I WAS TELLING YOU ABOUT, WITH WHICH I DISPERSED THE CLOUD-CREATURE!
AS THEY CONVERSE TOGETHER, ADAM AND ALANNA GUESS AT THE TRUTH...
IF AS YOU SAY, THIS WEAPON APPEARED FIRST-- THEN ALVA XAR AFTER IT--HE PROBABLY LET THE ZETA-BEAM HIT IT RATHER THAN HIMSELF. PROBABLY TO CHARGE IT WITH SOME PROPERTY OF THE ZETA-BEAM WE DON'T KNOW ABOUT!
FROM WHAT I'VE DETERMINED IT REMAINS INERT WHILE IN SOMEONE'S POSSESSION! I'VE THOUGHT ABOUT IT-- TESTED IT--AND HAVE COME TO THE CONCLUSION THAT THIS WEAPON GIVES A PERSO THE POWER OF MIND-OVER-MATTER!
WITH A DUPLICATE OF HIS WEAPON, YOU CAN FIGHT AND BEAT ALVA XAR!
SIDE BY SIDE, THE SWEETHEARTS OF TWO WORLDS JET TOWARD THE GREAT CAMP OUTSIDE PARMALEEN WHERE ALVA XAR HAS MADE HIS HEADQUARTERS...
I'LL LIFT EVERYTHING AWAY FROM THE IMMEDIATE VICINITY OF ALVA XAR AND SET IT DOWN GENTLY A MILE OR SO AWAY-- SO WE'LL HAVE A WIDE-OPEN FIELD FOR OUR DUEL!
IN THE NEXT INSTANT, ALVA XAR STANDS ALONE ON THE PLAIN OF PARMALEEN...
STAY BACK, ALANNA! I DON'T WANT ANYTHING TO HAPPEN TO YOU!
ADAM STRANGE! I'VE BEEN EXPECTING YOU--BUT I SHOULD WARN YOU THAT YOU'RE ONLY WASTING TIME IF YOU ARE GOING TO MAKE A FOOLHARDY ATTEMPT TO BEAT ME!

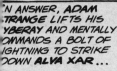

IN ANSWER, ADAM STRANGE LIFTS HIS CYBERAY AND MENTALLY COMMANDS A BOLT OF LIGHTNING TO STRIKE DOWN ALVA XAR...

TO MEET THAT GOLDEN SPEAR OF RAW DE-STRUCTION, THE DIKTATOR OF RANN SENDS OUT A STEEL ROD...

I DON'T UNDER-STAND! HOW COULD HE HAVE ACTED SO SWIFTLY TO COUNTERACT MY MOVE?

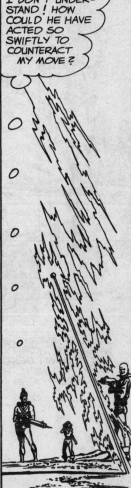

AGAIN THE YOUNG EARTHMAN SENDS OUT HIS MENTAL ORDERS-- AND A SHOWER OF HAILSTONES RAINS DOWN ON HIS FOE...

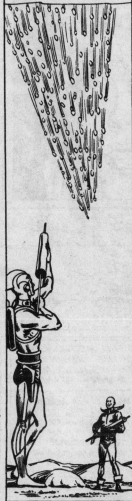

INSTANTLY, ALVA XAR CREATES AN UPDRAFT IN THE AIR, HURLING THE HAILSTONES UP AND AWAY...

IT'S AS IF HE ANTICIPATED MY MOVE! HE MUST BE READING MY THOUGHTS! HE KNOWS WHAT I INTEND TO DO-- AS SOON AS I DO!

RIGHT YOU ARE, ADAM STRANGE! MY HIDDEN MENTA-SCANNER ENABLES ME TO CATCH EVERY THOUGHT YOU HAVE!

THAT IS WHY I DO NOT FEAR YOU! IN THE PAST, YOU OVERCAME RANN'S ENEMIES BY OUT-THINKING THEM--BUT YOU CAN'T OUT-THINK SOMEBODY WHO KNOWS EVERY-THING YOU'RE THINKING ABOUT! YOU'RE BEATEN-- BEFORE YOU START!

CAN THIS BE? ADAM STRANGE HAS ALWAYS MANAGED TO THINK HIS WAY OUT OF TROUBLE!

HAS THE RANN CHAMPION FINALLY MET HIS MATCH?

23

TEARS RUN DOWN *ALANNA'S* CHEEKS AS SHE WATCHES HER SWEETHEART FACE THE MIGHTIEST OF ALL HIS FOES...

ADAM, DARLING! ÷ SOB÷ YOU'VE TRIED AS BEST AS YOU KNOW HOW BUT-- BUT IT ISN'T ANY USE!

DESPAIR SLUMPS *ADAM'S* SHOULDERS! WEARILY HE TOSSES ASIDE THE USELESS *CYBERAY*...

WHY FIGHT ANY MORE? I SURRENDER!

YOU DON'T FOOL *ME, ADAM STRANGE*! YOU AREN'T REALLY SURRENDERING! YOU'RE STILL HOPING TO OVERCOME ME BY A *TRICK*!

YOU'RE THINKING THAT NOW YOU'VE LET GO OF THE *CYBERAY*, THE CLOUD-CREATURE YOU OVERCAME ON EARTH WILL FORM AND DESTROY ME! BUT YOU FORGET THAT WITH MY *CYBERAY* I CAN DISPERSE IT JUST AS YOU DID BACK ON YOUR HOME PLANET!

BUT BEFORE HE CAN ISSUE THE MENTAL COMMAND WHICH WILL DESTROY THE SPAWN OF THE *CYBERAY*--ALVA XAR--AS WELL AS EVERY LIVING THING ON *RANN*--STANDS AS IF PETRIFIED!...

ONLY I AM NORMAL-- JUST AS HAPPENED ON EARTH! THE CLOUD-CREATURE CAN'T AFFECT MY BODY--BECAUSE IT'S BEEN CHARGED BY THE REGULAR *ZETA-BEAM*! *ALVA XAR* READ *SOME* OF MY THOUGHTS, BUT THE *MAIN ONE*-- THAT THE CLOUD-CREATURE CAUSED A SUSPENSION OF TIME--I KEPT OUT OF MY MIND!

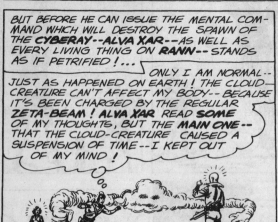

I KNEW BY CASTING AWAY THE *CYBERAY* FROM MY PERSON, THE MENACING CLOUD WOULD FORM AND OVERCOME *ALVA XAR*!

BEFORE *ALVA XAR* CAN RECOVER FROM THE SUSPENSION OF TIME THAT GRIPS HIM, I'LL REMOVE HIS MENTA-SCANNER AND MAKE HIM MY PRISONER!

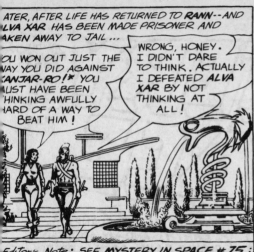

...ATER, AFTER LIFE HAS RETURNED TO *RANN*--AND *ALVA XAR* HAS BEEN MADE PRISONER AND TAKEN AWAY TO JAIL ...

...OU WON OUT JUST THE WAY YOU DID AGAINST *KANJAR-RO!** YOU MUST HAVE BEEN THINKING AWFULLY HARD OF A WAY TO BEAT HIM!

WRONG, HONEY. I DIDN'T DARE TO THINK. ACTUALLY I DEFEATED *ALVA XAR* BY NOT THINKING AT ALL!

Editor's Note: SEE MYSTERY IN SPACE #75: "THE PLANET THAT CAME TO A STANDSTILL!"

WE HAVE TWO TERRIBLE WEAPONS IN THESE *CYBERAYS.* BUT THE DANGER EXISTS THAT SOME DAY AN ENEMY-- A SPY OR A TRAITOR-- MIGHT GET HOLD OF THEM AND USE THEM AGAINST US!

IT SEEMS A SHAME-- BUT THERE'S ONLY ONE THING TO DO! WE MUST GET RID OF BOTH OF THEM!

...AND SO...

WE'LL MENTALLY COMMAND THEM TO DESTROY EACH OTHER!

THERE THEY GO! SINCE *ALVA XAR* WILL BE IN PRISON FROM NOW ON-- HE'LL NEVER BE ABLE TO CREATE ANY MORE!

THEN AS THE EFFECT OF THE **ZETA-BEAM** *WEARS OFF HER SWEETHEART...*

NOW, ADAM-- ABOUT THIS DOUBLE OF MINE ON EARTH! WAS SHE ⸴OH⸴ HE'S FADING AWAY! I'LL HAVE TO WAIT UNTIL NEXT TIME TO ASK HIM WHAT I WAS LIKE--ON EARTH!

The End

/25

SUPERMAN DC NATIONAL COMICS
MYSTERY IN SPACE
12¢
APPROVED BY THE COMICS CODE AUTHORITY
MAR. NO. 82
MY NATIVE PLANET EARTH-- AND MY ADOPTED PLANET RANN--EACH IN DEADLY PERIL! THERE'S ONLY TIME FOR ME TO SAVE ONE! WHICH SHALL IT BE?
WORLD WAR ON EARTH — and — RANN!

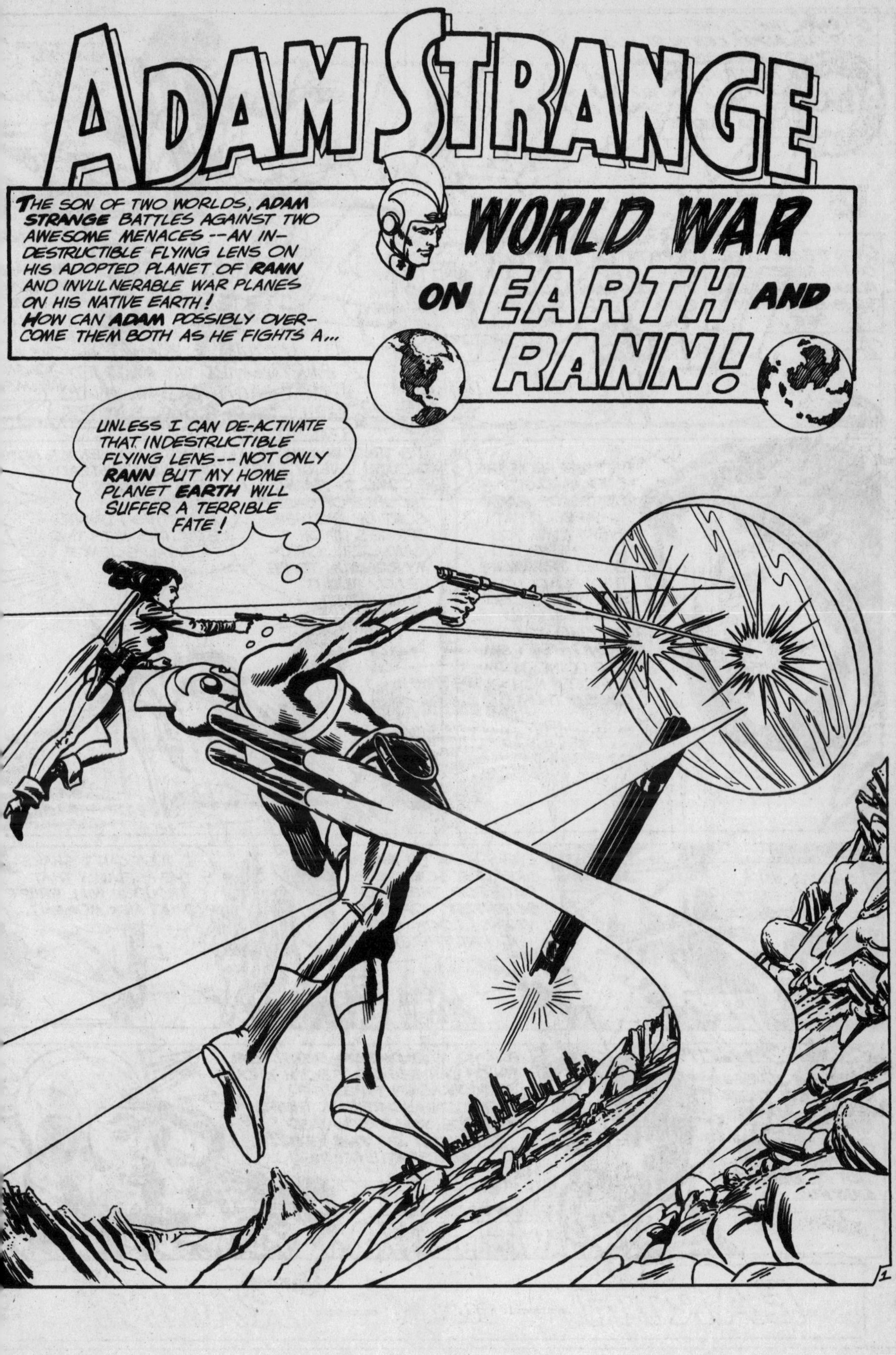
ADAM STRANGE
THE SON OF TWO WORLDS, ADAM STRANGE BATTLES AGAINST TWO AWESOME MENACES--AN INDESTRUCTIBLE FLYING LENS ON HIS ADOPTED PLANET OF RANN AND INVULNERABLE WAR PLANES ON HIS NATIVE EARTH! HOW CAN ADAM POSSIBLY OVERCOME THEM BOTH AS HE FIGHTS A...
WORLD WAR ON EARTH AND RANN!
UNLESS I CAN DE-ACTIVATE THAT INDESTRUCTIBLE FLYING LENS-- NOT ONLY RANN BUT MY HOME PLANET EARTH WILL SUFFER A TERRIBLE FATE!
1

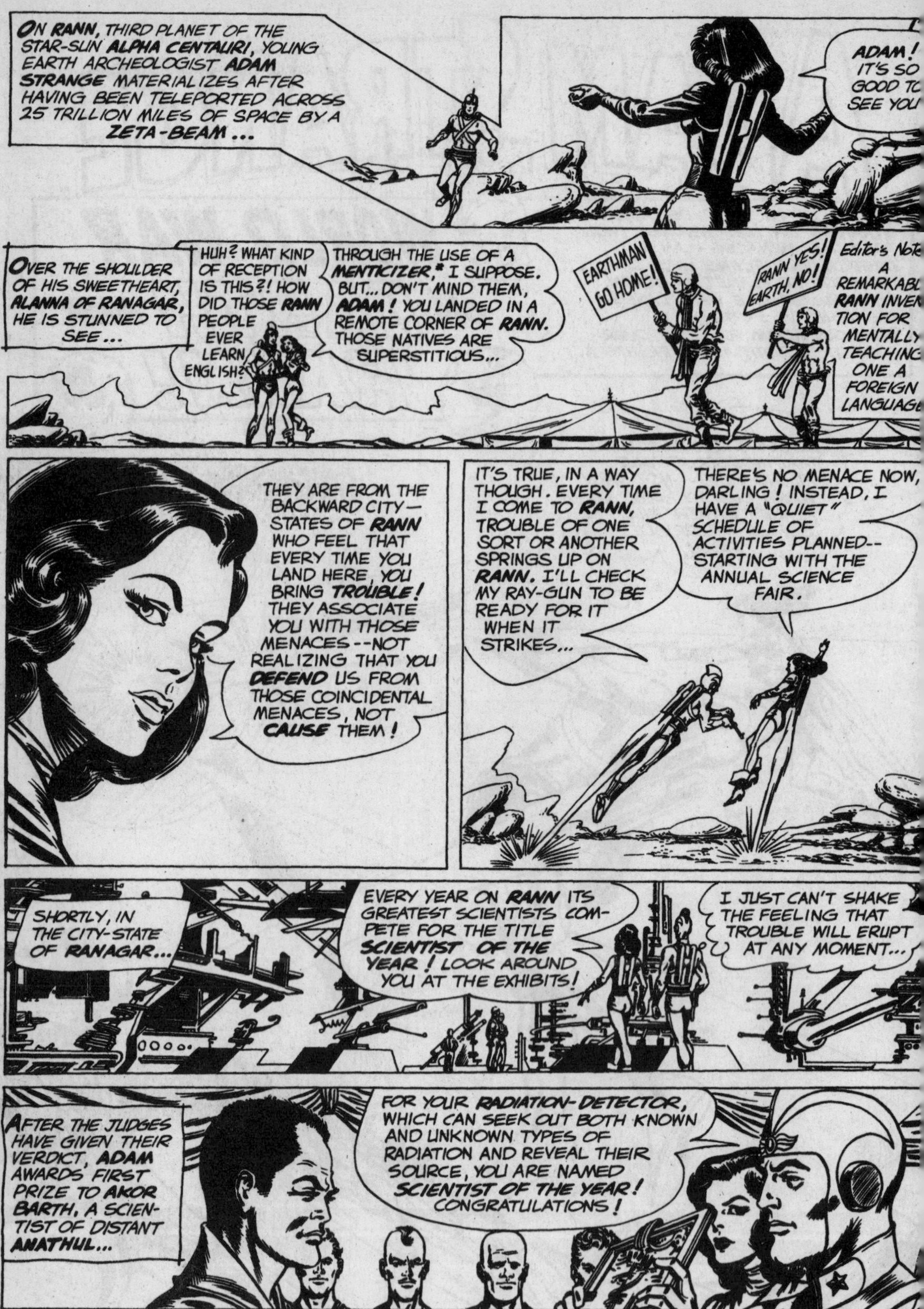
ON RANN, THIRD PLANET OF THE STAR-SUN ALPHA CENTAURI, YOUNG EARTH ARCHEOLOGIST ADAM STRANGE MATERIALIZES AFTER HAVING BEEN TELEPORTED ACROSS 25 TRILLION MILES OF SPACE BY A ZETA-BEAM...
ADAM! IT'S SO GOOD TO SEE YOU
OVER THE SHOULDER OF HIS SWEETHEART, ALANNA OF RANAGAR, HE IS STUNNED TO SEE...
HUH? WHAT KIND OF RECEPTION IS THIS?! HOW DID THOSE RANN PEOPLE EVER LEARN ENGLISH?
THROUGH THE USE OF A MENTICIZER,* I SUPPOSE. BUT... DON'T MIND THEM, ADAM! YOU LANDED IN A REMOTE CORNER OF RANN. THOSE NATIVES ARE SUPERSTITIOUS...
EARTHMAN GO HOME!
RANN YES! EARTH, NO!
Editor's Note: A REMARKABLE RANN INVENTION FOR MENTALLY TEACHING ONE A FOREIGN LANGUAGE
THEY ARE FROM THE BACKWARD CITY-STATES OF RANN WHO FEEL THAT EVERY TIME YOU LAND HERE, YOU BRING TROUBLE! THEY ASSOCIATE YOU WITH THOSE MENACES--NOT REALIZING THAT YOU DEFEND US FROM THOSE COINCIDENTAL MENACES, NOT CAUSE THEM!
IT'S TRUE, IN A WAY THOUGH. EVERY TIME I COME TO RANN, TROUBLE OF ONE SORT OR ANOTHER SPRINGS UP ON RANN. I'LL CHECK MY RAY-GUN TO BE READY FOR IT WHEN IT STRIKES...
THERE'S NO MENACE NOW, DARLING! INSTEAD, I HAVE A "QUIET" SCHEDULE OF ACTIVITIES PLANNED-- STARTING WITH THE ANNUAL SCIENCE FAIR.
SHORTLY, IN THE CITY-STATE OF RANAGAR...
EVERY YEAR ON RANN ITS GREATEST SCIENTISTS COMPETE FOR THE TITLE SCIENTIST OF THE YEAR! LOOK AROUND YOU AT THE EXHIBITS!
I JUST CAN'T SHAKE THE FEELING THAT TROUBLE WILL ERUPT AT ANY MOMENT...
AFTER THE JUDGES HAVE GIVEN THEIR VERDICT, ADAM AWARDS FIRST PRIZE TO AKOR BARTH, A SCIENTIST OF DISTANT ANATHUL...
FOR YOUR RADIATION-DETECTOR, WHICH CAN SEEK OUT BOTH KNOWN AND UNKNOWN TYPES OF RADIATION AND REVEAL THEIR SOURCE, YOU ARE NAMED SCIENTIST OF THE YEAR! CONGRATULATIONS!

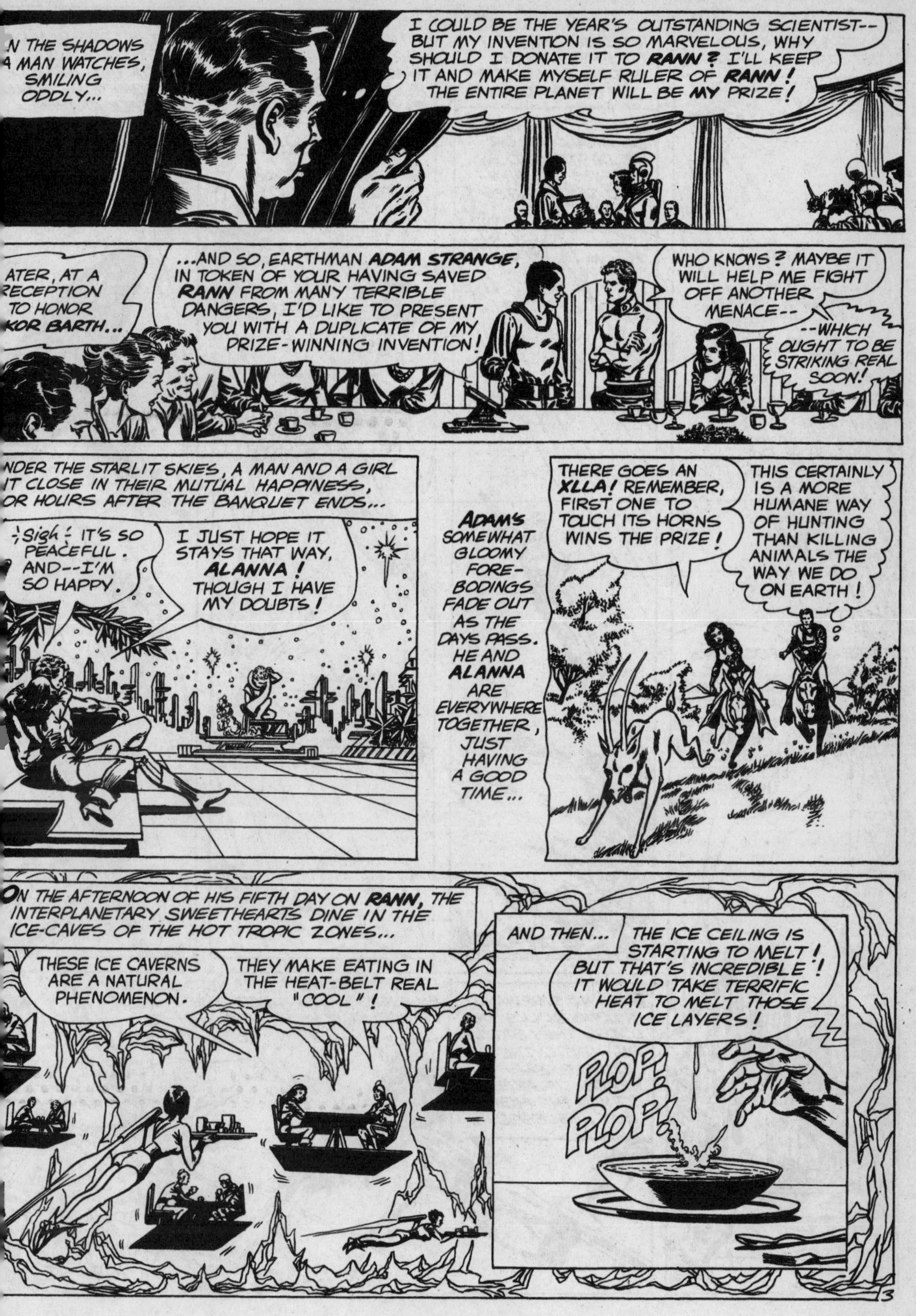
N THE SHADOWS A MAN WATCHES, SMILING ODDLY...
I COULD BE THE YEAR'S OUTSTANDING SCIENTIST-- BUT MY INVENTION IS SO MARVELOUS, WHY SHOULD I DONATE IT TO RANN? I'LL KEEP IT AND MAKE MYSELF RULER OF RANN! THE ENTIRE PLANET WILL BE MY PRIZE!
ATER, AT A RECEPTION TO HONOR KOR BARTH...
...AND SO, EARTHMAN ADAM STRANGE, IN TOKEN OF YOUR HAVING SAVED RANN FROM MANY TERRIBLE DANGERS, I'D LIKE TO PRESENT YOU WITH A DUPLICATE OF MY PRIZE-WINNING INVENTION!
WHO KNOWS? MAYBE IT WILL HELP ME FIGHT OFF ANOTHER MENACE--
--WHICH OUGHT TO BE STRIKING REAL SOON!
NDER THE STARLIT SKIES, A MAN AND A GIRL IT CLOSE IN THEIR MUTUAL HAPPINESS, OR HOURS AFTER THE BANQUET ENDS...
Sigh! IT'S SO PEACEFUL. AND--I'M SO HAPPY.
I JUST HOPE IT STAYS THAT WAY, ALANNA! THOUGH I HAVE MY DOUBTS!
ADAM'S SOMEWHAT GLOOMY FOREBODINGS FADE OUT AS THE DAYS PASS. HE AND ALANNA ARE EVERYWHERE TOGETHER, JUST HAVING A GOOD TIME...
THERE GOES AN XLLA! REMEMBER, FIRST ONE TO TOUCH ITS HORNS WINS THE PRIZE!
THIS CERTAINLY IS A MORE HUMANE WAY OF HUNTING THAN KILLING ANIMALS THE WAY WE DO ON EARTH!
ON THE AFTERNOON OF HIS FIFTH DAY ON RANN, THE INTERPLANETARY SWEETHEARTS DINE IN THE ICE-CAVES OF THE HOT TROPIC ZONES...
THESE ICE CAVERNS ARE A NATURAL PHENOMENON.
THEY MAKE EATING IN THE HEAT-BELT REAL "COOL"!
AND THEN...
THE ICE CEILING IS STARTING TO MELT! BUT THAT'S INCREDIBLE! IT WOULD TAKE TERRIFIC HEAT TO MELT THOSE ICE LAYERS!
PLOP! PLOP!
3

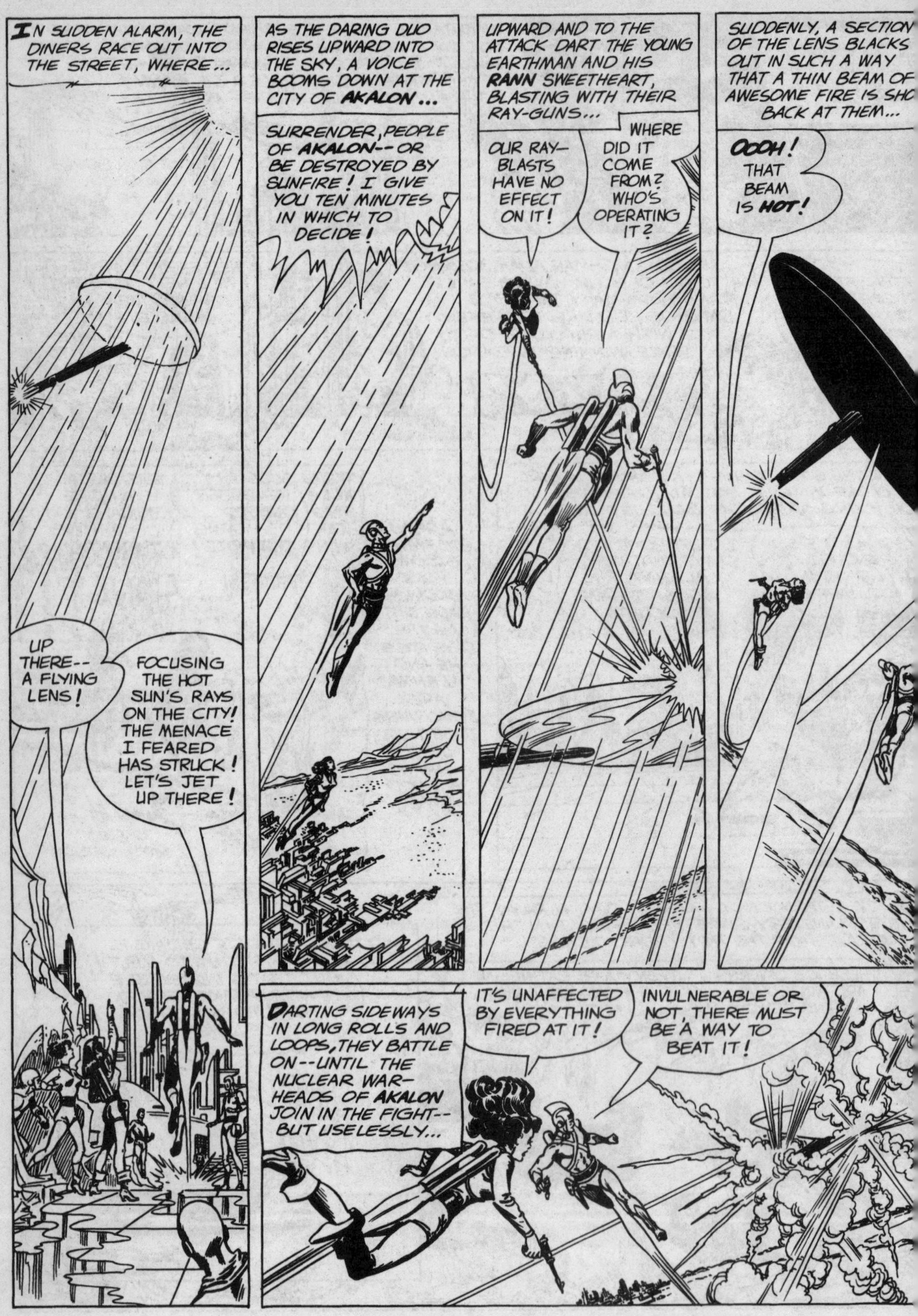
IN SUDDEN ALARM, THE DINERS RACE OUT INTO THE STREET, WHERE...
UP THERE-- A FLYING LENS!
FOCUSING THE HOT SUN'S RAYS ON THE CITY! THE MENACE I FEARED HAS STRUCK! LET'S JET UP THERE!
AS THE DARING DUO RISES UPWARD INTO THE SKY, A VOICE BOOMS DOWN AT THE CITY OF AKALON...
SURRENDER, PEOPLE OF AKALON-- OR BE DESTROYED BY SUNFIRE! I GIVE YOU TEN MINUTES IN WHICH TO DECIDE!
UPWARD AND TO THE ATTACK DART THE YOUNG EARTHMAN AND HIS RANN SWEETHEART, BLASTING WITH THEIR RAY-GUNS...
OUR RAY-BLASTS HAVE NO EFFECT ON IT!
WHERE DID IT COME FROM? WHO'S OPERATING IT?
SUDDENLY, A SECTION OF THE LENS BLACKS OUT IN SUCH A WAY THAT A THIN BEAM OF AWESOME FIRE IS SHO BACK AT THEM...
OOOH! THAT BEAM IS HOT!
DARTING SIDEWAYS IN LONG ROLLS AND LOOPS, THEY BATTLE ON--UNTIL THE NUCLEAR WAR-HEADS OF AKALON JOIN IN THE FIGHT-- BUT USELESSLY...
IT'S UNAFFECTED BY EVERYTHING FIRED AT IT!
INVULNERABLE OR NOT, THERE MUST BE A WAY TO BEAT IT!

S THE TEN-MINUTE ULTIMATUM XPIRES, MIGHTY GOLDEN BEAMS HOOT DOWN AT *AKALON*...

OHHH! THE LENS IS DESTROYING *AKALON* AND-- *ADAM'S ZETA-BEAM* IS WEARING OFF! HE'S BEING DRAWN BACK TO EARTH! WE'LL HAVE TO FIGHT ON-- WITHOUT HIM!

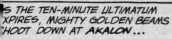
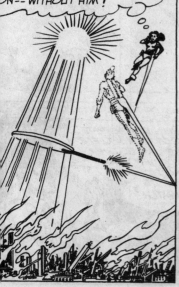

ON EARTH, AN INSTANT LATER...

USUALLY THE *ZETA-BEAM* WEARS OFF *AFTER* A MENACE HAS BEEN FOUGHT AND DE-FEATED-- NOT WHEN THE BATTLE HAS JUST BEGUN! IS *ALANNA* ALL RIGHT? CAN *RANN* DEFEAT THE LENS? HERE ON EARTH I'M HELPLESS TO AID THEM!

WORRIED, DISTRACTED, CLOSE TO THE EDGE OF DESPAIR, *ADAM STRANGE* TRAVELS TO HIS NEW YORK CITY APARTMENT. HE CANNOT WORK. ALL HE CAN DO IS THINK OF *ALANNA* AND THE DANGER TO *RANN*...

NO SENSE IN GOING TO THE MUSEUM. I'D ONLY BE IN THE WAY!

N THE EVENINGS HE TAKES LONG ALKS TO QUIET HIS NERVES...

ORTUNATELY THIS IS ONE OF THE HORTER INTERVALS BETWEEN ZETA-BEAMS-- OR I'D REALLY GO LOCO FROM ORRY! ARE YOU ALL RIGHT, *ALANNA*? DID THE LENS-- GET YOU?

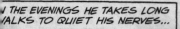

THE DAY BEFORE THE *ZETA-BEAM* IS DUE TO STRIKE, HE DONS HIS *RANN* GARMENTS...

I CAN'T WAIT HERE ANY LONGER! I'VE GOT TO DO SOMETHING! I'LL LISTEN TO A WEATHER REPORT, THEN FLY DOWN TO MY CONTACT-POINT AT NIGHT.

ATTENTION, PLEASE! A GROUP OF *FUTURISTIC* WAR PLANES HAS APPEARED OVER WASHING-TON, LONDON, MOSCOW, PARIS!

WHAT'S THIS? I'VE KEPT TO MYSELF SO MUCH I'M A LITTLE BEHIND ON THE LATEST EARTH NEWS!

A *VOICE* HAS CALLED ON THE NATIONS OF THE WORLD TO SURRENDER TO SCIENCE WIZARD *MANLO TALLIFA!* OR ELSE-- BE TOTALLY ANNIHILATED!

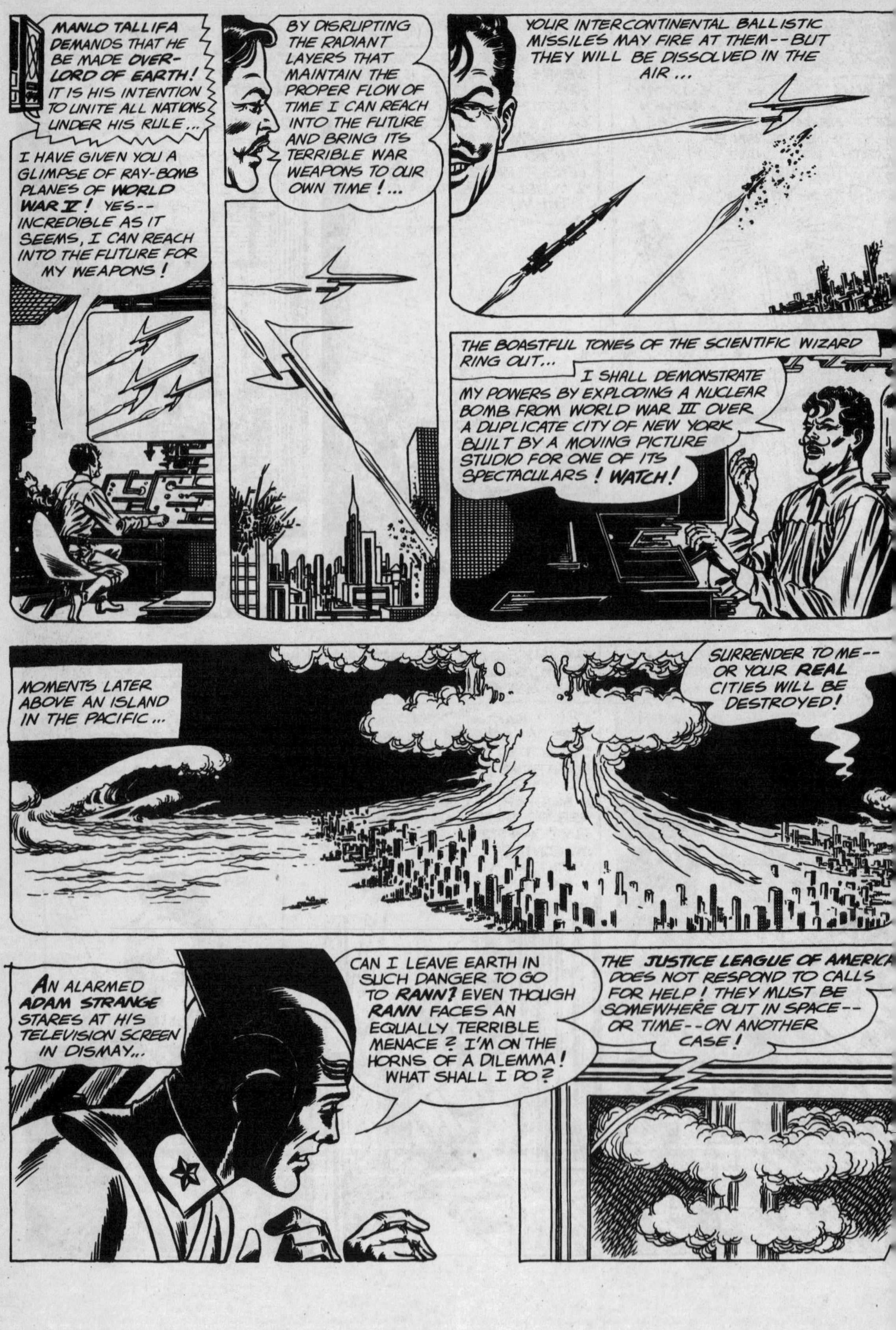
MANLO TALLIFA DEMANDS THAT HE BE MADE OVER-LORD OF EARTH! IT IS HIS INTENTION TO UNITE ALL NATIONS UNDER HIS RULE...
I HAVE GIVEN YOU A GLIMPSE OF RAY-BOMB PLANES OF WORLD WAR V! YES-- INCREDIBLE AS IT SEEMS, I CAN REACH INTO THE FUTURE FOR MY WEAPONS!
BY DISRUPTING THE RADIANT LAYERS THAT MAINTAIN THE PROPER FLOW OF TIME I CAN REACH INTO THE FUTURE AND BRING ITS TERRIBLE WAR WEAPONS TO OUR OWN TIME!...
YOUR INTERCONTINENTAL BALLISTIC MISSILES MAY FIRE AT THEM--BUT THEY WILL BE DISSOLVED IN THE AIR...
THE BOASTFUL TONES OF THE SCIENTIFIC WIZARD RING OUT...
I SHALL DEMONSTRATE MY POWERS BY EXPLODING A NUCLEAR BOMB FROM WORLD WAR III OVER A DUPLICATE CITY OF NEW YORK BUILT BY A MOVING PICTURE STUDIO FOR ONE OF ITS SPECTACULARS! WATCH!
MOMENTS LATER ABOVE AN ISLAND IN THE PACIFIC...
SURRENDER TO ME--OR YOUR REAL CITIES WILL BE DESTROYED!
AN ALARMED ADAM STRANGE STARES AT HIS TELEVISION SCREEN IN DISMAY...
CAN I LEAVE EARTH IN SUCH DANGER TO GO TO RANN? EVEN THOUGH RANN FACES AN EQUALLY TERRIBLE MENACE? I'M ON THE HORNS OF A DILEMMA! WHAT SHALL I DO?
THE JUSTICE LEAGUE OF AMERICA DOES NOT RESPOND TO CALLS FOR HELP! THEY MUST BE SOMEWHERE OUT IN SPACE--OR TIME--ON ANOTHER CASE!

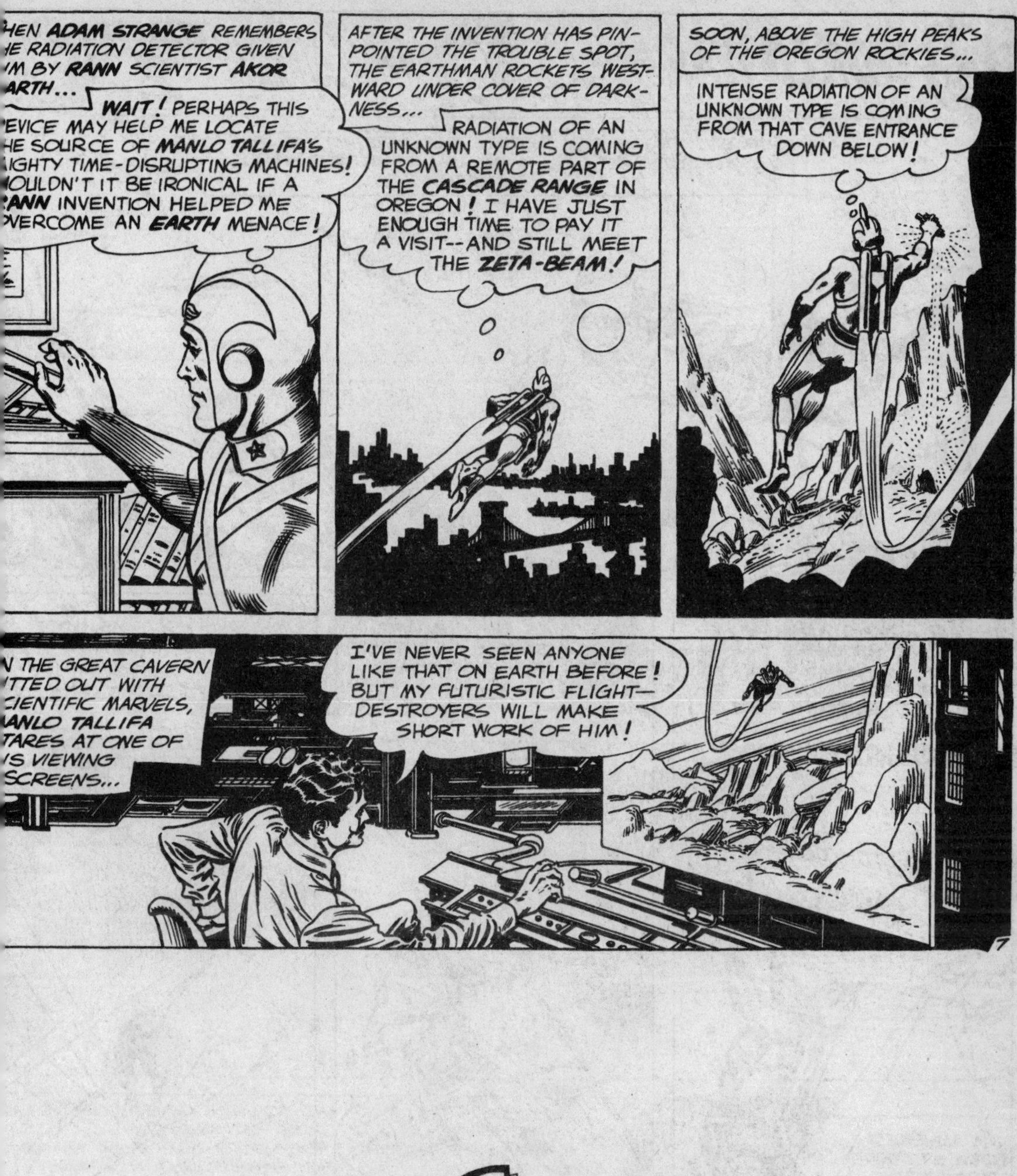
HEN ADAM STRANGE REMEMBERS HE RADIATION DETECTOR GIVEN IM BY RANN SCIENTIST AKOR ARTH...
WAIT! PERHAPS THIS EVICE MAY HELP ME LOCATE HE SOURCE OF MANLO TALLIFA'S IGHTY TIME-DISRUPTING MACHINES! OULDN'T IT BE IRONICAL IF A ANN INVENTION HELPED ME VERCOME AN EARTH MENACE!
AFTER THE INVENTION HAS PIN-POINTED THE TROUBLE SPOT, THE EARTHMAN ROCKETS WEST-WARD UNDER COVER OF DARK-NESS...
RADIATION OF AN UNKNOWN TYPE IS COMING FROM A REMOTE PART OF THE CASCADE RANGE IN OREGON! I HAVE JUST ENOUGH TIME TO PAY IT A VISIT--AND STILL MEET THE ZETA-BEAM!
SOON, ABOVE THE HIGH PEAKS OF THE OREGON ROCKIES...
INTENSE RADIATION OF AN UNKNOWN TYPE IS COMING FROM THAT CAVE ENTRANCE DOWN BELOW!
N THE GREAT CAVERN TTED OUT WITH CIENTIFIC MARVELS, ANLO TALLIFA TARES AT ONE OF S VIEWING SCREENS...
I'VE NEVER SEEN ANYONE LIKE THAT ON EARTH BEFORE! BUT MY FUTURISTIC FLIGHT-DESTROYERS WILL MAKE SHORT WORK OF HIM!
7

ADAM STRANGE

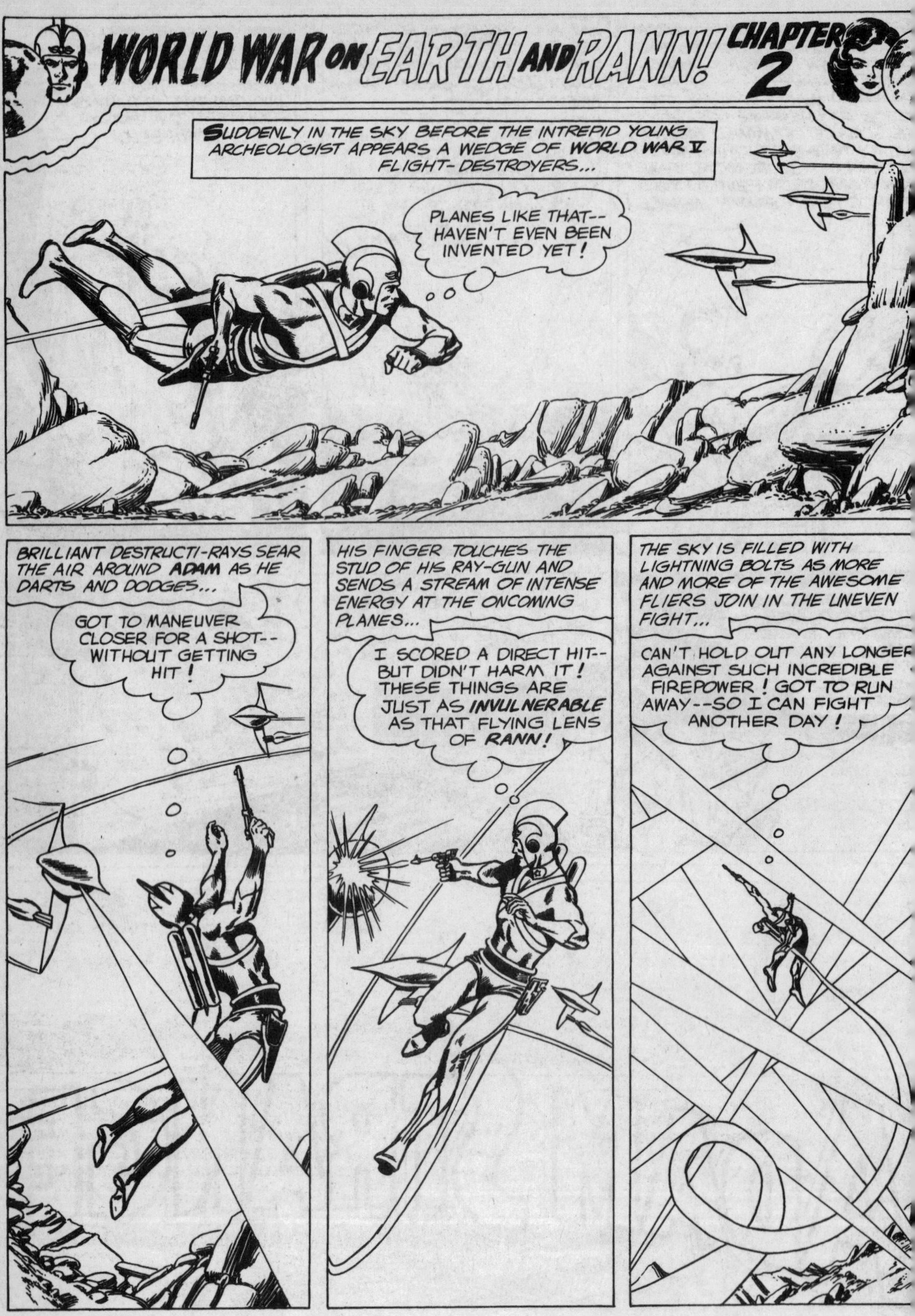
WORLD WAR ON EARTH AND RANN! CHAPTER 2
SUDDENLY IN THE SKY BEFORE THE INTREPID YOUNG ARCHEOLOGIST APPEARS A WEDGE OF WORLD WAR V FLIGHT-DESTROYERS...
PLANES LIKE THAT-- HAVEN'T EVEN BEEN INVENTED YET!
BRILLIANT DESTRUCTI-RAYS SEAR THE AIR AROUND ADAM AS HE DARTS AND DODGES...
GOT TO MANEUVER CLOSER FOR A SHOT-- WITHOUT GETTING HIT!
HIS FINGER TOUCHES THE STUD OF HIS RAY-GUN AND SENDS A STREAM OF INTENSE ENERGY AT THE ONCOMING PLANES...
I SCORED A DIRECT HIT-- BUT DIDN'T HARM IT! THESE THINGS ARE JUST AS INVULNERABLE AS THAT FLYING LENS OF RANN!
THE SKY IS FILLED WITH LIGHTNING BOLTS AS MORE AND MORE OF THE AWESOME FLIERS JOIN IN THE UNEVEN FIGHT...
CAN'T HOLD OUT ANY LONGER AGAINST SUCH INCREDIBLE FIREPOWER! GOT TO RUN AWAY--SO I CAN FIGHT ANOTHER DAY!

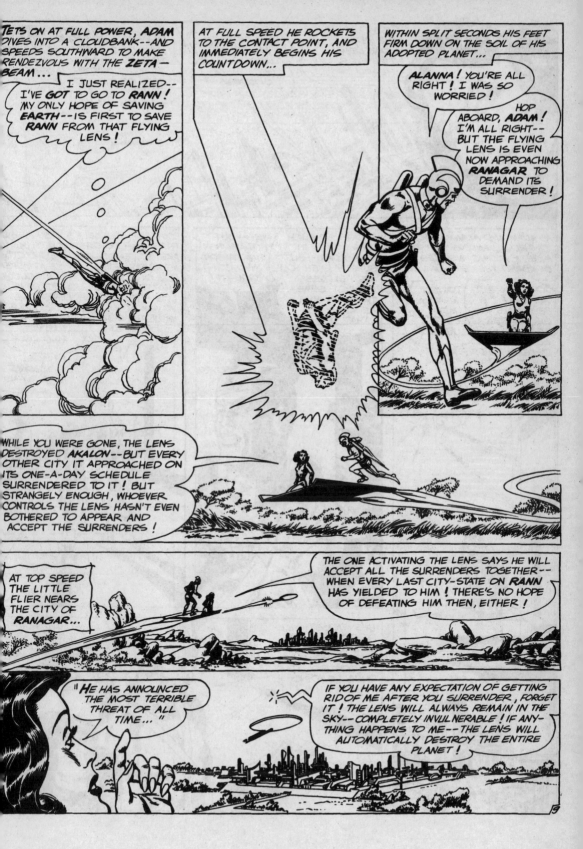

JETS ON AT FULL POWER, ADAM DIVES INTO A CLOUDBANK--AND SPEEDS SOUTHWARD TO MAKE RENDEZVOUS WITH THE ZETA--BEAM...

I JUST REALIZED-- I'VE GOT TO GO TO RANN! MY ONLY HOPE OF SAVING EARTH--IS FIRST TO SAVE RANN FROM THAT FLYING LENS!

AT FULL SPEED HE ROCKETS TO THE CONTACT POINT, AND IMMEDIATELY BEGINS HIS COUNTDOWN...

WITHIN SPLIT SECONDS HIS FEET FIRM DOWN ON THE SOIL OF HIS ADOPTED PLANET...

ALANNA! YOU'RE ALL RIGHT! I WAS SO WORRIED!

HOP ABOARD, ADAM! I'M ALL RIGHT-- BUT THE FLYING LENS IS EVEN NOW APPROACHING RANAGAR TO DEMAND ITS SURRENDER!

WHILE YOU WERE GONE, THE LENS DESTROYED AKALON--BUT EVERY OTHER CITY IT APPROACHED ON ITS ONE-A-DAY SCHEDULE SURRENDERED TO IT! BUT STRANGELY ENOUGH, WHOEVER CONTROLS THE LENS HASN'T EVEN BOTHERED TO APPEAR AND ACCEPT THE SURRENDERS!

THE ONE ACTIVATING THE LENS SAYS HE WILL ACCEPT ALL THE SURRENDERS TOGETHER-- WHEN EVERY LAST CITY-STATE ON RANN HAS YIELDED TO HIM! THERE'S NO HOPE OF DEFEATING HIM THEN, EITHER!

AT TOP SPEED THE LITTLE FLIER NEARS THE CITY OF RANAGAR...

"HE HAS ANNOUNCED THE MOST TERRIBLE THREAT OF ALL TIME..."

IF YOU HAVE ANY EXPECTATION OF GETTING RID OF ME AFTER YOU SURRENDER, FORGET IT! THE LENS WILL ALWAYS REMAIN IN THE SKY--COMPLETELY INVULNERABLE! IF ANY-THING HAPPENS TO ME--THE LENS WILL AUTOMATICALLY DESTROY THE ENTIRE PLANET!

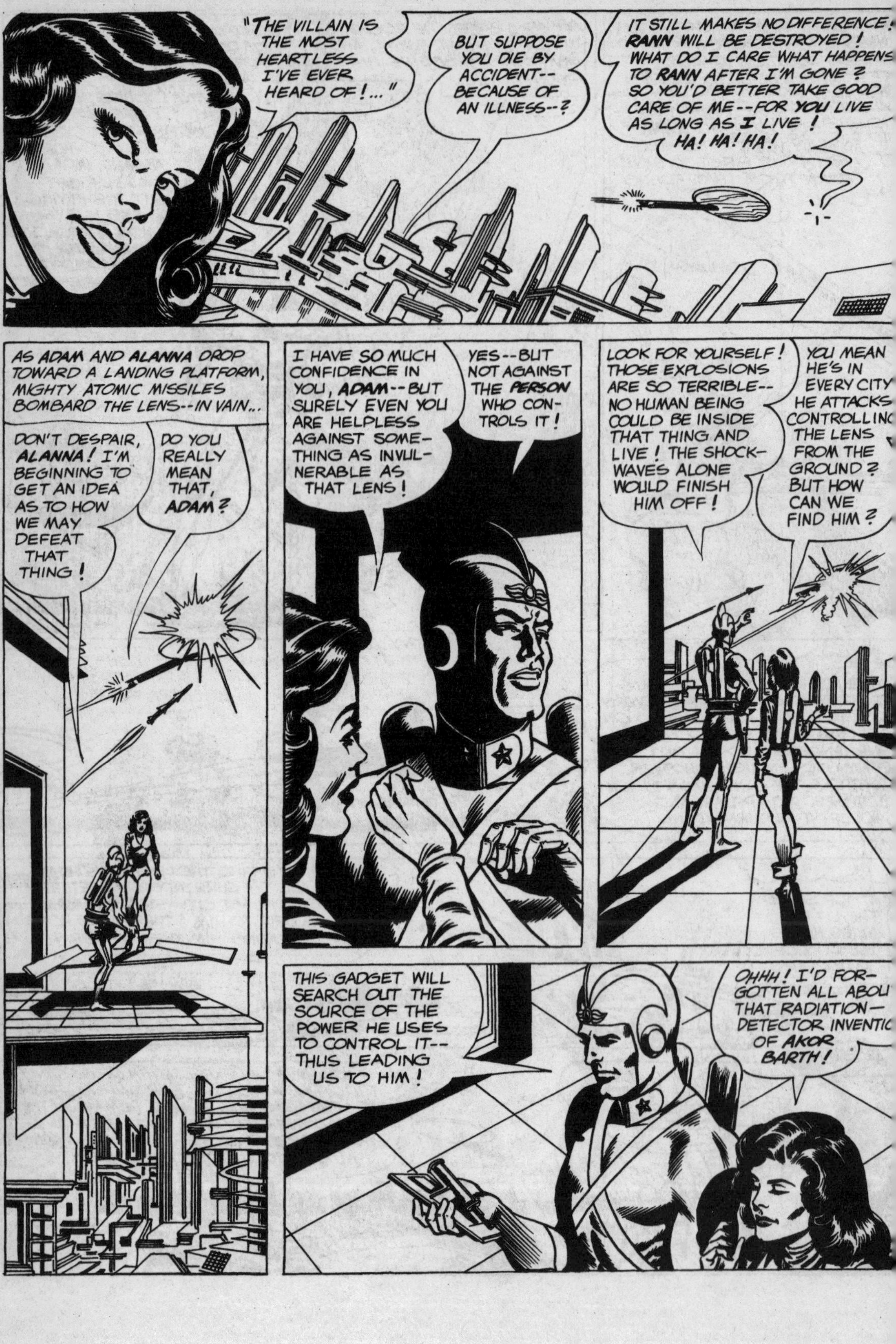
"THE VILLAIN IS THE MOST HEARTLESS I'VE EVER HEARD OF!..."
BUT SUPPOSE YOU DIE BY ACCIDENT--BECAUSE OF AN ILLNESS--?
IT STILL MAKES NO DIFFERENCE! RANN WILL BE DESTROYED! WHAT DO I CARE WHAT HAPPENS TO RANN AFTER I'M GONE? SO YOU'D BETTER TAKE GOOD CARE OF ME--FOR YOU LIVE AS LONG AS I LIVE! HA! HA! HA!
AS ADAM AND ALANNA DROP TOWARD A LANDING PLATFORM, MIGHTY ATOMIC MISSILES BOMBARD THE LENS--IN VAIN...
DON'T DESPAIR, ALANNA! I'M BEGINNING TO GET AN IDEA AS TO HOW WE MAY DEFEAT THAT THING!
DO YOU REALLY MEAN THAT, ADAM?
I HAVE SO MUCH CONFIDENCE IN YOU, ADAM--BUT SURELY EVEN YOU ARE HELPLESS AGAINST SOMETHING AS INVULNERABLE AS THAT LENS!
YES--BUT NOT AGAINST THE PERSON WHO CONTROLS IT!
LOOK FOR YOURSELF! THOSE EXPLOSIONS ARE SO TERRIBLE--NO HUMAN BEING COULD BE INSIDE THAT THING AND LIVE! THE SHOCK-WAVES ALONE WOULD FINISH HIM OFF!
YOU MEAN HE'S IN EVERY CITY HE ATTACKS CONTROLLING THE LENS FROM THE GROUND? BUT HOW CAN WE FIND HIM?
THIS GADGET WILL SEARCH OUT THE SOURCE OF THE POWER HE USES TO CONTROL IT--THUS LEADING US TO HIM!
OHHH! I'D FORGOTTEN ALL ABOUT THAT RADIATION-DETECTOR INVENTI OF AKOR BARTH!

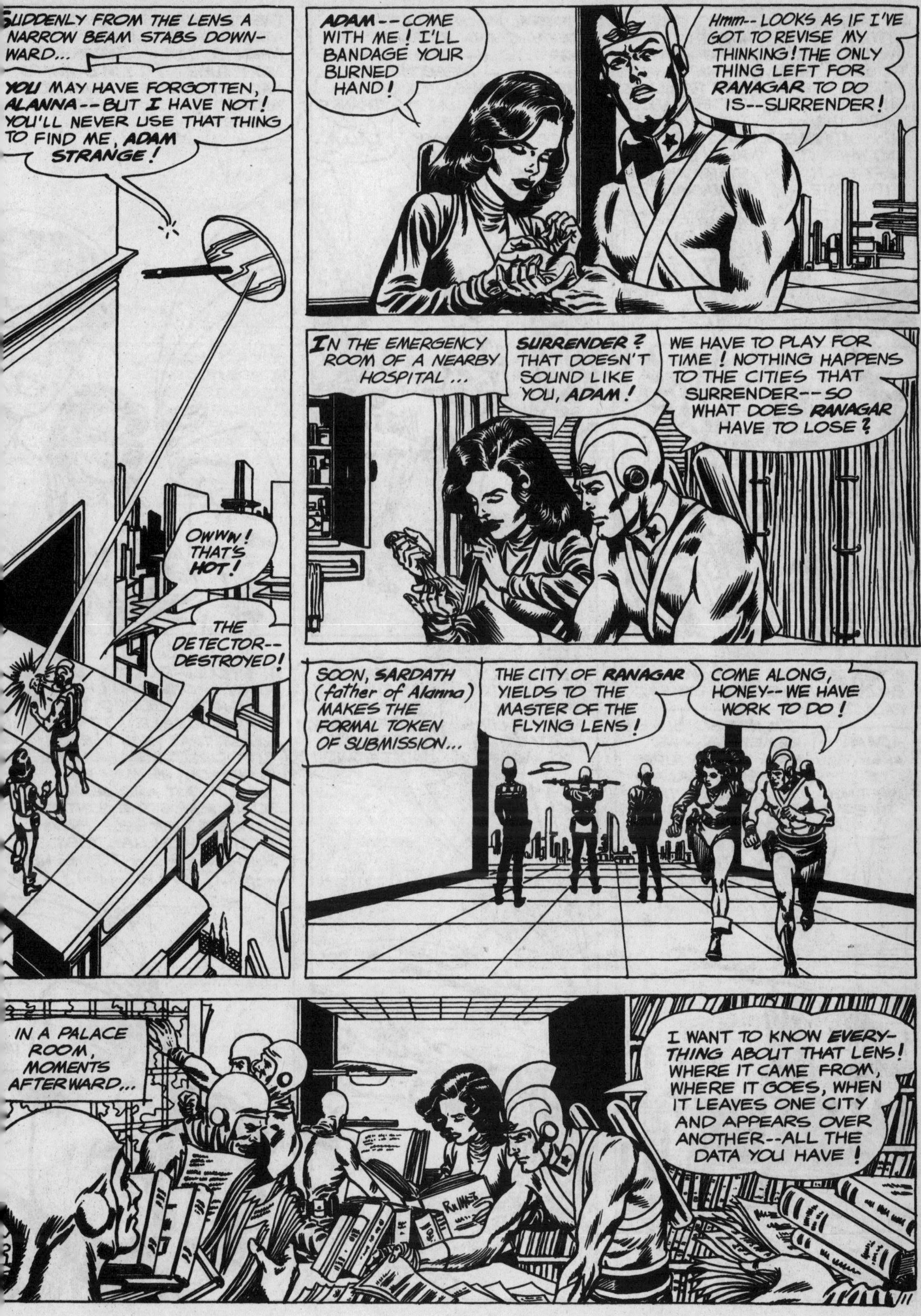
SUDDENLY FROM THE LENS A NARROW BEAM STABS DOWNWARD...
YOU MAY HAVE FORGOTTEN, ALANNA--BUT I HAVE NOT! YOU'LL NEVER USE THAT THING TO FIND ME, ADAM STRANGE!
OWWW! THAT'S HOT!
THE DETECTOR--DESTROYED!
ADAM--COME WITH ME! I'LL BANDAGE YOUR BURNED HAND!
Hmm--LOOKS AS IF I'VE GOT TO REVISE MY THINKING! THE ONLY THING LEFT FOR RANAGAR TO DO IS--SURRENDER!
IN THE EMERGENCY ROOM OF A NEARBY HOSPITAL...
SURRENDER? THAT DOESN'T SOUND LIKE YOU, ADAM!
WE HAVE TO PLAY FOR TIME! NOTHING HAPPENS TO THE CITIES THAT SURRENDER--SO WHAT DOES RANAGAR HAVE TO LOSE?
SOON, SARDATH (father of Alanna) MAKES THE FORMAL TOKEN OF SUBMISSION...
THE CITY OF RANAGAR YIELDS TO THE MASTER OF THE FLYING LENS!
COME ALONG, HONEY--WE HAVE WORK TO DO!
IN A PALACE ROOM, MOMENTS AFTERWARD...
I WANT TO KNOW EVERYTHING ABOUT THAT LENS! WHERE IT CAME FROM, WHERE IT GOES, WHEN IT LEAVES ONE CITY AND APPEARS OVER ANOTHER--ALL THE DATA YOU HAVE!

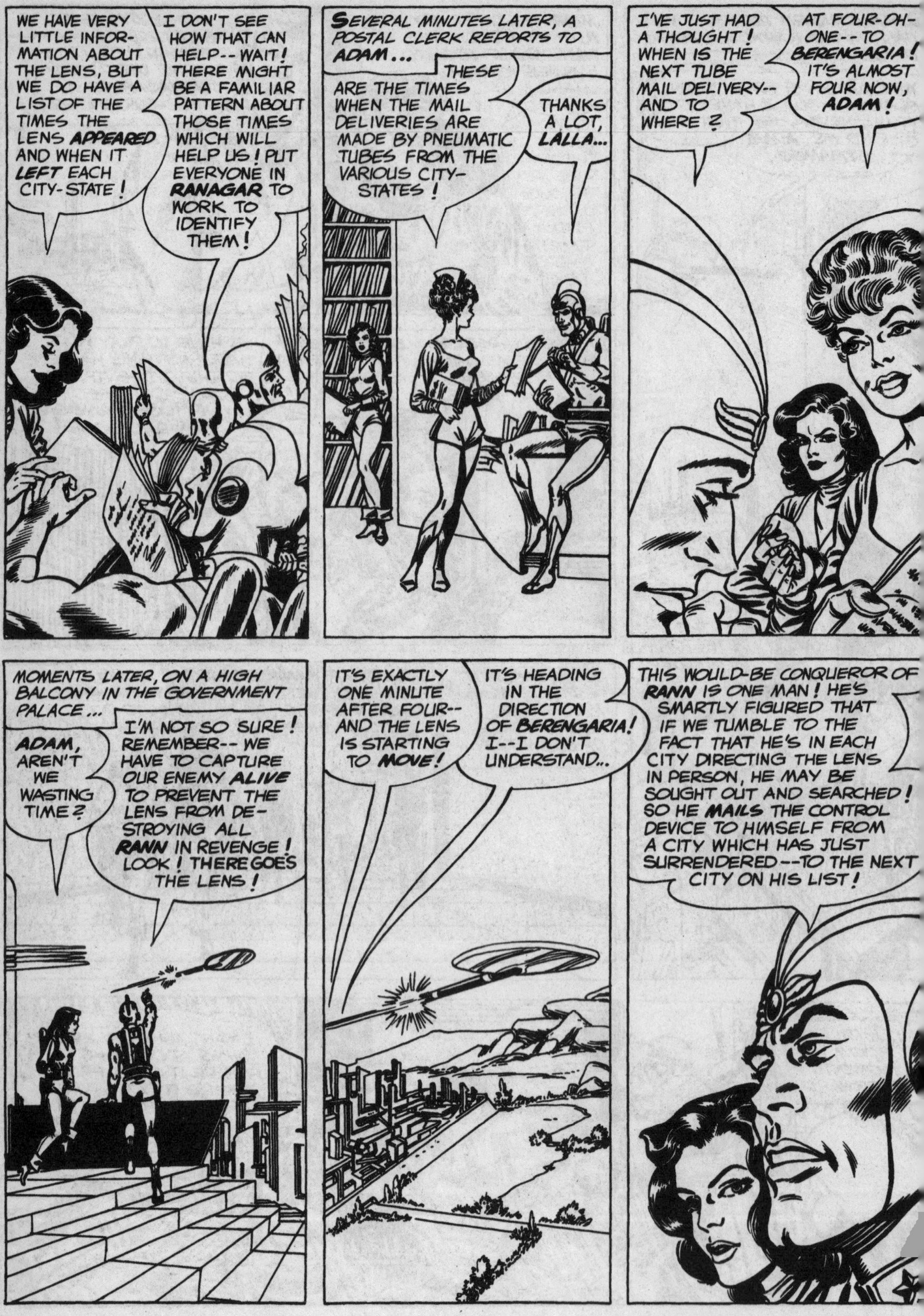
WE HAVE VERY LITTLE INFORMATION ABOUT THE LENS, BUT WE DO HAVE A LIST OF THE TIMES THE LENS APPEARED AND WHEN IT LEFT EACH CITY-STATE!
I DON'T SEE HOW THAT CAN HELP-- WAIT! THERE MIGHT BE A FAMILIAR PATTERN ABOUT THOSE TIMES WHICH WILL HELP US! PUT EVERYONE IN RANAGAR TO WORK TO IDENTIFY THEM!
SEVERAL MINUTES LATER, A POSTAL CLERK REPORTS TO ADAM...
THESE ARE THE TIMES WHEN THE MAIL DELIVERIES ARE MADE BY PNEUMATIC TUBES FROM THE VARIOUS CITY-STATES!
THANKS A LOT, LALLA...
I'VE JUST HAD A THOUGHT! WHEN IS THE NEXT TUBE MAIL DELIVERY-- AND TO WHERE?
AT FOUR-OH-ONE-- TO BERENGARIA! IT'S ALMOST FOUR NOW, ADAM!
MOMENTS LATER, ON A HIGH BALCONY IN THE GOVERNMENT PALACE...
ADAM, AREN'T WE WASTING TIME?
I'M NOT SO SURE! REMEMBER-- WE HAVE TO CAPTURE OUR ENEMY ALIVE TO PREVENT THE LENS FROM DESTROYING ALL RANN IN REVENGE! LOOK! THERE GOES THE LENS!
IT'S EXACTLY ONE MINUTE AFTER FOUR-- AND THE LENS IS STARTING TO MOVE!
IT'S HEADING IN THE DIRECTION OF BERENGARIA! I--I DON'T UNDERSTAND...
THIS WOULD-BE CONQUEROR OF RANN IS ONE MAN! HE'S SMARTLY FIGURED THAT IF WE TUMBLE TO THE FACT THAT HE'S IN EACH CITY DIRECTING THE LENS IN PERSON, HE MAY BE SOUGHT OUT AND SEARCHED! SO HE MAILS THE CONTROL DEVICE TO HIMSELF FROM A CITY WHICH HAS JUST SURRENDERED--TO THE NEXT CITY ON HIS LIST!

ADAM STRANGE PUTS IN A VIEW-CALL TO THE POSTAL AUTHORITIES OF BERENGARIA...

NOW LISTEN CLOSELY! THE SAFETY OF THE ENTIRE PLANET AND YOUR OWN CITY-STATE DEPENDS ON YOUR FOLLOWING MY INSTRUCTIONS!

MOMENTS LATER ADAM AND ALANNA ARE JETTING AT HIGH SPEED TOWARD BERENGARIA...

YOU SEE? THE LENS IS MOVING AT THE VERY SAME SPEED THE MAIL DELIVERIES ARE MOVING THROUGH THE UNDERGROUND PNEUMATIC TUBES--PROVING THE CONTROL DEVICE IN THE PNEUMATIC TUBES IS DIRECTING IT!

AT OUR PRESENT SPEED WE'LL PASS THE LENS AND ARRIVE IN BERENGARIA SOME MINUTES AHEAD OF IT!

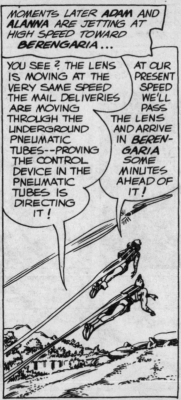

SHORTLY, IN THE CITY-STATE OF BERENGARIA...

I'VE INSTRUCTED THE POSTAL CLERKS TO X-RAY EVERY PACKAGE RECEIVED IN THE 4:01 SHIPMENT OF MAIL FROM RANAGAR-- AND SIGNAL ME WHEN SOMEONE CALLS FOR ANY ELECTRONIC DEVICE IN THAT MAIL!

SOON, IN THE MAIL DELIVERY ROOM...

:COUGH: :COUGH:

THERE'S OUR SIGNAL NOW!

LIKE A TIGER, ADAM MAKES HIS LEAP...

OHHH! HEY-- WHAT'S THE IDEA--

13

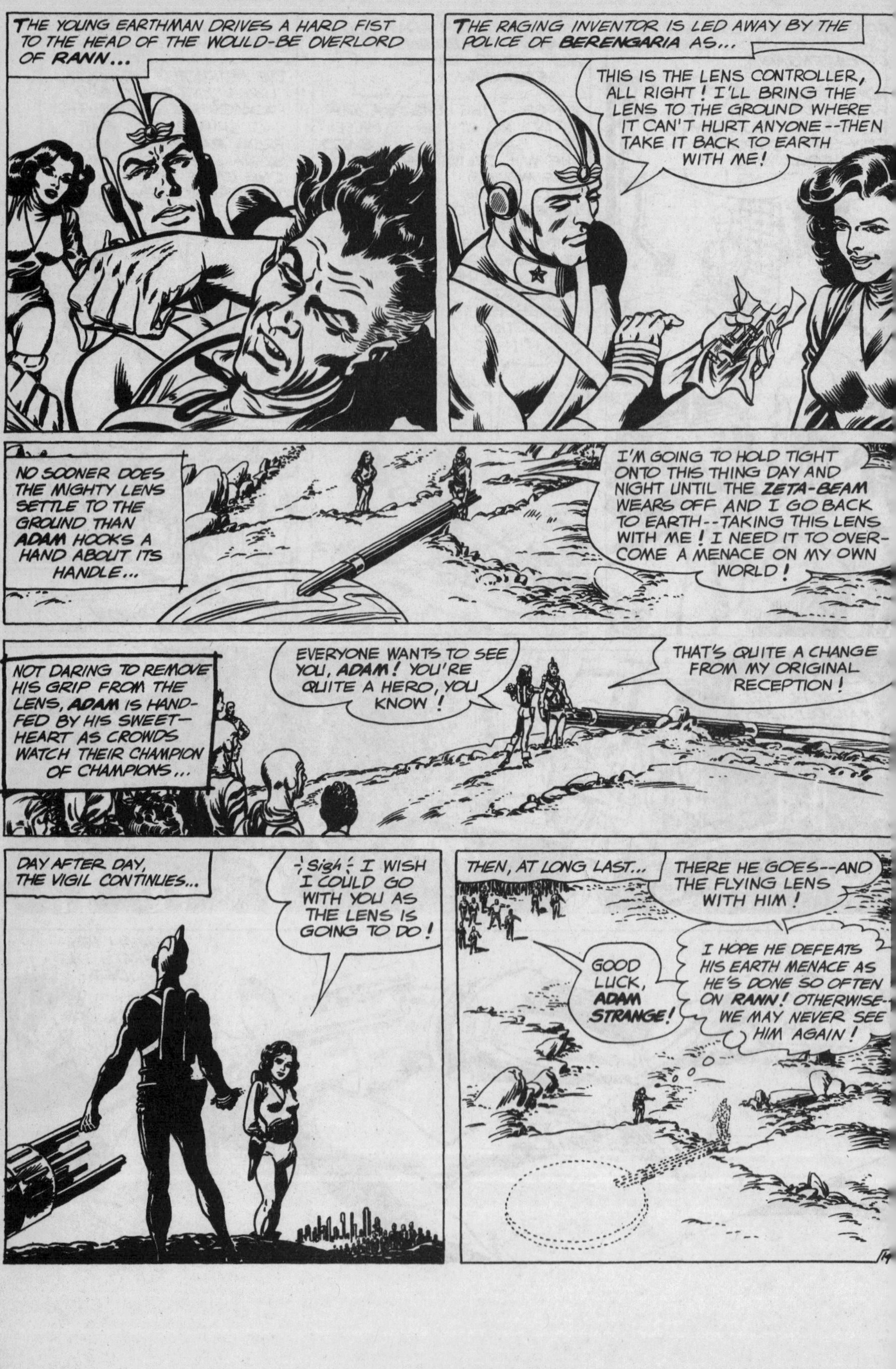
THE YOUNG EARTHMAN DRIVES A HARD FIST TO THE HEAD OF THE WOULD-BE OVERLORD OF RANN...
THE RAGING INVENTOR IS LED AWAY BY THE POLICE OF BERENGARIA AS...
THIS IS THE LENS CONTROLLER, ALL RIGHT! I'LL BRING THE LENS TO THE GROUND WHERE IT CAN'T HURT ANYONE--THEN TAKE IT BACK TO EARTH WITH ME!
NO SOONER DOES THE MIGHTY LENS SETTLE TO THE GROUND THAN ADAM HOOKS A HAND ABOUT ITS HANDLE...
I'M GOING TO HOLD TIGHT ONTO THIS THING DAY AND NIGHT UNTIL THE ZETA-BEAM WEARS OFF AND I GO BACK TO EARTH--TAKING THIS LENS WITH ME! I NEED IT TO OVERCOME A MENACE ON MY OWN WORLD!
NOT DARING TO REMOVE HIS GRIP FROM THE LENS, ADAM IS HAND-FED BY HIS SWEETHEART AS CROWDS WATCH THEIR CHAMPION OF CHAMPIONS...
EVERYONE WANTS TO SEE YOU, ADAM! YOU'RE QUITE A HERO, YOU KNOW!
THAT'S QUITE A CHANGE FROM MY ORIGINAL RECEPTION!
DAY AFTER DAY, THE VIGIL CONTINUES...
-Sigh- I WISH I COULD GO WITH YOU AS THE LENS IS GOING TO DO!
THEN, AT LONG LAST...
THERE HE GOES--AND THE FLYING LENS WITH HIM!
GOOD LUCK, ADAM STRANGE!
I HOPE HE DEFEATS HIS EARTH MENACE AS HE'S DONE SO OFTEN ON RANN! OTHERWISE--WE MAY NEVER SEE HIM AGAIN!

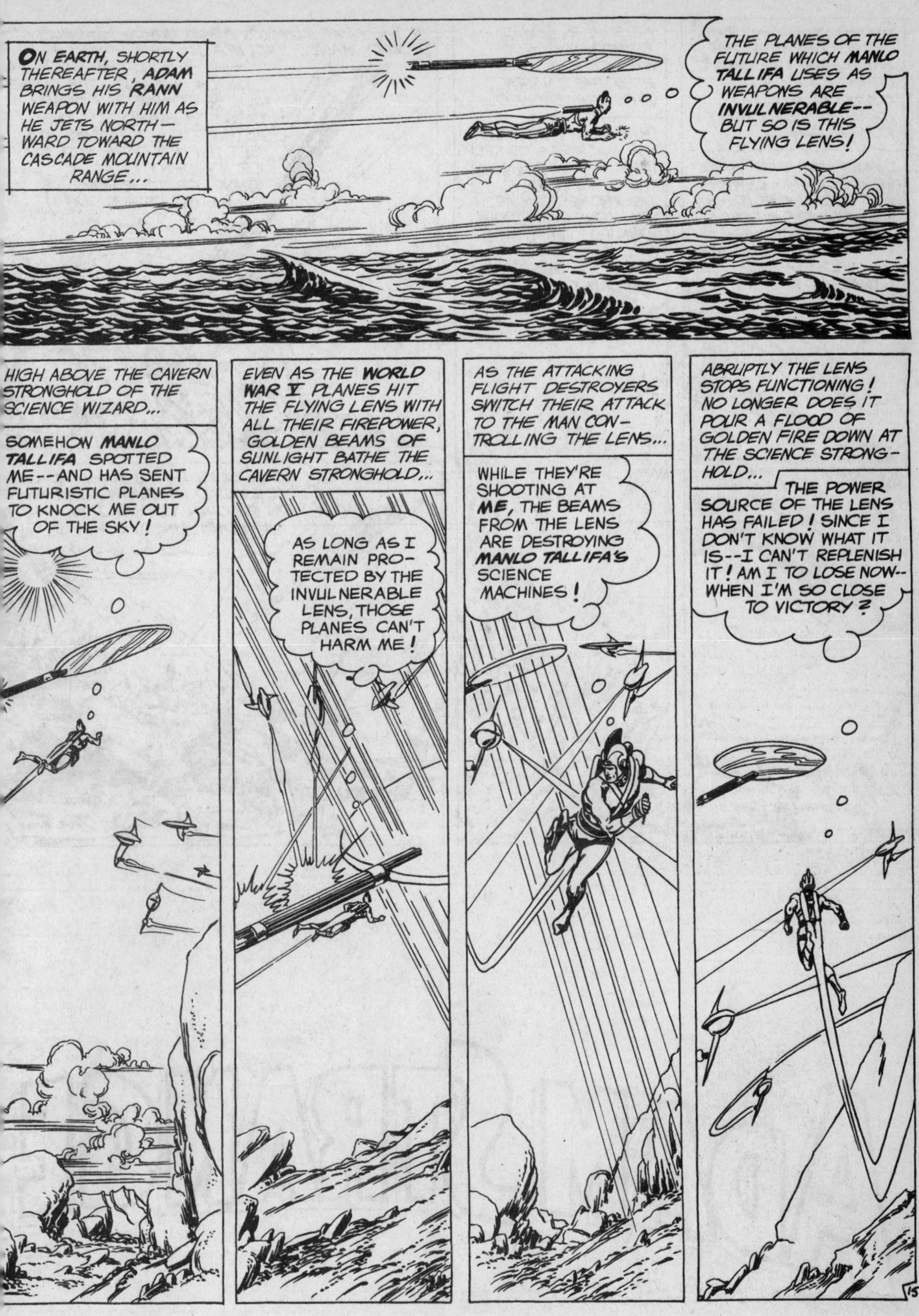
ON EARTH, SHORTLY THEREAFTER, ADAM BRINGS HIS RANN WEAPON WITH HIM AS HE JETS NORTH-WARD TOWARD THE CASCADE MOUNTAIN RANGE...
THE PLANES OF THE FUTURE WHICH MANLO TALLIFA USES AS WEAPONS ARE INVULNERABLE-- BUT SO IS THIS FLYING LENS!
HIGH ABOVE THE CAVERN STRONGHOLD OF THE SCIENCE WIZARD...
SOMEHOW MANLO TALLIFA SPOTTED ME--AND HAS SENT FUTURISTIC PLANES TO KNOCK ME OUT OF THE SKY!
EVEN AS THE WORLD WAR V PLANES HIT THE FLYING LENS WITH ALL THEIR FIREPOWER, GOLDEN BEAMS OF SUNLIGHT BATHE THE CAVERN STRONGHOLD...
AS LONG AS I REMAIN PRO-TECTED BY THE INVULNERABLE LENS, THOSE PLANES CAN'T HARM ME!
AS THE ATTACKING FLIGHT DESTROYERS SWITCH THEIR ATTACK TO THE MAN CON-TROLLING THE LENS...
WHILE THEY'RE SHOOTING AT ME, THE BEAMS FROM THE LENS ARE DESTROYING MANLO TALLIFA'S SCIENCE MACHINES!
ABRUPTLY THE LENS STOPS FUNCTIONING! NO LONGER DOES IT POUR A FLOOD OF GOLDEN FIRE DOWN AT THE SCIENCE STRONG-HOLD...
THE POWER SOURCE OF THE LENS HAS FAILED! SINCE I DON'T KNOW WHAT IT IS--I CAN'T REPLENISH IT! AM I TO LOSE NOW-- WHEN I'M SO CLOSE TO VICTORY?
15

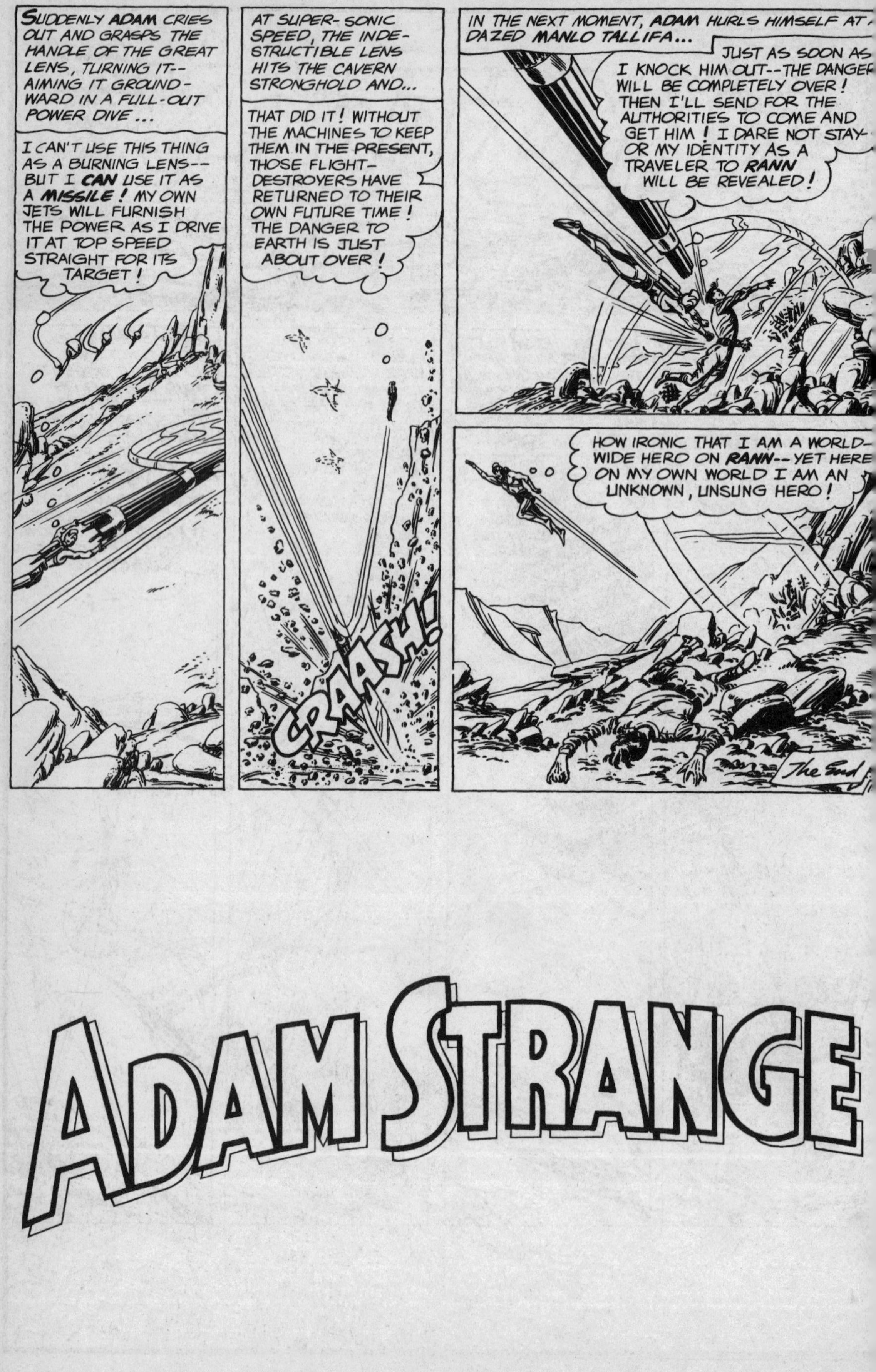
SUDDENLY ADAM CRIES OUT AND GRASPS THE HANDLE OF THE GREAT LENS, TURNING IT--AIMING IT GROUND-WARD IN A FULL-OUT POWER DIVE ...
I CAN'T USE THIS THING AS A BURNING LENS--BUT I CAN USE IT AS A MISSILE! MY OWN JETS WILL FURNISH THE POWER AS I DRIVE IT AT TOP SPEED STRAIGHT FOR ITS TARGET!
AT SUPER-SONIC SPEED, THE INDE-STRUCTIBLE LENS HITS THE CAVERN STRONGHOLD AND...
THAT DID IT! WITHOUT THE MACHINES TO KEEP THEM IN THE PRESENT, THOSE FLIGHT-DESTROYERS HAVE RETURNED TO THEIR OWN FUTURE TIME! THE DANGER TO EARTH IS JUST ABOUT OVER!
CRAASH!
IN THE NEXT MOMENT, ADAM HURLS HIMSELF AT A DAZED MANLO TALLIFA...
JUST AS SOON AS I KNOCK HIM OUT--THE DANGER WILL BE COMPLETELY OVER! THEN I'LL SEND FOR THE AUTHORITIES TO COME AND GET HIM! I DARE NOT STAY-OR MY IDENTITY AS A TRAVELER TO RANN WILL BE REVEALED!
HOW IRONIC THAT I AM A WORLD-WIDE HERO ON RANN--YET HERE ON MY OWN WORLD I AM AN UNKNOWN, UNSUNG HERO!
The End
ADAM STRANGE

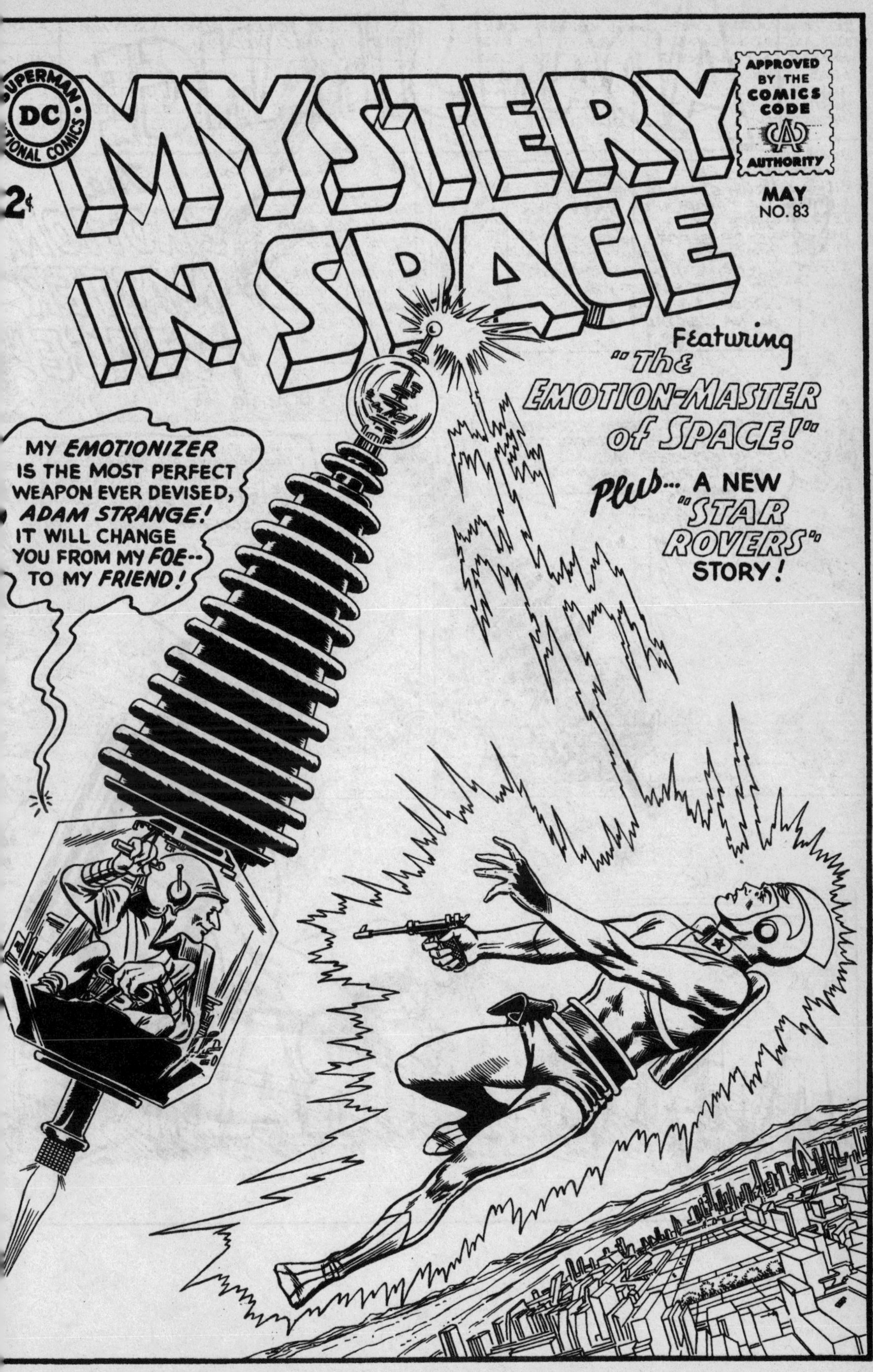
SUPERMAN DC NATIONAL COMICS
MYSTERY IN SPACE
APPROVED BY THE COMICS CODE AUTHORITY
2¢
MAY NO. 83
Featuring "The EMOTION-MASTER of SPACE!"
Plus... A NEW "STAR ROVERS" STORY!
MY EMOTIONIZER IS THE MOST PERFECT WEAPON EVER DEVISED, ADAM STRANGE! IT WILL CHANGE YOU FROM MY FOE-- TO MY FRIEND!

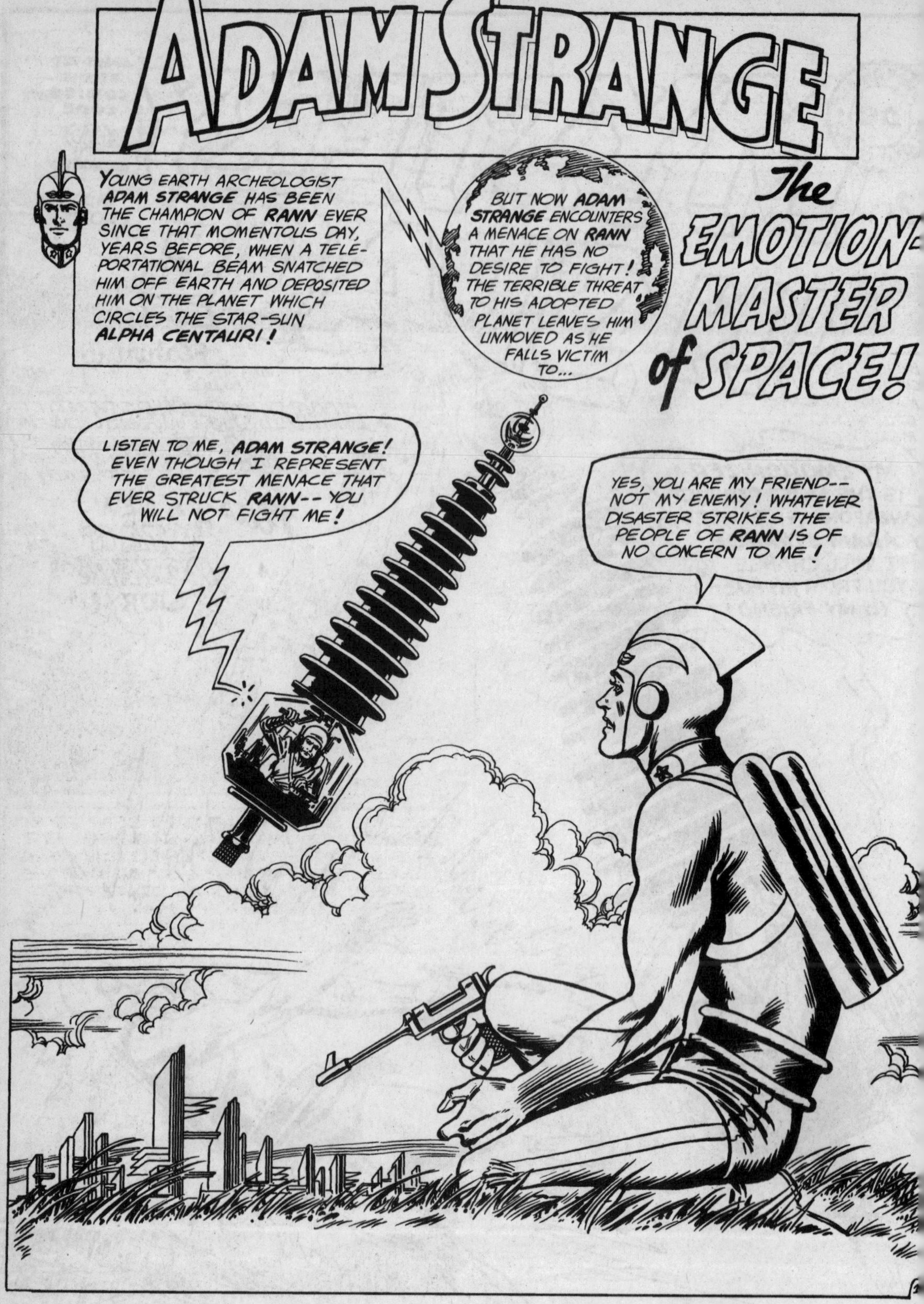
ADAM STRANGE
YOUNG EARTH ARCHEOLOGIST ADAM STRANGE HAS BEEN THE CHAMPION OF RANN EVER SINCE THAT MOMENTOUS DAY, YEARS BEFORE, WHEN A TELE-PORTATIONAL BEAM SNATCHED HIM OFF EARTH AND DEPOSITED HIM ON THE PLANET WHICH CIRCLES THE STAR-SUN ALPHA CENTAURI!
BUT NOW ADAM STRANGE ENCOUNTERS A MENACE ON RANN THAT HE HAS NO DESIRE TO FIGHT! THE TERRIBLE THREAT TO HIS ADOPTED PLANET LEAVES HIM UNMOVED AS HE FALLS VICTIM TO...
The EMOTION-MASTER of SPACE!
LISTEN TO ME, ADAM STRANGE! EVEN THOUGH I REPRESENT THE GREATEST MENACE THAT EVER STRUCK RANN-- YOU WILL NOT FIGHT ME!
YES, YOU ARE MY FRIEND-- NOT MY ENEMY! WHATEVER DISASTER STRIKES THE PEOPLE OF RANN IS OF NO CONCERN TO ME!

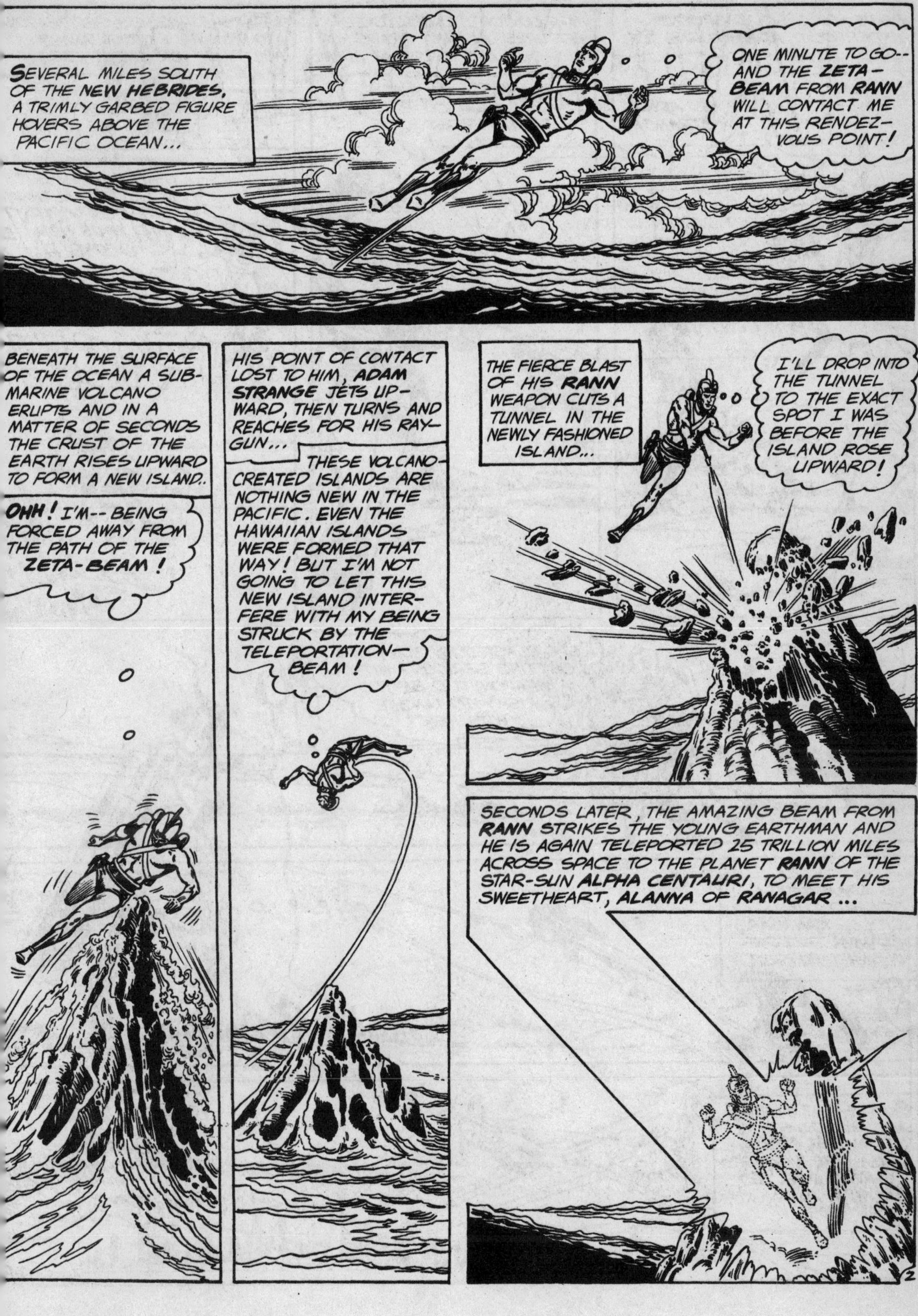
SEVERAL MILES SOUTH OF THE NEW HEBRIDES, A TRIMLY GARBED FIGURE HOVERS ABOVE THE PACIFIC OCEAN...
ONE MINUTE TO GO-- AND THE ZETA-BEAM FROM RANN WILL CONTACT ME AT THIS RENDEZ-VOUS POINT!
BENEATH THE SURFACE OF THE OCEAN A SUB-MARINE VOLCANO ERUPTS AND IN A MATTER OF SECONDS THE CRUST OF THE EARTH RISES UPWARD TO FORM A NEW ISLAND.
OHH! I'M-- BEING FORCED AWAY FROM THE PATH OF THE ZETA-BEAM!
HIS POINT OF CONTACT LOST TO HIM, ADAM STRANGE JETS UP-WARD, THEN TURNS AND REACHES FOR HIS RAY-GUN...
THESE VOLCANO-CREATED ISLANDS ARE NOTHING NEW IN THE PACIFIC. EVEN THE HAWAIIAN ISLANDS WERE FORMED THAT WAY! BUT I'M NOT GOING TO LET THIS NEW ISLAND INTER-FERE WITH MY BEING STRUCK BY THE TELEPORTATION-BEAM!
THE FIERCE BLAST OF HIS RANN WEAPON CUTS A TUNNEL IN THE NEWLY FASHIONED ISLAND...
I'LL DROP INTO THE TUNNEL TO THE EXACT SPOT I WAS BEFORE THE ISLAND ROSE UPWARD!
SECONDS LATER, THE AMAZING BEAM FROM RANN STRIKES THE YOUNG EARTHMAN AND HE IS AGAIN TELEPORTED 25 TRILLION MILES ACROSS SPACE TO THE PLANET RANN OF THE STAR-SUN ALPHA CENTAURI, TO MEET HIS SWEETHEART, ALANNA OF RANAGAR...
2

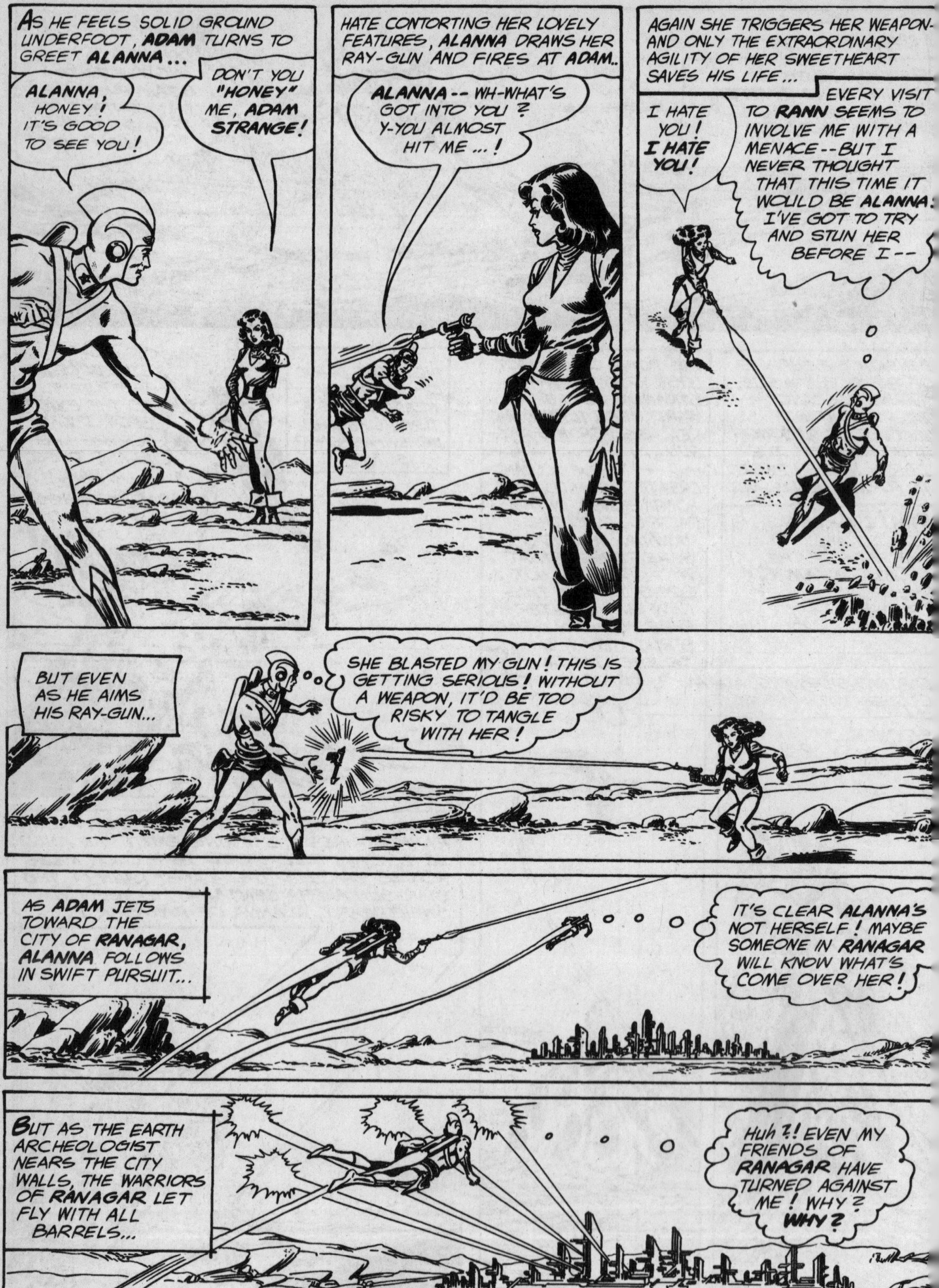
AS HE FEELS SOLID GROUND UNDERFOOT, ADAM TURNS TO GREET ALANNA...
ALANNA, HONEY! IT'S GOOD TO SEE YOU!
DON'T YOU "HONEY" ME, ADAM STRANGE!
HATE CONTORTING HER LOVELY FEATURES, ALANNA DRAWS HER RAY-GUN AND FIRES AT ADAM..
ALANNA-- WH-WHAT'S GOT INTO YOU? Y-YOU ALMOST HIT ME...!
AGAIN SHE TRIGGERS HER WEAPON-AND ONLY THE EXTRAORDINARY AGILITY OF HER SWEETHEART SAVES HIS LIFE...
I HATE YOU! I HATE YOU!
EVERY VISIT TO RANN SEEMS TO INVOLVE ME WITH A MENACE--BUT I NEVER THOUGHT THAT THIS TIME IT WOULD BE ALANNA! I'VE GOT TO TRY AND STUN HER BEFORE I--
BUT EVEN AS HE AIMS HIS RAY-GUN...
SHE BLASTED MY GUN! THIS IS GETTING SERIOUS! WITHOUT A WEAPON, IT'D BE TOO RISKY TO TANGLE WITH HER!
AS ADAM JETS TOWARD THE CITY OF RANAGAR, ALANNA FOLLOWS IN SWIFT PURSUIT...
IT'S CLEAR ALANNA'S NOT HERSELF! MAYBE SOMEONE IN RANAGAR WILL KNOW WHAT'S COME OVER HER!
BUT AS THE EARTH ARCHEOLOGIST NEARS THE CITY WALLS, THE WARRIORS OF RANAGAR LET FLY WITH ALL BARRELS...
Huh?! EVEN MY FRIENDS OF RANAGAR HAVE TURNED AGAINST ME! WHY? WHY?
3

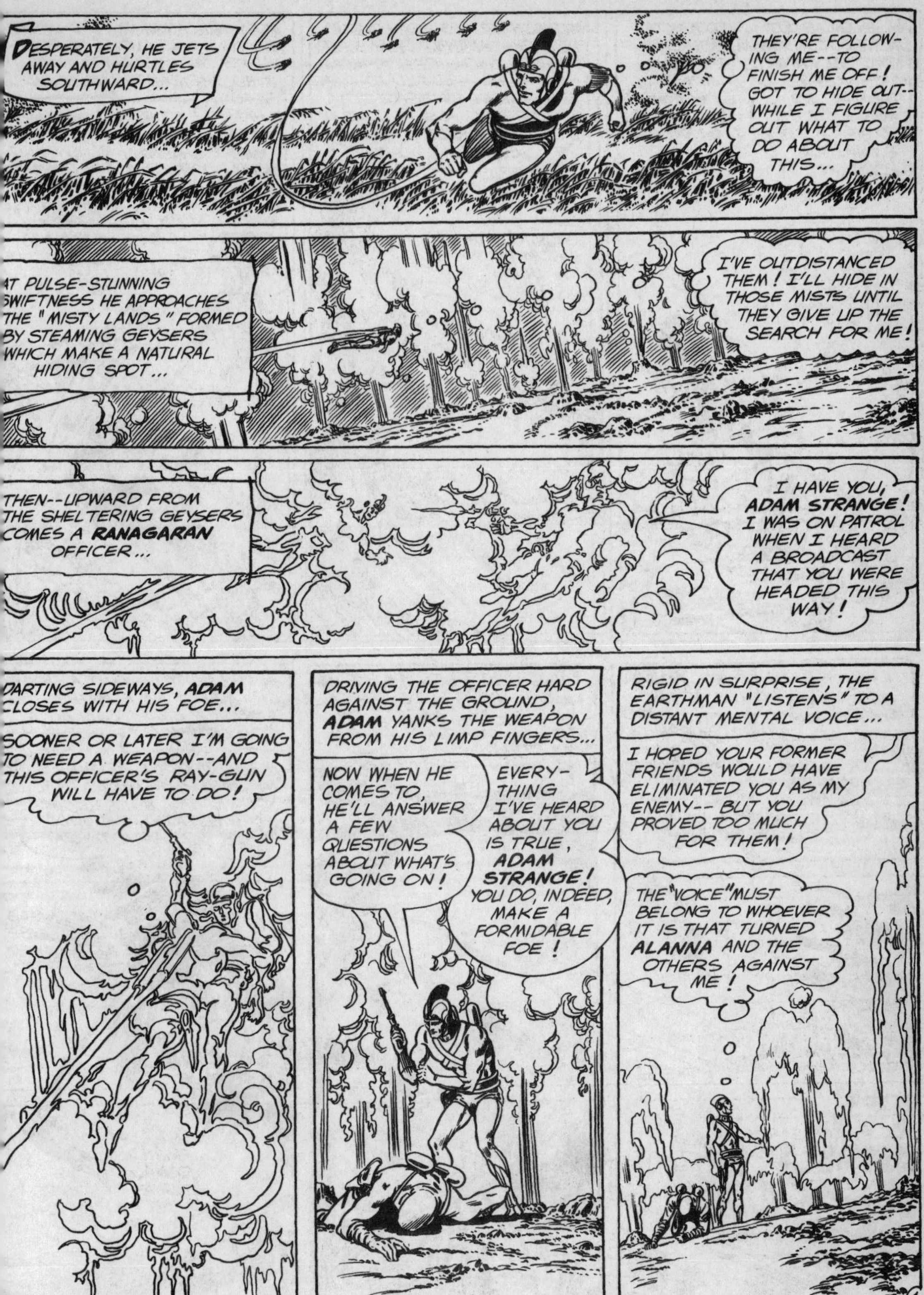
DESPERATELY, HE JETS AWAY AND HURTLES SOUTHWARD...
THEY'RE FOLLOWING ME--TO FINISH ME OFF! GOT TO HIDE OUT--WHILE I FIGURE OUT WHAT TO DO ABOUT THIS...
AT PULSE-STUNNING SWIFTNESS HE APPROACHES THE "MISTY LANDS" FORMED BY STEAMING GEYSERS WHICH MAKE A NATURAL HIDING SPOT...
I'VE OUTDISTANCED THEM! I'LL HIDE IN THOSE MISTS UNTIL THEY GIVE UP THE SEARCH FOR ME!
THEN--UPWARD FROM THE SHELTERING GEYSERS COMES A RANAGARAN OFFICER...
I HAVE YOU, ADAM STRANGE! I WAS ON PATROL WHEN I HEARD A BROADCAST THAT YOU WERE HEADED THIS WAY!
DARTING SIDEWAYS, ADAM CLOSES WITH HIS FOE...
SOONER OR LATER I'M GOING TO NEED A WEAPON--AND THIS OFFICER'S RAY-GUN WILL HAVE TO DO!
DRIVING THE OFFICER HARD AGAINST THE GROUND, ADAM YANKS THE WEAPON FROM HIS LIMP FINGERS...
NOW WHEN HE COMES TO, HE'LL ANSWER A FEW QUESTIONS ABOUT WHAT'S GOING ON!
EVERYTHING I'VE HEARD ABOUT YOU IS TRUE, ADAM STRANGE! YOU DO, INDEED, MAKE A FORMIDABLE FOE!
RIGID IN SURPRISE, THE EARTHMAN "LISTENS" TO A DISTANT MENTAL VOICE...
I HOPED YOUR FORMER FRIENDS WOULD HAVE ELIMINATED YOU AS MY ENEMY-- BUT YOU PROVED TOO MUCH FOR THEM!
THE "VOICE" MUST BELONG TO WHOEVER IT IS THAT TURNED ALANNA AND THE OTHERS AGAINST ME!
4

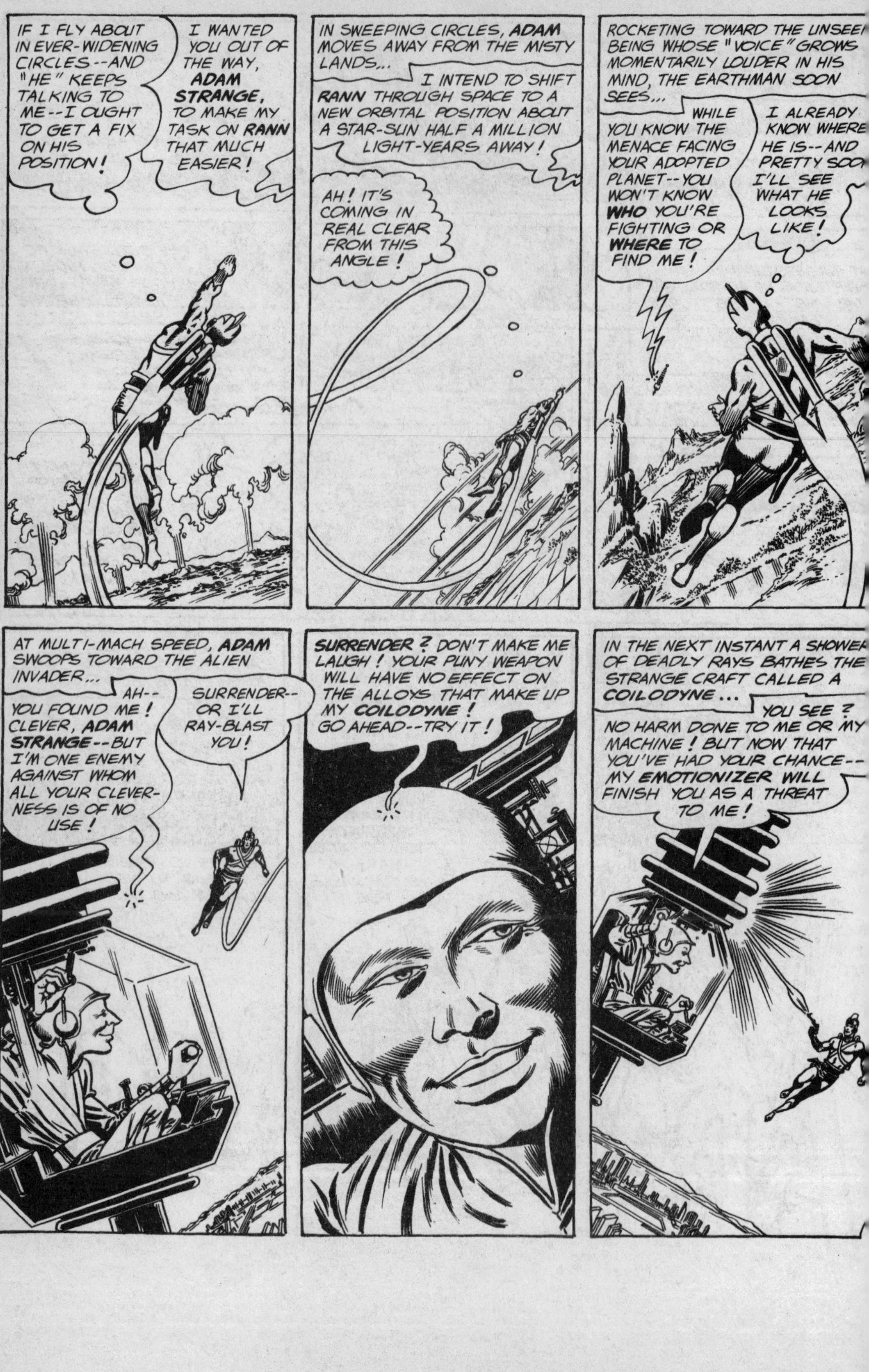
IF I FLY ABOUT IN EVER-WIDENING CIRCLES--AND "HE" KEEPS TALKING TO ME--I OUGHT TO GET A FIX ON HIS POSITION!
I WANTED YOU OUT OF THE WAY, ADAM STRANGE, TO MAKE MY TASK ON RANN THAT MUCH EASIER!
IN SWEEPING CIRCLES, ADAM MOVES AWAY FROM THE MISTY LANDS...
I INTEND TO SHIFT RANN THROUGH SPACE TO A NEW ORBITAL POSITION ABOUT A STAR-SUN HALF A MILLION LIGHT-YEARS AWAY!
AH! IT'S COMING IN REAL CLEAR FROM THIS ANGLE!
ROCKETING TOWARD THE UNSEEN BEING WHOSE "VOICE" GROWS MOMENTARILY LOUDER IN HIS MIND, THE EARTHMAN SOON SEES...
WHILE YOU KNOW THE MENACE FACING YOUR ADOPTED PLANET--YOU WON'T KNOW WHO YOU'RE FIGHTING OR WHERE TO FIND ME!
I ALREADY KNOW WHERE HE IS--AND PRETTY SOON I'LL SEE WHAT HE LOOKS LIKE!
AT MULTI-MACH SPEED, ADAM SWOOPS TOWARD THE ALIEN INVADER...
AH--YOU FOUND ME! CLEVER, ADAM STRANGE--BUT I'M ONE ENEMY AGAINST WHOM ALL YOUR CLEVERNESS IS OF NO USE!
SURRENDER--OR I'LL RAY-BLAST YOU!
SURRENDER? DON'T MAKE ME LAUGH! YOUR PUNY WEAPON WILL HAVE NO EFFECT ON THE ALLOYS THAT MAKE UP MY COILODYNE! GO AHEAD--TRY IT!
IN THE NEXT INSTANT A SHOWER OF DEADLY RAYS BATHES THE STRANGE CRAFT CALLED A COILODYNE...
YOU SEE? NO HARM DONE TO ME OR MY MACHINE! BUT NOW THAT YOU'VE HAD YOUR CHANCE--MY EMOTIONIZER WILL FINISH YOU AS A THREAT TO ME!

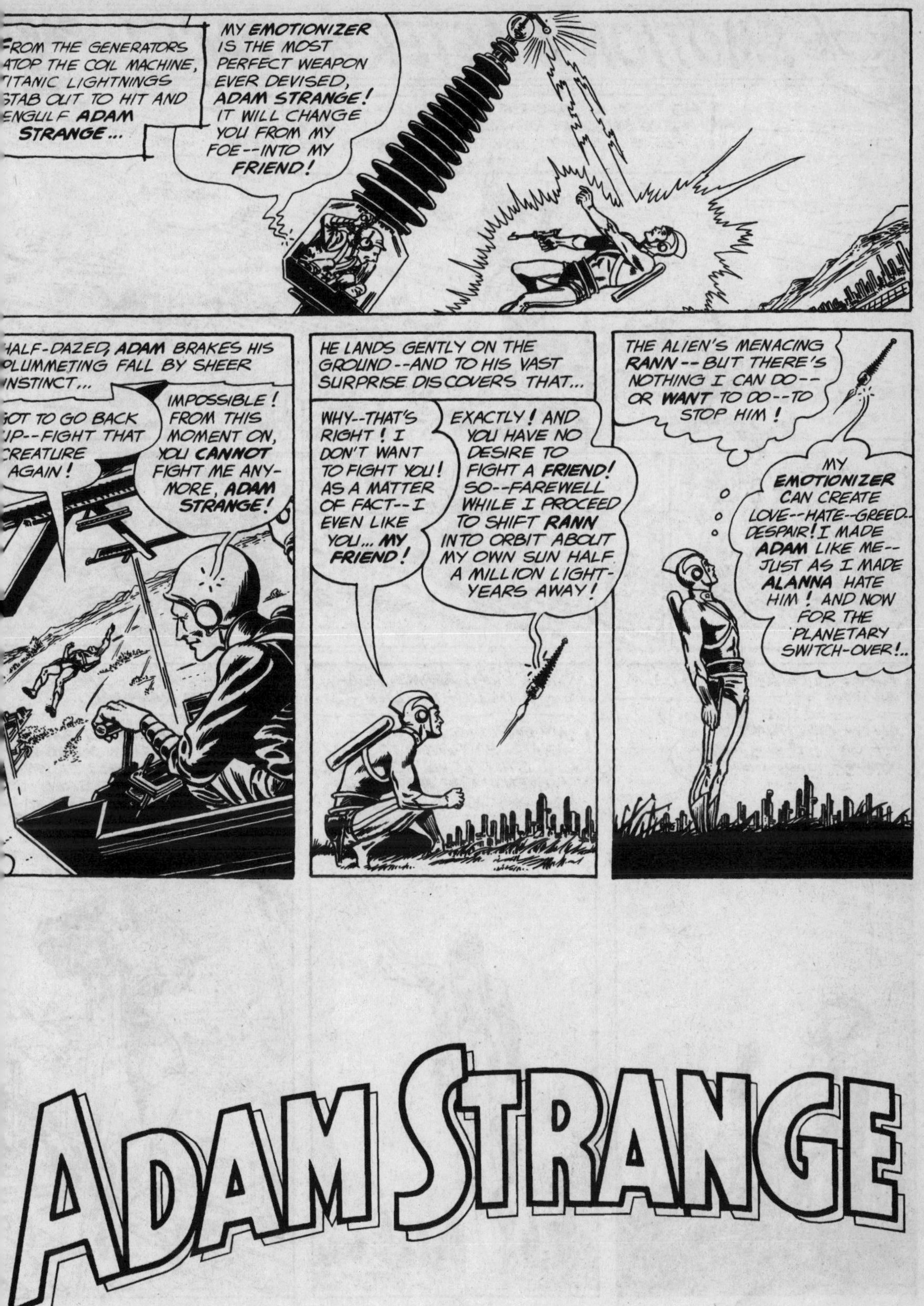
FROM THE GENERATORS ATOP THE COIL MACHINE, TITANIC LIGHTNINGS STAB OUT TO HIT AND ENGULF ADAM STRANGE...
MY EMOTIONIZER IS THE MOST PERFECT WEAPON EVER DEVISED, ADAM STRANGE! IT WILL CHANGE YOU FROM MY FOE--INTO MY FRIEND!
HALF-DAZED, ADAM BRAKES HIS PLUMMETING FALL BY SHEER INSTINCT...
GOT TO GO BACK UP--FIGHT THAT CREATURE AGAIN!
IMPOSSIBLE! FROM THIS MOMENT ON, YOU CANNOT FIGHT ME ANY-MORE, ADAM STRANGE!
HE LANDS GENTLY ON THE GROUND--AND TO HIS VAST SURPRISE DISCOVERS THAT...
WHY--THAT'S RIGHT! I DON'T WANT TO FIGHT YOU! AS A MATTER OF FACT--I EVEN LIKE YOU... MY FRIEND!
EXACTLY! AND YOU HAVE NO DESIRE TO FIGHT A FRIEND! SO--FAREWELL WHILE I PROCEED TO SHIFT RANN INTO ORBIT ABOUT MY OWN SUN HALF A MILLION LIGHT-YEARS AWAY!
THE ALIEN'S MENACING RANN -- BUT THERE'S NOTHING I CAN DO-- OR WANT TO DO--TO STOP HIM!
MY EMOTIONIZER CAN CREATE LOVE--HATE--GREED--DESPAIR! I MADE ADAM LIKE ME--JUST AS I MADE ALANNA HATE HIM! AND NOW FOR THE PLANETARY SWITCH-OVER!..

ADAM STRANGE

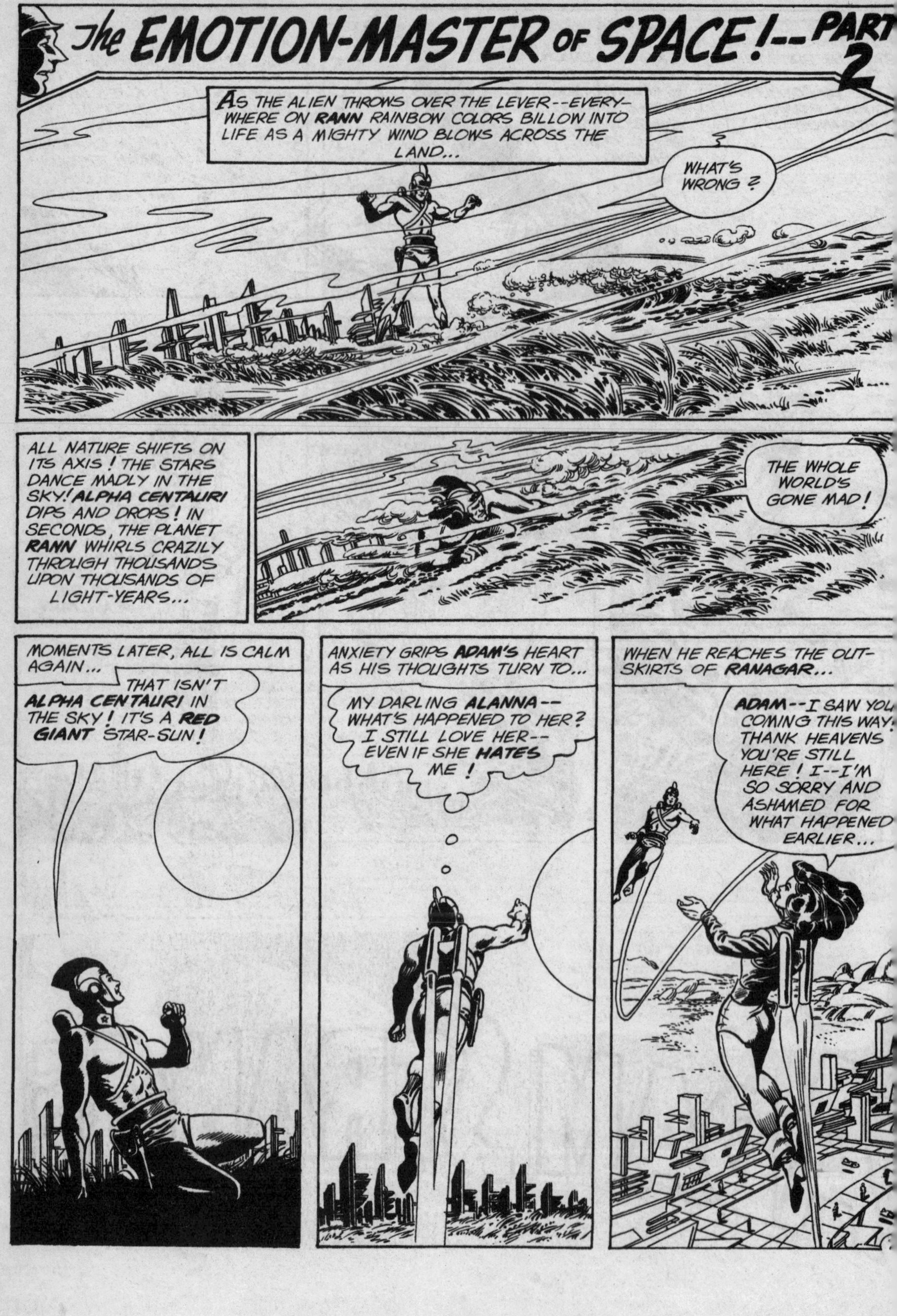

The EMOTION-MASTER OF SPACE!-- PART 2
AS THE ALIEN THROWS OVER THE LEVER--EVERYWHERE ON RANN RAINBOW COLORS BILLOW INTO LIFE AS A MIGHTY WIND BLOWS ACROSS THE LAND...
WHAT'S WRONG ?
ALL NATURE SHIFTS ON ITS AXIS ! THE STARS DANCE MADLY IN THE SKY! ALPHA CENTAURI DIPS AND DROPS ! IN SECONDS, THE PLANET RANN WHIRLS CRAZILY THROUGH THOUSANDS UPON THOUSANDS OF LIGHT-YEARS...
THE WHOLE WORLD'S GONE MAD !
MOMENTS LATER, ALL IS CALM AGAIN...
THAT ISN'T ALPHA CENTAURI IN THE SKY ! IT'S A RED GIANT STAR-SUN !
ANXIETY GRIPS ADAM'S HEART AS HIS THOUGHTS TURN TO...
MY DARLING ALANNA-- WHAT'S HAPPENED TO HER? I STILL LOVE HER-- EVEN IF SHE HATES ME !
WHEN HE REACHES THE OUTSKIRTS OF RANAGAR...
ADAM--I SAW YOU COMING THIS WAY. THANK HEAVENS YOU'RE STILL HERE ! I--I'M SO SORRY AND ASHAMED FOR WHAT HAPPENED EARLIER...

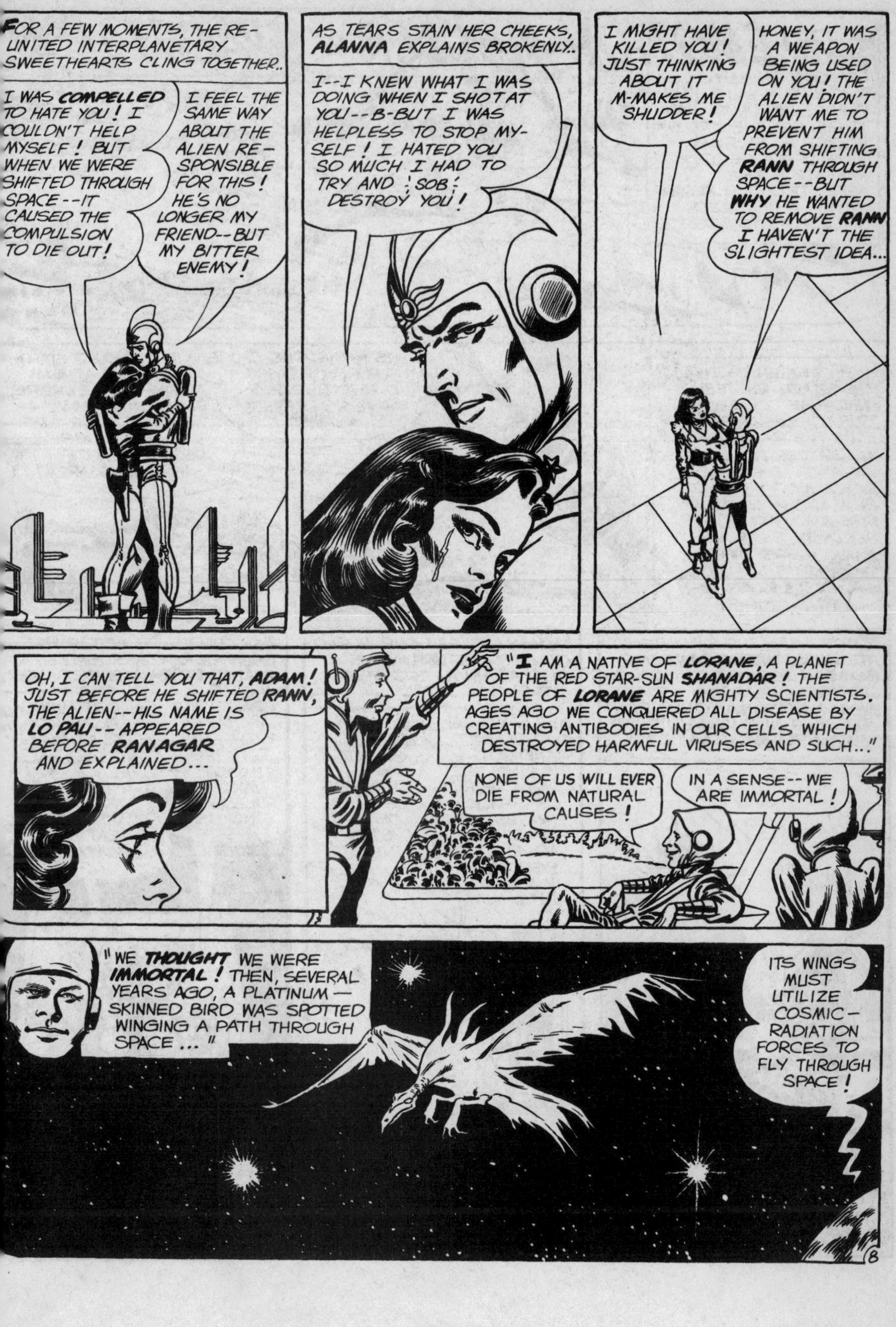
FOR A FEW MOMENTS, THE RE-UNITED INTERPLANETARY SWEETHEARTS CLING TOGETHER..
I WAS COMPELLED TO HATE YOU! I COULDN'T HELP MYSELF! BUT WHEN WE WERE SHIFTED THROUGH SPACE--IT CAUSED THE COMPULSION TO DIE OUT!
I FEEL THE SAME WAY ABOUT THE ALIEN RESPONSIBLE FOR THIS! HE'S NO LONGER MY FRIEND--BUT MY BITTER ENEMY!
AS TEARS STAIN HER CHEEKS, ALANNA EXPLAINS BROKENLY..
I--I KNEW WHAT I WAS DOING WHEN I SHOT AT YOU--B-BUT I WAS HELPLESS TO STOP MYSELF! I HATED YOU SO MUCH I HAD TO TRY AND :SOB: DESTROY YOU!
I MIGHT HAVE KILLED YOU! JUST THINKING ABOUT IT M-MAKES ME SHUDDER!
HONEY, IT WAS A WEAPON BEING USED ON YOU! THE ALIEN DIDN'T WANT ME TO PREVENT HIM FROM SHIFTING RANN THROUGH SPACE--BUT WHY HE WANTED TO REMOVE RANN I HAVEN'T THE SLIGHTEST IDEA...
OH, I CAN TELL YOU THAT, ADAM! JUST BEFORE HE SHIFTED RANN, THE ALIEN--HIS NAME IS LO PAU--APPEARED BEFORE RANAGAR AND EXPLAINED...
"I AM A NATIVE OF LORANE, A PLANET OF THE RED STAR-SUN SHANADAR! THE PEOPLE OF LORANE ARE MIGHTY SCIENTISTS. AGES AGO WE CONQUERED ALL DISEASE BY CREATING ANTIBODIES IN OUR CELLS WHICH DESTROYED HARMFUL VIRUSES AND SUCH..."
NONE OF US WILL EVER DIE FROM NATURAL CAUSES!
IN A SENSE--WE ARE IMMORTAL!
"WE THOUGHT WE WERE IMMORTAL! THEN, SEVERAL YEARS AGO, A PLATINUM-SKINNED BIRD WAS SPOTTED WINGING A PATH THROUGH SPACE..."
ITS WINGS MUST UTILIZE COSMIC-RADIATION FORCES TO FLY THROUGH SPACE!
8

"THE BEAST LANDED ON *LORANE* AND BEGAN FEASTING ON RAW PLATINUM IN WHICH THE PLANET ABOUNDS. AS IT DID SO, THE BIRD'S INGESTIVE SYSTEM GAVE OFF A DEADLY RADIATION THAT AFFECTED OUR PEOPLE WITHIN A HUNDRED MILES OF ITS SOURCE..."

"HAVING EATEN ITS FILL, THE BEAST RESTED WHILE WE COUNTED OUR LOSSES SUFFERED BY THE RADIATION..."

ITS RADIATIONS CAUSE A FORM OF DYING OUR ANTIBODIES HAVE NO DEFENSE AGAINST!

IF IT SHOULD START EATING PLATINUM AGAIN--SOMEWHERE ELSE ON *LORANE*--WE WON'T HAVE TIME TO REMOVE OUR PEOPLE OUT OF THE DANGER AREA!

"ONCE AGAIN THE BIRD-BEAST ATE WHILE WE *LORANEANS* BOMBARDED IT WITH LONG-DISTANCE WEAPONS--TO NO AVAIL! NOTHING COULD DENT THE PLATINUM CREATURE WE CALLED *KALULLA*..."

"*KALULLA* LEFT OUR WORLD ONLY TO RETURN AGAIN AND AGAIN AT TWO-YEAR INTERVALS, UNTIL..."

BY LIVING ON OUR PLANET AND NOT RISKING THE COSMIC PERILS OF SPACE-TRAVEL, WE HAVE MANAGED TO BECOME IMMORTAL... UNTIL NOW!

BUT NOW WE MUST GO INTO SPACE--OR PERISH BECAUSE OF THAT BIRD-BEAST!

WE COULD SHIFT OUR PLANET ELSEWHERE IN SPACE--TO ANOTHER STAR-SUN--BUT THE BEAST MIGHT FOLLOW AND FIND US!

NOT IF WE FOUND A PLANET LIKE OUR OWN--CONTAINING PLENTY OF *PLATINUM*--AND EXCHANGE PLACES WITH IT! *KALULLA* WOULD BE SATISFIED TO EAT *ITS* PLATINUM!

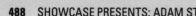

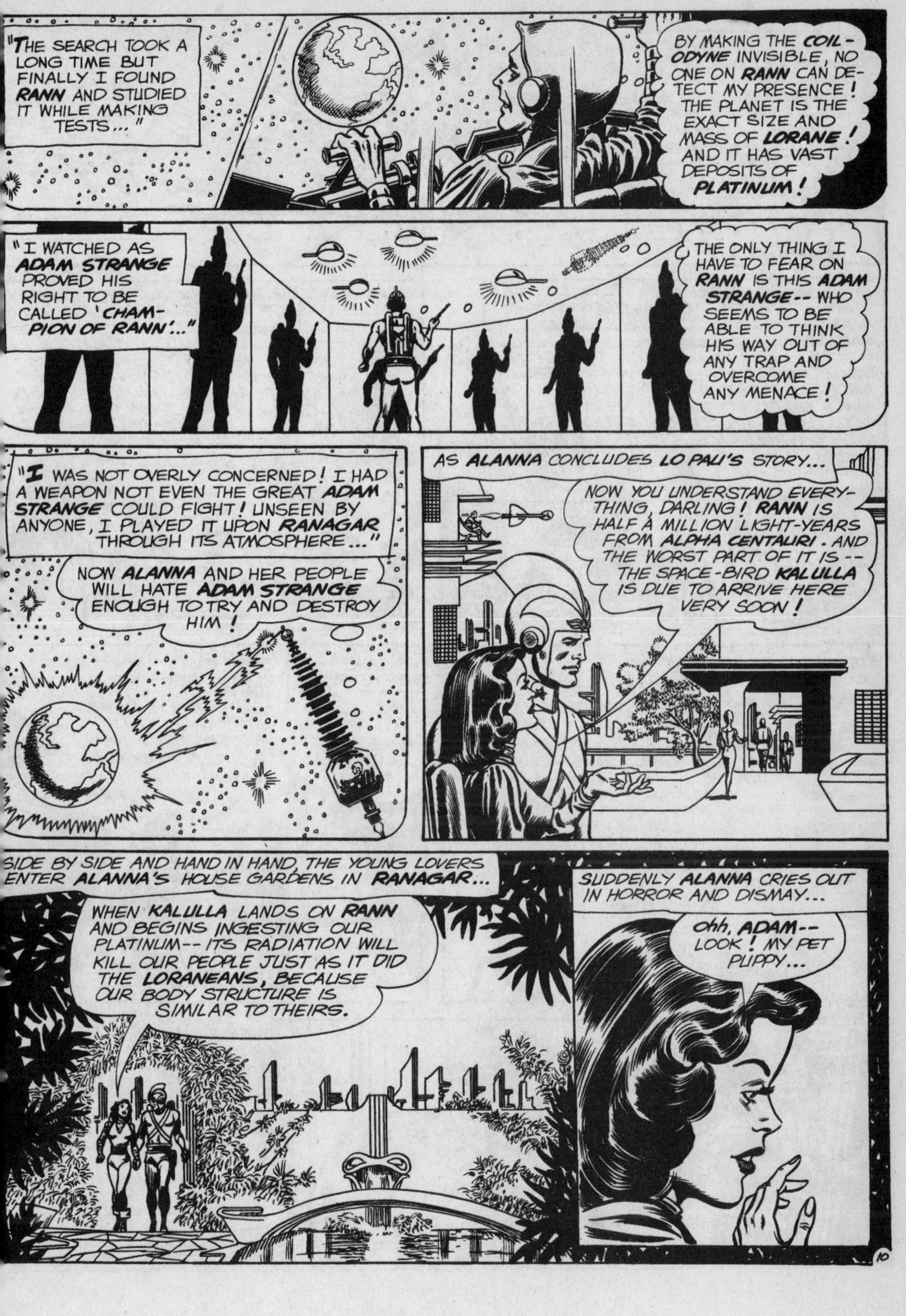
"THE SEARCH TOOK A LONG TIME BUT FINALLY I FOUND RANN AND STUDIED IT WHILE MAKING TESTS..."
BY MAKING THE COIL-ODYNE INVISIBLE, NO ONE ON RANN CAN DETECT MY PRESENCE! THE PLANET IS THE EXACT SIZE AND MASS OF LORANE! AND IT HAS VAST DEPOSITS OF PLATINUM!
"I WATCHED AS ADAM STRANGE PROVED HIS RIGHT TO BE CALLED 'CHAMPION OF RANN'..."
THE ONLY THING I HAVE TO FEAR ON RANN IS THIS ADAM STRANGE-- WHO SEEMS TO BE ABLE TO THINK HIS WAY OUT OF ANY TRAP AND OVERCOME ANY MENACE!
"I WAS NOT OVERLY CONCERNED! I HAD A WEAPON NOT EVEN THE GREAT ADAM STRANGE COULD FIGHT! UNSEEN BY ANYONE, I PLAYED IT UPON RANAGAR THROUGH ITS ATMOSPHERE..."
NOW ALANNA AND HER PEOPLE WILL HATE ADAM STRANGE ENOUGH TO TRY AND DESTROY HIM!
AS ALANNA CONCLUDES LO PALI'S STORY...
NOW YOU UNDERSTAND EVERYTHING, DARLING! RANN IS HALF A MILLION LIGHT-YEARS FROM ALPHA CENTAURI. AND THE WORST PART OF IT IS -- THE SPACE-BIRD KALULLA IS DUE TO ARRIVE HERE VERY SOON!
SIDE BY SIDE AND HAND IN HAND, THE YOUNG LOVERS ENTER ALANNA'S HOUSE GARDENS IN RANAGAR...
WHEN KALULLA LANDS ON RANN AND BEGINS INGESTING OUR PLATINUM-- ITS RADIATION WILL KILL OUR PEOPLE JUST AS IT DID THE LORANEANS, BECAUSE OUR BODY STRUCTURE IS SIMILAR TO THEIRS.
SUDDENLY ALANNA CRIES OUT IN HORROR AND DISMAY...
Ohh, ADAM-- LOOK! MY PET PUPPY...
10

FALLING TO HER KNEES, SHE GATHERS HER PET INTO HER ARMS...

IT...IS DEAD! WHAT COULD HAVE CAUSED IT...?

IT WAS EATING THIS HERB-- THE PLANT YOU CALL *ATHATALE* Hmmm--I WONDER?

WITHIN MINUTES, **ADAM** IS IN THE PRIVATE LABORATORY ATTACHED TO THE HOME OF **ALANNA** AND HER SCIENTIST FATHER, **SARDATH**...

THE SUDDEN SHIFT THROUGH INTERSTELLAR SPACE AFFECTED THE MOLECULAR STRUCTURE OF THE *ATHATALE*-- TURNED IT INTO A DEADLY POISON!

I--I'D BETTER WARN EVERYONE! AND--WE'LL MAKE TESTS OF THE OTHER PLANTS, TOO! M-MAYBE ALL OUR VEGETABLES AND PLANTS HAVE BEEN POISONED!

SOME HOURS LATER, WHEN THE FULL SCIEN-TIFIC GENIUS OF **RANAGAR** HAS BEEN CALLED INTO PLAY...

FORTUNATELY *ATHATALE* IS THE **ONLY** HERB THAT BE-CAME POISONOUS AS A RE-SULT OF THE TRANSFER IN SPACE! WHEN IT IS EATEN, IT KILLS **ALL** LIFE-FORMS...

...WHICH GIVES ME AN IDEA! IF WE SMEAR THIS POISON EXTRACTED FROM THE *ATHATALE* PLANTS OVER EVERY PLATINUM DEPOSIT ON **RANN**-- WHEN THE SPACE-BIRD COMES TO EAT--THE POISON WILL DESTROY IT! WE MUST MAKE A LOT OF THIS POISON AS FAST AS POSSIBLE!

BUT--BEFORE **ADAM'S** PLAN CAN BE CARRIED OUT...

I'VE CHECKED OUT ALL THE PLATINUM DEPOSITS AND...

ADAM, THERE'S NO TIME TO PUT YOUR PLAN INTO OPERATION! OUR ASTRONOMERS HAVE SIGHTED **KALULLA** FLYING THROUGH SPACE TOWARD **RANN**!

THEN I HAVE TO GO INTO SPACE TO HIT THE BIRD-BEAST WITH SPECIAL HARPOONS-- COATED ALL OVER WITH THAT POISON! I MUST TRY AND PREVENT IT FROM LANDING ON **RANN**! WE CAN'T WAIT UNTIL IT LANDS AND THEN COAT THE PLATINUM IT IS EATING BECAUSE WE'D BE IMMEDIATELY KILLED BY ITS INGESTIVE RADIATION!

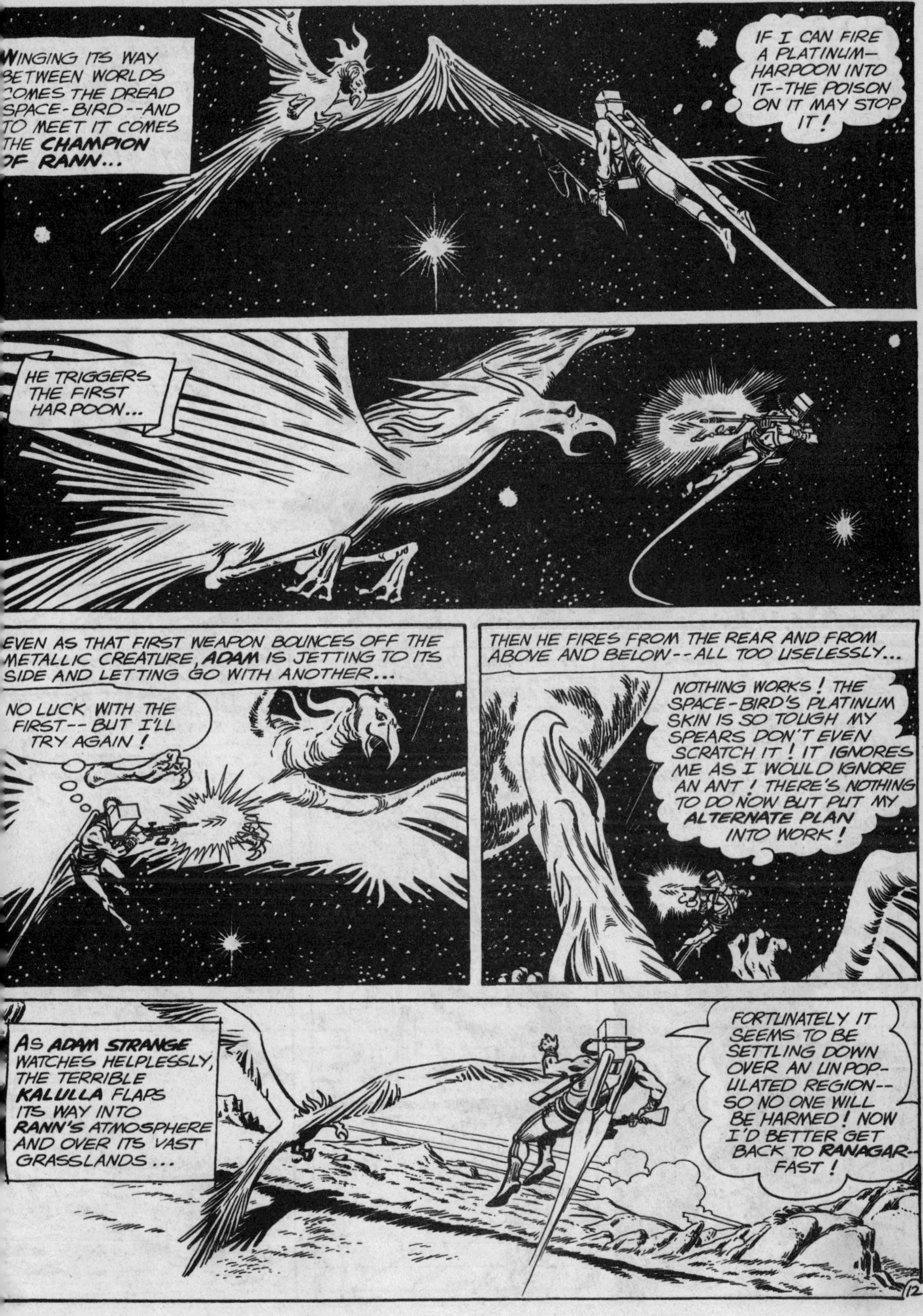
WINGING ITS WAY BETWEEN WORLDS COMES THE DREAD SPACE-BIRD--AND TO MEET IT COMES THE CHAMPION OF RANN...
IF I CAN FIRE A PLATINUM-HARPOON INTO IT--THE POISON ON IT MAY STOP IT!
HE TRIGGERS THE FIRST HARPOON...
EVEN AS THAT FIRST WEAPON BOUNCES OFF THE METALLIC CREATURE, ADAM IS JETTING TO ITS SIDE AND LETTING GO WITH ANOTHER...
NO LUCK WITH THE FIRST--BUT I'LL TRY AGAIN!
THEN HE FIRES FROM THE REAR AND FROM ABOVE AND BELOW--ALL TOO USELESSLY...
NOTHING WORKS! THE SPACE-BIRD'S PLATINUM SKIN IS SO TOUGH MY SPEARS DON'T EVEN SCRATCH IT! IT IGNORES ME AS I WOULD IGNORE AN ANT! THERE'S NOTHING TO DO NOW BUT PUT MY ALTERNATE PLAN INTO WORK!
AS ADAM STRANGE WATCHES HELPLESSLY, THE TERRIBLE KALULLA FLAPS ITS WAY INTO RANN'S ATMOSPHERE AND OVER ITS VAST GRASSLANDS...
FORTUNATELY IT SEEMS TO BE SETTLING DOWN OVER AN UNPOPULATED REGION--SO NO ONE WILL BE HARMED! NOW I'D BETTER GET BACK TO RANAGAR-FAST!
12

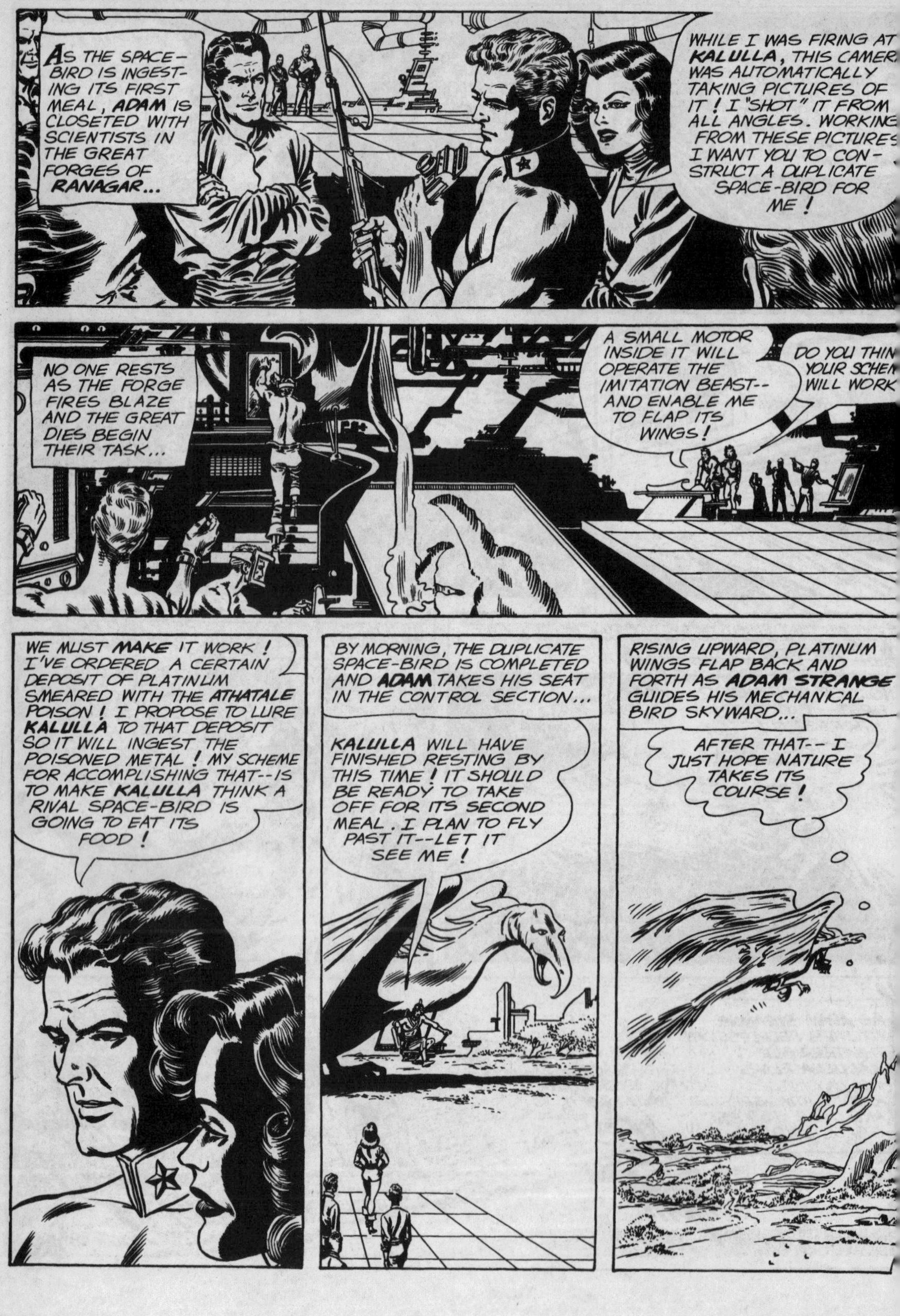
AS THE SPACE-BIRD IS INGESTING ITS FIRST MEAL, ADAM IS CLOSETED WITH SCIENTISTS IN THE GREAT FORGES OF RANAGAR...
WHILE I WAS FIRING AT KALULLA, THIS CAMER WAS AUTOMATICALLY TAKING PICTURES OF IT! I "SHOT" IT FROM ALL ANGLES. WORKING FROM THESE PICTURES I WANT YOU TO CONSTRUCT A DUPLICATE SPACE-BIRD FOR ME!
NO ONE RESTS AS THE FORGE FIRES BLAZE AND THE GREAT DIES BEGIN THEIR TASK...
A SMALL MOTOR INSIDE IT WILL OPERATE THE IMITATION BEAST--AND ENABLE ME TO FLAP ITS WINGS!
DO YOU THIN YOUR SCHEM WILL WORK
WE MUST MAKE IT WORK! I'VE ORDERED A CERTAIN DEPOSIT OF PLATINUM SMEARED WITH THE ATHATALE POISON! I PROPOSE TO LURE KALULLA TO THAT DEPOSIT SO IT WILL INGEST THE POISONED METAL! MY SCHEME FOR ACCOMPLISHING THAT--IS TO MAKE KALULLA THINK A RIVAL SPACE-BIRD IS GOING TO EAT ITS FOOD!
BY MORNING, THE DUPLICATE SPACE-BIRD IS COMPLETED AND ADAM TAKES HIS SEAT IN THE CONTROL SECTION...
KALULLA WILL HAVE FINISHED RESTING BY THIS TIME! IT SHOULD BE READY TO TAKE OFF FOR ITS SECOND MEAL. I PLAN TO FLY PAST IT--LET IT SEE ME!
RISING UPWARD, PLATINUM WINGS FLAP BACK AND FORTH AS ADAM STRANGE GUIDES HIS MECHANICAL BIRD SKYWARD...
AFTER THAT-- I JUST HOPE NATURE TAKES ITS COURSE!

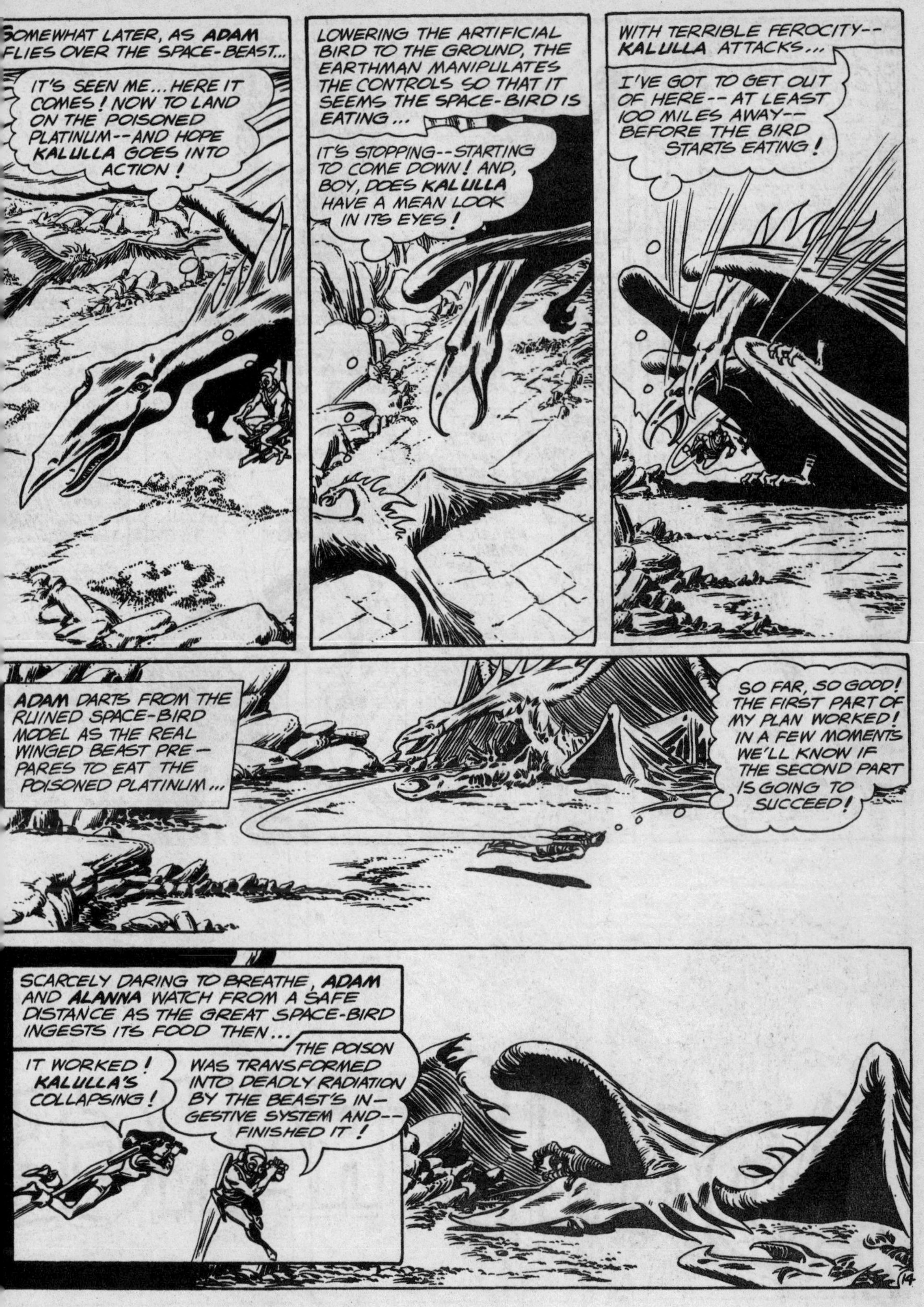
SOMEWHAT LATER, AS ADAM FLIES OVER THE SPACE-BEAST...
IT'S SEEN ME... HERE IT COMES! NOW TO LAND ON THE POISONED PLATINUM--AND HOPE KALULLA GOES INTO ACTION!
LOWERING THE ARTIFICIAL BIRD TO THE GROUND, THE EARTHMAN MANIPULATES THE CONTROLS SO THAT IT SEEMS THE SPACE-BIRD IS EATING...
IT'S STOPPING--STARTING TO COME DOWN! AND, BOY, DOES KALULLA HAVE A MEAN LOOK IN ITS EYES!
WITH TERRIBLE FEROCITY--KALULLA ATTACKS...
I'VE GOT TO GET OUT OF HERE--AT LEAST 100 MILES AWAY--BEFORE THE BIRD STARTS EATING!
ADAM DARTS FROM THE RUINED SPACE-BIRD MODEL AS THE REAL WINGED BEAST PRE-PARES TO EAT THE POISONED PLATINUM...
SO FAR, SO GOOD! THE FIRST PART OF MY PLAN WORKED! IN A FEW MOMENTS WE'LL KNOW IF THE SECOND PART IS GOING TO SUCCEED!
SCARCELY DARING TO BREATHE, ADAM AND ALANNA WATCH FROM A SAFE DISTANCE AS THE GREAT SPACE-BIRD INGESTS ITS FOOD THEN...
IT WORKED! KALULLA'S COLLAPSING!
THE POISON WAS TRANSFORMED INTO DEADLY RADIATION BY THE BEAST'S IN-GESTIVE SYSTEM AND--FINISHED IT!
14

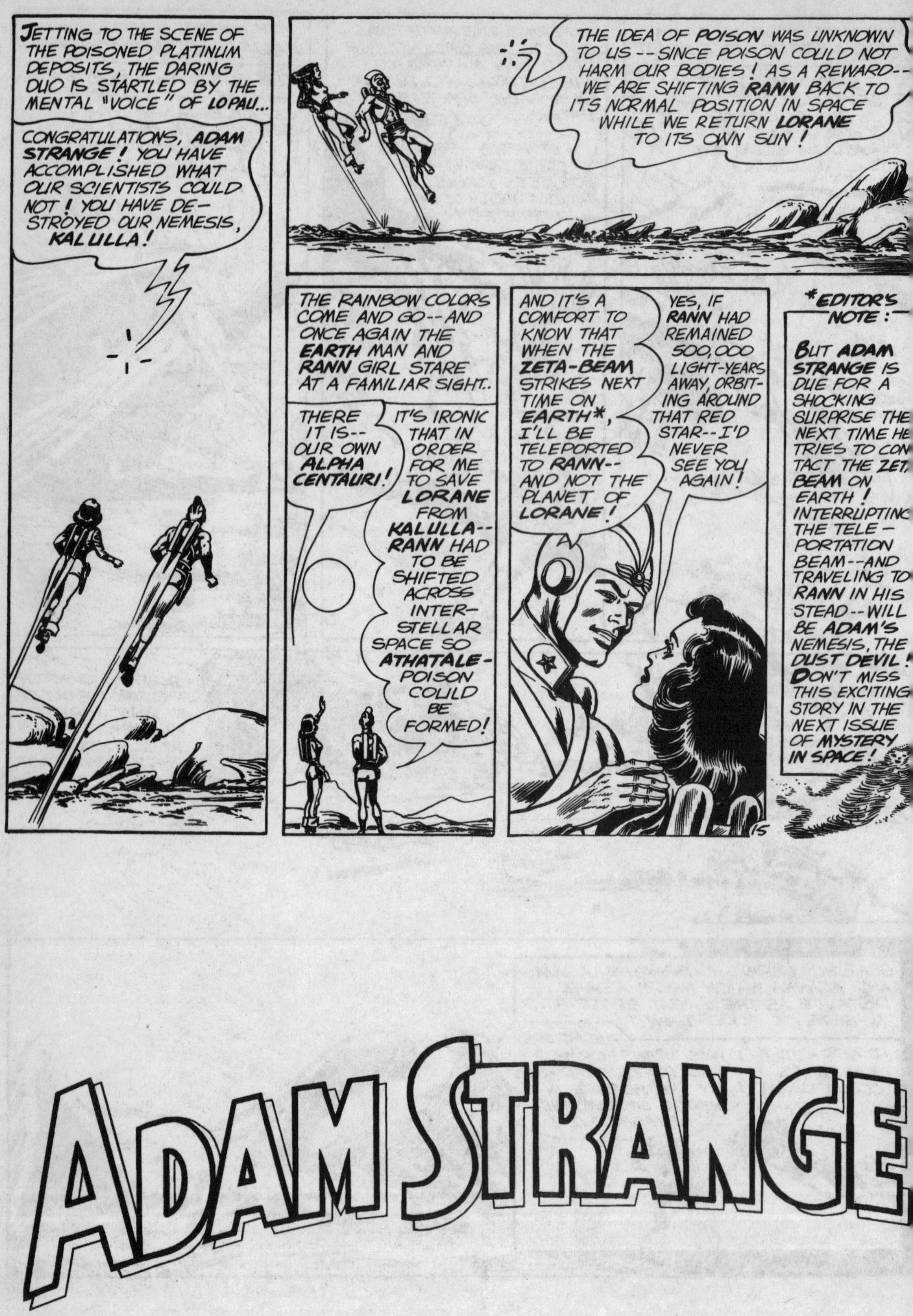
JETTING TO THE SCENE OF THE POISONED PLATINUM DEPOSITS, THE DARING DUO IS STARTLED BY THE MENTAL "VOICE" OF LOPAU...
CONGRATULATIONS, ADAM STRANGE! YOU HAVE ACCOMPLISHED WHAT OUR SCIENTISTS COULD NOT! YOU HAVE DESTROYED OUR NEMESIS, KALULLA!
THE IDEA OF POISON WAS UNKNOWN TO US -- SINCE POISON COULD NOT HARM OUR BODIES! AS A REWARD-- WE ARE SHIFTING RANN BACK TO ITS NORMAL POSITION IN SPACE WHILE WE RETURN LORANE TO ITS OWN SUN!
THE RAINBOW COLORS COME AND GO--AND ONCE AGAIN THE EARTH MAN AND RANN GIRL STARE AT A FAMILIAR SIGHT..
THERE IT IS-- OUR OWN ALPHA CENTAURI!
IT'S IRONIC THAT IN ORDER FOR ME TO SAVE LORANE FROM KALULLA--RANN HAD TO BE SHIFTED ACROSS INTERSTELLAR SPACE SO ATHATALE-POISON COULD BE FORMED!
AND IT'S A COMFORT TO KNOW THAT WHEN THE ZETA-BEAM STRIKES NEXT TIME ON EARTH*, I'LL BE TELEPORTED TO RANN--AND NOT THE PLANET OF LORANE!
YES, IF RANN HAD REMAINED 500,000 LIGHT-YEARS AWAY, ORBITING AROUND THAT RED STAR--I'D NEVER SEE YOU AGAIN!
15
*EDITOR'S NOTE: BUT ADAM STRANGE IS DUE FOR A SHOCKING SURPRISE THE NEXT TIME HE TRIES TO CON TACT THE ZET BEAM ON EARTH! INTERRUPTING THE TELE-PORTATION BEAM--AND TRAVELING TO RANN IN HIS STEAD--WILL BE ADAM'S NEMESIS, THE DUST DEVIL! DON'T MISS THIS EXCITING STORY IN THE NEXT ISSUE OF MYSTERY IN SPACE!

ADAM STRANGE

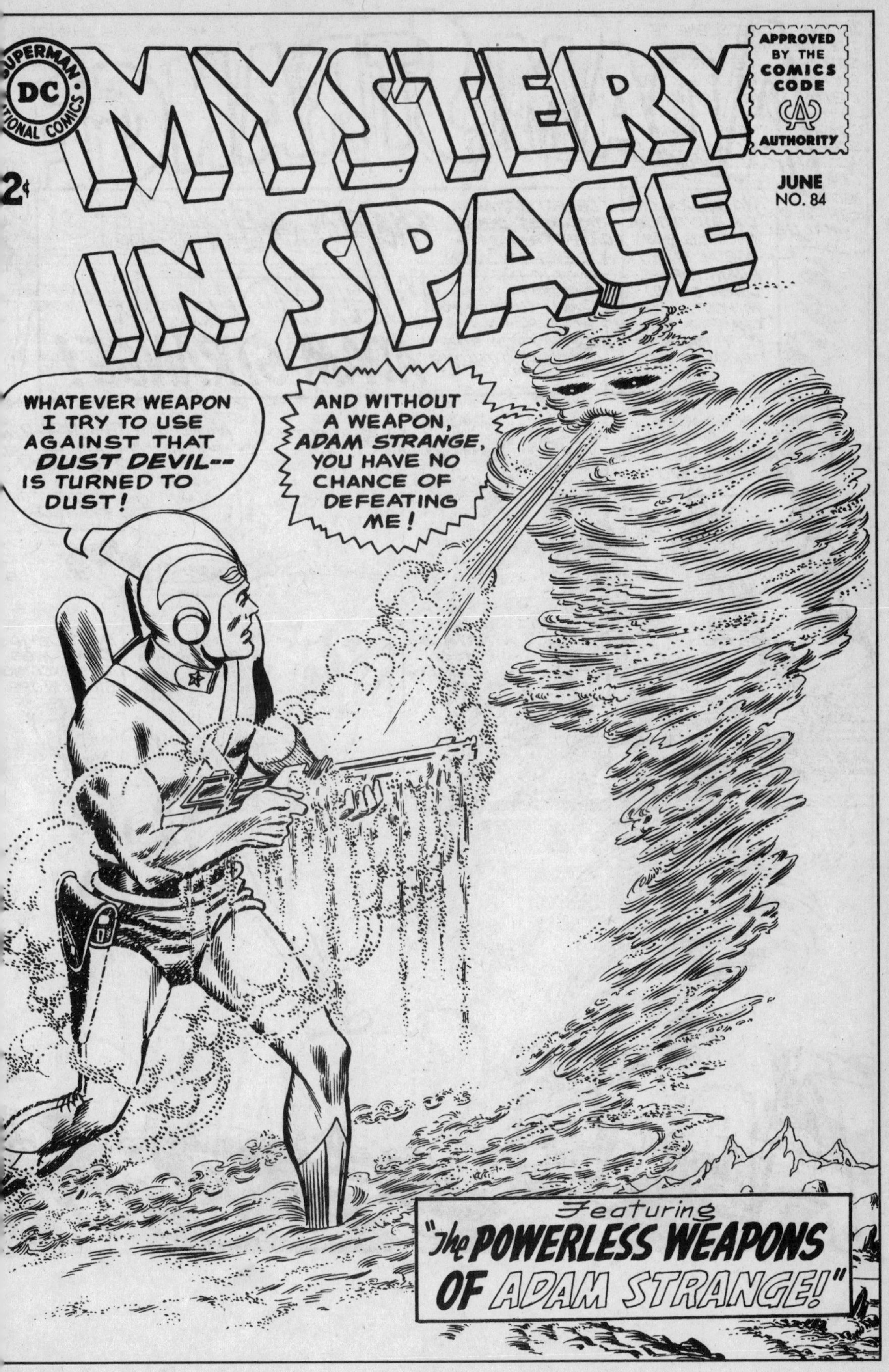
SUPERMAN DC NATIONAL COMICS
MYSTERY IN SPACE
APPROVED BY THE COMICS CODE AUTHORITY
2¢
JUNE NO. 84
WHATEVER WEAPON I TRY TO USE AGAINST THAT DUST DEVIL-- IS TURNED TO DUST!
AND WITHOUT A WEAPON, ADAM STRANGE, YOU HAVE NO CHANCE OF DEFEATING ME!
Featuring "The POWERLESS WEAPONS OF ADAM STRANGE!"

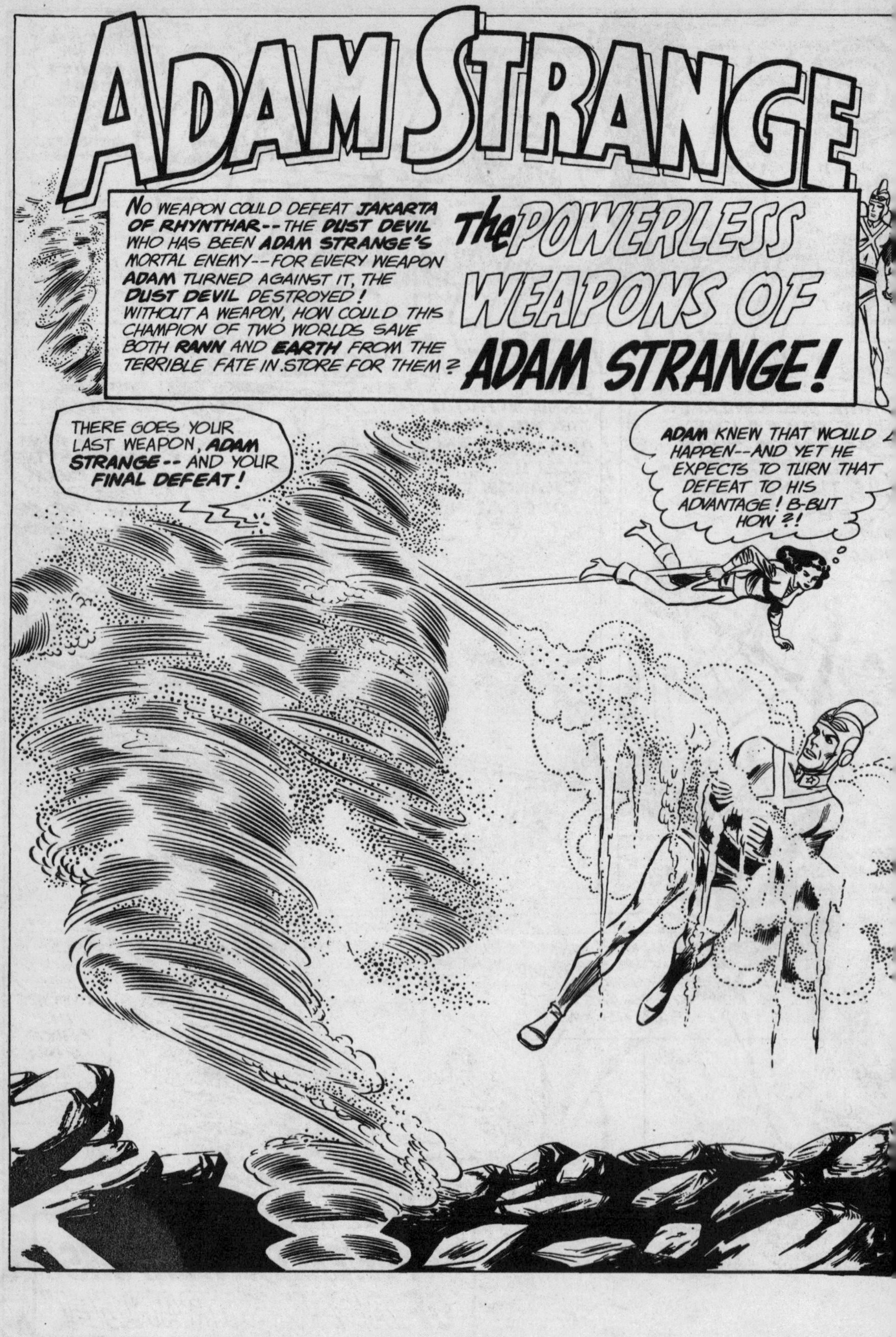
ADAM STRANGE
NO WEAPON COULD DEFEAT JAKARTA OF RHYNTHAR--THE DUST DEVIL WHO HAS BEEN ADAM STRANGE'S MORTAL ENEMY--FOR EVERY WEAPON ADAM TURNED AGAINST IT, THE DUST DEVIL DESTROYED! WITHOUT A WEAPON, HOW COULD THIS CHAMPION OF TWO WORLDS SAVE BOTH RANN AND EARTH FROM THE TERRIBLE FATE IN STORE FOR THEM?
The POWERLESS WEAPONS OF ADAM STRANGE!
THERE GOES YOUR LAST WEAPON, ADAM STRANGE--AND YOUR FINAL DEFEAT!
ADAM KNEW THAT WOULD HAPPEN--AND YET HE EXPECTS TO TURN THAT DEFEAT TO HIS ADVANTAGE! B-BUT HOW?!

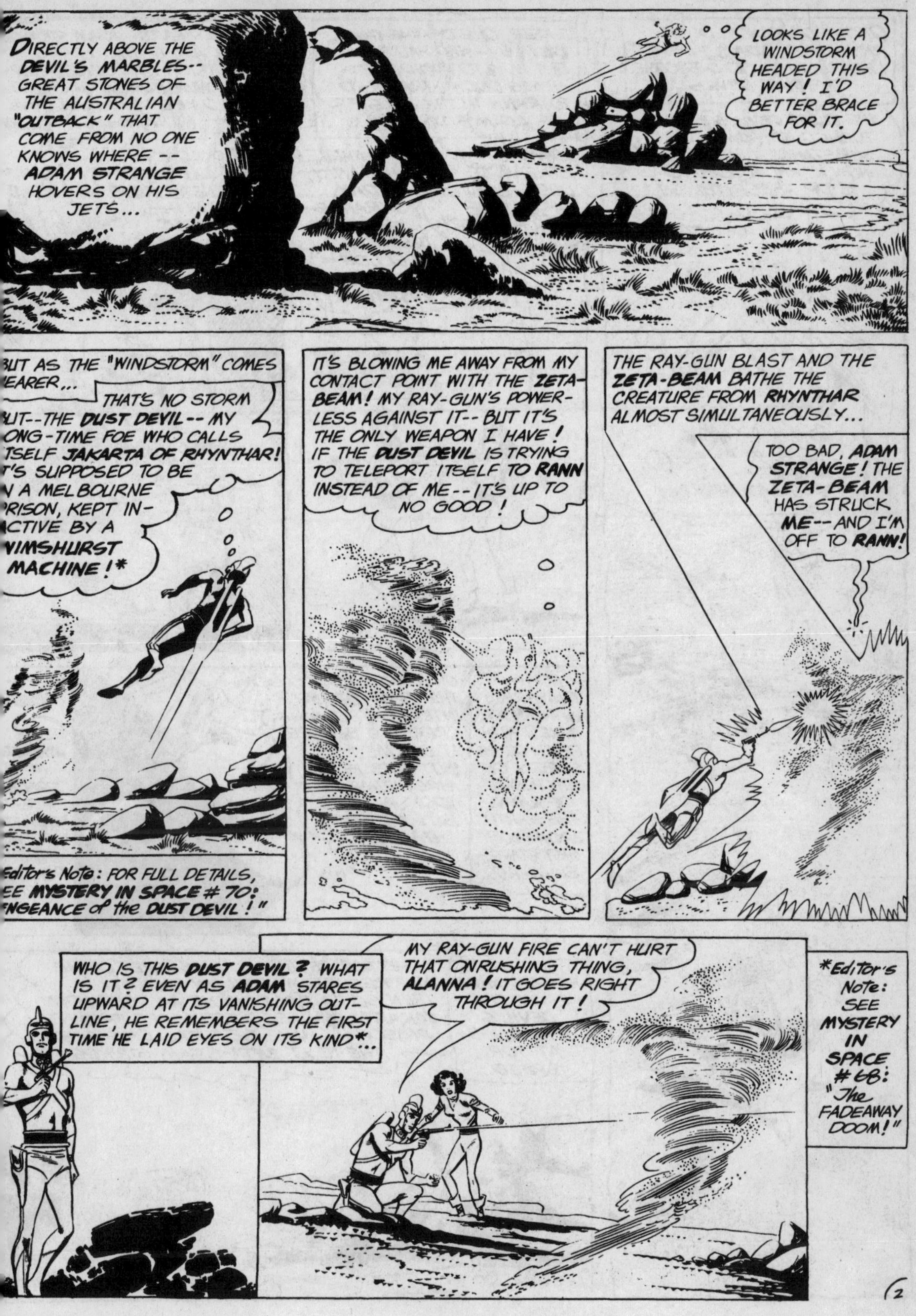
DIRECTLY ABOVE THE DEVIL'S MARBLES-- GREAT STONES OF THE AUSTRALIAN "OUTBACK" THAT COME FROM NO ONE KNOWS WHERE -- ADAM STRANGE HOVERS ON HIS JETS...
LOOKS LIKE A WINDSTORM HEADED THIS WAY! I'D BETTER BRACE FOR IT.
BUT AS THE "WINDSTORM" COMES NEARER...
THAT'S NO STORM BUT--THE DUST DEVIL-- MY LONG-TIME FOE WHO CALLS ITSELF JAKARTA OF RHYNTHAR! IT'S SUPPOSED TO BE IN A MELBOURNE PRISON, KEPT INACTIVE BY A WIMSHURST MACHINE!*
Editor's Note: FOR FULL DETAILS, SEE MYSTERY IN SPACE #70: "VENGEANCE of the DUST DEVIL!"
IT'S BLOWING ME AWAY FROM MY CONTACT POINT WITH THE ZETA-BEAM! MY RAY-GUN'S POWERLESS AGAINST IT-- BUT IT'S THE ONLY WEAPON I HAVE! IF THE DUST DEVIL IS TRYING TO TELEPORT ITSELF TO RANN INSTEAD OF ME--IT'S UP TO NO GOOD!
THE RAY-GUN BLAST AND THE ZETA-BEAM BATHE THE CREATURE FROM RHYNTHAR ALMOST SIMULTANEOUSLY...
TOO BAD, ADAM STRANGE! THE ZETA-BEAM HAS STRUCK ME--AND I'M OFF TO RANN!
WHO IS THIS DUST DEVIL? WHAT IS IT? EVEN AS ADAM STARES UPWARD AT ITS VANISHING OUTLINE, HE REMEMBERS THE FIRST TIME HE LAID EYES ON ITS KIND*...
MY RAY-GUN FIRE CAN'T HURT THAT ONRUSHING THING, ALANNA! IT GOES RIGHT THROUGH IT!
*Editor's Note: SEE MYSTERY IN SPACE #68: "The FADEAWAY DOOM!"
2

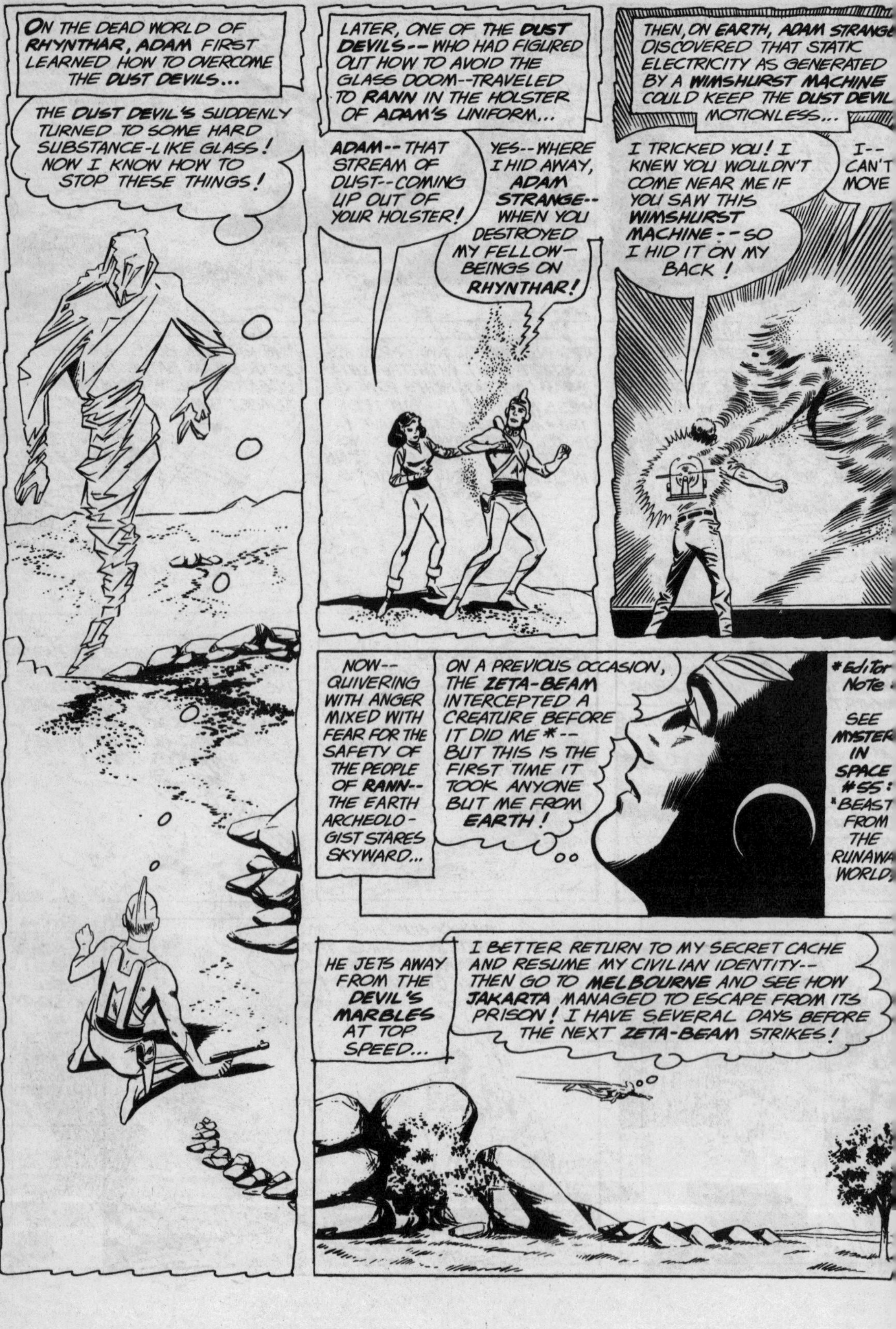

ON THE DEAD WORLD OF RHYNTHAR, ADAM FIRST LEARNED HOW TO OVERCOME THE DUST DEVILS...
THE DUST DEVIL'S SUDDENLY TURNED TO SOME HARD SUBSTANCE-LIKE GLASS! NOW I KNOW HOW TO STOP THESE THINGS!
LATER, ONE OF THE DUST DEVILS-- WHO HAD FIGURED OUT HOW TO AVOID THE GLASS DOOM--TRAVELED TO RANN IN THE HOLSTER OF ADAM'S UNIFORM...
ADAM-- THAT STREAM OF DUST--COMING UP OUT OF YOUR HOLSTER!
YES--WHERE I HID AWAY, ADAM STRANGE-- WHEN YOU DESTROYED MY FELLOW-BEINGS ON RHYNTHAR!
THEN, ON EARTH, ADAM STRANGE DISCOVERED THAT STATIC ELECTRICITY AS GENERATED BY A WIMSHURST MACHINE COULD KEEP THE DUST DEVIL MOTIONLESS...
I TRICKED YOU! I KNEW YOU WOULDN'T COME NEAR ME IF YOU SAW THIS WIMSHURST MACHINE--SO I HID IT ON MY BACK!
I-- CAN'T MOVE
NOW-- QUIVERING WITH ANGER MIXED WITH FEAR FOR THE SAFETY OF THE PEOPLE OF RANN-- THE EARTH ARCHEOLOGIST STARES SKYWARD...
ON A PREVIOUS OCCASION, THE ZETA-BEAM INTERCEPTED A CREATURE BEFORE IT DID ME *-- BUT THIS IS THE FIRST TIME IT TOOK ANYONE BUT ME FROM EARTH!
* Editor Note: SEE MYSTERY IN SPACE #55: "BEAST FROM THE RUNAWAY WORLD,
HE JETS AWAY FROM THE DEVIL'S MARBLES AT TOP SPEED...
I BETTER RETURN TO MY SECRET CACHE AND RESUME MY CIVILIAN IDENTITY-- THEN GO TO MELBOURNE AND SEE HOW JAKARTA MANAGED TO ESCAPE FROM ITS PRISON! I HAVE SEVERAL DAYS BEFORE THE NEXT ZETA-BEAM STRIKES!

FEW HOURS AFTERWARD, AT A LABORATORY-PRISON IN MEL-BOURNE, AUSTRALIA...

THERE WAS A POWER SHORTAGE HERE CAUSED BY AN ELECTRICAL STORM. SINCE THE *WIMSHURST MACHINE* THAT IMMOBILIZED THE *DUST DEVIL* WAS OPERATED BY ELECTRICITY, IT STOPPED WORKING-- ENABLING THE *DUST DEVIL* TO ESCAPE!

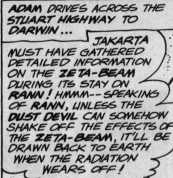

ADAM DRIVES ACROSS THE *STUART HIGHWAY* TO *DARWIN*...

JAKARTA MUST HAVE GATHERED DETAILED INFORMATION ON THE *ZETA-BEAM* DURING ITS STAY ON *RANN!* HMMM--SPEAKING OF *RANN*, UNLESS THE *DUST DEVIL* CAN SOMEHOW SHAKE OFF THE EFFECTS OF THE *ZETA-BEAM*, IT'LL BE DRAWN BACK TO EARTH WHEN THE RADIATION WEARS OFF!

FROM *DARWIN* HE TAKES A JET-PLANE TO *CAPETOWN, SOUTH AFRICA*...

THE *DUST DEVIL* WANTED TO TAKE OVER BOTH *RANN* AND *EARTH* IN THE PAST! IT PROBABLY STILL WANTS TO-- SO IT'LL HAVE TO FIGURE OUT A WAY BY WHICH IT CAN TRAVEL BACK AND FORTH BETWEEN BOTH WORLDS!

BY JEEP HE MOTORS NORTH-WARD ALONG THE *MOLOPO RIVER* TOWARD THE *KALAHARI DESERT*...

FOR ALL I KNOW, JAKARTA MAY OVERCOME RANN BEFORE I HAVE A CHANCE TO STOP IT! I HAVE ANOTHER WORRY, TOO! THE *DUST DEVIL* MAY RETURN TO *EARTH* AND CONQUER IT WHILE I'M ON *RANN!*

ABOVE THE SANDS OF *KALAHARI*, SOME DAYS LATER...

HERE COMES JAKARTA NOW! IT MUST HAVE RETURNED TO EARTH WHEN THE *ZETA-BEAM* WORE OFF! IT'S TRYING TO BEAT ME TO THE *ZETA-BEAM* AGAIN. BUT THIS TIME I'M READY FOR MY FOE!

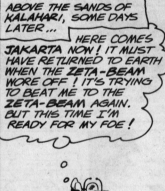

I'LL BATTLE IT HERE ON EARTH--AND PREVENT IT FROM RETURN-ING TO *RANN* TO COMPLETE ITS CONQUEST OF THAT PLANET! THIS *WIMSHURST MACHINE* I BROUGHT WITH ME WILL STOP JAKARTA COLD!

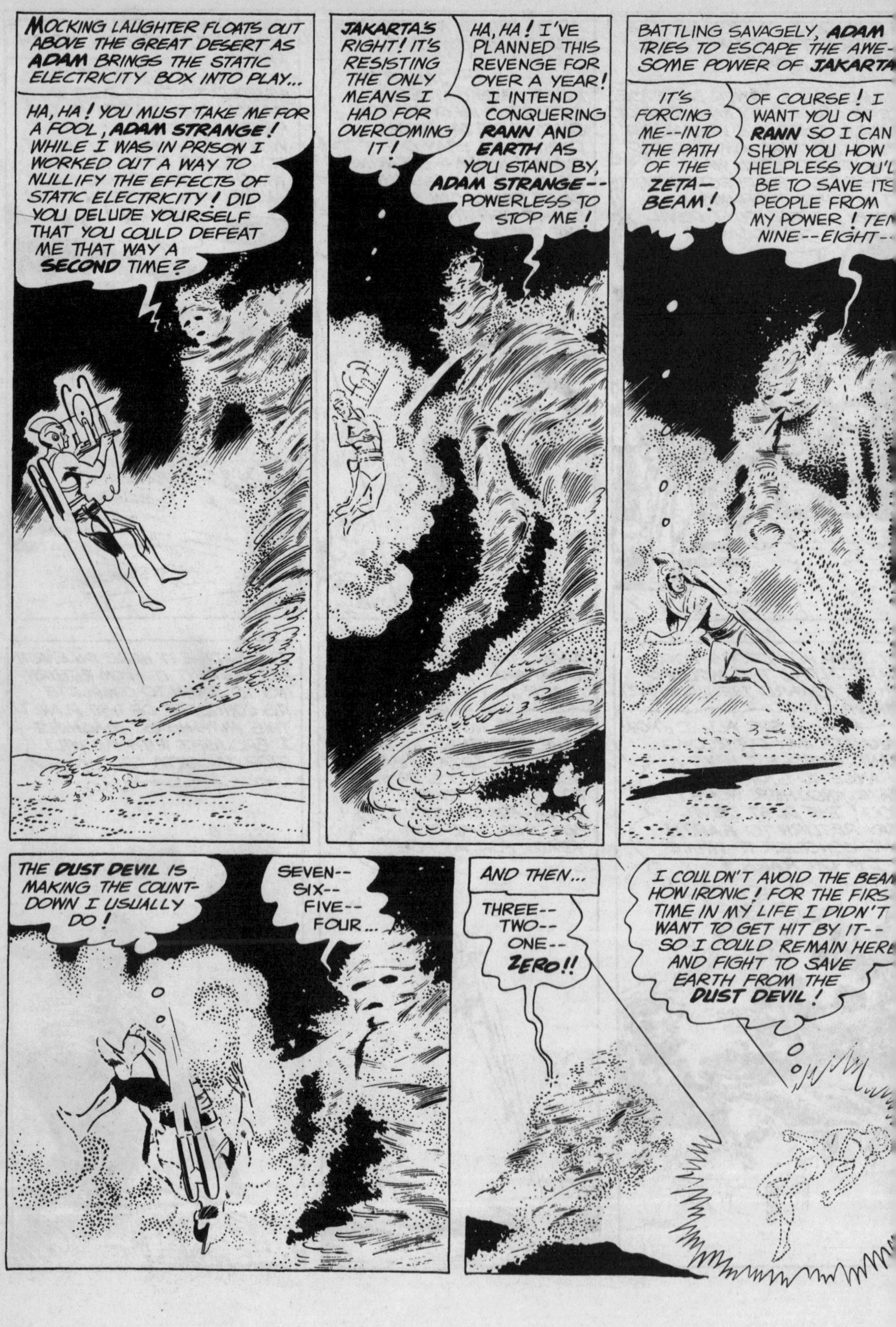
MOCKING LAUGHTER FLOATS OUT ABOVE THE GREAT DESERT AS ADAM BRINGS THE STATIC ELECTRICITY BOX INTO PLAY...
HA, HA! YOU MUST TAKE ME FOR A FOOL, ADAM STRANGE! WHILE I WAS IN PRISON I WORKED OUT A WAY TO NULLIFY THE EFFECTS OF STATIC ELECTRICITY! DID YOU DELUDE YOURSELF THAT YOU COULD DEFEAT ME THAT WAY A SECOND TIME?
JAKARTA'S RIGHT! IT'S RESISTING THE ONLY MEANS I HAD FOR OVERCOMING IT!
HA, HA! I'VE PLANNED THIS REVENGE FOR OVER A YEAR! I INTEND CONQUERING RANN AND EARTH AS YOU STAND BY, ADAM STRANGE--POWERLESS TO STOP ME!
BATTLING SAVAGELY, ADAM TRIES TO ESCAPE THE AWESOME POWER OF JAKARTA
IT'S FORCING ME--INTO THE PATH OF THE ZETA-BEAM!
OF COURSE! I WANT YOU ON RANN SO I CAN SHOW YOU HOW HELPLESS YOU'L BE TO SAVE ITS PEOPLE FROM MY POWER! TEN NINE--EIGHT--
THE DUST DEVIL IS MAKING THE COUNT-DOWN I USUALLY DO!
SEVEN--SIX--FIVE--FOUR...
AND THEN...
THREE--TWO--ONE--ZERO!!
I COULDN'T AVOID THE BEAM HOW IRONIC! FOR THE FIRS TIME IN MY LIFE I DIDN'T WANT TO GET HIT BY IT--SO I COULD REMAIN HERE AND FIGHT TO SAVE EARTH FROM THE DUST DEVIL!

INSTANTLY THE EARTHMAN IS TELEPORTED ACROSS 25 TRILLION MILES OF INTER-STELLAR SPACE TO THE PLANET *RANN* OF THE STAR-SUN *ALPHA CENTAURI*-- WHERE HE HAS GONE MANY TIMES BEFORE TO MEET HIS SWEETHEART *ALANNA OF RANAGAR* AND SHARE THE DANGERS THAT CONFRONT HER WORLD...

AS HE LANDS ON *RANN*, HE IS WARMLY GREETED BY *ALANNA*...

I MAY HAVE WANTED TO MISS THE *ZETA-BEAM*--BUT I SURE DIDN'T WANT TO MISS *THIS*!

HONEY, I LEFT THE *DUST DEVIL* BACK ON EARTH, BUT WHAT HAPPENED WHILE IT CAME TO *RANN* IN MY PLACE--?

Y-YOU LEFT IT BACK ON *EARTH*?! BUT, ADAM--THE *DUST DEVIL* IS STILL HERE ON *RANN*!

IN AMAZEMENT, *ADAM* SWINGS AROUND AS A MOCKING VOICE TELEPATHS TO HIM ...

YES, *ADAM STRANGE*--I AM HERE--AND ON EARTH TOO! WHEN I CAME TO *RANN* IN YOUR PLACE I REALIZED THAT I WOULD SOON BE DRAWN BACK TO EARTH WHEN THE *ZETA-BEAM* WORE OFF!

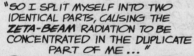

"SO I SPLIT MYSELF INTO TWO IDENTICAL PARTS, CAUSING THE *ZETA-BEAM* RADIATION TO BE CONCENTRATED IN THE DUPLICATE PART OF ME ..."

"WHEN THE *ZETA-BEAM* WORE OFF, MY 'OTHER' SELF WAS DRAWN BACK TO EARTH TO FORCE YOU TO COME TO *RANN*-- WHILE *I* REMAINED HERE TO OVERCOME YOU!..."

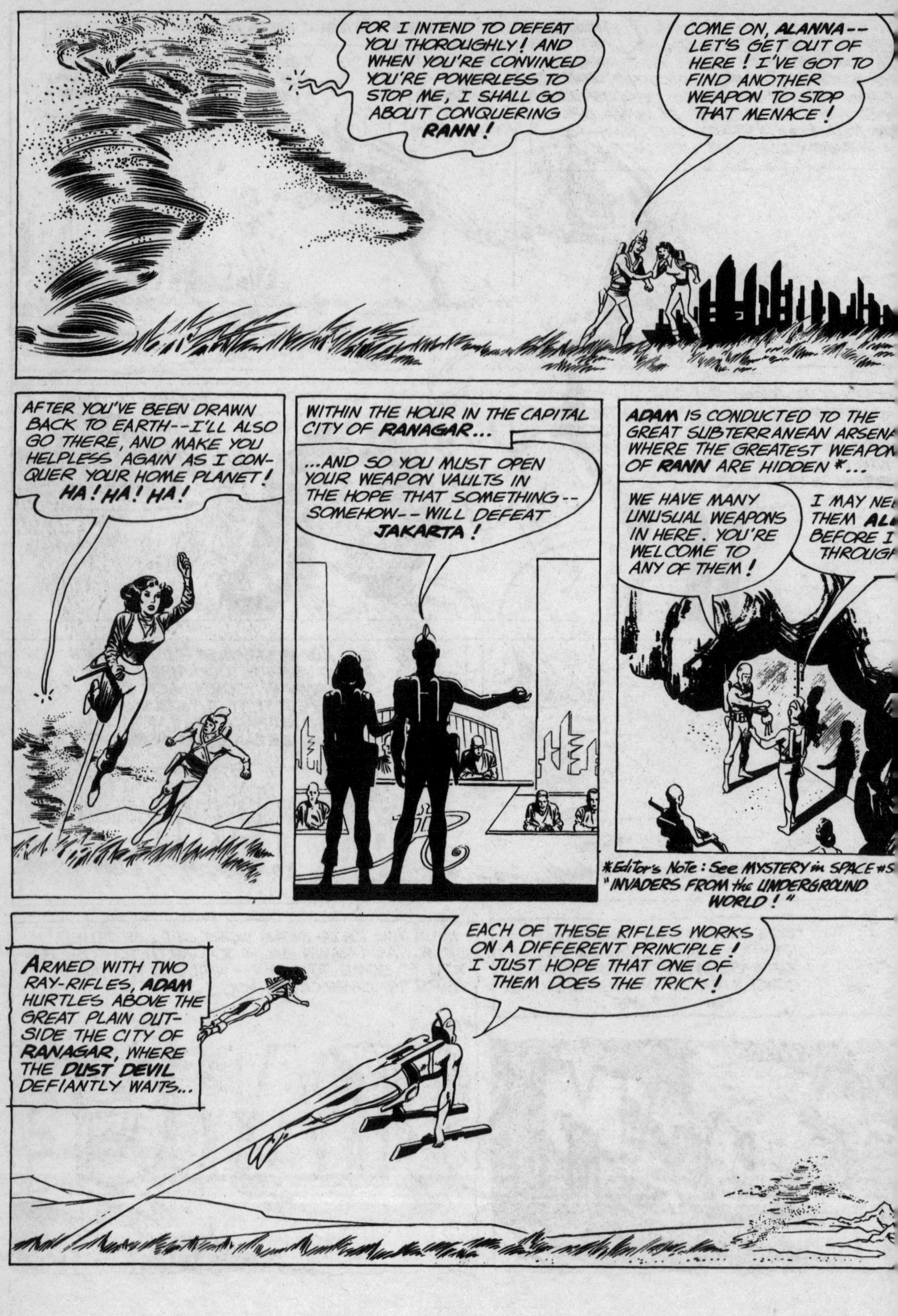
FOR I INTEND TO DEFEAT YOU THOROUGHLY! AND WHEN YOU'RE CONVINCED YOU'RE POWERLESS TO STOP ME, I SHALL GO ABOUT CONQUERING RANN!
COME ON, ALANNA-- LET'S GET OUT OF HERE! I'VE GOT TO FIND ANOTHER WEAPON TO STOP THAT MENACE!
AFTER YOU'VE BEEN DRAWN BACK TO EARTH--I'LL ALSO GO THERE, AND MAKE YOU HELPLESS AGAIN AS I CONQUER YOUR HOME PLANET! HA! HA! HA!
WITHIN THE HOUR IN THE CAPITAL CITY OF RANAGAR...
...AND SO YOU MUST OPEN YOUR WEAPON VAULTS IN THE HOPE THAT SOMETHING--SOMEHOW--WILL DEFEAT JAKARTA!
ADAM IS CONDUCTED TO THE GREAT SUBTERRANEAN ARSENA WHERE THE GREATEST WEAPON OF RANN ARE HIDDEN *...
WE HAVE MANY UNUSUAL WEAPONS IN HERE. YOU'RE WELCOME TO ANY OF THEM!
I MAY NE THEM AL BEFORE I THROUG
*Editor's Note: See MYSTERY in SPACE #5 "INVADERS FROM the UNDERGROUND WORLD!"
ARMED WITH TWO RAY-RIFLES, ADAM HURTLES ABOVE THE GREAT PLAIN OUTSIDE THE CITY OF RANAGAR, WHERE THE DUST DEVIL DEFIANTLY WAITS...
EACH OF THESE RIFLES WORKS ON A DIFFERENT PRINCIPLE! I JUST HOPE THAT ONE OF THEM DOES THE TRICK!

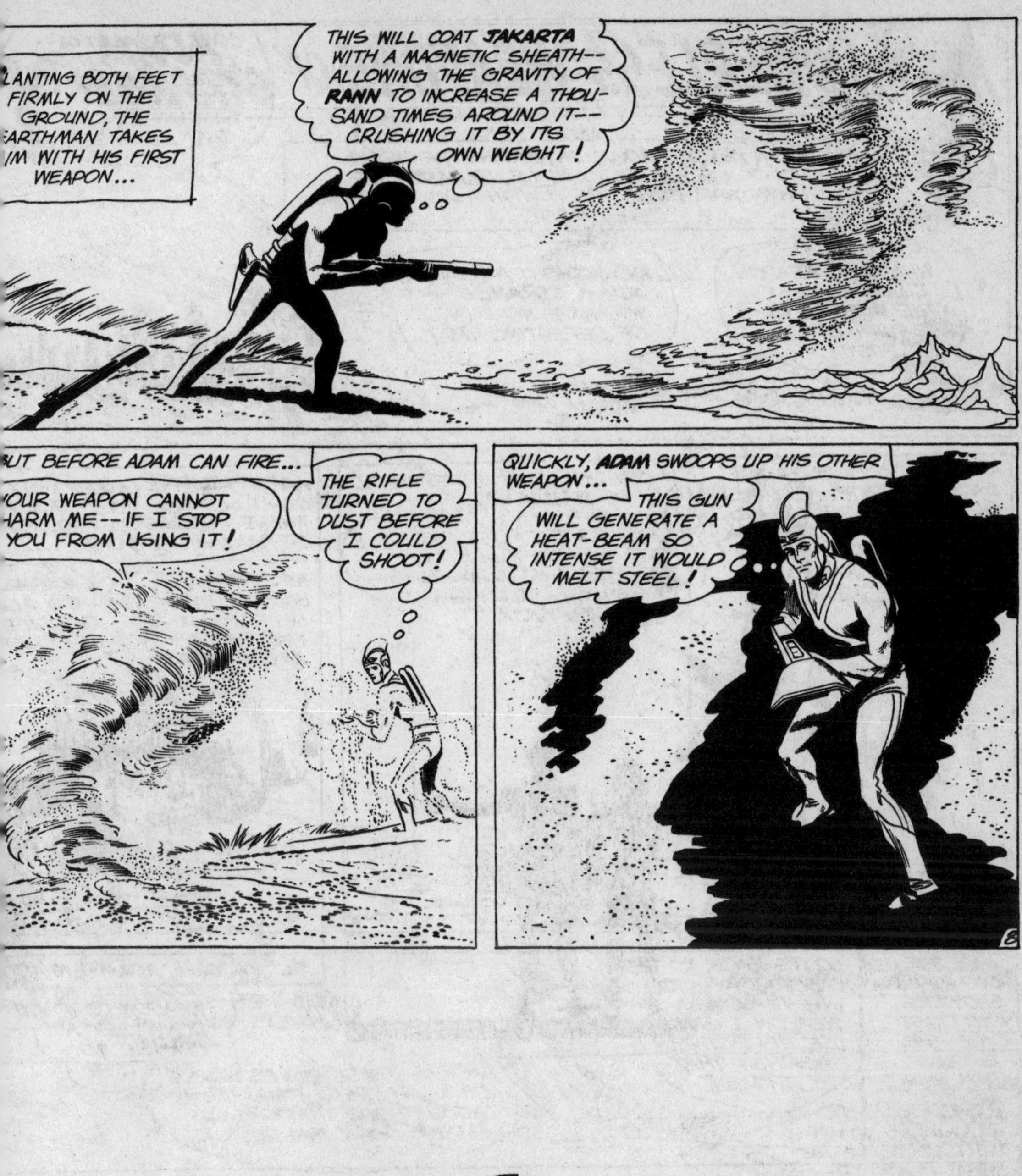
LANTING BOTH FEET FIRMLY ON THE GROUND, THE EARTHMAN TAKES IM WITH HIS FIRST WEAPON...
THIS WILL COAT JAKARTA WITH A MAGNETIC SHEATH-- ALLOWING THE GRAVITY OF RANN TO INCREASE A THOUSAND TIMES AROUND IT-- CRUSHING IT BY ITS OWN WEIGHT!
UT BEFORE ADAM CAN FIRE...
OUR WEAPON CANNOT HARM ME--IF I STOP YOU FROM USING IT!
THE RIFLE TURNED TO DUST BEFORE I COULD SHOOT!
QUICKLY, ADAM SWOOPS UP HIS OTHER WEAPON...
THIS GUN WILL GENERATE A HEAT-BEAM SO INTENSE IT WOULD MELT STEEL!
8

ADAM STRANGE

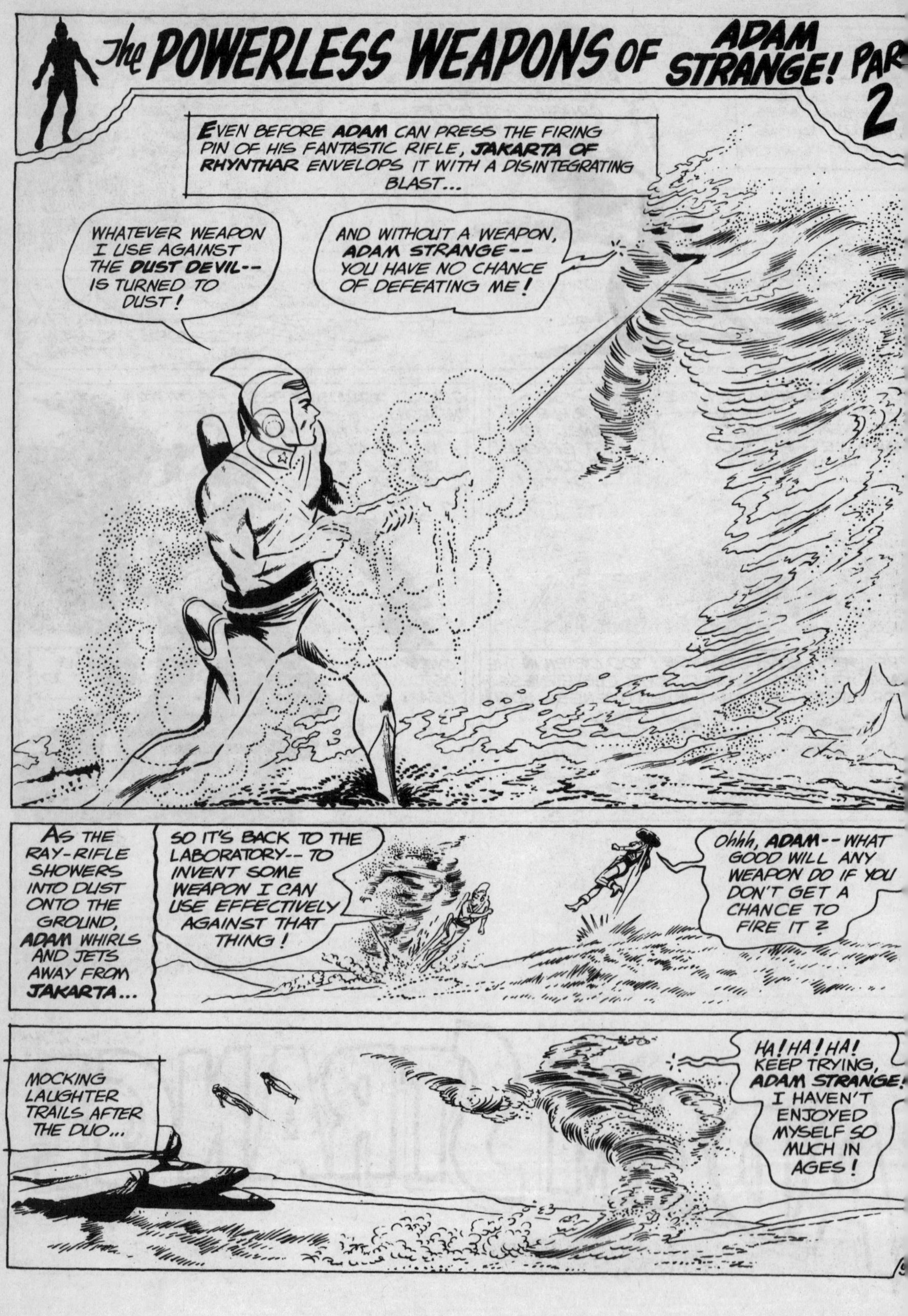
The POWERLESS WEAPONS OF ADAM STRANGE! PART 2
EVEN BEFORE ADAM CAN PRESS THE FIRING PIN OF HIS FANTASTIC RIFLE, JAKARTA OF RHYNTHAR ENVELOPS IT WITH A DISINTEGRATING BLAST...
WHATEVER WEAPON I USE AGAINST THE DUST DEVIL-- IS TURNED TO DUST!
AND WITHOUT A WEAPON, ADAM STRANGE-- YOU HAVE NO CHANCE OF DEFEATING ME!
AS THE RAY-RIFLE SHOWERS INTO DUST ONTO THE GROUND, ADAM WHIRLS AND JETS AWAY FROM JAKARTA...
SO IT'S BACK TO THE LABORATORY-- TO INVENT SOME WEAPON I CAN USE EFFECTIVELY AGAINST THAT THING!
Ohhh, ADAM--WHAT GOOD WILL ANY WEAPON DO IF YOU DON'T GET A CHANCE TO FIRE IT?
MOCKING LAUGHTER TRAILS AFTER THE DUO...
HA! HA! HA! KEEP TRYING, ADAM STRANGE! I HAVEN'T ENJOYED MYSELF SO MUCH IN AGES!

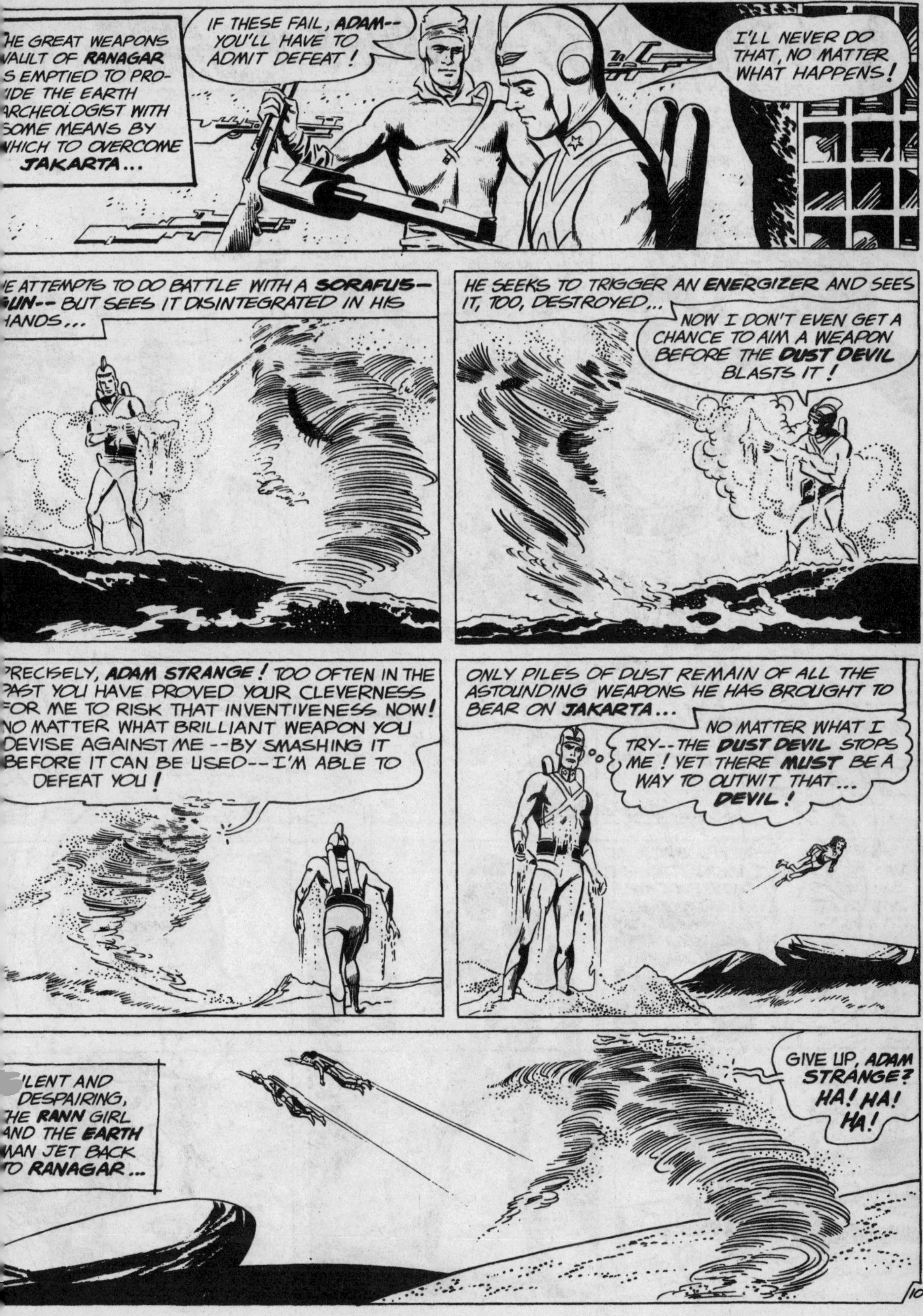
HE GREAT WEAPONS VAULT OF RANAGAR S EMPTIED TO PROVIDE THE EARTH ARCHEOLOGIST WITH SOME MEANS BY WHICH TO OVERCOME JAKARTA...
IF THESE FAIL, ADAM-- YOU'LL HAVE TO ADMIT DEFEAT!
I'LL NEVER DO THAT, NO MATTER WHAT HAPPENS!
HE ATTEMPTS TO DO BATTLE WITH A SORAFUS-GUN-- BUT SEES IT DISINTEGRATED IN HIS HANDS...
HE SEEKS TO TRIGGER AN ENERGIZER AND SEES IT, TOO, DESTROYED...
NOW I DON'T EVEN GET A CHANCE TO AIM A WEAPON BEFORE THE DUST DEVIL BLASTS IT!
PRECISELY, ADAM STRANGE! TOO OFTEN IN THE PAST YOU HAVE PROVED YOUR CLEVERNESS FOR ME TO RISK THAT INVENTIVENESS NOW! NO MATTER WHAT BRILLIANT WEAPON YOU DEVISE AGAINST ME --BY SMASHING IT BEFORE IT CAN BE USED-- I'M ABLE TO DEFEAT YOU!
ONLY PILES OF DUST REMAIN OF ALL THE ASTOUNDING WEAPONS HE HAS BROUGHT TO BEAR ON JAKARTA...
NO MATTER WHAT I TRY--THE DUST DEVIL STOPS ME! YET THERE MUST BE A WAY TO OUTWIT THAT... DEVIL!
SILENT AND DESPAIRING, THE RANN GIRL AND THE EARTH MAN JET BACK TO RANAGAR...
GIVE UP, ADAM STRANGE? HA! HA! HA!
10

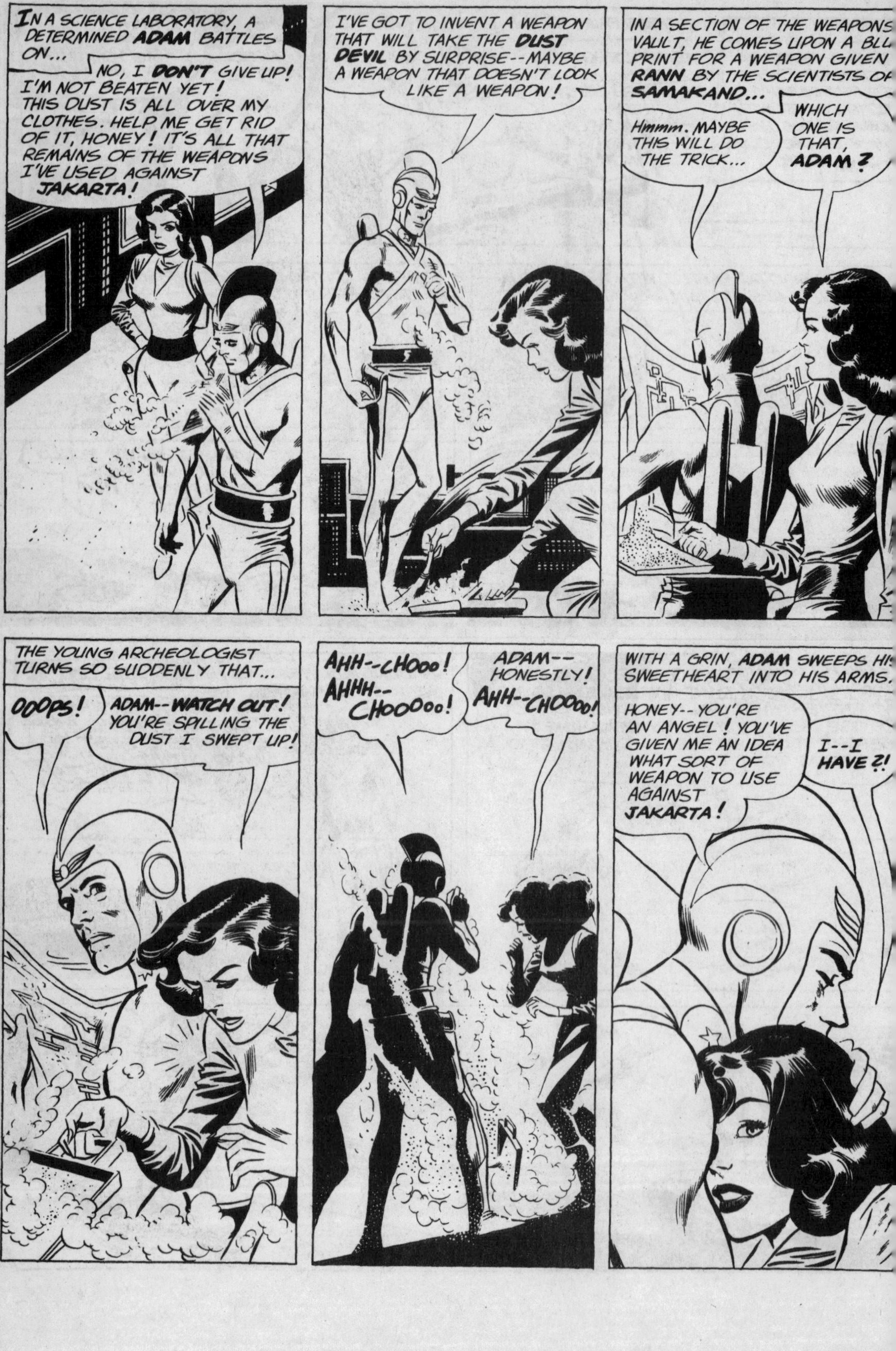
IN A SCIENCE LABORATORY, A DETERMINED ADAM BATTLES ON...
NO, I DON'T GIVE UP! I'M NOT BEATEN YET! THIS DUST IS ALL OVER MY CLOTHES. HELP ME GET RID OF IT, HONEY! IT'S ALL THAT REMAINS OF THE WEAPONS I'VE USED AGAINST JAKARTA!
I'VE GOT TO INVENT A WEAPON THAT WILL TAKE THE DUST DEVIL BY SURPRISE--MAYBE A WEAPON THAT DOESN'T LOOK LIKE A WEAPON!
IN A SECTION OF THE WEAPONS VAULT, HE COMES UPON A BLU PRINT FOR A WEAPON GIVEN RANN BY THE SCIENTISTS OF SAMAKAND...
Hmmm. MAYBE THIS WILL DO THE TRICK...
WHICH ONE IS THAT, ADAM?
THE YOUNG ARCHEOLOGIST TURNS SO SUDDENLY THAT...
OOOPS!
ADAM--WATCH OUT! YOU'RE SPILLING THE DUST I SWEPT UP!
AHH--CHOOO! AHHH--CHOOOOO!
ADAM-- HONESTLY! AHH--CHOOOO!
WITH A GRIN, ADAM SWEEPS HIS SWEETHEART INTO HIS ARMS.
HONEY--YOU'RE AN ANGEL! YOU'VE GIVEN ME AN IDEA WHAT SORT OF WEAPON TO USE AGAINST JAKARTA!
I--I HAVE?!

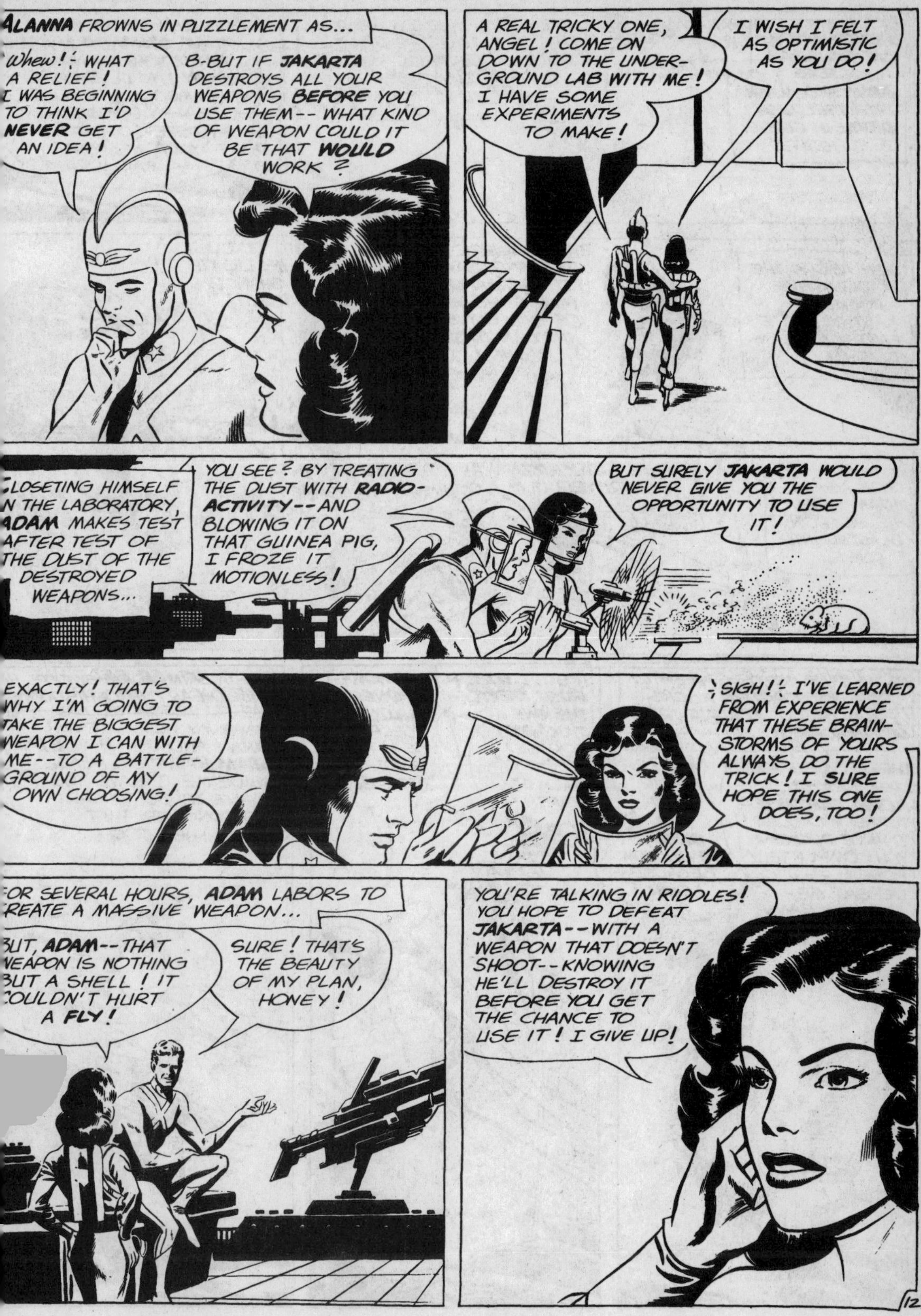
ALANNA FROWNS IN PUZZLEMENT AS...
Whew! -- WHAT A RELIEF! I WAS BEGINNING TO THINK I'D NEVER GET AN IDEA!
B-BUT IF JAKARTA DESTROYS ALL YOUR WEAPONS BEFORE YOU USE THEM -- WHAT KIND OF WEAPON COULD IT BE THAT WOULD WORK?
A REAL TRICKY ONE, ANGEL! COME ON DOWN TO THE UNDERGROUND LAB WITH ME! I HAVE SOME EXPERIMENTS TO MAKE!
I WISH I FELT AS OPTIMISTIC AS YOU DO!
CLOSETING HIMSELF IN THE LABORATORY, ADAM MAKES TEST AFTER TEST OF THE DUST OF THE DESTROYED WEAPONS...
YOU SEE? BY TREATING THE DUST WITH RADIO-ACTIVITY -- AND BLOWING IT ON THAT GUINEA PIG, I FROZE IT MOTIONLESS!
BUT SURELY JAKARTA WOULD NEVER GIVE YOU THE OPPORTUNITY TO USE IT!
EXACTLY! THAT'S WHY I'M GOING TO TAKE THE BIGGEST WEAPON I CAN WITH ME -- TO A BATTLE-GROUND OF MY OWN CHOOSING!
-SIGH!- I'VE LEARNED FROM EXPERIENCE THAT THESE BRAIN-STORMS OF YOURS ALWAYS DO THE TRICK! I SURE HOPE THIS ONE DOES, TOO!
FOR SEVERAL HOURS, ADAM LABORS TO CREATE A MASSIVE WEAPON...
BUT, ADAM -- THAT WEAPON IS NOTHING BUT A SHELL! IT COULDN'T HURT A FLY!
SURE! THAT'S THE BEAUTY OF MY PLAN, HONEY!
YOU'RE TALKING IN RIDDLES! YOU HOPE TO DEFEAT JAKARTA -- WITH A WEAPON THAT DOESN'T SHOOT -- KNOWING HE'LL DESTROY IT BEFORE YOU GET THE CHANCE TO USE IT! I GIVE UP!
12

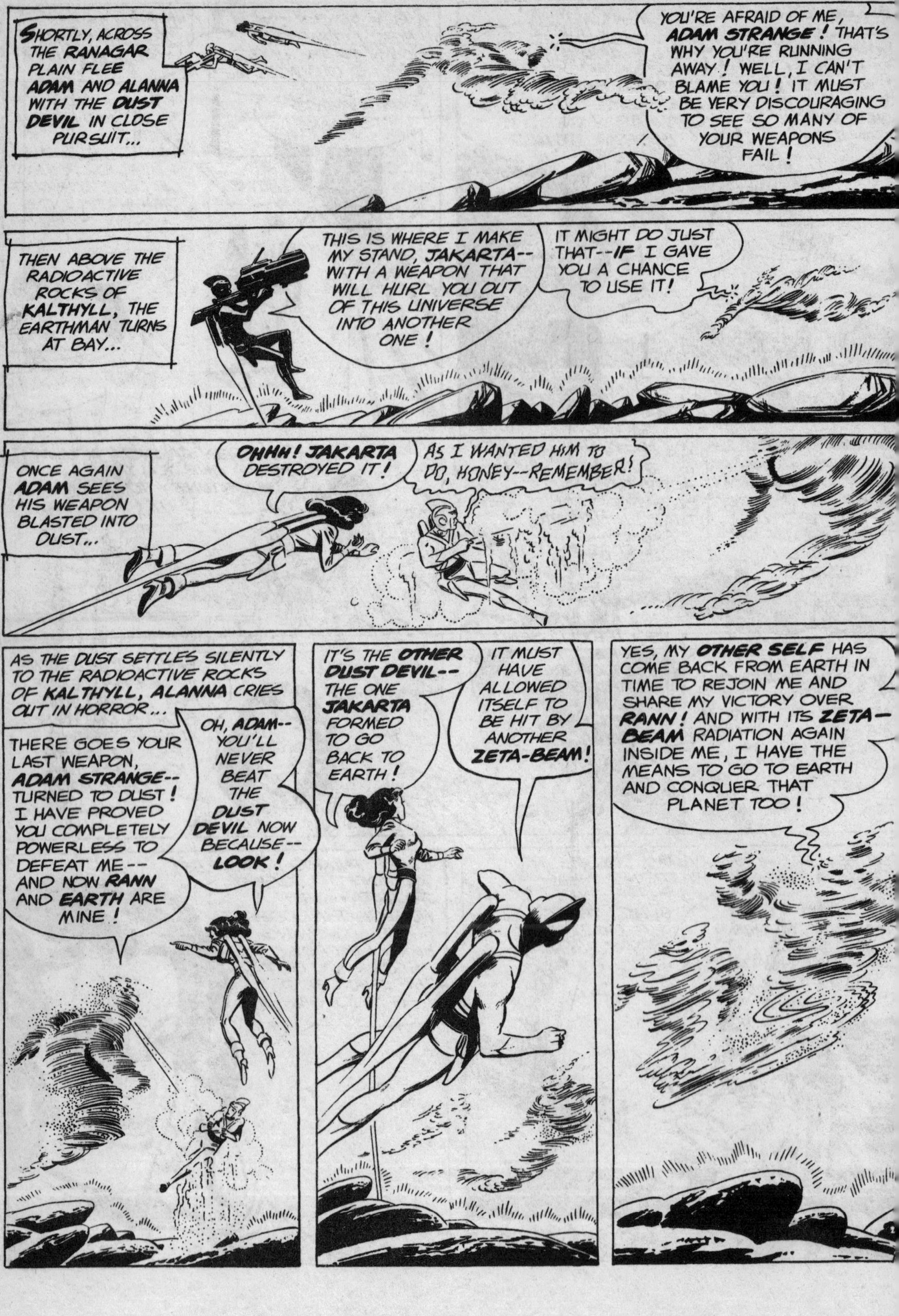
SHORTLY, ACROSS THE RANAGAR PLAIN FLEE ADAM AND ALANNA WITH THE DUST DEVIL IN CLOSE PURSUIT...
YOU'RE AFRAID OF ME, ADAM STRANGE! THAT'S WHY YOU'RE RUNNING AWAY! WELL, I CAN'T BLAME YOU! IT MUST BE VERY DISCOURAGING TO SEE SO MANY OF YOUR WEAPONS FAIL!
THEN ABOVE THE RADIOACTIVE ROCKS OF KALTHYLL, THE EARTHMAN TURNS AT BAY...
THIS IS WHERE I MAKE MY STAND, JAKARTA-- WITH A WEAPON THAT WILL HURL YOU OUT OF THIS UNIVERSE INTO ANOTHER ONE!
IT MIGHT DO JUST THAT--IF I GAVE YOU A CHANCE TO USE IT!
ONCE AGAIN ADAM SEES HIS WEAPON BLASTED INTO DUST...
OHHH! JAKARTA DESTROYED IT!
AS I WANTED HIM TO DO, HONEY--REMEMBER!
AS THE DUST SETTLES SILENTLY TO THE RADIOACTIVE ROCKS OF KALTHYLL, ALANNA CRIES OUT IN HORROR...
THERE GOES YOUR LAST WEAPON, ADAM STRANGE-- TURNED TO DUST! I HAVE PROVED YOU COMPLETELY POWERLESS TO DEFEAT ME-- AND NOW RANN AND EARTH ARE MINE!
OH, ADAM-- YOU'LL NEVER BEAT THE DUST DEVIL NOW BECAUSE-- LOOK!
IT'S THE OTHER DUST DEVIL-- THE ONE JAKARTA FORMED TO GO BACK TO EARTH!
IT MUST HAVE ALLOWED ITSELF TO BE HIT BY ANOTHER ZETA-BEAM!
YES, MY OTHER SELF HAS COME BACK FROM EARTH IN TIME TO REJOIN ME AND SHARE MY VICTORY OVER RANN! AND WITH ITS ZETA-BEAM RADIATION AGAIN INSIDE ME, I HAVE THE MEANS TO GO TO EARTH AND CONQUER THAT PLANET TOO!